Y0-CMM-118

C.F.A. Readings in Financial Analysis

C.F.A. Readings in Financial Analysis

The Institute of Chartered Financial Analysts

Second Edition

1970　RICHARD D. IRWIN, INC.　HOMEWOOD, ILLINOIS
　　　IRWIN-DORSEY LIMITED, Georgetown, Ontario

© THE INSTITUTE OF CHARTERED
FINANCIAL ANALYSTS, 1966 AND 1970

ALL RIGHTS RESERVED. No part of this publication may be reproduced, stored in a retrieval system, or transmitted, in any form or by any means, electronic, mechanical, photocopying, recording, or otherwise, without the prior written permission of the copyright holder.

SECOND EDITION
First Printing, September, 1970

Library of Congress Catalog Card No. 70-128705
Printed in the United States of America

FOREWORD

This collection of readings represents a part of the study materials required of financial analysts who are candidates for the professional designation *Chartered Financial Analyst (C.F.A)*. The publication of a second edition of readings is an indication of the continued advancement of financial analysis. On its part, the Institute will continue to review the literature and to revise the recommended articles every three or four years in a new book of readings. The annual Study Guides, which are a part of the examination material, will contain more topical references and will be used on an interim basis in order to keep the examination material as current as possible.

The Institute of Chartered Financial Analysts was formed in 1959 by The Financial Analysts Federation, an organization of over 11,000 members in 41 constituent societies located in major cities of the United States and Canada. The Institute has the following objectives:

1. To foster higher educational standards in the field of financial analysis.
2. To conduct examinations designed to test individual competence and skill in pertinent fields of knowledge.
3. To recognize with the professional designation *Chartered Financial Analyst* persons who have met the standards established by the Institute for the professional practice of financial analysis.
4. To insist upon the maintenance of professional ethical standards.
5. To stimulate research and the dissemination of educational materials.

The professional designation *Chartered Financial Analyst (C.F.A.)* is awarded to those candidates who have satisfactorily completed the examinations and other requirements established by The Institute of Chartered Financial Analysts. The candidate is required to pass three examinations: Examination I—Investment Principles; Examination II—Applied Security Analysis; and Examination III—Investment Management Decision Making. The main objective of the examination series is to assure the investing public, employers, and fellow analysts that a C.F.A. possesses at least the fundamental knowledge necessary to practice his profession. Passing a series of examinations, of course, does not necessarily indicate that a recipient of the C.F.A. designation will be a successful practicing analyst. It does, however, indicate that he is familiar with the basic body of knowledge that comprises the field of financial analysis. The success of the program to date is indicated by the fact that in the seven years since the

Institute has been giving examinations some 2,500 certificates have been awarded, and at the present time there are over 2,000 candidates registered in various stages of the examination program.

There are five basic subject-matter areas extending throughout the examination series: accounting, economics, financial analysis, portfolio management, and ethical standards. This book is divided into sections containing material in each of these areas. During the past several years, the Research and Publications Committee of the Institute has not only undertaken a thorough review of these five areas but has established preexamination requirements for candidates in each area and also has defined the level of knowledge that should be attained in each area. A general topical outline and a brief review of the five main subject areas are contained as an addendum to this foreword.

It is not expected that the articles in this book will provide an exhaustive review of all the areas of financial analysis. In the first place, financial analysis is a constantly growing profession; any list of articles or other readings can present only a snapshot at a point in time of the current state of professional knowledge. Secondly, the purpose of this book is to gather in one place articles to be used for study purposes. In addition to these articles, other books and study materials are used as a part of the program. In the third place, it is occasionally extremely difficult to find an article that will successfully cover a subject required for examination. In some instances, the Institute has had to commission articles or monographs in a particular area, or alternatively the Committee has had to settle for an article which, although not satisfactory in all respects, is the best that can be found. Finally, some areas like accounting are in such a state of change that it has been decided not to include certain articles that would quickly become outdated. Therefore, current articles for the examination have been included in the annual Study Guide.

An additional difficulty encountered has been the rapid advancement of the application of quantitative techniques to financial analysis. Although some articles on this subject are included in this collection, the treatment of quantitative techniques has not been nearly as extensive as might be expected. The primary difficulty here is that many of the candidates are several years removed from their academic acquaintance with quantitative techniques. Consequently, although a knowledge of quantitative techniques is considered essential for the practice of financial analysis, the background of many candidates is such that some more extensive review of methodology is necessary. This need has been met by other publications of the Institute.

The Institute is indebted to the C.F.A.s who over the last several years have worked so hard on the Research and Publications Committee to survey the current literature in the field of financial analysis and to assist in the final selection of articles. Our sincere appreciation is extended to the Institute's staff without whose untiring efforts this publication would not have been completed. Particular acknowledgment is due to Dr. C. Stewart Sheppard, Executive Director of the Institute, and his associates, Professor C. Ray Smith and Mr. Gerald J. MacFarlane.

The Institute also wishes to express its appreciation to the publishers and authors who have permitted us to reprint their materials. The Financial Analysts Federation has been especially cooperative in granting permission to reproduce a number of articles from its official publication, the *Financial Analysts Journal*.

August, 1970

EDMUND A. MENNIS, C.F.A.
Chairman, Research and Publications Committee
The Institute of Chartered Financial Analysts

THE C.F.A. PROGRAM—EXAMINATION CONTENT

The professional designation *Chartered Financial Analyst* (*C.F.A.*) is awarded to those candidates who have completed satisfactorily the examination and other requirements established by The Institute of Chartered Financial Analysts. Normally, the candidate will be expected to pass the three examinations: Examination I—Investment Principles; Examination II—Applied Security Analysis; and Examination III—Investment Management Decision Making.

The main objectives of the examination series is to assure the investing public, employers, and fellow analysts that a *C.F.A.* possesses at least the fundamental knowledge necessary to practice his profession. There are five basic subject-matter areas extending throughout the examination series: accounting, economics, financial analysis, portfolio management, and ethical standards. The *C.F.A.* program necessarily continues to be of an evolutionary nature, reflecting as it does the changing emphases and techniques of financial analysis and portfolio management in the dynamic economies of the United States and Canada. The logic and objectives of the program may best be illustrated by the following brief review of the five main subject areas. More specific examination guidance to candidates is provided in each of the three Study Guides published annually by the Institute.

AREA ONE—ACCOUNTING

PREEXAMINATION REQUIREMENTS

A candidate should have the equivalent of at least two years of academic accounting principles exposure.

EXAMINATION I

Questions at this examination level will be oriented to the application of accounting principles and basic techniques to financial analysis. A major objective is to test the candidate's ability to use published data in a meaningful analysis of corporate accounting statements.

EXAMINATION II

At this level, the candidate should be prepared to go beyond Examination I content into more controversial areas, such as acquisitions, mergers, and conglomerates. In such areas, the candidate will be expected to be familiar with recent Accounting Principles Board opinions.

EXAMINATION III

The candidate will be tested on his knowledge of accounting throughout the examination series. At this level, the treatment of accounting problems will be interrelated with the investment decision-making process. As such, emphasis will be placed on the applications of controversial accounting issues to financial analysis and portfolio management.

AREA TWO—ECONOMICS

PREEXAMINATION REQUIREMENTS

The candidate should be familiar with the basic principles of macroeconomics and the monetary system. Minimum knowledge should be at the level of an elementary economics textbook. The examination, however, will emphasize the practicalities rather than abstract economic theory.

EXAMINATION I

The main examination objective is to obtain assurance that the candidate is familiar with the tools and concepts of economic analysis. Primary emphasis in this area is placed upon the relevance and application of economics to the practice of financial analysis as related to securities investment.

EXAMINATION II

At this examination level, the candidate will be tested on his ability to apply the basic economic tools and concepts covered under Examination I, to the evaluation of specific industries and companies.

EXAMINATION III

A C.F.A. should be able to relate the impact of economic policies to the determination of investment policies. Accordingly, the candidate will be expected to interpret current economic issues and policies as they affect securities markets in order to arrive at a penetrating analysis of earnings trends of specific industries and companies.

AREA THREE—FINANCIAL ANALYSIS

PREEXAMINATION REQUIREMENTS

It is assumed that the candidate will have the equivalent of at least two years of academic exposure to business administration, including corporate finance and corporate financial policies. It is assumed further that the candidate has some knowledge of elementary mathematics and statistics.

EXAMINATION I

The candidate at this level is tested on his ability to prepare factual information to be used as a basis for investment decisions. In order to accomplish this objective, the candidate will be expected to acquire knowledge of sources of factual information, and to demonstrate the ability to select and evaluate relevant data in the analysis of different types of securities.

EXAMINATION II

This examination will test the candidate on the ability to apply financial principles to the analysis of corporate reports. By training and experience the candidate should be able to distinguish between facts, estimates, opinions, and conclusions in making an evaluation.

EXAMINATION III

At this level, financial analysis will be interrelated closely with problems of individual and institutional portfolio management. Primary emphasis will be placed on techniques of financial analysis used in the selection of securities to be included in individual and institutional portfolios under changing circumstances.

AREA FOUR—PORTFOLIO MANAGEMENT

PREEXAMINATION REQUIREMENTS

Practical experience is considered to be such an important requisite of professional portfolio management that no preexamination requirement is expected of the candidate.

EXAMINATION I

At this level, the candidate will be tested on basic principles of individual and institutional portfolio management. Primary emphasis will be placed upon the principal investment objectives of various financial institutions and the use of appropriate investment instruments to meet these objectives.

EXAMINATION II

Emphasis is placed upon problems of portfolio construction, with special attention being paid to security selection, diversification concepts, risk versus return, and variability and quality of rates of return.

EXAMINATION III

Based on the knowledge gained under Examinations I and II and the analyst's experience, this examination tests the candidate's ability to interrelate financial analysis and portfolio management, recognizing the skills and limitations of both analysts and portfolio managers. The investment decision-making process underlying portfolio management is the major concern of this examination.

AREA FIVE—ETHICAL STANDARDS

PREEXAMINATION REQUIREMENTS

All candidates for the *C.F.A.* designation will be required to show evidence of sound moral character. Character references are an integral part of the basic registration requirements. Furthermore, each candidate at the time of initial registration must agree, in writing, that he will abide by the *C.F.A. Code of Ethics* and *Guidelines* thereto. Violation of the *Code* and *Guidelines* may cause suspension from the program or rescission of the Charter.

Questions in this area will be included in each of the three examinations to assure the Institute that the candidate at least recognizes the ethical problems confronting him in his daily practice, and that he has acquired some competency in dealing with such problems.

Examination I

This examination, concerned primarily with the testing of the junior analyst, will contain a question or questions related to his dealings with the investing public, employers, and fellow analysts.

Examination II

At this examination level, the analyst with more experience has closer contact with clients and corporate management. Accordingly, examination questions will involve ethical considerations arising from the use of insider information, conflict of interests, and the professional stature of the financial analyst.

Examination III

At this further advanced level, the analyst is presumed to have sufficient experience to organize and supervise the activities of other analysts. Questions in this examination will revolve around the administration of ethical standards in terms of internal disciplinary control, together with recognition of the necessity to adhere to external controls imposed by regulatory authorities. In this examination, the Institute is concerned with the necessity to expose the candidate to the nature and basic concepts of financial professionalism.

ADDENDUM

THE C.F.A. PROGRAM—GENERAL TOPICAL OUTLINE

EXAMINATION
I　II　III

ACCOUNTING

Principles and Construction of Accounting Statements:
- balance sheet
- income statement
- sources and uses
- other

Analysis of Accounting Statements:
- income statement and balance sheet analysis
- comparative company analysis
- inventory evaluation
- depreciation accounting
- deferred tax accounting
- treatment of intangibles
- stock splits and dividends
- rights, warrants, convertibles
- ratio and coverage analysis
- other

Current Accounting Principles and Practices:
- AICPA opinions
- controversial areas
- acquisitions and mergers
- conglomerates

ECONOMICS

Basic Principles and Source Materials:
- GNP and national income accounts
- the monetary system
- the fiscal system
- the price system
- flow-of-funds
- input-output analysis
- aggregate profit measures
- indicator series analysis
- long-term trends in stock and bond prices

Economic Analysis and Forecasting:
- input-output applications
- corporate profits forecasting
- indicator series applications
- supply and demand of funds in the market
- economic fluctuations and long-term trends

Economic Policy:
- monetary policy
- fiscal policy
- balance of payments and international policy
- money supply
- antitrust legislation
- employment policy
- growth of the institutional investor

EXAMINATION
I　II　III

FINANCIAL ANALYSIS and PORTFOLIO MANAGEMENT

FINANCIAL ANALYSIS

Principles of Financial Analysis:
- sources of information
- financial instruments
- financial institutions
- common stock analysis
- fixed income security analysis
- management appraisal
- quantitative techniques

Applied Financial Analysis:
- industry appraisal and evaluation
- dividends and earnings evaluation and projection
- valuation techniques
- risk analysis - qualitative and quantitative
- market and price analysis and areas of speculation
- capital budgeting

PORTFOLIO MANAGEMENT

Objectives:
- individuals
- institutions -
  investment companies
  foundations and endowment funds
  pension funds and profit sharing plans
  trust funds
  fire and casualty insurance companies
  life insurance companies
  commercial banks
  hedge funds

Construction:
- security selection
- diversification
- marketability
- risk
- return

Timing and Formula Plans
Bond Portfolio Problems
Performance Measurement
Trading Problems
Tax Planning
Supervision
Quantitative Techniques for Portfolio Management
Computer Applications
Regulation

ETHICAL STANDARDS

C.F.A. Responsibilities:
- public
- customers and clients
- employers
- associates
- other analysts
- corporate management
- other sources of information

Professionalization
Administering Ethical Policy
Security Laws and Regulations

xiii

CONTENTS

List of Contributors and Index to Authors xix

Part One
FINANCIAL ACCOUNTING

1. Accounting Principles and Investment Analysis,
   Douglas A. Hayes, C.F.A. 3
2. Accounting for Inflation—A Field Test, *Paul Rosenfield* 24
3. Corporate Diversification and Financial Reporting,
   Leopold Schachner 34
4. Audits of Corporate Accounts, *One letter from correspondence between the American Institute of Accountants and the New York Stock Exchange* 47
5. New Rules for Determining Earnings per Share, *James E. Parker* . 54

Part Two
ECONOMICS

6. "Qui Numerare Incipit Errare Incipit," *Oskar Morgenstern* . . . 67
7. A Reply to "Qui Numerare Incipit Errare Incipit," *Julius Shiskin* . 80
8. Economics and Investment Management,
   Edmund A. Mennis, C.F.A. 83
9. The Flow of Funds Accounts: A Framework for Financial Analysis,
   Lawrence S. Ritter 92
10. Flow of Funds Analysis—Its Uses and Limitations,
    Stephen B. Packer 117
11. Aggregate Measures of Corporate Profits,
    Edmund A. Mennis, C.F.A. 131
12. Corporate Profits Data: Tax Returns versus Company Books,
    Vito Natrella 136
13. Corporate Earnings: A Record of Contrast and Change,
    Sidney Cottle 148
14. New Tools for Profits Analysis, *Edmund A. Mennis, C.F.A.* . . . 174
15. The Use of Input-Output Economics in Common Stock Analysis,
    Howard B. Bonham, Jr. 193

CONTENTS

16. The Role of Money and Monetary Policy, *Karl Brunner* 209
17. The Role of the Money Supply in Business Cycles, *Richard G. Davis* 237
18. Techniques for Forecasting Interest Rate Trends, *Sidney Homer* . 256
19. Long-Run Economic and Financial Projections, *John W. Kendrick* 271
20. How to Interpret the Balance of Payments Accounts, *Federal Reserve Bank of St. Louis* 281
21. New Trends in Institutional Investing, *Edmund A. Mennis, C.F.A.* 285

Part Three
FINANCIAL ANALYSIS

22. The Dimensions of Analysis: A Critical Review, *Douglas A. Hayes, C.F.A.* 299
23. SEC Filings—Their Use to the Professional, *Carl W. Schneider* . . 304
24. SEC Filings—Their Content and Use, *Carl W. Schneider* 315
25. Forecasting by Probabilities: Preface to Copper Industry Study, *Peter F. Way, C.F.A.* 327
26. The Copper Industry: Forecasting by Probabilities, *John A. Olsen, C.F.A. and Terry A. Blaney* 329
27. Caveats in Computer-Aided Financial Analysis, *Donald E. Stone* . 342
28. The Place of Book Value in Common Stock Evaluation, *Frank E. Block, C.F.A.* 352
29. Common Stock Valuation—Principles, Tables, and Application, *Nicholas Molodovsky, C.F.A., Catherine May, and Sherman Chottiner* 363
30. Recent Studies of P/E Ratios, *Nicholas Molodovsky, C.F.A.* . . . 400
31. "Recent Studies of P/E Ratios"—A Reply, *Paul F. Miller, Jr., C.F.A. and Thomas E. Beach* 414
32. Some Reflections on Techniques for Appraising Growth Rates, *Douglas A. Hayes, C.F.A.* 418
33. Current Growth Stock Valuation Methods: General Motors— An Illustration, *Paul F. Wendt* 431
34. Earnings Growth and Price Change in the Same Time Period, *Joseph E. Murphy, Jr., C.F.A.* 454
35. Random Walks in Stock Market Prices, *Eugene F. Fama* 459
36. Conceptual Foundations of Technical Analysis, *Robert A. Levy* . 469
37. Appraising Managements, *Townsend Hoopes* 482

38. The Financial Analyst and Management, *Harlow J. Heneman* . . 491

Part Four
Portfolio Management

39. Performance and Portfolio Management, *George C. Briggs, C.F.A.* 501
40. Elements of Portfolio Construction, *Frank E. Block, C.F.A.* . . . 509
41. Investment Policy for a Growing Pension Fund, *Edmund A. Mennis, C.F.A.* 522
42. Portfolio Selection and Investment Performance, *Irwin Friend and Douglas Vickers* 536
43. Risk and Performance, *Frank E. Block, C.F.A.* 562
44. How to Rate Management of Investment Funds, *Jack L. Treynor* . 578
45. Some Methods for Measuring Performance of a Pension Fund, *Randolph W. McCandlish, Jr.* 596
46. A Management Summary of Measuring the Investment Performance of Pension Funds—For the Purpose of Inter-Fund Comparison, *Bank Administration Institute* 607
47. Bond Investment Policy for Pension Funds, *Sidney Homer* . . . 615
48. Relative Price Performance among Coupon Areas in Corporate Bonds, *Neil Zaentz* 630
49. A Primer on Institutional Trading, *Carter T. Geyer* 648
50. Mathematical Analysis of Portfolio Selection: Principles and Application, *William J. Baumol* 666

Part Five
Ethical Considerations

51. Research Report Ethics, *Louis J. Zitnik, C.F.A.* 677
52. The Law of Corporate Information, *Alan R. Bromberg* 682
53. Corporate Disclosure and Insider Information—A Panel Interview, *Financial Analysts Federation* 694
54. Public Statement Concerning Corporate Disclosure and Inside Information, *Financial Analysts Federation* 714
55. Trouble at Quigby, *Financial Analysts Journal* 717

Index 735

LIST OF CONTRIBUTORS AND INDEX TO AUTHORS

AMERICAN INSTITUTE OF CERTIFIED PUBLIC ACCOUNTANTS
  Audits of Corporate Accounts, page 47
BANK ADMINISTRATION INSTITUTE
  A Management Summary of Measuring the Investment Performance of Pension Funds for the Purpose of Inter-Fund Comparison, page 607
WILLIAM J. BAUMOL, *Professor of Economics, Princeton University*
  Mathematical Analysis of Portfolio Selection: Principles and Application, page 666
THOMAS E. BEACH, *Security Analyst, Drexel Harriman Ripley Incorporated*
  'Recent Studies of P/E Ratios'—A Reply, page 414
TERRY A. BLANEY, *Analyst, First National City Bank*
  The Copper Industry: Forecasting by Probabilities, page 329
FRANK E. BLOCK, C.F.A., *Vice President, The Citizens and Southern National Bank of Georgia*
  Elements of Portfolio Construction, page 509
  Risk and Performance, page 562
  The Place of Book Value in Common Stock Evaluation, page 352
HOWARD B. BONHAM, JR., *Investment Analyst, Life & Casualty Insurance Company of Tennessee*
  The Use of Input-Output Economics in Common Stock Analysis, page 193
GEORGE C. BRIGGS, C.F.A., *Investment Counselor*
  Performance and Portfolio Management, page 501
ALAN R. BROMBERG, *Professor of Law, Southern Methodist University*
  The Law of Corporate Information, page 682
KARL BRUNNER, *Professor of Economics, The Ohio State University*
  The Role of Money and Monetary Policy, page 209
SIDNEY COTTLE, *Senior Financial Economist, Stanford Research Institute*
  Corporate Earnings: A Record of Contrast and Change, page 148
SHERMAN CHOTTINER, *Research Assistant, New York University Graduate School of Business Administration*
  Common Stock Valuation—Principles, Tables, and Application, page 363
RICHARD G. DAVIS, *Assistant Vice President, Federal Reserve Bank of New York*
  The Role of the Money Supply in Business Cycles, page 237
EUGENE F. FAMA, *Assistant Professor of Finance, The University of Chicago*
  Random Walks in Stock Market Prices, page 459
FEDERAL RESERVE BANK OF ST. LOUIS
  How to Interpret the Balance of Payments Accounts, page 281
FINANCIAL ANALYSTS FEDERATION
  Corporate Disclosure and Insider Information—A Panel Interview, page

Public Statement Concerning Corporate Disclosure and Inside Information, page 714

FINANCIAL ANALYSTS JOURNAL
Trouble at Quigby, page 717

IRWIN FRIEND, *Professor of Economics and Finance, University of Pennsylvania*
Portfolio Selection and Investment Performance, page 536

CARTER T. GEYER, *Trust Officer, Republic National Bank of Dallas*
A Primer on Institutional Trading, page 648

DOUGLAS A. HAYES, C.F.A., *Professor, The University of Michigan*
Accounting Principles and Investment Analysis, page 3
Some Reflections on Techniques for Appraising Growth Rates, page 418
The Dimensions of Analysis: A Critical Review, page 299

HARLOW J. HENEMAN, *Partner, Cresap, McCormick and Paget*
The Financial Analyst and Management, page 491

SIDNEY HOMER, *Partner, Salomon Brothers & Hutzler*
Bond Investment Policy for Pension Funds, page 615
Techniques for Forecasting Interest Rate Trends, page 256

TOWNSEND HOOPES, *Partner, Cresap, McCormick and Paget*
Appraising Managements, page 482

JOHN W. KENDRICK, *Professor, The George Washington University*
Long-Run Economic and Financial Projections, page 271

ROBERT A. LEVY, *School of Business Administration, The American University*
Conceptual Foundations of Technical Analysis, page 469

CATHERINE MAY, *White, Weld & Co.*
Common Stock Valuation—Principles, Tables, and Application, page 363

RANDOLPH W. MCCANDLISH, JR., *Senior Investment Adviser, Continental Illinois National Bank and Trust Company of Chicago*
Some Methods for Measuring Performance of a Pension Fund, page 596

EDMUND A. MENNIS, C.F.A., *Senior Vice President, Republic National Bank of Dallas*
Aggregate Measures of Corporate Profits, page 131
Economics and Investment Management, page 83
Investment Policy for a Growing Pension Fund, page 522
New Tools for Profits Analysis, page 174
New Trends in Institutional Investing, page 285

PAUL F. MILLER, JR., C.F.A., *President, Drexel Harriman Ripley Incorporated*
'Recent Studies of P/E Ratios'—A Reply, page 414

NICHOLAS MOLODOVSKY, C.F.A., *Vice President, White, Weld & Company Incorporated (deceased)*
Common Stock Valuation—Principles, Tables, and Application, page 363
Recent Studies of P/E Ratios, page 400

OSKAR MORGENSTERN, *Professor of Political Economy, Princeton University*
Qui Numerare Incipit Errare Incipit, page 67

JOSEPH E. MURPHY, JR., C.F.A., *Northwestern National Bank of Minneapolis*
Earnings Growth and Price Change in the Same Time Period, page 454

VITO NATRELLA, *Director, Statistics Division, Internal Revenue Service*
Corporate Profits Data: Tax Returns vs. Company Books, page 136

JOHN A. OLSEN, C.F.A., *Senior Metals Analyst, First National City Bank*
The Copper Industry: Forecasting by Probabilities, page 329

List of Contributors and Index to Authors

STEPHEN B. PACKER, *Economist, Continental Can Company, Inc.*
Flow of Funds Analysis—Its Uses and Limitations, page 117

JAMES E. PARKER, *Assistant Professor of Accounting, University of Missouri*
New Rules for Determining Earnings per Share, page 54

LAWRENCE S. RITTER, *Professor of Finance, New York University*
The Flow of Funds Accounts: A Framework for Financial Analysis, page 92

PAUL ROSENFIELD, *Project Manager, Research Division, American Institute of Certified Public Accountants*
Accounting for Inflation—A Field Test, page 24

LEOPOLD SCHACHNER, *Professor, The Bernard M. Baruch School of Business and Public Administration, City College of New York*
Corporate Diversification and Financial Reporting, page 34

CARL W. SCHNEIDER, *Partner, Wolf, Block, Schorr and Solis-Cohen, Attorneys*
SEC Filings—Their Content and Use, page 315
SEC Filings—Their Use to the Professional, page 304

JULIUS SHISKIN, *Chief Economic Statistician, Bureau of the Census*
A Reply to "Qui Numerare Incipit Errare Incipit," page 80

DONALD E. STONE, *Assistant Professor, The Amos Tuck School of Business Administration, Dartmouth College*
Caveats in Computer-Aided Financial Analysis, page 342

JACK L. TREYNOR, *Arthur D. Little, Inc.*
How to Rate Management of Investment Funds, page 578

DOUGLAS VICKERS, *Associate Professor, University of Pennsylvania*
Portfolio Selection and Investment Performance, page 536

PETER F. WAY, C.F.A., *Vice President, First National City Bank*
Forecasting by Probabilities: Preface to Copper Industry Study, page 327

PAUL F. WENDT, *Professor of Finance, University of California, Berkeley*
Current Growth Stock Valuation Methods: General Motors—An Illustration, page 431

NEIL ZAENTZ, *Vice President, Lionel D. Edie & Company Incorporated*
Relative Price Performance among Coupon Areas in Corporate Bonds, page 630

LOUIS J. ZITNIK, C.F.A., *Vice President, Mitchum, Jones & Templeton, Incorporated*
Research Report Ethics, page 677

Part One

Financial Accounting

1

ACCOUNTING PRINCIPLES AND INVESTMENT ANALYSIS*

Douglas A. Hayes, C.F.A.

In a broad sense, there are three major technical problems that surround the use of accounting data in investment analysis. The first is the *reliability* of the data within a given reporting period as an indication of the actual economic results pertaining to the period and of the financial position of the enterprise at the terminal date. The second is the problem of *consistency* in the determination of revenues, expenses, and the related asset values through time within a given corporate enterprise. The third is that of the *comparability* of the data offered by several similar firms within the same general industry area.

The accounting techniques that may distort or obscure actual economic results and financial position are probably of most importance to the nonprofessional investor since, for the most part, professional analysts can make the necessary adjustments from a penetrating appraisal of the statements and the notes appended thereto. Nonprofessionals, however, not trained to understand and interpret the significance of particular items, may find these adjustments beyond their competence.

I. THE IMPORTANCE OF CONSISTENCY IN THE APPLICATION OF "PRINCIPLES"

From the viewpoint of the professional analyst, a case can be made that the validity of the accounting principles applied during any given period to the determination of income and financial position are less important than consistency of application through time and their comparability within a given industry area. The reason is that a major objective of many investment analysis techniques is to obtain an insight into the probable pattern of future corporate performances and the relative performances of several firms within the industry group. For example, there is the very important question in investment appraisals of estimating the comparative

---

* Reprinted with permission from a symposium, "Accounting Principles and Investment Analysis," appearing in *Law and Contemporary Problems* (Vol. 30, No. 4, Autumn 1965), published by the Duke University School of Law, Durham, North Carolina. Copyright 1965 by Duke University.

rates of growth in earning power of different companies. In addition, the estimated range of fluctuations as a consequence of changing economic or industry conditions is of considerable significance.

If inconsistencies in accounting procedures produce arbitrary distortions in the pattern of reported earnings through time, the task of the investment analyst becomes considerably more difficult. Not only must the analyst reach decisions on the substantive economic issues, such as the probable growth in the demand for the products and prospective competitive conditions, but in addition it becomes necessary to ascertain the real quantitative impact of past developments in these matters via eliminating the effects of changes in earnings produced solely by variations in accounting techniques. As a result, the more penetrating treatises on investment analysis feel obliged to devote several chapters to the principal problem areas involved, to the means of eliminating the effects of accounting inconsistencies from the reported results, and to making comparable the reported results of two or more firms in the same general industry area.[1]

In some instances, it must be admitted, there may be a conflict between the desire for consistency in the application of accounting principles and the desire for obtaining the most accurate absolute portrayal of results for a given period in the light of emerging experience. It is an unfortunate fact that the incidence of important costs can only be roughly estimated at a given time, and future experience may indicate that serious errors were made in the estimation process. The annual accruals of depreciation expenses on plant assets and of the appropriate costs incident to the funding of pension programs are perhaps the major culprits on this score. If developments through time indicate that these costs have been estimated on the basis of projected data which experience now indicates to be in error, then corrections in the interest of "truth" in setting forth the current results would seem entirely justified.

It would be difficult indeed to argue with this proposition as stated. However, in many cases the revealed truth would also suggest the complete restatement of the past earnings reports for perhaps a decade or more. But conventional accounting practices usually extend only to the correction of the current year, or possibly one preceding year, and not to the complete series of past reports which theoretically would be affected by the new knowledge. The extensive effort involved in such restatements plus the belief that results for previous years are of only academic interest may be responsible for prevailing practice. However, when substantive corrections in the basis for major expense determinations have been made and the retroactive effects are ignored, then the comparability of the accounting data through time might be seriously impaired for investment

---

[1] See, *e.g.*, Douglas A. Hayes, *Investments: Analysis and Management 196–241* (1961); Benjamin Graham, David L. Dodd and Sidney Cottle, *Security Analysis 121–70* (4th ed. 1962).

analysis purposes. For example, the computation of meaningful long-term growth rates from such data may become exceedingly difficult if not impossible.

In connection with the above problem, the question might legitimately be raised as to whether the public accounting firms should not be charged with the duty to require restatement of the financial statements of prior years when experience suggests the need to revise the basis for the determination of significant expense items. The argument for raising the question would rest in the language of the conventional auditor's report pursuant to an unqualified opinion on the financial statements. Typically such a report includes the following language:

> In our opinion, the accompanying consolidated balance sheet and consolidated statements of income and retained earnings present fairly the financial position of the ——— Company as of [date] and the results of its operations for the year then ended, in conformity with generally accepted accounting principles applied on a basis *consistent* with that of the preceding year. [Emphasis added.]

Such language would seem to justify the supposition, for example, that if the percentage rates at which existing depreciable assets are charged off are changed, then the new rates would be retroactively applied to determine the depreciation expense of prior years to reflect the conditions that presumably induced the deviation in the write-off period. If the retroactive adjustments were not made, the language to the effect that accounting principles have been consistently applied through time hardly appears justified.

However, a convenient distinction has been developed in the accounting profession to distinguish between accounting *principles* and accounting *procedures*. Principles apparently are considered to be limited to the broad policy concepts related to the preparation of the financial statements; as an example take the idea that cost should be the primary measure of value of depreciable assets and that in some fashion the cost should be allocated against the revenue stream over the useful life of the assets. The example mentioned is generally regarded as the "cost principle." But the means used to implement this principle have been relegated to the status of procedures.[2] Therefore, if the estimates of useful life on given depreciable assets are changed due to new information, it is argued that retroactive adjustments are not required because there has merely been a change in procedure and not in the principle that an amortization of cost over the useful life should govern the write-off period.

Therefore, the fact that a company may radically revise its methods for determining depreciation rates, such as a change from a straight-line method to an accelerated method, is not considered to be a deviation from the consistent application of accounting principles. Moreover, under ex-

---

[2] Kemp, "Controversies on the Construction of Financial Statements," 38 *Accounting Rev.* 126, 128–29 (1963).

isting conditions in accounting practice, alternative procedures yielding widely different cost allocations in given years may be applied to identical assets by different firms, and all may receive an unqualified auditor's opinion that their statements have been prepared in conformity with generally accepted accounting principles.[3]

The semantic arguments that have been advanced in order to define and restrict the province of accounting "principles" as contrasted to that of "procedures" or "methods" seem strained and contrived for a presumably highly practical profession. As so defined and restricted, principles *per se* are not likely to raise problems of consequence to investment analysis. Therefore, for purposes of the subsequent discussion, a broader definition of accounting principles will be employed to include many of the problems of consistency and comparability that in a literal definitional sense may arise from differences in procedures or methods.

II. INCOME DETERMINATION: CONFLICT IN ACCOUNTING PRINCIPLES

The investment analyst is concerned only with an evaluation of the future return opportunities and risks within a given enterprise. Therefore, accounting data are useful only to the extent they provide clues to these opportunities and risks. As a consequence, it would be desirable for the income statements to reflect only that flow of revenues, costs, and related income that seems pertinent to future operations. Similarly, the balance sheet would be stated in a form to reflect clearly the financial obligations of the firm, the nature of the assets, and the equity of the shareholders. Then, as brought out above, from a series of such statements it is anticipated that an insight into the potential trends and fluctuations of these items can be obtained.

As a consequence of these objectives of investment analysis, it would follow that (1) transactions involving gains and losses to the firm that are unusual or nonrecurring in nature should be excluded from reported income and (2) all financial commitments related to future operations would be clearly presented in the balance sheet. Some generally accepted accounting principles, however, do not necessarily reflect these views on the preparation of financial statements.

With respect to the first concept, considerable controversy has existed within the accounting profession between those advocating the "all-inclusive" concept of net income and those advocating the "current operating performance" concept.[4] Proponents of the all-inclusive concept take the position that all items that increase or decrease the equity of the owners in

---

[3] *Id.* at 129.

[4] The terms are in current usage within the accounting profession. *E.g.*, Committee on Accounting Procedure, AICPA, *Restatement and Revision of Accounting Research Bulletins* 60 (Accounting Research Bull. No. 43, 1953).

the business, except dividend distributions and capital stock transactions, should be included in net income. In contrast, the current operating performance view is that net income should reflect only that flow of income incident to the actual operating conditions of the period.[5]

Clearly, it is the latter view that would be preferable for investment analysis purposes. However, the research committee of the American Institute of Certified Public Accountants unfortunately takes an equivocal position on the matter. It is first held that there should be a general presumption that all items of profit and loss recognized during a period should be included in determining net income; then it is stated that certain exceptions in the form of specified extraordinary items *may* be excluded; and finally it is stated that these items "*should* be excluded when their inclusion would impair the significance of net income so that misleading inferences might be drawn therefrom."[6] Moreover, to the distress of financial analysts, the Securities and Exchange Commission has taken a similarly equivocal position. It originally supported the view that all items of gain or loss should be reflected in the income statement and then subsequently compromised this position by allowing (not requiring) special items to be reported after arriving at the net income figure.[7]

The result of the indecisive posture of both the AICPA and the SEC has been a hodgepodge of treatment of special gains and losses both as between companies and within the same company. The SEC itself has made the damaging admission that its examination of reports to stockholders "reveals that some companies have a tendency to report favorable items in the income statement and unfavorable items as direct charges to earned surplus without adequate comment elsewhere."[8]

Table 1 provides an illustration of an inconsistent treatment of special gain and loss items and of the problems for investment analysis that ensue. These data show that the net income before federal taxes of Cowles Magazines and Broadcasting Inc. declined in 1964 from 1963 by more than $2 million. But, paradoxically, reported net income after taxes actually increased by $326,000 in 1964 from 1963 levels because of a decrease in the provision for income taxes of $2.3 million. While the corporate tax rate did decline modestly in 1964, a considerable portion of the greatly reduced tax accrual ($972,000) was due to tax recovery resulting from the liquidation of a subsidiary. This item could clearly be labeled a special gain item as it might be legitimately supposed that liquidations of subsidiaries are not a recurring and normal element in the operations. Therefore,

---

[5] For the detailed arguments advanced for each of these views, see *id.* at 60–62.

[6] *Id.* at 63.

[7] See statement prepared by the office of the chief accountant, SEC, filed by the Commission with the Subcommittee on Commerce and Finance, House of Representatives, Feb. 19, 1964, *J. Accountancy*, June 1964, p. 56, at 57–61.

[8] *Id.* at 59.

under the current operating performance concept of net income determination, the tax recovery would have been shown as a special addition to the statement subsequent to the determination of the net income figure.

Indeed, it can be noted that in 1964 the special loss item consequent to the revaluation of an investment in another corporation was in fact treated as a direct deduction from earned surplus rather than allowed to reduce reported net income. In short, it appeared that the all-inclusive concept of special items was applied to such gains while the current operating performance concept was applied to losses of a similar sort.

TABLE 1

COWLES MAGAZINES AND BROADCASTING INC.—CONDENSED INCOME AND SURPLUS STATEMENTS
(In Thousands of $)

	1963	1964
Revenues	$128,065	$133,302
Costs and expenses	120,690	127,940
Income before taxes	$ 7,375	$ 5,361
Federal taxes on income:		
Currently payable (after recoverable taxes in 1964 of $972,000 resulting from liquidation of a subsidiary)	2,993	741
Deferred taxes	897	809
Net income for year	$ 3,485	$ 3,811
Add: Earned surplus, beginning of year	8,522	10,173
Deduct:		
Appropriation for revaluation of investment in General Development Corporation to approximate market	—	2,384
Deficit of Star Publishing Co. as of January 1, 1963	694	—
Earned surplus, before dividends for year	$ 11,313	$ 11,600

SOURCE: Annual Report for 1964.

Finally, it might be mentioned that despite the apparent inconsistency in the treatment of these items, the company's statements received the standard unqualified opinion from a leading public accounting firm.

As suggested earlier, the major social impact of the inconsistent, and indeed sometimes conflicting, accounting principles applied to special gains and losses bear on the relatively unsophisticated investor. As adequate disclosures are usually made, the trained professional can adjust reported net income for such items without great difficulty. However, nonprofessionals more than likely accept net income and related earnings per share without a critical examination of their composition.[9] Moreover,

---

[9] In the statistical investment services—*Moody's Investors Service* and *Standard and Poor's Corporation Service*—the earnings per share of Cowles Magazine and Broadcasting Inc. were reported as $1.17 for 1963 and $1.28 for 1964 without comment. It might be presumed that the data presented in these services are widely used by nonprofessionals.

it may be conjectured that many, if not most, nonprofessional investors find the terminology and explanations of these items more confusing than enlightening. Disclosure is useful; but if an intelligent interpretation of the disclosed items depends upon a thorough knowledge of the subtleties of accounting theory, the objectives of disclosure, i.e., to promote intelligent decision making, may be largely forfeited. In short, the position taken by the SEC as to its power over accounting matters under the Securities Act of 1933,[10] that its role should be limited to requiring full disclosure of financial facts and that it should not regulate the form and method of disclosure, may be questioned if protection of the nonprofessional investor is considered to be among the SEC's primary social objectives.

III. INCOME DETERMINATION: RECOGNITION OF SUBSIDIARY EARNINGS

For legal, tax, or other reasons the modern corporate complex often includes a number of separate legal entities that typically operate as an integral group in the production and distribution of the product line. Under these conditions the investor in the parent company is primarily interested in the earning potential and financial soundness of the entire economic entity rather than in any particular legal component. The general view in investment analysis is that the composite earnings and obligations more appropriately measure the investment opportunities and risks within the enterprise. The only major exception would be where the security being evaluated occupies a creditor position against subsidiary operations without the guarantee of the parent. Such securities, however, are rarely found in the securities markets today.

By and large, generally accepted accounting principles agree with this view.[11] However, two difficulties arise in implementing the general principle. First, it is held that consolidation should take place only when there is "a controlling financial interest," which in turn is defined as ownership of more than fifty percent of the voting shares.[12] Second, on the ground that currency conversions may be restricted and devaluation risks may be great, the implementation recommendations are only permissive with respect to foreign subsidiaries.[13] It is notable that the bulletin with respect

---

[10] Section 19(a), 48 Stat. 85, as amended, 15 U.S.C. § 77s(a) (1964).

[11] The Committee on Accounting Procedure, AICPA, has gone on record as follows: "There is a presumption that consolidated statements are more meaningful than separate statements and that they are usually necessary for a fair presentation when one of the companies in the group directly or indirectly has a controlling financial interest in the other companies." Committee on Accounting Procedure, AICPA, "Consolidated Financial Statements 41" (*Accounting Research Bull.* No. 51, 1959).

[12] *Ibid.*

[13] Committee on Accounting Procedure, AICPA, "Foreign Operations and Foreign Exchange 29–31" (*Accounting Research Bull.* No. 4, 1939).

to foreign subsidiaries originally appeared in late 1939 when restrictions on the convertibility of currencies were widespread and the hostilities in Europe had begun. In view of the subsequent balance of payments difficulties of this country, the argument now appears considerably less persuasive if not obsolete; yet no evidence can be found that the 1939 statement on the recognition of foreign subsidiary earnings has been modified. Indeed, it was reiterated in the 1953 restatement of the Research Bulletins in essentially the same language.[14]

The view that more than fifty percent ownership should be the normal prerequisite to consolidation seems unduly rigid for investment analysis purposes. While this rule is perhaps in accord with literal legal theory,

TABLE 2

KIMBERLY–CLARK CORPORATION—ADJUSTMENT FOR EARNINGS OF AFFILIATES
(In Millions of $)

	1961	1962	1963	1964	% Increase 1961–64
Affiliate dividends to parent	$ 1.9	$ 1.9	$ 1.9	$ 2.3	
Equity in earnings of affiliates	2.1	.8	1.6	1.1	
Excess (deficiency) of earnings over dividends	$ .2	$(1.1)	$ (.3)	$(1.2)	
Reported earnings	$31.4	$31.5	$33.9	$35.8	14.2%
Add (deduct): Difference between earnings of affiliates and dividends received	.2	(1.1)	(.3)	(1.2)	
Adjusted earnings	$31.6	$30.4	$33.6	$34.6	9.4%

SOURCE: Annual Reports for 1961–1964.

control can in fact be exercised and the operations essentially integrated with the parent company when 50 percent or less of the voting stock is held, especially if a significant segment of the balance is held by friendly parties. When consolidation of affiliates (the usual term for companies actually controlled) is not effected, then the earnings of the parent company will include only dividends actually paid by the affiliates to the parent although supplementary disclosure of the parent's equity in the total earnings of such affiliates has been held desirable. Because the parent company may vary the proportion of affiliate earnings distributed in the form of dividends, the actual earnings performance of the entire corporate group, which is of primary concern to investors, may be significantly different than reported.

An example might be useful to clarify this important point. Table 2

[14] Committee on Accounting Procedure, AICPA, "Restatement and Revision of Accounting Research Bulletins 112" (*Accounting Research Bull.* No. 43, 1953).

shows the reported earnings for Kimberly–Clark Corporation, a leading producer of tissue and book papers, for the fiscal years 1961–64. These earnings, however, reflected only the actual amounts of dividends received from several Canadian affiliates that produce wood pulp and other raw materials mainly for the parent company. Therefore, the table also indicates the earnings that would have been reported had a full consolidation been effected of the affiliates' earnings, which would seem reasonable in view of the close operating relationships. While the differences between dividends received from these affiliates and the equity of Kimberly–Clark in their total earnings were not substantial in any given year, the fact that dividends received were less than such earnings in 1961 and greater in 1964 had a significant impact on the indicated growth rate. As reported, the company showed a growth in earnings of 14.2 percent from 1961 through 1964, but, when earnings were adjusted for differences in the proportion of affiliates' earnings declared as dividends, the earnings growth was only 9.4 percent. As the growth rate factor is a very important element in investment appraisals, it could be argued that reported earnings significantly distorted important data for investment decision purposes.

It is true that adequate disclosures of the data necessary for the adjustments were made in footnotes to the several annual reports. But each year was considered separately for this purpose, and the facts for prior years were not reported in each of the current years. Therefore, even professional analysts, unless extremely careful in their analytical procedures, might have failed to discern the true pattern of the earnings performance, especially as the differences in any one year did not appear significant in amount. As a solution to the problem, it might be recommended that the current income statement and the financial summaries of prior years show clearly in some fashion the total earnings performance of the entire operating group including closely allied affiliates prepared along the lines of Table 2.

Turning ourselves to the question of foreign subsidiaries, the prevailing recognized practice that earnings derived from foreign operations can either be fully consolidated or alternatively recognized only to the extent of dividends remitted to the parent company creates analytical problems both as outlined above and also with respect to the comparability of companies within a given industry area. For example, in the office equipment industry, foreign operations are usually of considerable importance to most leading companies in the field. Yet as shown in Table 3, Burroughs Corporation follows the practice of fully consolidating its worldwide operations whereas National Cash Register Company makes a deduction on its income statement for net earnings of foreign subsidiaries and branches not remitted to the United States. As a result, legitimate comparisons of these companies' performances—as to rates of return obtained on investment and earnings trends, for example—would require the adding back of the unremitted foreign earnings to the reported net income of National Cash Register.

As the full consolidation method used by Burroughs has become the preferred practice in recent years, it is, therefore, paradoxical to note that the data supplied by National Cash Register offer more complete information on the important matter of the geographic sources of net income than do the data supplied by Burroughs. For example, in investment appraisals, the value ascribed to net income derived from foreign sources may be quite different than that attached to domestic earnings because of greater political and economic uncertainties abroad.

TABLE 3

NATIONAL CASH REGISTER COMPANY VERSUS BURROUGHS CORPORATION—TREATMENT OF FOREIGN EARNINGS
(In Millions of $)

	1961	1962	1963	1964
National Cash Register Co.:				
Reported net income:				
Foreign subsidiary dividends	$10.0	$ 8.7	$10.8	$10.5
Domestic and Canadian	11.7	11.9	9.3	12.0
Total reported income	$21.7	$20.6	$20.1	$22.5
Unremitted foreign earnings	8.4	2.6	2.3	3.7
Total: full consolidation assumed	$30.1	$23.2	$22.4	$26.2
Burroughs Corporation:				
Reported net income: full consolidation	$10.5	$ 9.5	$ 8.5	$10.2
Foreign earnings; before U.S. taxes:[1]				
Foreign dividends received	7.3	4.4	.2	6.1
Unremitted foreign earnings	3.9	5.1	9.4	5.9
Total	$11.2	$ 9.5	$ 9.6	$12.0

[1] Computed from data provided in "Financial Review" section or footnotes to annual reports. Information not provided on income statements.
SOURCE: Annual Reports for 1961–64.

In the case of National Cash Register, the amounts of net income derived from each source after appropriate tax allocations were fully disclosed in the statements or footnotes thereto. However, neither in the body of its reports nor in the related discussion has Burroughs Corporation shown the proportion of after-tax net income derived from various sources. The amounts of foreign net earnings and gross dividends remitted were given in a "Financial Review" accompanying the income statement, but the U.S. income taxes payable on such dividends were not shown. As the income statement proper revealed net income only on a fully consolidated basis after all taxes, the proportion of net earnings derived from foreign sources could only be roughly estimated via making an assumption as to the amount of income taxes properly applied to foreign dividends. In short, for investment analysis purposes, effective comparability between companies with significant foreign operations would require that the principle of full consolidation be supplemented with disclosure as to the geographic sources of net income on some reasonable basis.

In order to make similar distinctions regarding the "quality" of earnings, a theoretically "ideal" income statement for investment analysis purposes would reveal the amounts of sales, expenses, and net income by major product lines. Wide diversification of product lines has become increasingly common through mergers and acquisitions in the postwar years. The Olin Mathieson Chemical Company complex of divisions and subsidiaries represents perhaps the extreme of such diversification, its products including chemicals, drugs, cement, metals, and firearms. As the growth and stability prospects for the several industry areas included in the product line may be quite different, an income statement showing the amounts of sales, and possibly earnings, derived from each would be quite helpful in an investment appraisal of such a company. But when requesting such information, the analyst is typically told that such breakdowns are not available for "competitive reasons."[15] As it has been alleged that competitors in one way or another often obtain much of this information about a given company, it is difficult to appraise the legitimacy of this reason for withholding disclosure. On the positive side, it may be mentioned that some leading companies with diversified product lines—for example, International Harvester and FMC Corporation—do reveal a breakdown of dollar sales by major product categories although not the amount of net income derived from each.

IV. TAX REGULATIONS AND ACCOUNTING PROCEDURES

The principle that statutory law and regulations thereunder pertaining to the computation of corporate taxable income should not necessarily determine the computation of net income reported to shareholders has been clearly stated in the AICPA's Research Bulletin No. 43 as follows: "Sound financial accounting procedures do not necessarily coincide with the rules as to what shall be included in 'gross income' or allowed as a deduction therefrom, in arriving at taxable net income."[16] Unfortunately, the language of this statement, like others found in the research bulletin guidelines, is permissive rather than strongly positive, possibly because it might be difficult to obtain consensus approval of a strong statement. Therefore, some companies, so far as can be determined from an analysis

---

[15] At a financial analysts meeting in Detroit a few years ago, the author pressed officials of the Ex-Cell-O Corporation for a breakdown in sales and profit margins by major product lines. The officials used "competitive reasons" as the grounds for refusing to disclose the information, and several practicing analysts stated that even in private interviews managements typically will give only very general intimations as to the relative importance of various product lines to sales and earnings.

[16] Committee on Accounting Procedure, AICPA, "Restatement and Revision of Accounting Research Bulletins 76" (*Accounting Research Bull.* No. 43, 1953).

of their annual reports, have departed from the recommended principle and have allowed the tax rules to control the determination of important expenses on the income statement, whereas others have used conventional accounting concepts to determine expense allocations when the tax rules diverge from such concepts.

The latter approach unquestionably is preferable for investment analysis purposes because considerations other than the objective of determining net income in a rational and consistent manner affect the tax rules. For example, national economic policy objectives to stimulate capital investment and to encourage the expansion of productive capacities deemed essential to national security have been incorporated into various tax provisions. Moreover, the tax rules have been notoriously unstable in certain respects, as frequent amendments to the tax statutes and the related regulations have become customary in recent years. The result has been a deplorable morass of questionable reliability of many income statements, inconsistencies through time in expense determination methods, and lack of comparability between companies within the same industry.

The expense deductions for depreciation and amortization have probably been the main problem area. But others could be cited—for example, whether foreign earnings should be considered subject to the federal income tax in the year earned or when remitted to the parent company, as the tax rules allow deferment of payment until actual remission is made. However, because of their dominant and general importance, the issues surrounding depreciation practices deserve special emphasis.

The major steel companies have been among those that have created considerable problems for investment analysts by allowing the tax rules to control the annual allowance for depreciation on their income statement supplied to shareholders. The consequent inconsistencies through time in the determination of this expense by these companies are suggested by the following statement by Inland Steel Company in its annual report for 1964:

Prior to 1962, Inland and its subsidiaries applied accelerated depreciation methods to property additions made since January 1, 1954, as permitted by the 1954 Revenue Code. For additions made before 1954, depreciation charges were calculated on a straight-line basis or on a sliding scale based on the rate of production. Depreciation charges for 1962, 1963, and 1964, are based on the guidelines issued by the Treasury Department in 1962, using accelerated depreciation methods for property additions made since January 1, 1954 and the straight-line method for assets acquired prior to 1954.[17]

Moreover, it may be noted that in the mid 1950's when 5-year amortization of a major portion of new facilities was permitted for national defense reasons, such amortization was also fully deducted as a normal operating expense on the income statements of Inland Steel.

---

[17] 1964 Inland Steel Co. Ann. Rep. 4.

The preposterous results ensuing from following the tax rules in determining depreciation charges are shown in Table 4. From the table, it can be noted that the average annual depreciation deduction on the income statement for the 1962–64 period was about $61.3 million as compared to $39.4 million in 1959–61, an increase of about 55 percent. The increase in depreciation charges in the single year of 1962 to $60.7 million from $42 million in 1961, or by 40 percent, was particularly remarkable as during that year gross plant assets subject to depreciation charges increased by only 4.3 percent. As a so-called "fixed expense" item in the short run, depreciation charges would ordinarily be expected to decline as a percentage of sales as sales increase, but between 1959 and 1964 the data show that annual sales increased from $705 million to $883 million, or by about

TABLE 4

INLAND STEEL COMPANY—ANALYSIS OF DEPRECIATION CHARGES: 1959–64
(In Millions of $)

	1959	1960	1961	1962	1963	1964
Depreciation	$ 35.2	$ 41.0	$ 42.0	$ 60.7	$ 60.6	$ 62.5
Gross plant assets	$822.5	$881.2	$896.7	$935.1	$1,017.3	$1,139.9
Depreciation as % of plant assets	4.2%	4.6%	4.6%	6.5%	6.0%	5.5%
Sales	$705.1	$747.1	$724.6	$760.1	$ 808.1	$ 883.0
Net income	$ 48.3	$ 47.0	$ 54.7	$ 52.5	$ 56.1	$ 71.1
Depreciation:						
% of net income	73.0%	87.0%	76.0%	114.0%	108.0%	88.0%
% of sales	5.0%	5.4%	5.8%	8.0%	7.5%	7.0%

SOURCE: Annual Reports for 1959–64.

25 percent, yet depreciation as a percentage of sales also moved upward from 5 percent to 7 percent.

Whether depreciation rates were too low in 1959–61 or too high in 1962–64 in relation to the effective useful lives of the plant assets could not be entirely determined. However, in its 1963 annual report, Inland Steel offered the following statement:

> It is encouraging that the Treasury Department through the guideline rules issued in 1962, recognized that numerous and rapid changes in technology in recent years have shortened the average economic life of steel mill equipment. Certain of the guideline lives are still excessively long. . . .

While this claim may be partially discounted as an attempt to secure more favorable tax treatment (which the stockholder might applaud), it represented at least some evidence that depreciation rates were excessively low prior to 1962 and that, as a consequence, true earnings were less than reported earnings in the earlier years.

But in any event, the important fact was that reported earnings prior to

1962 were not comparable for trend analysis purposes with those reported subsequently because of a discretionary increase in depreciation rates engendered by changes in the tax rules. As a solution to the problem, it might be suggested that when material changes are made in the basis for the determination of financial statement items, companies should be required to supply supplementary information as to these items adjusted to current practices for perhaps four or five prior years.

However, in the specific instance considered above, such retroactive adjustments would still not make the earnings comparable with other companies that have adopted the procedures recommended in Research Bulletin No. 43. In essence, the recommendation here is that companies should determine depreciation rates via a conventional method without regard to the tax rules and preferably maintain reasonable consistency in this method through time. Then if the allowable depreciation charges for tax purposes exceed those deducted for statement purposes, a deferred tax reserve should be established to equalize the tax accruals over the write-off period. Because comparability and consistency of reported earnings is maintained under this procedure, it can be regarded as highly preferable for investment analysis purposes.

V. THE INTERSTATE COMMERCE COMMISSION AND ACCELERATED DEPRECIATION

The jurisdiction of the Interstate Commerce Commission over the accounting practices of the railroads led many years ago to the prescription of a uniform system of accounts to be followed by all railroads in reporting to the ICC. For financial analysis purposes, some of the results were highly salutary. First, the railroads were required to disclose considerable detail with respect to their financial and physical operations. Second, the analyst obtained exact comparability in these data among all railroads. A major drawback, however, has emerged in recent years that can only be characterized as a lack of flexibility to adjust the accounting regulations to changes in the institutional factors bearing on appropriate accounting procedures, notably in the taxation area. For example, in 1956, the Commission denied a petition to modify the uniform system of accounts to require that provision be made for federal income taxes deferred as a result of deducting accelerated amortization of certain facilities for tax purposes but not on the statements submitted to stockholders.[18]

But finally, in 1962, the ICC issued an order that in substance permitted, but did not require, that financial statements submitted in annual reports could be prepared "in conformity with generally accepted accounting principles for which there is authoritative support," provided

---

[18] "Interstate Commerce Commission Jurisdiction Over Financial Statements in Reports to Stockholders," in 7 Arthur Andersen & Co., *Cases in Public Accounting Practice* 4 (1962).

variances from the prescribed procedures were disclosed.[19] Unfortunately, however, many if not most of the railroads have not yet taken advantage of this permissive order, and the result has been a serious overstatement of reported earnings in many cases. The overstatement results from the fact that plant facilities are being amortized more rapidly for tax purposes than on the published income statements, yet no provision is made for deferred tax liability that is clearly consequential to such a procedure. Most railroads have apparently taken the position that until the need for the deferred tax accrual is recognized in the uniform system of accounts, it will not be incorporated in their formal statements submitted to shareholders.[20]

For example, Table 5 shows selected items from the consolidated

TABLE 5

ATCHISON, TOPEKA & SANTA FE RAILWAY COMPANY—ADJUSTMENT FOR DEFERRED TAXES RESULTING FROM ACCELERATED DEPRECIATION
(In Millions of $)

	1961	1962	1963	1964
Per Statement:				
Net income before taxes	$92.1	$87.6	$82.5	$88.7
Income taxes	35.8	14.2	11.2	8.0
Reported net income	$56.3	$73.4	$71.3	$80.7
Supplementary information:				
Estimated tax adjustments (net)	6.2	25.3	24.8	26.8
Net income adjusted	$50.1	$48.1	$46.5	$53.9

SOURCE: Annual Reports for 1961–64.

income statements of the Atchison, Topeka & Santa Fe Railway Company, for the years 1961–64, and also the estimated annual provision for deferred taxes computed from information supplied in the body of the report to stockholders for each year. This information, it should be emphasized, was not referred to or shown in the financial statements themselves. Moreover, the explanations were phrased in rather technical language, which the ordinary investor would find quite difficult to understand. A thorough professional analyst, however, should have been able to make the indicated adjustments without great difficulty.

[19] Id. at 9.

[20] The following statement illustrates the policy of a major railroad in this regard: "Each Annual Report since 1951 has explained the variances in earnings that result because income statements to the Interstate Commerce Commission, and as shown in this report, do not correspond with the manner in which the reporting is made to the Internal Revenue Service for tax purposes." 1964 Atchison, Topeka & Santa Fe Ry. Ann. Rep. 4. The statement suggests that the company, despite the 1962 permissive order from the ICC, intends to continue to report to stockholders in accord with the uniform system of accounts.

But to allow, if not encourage, the preparation of income statements on a basis that permits a gross overstatement of reported net income plus a probably erratic and noncomparable flow of such income through time seems open to serious criticism. Therefore, unless the uniform system of accounts prescribed by the ICC becomes more responsible to new institutional conditions, particularly in the taxation area, it can only be concluded that the ICC regulation of accounting practices has operated to the serious disadvantage of investors. In fact, the current procedure in determining the effective tax liability incident to periodic income is so flagrantly misleading that it might conceivably support a charge of substantive deception.

VI. THE "INVESTMENT CREDIT" DILEMMA

Presumably in order to stimulate an increase in business expenditures for plant and equipment, the Revenue Act of 1962 provided for an "investment credit" deduction from currently payable income taxes equal to specified percentages of certain depreciable assets acquired after 1961.[21] The 1962 statute provided that the amount of the credit must be deducted from the cost basis of the facilities subject to subsequent depreciation for tax purposes, but in 1964 the statute was amended to eliminate the requirement that the investment credit be deducted from the cost basis of eligible properties.[22]

The Accounting Principles Board of the AICPA originally held that the investment credit should be interpreted as "a reduction in or offset against a cost otherwise chargeable in a greater amount to future accounting periods" and that, as a result, "the allowable investment credit should be reflected in net income over the productive life of acquired property and not in the year in which it is placed in service."[23] But in 1964 the APB modified its position to hold that while the same treatment "should be considered to be preferable, the alternative method of treating the credit as a reduction of federal income taxes of the year in which the credit arises is also acceptable."[24] Therefore, in full accord with authoritative statements on appropriate accounting principles, companies may follow quite different methods of treating the investment credit with the result that comparability of earnings amounts, trends, and rates of return both within and between companies may be seriously impaired. The problem appears particularly acute in those industries that tend to acquire large blocs of

---

[21] Int. Rev. Code of 1954, §§ 38, 46–48, added by Revenue Act of 1962, §§ 2(a)–(b), 76 Stat. 962.

[22] Int. Rev. Code of 1954, § 48(g), repealed by Revenue Act of 1964, § 203(a), 78 Stat. 33.

[23] Accounting Principles Board, AICPA, *Accounting for the "Investment Credit"* 2–3 (Opinion No. 2, 1962).

[24] Accounting Principles Board, AICPA, *Accounting for the "Investment Credit"* 2 (Opinion No. 4, 1964) (amending Opinion No. 2).

eligible assets in given years and little if any such assets in other years. The reason is that those companies following the practice of deducting the entire investment credit from taxes in the year in which the assets are acquired would have a large reduction in taxes in one year due to the credit and little such reductions in other years. As a result, substantial changes in the level of reported net income may arise solely due to the timing of equipment acquisitions and the consequent investment credits that become available.

For example, Pan American World Airways reported net income in the amount of $37.1 million in 1964 as compared to $33.6 million in 1963. However, in 1964, the company adopted the practice of reducing federal income taxes by the entire amount of the investment credit resulting from equipment acquisitions in that year, which increased earnings by $6 million alone.[25] In other words, if consistency had been maintained in the method of accounting for the investment credit, earnings would have declined in 1964 instead of showing a substantial growth as reported. If flight equipment acquisitions decline in 1965, it would seem entirely possible for reported earnings after taxes to decline even though pre-tax earnings increase, because of the reduced availability of the investment credit. It should be evident that obtaining an insight into the real economic trends of a firm's activities may become considerably more difficult under these conditions. Moreover, reported earnings are not comparable between firms treating the investment credit in different ways or even between firms with different timing in their equipment acquisitions.

The Accounting Principles Board gave two reasons for modifying its position with respect to the appropriate treatment of the investment credit.[26] The first was that, as modified in the 1964 Revenue Act, the credit could be logically construed as a rebate of taxes applicable to the year in which eligible facilities are acquired. As this reason is based on one plausible interpretation of the actual nature of the transaction, it can only be questioned on the basis that, nonetheless, an alternative interpretation is preferable for analysis purposes. The second reason advanced, however, is open to a more fundamental type of criticism. It was that a "significant number" of companies, and also, most unfortunately, the SEC, did not adopt the original recommendation for the treatment of the investment credit. Therefore, because the opinion did not receive general acceptability, the Board felt obliged to modify its position. This type of reasoning has disturbing general implications. It suggests that a position on an accounting principle is not necessarily based on whether its logical structure is actually correct or not but depends only on whether, regardless of a principle's logical foundations, its general acceptance is effectively

---

[25] *1964 Pan American World Airways Ann. Rep.* 20.

[26] Accounting Principles Board, AICPA, *Accounting for the "Investment Credit"*
2 (Opinion No. 4, 1964) (amending Opinion No. 2).

achieved in practice. Under this approach, it would seem that the Board's opinion on important principles may be based on an empirical review of what actually *does* exist in practice rather than what *should* exist as a consequence of conclusions derived from objective reasoning. Can one conclude that popularity rather than objective logic may determine the formulation of authoritative opinions on accounting principles and procedures?

VII. STATEMENTS OF FINANCIAL POSITION: OF LESSER SIGNIFICANCE

Attention has been concentrated on the accounting issues surrounding the determination of periodic net income because such income is the basic source of investment returns and economic values in most publicly held corporations. For investment analysis purposes, therefore, the statement of financial position (balance sheet) is of distinctly secondary importance in most cases. Exceptions might, of course, be noted, such as cases of companies in the process of liquidation or merger or perhaps more notably certain natural resource companies where estimated reserves of the particular resources may be of considerable importance in the determination of investment values.

In the typical corporation, statements of financial position are used in investment analyses in perhaps two principal functional ways. The first is largely negative in concept. It is to determine if the company may encounter temporary or permanent trouble because of excessive debt assumption or its equivalent. The second involves the use of the balance sheet as one element in measuring rates of return obtained on the total invested capital at the disposal of management or, alternatively, on the effective capital contributed to the enterprise by the shareholders (net worth).

Prevailing financial reporting procedures are adequate for the most part in achieving these objectives. The amounts of net worth and contractual liabilities on debt obligations are usually clearly disclosed and the final maturities, or their range, on long-term debt are indicated. Moreover, if certain liabilities are secured by a pledge of specific assets, the nature of the lien position is customarily indicated at least in general terms. Two issues, however, might be briefly mentioned in this respect. First, it is not customary in the statement, or in the footnotes thereto, to reveal compulsory or contingent sinking fund requirements under bond trust indentures or preferred stock contracts. Similarly, the detailed breakdown of serial maturities, if used on long-term debt, is not typically reported. As the timing and possible concentration of repayments on debt principal may be pertinent to a conclusion on the financial vulnerability of a company, this information would appear desirable. And, as a matter of fact, the stated position of the accounting profession holds that "whenever these stipulations are significant to an adequate interpretation of the financial statements they should be described in the face of the balance sheet or the notes thereto."[27] Therefore, the failure to disclose these data may be ascribed to a lack of implementation of an avowed recommendation in practice rather than to the accounting profession's silence or equivocation on the point.

The second issue is with respect to accounting for obligations under long-term lease commitments. With regard to such obligations, it should first be mentioned that the established position of both the accounting profession and the SEC is that the contractual amounts of minimum annual lease payments, as distinguished from contingent amounts, should be disclosed together with "the period over which the outlays will be made."[28] Therefore, the analysis issue is not with respect to disclosure. However, it might be suggested that, because a large portion of lease rentals often are the functional equivalent of interest charges (a contractual payment for capital provided to acquire the leased facilities), the minimum contractual annual lease rental payments should be shown on the income statement under a general caption "Interest Charges and Contractual Lease Rentals" with the amounts in each category then shown separately thereunder. This recommendation is made because it is the general and appropriate practice of financial analysts to include a portion, if not all, of minimum annual lease rentals in the computation of "fixed charges" used to compute the "times fixed-charges earned" ratio.[29] This ratio, it might be mentioned, is the principal quantitative measure of the investment quality of the debt obligations and the financial soundness of a company.

Apart from the form of disclosure, the remaining issue is whether a portion or all of the contractual long-term lease rentals should be capitalized at an appropriate rate and recognized as a liability in the statement of financial position matched by an equivalent recognition of the leased facilities in the property accounts. A research study, sponsored by the AICPA, concluded that rights to use leased properties are conceptually economic assets and that, to the extent that the assumption of contractual lease payments represents the acquisition of such rights, the present value of such payments should receive appropriate recognition in the assets and liabilities.[30] However, the official position of the accounting profession to date is that formal recognition in the statement of financial position of the

---

[27] Paul Grady, "Inventory of Generally Accepted Accounting Principles for Business Enterprises 285" (*AICPA Accounting Research Study* No. 7, 1965).

[28] Accounting Principles Board, AICPA, "Reporting of Leases in Financial Statements of Lessee 32" (*Opinion* No. 5, 1964).

[29] Graham, Dodd and Cottle, *op. cit. supra* note 1, at 402-03.

[30] John H. Myers, "Reporting of Leases in Financial Statements 38" (*AICPA Accounting Research Study* No. 4, 1962).

value of leased properties, along with the related liability, should occur only if the lease contract is in substance an installment purchase.[31]

In any event, it is clear that the accountants have oriented their discussion of the issue to theoretical legal or economic concepts. In contrast, investment analysis circles tend to debate the issue on the grounds of the need to achieve analytical comparability between different firms in the same industry, some of which lease a large portion of their facilities while others own them outright. One view is that "no valid comparison can be made between the bonds of the owning and those of the renting enterprises without a capitalization of all or some portion of the rentals paid."[32] The other view, held by the author, is that the basic determination of the relative and absolute investment qualities of bond issues and companies in general is obtained largely from an appraisal of the earnings protection afforded the contractual charges and not from balance sheet proportions of debt to equity. Therefore, elaborate techniques to establish such effective proportions are of dubious significance in reaching investment decisions. Moreover, the legal remedies for a default on lease payments are considerably different from those for a default on debt, so the view that capitalized lease rentals essentially represent a debt obligation seems to be of questionable validity. For these reasons, it is concluded that a recognition of a balance sheet liability implicit in lease contracts is not of major importance for investment analysis purposes.

VIII. CONCLUSION

The foregoing discussion had been largely concerned with certain specific issues in accounting principles and procedures that affect the usefulness of accounting data in appraising the quality and values of corporate securities. Therefore, it might be well to conclude by setting forth some broad guidelines that, if adopted generally in the preparation of accounting reports, would greatly improve their reliability and consistency and the comparability of financial statements generally. Along these lines, Professor Herbert E. Miller, a leading academic accountant, has suggested several basic guidelines for accounting principles that, if adopted, would undoubtedly make financial reports more useful and intelligible to investors. In summary, his points may be listed as follows.[33]

1. Financial statements should reflect an objective and impartial report on management's performance.
2. The accounting profession has the obligation to correct any deficien-

---

[31] Accounting Principles Board, AICPA, "Reporting of Leases in Financial Statements of Lessee 32" (*Opinion* No. 5, 1964).

[32] Graham, Dodd and Cottle, *op. cit. supra* note 1, at 361.

[33] Miller, "Audited Statements—Are They Really Management's?," *J. Accountancy*, Oct. 1964, p. 43.

cies in financial statements that impair an objective evaluation of managerial performances.
3. Disclosure of the use of unusual accounting principles or procedures in technical footnotes to the statements should not be regarded as alleviating the responsibility of the public accountant for their use in statements which receive unqualified opinions.
4. The accounting profession should not tolerate or advocate an "either-or" position on alternative procedures because of some uncertainty concerning which alternative is best. It should make a single choice from among the alternatives, even though some practitioners might dissent from the choice, in the interests of improved consistency and comparability.
5. Management's freedom of action in choosing alternative accounting procedures that have a material effect on the reported results should be strictly limited, if not eliminated, as there is a natural inclination for management to select the alternative that will make its position appear most favorable.
6. The outside auditor and *not* management should be in full control of the "ground rules" for the preparation of financial statements. Improved consistency and comparability cannot be achieved under the basic presumption that financial statements are primarily the responsibility of management, subject merely to modifying constraints of law and accepted principles in certain respects but with alternatives open for choice in many areas.

It would be sanguine to expect that the above guidelines will receive general implementation within the foreseeable future. Nevertheless, they do provide a clear and unequivocal framework for the development of more useful accounting data. Therefore, financial analysts would be well advised to support vigorously the above recommendations. The result may be at least evolutionary improvements in accounting standards to provide more reliable, consistent, and comparable financial statements.

2

ACCOUNTING FOR INFLATION—
A FIELD TEST*

Paul Rosenfield

Eighteen companies recently participated in a field test of general price-level accounting and many of the participants were surprised with the results. In spite of the modest rate of inflation in the United States in recent years, differences between financial statement amounts before and after restatement for general price-level changes were significant for many of the companies. The differences varied widely from company to company and even between years for the same company. Net income was a larger amount after restatement than before restatement for some companies and a smaller amount for others.

THE RESEARCH PROJECT

The field test is part of a program of the Accounting Principles Board to determine appropriate accounting under conditions of inflation. The program started in 1961 when the Board concluded that "the assumption in accounting that fluctuations in the value of the dollar may be ignored is unrealistic. . . ."[1] An accounting research study was authorized at that time in which "special attention was to be paid to the use of supplementary statements as a means of disclosure."[2]

The research study was published in 1963. It recommends that companies present supplementary financial statements in which all elements have been restated for changes in the general level of prices (inflation or deflation).[3] The study maintains that these "general price-level financial statements" should "provide a basis for a more intelligent, better informed allocation of resources. . . ."[4]

---

* Reprinted by permission of *The Journal of Accountancy* (June 1969). Copyright 1969, American Institute of Certified Public Accountants.

[1] Minutes of the Accounting Principles Board, April 28, 1961.

[2] *Ibid.*

[3] Accounting Research Study No. 6, *Reporting the Financial Effects of Price-Level Changes*, by the staff of the accounting research division (New York: American Institute of Certified Public Accountants, 1963). The conclusions of the study are summarized by Cecilia Tierney in "Price-Level Adjustments—Problems in Perspective," *JofA*, Nov. 63, pp. 56–60.

[4] ARS No. 6, p. 16.

GENERAL PRICE-LEVEL FINANCIAL STATEMENTS

General price-level financial statements deal with the problem of inflation (or deflation)—that is, with changes in the *general* level of prices. They do not deal with the problem of changes in *specific* prices of goods and services. They are based on the same generally accepted accounting principles as conventional ("historical-dollar") financial statements except that changes in the general purchasing power of money are recognized. All items in the restatements are given in a unit of measure which represents the same amount of general purchasing power—the general purchasing power of the dollar at the balance sheet date.

Changing the unit of measure does not change the bases of accounting. Assets are stated generally at cost and not at current value in general price-level balance sheets. The cost is restated for changes in the general purchasing power of the dollar but not for changes in the specific prices of the assets. The realization rule applies, and unrealized gains and losses are generally excluded from income in restated financial statements as they are in conventional statements.

General price-level financial statements contain one type of item not presented in historical-dollar statements—gains or losses of general purchasing power from holding money, receivables, payables, and other "monetary items" during inflation. Holders of monetary assets, such as cash, lose general purchasing power during inflation—for example, the value of cash in a checking account decreases as prices in general rise. Those who owe money gain during inflation because the debts can be paid off in "cheaper" dollars. These gains and losses may be called "general price-level gains and losses" because they are the direct result of changes in the general price level.[5] General price-level accounting brings to light these otherwise hidden results of doing business in an inflationary economy.

In short, general price-level financial statements are similar to conventional statements in that they preserve the cost basis and the realization rule, and they are different in two respects:

1. They present all financial statement items in a unit of measure that represents the same amount of general purchasing power—the general purchasing power of the dollar at the balance sheet date.
2. They report general price-level gains and losses that result from holding monetary assets and liabilities during inflation or deflation.

THE FIELD TEST

The Accounting Principles Board considered the accounting research study and comments on the study received from interested persons. It

---

[5] Gains and losses of this type are often called "purchasing power gains and losses" in discussions of general price-level accounting, but the term "general price-level gains and losses" is preferable to distinguish them from other gains and losses of general purchasing power experienced by business enterprises.

formed tentative conclusions and recommendations concerning voluntary disclosure of supplementary general price-level financial statements. These conclusions and recommendations were incorporated in 1968 in a "research draft" of a proposed pronouncement by the Board.

Actual prior application of general price-level principles and proce-

FIGURE 1

INFLATION IN THE UNITED STATES AS MEASURED BY GROSS NATIONAL PRODUCT IMPLICIT PRICE DEFLATORS
(1945–1967)

Year	Index Number (1958 = 100)	% Rate of Inflation (Deflation)
1945	59.7	2.6
1946	66.7	11.7
1947	74.6	11.8
1948	79.6	6.7
1949	79.1	(.6)
1950	80.2	1.4
1951	85.6	6.7
1952	87.5	2.2
1953	88.3	.9
1954	89.6	1.5
1955	90.9	1.5
1956	94.0	3.4
1957	97.5	3.7
1958	100.0	2.6
1959	101.6	1.6
1960	103.3	1.7
1961	104.6	1.3
1962	105.7	1.1
1963	107.1	1.3
1964	108.9	1.7
1965	110.9	1.8
1966	113.9	2.7
1967	117.3	3.0

SOURCE: United States Department of Commerce, *Survey of Current Business*, issued monthly.

dures in practice in the United States had been somewhat limited, however, and the Board felt that more knowledge of the practical effect of restatement was needed before moving ahead. A field test was therefore authorized which would test restatement procedures and give an indication of the effects of the inflation actually experienced in the United States in recent years. Eighteen companies were asked to restate their financial statements for changes in the general price level in accordance with guidelines recommended in the research draft. Managements of the companies were also asked to comment on the feasibility of general price-level restatement.

The companies involved in the field test vary in size and type. Most of them are listed on stock exchanges, but a few are relatively small or closely held. Industries represented by the companies include aircraft manufacture, airlines, automobile parts, chemicals, electronics, fabricated metal products, food processing, food retailing, finance companies, measuring devices, oils, packaging, paper, retail stores, and gas and electric utilities.

Each company restated the financial statement of its most recent fiscal year or its most recent two fiscal years; in general the statements cover 1966 and 1967.

Results of the field test should be evaluated in the context of the relatively moderate inflation of the recent past. Figure 1 presents yearly inflation since 1945. The amounts are based on the index of the general price level recommended for use in general price-level accounting (the Gross National Product Implicit Price Deflator).

The participating companies submitted their restated statements to the accounting research division of the AICPA. Figure 2 presents highlights of the results for the 18 companies (identified by the letters A to R). Five types of items are highlighted:

1. Net income (column 1).
2. General price-level gains and losses (column 2).
3. Federal income taxes (columns 3 and 4).
4. Cash dividends (columns 5 and 6).
5. Rate of return (columns 7 and 8).

NET INCOME

Several features concerning net income are brought out by the percentages in column 1:

Wide Variation. Differences between net income on the general price-level basis and on the historical-dollar basis varied widely. One company showed no difference while all but one other company showed differences of almost every magnitude from 4 percent to 31 percent. Several companies showed considerable variation in results between years.

Company D showed differences of 233 percent and 434 percent. These differences, however, should be interpreted in the light of the very small restated net income (.7 percent of average owners' equity for the second year—see column 7). If restated net income of Company D had represented a rate of return similar to that of the other companies in the field test, the same differences in amount would be much smaller percentages of restated net income.

The variations demonstrate that inflation does not affect financial statements alike, and that comprehensive restatement is needed to determine the effects on a particular company.

"Understatement" and "Overstatement." Using net income under general price-level accounting as the standard, the field test showed that ignoring inflation in historical-dollar statements results in understating net

FIGURE 2
GENERAL PRICE-LEVEL ACCOUNTING FIELD TEST
(Highlights of Results)

Company and year	Net income difference* (%) (Col. 1)	General price-level gains and (losses) % of restated net income (Col. 2)	Effective federal income tax rate (%) Restated (Col. 3)	Effective federal income tax rate (%) Historical (Col. 4)	Cash dividends (% of net income) Restated (Col. 5)	Cash dividends (% of net income) Historical (Col. 6)	Rate of return on owners' equity (%) Restated (Col. 7)	Rate of return on owners' equity (%) Historical (Col. 8)
A	4	4	39	38	61	58	14.2	16.7
B—1st year	0	19	44	43	52	50	n.a.	n.a.
2nd year	0	22	44	44	49	48	12.0	13.0
C—1st year	5	3	49	47	36	33	n.a.	n.a.
2nd year	14	5	50	47	50	44	13.2	15.8
D—1st year	233	(271)	75	47	n.d.	n.d.	n.a.	n.a.
2nd year	434	(542)	82	46	n.d.	n.d.	.7	3.7
E—1st year	(30)	50	31	38	54	74	9.3	10.3
2nd year	(25)	52	25	30	52	69	8.1	9.7
F	10	3	n.a.	n.a.	49	44	n.a.	n.a.
G	8	(1)	12	11	66	61	12.5	15.9
H—1st year	20	(5)	39	34	90	72	7.5	10.3
2nd year	18	(3)	41	37	86	72	7.9	10.5
I—1st year	11	8	50	46	63	54	n.a.	n.a.
2nd year	15	22	50	46	58	50	15.1	18.1
J—1st year	15	5	50	46	37	32	11.4	13.9
2nd year	29	8	56	49	65	50	6.4	8.8
K	12	7	41	38	49	43	12.6	16.1
L	13	9	36	34	92	80	n.a.	n.a.
M—1st year	(10)	13	35	38	21	22	n.a.	n.a.
2nd year	(9)	22	30	31	29	32	14.0	15.0
N—1st year	4	(7)	50	48	n.a.	n.a.	n.a.	n.a.
2nd year	12	(7)	48	45	n.a.	n.a.	n.a.	n.a.
O	28	(11)	57	50	78	60	n.a.	n.a.
P—1st year	(26)	49	31	36	48	62	n.a.	n.a.
2nd year	(31)	59	21	27	56	79	4.9	5.8
Q	(12)	36	37	39	24	27	n.a.	n.a.
R—1st year	21	20	52	46	37	29	n.a.	n.a.
2nd year	15	6	50	46	46	39	13.0	15.6

* Percent that historical-dollar net income is higher (lower) than restated net income in terms of restated net income.
Note: n.d. = no dividends; n.a. = not available.

income for some companies and overstating net income for other companies. In countries which have experienced severe inflation, understatement or overstatement of net income by ignoring inflation can be of such magnitude that it can cause historical statements to "lose their practical significance."[6]

"Ballooning" Effect. Inflation in the United States averaged about 2 percent per year in the 15 years to 1967, and did not exceed 3.7 percent in any year during that period. Nevertheless, 27 of the 29 differences in net income exceeded 3.7 percent, and many were several times as great as the most severe inflation in recent years. The results show that a ballooning effect causes relatively modest rates of inflation to be magnified in net income.

The ballooning effect has two causes. First, net income is a small amount in relation to many of the other amounts in a set of financial statements. Small changes in relatively large amounts in the statements, caused by moderate inflation, may be substantial in relation to net income. Large inventories stated at Fifo cost, for example, can cause this effect. To illustrate, a company on the historical-dollar basis has a net income of $900,000 during a year in which the general price level rises 2 percent, and has a $5 million inventory at the beginning and end of the year. The beginning inventory, a charge in the income statement, is restated by 2 percent more than the ending inventory, a credit. The 2 percent additional charge, which amounts to 2 percent × $5,000,000 = $100,000, is substantial in relation to the net income of $900,000.

Second, depreciation, depletion, and amortization are related, in many cases, to assets bought years before the balance sheet date. Restatement of the cost of the assets and the related depreciation involves the cumulative compound amount of inflation since the assets were purchased. According to the data in Figure 1, the inflation between 1957 and 1967 was $(117.3 - 97.5) \div 97.5 = 20.3$ percent. Depreciation in 1967 on an asset bought in 1957, therefore, would be restated by 20.3 percent, not by just the 3 percent inflation of 1967.

Crosscurrents. Restatement increases some amounts and decreases other amounts which are components of net income. Restating revenue in a period of inflation tends to increase the amount at which net income is stated, and restating expenses tends to decrease it. Furthermore, restatement may result in reporting a general price-level gain or loss on monetary items which is included as a component of net income in accordance with the Board's research draft.

These crosscurrents can cause restated net income to be approximately the same as historical-dollar net income, even though individual items in the income statement differ significantly on the two bases. For example, net income was unchanged for Company B although the company had

---

[6] *Accounting Research Bulletin* No. 43, chap. 9A, para. 13.

substantial general price-level gains (see column 2 in Figure 2) which offset higher restated expenses. The effect of restatement is magnified when most of the items reinforce rather than offset each other, as for Company D in the test (see Figure 2).

Nature of Company Operations. The complex way in which inflation affects companies and financial statements makes generalizations hazardous about the effect of restatement on the financial statements of companies in particular industries. Companies in any industry may have restated results that vary widely.

Certain observations may, however, be made concerning the effect of the nature of company operations on the restatement process. First, capital-intensive companies tend to be affected more by restatement than others. Depreciation charges are more substantial, and restatement of these charges for the inflation since acquisition of the assets is a major factor in these companies. Second, companies with rapid turnover and, consequently, with relatively low inventory in relation to sales are less affected than companies with expensive, slower moving inventory. Third, financing plays an important role. Debtors gain and creditors lose in an inflationary economy. Companies that must carry heavy receivables bear general price-level losses on them. Companies that finance their operations more heavily with debt gain more from inflation than those which rely more heavily on equity financing. General price-level gains on debt are offset, of course, by increasing interest rates as the rate of inflation rises. Borrowers in countries with severe inflation must pay high interest rates to compensate their creditors for losses the creditors suffer due to inflation. Only general price-level financial statements show the general price-level gains of the borrowers which tend to offset the high interest charges.

Comparisons Affected. The impact on a company of restatement for general price-level changes cannot be determined solely by examining the financial statements of the company. The most important impact is the effect of restatement on comparisons between companies. For example, historical-dollar net income is 30 percent lower than restated net income for Company E and 20 percent higher for Company H (see column 1 in Figure 2). If Companies E and H had the same net income on the historical-dollar basis, restated net income of E would be 171 percent of restated net income of H.[7] Even if a company's restated net income is the same as its historical-dollar net income, as was the case with Company B (see columns 3 and 4 in Figure 2), restatement would affect comparisons with other companies whose restated net income differs from their historical-dollar net income.

---

[7] Seventy percent of restated net income of Company E = 120 percent of restated net income of Company H. Therefore, restated net income of Company E = 171 percent of restated net income of Company H.

OTHER RESULTS

General Price-Level Gains and Losses. Column 2 of Figure 2 presents the general price-level gains and losses reported by the companies, as percents of restated net income. These gains and losses are the net results of holding monetary assets and liabilities during the inflation that occurred in the year covered by the statements and are not reported in historical-dollar accounting.

Twice as many companies had general price-level gains as had losses. Several companies, especially Companies E and P, had very substantial general price-level gains in relation to restated net income. Company D had substantial general price-level losses from holding monetary assets that practically eliminated income from other sources.

Federal Income Taxes. Columns 3 and 4 in Figure 2 indicate the effective federal income tax rates for the companies both on the historical-dollar and restated bases. The effective rates are found by dividing the tax expense by the net income before taxes.

The Internal Revenue Code gives no consideration to general price-level changes and taxes dollar profits regardless of whether or not the profits represent increases in general purchasing power. For example, a purchase of an asset for $100 and a later sale for $105 during a period in which there was 5 percent inflation results in a $5 taxable profit in spite of the fact that the transaction results in no increase in general purchasing power. An opportunity for tax reform exists here—recognizing the effects of inflation in the tax law would result in more equitable treatment of taxpayers.

Effective federal income tax rates were lower on the general price-level basis than on the historical-dollar basis for companies that reported larger restated net income amounts than historical-dollar amounts. For example, Company E had a 31 percent restated rate compared with a 38 percent unrestated rate—a substantial difference. Companies that reported smaller restated net income amounts than historical-dollar amounts showed larger effective rates on the restated basis than on the unrestated basis. Although the historical-dollar statements for Company D show that 47 percent and 46 percent of its pretax income was paid in taxes, the restated statements show that 75 percent and 82 percent of its realized increase in command over goods and services in general was paid out to the federal government in income taxes.

Cash Dividends. Columns 5 and 6 of Figure 2 present cash dividends as a percent of net income on both the historical-dollar and restated bases. All companies, except the four that had a higher net income on the restated basis, showed cash dividends as a larger percent of restated than historical-dollar net income.

Cash dividends typically are considerably less than historical-dollar net income for the year. Earnings are retained for expansion, for contingencies, and so forth. One reason often stated for the retention of earnings is to maintain capital in the face of increasing general price levels. The AICPA has advised companies to explain this "need for retention of earnings" to readers of financial statements.[8] To the extent that historical-dollar net income exceeds restated net income, the earnings which "need" to be retained for this purpose can be seen to be "unreal"—they are a reported increase in number of dollars that is not matched by an increase in general purchasing power.

Rate of Return. Columns 7 and 8 of Figure 2 present the rate of return for the companies on both the historical-dollar and restated bases. The rate of return is computed by dividing the net income by the average of the beginning and ending owners' equity for the year.

The rate of return on the restated basis was lower than on the historical-dollar basis for every company in the test for which the rate of return was available. The rate is net income divided by average owners' equity: $\frac{NI}{OE}$. Restating owners' equity results in larger amounts for the divisor which more than offset the larger restated net income reported by Companies E, M and P. Companies which reported lower restated net income had even more markedly lower restated rates of return.

FEASIBILITY

Feasibility of preparing general price-level financial statements was discussed at a meeting with representatives of the companies that participated in the field test. Some of the companies encountered practical problems that would not have been found if they had prepared for restatement in advance. Records which otherwise would be maintained in the most usable form were not available and had to be constructed after the fact. Furthermore, restatement for the first year is more time-consuming than for subsequent years because analyses prepared in the first year can be used in subsequent years. Other practical problems cited include the possible unavailability of required records in foreign subsidiaries necessitating estimates of ages of assets etc., and the necessity for initial restatement for pooled companies. Nevertheless, the participants in general agreed that with proper preparation, practical problems should not present a significant barrier to preparation of general price-level financial statements.

ACCOUNTING AND INFLATION

The field test sponsored by the Accounting Principles Board was a broad test of general price-level principles and procedures. Although

---

[8] *Accounting Research Bulletin* No. 43, chap. 9A, para. 17.

statistically valid generalizations are not warranted by the sample of 18 companies, the results nevertheless seem to support the view of Accounting Research Study No. 6 that presentation of supplementary general price-level financial statements would make available potentially useful information that otherwise is not disclosed.

3

CORPORATE DIVERSIFICATION AND FINANCIAL REPORTING*

Leopold Schachner

Compared with the history of accounting, not to mention that of business enterprise, diversification is a rather recent development. It had its beginnings in the 1920's, gained momentum immediately after World War II, and increased further in the second half of the 1950's.[1] It might, therefore, be of interest to inquire as to how it may affect accounting methods and procedures. After all, the late accounting issues concerning leases, pension funds, the price level, and goodwill are the result of recent economic and business developments.

Specifically, if diversification is a rather recent phenomenon, then one may wonder whether the standards of reporting which have evolved in a period of specialized enterprise are still valid for firms engaged in several fields of endeavor. The financial statements that a company published in the days it was still specialized offered a report on a single product line. It would appear that such a report is crucial to the decision-making process of the investor, and its absence is an excessive compression of data. Operating reviews and other narrative materials do not lend themselves to precise interpretation and are therefore not suited to the forming of definitive conclusions. Yet, "the problems in the field of accounting have increasingly come to be considered from the standpoint of the buyer or seller of an interest in an enterprise"[2] (i.e., investment decisions). Using such criteria, financial reporting (to be distinguished from general corporate reporting) has hardly kept pace with the gradual shift of the larger enterprises from specialization to diversification.

Before proceeding further, it will be necessary to clarify the terms "diversification" and "diversified operations." Diversification may be defined as an act or policy of entering a new basic area of specialization, with reference to both production and markets. A company would de-

---

* Reprinted by permission of *The Journal of Accountancy* (April 1967). Copyright 1967, American Institute of Certified Public Accountants.

[1] Alfred D. Chandler, Jr., *Strategy and Structure* (Cambridge, Mass.: The MIT Press, 1962), pp. 383–396.

[2] *Accounting Research and Terminology Bulletins*, Final Ed., *AICPA*, 1961, p. 7.

liberately enter a substantially new production or technological base, as well as a new market area requiring substantial resources for the development of the new market—without entirely abandoning its old line of products or its old markets. It may be noted that diversification so defined implies expansion and growth as new activities are being entered into and old ones are not abandoned.

The definition will be roughly met by an entry into a new four-digit industry, as classified by the Standard Industrial Classification Code.[3] Use of the SIC Code would give product-line reporting a measure of uniformity. SIC numbers have been established by the U.S. Bureau of the Budget to facilitate the collection and interpretation of business data. All goods and services produced in the United States are divided into major industry groups, each of which is assigned a two-digit SIC Code. Each digit added to a Code number defines the industry and product more specifically. For example, SIC No. 28 refers to "Chemicals and Allied Products"; SIC No. 281 refers to "Industrial Inorganic and Organic Chemicals"; and SIC No. 2812 refers to "Alkalis and Chlorine." Thus, when a firm engaged in the production and sale of alkalis and chlorine is similarly engaged in inorganic pigments (SIC No. 2816), it would be considered to be engaged in two *product lines,* hence in diversified operations. For present purposes, the same definition may be applied to the term "conglomerate."

(Webster's Unabridged Third New International Dictionary offers the following meanings for "conglomerate":

As an adjective—made up of parts from various sources or composed of various kinds.
As a verb—to gather or collect into a mass or coherent whole: amass, accumulate.
As a noun—a mixture gathered from various sources.
"Conglomeration"—collection.

When used in business and industry as a noun or adjective, the term conglomerate connotes much diversity, vast size, and extreme unrelatedness. Conceptually, however, as far as accountability is concerned, the issues involved are the same as for any diversified firm. The difference is in degree, not in kind.)

The four-digit SIC industry is a very useful bench mark. In most cases, but not in all, products contained within a four-digit industry are made of similar materials, by similar processes and with similar equipment—all largely exclusive to the industry. In addition, the producers usually compete with one another throughout such a four-digit industry, but with no other industry. Again, the four-digit industry is meant to serve only as a bench mark, to be used with judgment, inasmuch as the exacting

---

[3] U.S. Technical Committee on Industrial Classification, *Standard Industrial Classification Manual* (Washington, D.C.: U.S. Government Printing Office, 1957).

criteria are not always met. Yet, in most cases, the products within a four-digit industry will substantially meet the listed criteria.

Need for Product-line Breakdowns

It is generally agreed that the omission of product-line breakdowns in financial statements is a severe handicap to analysis and the forecasting of future results. The Chairman of the Securities and Exchange Commission went as far as to say that "the effect of diversification has been, at times, to obscure financial information." He pointed out that merger frequency speeds the process of deterioration, for, if one specialized manufacturer (say, of office equipment) merges with another specialized form (say, a housewares manufacturer), the stockholders of both become in short order the recipients of figures which tell them very little about anything.[4]

Anyone only vaguely familiar with the projections involved in the analysis of securities can easily appreciate the importance of knowing the base before proceeding with projections. Not only the sophisticated analyst but also the average investor, if he is to make a businesslike decision, would want to know the contributions of the various product lines to net income. (We would not venture to offer a valid distinction between the two.) This being readily apparent, it may be appropriate to examine now in some depth some further and related aspects of reporting for the diversified firm.

Reporting for the Diversified Firm

As a company diversifies into a new industry, it increases its productive resources, broadens them, becomes more flexible, and extends its productive opportunities. In general, the cost of the new resources sooner or later is reflected as expenses in the annual income statements, *whether or not the full potential of these resources is realized in those years.* Full potential is not realized in any year in which resources committed to a diversification activity contribute a negative or a disproportionately small amount to net income. The charges may be included in such accounts as cost of sales, salaries and wages, research and development, depreciation and amortization, and advertising and promotion.

Very little of the essence of this new potential can be seen on the asset side of the traditional balance sheet. The balance sheet never gives any expression, of course, to the vital human resources in the possession of the enterprise, such as technologically skilled labor, research personnel, engineering skills, marketing organization, management services, and the more subtle qualities of special knowledge, operating experience, and teamwork. Nevertheless, for a specialized firm, a listing of physical resources may convey at least some notion of the existing human resources and the

---

[4] Manuel F. Cohen, Chairman, Securities and Exchange Commission, "The SEC and Accountants: Co-operative Efforts to Improve Financial Reporting," *JofA*, Dec.66, pp. 58–59.

amount invested in physical assets. The heterogeneous and more complex nature of the resources available to a diversified firm, and the respective investments, cannot be inferred from an unclassified listing of assets.

One of the basic difficulties with the income statement is that it offsets losses in one industry against earnings in another, or that it spreads total earnings of the enterprise over all its diversified operations. As will be seen shortly, this may have a very adverse effect on the market value of the shares of a diversified company. The offsetting or spreading process is even more serious for the earlier years of a company's entry into a new industry.

Diversification is a long-term strategy, and improvement in earnings may not be expected in the short run. Experience shows that diversification is generally not profitable in the earlier years and is often even a drain on the profits of established operations. Technological problems must be worked out and considerable promotional expenses must be incurred for the initial entry into new markets. Diversification tends also to be associated with disproportionately large expenditures for research and development in the earlier years. In addition, there are considerable expenses for training personnel which, when combined with the unavoidable trial-and-error costs at all levels of the organization, can have a significant impact. The result is that, in the case of internal diversification, short-run improvement in earnings is almost precluded.

Depreciation may also be a factor. Diversification appears to be associated with excess capacity in the short run. It would be uneconomical to build less than a minimum-sized plant, yet such a plant may far exceed immediate sales volume. Furthermore, companies enter an industry with a view to grow in it and usually envision a progressive increase in sales. They will, therefore, construct a plant to meet what they believe to be their intermediate needs, as it would not be economical or practicable to enlarge the plant for every increment in volume. Intermediate goals are not easily achieved, however, as firms do not enjoy the same advantage in new industries as they do in their established ones. To this may be added another factor: Companies cannot evaluate very well the possible expansion programs of other firms. As a result, there may be significant depreciation charges on idle capacity which may last for a number of years. The use of accelerated depreciation methods would aggravate the situation further, since the heaviest depreciation charges become concentrated in the earlier years of the investment. A diversifying company is by definition an expanding company, but of a peculiar type.

The observation on the adverse effect of diversification on short-run profitability applies chiefly to internal diversification, yet not exclusively. In the case of external diversification, where it is achieved by merger and acquisition, the short-run situation may be less adverse but will bear down on profits nevertheless. First, there are expenses associated with integrating the acquired enterprise into the enlarged entity, pruning and relocation expenses, and temporary inefficiencies in the period of adjustment at all levels of the organization—all of which are not necessarily confined to only one fiscal year. Second, external diversification is usually followed by further internal expansion into that industry, since it is this which most often makes a merger feasible; i.e., it enables the buyer to meet the seller's price. External diversification followed up by internal expansion will bring about a good deal of the short-run problems encountered under internal diversification. (According to one research study, the typical practice was to support internal diversification by a subsequent acquisition and to support the acquisition by additional internal expansion.[5]) It should also be pointed out that where an acquisition is financed by an exchange of shares, the expected or "intrinsic" earnings of the acquired enterprise will generally not increase earnings per share of the enlarged entity. The approximate amount of these earnings, adjusted for the benefits to be derived from the merger, become permanently assigned to the stockholders of the acquired enterprise by means of the shares issued to them. Yet any temporary decline in these earnings will, of course, reduce earnings per share. On the other hand, if an acquisition is financed by cash or debt, amortization of goodwill will generally wipe out all intrinsic earnings of the acquired company during the amortization period.

UNPROFITABLE OPERATIONS IN THE EARLY STAGES

The effect that an unclassified income statement may have on the market value of the shares of a diversified or diversifying company is perhaps best demonstrated by means of an illustration. Pittsburgh Plate Glass Company entered the fiber glass industry late in 1952. Operations were unprofitable for nearly nine years. The company encountered considerable technological difficulties despite its extensive research and development activities, the acquisition of a fiber glass manufacturing enterprise, and its deep roots in glass technology. Market difficulties were also encountered. It was not until 1962 that the company reported "encouraging progress in sales and earnings."

In an appearance before the New York Society of Security Analysts in 1960, the president of the company stated, "We have a tremendous stake in the fiber glass business and have passed through some very dark days." On the basis of indirect estimates, that stake may have been as much as $100 million, or $10 per share. Assuming that fiber glass operations reduced earnings per share in some years by 67 cents, and assuming a price-earnings ratio of 15, the resulting price decline would have been $10—to the extent that stock prices are determined by price-earnings ratios. On these assumptions, when an investor purchased Pittsburgh Plate stock in those years, he paid nothing for the fiber glass business, as it made

---

[5] Stanley S. Miller, *The Management Problems of Diversification* (New York: John Wiley & Sons, Inc., 1963), p. 11.

no positive contribution to earnings. But since it made a negative contribution, he received, in addition, a reduction in price equal to his share of the company's investment in that business. (Earnings per share for the years 1959, 1960, and 1961 were $4.11, $4.44, and $3.23, respectively.)

Now, the question is whether this really resulted in a fair price. Was not the fiber glass business worth at least something? If fiber glass had been set up as a separate corporation with its stock traded in the market, would its shares sell for less than nothing? Furthermore, in view of the fact that diversification almost always makes an unsatisfactory contribution to profits in the early years, should not an adjustment be made on that account? Should a reduced level of earnings, to the extent that it is caused by diversification, be treated the same as that attributed to primary industry operations? An affirmative answer to the last two questions would bring increased instability to the stock market and would be generally absurd if offered in response to the first two questions.

Primary industry operations—or traditional operations—may, of course, also have some unprofitable segments, such as certain products, territories, types of customers, foreign markets, and domestic outlets. These, too, may have been gained only after a considerable investment of human and physical resources. There is, however, a significant difference. Due to full product-line policies, market share considerations, and joint costs, there is less likelihood that the loss segments, even if thought to be permanent, would be wound up and terminated. This either does not apply to a diversification activity at all, or it does apply but to a lesser degree. Furthermore, for the early years of entry into a new industry, every company *must* apparently pass through an unsatisfactory profit stage in that new field. In brief, we must give cognizance to all characteristics peculiar to diversifications; i.e., all the things that diversification is and primary industry expansion is not. As a minimum, whatever the sacrifice in earnings, diversification does increase flexibility; it does offer the corporation a means of survival beyond the life cycle of a single industry.

The willingness and readiness of a management to carry through a significant diversification program should reflect well on it, as it is not an easy task. Many a management clung to its sole industry until it became too late. In a forward-looking inquiry into a relevant framework for disclosure, it was pointed out that "the presence of uncertainty suggests a needed modification in our concepts of rational actions by managers," and that there is "the possibility that managements may attempt to achieve other goals, in addition to profit maximization":

> The existence of uncertainty may require a modification in our concept of managerial effectiveness in the sense that uncertainty may lead to the pursuit of diverse or multiple goals. This possibility develops when managements, in an attempt to decrease the likelihood of or the adverse effects of unexpected events, strive for flexibility and security. Flexibility, the ability to change to

alternative plans, reduces the consequence of adverse events. The necessary investments to achieve flexibility may, however, require the foregoing of greater profits.[6]

It is, therefore, fair to assume that investors would want to measure both flexibility achieved and its cost in terms of profits foregone in order to avoid undervaluation of their investment. To do this they would need an analysis of the balance sheet and the income statement by product line.

Product-line Sectors

A diversified company will tend to be a divisionalized company, but the number of product-line sectors will not necessarily coincide with the number of divisions. More than one division may be engaged in the production and sale of a given product line; e.g., under geographical dispersion. Some divisions may manufacture intermediate products only, in the context of an integrated enterprise. A divisionalized company need not necessarily be a diversified company.

Any sector or facet of business activity which is deemed desirable to analyze may be designated an accounting entity for the purpose of collecting and reporting accounting data. The delineation of an entity provides a basis for defining the area of coverage appropriate to a given set of records and reports. A product-line sector may mark off such an entity and may comprise several divisions, including integration divisions —no matter what entity classifications are used for internal accounting purposes, often defined by reference to responsibility. Profit measurement will be successful if each product-line sector is as independent as possible of operation and performance elsewhere in the company.

Product-line sectors will never be completely self-contained and are not expected to be. Some degree of interrelationship would have to exist, with each product sector contributing something to the others; otherwise the corporation would, in effect, be administering a portfolio of discrete investments. Various services and activities may be performed centrally, such as data processing, executive training, engineering design, insurance coverage, market research, and economic forecasting. Product research may be carried out in a central research laboratory, while process research and development may be assigned to the product sectors. In addition, central research will also be engaged in projects which do not fall clearly into the area of any product line. Again, institutional advertising may be a central function, and product advertising that of the appropriate sector. There is a great deal of variation in these matters from company to company. For example, all advertising may be handled by a central department in which there are sections assigned to each product sector. Finally, while less important for product-line accounting than for divi-

---

[6] Jacob G. Birnberg and Nicholas Dopuch, "A Conceptual Approach to the Framework for Disclosure," *JofA*, Feb.63, p. 57.

sional accounting, there may be some intermediate-product transfers between sectors.[7]

When product transfers are made, a portion of the revenue of one sector becomes a portion of the cost of another, so that the price at which transfers are made can influence reported earnings. Gordon Shillinglaw observed that "many transfer pricing problems would disappear if the division structure could be reorganized around product lines," and again that "divisional boundaries should be established in such a way as to reduce the number of interdivisional transfers and to permit effective market checks on the realism of transfer prices."[8] Where the transfers to other sectors represent only a minor portion of the supplying sector's output, there is no significant problem. Transfer prices may be essentially the same as the prices charged to other customers. Market price may be modified by deducting from it a margin estimated to cover the saving of selling and collection expenses and bad debts on internal transfers. In practice it is also modified for other pertinent factors to arrive at a kind of net realizable value. Where the transferred intermediates are of a type not regularly sold to customers, the outside competitive market price should be used, if available. Many intermediate products are, to a certain extent, unique and it may be necessary to use market-based prices, at some loss of accuracy.

Use of Market Prices for Transfer Pricing

Market-based prices are still useful and may be obtained by a resourceful solicitation of bids or by reference to the company's own selling price for related products. Market-based prices may take on added significance when they result, in addition, from bona fide negotiations between the respective product sectors. Independent public accountants might sometimes want to check these prices against the standard cost of the transferred product, plus a "fair" return on the capital employed in its production, with further recourse to analyses of cost-price relationships in related products. What is really needed here is not perfection but adequate reliability. Even market price is hardly ever a fully reliable basis for transfer pricing, since perfectly competitive conditions exist only very rarely. Objectivity should present no obstacle for product-line reporting. Any data which are considered useful in reflecting the entity events, provided they are substantiated or capable of being substantiated by another competent investigator, are accepted as objective by most accountants:

---

[7] For an extensive discussion of divisional accounting, see David Solomons, *Divisional Performance: Measurement and Control* (New York: Financial Executives Research Foundation, 1965). This book also contains an ample bibliography.

[8] Gordon Shillinglaw, *Cost Accounting: Analysis and Control* (Homewood, Ill.: Richard D. Irwin, Inc., 1961), pp. 747–748.

In summary, data still need to be impersonal in order to be objective. However, "impersonal" is now much more flexible in its application than under the strict construction. If the data are considered useful in reflecting the entity events (and this appears to be the first requirement), they need not result from a bargained exchange between independent parties, just so long as they would fall within the limits set by this test. The amount need not be accurately determined, just so long as it can be reasonably approximated. And the accounting entity need not be one of the negotiating parties, just so long as it can reasonably be assumed that the results are the same as though it had been.[9]

Transfer pricing for product-line financial reporting is not concerned with the motivating aspect of pricing, which is very important for internal purposes, in that it is expected to prompt the divisions to act in a manner which is conducive to the success of the corporation as a whole. It is this, in combination with the fact that transfers between product sectors are not expected to be significant, that takes much of the sting and complexity out of the transfer pricing problem. Should a sector's shipments to other sectors constitute a substantial portion of its output and market prices were not reliably available, profit measurement would weaken, because it would become dependent on the formulas used to transfer pricing, and it may become necessary to combine the supplying sector with its most significant transferee sector. In the extreme case, the supplying sector may have to lose its status and be assigned the position of a service center. Its function would then be to serve other sectors, but it would not make a profit. Any sales made to outside parties would be accounted for by the general sector.

The general sector is a very useful entity in product-line accounting. The launching of new product-line ventures, some of which may be at various experimental stages, may be accounted for by this sector without disclosing their specific nature, if not material. Where applicable, infant entry may alternatively be accounted for by the product sector in which it is housed. Companies often set up new diversification moves in existing plants, if they do not require extraordinary processing facilities, in order to spread overhead and avoid unnecessary duplication of services. Some new ventures would collapse if they did not have the initial support of existing plant space and production services.[10]

Generally, the assets directly traceable to one or another of the product-line sectors will in the aggregate not account for all the capital invested in the enterprise. The more thorough the decentralization achieved, the less important the nonsector assets. Some shared corporate assets will still remain and may be accounted for by the general sector. Holdings of government obligations and minority interests in other companies are a primary example. Corporate fixed assets which serve several or all sectors, or are used in connection with central administration, may

---

[9] Harold E. Arnett, "What Does 'Objectivity' Mean to Accountants?" *JofA*, May61, p. 68.

[10] Stanley S. Miller, *op. cit.*, pp. 118-119.

be allocated to given sectors only if the use of these assets can be directly attributed to them on an incremental basis. Shared assets, such as buildings, may be allocated on the basis of occupancy; shared service departments on the basis of proportionate usage of the facilities. The fixed assets so allocated would become a part of the total fixed assets of the respective sectors. Fixed assets for which no direct relationship can be established would be distributed to the general sector. Cash and marketable securities would be held by the general sector, whether or not cash collections are centralized. Accounts receivable would be identified with the originating sector, even if held centrally. Inventories clearly belong to a specific sector, although shared raw materials may on occasion require a minor apportionment effort. In addition, the general sector would of course account for any assets related to (minor) product-line operations and assigned to it. Presented in Exhibit I, below, is a suggested form for analysis of assets by product line, which should also help restore to the balance sheet a further measure of significance.

EXHIBIT I
ANALYSIS OF ASSETS BY PRODUCT LINE
(Zeroes Omitted)

	Product Line A	Product Line B	Product Line C	General Sector	Total
Cash				$ 32	$ 32
Marketable securities				19	19
Receivables, net	$ 72	$ 41	$ 29	5	147
Inventories	78	57	35	8	178
Prepaid expenses	8	5	3	2	18
Investments				61	61
Plants and equipment	270	110	50	45	
Less accumulated depreciation	(165)	(45)	(18)	(27)	220
Other assets	17	12	3	14	46
Total Assets	$280	$180	$102	$159	$721

This appears to provide an adequate analysis of the balance sheet and is concerned with total assets; i.e., total capital invested. With no attempt to ascertain where it came from (sources), it is assumed to flow from a common corporate pool. For this reason all financing, including current debt, is deemed to be handled at the corporate level. For analysis of the income statement by product line, the form which appears in Exhibit II, page 44, is suggested.

The calculation of incremental central expenses chargeable to the sectors should be made by the head office personnel most familiar with each expense. These expenses cover services which the sectors would have to purchase outside, if they were not provided by the staff or service departments located at corporate headquarters. The cost of these services

—such as data processing, engineering design, market research, executive development, and product advertising—can be charged to sectors in a manner that would roughly equate the charges made with the cost of the services rendered. These charges will be shown as "incremental central expenses" only if they were not already itemized as depreciation, research and development, advertising and promotion, and cost of sales. Research and development, as well as advertising, often represents a very important part of total costs, and, in addition, their extent is believed to be closely correlated with profitability and growth potential. Each sector will also show its part of the corporate income taxes, in proportion to the share of the company's *taxable* income earned by it. A product sector making a

EXHIBIT II
ANALYSIS OF INCOME STATEMENT BY PRODUCT LINE

	Product Line A	Product Line B	Product Line C	General Sector	Total
Sales					
Transfers to other sectors					
Total					
Cost of sales and transfers					
Transfers from other sectors					
Depreciation					
Research and development					
Advertising and promotion					
Other operating expenses					
Incremental central expenses					
Allocated central expenses					
Other charges (credits)					
Income taxes					
Total					
Net Income					

loss would receive a negative tax apportionment, as the tax figure is meant to reflect the approximate increment in the company's tax liability resulting from a sector's operations.

Allocated central expenses, theoretically not identifiably incremental, are charged to product sectors and to the general sector, although not directly related to their activities. These expenses must be covered before the company as a whole can earn a profit. Included here are such items as central administration, institutional advertising, certain research, and interest. The allocations being in the final analysis arbitrary, they are shown separately on the analysis schedule to avoid misinterpretation. Allocation methods and rationale were widely discussed in the literature published by the National Association of Accountants. Revenues and losses generated by assets held by the general sector would be attributed to that sector only. Thus, dividends and interest on corporate investments and gains or losses on the sale of investments, or on disposals of head office buildings, would be general sector items.

Technical details will not be discussed, but it should perhaps be pointed out that the elimination of intercompany profit in ending inventories would require an equal elimination in the accounts "transfers to other sectors" and "transfers from other sectors." The income of the supplying sector would be reduced to the extent that a portion of the transfer is still held by the transferee sector. Total "transfers to" will always be equal to total "transfers from."

Summary

Several general observations will be offered as concluding comments. It is commonplace that there is at present no uniformity in accounting methods and practices. But anyone arguing this point against product-line reporting will have to show that it is more crucial here than it is for conglomerate reporting. On the contrary, more detailed reporting will make it possible to indicate the accounting methods employed by the various product lines, so as to facilitate analysis of consequences.

The kind of product-line information needed for external reporting is generally accumulated anyway for managerial purposes. Depending upon internal accounting procedures, disclosure may require some reclassification but will not entail substantial effort or outlay.

Further study in expense allocation will be needed, as allocation methods would be put to a new use when employed for published statements in this manner. However, there is no reason to believe that independent public accountants will be unable to certify product-line reports without qualification, if the basis of allocation were disclosed.

The reason most frequently advanced against product-line disclosure is that it may result in competitive disadvantage and be injurious to the profit position of the firm. It was pointed out repeatedly, however, that competitors already know a great deal about one another and that competition is in fact an excellent place to obtain withheld operating data. Furthermore, the degree of detail outlined above would ordinarily not be sufficient to benefit competitors. The larger a firm's position in a given industry, the less likely is it to incur a competitive disadvantage by disclosure. Initial protection for infant entry into a new industry, if deemed desirable, can be afforded by the concept of materiality.

The suggested form for product-line analysis will go a long way to facilitate evaluation methods used by financial analysts. Knowledge of the relative profit contribution of each product line to net income, when used with caution, will enable them to apply several price-earnings ratios to a single company. Different industries command different price-earnings ratios.

In the limited space available it is not possible to deal with every conceivable criticism. One may not even be able, perhaps, to answer convincingly every conceivable objection. Yet, this need not necessarily negate the proposals made. A system must be evaluated in its totality, both for what it offers and for what it does not offer. Also, this applies not only to the proposed system; it applies equally to the one long in use.

Showing a loss for a product line for several years may very well cause some stockholders to demand its discontinuance, which may not be desirable from a long-term point of view. However, this appears to be merely another item in the program of educating stockholders. Furthermore, expected reaction may even be beneficial, in that it may discourage management from engaging in excessive industry-hopping. The yearning for the seemingly greener pastures of other industries is one of the more regrettable features of the diversification movement. Finally, it may encourage improvements in internal accounting procedures and refinement in measuring product-line earnings, so as to avoid subjecting management to unwarranted criticism that may result from inaccurate presentation of performance.

It will be necessary to establish materiality standards for product-line reporting. These standards should preferably not be oriented toward the "average prudent investor," or "reasonable person," the perennial unknowns. The frame of reference should rather be expected interpretation when applying the best methods of financial analysis. Accountants would have to study carefully the possible interpretations of the measuring devices normally derived from the data by security analysts.[11] Such an approach offers objective guideposts. The valuation of common stocks is no easy task even when employing the best theories and techniques of financial analysis. Financial statements are meant to be instrumental in the performance of this task.

---

[11] Donald Rappaport, "Materiality," *JofA,* Apr.64, pp. 42–48.

4
AUDITS OF CORPORATE ACCOUNTS*

Editorial Comments: The following letter is one of a series of exchanges between the then American Institute of Accountants (now the American Institute of Certified Public Accountants) Committee on Co-operation with Stock Exchanges and the Committee on Stock List of the New York Stock Exchange. The subject discussed in this letter is the annual reports of corporations, and while the letter is dated 1932, it discusses many items that are the subject of interest today, such as:
  the role of the balance sheet and the income statement, the role of individual judgment in accounting statements, the place of consistency and standardization in accounting statements.
  The Exhibits referred to in the text are omitted. Exhibit I included five detailed accounting guidelines which have been generally accepted. Exhibit II listed guidelines for adequate disclosure of the accounting methods used.
  The letter became one of the bases of the Security and Exchange Commission's original financial reporting and certification requirements.
  Other items of correspondence in the series include concurring letters by nine accounting firms and by the Controllers Institute of America.

AMERICAN INSTITUTE OF ACCOUNTANTS
Incorporated under the Laws of the District of Columbia

NOTE

The accompanying communication addressed by this committee to the Committee on Stock List of the New York Stock Exchange was placed in evidence by the chairman of that committee in a hearing before the United States Senate committee on banking and currency January 12, 1933, and is now circulated for the information of members of the Institute and others interested.

ARCHIBALD BOWMAN
ARTHUR H. CARTER
CHARLES B. COUCHMAN
SAMUEL D. LEIDESDORF
WILLIAM M. LYBRAND
GEORGE O. MAY, *Chairman*

Special Committee on Co-operation with Stock Exchanges

---

*Reprinted by permission of the American Institute of Certified Public Accountants.

SEPTEMBER 22, 1932.

THE COMMITTEE ON STOCK LIST,
  New York Stock Exchange,
    New York, N.Y.
DEAR SIRS:

In accordance with suggestions made by your Executive Assistant, this Committee has given careful consideration to the subject of the general line of development of the activities of the Exchange in relation to annual reports of corporations.

It believes that there are two major tasks to be accomplished—one is to educate the public in regard to the significance of accounts, their value and their unavoidable limitations, and the other is to make the accounts published by corporations more informative and authoritative.

The nature of a balance-sheet or an income account is quite generally misunderstood, even by writers on financial and accounting subjects. Professor William Z. Ripley has spoken of a balance-sheet as an instantaneous photograph of the condition of a company on a given date. Such language is apt to prove doubly misleading to the average investor—first, because of the implication that the balance-sheet is wholly photographic in nature, whereas it is largely historical; and, secondly, because of the suggestion that it is possible to achieve something approaching photographic accuracy in a balance-sheet which, in fact, is necessarily the reflection of opinions subject to a (possibly wide) margin of error.

Writers of text-books on accounting speak of the purpose of the balance-sheet as being to reflect the values of the assets and the liabilities on a particular date. They explain the fact that in many balance-sheets certain assets are stated at figures which are obviously far above or far below true values by saying that the amounts at which such assets are stated represent "conventional" valuations. Such statements seem to involve a misconception of the nature of a balance-sheet.

In an earlier age, when capital assets were inconsiderable and business units in general smaller and less complex than they are today, it was possible to value assets with comparative ease and accuracy and to measure the progress made from year to year by annual valuations. With the growing mechanization of industry, and with corporate organizations becoming constantly larger, more completely integrated and more complex, this has become increasingly impracticable. From an accounting standpoint, the distinguishing characteristic of business today is the extent to which expenditures are made in one period with the definite purpose and expectation that they shall be the means of producing profits in the future; and how such expenditures shall be dealt with in accounts is the central problem of financial accounting. How much of a given expenditure of the current or a past year shall be carried forward as an asset can not possibly be determined by an exericse of judgment in the nature of a valuation. The task of appraisal would be too vast, and the variations in appraisal from year to year due to changes in price levels or changes in the mental attitude of the appraisers would in many cases be so great as to reduce all other elements in the computations of the results of operations to relative insignificance.

Carrying the thought one stage further, it is apparent that the real value of the assets of any large business is dependent mainly on the earning capacity of the enterprise. This fact is fairly generally recognized by intelligent investors as regards capital assets such as plant and machinery, but it is not equally generally recognized that it is true, though to a lesser extent, in respect of such assets as inventories and trade accounts receivable. Those, however, who have had experience in liquidations and reorganizations realize that in many industries it becomes impossible to realize inventories or accounts receivable at more than a fraction of their going-concern value, once the business has ceased to be a going concern. To attempt to arrive at the value of the assets of a business annually by an estimation of the earning capacity of the enterprise would be an impossible and unprofitable task. Any consideration of the accounts of a large business enterprise of today must start from the premise that an annual valuation of the assets is neither practical nor desirable.

Some method, however, has to be found by which the proportion of a given expenditure to be charged against the operations in a year, and the proportion to be carried forward, may be determined; otherwise, it would be wholly impossible to present an annual income account. Out of this necessity has grown up a body of conventions, based partly on theoretical and partly on practical considerations, which form the basis for the determination of income and the preparation of balance-sheets today. And while there is a fairly general agreement on certain broad principles to be followed in the formulation of conventional methods of accounting, there remains room for differences in the application of those principles which affect the results reached in a very important degree.

This may be made clearer by one or two illustrations. It is a generally accepted principle that plant value should be charged against gross profits over the useful life of the plant. But there is no agreement on the method of distribution. The straight-line method of providing for depreciation which is most commonly employed by industrial companies, the retirement-reserve method used by utilities, the sinking-fund method, the combined maintenance-and-depreciation method, and others, are supported by respectable argument and by usage, and the charges against a particular year may vary a hundred per cent or more according as one or the other permissible method is employed.

Again, the most commonly accepted method of stating inventories is at cost or market, whichever is lower; but within this rule widely different results may be derived, according to the detailed methods of its application. For instance, at times like the present, cost of finished goods may be deemed to be the actual cost, as increased by subnormal operation, or a normal cost computed on the basis of a normal scale of operations. It may or may not include interest during the period of production or various kinds of overhead expenses. Market value may be either gross or net after deducting direct selling expenses. The choice between cost or market may be made in respect of each separate item or of classes of items or of the inventory as a whole. Frequently, whether a profit or a loss for the year is shown depends on the precise way in which the rule is applied. And since the conventions which are to be observed must, to possess value, be based on a combination of theoretical and practical considerations, there are few, if any, which can fairly be claimed to be so inherently superior in merit to possible alternatives that they alone should be regarded as acceptable.

Most investors realize today that balance-sheets and income accounts are largely the reflection of individual judgments, and that their value is therefore to a large extent dependent on the competence and honesty of the persons exercising the necessary judgment. The importance of method, and particularly consistency of method from year to year, is by no means equally understood.

In considering ways of improving the existing situation two alternatives suggest themselves. The first is the selection by competent authority out of the body of acceptable methods in vogue today of detailed sets of rules which would become binding on all corporations of a given class. This procedure has been applied broadly to the railroads and other regulated utilities, though even such classifications as, for instance, that prescribed by the Interstate Commerce Commission allow some choice of method to corporations governed thereby. The arguments against any attempt to apply this alternative to industrial corporations generally are, however, overwhelming.

The more practicable alternative would be to leave every corporation free to choose its own methods of accounting within the very broad limits to which reference has been made, but require disclosure of the methods employed and consistency in their application from year to year. It is significant that Congress in the federal income-tax law has definitely adopted this alternative, every act since that of 1918 having contained a provision that the net income shall be computed "in accordance with the method of accounting regularly employed in keeping the books of such taxpayer" unless such method does not clearly reflect income. In its regulations the Internal Revenue Bureau has said, "the law contemplates that each taxpayer shall adopt such forms and systems of accounting as are in his judgment best suited to his purpose." (Reg. 45, Art. 24.) The greatest value of classification such as those imposed on regulated utilities lies in the disclosure of method and consistency of method which they tend to produce.

Within quite wide limits, it is relatively unimportant to the investor what precise rules or conventions are adopted by a corporation in reporting its earnings if he knows what method is being followed and is assured that it is followed consistently from year to year. Reverting to the illustrations already used, the investor would not need to be greatly concerned whether the straight-line or the sinking-fund method of providing for depreciation were being employed by a given corporation, provided he knew which method was being used and knew that it was being applied in the same way every year. But if depreciation is charged in one year on the straight-line basis applied to cost and in another is charged on a sinking-fund basis applied to a valuation less than cost, the investor may be grossly deceived unless the change is brought to his notice. For this reason, the requirement of the Exchange that the depreciation policy of a company applying for listing shall be stated in the application is valuable, and it might well by amplified to include an undertaking to report to the Exchange and to stockholders any change of policy or any material change in the manner of its application.

Again, it is not a matter of great importance to investors whether the cost-or-market rule for stating inventories is applied to individual items or to the inventory as a whole, but it is very important to the investor that he should be advised if the test is applied to individual items at the beginning of the year and to the inventory as a whole at the close thereof.

It is probably fairly well recognized by intelligent investors today that the earning capacity is the fact of crucial importance in the valuation of an industrial enterprise, and that therefore the income account is usually far more important than the balance-sheet. In point of fact, the changes in the balance-sheets from year to year are usually more significant than the balance-sheets themselves.

The development of accounting conventions has, consciously or unconsciously, been in the main based on an acceptance of this proposition. As a rule, the first objective has been to secure a proper charge or credit to the income account for the year, and in general the presumption has been that once this is achieved the residual amount of the expenditure or the receipt could properly find its place in the balance-sheet at the close of the period, the principal exception being the rule calling for reduction of inventories to market value if that is below cost. But if the income account is to be really valuable to the investor, it must be presented in such a way as to constitute to the fullest possible extent an indication of the earning capacity of the business during the period to which it relates. This Committee feels that the direction of the principal efforts of the Exchange to improve the accounting reports furnished by corporations to their stockholders should be towards making the income account more and more valuable as an indication of earning capacity.

The purpose of furnishing accounts to shareholders must be not only to afford them information in regard to the results being achieved by those to whom they have entrusted the management of the business, but to aid them in taking appropriate action to give effect to the conclusions which they reach regarding such accomplishments. In an earlier day, stockholders who were dissatisfied with the results secured by the management could perhaps move effectively to bring about a change of policy or, failing that, a change of management. With the growth in magnitude of corporations and the present wide diffusion of stock holdings, any such attempt is ordinarily impracticable because of the effort and expenditure that it would entail. The only practical way in which an investor can today give expression to his conclusions in regard to the management of a corporation in which he is interested is by retaining, increasing or disposing of his investment, and accounts are mainly valuable to him in so far as they afford guidance in determining which of these courses he shall pursue.

There is no need to revolutionize or even to change materially corporate accounting, but there is room for great improvement in the presentation of the conclusions to which accounts lead. The aim should be to satisfy (so far as is possible and prudent) the investor's need for knowledge, rather than the accountant's sense of form and respect for tradition, and to make very clear the basis on which accounts are prepared. But even when all has been done that can be done, the limitations on the significance of even the best of accounts must be recognized, and the shorter the period covered by them the more pronounced usually are these limitations. Accounts are essentially continuous historical record; and, as is true of history in general, correct interpretations and sound forecasts for the future can not be reached upon a hurried survey of temporary conditions, but only by longer retrospect and a careful distinction between permanent tendencies and transitory influences. If the investor is unable or unwilling to make or secure an adequate survey, it will be best for him not to rely on the results of a superficial one.

To summarize, the principal objects which this Committee thinks the Exchange should keep constantly in mind and do its best gradually to achieve are:

1. To bring about a better recognition by the investing public of the fact that the balance-sheet of a large modern corporation does not and should not be expected to represent an attempt to show present values of the assets and liabilities of the corporation.

2. To emphasize the fact that balance-sheets are necessarily to a large extent historical and conventional in character, and to encourage the adoption of revised forms of balance-sheets which will disclose more clearly than at present on what basis assets of various kinds are stated (*e.g.*, cost, reproduction cost less depreciation, estimated going-concern value, cost or market whichever is lower, liquidating value, *et cetera*).

3. To emphasize the cardinal importance of the income account, such importance being explained by the fact that the value of a business is dependent mainly on its earning capacity; and to take the position that an annual income account is unsatisfactory unless it is so framed as to constitute the best reflection, reasonably obtainable, of the earning capacity of the business under the conditions existing during the year to which it relates.

4. To make universal the acceptance by listed corporations of certain broad

principles of accounting which have won fairly general acceptance (see Exhibit I attached), and within the limits of such broad principles to make no attempt to restrict the right of corporations to select detailed methods of accounting deemed by them to be best adapted to the requirements of their business; but—

(a) To ask each listed corporation to cause a statement of the methods of accounting and reporting employed by it to be formulated in sufficient detail to be a guide to its accounting department (see Exhibit II attached); to have such statement adopted by its board so as to be binding on its accounting officers; and to furnish such statement to the Exchange and make it available to any stockholder on request and upon payment, if desired, of a reasonable fee.

(b) To secure assurances that the methods so formulated will be followed consistently from year to year and that if any change is made in the principles or any material change in the manner of application, the stockholders and the Exchange shall be advised when the first accounts are presented in which effect is given to such change.

(c) To endeavor to bring about a change in the form of audit certificate so that the auditors would specifically report to the shareholders whether the accounts as presented were properly prepared in accordance with the methods of accounting regularly employed by the company, defined as already indicated.

This Committee would be glad to discuss these suggestions with you at any time, and to co-operate with the Exchange in any action it may see fit to take along the lines indicated.

Yours very truly,
GEORGE O. MAY,
Chairman.

5

NEW RULES FOR DETERMINING EARNINGS PER SHARE*

James E. Parker

In May 1969, the Accounting Principles Board (APB) of the American Institute of Certified Public Accountants issued Opinion 15 entitled "Earnings Per Share." The purpose of this article is twofold: (a) to direct attention to certain procedures that will be employed by major U.S. corporations when determining per share earnings, and (b) to warn of resulting potential pitfalls for the unwary user of these data.

Historical Background

Prior to the issuance of APB Opinion 9 (December 1966), the usual method of computing EPS was to divide the amount shown as net income (minus preferred stock dividends) by the weighted average of the number of common shares outstanding during the accounting period being reported upon. In Opinion 9 the APB recommended the reporting, where applicable, of four per share earnings figures, no one of which was to be determined in accordance with pre-Opinion 9 procedures. These were:

Income before extraordinary items per share of common stock or other residual security outstanding.

Income after extraordinary items per share of common stock or other residual security outstanding.

Pro forma per share income before extraordinary items, reflecting potential dilution.

Pro forma per share income after extraordinary items, reflecting potential dilution.

The presentation of these recommended amounts was illustrated in Opinion 9[1] as shown in Exhibit I.

Consider two of the several effects of Opinion 9 upon the practice of determining and reporting EPS for corporations with complex capital

---

* Reprinted by permission of the *Financial Analysts Journal* (January–February 1970).

[1] Accounting Principles Board, "Reporting the Results of Operations," Opinion No. 9 (New York: American Institute of Certified Public Accountants, December 1966), p. 139.

structures: First, "residual securities" other than common stock may enter into the computation of "earnings per share." Opinion 9 defined a residual security as follows:[2]

> When more than one class of common stock is outstanding, or when an outstanding security has participating dividend rights with the common stock, or when an outstanding security clearly derives a major portion of its value from its conversion rights or its common stock characteristics, such securities should be considered "residual securities" and not "senior securities" for purposes of computing earnings per share.

Second, pro forma EPS data reflecting potential dilution must also be furnished in annual reports to stockholders.[3]

EXHIBIT I

PRESENTATION OF PER SHARE DATA PER OPINION 9
(Preferably to Be Shown at the Bottom of the Income Statement)

	1967	1966
Per share of common stock:		
Income before extraordinary items	$1.73	$1.37
Extraordinary items, net of tax	(.34)	(.22)
Net Income	$1.39	$1.15
Pro forma per share of common stock,* reflecting conversion:		
Income before extraordinary items	$1.53	$1.21
Extraordinary items, net of tax	(.31)	(.19)
Net Income	$1.22	$1.02

* The pro forma per share data are based on the assumption that the 5½ percent convertible debentures outstanding at December 31, 1967 were converted into common shares at the conversion rate in effect at that date, reflecting the 800,000 shares issuable on conversion and eliminating the related interest on the convertible debentures (less applicable income tax) of $50,000.

Under certain circumstances, earnings per share may be subject to dilution in the future if existing contingencies permitting issuance of common shares eventuate. Such circumstances include contingent changes resulting from the existence of: (a) outstanding senior stock or debt which is convertible into common shares, (b) outstanding stock options, warrants or similar agreements, and (c) agreements for the issuance of common shares for little or no consideration upon the satisfaction of certain conditions (e.g., the attainment of specified levels of earnings following a business combination). If such potential dilution is material, supplementary pro forma computations of earnings per share should be furnished, showing what the earnings would be if the conversions or contingent issuances took place.

In Opinion 15 (dated May, 1969) the board recognized that the residual security concept as defined above has raised questions in its application and after further consideration concluded that modifications were desirable. Basically, Opinion 15 is both a modification and more detailed state-

---

[2] *Ibid.*, p. 120.
[3] *Ibid.*, p. 123.

ment of the "Earnings Per Share" section of Opinion 9 which it supersedes.

Before proceeding to more substantive matters, it is necessary to take note of some of the terminology changes effected in Opinion 15 (see Exhibit II). Opinion 15 terminology will then be used in the balance of this article.

EXHIBIT II
Comparison of Terminology Used in Opinions 9 and 15

Opinion 9	Opinion 15
Residual security	Common stock equivalent
Income after extraordinary items per share of common stock or other residual security outstanding	Primary earnings per share
Pro forma per share income after extraordinary items, reflecting potential dilution	Fully diluted earnings per share

Determination of Primary EPS Under Opinion 15

The determination of primary EPS is based on the outstanding common shares and those (and only those) common stock equivalents that have a dilutive effect of 3 percent or more. Thus, it is important to note that a common stock equivalent may or may not be reflected in the determination of primary EPS; to be included it must have the effect of reducing EPS.

What is a common stock equivalent? To apply the test of common stock equivalent status, it is first necessary to differentiate between (a) options and warrants and (b) convertible securities. Options and warrants "should be regarded as common stock equivalents at all times."[4] Convertible debt or convertible preferred stock "should be considered as a common stock equivalent at the time of issuance if, based on its market price, it has a cash yield of less than 66⅔ percent of the current bank prime interest rate."[5]

At least two characteristics of the test of common stock equivalent status are important to anyone using amounts reported as primary EPS. First, this test is made at the time of original issuance of the security in question and, once a security's status is determined, that status never changes. Consider Exhibit III. For Company B, the convertible debt is not considered as a common stock equivalent under Opinion 15 because its cash yield (3 percent) exceeded two thirds of the then current (1959) bank prime interest rate (4 percent). However, for Company A the

---

[4] Accounting Principles Board, "Earnings Per Share," Opinion No. 15 (New York: American Institute of Certified Public Accountants, May 1969), p. 230.

[5] *Ibid.*, p. 229.

convertible debt is considered as a common stock equivalent. Yet it is Company B's debt holders who would convert at present market prices in event of approaching maturity or of a calling of the bonds. The APB's belief "that the presentation of fully diluted earnings per share data adequately discloses the potential dilution which may exist because of changes in conditions subsequent to time of issuance"[6] is, in the opinion of this writer, in error for at least two reasons. First, it does not allow for comparability of EPS between companies that differ in the original issu-

EXHIBIT III
Hypothetical Examples of Primary EPS Determination Under Opinion 15 Where Convertible Debt is Outstanding

	Company A	Company B
Net income for 1969	$ 4,000,000	$ 4,000,000
Common shares outstanding	1,000,000	1,000,000
Market price of common—1969	$ 35	$ 40
Market price of common—1959	$ 15	$ 15
Data re convertible debt		
Par value of total issue	$10,000,000	$10,000,000
Coupon interest rate	3%	3%
Conversion price per common share	$ 50	$ 20
Original date of issuance	1/1/69	1/1/59
Assumed bank prime interest rate at date of issuance	6%	4%
Original issue price	$ 100	$ 100
* Primary earnings per share—1969	$ 3.46	$ 4.00

* Computation of primary earnings per share for Company A:

Net income for year		$ 4,000,000
Interest on debt (3% of $10,000,000)	$ 300,000	
Less related income taxes (50%)	150,000	150,000
Adjusted income		$ 4,150,000
Common shares outstanding		1,000,000
Common stock equivalent ($10,000,000 ÷ $50)		200,000
		1,200,000
Primary earnings per share ($4,150,000 ÷ 1,200,000)		$ 3.46

ance dates of their respective convertible securities. Secondly, it seems internally inconsistent that the less likely "potential" dilution is to be reflected in primary EPS, while the more likely case of dilution is reflected only in fully diluted EPS.

The second important characteristic of the test of common stock equivalent status as set forth by Opinion 15 is that it represents a change from the criteria of Opinion 9. Thus, it is to be expected that, beginning

---
[6] *Ibid.*, p. 227.

with the 1969 calendar year reports, there will be changes for some companies in the number of shares upon which primary EPS are based. This will result from reclassifications of certain convertible securities since Opinion 15 allows (but does not require—thus adding another potential inconsistency between companies) for the classification of previously issued securities as common stock equivalents even though such securities would not have been classified as residual securities under Opinion 9.

With respect to historical data included in annual reports, it is encouraging to note that where such reclassifications of previously issued securities are made in the determination of current year primary earnings per share, this basis must be applied for all periods presented. However, when making comparisons with the 1969 per share figures, analysts will still need to check the basis of any previously determined per share results or estimates.

Now consider the determination of primary EPS where there are warrants outstanding. As noted above, options and warrants are always regarded as common stock equivalents and therefore enter into the computation of primary EPS if and only if their inclusion has the effect of decreasing the per share amount. The "treasury stock" method is specified by the APB. "Under this method, earnings-per-share data are computed as if the options and warrants were exercised at the beginning of the period (or at a time of issuance, if later) and as if the funds obtained thereby were used to purchase common stock at the average market price during the period."[7] The use of this method is limited to 20 percent of the common shares outstanding. The method is illustrated in Exhibit IV.

Historical common share market prices are not relevant to the determination of primary EPS since (1) historical prices reflect *previously* held expectations which do not necessarily bear any ordered relationship to currently held expectations and (2) the amount reported as primary EPS is intended to reflect, on a pro forma basis, that potential dilution *currently* existing. From Exhibit IV it can be noted that Companies X and Y will report different amounts as primary EPS even though all obvious financial considerations are identical for the two companies. This situation is the result of the APB's procedure of basing the dilution computation on historical common stock market prices which may or may not approximate market prices at the time the analyst receives the annual report and thus may or may not reflect the dilution effect then existing. Thus, before using reported primary EPS figures the analyst would be wise to determine the effect, if any, resulting from changes in market prices. In this example using common market prices as of March 1, 1970, a recomputation of primary earnings per share yields $3.72 ($4,000,000 ÷ 1,075,000) for each company.

---

[7] *Ibid.*, p. 320.

The procedure of basing per share computations on the weighted average of the number of common shares actually outstanding during the period being reported is logical since the resources received upon issuance of the additional shares during the period are available for employment for a corresponding portion of the period. Thus, if the firm continued to earn exactly the same rate of return on stockholder's equity, the past period's earnings per share would exactly equal the following period's EPS except for the increase due to previous earnings retained. However,

EXHIBIT IV

HYPOTHETICAL EXAMPLES OF PRIMARY EPS DETERMINATION UNDER OPINION 15 WHERE WARRANTS ARE OUTSTANDING

	Company X	Company Y
Net income for 1969	$ 4,000,000	$ 4,000,000
Common shares outstanding	1,000,000	1,000,000
Warrants outstanding	200,000	200,000
Exercise price	$ 50	$ 50
Market price of common		
Average—1st quarter 1969	$ 40	$ 100
Average—2nd quarter 1969	$ 40	$ 80
Average—3rd quarter 1969	$ 70	$ 120
Average—4th quarter 1969	$ 60	$ 100
As of 3/1/70	$ 80	$ 80
Average—3rd and 4th quarters 1969	$ 65	
Average—year 1969		$ 100
Adjustment of shares outstanding:		
Assumed issued	200,000	200,000
Proceeds (200,000 × $50)	$10,000,000	$10,000,000
Reacquired:		
($10,000,000 ÷ $65)	153,846	
($10,000,000 ÷ $100)		100,000
Net increases in shares	46,154	100,000
Portion of year outstanding	50%	100%
Net adjustment	23,077	100,000
Actual outstanding	1,000,000	1,000,000
Adjusted shares outstanding	1,023,077	1,100,000
Primary earnings per share		
($4,000,000 ÷ 1,023,077)	$ 3.91	
($4,000,000 ÷ 1,100,000)		$ 3.64

there is no corresponding logical explanation for the APB's procedure of using a weighted average of the net number of shares that would have been added if the warrants had been converted since no additional net assets would have been received. Also, it must be remembered that these are only pro forma or "what if" computations. Thus, it would seem logical to base such computations on the total net increase in the number of shares outstanding that would result if conversion were to take place at current market prices. This was the procedure employed in recomputing the primary EPS figure of $3.72 above.

In the past, per share earnings figures covering a number of periods have often been used in assessing a firm's earning power and in forming opinions as to its potential. Opinion 15 introduces a new determinant of primary EPS which will (for companies with warrants outstanding) reduce their appropriateness for this use since changes in the level of a firm's common stock price will now directly affect the level of its reported primary EPS. Once the market price of the firm's common rises above the exercise price of any warrants outstanding, a still higher price will result in a lower reported primary EPS figure, whereas a lower price for the common will increase primary EPS.

Determination of Fully Diluted EPS Under Opinion 15

The APB's stated purpose in requiring the presentation of fully diluted EPS was "to show the maximum potential dilution of current earnings per share on a prospective basis."[8] Thus, it would seem that any and all contingent issuances of additional shares, no matter how remote, would be reflected if the realization of such contingency would have the effect of reducing EPS. However, this is *not* true under the procedure outlined by Opinion 15 with respect to outstanding options and warrants even though it is true with respect to convertible securities.

With respect to options and warrants, fully diluted EPS are calculated by means of the treasury stock method as described above except that the market price at the close of the reporting period is used in determining the number of shares assumed to have been repurchased if such market price is higher than the average price used in computing primary EPS. Therefore, if the exercise price exceeds both the period average and period end market prices, warrants and/or options outstanding will have no effect in the determination of reported fully diluted EPS. On the other hand, all noncommon stock equivalent convertible preferred stock and/or convertible debt (irrespective of conversion price) is used in determining fully diluted EPS in the same manner as illustrated in Exhibit III. In summary, from the viewpoint of a potential investor there are two undesirable aspects to fully diluted earnings per share figures as reported: (*a*) the complete omission of the potential dilution effect due to warrants and/or options whose exercise prices are in excess of market prices prevailing during the reporting period, and (*b*) the lack of any indication of the extent of remoteness associated with those dilution effects that are reflected in fully diluted EPS.

In order to overcome these undesirable aspects of fully diluted EPS figures as reported, an alternative procedure is presented in Exhibit V in the form of an example. Under this alternative the analyst would develop not one but a schedule of diluted EPS amounts where each amount is associated with a given potential future market price for the common stock. By employing this relationship between the common's market price

---

[8] *Ibid.*, p. 234.

EXHIBIT V
HYPOTHETICAL EXAMPLE OF FULLY DILUTED EPS DETERMINATION UNDER OPINION 15 AND WRITER'S SUGGESTED PROCEDURE

DATA

Net income for 1969	$4,000,000
Common shares outstanding	1,000,000
Market price of common during 1969	$35–$45
Assumed bank prime interest rate—1969	6%
Convertible 5% bonds—due 1980	$1,000,000
Conversion price	$ 50
12/31/69 market price	$ 100
Date issued	1960
Convertible 6% bonds—due 1985	$1,000,000
Conversion price	$ 50
12/31/69 market price	$ 120
Date issued	1965
A Warrants—expire 1990	100,000
Exercise price	$ 55
Date issued	1964
B Warrants—expire 1995	100,000
Exercise price	$ 70
Date issued	1967

PROCEDURE UNDER OPINION 15

Net income for 1969		$4,000,000
Interest on 5% bonds	$ 50,000	
Interest on 6% bonds	60,000	
	$ 110,000	
Tax savings	55,000	$ 55,000
Adjusted net income		$4,055,000
Actual common shares outstanding		1,000,000
Issuable on conversion of 5% bonds		20,000
Issuable on conversion of 6% bonds		20,000
Adjusted number of common shares		1,040,000
Fully-diluted EPS ($4,055,000 ÷ 1,040,000)		$ 3.90

PROCEDURE UNDER WRITER'S SUGGESTED ALTERNATIVE SCHEDULE OF DILUTED EPS

Market price of common	$40	$50	$60	$70	$80
EPS	$ 4.0	$ 3.95	$ 3.87	$ 3.82	$ 3.74

CALCULATIONS

Market Price of Common	Adjustments	Shares	Income	EPS
$40	None (Note 1)	1,000,000	$4,000,000	$4.00
$50	Conversion of 5% bonds (Note 2)	20,000	$ 25,000	
		1,020,000	$4,025,000	$3.95
$60	Conversion of 6% bonds and	20,000	$ 30,000	
	Exercise of A warrants (Note 3)	8,333	...	
		1,048,033	$4,055,000	$3.87
$70	Reversal	(8,333)	...	
	Exercise of A warrants (Note 4)	21,429	...	
		1,061,429	$4,055,000	$3.82

EXHIBIT V (*Continued*)

Market Price of Common	Adjustments	Shares	Income	EPS
$80	Reversal	(21,429)	...	
	Exercise of A warrants and	31,250	...	
	Exercise of B warrants (Note 5)	12,500	...	
		1,083,750	$4,055,000	$3.74

Explanatory Notes

Note 1 ($40 market price)

	5% Bonds	6% Bonds
Conversion value ($40 × 200,000)	$ 800,000	$ 800,000
Estimated premium	200,000	400,000
Estimated market value	$1,000,000	$1,200,000
Cash interest	$ 50,000	$ 60,000
Cash yield	5%	5%
Current bank prime rate	6%	6%

No adjustment is required since the cash yield for each bond is greater than 75% of the prime bank rate. (Note: this means of deciding whether to assume conversion is only one of several that could be employed. In this example the cash yield is related to 75% of the prime bank rate instead of 66-2/3% as specified in Opinion 15 solely for the purpose of emphasizing this point. The essential characteristic of any such test is that it should be related to the estimated market value of the bonds which is in turn based primarily on the assumed market price of the common.)

Note 2 ($50 market price)

	5% Bonds	6% Bonds
Conversion value ($50 × 200,000)	$1,000,000	$1,000,000
Estimated premium	150,000	300,000
Estimated market value	$1,150,000	$1,300,000
Cash interest	$ 50,000	$ 60,000
Cash yield	4.35%	4.62%
Current bank prime rate	6%	6%

Adjustment required for 5% bonds only
(Method of adjustment: same as under Opinion 15)

Note 3 ($60 market price)

	6% Bonds	A Warrants
Conversion value ($60 × 200,000)	$1,200,000	
Estimated premium	200,000	
Estimated market value	$1,400,000	
Cash interest	$ 60,000	
Cash yield	4.29%	
Current bank prime rate	6%	
Adjustment required for 6% bonds		
Shares issued		100,000
Proceeds (100,000 × $55)		$5,500,000
Shares repurchased ($5,500,000 ÷ $60)		91,667
Net increase in shares (100,000 ÷ 91,667)		8,333

Note 4 ($70 market price)

	A Warrants
Shares issued	100,000
Proceeds (100,000 × $55)	$5,500,000
Shares repurchased ($5,500,000 ÷ $70)	78,571
Net increase in shares (100,000 ÷ 78,571)	21,429

Note 5 ($80 market price)

	A Warrants	B Warrants
Shares issued	100,000	100,000
Proceeds		
(100,000 × $55)	$5,500,000	
(100,000 × $70)		$7,000,000
Shares repurchased		
($5,500,000 ÷ $80)	68,750	
($7,000,000 ÷ $80)		87,500
Net increase in shares		
(100,000 ÷ 68,750)	31,250	
(100,000 ÷ 87,500)		12,500

and the likelihood of actual conversion or exercise, the analyst will be able to determine the portion of the firm's current income that is likely to be attributed to a single share in the event of each of several different future occurrences.

SUMMARY

Opinion 15 specified the presentation of both primary and fully diluted EPS in annual reports to stockholders. It is the opinion of this writer that neither nor both of these amounts, as determined under the procedures outlined in Opinion 15, are adequate for evaluating the past earnings performance of a business in relation to the common shares held by a single individual where there is a complex capital structure. It is hoped that a basic understanding of the manner in which the reported per share amounts are determined will be of assistance to the analyst and other users of these data.

Part Two

Economics

6

"QUI NUMERARE INCIPIT ERRARE INCIPIT"*

Oskar Morgenstern

Although the natural sciences—sometimes called the "exact" sciences—have been concerned with the accuracy of measurements and observations from their earliest beginnings, they nevertheless suffered a great crisis when it became clear that absolute precision and certainty of important kinds of observations were impossible to achieve in principle. At least all sources of error that occur in the natural sciences also occur in the social sciences: or, in other words, the statistical problems of the social sciences cannot possibly be less serious than those of the natural sciences. But the social sciences pay far less attention to errors than the physical. This is undoubtedly one of the reasons why the social sciences have had a rather uncertain development.

In the physical sciences, when an error is not mentioned explicitly, it is because it can generally be assumed to be well known, or because the values have already entered into physical theories that determine an admissible error level, and their limitations are then those of the respective theory. To give an illustration, it may not be necessary to state every time the error in the measurement of the velocity of light because this value is indissolubly tied up with the theory of relativity. But when new measurements are made the error margin must always be stated. Thus exaggeration of the significance of the new results is avoided, and they assume their proper place in physical theory.

It ought to be clear a priori that most economic statistics should not be stated in the manner in which they are so often reported, pretending an accuracy that may be completely out of reach. Changes in consumers' total spending power down to the last billion or less (i.e., variations of less than one-half of 1 percent) are reported and taken seriously. Price indexes for wholesale and retail prices are shown to second decimals, even though there have been so many computing steps that the rounding-off errors alone may preclude such a degree of precision. Unemployment figures of

---

* Reprinted from the October 1963 issue of *Fortune* by special permission; © 1963 Time Inc.
  This article is an extract from the book *On the Accuracy of Economic Observations* (Princeton University Press, 1963).

several millions are given down to the last 1,000's (i.e., one-hundredths of 1 percent "accuracy"), when certainly the 100,000's or in some cases perhaps even the millions are in doubt. It will be seen later that national income and consumers' spending power probably cannot be known now in part without an error of plus or minus 10 to plus or minus 15 percent.

Business must be deeply concerned about these matters; its decisions are dependent upon statistical information. For example, wage agreements involving millions of workers are sometimes based on price indexes that record alleged changes of price levels up to one-tenth of 1 percent! Common price and cost-of-living indexes are reported in this form. They are splashed across the front pages of newspapers together with the most important political news of the day. These price changes are then interpreted as a measure of the success or failure of government policy and the existence or absence of inflation. In fact, these minute changes show nothing at all. The public in general and Congress in particular must be made to understand that there cannot be absolute accuracy, that there must be error, and that the important thing to do is to try to uncover, remove, or at least limit the error.

Do Errors Cancel Out?

People gathering statistics all too often face a deliberate attempt to hide information. In other words, economic and social statistics are frequently based on evasive answers and even deliberate lies. Lies arise principally from fear of tax authorities, from dislike of government interference, or from the desire to mislead competitors. Nothing of this sort stands in the path of the physical scientists. Nature may hold back information, is always difficult to understand, but it is believed that she does not lie deliberately. Einstein has aptly expressed this fact by saying: "*Raffiniert ist der Herr Gott, aber boshaft ist er nicht.*" ("The Lord God is sophisticated, but not malicious.")

In addition to deliberate lies and evasions there are many other sources of error in the data from which economic observations are made. Anyone familiar with the actual handling of statistical data at the primary level is aware of the great number of possible errors and mistakes and of the frequency with which they occur. The increasing use of machines in handling economic data does not eliminate the main sources of error. These are so deeply rooted that it is impossible, on purely theoretical-probabilistic grounds, to eliminate all of them all of the time. The problem is to appraise them and to reduce them to the minimum.

It is possible that the influence of one error that drives a number in one direction is exactly offset by the influence of another error doing the opposite. In that case, by coincidence, the errors could cancel out—if their "extent" or "strength" balance—and we obtain a "true" figure for our observation. But we have not *made* a true observation. The notion that errors do cancel out is widespread, and when not explicitly stated, it appears as the almost inevitable argument of investigators when they are pressed to say why their statistics should be acceptable. Yet any statement that errors cancel one another has to be proved. The world would, indeed, be even more of a miracle than it is if the influence of one set of errors offset that of another set of errors so conveniently that we need not bother much with the whole matter.

It is also widely believed that more recent statistics are more accurate and trustworthy than earlier ones. This is probably sound, in a vague, general way, but only when sufficiently large intervals of time are taken. There are, however, many instances where statistics produced today are probably no better—and are indeed worse—than statistics produced decades ago. It is obviously more difficult, for example, to describe statistically an economy in a state of vigorous development, signified by the introduction of many new products, changes in quality of existing products, and a rapidly advancing technology.

In particular, modern statistics of the value of foreign trade—an enormously important field—are virtually worthless where countries practicing discriminatory exchange rates are concerned; many nations do so right now and did not in earlier years. Domestic statistics do not necessarily improve either. Sometimes governments change rapidly and bring forth the deliberate falsifications associated with Nazi and Communist practices. Or "strategic" considerations play havoc with reliability.

How Old Is the River?

There is a tendency toward specious accuracy, a pretense that things have been counted more precisely than they can be—e.g., the U.S. Army published *enemy* casualties for the Korean war to 1/1,000 of 1 percent, at a time when our own losses were not well known even to the thousands of men! An even better example is given by the official publication of the Austrian Finance Administration, which states that the population of Salzburg Province in 1951 was 327,232 people—*4.719303 percent* of the entire population of Austria. The classical case is, of course, that of the story in which a man, asked about the age of a river, states that it is 3,000,021 years old. Asked how he could give such accurate information, the answer was that 21 years ago the river's age was given as three million years. There is a fair amount of this in economic (and other social) statistics.[1] Economic series, reported in billions, are often aggregated with others, reported in millions or thousands, by simple addition. The result is a new series which gives the impression that the aggregate has been

---

[1] Years ago an example made the rounds: in order to determine the precise height of the Emperor of China, whom none of his subjects has ever seen, it suffices to ask each of 300 million Chinese what he thinks the height is and average their opinions. This will necessarily give a very precise figure.

measured, counted, or determined to far more digits than is actually the case.

Another kind of specious accuracy is perhaps even more dangerous. It is functional speciousness. Here data are given that, even when they have only a very small margin of error, are nevertheless useless. This is the case, for example, when the exchange rate of a country with exchange control is given at the official rate (quite accurately to any desired number of decimals), although the vast majority of transactions take place at different rates that are not disclosed or cannot be determined.

The success or failure of a government's economic policy is often measured by the number of the nation's involuntary unemployed. "Full employment" is a national goal in most advanced nations. But as soon as one tries to discover when that desired condition has been reached, considerable difficulties are encountered. They are conceptual as well as statistical.

First, it is known that there is always some "unemployment" which may not be truly involuntary, because labor shifts from one place to another, young people enter the labor force, others more or less gradually slip from it because of age, ill health, emigration. These transitions take time for purely technological reasons, such as slow transmission and dissemination of knowledge, time needed to move to other places of employment, etc. This is then the so-called "frictional" unemployment, which is at some level unrelated to the state of the economy. There is also possibly a great deal of "hidden unemployment," e.g., when persons becoming unemployed in industry go back to farms for varying periods of time. There is a shift in occupations, for example, when skilled workers are displaced by machines and then have to find employment at lesser skills.

Second, because of the high political significance of unemployment figures, this area is charged with emotions, insinuations, assertions, etc. This applies in particular to times of great stress, of political upheavals and changes in the form of government. Some countries, such as the Soviet Union, flatly assert that they never have unemployment, this allegedly being impossible because of their political system. Others, such as Nazi Germany, "reduced" unemployment by drafting men into the army and thereby changed the statistics to their liking.

In the U.S. two distinct series of unemployment statistics are produced by the Bureau of Employment Statistics and the Census. The discrepancies between these series are enormous; the BES series has averaged lower than that of the Census in every year but 1946. It is not uncommon, indeed it is frequent, to find the government making strong statements about developments in unemployment over periods as short as *one* month. The nation's largest or most important newspapers play up a "drop" in the unemployment rate, say from 5.8 to 5.5 percent, as a highly significant event and the Secretary of Labor will not hesitate to make speeches on that occasion. All this is done on the basis of "seasonal correction" and dealing with figures given to four "significant" digits. It is clear, of course, that statements of this kind are completely devoid of the meaning attributed to them.

In the notion of a "national income," most difficulties of economics culminate. Neither the conceptual nor the statistical problems in this field have been resolved to anyone's satisfaction, though a great deal of progress has been made in both respects. The two areas are interdependent, since nothing can be measured for which there exist no good concepts, and concepts, no matter how precise, are of little practical value if the corresponding measurements cannot be performed.

National income is a total of composites that differ in reliability from sector to sector and year to year, and hence the error of the composite is, as economist Simon Kuznets has said, a "complex amalgam of errors in the parts whose magnitude is not easily determined." The National Income Division of the Department of Commerce provides no measure of the possible error, taking the position that "meaningful mathematical measures of reliability cannot be calculated for national income statistics; only a frank evaluation of the sources and methods underlying them can provide the understanding which is needed for their effective use in economic analysis." Any quantitative estimate is left to the user of the statistics, who must base his estimate on his knowledge of the sources and methods as provided by the U.S. Income and Output and 1954 National Income supplements. It is impossible for the user to determine with what confidence he may employ the data. The fact that little or nothing is said about accuracy is more dangerous than if the margins of error were frankly stated to be very high.

To throw the burden of estimating the errors and the reliability upon the user, though exceedingly convenient for the maker, is a totally inadmissible procedure. How can the individual user be expected to accomplish something where the government with its vast resources for compiling statistics fails?

Kuznets' study on margins of error in national-income estimates is the most important one that has been made so far. He considered the aggregate national income as composed of 520 cells (forty industries, thirteen income and employment categories). Then he and two of his co-workers attempted to classify each of these entries according to its margin of error. The possible margins of error were grouped into four categories:

I 5–10% with average of 7.5%
II 11–20% with average of 15%
III 21–40% with average of 30%
IV 41–80% with average of 60%

And for each cell each of these three investigators made independent classifications. An average was taken of the investigators' judgments and the deviation between them was noted. As a result, a measure was obtained of the general magnitude of errors in each of the component estimates of national income as well as of the aggregate itself. From this classification, Kuznets distinguished three groups of industries according to the relative margins of error judged to be present in their estimates. First, those with a margin of error well below 15 percent (in categories I and II above) were the basic manufacturing industries and public utilities —electric light and power, railroads, street railways, telephone, telegraph; second, with margins of error of about 15 percent but well below 30 percent, were agriculture, mining, manufactured gas, pipelines, trade, banking, insurance, and government—industries for which information is extensive but not complete; and third were industries with an error margin of about 30 percent and higher—construction, water transportation, real estate, direct service industries, and the miscellaneous division.

Textbooks on national income and macroeconomics and trade journals accept the statistics at face value and do not seem to be conscious of their severe limitations. But let us see what even a 5 percent difference in national income means. Assuming a gross national product of about $550 billion, a 5 percent error equals plus or minus $30 billion. This is far more than the total annual production of the entire electronics industry in the U.S. Yet a 10 percent error in national income is even more reasonable to assume than a 5 percent error. But 10 percent amounts to a plus or minus variation of about three times the total exports of the U.S. The possible differences are, of course, not concentrated in the manner of these illustrations; instead they are scattered in an unknown way throughout all activities producing the national income. On the other hand, the reader, like everyone else, has probably become conditioned to accept economic data as being so highly accurate that even an alleged mere 1 to 2 percent variation of national income is considered significant enough for making statements about "true" variations in the state of the economy.

Comparing One Nation with Another

There are two principal questions involved: the first is one referring to the comparability and applicability of concepts, and the second is one referring to the quality of the component data. Conceptually different situations arise for each class or category of countries. For example, home-consumed agricultural produce, which is an enormous part of the total in underdeveloped agricultural countries, is practically irrelevant in the U.S. Clearly, this is much more difficult to measure in the former than in the latter. Yet agricultural statistics in the U.S. are far from satisfactory. How, then, could the agricultural income of, say, Ceylon, the Congo, China, Bolivia, or Tibet be known at least as accurately? How can they be made comparable—e.g., on a per capita basis—when even the number of inhabitants in these countries is in far greater doubt than that in the U.S.?

International comparisons, however, are constantly being made. No doubt some information can be had from existing figures, and whether they are useful depends, as we shall not tire of repeating, on the purposes of the comparisons. To ascertain in a rather general manner the gross differences in the income of different nations, to show that they differ by large factors,[2] and to see whether these differences have changed over the years, etc., is one thing, but to believe that we can state this and much more reliably to two, three, or even four "significant" digits is an entirely different matter.

Defect of Soviet Statistics

A special problem is offered by the Soviet Union. The statistics of that country are exceedingly difficult to assess, but it is generally known that they are seldom what they purport to be. There has been a great deal of deliberate doctoring of statistics at many levels, in order, for example, to make production results appear better than they are or to receive assignments of raw materials that would not otherwise be allocated. Even Khrushchev has repeatedly referred to falsified accounts of various activities, especially in farming, and there is no reason to assume that statistical practices were better in Stalin's time. A particular trouble in measuring aggregates is (as in all other countries) the double counting, or rather the multiple counting. Double counting has apparently been a most serious defect of Soviet statistics, with the necessary result that accounts of national income have been exaggerated, and increasingly so in more recent times. This is the gist of criticism by S. G. Strumilin, a well-known Soviet economist. For example, in 1945 industrial output was, according to him, more than 30 percent below 1940, rather than only 8 percent, as the official statistics show. Again according to Strumilin, industrial production rose from 1945 to 1956 only threefold, rather than fourfold, as officially asserted. (Strumilin's own figure may, of course, still be an exaggeration.) Though industrial production is not identical with national income, it is a substantial component; its difficulties are illustrative for the larger aggregate and show how limited the value is of any "growth factor" based on such data.

Figures giving international comparisons of national incomes are among the most uncertain and unreliable statistics with which the public is confronted. The area is full of complicated and unsolved problems, despite great efforts to overcome them. This is a field where politics reigns supreme and where lack of critical economic appraisal is particularly detrimental.

---

[2] But probably not by as large factors as is suggested by the official statistics. As Kuznets has observed, if the frequently stated low figures were correct the inhabitants of the poorest countries would all have starved a long time ago.

The Accuracy of Growth Rates

In recent years there has been much concern about the rate of economic growth of the U.S. and other countries. In addition to the goals of maintaining a high level of employment and providing for general stability in the price level, a third goal, that of maintaining a satisfactory rate of economic growth, has been added to the responsibilities of fiscal and monetary authorities.

The value of a growth rate depends on the accuracy both of the figures for gross national product and of the prices going into the construction of the deflator indexes. The former are subject to considerable uncertainties; the latter depend on the precision with which actual prices, as distinguished from posted prices, list prices, etc., can be determined and applied to the correct sectors of gross national product.

A reliable growth rate of two significant digits is impossible to establish. Even the first digit is in grave doubt, as will be shown below. Yet the emphasis of the public discussion is on the second digit, usually the first decimal, and it is carried on in all seriousness as if a distinction between, say, 3.2 and 3.3 percent were really possible, and as if the transition, within a short time, from the former to the latter constituted an advance by the country. But a growth rate simply cannot be computed with the stated or demanded degree of refinement and reliability. This applies to the existing national income data of any country in the world.

We know that countries have grown and that, at periods, some have grown faster than others. But such observations and statements can be made with confidence only qualitatively and for longer periods. They are impossible to make for one year (or less), when a nation's growth is as imperceptible as the growth of a person's teeth in a month.

The table below shows growth rates as commonly computed, but for 1, 3, and 5 percent plus or minus variations of the underlying figures. We recall that the assumption of a plus or minus 5 percent accuracy of the non-deflated gross national product is conservative. The results of this simple computation should shake the confidence of anyone who thinks that the difference between, say, 3.2 and 3.3 percent is significant.

The computation is for a (hypothetical) change in U.S. gross national product from $550 billion in Period I to $560 billion in Period II. The first column lists the values of gross national product assuming the reported figure for Period I—i.e., $550 billion—to be subjected to the above-mentioned error of plus or minus 1 percent, 3 percent, and 5 percent. The top row carries the same assumption through for the Period II figures. The body of the table contains the growth rates obtained for all combinations of the assumed possible errors. When there is no error assumed or when an error of a given magnitude is exactly compensated by an error of the same magnitude and with the same sign, the growth rate is 1.8 percent. This rate would, according to current practices, be reported (and analyzed) as *the* rate. It is, of course, impossible that there be no errors at all, and most improbable that they always exactly compensate for each other. The table now shows clearly what happens when even the modest 1 percent or 3 percent errors are introduced. Magnitudes and even signs are affected. If we assume that the reported figure of 550 for Period I is 5 percent too high and the figure for Period II 5 percent too low, we arrive,

APPARENT RATE OF GROWTH FOR ±1, ±3, ±5 PERCENT ERRORS

A. Assuming Reported Gross National Product Figures 550 and 560 in Two Successive Periods

Period II GNP 560 ± Error		532.0	543.2	554.4	560.0	565.6	576.8	588.0
Period I GNP 550 ± Error	% Error	−5	−3	−1	0	+1	+3	+5
522.5	−5	1.8	4.0	6.1	7.2	8.2	10.4	12.5
533.5	−3	−.3	1.8	3.9	5.0	6.0	8.1	10.2
544.5	−1	−2.3	−.2	1.8	2.9	3.9	5.9	8.0
550.0	0	−3.3	−1.2	.8	1.8	2.9	4.9	7.0
555.5	+1	−4.2	−2.2	−.2	.8	1.8	3.8	5.9
566.5	+3	−6.1	−4.1	−2.1	−1.2	−.2	1.8	3.8
577.5	+5	−7.9	−5.9	−4.0	−3.0	−2.1	−.1	1.8

Computed rate of growth assuming the reported figures to be correct is $\frac{560-550}{550} = 1.8\%$.

B. Assuming Reported Gross National Product Figures 550 and 566.5 in Two Successive Periods

Period II GNP 566.5 ± Error		538.2	549.5	560.8	566.5	572.2	583.5	594.8
Period I GNP 550 ± Error	% Error	−5	−3	−1	0	+1	+3	+5
522.5	−5	3.0	5.2	7.3	8.4	9.5	11.7	13.8
533.5	−3	.9	3.0	5.1	6.2	7.3	9.4	11.5
544.5	−1	−1.2	.9	3.0	4.1	5.1	7.2	9.2
550.0	0	−2.2	−.1	2.0	3.0	4.1	6.1	8.2
555.5	+1	−3.1	−1.1	1.0	2.0	3.0	5.0	7.1
566.5	+3	−5.0	−3.0	−1.0	0.0	1.0	3.0	5.0
577.5	+5	−6.8	−4.8	−2.9	−1.9	−.9	1.0	3.0

Computed rate of growth assuming the reported figures to be correct is $\frac{566.5-550}{550} = 3.0\%$.

instead of at 1.8 percent, at 12.5 percent as the growth rate. If we reverse the signs, the growth rate is −7.9 percent. Suppose gross national product for the second year is only plus 1 percent off and gross national product for the preceding one is minus 1 percent off (a total error of only 2 percent), then the growth rate is 3.9 percent. But if the signs of the errors are reversed, the growth rate is −0.2 percent! It is in the essence of an error estimate that the occurrence of a positive and negative deviation has to be admitted. Surely, the assumption of only a 1 percent error for each period is a very mild one. The reader should contemplate what this trifling difference in our assumption entails. If our basic figures of 550 and

560 are more than 1.8 percent apart, say 3 percent, the results of a corresponding table are necessarily worse. For example, a minus 1 percent error in the first period and a plus 1 percent error in the second then give a growth rate of 5.1 percent, and if the signs are reversed a growth rate of 1 percent. With plus or minus 3 percent the corresponding figures are 9.4 percent and −3 percent.

The computations obviously apply to *any* situation where rates of change are involved and where the data are subject to error. In other words, *they apply to all economic data.* And it cannot be assumed without further proof that the errors remain constant over time, that they change uniformly over time, and that the signs of the errors never reverse themselves.

This simple arithmetical exercise combined with the indisputable fact that our final gross national product or national income data cannot possibly be free of error raises the question whether the computation of growth rates has any value whatsoever.

Pick Your Time

The usefulness of growth rates becomes even more dubious when revisions are considered. If the rate for the change from 1947 to 1948 was determined in February, 1949, when the first figures became available, it was 10.8 percent. In July, 1950, using officially corrected figures, it became 12.5 percent; in July, 1956, it fell to 11.8 percent—a full percentage point. All this for the growth from 1947 to 1948! Similar observations apply to the other years for which this computation has been made. There is no consistency in the changes. In stating what the growth rate of the country is, much depends, therefore, on the moment of time when a growth rate is computed. Though not surprising in the light of our previous investigations, this result is nevertheless noteworthy. And all this applies to figures where we have *abstracted* from the fact that they are necessarily afflicted with errors which, when low, must be at least 5 percent.

In addition to all these difficulties, there is the ambiguity in choosing the base year. The need for a base year arises from the desire to compare long periods by means of the compound rate. Such periods will often comprise a whole series of business cycles and therefore several decades. If a year with a high (or low) gross national product is chosen as base year, this will depress (or raise) the growth rate of subsequent years. Since there is no such thing as a "normal" year, the investigator has a great amount of freedom in determining a base year. An unscrupulous or politically oriented writer will choose that base year which produces the sequence of (alleged) growth rates best suited to his aims and programs. An advocate of government spending and inflation will pick a year with a high gross national product as base year in order to show a low rate of growth and thereby strengthen his argument in favor of inflation, government deficits, and the like. An opponent of such policies will choose a relatively poor gross national product as base year, thus obtaining a series of growth rates carrying the comforting message that the development of the country is progressing well. These are, of course, standard tricks, used, undoubtedly, ever since index numbers were invented.

Suppose a 3.5 percent growth is considered desirable: then the goal has been reached only when 1949 is chosen as a base year.

It is clear, furthermore, that in view of the high degree of unreliability of its basic national-income data, the growth rates for the U.S. are at best very shaky. From their relatively better quality we have to go over to the lesser and lesser quality of the national-income statistics of other countries. The computation, and hence the comparison, of international growth rates under these conditions is a most dubious undertaking.

It will always be necessary to supplement the rates by qualitative information. We emphasize again that there can be no doubt that countries develop at different speeds and that this fact is noticeable over longer periods of time, particularly when the initial level of economic activity is low and the state of technology is primitive. When big gaps exist, a comparison of change can be made with some confidence provided a sufficiently long time interval is admitted. When countries are very dissimilar in their structure, such comparisons become immeasurably more difficult and unreliable.

If there is any value at all in the notion that countries grow in characteristic patterns, depending on their history, technological age, geographic position, size, etc., then it is unlikely that a single simple number can state adequately (or at least not in a misleading sense) how they evolve relatively to each other. In this respect, the problems of finding a proper solution for describing the gross national product or the national income are compounded many times.

SWIMMING POOLS OR POWER PLANTS

There is also a conceptual problem that has to be taken care of even if the statistics are in good shape. Let us say country A expands by adding to its output of automobiles, refrigerators, swimming pools, etc., while country B increases its output of machine tools, power plants, mines, etc. B is laying the foundation for further output increase while A is not. Similar considerations apply when weapons and other tools for war are involved. The ordinary growth rate, computed for the big gross-national-product aggregate, covers up these profoundly different developments and would easily give entirely erroneous and misleading information about the relative development of these countries. Yet this is the figure commonly used to assess past progress and future tendencies. The answer would be to compute instead "power indexes" (of growth), which would have to be based on the information given by special aggregates made up of better related components.

To summarize: precise uses of "growth rates" are entirely inadmissible, whether for comparing different countries or short periods of the same country. Their computation is largely arbitrary. The concept itself is vague and unreliable.

An argument often heard is: "True, the statistics are not as good as we would want them to be, but what would we do without them?" This is, indeed, a dilemma. The answers, of course, are manifold. The primary consideration is to make the data better (admittedly easier said than done and involving costs and time delays, both of which may not be permissible; many statistics are needed precisely because decisions have to be made at the moment when the first estimates become available). The next point is to distinguish in what sense the data are unsatisfactory: Is it due to deliberate obstruction, lies, falsifications? Or is it due to inherent difficulties of measurement and observation, which otherwise have been carried out scrupulously?

In the first case there is but one answer: discard the data if the element of lying affects a significant part of the information or is suspected of doing so.

In the second case, where the data are unsatisfactory because of incomplete information or inherent difficulties of measurement, the only answer must be to say: modify the theory into which the poor data are to be fitted. Here the truth is that much of economic theory merely appears to be highly accurate and precise. It can maintain this appearance, like any theory, by virtue of being an abstraction. The problems arise therefore in the act of application; it is here that the difficulties have to be faced.

Abandon Old Views

Economics is not nearly so much of a science as the free use of allegedly accurate figures would seem to indicate. On the other hand, there is no reason to conclude that there cannot be or is no theory at all. The belief that we have to get more and more data, make more and more descriptions before we can formulate valid theories is entirely mistaken. A theory means a commitment, and in scientific life that is exactly what is wanted. When new facts come to light and new interpretations are needed, a new situation can arise. This may then call for abandoning the old views and for making a new decision.

There is, however, one definite action that is possible, though it will take time before desirable results will become visible. That is to stop important government agencies, such as the President's Council of Economic Advisers, the various government departments, the Federal Reserve Board, and other agencies, public and private, from presenting to the public economic statistics as if these were free from fault.

Perhaps the greatest step forward that can be taken, even at short notice, is to insist that economic statistics should not be released without an accompanying estimate of their error. Even if only roughly estimated, this would produce a wholesome and perhaps a profound effect. Makers and users of economic statistics both might refrain from making claims and demands that cannot be supported scientifically if the publication of error estimates became a general practice.

Eventually a new generation of economists will have learned to live with data of widely differing quality. In that they will emulate the physicists, who have created a magnificent and terrifying theory though their data range in accuracy from better than 1/100,000,000 percent to only 50 percent—that is, when they can measure at all. In appreciating the true condition of the data, economists cannot fail to develop economic theory in conformity with the high scientific standards set in the physical sciences.

7

A REPLY TO "QUI NUMERARE INCIPIT ERRARE INCIPIT"*

Julius Shiskin

To the Editors:

Despite factual mistakes and other shortcomings, Dr. Morgenstern's article ("Qui Numerare Incipit Errare Incipit," *Fortune*, October, 1963) is likely to have constructive effects because it is essentially a plea for better measures of economic change. There is hardly an economic statistician who would not support his proposal for additional information regarding the "errors" to which economic statistics are subject. The shortage of such information arises not from the lack of recognition of its importance, but rather from the difficulties and costs of obtaining and quantifying it. It is well known among economists and statisticians that the Bureau of the Census has under way an extensive program of measuring statistical errors and has long been publishing such data for many series.

The interest expressed in measures of the accuracy of economic statistics should not, however, be permitted to divert attention from a broader, though closely related kind of information needed to interpret economic statistics. To borrow language from the physical sciences, the kind of information required is that which distinguishes meaningful "signals" from random "noise." The critical question usually asked by the data user is whether various changes shown by statistics from one period in time to another are significant in an economic sense. Do they represent systematic movements in the economy or are they merely short-term irregular fluctuations?

The systematic movements in the economy—the true signals—reveal seasonal patterns, cyclical movements and long-term trends. On the other hand, the noise in economic statistics is a composite of two kinds of factors. First, there are errors of measurement—data collecting and processing errors, sampling errors, response errors, imperfect seasonal, trading-day, and holiday adjustments, and so on. Second, there are various

---

* "Letters to Fortune," *Fortune* (February 1964). Reprinted by permission of *Fortune* Magazine.

nonsystematic irregularities in the behavior of the economy—erratic real-world occurrences, such as strikes, unexpected political or international developments, and abnormal weather. The composite of these types of effects is usually described by economic statisticians as "irregular movements."

Hence, the critical problem in analyzing economic data involves not only measuring the extent of error inherent in each individual datum in an economic series, but even more importantly, it involves the ability to separate the total noise from the true signals as the series indicate changes in direction and magnitude over time. In recent years, especially with the availability of electronic computers, a substantial effort has been made in this direction by government agencies responsible for producing economic data. Thus, for all major time series now published by the Census Bureau, separate measures are provided which isolate and summarize the magnitude of irregular movements, the seasonal movements, and the trend-cycle movements inherent in a given economic series. Moreover, the relationships among these various measures are computed and a new measure, "MCD" (Months for Cyclical Dominance) has come into widespread use in recent years. Month-to-month changes in many economic series consist largely of irregular movements that obscure the underlying cyclical movements. However, over longer spans the effects of cyclical movements cumulate and become dominant over the irregular movements which tend to cancel one another. MCD provides an estimate of the appropriate time span over which to observe the cyclical movement in a monthly series.

Empirical studies using this analytical approach show that most month-to-month movements of seasonally adjusted economic series are not "cyclically significant." For most series, meaningful economic trends are revealed only by comparing changes over three-month or longer spans. For many important series, of course, month-to-month changes are typically, though, of course, not always significant, including such important series as the Federal Reserve index of industrial production, employment in nonagricultural establishments, personal income, the wholesale price index, and manufacturers' inventories. MCD and its family of related measures are more useful than a quantitative measure of "error" alone, because they provide the user with additional information needed to help determine whether a short-term change represents a true economic signal.

It is important to pursue the distinction between the irregular fluctuations which result from measurement error and those irregular fluctuations which accurately reflect erratic but real situations in the economic market place. Where the measurement error is known, it is possible to balance the costs of reducing it against the resulting gains in accuracy. For this reason, measurement errors should be compiled for each economic series and their relation to other elements of the irregular movements and underlying trends of the series should be analyzed. For some series, the significant economic signals can be brought out more clearly by reducing the errors of measurement. If this can be done at a reasonable cost, it is an obvious course to follow in collecting and processing the data. For other series, the measurement error is already relatively small and it may not be possible to reduce further the irregular movements to a point where month-to-month movements of a series are significant in an economic sense. For such series, further investments to reduce measurement errors may be a wasteful expenditure of limited public funds.

Such measures of economic significance are now available for a great many government series. Measures for the 65 principal business cycle indicators, for example, are published in the U.S. Census Bureau monthly report, "Business Cycle Developments," each month. They are also published in the monthly releases of the Census Bureau for 382 manufacturers' sales, orders, and inventories series; 30 wholesale trade series, 38 retail trade series, and 14 housing start series. These supplement measures of sampling and other types of errors that have also been compiled for many of these series.

It is to be emphasized that the availability of these measures does not eliminate the need for more and better measures of errors. It is also recognized that there is room for improvement in MCD and the related measures now published. In the light of the widespread availability of such measures at the present time, however, it does seem unwarranted to charge government statisticians with not trying to provide the necessary information required to judge the economic significance of the data they publish.

8

ECONOMICS AND INVESTMENT MANAGEMENT*

Edmund A. Mennis, C.F.A.

A significant development in the postwar period has been the growing use of economic analysis and the increased employment of professional economists in government and business. Certainly this trend has been helped by the greater availability of economic data and the improved analytical tools at the economist's disposal. Moreover, the increased role of the federal government in economic policymaking as well as a better understanding by both the professional economist and the businessman of how the economy operates have focused increasing attention on economic analysis as a guide to policy formulation and decision-making.

Economic analysis has been used in the investment field as well, particularly in the banking community, where interest rates and the money market require constant attention. However, more recently a marked increase has occurred in the use of economic analysis in common-stock investment. A good part of this application of economics undoubtedly stems from the growth in the number and size of institutional investment portfolios and the development of institutional research staffs in the financial community to serve these important clients.

It would be an overstatement, however, to claim that economic analysis has received widespread acceptance as a tool in common-stock investment. In the United States, the abundance of financial data on individual companies and the increasing willingness of corporate management to speak with financial analysts have made industry and company analysis the area of major concentration for financial analysts. A further difficulty facing the economist in the investment field is the characteristic lead of the turning points in stock prices ahead of the turning points in business. If the market leads business, what is the advantage of following business trends? Moreover, yesterday's stock prices are known and will not change. Business data, however, are invariably reported several weeks or months after the fact, with the perennial hazard of subsequent revision

---

* Reprinted by permission of the *Financial Analysts Journal* (November-December 1966).

and adjustment, so that it is difficult to determine where the economy has been recently, let alone where it is now and where it is going. For promptness in obtaining economic data, precision is sacrificed; for precision, revision is inevitable.

More important than all of these difficulties, in my opinion, is the problem of linking economic analysis to investment decisions. This problem might be compared to an hourglass, with a vast quantity of economic data on top and an equally vast array of corporate data on the bottom, and only a narrow channel of communication in between. It is frustrating, for example, to find that the traditional classification of industries used by the government in reporting economic information does not particularly match the conventional industry classifications of stock prices. The wealth of industry information provided by various federal government agencies, not to mention the gems that occasionally come to light in congressional hearings, are not used nearly enough by the financial analyst. The lack of familiarity with economic data and with the new methods of economic analysis, particularly among the older members of the financial analysts profession, also has prevented full utilization of the tools available. But the major obstacle lies not in the data but in the failure to find common ground where both the economist and the financial analyst can meet.

To reach this common ground, it is necessary to recognize that an investment is the purchase of future economic performance. The economist can provide information about the current or probable future economic environment, the analysis and projection of monetary and fiscal trends, international developments, and a variety of other economic information that can assist the investment manager and the financial analyst. However, unless this information is directed toward the goal of determining the profitability of the economy, a particular industry, or a company, the economist will not satisfy the needs of the financial analyst.

In the remaining sections of this paper I should like to discuss the various functions the economist can perform in an investment organization. Then I will describe how this information can be combined in a logical way so that you can see how economic analysis can be integrated into investment management.

THE BUSINESS FORECAST

Analysis of current economic developments and forecasting the future usually are considered the primary contribution of the economist in the investment field; sometimes this is his only function. The stock market may lead current business developments, but if you can forecast business accurately and sufficiently far ahead, presumably you can get a lead on the stock market.

In performing his forecasting function, the economist ordinarily provides quarterly estimates, usually for the succeeding year, of economic data such as Gross National Product and its components, industrial production, personal income, and aggregate corporate profits. These forecasts are presented in neat, tabular form, usually accompanied by a description of where the economy is, with perhaps a statement of the assumptions that underlie the projected figures. These forecasts most frequently are made toward the end of each calendar year. They may be revised at regular intervals, or they may be used until the next forecasting season rolls around, regardless of how they age in the interval. This approach assumes that the function of the economist is "to win the numbers game," that is, to provide in advance a set of numbers that will accurately project the future.

This practice does not seem to me to be the most advantageous use of the economist's talents. I consider it an unwarranted expectation that an economist or anyone else can provide even a reasonably precise numercial forecast four quarters or more in advance of what future business statistics will be. Periodic revisions of data, which, although necessary and desirable, place the economist in the difficult position of standing on a most shaky and uncertain platform as he launches into the future. Another reason for lack of enthusiasm for this approach is my belief that there is nothing magic in numbers. These neat, tabular presentations of economic data are no more than the quantifying of a large number of qualitative assumptions and evaluations that often change, sometimes quite suddenly. A perfect example of how abruptly business conditions can change materially was the sharp drop in automobile sales in the spring of 1966, when sales fell from a seasonally adjusted annual rate of 9.3 million domestically produced cars in the first quarter to an 8.0 million rate in April and a 7.5 million rate in May. Such an unexpected decline clearly calls for a reassessment not only of automobile demand but also of consumer buying attitudes generally. A forecast, therefore, is not something done by the calendar; rather it should be a daily reappraisal of the future as new information becomes available. In addition, many factors besides economic developments affect stock prices, so that even the best economic forecast may not provide the clue to stock price performance. The unusually sharp drop in stock prices in 1962, unaccompanied by a business contraction, is a good illustration.

How, then, do I believe economic forecasts should be used in the investment field? One suggestion, and not an insignificant one, would be to stop labeling such exercises "forecasts." The word "forecast" implies a prediction of what the future will be. Personally, I much prefer the word "assumption," which clearly announces that the economic information provided is not a prediction but rather an assessment of the most probable outcome based on what we know now and where we are today. Assumptions can be changed, but forecasts are expected to come true.

But if assumptions are not useful to predict stock prices, for they can at best be only part of the factors influencing stock prices, what purpose can they serve? In the first place, they describe the probable business environment in which investments will be made. Aided by this information, the investment manager is better able to appraise the investment climate; that is, in what kinds of investments is he most likely to make money? Should he be moving from bonds to stocks? Should he be more or less conservative in his equity selections? What industries should he favor? How should he balance his portfolio to take advantage of the most probable developments and also retain some hedges in case the assumptions have to be changed? In addition, the financial analyst is given guidelines to assess the profitability of the industries and companies he follows.

The nature of the assumptions is important also. The economist can provide a perspective far broader and for a longer time period than either the investment manager or the analyst is likely to have in his preoccupation with daily events. The economist's assumptions provide not only an overview but also can extend horizons out three to five years, indicating the trends as well as the dimensions of possible downturns during that period. With this background, the investment manager is better equipped to meet the challenge of sudden market movements or the distortions caused by overemphasis on near-term developments. For the large institutional investor, where the accumulation or sale of large positions takes time, the longer term view obviously is most important.

Flexibility and willingness to change are vital if the economist is to perform his function effectively. His usefulness is enhanced if he avoids the temptation to substitute his ideas of what should be for his best appraisal of what probably will be. The latter obviously is of greater importance. Moreover, a purely economic analysis is not nearly so effective as one which includes the political climate as well. Political decisions are often not economically based, but they can have an important influence on economic activity. Consumer attitudes also may not be economically rational, but they have an important impact on spending and investment. A properly trained and experienced economist will be aware of these requirements, all of which are necessary to make him a useful member of the investment team.

How should business assumptions be prepared? My own experience suggests that business assumptions should be prepared initially in the late summer to cover the remaining quarters of the current year and the four quarters of the succeeding year. In addition, it is extremely useful to have an estimate of the economy for a good business year about five years away as well as an estimate of the probable dimensions of any downturn in that period. This procedure provides not only a fairly detailed analysis of the year ahead but also the trend for the next several years and some measure of the possible pitfalls in between. The starting point for this work is a review of where the economy is believed to be and a qualitative evaluation of such critical areas as expected consumer durable demand, plant and equipment spending trends, the residential construction outlook, probable inventory developments, and federal government monetary and fiscal actions. With these essentials determined, a numerical forecast then can be prepared.

The data contained in these assumptions should include the details of Gross National Product and its components; the Federal Reserve Index of Industrial Production; plant and equipment spending; automobile sales, production, and inventories; housing starts; personal income and personal disposable income; and aggregate profits. The economic assumptions, together with assumptions about the money market and the stock market, summarize the most probable future investment environment and form the basis for investment policy. In addition, the results should be used uniformly by all of the industry analysts in preparing their company earnings estimates. This approach provides a consistent framework for investment decisions and avoids the internal conflict and confusion that might result if, for example, the steel analyst anticipated production of 130 million tons of steel, and the automobile analyst expected production of only 7 million cars.

Having prepared the detailed business assumptions, the monitoring process begins. Current economic information, both published and unpublished, should be gathered daily and analyzed in order to determine if the assumptions still are valid. When necessary, rather than at stated intervals, a new set of numbers should be prepared. While assumptions should not be changed unnecessarily, whenever substantial economic shifts occur the assumptions should be adjusted rapidly.

To summarize, then, economic assumptions may not be the best guide to future stock price movements. However, they should provide the broad perspective of the environment in which investments will be made and the fundamental ingredients to determine the relative profitability of particular industries and companies. Effective use of these services of the economist can, I believe, make a vital contribution to successful investment performance.

Money Market Trends

In addition to providing business analysis and assumptions about the future, there are other areas in which the economist can be effective. Although frequently considered a part of general economic analysis, the financial sector really deserves separate treatment, particularly where investment in fixed-income obligations is important. Money market trends must be followed because of their impact on the business picture, because of their impact on the timing and selection of bond purchases and sales, because of their influence on shifts in the equity ratio of a balanced investment portfolio and, finally, because of their influence on investment in financial institutions, the earnings of which depend fundamentally on the difference between the interest rates they must pay and the rates that they can earn.

In addition, money market analysis provides an important feedback to business analysis. The recent effect of high interest rates and tight money in the economy is a reminder that fiscal policy has not completely displaced monetary policy as an economic regulator. Tight money may cause a slowing of economic expansion and raise questions about future profits stability and growth. Tight money has an influence on investment attitudes and alters the yield relationships and relative attractiveness of bonds and stocks. The trend of commercial loans gives an indication of business demand. The pattern of institutional investors' forward investment commitments provides a clue to the willingness of businessmen to make future investments and to the strength of the housing market. Thus, you can see that the contribution of monetary analysis to business analysis is significant.

The specialized nature of the research in the money market area can be touched on only briefly. Fundamentally, this work requires an analysis of the supply and demand for funds. It includes a detailed evaluation of savings flows and the demand for funds by the business sector, the mortgage market, and the government sector—federal and state and local. An essential part of this research is an analysis of the attitudes, objectives, and actions of the Federal Reserve System and the U.S. Treasury, both of whom are critical forces in the money market. Federal, state, and local budgets and projected financing plans are other essential ingredients in effective money-market analysis. Not to be overlooked is the balance of payments, which in recent years has acted as an important inhibiting factor on the money managers from taking action that might otherwise have been indicated were only domestic considerations important. The result is not only an evaluation of the future course of interest rates, both long- and short-term, but also additional evidence from the financial side of current and prospective business activity and the investment climate.

International Developments

A good economics staff in the investment field also must be aware of what is happening in the world outside of a country. Analysis of foreign developments is essential for a variety of reasons. Money rates are affected by changes in the balance of payments and competitive interest rates abroad. Developments in the balance of payments can lead to restrictions on direct investment, such as the voluntary restraints on corporate investing abroad or indirect restrictions such as the interest equalization tax. Devaluation losses in foreign currencies can have a significant impact on the earnings of American corporations, sometimes eliminating one or two years growth in earnings. Devaluation of the dollar or the pound, whether actual or feared, will have important repercussions on domestic companies as well as an impact on security values, both short- and long-term. Foreign companies provide competition for American companies, which must be assessed. Wage and price developments abroad influence both the effectiveness of this competition and the operation of foreign subsidiaries of American companies. Finally, in spite of temporary inhibitions such as the interest equalization tax, investment is becoming more international, and securities of foreign companies will continue to find a place in the portfolios of American investors.

Obviously, the kind of research done in the international field is different and may not be as thorough as that done on the U.S. economy. Distance and the lack of available data make this type of analysis less comprehensive. Nevertheless, at a minimum economic and political developments abroad, foreign and the U.S. balance of payments, trends in prices and wages, and major industry and company developments should be followed. Foreign periodicals and statistical reports can be helpful, but much useful information also can be provided by reports from and personal contacts with research organizations and banks, both in the United States and abroad. This information should be integrated into the preparation of the economic assumptions and also be reported to the research staff to assist them in the evaluation of their industries and companies.

Corporate Profits Research

Although all of the information the economist can provide may be helpful, the most valuable contribution he can make is to focus and interpret this information as it bears on the outlook for corporate profits. The remaining section of this paper will indicate an approach for accomplishing this task of fully integrating economic analysis and investment management.

The detailed set of business assumptions described earlier can be used to outline for the analysts the probable business environment in which particular companies and industries will operate. These business assumptions are therefore a very helpful guide in making estimates of sales volume for the period ahead. Some industry sales are closely related to cyclical factors, others to aggregate activity, others are influenced by population and income trends, still others by financial forces. A skilled analyst will know which inputs are most useful.

In addition to help in estimating sales trends, the economist can also assist in estimating changes in factors affecting costs and prices and therefore profit margins. Aggregate data are available on trends in labor costs and productivity not only in broad areas of the economy but also in many specific industries. In addition, the economist has available a wide variety of data on price trends that cover the economy generally as well as many particular areas and products. More importantly, with his broader perspective he can evaluate the economic and political forces affecting prices and give valuable clues to future price trends. His perspective may help the analyst to determine whether a price change is in the offing or whether a given price change will stick.

An economist who is aware of the changing trends in the business scene and the political forces at work also can advise whether changes in the tax structure should be considered in making estimates. Economic assumptions have definite implications for the federal budget and the flow of funds into and out of the Treasury. This information combined with knowledge of the political attitude of the Administration and of Congress can be important determinants of fiscal policy, an area most financial analysts usually are willing to leave to someone well acquainted with this field.

With this information to guide him, coupled with his knowledge and experience and the additional benefit of contacts with companies, the analyst can now prepare earnings estimates for individual companies. However, this ordinarily is not the ultimate objective of an investment organization; from these individual earnings estimates an investment policy and program must emerge. Most institutional investment is done with some concept of relative investment values in mind rather than concentrating on the earnings and market value of individual securities taken in isolation. Consequently, some procedure must be used to obtain benchmarks against which any particular company can be compared.

Many analysts use the Dow-Jones Industrial Average as a yardstick, although the composition of this average does not make it particularly suitable for this purpose, in my opinion. The Standard and Poor's average would seem more useful, particularly since historical data are available covering a large number of industries. However, using the Standard and Poor's average requires making a great many individual company earnings estimates. My own experience suggests that earnings of the Standard and Poor's average can be approximated by a smaller sample of 125–150 companies. Individual earnings estimates can be aggregated by industry, by economic groupings and in total, in order to determine general earnings trends as well as trends in specific investment areas.

Here is another place the economist can be helpful. These earnings estimates can be compared with the economic assumptions in order to see if the estimates seem reasonable. They can also be compared with estimates of other broad aggregates of corporate profits that the economist can prepare, such as the Department of Commerce profits figures or those of the Federal Trade Commission-Securities and Exchange Commission in the manufacturing area.[1] Differences in the expectations for some of these broad profit aggregates and any sample of large, successful companies should not be surprising, because the profits performance of companies that are of primary investment interest usually is better than that of

---

[1] Such comparisons must be made with care, for these broad profit aggregates may be conceptually as well as statistically different from aggregates of shareholder profits. For a further discussion of this point, see Edmund A. Mennis, "Forecasting Corporate Profits," in *How Business Economists Forecast*," edited by William Butler and Robert Kavesh (Prentice Hall, 1966).

companies generally. However, comparison of trends and turning points is useful.

Two further steps can be taken. The first would be to aggregate data for particular industries into groups, the earnings of which are affected differently by changing economic conditions. A possible division might be cyclical, cyclical growth, growth and defensive industries. Others will occur to the sophisticated analyst. In this way, broad divergences in earnings trends can be ascertained that may indicate shifts in investment emphasis.

A second step would be to add data on prices in order to compute price-earning ratios and yields. This step provides a basis for relative value comparisons, because a stock can be compared with its industry, with the group of which it is a part, and also with a broad measure of the market in terms of the two fundamentals of security analysis, earnings, and their valuation. This comparison can be made at a point in time, and, if the historical data are available, a comparison may also be made with past relationships over time. This perspective provides invaluable insight for investment selection.[2] Admittedly, the historical data are not easily prepared, although the computer has simplified the task materially.

These last two steps are not necessarily the function of the economist. They have been described, however, in order to indicate the logical steps in investment decision-making and to show the flow from the broad economic assumptions to earnings to their valuation. Such a logical, step-by-step approach will give the framework in which investment policy is set. It also will assist in the investment program, that is, the selection and timing of individual security purchases and sales. At each point, critical judgments must be made, and a constant review is necessary in the light of the flow of new information. The economist, with his background and perspective, can play a key role in interpreting the information and assisting in making better investment decisions. I am convinced that more rather than less use of this kind of analysis will occur in the years ahead.

---

[2] For an outline of how such an analysis can be done, see Edmund A. Mennis, "Profit Trends and Values in Mid–1965," *Financial Analysts Journal*, July–August 1965, page 63 ff.

9
THE FLOW OF FUNDS ACCOUNTS: A FRAMEWORK FOR FINANCIAL ANALYSIS*

Lawrence S. Ritter

INTRODUCTION

Throughout most of its history, accounting has been concerned primarily with recordkeeping in the individual business firm. About a generation or so ago, however, economists started applying accounting principles and techniques to the whole economy: recordkeeping for the whole society. Out of such "social accounting" came the National Income Accounts of the Department of Commerce, which are by now well known. On the financial side, more recently, the Board of Governors of the Federal Reserve System developed the Flow of Funds Accounts.

The National Income Accounts are today familiar to every student who has taken even one course in economics, as well as to many who have not. Such concepts as consumer spending, investment spending, and gross national product (GNP) have become recognizable to millions. Every beginning economics textbook now devotes at least one chapter to the derivation and construction of the National Income Accounts, and newspapers and other media do not hesitate to report and discuss recent developments at considerable length.

The Flow of Funds Accounts have not yet acquired the widespread familiarity, even among economists, that has been attained by the National Income Accounts. And perhaps they never will. But they are as indispensable for understanding developments and interrelationships in financial markets as the National Income Accounts are for understanding trends in production and real output.

Strangely enough, the Department of Commerce's famous National Income Accounts do not contain even one reference to the financial aspects of the economy. Nothing about the money supply, about liquidity, about lending, borrowing, or hoarding. It would seem that the

---
* Reprinted by permission of *The Bulletin* (August 1968). Copyright 1968 by New York University.

National Income Accounts are constructed on the assumption that what happens in financial markets is not significant for what happens in the markets for goods and services. Be that as it may—and it is, of course, not likely—this has meant that financial analysts have had to construct their own social accounts, accounts which record such things as borrowing and lending in financial markets as well as the interrelationships between financial markets and goods markets. These are known as the Flow of Funds Accounts. The only prior knowledge which is necessary to understand them are some very elementary accounting priniples—namely, the concept of a balance sheet and an income statement.

Very briefly, the flow of funds is a system of social accounting in which (a) the economy is divided into a number of sectors, and (b) a "sources and uses of funds statement" is constructed for each sector. When all these sector sources and uses of funds statements are placed side by side, we obtain (c) the flow of funds matrix for the economy as a whole. That is the sum and substance of the matter, and most of the rest of this paper is devoted to explaining its meaning and implications.

DIVIDING THE ECONOMY INTO SECTORS

In geometry, the word "sector" refers to the area bounded by two radii and the included arc of a circle. It is a subdivision or a section of the circle. In the same sense, a sector in economics refers to a subdivision of the economy, in particular to a group of decision-making units within the economy that are more or less homogeneous in certain respects.

In the National Income Accounts, for example, the economy is usually divided into three main sectors: consumers, business firms, and government. In the Flow of Funds Accounts, financial institutions are separated from other business firms and grouped together in a sector of their own. The number of sectors into which the economy is divided is not especially important, providing the sectoring is done on some consistent basis. There should be more than one sector, of course, in order to be able to trace transactions between sectors. The maximum practical number of sectors depends on such factors as the relative homogeneity of groups of decision-making units within the economy, the availability of raw data and, perhaps most important, ease of handling. Too many sectors make it cumbersome to analyze interrelations among them. Thus, although we are well aware that all consumers are not really homogeneous, we still group them all together, and the same goes for commercial banks, nonfinancial business firms, etc. Whatever the number of sectors, it is important that they be exhaustive—i.e., that taken all together they encompass the whole economy.

A GENERALIZED SECTOR BALANCE SHEET

Our first objective, as mentioned in (b) above, is to construct a model sector "sources and uses of funds statement." This is a hybrid accounting statement that combines both the balance sheet and the income statement into one. It is the fundamental basis of the flow of funds accounts, and the explanation of its derivation will occupy much of the remainder of this paper.

As a first step in building a sector sources and uses of funds statement, let us begin with a model balance sheet, a balance sheet so general that its terminology would be applicable to *any* sector. Such a very general sector balance sheet would look like the following:

(1) A Generalized Balance Sheet for a Single Sector:

Assets	Liabilities and Net Worth
Financial Assets:	Liabilities:
1. Money	1. Short-term
2. Near-monies	2. Long-term
3. Other	
Real Assets	Net Worth
$\Sigma =$	Σ

A balance sheet similar to this can be drawn up for each sector. Since it is a balance sheet, it must balance—i.e., the sum of the sector's total assets must equal its liabilities plus net worth. Thus it contains, at the bottom, summation equality signs. The only difference between the balance sheets of the different sectors would be in the characteristic items that would appear under each heading. Under the heading "Real Assets," for example, business firms would typically include the value of inventories and plant and equipment, while consumers would list such items as clothing and furniture.

A crucial distinction in (1) is that between real assets and financial assets. A real asset is something which appears on only one balance sheet, that of its owner. It includes such items as inventories, plant and equipment, houses, automobiles, etc. A financial asset, on the other hand, is defined as a claim against someone else, an IOU of one sort or another. Every financial asset must appear on two balance sheets: on the balance sheet of its owner (as an asset, a *financial* asset) and also, simultaneously, on the balance sheet of whoever owes it to that owner (this time as a liability).[1]

While only some assets are financial assets (i.e., are claims against someone else), all liabilities are financial (i.e., they must involve a debt owed to someone else). This means that every liability listed on every balance sheet must necessarily imply the existence of a financial asset of equal amount on someone else's balance sheet.

If we attempt to reckon up the wealth (or net worth) of society as a whole, this correspondence between financial assets and liabilities has interesting consequences. It is well known that the net worth (or wealth)

---

[1] For example, if you owe $100 to the First National Bank, then the bank counts that $100 IOU of yours (which it owns) as one of its financial assets. But you list the same $100 on your balance sheet as a liability. No one can be owed money (and list it as his financial asset) unless someone owes it to him (and thus has a liability).

of any *one* entity is equal to its total assets minus its total liabilities. This could be expressed by saying that the net worth of any family or business firm is equal to its real assets plus its financial assets minus its liabilities. For society as a whole, however, every time a financial asset is entered for any firm or family, a corresponding liability has to be rung up on the balance sheet of some *other* firm or family.

Imagine a single lengthy balance sheet for the entire economy. We could theoretically construct such a balance sheet for society as a whole by entering all the assets and liabilities of every firm, every family, and every governmental unit on one huge balance sheet. However, every time we put down a financial asset for someone, we would sooner or later find ourselves putting down a liability of equal amount for someone else. Then, after all the records had been entered, if we tried to figure out the net worth of society as a whole—which, as with individuals, would be real assets plus financial assets minus liabilities—we would find that since the liabilities are equal to the financial assets these two would cancel each other out. For all of society taken as a whole, only real assets would be left.

The net worth of any one unit within society is equal to its real assets plus its financial assets less its liabilities, *but the wealth of society as a whole must be equal to just its real assets*. The difference between a single unit and society as a whole arises because for any one unit or sector its financial assets need not equal its own liabilities, but for society as a whole total financial assets *must* equal total liabilities.

This conclusion—that the net worth or wealth of society as a whole equals only its real assets—always pleases conservatives because it implies that printing money cannot in and of itself make a country richer. After all, money is a *financial* asset, and therefore appears on *two* balance sheets, as an asset of the holder but as a liability of the issuer. Most of our money is in the form of demand deposits, for example, and these are liabilities of commercial banks. The part of our money that is in the form of coin or currency is a liability of either the United States Treasury or the Federal Reserve, depending on which agency issued it. Thus, merely printing money can hardly make a nation richer, no matter how much it prints. Liabilities go up as much as assets. To become richer—to increase its net worth—a country must increase its output of *real* assets, its production of real goods and services. As conservatives are fond of pointing out, if we want to become wealthier we must work harder and produce more. Printing money, per se, will not do it.

By the same token, however, the exact same logic also implies that one of the favorite incantations of conservatives is equally false: namely, the belief that increasing the national debt makes a country poorer. Government bonds—the total outstanding being our national debt—are liabilities to the government but are financial assets to whoever owns them. If the national debt increases, as long as it is held within the country, someone's financial assets go up as much as the government's liabilities. A government bond is, after all, an asset for whoever buys it. The very term "national debt" is a half-truth. If it is a domestically held debt, it could just as well be called the "national credit." Both labels are half-truths. As with all liabilities, it is *both* a debt (to the borrower) *and* a credit (to the lender). To become poorer—to reduce its net worth—a country must reduce its holdings of real assets, curtail its production of *real* goods and services. Increasing the national debt, no matter how high it goes, will not in itself make a country poorer.[2] The equality between financial assets and liabilities for society as a whole turns out to be a two-edged sword.

Before leaving our generalized sector balance sheet, it will be helpful for later purposes to rearrange and consolidate the items. Thus:

(2) Rearranging Our Sector Balance Sheet:

A	L and NW
Real Assets	Net Worth
Financial Assets	Liabilities
Money	

$$\Sigma = \Sigma$$

Sector balance sheet (2) is identical with (1) except for some slight rearrangement and consolidation of the items. Since it is a complete balance sheet it must still "balance"; thus the summation equality signs are still below Assets and below Liabilities plus Net Worth. However, in this version "money" has been singled out for special treatment. Strictly speaking, money is a financial asset and it should, therefore, be considered as already taken into account under the heading of financial assets. However, economists have traditionally treated money as a rather special and unique sort of financial asset. Thus, we have given it a special pigeon-hole. From now on, therefore, the entry "financial assets" should be understood as really meaning "financial assets other than money."

FROM STOCKS TO FLOWS: BORROWING, LENDING, AND HOARDING

Balance sheets, of course, show all assets and liabilities at a *moment* in time. By definition, they show the values of assets and liabilities as of a

---

[2] The following article, "The Burden of the Debt: A Mathematical Proof," by Professor John M. Kuhlman, reprinted in its entirety from the March 1966 issue of the *American Economic Review* (page 188), makes the same point somewhat more succinctly:

A familiar proposition is that we owe the national debt to ourselves. However, this proposition has still not been rigorously proved. My intention is to provide such a proof.

The proposition that the national debt as a liability must just equal the total of the associated assets can be stated as follows:

(1) $\Sigma IOU's = \Sigma UOMe's$.

If we divide both sides of the equation by OU, we have:

(2) $\Sigma I's = \Sigma Me's$.

Q.E.D.

given date, say December 31, 1969. However, we are often more interested in a flow over a period of time than we are in stocks at a moment in time. In order to convert the stocks typically shown on balance sheets to flows, we can compare two balance sheets for the same sector, two balance sheets "snapped" at different points in time. Thus, we take the balance sheet of a household on December 31, 1969, and then again on December 31, 1970. By comparing the two and noting the *changes* that have taken place in each entry, we can in a sense convert stocks into flows. We can now tell how much furniture was purchased, or how many bonds were bought, during the year 1970.

If we confine ourselves to financial assets, money, and liabilities, ignoring real assets and net worth for the moment, such a comparative sector statement, indicating the *changes* that have taken place between two dates in our balance sheet (2), would look like this:

(3) A Sector Financial Sources and Uses of Funds Statement:

Financial Uses	Financial Sources
Δ Financial Assets Δ Money	Δ Liabilities

Such a statement is called a sector *financial* sources and uses of funds statement. It covers a *period* of time (say a year). It need not balance—thus no summation equality signs—since it is derived from partial rather than complete balance sheets (remember that we have not yet taken real assets and net worth into account), and it tells us the *net changes* that have taken place in each item between the start and the end of the time span it covers.

Notice that the headings of the columns have been changed somewhat compared with (2). Instead of "Assets" and "Liabilities" we now have "Financial Uses" and "Financial Sources." A financial source of funds for a sector is, by definition, an increase in its liabilities: households, business firms, governments, and financial institutions can obtain funds by increasing their liabilities (borrowing). A financial use of funds for a sector is—also by definition—an increase in its holdings of financial assets or of money: households, business firms, governments, and financial institutions can use their funds to buy financial assets (lending) or to build up their stock of money (which is usually called hoarding). Using these common terms, we could rewrite (3) as follows:

(3):

Financial Uses	Financial Sources
Δ FA (Lending) Δ M (Hoarding)	Δ L (Borrowing)

However, these possibilities—borrowing, lending, and hoarding—do not exhaust all the possible sources and uses of funds potentially available to a sector. For example, another possible source through which a family or a firm might acquire funds, other than borrowing, is by selling off some of its financial assets. Still another is by dishoarding. And another possible use of funds would be to repay one's debts.

These alternatives did not appear on (3) because only net changes were considered there, and it was assumed that these could only be positive. Potential negative changes should also be included in our financial sources and uses of funds statement if we are to make it complete:

(3′) Gross Form of (3):

Financial Uses	Financial Sources
ΔFA ⋀ (Lending)	ΔFA ⋁ (Selling Securities)
ΔL ⋁ (Repaying Debts)	ΔL ⋀ (Borrowing)
ΔM ⋀ (Hoarding)	ΔM ⋁ (Dishoarding)

Statement (3′) is the gross form of Statement (3). That is, in Statement (3) we implicitly netted out any pluses and minuses and assumed that the net result was a plus. In (3′), however, the gross form of a sector financial sources and uses of funds statements, there is space for either negative or positive changes, or for both.[3]

In Statement (3) we had only three possible sources or uses of funds—borrowing, lending, and hoarding. With (3′) we now have three additional alternatives—repaying one's debts, selling off financial assets, and dishoarding. These latter three are merely the negative form of the first three. An increase in liabilities, or borrowing, is a source of funds; a decrease in liabilities, or repaying one's debts, is a use of funds. An increase in holdings of financial assets—the purchase of government bonds, for example, or any other form of lending—is a use of one's funds; selling off some of those bonds to raise money is obviously a source of funds. Similarly, if hoarding is considered a use of one's funds, dipping into one's pool of cash so that one's money holdings decline (dishoarding) would have to be considered a source of funds. Thus the gross form of a sector's financial sources and uses of funds statement has room for negative as well as for positive changes, for possible decreases in L, FA, and M, as well as for increases.

A look at (3′) shows that lending and borrowing are not really opposites, as is usually assumed. Instead, the opposite of lending, which is the purchase of a financial asset, is the sale of a financial asset. And the

---

[3] Example: If during a year, a firm borrows $100 and *also* repays $40 of its previously outstanding debts, we would have entered only the net $60 under borrowing—a source of funds—if we used Statement (3), the net form. With gross statement (3′), however, we enter $100 under borrowing, a source of funds, *and* $40 under debt repayment (or negative borrowing), a use of funds. This is, of course, a much more complete description of the firm's transactions than merely entering a net $60 under borrowing.

opposite of borrowing, in which one's liabilities go up, is repayment of one's debts, which reduces one's liabilities.

Useful conceptually as (3') is, it is difficult to collect data on the gross basis needed for its proper construction. As a result, most published data are in the form of (3), with each pair netted. Because of this, we will return to (3) as we continue to construct a complete sources and uses statement. By convention, if the net change in any entry turns out to be negative over a period, it is kept on the side where it presently appears in (3) but preceded by a minus sign. If the net change in financial assets for a sector turned out to be minus, for example, it would be recorded on the uses side but preceded by a minus sign and referred to as a negative use.

INVESTMENT AND SAVING

We have thus far ignored the possibility of changes in the first pair of items on sector Balance Sheet (2), namely changes in real assets and in net worth. This is because up to now we have confined ourselves to considering only purely *financial* sources and uses of funds—to changes in only financial assets, money holdings, and liabilities. It is time to bring in the possibility of changes in the two remaining balance sheet entries, real assets and net worth.

In addition to purely financial sources and uses of funds, a sector is also likely to have "nonfinancial" sources and uses of funds, arising from the sale or purchase of *real* assets. These may involve transactions on *capital* account or transactions on *current* account. We will devote the remainder of this section to nonfinancial capital transactions and will turn to current receipts and expenditures in the next section.

Nonfinancial uses of funds on *capital* account (capital expenditures) refer to the purchase of real assets with an expected useful life of one year or longer. For a business firm, it could be the acquisition of plant or equipment. For a household, it could be the purchase of a house or a car. Nonfinancial transactions on *current* account—current expenditures—refer to the acquisition of real assets with an expected life of less than a year. This follows conventional accounting procedures, in which a distinction is made between capital expenditures, the purchase of durable real assets, and current expenditures, the purchase of nondurables, with an expected life of one year arbitrarily dividing the two.

The acquisition of real assets on capital account, or capital expenditures, is usually termed real investment, in contrast to financial investment, which refers to the purchase of financial assets. Indeed, when the term investment is used by itself, without a modifying adjective, it is usually understood in economics jargon to mean real investment, the purchase of capital goods, and that is the way we will use the term henceforth. If we want to use the term to refer to the purchase of financial assets—stocks or bonds—we will explicitly say *financial* investment. Used alone, the word investment stands for the purchase of real capital assets, and since this is obviously as much a use of funds as is the acquisition of financial assets we will have to include it as a potential use of funds on our sector sources and uses of funds statement.[4]

The change in a sector's net worth can now be derived as a residual. Net worth is defined as a sector's total assets minus its total liabilities. Any increase in net worth over a period must therefore be equal to the increase in the sector's total assets minus any increase in its liabilities. If we insert any change in real assets into (3), we will have accounted for changes in all assets and in liabilities. The difference between them must be in the change in net worth.

Just as an increase in real assets is called investment, an increase in net worth is what we mean when we use the term saving. Actually, a sector's saving is usually defined in terms of its current transactions rather than its capital transactions. Saving usually refers to the excess of a sector's current receipts over its current expenditures. But an excess of current receipts over current expenditures (flows) must necessarily imply either a buildup of (stocks of) total assets or a reduction of liabilities, or some combination of the two, exactly equal in amount to the excess of current receipts over current expenditures.

For example, if a household receives $100 in income and spends $80 of it on consumer goods, it has saved $20. If that $20 is merely held in the form of cash, money holdings will have risen. If it is used to buy bonds or real assets, either financial or real assets must have risen. Or it might be used to repay debts, in which case liabilities will have declined. In any case, total assets must rise or liabilities fall in an amount that is precisely equal to the sector's saving during the period. Since a sector's saving during a period must be equal to the increase in its total assets plus any decrease in its liabilities, which is exactly what we mean by a change in net worth, the two—saving and the change in net worth—must be identical.

The changes for a sector between two dates in real assets and net worth can thus be presented as follows:

(4) A Sector Nonfinancial Sources and Uses of Funds Statement on Capital Account:

Nonfinancial Uses on Capital Account	Nonfinancial Sources on Capital Account
Δ Real Assets (Investment)	Δ Net Worth (Saving)

Just as (3) did not have to balance since it was derived from some (rather than all) of the balance sheet items, neither is (4) likely to balance. An individual unit or sector may or may not invest—that is,

---

[4] Real investment may be recorded on either a net or a gross basis, in the sense that depreciation may or may not be deducted.

purchase real assets—in an amount just equal to its current saving. It may invest less than it saves, or more. If a unit or sector has investment equal to its saving it is called a balanced budget sector. If it saves more than it invests it is a surplus sector, and if it invests more than it saves it is a deficit sector. (How could a sector invest more than it saves? Simply by borrowing enough money to finance its deficit, or perhaps by dishoarding or selling off financial assets to raise the funds it needs.)

A COMPLETE SECTOR SOURCES AND USES OF FUNDS STATEMENT

Although neither (3) nor (4), taken alone, have to balance, if they are combined together then they must necessarily balance. This is because if they are combined together then the changes in *all* of the items on Balance Sheet (2) will have been taken into account:

(5) = (3) + (4) A Sector Sources and Uses of Funds Statement:

Uses	Sources
ΔRA (Investment)	ΔNW (Saving)
ΔFA (Lending)	ΔL (Borrowing)
ΔM (Hoarding)	
$\Sigma =$	Σ

Sector Statement (5) must balance—and thus it contains summation equality signs—because it includes changes in all of the items on Balance Sheet (2). If Balance Sheet (2) must balance on December 31, 1969, and also on December 31, 1970, then the changes that have occurred between the two dates—which is what (5) represents—must also balance.[5]

Because it *must* balance, Statement (5) shows clearly that a surplus sector, which saves more than it invests, *must* repay debts, lend, or hoard an amount equal to its surplus. And a deficit sector, which invests more than it saves, *must* finance that deficit by borrowing, selling off financial assets, or dishoarding in an amount equal to its deficit.[6] If they did not do one of these things, then Statement (5) would not balance. By definition, however, it must balance.[7]

---

[5] As would also be true if (3') and (4) were combined into one, which could be called (5'), the gross form of (5).

[6] A deficit sector may also finance its deficit by printing money. However, only two sectors are legally able to exercise that unique option—commercial banks (by creating demand deposits) and the government (by creating dollar bills). If they did so, it would be entered on their Statement (5) as an increase in their liabilities (borrowing). While money is an asset to whoever owns it, it is a liability to whoever issues it. Later we will examine some of the implications of borrowing via the issuance of liabilities that people use as money. For the moment, however, we will assume that the option is not exercised, that the money supply does not change.

[7] Statement (5) is also useful in providing a demonstration alternative to the usual textbook Keynesian one that, ex post, saving must equal investment for the economy as a whole. It was noted above, with respect to (1) and (2), that if *all* sector balance sheets were consolidated into one, the total of liabilities would equal the total of financial assets, so that the net worth of the economy as a whole must necessarily

Statement (5) is the most widely used form of sector sources and uses of funds statement and is frequently labeled so. However, strictly speaking, it is incomplete. It contains financial sources and uses of funds (3), and nonfinancial sources and uses on capital account (4), but it does not take explicit account of *current* transactions. That is, it does not include current receipts accruing during a period as a source of funds or current expenditures as a use, except insofar as the difference between the two (saving) is included as a source of funds on capital account. In other words, thus far we have neglected the crucial fact that current income is a most important source of funds for the average household, just as current sales receipts are for the business firm. And that current consumption expenditures are a significant household use of funds, as are payments for wages and raw materials by the typical business firm.

A truly complete sector sources and uses of funds statement should take account of such current transactions, just as much as it should take account of financial and nonfinancial capital transactions. To put it somewhat differently, up to now we have painstakingly taken balance sheet factors into account, but we have neglected the income statement. (Capital expenditures, discussed at length above, do not appear on an income statement, which is confined to current transactions.)

A typical sector income statement, general enough to apply to any sector, would, in skeleton form, look something like the following:

(6) A Generalized Income Statement for a Single Sector:

Nonfinancial Uses on Current Account	Nonfinancial Sources on Current Account
Current Expenditures Saving (Addition to NW)	Current Receipts

$$\Sigma = \Sigma$$

A sector income statement amounts to a statement of nonfinancial sources and uses of funds on current account. Current receipts—mainly current income where households are concerned, sales receipts for business firms, and tax receipts when government is involved—are of course a major source of funds in most instances. And current expenditures—on wages, salaries, raw materials, nondurable goods, services—are similarly usually the major use of funds for most economic units, be they households, business firms, or a governmental body.

Naturally, tax payments, a major current *use* of funds for households and business firms, are a current *source* of funds to governments. This is

---

equal the value of the real assets. It follows that, if *all* the sector sources and uses statements, such as (5), were consolidated into one, the total of borrowing would equal the total of lending plus hoarding, so that for the economy as a whole saving must necessarily equal investment. We will return to this point later.

not unusual, however: consumer expenditures (a household use of funds) are receipts (a source of funds) for the businessman who sells the goods and services to the consumers. And business spending on wages and salaries (a business use of funds) becomes income (a source of funds) to consumers. This is fundamentally no different than the fact that, as we have seen, every financial asset must also appear as a liability on someone else's balance sheet.

Any excess of current receipts over current expenditures is generally termed saving, although when it involves the government sector it is frequently called a budget surplus and when it applies to the business sector it is often labeled either retained earnings or addition to net worth. Saving is the balancing item on an income statement, just as net worth is on a balance sheet. Since saving is defined as equal to any difference between current receipts and current expenditures—just as net worth is defined as equal to any difference between total assets and total liabilities —an income statement must balance as much as a balance sheet must. Thus, our summation equality signs appear on Statement (6).

As a "use" of funds on current account, saving takes the form of non-spending, of retention or accumulation. As such, it represents an addition to one's wealth or net worth and becomes available as a source of funds for capital account. Saving may also be negative, of course, as when one spends more on current expenditures than one receives in income, in which case this "dissaving" represents a reduction in one's wealth or net worth, a drain on capital. In New England, it is said, the second greatest sin is to spend more on consumption than your income, thereby using up your capital. (What *the* greatest sin is appears to depend on just which section of New England one has in mind.)[8]

A truly complete sector sources and uses of funds statement—one which includes current nonfinancial sources and uses in addition to financial transactions and capital nonfinancial transactions—would combine Statements (5) and (6):[9]

---

[8] As investment, saving may be recorded on either a net or a gross basis in that depreciation charges may or may not be deducted from the addition to net worth. It should be noted, however, that even if depreciation is deducted, so that saving is measured on a net basis, depreciation would still be a source of funds for capital account, since it represents a non-cash expense rather than an actual current outlay of funds. For example, assume that a firm's current receipts exceed current expenditures by exactly the amount of depreciation charges, so that net saving (and the change in net worth) is zero. This zero change in net worth is not consistent with the fact that real assets must be written down by the amount of the depreciation; on this latter basis, net worth should be lower by the amount of depreciation. The firm must have, for example, "involuntarily" accumulated cash equal to the depreciation charges, which cash can be spent to restore real assets to their former value *or for any other purpose the firm chooses.*

[9] Or, in gross form, would combine (5') and (6) into what could be called (7'). See Statement (3') and the discussion related thereto and footnote 5.

(7) = (5) + (6) A Complete Sector Sources and Uses of Funds Statement:

Uses	Sources
Current Expenditures Saving (ΔNW)	Current Receipts
ΔRA (Investment) ΔFA (Lending) ΔM (Hoarding)	ΔNW (Saving) ΔL (Borrowing)

$$\Sigma = \Sigma$$

Since the income statement (above the dotted line) must balance, and the changes in the balance sheet (below the dotted line) must also balance, the summation of all the sources must equal the summation of all the uses of funds. Also, since saving (or the change in net worth) on the income statement must necessarily be the same as the change in net worth (or saving) on the balance sheet, saving could be deleted from both sides without disturbing the equality between total sources and total uses.

If saving were deleted from both sides, Statement (7) would simply express the logical imperative that the funds a sector receives during a period from current receipts and borrowing must be disposed of in some way—either by current expenditures, capital expenditures, lending or, if it does none of these, by hoarding, merely increasing its cash holdings. More precisely, in terms of Statement (7'),[10] the funds a sector receives during a period from all sources, including current receipts, borrowing, selling off financial assets, and dishoarding, must be disposed of in some way—by current spending, capital spending, lending, debt repayment, or hoarding.

Above, we defined a deficit sector as one which invests more than it saves, and a surplus sector as one with saving greater than investment. Statement (7) shows that an alternative definition of a deficit sector would be one which spends more on current and capital goods than it receives in current receipts. Its nonfinancial spending, in other words, exceeds its income. And a surplus sector could be defined as one with consumption plus investment spending less than its current receipts (or income).

This follows from the fact that saving is defined as the gap between income and current expenditures. If a sector's capital expenditures exceed that gap (i.e., exceed its saving), then its current plus capital expenditures must exceed its income. In brief, if a household's current income is $100 and its current expenditures are $80, it has saved $20. If it now makes a nonfinancial investment expenditure of $35, its *total* spending has exceeded its income by $15, precisely the same deficit margin that its investment exceeded its saving. Alternatively, if it had only spent $5 on

---

[10] See footnote 9.

investment goods, its total spending on consumption and investment would have been only $85, which is $15 less than its income. This $15 surplus is precisely the same as the margin by which its saving exceeded its investment.

A deficit sector can thus be defined as one where investment exceeds saving or, alternatively, as one which spends more on consumption plus investment than it earns. The amount of the deficit will be the same regardless of which definition is used. Likewise, a surplus sector can be defined as one where saving exceeds investment, or as one which spends less on consumption and investment than it earns, so that it is left with a surplus. The amount of the surplus will be the same regardless of which definition is used.[11]

In any case, the summation equality signs on Statement (7) reaffirm, as we have seen before, that a surplus sector must dispose of its surplus by repaying debts, hoarding, or lending an amount equal to its surplus. And a deficit sector must finance its excess spending by selling off financial assets, dishoarding, or borrowing an amount equal to its deficit.[12]

THE FLOW OF FUNDS MATRIX FOR THE WHOLE ECONOMY

Near the beginning of this paper the flow of funds accounts were described as "a system of social accounting in which (*a*) the economy is divided into a number of sectors, and (*b*) a sources and uses of funds statement is constructed for each sector. When all these sector sources and uses of funds statements are placed side by side, we obtain (*c*) the flow of funds matrix for the economy as a whole."

Having completed steps (*a*) and (*b*), all that remains is to place our sector sources and uses statements side by side in order to obtain (*c*), the flow of funds matrix for the economy as a whole. When the flow of funds matrix was first published by the Federal Reserve in 1955 it showed, side by side, the truly complete sector sources and uses of funds statements in the form of (7). Since 1959, however, it has consisted only of partial statements in the form of (5), i.e., only that part of (7) below the dotted line. Thus, current receipts and current expenditures are not shown explicitly by themselves in the presently published final matrix, but they are implicitly included in that the difference between them—saving—*is* shown.

Assuming a total of three sectors, and omitting some detail, the flow of funds matrix as presently published appears essentially as follows:

---

[11] Put succinctly, a sector's consumption (*c*) plus investment (*i*) spending comprise its total nonfinancial expenditure (x): $c + i = x$. Saving (s) is defined as its current income (y) less consumption spending (c): $s = y - c$, so that $c + s = y$.
Since $c + i = x$ and $c + s = y$, it follows that if i is greater than, equal to, or less than s, so will, by exactly the same amount, x be greater than, equal to, or less than y.

[12] A deficit sector might also cover its deficit by printing money, which is a form of borrowing. See footnote 6.

(8) Flow of Funds Matrix for the Whole Economy:

	Sector A		Sector B		Sector C		All Sectors	
	U	S	U	S	U	S	U	S
Saving (ΔNW)		s		s		s		S
Investment (ΔRA)	i		i		i		I	
Borrowing (ΔL)		b		b		b		B
Lending (ΔFA)	l		l		l		L + H	
Hoarding (ΔM)	h		h		h			
	$\Sigma = \Sigma$		$\Sigma = \Sigma$		$\Sigma = \Sigma$		$\Sigma = \Sigma$	

NOTE: The small letters within the matrix represent the data for sector saving (s), investment (i), borrowing (b), lending (l), and hoarding (h), and are placed in the appropriate space where such data would be entered. The large letters similarly represent the aggregate sum totals for the whole economy. Thus s+ s+ s = S, i+i+i= I, etc.

This complete matrix, or summary statement of the flow of funds through the economy, forms an interlocking, self-contained system. It shows, for a specified time period, the balanced sources and uses of funds for each sector; the interrelations among the sectors; and the aggregate totals of saving, investment, borrowing, lending, and hoarding for the economy as a whole.

For each individual sector, saving plus borrowing must equal investment plus lending plus hoarding. Since that is true for each individual sector, it is also true in summation for all the sectors taken together, i.e., for the economy as a whole. In addition, for the economy as a whole, though not necessarily for any one sector taken by itself, saving must equal investment.[13] This follows from the fact that, since one sector's liability is another sector's financial asset, for the whole economy borrowing must equal lending plus hoarding:

$$\text{For the whole economy} \quad S + B = I + L + H$$
$$\text{But} \quad B = L + H$$
$$\therefore \quad S = I$$

The conclusion that saving must equal investment applies only to the entire economy taken in the aggregate, not to any one sector taken by itself. Any one sector may borrow more or less than it lends, and save more or less than it invests:

$$\text{For any one sector} \quad s + b = i + l + h$$
$$\text{However} \quad b \text{ need not} = l + h$$
$$\therefore \quad s \text{ need not} = i$$

Since saving need not equal investment for any one sector, but must be equal for the whole economy, it follows that for each sector that invests

---

[13] See footnote 7.

more than it saves there must, somewhere, be other sectors which save correspondingly more than they invest. Since $s + s + s = S$, and $i + i + i = I$, and S must equal I, then for every sector where $i > s$ there must be other sectors where $s > i$.

Thus, deficit sectors, which invest more than they save, necessarily imply the existence of other surplus sectors, which save more than they invest. This is true not only because the economy-wide total of saving must equal investment, but also because a deficit sector must finance its deficit, as we have seen, by borrowing, selling off financial assets, or dishoarding.[14] This implies the existence of surplus sectors to do the lending, buying of the securities, or hoarding.

Similarly, surplus sectors, which save more than they invest, necessarily imply the existence of deficit sectors. A surplus sector must lend, repay debts, or hoard in an amount equal to its surplus. This, in turn, implies the existence of deficit sectors to borrow, reduce their financial assets, or dishoard.

FINANCIAL MARKETS AND GNP

The economic function of financial markets is to provide channels through which the excess funds of surplus units—who are spending less than their current income—can be transferred to the hands of potential deficit units—who want to spend more than their income. Those who can visualize and exploit potentially profitable investment opportunities are not always the same ones who are generating sufficient current saving to finance themselves. Financial markets are the conduits that link surplus and deficit units together, providing the means whereby, directly or indirectly, one can finance the other.

Without such markets, surplus units would be unable to do anything with their surpluses except hoard them, and deficit units would be unable to finance any spending over and above their current income except insofar as they were fortunate enough to have previously hoarded cash that they could now draw upon. Financial markets give surplus units additional options besides that of simply hoarding their surpluses: They

---

[14] Or, as we have noted before, by printing money (see footnote 6). If it occurred, this would be entered on the Flow of Funds Matrix in the bottom row (i.e., ΔM), but as a *source* of funds for the sector creating the monetary liability. This possibility could only apply to the commercial banking sector (creating demand deposits), the Federal Reserve (creating Federal Reserve Notes), or the government (creating other forms of coin or currency). These newly created liabilities of these sectors must then also be entered on the matrix as a *use* of funds for whichever sector winds up holding (hoarding) them.

As earlier we separated money from all other financial assets, here we are separating the creation of money from the creation of all other liabilities. Thus, just as lending means the purchase of financial assets other than money, similarly borrowing should mean the sale of liabilities other than monetary liabilities. None of this disturbs, in any way, any of the conclusions we have reached.

can, if they wish, *buy securities*[15] with the money. That is, they can lend their funds (by buying securities which represent the liabilities of others), or repay debts (by buying back securities which represent their own liabilities).

Similarly, through financial markets deficit sectors can finance their deficits even though they may not have a previously accumulated hoard of cash to draw upon: They can *sell securities* to raise the funds they need. That is, they can borrow the money (by selling securities representing their own liability), or dispose of some financial assets they had previously acquired (sell off securities which represent the liability of others).

The existence of highly developed, widely accessible, and smoothly functioning financial markets is thus of crucial importance in transmitting saved funds into the hands of those desiring to make investment expenditures. If the transmission mechanism is underdeveloped, inaccessible, or imperfect, the flow of funds from surplus units (or "ultimate lenders") to deficit units (or "ultimate borrowers") will be impeded and GNP will fall below the potential it might otherwise have attained. While it is true, as we have seen above, that for the whole economy saving must equal investment, ex post, this equality may take place at low or high magnitudes of saving and investment, implying consequent low or high magnitudes of GNP, production, and employment. The equality between realized or ex post saving and investment does not mean that all planned or ex ante saving must inevitably flow into or be matched by an equal volume of investment spending.

Assume, for example, that a significant portion of otherwise feasible investment plans is not undertaken because of lack of financing, due to the failure of financial markets to effectively channel funds from surplus units able to lend to potential deficit units anxious to borrow. The end result of such a curtailment of investment spending is likely to be a lower level of GNP, out of which will then be generated a reduced volume of saving. Realized or ex post saving and investment will be equal, after all is said and done, but at levels far below their potential and at a level of GNP also far below that which could have been reached had financial markets operated more effectively.

FINANCIAL MARKETS AND INTEREST RATES

In any market, whether for wheat, steel, or land, interaction between supply and demand determines the quantity of the product that will change hands and the price at which the exchanges will be made. Finan-

---

[15] The term "securities" includes any and all kinds of financial assets: bonds, stocks, mortgages, all kinds of loans, etc. These are all financial assets to whoever owns them; they are at the same time, of course, liabilities to whoever issued them. Equities (stocks) are not really liabilities of the issuer; in the flow of funds accounts, however, they are treated as though they were.

cial markets are no different. In financial markets the product is not wheat, steel, or land; it is credit, or what amounts to the same thing, *loanable funds*. And the price of the product, of loanable funds, is expressed not as so many dollars per bushel or per acre, but as the *rate of interest*—the amount per dollar per annum that the lender (or supplier of loanable funds) receives for parting with them for a specified time period, and which the borrower (or demander of loanable funds) must pay to acquire them. While the product in financial markets may be called loanable funds, and the price may be called the rate of interest, supply and demand are nevertheless just as important as in any other market in determining the quantity exchanged and the terms on which the exchanges will be made.

A useful perspective from which to analyze the sources of market supply and demand for loanable funds is from the point of view of the gross form of our complete sector sources and uses of funds statement. We have previously labeled this (7'):[16]

(7') A Complete Sector Sources and Uses of Funds Statement—Gross Form:

Uses	Sources
Current Expenditures	Current Receipts
Saving (Δ NW)	
Δ RA (Investment)	Δ NW (Saving)
Δ FA ↑ (Lending)	Δ FA ↓ (Selling Securities)
Δ L ↓ (Repaying Debts)	Δ LA ↑ (Borrowing)
Δ M ↑ (Hoarding)	Δ M ↓ (Dishoarding)
	$\Sigma = \Sigma$

Looking first at the sources side of Statement (7'), note that three of the five potential sources of funds available to a sector do not involve recourse to financial markets. Current income refers to funds received from the sale of goods or services on product or factor markets; saving refers to the non-spending of current income on consumption—to the retention or accumulation of the funds; and dishoarding involves drawing down cash already in the till.

The other two sources of funds, however, borrowing and selling off financial assets, both require resort to financial markets. Both involve the *sale of securities* in financial markets, either the sale of one's own liabilities (borrowing) or of someone else's (selling off financial assets). If a firm or a family acquires funds by selling securities, it thereby draws funds out of financial markets. While such transactions are a source of funds to those acquiring the money, they simultaneously involve the using of funds from financial markets. Any act of borrowing, then, any sale of securities, thus contributes to the *demand for loanable funds*.

---

[16] See Statement (3') and footnotes 3, 5, and 9.

Turning to the uses side of Statement (7'), again only two of the possible uses of funds involve financial markets, namely lending and repaying debts. Consumption and investment expenditures send the funds to a product market, not a financial market. And hoarding, of course, means the money is not released to anyone. However, the other two possible uses of funds both involve the *purchase of securities* in financial markets, either the purchase of someone else's liabilities (lending) or of one's own liabilities (repaying debts). If securities are bought, funds flow into financial markets. While such transactions are a use of funds for the unit spending the money, they simultaneously represent a source of funds to financial markets. Any act of lending, any purchase of securities, thus contributes to the *supply of loanable funds*.

Whether the rate of interest—the price of loanable funds—rises, falls, or remains stable naturally depends on the relative eagerness of demanders

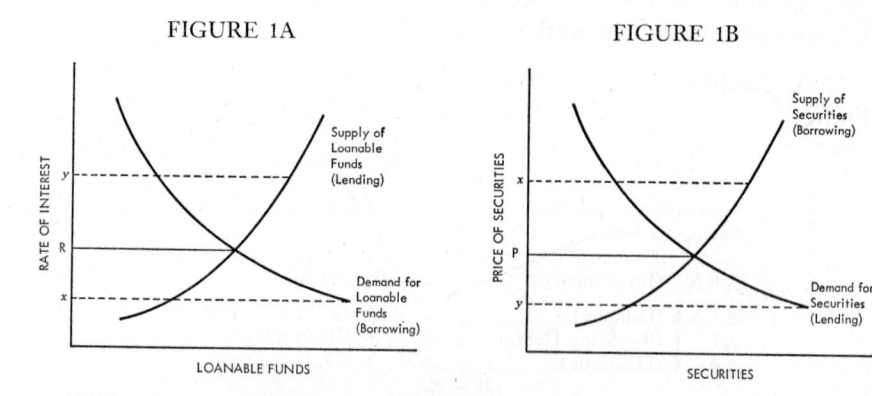

FIGURE 1A

FIGURE 1B

and suppliers of loanable funds. Given competitive conditions, the rate of interest will tend to move to equilibrium, where the amount of loanable funds demanded is equal to the amount supplied, as in any orthodox diagram illustrating price determination with supply and demand schedules (see R on Figure 1A).

If, at a particular rate of interest (say x on Figure 1A), borrowers—the demanders of loanable funds—are particularly anxious to borrow, and lenders rather reluctant to lend, then the rate of interest will rise. A large demand and a short supply inevitably lead to price increases. On the other hand, if the rate of interest were at y on Figure 1A, at which rate lenders —the suppliers of loanable funds—are more eager to lend than borrowers are to borrow, then the rate of interest is likely to fall.

Instead of talking about the demand and supply of loanable funds determining the rate of interest, we could alternatively have talked about the supply of securities and the demand for securities determining the price of securities (see equilibrium price P on Figure 1B). To demand loanable funds is equivalent to supplying securities (borrowing), and to supply loanable funds is the same as demanding securities (lending). Figure 1B illustrates that at price x relative eagerness to borrow (sell securities) would drive the price of securities down, just as Figure 1A shows that it would drive the rate of interest up. Relative eagerness to lend (buy securities), as at price y on Figure 1B, would drive the price of securities up, just as Figure 1A shows that it would drive the rate of interest down.

To analyze interest rate determination in terms of the supply and demand for loanable funds, or security prices in terms of the demand and supply of securities, amounts to one and the same thing. It is no accident that when securities prices fall, interest rates rise. The rate of interest (R) is *defined* as D/P, where D equals the annual dollar income return yielded by a security and P stands for its price. If the dollar income return is contractually fixed, as is usually the case with debt instruments, the effective rate of interest and the price of the security *must* move inversely. If, for example, a perpetual bond carrying a $5 income, contractually fixed, sells for $100, the rate of interest would be 5 percent. If the same bond rose in price to $200, the effective rate of interest would drop to 2½ percent. If you bought that bond for only $50, on the other hand, you would receive an effective yield of 10 percent.

To say that interest rates are determined by the supply and demand for loanable funds is helpful only up to a point. To analyze interest rate determination in any depth we would have to delve into the forces underlying the supply and demand for loanable funds, the factors which give rise to each. Although that is not our primary purpose in this paper, we can conclude by briefly indicating the nature of some of the elements involved in shaping the forces of supply and demand. Again, we can do it best with reference to our gross sector sources and uses Statement (7').

As Statement (7') shows, surplus sectors—which spend less than they earn—*must* hoard, repay debts, or lend an amount equal to their surplus. If they hoard, they do not supply loanable funds to anyone. But, if they repay debts or lend their surplus, they do supply loanable funds, in the one case by buying back securities representing their own liabilities and in the other case by buying securities that represent the debts of others. The net saving (over and above their investment) of surplus sectors, less their hoarding, thus constitutes the supply of loanable funds.

Deficit sectors—which spend more than they earn—*must* dishoard, sell off financial assets, or borrow an amount equal to their deficit. If they dishoard, they do not acquire loanable funds from anyone. But if they sell off financial assets or borrow to finance their deficit spending, they do acquire loanable funds from financial markets, in the one case by selling securities that represent the liabilities of others and in the other case by selling securities representing their own liabilities. The net investment (over and above their saving) of deficit sectors, less their dishoarding, thus constitutes the demand for loanable funds.

There is one exception to the above, which is an amplification more than an exception. If the sector involved happens to be the commercial banking sector, the Federal Reserve, or the United States Treasury, it can, under certain conditions, borrow by itself creating money.[17] If a sector's "borrowing" takes this form, the creation of new money, it obviously does not draw loanable funds out of financial markets. Indeed, it actually enlarges the pool of loanable funds. Such "borrowing" thus should either be subtracted from the demand for loanable funds (the same as dishoarding) or, as is usually done, added to the supply of loanable funds.

The supply of loanable funds thus depends upon the net saving (over and above their investment) of surplus sectors, less their hoarding, plus new money created during the period. The demand for loanable funds depends upon the net investment (over and above their saving) of deficit sectors, less their dishoarding.

Finally, a distinction should again be made between planned (ex ante) transactions and realized (ex post) transactions. Since one sector's financial asset is another sector's liability, it follows that for the whole economy, ex post, lending and hoarding must wind up equal to borrowing (including new money creation) and dishoarding. But this does not mean that the planned lending and hoarding of the surplus sectors need equal the planned borrowing and dishoarding of the deficit sectors.

Surplus sectors may be planning, at the start of a period, to lend very little. Deficit sectors may simultaneously be planning to borrow a great deal. Obviously, such plans are mutually inconsistent. As Figure 1A indicates, such a situation is likely to result in an increase in interest rates and, in light of the now higher interest rates, revisions in plans by both lenders and borrowers. If investment plans are then revised also, as borrowers find themselves unable to borrow as much as they had expected at the old level of interest rates, GNP will fall. With saving and investment decisions partially dependent on GNP, this is likely to alter the surplus or deficit position of various sectors and lead to additional revisions in borrowing and lending plans, with consequent further effects on interest rates and GNP.

Ex post, actual lending and hoarding for the whole economy will turn out to be equal to borrowing and dishoarding. They must. The same is true of saving and investment. But the dynamics of this adjustment process, through which initial ex ante inequalities at the start of a period are eventually resolved into ex post equalities—and the implications of this resolution for interest rates and GNP—are topics that would carry us well beyond the scope of this paper.

---

[17] See footnotes 6, 12, and 14. On Statement (7′) borrowing by the issuance of liabilities that constitute money should have an entry of its own ($\Delta M \blacktriangle$, Money Creation, under Sources of Funds). However, it can also be entered as an additional form of dishoarding, or as an addition to borrowing, both of which are also sources of funds.

APPENDIX
THE FLOW OF FUNDS MATRIX, FOURTH QUARTER OF 1967

The explanation of the construction of the flow of funds accounts culminated in Matrix (8), the Flow of Funds Matrix for the Whole Economy. Matrix (8) assumed a total of only three sectors and for purposes of clarity omitted a considerable amount of detail. Table 1 in this appendix is the actual Flow of Funds Matrix for the fourth quarter of 1967, as published in the *Federal Reserve Bulletin*.[18] Ex ante, it appears to bear little resemblance to (8); ex post, it turns out to be the same thing, merely more elaborate. The best way to see this is to relate Table 1 to Matrix (8), column by column and line by line.

First, the columns. Instead of only three sectors, the actual published matrix contains four major sectors—the private domestic nonfinancial sector, the United States government, the financial sector, and the rest of the world. These in turn are subdivided into a number of subsectors, eight in all. The names of each are self-explanatory, except perhaps for the "Monetary Authorities" sector. This consists of the Federal Reserve plus the United States Treasury's monetary accounts. (For some unexplained reason, the "State and Local Governments" sector is included under the *private* part of the economy. Some other miscellaneous observations: The "Household" sector includes nonprofit organizations within it; "Nonbank Finance" includes savings and loan associations, mutual savings banks, insurance companies, pension funds, mutual funds, credit unions, etc.)

The last two columns in Table 1 are new. Neither of them appeared in Matrix (8). The "Discrepancy" column results from the fact that deficiencies and inconsistencies often exist in the raw statistical data. Things often do not add up the way logic tells us they should. Borrowers report liabilities of x dollars, while lenders report they are owed y dollars. Errors in data collection, omissions, differences in coverage or classification, all give rise to inconsistencies in the data. The "Discrepancy" column is the statistician's way of reconciling such problems so that the accounts balance logically the way they are supposed to.

In Table 1, for example, we know that for "All Sectors" financial uses of funds (line 11) should equal financial sources (line 12). Thus, the difference between them (line 10) should be zero. However, financial uses of funds for "All Sectors" are $178.7 billion, and financial sources are

---

[18] *Federal Reserve Bulletin*, May 1968, p. A–66. See also pages A–67.1 and A–67.11 for additional data and individual sector sources and uses statements in greater detail.

For explanations of the actual construction and presentation of the accounts in greater depth than this appendix provides, see "Revision of Flow of Funds Accounts," *Federal Reserve Bulletin*, November 1965; "Flow of Funds Seasonally Adjusted," *Federal Reserve Bulletin*, November 1962; "A Quarterly Presentation of the Flow of Funds, Saving, and Investment," *Federal Reserve Bulletin*, August 1959; and *The Flow of Funds Approach to Social Accounting* (National Bureau of Economic Research, 1962).

TABLE 1

Summary of Flow of Funds Accounts for Fourth Quarter, 1967—Seasonally Adjusted Annual Rates
(In Billions of Dollars)

	Sector	Private domestic nonfinancial sectors											Financial sectors											Rest of the world		All sectors		Discrepancy	Natl. saving and investment	
		Households		Business		State and local govts.		Total		U.S. Govt.		Total		Monetary auth.		Com. banks		Nonbank finance								
	Transaction category	U	S	U	S	U	S	U	S	U	S	U	S	U	S	U	S	U	S	U	S	U	S	U		
1	Gross saving		127.6		76.6		−4.0		200.2		−14.2		3.0		.		2.1		.9		.9		187.1		189.0	1
2	Capital consumption		68.6		36.8				125.2				1.1		.5		.6				126.3		126.3	2
3	Net saving (1 − 2)		59.1		19.9		−4.0		75.0		−14.2		1.9				1.6		.3		−1.8		60.8		62.6	3
4	Gross investment (5 + 10)	125.3		72.9		−4.2		194.0		−12.9		2.7		.		2.1		.6		−1.2		182.7		4.5	185.4	4
5	Private cap. expend., net	92.4		90.9				183.3				.9				.4		.5				184.2		2.9	184.2	5
6	Consumer durables	72.1						72.1														72.1			72.1	6
7	Residential constr.	16.0		8.4				24.4														24.4			24.4	7
8	Plant and equipment	4.3		77.3				81.7				.9				.4		.5				82.6			82.6	8
9	Inventory change			5.2				5.2														5.2			5.2	9
10	Net financial invest. (11 − 12)	32.9		−18.0		−4.2		10.7		−12.9		1.8		.		1.7		.1		−1.2		−1.6		−1.6	−1.2	10
11	Financial uses, net	55.4		18.7		10.5		84.6		3.1		83.2		4.8		39.3		39.2		7.8		178.7			8.9	11
12	Financial sources		22.5		36.7		14.7		73.9		16.0		81.4		4.7		37.5		39.2		8.9		180.3		.7	7.8	12
13	Gold & off. U.S. fgn. exch.									.4		−.5		−.5						1.2		1.1				13
14	Treasury currency									−.7		−.5		.5								−.5		.2		14
15	Dem. dep. and currency	12.4		−1.5		.3		11.2				.7		3.0		11.6		.7				13.7	14.7			15
16	Private domestic									1.0		12.7		2.9		10.2						11.9	12.7	−.8		16
17	U.S. Govt.											1.2				.3						1.0	1.2	−.2		17
18	Foreign											.8				.8				.8			1.8			18
19	Time and svgs. accounts	32.4				2.4		39.0				40.8				23.8		.4				40.8	40.8			19
20	At coml. banks	15.8		4.1				22.6				23.8				23.8				1.3		23.8	23.8			20
21	At svgs. instit.	16.6						16.6				.4						17.0				17.0	17.0			21
22	Life insur. reserves	4.8						4.8				4.6						4.6				4.8	4.6			22
23	Pension fund reserves	14.3				4.1		14.3		1.6		8.5						8.5				14.3	8.5			23
24	Consol. bank items[1]									1.6		1.6		−.1		1.7		.				1.6	1.6			24
25	Credit mkt. instr.	−3.8	18.8	.4	37.2	7.8	10.5	4.4	66.4	4.5	2.2	73.1	2.2	4.8	.	34.8	.2	33.5	2.0	3.3	4.0	85.4	85.4			25
26	U.S. Govt. securities	−.9		−3.0		.9	10.1	−3.0	10.1		12.7	13.6	12.7	4.8		8.8				3.1		12.7	12.7			26
27	State and local oblig.	1.6				−.5	10.1	1.1	10.1			9.9				9.0	.3	8.9	.6			10.1	10.1			27
28	Corp. and foreign bonds			6.5	15.1			6.5	15.1		.9	8.8	.9			−.8		8.2	.9	2.1	1.3	10.2	17.2			28
29	Corp. stocks	−3.6		.8	2.3			−2.8	2.3			2.9						8.4	1.0	2.8		5.2	5.2			29
30	1- to 4-family mortgages	10.4						10.4	4.4	1.9		10.4	1.0			2.5		7.9				12.5	12.5			30
31	Other mortgages			.8	1.8			.8	1.8			8.5				2.2		6.9				9.4	9.4			31
32	Consumer credit	4.4		1.3				1.3	4.4			3.1				2.2						4.4	4.4			32
33	Bank loans n.e.c.	1.7			7.4			1.7	7.4			6.5				6.5				.2		6.5	7.4			33
34	Other loans	1.2		1.4	3.0	.3		2.9	4.5	1.8		3.9	−2.4			3.1		−.9	−.2	.2	3.0	7.3	6.5			34
35	Open market paper			1.4	1.7		.3	1.4	1.7			−2.4						−.1	−2.4	−.2	2.5		4.5	−.1		35
36	Federal loans			1.3			.3	1.8	1.8			2.9	−2.5						−2.5				1.8			36
37	Security credit	1.1	3.3	.		1.1		1.1	3.3		2.1	4.3	2.1			1.5		2.8	2.1	1		5.6	5.6			37
38	To brkrs. and dealers	1.1		.				1.1			2.1	.9	2.1			1.9			2.1			2.1	2.1			38
39	To others		3.3						3.3			3.5				.6		2.8			.2	3.5	3.5			39
40	Taxes payable		.1	5.1	−3.8			5.1	−3.8	−4.2		.9	−.5				−.3		−.2	1.1		−4.2	−4.3	−.1		40
41	Trade credit			8.7	5.5		.1	8.7	5.7	1.5	.6	.3						.3			.2	10.4	6.3	−4.1		41
42	Equity in noncorp. business	−7.3		7.0	−7.3			−.3	−7.3													−7.3	−7.3			42
43	Misc. financial trans.	1.5	.4		5.1			1.5	5.4	−.1	.4	2.7	7.2			1.2	2.2	1.5	5.1	1.1	3.7	12.1	16.7	−4.7		43
44	Sector discrepancies (1 − 4)	2.3		3.7		.2		6.2		−1.3		.3		.		.		.3		−.7		4.5		4.5	3.6	44

[1] Claims between commercial banks and monetary authorities: member bank reserves, vault cash, F.R. loans to banks, F.R. float, and stock at F.R. Banks.

$180.3 billion. They are *not* equal. So in the "Discrepancy" column we put a use of $1.6 billion. *Now* they balance. By convention, all discrepancies are entered on the uses side of the accounts, making them positive or negative as appropriate to create the equality that logic tells us should exist.

The last column, "National Saving and Investment," is merely a measure of *domestic* saving and investment. It consists of the "All Sectors" data for saving and investment, plus any discrepancies in those accounts, minus the "Rest of the World" sector. Also included here is any increase in net financial claims on foreigners.

Turning now to the lines (or rows), there are two main differences between Table 1 and Matrix (8): first, a slight rearrangement of the entries (including differences in terminology); and second, the presentation of considerably greater detail.

The first line in Table 1, "Gross Saving," corresponds to "Saving" on the first line of Matrix (8). Table 1 also gives an estimate of depreciation (capital consumption, line 2) and thus data for net saving as well (line 3). Line 5 on Table 1 corresponds to the entry "Investment" on our model matrix. Lines 6–9 are a breakdown by type of investment. Line 11 corresponds to "Lending" on Matrix (8) and line 12 to "Borrowing." Line 15[19] is roughly equivalent to what we have called "Hoarding"; on Table 1 it is not given a major entry of its own, but is included as a subcategory under "Financial Uses" of funds.

Thus, if we were to list the rows on Table 1 which correspond to the entries on Matrix (8)—Saving, Investment, Borrowing, Lending, and Hoarding—they would be, in the same order, lines 1, 5, 12, 11 minus 15, and 15.[20]

Line 10, called "Net Financial Investment," really refers to a sector's lending plus hoarding minus its borrowing, as we have been using these terms. And line 4, called "Gross Investment," refers to a sector's real investment plus lending plus hoarding minus its borrowing. To find whether a particular sector is a surplus or deficit sector we should compare the entry for that sector on line 1 with the entry on line 5. (Or, if we deducted depreciation from both saving and investment, we would compare the entry on line 3 with line 5 minus line 2.)

The remainder of Table 1, from line 13 down, consists of a detailed breakdown of the various forms of lending and borrowing by type of asset (or liability) involved. As an example, line 26 indicates that the United States government borrowed $12.7 billion by selling new bonds

---

[19] Line 15 technically should include the sum total of lines 16–18. If only one figure is shown for a sector in lines 16–18, however, it is not repeated again on the table in line 15. Our reference to line 15 is to what it technically should include.

[20] If a money-*issuing* sector were involved, this would become 1, 5, 12 minus 15, 11, and 15. Money creation is a financial source of funds to those who issue it. See footnotes 6, 14, and 17.

during the period. Households and business firms also sold government securities ($0.9 billion and $3.0 billion, respectively). Thus, a total of $16.6 billion of government securities was sold. Who bought them? Line 26 shows that state and local governments bought $0.9 billion, the monetary authorities acquired $4.8 billion, commercial banks purchased $8.8 billion, and foreigners bought $2.1 billion.

A final word should be said about the differences between the Federal Reserve's Flow of Funds Accounts and the Department of Commerce's National Income Accounts. Three differences are of special interest.

First, the National Income Accounts confine themselves exclusively to nonfinancial transactions. They contain no data on borrowing, lending, or hoarding. Second, the National Income Accounts confine all real investment to the business sector, except for home-building. With the exception of housing, neither consumers nor governments can invest. In the Flow of Funds Accounts, however, consumer purchases of durable goods are treated as (real) investments and are shown both gross and net of depreciation. This removes the purchase of consumer durables from the category of current (or consumer) expenditures and thereby greatly increases the volume of recorded household (and national) saving. Finally, the sectoring is more detailed in the Flow of Funds Accounts than in the National Income Accounts, making integration and reconciliation of the two a rather complicated affair. In principle, one should be able to move easily from one set of accounts to the other, but in practice the sectoring and the treatment of various transactions are so different as to make it awkward and cumbersome to do so.

The potential usefulness of the Flow of Funds Accounts as a tool of financial and economic analysis is still largely unrealized. In the flow of funds we now have a complete and internally consistent body of financial data interlocked with national income data. Data on financial markets are meshed with data on goods and services markets. However, in both cases these consist of ex post logical identities. Upon this foundation, we now need to proceed to the equally important job of testing alternative hypotheses regarding the interaction between financial and nonfinancial variables, with the ultimate objective of moving from ex post logical identities to the construction of a set of behavior relationships possessing ex ante explanatory value.

10

FLOW OF FUNDS ANALYSIS—ITS USES AND LIMITATIONS*

Stephen B. Packer

Flow of Funds Analysis—examination of the sources and uses of funds in the money and capital markets—has received considerable attention over the past decade as a tool for studying market conditions and forecasting interest rates. The basic analysis underlying this approach has been set forth by the Federal Reserve Board,[1] Freund,[2] in the *Journal of Finance*,[3] and elsewhere. It is the purpose of this article to examine the uses and limitations of flow of funds analysis in forecasting interest rates, and to suggest both techniques and potential pitfalls for the analyst or economist who may wish to set up a study of his own.

Who is likely to find flow of funds analysis most useful? Anyone whose duties involve forecasting interest rates and capital market conditions for more than a couple of months ahead must of necessity make certain assumptions about prospective money flows. He will probably find it useful to have at least some of them spelled out in detail. Economists for banks and other financial institutions, research people in bond houses, men with the responsibility for investing funds (particularly in fixed-income securities), and corporate executives charged with setting up a financing program fit most clearly into this category.

Offhand, the answer to this question would appear to be bond men in general. However, most people in the selling and trading end of the bond business are concerned largely with short-term movements, rather than with the broader swings for which the sources-uses approach is most useful. The near-term calendar of new offerings, inventories of unsold bonds and news developments influencing market psychology are of

---

* Reprinted by permission of the *Financial Analysts Journal* (July–August, 1964). Revised September, 1969.

[1] "Flow of Funds in the United States 1939–1953," by the Federal Reserve Board of Governors (1955).

[2] "An Appraisal of the Sources and Uses of Funds Approach to the Analysis of the Financial Markets," by William C. Freund. A paper read before the American Finance Association, December 29, 1967.

[3] "The Flow of Funds Accounts: A New Approach to Financial Market Analysis," a series of articles appearing in the *Journal of Finance*, May 1963.

greater concern in the short run. In some cases, undue concentration on what appear to be basic market trends, based on economic projections and flow of funds analysis, can work against the mental agility needed to take advantage of brief market fluctuations.

The money and capital markets are wrongly regarded as arid and unpromising territory by many equity-oriented security analysts. The availability and cost of borrowed funds, as well as the psychological impact of Federal Reserve Board moves and statements, can at times have a significant impact on economic activity and stock market performance. Interest rate levels and trends are important in evaluating the so-called "income" stocks, although the continued decline of stock yields relative to rates of return available from bonds suggests that this guideline has lost some of its validity in recent years.

A Number of Studies Available

There are a number of studies on the sources and uses of funds prepared at intervals. Some are generally available and others (often because they are prepared for internal use rather than general circulation) difficult or impossible to obtain. The three most authoritative and widely circulated are: The Federal Reserve Flow of Funds analysis (published regularly in the monthly *Federal Reserve Bulletin*); "The Investment Outlook," prepared annually by the Bankers Trust Company; and the "Supply and Demand for Credit," from Salomon Brothers and Hutzler.

The Federal Reserve study is the broadest in scope and offers the greatest amount of statistical detail. It aims to encompass all credit or money transactions in the economy that affect at least two separate economic units. The basic format includes interlocking financial flow statements for each of the 10 major sectors into which the economy is divided and balance sheets for these sectors. Both nonfinancial (payrolls, wages, interest, etc.) and financial (securities, mortgages, currency and deposits) statements are recorded. The financial transactions, reported in a separate table and summarized in a financial balance sheet, represent actual activity in the money and capital markets.

While no forecasting is attempted, the Federal Reserve Board flow of funds analysis is invaluable as a picture of the entire financial economy and as a source of statistics. It offers a matchless amount of detail and, unlike the other studies, appears quarterly and presents seasonally adjusted data. Inadequacy of the source data for some sectors has required the preparation of estimates. According to the Federal Reserve Board, some of these estimates have been relatively crude.

The Bankers Trust study is more directly relevant to the practical problems of interest rate forecasting. It is restricted to financial market transactions and instruments and actually attempts forecasts for the calendar year in which it appears (actually, about 10 months ahead). The study consists of a summary table comparing sources and uses of funds, two tables breaking the analysis down into investment and short-term funds and over twenty supporting tables setting forth the sources and uses of funds for each of the categories covered in the summary table.

This study can be used for forecasting in two different ways. Figures for the year ahead are projected for each of the categories in the summary and supporting tables. The "Individuals and Others" category is considered to represent residual investors whose participation in the market increases with rising interest rates. As a result, the residual is believed to be correlated with market conditions and interest rates—a rise in the residual for the year being forecast means an uptrend in rates, and vice versa. The concept of the residual and the different things used in it will be discussed in some detail toward the end of this article.

The Salomon Brothers and Hutzler study, which a few years ago was confined to the market for long-term funds, has been broadened in scope and now covers more or less the same ground as the Bankers Trust. In its published form, the Salomon Brothers effort is somewhat less comprehensive and detailed. However, the firm makes available its "Detailed Credit Estimates" on special request. In addition, while the formal "Supply and Demand for Credit" is published annually, the study is supplemented and updated in the firm's various bond market letters.

These three studies, and others that might have been included in the discussion, differ from each other in scope, detail, and emphasis. The Federal Reserve aims at providing the broadest possible statistical matrix for examining savings and investment flows throughout the national economy. Bankers Trust quite naturally places emphasis on the problems of commercial banks and related financial institutions; it takes a broad view, focusing on many types of investments and a broad range of maturities. Salomon Brothers and Hutzler, as a major dealer in securities, tends to place greater emphasis on the long-term capital market.

Although a substantial volume of material is available from outside sources, some analysts may find it worthwhile to prepare their own study of the sources and uses of funds. They may desire a more concise tabulation or wish to focus on special problems. People with responsibilities for making forecasts or planning investment programs may need the data before the published studies become available, even if it means making estimates of some recent totals. There is no better way to obtain a feel for these statistics and their fluctuations than to work with the actual numbers and make the forecasts.

The flow of funds tabulation presented in Table I was designed for an overall examination of the money and capital markets, rather than a look at any particular sector. As a practical matter both conceptual and statistical limitations assure that the categories in all these studies will be generally similar. The analyst must nevertheless make a number of choices. He must decide whether he wishes to concentrate on the entire market or on a particular sector. In some instances he will face the alternative of using a statistical series which is reasonably comprehensive but reported infrequently and after a long delay, and one which is narrower in coverage but available more promptly and at more frequent intervals. There is a need to avoid double counting (for example, to include a bank loan to a corporation and the corporation's re-lending of the funds as separate items).

A considerable proportion of the data in this tabulation can be obtained in some form from three widely available sources—*The Survey of Current Business* (particularly the annual tabulation of debt and the review of the sources and uses of corporate funds), *The Federal Reserve Bulletin*, and *The U.S. Treasury Bulletin*. In some instances these are not the primary sources for the information and more current data can be obtained from the originator. The material on corporate pension funds is obtained from an annual release by the SEC and that on credit unions from the monthly "Indicators" published by the Department of Health, Education, and Welfare.

Some of the statistics in this tabulation—state and local net debt, state and local non-government security holdings and assets of fire and casualty companies—are available only annually and with considerable time lag. Estimates of current data must be made. The Federal Reserve flow of funds analysis provides an alternative means of obtaining the state and local figures on a more current basis. The FRB analysis does not provide a separate breakdown for fire and casualty companies.

In using the flow of funds analysis for forecasting, it must be remembered that, as a rule, there are one or two key sectors on both the sources and uses sides which really determine one's projections of market conditions, either because the sectors themselves are subject to large year-to-year fluctuations or because judgments about them affect other series which undergo big year-to-year shifts. The other areas will usually be of subsidiary importance, either because they show smaller fluctuations or because changes in them are more the result than the cause of basic market conditions. The uptrend in net mortgage borrowing from 1961 through 1963, for example, was believed to reflect the relaxation of lending standards in the face of record savings inflows as well as a large basic demand for housing. The sharp drop in mortgage borrowing shown for 1966 was the result of a credit "crunch," during which fund inflows of savings institutions contracted sharply, and came at a time when the basic demand for homes was generally believed to be rising.

This is another way of saying that interest rates and money market conditions in the U.S. economy of the 1960's are determined by official policies, aiming at certain objectives and taking into account the anticipated private supply and demand for funds (which is itself influenced strongly by these policy decisions), rather than by the supply and demand for funds considered as an independent variable. This statement is less completely true in the long-term market than in the short-term area, but even here the forecast of market conditions must usually be dominated by one's forecast of economic activity and the anticipated FRB Treasury reactions rather than by projections of supply and demand in themselves. These assumptions, rather than the statistics, determine the answers.

The pivotal importance of factors outside the actual statistics is at once a strength and a weakness in flow of funds analysis. On the one hand, it permits the analyst to make his basic decisions on the basis of a few key considerations without getting bogged down in detail. On the other hand, the existence of these few vital factors may make it appear unnecessary to work through all the numbers before forecasting market conditions. To rebut the latter statement, it is sufficient to observe that the money and capital markets are complex and detailed. Conditions and yield trends in the various sectors can diverge from each other for a substantial period of time. Oversimplification has been a major cause of incorrect capital market analysis.

On the sources side, the dominant factor is Federal Reserve policy, reflected in the asset totals of commercial banks. During periods of easy money, loans and investments can be expanded simultaneously. When policy is tighter, loans often grow faster but funds are provided through the liquidation of investments; growth in total assets slows down. Techniques employed by the commercial banks to mitigate the effects of tight money policy, such as the heavy Eurodollar borrowing of 1969, can sometimes dilute the effects of policy for a time, but the Federal Reserve can usually overcome these devices through use of available policy tools or changes in regulations.

Year-to-year shifts in the asset growth of savings institutions are usually quite gradual (as can be seen in Table I). When these shifts are abrupt, as was the case for savings and loan associations in 1966, the reason is usually related in some way to changes in Federal Reserve policy and the money market environment. The other sources of funds tend to be of lesser importance.

On the uses side, changes in the federal government's net debt is the pivotal item, along with Treasury decisions (not reflected in the statistics) relating to the timing of financing decisions and the selection of maturities. The Treasury is almost constantly in the market and the total volume of its operations—including refundings, which cause little or no change in the net debt but can have a substantial market impact—dwarfs all others.

Apart from the Treasury's actual demand for funds, the federal government's budget position exerts a considerable influence on money policy and thus on the money and capital markets. One of the Federal Reserve's major aims is to insure an orderly market for Treasury securities. As was demonstrated in 1967–68, a big federal deficit can hamper the FRB when it comes at a time when money policy is directed towards curbing price inflation.

TABLE I
Sources and Uses of Funds
(Billions of Dollars)

	1963	1964	1965	1966	1967	1968†
Sources:						
Life insurance companies	7.8	8.3	9.4	8.1	10.3	10.3
Mutual savings banks	3.6	4.5	4.0	2.7	5.4	4.8
Savings & loan associations	14.0	11.8	10.2	4.4	9.6	9.3
Corporate pension funds	4.7	5.4	6.2	6.4	7.4	8.6
Fire & casualty companies	1.3	1.1	0.9	1.6	2.2	2.7
State & local funds	2.4	2.8	3.0	3.6	3.9	4.4
Federal reserve system	2.8	3.4	3.9	3.5	4.8	3.7
Federal agencies	−0.8	0.4	0.2	3.5	4.2	3.8
Commercial banks	18.8	21.5	27.9	16.1	36.6	38.9
Business corporations:						
U.S. governments	.5	−1.4	−2.1	−1.2	−3.0	1.7
Other assets	6.2	3.9	9.9	6.7	7.7	9.1
Credit unions	0.7	0.9	1.1	1.0	0.8	1.4
Foreign capital inflow	0.8	0.8	−0.2	−1.8	2.1	1.2
Total	62.8	63.4	74.4	54.6	92.0	99.9
Residual*	9.1	7.3	7.0	31.2	5.1	15.2
Total	71.9	70.7	81.4	85.8	97.1	115.1
Uses:						
Federal government	3.7	5.5	1.7	2.2	8.2	9.8
Federal agencies	1.6	1.4	2.1	5.3	3.9	5.6
State & local governments	7.6	7.7	7.5	7.2	10.8	10.7
Business corporations:						
Bonds	3.9	4.0	5.4	10.2	15.1	12.9
Net new stock issues	−0.3	1.4	0.0	1.2	2.3	−0.4
Other debt (except mortgage)	7.4	6.7	14.8	16.0	12.0	18.3
Real estate mortgages:						
Farm	1.6	2.1	2.3	2.1	2.2	2.0
1–4 family home	15.7	15.4	15.3	10.7	12.5	15.1
Multi-family & commercial	8.4	8.3	8.0	8.9	8.2	10.0
Corporate trade debt†	6.0	3.4	7.4	7.8	3.1	10.0
Farm production loans	1.4	0.7	1.0	1.0	3.7	−0.1
Non-corporate commercial	2.2	2.0	3.5	3.9	4.2	3.5
Consumers	7.9	8.6	10.0	7.2	4.6	11.1
Non-corporate financial	2.5	0.7	1.2	1.6	4.8	5.5
Foreign capital outflow	2.3	2.8	1.2	0.5	1.5	1.1
Total	71.9	70.7	81.4	85.8	97.1	115.1

* Uses less sources: Includes individuals, corporate receivables, miscellaneous.
† Partly estimated.

In the long-term bond market, the predominance of Treasury finance is perhaps less clear than was the case during the 1950's. The Treasury has been shouldered out of the market for long-term funds in recent years by the 4¼ percent statutory interest rate ceiling on long-term government issues (now defined as those maturing in more than 10 years) and by difficult capital market conditions. Meanwhile, corporate long-term borrowing has shown marked growth. The rise in capital spending during recent years has outstripped the increase in internally generated funds. These sharp increases—triggered by exogenous forces, such as accelerating technological change, bright prospects for long-term economic growth, and more pervasive expectations of continued price inflation—have exerted a growing influence on bond market trends in the past few years.

Among other long-term borrowers, year-to-year changes in net municipal borrowing are surprisingly small, although there was a marked jump in 1967 and 1968; the municipal market, moreover, is somewhat insulated from other bond markets because tax exemption alters the structure of demand. The mortgage market is statistically larger than either the corporate or municipal segments but the tendency of mortgage borrowing to reflect rather than cause market conditions has apparently been accentuated in the past few years. Mortgage rates are relatively rigid over interest rate cycles, and during periods of high rates and shortage of funds this sector is customarily starved for funds.

The treatment of federal agency operations in future years, and the attainment of consistency with past figures, will present some special complications and require careful treatment. There have been statutory changes in the structure and function of these agencies, affecting the Federal National Mortgage Association, the Federal Intermediate Credit Banks, the Banks for Cooperative, etc. While operations of these agencies do not bulk too large in the overall capital market picture, the magnitude of funds involved is sufficient to produce noticeable distortions in the accounts if year-to-year inconsistencies in what is included and what is excluded are allowed to develop.

The corporate payables and consumer credit sectors are both subject to substantial shifts, caused by fluctuations in business activity and by the availability of bank loans. These two sectors are dependent on bank credit.

There are a number of special problems, some statistical and some analytical, of which anyone preparing a flow of funds analysis should be aware. Perhaps most important, there is no easy way to forecast most of these sectors. In the case of federal debt, budget estimates and Treasury financing plans are of considerable help but neither are unfailingly accurate. In most other cases the best approach is to consult with experts in the particular fields and to tabulate past data, get a feel for the historical pattern and the factors that seem to cause it, and keep any current data on the series and the causal factors as up to date as possible.

This approach is admittedly inexact, especially since actual data for some of these series (such as fire and casualty companies) are available on an annual basis only and interim figures are likely to be estimates. Many of these series are quite difficult to project, even for brief periods ahead. It is possible to forecast the increase in consumer credit outstanding and commercial bank loans for a particular year a few weeks before year-end and err significantly.

Some analysts may wish to perform their analysis on a quarterly or semiannual basis, rather than using the annual time period found in a majority of the regularly available studies (apart from the FRB flow of funds). It is necessary to proceed with caution when using time periods of less than one year. Using the raw data, it is possible for the analyst to make year-to-year comparisons of comparable quarters or half-years, but more difficult to compare consecutive quarters or half-years with each other. Some of the statistical series have a seasonal pattern, of which the majority reach a peak late in the year. There has been in the past a certain tendency for interest rates to fluctuate seasonally, but in recent years, the Federal Reserve and Treasury have moved to minimize such movements, particularly the tendency for rates to dip in January.

For those who wish to use them, the Federal Reserve provides seasonally adjusted quarterly figures in its flow of funds study. As an alternative approach, if the analyst is using a residual or similar device for forecasting purposes, it might be possible to use unadjusted data for the various sectors and seasonally adjust the residual—which is easy enough to do on a quarterly or semiannual basis.

The writer does not feel as confident about doing the entire job on a seasonally adjusted basis. Some of the series do not have a clear-cut seasonal pattern and thus are not really suited to adjustment. Use of the raw data, with its seasonal peaks and valleys, can at times give the analyst a better feel for the way the money and capital markets actually function and for what the policymakers are attempting to accomplish. While some of the monthly statistics (e.g., consumer credit outstanding) are available seasonally adjusted, many of them are not, and the user of seasonally adjusted data will find himself dependent on the quarterly FRB figures and without the up-to-date feel provided by weekly and monthly numbers.

Interest Rate Trends Diverge

Long and short-term interest rates are reported by a number of sources and are generally adequate in scope. One of the principal statistical limitations is that there seems to be no way of constructing a new issues yield index for either corporate or municipal bonds, in view of differences in the indenture and the prestige of the "name" for each individual issue. The indexes usually quoted are for outstanding (and in some cases inactively traded) bonds. The spread between new and seasoned bond yields varies substantially over time, tending to be greatest during periods of market weakness.

Another more theoretical problem is that in some sectors interest rates are relatively sticky and lenders adjust to changing market conditions by shifting standards for credit-worthy borrowers, i.e., amounts they will lend and other loan terms (maturity, compensating balance requirements, etc.), which are not reflected in interest rates.

While interest rates in the various markets tend to follow the same overall pattern, there can be substantial divergences in movements for a period of time. For example (as is shown in Table II), Standard & Poor's index of municipal bond yields averaged .02 percent lower in 1964 than in 1963, while Moody's index of corporate Aaa-rated yields rose 0.14 percent for that year and yields on three-month Treasury bills rose 0.39 percent. In 1967 yields on the shorter term issues in Table II averaged lower than in 1966; three-month Treasury bills were 0.56 percent lower and Treasuries maturing in 3 to 5 years fell .09 percent. On the other hand, average yields of long-term Treasuries were 0.19 percent higher in 1967 than in 1966, while the Moody's Aaa corporate yield index was 0.38 percent higher.

There can also occur divergences in trend between differently rated bonds of the same type. Over the business cycle, there is variation in the premium investors demand for increased risks. Also, there can be changes in the relative supply of bonds in the different quality ratings.

Divergences between movements in short and long-term yields and between the various long-term market sectors cannot easily be projected in an overall flow of funds approach, and some analysts may be interested in particular segments of the market (for example, those for corporate or municipal bonds). It is possible to prepare separate flow of funds analyses, in as much detail as is desired, for the various individual sectors. The Bankers Trust Company study does this in its many supporting tables and Atkinson[4] has also done much work on the long-term market sectors, although his work is not circulated at regular intervals.

Analysis of individual market sectors without use of an overall approach, although valuable as a review of the past, can be misleading as a forecasting device. The flow of funds into each market sector depends on conditions in the others and on general market. There is a back and forth feedback, with financing volume affecting interest rates and the availability of funds, and the reverse also taking place.

In some market sectors, the analyst must decide how fine his breakdown need be. For example, in the corporate market the demand for public and private placements are from sufficiently different sources so that the two types of issues are not directly competitive with each other. Pension funds (corporate, state, and local) are the largest buyers of public issues while insurance companies are dominant in the private placement field. Interest rates for private placements have usually been higher than for comparable public offerings and indenture provisions often more

---

[4] Statistical Supplement to "The Outlook for Corporate Bonds in 1964," by Thomas R. Atkinson. An address before the American Finance Association, December, 1963.

restrictive. The rate differential has narrowed over the years, and rates and terms in the two markets are kept from drifting too far apart by the flexibility of borrowers in choosing which way to sell their bonds. To look at the corporate market without distinguishing between the public and private sectors is incomplete—as an illustration, the relative shortage of public offerings during the early months of 1963 helped keep their yields down despite a large volume of private placements. To consider one segment of the corporate market without allowing for developments in the other is unrealistic.

The Effects of Equity Price Changes

The treatment of equities in the flow of funds accounts presents two special problems. First, the question of whether the asset is valued at book or market is far more critical in the case of stocks than with bonds or other financial instruments. The equity holdings of most institutions are not a sufficiently large proportion of their total assets to distort year-to-year changes markedly, and, in addition, it is their usual tendency to use book values, which minimize the distortions resulting from stock price fluctuations. The most prominent exception is the case of fire and casualty companies, where equities comprise over 25 percent of holdings.

A more important source of potential distortion is the marked increase in the total value of stock outstanding, stemming from the appreciation in equity prices, that has occurred over the years. Net new stock issues are a relatively minor item in the flow of funds. Fluctuations in the value of outstanding stocks typically amount to many times the value of the net new issues.

Much of this churning of values, although of prime importance to stock market traders and investors, is not reflected in the capital markets as long as the money remains in equities. When stocks are sold and the appreciation realized, the capital markets are influenced to the extent that these profits are returned to the market as a source of funds.

Sidney Homer[5] has pointed out that in recent years institutions have been net buyers and individuals net sellers of equities. To the extent that individuals have invested these profits directly (in mortgages, bonds, etc.) the "Individuals and Others" item that is sometimes counted as part of the residual on the sources side and used as a forecasting device is swelled. When these funds flow into time and savings deposits they are counted with institutional sources and not reflected in the residual.

The appreciation of stocks may have introduced minor distortions into the flow of funds figures because it is to some extent reflected in the valuations of holdings and thus is counted as an inflow on the sources side when it really isn't. It is not believed that the amount of such distortion is

---

[5] "A Bond Man Takes Another Look at the Stock Market," a talk delivered by Sidney Homer before the Boston Economic Club, April 15, 1964.

significant. The appreciation has swelled actual capital market inflows only to the extent that the profits resulting have actually been invested in capital instruments (as opposed to being spent for goods and services).

What Is the Residual?

Webster's Dictionary defines the word residual as "a remainder." In some flow of funds studies the remainder (difference between sources and uses of funds) is called what it is—the residual. In the Bankers Trust study, the category "Individuals and Others," built up from the individual market sectors where it is in some cases a true residual and sometimes derived from actual data, is only partly composed of remainders but is called the residual.

Historically, the sources and uses of funds are necessarily equal. In forecasting, there is a need to make them so. The residual item, however labelled, is for past years the balancing item—all the sources of funds in the market which could not be specifically identified but must have come from somewhere in order to make the total equal the uses. The residual projected in the forecast period serves the same purpose. Some analysts feel that the residual is useful in forecasting market conditions—that changes in the residual signal changes in supply-demand relationships and interest rates.

The residuals presented in the various flow of funds studies are composed of two basic categories of items—the unavoidable and the deliberate. In the first group one may include statistical errors, valuation inconsistencies, and asset changes for smaller institutions (such as college endowment funds) for which incomplete or no figures are available. Investments of individuals are usually included for both reasons. They are not reported for all categories (the SEC savings tabulation does not include such things as second mortgages, trade credit of proprietorship-type businesses, etc.) and it is felt that fluctuations in individuals' investments are related to interest rate changes.

Among the items suggested for deliberate inclusion in the residual are foreign investments in the U.S., on the grounds that they tend to increase as interest rates rise, and commercial bank loans and investments, where the net increase is related to Federal Reserve policy.

The logical basis for using a residual in forecasting does not appear completely sound. There is no justification for using the portion that consists of statistical errors and discrepancies and the inclusion of small institutions and other miscellaneous unknowns is simply an unavoidable confession of ignorance.

There is some foundation for believing that direct investments by individuals increase during periods of relatively high interest rates. However, their shift from liquidity to interest-bearing investments, which is the theoretical underpinning of the residual approach, is probably far outweighed by another effect. Interest rates paid by savings institutions fluctuate less than returns available in direct investments, so that deposits are relatively more attractive when rates are low and less attractive when rates are high. Under these circumstances the "Individuals and Others" residual probably reflects more than anything else the shift of funds between savings institutions and direct investments, rather than a net increase in total holdings of capital market instruments.

It may also be that the "Individuals and Others" category is swelled when individuals are realizing profits on stocks and placing these funds directly in other investments. It may be that investments from this source have in the past shown a rough relationship with interest rates and market conditions, and that higher rates have been one reason for the shift, but anybody using the "Individuals and Others" residual for forecasting should be aware that the reasons for this correspondence are not as set forth in the usual formulation of the theory behind the residual.

Inclusion of foreign investments in the U.S. as part of the residual also rests on apparently dubious ground. The increase in foreign holdings would appear to be based on relative faith in the dollar versus other currencies, relative interest rates in the U.S. and elsewhere, and relative prospects in the U.S. and other equity markets. The assumption that foreign investments here are related to the absolute level of U.S. rates, and that an increase in one means an increase in the other, does not seem completely accurate.

The use of commercial banks as the residual seems hard to justify either mechanically or logically. These figures are readily obtainable and those for individuals and some other groups are not. Furthermore, commercial bank activity is not a balancing item—the total of loans and investments usually rises most when interest rates are low and least when they are high. This is opposite to the way a residual should behave, since it is supposed to consist of investors who "fill the gap" during periods when investment funds are in short supply.

The residual employed in Table I consists of the unavoidable errors and discrepancies, individuals and corporate receivables. The latter was included on the grounds that receivables tend to rise with business activity (thus, usually, when interest rates are relatively high), that receivables include some double counting of bank loans reloaned by the corporation as credit (so that including them among the sources would result in distortions) and that there is no nonbank trade credit item on the uses side due to the absence of reliable statistics in this sector.

As Table II shows, neither this nor any other residual is useful in any more than a rough way. They do not correspond too closely with interest rates and besides the various interest rates do not always move together. It is the writer's opinion that this or any other residual should be used for forecasting only with caution and by someone sophisticated enough to be aware of its limitations. If a residual is to be used, a more specific and limited one, balancing a relatively few sources and uses against each other, seems safer than ones which are more inclusive and less definite, if only because the logic will tend to be clearer and the statistical underpinning more reliable.

TABLE II
Flow of Funds Residuals vs. Interest Rates

| Year | Residuals (Billions of Dollars) ||| Treasuries ||| Interest Rates (Percent) ||
	Table I*	Bankers Trust*	Salomon Brothers & Hutzler*	91-Day Bills	3-5 Year Issues	Long Term Bonds	Moody's Aaa Corporates	Standard & Poor's Municipals
1963	9.1	−1.7	4.1	3.16	3.72	4.00	4.26	3.24
1964	7.3	3.3	6.5	3.55	4.06	4.15	4.40	3.22
1965	7.0	0.8	7.1	3.95	4.22	4.21	4.49	3.27
1966	31.2	10.2	15.1	4.88	5.16	4.66	5.13	3.82
1967	5.1	−2.9	6.3	4.32	5.07	4.85	5.51	3.96
1968	15.2	0.4	11.4	5.34	5.59	5.25	6.18	4.51

* Individuals and Others.

Conclusions

While a number of highly proficient published studies are available, analysts whose duties require some familiarity with the money and capital markets are advised to attempt at least a sketchy and concise flow of funds analysis on their own. Working with the actual data is the best way to gain familiarity with the statistics and a feel for the market. One's own analysis can be more readily kept up to date and can be prepared as it is needed.

There are some problems. Some statistics are reported infrequently and tardily. Most projections must be made on pretty much a seat-of-the-pants basis and a number of the sectors are difficult to forecast. Interest rate changes are sometimes caused by psychological factors not directly reflected in the statistics. Different market sectors can experience divergent interest rate trends for periods of time. It must be remembered that the key considerations in making the forecast are largely qualitative. These include business conditions, the balance of payments and confidence in the dollar, Federal Reserve policy, volume of savings, and the expectations of borrowers and lenders.

Flow of funds analysis is too cumbersome to pick up really short-term movements. It is a useful tool for analyzing and projecting developments for about 3 to 18 months ahead. It provides a good statistical base for analysis, particularly when one realizes that anyone who is projecting capital market conditions is implicitly using such an analysis. Some residuals are roughly correlated with interest rates, but holes in the statistics and in the logic underlying their composition makes it advisable to use them only with great caution.

11

AGGREGATE MEASURES OF CORPORATE PROFITS*

Edmund A. Mennis, C.F.A.

Frequently Financial Analysts need to appraise the financial performance of an industry or to examine the trend of profits in general. For this purpose, several aggregate measures of profits are often used, and five of them are examined in the accompanying table. These reports are the compilations of corporate tax returns in the *Statistics of Income* prepared by the Internal Revenue Service, the industry profit compilation of all corporations prepared by the Department of Commerce for the national income accounts, the *Quarterly Financial Report for Manufacturing Corporations* prepared by the Federal Trade Commission-Securities and Exchange Commission, the quarterly compilations in the *Monthly Economic Letter* of the First National City Bank of New York, and the quarterly reports of large corporations published in the *Federal Reserve Bulletin*.

DESCRIPTION OF PROFIT SERIES

As indicated in the table, two of the reports (Statistics of Income and Department of Commerce) are based on income tax returns; the other three are based on company reports to shareholders. For purposes of financial analysis, compilations of tax returns are of limited usefulness to measure trends in shareholder-reported profits, because information on a tax basis is rarely available to the analyst and because tax reports frequently differ from shareholder reports, primarily because of different methods of consolidation and depreciation treatment.

The industry detail in many of the reports is based on the industry classifications given in the *Standard Industrial Classification Manual* published by the U.S. Bureau of the Budget. The structure of industrial classification in this manual is in progressively more detailed categories, using two-digit, three-digit, and four-digit numbers as bases. Ordinarily, a two-digit classification is so broad it has limited use for financial comparisons of industries. Moreover, definitions of industry classifications have been changed several times in the postwar period, so that comparability over time cannot be made in some instances.

---

* Reprinted by permission of the *Financial Analysts Journal* (January–February 1964). Revised May, 1966.

The consistency of the sample over time involves the question of whether the sample is composed of the same group of companies or whether changes in the sample may result from the shifting composition of the sample itself. The Department of Commerce series and the Statistics of Income series are so broadly based that, for all practical purposes, they reflect the activities of all corporations. The FTC-SEC sample changes each quarter, so that, although it represents the entire manufacturing sector, quarterly totals are not strictly additive to obtain annual results. In addition, mergers, especially of large companies in different industrial classifications, may affect the comparability of data for particular industries from quarter to quarter if a major company has been moved from one classification to another. The First National City Bank series covers companies that publish regular financial reports, and those companies included are only those whose reports are available when the bank's *Monthly Economic Letter* goes to press. Consequently, the series is not consistent from quarter to quarter, although the bank has prepared a seasonally adjusted link-relative index of net income on a quarterly basis, which is available to anyone interested. The Federal Reserve series is the only one that contains the same companies over the period for which it is is available.

Limitations of Series for Financial Analysis

For the Financial Analyst, the limitations of these five series would seem as follows:

1. The Statistics of Income and Department of Commerce series are based on tax returns, which differ materially from compilations of shareholder reports.
2. The time lag in the availability of the compilations is considerable for most of the reports. Only the First National City Bank series and the Federal Reserve series are reasonably prompt.
3. The accounting detail of the reports is limited in the case of the First National City Bank series. Only the FTC-SEC and the Statistics of Income series provide balance sheet data.
4. Only the First National City Bank series is directly comparable to shareholder reports; the other series make accounting adjustments that affect this comparability.
5. The industry detail is limited except for the First National City Bank series and the FTC-SEC series.

Recommendations for the Analyst

A review of the major profit series available for financial comparison suggests that, as a minimum, an understanding of the series used together with its advantages and limitations, is an essential prerequisite. For the purpose of comparing a company's profits with those of some industry aggregate, the First National City Bank series or the FTC-SEC series in the manufacturing area would seem the most useful of those considered here. For measuring broad profit trends, the First National City Bank series is again the most helpful, and it would be even more valuable if the bank would regularly publish the seasonally adjusted link-relative series that indicates the trends of corporate profits over time. Although widely used, the quarterly profit totals of the Department of Commerce series do not seem particularly useful to measure current profit trends. In the first place, the quarterly series is based on estimates of tax returns, not shareholder reports. Secondly, through no fault of the compilers, the preliminary estimates are frequently revised significantly until the actual tax returns become available several years later.

One further source of comparative data should be mentioned that is of interest to the Financial Analyst. Standard & Poor's Corporation has published annual earnings per share data for their industrial stock average, railroad average, utility average, and composite average from 1926 to date. For these same series, quarterly earnings per share, unadjusted and seasonally adjusted, are available since 1935. The data are published in Standard and Poor's *Trade and Securities Statistical Manual*. Earnings per share are generally taken as reported by the company and are comparable to the company figures in the Standard and Poor's *Corporation Records*.

An even more useful analytical tool is the Standard & Poor's *Analysts Handbook*, which provides composite balance sheet and income account items constructed in such a way as to maintain maximum continuity over the years and to relate these items directly to the identical stock groups for which price indexes are available.

The items reported, all in terms of a constant unit of stock, are: sales, operating profit, depreciation, Federal income taxes, capital expenditures, book value, working capital, earnings, and dividends, all related to stock prices. In addition to the above, six significant ratios are included, namely, profit margins, earnings as a percentage of sales, dividend payout ratios, percentage return on book value, price-earnings ratios, and dividend yields.

All of these items are available for 84 individual industrial groups in addition to a composite of 425 industrial stocks for the period 1946 to date. On the whole, the individual group series have fairly good continuity, enabling the analyst to compare company performance over the years with these composite measures. Where substitutions or a radical change in a company's activity affects the group composite it is noted on the tables.

Most of the items in the *Handbook* are reported annually only. A monthly supplement is published which updates sales, taxes, earnings, and dividends, on a quarterly basis, with the same ratios based on the available items as appear in the *Handbook*. The monthly supplements also report S & P's estimates of composite per share earnings, by groups, for the current year, and these estimates are revised every month. Current dividend yields

COMPARISON OF REPORTS OF CORPORATE PROFITS

	Statistics of Income	Department of Commerce	FTC-SEC	First National City Bank	Federal Reserve
Basis of reports	Income tax returns	Income tax returns	Shareholder reports	Shareholder reports	Shareholder reports
Coverage	All companies	All companies	All manufacturing companies	Quarterly—about 900. Annually—about 3,800 leading companies	180 large manufacturing companies; all railroads; utilities; Bell Telephone System
Frequency	Annually	Annually*	Quarterly	Quarterly	Quarterly
Time lag	2 years	2 years	3–4 months	1–2 months	3 months
Industry classification	Mostly 2-digit SIC basis	2-digit SIC basis	2 to 4-digit SIC basis	Primarily 3-digit SIC basis	6 major manufacturing groups, rails, utilities, banks, telephone
Consistent sample over time	No	No	No	No	Yes
Accounting detail	Income a/c and balance sheet	Sales, pretax, taxes, net dividends, depreciation	Income a/c and balance sheet	Net income, net assets	Sales, pretax, net dividends
Accounting treatment of:					
Capital gains & losses	Included	Excluded	Excluded	Included	Excluded
Special reserves	Excluded	Excluded	Excluded	Included	Excluded
Foreign earnings	Dividends only	Excluded†	Included as reported	Included as reported	Included as reported
Intercorporate dividends	Included	Excluded	Included	Included	Excluded if identified

* Estimates of seasonally adjusted annual rates of total corporate profits are also available quarterly with a three- to four-months time lag.
† Although not shown by industry, a "Rest of the World" adjustment indicates the net effect of corporate profits and dividends received from abroad by both corporations and individuals in the United States, less corporate profits and dividends paid abroad.

also are shown, based on the latest indicated payment and the latest stock price index.

Moody's also publishes annual aggregates of sales and earnings for 50 individual industries based on data from 357 companies. The data are available annually from 1947 to date. Similar figures are also available for a total of 452 industrial companies, Class I railroads, the airline industry, and electric, telephone, telegraph, and gas utilities. These figures are printed in the *Moody's Manuals*, so that a time lag in their availability occurs until the manuals are published.

12

CORPORATE PROFITS DATA: TAX RETURNS VERSUS COMPANY BOOKS*

Vito Natrella

Since 1909 the United States has been taxing the profits of corporations. As a consequence of the income tax laws, corporations have been filing tax returns containing comprehensive data on their financial position. What kind of data are these and how can they be used by financial analysts, economists, and businessmen?

STATISTICS OF INCOME

Statistics on profits of corporations based on tax return data have been published by the Internal Revenue Service for over 50 years in a publication known as *Statistics of Income*. These compilations have certain advantages over others. For one thing, they represent the complete corporate universe—large and small—profitable and unprofitable. This is because all corporations are required to file tax returns as compared with individuals where only those above a certain but variable level of income file. For 1966 approximately 1½ million corporate returns were filed.

Statistics of Income also has the advantage of being based on an administrative record—the tax return. One of the complaints of businessmen heard most often is about the expense of filling out the many reports and questionnaires requested by the government for statistical purposes. The tax return as a statistical document not only saves money for the respondent, directly, but also is economical for the government. Surveys are not only expensive to conduct but are subject to greater errors due to nonresponse and inaccurate figures.

Another important characteristic of the *Statistics of Income* program is its flexibility. A basic program of regular tables is supplemented by special tabulations reflecting new laws or current needs.

There are, unfortunately, a number of problems and disadvantages to the use of *Statistics of Income*. Reference is often made to the long delays in issuing the data. While the processing problems do contribute to the delay, the tax return filing procedures should be kept in mind. Returns for

---

* Reprinted by permission of the *Financial Analysts Journal* (March–April 1969).

companies on a calendar year basis are supposed to be filed by March 15. However, many of the larger corporations get extensions to September 15. The income year we use is defined to cover accounting periods ending July of one year through June of the next. Therefore, the delay is further prolonged for companies with June fiscal years, so that, in some cases, returns for our use are not filed until a year and a quarter after the close of the calendar year to which the data primarily relate.

A limitation which has been much discussed, but about which not too many data have been available, is the noncomparability of tax income with book income. The Commerce Department uses both, making necessary adjustments to arrive at the National Income concept of corporate profits. Many of the differences come about because of the peculiar nature of the tax laws or of the IRS regulations. It stands to reason that the taxpayer tries to minimize his income and his taxes by practices which, while legal, are not always the way he wants to report the same transaction to his stockholders. On the other hand, we have the IRS which, understandably, has the responsibility for collecting as much of the legitimate tax as possible and thus works to maximize the company profits. As a result there has developed a complicated body of tax laws and tax practices which call for a somewhat different income concept than would be applicable for stockholder reporting.

Differences in Income Concepts

For the most part, tax law is in agreement with general accounting principles. However, there are situations where the law requires or permits special accounting for certain kinds of income and deductions. Notable differences relate to depreciation, depletion, installment sales, and gains and losses on property transactions.

Differences due to depreciation arise when depreciation methods and property lives differ for book and tax purposes, or when the base used for depreciation differs. Asset revaluations as they affect the depreciation base are not recognized for tax purposes. In addition, property that may long since have been written off in the tax accounts as emergency facilities may still be subject to depreciation on the books. There are other variations when certain items in some industries are capitalized and recovered through depreciation on the corporate books, but expensed currently on the tax return. The net effect of all of these differences is generally a larger deduction on the tax return than on the books and, if depreciation were the only difference, a lower net income figure for tax purposes.

Differences due to depletion are based chiefly on the widespread use of percentage depletion for tax purposes and cost (or perhaps a variation of cost, or no depletion at all) for commercial accounting purposes. Unlike depreciation differences which, theoretically at least, can wash out over a period of years, percentage depletion results in permanent and frequently substantial differences between book and tax profits.

Profits on installment sales is another major reason why book and tax profits diverge. Profits are accrued on the books when the sale is recorded, but for tax purposes are reported only as they are actually collected over the term of the contract.

Other differences result when provisions of law recognize (or partially recognize) income and deductions while the books do not, and vice versa. Under these two broad categories would fall tax-exempt interest, certain taxable undistributed foreign profits, disallowed expenditures for lobbying or for political contributions, unrecognized additions to contingency reserves, and the various items subjects to statutory limitations. Still other differences result when law provisions specifically deny recognition to certain accounting practices, such as some of those involved in valuing inventories.

Generally, it may be said that under some circumstances, tax law requires that income be reported at an earlier date than normal accounting methods sanction. Expenses, on the other hand, are typically not recognized under the law until the amount involved can be accurately determined. In the first instance, prepaid income may be taxable so long as a claim of right to its receipt has been established. In the second instance, additions to contingency reserves to cover expected future losses or expenditures are, with the exception of bad debt losses, not recognized under the tax code. Of course, a timing difference is also involved whenever the law imposes a ceiling on recognized losses or deductions but allows the excess to be carried over to other years. Examples are capital losses and charitable contributions. The very complicated subject of property basis also has timing implications. Suffice it to say here that under specified conditions, tax law may postpone recognition of the gains and losses realized on property sales.

This brings us to another type of difference between the two sets of profits. The gains and losses on property sales that are recognized under the law may not be recognized at all as book income or loss. Instead they may be charged directly to retained earnings because they represent a nonrecurring or extraordinary item. The same treatment may also be applied to other situations, such as when assets are completely written off as obsolete or when they are expropriated. It should be noted though that such treatment is now being discouraged by accounting authorities.

Treatment of foreign profits and the degree of consolidation used in reporting for related corporations also have a bearing on profits data. Despite incentives to consolidated reporting contained in the Revenue Act of 1964, many related corporations continue to file separate tax returns for each affiliate while reporting to their stockholders on a consolidated basis. However, differences due to consolidation have only a limited effect on tax return statistics for book income. This is because it is convenient for corporations to use the tax reporting unit as the basis for comparing book and tax profits in the reconciliation statement of the tax return. Therefore, the statistics for net income per books of account are on the same, generally nonconsolidated, basis as the statistics for net income per tax law. As a result, book net income for a given industry may not be directly comparable with the more consolidated data published by the SEC, for example. Presumably though, most of the differences due to consolidation disappear in aggregated national totals for book income less deficit.

The varying treatment of foreign earnings continues to present problems when making statistical comparisons. Income under the tax code excludes foreign subsidiary earnings until they are repatriated. This has been the rule. But the statutory exceptions and modifications of 1962 mean that to some extent undistributed profits (as well as the foreign tax "gross-up" on most foreign dividends) are also reported as income items in determining tax return profits. Book treatment of foreign profits may vary depending on the company. In the past, foreign profits tended to be excluded until remitted, although in more recent years there has been a move to include them even if unremitted. The "gross-up" is, of course, strictly a creature of the law.

Analysis of profits may be made either before or after tax. The amount used as federal income tax reflects the composite effect of the differences in computing pretax profits. On the tax return it is the actual liability for the year; on the books it is frequently an estimate, based on the income and expenditures recorded that year. This leads to another difference in profits data, at the after-tax level. In many cases it reflects the different accounting for accelerated depreciation.

Measurement of Differences

Prior to 1963, the tax return called for reconciling the opening and closing retained earnings account for the year. Net income per books of account was not required as such in this reconciliation and it was beyond our capabilities to reconstruct it, given the variety of taxpayer reporting methods and the variety of items involved.

A redesign of the 1963 tax return separated the reconciliation statement in two: Schedule M-1 for profits and, the other more encompassing one, Schedule M-2 for retained earnings. Present plans are to include the book profit figure in *Statistics of Income* each year beginning with 1963. A complete statistical study of the reconciliation itself is tentatively scheduled to take place during the next few years. Thereafter, the intention is to repeat the study periodically, though not annually. Even here though, most of the statistics, based on the lines in the return, will be presented in broad aggregates of income and deductions, i.e., on the books but not on the return, on the return but not on the books. However, a change made on the 1965 forms will enable separate data to be obtained on the depreciation and depletion differences and also facilitate tabulation of tax-exempt interest.

Actually 1963 is not the first year that statistics on book income were obtained from the tax return. Tax returns for years prior to 1938 provided for the separate reporting of book profits. As part of a Works Project at Philadelphia during the 1930's, the data were tabulated for 1929-36 although they were not published in *Statistics of Income*. Some of the results were used and analyzed in one of the classic studies on the subject, *Taxable and Business Income*, by Dan Throop Smith and J. Keith Butters.

In analyzing a sample of returns, Smith and Butters concluded that although there were some wide variations by industry, on the overall there was little difference (less than 10 percent) between book and tax profits and that, in general, there appeared to be little variation by size of company.

By 1964, the statistics show that the overall difference in profits had increased to 34 percent and that the difference did increase with the size of the company. The variations by industry are now even wider. Changes in the law as well as in the economy and in accounting practices have all combined to contribute to the growing size of the difference.

Many of the basic causes that applied 30 years ago still apply today, although with some variations. The special problems associated with accounting for installment sales and construction contracts, the rules governing the timing of receipts and expenses and of gains and losses, and the tax exemption granted interest on state and local government obligations, help explain the differences of the 1930's and also the differences of the 1960's.

Depreciation and depletion continue to be major contributing factors to the difference in profits, but because of law changes their impact on profits has no doubt increased. The widespread use and recognition by the tax law of accelerated methods and the adoption of the depreciation guidelines are all fairly recent phenomena. The depletion differences of the 1930's were due as much to "discovery depletion" (which was more liberal than "cost depletion") as to "percentage depletion" (which was more liberal than "discovery depletion"). Nowadays percentage depletion is widely used for tax purposes and discovery depletion has, in fact, been repealed.

Accounting for foreign income and its effect on corporate profits for both book and tax purposes has taken on added significance in recent years as foreign operations have become more extensive. The evaluation of business accounting practices and the tax law changes of 1962 have already been alluded to.

Book accounting now has to cope with such tax related problems as how the investment credit should be reflected in corporate profits. It also has to cope with changes in commercial accounting principles, such as how unusual or nonrecurring items should be treated with respect to income.

These are just a few examples that come to mind, but the growing divergence in profits data must be considered in light of factors such as these.

Findings for 1964

Data on book profits from Schedule M-1 of the corporate tax return have been compiled for 1963 and 1964. Since both years show the same pattern, I will restrict the discussion to 1964, which is more complete in coverage.

For tax year 1964, tax net income amounted to $34.3 billion compared with $46.1 billion of book income tax, a gap of almost $12 billion (Table 1). Since both income figures come from the tax return for the same entity, there should be few problems of differences in coverage.

Without expensive analysis and digging into the schedule, it is not possible to quantify the reasons for the discrepancy. However, an industry distribution can suggest explanations. For instance, the crude petroleum and natural gas industry had book profits after taxes equal to 2½ times tax income (after tax), a difference of $500 million. The petroleum refining industry had a gap of $3.3 billion with book income 3 times tax income. In both of these industries, we can be sure percentage depletion accounted for a very large part of the discrepancy. The practice of expensing intangible drilling costs for tax purposes will also contribute.

Differences in depreciation methods can largely account for the gap for transportation and electric and gas utility industries. Transportation companies showed after-tax book income $600 million above tax income, while public utility book income was higher by $1.1 billion. These heavy fixed capital industries are required to use straight-line depreciation on their books, but use some form of accelerated depreciation for tax purposes. While, in theory, this type of discrepancy should have an offset in the future as property becomes fully depreciated for tax purposes, in actual practice, with ever expanding capital investment, the offsetting years are rarely reached.

The finance industry showed a substantial excess of book profits over tax profits. The largest discrepancy in this area was for banks and trust companies with $1.3 billion more in profits on their books, which were more than double profits for income tax purposes. This reflects approximately $900 million of interest on state and local government securities. The situation was similar for the insurance industry with about half of their $1 billion discrepancy accounted for by tax-exempt interest.

Credit agencies, other than banks, also indicated a wide divergence between book and tax income. The difference amounted to almost $900 million with book profits almost three times tax profits. Most of the discrepancy was in the savings and loan segment of the industry. The tax definition of bad debt charges for savings institutions allows for larger deductions on the tax return. Differences in treatment of installment sales

TABLE 1

Number of Returns and Net Income Per Internal Revenue Code and Per Books of Account, by Selected Industries, 1964
(millions of dollars)

	Total active corporation returns			Returns showing net income or deficit per books of account			
Selected industries	Number of returns	Net income less deficit after tax (per Internal Revenue Code) (million dollars)	Number of returns	Net income less deficit after tax (per Internal Revenue Code)* (million dollars)	Net income less deficit after tax (per books of account) (million dollars)	Percent by which net income per books of account exceeds net income per Internal Revenue Code (col. 5 ÷ col. 4)
	(1)	(2)	(3)	(4)	(5)	(6)
All industrial groups	1,373,517	35,036.7	1,221,035	34,350.5	46,099.4	34.2
Agriculture, forestry, and fisheries	25,933	51.8	22,048	46.1	89.5	94.1
Mining	14,487	634.6	12,373	654.5	1,336.9	104.3
Crude petroleum and natural gas	7,027	267.7	6,215	293.0	714.7	143.9
Contract construction	104,134	549.4	92,768	553.6	642.3	16.0
Manufacturing	184,961	17,752.5	171,836	17,545.3	23,087.8	31.6
Petroleum refining and related industries	1,072	1,662.6	1,023	1,659.3	4,961.5	199.0
Primary metal industries	4,421	1,375.2	4,153	1,362.1	1,707.9	25.4
Machinery except electrical	20,389	1,777.3	18,809	1,740.9	2,219.0	27.5
Transportation, communication, electric, gas, and sanitary services	56,338	5,393.7	49,222	5,249.9	6,986.6	33.1
Transportation	42,908	1,024.8	37,747	922.9	1,521.9	64.9
Electric, gas, and sanitary services	6,369	2,326.6	5,385	2,285.8	3,374.3	47.6
Wholesale and retail trade	421,553	3,890.0	379,873	3,798.0	4,238.2	11.6
Finance, insurance, and real estate	383,727	6,161.9	338,285	5,879.2	9,045.0	53.8
Banks and trust companies	15,402	1,270.8	14,306	1,213.2	2,494.0	105.6
Credit agencies other than banks	48,527	512.0	43,520	526.5	1,398.2	165.6
Insurance carriers	5,335	869.8	3,517	701.5	1,656.6	136.2
Services	176,902	606.5	150,989	626.2	679.6	8.5
Nature of business not allocable	5,482	3.8†	3,641	2.3†	6.4†	178.2

* Net income or deficit after tax includes tax from recomputing prior year investment credit and is after current year investment credit. Foreign tax credit is not taken into account.
† Net deficit.

Source: Preliminary data to be included in Statistics of Income—1964, Corporation Income Tax Returns with accounting periods ended July 1964–June 1965. Internal Revenue Service, Statistics Division, June 1968.

and, to a lesser extent, bad debts could also account for the $400 million discrepancy in trade.

Many other industries showed book profits in excess of profits for tax purposes. In these industries it is not possible to draw any conclusions as to major reasons for the differences. It is logical to assume that differences in depreciation accounted for a large part of the discrepancies in manufacturing industries. The primary metal industries showed excesses of 25 percent or $300 million in favor of book profits. Non-electrical machinery had a larger discrepancy, about one half billion dollars. Generally, there was a tendency for most industrial groups to show larger book profits.

Of the $11.7 billion discrepancy of book over tax profits, $8.5 billion was by corporations with $100 million or more in assets (Table 2). Corporations in the top size group averaged net income as shown on the books about 40 percent above tax profits. Corporations with $10 million in assets up to $100 million had book profits about a third higher than tax profits, while the next two smaller size groups showed excesses of 18 and 7 percent. The very smallest size group, those companies with assets under $100 thousand in assets, had the largest percent excess of all, 84 percent. This may reflect the large number of deficit companies in this group, which generally had larger relative discrepancies as well as the peculiar character of the group of companies we classify as having zero assets.

Pilot Study of Schedule M-1

As yet it has not been possible to devote the resources to a full scale study of the reasons for differences between net income as shown on company books and net income according to tax law. However, in anticipation of such a study, a small pilot was undertaken for 1963, the first year of the new schedule, based on returns filed in the IRS Mid-Atlantic Region. This region includes the states of Pennsylvania, New Jersey, Maryland, Delaware, and Virginia. The study was generally limited to corporations with total assets of $50 million or more. There were 346 corporations in the group for which tabulations could be prepared. These companies represented about 12 percent of returns or assets in the size class for the country as a whole. Representation was slightly higher than average for manufacturing and mining, slightly lower than average for transportation, public utilities, and trade, and about average for finance (Tables 3 and 4).

The pilot study indicates that for manufacturing, depreciation and depletion accounted for all the $460 million excess of book income before tax over tax income. Depreciation as shown on the books was about $110 million lower than depreciation charges on the tax return. Reflecting petroleum refiners depletion charges contributed $350 million to the discrepancy. Depletion on corporation books was only 10 percent of the amount shown for tax purposes.

TABLE 2

Number of Returns and Net Income Per Internal Revenue Code and Per Books of Account, by Size of Total Assets, 1964
(millions of dollars)

Size of total assets	Total active corporation returns		Returns showing net income or deficit per books of account			
	Number of returns	Net income less deficit after tax per Internal Revenue Code (million dollars)	Number of returns	Net income less deficit after tax per Internal Revenue Code* (million dollars)	Net income less deficit after tax per books of account (million dollars)	Percent by which net income per books of account exceeds net income per Internal Revenue Code (col. 5 ÷ col. 4)
	(1)	(2)	(3)	(4)	(5)	(6)
Total.............	1,373,517	35,036.7	1,221,035	34,350.5	46,099.4	34.2
Under $100,000†.......	823,641	262.8	701,425	361.8	665.0	83.8
$100,000 under $1,000,000.....	468,200	3,933.7	442,284	3,897.5	4,178.7	7.2
$1,000,000 under $10,000,000.....	68,619	3,934.0	65,086	3,908.7	4,616.4	18.1
$10,000,000 under $50,000,000.....	9,846	3,356.2	9,261	3,282.5	4,378.5	33.4
$50,000,000 under $100,000,000.....	1,453	1,957.7	1,349	1,885.8	2,425.5	28.6
$100,000,000 or more........	1,758	21,592.3	1,630	21,014.2	29,529.9	40.5

*Net income or deficit after tax includes tax from recomputing prior year investment credit and is after current year investment credit. Foreign tax credit is not taken into account.
†Includes zero assets.
SOURCE: Preliminary data to be included in Statistics of Income—1964, Corporation Income Tax Returns with accounting periods ended July 1964–June 1965. Internal Revenue Service, Statistics Division, June 1968.

TABLE 3

SELECTED CORPORATION INCOME TAX RETURNS WITH TOTAL ASSETS OF
$50 MILLION OR MORE: RECONCILIATION OF PROFITS BEFORE TAX PER
BOOKS OF ACCOUNTS AND PER TAX LAW, AND RELATED DATA, 1963
(millions of dollars)

Item	Manufacturing	Transportation, communication, electric, gas, and sanitary services	Finance, insurance, and real estate
Number of returns	86	30	208
A. Reconciliation of book and tax profits—			
Profits before tax, per books of account	2,914.1	655.5	677.7
Add:			
Excess of income on tax returns, over income on books	107.0	3.9	31.8
Excess of expenses on books over expenses on tax returns:			
Total	458.3	35.8	73.0
Excess depreciation	35.2	.5	.6
Excess depletion	.1	.0	
Other	423.0	35.3	72.4
Subtract:			
Excess of income on books over income on tax returns	144.6	14.8	150.5
Excess of expenses on tax returns over expenses on books:			
Total	882.9	189.6	88.5
Excess depreciation	149.6	103.4	8.3
Excess depletion	346.1	.7	3.3
Other	387.2	85.5	76.9
Equals:			
Profits before tax, per tax law	2,451.9	490.8	543.5
Profits per books as a percent of profits per tax law	118.9	133.6	124.7
B. Information items—			
Depreciation, per tax law	1,366.5	452.7	51.1
per books of account	1,252.1	349.8	43.4
Depletion, per tax law	386.0	5.6	27.1
per books of account	40.0	4.9	23.8
Book depreciation as a percent of tax depreciation	91.6	77.3	84.9
Book depletion as a percent of tax depletion	10.4	87.5	87.8

NOTE: Represents returns processed in Mid-Atlantic Service Center of the Internal Revenue Service. This center processed returns filed in the following district offices: Baltimore, Maryland; Newark, New Jersey; Philadelphia and Pittsburgh, Pennsylvania; Richmond, Virginia; and Wilmington, Delaware.

SOURCE: Special study based on selected corporation income tax returns for 1963 covering accounting periods ended July 1963–June 1964. Internal Revenue Service, Statistics Division, June 1968.

About two-thirds of the $160 million discrepancy in the transportation and public utility industry was accounted for by faster depreciation on the tax return than permitted on the books. Book depreciation amounted to about three-fourths of the amount taken for tax purposes. Other

TABLE 4

Selected Corporation Income Tax Returns With Total Assets of $50 Million or More: Summary of Differences Between Profits Before Tax Per Books of Accounts and Profits Per Tax Law, 1963
(millions of dollars)

Item	Manufacturing	Transportation, communication, electric, gas, and sanitary services	Finance, insurance, and real estate
Profits before tax, per books of account	2,914.1	655.5	677.7
Net difference:			
due to income	−37.6	−10.9	−118.7
due to depreciation	−114.4	−102.9	−7.7
due to depletion	−346.0	−.7	−3.3
due to other expenses	+35.8	−50.2	−4.5
Equals:			
Profits before tax, per tax law	2,451.9	490.8	543.5

Note: See Table 3.
Source: Internal Revenue Service, Statistics Division, June 1968.

expenses contributed $150 million to the discrepancy. It was not possible to further pinpoint these.

In the finance group, additional income on the books was responsible for practically all the $130 million discrepancy. This probably reflects the large investments in tax-exempt bonds by banks and insurance companies.

CONCLUSION

Statistics of Income constitute the most complete and detailed measure of the income of corporations. Data are presented regularly in *Statistics of Income* for such items as depreciation, depletion, tax-exempt interest, and capital gains and losses, so that adjustments are being made to tax income to arrive at a measure of economic income. When comparing statistics on book and tax income it should be pointed out that the net income reported for tax purposes is likely to be more uniformly determined because of the necessity to conform with provisions of the Code, than the net income reported for book purposes.

This paper has pointed out the growth in the difference between tax income and book income. It has tried to show that some of the items currently tabulated constitute extremely important adjustments and confirms the desirability of making them. It is hoped that further investigations along these lines will quantify other adjustments and improve our understanding of the ones now being made, thus making *Statistics of Income* even more useful.

SELECTED REFERENCES

Dan Throop Smith and J. Keith Butters, "Taxable and Business Income," National Bureau of Economic Research, 1949.

Corporation Income Tax Returns, "Statistics of Income—1963."

Vito Natrella, "Tax Returns as a Source of Data," *Financial Analysts Journal*, July–August, 1965.

Bureau of National Affairs, Tax Management Portfolio, 31-2nd T.M., Preparation and Use of Schedule M.

13
CORPORATE EARNINGS: A RECORD OF CONTRAST AND CHANGE*

Sidney Cottle

Contrasts dominate today's corporate earnings picture. Profits have been in a cyclical upswing since 1961 and by 1964 the dollar amount earned by all manufacturing corporations reached a record high that was 58 percent above the 1961 low. Yet in 1964 there were crosscurrents. The profit margin for 120 major manufacturing corporations—aided by a reduction in Federal income taxes—rose substantially from the 1961 low and by 1964 was well above the postwar average. In contrast, the amount of sales produced per dollar of invested capital—the turnover ratio—recovered only moderately from the 1961 low and remained below its 1947–64 level. As a result, the return earned on total capital did not quite reach its postwar level.

These contrasting facts raise two important questions. First, how profitable were U.S. manufacturing corporations in 1964? Second, what changes have occurred in profit margins and the turnover of invested capital and in their relationship? The first question is concerned with the level of profits; the second with the structure of profits. To the extent that these questions can be answered, our ability will be increased not only to interpret today's earnings but also to anticipate tomorrow's.

OBJECTIVE

To seek answers to these questions, we must undertake a long-run analysis in depth. The objective of this article, therefore, is to probe the record so that the present may be brought into perspective and a basis may be established for assessing the future. In this manner, we can determine where we are and how we got here; then we can more effectively anticipate where we are going.

To accomplish this objective, our analysis of the record is divided into two major parts. The first pertains to the level of earnings and comprises the following steps:

1. To provide an overview, the profitability of *all* manufacturing

---

* Reprinted by permission of the *Financial Analysts Journal* (November–December 1965).

corporations is examined in terms of both dollar earnings and return on total capital.

2. To place the postwar period in long-run perspective, the return on net worth for a large sample of manufacturing corporations is analyzed over the 40-year span, 1925–64.

3. To interpret more fully the present, the postwar composite performance of manufacturing corporations is disaggregated and examined in terms of the principal industrial segments.

The second part of our analysis is concerned with long-run changes in the structure of profits. This examination is in terms of expense ratios, profit margins, and turnover ratios.

In undertaking this research, earnings data from government agencies, the First National City Bank, and Stanford Research Institute (SRI) are used. The detailed analysis of the four postwar earnings periods is based on the substantial body of financial information maintained by SRI[1] on 120 major manufacturing corporations representing a cross section of industry. These statistics cover the 30-year span, 1935–64. In 1964, the 120 firms had total sales of $156 billion, or 35 percent of the aggregate sales for all manufacturing corporations.[2] By using the SRI series, the profit experience of the manufacturing sector can be probed in more detail than would otherwise be possible. The analysis begins, however, with the more comprehensive figures for all U.S. manufacturing corporations collected by the government.[3]

THE LEVEL OF PROFITS: ANALYSIS OF DOLLAR EARNINGS

We will examine the level of profits in terms of, first, the dollar amount of profits and, second, the rate of return on invested capital. Since rate-of-return analysis provides more penetrating insight into profitability, the examination of dollar earnings is confined to only major considerations.

Amount Earned by All Manufacturing Corporations

During the 1961–64 period, dollar earnings after taxes rose from less than $11 billion to nearly $17 billion. This represents an average annual increase in excess of 16 percent and constitutes the most pronounced cyclical rise in the postwar period. But the 1964 level of earnings cannot

---

[1] The SRI compilation is an extension of a series developed a number of years ago. See Cottle and Whitman, *Corporate Earning Power and Market Valuation* (Durham, N.C.: Duke University Press, 1959).

[2] The SRI data do not purport to represent the average experience of all corporations either in the manufacturing sector of the economy or in the individual industries. Rather, they are a barometer of the performance of those corporations that are primarily the largest units in their respective industries. Nevertheless, the return on net worth for the SRI compilation compares closely with those of three other series covering a much larger number of companies.

[3] As reported in the *Survey of Current Business*, U.S. Department of Commerce, Office of Business Economics, and in *Statistics of Income . . . Corporation Income Tax Returns*, U.S. Department of the Treasury, Internal Revenue Service.

be judged solely in terms of performance since 1961. It must also be considered with respect to the long-run record.

The record of earnings over the long run is distorted by depression, war, inflation, and the other economic abnormalities that are the aftermath of war. It is also distorted by changes in income tax rates, depreciation, and accounting practices. Accordingly, the annual dollar amounts of earnings after taxes over the 1929–64 span do not present a consistent pattern of growth (see Exhibit I). Even if we put aside the period of violent fluctuations—1929–34—and compare the growth rates for selected periods of the remaining 30 years, the absence of consistent growth is still evident.[4]

EXHIBIT I

Profits after Taxes of All Manufacturing Corporations and Growth Rates for Selected Periods
1929–64

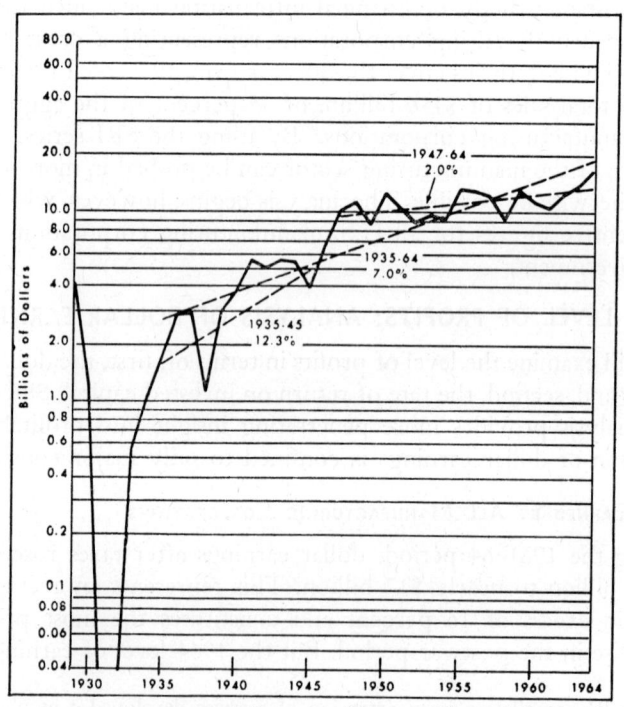

Source: Department of Commerce, "Survey of Current Business."

Period	Annual Growth Rate
1961–64	16.3%
1947–64	2.0
1947–62	1.2
1945–47	55.0
1935–45	12.3
1935–64	7.0

---

[4] The growth rates are mathematically computed by fitting trends by the least squares method.

1935–45 and 1945–47. The marked growth in earnings over the 1935–45 span is not surprising. This period is characterized by the recovery from the Great Depression and by the forced-draft activity of the war years. The sharp 1945–47 rise resulted from the removal of price controls, the pent-up demand for goods in the United States, the urgent reconstruction needs of our wartime allies, and the almost rampant inflation.

1947–62. In contrast to the 1945–47 period, the dollar amount of reported earnings for all manufacturing corporations over the 1947–62 span grew at only 1.2 percent per annum. Significant distortion exists in the data, however, particularly in the early years of the period. From 1947 through 1951, reported earnings were substantially overstated relative to *real* earnings because of marked inflation and the inadequacy of government allowed depreciation.

To determine the impact of these two factors, we adjusted reported earnings for the 1947–62 period for inventory profits and losses and for the rate of depreciation actually taken in 1958–62. On this adjusted basis, the 1947–62 growth rate was increased to 3 percent. Although this is a decided increase, the adjusted growth rate still remains well below the 1947–62 growth rate of 5.7 percent for GNP.[5] Moreover, if full adjustment for depreciation were made through placing fixed assets on a current price basis, the growth in earnings would quite probably still lag the growth in GNP.[6]

Does this drop in earnings relative to GNP indicate that the manufacturing sector was providing a significantly decreasing proportion of the nation's total output over the 1947–62 period?

An examination of the relationship to GNP of both manufacturers' sales and manufacturing gross product[7] indicates that only a little slippage occurred. Since sales and manufacturing gross product declined only slightly relative to GNP, the substantial lag between earnings and GNP must have resulted from a pronounced decline in profit margins over most

---

[5] Since the completion of this research, certain revised data have appeared in the August and September issues of the *Survey of Current Business.* Only the revised pretax earnings for all manufacturing corporations have been released to date. The 1947–62 growth rates for both the revised GNP and pretax earnings series show a minor increase over the rates for the unrevised series. However, the level of the earnings data is raised slightly, whereas for the full span the level of the GNP data is unchanged. As a result, pretax earnings are a slightly higher percent of GNP than shown on the unrevised basis.

[6] Earnings data for all corporations (finance, retail trade, manufacturing, etc.) from 1947–62 have been adjusted by Murray Brown for inventory profits and losses and for straight-line depreciation based on estimated current cost of fixed assets. On the reported basis, the 1947–62 annual growth rate was 2.7 percent; on the adjusted basis it was 4.4 percent. This adjusted rate is still considerably below that for GNP. Murray Brown, "Depreciation and Corporate Profits," *Survey of Current Business,* October, 1963.

[7] The gross product of the manufacturing sector is the value of output less principally purchases of raw materials from other sectors of the economy.

of the 1947–62 period. Our subsequent analysis of profit margins will confirm this.

1964. The dollar amount earned in 1964 was well above the 1947–64 trend line (Exhibit I). In fact, this departure was in excess of that for any other postwar year. Therefore, measured in this manner, 1964 stands out as a good year.

Another measure of the relative level of profits in the manufacturing sector of the economy in 1964 is a long-run comparison of the relationship of earnings to GNP. The tabulation below shows that the 1964 earnings/GNP relationship was substantially above that for the 1958–62 period. Furthermore, it was only slightly below the much higher 1952–57 average on the basis of reported earnings and was identical to both the adjusted 1952–57 and 1947–64 levels. Accordingly, 1964 also compares favorably with the record in terms of the historic earnings/GNP relationship.

Earnings of Manufacturing Corporations as a Percent of GNP

Period	Reported	Adjusted*
1964	2.7%	2.7%
1958–62	2.3	2.3
1952–57	2.8	2.7
1947–51	3.9	3.2
1947–64	2.9	2.7

* Data for 1947–62 adjusted for inventory profits and losses and for level of depreciation taken in 1958–62. Data for 1964 adjusted only for inventory profits.

Dollar aggregates are essential in appraising the growth of earnings and in deriving the earnings/GNP relationship, which is important from state-of-the-nation and public policy standpoints. But dollar amounts do not measure profitability in terms that are most useful to the individual and institutional investor or to the corporate manager.

The Level of Profits: Rate-of-Return Analysis. To appraise the earnings performance of a manufacturing enterprise, the investor, as well as the corporate manager, must be informed as to the rate of return earned on the capital invested. Profitability measured in this manner may be significantly different from that measured in terms of dollar earnings. This is also true when appraising the level of profits for the manufacturing sector as a whole or for a cross section of manufacturing corporations.

In the present study, the rate of return earned by manufacturing corporations is analyzed in terms of return on total capital for the government and SRI data and in terms of return on net worth for the longer-run First National City Bank series. The definitions used in return on total capital are not as familiar as those used in return on net worth. Accordingly, to assure a common understanding and interpretation of the data, summary definitions are given in footnote eight.[8]

RETURN EARNED BY ALL MANUFACTURING CORPORATIONS: 1947–64

The marked contrast between the earnings performance for all manufacturing corporations measured in dollars and in return on total capital is shown in Exhibit II. It may be seen from the upper field of the exhibit that dollar earnings rose over the postwar period. However, because a substantial increase in capital investment was needed to produce these earnings, an irregular—but pronounced—decline in the rate of return until 1961 can be seen.

The lower field indicates that—in terms of the level of return earned on total capital—there are four relatively distinct postwar earnings "eras": 1947–51, 1952–57, 1958–62, and 1963–64. Although these intervals do not coincide with the business cycles charted in Exhibit II, they represent reasonably discrete economic periods. The 1947–51 span—with its inordinately high level of return, due to a considerable degree to inflation and inadequate depreciation—ends with the subsiding effects of the Korean war. The 1952–57 span—with its heavy expenditures for durables in the mid 1950's—ends with the last good postwar year prior to 1964. The 1958–62 span—with its comparative economic sluggishness and excess capacity—ends with the first year of recovery in return on invested capital. The remaining era is 1963–64—the years of pronounced recovery. Although our primary concern is with 1964, information for 1963 is presented to complete the record.

The substantial difference in the return earned in each postwar era is emphasized by the following tabulation.

---

[8] *Total capital* is the sum of the net worth, all long-term debt, and any minority interest in the equity of a consolidated subsidiary. The objective is to measure the return earned on the capital committed on a long-term basis (invested in manufacturing corporations) and, therefore, excludes short-term obligations—current liabilities.

Earnings available for total capital is the sum of net income after taxes, plus minority interest in earnings of consolidated subsidiaries, plus tax-adjusted interest on long-term debt. The tax adjustment consists of subtracting from the interest expense each year an amount determined by applying to the interest payment the Federal income tax rate (normal and surtax) in effect that year. This procedure puts interest paid on long-term debt on roughly the same basis as income available for stock equity and thereby substantially reduces the influence of differences in capital structure on the rate of return. Government earnings data are adjusted by estimating interest on long-term debt, where appropriate to provide greater consistency with the SRI series.

Earnings margin is the ratio obtained by dividing earnings available for total capital by sales. *Profit margin* pertains to the ratio of net profits after taxes to sales.

Capital turnover is the ratio of sales to total capital.

Rate of return on total capital is obtained by dividing the annual earnings available for total capital by the annual average total capital. It can also be expressed as the product of (*a*) the amount of each sales dollar that remains for total capital, i.e., the earnings margin, and (*b*) the amount of sales per dollar of the total capital, i.e., capital turnover. Consequently, the three key ratios are (*a*) return on total capital, (*b*) earnings margin, and (*c*) capital turnover.

Period	Return on Total Capital*
1964†	7.9%
1963†	6.8
1958–62†	6.2
1952–57	7.9
1947–51	11.3

* Based on reported data.
† Years 1962–64 partially estimated.

By comparing these earnings eras, we can see more clearly the broad sweep of profit performance across the entire postwar span and appraise more effectively the profitability of manufacturing corporations in 1964.

We must emphasize that the figures for 1962–64 will be subject to revision when all the data become available, and that the era comparisons are distorted to varying degrees by inflation and major changes in tax-

EXHIBIT II

PROFITABILITY OF ALL MANUFACTURING CORPORATIONS
AND RELATED BUSINESS CYCLES
1947–64 and Selected Period Averages

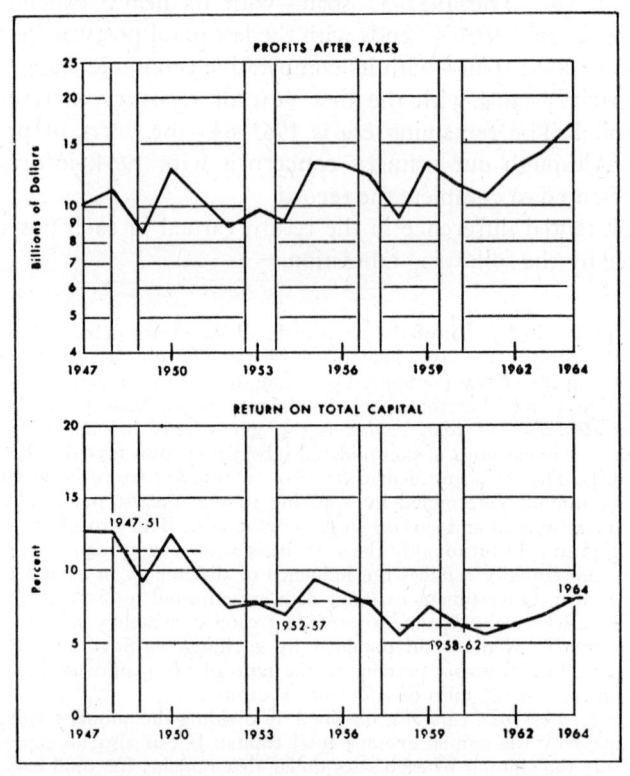

SOURCES: Department of Commerce, "Survey of Current Business" and "Business Cycle Developments;" Department of the Treasury, "Statistics of Income;" Stanford Research Institute. 1962–64 partially estimated.

allowable depreciation. This is particularly true when comparing rates of return, because inflation—and to a lesser degree changes in depreciation—cause distortions in the balance sheet as well as in the income statement. To adjust fully for these factors is extremely difficult and not feasible within the present undertaking. However, rough adjustments for the impact of inflation and changes in depreciation on the postwar rate of return are possible.[9]

If we eliminate the effect of inventory profits and losses and charge depreciation at the average effective rate over the 1958–62 span,[10] the computed return on total capital would be changed as shown below.

	Return on Total Capital				
	1947–51	1952–57	1958–62*	1963*	1964*
Computed from government data	11.3%	7.9%	6.2%	6.8%	7.9%
Adjusted	9.3	7.5	6.2	—†	—†

* Years 1962–64 partially estimated.

† Because of the lack of available information, 1963 and 1964 cannot be adjusted in the same manner. If the data are adjusted solely for inventory profits, however, the return would be reduced to 6.7 percent and 7.8 percent, respectively. Thus, 1964 would remain above the adjusted 1952–57 figure.

These rough adjustments demonstrate that the rate-of-return data for the 1947–51 period considerably overstate the *real* earnings performance. If all necessary adjustments were made, the decline in return earned between 1947–51 and 1958–62 would be considerably less drastic than the reported data indicate,[11] but a period-by-period decline would still exist.

In contrast to the foregoing decline, the estimated return on total capital for 1964 (7.9 percent) equaled the 1952–57 average on a reported basis, exceeded our adjusted 1952–57 figure (7.5 percent), and was above the adjusted 1947–64 average (7.6 percent). Therefore, the rate earned in 1964 represented a significant improvement in profitability over 1958–62 and compared favorably with the postwar record.

Long-term Perspective

Let us bring the return earned by manufacturing corporations over the postwar period into long run perspective. This can be done by using the

---

[9] The indicated adjustments have been applied only to the income side. Full adjustment for inflation would also require changes in the balance sheet. Since much of the plant and equipment, particularly in 1947–51, consisted of low-cost prewar facilities, a substantial increase in the book value (write-up) of fixed assets (and capital) would be necessary to provide for the significant postwar price changes. This increase, in turn, would require a further increase in depreciation charges.

[10] The effective 1958–62 rate was derived by dividing total depreciation charges reported in the *Survey of Current Business* by the total "depreciable assets" reported in *Statistics of Income . . . Corporation Income Tax Returns*. Total depreciable assets for 1962 were estimated.

[11] If the experience of manufacturing firms is comparable to that of all corporations, the extent of the adjustment may be inferred from the fact that Brown's adjustments reduced 1947–51 dollar earnings for all corporations by nearly 25 percent. Since total capital would need to be increased by the amount of the write-up of net fixed assets to current prices under his computations, the return on total capital for all corporations would be reduced by more than 25 percent. Our calculations decreased the 1947–51 return on total capital for manufacturing corporations by 18 percent.

return on net worth data compiled by the First National City Bank. This well-known series covers four decades.

The annual rates of return on net worth from 1925 through 1964 are shown in the upper field of Exhibit III.[12] The lower field provides a more simplified 40-year view of corporate profits. Selected period averages are used so that the major changes in the *level* of profitability can be readily

EXHIBIT III
Return on Net Worth
Leading Manufacturing Corporations,
1925–64 and Selected Period Averages

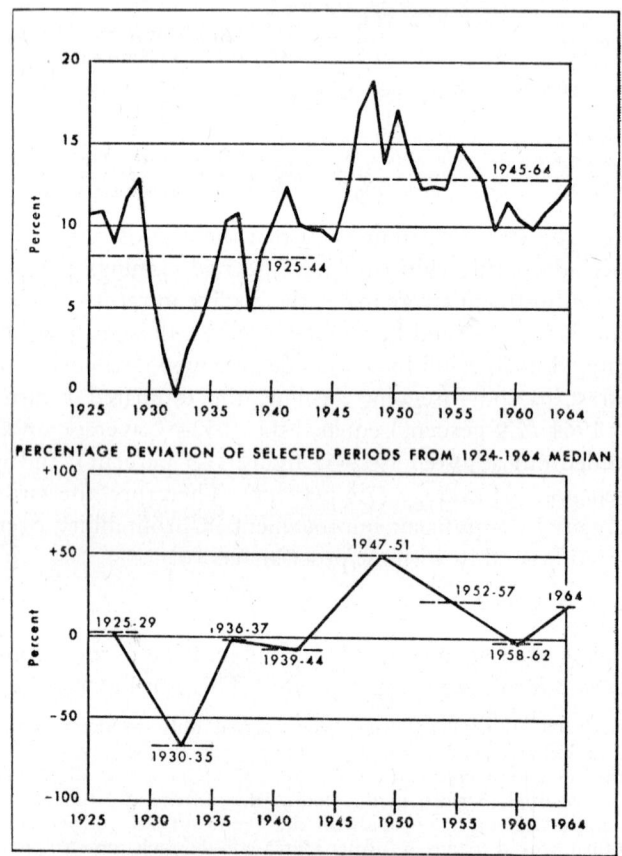

Source: First National City Bank.

seen, without the distraction of year-to-year fluctuations. Each period average is plotted in terms of its percentage deviation from the median return for the entire 1925–64 span (10.8 percent). Thus, prewar and postwar profit performance can be visually compared.

[12] The First National City Bank data cover a smaller number of firms than the government series, pertain only to the larger manufacturing corporations, and reflect the effect of leverage. Nevertheless, the return on net worth has the same general configuration as the return on total capital developed from the *Survey of Current Business* and *Statistics of Income* data.

The 40-year span can be divided into two distinct earnings eras of about 20 years each (Exhibit III). Despite the distortions inherent in such a long-run series, the return on net worth in the 1945–64 span fluctuated around a level significantly above that for the preceding 20 years (12.9 percent versus 8.2 percent).[13] Even if the distortions were remedied, the difference between the earnings levels would still be substantial; certainly, the postwar earnings environment constitutes an impressive departure from that of the preceding two decades. Although interrupted by recoveries in 1950 and 1955, the secular decline from the onset of the postwar period to 1961 is evident. Furthermore, since 1961 the return on net worth for manufacturing corporations has risen considerably. The significant improvement in profitability by 1964 indicated by our estimates developed from government data is confirmed by the First National City Bank series.

Return Earned by SRI Sample: 1947–64

The postwar rate-of-return experience of manufacturing corporations derived from government and First National City Bank data is reaffirmed by examining the return on total capital compilations of SRI shown in Exhibit IV.

The lower field of the exhibit sharply defines the extended postwar decline, the low earnings period of 1958–62, and the improved level of profitability in 1964 by showing the percentage deviation of the return earned in each selected postwar period from the 1947–64 average (11.5 percent). To facilitate period comparisons, this average is used throughout our examination of the earnings eras as a common base.[14] It should not be considered as a norm.

Profitability of Manufacturing Groups and Industries

Examination of the composite performance of manufacturing corporations has made possible a broad appraisal of the 1964 level. But aggregate data represent average experience and, therefore, may cover up marked differences in the performance of major components of the aggregate. Accordingly, to interpret more fully the earnings situation in 1964, we need to disaggregate composite performance and examine postwar experience in terms of the principal industrial segments comprising the manufacturing sector. This is accomplished by dividing manufacturing into

---

[13] In 1945 and 1946, earnings were disrupted by the cessation of World War II hostilities, termination of war contracts, problems of reconversion, and labor strikes. Therefore, in the more intensive analysis that follows, the 1947–64 span is treated as the postwar period.

[14] Arguments may be advanced for the use of a period average that excludes some of the particularly abnormal years at the onset of the postwar period. The logic in selecting some period other than 1947–64 would be to designate a level that is considered to be representative of the future. However, this is not the objective of the present study.

EXHIBIT IV
Return on Total Capital
SRI Manufacturing Sample, 1947–64 and Selected Period Averages

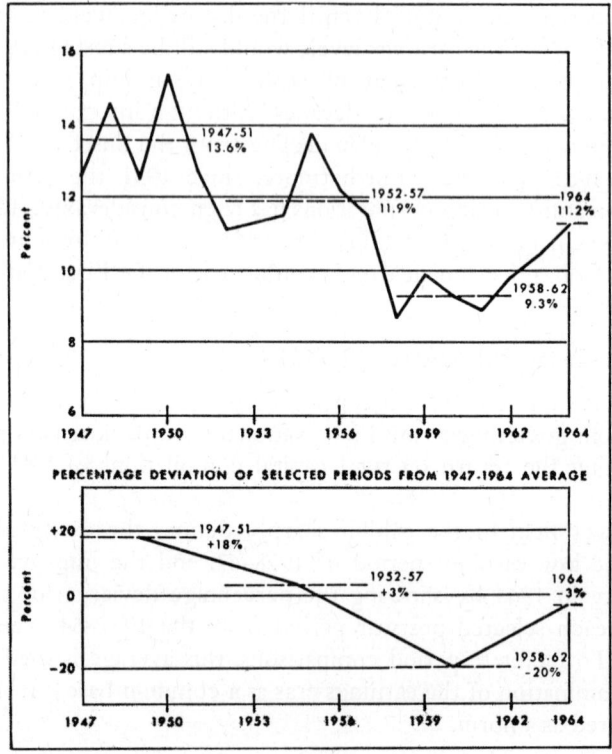

PERCENTAGE DEVIATION OF SELECTED PERIODS FROM 1947-1964 AVERAGE

Source: Stanford Research Institute.

two groups—durable and nondurable goods industries (see Exhibit V). The groups are then subdivided into major components on the basis of product demand and, to a somewhat lesser degree, of earnings performance. The components, in turn, are broken down into familiar industry classifications.

Comparative Performance of Durable and Nondurable Groups. Over the entire postwar span and in three of the four selected periods, the composite return earned on total capital by the durable goods group of industries exceeds that for the nondurables, as shown in the following tabulation and Exhibit VI.

	Return on Total Capital	
Period	Durables	Nondurables
1964	12.5%	10.4%
1958–62	9.3	9.3
1952–57	13.0	11.1
1947–51	14.6	12.9
1947–64	12.3	11.0

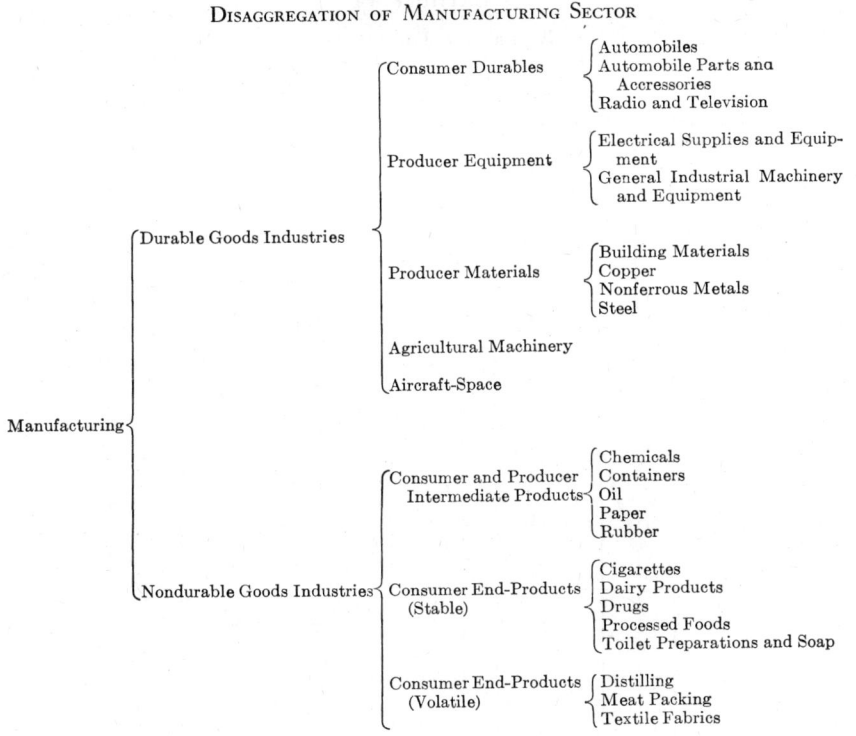

EXHIBIT V
Disaggregation of Manufacturing Sector

Manufacturing:

- **Durable Goods Industries**
  - Consumer Durables
    - Automobiles
    - Automobile Parts and Accessories
    - Radio and Television
  - Producer Equipment
    - Electrical Supplies and Equipment
    - General Industrial Machinery and Equipment
  - Producer Materials
    - Building Materials
    - Copper
    - Nonferrous Metals
    - Steel
  - Agricultural Machinery
  - Aircraft-Space
- **Nondurable Goods Industries**
  - Consumer and Producer Intermediate Products
    - Chemicals
    - Containers
    - Oil
    - Paper
    - Rubber
  - Consumer End-Products (Stable)
    - Cigarettes
    - Dairy Products
    - Drugs
    - Processed Foods
    - Toilet Preparations and Soap
  - Consumer End-Products (Volatile)
    - Distilling
    - Meat Packing
    - Textile Fabrics

The return earned by the durables group also fluctuates more widely. However, the long-run postwar decline in the rate of return and the subsequent pronounced recovery observed for the all-manufacturing composite dominate both the durable and the nondurable goods groups. The decline and recovery are accentuated in the case of the more volatile durables group. By 1964, the rate of return for the durable goods industries was above the 1947–64 average, whereas the return for the nondurables group was still below the postwar average.

Comparative Performance by Major Component. Do the rates of return earned by the major components of each group conform closely to the group return, or are there wide variations in the levels of return and in stability? Did some of the components even move in opposite directions?

In terms of both stability and the level of return, much wider differences exist between the components of the durables than those of the nondurables groups (see Exhibits VII and VIII). For example, the 1947–64 average for the highest earning segment in durables (consumer durables) was more than 125 percent above the return for the lowest earning segment (agricultural machinery), whereas the postwar average return for the highest earning segment in nondurables (consumer end-products—stable) was scarcely 65 percent above that for the lowest earner (consumer end-products—volatile).

Similarly, earnings fluctuations are greater among the individual com-

EXHIBIT VI

Return on Total Capital
Durable and Nondurable Goods Groups
SRI Manufacturing Sample, 1947–64

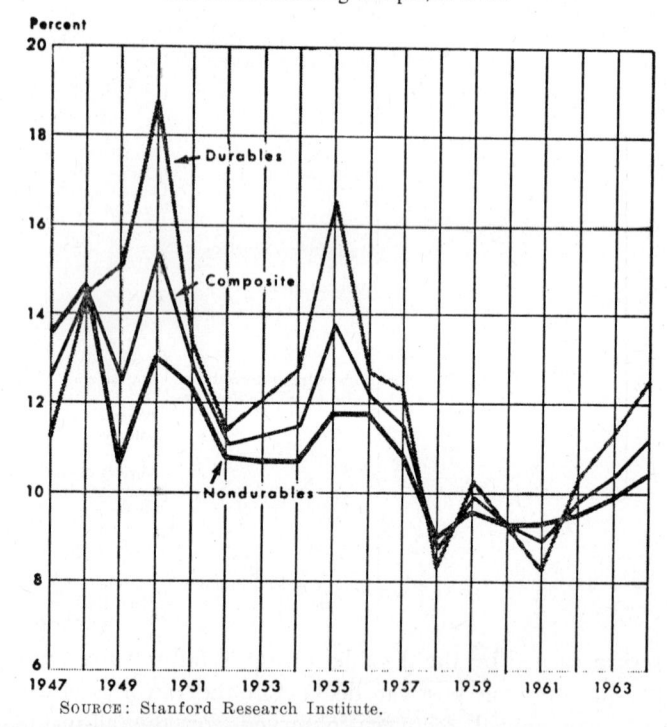

Source: Stanford Research Institute.

ponents of the durable goods group. Over the postwar period, returns for agricultural equipment, aircraft-space, and consumer durables fluctuated markedly, but the producer equipment and producer materials components fluctuated surprisingly little.

Two of the three major segments of the nondurable goods group—consumer-producer intermediate goods and consumer end-products (stable)—were much less volatile than the most stable segments of the durables group. The returns earned by the consumer end-products (volatile) component fluctuated widely during the postwar years. Subsequently, there was a significant dampening down of these fluctuations.

With the exception of aircraft-space and consumer end-products (stable), all the segments of both groups show a long-run decline from the beginning of the postwar span to the 1958–62 period. The virtual cessation of government procurement caused the aircraft-space industry to suffer an operating loss in 1947 and a very low return in 1948. This profit experience was repeated again in 1960–61 as a result of the commercial jet programs. The rate-of-return configuration for the consumer end-products (stable) component—cigarettes, dairy products, drugs, processed foods, and toilet preparations and soap—is entirely different from those of

EXHIBIT VII

Return on Total Capital
Durable Goods Subgroups
SRI Manufacturing Sample, 1947–64

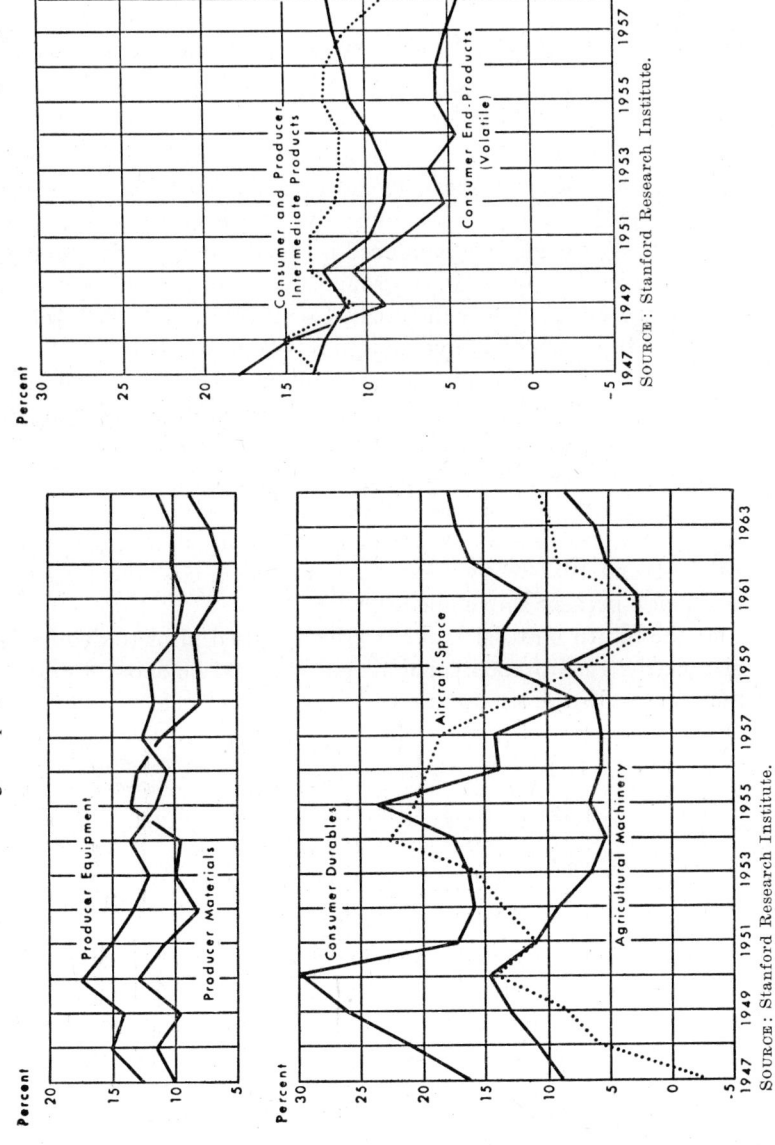

Source: Stanford Research Institute.

EXHIBIT VIII

Return on Total Capital
Nondurable Goods Subgroups
SRI Manufacturing Sample, 1947–64

Source: Stanford Research Institute.

all other components. The postwar low occurred in 1953 and was followed by a remarkable rising trend through 1960 and by almost a plateau since then.

Let us next analyze period-by-period the postwar experience of the major components of the nation's manufacturing sector. For ease of comparison, the discussion of each period is set forth below the respective graph in Exhibit IX.

How Profitable Were U.S. Manufacturing Corporations in 1964?

Can we now answer the question, "How profitable were U.S. manufacturing corporations in 1964?"

In terms of the record, 1964 was certainly a good year—a prosperous year. The duration, magnitude, and breadth of the recovery in earnings between 1961 and 1964 were impressive. Cyclical improvement, as might be expected, was more pronounced in the durable goods group of industries than in the nondurables group. The return on total capital for all industries except building materials was above the 1958–62 average and in a number of instances recovered to the 1947–64 level.

Whether 1964 was an excellent year depends on the standard of excellence adopted. If inflation and depreciation adjustments for the SRI series were proportional to those for the government series, the 1964 return of 11.2 percent would be above the 1947–64 average. Moreover, if the average return for the last 10 years (10.6 percent based on reported earnings) were arbitrarily taken as a test of normal earnings—the 1954–64, 1953–64, and 1952–64 averages are nearly identical—the 1964 rate would be about 6 percent above normal.

If the return on total capital were computed prior to deducting depreciation, the 1964 predepreciation return would be about 4 percent above the average for the last 10 years.

Period	Return on Total Capital before Depreciation
1964	17.7%
1952–64	17.1
1953–64	17.1
1954–64	17.1
1955–64	17.0

To provide further assistance in appraising the 1964 level of earnings, composite rates of return for 1965 have been derived for SRI's 120 companies from the earnings and dividend estimates of a well-known financial service and several major financial institutions. (These estimates were obtained in July, 1965.) Using the estimate of the financial service and the median institutional forecast, the resulting range in the anticipated return on total capital is from 11.2 percent to 11.5 percent. The lower figure is identical to the 1964 rate, and the higher is an improvement of about 3 percent. On the basis of these midyear forecasts, 1965 will represent at least as good a year as 1964 and will quite possibly exceed it.

Corporate Earnings: A Record of Contrast and Change

EXHIBIT IX
ANALYSIS OF RETURN ON TOTAL CAPITAL FOR SELECTED POSTWAR PERIODS
Major Groups and Subgroups, SRI Manufacturing Sample

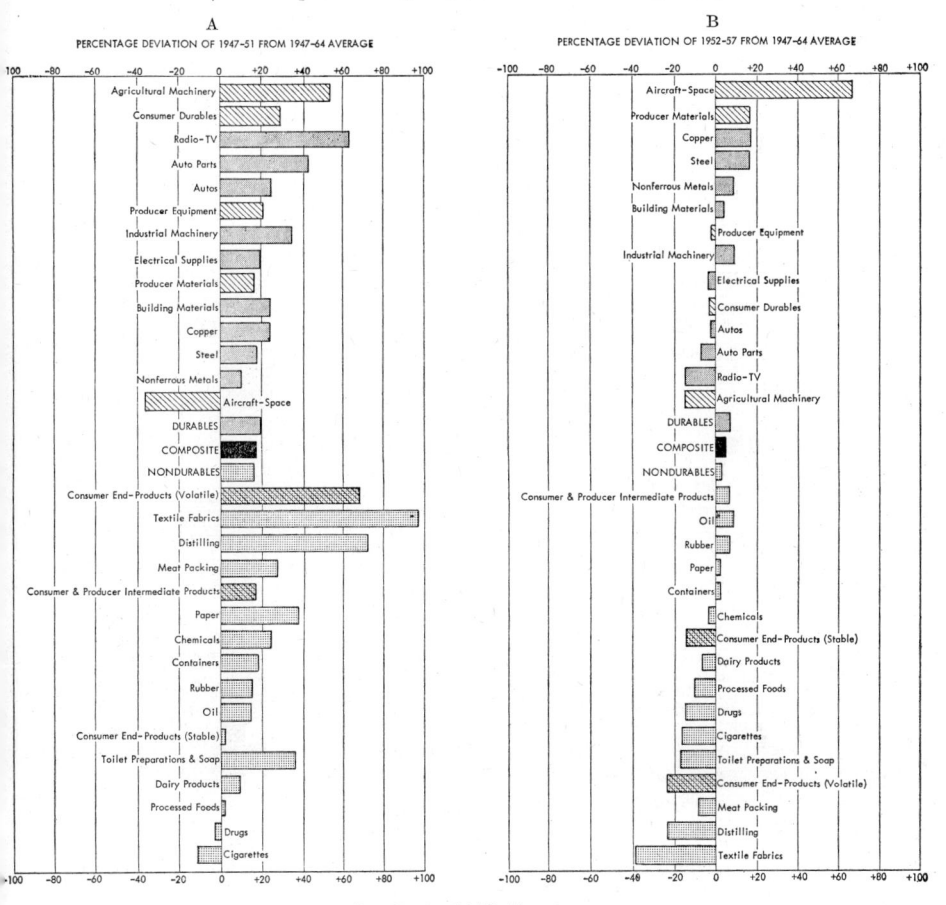

A — PERCENTAGE DEVIATION OF 1947–51 FROM 1947–64 AVERAGE

B — PERCENTAGE DEVIATION OF 1952–57 FROM 1947–64 AVERAGE

PANEL A—1947–51

The composite return on total capital was well above that for any other postwar span. Did all segments participate equally in this prosperity? In terms of the two main divisions—durables and nondurables—the experience was comparable. Moreover, with the exception of aircraft-space, the return earned by every major component was above the postwar average. Wide variations, however, existed between the profitability of both major components and individual industries. In the durable goods group, radio-TV, agricultural machinery, and auto parts were far above the group average, whereas nonferrous metals and steel lagged significantly and aircraft-space was even below its 1947–64 level. In nondurables, textile fabrics and distilling substantially exceeded the group average whereas the drug and cigarette industries were below their postwar averages.

PANEL B—1952–57

Between 1952 and 1957, inflation subsided and the supply and demand situation relative to both consumer durables and nondurables came into better balance. As a result, a striking change took place in the profits of the consumer components of both the durable and nondurable goods groups. Although the rates of return for both groups declined, their 1952–57 averages remained above those for 1947–64. Durables experienced the smaller decline. Although other industries showed a decline, the pervasiveness and extent of the decline in the consumer goods industries is notable. They suffered an aggregate drop of 23 percent in the rate of return, or more than double the decline for all other industries. With the exception of agricultural equipment, the demand for producer goods and materials was strong throughout most of the period.

EXHIBIT IX (Continued)
ANALYSIS OF RETURN ON TOTAL CAPITAL FOR SELECTED POSTWAR PERIODS
Major Groups and Subgroups, SRI Manufacturing Sample

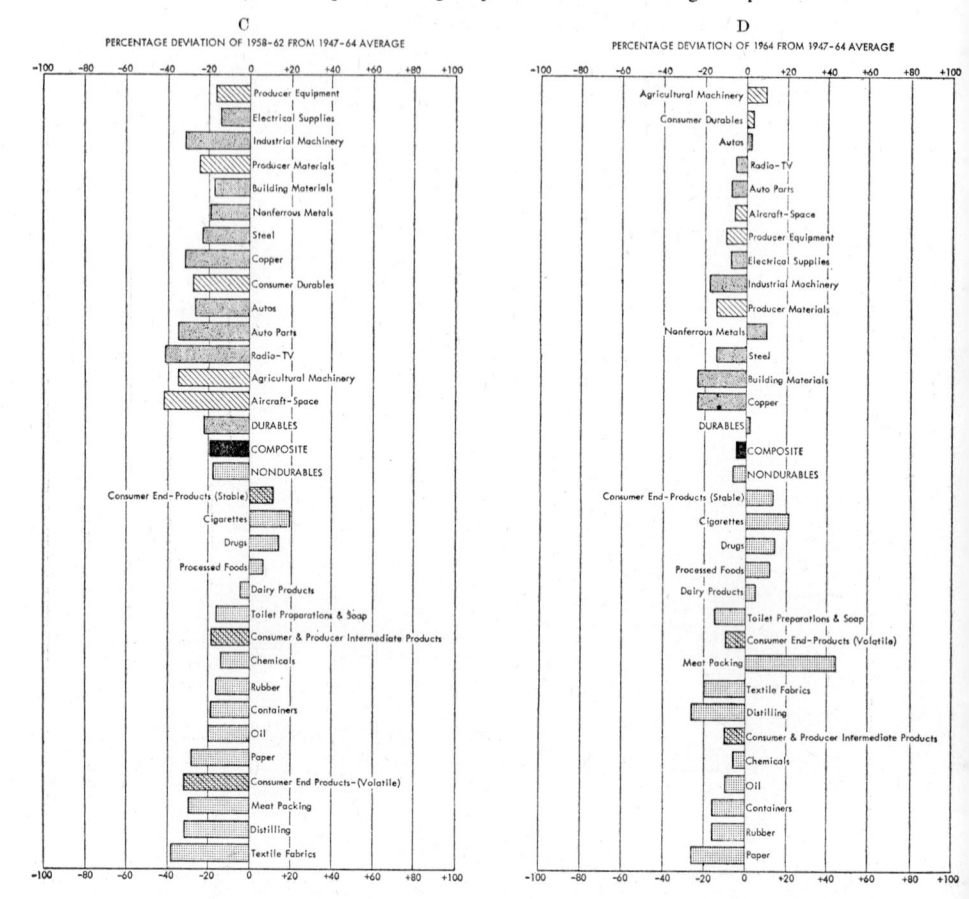

C — PERCENTAGE DEVIATION OF 1958–62 FROM 1947–64 AVERAGE

D — PERCENTAGE DEVIATION OF 1964 FROM 1947–64 AVERAGE

PANEL C—1958–62

The sharpness and breadth of the decline in the return between 1952–57 and 1958–62 is impressive. The durable goods industries felt the full force of the marked reduction in spending for plant and equipment by business—and for autos, washing machines, and other durables by consumers. The return on total capital for the group declined heavily. Coincidentally, the nondurables fell to exactly the same rate of return (9.3 percent) as the durables. Since they were somewhat lower in 1952–57 than the durables, the percentage decline was less. The decline was felt by every industry in the durables category. The nondurables situation is quite different. The returns earned by two major components declined, but the consumer end-product (stable) group enjoyed a higher return than in 1952–57 and actually stood above its postwar average.

PANEL D—1964

In 1964, the return earned on invested capital by every major component and every industry except one—building materials—was above its 1958–62 level. The recovery in durables was the most pronounced, particularly in agricultural equipment, consumer durables, and aircraft-space. Nondurables also participated in the recovery, but to a more limited degree. Consumer end-products (stable) rose slightly from their 1958–62 high. Although the return earned by consumer end-products (volatile) increased, it was still below its 1947–64 average. The business recovery is nearly four and one-half years old at the time of this writing (August, 1965) and is generally considered to have been well balanced. Improved profitability exists in nearly every segment of manufacturing. The durable goods group, however, has enjoyed the greatest recovery in return.

THE STRUCTURE OF EARNINGS:
ANALYSIS OF EARNINGS MARGIN AND TURNOVER RATIOS

The second question raised at the outset pertained to the structure of profits. As we noted at that point, the profit margin has improved significantly since 1961. (The term "earnings margin" is used hereafter to distinguish the ratio obtained through dividing earnings available for total capital by sales from the more familiar "profit margin" which is typically computed through dividing net income after taxes by sales.) In contrast to this pronounced improvement, the turnover ratio for total capital—amount of sales per dollar of total capital—has risen considerably less. As a result, the return earned on total capital did not rise as much as might have been anticipated solely from an examination of the earnings margin. This fact stresses the importance of considering the structure of profits—the earnings margin and the turnover ratio and their relationship. To the extent that changes in these two factors and the forces behind them can be probed and understood, the present earnings situation can be more effectively interpreted and the future significance of these structural changes can be more adequately appraised.

Earnings Margin and Turnover of Total Capital

Our structural analysis begins with the two key determinants of the return on total capital—the earnings margin and turnover of total capital.[15] If we examine these determinants over the 30-year span, 1935-64, two important and contrasting facts emerge.

First, the earnings margin declined over much of the last 30 years (see Exhibit X). In spite of the marked prosperity at the onset of the postwar period, the earnings margin did not recover to the 1936-37 level in any year. In fact, it did not reach even the significantly lower 1935-39 average. Since 1961, the earnings margin has risen significantly (from 6.2 percent to 7.2 percent). In 1964, it exceeded the average for the entire postwar span and for each intervening period except the somewhat distorted 1947-51 era. Nevertheless, it remains far below the prewar level.

Second, in marked contrast, the turnover of total capital has substantially exceeded the 1936-37 level in every postwar year (Exhibit X). For the entire postwar period, turnover averaged 1.65 times ($1.65 of sales for every dollar of invested capital) whereas in 1936-37 the turnover ratio was only 0.97 times (97¢ of sales per dollar of capital).

The following period averages for the earnings margin and turnover ratio show clearly the pronounced change in the *structure* of profits over the last three decades.

The importance of the increased turnover can be readily demonstrated.

---

[15] The return on total capital is the product of (*a*) the earnings margin and (*b*) the capital turnover. Thus, if the earnings margin were 5 percent and turnover were 2 ×, the rate of return would be 10 percent.

Period	Earnings Margin	Turnover of Total Capital	Return on Total Capital
1964	7.2%	1.54×	11.2%
1963	6.9	1.52	10.4
1958–62	6.3	1.48	9.3
1952–57	6.8	1.74	11.9
1947–51	7.7	1.75	13.6
1936–37	10.2	0.97	10.0

EXHIBIT X
Key Profitability Ratios
SRI Manufacturing Sample, 1935–64

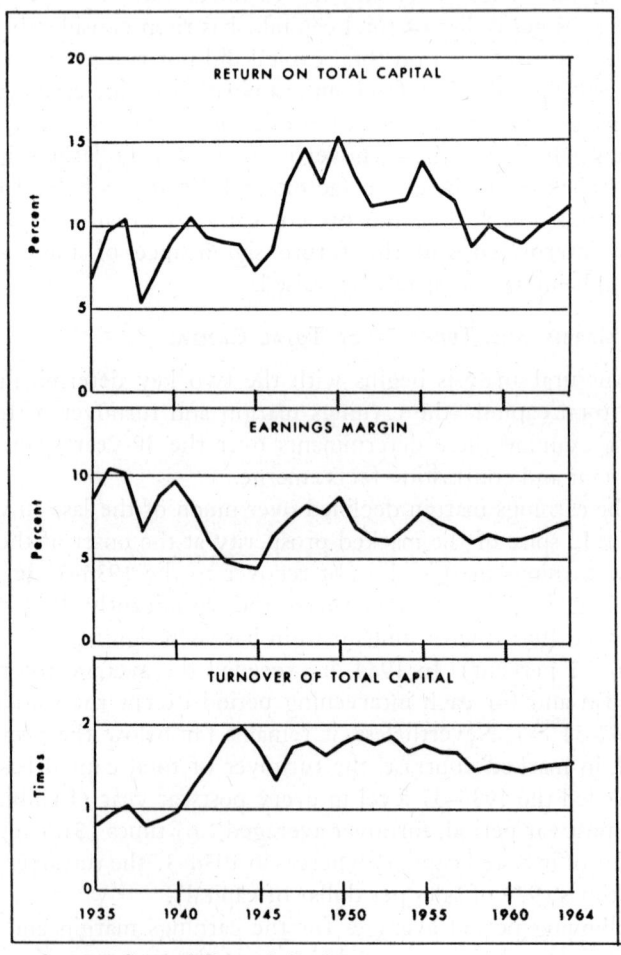

Source: Stanford Research Institute.

If the 1936–37 turnover had prevailed in 1964, the return on total capital —based on the 1964 earnings margin—would have been 7.0 percent instead of 11.2 percent. Turnover of total capital, of course, is no more important than earnings margin in determining the return earned on total capital. Nevertheless—taking the postwar earnings margin as the given factor—manufacturing corporations in the postwar period would have been far from prosperous if the prewar level of turnover had prevailed.

Thus, increased efficiency in the employment of capital has been a dominant factor in the postwar financial performance of U.S. manufacturers. In 1958–62, however, the ratio of sales to capital fell substantially below that in the earlier postwar periods. As a result, instead of being a support factor against the earnings margin squeeze—as in earlier periods—it now had an adverse and compounding effect on the rate of return. The sharp 1957–58 decline in the return on total capital occurred because a pronounced drop in the earnings margin was accompanied by a significant drop in turnover.

Turnover has increased modestly during the present recovery. In 1964, turnover (1.54×) was still 8 percent below the 1956–57 average (1.68×), but capacity utilitization in the manufacturing sector was reported to have returned to the 1956–57 level. It should be recognized that capacity utilization series are imprecise measures and therefore that precise conclusions cannot be drawn from them. Nevertheless, the lag in recovery emphasizes the need for examining turnover. The factors that resulted in the higher postwar turnover of total capital and in the subsequent drop, as well as the recovery to date in turnover, must be probed as carefully as the factors behind the postwar squeeze and the subsequent improvement in the earnings margin.

Unfortunately, there is a decided tendency for financial analysts to treat the turnover factor too lightly or to ignore it altogether. In our opinion, this approach is hazardous and omits a vital part of the earnings picture. To stress the importance of turnover ratios, we will examine them and their effect on the structure of earnings before considering the earnings margin further.

Turnover of Total Capital. Why has the turnover of total capital (sales to total capital) been much higher in the postwar period than it was before World War II? Why did it slow down significantly in 1958–62? And why, in 1964, has it not recovered to its former level?

An increase in the turnover of total capital can only result from a decline in total capital relative to total assets, an increase in the turnover of total assets, or a combination of the two. Conversely, a drop in the turnover of total capital would be due to a reverse situation.

In 1936–37, total capital averaged 87 percent of total assets; in 1947–64, it averaged 81 percent. This modest reduction in total capital was sufficient to increase the postwar turnover of total capital by only 7 percent, whereas the actual increase in turnover was 10 times that figure, or 70 percent. (Turnover rose from 0.97× in 1936–37 to 1.65× in 1947–64.) Accordingly, the much improved postwar turnover of total capital is due almost entirely to a substantial increase in the ratio of sales to total assets.

But what caused the 1958–62 decline in turnover? And the modest recovery by 1964? Again, we must look at the turnover of assets for our answer, because the total capital/total assets relationship has been strikingly consistent throughout the postwar period. The balance of the turnover analysis is, therefore, devoted to an examination of the 1947–64 relationship of sales to the principal asset categories.

Turnover of Principal Asset Categories. Net fixed assets (principally land, plant, and equipment) and current assets consistently aggregated in excess of 90 percent of total assets over the entire postwar period. The remaining 10 percent consisted primarily of investments, advances to subsidiaries, and similar items that are usually carried in "other assets."

Turnover of current assets, as a whole, has been relatively stable over the postwar period as can be seen in the tabulation below. This stability is impressive in view of the divergent turnover experience of cash, receivables, and inventory. The 1958–62 decline was modest, and in 1964 turnover was close to the 1947–57 average and identical to the 1947–64 level.

Period	Turnover of Current Assets	Turnover of Net Fixed Assets
1964	2.68×	2.66×
1963	2.64	2.64
1958–62	2.60	2.51
1947–57	2.72	3.29
1947–64	2.68	3.00

The turnover record for net fixed assets is significantly different. Because fixed assets do not fluctuate with the volume of business transacted as do current assets and because in the case of fixed assets a lag exists —in periods of rising prices—between price at time of installation of a stock of fixed assets and the current price of output, the turnover experience of net fixed assets and current assets can vary substantially.

The turnover ratio for net fixed assets was at an unsustainable level during the 1947–57 period, primarily as a result of the high utilization of capacity, the existence of a substantial investment in facilities purchased at prewar prices, and the rapid rise in sales prices over much of the period. The marked slowdown in the turnover of fixed assets caused most of the 1958–62 decline in the turnover of total assets and, in turn, of total capital.

As noted above, capacity utilization figures indicate that in 1964 manufacturing corporations were operating at about the same percent of capacity as in 1956–57. But the turnover ratio for net fixed assets (2.66×) was below that for 1956–57 (2.93×). Why did this occur?

Unfortunately, experts differ on a key consideration: whether, in the manufacturing sector, output relative to the investment in fixed capital (the output-fixed capital ratio) has risen over the full postwar period and, more specifically, in recent years. An increase in the output-capital ratio would mean—everything else being equal—a rise in our turnover ratio. A decline in the output-capital ratio would, of course, mean the reverse.

With this basic factor unresolved, any attempt to answer the above question is fraught with uncertainty.

Some crosscurrents, however, can be noted. In 1964 net fixed assets were a lower percentage of gross fixed assets than in 1956–57 (49 percent versus 53 percent), i.e., depreciation reserves were higher. This fact would argue for a higher turnover of net fixed assets in 1964. On the other hand, several factors may help to explain why the turnover of net fixed assets was not higher in 1964.[16] These include:

1. The constant problem of changes in accounting practices, as well as the increased consolidation of subsidiaries.
2. The further vertical integration of manufacturing corporations, particularly such major firms as those covered by the SRI sample.
3. The impact of price changes on the cost of plant and equipment.
    a. In 1964, over 80 percent of the equipment and 50 percent of the plant were purchased at postwar prices, whereas in 1956–57, the proportions were closer to 70 percent and 35 percent, respectively.
    b. Although price indexes may be challenged and although they do not compensate for technological progress, they indicate that the price of plant and equipment has risen more rapidly than the price of manufactured goods.
4. The reduced use of government-financed facilities in defense industries.

Earnings Margin. The final step in our analysis is to examine the other half of the rate-of-return equation—the earnings margin. In broad terms, the earnings margin is the amount of the sales dollar that remains after deducting all expenses (except tax-adjusted interest on long-term debt) and income taxes. It is determined by the price at which output is sold and the cost of manufacturing and distributing that output (plus income taxes). A full analysis of the earnings margin would, therefore, involve a consideration of both prices and expenses. However, we will confine our analysis to the major expense and income ratios. An examination of supply, demand, and other factors that determine the prices of manufactured goods is beyond the scope of this article.

Total Operating Expense Ratio. Period by period, the ratio of total operating expenses to sales rose until 1963–64, when it declined (Exhibit XI). If depreciation is deducted, the postwar rise in the expense ratio is reduced somewhat. However, the 1963–64 decline is approximately the same on either a before- or an after-depreciation basis.

The two broad components of total operating expenses are (1) cost of goods sold and (2) selling, general, and administrative expenses (SG&A). Companies in 4 of the 24 industries in the SRI sample do not release information on these two broad expense categories, but data have been compiled for the remaining industries, which in 1964 constituted about 90 percent of aggregate sales for the sample. These data were examined to

---

[16] Change in industry composition does not appear to be a factor. Our data do not indicate that the capital intensive industries constituted a heavier proportion of sales in 1964 than they did earlier in the postwar period.

EXHIBIT XI

EXPENSE AND INCOME RATIOS
SRI Manufacturing Sample, 1947–64

Year	Total Operating Expenses Including Depreciation	Total Operating Expenses Excluding Depreciation	Depreciation, Depletion, and Amortization	Net Operating Income	Earnings Margin
1947	88.4%	85.7%	2.7%	11.6%	7.3%
1948	87.2	84.3	2.9	12.8	8.2
1949	88.2	85.0	3.2	11.8	2.7
1950	84.5	81.5	3.0	15.5	8.7
1951	85.1	82.2	2.9	14.9	6.8
1952	87.8	84.6	3.2	12.2	6.2
1953	87.8	84.4	3.4	12.2	6.0
1954	88.5	84.6	3.9	11.5	6.8
1955	86.3	82.4	3.9	13.7	7.8
1956	87.8	83.7	4.1	12.2	7.2
1957	88.4	84.2	4.2	11.6	6.8
1958	90.2	85.7	4.5	9.8	6.0
1959	89.2	84.9	4.3	10.8	6.5
1960	89.9	85.6	4.3	10.1	6.2
1961	90.0	85.6	4.4	10.0	6.2
1962	89.3	84.8	4.5	10.7	6.5
1963	88.5	84.2	4.3	11.5	6.9
1964	88.5	84.3	4.2	11.5	7.2
1963–64	88.5	84.2	4.2	11.5	7.0
1958–62	89.7	85.3	4.4	10.3	6.3
1952–57	87.8	84.0	3.8	12.2	6.8
1947–51	86.7	83.8	2.9	13.3	7.7
1947–64	88.1	84.3	3.8	11.9	7.0

SOURCE: Stanford Research Institute.

determine the postwar performance of the two major components of total operating expenses.

Cost of Goods Sold. The cost of goods sold, before allowing for depreciation, actually edged down as a percent of sales on a period basis across the postwar span and in 1963–64 reached a postwar low.

How can this lower ratio be explained? One of the major contributing factors is the corporate belt tightening that has occurred since 1957 in the form of cost-cutting and increased efficiency. Another is the continued increase in the amount of capital per worker—an important factor in reducing labor costs relative to output. Annual averages computed from the index of labor cost per unit of output, published in *Business Cycle Developments*,[17] indicate a decline in labor cost relative to output since 1960.

Depreciation. We are using the term "depreciation" in its broader

---

[17] *Business Cycle Developments*, U.S. Department of Commerce, Bureau of the Census.

sense to include also depletion and amortization. Depreciation, depletion, and amortization charges—most of which relate to the cost of goods sold—amounted to a larger percent of the sales dollar in 1963–64 than in the first 10 years of the postwar period. This occurred not because depreciation charges increased relative to gross fixed assets but because gross fixed assets increased relative to sales—that is, the turnover of gross fixed assets slowed down. These relationships are shown in the following tabulation.

Period	Depreciation Charges as a Percent of Gross Fixed Assets	Sales to Gross Fixed Assets (turnover ratio)
1964	5.5%	1.30×
1963	5.6	1.30
1958–62	5.6	1.29
1952–57	6.3	1.66
1947–51	5.3	1.78

The higher ratio of depreciation to gross fixed assets in the 1952–57 span is due principally to the 5-year amortization allowed under Certificates of Necessity in connection with the Korean war and to changes in the tax-allowable depreciation on assets acquired during and after 1954.

The rise in depreciation charges as a percentage of sales, therefore, results from a decline in the turnover ratio for gross fixed assets. Note from the above tabulation that sales dropped from $1.78 per dollar of gross fixed assets in 1947–51 to $1.29 in 1958–62—a 28 percent decline.

Selling, General, and Administrative Expenses (SG&A). The SG&A expense ratio has also risen over the postwar period. On the basis of the experience of the 20 industries, these expenses amounted to 7.9 percent of the sales dollar in 1947–51, 8.6 percent in 1952–57, and 10.4 percent in 1958–62. Even with the substantial increase in sales in 1963 and 1964, the ratio edged higher. This increase resulted from intensified competition—particularly since 1957—which has required significantly greater sales effort than in the earlier postwar years, and from such factors as the increasing complexity of business, the growth of nonproduction functions (e.g., accounting and personnel administration), and the substantial expansion of research and development. The allocation of R & D expense between cost of goods sold and SG&A varies among companies. Consequently, we cannot assume that all increases in R & D costs are—or should be—charged to SG&A.

Putting aside price considerations, this analysis of expense ratios has determined (1) that the postwar rise in the total operating expense ratio resulted primarily from rises in the depreciation and SG&A expense ratios and (2) that the improvement in 1963–64 was due basically to a decline in the cost of goods sold ratio before allowance for depreciation charges.

Net Operating Income Ratio. With the 1963–64 decline in the amount of each dollar of sales needed to meet operating expenses, the net operating income ratio rose. The ratio in 1963–64 was well above the 1958–62 level, but note from the figures shown in the following tabulation that it was identical in 1963 and 1964.

Period	Net Operating Income Ratio
1964	11.5%
1963	11.5
1958–62	10.3
1952–57	12.2
1947–51	13.3

The pretax earnings margins in 1963 and 1964 were also identical. Accordingly, if financial data were completely consistent from one year to the next, the 1964 improvement in the earnings margin could be attributed entirely to a reduction in corporate income taxes. However, the degree of consistency necessary to such a conclusion cannot be claimed for this—or probably any other—body of earnings data. Nevertheless, the figures do imply that the reduction in corporate income taxes was a major factor in the 1964 increase in the earnings margin and, therefore, that the increase in the return earned on total capital by manufacturing corporations in 1964 was due more to public policy than to an improvement in business.

What Changes Have Occurred in the Structure of Profits?

The second question posed at the outset of this study pertained to changes in the structure of profits. In seeking to answer this question, our analysis has developed several major points.

First, the earnings margin has been characterized by a pronounced decline over much of the last three decades. In even the most prosperous years of the postwar period, the earnings margin was below the prewar level.

Second, in marked contrast, the turnover of total capital throughout the postwar period has substantially exceeded the prewar average. This increased efficiency in the employment of capital has been a dominant factor in the postwar financial performance of manufacturing corporations.

Third, during the present recovery, the earnings margin has risen markedly. By 1964, it exceeded the postwar average as well as the average of each intervening period except that of the distorted 1947–51 era. The turnover of total capital, however, has experienced only a limited increase. This is attributable primarily to the lagging improvement in the turnover of net fixed assets.

In our opinion, the turnover of fixed assets presents today one of the most challenging factors in the earnings picture. It is doubtful whether the turnover of current assets will accelerate much further over the next 5 to 10 years. As a result most of the burden for a higher asset and total capital turnover must rest on net fixed assets. But recent data raise a question as to the extent such an increase may be anticipated. If the turnover ratio for net fixed assets and, in turn, total capital should remain relatively constant over the next decade, the maintenance of profit margins will be doubly important. Therefore, the turnover factor merits close attention in appraising today's earnings and assessing the outlook for tomorrow's.

14

NEW TOOLS FOR PROFITS ANALYSIS*

Edmund A. Mennis, C.F.A.

Financial analysis cannot be done in a vacuum. An analyst spends the bulk of his time working on companies and industries, but his conclusions must be affected by the economic environment in which industries or companies operate. The portfolio manager must set investment policy and make security selections in the same economic environment. As a result, the analyst tries to follow changing business conditions, constantly asking the critical question of what these developments will mean for the profits of the companies in which he is interested. His tools are crude and not well organized, however, and the link between the economic environment and the profits outlook is an elusive one.

Fortunately, new material recently published and updated regularly by the Department of Commerce has improved and deepened our understanding of the important economic variables affecting corporate profits. With this information, our ability to follow profit performance is enhanced, and our tools for forecasting the implications of changes in the economy on profits is better than it has been heretofore. This new information was published originally in the May 1967 *Survey of Current Business* and is updated regularly in each monthly *Survey* as Table 9, Corporate Gross Product, in the National Income and Product Tables. The purpose of this article is to describe and chart some of the new information made available, to indicate its usefulness for the analysis of historical profit performance, and to suggest a method of using the data to prepare an estimate of future corporate profits.

DEFINITIONS

At the outset, it should be understood that the profits described herein are those reported as a part of the national income and product accounts published regularly by the Department of Commerce. In this series corporate profits are *not* an aggregate of the profits reported to shareholders by the corporations in the United States. In national income terminology, corporate profits represent the accrual to the account of the residents of

---

* Reprinted by permission of the *Financial Analysts Journal* (January-February 1969).

the nation of the earnings of domestic and foreign corporations, which are a portion of the aggregate earnings of labor and property arising out of current production. As a part of national income, profits are viewed as measured by the recipient rather than the originator. These profits arise from current production, so that inventory profits and capital gains and losses are excluded. This profit series is statistically based on profits as reported for tax purposes, which, as any financial analyst knows, may well differ in several respects from profits reported to shareholders.[1] Nevertheless, this profit series does have a relationship to shareholder profits in that their broad, general moves and cyclical turning points, over a period of years, are quite similar. Moreover, the new data permit a better analysis of the economic factors affecting profits than any information elsewhere.

The new data provided by the Commerce Department cover gross corporate product quarterly since 1948 and also gross corporate product originating in the nonfinancial sector of the economy (NFGCP). In addition to NFGCP in current dollars, the series provides a price deflator, which enables NFGCP to be stated in constant 1958 dollars. NFGCP is further divided into its components of costs and profits and also unit costs and unit profits. The most effective way of utilizing this series is to concentrate on the NFGCP sector and treat the financial sector separately.

Most of the terms used are not familiar and require some clarification. The first question, therefore, is what is NFGCP? This series reflects the contribution of the domestic operations of nonfinancial corporations to gross national product. Excluded from the nonfinancial area are the results of financial corporations: commercial banks, mutual savings banks, savings and loan associations, credit unions, financial companies, securities and commodity brokers, regulated investment companies, and insurance carriers.

NFGCP can be considered in two ways. Just as the national income accounts have both an income and product side, NFGCP has both a sales or product side and a balancing income or factor cost side. On one hand it can be looked upon as the sale of nonfinancial firms to other businesses, consumers, government and foreigners, plus inventory change, less purchases from other firms, both domestic and foreign. NFGCP can also be defined as the sum of incomes and charges to this gross product. From this latter viewpoint, it is therefore the sum of: (1) capital consumption allowances; (2) indirect business taxes less subsidies plus business transfer

---

[1] For a further discussion of these measures, see "Different Measures of Corporate Profits," by Edmund A. Mennis, *Financial Analysts Journal*, September–October 1962; "Corporate Profits Data—Tax Returns vs. Company Books" by Vito Natrella (see p. 136) and "Profit Measures Published by the Department of Commerce" by John A. Gorman, two papers given at the Federal Statistical Users Conference in Cleveland, Ohio on June 12, 1968.

payments; (3) compensation of employees; (4) net interest; and (5) corporate profits before taxes and inventory valuation adjustment. Capital consumption allowances in national income terminology include depreciation and accidental damage to fixed capital. Indirect business taxes represent primarily sales, excise, and property taxes. Business transfer payments would include gifts to nonprofit organizations and consumer bad debts. Employee compensation includes monetary remuneration plus supplements, such as contributions to social insurance, pension, health, welfare and unemployment funds and compensation for injuries.

In addition to the figures for NFGCP and its factor cost components in current dollars, Commerce also provides data for NFGCP in 1958 prices together with implicit price deflators. The price deflator for NFGCP reflects the current cost per unit of 1958 dollar NFGCP, that is, the costs incurred and the profits earned in producing one 1958 dollar's worth of output in the current period. The current factor costs of capital consumption allowances, indirect business taxes, net interest, employee compensation, and profits have also been related to NFGCP in 1958 dollars, so that we have not only the dollar costs but also unit labor costs, unit nonlabor costs, and unit profits. This additional information is a significant contribution to the field of profits analysis.

Historical Analysis

Several charts have been prepared that show the historical record of a number of the series described above, arranged in a way that facilitates their use for profits analysis. Chart I plots NFGCP in current dollars against gross national product (GNP) and also shows the implicit price deflators for both series. The data are plotted on a semilogarithmic grid, so that rates of change, rather than absolute values, are stressed. In addition, the cyclical peaks and troughs of the postwar period as defined by the National Bureau of Economic Research are shown on the chart to assist in the analysis.

As the two lines toward the top of the chart indicate, NFGCP, which accounts for about 55 percent of GNP, follows the pattern of GNP fairly closely, although it is more volatile. Its peaks and troughs have in almost all instances coincided with peaks and troughs in GNP. With respect to price changes, the movement of the price deflator of both GNP and NFGCP were quite similar until 1958. Since that time, the price deflator for GNP has moved up more rapidly than for NFGCP, presumably reflecting the more rapid price increases in the service component and government sectors of GNP.

Chart II plots NFGCP in current dollars and nonfinancial corporate profits before taxes and inventory valuation adjustment. (The tax factor and the adjustment for inventory profits will be discussed later.) These two series represent the sales and the pretax profits emerging from those sales in the nonfinancial sector of the economy. At the bottom of the chart we have shown profits per unit of real NFGCP, which is a measure of profit margins. However, this measure is not exactly comparable with pretax margins as ordinarily computed by the financial analyst. Pretax margins normally reflect the proportion of pretax dollars to sales dollars. Unit profits represent the percent that current dollar pretax profits are of

CHART I

Gross National Product, Nonfinancial Gross Corporate Product and Price Deflators
(1948–1968)

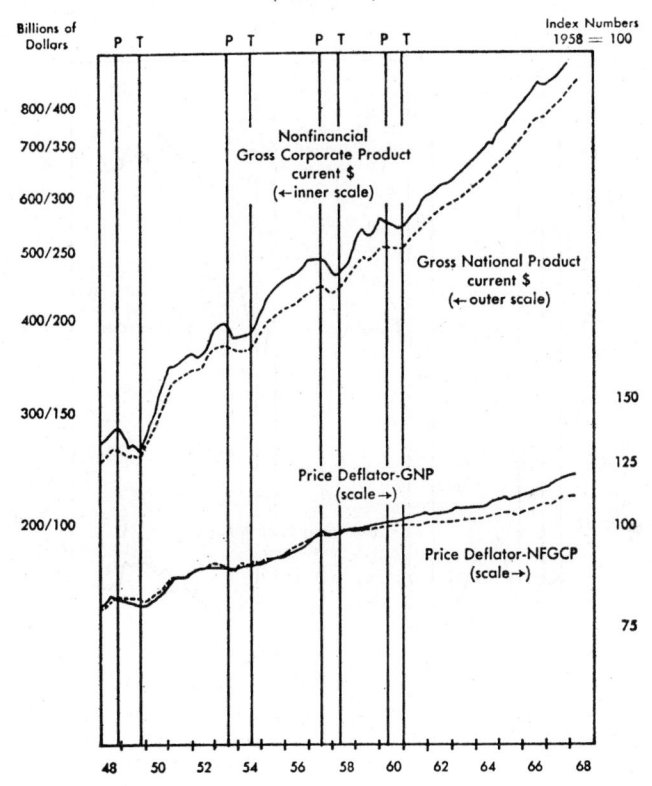

current output measured in 1958 prices. In other words, unit profits relate to profits per unit of real output rather than current dollar sales.

Examining the lines at the top of the chart, the strong growth trend in NFGCP is clearly evident. Moreover, this growth trend accelerated and has been much smoother beginning in 1961. The impact of this sales pattern on profits is seen in the second line. The cyclical fluctuations in corporate profits are quite pronounced and the general growth trend from 1948 to 1961 is substantially slower than the growth in NFGCP. As shown in the third line on the chart, unit profits were in a declining trend and also had substantial cyclical fluctuations in the period 1948 through 1960.

A major change occurred in profits beginning in 1961. Not only was their recovery from the 1960–61 business decline pronounced, but the growth through 1966 was the longest in the postwar period. This can be

CHART II

NONFINANCIAL GROSS CORPORATE PRODUCT, PRETAX PROFITS AND UNIT PROFITS
(1948–1968)

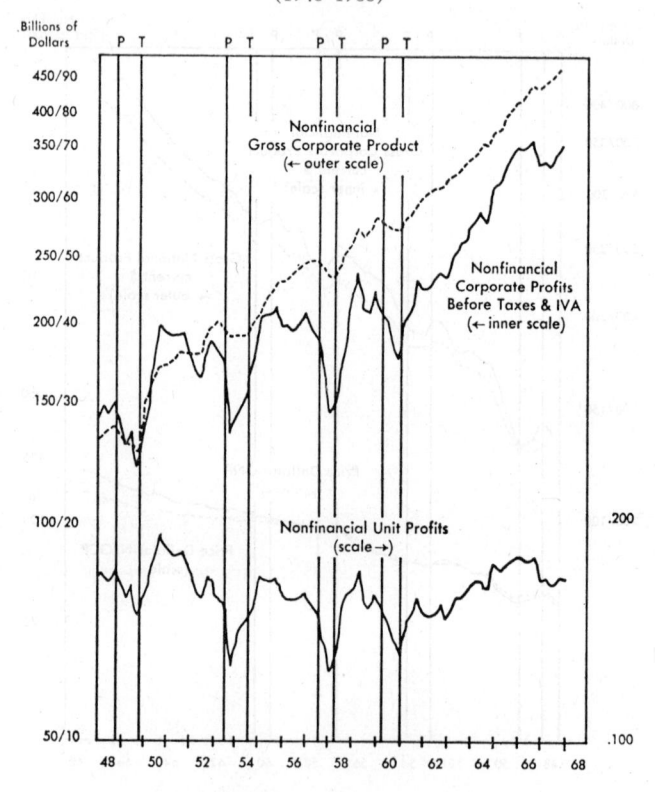

attributable, in part, to the sustained volume rise uninterrupted by cyclical fluctuations from 1961 to 1966. A good portion of the profits improvement was due not just to rising sales volume but also to a significant change in the trend of unit profits. It is also interesting to note that the 1967 decline in profits was quite pronounced considering the brief and moderate decline in sales volume. In fact, unit profits in 1966–67 have reacted more than the sales decline would suggest. The new data supplied by the Commerce Department can be helpful in understanding the behavior of unit profits and the cost factors associated with them.

Cost Analysis

A breakdown of 1967 costs and profits for nonfinancial corporations is contained in the table below:

	Billions of Dollars	Percent
Nonlabor costs:		
Capital consumption allowances	$ 42.2	9.7%
Indirect business taxes, etc.	38.8	9.0
Interest	8.5	2.0
Total nonlabor costs	$ 89.5	20.7%
Labor costs	277.0	64.0
Total costs	$366.5	84.7%
Corporate profits before tax and IVA	66.4	15.3
Nonfinancial gross corporate product	$432.9	100.0%

As indicated in the table, nonlabor costs (capital consumption allowances, indirect business taxes and interest) accounted for about 21 percent of NFGCP in 1967, labor costs accounted for 64 percent and profits, which is the remaining factor cost, about 15 percent. A substantial portion of the nonlabor costs are relatively inflexible, while other costs will vary with sales volume.

Chart III plots unit nonlabor costs and unit labor costs quarterly from 1948 through the second quarter of 1968. If we can get a better understanding of these two components of cost, we shall be able to understand the movement of the total unit cost line.

As indicated on the chart, unit labor costs moved up fairly steadily from 1948 to 1961, although a reduction in unit labor costs was fairly characteristic of the periods shortly after a business cycle peak until early in the recovery after the cyclical trough. The experience after the 1961 cyclical trough was unusual, however, because unit labor costs trended downward until 1965. The rise from 1966 to mid-1968 was quite marked.[2]

Unit nonlabor costs moved up even more steeply than unit labor costs, reaching a peak in 1962. Thereafter, unit nonlabor costs flattened out, actually declined in 1965 and 1966, but rose sharply in 1967. Thus, the sharp rise in unit profits in 1961–1966 shown in Chart II was accounted for by the changed direction of both unit labor costs and unit nonlabor costs beginning in 1961.

Chart IV takes the analysis one step further by examining both the numerator and the denominator of each unit cost line. NFGCP is plotted in 1938 dollars, which provide a stable unit of measurement for the

---

[2] This series is similar to the monthly unit labor cost ratio in manufacturing, which is published regularly as Series 62 in the Department of Commerce publication, *Business Cycle Developments*. However, this series covers the entire nonfinancial area and thus includes a broader sector of the corporate universe.

denominator of each of the two unit cost ratios. Then labor costs and nonlabor costs are plotted in current dollars.

As the chart indicates, nonlabor costs have moved up rather steadily during the entire postwar period, and from 1948 to 1961 the rate of increase was more rapid than NFGCP. Consequently, unit nonlabor costs

CHART III
EMPLOYEE COMPENSATION AND NONLABOR COSTS PER UNIT
OF 1958 NFGCP
(1948–1968)

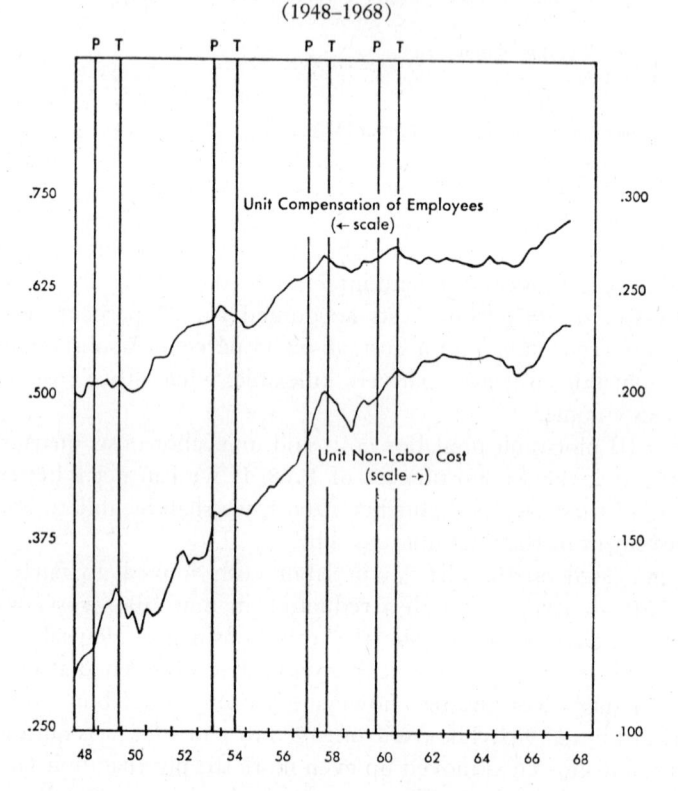

increased. From 1961 to 1965, the two lines moved in parallel, and the unit nonlabor cost ratio flattened out. A slowing in the gain in NFGCP since 1966, however, has resulted once more in an upward movement of the unit nonlabor cost line.

The relationship of labor costs and NFGCP is similar to that of nonlabor costs and NFGCP. Labor costs moved up more rapidly prior to 1961, paralleled the growth in real output from 1961 to 1965, and moved upward more rapidly since. For a better understanding of unit labor costs, however, a deeper analysis of its components is necessary.

Labor costs per unit of output are calculated as the ratio of employee compensation (in current dollars) to NFGCP (in constant 1958 dollars). In order to provide a more useful analytical framework, both the numerator and denominator of this ratio can be divided by manhours, making unit labor costs equal to the ratio of compensation per manhour and output per manhour. Thus, changes in unit labor costs can be analyzed

CHART IV

Nonfinancial Gross Corporate Product in 1958 Dollars
Labor and Nonlabor Costs in Current Dollars
(1948–1968)

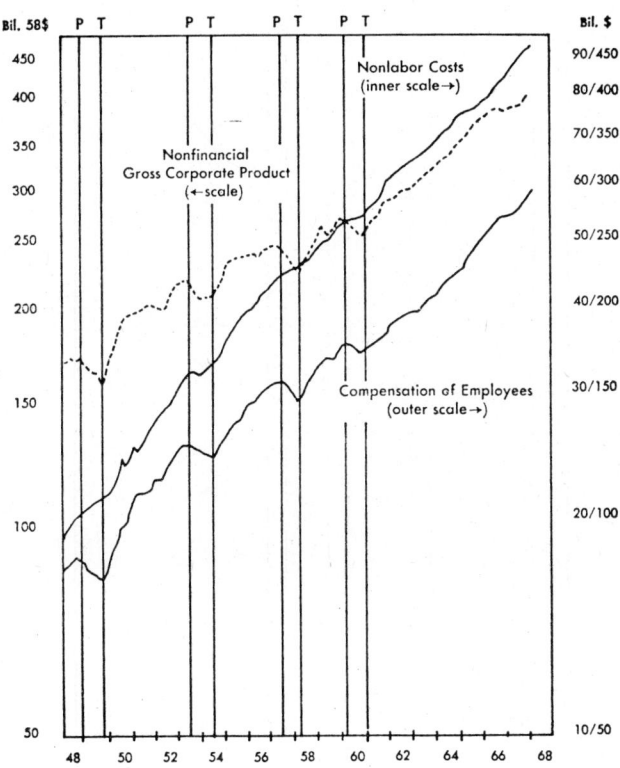

from the interaction of two key factors: hourly wage rates (including salaries and fringe benefits) and labor productivity. When wages advance more rapidly than output per manhour, unit labor costs increase. When productivity gains exceed increases in wage rates, unit labor costs decline. Violating arithmetic principles only slightly, the present change in unit labor costs can be calculated as the difference between the percent changes in hourly compensation and output per manhour. For example, a 4 percent increase in wage rates and a 3 percent advance in productivity result in a rise of 1 percent in unit labor costs.

Unfortunately, the Commerce data on NFGCP do not provide information on manhours and compensation per manhour, and therefore output per manhour cannot be calculated. However, an acceptable substitute for this information is published quarterly by the Bureau of Labor Statistics in their quarterly release "Wages, Prices and Productivity in the

CHART V

INDEXES OF OUTPUT, MANHOURS AND OUTPUT PER MANHOUR
PRIVATE NONFARM SECTOR 1947–1968
(1957–1959 = 100)

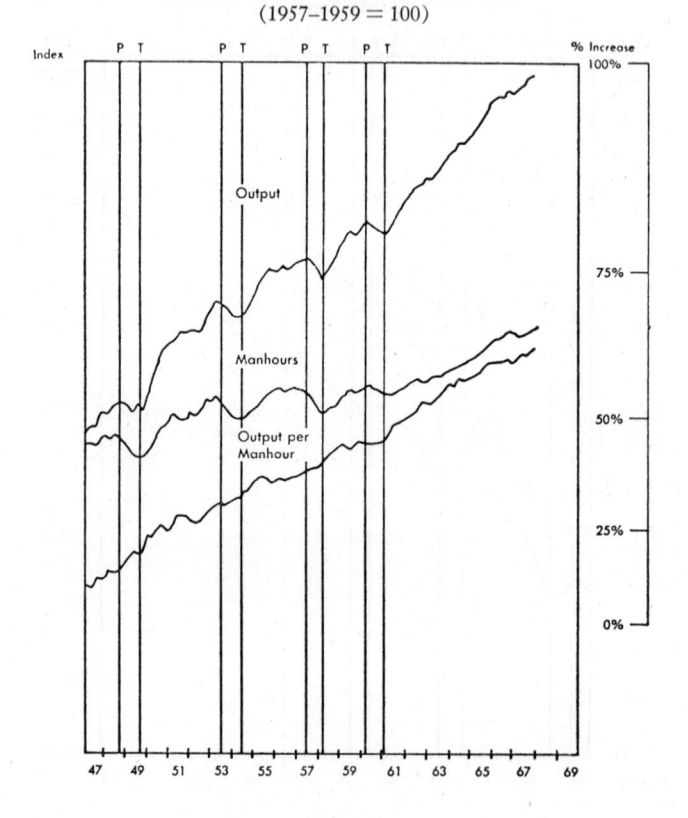

Private Nonfarm Sector." Although not precisely comparable, the movement of unit labor costs in the BLS series and in the Commerce series has been quite similar. Charts V and VI plot the various components of unit labor costs in the BLS series.

As Chart V indicates, output has increased faster than manhours in the postwar period and, consequently, output per manhour has moved upward. The gain in output relative to manhours was particularly pronounced in the 1961–1965 period, partly due to unused resources and available labor supply. In 1966–1967, the rate of gain in output slowed as the economy moved to full utilization of its labor force, and demand also slackened. Consequently, productivity gains slowed and only recently have begun to pick up again.

Chart VI repeats the line showing output per manhour, shows employee compensation per manhour, and finally shows the result of those two forces in the unit labor cost line. One interesting fact shown on the chart is the fairly steady increase in employee compensation, with the trend accelerating beginning in 1965. The rate of gain also shows some-

CHART VI

Indexes of Output Per Manhour, Hourly Compensation and Unit Labor Costs Private Nonfarm Sector 1947-1968
(1957-1959 = 100)

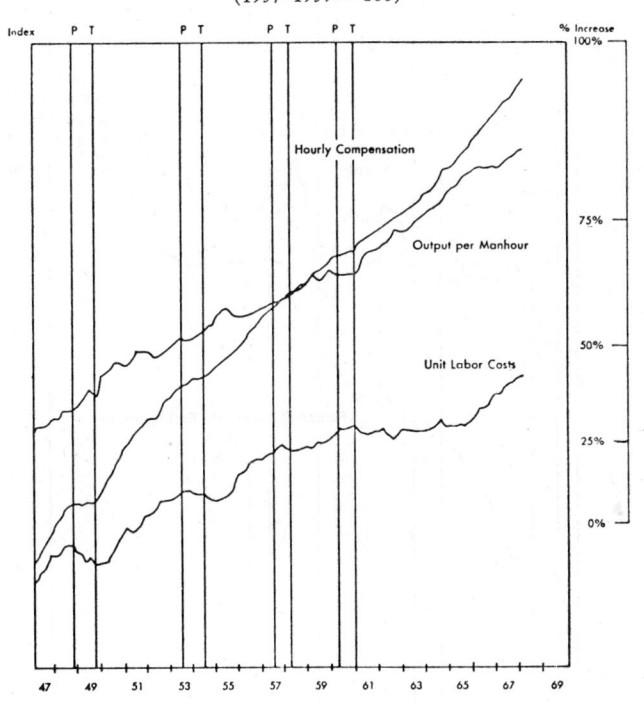

what during periods of cyclical contraction. The slower rate of growth in output per manhour relative to hourly labor costs from 1947 to 1961 accounted for the rising unit labor cost line during that period. The faster rise in productivity, which roughly paralleled hourly compensation from 1961 to 1965, resulted in the leveling of unit labor costs. Since 1966, the acceleration in employee compensation and the slowing in productivity gains have resulted in one of the sharpest rises in unit labor costs in the postwar period.

Domestic Corporate Profits

Thus far we have examined domestic corporate profits in the nonfinancial sector and the underlying component costs. The profits squeeze of the past three years has been identified as caused by some slowing in the growth of output, a consequent rise in unit nonlabor costs, and also a combination of accelerated hourly compensation and slower productivity gains, which together caused unit labor costs to advance. Price increases,

CHART VII
DOMESTIC CORPORATE PROFITS BEFORE TAXES AND IVA TOTAL,
NONFINANCIAL AND FINANCIAL
(1948–1968)

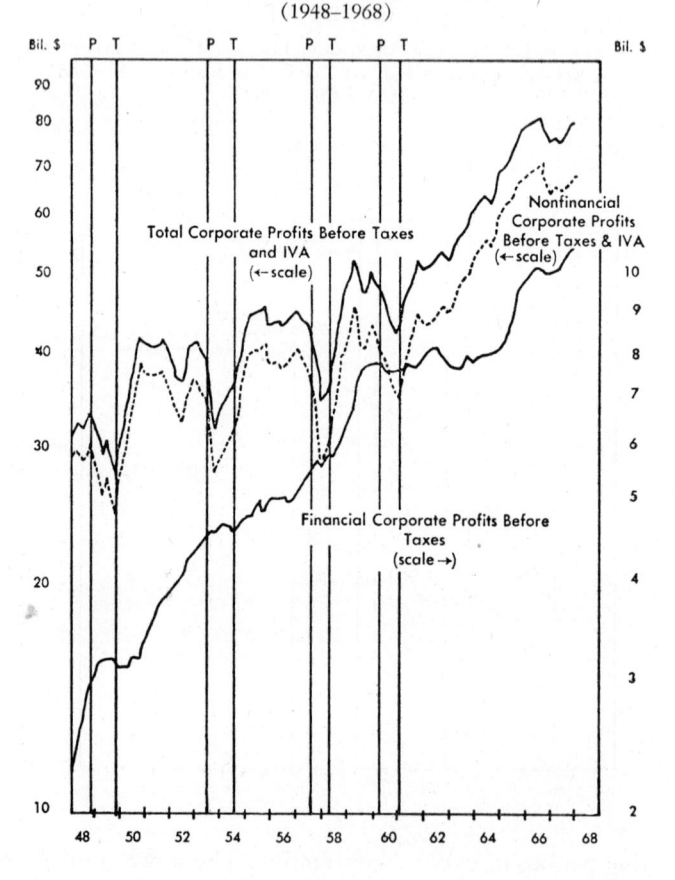

which are the offsetting factor to rising costs, have been sufficient to hold unit profits about level after a sharp drop in the first quarter of 1967.

The last three charts summarize the remaining components that must be included to get a picture of total corporate profits. Chart VII plots total domestic corporate profits before taxes and inventory valuation adjustment and its two components, nonfinancial and financial profits. Nonfinancial corporate profits have been analyzed in some detail because, as the chart indicates, their path closely parallels the path of total domestic profits. The pattern of financial profits is much different, but it has less influence on the total because it represents only about 12 percent of total domestic profits.

The financial component of profits is heavily weighted by the banks, which in the past five years have accounted for from 58 percent to 62 percent of total financial profits. The remainder is accounted for by insurance carriers, security and commodity brokers, and credit agencies and regulated investment companies. The trend in bank earnings has been upward since 1948, although a sharp decline was experienced in 1961 and the growth rate since that time has been slower than the 1948–1960 rate due to higher interest charges and a growing proportion of time deposits. Insurance carriers account for about 17 percent of financial pretax profits, but their impact on changes in financial profits is significant because of their volatility. The fluctuations are due to the wide swings in the profits of nonlife insurance carriers, accounted for by their insurance operations rather than their investment results.[3] The leveling of financial profits in 1961–1964 was due to the decline in bank profits in 1961 and to the decline in insurance carrier profits in the other years. In 1967 the decline was centered in the insurance carriers.

Total Corporate Profits

Two other adjustments are necessary to the domestic corporate profit figures in order to obtain the aggregate measures of corporate profits provided by the Commerce Department. These two adjustments reflect the inventory valuation adjustment and the adjustment for the "rest of the world."

Chart VIII shows the pattern of the inventory valuation adjustment and the rest of the world adjustment on a quarterly basis since 1948. The inventory valuation adjustment is necessary because inventory profits are not considered a part of the profits arising from current production and, consequently, are excluded in the national income account profits component. The IVA measures the excess of the change of the physical volume of nonfinancial inventories valued at the average prices during the period over the change in book value as recorded by corporate accountants. As the chart indicates, the inventory valuation adjustment has fluctuated from positive to negative and has ranged from as much as $-9 billion to as much as $+4 billion. (A negative figure means that inventory profits have been included in book profits for a period.) It is interesting to note that, during the period 1958 through 1964, inventory valuation adjustments were rather modest, reflecting the price stability of that period. Inventory valuation adjustments have increased considerably since then and by the first quarter of 1968 they had reached the large sum of $5.1

---

[3] I am grateful to John Gorman, Associate Chief, National Income Division, Office of Business Economics, Department of Commerce for unpublished data and comments on the profit trends of financial companies.

billion at a seasonally adjusted annual rate. In only two quarters since 1948, during the Korean War, have inventory profits been so large.

The rest of the world adjustment is an allowance for the net receipt of dividends and branch profits from abroad. These receipts may be by either corporations or individuals in the United States. As can be seen, this has been a plus figure since the end of World War II and has been growing fairly significantly, particularly since 1961.

CHART VIII

REST OF WORLD AND INVENTORY VALUATION ADJUSTMENT
(1948-1968)

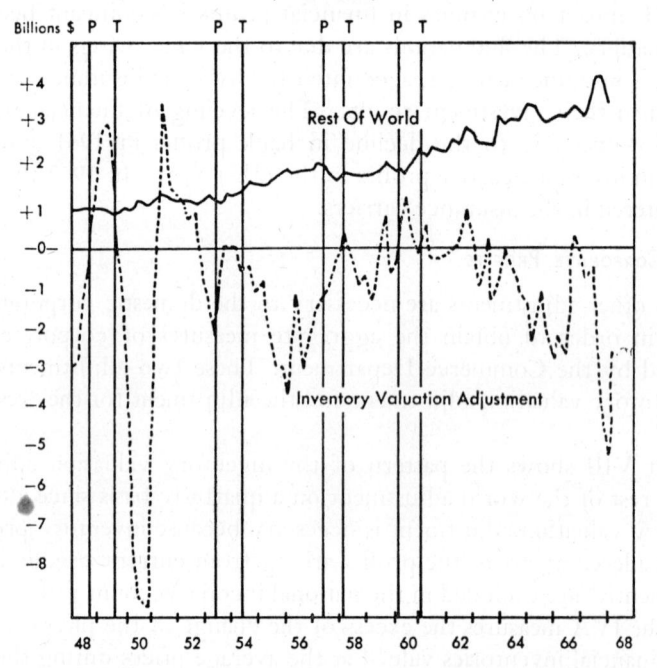

Chart IX plots the usually reported and more familiar profits figures: corporate profits before taxes (including inventory profits), the tax liability, and corporate profits after taxes. These are the figures regularly reported in the financial press.

ESTIMATING FUTURE PROFITS

Thus far we have analyzed in some detail the new profits data recently made available, which consider profits as the difference between receipts and costs. Receipts are treated as the product of prices times output, and costs are apportioned among nonlabor costs and labor costs. Costs have been examined on a unit cost basis, with unit labor costs the result of the

New Tools for Profits Analysis

CHART IX
TOTAL CORPORATE PROFITS BEFORE TAXES AND AFTER TAXES AND TAX LIABILITY

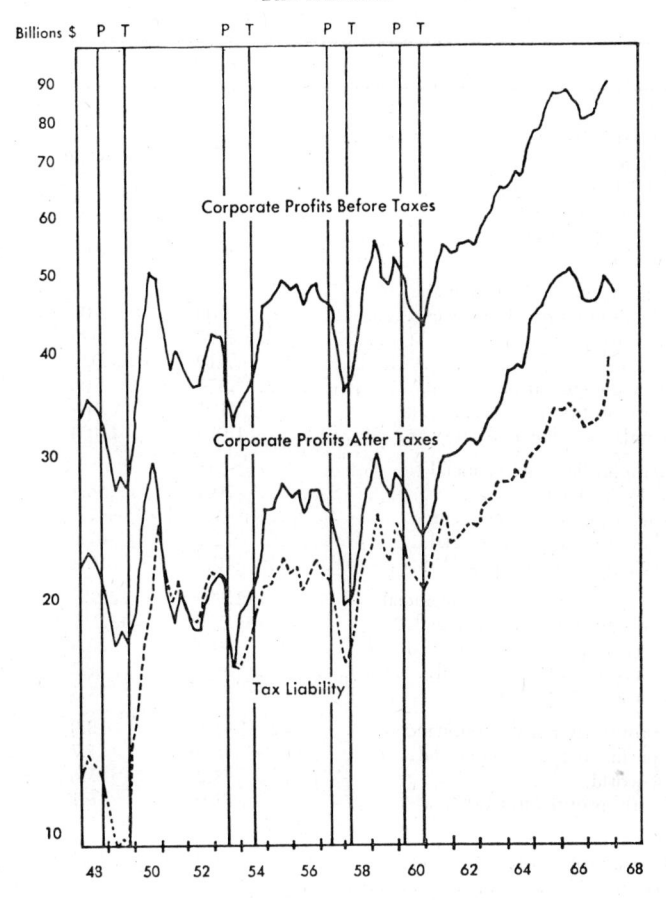

interaction of hourly wage rates and output per manhour.[4] It may be helpful now to organize this information in a form that will facilitate either estimating the profits implications of certain economic assumptions or analyzing the quarterly pattern of profits.

The purpose here is to provide a relatively simple and consistent framework for analysis and the preparation of future estimates. Of course, forecasting the future of the economy and of profits is not a simple task. Relatively elaborate and sophisticated econometric models

---

[4] For a further discussion of this analytical approach, an excellent reference is *Profits, Profit Markups and Productivity*, by Edwin Kuh, Study Paper No. 15, Study of Employment, Growth and Price Levels, Joint Economic Committee, Congress of the United States (Washington, D.C.: U.S. Government Printing Office, January 25, 1960).

TABLE I

Actual and Estimates of Corporate Profits
Department of Commerce Basis
(Dollars in Billions)

	1966 A	1967 A	1968 E
1. Gross National Product	$747.6	$789.7	$859.0
Gross Corporate Product—nonfinancial			
2. Actual	413.8	433.0	
3. Computed*			473.1
4. Price deflator NFGCP	107.4	110.4	113.8
5. Gross Corporate Product—			
nonfinancial—1958 $	385.5	392.3	415.7
Unit costs and profits—nonfinancial:			
6. Capital consumption allowances	.100	.108	.111
7. Indirect business taxes, etc.	.095	.099	.102
8. Interest	.019	.022	.022
9. Employee compensation	.677	.706	.729
10. Corporate profits + IVA	.183	.169	.173
11. Total (= Line 4 ÷ 100)	1.074	1.104	#1.138
12. Corporate profits—nonfinancial			
+ IVA (10 × 5)	70.4	66.4	71.9
13. Inventory valuation adjustment	−1.7	−1.2	−3.4
14. Corporate profits—nonfinancial	72.2	67.6	75.3
15. Corporate profits—financial	10.2	10.4	11.4
16. Tax rate—corp. profits, nonfinancial	42.1%	42.6%	46.3%
17. Tax rate—corp. profits, financial	41.2%	45.2%	48.2%
18. Taxes—corp. profits, nonfinancial	30.4	28.8	34.9
19. Taxes—corp. profits, financial	4.2	4.7	5.5
20. Taxes—total	34.6	33.3	40.4
21. Corp. profits after tax—nonfinancial	41.8	38.8	40.4
22. Corp. profits after tax—financial	6.0	5.7	5.9
23. Rest of world	3.2	3.6	3.5
24. Total corp. profits after tax	51.0	48.1	49.8
Recap:			
25. Total corp. profits after tax (line 24)	51.0	48.1	49.8
26. Plus tax (line 20)	34.6	33.5	40.4
27. Corp. profits before tax	85.6	81.6	90.2
28. Plus or minus inv. val. adj. (line 13)	−1.7	−1.2	−3.4
29. Corp. profits before tax + IVA	83.9	80.4	86.8

*NFGCP = $−10.04 billion + .562 GNP; r^2 = .998, Sy = $3.26 billion.
#Does not add due to rounding.

have been constructed for this purpose[5] and a variety of other forecasting techniques are used. However, for the analyst who lacks the time or the

---

[5] An excellent example of an econometric model that includes a profits equation has been prepared by the Department of Commerce and is described in the May 1966 *Survey of Current Business*. In the model, pretax corporate profits excluding inventory profits are made to vary positively with corporate sales and negatively with the ratio of money wage rates to the overall price deflator, manhours per unit of output, and the ratio of capacity to actual output.

desire to engage in the more complex aspects of forecasting, the approaching discussed below may be useful.

Table I provides the actual data for 1966 and 1967 and the writer's estimate for 1968 of corporate profits on a national income basis. Although analysis and preparation of future estimates are usually facilitated by working with the quarterly figures, the annual data are more familiar and the procedures used are the same.

The starting point in any profits estimate is some assumption about overall economic activity or GNP. Such an estimate can be prepared by the analyst himself or estimates by both private and government economists are often available. From this GNP estimate, an estimate of NFGCP is derived. As indicated in the table, using an estimate of $859 billion of GNP for 1968 results in an estimate of $473.1 billion of NFGCP, using the correlation equation given in the footnote of the table. This equation reflects the relationship between these two variables that has prevailed for the 1948–67 period. The r^2 is relatively high at .998 and the deviations of the actual from the computed figure fall within $3.26 billion about two-thirds of the time.[6]

The second step in the analysis is to make an assumption about the movement of prices in the NFGCP area. In this connection the forecaster can be materially helped by either plotting the price deflator on a semilogarithmic grid, as in Chart I, or alternatively by analyzing the quarter-to-quarter changes in this time series and combining this analysis with a general consideration of the pricing environment.

Line 5 is derived by dividing the current dollar NFGCP figure in line 3 by the price deflator in line 4, thereby obtaining NFGCP in constant 1958 dollars.

The next step in the analysis is to determine unit costs. Lines 6, 7, and 8 reflect the nonlabor costs and are relatively easy to estimate, assuming no changes in either depreciation practices or in excise tax laws. If capital consumption allowances, indirect business taxes, and interest in current dollars are plotted on a semilogarithmic grid, it will be seen that they fluctuate relatively little. Consequently, the analyst can, with a fair degree of safety, merely extrapolate recent trends over the forecast period. Having derived the dollar amounts for each factor, they can be divided into NFGCP on line 5 in order to derive the respective unit costs.

The unit employee compensation figure is somewhat more difficult to estimate and also is a more critical figure because of its size. The easiest procedure for the analyst is to make his own independent judgment of

---

[6] As Chart I indicates, NFGCP is more volatile than GNP and thus the equation, which is linear, tends to be less accurate at turning points. However, the regression was run on a percentage change basis and a first difference basis, but the percentage of variance explained and the standard error were inferior to the equation being used. Other unsuccessful attempts to improve the regression include removing from GNP certain components which may not be related to NFGCP.

what increases in productivity and hourly labor costs he anticipates for the forecast period. For example, an increase of 6 percent in hourly compensation and 3 percent in productivity would result roughly in a 3 percent increase in unit labor costs. As an alternative, the BLS data referred to earlier show quarter-to-quarter increases in output, manhours, output per manhour, hourly compensation, and unit labor costs. These data coupled with knowledge of the current labor scene should enable the forecaster to come up with a reasonable estimate of unit labor cost.

When these four computations are completed, corporate profits plus inventory valuation adjustment (line 10) can be derived by subtracting the total of these four unit costs from the price deflator, with the decimal point moved two places to the left. The corporate profits per unit can then be multiplied by real NFGCP (line 5) in order to derive the dollar corporate profits in the nonfinancial sector plus inventory valuation adjustment (line 12).

To this figure must be added an estimate of the inventory valuation adjustment, which can be done most simply by a rough approximation based on recent wholesale price changes and also the recent pattern of the IVA as shown in Chart VIII. The addition or subtraction of the inventory valuation adjustment produces an estimate of nonfinancial corporate profits (line 14), to which can then be added an estimate of corporate profits in financial sector (line 15). This figure can be estimated either by a rough approximation of recent profit trends in banks and other major financial institutions, or, alternatively, by extrapolating recent quarter-to-quarter increases in these profits as published by the Commerce Department. Unfortunately, the uncertainty of future underwriting losses in the nonlife insurance carriers referred to earlier introduces an element of unpredictability in this estimate, but the relatively small size of their contribution to total profits minimizes their impact on the total estimate.

With respect to taxes, the tax rate in the nonfinancial and financial areas should be treated separately because the implicit tax rates are different. The usual procedure is to extrapolate the implicit tax rate used by Commerce in the quarterly profits reports. For 1968 the rate reflects the surcharge of 10 percent, effective January 1. Having computed the appropriate taxes for the nonfinancial and financial area, corporate profits after taxes are derived for each of these sectors. To this computation must be added an estimate of rest of the world profits, which then gives the answer of total corporate profits after tax. This rest of the world estimate can best be made by extrapolating recent trends, although consideration must be given to such developments as the impact of government programs to improve the balance of payments.

The last five lines of Table I indicate a way to derive the usual published estimates of corporate profits. To total corporate profits after tax (line 25) must be added the tax on domestic profits (line 20), which gives total corporate profits before tax; from this total can be added or subtracted the inventory valuation adjustment (line 13). The result will be total corporate profits before taxes and inventory valuation adjustment.

Additional Uses of New Profits Data

The foregoing description indicates a method of forecasting corporate profits that insures the inclusion of all pertinent factors and also simplifies the judgments that must be made. The most critical factors are the estimates for GNP, the price deflator for NFGCP, and the estimate of unit labor costs. Most of the other variables perform in a relatively predictable fashion over the short term and can be readily estimated from a chart plotting their quarterly movements.

A second advantage of the suggested analysis is that it facilitates testing profits results for various assumptions about GNP, price changes, or unit labor costs. The nonlabor costs and other profits components would not be materially affected. For example, if the price deflator assumed for NFGCP in 1968 were 4 percent above that of 1967 instead of the 3.1 percent increase assumed in Table I, line 4 on the table would be 114.8 and NFGCP in 1958 dollars (line 5) would be $412.1 billion. Unit profits (line 10) would rise to .184 and nonfinancial corporate profits plus IVA (line 12) would be $75.8 billion. The IVA (line 13) would be somewhat larger and working the figures down to profits after taxes (line 24), profits would be about $2.5 billion higher, or 5 percent, more than the $49.8 billion estimated for 1968. Similarly, if unit labor costs (line 9) were up 4 percent in 1968 compared with 1967 instead of the 3.3 percent increase estimated on the table, unit profits (line 10) would be .169 and profits after taxes (line 24) would be about $800 million less. As a result of the availability of the new data and the procedure outlined in the table, it is relatively easy now to experiment with the impact of various economic assumptions on profits.

A third advantage of the suggested analysis is that, using the tabular format provided, an analyst can readily follow the quarterly changes in factors affecting profits. For example, an examination of recent quarterly profits data reveals that, beginning in the fourth quarter of 1967, inventory profits have once again become a significant contributor to total profits. As another example, unit profits in the second quarter of 1968 rose 4.7 percent from the first quarter, after five quarters of relative stability. This improvement was caused by the stability of unit labor costs coupled with an 0.9 percent price increase. An examination of the BLS data indicates that the rise in hourly compensation in the second quarter was offset by a comparable increase in productivity. A continuation of this trend is by no means certain, but the evidence is worth following because it is contrary to the generally accepted opinions of what is occurring in the profits area.

For the financial analyst, this information does not readily translate into forecasts for individual companies, which are affected not only by the economic environment but also by competitive factors, material costs, and other developments of a more particular nature. The analyst must extend his analysis to industries and companies and determine whether their sales and costs patterns differ from the economic environment in which they operate. However, the approach described above does give the analyst a better understanding of the broad economic forces that influence profits, thus helping to bridge that elusive gap between economics and investment management.

15

THE USE OF INPUT-OUTPUT ECONOMICS IN COMMON STOCK ANALYSIS*

Howard B. Bonham, Jr.

One of the most useful macroeconomic tools available for measuring the effects on equity investments of dynamic product flows within an economic structure is input-output analysis. Indeed, at this point in its development, one eminent American economist considers the concept second only to the national accounts system as a modern development in quantitative economics;[1] yet future applications to be made possible by more continuous data should increase the utility of the concept even more.

INPUT-OUTPUT TERMINOLOGY

Initially it would be useful to establish the meaning of several terms used within the context of this article. First, *final demand* is composed of the purchases of goods and services by consumers, investors (capital goods), foreigners, and governments; *input* is the value of each industry's consumption of the raw materials, semi-finished products, and services of other industries; *output* is the value of goods and services delivered to other industries, which is *intermediate output*, or to final demand; and *value added* is the sum of compensation of employees, profits and proprietors' income, depreciation allowances, etc., which industries include in their product prices.

An intput-output system is the calculation of the values of industry product flows as goods and services pass through an economy, including those received by intermediate fabricators who add value to the products, towards their final consumption. Thus, for the United States economy, the intput-output system reflects in dollar terms the demands on our industries caused by specific magnitudes of final demand as represented by the following national accounts: personal consumption expenditures;

---

* Reprinted by permission of the *Financial Analysts Journal* (January–February 1967).

[1] John Kenneth Galbraith, quoted in advertisement by Oxford University Press appearing in *Saturday Review*, June 11, 1966.

gross private fixed capital formation; net inventory change; net exports; federal government purchases, and state and local government purchases.

The Applications of the Concept

The calculations symbolize mathematically the structure of the flows of goods or services in an economy for a selected year based on aggregate financial records of disbursements and receipts in that economy. The quantification of such a structure lends itself to several purposes: It can offer insights into imbalances in national economic development;[2] it can aid in business forecasting;[3] it can reflect changes in the technology of an economy;[4] and finally, it can indicate results on industry sales of static or dynamic levels of final demand—its primary application in stock analysis and the essence of this paper.

Input-output analysis is not a new concept. It has evolved from the work of Professor Wassily Leontief of Harvard University. He prepared studies of the United States economy for 1919 and 1929 and collaborated with officials of the Bureau of Labor Statistics in a 1939 study. This was used by W. Duane Evans, Jerome Cornfield, and Marvin Hoffenberg to investigate the American economy after World War II.

Recently an article[5] and his most recent book[6] have verified Professor Leontief's preeminence in this concept. His efforts are currently continued by the Research Project on the Structure of the American Economy at Harvard University and the Office of Business Economics of the Department of Commerce. The latter organization has constructed the tables for the 1958 economy reproduced for this article and is responsible for the periodic development of input-output tables for the United States. The OBE tables are the first to be integrated with the national accounts.[7]

---

[2] Wassily Leontief, "The Structure of Development," in *Technology and Economic Development* by the Board of Editors of *Scientific American* (New York: Alfred A. Knopf, 1963), pp. 105–124.

[3] There have been three recent papers setting forth the uses and limitations of input-output analysis in business forecasting: Morris R. Goldman's "Some Observations on the 1958 Input-Output Study and Its Uses" (paper presented to the Seminar on Sources and Techniques for Analyzing Financial Markets of the National Association of Business Economists, New York City, May 7, 1965); The Machinery & Allied Products Institute's "Use of Input-Output Analysis as an Aid in Forecasting in the Capital Goods Industries" (Washington, D.C., Memorandum of May 10, 1965); James R. Cambern's "Input-Output: A Market Analysis Tool," *Construction Review*, February 1966.

[4] Anne P. Carter, "The Economics of Technological Change," *Scientific American*, April 1966, pp. 25–31.

[5] Leontief, "The Structure of the U.S. Economy," *Scientific American*, April 1965.

[6] Leontief, *Input-Output Economics* (New York: Oxford University Press, 1966).

[7] Within the Office of Business Economics, responsibility for the estimates centered in the National Economics Division with important assistance from the staff of the National Income Division. Also, important contributions were made by the staff in the Farm Income Branch of the Department of Agriculture's Economic Research Service and in the Division of Economic Analysis of the Bureau of Mines.

Also, the Bureau of Labor Statistics completed in 1952 a model for the 1947 economy and is currently doing research work as is the National Planning Association.

Basic Methodology

The basic methodology of the system, as presently conceived for the 1958 economy by the Office of Business Economics, employs tables arranged as matrices.[8] Table 1, the "Interindustry Transactions, 1958," measures the value in dollars at producers' prices of product flows between 86 industries and final demand (Exhibit I). Tables 2 and 3, "Direct Requirements Per Dollar of Gross Output, 1958" and "Total Requirements (Direct and Indirect) Per Dollar of Delivery to Final Demand, 1958," respectively, measure the value of direct and total product requirements of each of these industries relative to: (1) the value of the gross output of the others (Exhibit II), and (2) relative to the value of deliveries of each to final demand segments of the economy (Exhibit III).

Each matrix is composed of a left-hand list of numbered industries identifying the rows and an overhead arrangement of the same and identically numbered industries forming the columns. The division of the economy into industrial sectors is the Standard Industrial Classification prepared by the Office of Statistical Standards in 1957 and issued by the Bureau of the Budget. As certain industries diminish or change in nature and others develop in economic importance, the components of these categories are revised to keep them keyed to our changing technology.

By tracing down a column within any matrix, the value of inputs to the industry heading the column is found. These inputs represent outputs from each of those industries comprising the rows. By observing the number at an intersection or cell, the input value is identifiable. This value is either absolute or relative depending on the orientation of the table. The number is an input for the industry heading the column and an output for the industry heading the row.

In the table of interindustry flows (Exhibit I), after including the value added and some adjusting entries, each industry column of inputs results in the same total as the row of intermediate outputs of that industry added to the value of its product delivered directly to final demand.

Tracing Product Flows

In Exhibit I, column 1 represents the inputs to the industry "Livestock & Livestock Products" by each industry forming the rows: Thus, $4,153 million of inputs was derived from the first row or "Livestock & Livestock Products" (interindustry sales); $6,600 million from "Other Agricultural Products," moving down; none from "Forestry & Fishery Prod-

---

[8] "The Transactions Table of the 1958 Input-Output Study and Revised Direct and Total Requirements Data," *Survey of Current Business*, September 1965, pp. 33–49, 56.

EXHIBIT I

EXTRACT OF TABLE 1—INTERINDUSTRY TRANSACTIONS, 1958
(In Millions of Dollars at Producers' Prices)

For the distribution of output of an industry, read the row for that industry.
For the composition of inputs to an industry, read the column for that industry.

	Livestock and livestock products (1)	Other agricultural products (2)	Intermediate outputs, total	Personal consumption expenditures	Gross private fixed capital formation	Net inventory change	Net exports¹	Federal Government purchases	State and local government purchases	Total final demand	Total
1. Livestock & Livestock Products	4,153	1,705	23,565	2,111		601	38	−3	11	2,758	26,322
2. Other Agricultural Products	6,600	708	17,624	2,429		428	1,813	1,073	27	5,770	23,395
3. Forestry & Fishery Products			1,257	281		19	30	−137	(*)	194	1,451
4. Agricultural, Forestry & Fishery Services	493	878	1,563			20	3	45	−68		1,564
5. Iron & Ferroalloy Ores Mining			1,227			−23	41			18	1,245
6. Nonferrous Metal Ores Mining			1,156			−32	4	192		163	1,319
7. Coal Mining	6	1	2,120	261		−22	332		61	631	2,752
8. Crude Petroleum & Natural Gas			10,865			−40	28			−12	10,852
9. Stone and Clay Mining and Quarrying	1	67	1,583	17		4	23	10	−12	41	1,624
10. Chemical & Fertilizer Mineral Mining		28	485	1		−1	55	11	12	78	563
11. New Construction					36,957		2	3,388	12,069	52,416	52,416
12. Maintenance & Repair Construction	234	377	12,455	158		84		1,081	3,339	4,420	16,875
13. Ordnance & Accessories		3	2,136				17	2,270	4	4,669	4,669
14. Food & Kindred Products	2,964		17,536	45,759		248	1,298	53	272	47,629	65,165
15. Tobacco Manufactures			1,284	4,250		−26	436			4,661	5,945
16. Broad & Narrow Fabrics, Yarn & Thread Mills	6	7	10,008	712		−104	210	50	(*)	878	10,886
17. Miscellaneous Textile Goods & Floor Coverings		27	1,690	743	45	−27	46	4	9	812	2,502
18. Apparel			2,982	11,165		−123	140	40	1	11,314	14,296
19. Miscellaneous Fabricated Textile Products	8	35	1,068	1,101		−1	18	103	92	1,221	2,290
20. Lumber & Wood Products, Except Containers	2	2	8,116	149	6	62	110	−6	(*) 1	323	8,439
81. Business Travel, Entertainment & Gifts	18	27	6,611								6,611
82. Office Supplies	1	2	1,154	−14		−206	209	74	132	−207	1,360
83. Scrap, Used & Secondhand Goods			1,768					117	342	−374	1,394
84. Government Industry				−1,153			4,020	19,951	19,078	39,029	39,029
85. Rest of the World Industry				3,503				−307		2,560	2,560
86. Household Industry										3,503	3,503
87. Inventory Valuation Adjustment						−311				−311	−311
I. Intermediate Inputs, Total	17,298	11,573									
V.A. Value Added	9,024	11,822		290,069	62,392	−1,491	2,206	53,594	40,564	447,334	447,344
T. Total	26,322	23,395									
TR. Transfers²		561									

EXHIBIT II

EXTRACT OF TABLE 2—DIRECT REQUIREMENTS PER DOLLAR OF GROSS OUTPUT, 1958
(Producers' Prices)

For the composition of inputs to an industry, read the column for that industry.	1. Livestock and livestock products	2. Other agricultural products	3. Forestry and fishery products	4. Agricultural, forestry and fishery services	5. Iron and ferroalloy ores mining	6. Nonferrous metal ores mining	7. Coal mining	8. Crude petroleum and natural gas	9. Stone and clay mining and quarrying	10. Chemical and fertilizer mineral mining	11. New construction	60. Aircraft and parts
1. Livestock & Livestock Products	0.15974	0.07289	0.05163	0.13924								
2. Other Agricultural Products	.25073	.03026	.11284	.35129								
3. Forestry & Fishery Products	.01871		.01102									
4. Agricultural, Forestry & Fishery Services		.03755	.01203	.00105								
5. Iron & Ferroalloy Ores Mining					.05144	.00966			.00025	.00063		
6. Nonferrous Metal Ores Mining					.03217	.17547			.00059	.00053		
7. Coal Mining	.00023	.00002			.00375	.00096	.17116	0.00002	.00162	.00083		0.00018
8. Crude Petroleum & Natural Gas				(*)			.00051	.02225	.00727	.00213	(*)	
9. Stone & Clay Mining & Quarrying	.00003	.00285	.00005			.00006	.00002		.00041	.01642	.01193	
10. Chemical & Fertilizer Mineral Mining		.00121				.00092				.05875		
11. New Construction	.00889	.01612	.00023	.00127	.00053	.00692	.00088	.00039	.00122	.00059	.00013	.00178
12. Maintenance & Repair Construction											.00010	.05150
13. Ordnance & Accessories		.00012	.01706	.00482		.00138				.00010	.00032	
14. Food & Kindred Products	.11205						.00067	.00020	.00003	.00033		.00015
15. Tobacco Manufactures												.00049
16. Broad & Narrow Fabrics, Yarn & Thread Mills	.00022	.00030	.00801	.00761	.00012						.00007	.00089
17. Miscellaneous Textile Goods & Floor Coverings		.00114										
18. Apparel	.00032	.00149				.00101	.00683	.00053	.00002	.00041	.00001	.00170
19. Miscellaneous Fabricated Textile Products	.00007	.00007			.00482						.06258	
20. Lumber & Wood Products, Except Containers												
81. Business Travel, Entertainment & Gifts	.00067	.00115	.00085	.00078	.00393	.00413	.00398	.00626	.00480	.00921	.00429	.00409
82. Office Supplies	.00003	.00009	.00033	.00007	.00017	.00018	.00022	.00026	.00022	.00042	.00026	.00077
A. Adjustment for Scrap and By-Products [1]	−.00142				+.00232	+.00042	+.00194	+.01015	+.00250	+.00140	+.00139	−.00171
V.A. Value Added	.34281	.50633	.38995	.44650	.35331	.33927	.58310	.61468	.57272	.62593	.35493	.47004
T. Total	1.00000	1.00000	1.00000	1.00000	1.00000	1.00000	1.00000	1.00000	1.00000	1.00000	1.00000	1.00000

EXHIBIT III

Extract of Table 3—Total Requirements (Direct and Indirect) Per Dollar of Delivery to Final Demand, 1958
(Producers' Prices)

Each entry represents the output required, directly and indirectly, from the industry named at the beginning of the row for each dollar of delivery to final demand by the industry named at the head of the column.

	Livestock and live-stock products	Other agricultural products	Forestry and fishery products	Agricultural, forestry and fishery services	Iron and ferroalloy ores mining	Nonferrous metal ores mining	Coal mining	Crude petroleum and natural gas	Stone and clay mining and quarrying	Chemical and fertilizer mineral mining	New construction	Aircraft and parts
	1	2	3	4	5	6	7	8	9	10	11	60
1. Livestock & Livestock Products	1.28150	.10857	.09097	0.21960	0.00325	0.00311	0.00281	0.00448	0.00289	0.00320	0.00540	0.00290
2. Other Agricultural Products	.36998	1.08008	.15396	.43231	.04426	.04394	.00378	.00567	.00344	.00344	.01289	.00337
3. Forestry & Fishery Products	.00116	.00071	1.01169	.00052	.00091	.00048	.00029	.00029	.00040	.00043	.00898	.00070
4. Agricultural, Forestry & Fishery Services	.03774	.04278	.01976	1.02150	.00031	.00030	.00032	.00036	.00029	.00028	.00101	.00028
5. Iron & Ferroalloy Ores Mining	.00069	.00094	.00558	.00056	1.05666	.01696	.00226	.00053	.00181	.00333	.00676	.00525
6. Nonferrous Metal Ores Mining	.00060	.00098	.00042	.04203	.04203	1.21532	.00200	.00056	.00608	.00221	.00533	.00767
7. Coal Mining	.00196	.00201	.00130	.00727	.00727	.00616	1.20977	.00116	.02277	.00546	.00639	.00442
8. Crude Petroleum & Natural Gas	.01475	.03043	.01454	.01460	.01192	.01243	.01370	1.02947	.01274	.01802	.01982	.00666
9. Stone & Clay Mining & Quarrying	.00176	.00410	.00092	.00180	.00060	.00129	.00143	.00044	1.01274	.01835	.01916	.00126
10. Chemical & Fertilizer Mineral Mining	.00146	.00372	.00083	.00160	.00070	.00295	.00105	.00033	.00152	1.05399	.00127	.00052
11. New Construction	.02869	.03294	.01267	.01920	.01603	.01315	.01009	.01790	.01125	.01240	1.00000	.00940
12. Maintenance & Repair Construction	.00013	.00017	.00012	.00010	.00018	.00019	.00017	.00013	.00018	.00019	.01198	.06814
13. Ordinance & Accessories	.17689	.01977	.03662	.03865	.00461	.00586	.00531	.00497	.00575	.00765	.00060	.00676
14. Food & Kindred Products	.00018	.00019	.00016	.00014	.00021	.00027	.00026	.00026	.00028	.00039	.00963	.00037
15. Tobacco Manufactures	.00249	.00364	.00411	.00409	.00110	.00377	.00283	.00091	.00244	.00192	.00042	.00361
16. Broad & Narrow Fabrics, Yarn & Thread Mills	.00199	.00304	.01040	.00993	.00051	.00084	.00132	.00081	.00208	.00098	.00351	.00232
17. Miscellaneous Textile Goods & Floor Coverings	.00042	.00037	.00033	.00029	.00028	.00037	.00040	.00025	.00043	.00035	.00200	.02212
18. Apparel	.00166	.00228	.00076	.00116	.00028	.00041	.00035	.00025	.00043	.00042	.00091	.00045
19. Miscellaneous Fabricated Textile Products	.00361	.00539	.00372	.00318	.00883	.00376	.01383	.00237	.00327	.00310	.00070	.00028
20. Lumber & Wood Products, Except Containers											.09396	
79. State & Local Government Enterprises	.00424	.00446	.00270	.00293	.00654	.00791	.00683	.00415	.00767	.01093	.00624	.00405
80. Gross Imports of Goods & Services	.03506	.03962	.21089	.02224	.32084	.24310	.01288	.09568	.07829	.12270	.03111	.02500
81. Business Travel, Entertainment & Gifts	.00664	.00692	.00586	.00494	.00777	.01000	.00961	.00943	.01050	.01463	.01546	.01385
82. Office Supplies	.00115	.00137	.00192	.00090	.00092	.00113	.00108	.00118	.00118	.00135	.00224	.00200

ucts"; and $493 million from "Agricultural, Forestry & Fishery Services," etc. At the foot of the column is the total value of these intermediate inputs, $17,298 million. Next is the "Value Added" of $9,024 million, making a total product value of $26,322 million. The $237 million in italics represents imports and the value of identical output emanating from other industries as a secondary product but attributed to "Livestock & Livestock Products." Technically, these should be deducted because the imports are not part of the domestic United States interindustry flow and the secondary products are not supplied by the prime producer.

In the same table, tracing across the first row we find the "Livestock & Livestock Products" industry shipped products valued at $4,153 million to itself; $1,705 million to "Other Agricultural Products," etc., moving laterally. On the last page of the tables, we find these intermediate outputs totaled $23,565 million and that final demand components received the following deliveries: "Personal Consumption Expenditures," $2,111 million; "Net Inventory Change" or increments or decrements to stock in trade, $601 million; "Net Exports," $38 million; "Federal Government Purchases," −$3 million; "State & Local Government Purchases," $11 million—making "Total Final Demand" of $2,758 million, and Total Output of $26,322 million. (Note, this total agrees with columnar inputs plus values added).

1958 STUDY INTEGRATED WITH NATIONAL ACCOUNTS

In this most recently published United States study, the interindustry input-output computations are statistically and conceptually integrated with the national income and product accounts, so that total value of final demand categories is equal to the corresponding components of Gross National Product.

DIRECT COEFFICIENTS MEASURE DEMAND

In the cells of Exhibit II are direct coefficients representing the ratios of inputs by the industries heading the rows to each dollar of gross output by the industries atop the columns. For example, industry column 1, "Livestock & Livestock Products," received $0.15974 as product inputs from itself for each dollar of gross output. Continuing down column 1, we find this industry received $.25073 from the "Other Agricultural Products" industry and $.01871 from "Agricultural, Forestry & Fishing Services," etc. Then at the foot of the column we see that $.00142 was subtracted as scrappage during the materials assimilation and manufacturing processes and $.34281 of the dollar of gross output was accounted for by "Value Added."

INVERSE COEFFICIENTS MEASURE TOTAL DEMAND

To show the cumulative effects throughout the industrial structure which various levels of final demand have is the function of the Leontief inverse coefficients in Exhibit III. For instance, under column 1 we see that for every dollar of delivery to final demand by "Livestock & Livestock Products," $1.28150 was required from the industry itself. This seeming paradox of a greater input than output ($1.28 to $1.00) results from the table's measurement of direct and indirect demand for the industry's products caused by a dollar of its sales to final demand and represents primarily the sales of the industry to itself to produce its output. These coefficients measure the aggregate demand on each industry row from a dollar's worth of delivery to final demand by each industry column as an interindustry buying chain reaction is triggered. For "Livestock & Livestock Products," the $1.28150 also results from the sale of livestock products that are required by other industries as products ancillary to the delivery to final demand of $1.00 of products by "Livestock & Livestock Products." Continuing down column 1, we find cumulative demand on "Other Agricultural Products" of $.36098.

As we shall see later, it is these coefficients which provide the most pragmatic aid in stock analysis, or more aptly, stock analysis as derived from industry analysis.

Background for Input-Output Study

This study by the Office of Business Economics is one of considerable magnitude. Its genesis and objectives are summarized in the following text:

> The 1958 study is part of a major new program of the Office of Business Economics which involves the periodic preparation of a set of interindustry (input-output) tables as part of an integrated system of national accounts. Such an expanded system of integrated national accounts permits a much more comprehensive understanding of the interaction between the various industries and final markets of the economy.
>
> The program was instituted in the latter half of 1959 in response to a recommendation of the National Accounts Review Committee which was set up at the request of the Bureau of the Budget to evaluate the national accounts work of the United States. One of the principal recommendations made by the Review Committee was that input-output accounts be prepared regularly as an important and integral component of the national accounts. . . .[9]

The Application to Stock Analysis

As we delve into the application of the input-output concept to stock analysis, a word is in order concerning the tabular structure we have been discussing and which we will be using. The relationships manifested in the study are for 1958 and do not take account of price changes since then, or technical changes which have altered the mix of product flows. Of course, we could adjust matrix results for price changes in the modern period by inflating or deflating demand values by price changes in each industrial

---

[9] Morris R. Goldman, et al., "The Interindustry Structure of the United States: A Report on the 1958 Input-Output Study," *Survey of Current Business*, November 1964, pp. 10–29.

segment in relation to a general price index. Essentially, this technique would reflect roughly the current flow structure caused by producers' price changes; in the economic processing to meet current demand magnitudes, inflation has altered the 1958 process, and some products are now more expensive and should be mathematically inflated with compensatory decreases to more stable ones to maintain valid relationships.[10] For rapid estimating, however, such an adjusting rationale might be cumbersome. Also, it would be questionable considering the inadequacies of price indexes.

The measure of technological effects on interindustry flows requires more sophistication and is taken up briefly in another section.

These qualifications are not meant to mollify the application to common stock analysis; for the maturity of our economic system means mutations in manufacturing and distribution patterns will be gradual; the basic interindustry structure currently should be very similar to the 1958 model except for the Vietnam military disruptions. Nevertheless, later models for the 1961 and 1963 economies being constructed by the Office of Business Economics will reflect price and technological changes and will add validity to the application. The full-scale study of 1963, with 1967 as the target date for completion, especially will enhance the concept as an analytical tool because the economic patterns caused by the scientific product proliferation of the 1960's will have registered.

There are two major uses of input-output data in stock analysis: (1) the observance of long-term technological change and an interpretation of its effect on common stock earnings; and (2) the anticipation of short-term effects on stock earnings caused by expected changes in final demand components.

---

[10] The following mathematical system could be employed to adjust coefficients for price changes in each industry; the adjustment also could be made on absolute values obtained with direct or indirect coefficients. Using column 1 in Exhibit III, we can construct the hypothetical model below showing adjusted total demand coefficients for each dollar of delivery to final demand.

Industry Inputs	Per Dollar of Delivery By "Livestock & Livestock Products"	
	1958	196—
(1) "Livestock & livestock products"................	1.28150 ($\times$1.05)	1.34558
a. Industry price index.......100		110
b. General industrial price index............100		−105
		0.05
(2) "Other agricultural products".................	.36098 ($\times$.97)	.35105
a. Industry price index.......100		102
b. General industrial price index............100		−105
		−0.03

Long-Term Technological Change

The first application is lucidly suggested in a recent article by Anne P. Carter.[11] In the article, she explains a study she and her colleagues at the Harvard Research Project on the Structure of the American Economy conducted to detect technological changes affecting interindustry flows. This was accomplished with the aid of the 1947 and 1958 tables. With the 1947 matrix, the group derived the outputs of total goods and services required to fulfill the 1958 final demand based on the 1947 technology. These hypothetical outputs were then compared with the actual ones which satisfied 1958 final demand to detect changes in 1947–1958 product flows relative to the 1958 economic requirements.

The results showed several salient points for stock analysts. First, in constant dollars it cost about $14 billion more to satisfy 1958 final demand with 1958 technology than it would have with 1947 technology. Since the difference was accounted for by interindustry transactions, the conclusion was that our manufacturing and distributive processes have become more circuitous. Picking up this thought, it would seem this phenomenon reflects more specialization in fabrication, and conversely less economic centralization in certain industries, than is generally suspected. Therefore, the analyst would be well advised to be cognizant of attractive corporations that exist to embellish a product in modern capitalism's state of quality competition as opposed to the price competition of classical economics. The product sophistication of the automobile and aerospace industries, both amassing components from spawning peripheral manufacturers, would be examples of equity opportunities revealed by the observation. Also, the study indicated that *demands for services* are contributing to the "round-about" distribution process which opens up another investment facet discussed later.

Another area illuminated by the study is labor productivity. About 33 percent more labor would have been required by the 1947 technology in satiating 1958 final demand than was actually used in the latter year, indicating real investment increased labor efficiency approximately that amount. Picking up the idea again, since composite wages and salaries increased considerably more during the period, we observe what could be the incipient stages of cost-push inflation and the consequential corporate modernization programs of the 1960's to cope with the cost problem. This suggests analysts should emphasize those corporations continuing plant and equipment modernization in the effort to maximize labor output in relation to labor costs.

Changing Structure of Inputs

Perhaps the most important of the project's signals to stock analysts was the changing structure of inputs in the technological comparisons.

---

[11] Carter, *op. cit.*

TABLE I

General inputs:	% Change
Business services	+42
Communications (including radio & television)	+33
Electricity, gas, & water	+30
Finance, insurance, real estate, & rentals	+11
Paper products & containers	+ 5
Petroleum refining	+ 4
Wholesale & retail trade	+ 4
Printing & publishing	+ 4
Metal containers	+ 2
Materials inputs:	
Primary iron & steel mfg.	−27
Lumber & wood products (except containers)	−26
Primary nonferrous metal mfg.	−23
Agricultural products (other than food)	−14
Glass & glass products	−13

Comprehensively, the study estimated that, as a proportion of total inputs, material inputs declined 9 percent while general inputs increased 6 percent from 1947 to 1958. This means businessmen required less traditional structural materials and more business and financial services, packaging materials, warehousing, and other general inputs in relation to total requirements.

Table I shows selected general inputs with positive changes and materials inputs with negative changes when product demands on the 1947 technology were compared with 1958. Obviously, the expanding GNP is being restructured so that industries in the general category have greater investment potential than the historically dominant material class.

In the interest of objectivity, however, Table II shows that several material sectors advanced markedly as well as industries of the metalworking and chemical sectors. But even the ascendance of these sectors accentuates the atrophy of "basic-industry" giants and shows the economic dynamics caused by our evolutionary technology.

These figures certainly reflect the pervasive influence even as early as 1958 of the scientific diffusion into United States technology fostered by service industries which have financed, distributed, and maintained the sophisticated technology. Judging from industrial production indices through 1965, these trends have continued and indications are they will

TABLE II

Materials inputs:	% Change
Plastics & synthetic materials	+41
Stone & clay products	+28
Rubber & plastic products	+11
Livestock & livestock products	+10
Metalworking inputs:	
Electronic components & accessories	+82
Scientific & controlling instruments	+16
Chemical inputs:	
Chemicals & selected chemical products	+31

accelerate. (It is just this sort of intuitive reasoning that could be verified or rejected by continuous input-output data.)

INPUT-OUTPUT TABLES MEASURE TECHNOLOGICAL CHANGES

The industry analyst can use input-output tables to measure long-term technological demand changes also, particularly to gauge the status of his industry in relation to final demand dynamism. It would appear from the results of the Harvard studies cited above that a comparison of Leontief inverse coefficients for 1947 and 1958 would show the industry products included in the declining materials inputs listed in Table I as comprising a smaller portion of each dollar of delivery to final demand by other industries in the economy. Such an observation would put on guard analysts following "Primary Iron & Steel Mfg."; "Lumber & Wood Products (except containers)"; "Primary Nonferrous Metals Mfg."; "Agricultural Products (other than food)"; and "Glass & Glass Products."

Furthermore, compensatory beneficiaries of these material attritions appear to be included in the material inputs increments listed in Table II: namely, "Plastics & Synthetic Materials"; "Stone & Clay Products"; "Rubber & Plastic Products"; and "Livestock & Livestock Products." Since these increments would appear in input-output tables as greater coefficients, analysts following industries in these sectors would become more sanguine vis-à-vis the decrements in the traditionally "basic industries," provided a continuation of the trend has occurred. Again we are frustrated by the absence of current models, but when future tables are available, basic industry trends in the technological mix can be discerned objectively.

However, the assumption of a continuation in these trends seems reasonable when one considers the apparent inroads plastic extrusions, aluminum, and chemicals have made on primary metals and agricultural products since 1958.[12]

SHORT-TERM EFFECTS OF PURCHASES BY FINAL DEMAND

For a preview of the short-term effects on industry sales of purchases within the final demand sector, the Leontief inverse coefficients are ideal. The anticipation of additional equity profits is the essence of advanced stock analysis and these coefficients provide variables for equations which estimate incremental revenue flows throughout the industrial complex resulting from stimuli to final demand components. This technique is especially useful where large purchasing power is manifest. By constructing an equation deriving the revenue flows to an industry and expanding this formula to include a certain corporation's estimated portion of these sales, a calculus is available to translate macroscopic input-output flows

---

[12] For a recent article on the competition between plastic and steel for certain key markets, see Charles B. Camp, "Plastics Make Inroads in Key Steel Markets, Draw Counterattacks," *Wall Street Journal*, Sept. 19, 1966, p. 1, col. 6.

into microscopic corporate revenue flows. The following general equation can be used to this end.

$$R = P \times C \times M.$$

where: R = The Estimate of Additional Revenues for a Corporation.
P = Total Purchases by a Final Demand Component from an Industry Buying Goods or Services from the Industry Represented by R.
C = Leontief Inverse Coefficient for the Industry Represented by R Selling to the Industry Satisfying the Final Demand in P.
M = Expected Proportion of the Sales to the Industry Purchases in P Attributable to the Corporation Represented by R.

For example, the annual rate of new construction of residential and business structures during the first quarter of 1966 was $55.1 billion.[13] Assuming this figure will be the actual rate of new construction for the year, we can solve a series of equations using $55.1 billion as the constant P. "New Construction" purchases can be used as a Final Demand component because it is included in "Gross Private Fixed Capital Formation" statistically. Table III indicates the 10 industrial sectors which would be the largest suppliers in 1966 to "New Construction" (Industry 11, Exhibit III) derived from the following abbreviated version of the formula:

$$RI = P \times C.$$

where: RI = Estimated Revenues to a Selected Industry.
P = Total Purchases by a Final Demand Component from an Industry Buying Goods or Services from the Industry Represented by RI.
C = Leontief Inverse Coefficient for the Industry Represented by RI Selling to the Industry Satisfying the Final Demand in P.

Such solutions can be expanded into the first general equation ($R = P \times C \times M$) to include the revenue flows to a corporation following this rationale. Suppose historical analysis indicates Company XYZ supplies 5 percent of the construction market for "Primary Iron & Steel Manufacturing." This ratio is inserted in the general equation, converting it into a special equation thusly:

$$R_1 = P_1 \times C_1 \times M_1$$
$$R_1 = 55.1 \times .11 \times .05$$
$$R_1 = 6.06 \times .05$$
$$R_1 = \$.333 \text{ billion}$$

By way of summation, the solution of the equation estimates that XYZ Corporation will receive orders valued at $333 million as a result of the

---

[13] Derived by the author from table entitled, "Recovery Profile: National Output and Expenditures," prepared by the Conference Board, May 16, 1966.

chain reaction triggered by final demand of $55.1 billion in new construction activity.

Referring to Table III showing the 10 industries most sensitive to changes in construction activity, several are vitally affected by levels of new construction, and this is an example of a situation in which input-output analysis is especially useful—in detecting revenue flows to smaller industries. By isolating industries reliant on only a few industrial customers, a supplementary forecasting technique can be developed. For instance, in Table III, "Primary Iron & Steel Manufacturing"; "Heating, Plumbing & Structural Metal Products"; "Lumber & Wood Products,

TABLE III

Industry	RI (Industry Sales) Billions	=	P (Final Demand) Billions	×	C (Leontief Inverse Coefficient)*
New construction	$55.10		$55.10		1.00
Wholesale & retail trade	7.71		55.10		.14
Primary iron & steel mfg	6.06		55.10		.11
Heating, plumbing, & structural metal products	5.51		55.10		.10
Lumber & wood products (except containers)	4.96		55.10		.09
Transportation & warehousing	4.41		55.10		.08
Business services	3.86		55.10		.07
Primary nonferrous metals mfg	2.76		55.10		.05
Petroleum refining & related industries	2.20		55.10		.04
Real estate & rental	1.65		55.10		.03

* Rounded to nearest hundredth.

except Containers"; and "Business Services" are significantly dependent on the "New Construction" market as comparisons of their total sales and sales derived from new construction will bear out.[14] By solving a series of equations estimating their sales to each final demand component, an industry sales forecast can be constructed.

THE $525 MILLION PAN AMERICAN CONTRACT

Another estimating application of input-output can be employed in translating voluminous capital equipment orders into corporate revenue flows. Pan American World Airways recently ordered 25 gigantic model 747 airliners from Boeing Co. for $525 million including spare parts for delivery in September, 1969. The same series of equations using total demand coefficients can be devised as in the new construction example to

---

[14] For a more thorough treatment of the effects on industries of new construction activity, see Norman Frumkin's "Construction Activity in the 1958 Input-Output Study," *Survey of Current Business*, May 1965, pp. 13–24.

derive various industrial and corporate revenue flows. The rationale employed is that the sale of the model 747 airliners is a delivery by Boeing to a Final Demand component, "Gross Private Fixed Capital Formation," since Pan American's purchase represents a capital expenditure. Therefore, the revenues to each of Boeing's suppliers can be derived from the equation, $RI = P \times C$ (where RI = Industry Revenue; P = $525 million; and C = the Leontief Inverse Coefficient for Each Industry in the Matrix Selling to the "Aircraft & Parts" Industry). Obviously, Boeing represents a buyer in that industry.

In order to show the variance in measurement of the direct and total requirements, Table IV has been set up using the direct coefficients and Leontief inverse coefficients, respectively, as multipliers for the $525 million to indicate Boeing's leading suppliers in making delivery under the $525 million contract.

TABLE IV

| | Requirements | |
Industry	Direct (Millions)	Total (Millions)
Aircraft and parts	$100.0[15]	$657.0[15]
Ordnance and accessories	26.2	36.7
Primary iron and steel mfg.	15.9	47.2
Primary nonferrous metals mfg.	15.8	42.0
Wholesale and retail trade	11.0	26.2
Radio, television, and communication equipment	15.8	21.0

Criticism of Input-Output Analysis

Morris R. Goldman has pointed out two problems in using input-output data for short-term analysis:[16] the problem of inventory and the problem of timing.

The inventory problem arises because input-output models reflect consumption of industry products. However, this consumption might come from current production *or from business inventories;* if the source is the latter no productive interindustry flows are energized (unless to replenish inventory); in fact, the system normally has already reflected the delivery to inventory since it is a component of final demand. Goldman suggests that to prevent the production distortion caused by inven-

---

[15] Based on public statements by Boeing officials, there is evidence both the Direct Requirements and Total Requirements would be higher because of subcontracting intentions by Boeing on the model 747. The author feels a direct coefficient of .21000 and a total coefficient of 1.39000, producing approximate Direct Requirements of $111,400,000 and Total Requirements of $729,000,000 respectively, would be realistic levels in this situation.

[16] *Op. cit.*, Footnote 3.

tory usage, the inventory depletion of each industrial class of products must be entered as a negative in final demand. Ideally, he asserts, the final demand should be adjusted to show the net of inventory depletion and repletion for each class of products which should be used to reduce or increase, respectively, final demand. For example, demand for an airplane will not trigger the normal reactions in steel production if the aircraft manufacturer uses sheet steel inventory which has been bought in anticipation of the order.

The second problem Goldman presents in short-term application is that of timing, although the inventory admonishment also seems to be a question of timing ultimately. He reminds us that in the normal static input-output analysis the sequence of causality between delivery of final products and demand for inputs is ignored, so that interindustry flows are assumed to take place within the period being analyzed, usually one year. Actually, this is not the case, and products might not find their way into a finished, deliverable form for several quarters although input requirements have been fulfilled. This situation would seem to be especially true in the delivery of components and replacement parts of the sort included in the Pan American contract alluded to earlier.

Conclusion

In spite of the shortcomings of the input-output applications, however, the system presents the most incisive look at an economy's industrial structure yet accomplished. More sophisticated techniques and regular constructs will increase the validity of applications. Already over 50 countries have adopted input-output analysis as aids in understanding better their economic structures. It is not difficult to envision an input-output study of the world which will someday serve as a guide for international monetary and fiscal policies and coordinated economic development.

Finally, because of variations in consumer tastes, extraordinary events like wars and technological changes, the structure of product flows in the American economy is constantly in a state of flux. For this reason, corporate revenue flows calculated by using input-output analysis should be considered estimates which need refining through direct inquiry or research of historical patterns; but, used judiciously, this concept, emphasizing the inherent order of the economy, can establish logical magnitudes of revenue flows to industries, and deductively to companies, from the immense buying power in the United States economy today.

16
THE ROLE OF MONEY AND MONETARY POLICY*

Karl Brunner [†]

The development of monetary analysis in the past decade has intensified the debate concerning the role of money and monetary policy. Extensive research fostered critical examinations of the Federal Reserve's traditional descriptions of policy and of the arrangements governing policymaking. Some academic economists and others attribute the cyclical fluctuations of monetary growth and the persistent problem concerning the proper interpretation of monetary policy to the established procedures of monetary policy and the conceptions traditionally guiding policymakers.

The critique of established policy procedures, which evolved from this research into questions concerning the monetary mechanism, is derived from a body of monetary theory referred to in this paper as the Monetarist position. Three major conclusions have emerged from the hypotheses put forth. First, monetary impulses are a major factor accounting for variations in output, employment, and prices. Second, movements in the money stock are the most reliable measure of the thrust of monetary impulses. Third, the behavior of the monetary authorities dominates movements in the money stock over business cycles.

A response to the criticisms of existing monetary policy methods was naturally to be expected and is welcomed. Four articles which defend present policy procedures have appeared during the past few years in various Federal Reserve publications.[1] These articles comprise a counter-

---

* Reprinted by permission of *Review* of the Federal Reserve Bank of St. Louis (July 1968).

† This paper owes a heavy debt to my long and stimulating association with Allan H. Meltzer. I also wish to acknowledge the editorial assistance of Leonall C. Andersen, Keith M. Carlson, and Jerry L. Jordan of the Federal Reserve Bank of St. Louis.

[1] Lyle Gramley and Samuel Chase, "Time Deposits in Monetary Analysis," Federal Reserve *Bulletin*, October 1965. John H. Kareken, "Commercial Banks and the Supply of Money: A Market Determined Demand Deposit Rate," Federal Reserve *Bulletin*, October 1967. J. A. Cacy, "Alternative Approaches to the Analysis of the Financial Structure," *Monthly Review*, Federal Reserve Bank of Kansas City, March 1968. Richard G. Davis, "The Role of the Money Supply in Business Cycles," *Monthly Review*, Federal Reserve Bank of New York, April 1968.

critique which argues that monetary impulses are neither properly measured nor actually transmitted by the money stock. The authors reject the Monetarist thesis that monetary impulses are a chief factor determining variations in economic activity, and they contend that cyclical fluctuations of monetary growth cannot be attributed to the behavior of the Federal Reserve authorities. These fluctuations are claimed to result primarily from the behavior of commercial banks and the public.

The ideas and arguments put forth in these articles deserve close attention. The controversy defined by the critique of policy in professional studies and the countercritique appearing in Federal Reserve publications bears on issues of fundamental importance to public policy. Underlying all the fashionable words and phrases is the fundamental question: What is the role of monetary policy and what are the requirements of rational policymaking?

The following sections discuss the major aspects of the countercritique. These rejoinders may contribute to a better understanding of the issues, and the resulting clarification may remove some unnecessary disputes. Even though the central contentions of the controversy will remain, the continuous articulation of opposing points of view plays a vital role in the search for greater understanding of the monetary process.

A SUMMARY OF THE COUNTERCRITIQUE

The four articles relied on two radically different groups of arguments. Gramley–Chase, Kareken and Cacy exploit the juxtaposition "New View versus Traditional View" as the central idea guiding their countercritique. The analytical framework developed by the critique is naturally subsumed for this purpose under the "Traditional View" label. On the other hand, Davis uses the analytical framework developed by the critique in order to organize his arguments.

Gramley–Chase describe their general argument in the following words:

> (New) developments have reaffirmed the bankers' point of view that deposits are attracted, not created, as textbooks suggest. In this new environment, growth rates of deposits have become more suspect than ever as indicators of the conduct of monetary policy.... A framework of analysis [is required] from which the significance of time deposits and of changing time deposits can be deduced. Traditional methods of monetary analysis are not well suited to this task. The 'New View' in monetary economics provides a more useful analytical framework. In the new view, banks—like other financial institutions—are considered as suppliers of financial claims for the public to hold, and the public is given a significant role in determining the total amount of bank liabilities.... Traditional analysis ... fails to recognize that substitution between time deposits and securities may be an important source of pro-cyclical variations in the stock of money even in the face of countercyclical central bank policy.[2]

---
[2] Gramley–Chase, pp. 1380, 1381, 1393.

This general argument guided the construction of an explicit model designed to emphasize the role of the public's and the banks' behavior in the determination of the money stock, bank credit, and interest rates.

Kareken's paper supplements the Gramley–Chase arguments. He finds "the received money supply theory" quite inadequate. His paper is designed to improve monetary analysis by constructing a theory of an individual bank as a firm. This theory is offered as an explanation of a bank's desired balance sheet position. It also appears to form the basis of a model describing the interaction of the public's and the banks' behavior in the joint determination of the money stock, bank credit, and interest rates. The whole development emphasizes somewhat suggestively the importance of the public's and banks' behavior in explanations of monetary growth. It is also designed to undermine the empirical hypotheses advanced by the Monetarist position. This is achieved by means of explicit references to specific and "obviously desirable" features of the model presented.

Cacy's article develops neither an explicit framework nor a direct critique of the basic propositions advanced by the Monetarist thesis. However, he provides a useful summary of the general position of the countercritique. The Monetarist analysis is conveniently subsumed by Cacy under a Traditional View which is juxtaposed to a New View of monetary mechanisms: "The new approach argues . . . that there is no essential difference between the manner in which the liabilities of banks and nonbank financial institutions are determined. Both types of institutions are subject in the same way to the portfolio decisions of the public."[3] The new approach is contrasted with the Traditional View, which "obscures the important role played by the public and overstates the role played by the central bank in the determination of the volume of money balances."[4] The general comparison developed by Cacy suggests quite clearly to the reader that the Traditional View allegedly espoused by the Monetarist position cannot match the "realistic sense" of the New View advocated by the countercritique.

In the context of the framework developed by the critique, Davis questions some basic propositions of the Monetarist position:

> In the past five to ten years, however, there has come into increasing prominence a group of economists who would like to go considerably beyond the simple assertion that the behavior of money is a significant factor influencing the behavior of the economy. . . . In order to bring a few of the issues into sharper focus, this article will take a look at some evidence for the 'money supply' view. . . .
> It confines itself to examining the historical relationship between monetary cycles and cycles in general business. The article concludes that the relationship between these two kinds of cycles does not, in fact, provide any real support

---

[3] Cacy, pp. 5 & 7.
[4] *Ibid.*, p. 7.

for the view that the behavior of money is the predominant determinant of fluctuations in business activity. Moreover, the historical relationship between cycles in money and in business cannot be used to demonstrate that monetary policy is, in its effect, so long delayed and so uncertain as to be an unsatisfactory countercyclical weapon.[5]

AN EXAMINATION OF THE ISSUES

A careful survey of the countercritique yielded the following results. The Gramley–Chase, Kareken, and Cacy papers parade the New View in order to question the status of empirical theories used by the Monetarist critique in its examination of monetary policy. The Davis paper questions quite directly, on the other hand, the existence and relevance of the evidence in support of the Monetarist position, and constitutes a direct assault on the Monetarist critique. The others constitute an indirect assault which attempts to devalue the critique's analysis, and thus to destroy its central propositions concerning the role of money and monetary policy.

The indirect assault on the Monetarist position by Gramley–Chase, Kareken, and Cacy requires a clarification concerning the nature of the New View. A program of analysis must be clearly distinguished from a research strategy and an array of specific conjectures.[6] All three aspects are usually mixed together in a general description. It is important to understand, however, that neither research strategy nor specific empirical conjectures are logical implications of the general program. The explicit separation of the three aspects is crucial for a proper assessment of the New View.

Section A examines some general characteristics of the countercritique's reliance on the New View. It shows the New View to consist of a program acceptable to all economists, a research strategy rejected by the Monetarist position, and an array of specific conjectures advanced without analytical or empirical substantiation. Also, not a single paper of the countercritique developed a relevant assessment of the Monetarist's empirical theories or central propositions.

In sections B and C detailed examinations of specific conjectures centered on rival explanations of cyclical fluctuations of monetary growth are presented. The direct assault on the Monetarist position by Davis is discussed in some detail in Section D. This section also states the crucial propositions of the Monetarist thesis in order to clarify some aspects of

---

[5] Davis, pp. 63–64.

[6] These three aspects of the New View will subsequently be elaborated more fully. Their program of analysis refers to the application of relative price theory to analysis of financial markets and financial institutions. Their research strategy refers to a decision to initiate analysis in the context of a most general framework. Their specific conjectures refer to propositions concerning the causes of fluctuation of monetary growth and propositions about proper interpretation of policy.

this position. This reformulation reveals that the reservations assembled by Davis are quite innocuous. They provide no analytical or empirical case against the Monetarist thesis. Conjectures associated with the interpretation of monetary policy (the "indicator problem") are presented in Section E.

A. The New View

The countercritique has apparently been decisively influenced by programmatic elaborations originally published by Gurley–Shaw and James Tobin.[7] The program is most faithfully reproduced by Cacy, and it also shaped the arguments guiding the model construction by Kareken and Gramley–Chase. The New View, as a program, is a sensible response to a highly unsatisfactory state of monetary analysis inherited in the late 1950's. A money and banking syndrome perpetuated by textbooks obstructed the application of economic analysis to the financial sector. At most, this inherited literature contained only suggestive pieces of analysis. It lacked a meaningful theory capable of explaining the responses of the monetary system to policy actions or to influences emanating from the real sector. The New View proposed a systematic application of economic analysis, in particular an application of relative price theory, to the array of financial intermediaries, their assets and liabilities.

This program is most admirable and incontestable, but it cannot explain the conflict revealed by critique and countercritique. The Monetarist approach accepted the general principle of applying relative price theory to the analysis of monetary processes. In addition, this approach used the suggestions and analytical pieces inherited from past efforts in order to develop some specific hypotheses which do explain portions of our observable environment. The New Viewers' obvious failure to recognize the limited content of their programmatic statements only contributes to maintenance of the conflict.

A subtle difference appears, however, in the research strategy. The New View was introduced essentially as a generalized approach, including a quite formal exposition, but with little attempt at specific structuring and empirical content. The most impressive statements propagated by the New View were crucially influenced by the sheer formalism of its exposition. In the context of the New View's almost empty form, little remains to differentiate one object from another. For instance, in case one only admits the *occurrence* of marginal costs and marginal yields associated with the actions of every household, firm, and financial intermediary, one will necessarily conclude that banks and non-bank financial

---

[7] John G. Gurley and Edward F. Shaw, *Money in a Theory of Finance*, (Washington: Brookings Institute, 1960). James Tobin, "Commercial Banks as Creators of Money," *Banking and Monetary Studies*, ed. Deane Carson (R. D. Irwin, 1963).

intermediaries are restricted in size by the same economic forces and circumstances. In such a context there is truly no essential difference between the determination of bank and non-bank intermediary liabilities, or between banks and non-bank intermediaries, or between money and other financial assets.

The strong impressions conveyed by the New View thus result from the relative emptiness of the formulation which has been used to elaborate their position. In the context of the formal world of the New View, "almost everything is almost like everything else." This undifferentiated state of affairs is not, however, a property of our observable world. It is only a property of the highly formal discussion designed by the New View to overcome the unsatisfactory state of monetary analysis still prevailing in the late 1950's or early 1960's.[8]

Two sources of the conflict have been recognized thus far. The Monetarists' research strategy was concerned quite directly with the construction of empirical theories about the monetary system, whereas the New View indulged, for a lengthy interval, in very general programmatic excursions. Moreover, the New Viewers apparently misconstrued their program as being a meaningful theory about our observable environment. This logical error contributed to a third source of the persistent conflict.

The latter source arises from the criticism addressed by the New Viewers to the Monetarists' theories of money supply processes. Three of the papers exploit the logically dubious but psychologically effective juxtaposition between a New View and a Traditional View. In doing this they fail to distinguish between the inherited state of monetary system analysis typically reflected by the money and banking textbook syndrome and the research output of economists advocating the Monetarist thesis. This distinction is quite fundamental. Some formal analogies misled the New Viewers and they did not recognize the logical difference between

---

[8] Adequate analysis of the medium of exchange function of money, or of the conditions under which inside money becomes a component of wealth, was obstructed by the programmatic state of the New View. The useful analysis of the medium-of-exchange function depends on a decisive rejection of the assertion that "everything is almost like everything else." This analysis requires proper recognition that the marginal cost of information concerning qualities and properties of assets differs substantially between assets, and that the marginal cost of readjusting asset positions depends on the assets involved. The analysis of the wealth position of inside money requires recognition of the marginal productivity of inside money to the holder. Adequate attention to the relevant differences between various cost or yield functions associated with different assets or positions is required by both problems. The blandness of the New View's standard program cannot cope with these isssues. The reader may consult a preliminary approach to the analysis of the medium of exchange function in the paper by Karl Brunner and Allan H. Meltzer, in the *Journal of Finance*, 1964, listed in footnote 9. He should also consult for both issues the important book by Boris Pesek and Thomas Saving, *Money, Wealth and Economic Theory*, The Macmillan Company, New York, 1967, or the paper by Harry Johnson, "Inside Money, Outside Money, Income, Wealth and Welfare in Monetary Theory," in *The Journal of Money, Credit and Banking*, December 1968.

detailed formulations of empirical theories on the one side and haphazard pieces of unfinished analysis on the other side.[9]

A related failure accompanies this logical error. There is not the slightest attempt to assess alternative hypotheses or theories by systematic exposure to observations from the real world. It follows, therefore, that the countercritique scarcely analyzed the empirical theories advanced by the Monetarist critique and, consequently, failed to understand the major implications of these theories.

For instance, they failed to recognize the role assigned by the Monetarist view to banks' behavior and the public's preferences in the monetary process. The objection raised by the New View that "the formula [expressing a basic framework used to formulate the hypothesis] obscures the important role played by the public" has neither analytical basis nor meaning. In fact, the place of the public's behavior was discussed in the Monetarist hypotheses in some detail. Moreover, the same analysis discussed the conditions under which the public's behavior dominates movements of the money stock and bank credit.[10] It also yielded information about the response of bank credit, money stock, and time deposits to changes in ceiling rates, or to changes in the speed with which banks adjust their deposit-supply conditions to evolving market situations. Every single aspect of the banks' or the public's behavior emphasized by the countercritique has been analyzed by the Monetarist's hypotheses in terms which render the results empirically assessable. Little remains, consequently, of the suggestive countercritique assembled in the papers by Gramley–Chase, Kareken, and Cacy.[11]

---

[9] As examples of the empirical work performed by the Monetarists, the reader should consult the following works: Milton Friedman and Anna Jacobson Schwartz, *A Monetary History of the United States, 1867–1960*, (Princeton: Princeton University Press, 1963). Philip Cagan, *Determinants and Effects of Changes in the Stock of Money*, (Columbia: Columbia University Press, 1965). Karl Brunner and Allan H. Meltzer, "Some Further Investigations of Demand and Supply Functions for Money," *Journal of Finance*, Volume XIX, May 1964. Karl Brunner and Allan H. Meltzer, "A Credit-Market Theory of the Money Supply and an Explanation of Two Puzzles in U.S. Monetary Policy," *Essays in Honor of Marco Fanno*, 1966, Padova, Italy. Karl Brunner and Robert Crouch, "Money Supply Theory and British Monetary Experience, *Methods of Operations Research III—Essays in Honor of Wilhelm Krelle*, ed. Rudolf Henn (Published in Meisenheim, Germany, by Anton Hain, 1966). Karl Brunner, "A Schema for the Supply Theory of Money," *International Economic Review*, 1961. Karl Brunner and Allan H. Meltzer, "An Alternative Approach to the Monetary Mechanism," *Subcommittee on Domestic Finance, Committee on Banking and Currency, House of Representatives*, August 17, 1964.

[10] The reader will find this analysis in the following papers: Karl Brunner and Allan H. Meltzer, "Liquidity Traps for Money, Bank Credit, and Interest Rates," *Journal of Political Economy*, April 1968. Karl Brunner and Allan H. Meltzer, "A Credit–Market Theory of the Money Supply and an Explanation of Two Puzzles in U.S. Monetary Policy," *Essays in Honor of Marco Fanno*, Padova, Italy, 1966.

[11] The reader is, of course, aware that these assertions require analytic substantiation. Such substantiation cannot be supplied within the confines of this article. But the reader could check for himself. If he finds, in the context of the countercritique, an analysis of the Monetarists' major hypotheses, an examination of implication, and

B. A Monetarist Examination of the New View's Money Supply Theory

Three sources of the conflict have been discussed thus far. Two sources were revealed as logical misconstruals, involving inadequate construction and assessment of empirical theories. A third source pertains to legitimate differences in research strategy. These three sources do not explain all major aspects of the conflict. Beyond the differences in research strategy and logical misconceptions, genuinely substantive issues remain. Some comments of protagonists advocating the New View should probably be interpreted as conjectures about hypotheses to be expected from their research strategy. It should be clearly understood that such conjectures are not logical implications of the guiding framework. Instead, they are pragmatic responses to the general emphasis associated with this approach.

A first conjecture suggests that the money stock and bank credit are dominated by the public's and the banks' behavior. It is suggested, therefore, that cyclical fluctuations of monetary growth result primarily from the responses of banks and the public to changing business conditions. A second conjecture naturally supplements the above assertions. It is contended that the money stock is a thoroughly "untrustworthy guide to monetary policy."

Articles by Gramley–Chase and Kareken attempt to support these conjectures with the aid of more explicit analytical formulations allegedly expressing the general program of the New View. The paper contributed by Gramley–Chase has been critically examined in detail on another

---

exposure to observations, I would have to withdraw my statements. A detailed analysis of the banks' and the public's role in the money supply, based on two different hypotheses previously reported in our papers, will be developed in our forthcoming books. This analysis, by its very existence, falsifies some major objections made by Cacy or Gramley–Chase. Much of their criticism is either innocuous or fatuous. Gramley–Chase indulge, for instance, in modality statements, i.e., statements obtained from other statements by prefixing a modality qualifier like "maybe" or "possibly." The result of qualifying an empirical statement always yields a statement which is necessarily true, but also quite uninformative. The modality game thus yields logically pointless but psychologically effective sentences. Cacy manages, on the other hand, some astonishing assertions. The New View is credited with the discovery that excess reserves vary over time. He totally disregards the major contributions to the analysis of excess reserves emanating from the Monetarists' research. A detailed analysis of excess reserves was developed by Milton Friedman and Anna Schwartz in the book mentioned in footnote 9. The reader should also note the work by George Morrison, *Liquidity Preferences of Commercial Banks*, (Chicago: University of Chicago Press, 1966), and the study by Peter Frost, "Banks' Demand for Excess Reserves," an unpublished dissertation submitted to the University of California at Los Angeles, 1966. The classic example of an innocuous achievement was supplied by Cacy with the assertion: ". . . the actual volume of money balances determined by competitive market forces may or may not be equal to the upper limit established by the central bank" (p. 8). Indeed, we knew this before the New View or Any View, just as we always knew that "it may or may not rain tomorrow." The reader should note that similar statements were produced by other authors with all the appearances of meaningful elaborations.

occasion,[12] and only some crucial aspects relevant for our present purposes will be considered at this point. Various aspects of the first conjecture are examined in this and the next section. The second conjecture is examined in sections D and E.

A detailed analysis of the Gramley–Chase model demonstrates that it implies the following reduced form equations explaining the money stock (M) and bank credit (E) in terms of the extended monetary base (B^e),

$$M = g(B^e, Y, c) \quad g_1 > 0 < g_2,$$
$$E = h(B^e, Y, c) \quad h_1 > 0 > h_2, \text{ and } h_1 > g_1 {}^{13}$$

the level of economic activity expressed by national income at current prices (Y), and the ceiling rate on time deposits (c).[14]

The Gramley–Chase model implies that monetary policy does affect the money stock and bank credit. It also implies that the money stock responds *positively* and bank credit *negatively* to economic activity. This model thus differs from the Monetarist hypotheses which imply that both bank credit and the money stock respond *positively* to economic activity. The Gramley–Chase model also implies that the responses of both the money stock and bank credit to monetary actions are independent of the general scale of the public's and the banks' interest elasticities. Uniformly large or small interest elasticities yield the same response in the money stock or bank credit to a change in the monetary base.

A detailed discussion of the implications derivable from a meaningfully supplemented Gramley–Chase model is not necessary at this point. We are foremost interested in the relation between this model and the propositions mentioned in the previous paragraph. The first proposition can be interpreted in two different ways. According to one interpretation, it could mean that the marginal multipliers g_i and h_i (i = 1, 2) are functions of the banks' and the public's response patterns expressing various types of substitution relations between different assets. This interpretation is, however, quite innocuous and yields no differentiation relative to the questioned hypotheses of the Monetarist position.

A second interpretation suggests that the growth rate of the money stock is dominated by the second component (changes in income) of the differential expression:

$$\Delta M = g_1 \Delta B^e + g_2 \Delta Y$$

---

[12] The reader may consult my chapter "Federal Reserve Policy and Monetary Analysis" in *Indicators and Targets of Monetary Policy*, ed., by Karl Brunner, to be published by Chandler House Publishing Co., San Francisco. This book also contains the original article by Gramley–Chase. Further contributions by Patric H. Hendershott and Robert Weintraub survey critically the issues raised by the Gramley–Chase paper.

[13] In the Gramley–Chase model, g_3 and h_3 are indeterminant.

[14] This implication was demonstrated in my paper listed in footnote 12. The monetary base is adjusted for the accumulated sum of reserves liberated from or impounded into required reserves by changes in requirement ratios.

This result is not actually implied by the Gramley–Chase model, but it is certainly consistent with the model. However, in order to derive the desired result, their model must be supplemented with special assumptions about the relative magnitude of g_1 and g_2, and also about the comparative cyclical variability of ΔB^e and ΔY. This information has not been provided by the authors.

Most interesting is another aspect of the model which was not clarified by the authors. Their model implies that policymakers could easily avoid procyclical movements in ΔM. This model exemplifying the New View thus yields little justification for the conjectures of its proponents.

A central property of the Gramley–Chase model must be considered in the light of the progammatic statements characterizing the New View. Gramley–Chase do not differentiate between the public's asset supply to banks and the public's demand for money. This procedure violates the basic program of the New View, namely, to apply economic analysis to an array of financial assets and financial institutions. Economic analysis implies that the public's asset supply and money demand are distinct, and not identical behavior patterns. This difference in behavior patterns is clearly revealed by different responses of desired money balances and desired asset supply to specific stimuli in the environment. For instance, an increase in the expected real yield on real capital *raises* the public's asset supply but *lowers* the public's money demand. It follows thus that a central analytical feature of the Gramley–Chase model violates the basic and quite relevant program of the New View.

Kareken's construction shares this fundamental analytical flaw with the Gramley–Chase model, but this is not the only problem faced by his analysis. The Kareken analysis proceeds on two levels. First, he derives a representative bank's desired balance sheet position. For this purpose he postulates wealth maximization subject to the bank's balance sheet relation between assets and liabilities, and subject to reserve requirements on deposits. On closer examination, this analysis is only applicable to a monopoly bank with no conversion of deposits into currency or reserve flows to other banks. In order to render the analysis relevant for a representative bank in the world of reality, additional constraints would have to be introduced which modify the results quite substantially. It is also noteworthy that the structural properties assigned by Kareken to the system of market relations are logically inconsistent with the implications one can derive from the author's analysis of firm behavior developed on the first level of his investigation.

This disregard for the construction of an economic theory relevant for the real world is carried into the second level of analysis where the author formulates a system of relations describing the joint determination of interest rates, bank credit, and money stock. A remarkable feature of the Kareken model is that it yields no implications whatsoever about the response of the monetary system to actions of the Federal Reserve. It can say nothing, as it stands, about either open market operations or about discount rate and reserve requirement actions. This model literally implies, for instance, that the money stock and the banking system's deposit liabilities do not change as a result of any change in reserve requirement ratios.

None of the conjectures advanced by the countercritique concerning the behavior of the money stock and the role of monetary policy find analytical support in Kareken's analysis. To the extent that anything is implied, it would imply that monetary policy operating directly on bank reserves or a mysterious rate of return on reserves dominates the volume of deposits—a practically subversive position for a follower of the New View.[15]

C. Alternative Explanations of Cyclical Fluctuations in Monetary Growth

The examination thus far in this article has shown that even the most explicit formulation (Gramley–Chase) of the countercritique, allegedly representing the New View with respect to monetary system analysis, does assign a significant role to monetary policy. This examination also argued that the general emphasis given by the New View to the public's and the banks' behavior in determination of the money stock and bank credit does not differentiate its product from analytical developments arising from the Monetarist approach. It was also shown that the only explicit formulation advanced by the New Viewers does not provide a sufficient basis for their central conjectures. It is impossible to derive the proposition from the Gramley–Chase model that the behavior of the public and banks, rather than Federal Reserve actions, dominated movements in the money supply. But the declaration of innocence by the countercritique on behalf of the monetary authorities with respect to cyclical fluctuations of monetary growth still requires further assessment.

The detailed arguments advanced to explain the observed cyclical fluctuations of monetary growth differ substantially among the contributors to the countercritique. Gramley–Chase maintain that changing business conditions modify relative interest rates, and thus induce countercyclical movements in the time deposit ratio. These movements in

---

[15] Two direct objections made to the Brunner–Meltzer analysis by Kareken should be noted. He finds that the questioned hypotheses do not contain "a genuine supply function" of deposits. Accepting Kareken's terminology, this is true, but neither does the Gramley–Chase model contain such a supply function. But the objection has no evidential value anyway. If a hypothesis were judged unsatisfactory because some aspects are omitted, all hypotheses are "unsatisfactory." Moreover, the cognitive status of an empirical hypothesis does not improve simply because an "analytical underpinning" has been provided. Kareken also finds fault with our use of the term "money supply function." Whether or not one agrees with his terminological preferences surely does not affect the relation between observations and statements supplied by the hypothesis. And it should be clear that the status of a hypothesis depends only on this relation, and not on names attached to statements.

demand and time deposits generate cyclical fluctuations in monetary growth. On the other hand, Cacy develops an argument used many years ago by Wicksell and Keynes, but attributes it to the New View. He recognizes a pronounced sensitivity of the money stock to variations in the public's money demand or asset supply. These variations induce changes in credit market conditions. Banks, in turn, respond with suitable adjustments in the reserve and borrowing ratios. The money stock and bank credit consequently change in response to this mechanism.

Davis actually advances two radically different conjectures about causes of cyclical fluctuations of monetary growth. The first conjecture attributes fluctuations of monetary growth to the public's and banks' responses. Changing business conditions modify the currency ratio, the banks' borrowing ratio, and the reserve ratio. The resulting changes generate the observed movements in money. His other conjecture attributes fluctuations in monetary growth to Federal Reserve actions: "The state of business influences decisions by the monetary authorities to supply reserves and to take other actions likely to affect the money supply."[16]

The various conjectures advanced by Gramley–Chase, Cacy, and Davis in regard to causes of movements in money and bank credit can be classified into two groups. One set of conjectures traces the mechanism generating cyclical fluctuations of monetary growth to the responses of banks and the public; the behavior of monetary authorities is assigned a comparatively minor role. The other group of conjectures recognizes the predominant role of the behavior of monetary authorities.

In the following analysis the framework provided by the Monetarist view will be used to assess these conflicting conjectures. The emphasis concerning the nature of the causal mechanisms may differ between the various conjectures regarding sources of variations in money, but the following examination will be applied to an aspect common to all conjectures emphasizing the role of public and bank behavior.

In the context of the Monetarist framework, the money stock (M) is exhibited as a product of a multiplier (m) and the monetary base (B), (such that $M = mB$). This framework, without the supplementary set of hypotheses and theories bearing on the proximate determinants of money summarized by the multiplier and the base, is completely neutral with

---

[16] Davis, p. 66. One argument about monetary policy in the same paper requires clarification. Davis asserts on p. 68 that the money supply need not be the objective of policy, and "given this fact, the behavior of the rate of growth of the money supply during the period cannot be assumed to be simply and directly the result of monetary policy decisions alone." This quote asserts that the money supply is "simply and directly the result of policy alone" whenever policy uses the money supply as a target. This is in a sense correct. But the quote could easily be misinterpreted due to the ambiguity of the term "policy." This term is frequently used to designate a strategy guiding the adjustment of policy variables. It is also frequently used to refer to the behavior of the policy variables or directly to the variables as such. The quote is quite acceptable in the first sense of "policy," but thoroughly unacceptable in the second sense.

respect to the rival conjectures; it is compatible with any set of observations. This neutrality assures us that its use does not prejudge the issue under consideration. The Monetarist framework operates in the manner of a language system, able to express the implications of the competing conjectures in a uniform manner.

The first group of conjectures advanced by the countercritique (behavior of the public and banks dominates movements in money) implies that variations in monetary growth between upswings and downswings in business activity are dominated by the variations in the monetary multiplier. The second group (behavior of monetary authorities dominates movements in money) implies that, in periods with unchanged reserve requirement ratios and ceiling rates on time deposits, variations in the monetary base dominate cyclical changes in monetary growth. The movements of the monetary multiplier which are strictly attributable to the changing of requirement ratios can be separated from the total contribution of the multiplier and combined with the monetary base. With this adjustment, the second group of conjectures implies that the monetary base, supplemented by the contribution of reserve requirement changes to the multiplier, dominates variations in the money stock.

In this examination of contrasting explanations of monetary fluctuations, values of the money stock (M), the multiplier (m), and the monetary base adjusted for member bank borrowing (B) are measured at the initial and terminal month of each half business cycle (i.e., expansions and contractions) located by the National Bureau of Economic Research. We form the ratios of these values and write:

$$\frac{M_1}{M_0} = \frac{m_1}{m_0}\frac{B_1}{B_0}; \text{ or } \mu = \alpha\beta$$

The subscript 1 refers to values of the terminal month and the subscript 0 to values of the initial month. These ratios were measured for each half cycle in the period March 1919 to December 1966. They were computed for two definitions of the money stock, inclusive and exclusive of time deposits, with corresponding monetary multipliers.

Kendall's rank correlation coefficients between the money stock ratios (μ) and the multiplier ratios (α), and between (μ) and the monetary base ratio (β) were computed. We denote these correlation coefficients with $\rho(\mu, \alpha)$ and $\rho(\mu, \beta)$. The implications of the two rival conjectures can now be restated in terms of the two coefficients. The first group of conjectures implies that $\rho(\mu, \alpha) > \rho(\mu, \beta)$; while the second group implies that in periods of unchanged reserve requirement ratios and ceiling rates on time deposits, the coefficient $\rho(\mu, \beta)$ exceeds the coefficient $\rho(\mu, \alpha)$. The second group implies nothing about the relation of the two coefficients in periods of changing reserve requirements and ceiling rates on time deposits. It follows, therefore, that observations yielding the inequality $\rho(\mu, \beta) > \rho(\mu, \alpha)$ disconfirm the first group and confirm the second group.

The correlations obtained are quite unambiguous. The value of $\rho(\mu, \beta)$

is .537 for the whole sample period, whereas $\rho(\mu, \alpha)$ is only 0.84. The half-cycle from 1929 to 1933 was omitted in the computations, because movements in the money stock and the multiplier were dominated by forces which do not discriminate between the rival conjectures under consideration. The sample period, including 1929 to 1933, still yields a substantially larger value for $\rho(\mu, \beta)$. The same pattern also holds for other subperiods. In particular, computations based on observations for 1949 to 1966 confirm the pattern observed for the whole sample period. The results thus support the second group of conjectures but not the first group. These results also suggest, however, that forces operating through the multiplier are not quite negligible. The surprisingly small correlation $\rho(\mu, \alpha)$ does not adequately reveal the operation of these forces. Their effective operation is revealed by the correlation $\rho(\mu, \beta)$, which is far from perfect, even in subperiods with constant reserve requirement ratios. This circumstance suggests that the behavior of the public and banks contributes to the cyclical movements of monetary growth. The main result at this stage is, however, the clear discrimination between the two groups of conjectures. The results are quite unambiguous on this score.

Additional information is supplied by Table I. For each postwar cycle beginning with the downswing of 1948–49, the average annual growth rate of the money stock was computed. The expression $M = mB$ was then used to compute the contribution to the average growth rate of money from three distinct sources: (*a*) the behavior of monetary authorities (i.e., the monetary base and reserve requirement ratios), and the public's currency behavior; (*b*) the time deposit substitution process; and, (*c*) the variations in the excess reserve and borrowing ratios of commercial banks (Wicksell–Keynes mechanism).

The rank correlations between each contribution and the average growth rate of the money stock over all postwar half-cycles clearly support the conclusion of the previous analysis that cyclical movements in the money stock are dominated by Federal Reserve actions.

Table I also presents the results of a similar examination bearing on causes of movements in bank credit. The reader should note the radical difference in the observed patterns of correlation coefficients. The behavior of monetary authorities, supplemented by the public's currency behavior, does not appear to dominate the behavior of bank credit. The three sources contributing to the growth rate of money all exerted influences of similar order on bank credit. It appears that bank credit is comparatively less exposed to the push of Federal Reserve actions than was the money stock. On the other hand, the money stock is less sensitive than bank credit to the time-deposit substitution mechanism emphasized by Gramley–Chase, and the Wicksell–Keynes mechanism suggested by Cacy. Most astonishing, however, is the *negative* association between the average growth rate of bank credit and the Wicksell–Keynes mechanism emphasized by Cacy.

TABLE I

A Comparison of Alternative Contributions to the Average Annual Growth Rate of the Money Stock and Bank Credit

	Rank Correlations	
Contribution made by:	Money	Bank Credit
Public's currency and authorities' behavior	.905	.333
Time deposit substitution mechanism	.048	.381
Wicksell–Keynes mechanism	.143	−.333

REMARKS: The figures listed state the rank correlation between the average growth rate of the money stock and bank credit with three different contributing sources.

It should also be noted that the average growth rate of money conforms very clearly to the business cycle. Such conformity does not hold for bank credit over the postwar half-cycles. This blurring occurred particularly in periods when the ceiling rate on time deposits was increased. These periods exhibit relatively large contributions to the growth rate of bank credit emanating from the time deposit substitution mechanism.

A regression analysis (Table II) of the reduced form equations derived from the Gramley–Chase model confirms the central role of the monetary base in the money supply process. Estimates of the regression coefficient

TABLE II

Regressions of the Money Supply On the Monetary Base and Gross National Product*

	Regression Coefficients For:			
	Monetary Base		Gross National Product	
Cycle	First Differences	Log First Differences	First Differences	Log First Differences
IV/48 to II/53	2.03 (9.80) .92	.77 (10.02) .93	.04 (3.12) .62	.11 (3.39) .65
II/53 to III/57	1.75 (1.89) .44	.63 (1.96) .45	.02 (1.02) .26	.07 (1.23) .30
III/57 to II/60	4.59 (11.76) .97	1.66 (11.81) .97	.06 (5.10) .86	.19 (5.34) .67
II/60 to III/65	2.76 (7.56) .87	1.08 (8.54) .89	−.01 (−.33) −.08	−.03 (−.27) −.07

* The monetary base was adjusted for reserve requirement changes and shifts in deposits. All data are quarterly averages of seasonally adjusted figures. The first entry in a column for each cycle is the regression coefficient, t-statistics are in parentheses, and partial correlation coefficients are below the t-statistics.

relating money to income are highly unstable among different sample periods, relative to the coefficient relating money to the monetary base. Furthermore, estimates of regression coefficients relating money to income occur in some periods with signs which contradict the proposition of Gramley–Chase and Cacy, or exhibit a very small statistical significance. These diverse patterns of coefficients do not occur for the estimates of coefficients relating money and the monetary base. It is also noteworthy that the average growth rate of the monetary base (adjusted

TABLE III

Spectral Correlation Between the Monetary Base, Federal Reserve Credit and Other Sources of the Base

Period in Months	Monetary Base and Federal Reserve Credit	Monetary Base and Other Sources of the Base
∞	.65	.24
120	.69	.61
60	.74	.71
40	.74	.45
30	.73	.25
24	.71	.18
20	.60	.11
17.14	.43	.11
15	.51	.07
13.33	.82	.48
12	.94	.71
6	.91	.21
4	.92	—
3	.90	—

Remarks: The monetary base equals Federal Reserve Credit plus other sources of the base. The spectral analysis is based on first differences between adjacent months. The data used were not seasonally adjusted.

for changes in reserve requirement ratios), over the upswings, exceeds without exception the average growth rate of adjacent downswings. This observation is not compatible with the contention made by Gramley–Chase that policy is countercyclical.

Additional information is supplied by Table III, which presents some results of a spectral analysis bearing on the monetary base and its sources. Spectral analysis is a statistical procedure for decomposing a time series into seasonal, cyclical, and trend movements. After such an analysis was conducted on the monetary base and its sources, a form of correlation analysis was run between movements in the monetary base and movements in its various sources. The results of this procedure (Table III) indicate that movements in Federal Reserve credit dominate seasonal and cyclical movements in the monetary base.

In summary, preliminary investigations yield no support for the contention that the behavior of banks and the public dominates cyclical movements in the money stock. The conjectures advanced by Gramley–Chase or Cacy are thus disconfirmed, whereas Davis' second conjecture that fluctuations in monetary growth may be attributed to Federal Reserve actions seems substantially more appropriate. However, further investigations are certainly useful.

D. Relevance of Money and Monetary Actions With Respect to Economic Activity

At present, a broad consensus accepts the relevance of money and monetary policy with respect to economic activity. But this consensus concerning the relevance of money emerges from two substantially different views about the nature of the transmission mechanism. One view is the Keynesian conception (not to be confused with Keynes' view), enshrined in standard formulations of the income–expenditure framework. In this view, the interest rate is the main link between money and economic activity. The other view rejects the traditional separation of economic theory into parts: national income analysis (macroeconomics) and price theory (microeconomics). According to this other view, output and employment are explained by a suitable application of relative price theory. With regard to discussions of the impact of money and monetary actions on economic activity, this latter view has been termed the Monetarist position. This position may be divided into the weak Monetarist thesis and the strong Monetarist thesis. In a sense, both the New View and the Monetarist extension of the traditional view are represented in the weak Monetarist position.

The following discussions develop the weak and the strong Monetarist thesis. The weak thesis is compared with some aspects of the income–expenditure approach to the determination of national economic activity. The strong thesis supplements the weak thesis with special assumptions about our environment, in order to establish the role of monetary forces in the business cycle.

1. The Weak Monetarist Thesis. According to the weak Monetarist thesis, monetary impulses are transmitted to the economy by a relative price process which operates on money, financial assets (and liabilities), real assets, yields on assets and the production of new assets, liabilities, and consumables. The general nature of this process has been described on numerous occasions and may be interpreted as evolving from ideas developed by Knut Wicksell, Irving Fisher, and John Maynard Keynes.[17]

The operation of relative prices between money, financial assets, and real assets may be equivalently interpreted as the working of an interest

---

[17] The reader may consult the following studies on this aspect: Milton Friedman and David Meiselman, "The Relative Stability of Monetary Velocity and the Investment Multiplier in the United States, 1897–1958," in *Stabilization Policies,* prepared

rate mechanism (prices and yields of assets are inversely related). Monetary impulses are thus transmitted by the play of interest rates over a vast array of assets. Variations in interest rates change relative prices of existing assets, relative to both yields and the supply prices of new production. Acceleration or deceleration of monetary impulses are thus converted by the variation of relative prices, or interest rates, into increased or reduced production, and subsequent revisions in the supply prices of current output.

This general conception of the transmission mechanism has important implications which conflict sharply with the Keynesian interpretation of monetary mechanisms expressed by standard income–expenditure formulations.[18] In the context of standard income–expenditure analysis, fiscal actions are considered to have a "direct effect" on economic activity, whereas monetary actions are considered to have only an "indirect effect." Furthermore, a constant budget deficit has no effect on interest rates in a Keynesian framework, in spite of substantial accumulation of outstanding government debt when a budget deficit continually occurs. And lastly, the operation of interest rates on investment decisions has usually been rationalized with the aid of considerations based on the effects of borrowing costs.

These aspects of the income–expenditure approach may be evaluated within the framework of the weak Monetarist thesis. The effects of fiscal actions are also transmitted by the relative price mechanism. Fiscal impulses (i.e., government spending), taxing, and borrowing, operate just as indirectly as monetary impulses, and there is no *a priori* reason for believing that their speed of transmission is substantially greater than that of monetary impulses. The relative price conception of the transmission mechanism also implies that a constant budget deficit exerts a continuous influence on economic activity through persistent modifications in relative prices of financial and real assets. Lastly, the transmission of monetary impulses is not dominated by the relative importance of borrowing costs.

---

by the Commission on Money and Credit, Englewood Cliffs, 1963. The paper listed in footnote 21 by James Tobin should also be consulted. Harry Johnson, "Monetary Theory and Policy," *American Economic Review*, June 1962. Karl Brunner, "The Report of the Commission on Money and Credit," *The Journal of Political Economy*, December 1961. Karl Brunner, "Some Major Problems of Monetary Theory," *Proceedings of the American Economic Association*, May 1961. Karl Brunner and Allan H. Meltzer, "The Role of Financial Institutions in the Transmission Mechanism," *Proceedings of the American Economic Association*, May 1963. Karl Brunner, "The Relative Price Theory of Money, Output, and Employment," unpublished manuscript based on a paper presented at the Midwestern Economic Association Meetings, April 1967.

[18] The paper on "The Effect of Monetary Policy on Expenditures in Specific Sectors of the Economy," presented by Dr. Sherman Maisel at the meetings organized by the American Bankers Association in September 1967, exemplifies very clearly the inherited Keynesian position. The paper will be published in a special issue of the *Journal of Political Economy*.

In the process, marginal costs of liability extension interact with marginal returns from acquisitions of financial and real assets. But interest rates on financial assets not only affect the marginal cost of liability extention, but also influence the substitution between financial and real assets. This substitution modifies prices of real assets relative to their supply prices and forms a crucial linkage of the monetary mechanisms; this linkage is usually omitted in standard income–expenditure analysis.

The description of monetary mechanisms in Davis' article approaches quite closely the notion developed by the weak Monetarist thesis. This approximation permits a useful clarification of pending issues. However, the criticisms and objections advanced by Davis do not apply to the weak Monetarist position. They are addressed to another thesis, which might be usefully labeled the *strong Monetarist thesis*.

2. *The Strong Monetarist Thesis.* If the theoretical framework of the weak Monetarist thesis is supplemented with additional and special hypotheses, the *strong Monetarist thesis* is obtained. An outline of the strong thesis may be formulated in terms of three sets of forces operating simultaneously on the pace of economic activity. For convenience, they may be grouped into monetary forces, fiscal forces, and other forces. The latter include technological and organizational innovation, revisions in supply prices induced by accruing information and expectation adjustments, capital accumulation, population changes, and other related factors or processes.

All three sets of forces are acknowledged by the strong thesis to affect the pace of economic activity via the relative price process previously outlined. Moreover, the strong Monetarist point of view advances the crucial thesis that the variability of monetary forces (properly weighted with respect to their effect on economic activity) exceeds the variability of fiscal forces and other forces (properly weighted). It is argued further that major variabilities occurring in a subset of the other forces (e.g., expectations and revisions of supply prices induced by information arrival) are conditioned by the observed variability of monetary forces. The conjecture thus involves a comparison of monetary variability with the variability of fiscal forces and independent "other forces." According to the thesis under consideration, the variability of monetary impulses is also large relative to the speed at which the economy absorbs the impact of environmental changes. This predominance of variability in monetary impulses implies that pronounced accelerations in monetary forces are followed subsequently by accelerations in the pace of economic activity, and that pronounced decelerations in monetary forces are followed later by retardations in economic activity.

The analysis of the monetary dynamics, using the relative price process, is accepted by both the weak and the strong Monetarist theses. This analysis implies that the regularity of the observed association between accelerations and decelerations of monetary forces and economic activity depends on the relative magnitude of monetary accelerations (or decelerations). The same analysis also reveals the crucial role of changes in the rate of change (second differences) of the money stock in explanations of fluctuations in output and employment. It implies that any pronounced deceleration, occurring at any rate of monetary growth, retards total spending. It is thus impossible to state whether any particular monetary growth, say a 10 percent annual rate, is expansionary with respect to economic activity, until one knows the previous growth rate. The monetary dynamics of the Monetarist thesis also explains the simultaneous occurrence of permanent price-inflation and fluctuations in output and employment observable in some countries.

The nature and the variability of the "Friedman lag" may also be analyzed within the framework of the Monetarist thesis. This lag measures the interval between a change in sign of the *second* difference in the money stock and the subsequent turning point located by the National Bureau. In general, the lag at an upper turning point will be shorter, the greater the absorption speed of the economy, and the sharper the deceleration of monetary impulses relative to the movement of fiscal forces and other forces. Variability in the *relative* acceleration or deceleration of monetary forces necessarily generates the variability observed in the Friedman lag.

What evidence may be cited on behalf of the strong Monetarist thesis? Every major inflation provides support for the thesis, particularly in cases of substantial variations of monetary growth. The attempt at stabilization in the Confederacy during the Civil War forms an impressive piece of evidence in this respect. The association between monetary and economic accelerations or decelerations has also been observed by the Federal Reserve Bank of St. Louis.[19] Observations from periods with divergent movements of monetary and fiscal forces provide further evidence. For instance, such periods occurred immediately after termination of World War II, from the end of 1947 to the fall of 1948, and again in the second half of 1966. In all three cases, monetary forces prevailed over fiscal forces. The evidence adduced here and on other occasions does not "prove" the strong Monetarist thesis, but does establish its merit for serious consideration.

Davis' examination is therefore welcomed. His objections are summarized by the following points: (*a*) Observations of the persistent association between money and income do not permit an inference of causal direction from money to income; (*b*) the timing relation between money and economic activity expressed by the Friedman lag yields no evidence in support of the contention that variations in monetary growth cause fluctu-

---

[19] *U.S. Financial Data*, Federal Reserve Bank of St. Louis, week ending February 14, 1968. Also see "Money Supply and Time Deposits, 1914–1964" in the September 1964 issue of this *Review*.

ations in economic activity; (c) the correlation found in cycles of moderate amplitude between magnitudes of monetary and economic changes was quite unimpressive; (d) the length of the Friedman lag does not measure the interval between emission of monetary impulse and its ultimate impact on economic activity. Furthermore, the variability of this lag is due to the simultaneous operation and interaction of monetary and non-monetary forces.

Davis' first comment (a) is, of course, quite true and well known in the logic of science. It is impossible to derive (logically) causal statements or any general hypotheses from observations. But we can use such observations to confirm or disconfirm such statements and hypotheses. Davis particularly emphasizes that the persistent association between money and income could be attributed to a causal influence running from economic activity to money.

Indeed it could, but our present state of knowledge rejects the notion that the observed association is essentially due to a causal influence from income on money. Evidence refuting such a notion was presented in Section C. The existence of a mutual interaction over the shorter-run between money and economic activity, however, must be fully acknowledged. Yet, this interaction results from the conception guiding policymakers which induces them to accelerate the monetary base whenever pressures on interest rates mount, and to decelerate the monetary base when these pressures wane. Admission of a mutual interaction does not dispose of the strong Monetarist thesis. This interaction, inherent in the weak thesis, is quite consistent with the strong position and has no disconfirming value. To the contrary, it offers an explanation for the occurrence of the predominant variability of monetary forces.

The same logical property applies to Davis' second argument (b). The timing relation expressed by the Friedman lag, in particular the chronological precedence of turning points in monetary growth over turning points in economic activity, can probably be explained by the influence of business conditions on the money supply. Studies in money supply theory strongly suggest this thesis and yield evidence on its behalf. The cyclical pattern of the currency ratio and the strategy typically pursued by monetary policymakers explain this lead of monetary growth. And again, such explanation of the timing relation does not bear negatively on the strong conjecture.

The objection noted under Davis' point (c) is similarly irrelevant. His observations actually confirm the strong thesis. The latter implies that the correlation between amplitudes of monetary and income changes is itself correlated with the magnitude of monetary accelerations or decelerations. A poor correlation in cycles of moderate amplitude, therefore, yields no discriminating evidence on the validity of the strong thesis. Moreover, observations describing occurrences are more appropriate relative to the formulated thesis than correlation measures. For instance, observations tending to disconfirm the strong Monetarist thesis would consist of occurrences of pronounced monetary accelerations or decelerations which are *not followed* by accelerated or retarded movements of economic activity.

Point (*d*) still remains to be considered. Once again, his observation does not bear on the strong Monetarist thesis. Davis properly cautions readers about the interpretation of the Friedman lag. The variability of this lag is probably due to the interaction of monetary and non-monetary forces, or to changes from cycle to cycle in the relative variability of monetary growth. But again, this does not affect the strong thesis. The proper interpretation of the Friedman lag, as the interval between reversals in the rate of monetary impulses and their prevalence over all other factors simultaneously operating on economic activity, usefully clarifies a concept introduced into our discussions. This clarification provides, however, no relevant evidence bearing on the questioned hypotheses.

In summary, the arguments developed by Davis do not yield any substantive evidence against the strong Monetarist thesis. Moreover, the discussion omits major portions of the evidence assembled in support of this position.[20]

E. COUNTERCYCLICAL POLICY AND THE INTERPRETATION OF MONETARY POLICY

The usual assertion of the New View, attributing fluctuations of monetary growth to the public's and the banks' behavior, assumed a strategic role in the countercritique. The countercritique denied, furthermore, that monetary actions have a major impact on economic activity. With the crumbling of these two bastions, the monetary policymakers' interpretation of their own behavior becomes quite vulnerable. In a previous section, the substantial contribution of the monetary base to the fluctuations of monetary growth has been demonstrated. These facts, combined with repeated assertions that monetary policy has been largely countercyclical, suggest the existence of a pronounced discrepancy between actual behavior of the monetary authorities and their interpretation of this behavior.

A crucial question bearing on this issue pertains to the proper measure

---

[20] Milton Friedman's summary of the evidence in the *Forty-fourth Annual Report of the National Bureau of Economic Research* is important in this respect. Davis overlooks in particular the evidence accumulated in studies of the money supply mechanism which bears on the issue raised by point (*a*) in the text. A persistent and uniform association between money and economic activity, in spite of large changes in the structure of money supply processes, yields evidence in support of the Monetarist theses.

The reader should also consult Chapter 13 of the book by Milton Friedman and Anna Schwartz listed in footnote 9; *Studies in the Quantity Theory of Money*, edited by Milton Friedman, University of Chicago Press, 1956; and a doctoral dissertation by Michael W. Keran, "Monetary Policy and the Business Cycle in Postwar Japan," Ph.D. thesis at the University of Minnesota, March 1966, to be published as a chapter of a book edited by David Meiselman.

summarizing actual behavior of the monetary authorities. Two major facts should be clearly recognized. First, the monetary base consists of "money" directly issued by the authorities, and every issue of base money involves an action of the monetary authorities. This holds irrespective of their knowledge about it, or their motivation and aims. Second, variations in the base, extended by suitable adjustments to incorporate changing reserve requirement ratios, are the single most important factor influencing the behavior of the money stock. And this second point applies irrespective of whether Federal Reserve authorities are aware of it or wish it to be, or whatever their motivations or aims are. Their actual behavior, and not their motivations or aims, influences the monetary system and the pace of economic activity. Thus, actual changes in the monetary base are quite meaningful and appropriate measures of actual behavior of monetary authorities.[21]

The information presented in Table IV supports the conjecture that monetary policymakers' interpretation of their own behavior has no systematic positive association with their actual behavior. Table IV was constructed on the basis of the scores assigned to changes in policies, according to the interpretation of the Federal Open Market Committee.[22] Positive scores were associated with each session of the FOMC which decided to make policy easier, more expansionary, less restrictive, less tight, etc., and negative scores indicate decisions to follow a tighter, less expansionary, more restrictive course. The scores varied between plus and minus one, and expressed some broad ordering of the revealed magnitude of the changes.

An examination of the sequence of scores easily shows that the period covered can be naturally partitioned into subperiods exhibiting an overwhelming occurrence of scores with a uniform sign. These subperiods are listed in the first column of Table IV. The second column cumulated the scores over the subperiods listed in order to yield a very rough ranking of the policymakers' posture according to their own interpretation.

Table IV reveals that the FOMC interpreted the subperiods from August 1957 to July 1958, and from July 1959 to December 1960 as among the most expansionary policy periods. The period from November 1949 to May 1953 appears in this account as a phase of persistently tight or restrictive policy. The next two columns list the changes of two important variables during each subperiod. The third column describes

---

[21] The reader may also be assured by the following statement: ". . . monetary policy refers particularly to determination of the supply of (the government's) demand debt . . ." This demand debt coincides with the monetary base. The quote is by James Tobin, a leading architect of the New View, on p. 148 of his contribution to the Commission on Money and Credit, "An Essay on Principles of Debt Management," in *Fiscal and Debt Management Policies,* Prentice Hall, Englewood Cliffs, 1963.

[22] The scores were published as Appendix II to "An Alternative Approach to the Monetary Mechanism." See footnote 9.

TABLE IV

The Association between Policymakers' Interpretation of Policy, Changes in the Monetary Base and Changes in Free Reserves

Periods	Cumulative Scores of Policymakers' Interpretation over the Period	Changes in Free Reserves over the Period in $ Million	Changes in the Monetary Base over the Period in $ Million
11/49– 5/53	−4.75	−1030	+5216
6/53–11/54	+2.63	+ 286	+1321
12/54–10/55	−3.37	− 818	+ 345
11/55– 7/56	+1.12	+ 352	+ 399
8/56– 7/57	−1.00	− 44	+ 657
8/57– 7/58	+3.50	+1017	+1203
7/58– 6/59	−2.12	−1059	+ 531
7/59–12/60	+2.62	+1239	− 53
1/61–12/62	− .63	− 428	+3288

changes in free reserves, and the fourth column notes changes in the monetary base. A cursory examination of the columns immediately shows substantial differences in their broad association. The rank correlation between the various columns is most informative for our purposes.

These rank correlations are listed in Table V. The results expose the absence of any positive association between the policymakers' own interpretation or judgment of their stance and their actual behavior, as indicated by movements in the monetary base. The correlation coefficient between the monetary base and cumulated scores has a *negative* value, suggesting that a systematic divergence between stated and actual policy (as measured by the monetary base) is probable. On the other hand, the correlation between the policymakers' descriptions of their posture, and the movement of free reserves, is impressively close. This correlation confirms once again that the Federal Reserve authorities have traditionally used the volume of free reserves as an indicator to gauge and interpret prevailing monetary policies. Yet little evidence has been developed which establishes a causal chain leading from changes in free reserves to the pace of economic activity.

Another observation contained in Table IV bears on the issue of policymakers' interpretation of their own behavior. Changes in the cumulated scores and free reserves between the periods listed always move

TABLE V

Rank Correlation Between Changes in the Monetary Base, Changes in Free Reserves and the Cumulated Scores of Policymakers' Interpretations

Cumulated scores and base	−.09
Cumulated scores and free reserves	+.70
Free reserves and base	−.26

together and are perfect in terms of direction. By comparison, the co-movement between cumulated scores and changes in the monetary base is quite haphazard; only three out of eight changes between periods move together. This degree of co-movement between cumulated scores and the monetary base could have occurred by pure chance with a probability greater than .2, whereas the probability of the perfect co-movement between cumulated scores and free reserves occurring as a matter of pure chance is less than .004. The traditional selection of free reserves or money market conditions as an indicator to interpret prevailing monetary policy and to gauge the relative thrust applied by policy, forms the major reason for the negative association (or at least random association) between stated and actual policy.

Attempts at rebuttal to the above analysis often emphasize that policy-makers are neither interested in the monetary base, nor do they attach any significance to it. This argument is advanced to support the claim that the behavior of the monetary base is irrelevant for a proper examination of policymakers' intended behavior. This argument disregards, however, the facts stated earlier, namely, movements in the monetary base are under the direct control and are the sole responsibility of the monetary authorities. It also disregards the fact that actions may yield consequences which are independent of motivations shaping the actions.

These considerations are sufficient to acknowledge the relevance of the monetary base as a measure summarizing the actual behavior of monetary authorities. However, they alone are not sufficient to determine whether the base is the most reliable indicator of monetary policy. Other magnitudes, such as interest rates, bank credit, and free reserves, have been advanced with plausible arguments to serve as indicators. A rational procedure must be designed to determine which of the possible entities frequently used for scaling policy yields the most reliable results.

This indicator problem is still very poorly understood, mainly because of ambiguous use of economic language in most discussions of monetary policy. The term "indicator" occurs with a variety of meanings in discussions, and so do the terms "target" and "guide." The indicator problem, understood in its technical sense, is the determination of an optimal scale justifying interpretations of the authorities' actual behavior by means of comparative statements. A typical statement is that policy X is more expansionary than policy Y, or that current policy has become more (or less) expansionary. Whenever we use a comparative concept, we implicitly rely on an ordering scale.

The indicator problem has not been given adequate treatment in the literature, and the recognition of its logical structure is often obstructed by inadequate analysis. It is, for instance, not sufficient to emphasize the proposition that the money supply can be a "misleading guide to the proper interpretation of monetary policy." This proposition can be easily demonstrated for a wide variety of models and hypotheses. However, it establishes very little. The same theories usually demonstrate that the rate of interest, free reserves, or bank credit can also be very misleading guides to monetary policy. Thus, we can obtain a series of propositions about a vast array of entities, asserting that each one can be a very misleading guide to the interpretation of policy. We only reach a useless stalemate in this situation.

The usual solution to the indicator problem at the present time is a decision based on mystical insight supplemented by some impressionistic arguments. The most frequently advanced arguments emphasize that central banks operate directly on credit markets where interest rates are formed, or that the interest mechanism forms the centerpiece of the transmission process. Accordingly, in both cases market interest rates should obviously emerge as the relevant indicator of monetary policy.

These arguments on behalf of market interest rates are mostly supplied by economists. The monetary authorities' choice of money market conditions as an indicator evolved from a different background. But in recent years a subtle change has occurred. One frequently encounters arguments which essentially deny either the existence of the indicator problem or its rational solution. A favorite line asserts that "the world is very complex" and, consequently, it is impossible or inadmissible to use a single scale to interpret policy. According to this view, one has to consider and weigh many things in order to obtain a realistic assessment in a complicated world.

This position has little merit. The objection to a "single scale" misconstrues the very nature of the problem. Once we decide to discuss monetary policy in terms of comparative statements, an ordinal scale is required in order to provide a logical basis for such statements. A multiplicity of scales effectively eliminates the use of comparative statements. Of course, a single scale may be a function of multiple arguments, but such multiplicity of arguments should not be confused with a multiplicity of scales. Policymakers and economists should therefore realize that one either provides a rational procedure which justifies interpretations of monetary policy by means of comparative statements, or that one abandons any pretense of meaningful or intellectually honest discussion of such policy.

Solution of the indicator problem in the technical sense appears obstructed on occasion by a prevalent confusion with an entirely different problem confronting the central banker—the target problem. This problem results from the prevailing uncertainty concerning the nature of the transmission mechanism and the substantial lags in the dynamics of monetary processes.

In the context of perfect information, the indicator problem becomes trivial and the target problem vanishes. But perfect information is the privilege of economists' discourse on policy; central bankers cannot afford this luxury. The impact of their actions are both delayed and uncertain. Moreover, the ultimate goals of monetary policy (targets in the

Tinbergen–Theil sense) appear remote to the manager executing general policy directives. Policymakers will be inclined under these circumstances to insert a more immediate target between their ultimate goals and their actions. These targets should be reliably observable with a minimal lag.

It is quite understandable that central bankers traditionally use various measures of money market conditions, with somewhat shifting weights, as a target guiding the continuous adjustment of their policy variables. This response to the uncertainties and lags in the dynamics of the monetary mechanism is very rational indeed. However, once we recognize the rationality of such behavior, we should also consider the rationality of using a particular target. The choice of a target still remains a problem, and the very nature of this problem is inadequately understood at this state.

This is not the place to examine the indicator and target problem in detail. A possible solution to both problems has been developed on another occasion.[23] The solutions apply decision theoretic procedures and concepts from control theory to the determination of an optimal choice of both indicator and target. Both problems are in principle solvable, in spite of the "complexity of the world." Consequently, there is little excuse for failing to develop rational monetary policy procedures.

CONCLUSION

A program for applying economic analysis to financial markets and financial institutions is certainly acceptable and worth pursuing. This program suggests that the public and banks interact in the determination of bank credit, interest rates, and the money stock, in response to the behavior of monetary authorities. But the recognition of such interaction implies nothing with respect to the relative importance of the causal forces generating cyclical fluctuations of monetary growth. Neither does it bear on the quality of alternative empirical hypotheses, or the relative usefulness of various magnitudes or conditions which might be proposed as an indicator to judge the actual thrust applied by monetary policy to the pace of economic activity.

The Monetarist thesis has been put forth in the form of well structured hypotheses which are supported by empirical evidence. This extensive research in the area of monetary policy has established that: (*a*) Federal Reserve actions dominate the movement of the monetary base over time; (*b*) movements of the monetary base dominate movements of the money supply over the business cycle; and, (*c*) accelerations or decelerations of the money supply are closely followed by accelerations or decelerations in economic activity. Therefore, the Monetarist thesis puts forth the

---

[23] The reader may consult the chapter by Karl Brunner and Allan H. Meltzer on "Targets and Indicators of Monetary Policy," in the book of the same title, edited by Karl Brunner. The book will be published by Chandler House Publishing Co., Belmont, California.

proposition that actions of the Federal Reserve are transmitted to economic activity via the resulting movements in the monetary base and money supply, which initiate the adjustments in relative prices of assets, liabilities, and the production of new assets.

The New View, as put forth by the countercritique, has offered thus far neither analysis nor evidence pertaining relevantly to an explanation of variations in monetary growth. Moreover, the countercritique has not developed, on acceptable logical grounds, a systematic justification for the abundant supply of statements characterizing policy in terms of its effects on the economy. Nor has it developed a systematic justification for the choice of money market conditions as an optimal target guiding the execution of open market operations.

But rational policy procedures require both a reliable interpretation and an adequate determination of the course of policy. The necessary conditions for rational policy are certainly not satisfied if policies actually retarding economic activity are viewed to be expansionary, as in the case of the 1960–61 recession, or, if inflationary actions are viewed as being restrictive, as in the first half of 1966.

The major questions addressed to our monetary policymakers, their advisors and consultants remain: How do you justify your interpretation of policy, and how do you actually explain the fluctuations of monetary growth? The major contentions of the academic critics of the past performance of monetary authorities could possibly be quite false, but this should be demonstrated by appropriate analysis and relevant evidence.

17
THE ROLE OF THE MONEY SUPPLY IN BUSINESS CYCLES*

Richard G. Davis

Most, if not quite all, economists are agreed that the behavior of the quantity of money makes a significant difference in the behavior of the economy—with "money" usually defined to include currency in circulation plus private demand deposits, but sometimes to include commercial bank time deposits as well.[1] Most economists, for example, setting out to forecast next year's gross national product under the assumption that the money supply would grow by 4 percent, would probably want to revise their figures if they were to change this assumption to a 2 percent decrease.

In the past five to ten years, however, there has come into increasing prominence a group of economists who would like to go considerably beyond the simple assertion that the behavior of money is a significant factor influencing the behavior of the economy. It is not easy to characterize with any precision the views of this group of economists. As is perhaps to be expected where complex issues are involved, their statements about the importance of monetary behavior in determining the course of business activity encompass a variety of individual positions, positions which may themselves be undergoing change. Moreover these positions are rarely stated in quantitative terms. More frequently, the importance of money as a determinant of business conditions will be characterized as "by far the major factor," "the most important factor," "a primary factor," and by similar qualitative phrases inescapably open to various interpretations.

Of course as one moves from the stronger phrases to the weaker, one comes closer and closer to the view that money is simply "a significant factor," at which point it becomes virtually impossible to distinguish their views from those of the great majority of professional opinions. In order to bring a few of the issues into sharper focus, this article will take a look

---

* Reprinted by permission of the *Monthly Review* of the Federal Reserve Bank of New York (April 1968).

[1] More rarely, other types of liquid assets, such as mutual savings bank deposits, are also included in the definition of money.

at some evidence for the "money supply" view of business fluctuations in one of its more extreme forms. Without necessarily implying that all the following positions are held precisely as stated by any single economist, an extreme form of the money supply view can perhaps be characterized somewhat as follows: The behavior of the rate of change of the money supply is the overriding determinant of fluctuations in business activity. Government spending, taxing policies, fluctuations in the rate of technological innovation, and similar matters have a relatively small or even negligible influence on the short-run course of business activity. Hence, to the extent that it can control the money supply, a central bank, such as the Federal Reserve System, can control ups and downs in business activity. The influence of money on business operates with a long lag, however, and the timing of the influence is highly variable and unpredictable. Thus, attempts to moderate fluctuations in business activity by varying the rate of growth of the money supply are likely to have an uncertain effect after an uncertain lag. They may even backfire, producing the very instability they are designed to cure. Consequently, the best policy for a central bank to follow is to maintain a steady rate of growth in the money supply, year in and year out, at a rate which corresponds roughly to the growth in the economy's productive capacity.

The implications of these views are obviously both highly important and strongly at variance with widely held beliefs. Thus, they deny the direct importance of fiscal policy (except perhaps in so far as it may influence monetary policy), while they attribute to monetary policy a virtually determining role as regards business fluctuations. At the same time, they deny the usefulness of discretionary, countercyclical monetary policy. The issues involved are highly complex and cannot possibly be adequately treated in their entirety in a single article.[2] The present article, therefore, confines itself to examining the historical relationship between monetary cycles and cycles in general business. The article concludes that the relationship between these two kinds of cycles does not, in fact, provide any real support for the view that the behavior of money is the predominant determinant of fluctuations in business activity. Moreover, the historical relationship between cycles in money and in business cannot be used to demonstrate that monetary policy is, in its effects, so long delayed and so uncertain as to be an unsatisfactory countercyclical weapon.

The first section shows how proponents of the money supply view have measured cycles in money and examines the persistent tendency of turning points in monetary cycles, so measured, to lead turning points in general business activity. It argues that these leads do not necessarily point

---

[2] Among the many interesting and relevant issues not discussed are the advantages and disadvantages of the money supply as an immediate target of monetary policy or as an indicator of the effects of policy, the proper definition of the money supply, and the nature and stability of the demand for money.

to a predominant causal influence of money on business. A second section suggests that the cyclical relationship of money and business activity may be as much a reflection of a reverse influence of business on money as it is of a direct causal influence running from money to business. A third section indicates why, for some periods at least, the tendency for cycles in money to lead cycles in business may reflect nothing more than the impact on money of a countercyclical monetary policy. Next, the relative amplitudes of monetary contractions and their associated business contractions are examined. Again it is argued that these relative amplitudes fail to provide any clear evidence for a predominant causal influence of money. A fifth section examines the timing of turning points in money and in business for evidence that the influence of money operates with so long and variable a lag as to make countercyclical monetary policy ineffective. A final section suggests that there may well be better ways to evaluate the causal influence of money on business than through the examination of past cyclical patterns.

CYCLES IN MONEY AND CYCLES IN BUSINESS ACTIVITY

As already implied, proponents of the money supply school have argued that the historical relationship between cycles in money and cycles in general business activity provides major support for their views on the causal importance of money in the business cycle. For the most part, these economists have delineated cycles in the money supply in terms of peaks and troughs in the percentage rate of change of money (usually including time deposits), while cycles in business have been defined in terms of peaks and troughs in the *level* of business activity as marked off, for instance, by the so-called "reference cycles" of the National Bureau of Economic Research (NBER).[3] They have argued that virtually without exception every cycle in the level of business activity over the past century of United States experience can be associated with a cycle in the rate of growth of the money supply. The exceptions that are observed occurred during and just after World War II—although the events of 1966–67 may also be interpreted as an exception, since an apparent cyclical decline in monetary growth was not followed by a recession but only by a very brief slowdown in the rate of business expansion.[4] The money

---

[3] See, for example, Milton Friedman and Anna J. Schwartz, "Money and Business Cycles," *Review of Economics and Statistics* (February 1963, supplement), pp. 34–38. While the procedure of these economists in comparing percentage rates of growth of money with levels of business activity can certainly be defended, it is by no means obvious that this is the most appropriate approach, and there are many possible alternatives. Thus, for example, cycles in the rate of growth of money could be compared with cycles in the rate of growth, rather than the level, of business activity. For some purposes the choice among these alternatives makes a considerable difference, as is noted later in connection with measuring the length of the lags of business-cycle turning points relative to turning points in the monetary cycle.

[4] Granting the difficulties of dating specific cycle turning points for series as erratic as the rate of growth of the money supply, a peak (for the definition of

supply school also finds that cycles in business activity have lagged behind the corresponding cycles in the rate of growth of the money supply, with business peaks and troughs thus following peaks and troughs in the rate of monetary change.

While the evidence supporting these generalizations is derived from about a century of United States data, the nature of the measurements and some of the problems of interpretation can be illustrated from the postwar experience represented in Chart I. The chart shows monthly percentage changes in the money supply, defined here to include currency in the hands of the public plus commercial bank private demand and time deposits, on a seasonally adjusted daily average basis.[5] The shaded areas represent periods of business recession as determined by the NBER. The first point to note is the highly erratic nature of month-to-month movements in the rate of change of the money supply. Indeed, the reader might be excused if he found it difficult to see any clear-cut cyclical pattern in the chart. The erratic nature of the money series, which partly reflects short-run shifts of deposits between Treasury and private accounts, does make the precise dating of peaks and troughs in the money series somewhat arbitrary. This introduces a corresponding degree of arbitrariness in measuring timing relationships relative to turning points in business activity. Waiving this difficulty, however, peaks and troughs in the money series as dated in one well-known study of the problem are marked on the chart for the 1947-60 period.[6] As can be seen, each monetary peak occurs during the expansion phase of the business cycle and thus leads the peak in business. Similarly, there is a monetary trough marked during three of the four postwar recessions acknowledged by the NBER. A fourth monetary trough, however, in February 1960 occurs somewhat before the onset of recession three months later.

The leads of the peaks in the money series with respect to the subse-

---

money that includes time deposits) seems to have occurred in October 1965, with a trough in October 1966. While there was a slowdown in the rate of growth of business activity in the first half of 1967, there was clearly no business cycle peak corresponding to the peak in the money series. Indeed, the current dollar value of GNP moved ahead in the first two quarters of 1967, although at a reduced rate. The 1965-66 decline in the rate of growth in the money supply was relatively short (twelve months). In amplitude it was clearly among the milder declines, but it was nevertheless still nearly twice as steep as the mildest of past contractions in the rate of monetary growth (November 1951 to September 1953). In any case, the 1965-66 decline does appear to represent a specific cycle contraction for the rate of monetary change under the standard NBER definition. See Arthur F. Burns and Wesley C. Mitchell, *Measuring Business Cycles* (National Bureau of Economic Research, 1946), pp. 55-66.

[5] While, as noted, many analysts would prefer to define the money supply to exclude commercial bank time deposits, such an exclusion would not materially affect the general picture, at least not for the period illustrated by the chart.

[6] The dates used are essentially those presented in Milton Friedman and Anna J. Schwartz *op. cit.*, p. 37, Table I. Minor modifications of the Friedman-Schwartz dates have been made when these seemed obviously dictated by revisions in the data subsequent to publication of their work.

CHART I

CHANGES IN MONEY SUPPLY PLUS TIME DEPOSITS
(Month-to-Month Percentage Changes; Compound Annual Rates)

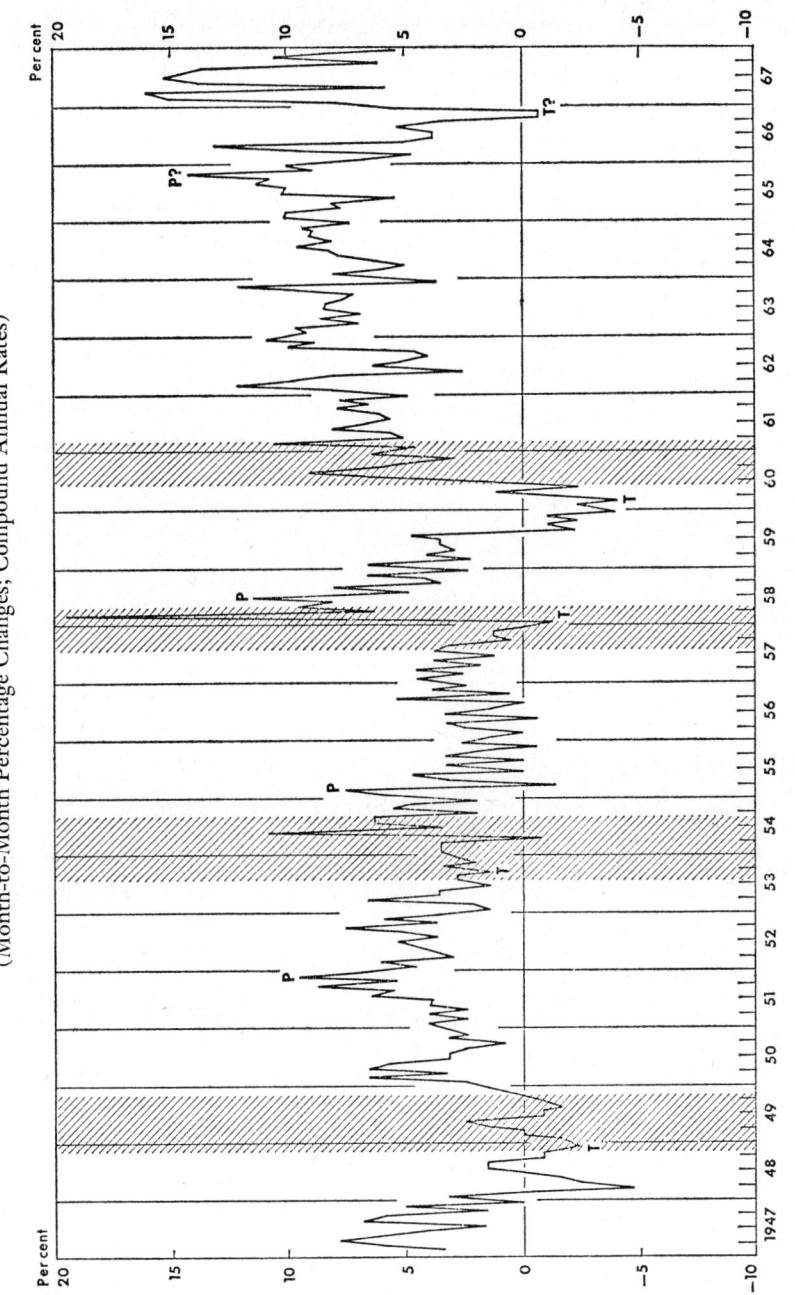

NOTE: Percentage changes are based on seasonally adjusted data. Shaded areas represent recession periods, according to National Bureau of Economic Research chronology.
SOURCE: Board of Governors of the Federal Reserve System.

quent peaks in business activity are, it should be emphasized, quite variable, ranging from 20 months to 29 months for the period covered in the chart and from 6 months to 29 months for the entire 1870 to 1961 period. The corresponding range of leads of money troughs relative to subsequent troughs in business cycles varies from 3 months to 12 months for the charted period and up to 22 months for the longer period.

The significance, if any, of these leads in assessing the importance of cycles in money in causing cycles in business is highly problematical. Firstly, chronological leads do not, of course, necessarily imply causation. It is perfectly possible, for example, to construct models of the economy in which money has *no* influence on business but which generate a consistent lead of peaks and troughs in the rate of growth of the money supply relative to peaks and troughs in general business activity.[7] Secondly, the extreme variability of the length of the leads would seem to suggest, if anything, the existence of factors other than money that can also exert an important influence on the timing of business peaks and troughs. Certainly even if a peak or trough in the rate of growth of the money supply could be identified around the time it occurred, this would be of very little, if any, help in predicting the timing of a subsequent peak or trough in business activity. Thirdly, there is a real question as to whether anything at all can be inferred from the historical record about the influence of money on business if, as is argued in the next section, there is an important reverse influence exerted by the business cycle on the monetary cycle itself.

THE INFLUENCE OF BUSINESS ON MONEY

Although the persistent tendency of cycles in monetary growth rates to lead business activity does not, as noted, necessarily imply a predominant causal influence of money on business, this tendency has nevertheless seemed to the money supply economists to be highly suggestive of such an influence. Certainly the consistency with which these leads show up in cycle after cycle is rather striking and does suggest that cycles in money and cycles in business are related by some mechanism, however loose and unreliable. Nevertheless, it is important to recognize that this mechanism need not consist entirely or even mainly of a causal influence of money on business. It might, instead, reflect principally a causal influence of business on money, or it could reflect a complex relationship of mutual interaction. As noted earlier, virtually all economists believe that there is, in fact, at least *some* causal influence of money on business, and it may be that this influence alone is enough to explain the existence of some degree of consistency, albeit a loose one, in the timing relationships of peaks and troughs in business and money. However, the existence of a powerful

---

[7] See James Tobin, "Money and Income: Post Hoc Propter Hoc?," to be published.

reverse influence of the business cycle itself on the monetary cycle would have important implications. By helping to explain the timing relationships of the money and business cycles, the existence of such an influence would certainly tend to question severely any presumption that these timing relationships are themselves evidence for money as the predominant cause of business cycles.

There are, in fact, a number of important ways in which changing business conditions can affect, and apparently have affected, the rate of growth of the money supply over the 100 years or so covered by the available data. First, the state of business influences decisions by the monetary authorities to supply reserves and to take other actions likely to affect the money supply—as is discussed in detail in the next section. Business conditions can also have a direct impact on the money supply, however. For example, they may affect the balance of payments and the size of gold imports or exports. These gold movements, in turn, may affect the size of the monetary base—the sum of currency in the hands of the public and reserves in the banking system. Various official policies have tended to reduce or offset this particular influence of business on money, but at least prior to the creation of the Federal Reserve System it may have been of considerable significance.

Second, business conditions may influence the money stock through an influence on the volume of member bank borrowings at the Federal Reserve. While the size of such borrowings is, of course, importantly conditioned by the terms under which loans to member banks are made, including the level of the discount rate, it may also be significantly affected by the strength of loan demand and by the yields that banks can obtain on earning assets. These matters, in turn, are clearly related in part to the state of business activity.

A third influence of business on money operates through the effects of business on the ratio of the public's holdings of coin and currency to its holdings of bank deposits. A rise in this ratio, for example, tends to drain reserves from banks as the public withdraws coin and currency. Since one dollar of reserves supports several dollars of deposits, the loss of reserves leads to a multiple contraction of deposits which depresses the total money supply by more than it is increased through the rise in the public's holdings of cash. While no one is very sure as to just what determines the cyclical pattern of the currency ratio, a pattern does seem to exist which in some way reflects shifts in the composition of payments over the business cycle as well as, in the historically important case of banking panics, fluctuations in the public's confidence in the banks themselves.[8]

---

[8] It might be noted that while the Federal Reserve has for many years routinely offset the reserve effects of short-term movements in coin and currency, such as occur around holidays, for example, the ratio of coin and currency in the hands of the public to deposits has apparently continued to show some mild fluctuations of a cyclical nature.

A final avenue of influence of business on money is through the influence of business conditions on the ratio of bank excess reserves to deposits. When the ratio of excess reserves to deposits is relatively high, other things equal, the money supply will be relatively low since banks will not be fully utilizing the deposit-creating potential of the supply of reserves available to them. Business conditions can affect the reserve ratio in various ways. Thus, they can influence bank desires to hold excess reserves through variations in the strength of current and prospective loan demand, through variations in the yields on the earning assets of banks, and through variations in banker expectations. When business is rising, loan demand is apt to be strengthening, yields on earning assets are apt to be rising, and banker confidence in the future is likely to be increasing. Thus, excess reserves are apt to decline, with the reserve ratio rising and thereby exerting an upward influence on the money supply.

The influence of business on money—acting through its influence on the growth of the monetary base, the currency ratio, and the excess reserve ratio—is extremely complex and is not necessarily stable over time. The cyclical behavior of the monetary base and the currency and reserve ratios have in fact varied from cycle to cycle. Moreover the relative importance of these three factors in influencing the cyclical behavior of money has varied over the near 100-year period for which data are available. In part, these variations have reflected the effects of the creation and evolution of the Federal Reserve System. A detailed examination of the behavior of the monetary base, the currency and reserve ratios, and the role of business conditions in fixing their cyclical patterns is beyond the scope of this article. Recently, however, a very thorough analysis of the problem has been done for the NBER by Professor Phillip Cagan of Columbia University. He finds that "although the cyclical behavior of the three determinants [of the money stock] is not easy to interpret, it seems safe to conclude that most of their short-run variations are closely related to cyclical fluctuations in economic activity. . . . Such effects provide a plausible explanation of recurring cycles in the money stock whether or not the reverse effect occurred."[9]

The fact that the business cycle itself has an important role in determining the course of the monetary cycle seriously undermines the argument that the timing relationships of monetary cycles and business cycles point to a dominant influence of money on business. By the same token, ample room is left for the possibility that many other factors, such as fiscal policy, fluctuations in business investment demand, including those related to changes in technology, fluctuation in exports, and replacement cycles

---

[9] Phillip Cagan, *Determinants and Effects of Changes in the Stock of Money, 1875–1960* (National Bureau of Economic Research, 1965), p. 261.

in consumer durable goods, may also exert important independent influences on the course of business activity.

MONETARY POLICY AND THE CYCLICAL BEHAVIOR OF MONEY

One important, though perhaps indirect, influence of business on money requires special mention, namely the influence it exerts via monetary policy. The relevance of monetary policy to the behavior of monetary growth during the business cycle was perhaps especially clear during the period beginning around 1952 and extending to the very early 1960's. In this period, policy was more or less able to concentrate on the requirements of stabilizing the business cycle relatively (but not entirely) unimpeded by considerations of war finance, the balance of payments, and possible strains on particular sectors of the capital markets. The ultimate aim of stabilizing the business cycle is, of course, to prevent or moderate recessions and to forestall or limit inflation and structural imbalances during periods of advance. The tools available to the Federal Reserve, however, such as open market operations and discount rate policy, influence employment and the price level only through complex and indirect routes. Hence, in the short run, policy must be formulated in terms of variables which respond more directly to the influence of the System. Some possibilities include, in addition to the rate of growth of the money supply, the growth of bank credit, conditions in the money market and the behavior of short-term interest rates, and the marginal reserve position of banks as measured, for example, by the level of free reserves of member bank borrowings from the Federal Reserve. It is clear that the money supply need not always be the immediate objective of monetary policy, and indeed it was not by any means always such during the 1950's. Given this fact, the behavior of the rate of growth of the money supply during the period cannot be assumed to be simply and directly the result of monetary policy decisions alone.

Nevertheless, it is clear that the current and prospective behavior of business strongly influenced monetary policy decisions, given the primary aim of moderating the cycle, and that these decisions, in turn, influenced the behavior of the rate of growth of the money supply. Thus, for example, as recoveries proceeded and threatened to generate inflationary pressures, monetary policy tightened to counteract these pressures. Regardless of what particular variable the System sought to control—whether the money supply itself, conditions in the money market, or bank marginal reserve positions—the movement of any of these variables in the direction of tightening would, taken by itself, tend to exert a slowing influence on the rate of monetary expansion. In this way, the firming of monetary policy in the presence of cumulating expansionary forces would no doubt help to explain the tendency of the rate of monetary growth to peak out well in advance of peaks in the business cycle. Similarly, the easing of policy to counteract a developing recession would help to produce an upturn in the rate of monetary growth in advance of troughs in business activity.

In addition to the feedback from business conditions to policy decisions and thence from policy to the money supply, there are circumstances in which developments in the economy can react on the money supply even with monetary policy unchanged. Consider, for example, a situation in which the focus of policy is on maintaining an unchanged money market "tone"—a phrase that has been interpreted to imply, among other things, some rough stabilization of the average level of certain short-term interest rates, such as the rate on Federal funds. Now a speedup in the rate of growth in economic activity would ordinarily accelerate the growth of demand for bank credit and deposits. This, in turn, would normally result in upward pressure on the money market and on money market interest rates. Maintaining the stability in money market tone called for by such a policy would require, however, under the assumed circumstances, supplying more reserves to the banks in order to offset the upward pressures on money market rates. Thus, with unchanged policy, an acceleration in the rate of business expansion could generate an acceleration in the rate of growth of reserves, and thence in the money supply. Similarly, a tapering-off in the rate of business expansion could, in these circumstances, generate a tapering-off in the rate of monetary expansion well before an absolute peak in business activity occurred. It should be emphasized that unchanged monetary policy could be perfectly consistent with countercyclical objectives under these conditions if the slowdown (or speedup) in the rate of business advance either were expected to be temporary or were regarded as a healthy development.

The reaction of monetary policy to changing business conditions and the reaction of the money supply to monetary policy undoubtedly help explain the tendency of peaks and troughs in the rate of growth of the money supply to precede peaks and troughs in the level of economic activity during this period. The resulting monetary leads, however, cannot then be interpreted as demonstrating a dependence of cycles in business on cycles in monetary growth. These leads would very likely have existed even if the influence of money on business were altogether negligible.

SEVERITY OF CYCLICAL MOVEMENTS

Apart from matters of cyclical timing, some proponents of the money supply school have also regarded the relationship between the severity of cyclical movements in money and the severity of associated cyclical movements in business as suggesting a predominant causal role for money. They argue, perhaps with some plausibility, that, if the behavior of money were the predominant determinant of business fluctuations, the relative sizes of cyclical movements in business and roughly contemporaneous cyclical movements in money should be highly correlated. For example, the severity of a cyclical decline in the rate of growth of the money supply should be closely related to the severity of the associated business recession or depression. The evidence for such a correlation, however, is actually rather mixed.

Cyclical contractions in the monetary growth rate can be measured by computing the decline in the rate of monetary growth from its peak value to its trough value.[10] On the basis of these computations, monetary contractions can be ranked in order of severity. Similarly, the severity of business contractions can be ranked by choosing some index of business activity and computing its decline during each business contraction recognized and dated by the NBER. If the resulting rankings of monetary contractions are compared with the rankings of their associated business declines for 18 nonwar business contractions from 1882 to 1961, the size of monetary and business contractions proves to be moderately highly correlated.[11] It turns out, however, that this correlation depends entirely on the experience of especially severe cyclical contractions. Among the 18 business contractions experienced during the period, six are generally recognized as having been particularly deep. They include three pre-World War I episodes and the contractions of 1920–21, 1929–33, and 1937–38. In the latter three declines, the Federal Reserve Board's industrial production index fell by 32 percent, 52 percent, and 32 percent, respectively, compared with a decline of only 18 percent for the next largest contraction covered by the production index (1923–24).

These six most severe contractions were in fact associated with the six most severe cyclical declines in the rate of growth of the money supply, though the rankings within the six do not correspond exactly. As was argued earlier, business conditions themselves exert a reverse influence on the money supply, and it seems probable that particularly severe business declines may tend to accentuate the accompanying monetary contractions. Thus, for example, the wholesale default of loans and sharp drops in the value of securities that accompanied the 1929–33 depression helped lay the groundwork for the widespread bank failures of that period. These failures were in part caused by, but also further encouraged, large withdrawals of currency from the banking system by a frightened public. By

---

[10] Generally, three-month averages centered on the specific cycle turning point months have been used to reduce the weight given to especially sharp changes in the peak and trough months themselves.

[11] The Spearman rank correlation, for which satisfactory significance tests apparently do not exist when medium-sized samples ($10 < n < 20$) are involved, is .70. The Kendall rank correlation coefficient, adjusted for ties, is .53 and is significant at the 1 percent level. Rankings of business contractions are based on the Moore index. See Friedman and Schwartz, *op. cit.*, Table 3, p. 39.

contracting the reserve base of the banking system, in turn, these withdrawals results in multiple contractions of the deposit component of the money supply.

Developments of this type help to explain the association of major monetary contractions with major depressions but do not seem to account fully for it.[12] Thus, it may be that catastrophic monetary developments are in fact a precondition for catastrophic declines in business activity. In any case, for more moderate cyclical movements, the association between the severity of monetary contractions and the severity of business contractions breaks down completely. There is virtually no correlation whatever between the relative rankings of the 12 nonmajor contractions in the 1882–1961 period and the rankings of the associated declines in the rate of monetary growth.[13] Certainly this finding does not support the theory that changes in the rate of monetary growth are of predominant importance in determining business activity.

MEASURING LAGS IN THE INFLUENCE OF MONEY ON BUSINESS

Despite their belief in the crucial role of the money supply in determining the cyclical course of business activity, some members of the money supply school nevertheless argue, as suggested at the beginning of this article, that discretionary monetary policy is a clumsy and even dangerous countercyclical weapon. The starting point for this view is again the fact that peaks and troughs in the level of business activity tend to lag behind peaks and troughs in the rate of change of the money supply—in particular, the fact that these lags have tended to be quite long on average and highly variable from one cycle to another. Thus, long average lags of about 16 months for peaks and 12 months for troughs have suggested to these economists that the impact of monetary policy is correspondingly delayed, with actions taken to moderate a boom, for example, having their primary impact during the subsequent recession when precisely the opposite influence is needed. Moreover, the great variability from cycle to cycle of the lags as measured by the money supply school has suggested that the timing of the impact of monetary policy is similarly variable and unpredictable. For this reason, they argue, it will be impossible for the monetary authorities to gauge when their policy actions will take effect and therefore whether these actions will turn out to have been appropriate.

It is true, of course, that monetary policy affects the economy with a lag. The full effects of open market purchases on bank deposits and credit, for example, require time to work themselves out. More important, additional time must elapse before businessmen and consumers adjust their spending plans to the resulting changes in the financial environment. For

---

[12] See Phillip Cagan, *op. cit.*, pp. 262–68.

[13] The Kendall coefficient for the 12 nonmajor contractions is a statistically insignificant .03, while the corresponding Spearman coefficient is .01.

this reason, the pattern of spending at any given time will to some degree reflect the influence of financial conditions as they existed several months or quarters earlier. Hence, it is certainly possible, for example, that some of the effects of a restrictive monetary policy could continue to be felt during a recession even though the current posture of monetary policy were quite expansionary.

The fact that such lags do exist, however, shows only that monetary policy cannot be expected to produce immediate results. Like fiscal policy, its effectiveness depends in part on the ability to anticipate business trends so that policy actions taken today will be appropriate to tomorrow's conditions. Of course, the longer the lags in the effects of policy prove to be, the further out in time must such anticipations be carried and the greater is the risk that policy actions will prove to be inappropriate. Moreover, if the lengths of the lags are highly variable and thus perhaps unpredictable, the risks of inappropriate policy decisions are obviously increased and the need for continuous adjustments in policy is apt to arise.

The timing of cycles in money and cycles in business, however, provides absolutely no basis for believing that the lags in the effects of monetary policy are so long or so variable as to vitiate the effectiveness of a countercyclical policy. First, there are many reasons for doubting that the lag in the effects of monetary policy should be measured by comparing the timing relationships between cyclical turns in money and in business. It has been argued, for example, that other variables more directly under the control of policymakers, such as member bank nonborrowed reserves, or variables more clearly related to business decisions, such as interest rates, must also be taken into account. Yet, even if the behavior of the money supply be accepted as the indicator of policy, there are many alternative ways in which the lag between monetary and business behavior can be measured, and it makes a great deal of difference which measure is used. If, for example, the rate of change in the money supply is replaced by deviations in the level of the money supply from its long-run trend, the average lag between monetary peaks so measured and peaks in general business apparently shrinks from the 16 months previously cited to a mere 5 months.[14] Alternatively, it can be plausibly argued that the appropriate measure is the lag between the rate of change in the money supply, and the *rate of change*, rather than the level, of some measure of business activity, such as gross national product (GNP) or industrial production. When peaks and troughs for money and business are compared on this basis, the lead of money over business appears to be quite short.[15] The near simultaneity, in most cases, of peaks and troughs in

---

[14] This estimate is presented by Milton Friedman in "The Lag Effect in Monetary Policy," *Journal of Political Economy*, October 1961, p. 456.

[15] See John Kareken and Robert Solow, "Lags in Monetary Policy," *Stabilization Policies* (Commission on Money and Credit, 1963), pp. 21–24.

CHART II

Changes in Gross National Product and in Money Supply Plus Time Deposits
(Quarter-to-Quarter Percentage Changes; Compound Annual Rates)

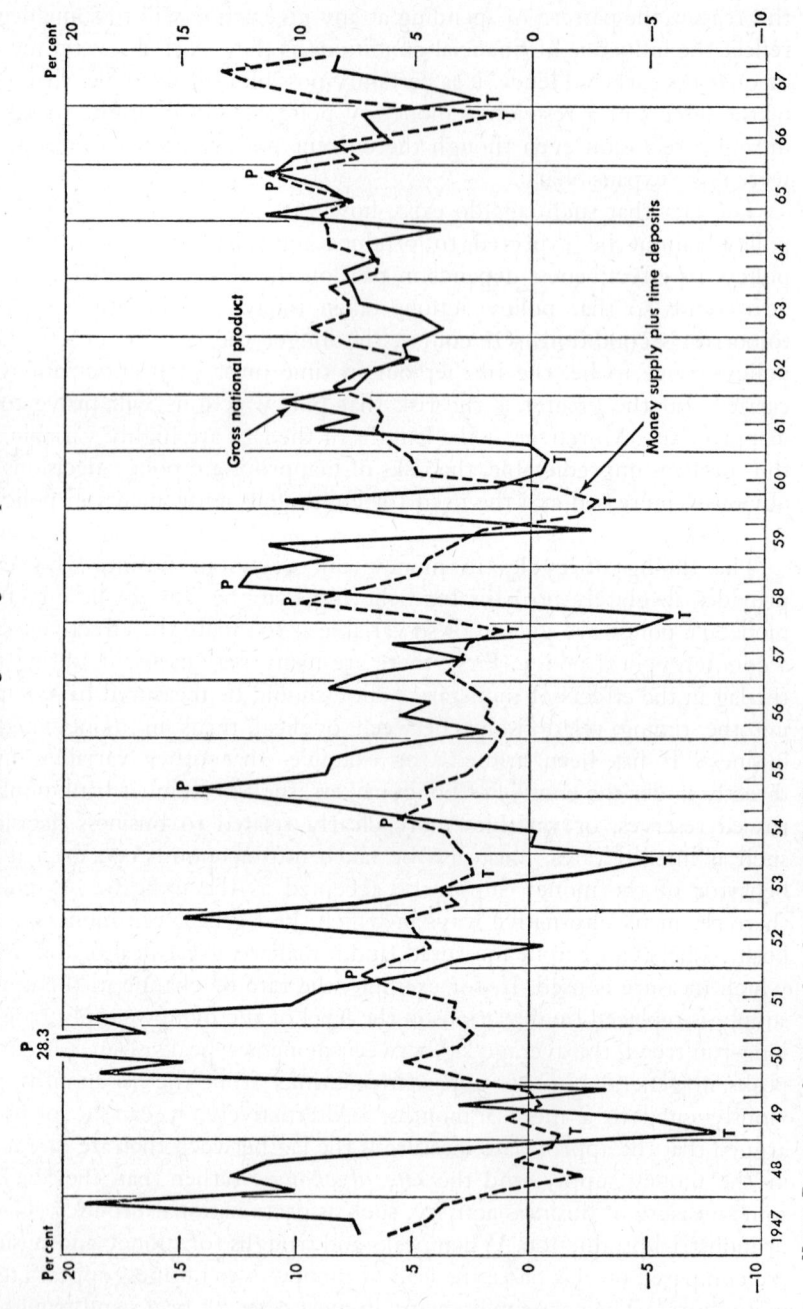

NOTE: Percentage changes are based on seasonally adjusted data.
SOURCES: Board of Governors of the Federal Reserve System; United States Department of Commerce.

the rates of change of the money supply and of GNP during the post-World War II period can be seen in Chart II. To be sure, movements in the two series are quite irregular, so that the decision on whether to treat a particular date as a turning point is sometimes rather arbitrary. Nevertheless, the lead of peaks and troughs in the rate of growth of money over peaks and troughs in the rate of growth of GNP appears to average about one quarter or less.[16]

The point of these various comparisons is not to prove that the lag in monetary policy is necessarily either very long or very short, but rather to illustrate how hard it is to settle the matter through the kind of evidence that has been offered by the money supply school. Similar difficulties, as well as others, beset attempts to measure the *variability* of the lag in the influence of money on business by comparisons of cyclical peaks and troughs in the two. However the turning points are measured, the resulting estimates may seriously overstate the true variability of the lag in the influence of money on business. The reason is that observed differences from cycle to cycle in the timing of turning points in money relative to turning points in business are bound to reflect a number of factors over and beyond any variability in the influence of money on business.[17] These "other" sources of variability include purely statistical matters, such as errors in the data and the arbitrariness involved in assigning precise dates to turning points in money and in business. More fundamentally, the fact that there exists a reverse influence of business on money, an influence that is probably uneven from one cycle to the next, imparts a potentially serious source of variability to the observed lags. Moreover, if there are important influences on the general level of business activity other than the behavior of money, these factors would also increase the variability of the observed timing relationships between turning points in money and in business. Taking all these possibilities into account, it seems fair to say that whatever the true variability in the impact of money on business, its size is overstated when it is measured in terms of the variability of the lags in cyclical turning points.

WAYS IN WHICH MONEY MAY INFLUENCE BUSINESS

If there is a broad conclusion to be drawn from a study of the historical pattern of relationships between cycles in money and cycles in business, it is that there are distinct limits to what can be learned about the

---

[16] When quarterly dollar changes in the money supply are correlated with quarterly dollar changes in GNP experimenting with various lags, the highest correlation is achieved with GNP lagged two quarters behind money. (For the 1947–II to 1967–III period the R^2 is .34.) The correlation with a one quarter lag is almost exactly as high, however ($R^2 = .33$). When percentage changes in the two series are used instead, the correlation virtually disappears, no matter what lag is used.

[17] Other sources of variability are discussed in some detail by Thomas Mayer in "The Lag in the Effect of Monetary Policy: Some Criticisms," *Western Economic Journal* (September 1967), pp. 335–42.

influence of money on business from this kind of statistical analysis. Perhaps this should not be surprising. During the business cycle, many factors of potential importance to the subsequent behavior of business activity undergo more or less continuous change. At the same time, the business cycle itself feeds back on the behavior of these factors. Hence, it is extremely difficult to isolate the importance of any single factor, such as the behavior of money, and *post hoc, propter hoc* reasoning becomes especially dangerous. In these circumstances there appears to be no substitute for a detailed, and hopefully quantitative, examination of the ways in which changes in the money supply might work through the economy ultimately to affect the various components of aggregate demand. Some brief and tentative sketches aside, the proponents of the monetary school have not attempted such an analysis.

The possible ways in which an increase, for example, in the money supply might stimulate aggregate demand can be separated into what are sometimes called "income effects," "wealth effects," and "substitution effects." Income effects exist when the same developments that produce an increase in the quantity of money also add directly to current income. Examples would be increases in bank reserves and deposits resulting from domestically mined gold or an export surplus. Similarly, a wealth effect occurs when a process increasing the money supply also increases the net worth of the private sector of the economy. A Treasury deficit financed by a rundown of Treasury deposit balances might be regarded as an example of such a process, since the resulting buildup of private deposits would represent an increase in private wealth.

Far more important than the income or wealth effects in the present-day United States economy are substitution effects such as result when the Federal Reserve engages in open market operations and banks expand loans and investments.[18] When the Federal Reserve buys government securities from the nonbank public, the public, of course, acquires deposits and gives up the securities. There is no direct change in the public's net worth position,[19] or in its income; rather there is a substitution of money for securities in the public's balance sheet. The same is true when the banks expand the money supply by buying securities from the nonbank public: The public substitutes money for securities, but neither its wealth nor its income is directly changed by the transaction. Similarly, when banks expand deposits by making loans, the monetary assets of the borrowers rise, but their liabilities to the banking system rise by an equal amount and their net worth and income are unchanged.

Since these substitution effects associated with open market operations

---

[18] These substitution effects are sometimes also known as "portfolio balance" or "liquidity" effects.

[19] This statement has to be modified to the extent that the Federal Reserve's buying activity bids up the market value of the public's holdings of government securities. The significance of this wealth effect is probably minimal and is further limited in its consequences by the tendency of many holders to value governments at original purchase price or at par rather than at current market value.

and with the expansion of bank deposits are by far the most important operations by which the money supply is changed, it seems especially relevant to study the ways in which these effects may influence economic activity. The main avenues appear to be through changes in interest rates on the various types of assets and changes in the availability of credit. When the Federal Reserve or the commercial banks buy securities from the nonbank public in exchange for deposits, funds are made available for the public to purchase, in turn, a wide variety of private securities, such as mortgages, corporate bonds, or bankers' acceptances.[20] The increased demand for these securities tends to push rates on them down. And with borrowing costs down, business firms may be induced to expand outlays on plant and equipment or inventory while consumers may increase spending on new homes. In most cases, the effects of lower interest rates on capital spending probably stem from the fact that external financing has become cheaper. In some cases, however, lower market yields on outstanding government and private securities might induce business holders to sell such assets in order to purchase higher yielding capital goods and thus, in effect, to make direct substitution of physical capital for financial assets in their "portfolios." Finally, lower interest rates on securities may reduce consumer incentives to acquire and hold financial assets while tempting them to make more use of consumer credit, thereby reducing saving out of current income and increasing consumption purchases.[21]

---

[20] The newly created deposits may, of course, in principle be used immediately to buy goods rather than financial assets, thus tending directly to stimulate business activity. Even in this case, however, the effects of the money-creating operations work through and depend upon reactions to interest rates. When the Federal Reserve or the commercial banks enter the market to buy securities, their bids add to total market demand, making market prices for securities higher (and yields lower) than they otherwise would have been. Indeed, it is these relatively higher prices (lower yields) that induce the nonbank public to give up securities in exchange for deposits. If the deposits are in fact immediately used to purchase goods, then the process can be regarded as one in which lower market interest rates on securities stemming from bids by the Federal Reserve or the commercial banks have induced the public to give up securities in exchange for goods. The extent to which such switching will occur obviously depends upon the sensitivity to interest rates of business and consumer demands for goods.

[21] While there is little general agreement that such direct effects on consumption are important, a recent study of the problem has in fact found a significant influence of interest rates on consumer demand for automobiles and other durables. (See Michael J. Hamburger, "Interest Rates and the Demand for Consumer Durable Goods," *American Economic Review*, December 1967.) In general, proponents of the monetary school feel that analyses of the role of interest rates in consumer demand undertaken to date have neglected to take into account certain important factors. In particular, they think that the most relevant interest rates may not be the ones usually studied, namely the rates on financial instruments, but rather the interest rates "implicit" in the prices of the durable goods themselves—i.e., where the value of the services yielded by a consumer durable, such as an auto or a washing machine, is treated as analogous to the coupon or dividend yielded by a bond or stock. The obvious difficulties of defining and measuring the value of such services have probably been responsible for the notable dearth of research into this possibility, however, and the issue must be regarded as completely unsettled.

With regard to bank lending, open market purchases of government securities increase bank reserves and may ease the terms on which banks are willing to make loans. Changes in lending terms other than interest rates, which include repayment procedures, compensating balance requirements, and the maximum amount a bank is willing to lend to a borrower of given credit standing, are often bracketed as changes in "credit availability." Such changes are regarded by many analysts as being more important influences on many types of spending than are changes in interest rates. Moreover, changes in credit availability related in part to changes in the money supply are not confined to lending by commercial banks, as was dramatically illustrated in 1966 with regard to nonbank mortgage lenders. In any case, an increased availability of funds permits and encourages potential borrowers to increase their loan liabilities, thereby providing funds which can be used to build up financial assets (perhaps mainly money market instruments) or to purchase physical assets in the form of business capital goods, inventories, or consumer durables. Stepped-up purchases of financial assets add to downward pressures on interest rates, stimulating spending through the processes already described, while additional demand for physical assets stimulates business activity directly.

Studies of the influence of changes in interest rates and the availability of credit on spending in the various sectors of the economy have appeared with increasing frequency in the post-World War II period, especially within the past few years. Some of these studies have taken the form of interviews of businessmen and consumers with regard to the influence of credit cost and availability conditions on their spending decisions. Other studies have employed modern statistical and computer technology in an attempt to extract such information from data on past behavior.[22] With regard to spending on housing, there has been general agreement that the cost and availability of credit are highly important. A number of studies have also found varying degrees of influence on business spending for plant and equipment and for inventories as well as on consumer spending for durable goods, such as autos and appliances. All these studies, however, have also found factors other than cost and availability of credit to be highly important. Moreover, a large degree of disagreement exists with regard to the exact quantitative importance of the financial factors.

Given the serious technical problems that surround these studies, major areas of disagreement are virtually certain to exist for some time to come. Nevertheless, studies of the type referred to here appear to offer the hope at least that firmly grounded and widely accepted conclusions on the

---

[22] For a summary of some of these studies, see Michael J. Hamburger, "The Impact of Monetary Variables: A Selected Survey of the Recent Empirical Literature" (Federal Reserve Bank of New York, July 1967). Copies of this paper are available on request from Publications Services, Division of Administrative Services, Board of Governors of the Federal Reserve System, Washington, D.C. 20551.

importance of money in the business cycle may ultimately be reached. Of particular interest are large-scale econometric models which attempt to provide quantitative estimates of the timing and magnitude of the effects of central bank actions on the money supply and other financial magnitudes and the subsequent effects, in turn, of these variables on each of the various major components of aggregate demand. One such model is currently under construction by members of the Federal Reserve Board staff in cooperation with members of the Economics Department of the Massachusetts Institute of Technology.[23] Granting the major technical problems still unresolved, projects of this kind appear promising as a means of eventually tracking down the importance of money in explicit, quantitative terms.

---

[23] Some preliminary results of this work are discussed in "The Federal Reserve-MIT Econometric Model" by Frank deLeeuw and Edward Gramlich, *Federal Reserve Bulletin* (January 1968), pp. 9–40.

18

TECHNIQUES FOR FORECASTING INTEREST RATE TRENDS*

Sidney Homer

The most successful forecaster in all of history was undoubtedly the Delphic Oracle. She maintained her preeminence for over three hundred years. In the course of these three centuries she numbered among her clients virtually all the moneyed aristocracy of the Mediterranean world. Her system, as I understand it, ran somewhat as follows:

First, she collected her fee, always in advance, always in gold or silver. It was often extraordinarily large (for example, at times all the metallic wealth of a kingdom).

Second, she descended deep into the cave at Delphi, and when there she inhaled intoxicating vapors.

Third, she uttered her prophecy, always in riddles.

Fourth, she never put a date on her prophecies.

Today, alas, all we have left to us of this beautiful system is the intoxicating vapors. The gold and silver are gone, caves are not accessible, riddles are infra dig, and everybody asks "when?". Just in case any modern forecaster tries to get away with anything, we have invented the question and answer period.

I have seen no record of the Delphic Oracle's success in forecasting the trends of ancient interest rates and commodity prices. However, we can assume that she was generally wrong because we know her temple accumulated one of the greatest hoards of gold and silver in antiquity at a time when the purchasing power of these metals was declining spectacularly and at a time when interest rates were also declining. However, the beauty of the system was that the Oracle's reputation and income were not at all related to the validity of her prophecies. We here today could well envy the Delphic Oracle.

By comparison our task is formidable. Believe it or not, we modern forecasters are actually supposed to tell the customers just what is going

---

* An Address given before the Annual Forecasting Conference of the Chicago Chapter of the American Statistical Association on June 14, 1966.

to happen and when. I have always liked the true story of the little lady who many years ago walked in on her investment advisor and asked him a very simple question: "Mr. Scudder," she said, "next week I am going abroad for the summer. I shall have to sell a few stocks to pay for the trip, but I can wait until fall. Between now and September will the stock market go up or go down?" Of course, he gave her that long talk you all know, the gist of which was that he didn't know. "You don't know what the market is going to do this summer?" she said in some surprise, "then why don't you ask somebody?"

Now down to business. My topic today is Techniques for Forecasting Interest Rate Trends. Most bond market fluctuations can be arbitrarily broken down into three principal types according to duration: (1) short-term, sometimes seasonal, trends which last a few weeks or months; (2) medium-term trends, usually called cyclical trends, which last from one to three or four years and frequently coincide roughly with the trends of the business cycle; and (3) long-term secular trends which embrace at least two business cycles and frequently last several decades. Today I shall discuss primarily the medium-term cyclical trends. When most of us are asked our opinion of the bond market, the question usually refers to a period of not more than a year or so ahead and, thus, is very largely answerable in terms of cyclical analysis.

Unfortunately, however, we can never altogether ignore the great long-term secular swings of interest rates. Indeed, one of the most baffling problems to the forecaster is how to weigh these longer term influences against medium-term business developments. For example, in 1962, 1963, or 1964, when cyclical pressures on the economy were mild, cyclical analysis was misleading and the trend of the bond market was best analyzable in terms of long-term fundamentals. However, in years like 1959 or 1966, when cyclical forces are powerful, they deserve the forecaster's main attention. As a useful generality, I would suggest that at extremes of the business cycle, that is to say, in times of depression or boom, the forecaster can pretty well ignore long-term fundamentals and look closely at medium-term cyclical prospects. At other times, he would be well advised to divide his attention between these two sometimes highly divergent sets of forces.

SECULAR TRENDS

Therefore, before I attempt my discussion of cyclical trends I should like to say a word about those broader, more fundamental, long-term influences which are summed up in the term secular trend. I refer you to Chart I dating back to 1800. Although the earlier data is imperfect and has to be sketched together from a variety of sources, the chart clearly shows a succession of dominating trends towards lower or higher bond yields each one lasting at least a decade and several of them for much longer periods. Looking only at this century, we can see the great bear bond

CHART I
Inverted Yields of Long-Term High Grade American Bonds

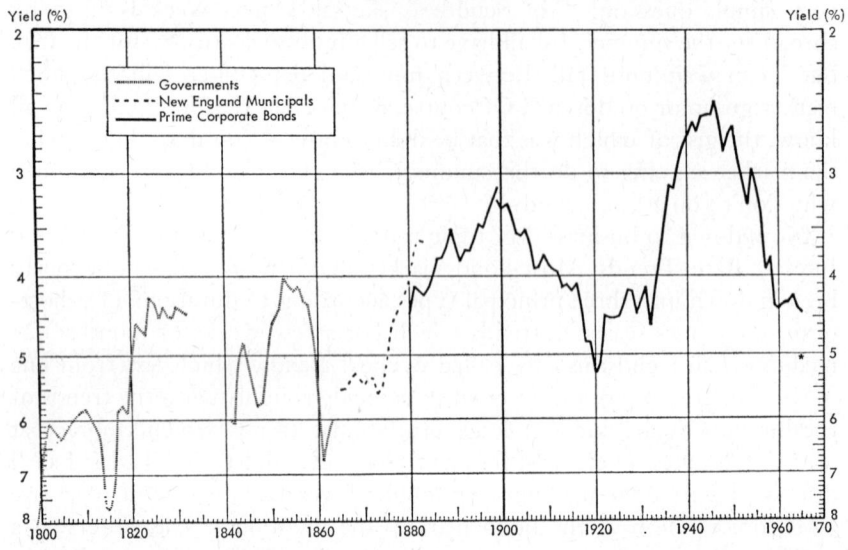

- Governments
- New England Municipals
- Prime Corporate Bonds

* Approximate current level.

market of 1900 to 1920, the bull bond market of 1920 to 1946, and finally the greatest of all bear bond markets, that of 1946 to date, which seemed for a while to have stopped in 1960 but which lately has resumed. The chart demonstrates that these secular trends are not rhythmic: Their time spans are highly diverse.

We see plainly the dominance of these great secular trends. They indeed swamp the cyclical trends which every few years run counter to them. Of course, since the chart is in annual averages, it obscures the full range of inter-year cyclical fluctuations which I shall discuss later, but nevertheless, a cyclical bull market in a bear secular trend is apt to be small and brief as is a cyclical bear market in a bull secular trend. I venture to say that many errors in cyclical interest rate analysis stem from ignoring these overriding secular trends, or from erroneous analysis of their direction. These great persistent sweeps up and down make our short-range cyclical markets seem indeed like chips in a great tide.

One or two brief observations on these secular trends of bond yields might help us to understand how formidable is the task of forecasting them. Throughout the financial history of the United States from Alexander Hamilton all or almost all the great periods of rising rates have been associated with major wars. One such bear bond market centered around 1812, one around the Civil War, the next centered around World War I, and the latest (postponed, no doubt, by controls) immediately followed

World War II and may also be in some measure associated with the Cold War and its occasional heatings. We have scarcely ever had a sustained bear bond market during peacetime. Secondly, all of the sustained inflations of wholesale commodity prices in the economic history of the United States have been roughly associated with the same wars. Therefore, our bear bond markets have roughly correlated with our inflations.

This correlation of interest rate trends with wars suggests that my topic today is bigger than its title seems to suggest. Indeed the long range bond market forecaster must be first of all a forecaster of international political trends, and this is a tall order. I could go even further. Every major military, political, sociological, technological, or economic event on the face of the globe can influence American bond yields. No wonder we bond men read the papers carefully day-by-day; no wonder we have a worried abstracted air; no wonder we hem and haw and love phrases like: "on the other hand," "however," "provided," and "all things else being equal."

I simply don't know what is going on in Peking today, but I do know that whatever it is will be potentially crucial to my bond market—much more so than Mr. Martin's policy preferences or Mr. Johnson's economic programs. I suspect that the biggest event so far this year potentially affecting the future of American bond yields was not the escalation in Viet Nam, but the counter-revolution in Indonesia. Also vital to the outlook is the development of political policy in the Kremlin and of economic policy in London. How about de Gaulle? When will the Germans seek a solution of their partition? How long will the consensus in our policies hold? These are the kinds of questions which must be asked at the outset if we are to consider the long range future of American interest rates. In weighing all these baffling questions of world politics and international economics, we are, however, in each case seeking to solve just one simple equation: Will American productivity in the long run usually be greater than or less than the demands put upon it?

Fortunately your management did not ask me to come to Chicago to provide all the answers. However, if we keep these long-range forces in mind we will understand the limitations of the sort of narrow cyclical analysis of interest rate trends which I shall now discuss.

Cyclical Trends

The process of cyclical analysis usually begins somewhat as follows: First, we freeze the international situation at about where it is. Then we select an economic model for the year ahead which seems to fit into recent economic trends and known government policies. Thus far, all we have is a picture of what will happen if nothing happens.

I do not use this expression critically. This is a useful first step. It permits us to isolate the effect of disturbing events as they occur or as we expect them to occur.

My proposed procedure for analysis of cyclical interest rate trends falls conveniently into four steps as follows:

1. The selection of a tentative economic model for the year ahead.
2. A judgment on the effect of this economic model on: (*a*) commodity prices and (*b*) employment.
3. The construction of a corresponding financial model estimating the supply and demand for credit which is implicit in the economic model.
4. An estimate of the effect of steps 1, 2, and 3 above on monetary and fiscal policy.

Step Number One: Bond Yield Trends and the Business Cycle

An article of faith among most financial men is the proposition that business depressions bring low interest rates and business booms bring high interest rates. However, this creed often goes a big step further and affirms that fluctuations in business of less importance than booms or depressions promise corresponding, if milder, increases or decreases in interest rates. If this were automatically true, the future of bond yields would be directly forecastable from any economic model; the validity of both forecasts would be inseparable.

In order to test the correlation of prime bond yield trends with the business cycle, I have prepared two charts. Chart II is a simple unadjusted inverted yield chart of prime corporate bonds plotted monthly from 1902 to date and then cut up with scissors at the peak of each business cycle so that each little box pictures the price trends of bonds during a complete business cycle from boom to boom. I think one glance will convince you there was very little uniformity. It would be very hard to prove from this chart that the bond market follows a reasonably uniform cyclical pattern. The reason is that these markets are simultaneously reflecting three trends: a long-term secular trend, and a medium-term cyclical trend, and temporary short-term swings based on transitory events. What the charts show us is a synthesis of the three trends.

In an attempt to isolate the cyclical trends from the secular trends, I have prepared another chart, Chart III. This is based on exactly the same data and is broken up into the same business cycles, but it is adjusted in three ways.

1. The secular trend during each cycle is eliminated in equal monthly installments so that the inverted yield curve (i.e., bond price index) seems to end each cycle at precisely the same level where it began.
2. Although the range of yields within each cycle varied importantly, they are all plotted to occupy approximately the same space up and down within each cycle.
3. Although the time spans of recessions and recoveries were enormously diverse, they are all plotted as though they were identical with the first half of each chart representing the business recession divided into five equal time spans, and the second half of each chart representing the business recovery and again divided into five equal time spans.

CHART II

Fluctuations of High Grade Corporate Bond Prices During Industrial Production Cycles*

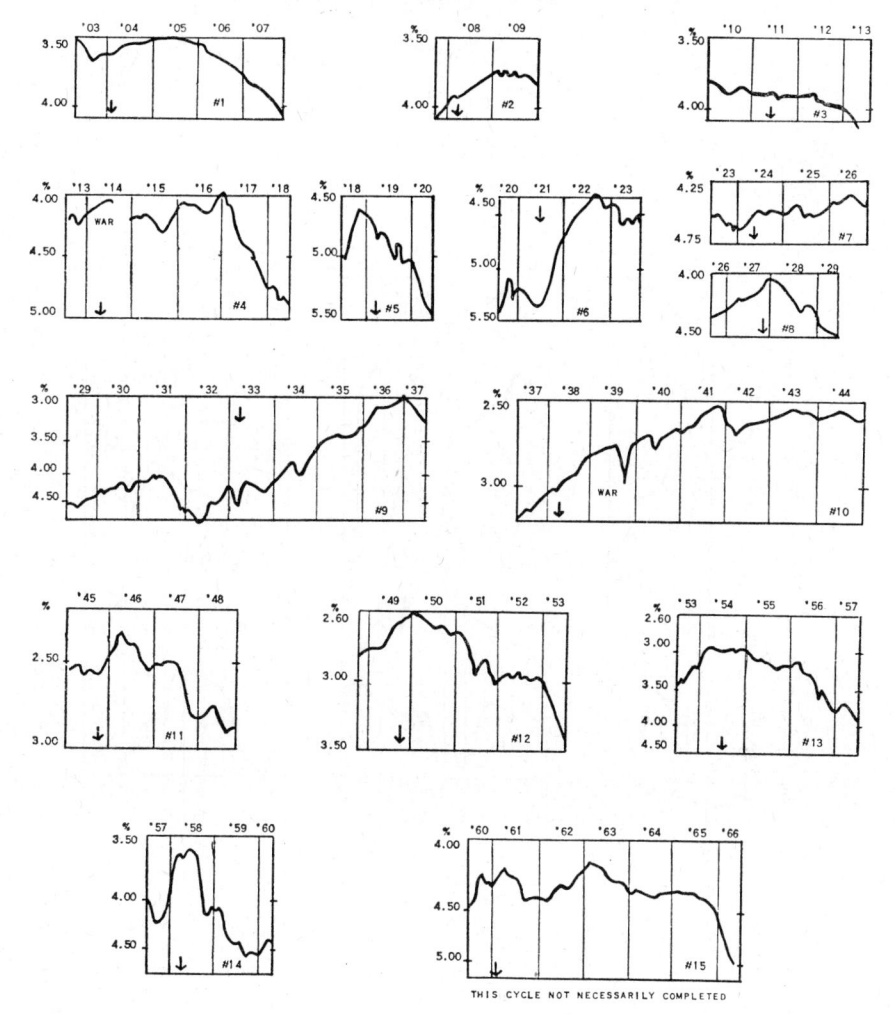

* Inverted yields plotted monthly on ratio scale using Durand 30–year prime corporate bonds. Each chart starts and ends with a peak in industrial production: The intervening trough is indicated by ↓.

The net result is a pattern of cyclical and transitory price fluctuations. When the line is rising, it merely means that the bond market was then doing that much better than its average monthly performance for that cycle; when the line is falling, it means that the bond market was then doing that much worse than its average performance for the cycle.

These charts are merely rough preliminary sketches for a cyclical analysis that we are in process of developing. While I do not have time here to discuss this analysis in detail, I think you will agree that this picture of 15 cycles does in fact show repetitive cyclical patterns. The first half of 12 out of the 15 cyclical charts shows a rising line which means that the bond market was doing better than average during the recession. This rising line very often, but not always, continued into the earlier stages of business recovery. The latter stages of recovery, which were often booms, were marked by sharp relative bond price declines in

CHART III

CYCLICAL PATTERNS OF HIGH GRADE CORPORATE BOND PRICE FLUCTUATIONS
DURING INDUSTRIAL PRODUCTION CYCLES*

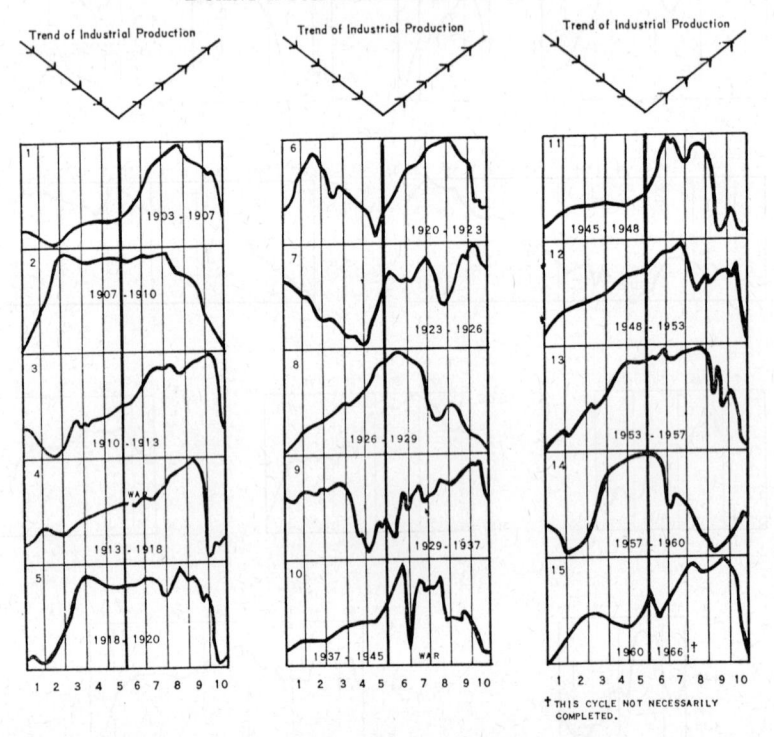

† THIS CYCLE NOT NECESSARILY COMPLETED.

* Inverted yields of prime 30-year corporate bonds adjusted to eliminate secular yield trend and charted so that yield range within each cycle appears identical.

Plotted to coincide with major trends in industrial production. The first half of each chart covers a downtrend in industrial production from cyclical peak to trough in 5 equal time segments, and the second half covers the succeeding uptrend in industrial production from trough to the next peak, also in 5 equal time segments.

13 out of the 15 cycles. In a few cases like 1957–60, the bond market, nevertheless, tended to do better a few months before the actual crest of the boom. I cannot here discuss the interesting leads and lags indicated by this chart and the significant variety of patterns shown at mid-cycle.

The net of it is, however, that there is indeed a nucleus of truth in the popular belief that bond yields tend to fluctuate with the business cycle. This study suggests, however, that such correlation can only be relied upon in periods when cyclical forces are powerful, such as at the peaks of booms or recessions, and that at other times the bond market is capable of a wide variety of patterns which do not correlate with business trends and are influenced no doubt partly by long-term secular fundamentals and partly by transitory political or economic events. The pattern of the five postwar cycles supports these generalizations. The fallacy of assuming automatically that business recovery must lead to a larger than average rise in yields was amply demonstrated in 1950, 1952, 1955, 1962, and 1964, and the early part of 1965. The validity of the correlation between the bond market and extreme cyclical pressures was, however, often demonstrated again during the past 12 months when recovery turned into a genuine boom and the bond market followed its traditional pattern and collapsed.

The cyclical chart of the current cycle is necessarily constructed as if the cycle is just now ended. I am sorry to say this procedure is not intended to be an overt or implicit forecast. It is a statistical necessity. We can observe, however, that the cyclical pattern of this cycle so far is not unlike many others such as 1903, 1910, 1913, and 1953 in that the price index rose well into the recovery period and then collapsed sharply only very late in the cycle (so far). It is very unlike the pattern of 1907–1926–1937–1945–1957 when bond prices started to do relatively badly soon after recovery began. The unusually favorable action of bond prices in the recovery years of 1962, 1963, 1964 led some analysts including myself, to suspect that perhaps the underlying secular trend had turned up in 1960 after 15 years of decline. Subsequent events late in 1965 and early 1966 have, however, disproved this supposition.

Step Number Two: Commodity Prices and Employment

We have seen above that business trends alone often do not give us a useful forecast of bond market trends. For example, recoveries sometimes bring with them bear bond markets in their early stages, i.e., 1958, and sometimes have very little effect on the bond market until the late or boom stages, as in 1962–66. An important help for judging the effect of any economic model on bond yields should be estimates of the effect of the economic model on commodity prices and on unemployment. The trend of commodity prices should provide an important clue to monetary policy and perhaps even to fiscal policy, while the trend of employment or unemployment should also importantly influence both areas of government policy. If commodity prices are stable or sloppy, monetary and fiscal policy are both free to promote economic growth without fear of inflation and they are very apt to do so if unemployment is substantial. Under this environment a model even of rapid growth need not imply rising bond yields and in fact could be consistent with declining bond yields. On the other hand, in an environment of low unemployment and rising commodity prices, it is probable that an economic model showing any economic growth will promptly bring with it a declining bond market and rising yields.

Step Number Three: Supply and Demand for Credit

The next step is to look at the financial implications of the model in terms of supply and demand for credit. In this way we can try to answer the questions—"How will the model be financed?" "Where is the money coming from?" "What are the volume implications for the different departments of the capital markets?" I refer you to a summary sheet showing estimates of supply and demand each year since 1957.

The demand side shows the net annual increase of outstanding credit in each important department of the money and bond markets. The supply side shows the net acquisitions of these same credit instruments by various investor groups. Again, time will not permit me to go into detail on the use of this very interesting tool for money market forecasting. Indeed, we are just now preparing an exhaustive and exhausting review of this entire subject back to the war which may or may not be completed late this year.

For over two decades I have worked in this area, creating just such supply and demand for credit models. While by themselves they rarely forecast interest rates, I have found them extremely useful in many ways: In the first place, they show which type of credit demand is dynamic and which is stable. For example, in 1965 and 1966 obviously corporate bonds were the dynamic area, while in an earlier credit squeeze in 1959 Treasury debt was dynamic and corporate finance was not. At other times, like 1963, it was real estate mortgages which were eating up most of the available credit. Similarly, the model shows which sources of credit are expanding and which are contracting. It shows, for example, that commercial banks alone have financed a very large part of the present credit boom, but they were smaller factors in earlier booms. It shows the sharp rise and recent fall of savings and loan associations, the steady persistent growth of new funds flowing to retirement funds, and the volatile role of individuals as direct purchasers of bonds. Individuals are usually negligible direct suppliers of credit, but every now and then they leap to dominating importance. This usually occurs during periods of high interest rates. The recent models also seem to show the increased mobility of our capital markets both on the demand and on the supply side. For example, funds are at present apparently being diverted from real estate mortgages to corporate bonds to help finance the urgent demand for plant and equipment, whereas in 1959 the great pressure on the capital markets did not prevent a further rise in mortgage formation. We see a corresponding flexibility in supply with funds being diverted from specialized savings institutions to commercial banks which are in a position to use them to fill almost any form of demand.

Thus, supply and demand analysis provides a useful picture of the dramatis personae of the bond market: who is borrowing the most money and who is lending the most money. It tells us which market and which institutional group to watch carefully, and this is often highly useful.

However, I would caution you against the use of these credit statistics as a simple guide to interest rate trends. For example, it is often erroneously assumed that a very large expansion in the grand total of credit implies rising interest rates. It did in 1959, but it did not in 1961, 1962, 1963; it did in 1965. This poor correlation is because the total of credit expansion can never be larger than the total demand or the total supply, whichever is smaller. Thus, a small total of credit expansion can be due to a severe shortage of funds (tight money), or can be due to a deficiency of demand (easy money). A large total expansion can be due to a surplus of loanable funds (easy money), or a large total can be due to excessive demand (tight money).

Again, it has sometimes been useful to subtract the total institutional supply of new funds from the grand total of new demands, coming up with a residual which must be financed by individuals and miscellaneous investors. When this residual is large, it often means that demand is excessive and money is tight. However, this tool, like all such statistical tools, is not infallible because individuals and miscellaneous investors might, for unrelated reasons, suddenly prefer the bond market and invest large sums in a period of comparatively easy money or might simply not have the money to buy bonds at high rates. Again, it is sometimes argued when the commercial bank contribution jumps up rapidly, as in 1958, this implies that the bond market is vulnerable because such a large growth in bank credit cannot be repetitive. With this in mind when bank credit grew by a record amount in 1962, many argued that higher interest rates were in prospect. However, for several years thereafter bank credit expansion grew even larger and bond yields did not rise. Finally, in 1965 large growth in bank credit was followed by a rise in interest rates.

Therefore, to be really useful as a forecasting tool, these supply and demand statistics are best read against a background of commodity price trends and employment trends. If there is a large surplus of goods and services and, therefore, stable to declining commodity prices, this implies an adequacy of real savings, which in turn leaves monetary and fiscal authorities free to permit or even encourage a large expansion of bank credit and thus maintain stable to easy interest rates. Something like this was the situation in the many years of firm bond markets from 1961 through 1964. However, if commodity prices are rising and the labor supply is not redundant, monetary policy is limited in its scope and is forced to turn restrictive, thereby depriving the credit market of needed funds. This necessarily creates higher interest rates.

Step Number Four: Monetary and Fiscal Policy

If our analysis is correct so far, that is to say, if we have the right economic model and have correctly judged its effect on commodity prices and unemployment and have correctly estimated its implications

TABLE I
Summary of Demand and Supply for Credit
(billions of dollars)

	See Table	1957	1958	1959	1960	1961	1962	1963	1964	1965E	1966E
Net investment demand											
Real estate mortgages	II	10.8	14.9	16.8	14.8	18.9	24.9	30.2	30.2	29.4	27.0
Corporate bonds	III	7.0	5.9	4.1	5.0	5.1	4.9	5.6	6.6	8.1	11.0
Bank term loans (SB&H est.)	VIII	0.8	0.5	0.9	0.9	1.0	1.4	2.0	2.8	5.3	5.0
State and local securities	IV	4.6	5.1	4.9	4.0	5.0	5.3	6.3	5.6	6.8	6.6
Foreign and int'l. bank bonds	VII	0.5	1.2	0.5	0.6	0.5	0.9	1.0	0.7	0.9	0.8
Total net investment demand		23.7	27.6	27.2	25.3	30.5	37.4	45.1	45.9	50.5	50.4
Net other demand											
Other bk. loans (ex term & mtge.)	VIII	2.3	1.6	9.0	5.1	4.6	8.6	9.1	10.8	15.0	14.7
Publicly held treasury debt	V	−2.2	6.7	8.3	−2.7	5.2	4.5	0.9	2.6	−2.4	0.0
Publicly held fed. agcy. debt	VI	2.2	−0.5	2.2	0.0	0.6	1.6	1.6	0.6	2.9	3.0
Total net other demand		2.3	7.8	19.5	2.4	10.4	14.7	11.6	14.0	15.5	17.7
Total net demand for funds		26.0	35.4	46.7	27.7	40.9	52.1	56.7	59.9	66.0	68.1
Net supply*											
Mutual savings banks	VIII	1.7	2.3	1.2	1.6	2.2	3.0	3.6	4.1	3.6	3.5
Savings & loan associations	VIII	4.7	6.1	8.2	7.2	9.4	10.4	13.0	10.9	9.3	8.0
Life insurance companies	VIII	4.5	4.8	4.6	4.5	4.9	5.3	5.9	6.4	7.1	7.7
Fire & casualty ins. companies	VIII	0.6	0.7	1.3	1.0	0.9	0.9	0.9	0.8	0.7	0.9
Private non-ins. pension funds	VIII	1.8	1.7	1.7	1.9	1.5	1.7	1.9	2.2	2.4	2.8
State & local-retirement funds	VIII	1.5	1.5	1.7	1.9	2.1	2.2	2.5	2.7	3.0	3.3
Open-end mutual funds	VIII	0.1	0.4	0.4	0.3	0.2	0.7	−0.1	0.4	−0.1	0.5
Commercial bank long-term funds	VIII	2.5	5.2	3.8	1.9	5.6	10.1	11.8	11.1	15.5	12.4
Total net long inst'l. supply		17.4	22.7	22.9	20.3	26.8	34.3	39.5	38.6	41.5	39.1
Other commercial bank funds	VIII	2.6	9.9	1.6	7.1	10.3	9.1	7.0	10.4	11.4	12.1
Total net inst'l. supply		20.0	32.6	24.5	27.4	37.1	43.4	46.5	49.0	52.9	51.2
Nonfinancial corporations	IX	−0.1	0.8	6.9	−5.2	0.7	0.8	1.4	−0.6	−1.1	−0.5
State & local governments	IX	0.9	−0.5	0.8	−0.2	−0.4	0.5	0.6	−0.3	2.1	1.2
Foreigners	IX	−0.2	0.1	4.4	1.0	0.4	1.9	0.6	0.8	−0.2	0.0
Sub total		20.6	33.0	36.6	23.0	37.8	46.6	49.1	48.9	53.7	51.9
Individuals & miscellaneous	IX	5.4	2.4	10.1	4.7	3.1	5.5	7.6	11.0	12.3	16.2
Total net supply of funds		26.0	35.4	46.7	27.7	40.9	52.1	56.7	59.9	66.0	68.1

		5.1	15.1	5.4	9.0	15.9	19.2	18.8	21.5	26.9	24.5
Note: Total commercial bk. funds											
Memo on gross demands:											
Real estate mortgages	II	21.6	25.8	30.5	28.5	33.0	40.0	45.2	47.8	49.0	48.2
Corporate bonds	III	9.6	9.7	7.1	8.2	9.2	8.6	10.6	10.7	12.7	16.0
State & local securities	IV	7.5	8.4	8.8	8.1	9.4	9.7	11.0	10.5	12.0	12.3
Total		38.7	43.9	46.4	44.8	51.6	58.3	66.8	69.0	73.7	76.5
Amortization, retirements & purchases by											
U.S. agencies		16.3	18.0	20.6	21.0	22.6	23.2	24.7	26.6	29.4	31.9
Net Demands for Above		22.4	25.9	25.8	23.8	29.0	35.1	42.1	42.4	44.3	44.6

* Excludes funds for equities, cash, and miscellaneous demands not tabulated above.
  March 1966.

for the supply and demand for credit, then we probably have a good general idea of the prospects for monetary and fiscal policy in the year ahead. The policy decisions of the agencies of our government are, of course, vital to interest rate trends, but these decisions are not made in a vacuum. In some measure they are what economists call "dependent variables," which means that they are forecastable if we have an accurate preview of the environment in which policy will operate.

While this is true in very general terms, it is far from universally true because of the human element involved and the element of politics. Even though we are entirely clear on the future economic environment, officials of the government have a measure of choice, and we must take into account personal preferences and political considerations. Thus, we might have accurately forecast that restraint would be required in 1966 and accurately expected that both fiscal and monetary policy would move towards restraint, but this did not tell us how the burden of restraint would be shared between fiscal and monetary policy. It is probable that the area of official discretion is not too large, but there is an unpredictable area, and this forces the forecaster to mind reading which is, no doubt, a most difficult but unavoidable task.

It is probably at just this point in our analysis that pressures growing out of our balance of payments should be considered. While they may not exert a powerful influence on our economic model, or on commodity price trends, or on capital market statistics, they could exert a powerful influence on monetary policy and, hence, on interest rate trends. Something like this occurred in 1961, 1962, 1963, and 1964. At present, the capital markets of the world are pretty well compartmentalized by the direct intervention of governments, but if and when a better balance of payments is achieved free market forces might be allowed to reassert themselves. If so, monetary authorities might again have to consider international short-term interest rate differentials.

The Present Situation

Up to this point, I have been talking only in generalities and about forecasting techniques, not forecasts. It would be very comfortable indeed if I could let it go at that. However, your management has insinuated that at some point or other I should relate these techniques to the bond market in 1966.

It looks as though 1966 is one of those rarely interesting years in which the economic model itself is challenged by its financial consequences. During the great majority of years, the supply and demand for credit estimates do not suggest changes in a reasonable economic model. However, in times of major booms or major recessions, credit estimates do sometimes suggest modifications in the economic model.

For example, in years like 1963 and 1964 when the economy was operating far below its resources, the question of finance was hardly pertinent to the economic model—there was sure to be ample funds to finance any reasonable model. However, the redundancy of resources and, hence, of savings then had significance for the bond market outlook because they provided assurance that monetary policy would not be used to brake growth and offset fiscal stimulation. At that time, no problem of inflation or overemployment interfered with a policy of credit expansion.

In the boom year of 1966, however, the questions of inflation and of finance are highly pertinent to the economic model itself. Commodity prices started up in 1965 and the standard 1966 model promised further upward price pressure. This fact promised to limit monetary expansion. However, without an even larger credit expansion than in 1965, the boom model itself would be hard to finance. If so, it might be necessary to ration credit and resources. Therefore, some programs might have to be cut back from sheer lack of savings (the same thing as a deficit in physical resources) and this would reduce the model.

A glance at this year's optimistic business forecasts and their financial corollaries will demonstrate my point. I have often wished that economic model builders would regularly construct consistent financial models so that we could see just how the assumed production and consumption might be financed.

As long ago as last fall we at SB&H began making financial models to fit the boomtime economic models which then began to be generally accepted. Even then it seemed highly unlikely that such a boom could be readily financed. Then last January when expectations became even rosier, we did the formal job which you have on the credit requirements of the boom. The gap between available savings and prospective credit requirements was enormous, perhaps in the range of $10 billion or larger. In the table the gap is to be found in the reduced commercial bank contribution, and in the large jump in the residual to be provided by individuals and miscellaneous. It seemed evident that the full requirements of the expected boom could not readily be financed.

Given then a model which promised rising commodity prices, falling unemployment, and a large excess of credit demands, there could be little doubt about the impact of all of this on monetary and fiscal policy. In fact the direction of both policies had become evident by January—the direction was restraint—but the degree and form of restraint and the timing of policy shifts could not be answered by such an analysis. The analysis showed clearly enough the environment immediately ahead under the economic model, but did not tell us how or how quickly our authorities would react.

This form of analysis does, nevertheless, provide some further guidance to the contingencies which lie ahead. I have mentioned a large gap between the volume of credit necessary to finance the model, and the amount of credit apt to be available. How will the gap be closed? Four ways suggest themselves:

1. An expansionary monetary policy could provide $10 billion or so

more bank credit than the large $24.5 billion of new bank credit that we forecast. With rising commodity prices and a shortage of real savings and a balance of payments problem, such a monetary policy seems most unlikely.

2. A mildly restrictive monetary policy, such as we assumed and such as we have had, and few fiscal restraints would leave the problem of credit rationing entirely to the market. This is the present situation. Lending institutions are severely pinched and unable to meet all the demands of their customers. This form of credit rationing could well lead to large areas of disappointment—projects which simply cannot be financed. It might also lead to financial difficulties where weak borrowers are unable to renew or to fund their short-term debt. As this year progresses, this process of credit rationing could dampen down the model itself. In peacetime, this is the classical prelude to recession.

3. Fiscal policy seems to hold the key to this dilemma. A tax increase or a reduction in government expenditures would dampen down credit demands both directly by reducing federal borrowing and indirectly by reducing private borrowing. Furthermore, the upward pressures on commodity prices and employment might relax and as a result monetary policy could permit somewhat more private credit expansion, thus closing the gap and removing pressures on liquidity and even solvency.

4. Finally, there is unfortunately the alternative of direct government intervention to close the gap by credit rationing or resource rationing, or by control of credit terms, or in a variety of ways. If Viet Nam escalates, such measures may be proposed and even combined with an increase in taxes.

I have used the situation in 1966 as an illustration of money market forecasting both because it is of current interest and also because it is a harshly one-sided picture and thus provides a vivid illustration of a model which, by itself, may be modified by its own financial implications. My analysis does not even touch on the fundamentals: the course of the war, and of the international political scene. It does not anticipate the policy decisions of our authorities. It does present a picture of the pressures of rising interest rates immediately ahead of the market if there is no change in the rapid rate of economic growth, or in programs and policies. However, it suggests that the present period of pressure may soon end in one of three ways: (1) an economic levelling off or downturn based partly on the abandonment of unfinanceable projects; or (2) a tax increase having a similar effect; or (3) direct government intervention in the credit markets to ration credit in accordance with national needs. All three contingencies imply a reduction of present money market pressures later this year.

19

LONG-RUN ECONOMIC AND FINANCIAL PROJECTIONS*†

John W. Kendrick

It is of value periodically to appraise the long-run economic and financial outlook. Not only do most of us make at least some investments for the long pull, but it lends perspective to short-term developments to have a clear notion of longer range probabilities.

PREVIEW

Since equity values depend fundamentally on variables—particularly on expected sales, net earnings, and discount rates—appraisal of the financial outlook must be based on projections of the relevant economic variables. At the aggregate level, the broadest measure of sales is the gross national product (GNP)—the market value of all final goods and services produced in the nation's economy, including plants and equipment financed out of depreciation reserves. So we shall start with a projection to 1975 of GNP in constant prices (Chart 1), and then inflate the estimate for probable price changes. From there, we go to corporate profits in aggregate and the average profits per share of common stock. Then we are in a position to consider the appropriate capitalization rate—the most sensitive part of the projection—to apply to net earnings in order to arrive at a forecast of stock market averages. Although my chief assignment is to cover the overall picture, I shall conclude with some comments on factors to be considered in appraising the outlook for individual industry groups.

All projections involve certain assumptions, of course—such as avoidance of world war, a more or less orderly evolution of social institutions, and the persistence of basic economic trends and relationships. As a matter of fact, there has been a remarkable continuity of economic development, and long-run macroprojections have proved to be quite

---

* Reprinted by permission of *The Commercial and Financial Chronicle* (May 25, 1967).

† A presentation by Dr. Kendrick before the Institute of Investment Banking of the Investment Bankers Association of America, Philadelphia, Pa., March 22, 1967.

CHART 1

Economic and Financial Projections to 1975
(with comparisons for 1950 and 1965–66)

Line	Supply Factors	1950	Actual 1965	1966	Projected 1975	Average annual % rates of change 1950–65	1965–75
1.	Total labor force (millions)	65.1	77.2	78.9	92.0	1.1	1.8
2.	Civilian labor force	63.4	74.4	75.8	89.5	1.1	1.9
3.	Unemployment	3.4	3.4	2.9	3.0	0.0	−1.0
4.	Employment	60.1	71.0	72.9	86.5	1.1	2.0
5.	Government	5.5	10.1	10.8	13.7	4.1	3.1
6.	Private	54.6	60.9	62.1	72.8	0.7	1.8
7.	Average hours worked per week	41.0	39.3	39.4	37.5	−0.3	−0.5
8.	Total manhours (billions)	116.5	124.4	127.2	141.9	0.4	1.3
9.	Real private GNP per man-hour (1965 dollars)	3.03	4.93	5.08	6.73	3.3	3.2
10.	Real private GNP (billions)	352.6	613.4	646.0	953.5	3.8	4.5
11.	Real government GNP	41.4	67.8	72.2	84.6	3.5	2.2
12.	Total real GNP	393.9	681.2	718.1	1038.1	3.7	4.3
13.	GNP price index (1965=100)	72.3	100.0	103.0	124.7	2.2	2.2
14.	Private economy	74.8	100.0	102.7	122.2	2.0	2.0
15.	Government	50.5	100.0	105.5	153.7	4.7	4.5
16.	GNP, current dollars (billions)	284.8	681.2	739.5	1295.0	6.0	6.6
17.	Private economy	263.9	613.4	663.3	1165.0	5.8	6.6
18.	Government	20.9	67.8	76.2	130.0	8.2	6.8
19.	Corporate profits, adjusted (billions)	37.7	74.2	80.0	130.5	4.6	5.8
20.	Percent of private GNP	14.3	12.1	12.1	11.2	...	...
21.	Corporate profits, reported	42.6	75.7	82.1	133.1	3.9	5.8
22.	After tax	24.8	44.5	48.3	78.5	4.0	5.8
	Standard & Poor's 500 stocks:						
23.	Net earnings per share	2.78	5.19	5.56	9.0	4.2	5.7
24.	Price/earnings ratio	6.63	17.1	14.8	...	...	...
25.	14xE projected	(14xE)			126.0	...	3.8
26.	Average price* 18xE projected	18.4	88.65	82.29	162.0	10.8	5.7
27.	22xE projected	(22xE)			199.0	...	7.1
28.	Dividend yield (at 18 P/E), %	6.6	3.0	3.4	3.0	−5.4	0.0
29.	Aaa bond yield (Moody's), %	2.6	4.5	5.1	4.5	3.7	0.0
30.	Dow-Jones industrials (projected at 18x earnings)	216.3	910.9	873.6	1665.0	10.1	5.7

* Actual through 1966; projected at the three P/E ratios for 1975.

accurate—more so than short-run projections that are dominated by fluctuations in demand.

The long-term projection is based on the probable course of the supply factors influencing productive capacity, chiefly the labor force, manhours worked, and productivity. It is assumed that in the target year, in this case 1975, aggregate demand will be sufficient to provide relatively full employment. Even if in that year the federal government were not able to fulfill its obligations under the Employment Act of 1946, a shortfall of total demand of a few percentage points would make very little difference in the long-term average growth rate. And even if 1975 were not a full-employment year, it is likely that 1976 or 1977 would be back in the high-level trend line.

BASIC GROWTH FORCES

In any economy, regardless of its type of organization, the physical volume of final production (*real* GNP) will grow only as the supply of labor (manhours) and its productivity (output per manhour) grows. The productivity factor is, of course, a catchall, and is influenced by the growth in the quantity of capital-goods per worker as well as by the rate of technological and organizational progress. We give all these forces due weight, although the following discussion is necessarily brief. It is keyed in to the accompanying table, by line number.

Labor Supply

The labor force can be projected quite accurately for at least 14 years ahead, since all the persons who then will be labor force members are now living. The projections in lines 1 and 2 are based on a U.S. Department of Labor study, in which the population 14 years of age and over is projected by age-sex groups, and projected labor force participation ratios applied to these numbers. Trends in labor force participation ratios for the various groups have been quite smooth, and largely offsetting in aggregate. As shown by the table, in the decade 1965–75, the labor force is expected to grow by an average of 1.5 million workers per year, compared with 0.8 1950–65, an increase of over 50 percent in the growth *rates* shown in the last two columns.

Unemployment is projected at 3 million in 1975 (line 3), about the normal fractional percentage of the labor force. The resulting employment estimates (lines 5, 6, 7) are broken down between private and government, since in estimating real government product the Commerce Department assumes no change in productivity of government employees (!), and in any case our profit estimates are necessarily derived from estimates of gross private product.

Average hours worked per week and per year in private industry (line 7) are assumed to continue their downward trend. But since this trend also affected past periods, total manhours worked (line 8) also show a marked acceleration 1965–75 compared with 1950–65.

Productivity and Total Real GNP

Even more important than expansion of labor supply in economic growth is productivity advance. We have projected a continuation of the

3.2 percent a year average increase in real private product per manhour (line 9) which has prevailed in the post-war period: Productivity advance reflects innovations in the instruments, processes, and organization of production. Some people predict an acceleration of productivity gains, pointing to increases in research, development, and educational and training expenditures, which help create and disseminate new knowledge and know-how. They also stress dramatic developments in automation and other new technology. But expenditures for R. and D., and for education and training have been rising rapidly in relation to GNP for decades. If productivity advance is to accelerate, there would have to be an acceleration in such expenditures. If anything, the outlook is for a deceleration in the growth of these "intangible investments." Also, it is doubtful if the volume of tangible capital per worker can grow as fast in the decade ahead as during the period 1950–65, given the current acceleration in labor supply but with no apparent tendency for the proportion of GNP devoted to saving and investment to increase. As to automation, it takes time for any new technological developments to spread. In any case, our past rate of productivity advance depended on many new inventions which were at the time just as impressive as automation is today. So I believe we are not being unduly conservative in projecting the past record of productivity advance into the future. It is a good record, and we shall be doing well to maintain it.

This means that total real GNP (line 12) will accelerate in line with the accelerated growth of labor supply. We may expect an average annual growth rate of close to 4½ percent, compared with 3.7 percent in 1950–65. An acceleration of this magnitude is also projected by the staff of the Joint Economic Committee of Congress, the National Planning Association, and other groups experienced in economic projection work.

PRICES, SALES, AND PROFITS

Profits depend on sales at market prices, not on the GNP in constant dollars. To translate the GNP from constant to current dollars, we must project the general price level (lines 13, 14, 15). Unfortunately, in our predominantly free enterprise economy, since World War II, relatively full employment has been associated with an upward creep of prices that has averaged around 2 percent a year. In good years, labor has been getting average hourly wage increases of 5 to 6 percent, compared with the increases in output per manhour of 3.2 percent. This pushes the labor cost per unit of output up by around 2 percent a year, assuming that profit margins are maintained, and that the Federal Reserve Board increases the money supply sufficiently to accommodate the inflation. This pattern reemerged with new vigor in the period 1965–67. Despite some slowing down in recent months, I would expect the same basic pattern to continue in the coming decade, with price rises continuing to average around 2 percent a year in the private economy (line 14). It will be somewhat greater in the economy as a whole (line 13) since the government product in current prices reflects the increasing average wages and salaries of government employees (line 15).

Thus, the GNP in current dollars, which reflects both real growth and inflation, may be expected to grow by at least 6½ percent in the decade ahead (line 16). This is a 10 percent faster growth rate than that of the past 15 years—and it would be even greater if inflation speeded up.

Corporate profits are unlikely to grow as fast as GNP in current prices, as can be seen in lines 19 and 20. This is not due to any assumed decline in the rate of return to capital investment. That rate will have to be maintained to stimulate enough new investment to support full employment. Rather, the slower growth of profits reflects the fact that the stock of invested capital will not grow as fast as GNP, given present saving patterns.

Nevertheless, a marked acceleration in the growth of profits 1965–75 compared with 1950–65 is implied. This is because the rate of return *did* drop from the abnormally high levels of 1948–50, which reflected the postwar capital shortage. We assume a continuation of the same corporate income tax rate, so that after-tax profits are also expected to increase at the average annual rate of 5.8 percent (line 22). It is possible that there will be another round of tax-cuts in a few years, however, if revenues continue to rise faster than GNP and if our foreign commitments can eventually be reduced. Total after-tax profits are translated to a per-share basis on line 23, based on the past relationship.

CAPITALIZATION RATES AND STOCK PRICES

The most critical aspect of a stock-market projection lies in the price-earnings (P/E) ratio the analyst selects to apply to projected earnings. In past high-level years prior to 1958, such as 1929, 1937, 1945, and 1957, ratios of average stock prices to earnings averaged a bit better than 14 to 1. Since 1958, however, P/E ratios have averaged around 18 to 1, hitting a high of around 22 to 1 in 1962. I have chosen the three ratios just cited to give the range within which I consider it probable that the average per-share earnings of 1975 will be valued.

Needless to say, I consider the middle of the range, 18:1, to be the most probable average P/E ratio. Beginning with my first lecture at the IBA's Institute of Investment Banking at the Wharton School in 1959, I have consistently argued that multiples of around 18:1 were a new "norm," and not just a temporary aberration. The persistence of the higher multiples since then helps lend credibility to this thesis.

It is based on two main factors: (1) stronger expectations among investors of sustained income growth in the U.S. economy, and (2) a lowering of the discount rate, reflecting a reduced risk premium, at which expected future earnings are capitalized.

With regard to the first factor, investors have become more "growth-minded" in recent years. Economic statistics have improved since the war, long historical series have been developed, and long-term growth projections have become commonplace. Further, with the demonstrated ability of the "built-in stabilizers" and economic policy to hold cyclical revision to mild proportions during the first dozen years after the war, even the skeptical became convinced that a major postwar depression was not in the cards. Instead, it seemed increasingly probable that the 1960's would witness an accelerated rate of growth, for the reasons adduced above. Finally, the expectation of continuing creeping inflation had become widespread by 1958 reinforced by the fact that even during the recession of 1957–58, the general price level continued to rise. This factor further strengthened expectations concerning the future growth of income, which is compounded of both physical volume and price increases.

Associated with the upward shift of income expectations was an apparent downward revision of the average discount rate at which expected future income streams are discounted. The lower the discount rate, the greater the present value of future income, and thus the higher the ratio of stock prices to a given current income. As stock prices began their long ascent in 1949, carrying P/E ratios from less than 7 to their old high of 14 in 1957, and then on up to new levels of around 18 in 1958, it was apparent that there had been a major reduction of the discount rate applied to expected income from equities. And here I should add that the income I am referring to is total per-share income after tax, not just the portion paid out in dividends. The evidence has become rather clear that it is total net income that is discounted. In any case, the average proportion paid out in dividends has not changed greatly over the postwar period.

The discount rate consists of two major elements: the "pure" interest rate, and the risk premium. The interest rate fluctuates to some extent, and describes "long swings," but has not exhibited any pronounced long-run trend. Insofar as it reflects the basic rate of return on capital generally, it can be argued that there is a built-in mechanism that tends to bring interest rates back to a norm. That is, higher rates of return and interest stimulate saving and investment, which tends gradually to lower rates. Conversely, low rates tend to reduce capital formation, which eventually results in capital-shortage and rising rates.

Be that as it may, over the period we are discussing, interest rates on governments and Aaa bonds (see line 30) were gradually moving up, with occasional interruption. It is apparent, then, that the decline in the discount rate was due to a substantial reduction in the risk premium.

Probably the major factor behind the falling risk premium was the one discussed earlier as also enhancing growth prospects—the reduction in the amplitude of cyclical fluctuations in the U.S. economy. In particular, it has become widely believed that a major depression or period of relative stagnation, such as the 1930's, is now virtually impossible, given the built-in stabilizers, such as the unemployment insurance system, institutional bulwarks provided by agencies such as the Securities and Exchange Commission, and the Employment Act of 1946. Policies to implement the Employment Act are based on considerably more sophisticated understanding than existed before the war of the determinants of national income and appropriate measure for maintaining a high-level economy. The reduced risk of cyclical fluctuations has been reflected particularly in the rising P/E ratios accorded stocks of cyclically sensitive companies, such as the steels.

The growing relative importance of pension funds, trust funds, and other institutional purchasers of stocks has also tended to decrease the average risk-premium, as well as to broaden the market. That is, the risk of capital depreciation is less in the case of diversified holdings which can be held over long periods of time than in the case of narrow holdings of individuals which may have to be sold on short notice. The growth of income and wealth of individuals generally would also help reduce the risk element in equity holdings, and increase in relative demand for stocks.

I would expect that the higher average P/E ratios of recent years would continue into the foreseeable future, since I believe the shifts of the underlying factors were of a permanent nature. That is, we shall continue to be more growth-conscious, and shall require a lower risk-premium now that the 1930's are a fading memory and the economy promises to pursue a steadier growth path. This does not mean that there will not be occasional rises in discount rates and corresponding drops in P/E ratios, such as occurred last year. The 1966 drop in the stock market was, I believe, due largely to the sharp increases in the interest rate and to expectations of an economic readjustment and a decline in profits in later 1966 and 1967—expectations that are now being borne out by events. Although my topic is the long-run outlook, I should like to add that now the readjustment is upon us, I would expect the stock market recovery to continue, reflecting the reductions in interest rates in recent months and expectations of renewed economic advance in latter 1967 and 1968.

There will also be times when over-optimism and speculative excesses will develop, as in 1961, when the average P/E ratio got up above 22:1. I have the same reaction to such multiples as I did at the time, when I wrote the following words a few months before the severe correction of early 1962:[1]

> Remember that the higher the market relative to its earnings base, the more vulnerable it is to shock—and despite the bright outlook for strong growth, risks will always be with us. Further, as the P/E ratio rises, the dividend yield falls and at some point the bond yield will exert an upward pull and thus tend to restrain the rise in stock prices as more investors shift to bonds . . . The better than 6 percent rate of growth of sales anticipated in the 1960's means

---

[1] J. W. Kendrick, "Investment Implications of Long-Run Economic Trends," *Financial Analysts Journal*, September–October 1961.

that more new capital will have to be raised. The relatively cheaper cost of equity capital means that an increasing proportion of the increasing volume of new funds will probably come from new stock issues. This increases the supply of stock, which will also tend to prevent prices from continuing to rise in relation to earnings, and the increasing relative scarcity of bonds will help stabilize the bond-stock ratio.

It seems unlikely that the upward trend of the ratio will set new norms significantly above the 22:1 ratio suggested by 1961 market action. Certainly further upward movement will meet increasingly strong resistance. But we are dealing with valuations that are, in the last analysis, rooted in psychological elements. Further spread of a 'new era' psychology could conceivably support price-earnings ratios of 25:1 or better—until an unexpected major shock to confidence served to deflate expectations and capitalization rates. The increasing risk of a downward revaluation as capitalization rates mount is itself a major reason why we have not stretched the projected range further on the high side.

MARKET OUTLOOK

If we apply the 18:1. P/E ratio to the per share earnings projection, we come up with the Standard and Poor's 500 stock average at 162 in 1975 compared with 88.65 in 1965 and 82.29 in 1966 (line 26). The Dow-Jones industrials would hit 1665 in 1975, compared with averages of 911 in 1965 and 874 in 1966 (line 30). These levels would represent an average annual rate of appreciation of 5.7 percent over the decade 1965-75.

Even at the lower 14:1 P/E ratio in 1975, the average annual rate of appreciation would be almost 4 percent (line 25). At the higher 22:1 multiple, the price rise would average about 7 percent a year (line 27).

When combined with the projected dividend yield of 3 percent (line 28), the total return from equity holdings would average a better than 8½ percent a year over the decade 1965-75, assuming the 18:1 price-earnings ratio. If this figure approximates the discount rate, as some analysts maintain,[2] and the average interest rate is projected at between 4½ and 5 percent over the decade, then it is apparent that the risk premium alone is in the neighborhood of 4 percent. This would seem to be a generous allowance for the average risk of equity holdings as compared with debt ownership.

It is true that the total return from stocks would be significantly less than was realized during the decade 1950-1960, when the P/E ratio more than doubled. A decline in the discount rate of this magnitude is unlikely to repeat itself. But the projected return compares very favorably with the average of 9 percent for the period 1926-1960 calculated by University of Chicago researchers under a grant from Merrill Lynch. All in all, it may be concluded that common stocks will continue to be a very attractive investment in the years ahead.

ANALYZING THE OUTLOOK FOR INDUSTRIES

I shall conclude with a few observations on possible techniques for analyzing the outlook for average prices of stocks of companies in various

---

[2] See "Why the Stock Market Acts That Way," *Fortune*, November, 1966.

industry groups. One starts with overall GNP projections, as discussed above. Then you can project the sales of a particular industry based on their past relationship to GNP, or relevant segments of product, modified by projections of other variables believed to be relevant, such as relative prices, new product developments, or the relative growth of particular segments of the market important for the given industry.

A more sophisticated and costly approach to sales projections is available if one is interested in deriving consistent projections of sales of all industries. This involves breaking projected GNP down into its various detailed product classes, and assigning these to industry of origin. Then, by use of so-called input-output tables, showing interindustry sales and purchase relationships, the sales of each industry, comprising both final and intermediate products, can be projected. This method has been used by the federal government in its recent report, *Projections 1970: Interindustry Relationships, Potential Demand, Employment*[3] and by some private investigators.[4]

From the sales figures, net income projections can be derived by techniques analogous to those discussed for the private economy as a whole. It will be recalled that it is useful to deal with invested capital—sales ratios and rates of return separately. Projected net income must then be related to per-share earning for the corresponding industry groupings of average stock prices.

Then, as for the economy as a whole, one should look at past discount rates and associated P/E ratios on an industry basis. Before deciding on the appropriate capitalization rates to apply to projected earnings, it should be kept in mind that the higher the projected growth rate, the greater the risk premium, due to the possibility that the growth of sales and net income may decelerate. Nevertheless, other things equal, the higher the projected growth rate, the higher the ratio of price to current earnings. The critical, judgmental factor is deciding whether the market is according too high or too low a discount rate to future earnings—which will also reflect whether our own earnings projection is below or above that implicit in the composite market appraisal.

The company analyst has the hardest job of all, of course, because he must go through the economy and industry projections before he has a basis for the company projection. Then he must add the crucial judgment as to the probable quality of particular managements in future years with respect to market shares, and control of costs.

CONCLUSION

In the last analysis, forecasting remains an art, the more so the greater the degree of disaggregation. But the scientific element in financial projection is being expanded by the research going on at institutions, such

---

[3] U.S. Department of Labor *Bulletin* No. 1536.

[4] See especially Clopper Almon, Jr. The American Economy to 1975: An Interindustry Forecast.

as the University of Chicago and the Wharton School, which is financed by investment banking firms, and by the research being carried on within these firms themselves—such as Bankers Trust, Smith, Barney & Company —and by institutions such as the College Retirement Equities Fund.

I am convined that basic financial research should be expanded considerably. It will help our financial institutions and markets do a better job, as well as help the average individual achieve better results. But the element of personal judgment and intuition of the security analyst will always remain. Yet we can take comfort from the fact that even if some of our judgments are faulty, adequate diversification plus the overall growth trends, which can be projected with far more certainty than individual situations, will bail us out in the long-run!

20

HOW TO INTERPRET THE BALANCE OF PAYMENTS ACCOUNTS*

Federal Reserve Bank of St. Louis

The Balance of Payments Accounts is a double entry record of real and financial transactions between U.S. and foreign residents. Because it is based on double entry bookkeeping principles, the balance of payments always balances in the sense that receipts always equal payments. The double entry nature of the Balance of Payments Accounts is shown on the left-hand side of the accompanying table. This strictly accounting balance must not be confused, however, with a meaningful economic balance, because the economic behavior underlying some of these transactions may not be sustainable. For example, the receipt of $1.2 billion in 1967 from the sale of the U.S. gold stock (IV.3.a) can only continue as long as our gold stock lasts. There are two officially accepted measures of our economic Balance of Payments, the *Liquidity Balance* and the *Official Settlements Balance*, which are shown on the right-hand side of the table.

To understand the bookkeeping aspect, it is convenient to divide the Balance of Payments Accounts into four categories: Goods and Services, Private Capital, Government, and Other. These accounts are, of course, linked to one another; an export could be financed by a private bank loan, by a government grant, or by a private gift.

I. Goods and Services. Merchandise exports and imports are a measure of physical goods which cross national boundaries. Service exports and imports measure purchases and sales of services by U.S. residents to foreign residents. Sales of military equipment are included in service exports, and U.S. military purchases abroad are included in service imports (I.2.a). Investment income from the large volume of U.S. direct and portfolio investment abroad is the largest surplus item in the service category (I.2.b). Next to military, travel is the largest deficit item in the Goods and Services category (I.2.c).

II. Private Capital. For long-term capital, this records all changes in U.S. private assets and liabilities to foreigners. Net increases in U.S. assets are measured as payments of dollars abroad, and net increases in U.S.

---

* Reprinted by permission of the Federal Reserve Bank of St. Louis.

liabilities are measured as receipts of U.S. dollars from abroad. Direct investment (II.1.a) by Americans abroad is much larger than direct investment by foreigners in the United States. However, portfolio investment (II.1.b) is about evenly divided. For short-term capital, payments represent changes in all private U.S. assets, while receipts represent only changes in nonbank short-term liabilities. Changes in U.S. bank short-term liabilities are listed under IV.4 along with short-term liabilities of U.S. official monetary institutions.

III. Government. Gross outflow of loans, grants, and transfers for the government were $5.6 billion, and the net outflow was $4.2 billion in 1967. A large share of government loans and grants is tied to purchases in the United States. To the extent that tied purchases would not have been made without the government loan or grant, this results in an increase in exports of U.S. goods and services. Thus, the $4.2 billion deficit somewhat overstates the government's real impact on the overall Balance of Payments deficit.

IV. Other. Private Transfers represents gifts and similar payments by American residents to foreign residents. Errors and Omissions is the statistical discrepancy between all specifically identifiable receipts and payments. It is believed to be largely unrecorded short-term capital movements. Changes in U.S. Reserve Assets represent official transactions of the U.S. government with foreign governments and the International Monetary Fund. Changes in U.S. Liquid Liabilities represent increased foreign holdings of liquid dollar liabilities of U.S. private and official monetary institutions (banks, the U.S. Treasury, and the Federal Reserve).

BALANCE OF PAYMENTS MEASURES

Two economic measures of the balance of payments are represented in the table. The Net Balance column shows the source and overall size of the deficit or surplus, while the Financing column shows how the deficit is financed or the surplus disposed.

The major difference between these two measures is the way foreign holdings of U.S. bank and Treasury liabilities are handled. The underlying assumption about economic behavior in *Liquidity Balance* is that all foreign holdings of dollar liabilities which mature in one year or less (Liquid Liabilities) are a real claim on the U.S. gold stock. As such, the Liquidity Balance measures the actual decline in the U.S. gold stock and other reserve assets of the U.S. government and increases in all U.S. liquid liabilities to foreigners.

The underlying economic rationale of the *Official Settlements Balance* is that only foreign official holdings of dollars represent a real claim on the gold stock. Foreign private holders and international organizations have a demand for dollar balances as an international currency in the same way as they may have a demand for any U.S. services. Thus, an increase

Balance of Payments Measures

Transactions	Balance of Payments Accounts			Liquidity Balance		Official Settlements Balance	
	Receipts	Payments	Balance	Net Balance	Financing of Net Balance	Net Balance	Financing of Net Balance
I. Goods and Services............	45.8	41.0	+ 4.8	+ 4.8	....	+ 4.8	....
1. Mdse. Trade (goods)......	30.5	27.0	+ 3.5	....	....	....	....
2. Services..................	15.3	14.0	+ 1.3	....	....	....	....
a. Military...............	1.2	4.3	— 3.1	....	....	....	....
b. Investment Income......	6.9	2.3	+ 4.6	....	....	....	....
c. Travel.................	1.7	3.2	— 1.5	....	....	....	....
d. Other.................	5.5	4.2	+ 1.3	....	....	....	....
II. Private Capital..............	2.7	5.5	— 2.8	— 2.8	....	....	....
1. Long term..................	2.3	4.3	— 2.0	....	....	....	....
a. Direct Investment.......	.2	3.0	— 2.8	....	....	— 2.8	....
b. Portfolio Investment.....	1.0	1.3	— .3	....	....	— .3	....
c. Bank and Other Loans (Net).	1.1	.0	+ 1.1	....	....	+ .3	+ .8
2. Short term................	.4	1.2	— .8	....	....	— .8	....
III. Government (non-military)......	1.4	5.6	— 4.2	— 4.2	....	....	....
1. Loans.....................	1.4	3.4	— 2.0	....	....	— 2.5	+ .5
2. Grants and Transfers........	....	2.2	— 2.2	....	....	— 2.2	....
IV. Other........................			.8	.8	....	.8	....
1. Private Transfers...........	....	.8	— .8	— .8	....	— .8	....
2. Errors and Omissions........	....	.5	— .5	— .5	....	— .5	....
3. Changes in U.S. Reserve Assets	1.2	1.1	+ .1	....	+ .1	....	+ .1
a. Gold (outflow is receipt)..	1.2	....	+ 1.2	....	....	....	....
b. Convertible Currencies...	....	1.0	— 1.0	....	....	....	....
c. I M F Gold Tranche Position..	....	.1	— .1	....	....	....	....
4. Changes in U.S. Liquid Liabilities.................	3.7	.2	+ 3.5	....	+ 3.5	....	....
a. Foreign Official Holders...	2.0	....	+ 2.0	....	....	....	+ 2.0
b. Foreign Prvt. Holders.....	1.7	....	+ 1.7	....	....	+ 1.7	....
c. Int'l. Organizations other than I M F........	....	.2	— .2	....	....	— .2	....
Total................	54.8	54.8	.0	— 3.6*	+ 3.6	— 3.4*	+ 3.4

* Figures do not add because of rounding.

in foreign private holdings of dollars is treated in a manner similar to that of a capital inflow; i.e., included in the Net Balance column rather than in the Financing column. The Official Settlements Balance measures changes in U.S. reserve assets, and changes in foreign official holdings of dollars both liquid and nonliquid. Thus, long term U.S. bank liabilities of $.8 billion and U.S. Treasury liabilities of $.5 billion purchased by foreign governments are in the Financing column.

21

NEW TRENDS IN INSTITUTIONAL INVESTING*

Edmund A. Mennis, C.F.A.

In a very perceptive book written in 1959,[1] Paul Harbrecht pointed out the changing attitude of the individual toward property in our capitalist society. As corporations have grown in size and as ownership has become more diffused, the individual is less interested in his legal property rights and more interested in the income from his investments and their liquidity, that is, their transferability to others. Because the individual now is primarily interested in the results from his investments rather than the responsibilities of ownership and management, a further separation has developed between the productive property and the ultimate beneficiary. Large financial institutions—pension and profit sharing funds, investment companies, insurance companies, and bank administered trusts—themselves gather the evidences of ownership, manage them for their income producing function, and distribute the benefits to the ultimate owners in turn.

The growth of this so-called "institutional investor" has been accompanied by increased competition for the savings dollar of the individual investor, and this competition has taken the form not just of services rendered but of investment results obtained. Among other areas affected, these trends have had a significant impact on investment patterns, on stock exchange institutions, and on the capital markets. Each of these is worthy of some comment.

IMPORTANCE OF INSTITUTIONAL INVESTORS

The size of the funds held by institutional investors is indeed impressive. Based on data from a number of sources, the market value of their security holdings at the end of 1966 has been estimated at about $600 billion, divided among mutual funds, bank trust funds, eleemosynary institutions, insurance companies, and pension funds, both public and

---

* Reprinted by permission of the *Financial Analysts Journal* (July–August 1968).

[1] *Pension Funds and Economic Power*, Paul Harbrecht, Twentieth Century Fund (New York), 1959, especially Chap. 10.

private.[2] The value at the end of 1967 undoubtedly was considerably larger. The New York Stock Exchange has estimated that at the end of 1967 institutions held one third of the market value of stocks traded on the Exchange.[3] More importantly, institutional volume on the New York Stock Exchange as a percent of total public volume has increased from 25.4 percent in March 1956 to 42.9 percent in October 1966, the latest date available.[4] Net money flows into the capital markets by mutual savings banks, insurance companies, pension funds, mutual funds, and savings and loan associations have more than quadrupled in the postwar period to over $36 billion in 1967, and shifts in investment emphasis by these institutions have had a significant impact on savings patterns and the capital markets.[5]

COMPETITION

As the institutionalization of savings has grown, so has competition among the various institutions. Life insurance companies have entered the mutual fund field, either through the use of variable annuities or by the actual purchase of mutual fund management organizations. Mutual funds have purchased or formed life insurance subsidiaries. Banks have become active competitors of life insurance companies in the pension field, and life insurance companies have been permitted by law to set up segregated accounts that permit higher equity holdings for such funds. Rather than insure or trustee their pension plans, many corporations have chosen to self administer their plans. Investment management companies have broadened their activities to include many types of funds and also have added investment counseling services. Investment counseling firms as well as stock exchange firms have entered the mutual fund field, and banks are trying to overcome the legal obstacles to do the same. No longer are the lines of demarcation clear; every type of institutional investor is an actual or potential competitor for the individual and corporate savings dollar.

PERFORMANCE

Because of the aggressive competition for the savings dollar, the investor has quite understandably asked what his rewards will be if he entrusts his money to a particular investment manager. As a result, "performance"

---

[2] Sources: Investment Company Institute, National Banking Review, SEC, Institute of Life Insurance, Bests, Pension Research Council, as gathered by Smith, Barney & Co., New York.

[3] *Institutions and the Stock Market*, New York Stock Exchange (New York), March 1968.

[4] Release 8239, Securities Exchange Act of 1934, Securities and Exchange Commission (Washington, D.C.), January 26, 1965, p. 2.

[5] See Sidney Homer, *The Impact of Corporate Pension Funds on the Capital Markets*, a talk at the Financial Conference of the National Industrial Conference Board, February 16, 1967. Detailed statistical data provided by Salomon Bros. and Hutzler.

has emerged as the most used and abused word in the investment lexicon in the past several years. Institutions have devised ingenious methods to demonstrate their accomplishments and suggest their potential in the future.

It might be worthwhile for a moment to examine the current generally accepted meaning of performance. Originally, performance measurement was an examination of the investment results over a period of time in order to determine whether the objectives of a particular investment fund had been met. Investment objectives generally included meeting some designated income requirements, conserving the dollar principal of the account, or achieving some degree of capital appreciation to offset moderate inflationary trends. A fundamental consideration was always the degree of risk that could be assumed in a particular account. The primary questions asked were what was the investment account designed to accomplish and then how did the investment results and the risks taken meet these goals.

In recent years, however, performance has come to mean something quite different. Performance now relates almost exclusively to capital appreciation, that is, how much did an account gain absolutely or relative to some market average or some other fund. A "high-performance" investment fund is one designed to maximize capital appreciation, and the risk assumed is rarely discussed or measured. Moreover, the period over which this performance is attained has become shorter and shorter, as accomplishments are measured and compared not over several years but rather annually, monthly, and weekly. Funds are shifted on the basis of recent appreciation results, and risks assumed or objectives sought are given secondary consideration.

It is not my purpose here to object to emphasis on performance. Certainly it could be argued that in years past some institutional investors have not been sufficiently sensitive to the investor's needs, so that overly conservative attitudes were adopted with one eye on the experiences of the Great Depression and the other on the fear of possible suit or surcharge. But perhaps the pendulum has swung too far on the other side, and too many investors are now concerned primarily with how much their stocks have appreciated recently. This prevailing attitude and the demand that institutional investors meet certain performance requirements in a competitive environment have markedly altered investment patterns.

INSTITUTIONAL INVESTMENT PATTERNS

The most noticeable trend in institutional investing is the movement to higher and higher common stock ratios in portfolios. Corporate pension funds, which originally were invested almost entirely in bonds, now have average stock ratios of 55 percent, and many go much higher. Similar or higher ratios are seen in many bank trust funds. Many life insurance company portfolios, with the permission of state legislatures, now have about 5 percent of their admitted assets in stocks, and fire and casualty company stock ratios run 35 percent or more. Large university endowment funds, faced with expenses rising faster than income, hold over 50 percent of their portfolios in common stocks. Even state and local government pension funds, the last bastion of fixed-dollar securities, are now moving modestly to common stocks with the permission of state legislatures. Of course, mutual funds are a mixed breed, but the flow of new money has been strongly in favor of the all common stock fund, particularly the aggressively managed funds, while the balanced fund has lost investor attraction.

The rationale behind the greater use of equities stems originally from a conviction that the greatest investment risk in the postwar period has been not the financial risk of a sharp and prolonged decline in corporate earnings but rather the risk of decreasing purchasing power and loss of principal in fixed income securities as interest rates have moved up. With an expanding economy postwar contrasted with the heavily cyclical economy from 1919–1939, with the growth of professional financial analysis, and with the greater disclosure of corporate information, the financial risk has been minimized. However, the inflation risk is caused by political and economic forces over which the investor has little control, and this risk can be offset by selection of appropriate investment media as well as by careful security analysis.

As higher common stock ratios have gained in acceptance, however, the reasons for owning stocks have shifted in the view of many investors. No longer are they looked upon as a means of protection against decreasing purchasing power and of participating in the long-term growth of the American economy. Rather the emphasis has shifted to their appreciation potential, and stocks are purchased for the capital gains they might provide. This shift in emphasis has inevitably led many investors to assume greater risk and more recently to engage in a form of speculation in equities that has not been seen for some time. The necessity for producing a successful investment performance has led to substantial changes in the types of equities favored by institutional buyers.

One of the characteristics of institutional stock holdings is concentration in a relatively small number of issues. For example, the Wharton Report found that during 1953–58 a relatively large portion of mutual fund assets was concentrated in 30 favored stocks. As of September 1958, investments in these 30 stocks accounted for 19.1 percent of the funds' net assets and for 23.5 percent of the value of their common stock portfolios. The SEC added that the tendency of mutual funds to concentrate their investments in relatively few securities does not differ from the investment pattern of other institutional investors.[6] A report of Vickers Asso-

---

[6] *Public Policy Implications of Investment Company Growth,* Report of the Securities and Exchange Commission, December 2, 1966 (Washington, D.C.), U.S. Government Printing Office, p. 291.

ciates as of December 31, 1967 indicated that the 50 favorite stocks held by 550 investment companies with assets of approximately $60 billion represented a market value of $16.3 billion, or 27 percent of the total.[7]

Concentration in institutional portfolios is not surprising; it is almost inevitable considering the size of funds invested and the marketability problems of stocks with a small floating supply. However, shifts in these concentrations, especially if they are accomplished rapidly, may influence the prices and price-earnings multiples of particular industries and stocks. The evidence on shifts and increased portfolio turnover suggests this can happen. The report by Vickers shows a major shift in industry emphasis in mutual fund portfolios over the past 11 years. From December 31, 1957 to December 31, 1967 high growth industries, such as office equipment, electronics, leisure time, and airlines, have increased from 10 percent of the total market value of the "Favorite 50" to 51 percent. In contrast, other industry concentrations have declined significantly. Utilities fell from 11 percent to 4 percent, oil and natural gas from 35.4 percent to 21.8 percent, chemicals and drugs from 10.0 percent to 6 percent. Although data for other institutional holdings are not available, similar shifts in their portfolios undoubtedly have occurred. The trend to growth stocks and away from the more conventional "blue chips" is clearly evident, spurred no doubt by the desire to improve investment performance. These shifts affected both prices and price-earnings ratios. A study by The Republic National Bank of Dallas at the end of 1967 indicated that a large group of high-growth stocks was selling close to the highest price-earnings ratio relative to the market in the postwar period, while a group of moderate-growth and basic industry stocks were near the lowest relative price-earnings ratios.

An additional trend that has developed in institutional investing is the increasing turnover of holdings in investment portfolios. As computed by the New York Stock Exchange for the third quarter of 1967, open-end mutual fund portfolio turnover was at an annual rate of 40.8 percent, noninsured private pension funds 16.0 percent and life insurance companies 18.4 percent. All of these figures are substantially higher than they were several years ago. In 1955 the comparable ratios were 15.9 percent for open-end mutual funds, and 11.8 percent for both noninsured private pension funds and life insurance companies.[8]

A corollary of increased turnover has been higher trading volume on the New York Stock Exchange and a growing number of large block transactions. In 1967 trading volume reached a record daily average of 10.1 million shares, and the rate in the first 14 days of 1968 was an average of 12.7 million shares daily. Although this volume was handled on the floor of the Exchange, the "back office" work was so far behind that

---

[7] *Vickers Favorite Fifty*, published by Vickers Associates (New York), December 31, 1967.

[8] *Institutions and the Stock Market*, New York Stock Exchange (New York), March 1968 and June 1967.

curtailed trading days were necessary for six weeks, and extension of the settlement period was required.

A further measure of the influence of the institutional investor is the increased trading of large blocks of securities. In 1967 a record total of 6,685 blocks of 10,000 shares or more were traded on the New York Stock Exchange, 85 percent more than the blocks traded in 1966 and more than triple the 1965 number. Moreover, the market value of these large blocks amounted to 6.7 percent of the Exchange's reported volume for the year.[9]

As a matter of personal observation, the stock market at this time could be divided into three parts: the traditional blue chips, representing the larger industrial corporations; the quality growth stocks; and smaller, more speculative stocks. This latter area has received increasing attention in the past few years, again stemming from the search for short-term performance. At times, stocks with a relatively limited number of shares are said to be subjected to aggressive trading practices in order to affect their prices favorably.[10] This sort of investment has had many imitators among individual investors and has led the Chairman of the Federal Reserve Board to comment that "practices of this nature contain poisonous qualities reminiscent in some respects to the old pool operations of the 1920's."

The growing importance of the institutional investor and his influence on the securities markets is obvious. The result of all of these developments has been a significant increase in market volatility in securities where institutional investors own a large percent of the outstanding shares of a particular company. Institutions have long boasted of their stabilizing influence on securities market, because their unemotional judgments are supposed to support declining markets and prevent speculative excesses in rising markets. The performance of the last year, however, raises the question of whether this statement still can be considered accurate, especially in stocks where institutions hold a substantial number of shares. The effects of such volatility on the smaller, relatively less well-informed investor are hardly favorable. Moreover, there is some argument, at least, whether this increased activity has resulted in better performance.[11]

Impact on Stock Exchange Institutions

As the size and importance of the institutional investor has grown, so has the influence of the brokerage firms that serve this market. This development has obviously had a major effect on the older stock exchange

---

[9] *Ibid.*, March 1968.

[10] "In and Out Traders," *Wall Street Journal*, September 14, 1967, p. 1 and "Thin Stocks Due to Get New Rule," *New York Times*, October 8, 1967, sec. 3, p. 1.

[11] See Arthur M. Jones, "Those Go-Go Funds May Be Going Nowhere," *Fortune*, November 1967, p. 143 ff. Also see, Robert A. Levy, "Is Performance Fund Trading Gainful or Wasteful," *The Institutional Investor*, December 1967, p. 36 ff., and the rejoinder in *Fortune*, March 1968, pp. 199–200.

firms, which have had to adjust to the new character of the market. In addition, many new firms have been established in recent years that cater exclusively to institutional customers. The type of research provided for institutional consumption is considerably different from that used for retail purposes. The institutional client usually has his own professional staff. In addition, decision-making is shifting from large committees to one professional manager or to a small professional group in order to facilitate prompt action. Therefore, serving this sophisticated market requires more specialized services, such as economic and technical analysis, more in-depth studies of industries and companies, and more contact and personal attention. Moreover, because of the significant buying power of their customers, recommendations to buy or sell by their firms can have an important effect on the price of a stock. It has been reported that prospective recommendations are often communicated by telephone to certain customers before a report is written, which can give certain investors a market advantage.[12]

Because a relatively few institutions account for a substantial portion of the trading on the securities exchanges and because their trading ordinarily is in blocks of stock substantially larger than that of the retail customer, many stock exchange firms have set up trading departments to service these special customers. Institutional trading is significantly different from trading smaller amounts of stock because the customer usually has his own sophisticated trader with fairly specific ideas about the price he has in mind and the efficiency he expects in executions.

In addition to the growing volume of transactions on the New York Stock Exchange, the increase in institutional business had led to a revival in activity on regional stock exchanges and also the development of the so-called "third market." The regional exchanges were originally established to provide local markets for local securities. However, their growth in recent years can be attributed in a large part to their ability to provide additional markets for securities traded on the New York Stock Exchange. These regional exchanges have been used by institutional investors either to facilitate executing large orders without drawing undue attention to their activities or, more importantly, to take advantage of the more flexible commission rate structure on the regional exchanges. This point is discussed in greater detail below.

Trading by institutional investors has also encouraged the substantial growth of the third market, conducted by securities firms that are not members of any exchange and that deal in listed securities over-the-counter, both as principal and agent. The dollar volume of such activity has about doubled in the past three years and represents about 3 percent of the market value of activity on the New York Stock Exchange.[13] These firms often are able to execute orders at rates substantially below mini-

---

[12] "In and Out Traders," *Wall Street Journal*, September 14, 1967, p. 1.

[13] *Institutions and the Stock Market*, New York Stock Exchange (New York), December 1967.

mum commission rates on the exchanges and, consequently, are used by institutions where possible to lower the cost of transactions.

The subject of the large amount of commission business generated by institutional investors is quite complex. The peculiar rigid structure of commission rates allows no volume discount or reduced fee for larger orders, although the economies of scale are obvious. Consequently, the commission charged on a 10,000 share order is 100 times as great as that charged on a 100 share order. As a result of the substantial profit in large orders, they are eagerly sought by stock exchange firms. In fact, these executing firms are willing to "give up" a portion of their commission to other broker-dealers, either on their own initiative or most often at the request of the institutional customer. Institutional investors use these give-ups as a reward for research services. Managers of mutual funds also direct such give-ups to broker-dealers who have sold fund shares. New York Stock Exchange firm members may give up commissions only to other members of the Exchange. Some regional exchanges, on the other hand, permit give-ups not only to members of the particular exchange but also to any member of the National Association of Securities Dealers. Thus, institutional investors trading on regional exchanges have much greater flexibility in directing a portion of their commissions to firms who render other services and still do the bulk of their trading with a few lead brokers who render an exceptional trading service.

It should be no surprise that the disposition of commissions should be of interest to the regulatory authorities. The Securities and Exchange Commission now has under consideration a new rule stating that giving up a commission at the direction of a registered investment company or its affiliates is illegal unless the portion of the commission given up is either paid to the registered investment company or the fees charged that company are reduced by the amount of the commissions.[14] The New York Stock Exchange has made an alternative proposal that would give volume discounts for large orders and also limit the amount of give-ups, prevent regional exchanges from offering more liberal give-up arrangements, and prevent affiliates of institutional investors from becoming members of exchanges in order to receive give-ups and reciprocal business.[15] The outcome of these proposals is difficult to anticipate, but whatever changes are made will have a significant impact on the nature and profitability of many stock exchange institutions.

Impact on the Capital Markets

The increasing flow of institutional funds into the capital markets and the greater emphasis on equity securities versus debt instruments has had a

---

[14] Source cited in footnote 4 above.

[15] Letter to Members and Allied Members, New York Stock Exchange, Mr. Robert W. Haack, President, New York Stock Exchange, January 2, 1968, subject: Commission Rate Structure Proposal.

marked impact on the capital markets. Most of the external long term financing of business and the real estate industry is done by debt, yet the trend in institutional investing is toward purchase of equities. A continuation of these trends has implications for the flow of savings and the future growth of the economy.

A recent analysis by Salomon Brothers and Hutzler[16] indicates that financial intermediaries (mutual savings banks, insurance companies, private noninsured pension funds, state and local retirement funds, and open-end mutual funds) accounted for $6.1 billion, or 87 percent, of annual net purchases of corporate bonds in 1957, and, although this figure rose to $12.0 percent billion in 1967, it represented only 74 percent of annual net purchases. State and local retirement funds and life insurance companies accounted for two thirds of these purchases, and these institutions are among the leaders in reexamining the traditional high debt ratios in their portfolios.

With respect to annual net purchases of corporate stocks, these financial intermediaries have increased their purchases from $2.7 billion in 1957 to $9.1 billion in 1967. Inasmuch as the net new sale of corporate stock was about the same in both periods ($2.7 billion in 1957 and $2.2 billion in 1967), financial intermediaries have been buying on balance from individual and miscellaneous investors. In 1967 this net sale by individuals (which has continued without interruption since 1957) reached a record of $7.2 billion. The analysis also indicates that, of the financial intermediaries, pension funds are the largest and steadiest purchasers of common stocks, generally representing about 55–57 percent of net stock purchases each year in the 11-year period. It might appear that stock ownership is becoming increasingly institutionalized and that price-earnings multiples will continue to trend higher as institutions bid more and more for a dwindling supply of stocks held by individuals.

No doubt institutional stock ownership has grown and is an important factor in affecting security prices. However, the seriousness of the supply-demand equation is not so great as the raw statistics would suggest. The net new offerings of common stocks represent the money flows but not the net addition to market values. Presumably the plowback of earnings retained by corporations provides additional profits which support higher market values. In addition, if an individual investor held a certain amount of common stock for several years and market prices have risen since (which by and large has been the case), he can continue to sell a portion of his stocks and still have a significant investment in equities.[17] Nevertheless, the institutional investor is a persistent and increasingly dominant factor in the stock market, and his search for inflationary

---

[16] Source cited in footnote 5 above.

[17] I am indebted to Frank Block, Vice President of Citizens and Southern Bank of Atlanta, for these observations on the apparent net liquidation of individual security holdings.

protection or investment performance, neither of which is supplied by debt instruments, will direct the areas to which his capital will flow.

Future Trends

Predicting the future is always hazardous. However, some guesses about the future trends of institutional investing and their meaning for individual investors may be of interest.

Institutions will continue to grow, and the trend toward concentration of savings in institutional versus individual portfolios will continue.

Competition among institutional investors will increase. Diversification into offering more than one type of investment service and the emergence of "department stores" of finance is only beginning and will expand significantly. It is certain that the form of financial institutions will be different; it is difficult to predict what forms these institutions will take.

Many more individual investors will turn their investment problems over to institutions because of the increased and better services offered and the growing inability of the individual investor to be successful in an increasingly complex field.

Unless a reversal occurs in the growth of the economy, accompanied by a substantial moderation of inflation (both of which seem unlikely), the trend to large proportions of equities in institutional portfolios will continue. The decreasing interest of institutional investors in debt securities suggests that higher and higher yields will be necessary to attract their purchases, especially if the recent inflationary trends in the economy persist. Additional use of convertible securities probably will grow. Moreover, the implications for the mortgage market are even more serious. Savings and loan associations and life insurance companies are the chief sources of funds for mortgages. The former will have difficulty competing for the individual's savings unless mortgage rates are increased, and the latter may well find the corporate bond market more attractive. Methods of packaging mortgages and increasing their marketability also will be necessary if institutional funds are to be attracted to this area. The long-term implications for interest costs in the construction industry, competition for fixed-dollar savings and trends in residential construction are apparent.

Individual investors are also growing more sophisticated in evaluating these trends, and their investment patterns may shift even more rapidly from fixed dollar to equity investments.

To serve the expanding institutional market, stock exchange firms will have to expand their trading and research services. It is difficult to anticipate the outcome of the new regulatory proposals, but their effects on the securities business will be far-reaching. It seems logical that some form of volume discount will emerge, so that institutional investors and their beneficiaries will receive the benefits of the economies of scale derived from their larger buying and selling power. It also seems likely that give-ups will be regulated in some fashion so that the institutional investor and its beneficiaries will receive either reduced fees or increased services. Depending on the outcome of the proposals, the New York and regional stock exchanges may be strengthened or weakened. Selling practices of mutual funds could be substantially affected and the growth of dealer-distributed funds reduced. Institutional investors may or may not seek membership on regional exchanges. If the use of give-ups is drastically curtailed, institutional investors may restrict their business to firms that combine a strong trading capability and outstanding research, thus affecting the future of smaller firms, both in leading financial centers and elsewhere. Whatever the outcome, significant changes are ahead in stock exchange institutions that can be attributed in large part to the growing importance of the institutional investor.

Increasing interest by the regulatory authorities in the activities of institutional investors is inevitable. Certain rapidly growing areas especially, such as pension and profit sharing funds, will be subject to various forms of federal regulations covering vesting, funding, and investing.

Because of the size of large institutional portfolios, their trading activities will continue to have a significant effect on the trend and volatility of security prices. Because of their concentration in a relatively few securities, their shifts in investment emphasis from one area to another will have an important influence on stock price trends within the broad patterns of the market. Moreover, if the securities markets are an important factor in determining the allocation of savings within the economy, decisions by a relatively few investment managers rather than individual decisions by millions of small investors will become increasingly important.

The emphasis on measuring performance of an investment account will continue. Hopefully, this emphasis will shift back to the more rational consideration of how an account has met the objectives of the investor and shift away from the current stress on short-term capital appreciation. To the extent that the investor strives to achieve substantially more than the long-term growth trend of the economy will accommodate, he must assume greater risks, and failure to consider these risks, historically at least, has led to losses rather than gains. Financial analysis and investment management have grown enormously in sophistication since the 1920's, but they have not yet discovered a magic formula to provide a rapid path to untold wealth for all.

Part Three

Financial Analysis

22
THE DIMENSIONS OF ANALYSIS: A CRITICAL REVIEW*

Douglas A. Hayes C.F.A.

The process of selecting individual securities, and particularly common stocks, for investment portfolios has several dimensions. But while the basic structure of the portfolio selection process is fairly well established, considerable controversy seems to exist as to the means by which these dimensions should be implemented. It is our purpose to review critically a few major areas of conflict currently extant in investment analysis. Hopefully, this might enable practicing analysts to identify more clearly the issues involved and the possible implications of the alternative points of view.

For example, it is generally agreed that the process should be oriented to and conditioned by specific portfolio objectives, such as growth, income requirements, quality limitations, and diversification targets. But as these matters are essentially in the domain of overall portfolio strategy rather than security analysis per se, they are regarded as outside the scope of this review. However, it might be noted that considerable controversy currently exists in this areas as to the usefulness of computer programs to suggest and delineate the characteristics of efficient or optimum portfolios. It is my tentative opinion that existing models for portfolio structures are likely to be of very limited practical use as they seem to involve some highly questionable assumptions in order to obtain required quantifications, such as that the entire spectrum of risk factors can be adequately measured by the relative price volatility of individual issues.

A second crucial dimension of security selection is concerned with appraising the potential economic values (primarily prospective earnings and dividend flows and the risks surrounding their achievement) embodied in the industries and related companies that appear eligible to meet the portfolio requirements. The content of most of the literature, as well as of our series of C.F.A. examinations, suggests that mastery of this broad area is considered to be of prime importance to the professional development of financial analysts and portfolio managers. And rightly so. For while the

---
* Reprinted by permission of the *Financial Analysts Journal* (September–October 1966).

random walk theory of security prices may be convincing with respect to the problem of obtaining short-term trading results, this theory does not conflict with the proposition that long-term investment returns will largely be a function of the long-term economic performance of particular industries and companies.

Although the concept that investment results are likely to be heavily related to corporate performance in a long-term sense is generally accepted, some recent contributions to the field have alleged that the implementation methodology should be completely revolutionized. For example, Lerner and Carleton allege that a critical investigation of the past financial statements to reveal potential problems of consistency and comparability of reported income and balance sheet data can be largely discarded because accounting and disclosure standards have improved to the point where the underlying data require no critical review.[1] Moreover, they allege that financial risk factors no longer require appraisal because of the greatly improved stability features of the economy; in lieu thereof, they suggest elegant mathematical techniques to develop the theoretical effects of assumed patterns of various management decisions and economic data on security values.[2]

However, the empirical evidence would suggest that these allegations are seriously in error. Largely because of recurrent tinkering with the tax rules for national economic policy reasons, a strong case can be made that the reported income of many, if not most, corporations have become subject to increased problems of consistency and comparability rather than less.[3] Again, while there is no doubt that general economic stability has been greatly improved through the development and vigorous application of modern fiscal and monetary concepts, individual industries and companies continue to record wide variations in revenues and net income. The earnings collapse of the cement companies, despite generally favorable conditions in the construction industry, can be cited as a case in point. In a dynamic and highly competitive private economy, it is entirely possible for a condition of general stability and growth on a macroeconomic basis to be accompanied by wide fluctuations and divergent trends on a microbasis. Therefore, the position that techniques designed to estimate potential risks arising from potential earnings instability are entirely obsolete because severe general depression conditions are highly unlikely appears open to serious question.

In short, the argument that a large portion of conventional analysis

---

[1] Lerner and Carleton, *A Theory of Financial Analysis*, Harcourt, Brace, and World, Inc., New York: 1966, pp. 3–4.

[2] *Ibid.*, pp. 37–126.

[3] For documentation see the symposium issue of articles on "Uniformity in Financial Accounting," *Law and Contemporary Problems*, Duke University, Autumn, 1965 and particularly my own article entitled "Accounting and Investment Analysis," pp. 752–771.

techniques should be discarded in favor of elaborate mathematical models does not appear convincing for practical purposes in the present stage of the arts. However, continued experimentation with such models undoubtedly will continue. Moreoever, it is entirely possible that they will prove to be valuable supplements in the complex process of appraising the relative investment merits of individual companies. But at the same time, it is doubtful if they will completely replace orthodox techniques because of the necessity to introduce highly simplifying assumptions in order to reduce the models to manageable proportions.

A third dimension involved in investment decisions consists of placing some estimate of value on the potential stream of earnings and dividends. The various concepts and techniques for implementing this task have probably been explored more widely in recent years than any other phase of investment analysis. The result has been both a proliferation of techniques and serious differences in fundamental viewpoints. Because of space limitations, only a few of the conflicts can be cited herein; a worthwhile research project would certainly be a critical comparative analysis of this entire area.

First, a fundamental difference exists as to whether values should be established in absolute or relative terms. The "abolutists" hold that multipliers or capitalization rates should have a firmly established range which should change only slowly through time if at all.[4] Only in this way, it is argued, can commitments be restrained at overvalued market levels and encouraged at more attractive price levels. The "relativists," on the other hand, hold that investment decisions essentially represent a choice among the alternatives available at any existing point in time. The relative levels of bond and stock prices, along with other considerations (the estimated inflationary bias of the economy, for example), are the basis for determining the proportions of the portfolio within each area. But once this decision is reached, the multipliers on individual stocks should relate only to those currently prevailing in the market as represented by a general index of stocks or a qualified list of alternatives.[5] Otherwise, it is argued, the valuation process may decide not *which* stocks to buy but whether *any* stocks should be bought, and thus cancel out the basic portfolio strategy already presumably determined.

A second area of conflict relates to the usefulness of present-value theory and related techniques in determining common stock values. One group holds that such techniques are highly desirable to provide a more rigorous framework for making selection decisions and that their use may also sharpen greatly comparative value estimates. On the other side, it is argued that because of recurrent dynamic changes within the economy

---

[4] Graham, Dodd, and Cottle, *Security Analysis*, 4th ed., McGraw-Hill, New York, 1962, Chap. 37.

[5] For a more complete discussion of this view, see Bing, "Appraising our Methods of Stock Appraisal," *Financial Analysts Journal*, May–June, 1964, pp. 118–124.

and individual industries, the long-term earnings forecasts required under the present-value approach have little actual validity. As a consequence, it is concluded that what appears to be a scientific and precise method of valuation is merely a theoretical exercise at best and misleading at worst.[6]

An intermediate position here would seem desirable. Certainly the use of these techniques to obtain comparative *estimates* of *relative* values can be defended. The tables of growth yields, constructed by Soldofsky and Murphy, and the series of iso-yield curves, developed by David Eiteman, are fairly recent technical contributions incorporating present-value theory which appear to have considerable promise in this connection.[7] On the other hand, when present-value techniques are used to compute *precise* values for given stocks without qualification, then they may render a misleading impression of accuracy. Moreover, used in this way they may lead to a decision to reject most qualified stocks unless flexibility in the choice of discount and growth rates is maintained.

While the need to consider portfolio objectives, prospective earnings, and dividend flows, and to estimate appropriate values for such flows are generally accepted dimensions of security selection, there is a fourth dimension which is highly controversial as to whether it should have any role at all. Reference here is to an analysis of the prospective price performance that might be anticipated over the following year or so.

The arguments in favor of considering this factor seem to be primarily based on pragmatic and operating considerations rather than on investment theory and principles. First, it can be observed that highly favorable portfolio returns in recent years could often have been obtained by acquiring stocks which had a strong visible following among investors and speculators. The results on stocks in the airline and color television industries cannot easily be ignored. Second, some portfolio managers, like it or not, operate in a competitive environment, and the quarterly or annual relative market results may be quite significant in obtaining (or retaining) clients. As is well known, mutual funds and some pension funds seem to be particularly exposed to competitive price performance criteria over fairly short time periods. Therefore, they may correctly argue that even if in principle this dimension should be secondary to long-term value criteria, as a practical matter they cannot afford to disregard it.

On the other side, it is clear that the analytical factors in this area are often really behavioral in character rather than economic or financial. As the education and training of most analysts have largely been in econom-

---

[6] The exchanges between Messrs. Molodovsky and Bing in the *Financial Aanlysts Journal*, May–June, 1964, pp. 118–128 and continued by Bing in the July–August issue, pp. 109–111 are representative of the differences here.

[7] Soldofsky and Murphy, *Growth Yields on Common Stocks: Theory and Tables*, Bureau of Business Research, State University of Iowa, Iowa City, 1961; and David Eiteman, "A Graphic Framework for Growth Stock Selection," *California Management Review*, Winter, 1965, University of California, pp. 39–50.

ics and finance rather than in psychology, a legitimate question of competence to evaluate behavioral factors can be raised.

The eminent economist, John Maynard Keynes, had a lively section in his famous *General Theory* on this point wherein he concludes by observing that many professional investors become involved in the rather vague game of "devoting our intelligences to anticipating what average opinion expects the average opinion to be" rather than selecting the investments which appear to have the "best genuine long-term expecations."[8] In short, Keynes raised a fundamental question that is quite pertinent today: May not a preoccupation with prospective market popularity in reaching investment decisions detract from the desired degree of attention to the basic value elements which are most likely to be pertinent to favorable long-term results? Keynes' comments, it might be noted, were not those of a purely academic theoretician; he was known to have accumulated a sizeable fortune through investment activities. My opinion for investors not confronted by short-term competitive performance criteria is on the record as follows: "After an investment decision has been reached, subsequent review should focus primarily on the corporate performance rather than on the market action of the stock."[9]

---

[8] Keynes, *The General Theory of Employment, Interest and Money*, Harcourt, Brace and Co., New York, 1936, p. 156.

[9] Hayes, *Investments: Analysis and Management*, 2d ed., Macmillan Co., New York, 1966, p. 81.

23

SEC FILINGS—THEIR USE TO THE PROFESSIONAL*

Carl W. Schneider

The material contained in this article and the article which follows, "SEC Filings—Their Content and Use," may not be current in light of recent developments. The SEC has recently completed a comprehensive study of the Securities Act entitled Disclosure to Investors, A Reappraisal of Administrative Policies Under the '33 and '34 Securities Acts—"The Wheat Report."

Some of the proposals made in this report have been adopted and, in all probability, more will be adopted. However, these changes do not detract from the importance of these articles, but rather point out the necessity for analysts to be aware of the SEC reports and the material contained therein.

This is one of two related articles dealing generally with information filed with the Securities and Exchange Commission by issuers of publicly owned securities. This article deals with the use of official filings which can be made by broker-dealers, security analysts, investment advisers—the professionals—who make investment recommendations on which others will rely. It also discusses the responsibilities of the professional to avail himself of this source of information. A companion article, describing the SEC filing requirements and the methods of using such material, will appear in the March–April issue of this Journal.

In the recent past, two events have taken place to cause increased interest in SEC filings. First, the SEC's recent comprehensive Report of the Special Study of Securities Markets commented adversely on the research practices of some professionals, and recommended that more extensive use should be made of officially filed material.[1] Second, the Securities Acts Amendments of 1964 extended various SEC filing require-

---

* Reprinted by permission of the *Financial Analysts Journal* (January–February 1965). Reprinted by Leasco Systems & Research Corporation as edited and updated by the author, November 1968.

[1] See notes 5, 6 and 7, *infra,* and text thereat.

ments to a great many over-the-counter companies.[2] For many of these new companies, the SEC filings will constitute a relatively more important information source than they do for the companies previously subject to the reporting requirements. The 1964 Amendments will apply principally to middle-size publicly owned concerns for which other sources of information, such as the financial press, the broad tape, market reports, etc., may not provide such extensive coverage as they do for the larger listed companies.

It is now recognized that a broker-dealer or investment adviser must have a reasonable basis for his recommendations.[3] The Commission has established, in its releases and broker-dealer disciplinary opinions, that a recommendation under many circumstances requires an investigation taking into account all reasonably ascertainable information. To offer a recommendation, prediction, or opinion without a reasonable basis constitutes a fraud.[4] The New York Stock Exchange, through its advertising and public relations program, stresses the need for getting information before investing, and emphasizes the ability of its member firms to supply data on specific securities in which a customer is interested.

The recent comprehensive Report of the Special Study of Securities Markets was critical of the research underlying investment advice given by some professionals.[5] The report noted that the public gets only "modest protection from government and industry controls over the form and

---

[2] P.L. 88–467. The coverage of the 1964 Amendments will be considered briefly in the companion article which will appear in the next issue of this Journal.

[3] A New York Stock Exchange guidepost provides: "A recommendation ... must have a basis which can be substantiated as reasonable. When recommending the purchase, sale, or switch of specific securities, supporting information should be provided or offered." Guide, para. 2474A.10(1). An NASD interpretative guide to its Rules of Fair Practice provides that: "Informative sales literature must provide a fair basis for evaluating the facts presented.... No material fact of qualification may be omitted if the omission, in the light of the context of the material presented, would cause the advertising or sales literature to be misleading." Manual G-19.

A registered investment adviser is required to retain a written memorandum indicating the reasons for any recommendation distributed to 10 or more persons to purchase or sell a specific security, if the reasons for the recommendation are not stated therein. Rule 204–2(a) (11), 17 C.F.R. 275.204–2(a) 11).

Note *New and Comprehensive Duties of Securities Sellers To Investigate, Disclose, and Have an "Adequate Basis" for Representations*, 62 MICH. L. REV. 880 (1964); Kennedy, *Symposium*, 18 BUSINESS LAWYER 27, 72–74 (1962).

Representative among recent decisions are—Berko v. SEC, 316 F. 2d 137 (C.A. 2, 1963), aff'g. Mac Robbins & Co., SEA Rel. 6846 (1962); SEC v. F. J. Johns & Co., 207 F. Supp. 566 (D.N.J. 1962); Idaho Acceptance Corp., SEA Rel. No. 7383 (1964); Heft, Kahn & Infante, Inc., SEA Rel. No. 7020 (1963); Alexander Reid & Co., SEA Rel. No. 6727 (1962); SEA Rel. No. 6721, p. 3 (1962); Barnett & Co., SEA Rel. No. 6466 (1961); N. Pinsker & Co., SEA Rel. No. 6401 (1960); Best Securities, Inc., SEA Rel. No. 6282 (1960); Leonard Burton Corp., SEA Rel. No. 5978 (1959).

[4] See decisions cited in note 3, *supra*, and notes 12 and 25, *infra*.

[5] *Report of Special Studies of Securities Markets of the Securities and Exchange Commission*, H.R. Doc. No. 95, 88th Cong. 1st Sess. (1963) (herein referred to as the "Special Study Report"), Part 3, p. 59. See also Part 1, pp. 330–87.

content of investment advice and the manner in which it is disseminated." At the time of the study, industry guideposts were not always being followed and self-regulation was not vigorous in this area.[6]

The appropriate use to be made of official filings is a subject of some controversy. The Special Study Report recommended that:

> the reservoir of filed information about an issuer . . . should be required to be used to a greater extent in research, advisory, and selling activities, and that the obligations of broker-dealers and investment advisors in this regard should be appropriately defined from time to time by the Commission and other regulatory authorities. It is suggested, for example, that broker-dealers and investment advisers who sell or recommend specific securities ought to be under an appropriately described obligation to consult officially filed information where available and to make copies available to their customers.[7]

Industry comments on these recommendations were essentially negative. The industry noted with much justification, as did the Special Study Report itself,[8] that the relative inaccessibility of official filings significantly limits their usefulness as a source of information. An industry committee further stated:

> We recognize fully the responsibilities the industry has, with respect to the accuracy and completeness of information, used in selling activities. The means available for obtaining and checking the necessary data are many. Official documents are only one of them and they are not the only sources even for the information they contain. Others include annual and interim reports published by the corporations themselves, statistical services, discussions with company officials and others in the same industry, trade and governmental publications, and press reports. Any important information in an officially filed report will invariably be picked up by the financial services and reprinted or abstracted in current statistical publications. The industry does not need to be told what sources to use. It is competent to select among them and it uses the official data when and to the extent appropriate and practical.[9]

No doubt the scope of the investigation which should be made by a professional varies with the circumstances. Broker *A* may be asked by a customer whether the purchase of a particular stock at the prevailing price is recommended. Broker *B* may be preparing a detailed report recommending the same stock. The report will cover the company's background, an appraisal of its prospects, predictions of future earnings and dividends, and a suggested maximum price up to which purchases are recommended to satisfy a particular investment objective. Obviously *B* will need considerably more information to support his opinion than *A* will require. Of the various recurring situations, the duty to make the

---

[6] *Id.* Part 1, p. 385. See note 3, *supra*, for guideposts of the NYSE and the NASD.

[7] Part 3, Special Study Report, p. 59. See also Part I, pp. 329, 387.

[8] *Id.* Part 3, pp. 59–60, 64.

[9] Part 2, *Hearings before a House Subcommittee of the Committee on Interstate and Foreign Commerce on H.R. 6789, H.R. 6793, S. 1642,* 88th Cong. 1st Sess., pp. 702–03 (1964). As noted below the author challenges the assertion that important information "invariably" is available from other public sources.

most extensive investigation should be imposed on an underwriter.[10] At the other end of the spectrum is the registered representative who is answering an unsolicited inquiry about a security which neither he nor his firm is actively recommending.

It is impossible to specify in precise quantitative terms the amount of information necessary for each purpose. A recommendation to buy at the current price given in immediate response to a telephone inquiry represents, at the least, a general familiarity with the stock. By contrast, if a professional distributes a detailed report with a research department by-line, there is an implied representation that due consideration has been given to all reasonably available information relevant to the recommendation, considering its nature and scope. The controlling principle is the same in each case. By making any recommendation, a professional represents that he has a reasonable basis for it. If he does not have such a basis, he should decline to make any comment without checking further.[11] Nor may he avoid responsibility for a baseless recommendation by stating it in terms of an "opinion," even if he honestly holds the opinion.[12]

The basis used in formulating a recommendation constitutes another variable bearing on the duty to investigate the issuer. For example, it is sometimes clear that a recommendation has been ground on "technical" factors, such as market price patterns or other criteria unrelated to "fundamental" information about the company. Though such a recommendation carries the representation that it has a reasonable basis, there is not the further representation that all reasonably available data about the company has been evaluated. However, even in such cases it may be unwise to ignore fundamental information entirely, especially if it is adverse or if the security is speculative or unseasoned. The fact that the market price does increase to a level which had been predicted without adequate basis may reflect nothing more than the success of a fraudulent sales campaign.[13] Normally, it would seem desirable for any detailed

---

[10] Amos Treat & Co., SEA Rel. No. 7341 (1964). See Israels, *Recent Developments in Securities Regulation,* 63 COLUM. L. REV. 856, 865 (1963).

[11] Even if a professional does not initiate a transaction by a recommendation, it may be dangerous for him merely to effect transactions in a security for which there is *no* available information, unless he warns his customer of that fact. The Commission's view was expressed in a release relating to, Volkswagonwerk A.G., a foreign security which was then being traded in this country. After noting the apparent absence of "that information generally available for most securities traded in this country," it stated:

"Persons effecting transactions in these securities, particularly brokers and dealers, should be careful to avoid misstatements with respect to the securities and the company, and if, as appears, there is an unusual lack of pertinent information necessary to reach an informed judgment as to the value of the securities, this fact would be a material fact within the meaning of the anti-fraud provisions mentioned." SEA Rel. No. 4352 (1961).

See also B. Fennekohl & Co., SEA Rel. No. 6898 (1962).

[12] *E.g.,* Robert Edelstein Co., SEA Rel. No. 7400 (1964).

[13] Berko v. SEC, 297 F.2d 116 (C.A. 2, 1961), *subseq. op.,* 316 F. 2d 137 (1963); *cf.* Wright, Myers & Bessell, Inc., SEA Rel. No. 7415 (1964).

report to make clear the basis for the recommendations.[14] A reader is probably entitled to assume that reasonably available information about the issuer has been duly considered, unless the opposite is made clear.

The author does not suggest that official filings with the Commission are the only reliable source of information or that they must be consulted whenever a professional makes a recommendation. A great deal of useful information, including much that is contained in official filings, may be obtained from other reliable sources, such as standard financial manuals, stockholder reports, press releases, and other information disseminated by companies themselves. However, there are many circumstances when a responsible research job should include an examination of official filings.[15]

A number of studies have been made of voluntary company reporting, aside from filings with the SEC.[16] There is general agreement that serious deficiencies exist in the reporting of many companies. While standards vary widely, the larger companies, especially those with securities listed on the New York Stock Exchange, were much better as a group than the over-the-counter companies.

SEC filings contain much of the necessary information which is omitted from voluntary reports. Standard financial manuals are the only other generally available source which may reflect the filed information not included in voluntary reports. However, the manuals do not include all of the filed information. Nor do they cover all of the companies which have made filings with the SEC in the past (or even all of the companies which are currently filing periodic reports). The 1964 Amendments should increase the number of companies required to file periodic SEC reports but which are not covered by the major manuals.

To be specific, the following are subjects about which there is important detail commonly found in SEC filings but not included in voluntary reports or the principal manuals—detail which may not interest the casual unsophisticated investor but which may be highly significant in formulating a recommendation by a professional:[17] expenses (rentals, maintenance,

---

[14] See, e.g., the Commission's investment adviser rule cited in note 3, *supra*.

[15] See generally Graham, Dodd and Cottle, *Security Analysis* Ch. 6 (4th ed. 1962).

[16] Part 3, Special Study Report, pp. 10–12 (analyzing various studies made by the SEC of over-the-counter reporting); Corliss Anderson, *Corporate Reporting for the Professional Investor* (1962) (sponsored by the Financial Analysts Federation); Robert A. Cerf, *Corporate Reporting and Investment Decisions* (Univ. of Calif. Public Accounting Research Program, 1961).

[17] Rappaport, SEC *Accounting Practice and Procedure* Ch. 3 (2d ed. 1963), a leading authority on SEC accounting, also mentions the following more unusual situations in which financial statements filed with SEC may differ from others: accounting for property acquired for stock or services, valuations based upon appraisals, sale and leaseback transactions, accounting for noninterest bearing obligations, certain real estate transactions, contingent payments based on profits following an acquisition, recapitalizations, "quasi-reorganizations" and release of a company obligation upon payment of a consideration by a principal shareholder. See also Cerf, *supra*, pp. 77–105 and Appendix II.

repairs, royalties, interest, etc.); receivables, inventories (classification, method or valuation, etc.); source and application of funds;[18] depreciation, depletion, amortization; tax accounting (accounting the investment credit, information on loss carryovers, deferred taxes, etc.); employment costs (pensions, etc.); backlogs; information on significant unconsolidated subsidiaries; additions and retirements of fixed assets; treatment of nonrecurring "special items";[19] commitments (for capital expenditures, guarantees, long-term leases, etc.); investments in subsidiaries; reserves; management (direct and indirect compensation, options, bonuses, pensions, etc.); and wasting assets. These subjects relate principally to financial statement disclosures. Of course, there is a great deal of other material in filings which is not in any other source (the manuals tending to concentrate on financial data). For example, filings may be the exclusive source of information on control, background of management, and stockholding of and transactions with insiders.

A professional analyst has an obligation to know the scope and content of the disclosure requirements in official filings. As a minimum, filings should be consulted if there is reason to believe that they may contain relevant information which is not available from another source. Of course, the relevance of filed information to any particular recommendation will depend on the nature and the basis of the recommendation. Information bearing on the liquidation value of assets is crucial if a security is being recommended in contemplation of the company's liquidation. On the other hand, such information would be irrelevant in the case of a low-book-value security of a service enterprise being recommended solely on the basis of proven earning power.

The following are illustrations of recurring situations in which official filings may provide the best or only available source for relevant information:[20]

Example. Filed financial statements often give important information which cannot be found elsewhere. For many companies officially filed financial statements include consolidated statements as well as separate statements for the parent company only. Other available material may contain only consolidated statements, or may follow different principles

---

[18] A cash flow statement as such is not required except from certain real estate companies. However, the filings contain the data from which such a statement can be compiled.

[19] The controversy on this matter is discussed in *Fortune*, p. 77 (August 1964).

[20] In addition to examples cited in the text, a recent Commission decision provides still another illustration of a professional's obligation to use official filings, although in a slightly different context. Broker-dealers published quotations in a manner which was illegal under the circumstances because a distribution under Regulation A was then in process. In defense, they asserted reliance on the statements by the underwriter that the distribution had been completed. Rejecting this defense, the Commission noted that they knew or should have known that Regulation A requires the filing of a final report on the completion of the offering, and that no such report had been filed until after the time in question. Sidney Tager, SEA Rel. No. 7368 (1964).

of consolidation. Filings often give more information than other sources on unconsolidated subsidiaries. Likewise, the compliance notes and schedules in filed financial statements may contain important details on matters not otherwise publicly reported. In many cases, there is more than one accepted accounting principle which may be employed. In such cases, the SEC does not require use of any particular principle. However, it does require disclosures, to an extent not always found in other statements, of the principles which have been followed.[21]

Example. Most financial statements available to the public (including official filings) do not include the separate statements for individual subsidiaries or divisions. However, separate financial statements for a business acquired from others may be included for the period preceding the acquisition in a proxy statement relating to the acquisition (assuming it required a stockholder vote) or in a Form 8-K report relating to the acquisition.

Example. Many analysts consider insider securities transactions to be a key index of management's own appraisal of the company's future. Such analysts should consult the filed ownership reports relating to trading by insiders.[22] Of all the SEC publications, including free ones, the widest circulation by far is enjoyed by the monthly Official Summary of insider trading reports, which is sold on a subscription basis.

Example. Where an analyst stresses cash flow, there may be important information, not otherwise available, in the notes to the filed financial statement dealing with depreciation policy; or in the filed supplemental schedules relating to depreciation or to additions and retirements of property, plant, and equipment.

Example. It may be significant to know the precise terms of an exhibit, such as the dividend or working capital limitations in an indenture, the terms of a preferred stock sinking fund, or the formula in a lease providing for a rental based on profits. These provisions are often too involved to be summarized adequately in other available materials. They may be referred to in a manner which gives their present effect but which makes it difficult to ascertain their future significance, for example: "The indenture imposes certain restrictions on the payment of dividends. At this time, $100,000 of earned surplus is restricted and not available for dividend payments." Such a statement tells very little about the applicability of the dividend restriction to earnings in future years. The amount of surplus to be frozen by the indenture may very well increase, or decrease, with the passage of time or changes in earnings.

Example. Where there has been a change in management, official

---

[21] See a statement of the Commission's Chief Accountant in Hearings, note 9 *supra*, pp. 1299–1305.

[22] A description of the reporting requirements relating to insider trading will be considered in the companion article to appear in the next issue of this Journal.

filings may reveal a significant change in management salaries or insider-company relationships before the results of such changes are reflected in the profit and loss statement. The official filings may reveal, for instance, that substantial salaries will continue to be paid under employment contracts to old officers whose work is being done currently by new equally highly paid executives.

In formulating recommendations the professional should realize that all information available to him is not of equal quality. While many companies conduct financial public relations programs which are unimpeachable in terms of reliability, the professional must recognize that others fall below this standard. There is no assurance that any particular source of information is accurate and complete. However, official filings with the SEC may be more reliable in some cases than any other source.

A manufacturer selling his wares usually feels no compulsion to elaborate reasons for rejecting his product. He may refrain from misstatements in what he says. However, he will not normally volunteer adverse information, such as the difficulty in getting replacement parts. In certain commercial contexts there is a tendency to tell less than the whole truth, to omit balancing the adverse factors against the favorable ones. This tendency may be noted in the financial public relations activities of some companies. This Special Study Report found some evidence of deliberate misrepresentation. However, most of the inaccurate publicity seemed to have some basis in fact but erred in being overly optimistic. A related problem was the withholding of adverse information which should have been published.[23]

By contrast, a company selling its securities to the public must make *full* disclosure of all relevant information on specified subjects, favorable or not. One of the purposes of the Securities Act was to modify the standard of *caveat emptor*, let the buyer beware, which prevails even today in many business relationships. It is not uncommon to find the beginning pages of a prospectus devoted to an "introductory statement" which collects at the outset the speculative or other adverse factors militating *against* the purchase of the security. This philosophy of full disclosure pervades all of the official filings. There are serious penalties as well as civil liabilities not only for misstatements but also for material omissions. There is not the same toleration for "sales talk" or "mere puffing" which is still accepted in other commercial situations, and which carries over into some voluntary company reporting. In addition, the SEC often suggests changes which are reflected in the final form of official filings. It is not uncommon for modifications to be made in response to SEC comments, even in certified financial statements. The Commission's

---

[23] Part 3, Special Study Report, 101. See *id.*, 65–102 for a review of corporate publicity generally. See also Comment, *Current Problems in Securities Regulation*, 62 Mich. L. Rev. 680, 700–16 (1964).

expertise is very helpful in rendering the filings more informative than voluntary reports from the investor's point of view.[24]

Where the analyst has any reason to question the accuracy or completeness of data otherwise available to him, he should turn to filings. This point was illustrated by a recent Commission disciplinary case. The Commission held a broker-dealer's research analyst personally responsible as a participant in a fraud because he prepared a false and misleading market letter. In rejecting the analyst's defense that he relied in good faith on material supplied by his employer, the Commission emphasized the responsibilities assumed by the person preparing a market letter:

> A member of the research staff of a broker-dealer may well be entitled to rely, so far as he personally is concerned, upon materials concerning a going business supplied by an issuer or by his employer *absent facts and circumstances which would raise doubts in the mind of a careful and responsible analyst as to the reliability of the materials or the propriety of their use for a particular purpose.* In the circumstances of this case, however, we think that [the analyst's] defense that he followed the instructions of his employer is unavailing. By proceeding with the preparation of the false and misleading market letter notwithstanding his knowledge of the *absence of supporting facts and in light of the all-too-evident warnings of irregularities* and the indicated irresponsibility and lack of diligence on the part of the principals of [his employer and the issuer of the stock], he became an important part of an apparatus perpetrating a fraud. Under these facts, if a salesman had made these statements orally to his customer, we would have no hesitancy in finding him a cause of our order or revocation. In his fabulist role, [the analyst's] activities were no less reprehensible and no less willful; indeed, the market letter was designed to reach a much wider audience than the oral statements of a salesman."[25]

In another illustrative case, a so-called financial public relations counsel was held to have violated the anti-fraud provisions by disseminating false information to broker-dealers. The court rejected the defense that the information was supplied by a company officer. It noted that the securities were to pass to the public as a result of the defendant's representations and held that he had a duty to investigate further.[26]

Certain practical suggestions can be offered to the analyst making securities recommendations on which others will rely. He should have ready access to copies of the Commission's accounting Regulation S-X and Forms 8-K, 9-K and 10-K, plus copies of any other forms used by special classes of issuers in which he is interested. He will thereby be able to ascertain quickly whether a particular item of information which

---

[24] However, it is important to remember that the Commission does not itself approve or disapprove securities or pass upon the accuracy or adequacy of information in filings. Every prospectus must bear a bold face legend to this effect which includes the further statement that any representation to the contrary is a criminal offense. As a general matter the Commission does not verify by its own independent investigation the information disclosed in a filing.

[25] Heft, Kahn & Infante, Inc., SEA Rel. No. 7020, p. 10 (emphasis supplied, footnote omitted) (1963). See also Idaho Acceptance Corp., SEA Rel. No. 7383 (1964).

[26] SEC v. Chamberlain Associates, Fed. Sec. L. Rep. para. 91228, (S.D.N.Y. 1963).

interests him should appear in filed material. He would do well to review all prospectuses and proxy statements of companies in which he has a continuing interest, so that he becomes familiar with the form and content of information given. He should develop a working familiarity with proxy statements relating to mergers, recapitalizations, option plans and other types of transactions beside the routine election of directors. On a selective basis for companies in which he is interested, the professional should also review full Securities Act registration statements (preferably including all amendments but at least the first filing and the final prospectus), and Form 10-K reports. Special attention should be given to proxy statements and Form 8-K reports (except those relating to routine annual meetings). Normally these filings relate to significant events out of the ordinary course and may contain important detail or background information not otherwise available.[27]

In many cases, copies of filed documents may be obtained free of charge upon request to the company and/or the underwriter (for Securities Act registration statement). Extra copies of these materials as well as proxy statements are normally available at the time they are being distributed. Some companies will even supply copies of their periodic filings upon request.

By reviewing filings first hand, the analyst will absorb their flavor. He should sharpen his research techniques, thereby learning to sense those situations where a filing will contain relevant information which cannot be found in other accessible sources. Through experience he will learn to judge when and to what extent a reasonable investigation must include official filings.

In most situations, there is no dearth of available information. Rather, in light of the recent "investment information explosion,"[28] the analyst faces a different problem—separating the kernels of useful and reliable data from the mountain of chaff. For any significant research project, such as a report in depth on a particular company, the Form 10-K reports for the recent years might provide a logical starting point. Form 10-K

---

[27] A description of the materials referred to will appear in the companion article to appear in this Journal.

This article has focused upon the advisability of examining official SEC filings. Many other governmental bodies require information to be filed which is available for public inspection. A professional recommending a bank, insurance, or utility stock, for example, may have an equivalent obligation to consult official filings with other public agencies. There is an important difference between filings with the SEC compared with most other public sources of information, however. SEC filings are especially designed for the use of investors and require disclosures relevant to this purpose. Other public filings are designed for unrelated regulatory purposes, such as rate making or consumer protection, and the information may not be complete or in particularly useful form from the security analysts' point of view. Filings with state securities agencies and stock exchanges, on the other hand, may be very useful to the security analyst.

[28] The phrase was used by Babson, *Financial Analysts Journal*, Vol. 20, No. 4, p. 33 (July–August 1964).

reports are specifically designed to highlight the most important data from the security analysts' point of view. Considering a delay of less than a week and an estimated average cost of $3.00 to $5.00 for a single Form 10-K report (the maximum would rarely exceed $8.00), the burden of ordering this material for a few years from the SEC in connection with a substantial research undertaking is not unreasonable. On the other hand, it must be acknowledged that the lack of periodic synthesis makes the official filings a less than ideal research source. It is often difficult to get a composite picture from a series of unrelated filings.[29]

This article deals with the adequacy of the investigation which must underlie a recommendation. There are two related matters not dealt with herein for the professional to consider in organizing his research and advisory activities: (1) under what circumstances must he make the underlying information available to his customer;[30] and (2) to what extent must he ascertain the "suitability" of the recommended security to the investment needs of the particular customer.[31]

Conclusion

The investor protection goal of the Securities Act is implemented through the disclosure mechanism. Much information becomes available through stockholder reports and other company communications directly to the investing public. Indeed, the long-term improvements which have taken place in stockholder reports and other direct public reporting are no doubt attributable in part to the existence of the official filing requirements and the acceptance of the disclosure philosophy by the business community. Much, but by no means all, of the additional information in filings is reflected in the standard financial manuals. However, there is additional important information which is available to the public only through official filings. The average investor cannot be expected to tap this reservoir effectively. The professional advisers to the investing public must serve as the conduit if the market place is to be fully informed. The filing scheme has been tailored with the needs of the professionals in mind. The Commission has always welcomed their suggestions for improvements.

---

[29] See Heller, *Integration of the Dissemination of Information*, 29 LAW & CONTEMP. PROB. 749, 759 (1964). The filings are probably weakest in the area of the business description. On the other extreme, information on management is restated rather fully on an annual basis.

[30] See the NYSE and NASD guideposts note 3, *supra;* N. Pinsker & Co., SEA Rel. No. 6401, p. 7 (1960); Note, *A Symptomatic Approach to Securities Fraud*, 72 YALE L. J. 1411 (1963).

[31] See C. Gilman Johnston, SEA Rel. No. 7390 (1964); NASD Rules of Fair Practice, Art. III, Sec. 2; Part 1, Special Study Report, pp. 311–12. The New York Stock Exchange public relations program also stresses the ability of its member firms to tailor investment advice to the individual financial requirements of their customers.

24

SEC FILINGS—THEIR CONTENT AND USE*

Carl W. Schneider

This article surveys the various SEC filing and reporting requirements applicable to issuers of publicly owned companies. It deals with information available about such issuers through the "official filings" which they make with the Commission. It also discusses means by which this source of information may be utilized. A companion article, which appeared in the January–February issue of this Journal, discussed the uses which can be made and which should be made of this reservoir of information by broker-dealers, investment advisers, security analysts, and other professionals who make investment recommendations.

The various statutes administered by the Commission relating to publicly owned companies are essentially disclosure statutes.[1] These acts do not generally govern the merits of securities which may be distributed to or traded by the public. Rather, they require disclosure of certain information which should serve as the basis for investment decisions. The Securities Act relates principally to the distribution of securities, directly or through underwriters, by issuers or controlling persons. The Exchange Act deals principally with the trading of securities and also grants the Commission power to regulate proxy solicitation.

SECURITIES ACT REGISTRATION STATEMENTS

The registration statement is the basic disclosure document in connection with a public distribution of securities registered under the Securities Act. It is made up of two parts. The prospectus, the first section, is the

---

* Reprinted by permission of the *Financial Analysts Journal* (March–April 1965). Reprinted by Leasco Systems & Research Corporation as edited and updated by the author November 1968. Since this editing and updating by the author the SEC has published *The Wheat Report*. *The Wheat Report* proposes many changes in reporting policies of the SEC Commission under the 1933 and 1934 Acts.

[1] The principal statutes administered by the Commission relating to publicly owned companies are the Securities Act of 1933, 15 U.S.C. 77a to 77aa (Securities Act) and the Securities Exchange Act of 1934, 15 U.S.C. 78a to 78jj (Exchange Act). Other statutes administered by the Commission are the Public Utility Holding Company Act of 1935, 15 U.S.C. 79 to 79z-6; Trust Indenture Act of 1939, 15 U.S.C. 77aaa to 77bbbb; Investment Company Act of 1940, 15 U.S.C. 80a-1 to 80a-52; and Investment Advisers Act of 1940, 15 U.S.C. 80b-1 to 80b-21. The Commission also has advisory powers in Ch. X bankruptcy proceedings.

only part which is generally distributed to the public. Frequently, the prospectus is distributed, especially to broker-dealers, in preliminary or "red herring" form. Such a preliminary prospectus is subject to correction if deficient. The final prospectus should be checked for changes on any relevant point. In the normal course, each buyer receives a final prospectus with or preceding the confirmation of his purchase.

Part II of the registration statement contains information of a more technical nature dealing with such matters as marketing arrangements, the expenses of the distribution, relationships between the registrant and certain experts, sales of securities to special parties, recent sales of unregistered securities, a list of subsidiaries, treatment of proceeds from stock being registered, etc. In addition, Part II contains signatures and financial schedules and historical financial information not required in the prospectus. Filed with the registration statement are exhibits, such as contracts relating to the underwriting; the charter and bylaws of the registrant; specimen copies of securities; instruments relating to long-term debt, option agreements, pension plans, retirement plans, and deferred compensation plans; an opinion of counsel; material foreign patents; and certain material contracts not made in the ordinary course of business.[2]

Securities Act registration statements are filed with the Commission's principal office in Washington. Copies of the final prospectus, but not the other parts of the registration statement, are available for examination in all regional offices. For registrants with securities listed on a national securities exchange, the principal parts of the registration statement are usually available for inspection at the exchanges on which the company has securities listed.

Regulation A Filings Under the Securities Act

The Securities Act provides a conditional exemption, which the Commission has implemented through Regulation A, for offerings not exceeding $300,000. For issues exceeding $50,000,[3] a company relying on this exemption must prepare and distribute to offerees an offering circular which is equivalent to a simplified prospectus, except that the financial statements need not be certified. Prior to the offering, a notification on

---

[2] The text above describes the basic registration form on Form S-1 which is applicable in all cases, except foreign governments or other situations for which another form is authorized. Other forms include: S-2, for certain companies in the developmental stage; S-3, for certain mining ventures; S-4, S-5 and S-6, for various types of registered investment companies; S-7 for companies meeting certain financial, continuous reporting, and other tests; S-8, for certain offerings to employees under stock option, purchase, savings, or similar plans; S-9, for certain high-grade debt securities; S-10 for certain oil and gas interests offered by individuals; S-11, for certain real estate companies; S-12, for American depository receipts; S-14, for securities issued in certain acquisition transactions; and F-1, for voting trust certificates.

[3] Newly organized issuers, those which have not had net income from operations and those selling assessable stock, must use an offering circular even for offerings smaller than $50,000.

Form 1-A containing certain additional information must be filed relating principally to details of the offering and background of insiders and underwriters. Semi-annual reports on the progress of the offering must be made on Form 2-A until the offering is completed or terminated.

Regulation A filings are made with the main regional office of the Commission for the region in which the issuer's principal business operations are conducted.[4]

COVERAGE OF EXCHANGE ACT REQUIREMENTS

The Exchange Act has four types of disclosure requirements, all more fully discussed below, relating to registration, periodic reporting, proxy solicitation, and insider trading. The following are the three classifications of companies subject to some or all of these requirements:

(1) "Listed Companies." Those with any class of security listed and registered on a national securities exchange.[5] Listed companies are subject to all four types of Exchange Act disclosure requirements.

(2) "OTC Registered Companies." Those covered by the OTC registration requirements added by the Securities Acts Amendments of 1964 ("1964 Amendments").[6]

The 1964 Amendments generally require issuers with total assets exceeding $1,000,000 to register any class of "equity security" (generally a stock; security convertible into stock; or right, warrant, or option to purchase stock), traded over-the-counter which is held of record by 500 or more persons. The applicability of the registration requirement is determined as of the issuer's fiscal year end commencing with its first fiscal year end occurring after July 1, 1964. Once registered, a class of security must remain registered unless the number of holders of record is reduced to less than 300.

OTC registered companies are subject to the periodic reporting, proxy, and insider trading requirements of the Exchange Act. The effect of the 1964 Amendments was to extend to OTC registered companies all of the investor protections provisions applicable to listed companies. It should be noted that the 1964 Amendments extended the Exchange Act's obligations to some publicly owned companies which have never made any previous filings with the SEC—for example, companies which became publicly

---

[4] Regional offices (and branches of regional offices) are maintained in New York City, Boston, Atlanta (Miami), Chicago (Cleveland, Detroit, St. Louis), Fort Worth (Houston), Denver (Salt Lake City), San Francisco (Los Angeles), Seattle, and Washington, D.C.

[5] There are securities trading on exchanges which have "unlisted trading privileges." Although such securities are considered as "registered" under the Exchange Act, the issuer is not a "listed company" as used herein unless the same class of security is listed on another exchange or it has another class listed on an exchange. However, most of these companies with unlisted trading privileges (except for foreign issuers) will become "OTC registered" and will thereby become subject to all of the Exchange Act requirements applicable to listed companies.

[6] P. L. 88-467.

owned through intrastate offerings exempt from Securities Act registration requirements, or publicly owned companies which have made no public offerings since the passage of the Securities Act in 1933.

(3) *"Section 15(d) Companies."* Prior to the 1964 Amendments, the larger over-the-counter companies which had filed Securities Act registration statements were required to file periodic reports under Section 15(d) of the Exchange Act. Many of these companies became OTC registered. However, those Section 15(d) companies which do not meet the 1964 Amendments tests for OTC registration will continue to be subject to the periodic reporting requirements of the Exchange Act, but not to the registration, proxy, or insider trading provisions.

Very generally, and eliminating many refinements, Section 15(d) companies are those which have no securities listed or OTC registered and which have filed a registration statement under the Securities Act if, but only so long as, the registered class is owned by 300 or more persons. In addition, if the registration statement was filed subsequently to August 20, 1964, the periodic reports are due for the balance of the fiscal year in which the filing was made, regardless of the number of security holders. On the other hand, if the last Securities Act registration statement was filed before August 20, 1964, there are other applicable tests having the general effect of limiting the filing requirements to the larger over-the-counter companies.

Exchange Act Registration

The Exchange Act requires registration of any class of security listed on a national securities exchange. Under the 1964 Amendments, the act also requires "OTC registration" for securities traded over-the-counter if the above described tests of total assets and number of record holders are met. The Exchange Act's registration requirements are different from those under the Securities Act, and a security can be registered under either act without being registered under the other.

Form 10 is the basic Exchange Act registration form for issuers with no other class of security registered under the Exchange Act. It covers essentially the same information as is covered in a Securities Act registration statement, including the prospectus but omitting, of course, information in the latter type of registration statement relating to the terms of the registered offering and the use of proceeds. The provisions on financial statements and exhibits are similar for registration under either act.[7] There is a brief notice form, Form 8-A, for registration of securities by issuers already subject to the Exchange Act reporting requirements described below.

Exchange Act registration forms are filed with the Commission's prin-

---

[7] Prior to the 1964 Amendments, the exhibit provision on material contracts under the Exchange Act was more limited.

Periodic Reports

Listed, OTC registered, and Section 15(d) companies are all required to file certain periodic reports. The three most important of these reports are Forms 8-K, 9-K and 10-K.[8]

Form 8-K is a current report which is filed for each calendar month during which an event occurs which requires reporting. The report is due by the 10th day of the following month. The various events to be reported on Form 8-K include the following items: (1) changes in control of registrant; (2) acquisition or disposition of assets; (3) legal proceedings; (4) changes in securities (5) changes in security (i.e., collateral) for registered securities; (6) defaults upon senior securities; (7) increase in the amount of securities outstanding; (8) decrease in the amount of securities outstanding; (9) options to purchase securities; (10) revaluation of assets or restatement of capital share account; (11) submission of matters to a vote of security holders; (12) other materially important events; and (13) financial statements and exhibits. When a business of significant size is acquired, the registrant is required to file financial statements of the acquired business. The exhibits required by Form 8-K generally relate to the transactions or events otherwise reported by the form.

Form 9-K includes certain unaudited financial information for the first six months of each fiscal year. It is due within 45 days after the end of the period covered. The report is a very simple one containing these key figures: gross sales (less discounts, returns, and allowances), operating revenues, extraordinary items, net income or loss before taxes on income, provision for taxes on income, net income or loss, special items, and earned surplus items.

Form 10-K is an annual report which is due 120 days after the end of each fiscal year. The items in Form 10-K which must be answered by all reporting companies relate to the number of security holders for each class, increases and decreases in outstanding equity securities, and the identification of parents and subsidiaries of the registrant. The Form 10-K report contains certified financial statements including a balance sheet, a profit and loss statement for the fiscal year covered by the report, an analysis of surplus, and the supporting schedules. The report also requires such exhibits as would be required to an original Exchange Act registration which are necessary to update the exhibits previously filed.

---

[8] In addition, a quarterly "cash flow" report on Form 7-K is required of certain real estate companies.

Several of the items of Form 10-K require substantially the same information as is required in a proxy statement. These items of information need not be answered in the Form 10-K report by companies which also solicit proxies under the proxy rules. As a result of the 1964 Amendments, these overlapping items will be applicable only to Section 15(d) companies. The items of Form 10-K which overlap with the proxy statement deal with directors, nominees, officers, principal holders of voting securities, and certain associates of the foregoing.

Another item in Form 10-K deals with changes in the business during the fiscal year covered by the report. Though it has no counterpart in the proxy statement, this item need not be answered in the Form 10-K by any companies except Section 15(d) companies. It is apparently the Commission's expectation that the annual reports to security holders will cover this topic adequately for listed and OTC registered companies.[9]

The periodic reports are filed at the principal office of the SEC. A listed company also files copies with the exchange on which its securities are listed. The Commission itself transmits copies of the Form 8-K and 10-K reports to its regional offices in the same manner as the Form 10 registration statements are distributed.

Proxy Requirements

No person, whether or not associated with management, may solicit proxies from holders of listed or OTC registered securities without supplying them with a proxy statement meeting the requirements of Regulation 14. The proxy statement is the disclosure document containing information on matters to be acted upon. If there is an election contest, detailed information must be filed with the Commission about the participants in the contest.

For a routine annual meeting, the proxy statement identifies and makes certain disclosures about directors, nominees, officers, principal holders of voting securities, and certain associates of the foregoing. Shareholdings and principal occupations are given for directors and nominees. For directors and officers, information is given as to direct and indirect remuneration, options to purchase securities from the company, and indebtedness to the company. Certain transactions between the company and the insiders also must be disclosed.

Where other substantive matters are to be acted upon at a meeting, the proxy statement must contain all of the information necessary for the shareholder to make an informed decision. For instance, in a proxy statement dealing with a merger, there is information about both the company and the other party to the merger which is equivalent to the

---

[9] See SEA Rel. No. 7508 (1965). It may be anticipated that the provisions of the new Rule 14a-3(b), text at note 13, *infra*, will improve the annual reports of over-the-counter companies.

information which would appear in prospectuses relating to the two businesses.

Under a provision added to the Exchange Act by the 1964 Amendments,[10] if management of a listed or OTC registered company does not solicit proxies in connection with a stockholders meeting, it must, nonetheless, supply an "information statement" to security holders containing information substantially equivalent to the information in a proxy statement.

Copies of proxy material are on file at the principal office of the Commission and, for listed companies, at the exchange. Section 15(d) companies are required to furnish to the Commission "information" copies[11] of proxy materials sent to more than 10 stockholders.

INSIDER TRADING

The insider trading and reporting provision of the Exchange Act applies to all directors, officers, and beneficial owners of more than 10 percent of any class of equity security which is listed or OTC registered. Any such insider realizing a "short-swing" profit within a six-month period on a purchase and sale or a sale and purchase of any equity security, whether or not of a registered class, must turn such profits over to the company.

All insiders subject to liability for short-swing profits must file individual reports with respect to their beneficial holdings of all equity securities whether or not the class is registered. There are two basic ownership reports. Form 3 is an initial statement of ownership which is due at the time of registration or within 10 days after the event which subjects the individual to the reporting requirement. Form 4 is a statement of changes in ownership. It indicates the amounts of the security acquired and disposed of during the calendar month, and the amount owned at the end of the month. It is required to be filed within 10 days after the close of the month for any calendar month during which a change takes place. The ownership reports are filed with the Commission's principal office and also with the exchange in the case of a listed company.

FINANCIAL STATEMENTS

The Commission's Regulation S-X governs the form and content of most of the financial statements required to be filed with the Commission. The Regulation sets out in detail the items which must be covered. It also deals with such matters as certification and consolidation.

Financial statements prepared in compliance with Regulation S-X, and particularly the notes to the statements, often give substantially more information than other financial statements distributed by issuers. For

---

[10] Section 14(c). This provision has been implemented by Regulation 14C.
[11] See text at note 12, *infra*.

instance, Regulation S-X requires the notes to contain certain details on long-term leases, funded debt, management stock options, classification of inventories, and basis for computing depreciation which often do not appear in other financial statements. The notes covering these topics are sometimes referred to by accountants and others as "compliance notes" as distinguished from other notes furnished in reports to security holders.

Regulation S-X also requires supplemental schedules to complete the financial statements, unless the information is inapplicable or is otherwise disclosed in the financial statements. The information in these schedules almost never appears in financial statements which are distributed to the public. Sometimes such information is included in standard manuals, but rarely in full detail. Even in a Securities Act registration, most of the schedules are included in Part II and are omitted from the prospectus which is distributed to the public. Although the schedules may be of secondary interest to the average investor, they contain a great deal of supplemental information which may be extremely valuable for study in depth by a serious analyst or professional investor. They cover such matters as details on marketable securities held; amounts due from insiders; investment in and indebtedness of affiliates; property, plant, and equipment; reserve for depreciation, depletion, amortization, and other purposes; bonds, mortgages, and similar debt; and earnings of and dividends received from affiliates.

Financial statements in full S-X form, including schedules, appear in registration statements under the Securities Act and the Exchange Act, and in annual reports on Form 10-K. They appear without schedules (except for surplus, profit, and loss information), in an 8-K report or proxy statement relating to an acquisition or other transaction which can not be disclosed fully without such financial statements. Where a filing relates to an acquisition or other transaction which will change the financial picture of the company materially, the filing may also include pro forma statements showing the results of the transaction.

ANNUAL AND OTHER REPORTS TO SECURITY HOLDERS

Companies subject to Exchange Act reporting requirements must furnish to the Commission "for its information" copies of their annual reports to security holders. These information copies are not considered technically "filed," meaning that they are not subject to certain statutory liabilities which attach only to material "filed" under the act. Such materials furnished for the Commission's information are available for inspection at the principal office of the Commission.

The Commission has encouraged communication directly with security holders and other members of the public, and it does not generally regulate the form or content of such information.[12] However, the proxy

---

[12] Special considerations are applicable during the period of a public offering. See SA Rel. Nos. 4697 (1964) and 3844 (1957). For example, serious consequences may result if an annual report immediately preceding a public offering attempts to con-

rules do require that, for an annual meeting at which directors are to be elected, the proxy or information statement must be accompanied or preceded by an annual report to security holders containing financial statements for the last fiscal year. Consolidated statements must be included if they are necessary to reflect adequately the position and results of operations of the issuer and its subsidiaries. The statements must be certified unless the issuer is of a special class (e.g., insurance companies) which are not required to include certified statements in their annual reports to the Commission. The financials sent to security holders need not comply with Regulation S-X. However, they must, in the opinion of management, adequately reflect the financial position and results of operations of the issuer and its subsidiaries. They must include any material information necessary to a fair presentation or to make the financial statements not misleading. Certain differences between the financial statements in the report to security holders and the financial statements filed with the Commission must be noted and the effect thereof reconciled or explained in the report to security holders.

The principal stock exchanges also maintain copies of communications with security holders which are available for inspection.

Special Classes of Issuers

The foregoing discussion deals with conventional issuers to which no special provisions are applicable. There are several classes of issuers which are exempt from some or all of the provisions administered by the Commission—for example, certain nonprofit institutions, governmental agencies, foreign issuers, and issuers regulated by other federal agencies. For nonexempt issuers separate rules and forms apply to voting trusts; undivided interests in oil or gas rights; certificates of deposit issued in reorganizations; and employees' stock purchase, savings, and similar plans.

Still other reporting rules and forms have been devised for two classes of issuers regulated by the Commission under specific statutes: investment companies (including mutual funds, small business investment companies, etc.), and public utility holding companies (and subsidiaries) which are registered under the Investment Company Act and the Public Utility Holding Company Act, respectively. Registered investment companies and registered public utility holding companies are subject to the Commission's proxy rules. Certain insiders of registered closed-end investment companies and registered public utility holding companies are subject to the Commission's insider trading and reporting provisions.

Special treatment is accorded to banks and insurance companies under the Exchange Act. Insurance companies registering under the Securities Act are subject to the same periodic reporting requirements as other companies. Listed insurance companies are subject to the same require-

---

dition the market. Furthermore, false or misleading statements in communications to stockholders or other members of the public may give rise to certain liabilities under the Securities Acts.

ments as other listed companies. On the other hand, over-the-counter insurance companies are exempt from the OTC registration requirements if they are subject to similar regulatory pattern under state law. Therefore, assuming the existence of a state regulatory pattern, most insurance companies will be complying with state rather than federal law relating to proxy solicitation and insider trading. With respect to banks, the registration, periodic reporting, proxy, and insider trading provisions of the Exchange Act are administered by one of the three federal bank regulatory agencies, depending on the type of bank, rather than the SEC. Bank securities are exempt entirely from the registration requirements of the Securities Act.

Regulation S-X has special provisions applicable to financial statements of various types of investment companies, various types of insurance companies, and bank holding companies and banks. There are special forms to be used by companies reporting to the Federal Power Commission, the Interstate Commerce Commission, or the Federal Communications Commission.

Inspecting or Obtaining Copies of Filed Information

All officially filed information (not including correspondence, preliminary—as opposed to definitive—proxy material, or material accorded "confidential treatment") may be inspected at the Commission's office with which it was filed. Also, as noted above, certain information filed with the principal office is also available for inspection at regional offices or exchanges.

Reproductions of any information in the public files of the Commission's principal office may be ordered through the Commission's Public Reference Section, 425 Second Street, N.W., Washington, D.C. 20549. At the present time, the price per page ranges from 8 cents to 40 cents depending on size, plus postage. There is an additional $2.00 charge for an official certification, if desired. Orders are normally filled within five days of receipt and an invoice is included with the mailing. Cost estimates are supplied on request. An order may cover only a particular part of a filing, such as a specified item or schedule, if it is reasonably identified.

There is coin-operated photocopy equipment for the convenience of the public in the Public Reference Section of the Commission's principal office and New York Regional Office. Copies of most material can be made immediately at a cost of 25 cents per page.

The Commission is aware that the relative inaccessibility of official filings limits their practical utility. It has been studying various methods for making this material more available to the public in general and the financial community in particular.

Other Material Available

There is a great deal of material which is made available to the public to assist in disseminating officially field information. In this context, there are three SEC publications series of particular interest which may be ordered from the Superintendent of Documents, Government Printing Office, Washington, D.C. 20402:

The SEC *News Digest* is published and mailed daily. The annual cost is $15.00, plus $16.80 additional for air mail, if desired. The *News Digest* briefly summarizes all new financing proposals covered by registration statements filed under the 1933 Act and announces their effective dates. It also summarizes other important decisions and orders of the Commission under its various acts. In March 1964 the *News Digest* commenced the announcement of filings on Form 8-K. The *Digest* indicates the name of the issuer, the month for which the report was filed, and the number of the item or items covered by the report.

The *Official Summary* is a monthly publication summarizing security transactions and security holdings of directors, officers, and 10 percent stockholders of companies subject to insider trading provisions. It is, essentially, a compilation of the information reported on Forms 3 and 4. The cost is 15 cents per issue or $1.50 per year, plus 75 cents additional for foreign mailing.

The *Directory of Companies Filing Annual Reports with the Securities and Exchange Commission under the Securities Exchange Act of 1934* is published annually at $2.25 per copy. The *Directory* lists companies alphabetically and also by industry classifications.

There are also available from the Superintendent of Documents copies of various acts, rules, and regulations administered by the Commission, general statistical and financial report series, the Commission's Annual Reports to Congress, and its decisions.

The Commission itself distributes free of charge a number of release series as well as copies of its forms. There is a separate release series under each of the acts which it administers. It also maintains a special mailing list for releases of interest to different categories of persons.

Additional information concerning mailing lists maintained by the Commission and various materials distributed by it or through the Government Printing Office may be obtained from the Commission's Office of Records and Service.

Canadian Restricted List

The Commission published from time to time a "Canadian Restricted List." It names Canadian companies whose securities, the Commission has reason to believe, have been or apparently are being distributed in the United States in violation of the registration requirements of the Securities Act. The primary purpose of the list is to put American broker-dealers on notice that securities of the named Canadian companies appear to be the subject of illegal distributions in this country, because of nonregistration. The list warns broker-dealers to satisfy themselves that they are not participating in an unlawful distribution if they handle such securities.

APPENDIX
DESCRIPTION OF COMMONLY USED SEC FORMS

No.	Description or Contents	Due	Where Available*
	Securities Act Forms†		
S-1‡	Registration statement forms.	At time of registration.	P
	Final prospectus.	"	P, RO
1-A	Letter of notification under Reg. A.	At time of offering.	Local RO, P
2-A	Report on progress of sale under Reg. A.	"	Local RO, P
	Final offering circular under Reg. A.	"	Local RO, P
	Exchange Act Registration Forms		
10	Basic registration form.	120 days after f.y. end for OTC registration. At time of listing for exchange listing.	P, E, RO
8-A	Short forms for various		
8-B	classes of issuers for		
8-C	which current basic information is already on file.		
	Exchange Act Periodic Reports§		
10-K	Annual rept, including full S-X financials.	120 days after f.y. end.	P, E, RO
9-K	Summary profit, loss, and earned surplus, plus information for first half of f.y.	45 days after the end of the period covered.	P, E, RO
8-K	Description of important events.	10th day of mo. following mo. covered by rept.	P, E, RO
7-K	Quarterly cash flow information for real estate companies.	60 days after end of first 3 fiscal quarters and 120 days after end of last quarter.	P, E, RO
	Exchange Act Ownership Reports(‖)(¶)		
3	Initial statement of ownership.	10 days after event subjecting person to reporting requirement.	P, E
4	Change in ownership.	10 days after end of any calendar month during which there is a change.	P, E
	Exchange Act Proxy Material(‖)		
	Proxy statements, etc.	Prior to distribution.	P, E†

* Code for places where material is available for inspection:
P—Principal office in the SEC in Washington, D.C.
E—Each exchange on which company has securities listed, except that, for a company with multiple listings, the ownership reports need be filed with one exchange only.
RO—SEC regional office—in Chicago if company files reports with New York, American, or National Stock Exchanges, otherwise in New York—except that final prospectuses are filed in all regional offices (but not branch offices). The preceding sentence describes present practice although the Commission has indicated its intention to distribute the material more broadly throughout its regional offices in the future. See footnote 4 in the text of the article for a list of regional offices.
† There is no requirement for filing Securities Act material with exchanges although listed companies often transmit such material, at least final prospectuses, to the exchange. Proxy material is normally filed with exchanges pursuant to exchange requirements.
‡ See footnote 2 in the text of the article for a list of other registration forms.
§ Applicable to listed, OTC registered and Section 15(d) companies.
‖ Applicable to listed and OTC registered companies.
¶ To be filed by individual directors, officers and equity security holders of more than 10 percent.

25

FORECASTING BY PROBABILITIES: PREFACE TO COPPER INDUSTRY STUDY*

Peter J. Way, C.J.A.

The Copper Industry Study, prepared in July and August and first presented in September of 1967, reflects two significant accomplishments within our profession. It is the first actual *use* of probabilistic forecasting in investment analysis that has been displayed publicly in any of the professional literature. Second, and just as significant, the approach was chosen, the models developed, and the analysis performed *by the security analysts themselves*. The authors selected this method because they believed it best filled their needs to evaluate the situation and communicate their conclusions to the customers—in this case, a group of sophisticated, institutional portfolio managers.

The approach used recognizes the analyst's real-life forecasting problems and helps him to do a much better job of grappling with them than does the conventional single-point estimate approach. Every competent analyst recognizes that a wide range of earnings possibilities exists for nearly every company under study. Why then do we typically put our "best" assumptions together, scratch our head and swallow hard, and produce one estimate to be inevitably revised at a later date? One of the most unfortunate aspects of this procedure is that the revision will be done the same way and may communicate little or no more than did the first forecast.

It has never been adequate for us as analysts to merely indicate the *quantity* of future earnings for a company without indicating the *quality* of that potential. As a result, our profession has devised a myriad of ratios and tests which are often treated as though they were completely unrelated to one another. Typically, the ratios are used as arguments in themselves, apparently in the belief that they will communicate to the customer all the nuances and subtleties that they conveyed to the analyst. It is a rare study that assembles these bricks, beams, and joists of analysis

---

* Reprinted by permission of the *Financial Analysts Journal* (March–April 1968).

into an integrated structure which clearly shows what the analyst has planned, how it has been put together, and where its strongest timbers are. Forecasting by means of probabilistic models provides just that capability, since the outcome is a range of forecasts reflecting the analyst's judgment of what is most likely to occur.

Beside providing the analyst with a good tool for integrating and communicating qualitative information, models support the flexible revision of previous forecasts. Because the structure of the analysis has previously been made clear, changes in either the size of the structural elements, or the way the analyst (or any other forecaster) feels about them can quickly and easily be transformed into a new range of expectations. Thus, the analyst is encouraged to make more frequent, smaller revisions than he might conventionally. This allows the customer or portfolio manager to follow the analyst's changes in attitude more closely.

A word about the authors' training is in order. Neither has had any special background in mathematics or computer programming. Both have had unrestricted access to time-sharing computer systems, and the consulting support of an analytical systems and procedures group located within the Investment Research Department. Each of the authors has attended a one-day session available to all research department analysts and trainees on how to use the computer and how to write programs in the simple BASIC language.

Please read the copper study with more attention to the approach than the conclusions. Events to date have closely paralleled that first forecast made last fall. It is now obviously dated, and more current analysis reflects events which have occurred in the interim.

26

THE COPPER INDUSTRY: FORECASTING BY PROBABILITIES*

John A. Olsen, C.F.A. and Terry A. Blaney

The key to investments in the copper industry is an ability to anticipate changes in copper prices. Experience has shown that swings in the earnings of copper companies are influenced three to four times as much by copper prices as they are by changes in the physical volume of copper processed. Our approach to this industry, then, will be to establish an understanding of the supply and demand factors influencing copper prices so that we can make a forecast of prices. These price forecasts, in turn, will be instrumental in producing company earnings forecasts.

SUPPLY–DEMAND ELEMENTS

Listed below are the major supply-demand elements in the copper industry.

CHART I

Supply	Demand
Mine capacity	Economic activity
Production disruptions	Substitution
Scrap recovery	Vietnam war
Government stockpile	Government stockpiling
Inventories	Inventorying

The first two elements of supply, when netted against each other, usually result in mine production. There have been very few times in the past two decades when producers voluntarily idled mine capacity. As illustrated in Chart II, a major portion of copper supplies come from emerging nations which, coupled with poor labor relations and the uncertainties associated with the mining business, produce frequent supply interruptions.

These stoppages, which could be caused by anything from an industry-wide strike in the United States to civil war in the Congo, are

---

* Reprinted by permission of the *Financial Analysts Journal* (March–April 1968).

CHART II
Free World Copper Production by Geographic Origin

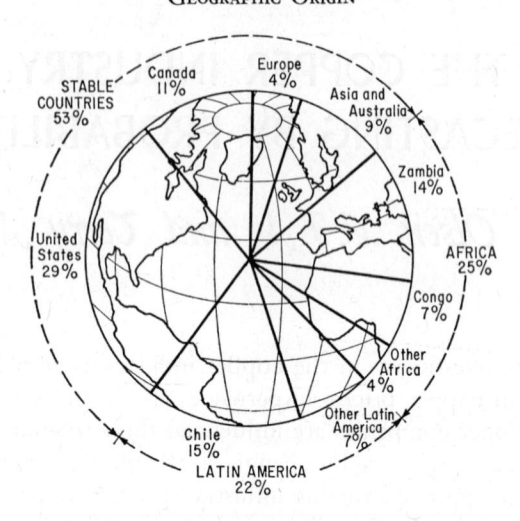

- STABLE COUNTRIES 53%
- Canada 11%
- Europe 4%
- Asia and Australia 9%
- Zambia 14%
- AFRICA 25%
- Congo 7%
- Other Africa 4%
- Other Latin America 7%
- Chile 15%
- LATIN AMERICA 22%
- United States 29%

essentially unpredictable. While the timing and extent of supply interruptions cannot be predicted with accuracy, it is a safe assumption that *some* interruption will take place during the course of any one year.

As the most unpredictable of the supply-demand elements, supply interruptions has been treated separately at the end of our analysis. We can now focus our efforts on the more predictable elements of copper supply and demand.

"Mine Needs"

Since the companies considered are producers of primary copper, we want to determine the amount of primary copper required to equate supply with demand. We call this "mine needs," and it appears on the chart as a triangle.

Chart III is merely a mathematical representation of the supply-demand elements (excluding production interruptions) illustrated in Chart I.

The most critical step in providing values for each of these elements is establishing a relationship between the level of economic activity and copper consumption both here and abroad. By the use of regression techniques, we were able to establish the fit illustrated in Chart IV.

In Chart IV the solid line represents actual copper consumption while the dotted line represents copper consumption as estimated by regression techniques using economic data as the input. We felt we had a reasonably good ability to translate an economic forecast into a forecast of copper consumption.

CHART III
INGREDIENTS FOR A COPPER FORECAST

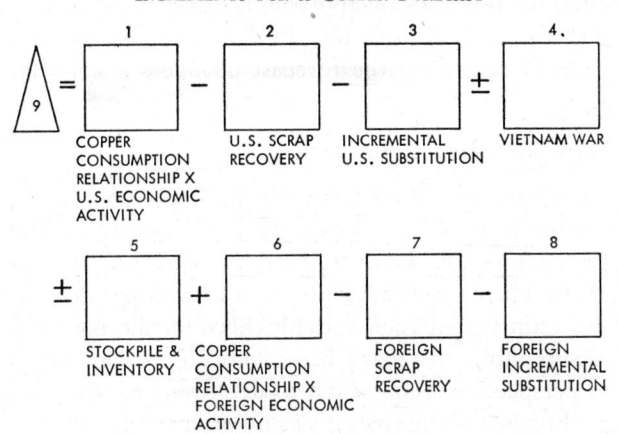

1	2	3	4
COPPER CONSUMPTION RELATIONSHIP X U.S. ECONOMIC ACTIVITY	U.S. SCRAP RECOVERY	INCREMENTAL U.S. SUBSTITUTION	VIETNAM WAR

$\triangle_9 =$ box 1 − box 2 − box 3 ± box 4

5	6	7	8
STOCKPILE & INVENTORY	COPPER CONSUMPTION RELATIONSHIP X FOREIGN ECONOMIC ACTIVITY	FOREIGN SCRAP RECOVERY	FOREIGN INCREMENTAL SUBSTITUTION

± box 5 + box 6 − box 7 − box 8

CHART IV
ACTUAL COPPER CONSUMPTION VERSUS ESTIMATED COPPER DEMAND
(Thousands of Tons)

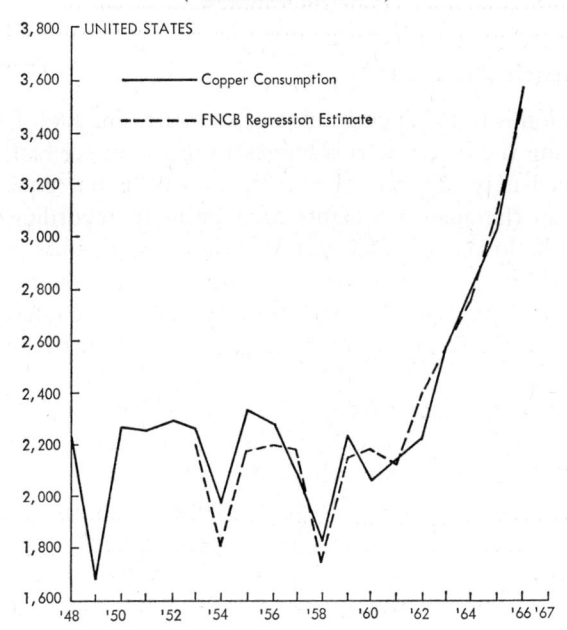

UNITED STATES

——— Copper Consumption
– – – FNCB Regression Estimate

[Line chart from '48 to '67, y-axis 1,600 to 3,800]

THE TRADITIONAL APPROACH

In the past, analysts have made mine needs forecasts by what we call the "single point" technique. This approach requires that the analyst place a single estimate of copper tonnage in each of the boxes in Chart III. The analyst derives these values either by using statistical relationships, as we have suggested for Box 1, or by applying his specialized knowledge of the industry as he evaluates each factor. The use of single estimates for each factor considered in making the forecast produces a single outcome for mine needs.

Problems With Traditional Approach

There are three major problems with the single point approach. First, while the customer intuitively knows that the analyst will be wrong to some degree in his single estimate, he does not know the extent of the expected error. The customer has no idea of how confident the analyst is in any of his estimates of each variable. Second, the customer is seldom given the assumptions that have been incorporated in the forecast and thus has no perspective from which to determine his own confidence in the estimate. Further, if the analyst's assumptions differ from those of the customer, the customer will tend to reject the entire forecast. Third, since the analyst is tied to one forecast, which will undoubtedly prove incorrect to some degree, he resorts to so many qualifications that no one really knows where he stands. All of these problems have one common factor, they result directly from the use of single point estimates of future events.

The Probabilistic Approach

The solution is to produce a range of estimates for each factor considered in making the forecast, as is suggested in the upper half of Chart V.

It is immediately apparent that each estimate is not equally likely to occur, and so the analyst weights each estimate according to his own judgment. The lower half of Chart V shows how this has been done for each of the elements in the mine needs forecast for 1968. Since there is a 100 percent probability of occurrence assumed over the range of estimates for each factor, the weightings for each estimate in the range will total to 1.00.

As an example of methodology, let us consider item No. 5, stockpile and inventory. We felt there was a high probability (.80) that copper inventories would be sharply rebuilt next year as a result of the present copper strike and the higher level of economic activity expected. Or consider No. 4, the Vietnam war. We felt there was a 50 percent chance that the war would escalate by a factor of one third and end by mid-1969, a 40 percent chance that the war would continue on at about the present level through 1971, and thus not affect our forecast, and a 10 percent probability that a dove would be elected to the White House. Continuing this method for each ingredient involved and combining every possibility with every other possibility, we produced approximately 4,000 individual forecasts of mine needs.

CHART V
Ingredients for a Copper Forecast

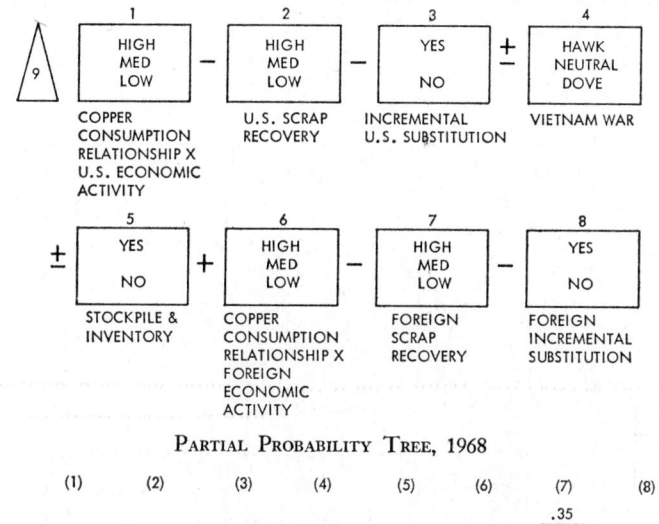

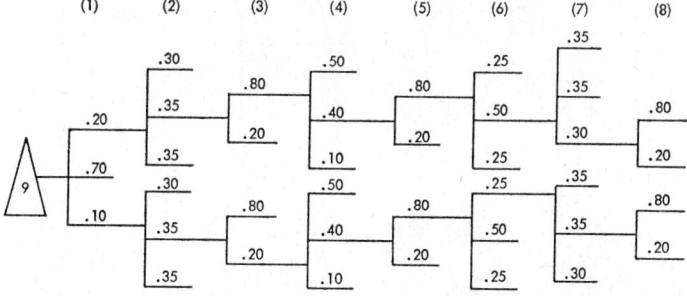

1	2	3	4
HIGH / MED / LOW	HIGH / MED / LOW	YES / NO	HAWK / NEUTRAL / DOVE
COPPER CONSUMPTION RELATIONSHIP X U.S. ECONOMIC ACTIVITY	U.S. SCRAP RECOVERY	INCREMENTAL U.S. SUBSTITUTION	VIETNAM WAR

5	6	7	8
YES / NO	HIGH / MED / LOW	HIGH / MED / LOW	YES / NO
STOCKPILE & INVENTORY	COPPER CONSUMPTION RELATIONSHIP X FOREIGN ECONOMIC ACTIVITY	FOREIGN SCRAP RECOVERY	FOREIGN INCREMENTAL SUBSTITUTION

Partial Probability Tree, 1968

Total Number of Forecasts 3,888

The Results

Having many forecasts, each with a probability attached, the analyst is now in a better position to communicate his opinions. As illustrated in Chart VI, the analyst is able to show the minimum and maximum reasonable expectations produced by his forecast. Since each forecast has a probability of occurrence associated with it, we can exclude the extreme values on either end of the distribution, leaving a more limited area in which there is a 75 percent probability that the actual result will fail. We call this area our 75 percent confidence limits. The horizontal lines on Chart VI represent the mean or expected value; this is really the center of gravity of the probabilities in each distribution.

Because the entire distribution in Chart VI is too wide to be useful, we confine ourselves in Chart VII to the area of the 75 percent confidence limits and the expected values.

CHART VI
PRIMARY COPPER NEEDS—1967–1971

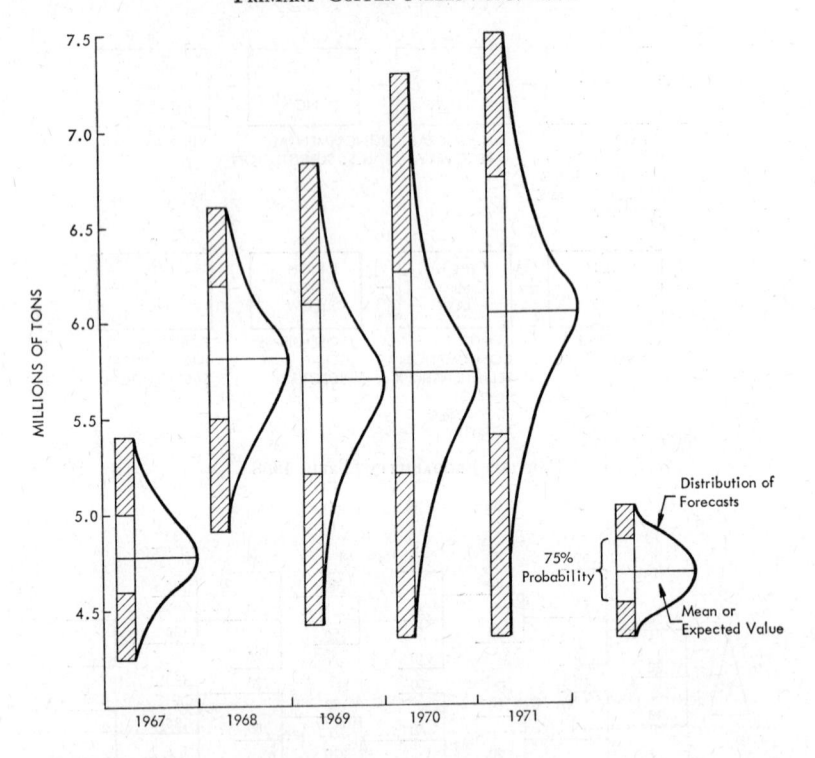

On Chart VII, we show historic mine production through 1966, and the 75 percent confidence limits of mine needs from 1967 through 1971. Mine needs jump very sharply in 1968, primarily reflecting a favorable economic outlook coupled with a strong likelihood of an inventory buildup and no further sales from the U.S. government stockpile. Mine needs tend to level out in 1969 and 1970 reflecting the increased importance of the substitution of other materials for copper.

If we continue to ignore the element of supply interruptions, we would expect production in each year to equal mine needs, that is, to fall within the 75 percent confidence limits shown on Chart VII. A glance at Chart VII, however, reveals this to be an unrealistic assumption; production has consistently fallen below capacity because of supply interruptions. This gap between production and capacity has averaged approximately 10 percent during the past decade, indicating that on average a 10 percent reserve capacity has been needed to offset these supply interruptions. Reflecting the sharp jump in mine needs, the amount of reserve capacity narrows sharply in 1968. This gap begins to widen in 1969 and 1970, as capacity continues to be added in the face of relatively level demand.

CHART VII
Mine Capacity versus Mine Needs

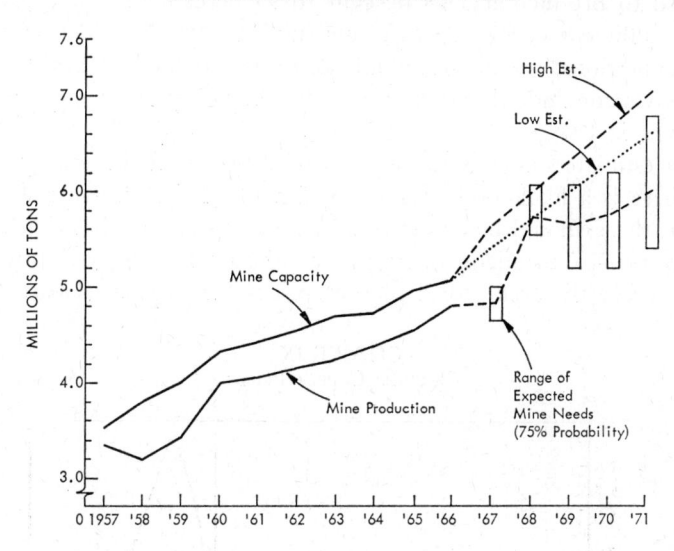

We can develop this analysis one step further by drawing an imaginary line between the two capacity forecasts and comparing this line to the expected values of mine needs. What results is an "operating rate." The 10 percent average reserve capacity during the past 10 years appears more vividly on Chart VIII.

In 1967 the operating rate will be somewhat lower because of the

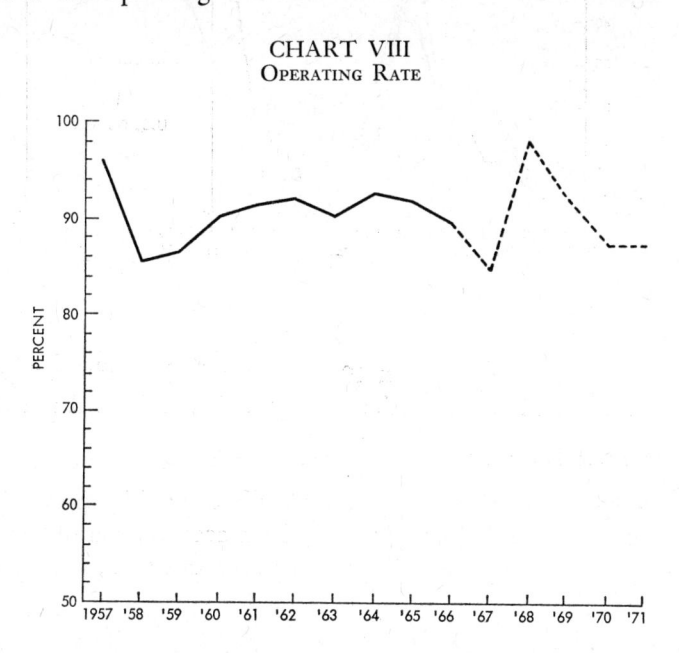

CHART VIII
Operating Rate

extended copper strike. In Chart VIII we are suggesting that the industry will need to produce at a 98 percent to 99 percent rate of capacity to provide sufficient copper to meet demand in 1968. Considering present world conditions, we do not think that such a result is likely. Consequently, we conclude that there is a high probability of a copper shortage developing in 1968.

Since estimated copper needs are not expected to be totally met in 1968, there is a likelihood of some spill-over of demand into 1969. By 1970–71, there should be ample reserve capacity and at that time copper could return to an adequate supply condition. In terms of prices, we would expect the free world market prices for copper (Chart IX) to

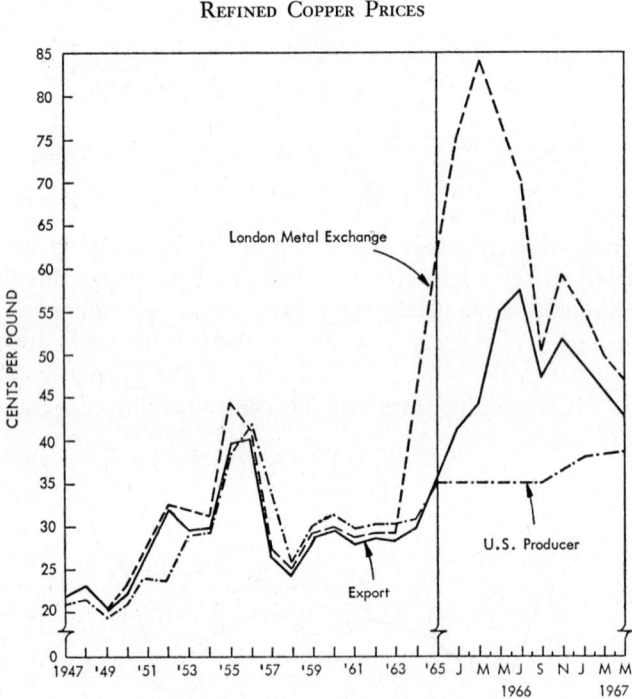

CHART IX
REFINED COPPER PRICES

average 50–55 cents a pound in 1968, with a U.S. producers' price of 40–42 cents a pound as soon as the strike is settled at the U.S. mines.

EFFECT OF PRICE FORECAST

Implicit in a forecast of a sharp increase in free-world copper prices and a more moderate rise in domestic prices is an accentuation of the present split price in world copper markets. Therefore, our price forecast affects companies differently depending upon the geographic origin of their copper and upon the form in which the copper is sold (since fabricated product prices tend to move with free-world primary copper prices).

CHART X
EARNINGS BREAKDOWN 1964 VERSUS 1966
($ millions)

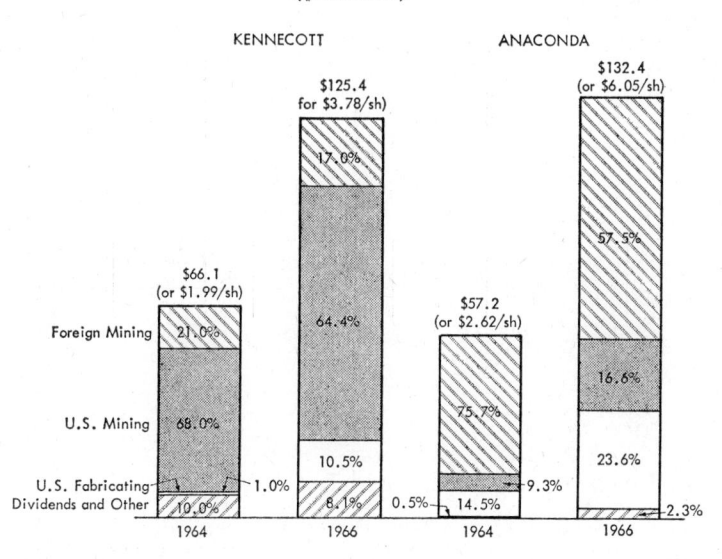

KENNECOTT — 1964: $66.1 (or $1.99/sh); 1966: $125.4 (for $3.78/sh)
- Foreign Mining: 21.0% (1964), 17.0% (1966)
- U.S. Mining: 68.0% (1964), 64.4% (1966)
- U.S. Fabricating: 1.0% (1966)
- Dividends and Other: 10.0% (1964), 8.1% (1966), with 10.5% segment in 1966

ANACONDA — 1964: $57.2 (or $2.62/sh); 1966: $132.4 (or $6.05/sh)
- Foreign Mining: 57.5% (1966)
- U.S. Mining: 75.7% (1964), 16.6% (1966), 23.6%
- U.S. Fabricating: 0.5% (1964), 9.3%, 2.3% (1966)
- Dividends and Other: 14.5% (1964)

As illustrated in Chart X, a company such as Anaconda, which derives the bulk of its earnings from foreign mining activities and fabricated products, should benefit to a much greater degree from higher copper prices than Kennecott, which derives the bulk of its earnings from domestic mining activities. The differing impact of the various copper prices must be recognized in making earning power estimates of the major companies. This can be accomplished by treating a company's copper operations as three separate businesses: foreign mining, domestic mining, and fabricating.

EARNINGS FORECASTS BY PROBABILITIES—THE METHOD

We can further refine our earnings forecasts by adapting the probabilistic technique, as illustrated in Chart XI. As in our price forecast, we use a range of forecasts for each variable, utilizing the conclusions of the price forecast to determine the weights of the three copper prices (foreign price, U.S. price and fabricating profit margin). It should be pointed out that Chart XI represents the general model, with some modification made for each company to reflect their structural differences. This is especially true for American Smelting & Refining.

CHART XI
Ingredients for an Earnings Forecast

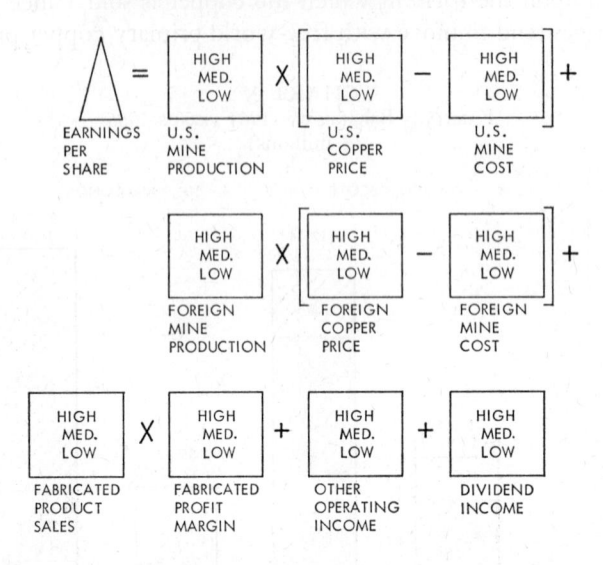

$$\triangle = \begin{bmatrix} \text{HIGH} \\ \text{MED.} \\ \text{LOW} \end{bmatrix} \times \begin{bmatrix} \text{HIGH} \\ \text{MED.} \\ \text{LOW} \end{bmatrix} - \begin{bmatrix} \text{HIGH} \\ \text{MED.} \\ \text{LOW} \end{bmatrix} +$$

EARNINGS PER SHARE | U.S. MINE PRODUCTION | U.S. COPPER PRICE | U.S. MINE COST

$$\begin{bmatrix} \text{HIGH} \\ \text{MED.} \\ \text{LOW} \end{bmatrix} \times \begin{bmatrix} \text{HIGH} \\ \text{MED.} \\ \text{LOW} \end{bmatrix} - \begin{bmatrix} \text{HIGH} \\ \text{MED.} \\ \text{LOW} \end{bmatrix} +$$

FOREIGN MINE PRODUCTION | FOREIGN COPPER PRICE | FOREIGN MINE COST

$$\begin{bmatrix} \text{HIGH} \\ \text{MED.} \\ \text{LOW} \end{bmatrix} \times \begin{bmatrix} \text{HIGH} \\ \text{MED.} \\ \text{LOW} \end{bmatrix} + \begin{bmatrix} \text{HIGH} \\ \text{MED.} \\ \text{LOW} \end{bmatrix} + \begin{bmatrix} \text{HIGH} \\ \text{MED.} \\ \text{LOW} \end{bmatrix}$$

FABRICATED PRODUCT SALES | FABRICATED PROFIT MARGIN | OTHER OPERATING INCOME | DIVIDEND INCOME

Earnings Forecasts by Probabilities—The Result

Upon weighting each estimate, the analyst can now obtain the range, 75 percent confidence limits, and the expected value of a company's earnings for each year.

The result, as shown in Chart XII, is a portrayal of the *earning power* of a company. In the case of Anaconda, Chart XII shows an earning power of $4.50 to $10.00 a share in 1968. We narrow this wide range by saying that we are 75 percent confident earnings will fall between $5.40 and $8.75 per share. If a single point estimate is required, we will reluctantly suggest $7.75 a share.

As is true of all copper companies, Anaconda's earnings are expected to jump sharply next year reflecting the resumption of U.S. mine production and the heavy weight given to higher free-world copper prices.

The same pattern prevails for Kennecott Copper (Chart XIII), a strong jump in earnings in 1968 reflecting higher prices and a resumption of U.S. mining activities.

Chart XIII is unfair to Kennecott. The gradual decline in earning power through 1970 and a sharp drop in 1971 is produced by the weight given to gradually rising U.S. mine costs and a lower U.S. copper price in 1971. Had we included 1972 on Chart XIII, Kennecott would have shown a good increase in earning power since several new mining properties are scheduled to come on stream in that year.

Phelps Dodge (Chart XIV) also benefits from high fabricated profit margins and a resumption of production at the company's U.S. properties

The Copper Industry

CHART XII
ANACONDA EARNINGS—1959–1971

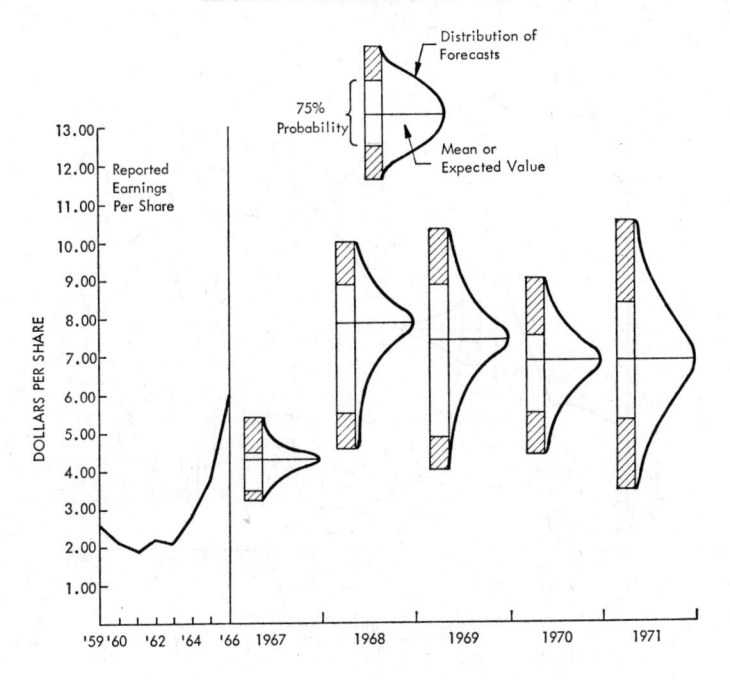

CHART XIII
KENNECOTT COPPER EARNINGS—1959–1971

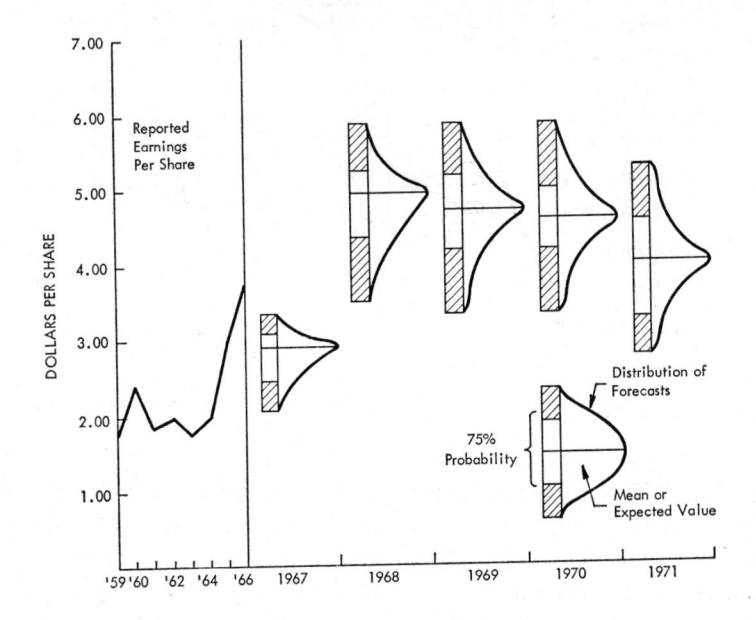

CHART XIV
Phelps Dodge Earnings—1959–1971

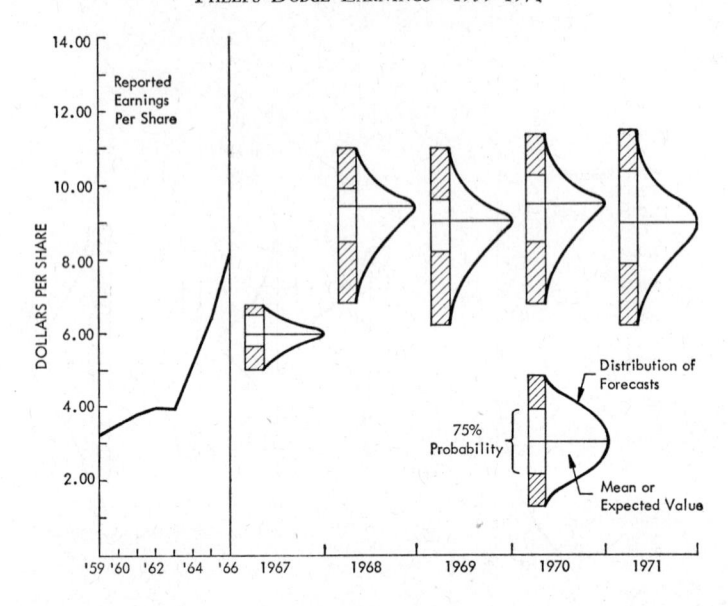

CHART XV
American Smelting & Refining Earnings—1959–1971

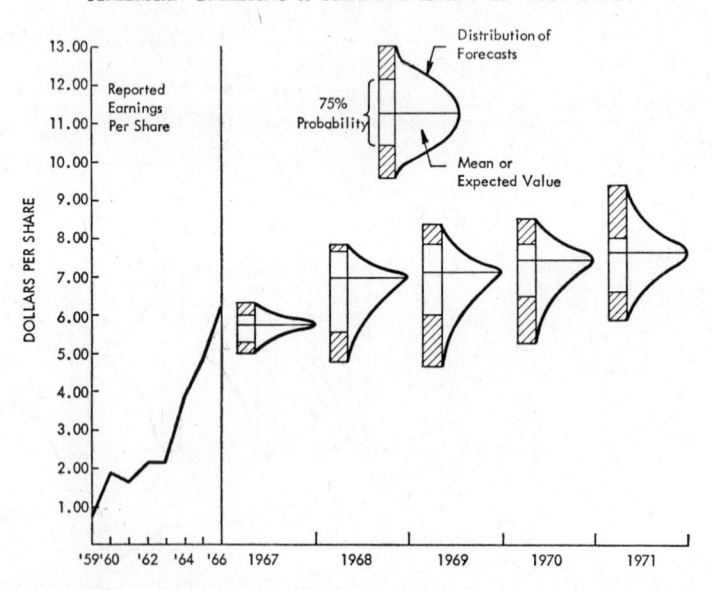

in 1968. P.D. is fortunate because a new copper mine is expected to be developed by 1970, in time to offset an expected decline in fabricated profit margins. The result is that Phelps Dodge's earning power should remain about level throughout our forecast period. With copper less important, American Smelting & Refining (Chart XV) does not show as great an expected earnings jump in 1968 as do the other companies. There is an interesting phenomenon on this chart. We show wider earning power distributions in 1968 and 1969 than we do in 1970 and 1971, implying that we are more confident about our 1971 forecast than we are about 1968. American Smelting derives a substantial portion of its earnings from dividend income from the Southern Peru Copper Company. There is some question whether Southern Peru will be able to continue its dividend over the next two years because of the financing of a new mine. If there is a reduction in the dividend, we could expect American Smelting's earnings to fall in the lower part of our range in either 1968 or 1969, or both. If the dividend is maintained, we could expect earnings to fall in the higher end of this range in either or both of these years. We think the question of the new mine will be settled one way or the other by 1970 and 1971.

Summary

Through the use of the computer, we have been able to adapt the probability technique to investment analysis. This technique has two advantages for our customers. First, we are able to display our assumptions in explicit, easy-to-understand form for both ourselves and our customers. Second, we can show how confident we are of the forecasts, the range over which these forecasts fall, and the degree of certainty within that range. It is, then, possible to compare degrees of confidence among companies.

For the security analyst, we think forecasting by probabilities offers three advantages. First, the analyst can pinpoint areas of weakness in his forecast; areas to be improved upon the next time. Second, he can quickly adjust his forecast to changing conditions by merely changing the weights used. Third, and possibly the most important, the analyst is no longer afraid to read the earnings report in the paper. He made 5,000 to 6,000 forecasts on an individual company's earnings ranging from maybe $4 to $10 a share; no matter where they came out, he hit it right on the button.

27
CAVEATS IN COMPUTER-AIDED FINANCIAL ANALYSIS*

Donald E. Stone

A considerable amount of enthusiasm over the potential of computer-aided financial analysis has been evident in recent articles in the *Financial Analysts Journal*.[1] This article is not a rebuttal to these prophetic works, but rather a word of caution. The marriage of the analyst's skills with the computer's speed and computational power is undoubtedly going to be fruitful, but certain elements of the proposed man-machine interactive environment produce potential pitfalls for the unwary.

COMPUTER-AIDED FINANCIAL ANALYSIS

In addition to the constantly improving computer hardware which is now a familiar aspect of the business environment, two significant developments are providing impetus to the application of computers to investment analysis problems. One of these, the development of problem-oriented computer languages which are readily understood and mastered by financial analysts, has been well presented in the two recent articles cited in footnote (1). These articles describe specifically two languages, LAFFF—*L*anguage for the *A*id of *F*inancial *F*act *F*inders and FFL—*F*irst *F*inancial *L*anguage. The other significant development, which is fundamental to both language systems described in these articles, is the compilation and commercial distribution of a comprehensive, machine-accessible data base containing financial and statistical data on a large number of major corporations.

Actual and proposed applications of computer-aided financial analysis utilizing a mass data base fall into four general areas: data retrieval,

---

* Reprinted by permission of the *Financial Analysts Journal* (January–February 1968).

[1] R. S. Bower, C. E. Nugent, J. P. Williamson, and B. C. Meyers, "A Language for the Aid of Financial Fact Finders," *Financial Analysts Journal* (January–February 1967), pp. 121–129.

Joseph J. Gal, "Man-Machine Interactive Systems and Their Application to Financial Analysis," *Financial Analysts Journal* (May–June 1966), pp. 126–135.

security valuation and selection, portfolio management, and research.[2] Of these, data retrieval, offering the most immediate cost savings, is the most widespread of actual applications[3] and will probably continue to be the "bread and butter" application for some time in the future.

Data Retrieval

Data retrieval operations range from generation of relatively simple reports[4] to far more complex selection routines employing multiple screening and sophisticated computational techniques which can limit data retrieval to those companies meeting criteria specified by the user and create information in a form designed to meet his specific needs. In the former example the analyst is using the computer as a high speed junior research assistant; in the latter the computer is also making a number of programmed decisions specified in advance by the analyst. In all data retrieval operations, the effectiveness and value of the system will be heavily dependent on the quality and comprehensiveness of the data base.

Stock Valuation and Selection

Stock valuation and selection is an extension of the more sophisticated data retrieval applications involving multiple screens and programmed decision rules. However, the analytical techniques employed are likely to call for more detailed and voluminous information for specific investment candidates and the impact of the decision reached is more critical (investment decision versus inclusion/exclusion from further consideration). For these reasons the demands on the data base in terms of reliability and comprehensiveness are likely to be more acute.

Portfolio Management

While a great deal of research has been done in the area of portfolio management, few, if any, computer-aided applications are commercially operational. The data inputs for most of the suggested models are quite stringent, and the results often highly sensitive to subtle changes in the input data. In any portfolio selection application utilizing a computer/data bank system, the effectiveness and quality of the results will be highly dependent on the quality, comprehensiveness, and reliability of the data bank.

---

[2] For some current examples, see: *Computer Applications in Investment Analysis*, a collection of articles published in September 1966 by The Amos Tuck School of Business Administration, Dartmouth College, Hanover, New Hampshire.

[3] Cited in a speech by Russell H. Morrison, the new president of Standard & Poor's Corporation, given at The Amos Tuck School of Business Administration, Dartmouth College, on June 21, 1966.

[4] See Gal, *op. cit.*, p. 131, for an example including both the man-machine dialogue and the resulting computer output.

Research

The availability of computers and the data bank has greatly extended the power of the researcher in the area of financial analysis. Naturally, the results of such research are limited by, and partially dependent upon, the quality and comprehensiveness of the data base.

DATA BASES FOR COMPUTER-AIDED FINANCIAL ANALYSIS

The preceding paragraphs have indicated that a machine-accessible comprehensive data base is both fundamental to the development of man-machine interactive systems and critical to the use of such systems in all areas of financial analysis.

To this writer's knowledge only one such data base has been developed that is currently commercially available to interested users.

The Compustat Data Base

This data base, marketed under the name of COMPUSTAT,[5] presently contains 60 items per year of annual data for 1800 major industrial and 100 utility corporations covering the most recent 20-year period, and a less comprehensive set of quarterly data on industrials covering the most recent 5-year period. Major expansions of this data base in terms of number of companies covered in each category, items covered, and related economic and environmental data are planned and some may be effected by the time this article is published.

COMPUSTAT represents a significant contribution to the development of computer applications in investment analysis, for without it each analyst wishing to use the computer in his work would first have to create his own data base, a tremendously expensive and time-consuming job. However, certain characteristics of the data base and its use in computer-aided analysis could create some problems that might not exist in analysis utilizing traditional data sources and manual techniques. This is not a condemnation of the systems that have been developed nor of COMPUSTAT; both are remarkable and potentially very beneficial. It is, rather, something inherent in the compromises that had to be made to achieve a computer-aided analysis system that works at a reasonable cost.

LIMITATIONS OF THE DATA BASE

It is important that the user be aware of the limitations contained in the present systems, since they can influence and possibly even distort the results of computerized analysis and decisions based on such analysis.

Limitations in the data base can be traced to three distinct causes:

---

[5] COMPUSTAT is the trade name for a set of services provided by Standard Statistics, Inc., a subsidiary of Standard & Poor's Corp. A detailed description of this service is available in *Compustat Information Manual* "COMPUSTAT," privately published by Standard & Poor's Corporation, New York, N.Y. in August 1966.

1. The Source Data.
2. The Reporting Format.
3. Definitions and Compilation Procedures.

THE SOURCE DATA

The principal sources of data for the COMPUSTAT annual industrial data service[6] are published corporate annual reports and reports filed with the SEC (primarily Form 10K). Information is also obtained from other sources including the financial press and direct correspondence with the reporting company.

The compilers do make a number of adjustments to the source data in order to achieve a standardized reporting format, as will be discussed later. However, COMPUSTAT data are basically the same as the data contained in annual reports and SEC Form 10Ks, subject to all the limitations, weaknesses, and lack of comparability so frequently cited in the literature. For example, in the airline industry two of the seven major carriers amortize the investment credit while five follow flow-through accounting. COMPUSTAT data on the industry will be subject to the same lack of inter-firm comparability due to alternative accounting methods that is found in the traditional hard copy data sources. Other examples could be cited including LIFO versus FIFO, accelerated versus straight-line depreciation methods, capitalization versus expensing of R & D expenditure. The accounting and financial literature has amply documented the shortcomings caused by alternative accounting methods. The chronic problem of different accounting practices has not been solved by the compilers of COMPUSTAT. Nor would it be fair to expect them to find a solution. That problem rests squarely on the accounting profession.

An interesting sidelight is that increasing acceptance and use of a computer-accessible data bank, such as COMPUSTAT, may produce subtle or even pronounced pressures towards increased uniformity in disclosure and accounting methods. Already, several companies have volunteered information for the COMPUSTAT tapes which was not available in any other published source.[7] And the treatment of net income and extraordinary items recommended in *APB No. 9*,[8] in 1967, is quite similar to the treatment used in the COMPUSTAT tapes since 1962.

THE REPORTING FORMAT

The present reporting format for the COMPUSTAT annual industrial tapes can be viewed as a three-dimensional matrix. Along one axis are the

---

[6] Throughout this paper, comments and examples will be based on COMPUSTAT's annual industrial tapes. The other services (annual utilities and quarterly tapes) have not been reviewed as extensively by the writer, but it is felt that the annual industrial service is representative of all the sets of data.

[7] Morrison, *op. cit.*

[8] *Reporting the Results of Operations*, Opinion of the Accounting Principles Board No. 9 (New York: American Institute of Certified Public Accountants, 1967).

1800 companies presently covered by the service. Along the second axis are the most recent 20 years. Along the third axis are 60 standardized categories of corporate financial and statistical data. The user obtains access to this data bank by designating through the computer the location of the cell or cells within this 2,160,000 (1800x20x60) cell matrix which are of interest to him.

The real power in this format, and at the same time the source of the major limitations in a system utilizing this data base, lies in the standardization of definitions. In order to achieve the benefits of mass screening and data retrieval through programmed computer routines, it is essential that data for each company be in a standardized format. The 60 items of information included in COMPUSTAT have been carefully selected and rigorously defined to provide a maximum amount of useful information in a form which facilitates a wide variety of possible uses of the information.[9]

COMPARABILITY AND UNIFORMITY

One potential danger in this format is that the standardized reporting format creates the appearance of absolute uniformity for each of the 1800 items covered in the tapes. In other words, the COMPUSTAT set of data for Allied Supermarkets *looks* identical in form to that of Bethlehem Steel, Delta Airlines, and Reynolds Tobacco, etc. Yet, as has already been discussed, the wide variety of accounting methods found in the source data and the noncomparability inherent between firms in widely differing industries are not eliminated in the compilation of the machine-accessible data base. What may appear to the user to be absolute uniformity is, in reality, a uniformity of classification only and not a uniformity of accounting methods. This illusory uniformity could prove to be deceptive to the unwary user.

Because the data base enables the analyst to "look at" a great number of companies, some relatively unfamiliar, and manipulate the data through the computer, it is possible and even likely that he will never see the basic source data, but only the computational results of his analytical techniques. Even if he did see the basic elements in the data base, he could not always ascertain from COMPUSTAT what accounting methods were followed in determining the basic data since such qualitative disclosures are not generally contained in the reporting format. Exceptions are inventory costing and valuation methods which are indicated by code. For these reasons there is a greater possibility for the computer-aided analyst to be misled by noncomparable data than is the case when he uses hard copy sources and manual methods.

---

[9] Companies with financial data not fitting COMPUSTAT's standardized definitions are footnoted on the tapes and the user is referred to a discussion of the special treatment in the *Compustat Information Manual*.

Non-Quantitative Disclosures

Another significant limitation resulting from the format is the lack of qualitative and descriptive disclosures. The increasing complexities of modern corporations make it difficult, if not impossible, to provide investors with all the relevant data in a single set of financial statements devoid of footnotes and descriptive account titles. This is documented by the increasing numbers of footnotes found in recent annual reports.

Important as these qualitative disclosures are, it is not at present feasible to include most of them on a computer-accessible data base. To do so would either sacrifice the mass screening and analysis potential of such a system or cause it to be so bulky and expensive that no user could afford it. However, the absence of such disclosures can present problems to the user.

For example, the 1965 reported earnings for West Virginia Pulp and Paper, inflated 22½ percent by a change in depreciation method, appears in COMPUSTAT without any footnote or other indication of this inconsistency in accounting method. In Standard Kollsman's 1965 Annual Report their auditors took exception to a questionable accounting treatment given contingent claims for reimbursement on government contracts.[10] No similar warning is found in the tapes. The analyst who is aware of such information might choose to adjust the data or modify his analytical techniques. The computer-aided analyst utilizing COMPUSTAT would not be aware of such information unless it were obtained from a source outside the system.

Several similar examples could be given, such as GE's significant retroactive shift in consolidation policy in 1965[11] or ITT's intention to utilize 2,823,058 shares of Cumulative Convertible Preference Stock (Participating) in connection with their proposed merger with American Broadcasting Companies, Inc.[12] Such information, even though contained in traditional data sources, such as the annual report, might be overlooked by an analyst utilizing these sources and manual methods. However, it is *more likely* to be overlooked by the computer-aided analyst who is screening a large number of companies, some quite unfamiliar, to find those companies which meet certain selection criteria he has established. Such oversight might not be too serious in mass screening techniques, but it might be very serious indeed in the detailed analysis of selected firms for investment decisions. Perhaps computer-aided analysis is at present better suited to the mass screening types of operations than to detailed analysis. In any event, the computer-aided analyst cannot afford to ignore information available from conventional sources in his detailed analyses.

---

[10] AICPA, *Accounting Trends and Techniques*, 20th ed. (New York: American Institute of Certified Public Accountants, 1966), p. 300.

[11] General Electric, *1965 Annual Report*, p. 22.

[12] International Telephone and Telegraph Corporation *1966 Annual Report*, p. 27.

Comprehensiveness

Format constraints also limit the number of items of quantitative data that can be disclosed. With 1800 companies and 20 years of data on each tape, the addition of just one new item to the present 60 would involve approximately 36,000 new entries into the tape. Such additions must demonstrate both a general availability of source data and a significant potential use-value to justify the effort and expense involved. As a result, such information as divisional breakdowns for sales and profit, currently receiving so much publicity, probably could not be included in the present reporting format even if it became generally available in corporate reports.

Lest a wrong impression be created, it should be pointed out that the 60 items currently included in the COMPUSTAT tapes have been very carefully chosen and give the analyst a very powerful and versatile data base with which to work. These items are "basic building blocks" of corporate information rather than traditional financial statements and common financial ratios. With them, a competent analyst can develop an almost infinite variety of reports and measures to meet his own unique needs.

Definitions and Compilation Procedures

COMPUSTAT definitions have been carefully developed and reviewed by CPAs prior to their adoption.[13] These definitions must be precise and collectively all-inclusive for it is through them that the standardized reporting format is achieved. Some of the definitions are a bit different from what is found in prevailing corporate reporting practice and a few are in possible conflict with generally accepted accounting principles. Most of the differences are readily reconcilable and do not create any significant distortions or problems *if the analyst is familiar with the definitions.*

For example, "Cost of Goods Sold" as a COMPUSTAT category excludes depreciation while if such a figure is given in the annual report it generally includes depreciation. Exclusion of depreciation from "Cost of Goods Sold" is not a generally accepted accounting principle.[14] An analyst using COMPUSTAT to develop the ratio "Cost of Goods Sold/Sales," or its inverse, Gross Profit/Sales, and considering the ratio by conventional standards would be at least surprised and possibly misled by the results obtained. However, the amount of depreciation is stated separately in

---

[13] Speech by Russell Morrison, President of Standard & Poor's Corporation, delivered at The Amos Tuck School of Business Administration, Dartmouth College, on June 21, 1966.

[14] Paul Grady, *Inventory of Generally Accepted Accounting Principles for Business Enterprises,* Accounting Research Study No. 7 (New York: American Institute of Certified Public Accountants, 1965), pp. 244–251.

COMPUSTAT and a fairly reliable estimate of "Cost of Goods Sold" including depreciation can be obtained from COMPUSTAT by adding the two figures together.

Other COMPUSTAT categories which may be unusual or different from categories commonly found in traditional hard copy sources include "Operating Income" ("net sales less cost of sales and operating expenses *before deducting depreciation, amortization,* etc.")[15] and "Common Equity" ("Surplus, Surplus Reserves, *Unamortized Debt Premiums,* and Capital Stock Premiums less Common Treasury Stock, *Intangibles, Unamortized Debt Discounts, Capital Stock Expense,* Accumulated Unpaid Preferred Dividends, and Excess of Involuntary Liquidating Value of Outstanding Preferred Stock over Carrying Value").[16]

While these definitions do not introduce any significant differences in the accounting methods followed by reporting firms in the development of the source data, they do involve a number of reclassifications of annual report data so that they can be converted into COMPUSTAT's standardized reporting format. In certain instances, the COMPUSTAT data represent a qualitative improvement in the reporting of corporate financial information. For example, a significant lack of comparability is introduced into annual reports of firms in the distilling industry by alternative treatments of federal excise taxes. Some companies include excise taxes in both sales and cost of sales figures; others omit these taxes from both calculations. Since these taxes usually amount to a very significant percentage of net sales, this lack of comparability could seriously distort comparative analysis even though net income is the same figure under both reporting methods. In COMPUSTAT, federal excise taxes are eliminated for all companies, thus establishing a greater comparability than that achieved by the voluntary efforts of the distilling industry in their annual reporting practice.

Reliability

The compilation and updating procedures followed with COMPUSTAT are sound and well controlled. Through a well-designed system of computerized syntactic checking, editing, and proofreading procedures, COMPUSTAT data are quite reliable and free from material errors in the transcription and adjustment of source data.

The handling of retroactive changes in accounting policies presents a problem to the compilers of COMPUSTAT and a possible bias to the data which could mislead the unwary user. The general policy is to restate prior year data when an accounting change has been made, if the company makes such data available. However, quite often companies provide

---

[15] Standard & Poor's Corporation, *op. cit.,* pp. 5–10, August 1966, emphasis not in original.

[16] *Ibid.,* pp. 5–8, August 1966, emphasis not in original.

complete recast data only for the year previous to the accounting change. They often adjust the multi-year summary to reflect the new accounting method, but these summaries just contain key accounts. While these adjusted data in the annual report may be sufficient to enable the analyst to cope with the effects of the accounting policy change, they are not sufficient for an adjustment of the COMPUSTAT figures.[17] For example, when General Electric shifted from a policy of partial consolidation to full consolidation in 1965, they recast their 1964 statements to reflect this. They also adjusted their 10-year summary for this change, giving such key figures as sales, net earnings, and earnings per share. If an analyst wished to compute a growth rate for GE sales over the years 1961–1965 (a very simple operation in a computer-aided system such as LAFFF),[18] using the COMPUSTAT data base he would get a compound growth rate of 8.3 percent. If he used the annual report as a data source and thus used data based on comparable accounting methods for all five years, the growth rate would be 6.8 percent. In dollar terms, at the end of a five-year extrapolation this 1.5 percent difference could amount to approximately a $600,000,000 difference in estimated sales for the fifth year. This possible distortion could be buried in the output of a sophisticated probabilistic simulation model.

IMPLICATIONS FOR COMPUTER-AIDED ANALYSIS

The new man-machine interactive systems, in placing the power of the computer and a mass data bank in the hands of the analyst, are a powerful tool which can greatly extend one's ability both to consider a far greater number of investment alternatives and to employ more complex analytical techniques to the analysis of these alternatives than were possible with manual methods and traditional hard copy data sources. As is the case with all powerful tools, the user must be aware of both the potential and the pitfalls if he is to make effective use of this tool.

The following observations are based on the preceding analysis of the power and limitations in the present computer-aided analytical systems:

1. Present systems seem to offer the greatest benefit in the area of mass screening and data retrieval on a large set of investment alternatives. Such applications take advantage of both the computer's great speed and ability to consistently follow user-specified screening criteria and decision rules and the data bank's ability to provide almost instantaneous data on a large number of corporations. Present systems seem less applicable to security valuation and portfolio management applications because of their more stringent input requirements. In the latter applications the analyst will

---

[17] Since a number of interrelationships exist between COMPUSTAT figures for a company in a given year, it is impossible to change only key figures, such as sales and net income, and not others, such as operating income or accounts receivable.

[18] Bower, et al., *op. cit.*, pp. 123–124.

often have to supplement the data base with information drawn from other sources before completing his final analysis.

2. It is vitally important that the user be familiar with the definitions employed in the compilation of the data base and how they differ from traditional accounting definitions. Also important is the realization by the user that data obtained through the system are subject to the same basic lack of comparability (caused by divergent accounting methods) found in traditional data sources.

3. The use of such a system does not obviate the analyst's consideration and use of data from traditional sources. Often such data can be manually entered by the analyst allowing him to retain the computational advantages offered by the computer.

4. The computer-aided analyst must guard against the apparent accuracy of computer-aided analysis. The results obtained through the system will only be as valid as the analytical techniques employed. Data which are fundamentally noncomparable or inappropriately used remain so even though the computational work is done by a computer.

28

THE PLACE OF BOOK VALUE IN COMMON STOCK EVALUATION*

Frank E. Block, C.F.A.

This article is written to review certain fundamental aspects of book value per share as it relates to the evaluation of common stocks. Though once considered among the most important determinants of common stock prices, book value is now mentioned in hardly a tenth of the investment reports we read.

Book value was watered in the 1920's, written down in the 1930's, and distorted by inflation after World War II. Its record has been so bad for so long that analysts are embarrassed to admit that they even consider it.

After World War II, book value and its equally shady companion, percent earned on book value, were badly distorted by inflation and inadequate depreciation. In 1948, depreciation was barely a third of corporate earnings and was far below the amount necessary for replacement of exhausted and obsolete plant and equipment. Thus, earnings were overstated. The low price/earnings ratios of that time may have been partly a reflection of investor distrust of reported earnings figures. Today, earnings dollars are bolstered by an equal or greater number of depreciation dollars and are further strengthened by the hidden values of research and technological advancement.

Book values in the early postwar years were distorted by failure to reflect the true value of inventories, land, plant, and equipment. There was no easy way to adjust book value for wartime and early postwar inflation. Calculations of percent earned on book value in the late 1940's resulted in overstated figures because the numerator was too large and the denominator was too small.

Today's book values stand up better under analysis. Inventories are 78 percent higher than they were in 1948 and, therefore, contain a larger portion of goods of up-to-date value and a lesser proportion of understated goods. Much of our plant and equipment is new and is stated at approximately current values. Prewar plant and equipment, while understated in terms of replacement costs, are probably stated fairly when

---

*Reprinted by permission of the *Financial Analysts Journal* (March–April 1964).

obsolescence factors are considered. Most of the rest of the balance sheet is expressed in current dollars so that any major understatement of assets is probably found in land values. Thus, today's book value is more realistic than it was and, despite a bit of tarnish here and there, deserves reconsideration. Calculations of percent earned on book value, using current figures, are probably about as sound as the analyst can hope for—assuming that he makes the usually required adjustments.

True Long-term Growth

Over a short period of time a company's earnings may fluctuate widely because of variations in profit margins, disasters, windfalls, and other nonrecurring events. True *long-term* growth can result only from growth in sales. As sales grow a company will need increases in working capital and fixed assets to support this growth. The asset side of the balance sheet must grow roughly in proportion to sales. Similarly, liabilities and the capital structure must increase in order to provide these assets.

The common stock equity is the foundation of the capital structure. A certain minimum proportion of the capital structure must be common stock equity if the company is to maintain its credit and investment standing.

The concept of roughly proportionate growth of sales, income statement, earnings, balance sheet, and common stock equity is essential to an understanding of the manner in which a company grows over the long term. It is also a concept which is necessary to grasp the reasons why book value per share must grow if earnings per share are to grow over the long term.

The rate of return earned on the common stock equity and the portion of those earnings which is retained are basic to the analysis of common stocks because the retention of a part of earnings is the most common way in which book value is increased. The rate at which book value per share grows tends to set a long-term limit on the rate at which earnings per share can grow.

Rescuing Book Value from Limbo

From the beginning young securities analysts are taught that common stock prices are dependent on earnings, dividends, future growth rates, and certainty of such growth rates, quality, and similar considerations. Only in cases of possible merger or liquidation is the analyst encouraged to consider book value. It is not surprising that book value gathers dust on the back row of the analyst's set of tools, to be used only in cases of utter desperation.

In an effort to rescue book value from limbo, the reader is asked to consider three hypothetical new utility companies. We shall make some assumptions that simplify the example in order to make our point. We shall assume sufficient demand for our purposes, 100 percent common stock capitalization, 50 percent dividend payout policy, 16 times price/earnings ratios for the stocks, and rates of return on invested capital of 5 percent, 6¼ percent, and 7½ percent.

So-So, Ltd., sells at book value because its return on book value equals the earnings yield demanded by the market. (The earnings yield demanded by the market is 6¼ percent, or the reciprocal of the assumed

TABLE I

	Bonanza Corp.	So-So. Ltd.	Dreary Co.
Book Value	$100	$100	$100
Allowed Rate of Return	7½%	6¼%	5%
Earnings per Share	$7.50	$6.25	$5.00
Dividend	$3.75	$3.12½	$2.50
Dividend Payout Policy	50%	50%	50%
P/E Ratio	16	16	16
Market Price	$120	$100	$80
Yield	3.125%	3.125%	3.125%
Ratio of Market Price to Book Value	1.2 to 1	1 to 1	0.8 to 1

price/earnings ratio of 16.) Bonanza Corp. sells 20 percent above book value because it earns 20 percent more than the market requires for these companies to sell book value. Similarly, Dreary Co.'s 5 percent return is 20 percent below the level demanded by the market.

In our example, the ratio of market price to book value is equal to the ratio of the *percent earned on book value* to *the earnings yield* demanded by the market. This is true in our hypothetical case because we are using the same price/earnings ratio for all three stocks.

At the end of one year, the picture is changed somewhat because of the varying rates of return and the number of dollars added back to book value.

TABLE II
SECOND YEAR

	Bonanza Corp.	So-So, Ltd.	Dreary Co.
Book Value	$103.75	$103.125	$102.50
Allowed Rate of Return	7½%	6¼%	5%
Earnings per Share	$7.78	$6.45	$5.125
Assumed P/E Ratio	16	16	16
Market Price	$124.50	$103.125	$82.00
Percent Appreciation from Previous Year	3.75%	3.125%	2.50%
Ratio of Market Price to Book Value	1.2 to 1	1 to 1	0.8 to 1
Dividend	$3.89	$3.22	$2.56
Yield	3.125%	3.125%	3.125%
Dollar Increase in Market Price from 1st Year	$4.50	$3.125	$2.00

While in all three cases market value rose, the capital gains were not proportionate to the reinvested dollars. A dollar of retained earnings for Bonanza Corp. resulted in $1.20 in increased market price ($4.50/$3.75 = 120%). A dollar of retained earnings resulted in a dollar of capital gain for So-So, and 80¢ for Dreary. Thus, the market value of retained earnings dollars increases or decreases proportionately with changes in the rates of return at which those dollars can be reinvested.

In our oversimplified case which held price/earnings ratios fixed, three relationships turned out to be identical: (1) the ratio of the *rate of return* at which a dollar of retained earnings could be reinvested to the *earnings yield* demanded by the market, (2) the ratio of the *market price* to *book value*, and (3) the ratio of the *incremental market value of a dollar of retained earnings* to *a dollar of reported earnings*. The fact that the latter two ratios were the same should not be surprising, since retained earnings become book value and presumably would deserve the same price per dollar as the previous book value.

Growth in Earnings and Market Price

The growth in market price was a result of an identical percentage growth in earnings and dividends. Retaining 50 percent of Bonanza's 7½ percent return on common equity resulted in growth of 3¾ percent. If no dividend had been paid by Bonanza Corp., the growth in earnings and market price would have been the full 7½ percent return on equity. It is easy to see that for each of our three companies the growth rate would equal the percent of earnings retained multiplied by the allowed rate of return on book value.

For companies which have predictable average rates of return on equity the following formula should be true over the long term:

$$G = R(1 - A) \qquad [1]$$

G = Earnings growth rate
R = Expected rate of return on equity
A = Dividend payout ratio

From this, one might generalize that the retained portion of the rate of return on equity tends to place a limit on earnings growth, unless the company manipulates its capital structure—perhaps by buying or selling shares of stock at prices other than book value. This formula echoes the earlier argument that book value must grow along with the balance sheet and the income statement.

Effect of Dividend Payout on Returns

We have shown that dollars of retained earnings are not equally valuable, but we may assume temporarily that all dividend dollars are equally valuable, regardless of which of our three companies pays them.

The table below shows the effect of dividend payout on the total return to the investor in dividends plus appreciation.

At 100 percent payout there is no growth, and the return is equal to the earnings yield. The total return for Dreary Co. is maximized by 100 percent payout, while for Bonanza Corp. the return is maximized by 0 percent payout.

TABLE III
TOTAL RETURN

	Bonanza Corp.	So-So, Ltd.	Dreary Co.
100% Payout	6.25%	6.25%	6.25%
50% Payout	6.875	6.25	5.625
0% Payout	7.50	6.25	5.00

This can be expressed another way which will lead to conclusions which many analysts will accept in theory, at least.

$$\text{Total Return} = \frac{\text{Dividend} + \text{Appreciation}}{\text{Price}}$$

$$= \frac{AE + R/Y\,(1-A)\,E}{P} \qquad [2]$$

$$= E/P\,[A\,(1 - R/Y) + R/Y] \qquad [3]$$

Where R = Rate of return on equity
Y = Earnings yield demanded by the market
E = Earnings per share
P = Price of stock
A = Dividend payout ratio

When R is greater than Y, the expression $1 - R/Y$ is negative and, therefore, the return is increased by a zero payout ratio. Negative dividends (that is, selling additional shares of common stock at a premium above book value) would be even more desirable.

When $R = Y$, $(1 - R/Y)$ becomes zero, and therefore dividend payout has no effect on the total return to the investor.

When R is less than Y, the total return is maximized by a maximum payout—even including liquidation, if it can be done at or near book value—or by purchasing shares below book value in the open market.

Actual dividend policies are determined by such considerations as tradition, investor preferences, internal needs for cash, and the like. Certainly no management would change its dividend policy on a basis of transitory fluctuations in the price/earnings ratio (the reciprocal of which is Y). However, where R/Y is substantially less than one for many years and shows little hope of improving, look out for raiders. When R/Y is two, three, or more, management probably sees too many opportunities to invest money at delightful rates of return to pay much in dividends, and rights to purchase additional stock are a likely prospect!

Equal Price/Earnings Ratios Unrealistic

In a theoretical sense, the price/earnings ratio reflects the present value of the future stream of dividends. Since we have determined that earnings and thus dividends of our three companies grow at different rates, it is obvious that our assumption of equal price/earnings ratios is not realistic. Table IV shows a recalculation of the figures on our three hypothetical utility companies assuming price/earnings ratios of 18 for Bonanza Corp., 16 for So-So, Ltd., and 14 for Dreary Co.

TABLE IV

First Year

	Bonanza Corp.	So-So, Ltd.	Dreary Co.
Book Value per Share	$100	$100	$100
Allowed Rate of Return	7.5%	6.25%	5.00%
Earnings per Share	$7.50	$6.25	$5.00
Dividend	$3.75	$3.125	$2.50
Percent Dividend Payout	50%	50%	50%
Price/Earnings Ratio	18	16	14
Market Price	$135	$100	$70
Ratio of Market Price to Book Value	1.35 to 1	1 to 1	0.7 to 1

Second Year

	Bonanza Corp.	So-So, Ltd.	Dreary Co.
Book Value	$103.75	$103.125	$102.50
Earnings per Share	$7.78	$6.45	$5.13
Dividend	$3.89	$3.22	$2.56
Dividend Payout Ratio	50%	50%	50%
Price/Earnings Ratio	18	16	14
Market Price	$140.06	$103.13	$71.75
Ratio of Market Price to Book Value	1.35 to 1	1 to 1	0.7 to 1
Dollar Appreciation over 1st year	$5.06	$3.13	$1.75
Percent Appreciation over 1st Year	3.75%	3.125%	2.50%
Dollar Appreciation over 1st year per $1 of Retained Earnings	$1.35	$1.00	$0.70

Here a dollar of Bonanza Corp.'s retained earnings resulted in $1.35 of appreciation. In our earlier case (Tables I and II), we found that a dollar of Bonanza's retained earnings should be worth $1.20 in the market because Bonanza earned 20 percent more on equity than the earnings yield required by the market. The additional $0.15 is due to the 18 times price/earnings ratio. Since the ratio of (1) the 18 times price/earnings ratio assumed for Bonanza Corp. to (2) the 16 times price/earnings ratio demanded by the market was 112.5%, the $1.20 should be raised 12.5%. This adjustment raises the $1.20 to $1.35.

The reader has probably already anticipated this relationship since it is obvious that:

$$P/B = P/E \times E/B \qquad [4]$$

Where P = Price
E = Earnings per share
B = Book value per share
P/E = Price earnings ratio
E/B = Return on equity

(Actually Formula 4 is $\dfrac{P/E}{1/Y} \times \dfrac{E/B}{Y}$ where the price/earnings ratio of the company, P/E, is being related to $1/Y$, the price/earnings standard demanded by the market. E/B is being compared with the earnings yield Y demanded by the market. The multiplication cancels out the Y and $1/Y$ and we are left with $P/B = P/E \times E/B$.)

It now seems that the value of a dollar of retained earnings is equal to the rate of return at which it may be put to work multiplied by the price/earnings ratio which is or will be applicable to the earnings. Much confusion has existed about the value of retained earnings simply because the market value of retained earnings is determined by the product of two factors. One of these factors is determined by the *internal* operations of the company and the other is entirely *external*, consisting of the market's appraisal of these operating results. As a result, it is not possible to predict a price to book value ratio without making assumptions about both future internal operations and stock market multipliers. If we fail to consider either factor, any estimate of future price to book value ratios is probably headed for trouble.

In short, the ratio of price to book value is two-faceted, involving both *internal* and *external* factors, and this complicated nature of the ratio is probably partly accountable for the lack of interest among analysts in the price to book value relationship.

Price/Earnings Ratios Viewed in New Light

If it is clear now that the value of dollars of retained earnings generally differs between one company and another, then it should be equally clear that they are not equal in value to dollars which are paid out as dividends, except in unique cases. If retained earnings and paid-out earnings are generally not equal, we must consider price/earnings ratios in a new light.

Even though we might assume that capital gains and dividends are equally desired by investors, we must recognize the difficulty of comparing price/earnings ratios for companies with different payout policies and different returns on equity.

Under the traditional concept, earnings are earnings and that's all there is to it! The price/earnings ratio is viewed simply as a valuation of total earnings per share, without regard for possible differences in value of the dividend portion and the retained portion of earnings. Thus, the most popular multiplier, the price/earnings ratio, has a structural weakness as a measure of the present value of the expected future stream of dividends.

An interesting variation of the price/earnings ratio would be:

$$\frac{\text{Price}}{\text{Adjusted Earnings}} = \frac{P}{E\,[A + K\,(1 - A)]} \qquad [5]$$

In this formula EA is the dividend and $E(1 - A)$ is retained earnings. The symbol K is an acceptable ratio of price to book value, derived from the $P/E \times E/B$ relationship. The symbol K could be greater or less than one, and the value of adjusted earnings would therefore depend heavily at times on the payout ratio, A.

If the analyst felt that capital gains and dividends were not equally desirable, additional constants could be put into Formula 5.

Formula 5 is an effort to equalize earnings of companies for comparative purposes. A price/earnings ratio is generally used as the relationship of current market price to current earning power, or perhaps, near-term earning power. In a sense it is like a photograph, giving an instantaneous picture of the relationship, but with no hint of what went on before or afterwards. There is no way to tell at a glance whether I.B.M. at 38 times earnings is more or less attractive than American Telephone and Telegraph at 21 times earnings.

The following example will show that even Formula 5 has its pitfalls:

For the years 1958–62 I.B.M. sold at 10.8 times book value and paid out an average dividend of 24.2 percent of earnings. The comparable figures for American Telephone and Telegraph were 1.87 times and 61.8 percent. If we substitute these two figures for K and A in the above formula, and estimate 1963 earnings of $6.00 for American Telephone and Telegraph and $12.80 (consolidated) for I.B.M., we reach the astonishing adjusted earnings figures of $107.89 for I.B.M. and $7.99 for American Telephone and Telegraph. From this it would appear that at 488 I.B.M. is selling at 4.5 times adjusted earnings and at 133 American Telephone and Telegraph is selling at 16.6 times adjusted earnings! Thus, I.B.M. appears to be three times as cheap as American Telephone and Telegraph.

This extreme example is presented for its "shock effect" since there is immense danger in assuming that an unusually high or low price to book value ratio (K in Formula 5) can be projected far into the future. While many security analysts are confident that I.B.M. will continue to grow at a rapid rate for several more years, most would feel that an eventual tapering off is to be expected, and that at some point in the future I.B.M.'s growth rate will be about in line with the growth in Gross National Product. At that time a saturated market and the resulting competitive conditions will no longer permit I.B.M. to earn a return on equity equal to the 24.9 percent average of 1958–62. It is not unreasonable for the analyst to assume that I.B.M. will earn 25¢ in 1964 for a dollar of 1963 retained earnings. It is illogical for the analyst to assume that I.B.M. will still be earning 25¢ on *that* dollar of its equity, say, 50 years from now. Certainly I.B.M.'s K factor should be higher than that for a company with only average growth prospects, but it should not be placed at an absurdly high figure. K should have been based not on the past, but on estimates of future average P/E and E/B ratios.

Perhaps future computer studies on the price to book value relationship will be helpful in guiding analysts in the adjustment of earnings. While the writer has no helpful suggestions at the moment to solve this dilemma, we must still face the fact that earnings of diverse companies are not equal in value.

The "Fundamentalist" Approach

We have discussed above the use of standards set by the market as a determinant of the factors creating the price to book ratio. To a "fundamentalist" investor who is concerned primarily with the "value approach," this is a cardinal sin. The "fundamentalist" never measures the attractiveness of a stock by the fickle standards of the market place, but rather determines the price at which he is willing to invest and then turns to the market place to see if his stock is selling at the required price.

Those who approach common stock investments from the viewpoint of attractiveness relative to the market as a whole, without giving any regard to the level of the market, will not be disturbed by the use of the ephemeral standards of the market.

It is certain that we lack sufficient knowledge of market preferences for dividends and retained earnings. Even if we were able to measure the market's exact preferences as of last Tuesday, could we count on their being the same five or ten years from now? We are not even sure that a dollar of dividends from American Telephone and Telegraph is just as desirable as a dollar of dividends from I.B.M. The class of investors which purchases American Telephone and Telegraph is probably quite different from the class which buys I.B.M. The relative desires of these two classes for dividends and retained earnings seem likely to be different. With such an abundance of ignorance about the market, the "attractive relative to the market" investor seems at more of a disadvantage as to market standards than the "fundamentalist." The fundamentalist with his value approach need not concern himself with what the market wants at the moment, but can set his own standards of desirability for dividends and retained earnings with the hope that, over the years, his standards and the market's standards will tend to be reasonably close.

If the fundamentalist uses a single multiplier for earnings (implying that dividends and capital gains are equally desirable) he may adjust retained earnings for the average rate at which they can be reinvested over the years and the expected average price/earnings ratio. He might do this by use of the constant K, as in the following formula:

$$\text{Value} = M \text{ (Dividends} + K \times \text{Retained Earnings)}$$
$$V = ME\,[A + K\,(1 - A)] \qquad [6]$$

Where V = Value of stock
M = A suitable multiplier for *adjusted* earnings
E = Unadjusted earnings
A = Payout ratio
K = An appropriate ratio of price to book value

Note that M is a multiplier for adjusted earnings and not an ordinary price/earnings ratio. On the other hand, K is an appropriate price/book ratio and is developed from assumptions made about future P/E and E/B ratios.

If dividends and capital gains are assumed not to be equal in value, separate multipliers would be in order.[1]

Formula 6 offers an unsettling thought. The multiplier M is a function of stability or volatility of earnings, financial strength, growth prospects, payout ratio, quality and depth of management, and a host of other elements. Many of these are reflected in the company's past earnings record and are included in future earnings projections. In the right-hand portion of the formula, $K\,(1 - A)$ contains the same elements found in Formula 1, thereby introducing growth rates directly into Formula 6. An earnings multiplier is partially a function of earnings, dividends, and growth, and if our formula calls for M to be multiplied by these factors, it seems likely that earnings, dividends, and growth are partially exponential rather than linear elements in the value of common stocks. This suggests a reason for the great difficulty analysts have in developing simple linear valuation formulae for common stocks.

Conclusion

In conclusion, it appears that book value plays both a direct and an indirect part in common stock valuation. The ratio of price to book value is the product of the price/earnings ratio and the percent earned on book value. The price/earnings ratio is a reflection of the company's image as an investment, including its expected growth rate, dividend payout ratio, quality, and other factors important to the stock market.

Percent earned on invested capital reveals what management is able to do with all of the assets available to it. It is the logical place to start a

---

[1] The reader may have noticed a similarity between Formula 6 and the Graham & Dodd formula, $V = M(D + \frac{1}{3}E)$. Those authors maintain that for below-average industrial stocks and railroad stocks their formula is sound except where asset values require an upward adjustment. They point out that their formula places four times as much value on dividends as on retained earnings. This would require Formula 6 to use a K of one-fourth and a multiple M of four-thirds the Graham & Dodd multiple; or separate weights could be applied to the dividend and retained earnings portions of Formula 6. In either event, the formulae would produce identical values. See Graham, Dodd and Cottle, *Security Analysis* (New York: McGraw-Hill Book Co., 1962), pp. 517–18.

study of rates of return. Return on book value, however, is more of an acid test, in that it shows the return the management is able to bring down to the stockholders' equity.

The ratio of price to book value is the final test of management's ability. It shows not only the rate of return on equity from which growth and dividends are created, but the premium in the market which is caused by expectations concerning the management's efforts (1) to operate the company, (2) to manage its financial affairs, and (3) to develop a favorable image among investors. These three factors create a price/earnings ratio which partially determines the premium over (or discount from) book value. This premium is a measure of both the company and its management and is of considerable importance to the investor.

This article is written neither to offer easy nostrums to the analyst nor to overemphasize the place of book value in stock valuation. The intention is merely to review and bring into proper focus the normal place of book value in common stock analysis and to expose a few perhaps debatable but interesting ideas which tend to develop naturally as side avenues from the main course of the review.

29

COMMON STOCK VALUATION—PRINCIPLES, TABLES, AND APPLICATION*

Nicholas Molodovsky, C. F. A., Catherine May, and Sherman Chottiner

The Tables in the Appendix are stock valuation tables of a new type.

There exists an obvious need for stock value tables. Common stocks have no maturity. An infinite perspective is needed for their valuation. The interactions of future earnings and dividend growth rates weighted by time and rates of investment returns cannot be grasped by the unaided brain. Computer generated valuation tables serve as a focus which brings the complex stock investment factors into a single value figure.

Our Tables are based on a dividend model. Assuming long-term investment, dividends are the only returns from stocks; but future dividends cannot be estimated without estimating future earnings. To make the Tables operationally more effective, statistical relations were developed which allowed earnings projections to serve directly as the input.

Attempts have been made by other analysts to construct stock value tables by imitating bond yield tables. Stocks were conceptually broken up into a series of payments over a period of years and a resale price. However, this approach calls for assumptions concerning rates of future dividend payouts and price at the date of the hypothetical future resale, thereby injecting additional unknowns into the problem. It also distorts the true nature of stocks.

VALUATION PRINCIPLES

The theoretical structure of our Tables rests on the foundation that the value of a common stock is the present worth of its future stream of dividends. Mathematically, value (V) is:

$$V = D_0 + \frac{D_1}{1+k} + \frac{D_2}{(1+k)^2} + \cdots + \frac{D_n}{(1+k)^n} + \cdots$$

Where: D_0 is the dividend initially.
D_n is the dividend in the nth year.
k is the discount rate, or the desired rate of return.

---

* Reprinted by permission of the *Financial Analysts Journal* (March–April 1965).

The model assumes dividend projections taken out to infinity. Fortunately, economic infinity is not as forbidding as it may sound. This is because the discount factor becomes so large in the distant future that contributions to value become negligible. For example, a dollar of dividends discounted at the average historical rate of 8 percent has a present value of only one cent if it is to be collected in 59 years. If the payment of $1 is 200 years off, its present value falls to 20 millionths of a cent.

The discount rate, k, is the desired rate of return on the common stock investment. Its setting by the investor should be guided by returns on alternative investments and historical stock market returns. One can get an understanding of the latter factor from two historical studies. Molodovsky found the average return on common stocks since 1871 to be slightly less than 8 percent.[1] Fisher and Lorie found it to be 9 percent for the period 1926 to 1960.[2]

The variability of k indicates that the notion of value is not fixed. Investors projecting identical future earnings would find different values if their desired rates of return were different.

Operational Model

To make the model operational, as well as theoretically sound, a relationship between dividends and earnings had to be found to make the latter become the basic input for the model. Such a link exists. This is best realized when the dynamics of the firm are brought into perspective. Corporate earnings can either be paid out as dividends or reinvested in the company. The relative mix is primarily a function of the investment opportunities of the firm.

Low dividend payouts are a result of high investment return, which in turn causes high earnings growth. High dividend payouts are a result of low investment return, which in turn causes low earnings growth. Our Tables are computed by using the hypothesis that the payout ratio is a function of earnings growth. An equation was applied to the Cowles Commission data and the Standard and Poor's 500 for the period 1871 to 1962. Using the least-squares criterion, a multiple regression was obtained expressing the relation between payout ratios and current and lagged earnings growth rates.[3]

---

[1] Nicholas Molodovsky, "Stock Values and Stock Prices—Part One," *Financial Analysts Journal*, May–June, 1960. The figures used in the present article result from further extension of the period. The secular average earnings growth rate of the Standard & Poor's 500 Index, spliced to the Cowles Commission Indexes, which was 2.58 for the period 1871–1959, is now coming closer to 2.74.

[2] Lawrence Fisher and James H. Lorie, "Rates of Return on Investments in Common Stocks," *The Journal of Business*, Graduate School of Business, University of Chicago, January, 1964.

[3] Eugene M. Lerner, *Readings in Financial Analysis and Investment Management*, pp. 267–68. Published for The Institute of Chartered Financial Analysts by Richard D. Irwin, Inc., 1963. The study referred to appeared originally in the February, 1959, issue of the *Financial Analysts Journal*.

Common Stock Valuation—Principles, Tables, and Application

This statistical transformation having been performed, it became possible to use earnings growth rates in a basic dividend model. Earnings growth projections should be made by the user, but the corresponding entries in the Tables show the present worth *not* of earnings, but of *dividends* which correlation analysis allocates to the earnings growth rates in question.

GROWTH PATTERN USED IN TABLES

One should not expect a table to evaluate all growth patterns; the possibilities are infinite. Evaluation without a reasonable accuracy of projected future growth trends is meaningless. Our Tables can be used to evaluate a growth pattern illustrated by Figure 1.

FIGURE 1
PATTERN OF EARNINGS GROWTH EVALUATED BY TABLES

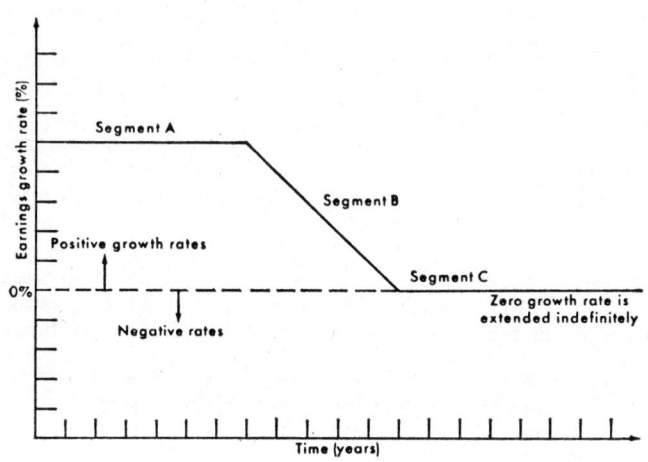

Figure 1 describes companies with established products and markets. Past growth, tempered or accelerated by emerging factors, should suggest an earnings growth projection into the future at some constant average rate (Segment A). Our statistical conscience will not allow us to extend this rate too far into the future. At some point, each company is likely to face the moment of truth when growth begins to taper off.

Of course, the transition from a given rate of growth to zero growth will not be sudden in most cases. This may be a period where markets are becoming saturated or competition is becoming keener. A linear function (Segment B) is an approximation of the dynamics of growth in this phase. As such, the decline of growth from 10 percent to 0 percent in 10 years would be accomplished by 9 percent growth in the first year, 8 percent growth in the second year . . . 1 percent in the ninth year. At some point, growth may completely subside. Segment C is the period, extending to infinity, of zero earnings growth, i.e., of stable earnings.

Our Tables are based on the earnings growth pattern of Figure 1. A constant earnings growth rate is projected for a period of years. A transition period brings earnings growth down to zero in linear fashion. From then on, earnings remain unchanged.

Considering the uncertainties of the industrial world, our Tables do not provide for growth projections beyond the 50th year.

Use of Tables

Investment value of a share of common stock is determined from the Tables once the following *hypotheses* are made:

1. *Normal Earnings*

The Tables are based on a normal earnings figure of $1.00 per share. Value for a security is therefore the Table entry times the normal earnings for that year.

Normal earnings are not a precise figure. They may be found by trend-line analysis using the least-squares criterion. Even so, judgment must enter in the selection of trend periods.

A less satisfactory but still acceptable approach is to determine normal earnings by averaging last year's earnings, the current level of earnings, and next year's expected earnings.

2. *Projected Growth Rate of Earnings*

This may be the same as the growth rate of earnings in the immediate past, or it may be higher or lower depending on circumstances which may alter the earnings trend.

Assuming a continuation of past growth rates, the projected rate may be approximated as follows. Take current earnings and divide by earnings 10 years ago (e.g., 1964 Earnings/1954 Earnings). Calling this ratio "r," the growth rate "g" in the past 10 years can be found in the following table.

r	g	r	g	r	g
1.105	1%	1.791	6%	2.839	11%
1.219	2	1.967	7	3.106	12
1.344	3	2.159	8	3.394	13
1.480	4	2.367	9	3.707	14
1.629	5	2.594	10	4.045	15

The Tables list projected earnings growth rates from 1 percent to 20 percent.

3. *Constant Growth Period*

This is the number of years in which the projected constant growth rate of earnings is expected to be maintained. An estimate of its length would be suggested from the same analytical considerations as used to estimate the projected growth rate.

The Tables list this period from 2 to 30 years in steps of 2 years.

4. *Diminishing Growth Period*

This is the number of years—after the expiration of Item 3 above—during which earnings growth may be expected to decline to zero. It also depends on the special characteristics of the company in question. For example, a company with brilliant promise of growth far into the future might be allowed quite a long period of declining growth. Alternatively, a firm with dull prospects might be assigned a suitable low growth rate for a short period of time followed by a rapid decline to zero growth.

The Tables list entries of 2 to 20 years in steps of 2 years.

5. *Rate of Return*

This is the investor's desired rate of return from long-term common stock investments. It should bear some relation to the returns available from alternative investments, e.g., real estate, proprietary business, bonds, savings accounts, etc. Historical average returns in the stock market of 8 percent to 9 percent should also serve as a guide to its determination.

For reasons of printing economy, the Appendix contains only the 6 percent to 9 percent rates.

Some Practical Illustrations

The mechanics of using the Value Tables may be demonstrated by a few examples.

Example 1

The common stock of Company A is currently selling at 78. Determine the investment value of its stock on the basis of the following hypotheses:

Normal Earnings............................ $5.00
Projected Earnings Growth Rate............... 6%
Constant Growth Period...................... 8 Yrs.
Diminishing Growth Period...................10 Yrs.
Rate of Return............................. 8%

Take the 8 percent return Tables. Under 6 percent projected growth rate of earnings, find the capitalizer corresponding to eight years at constant growth and 10 years at diminishing growth. This is 14.5, which corresponds to $1.00 normal earnings. Since actual normal earnings are $5.00, investment value is (14.5) (5.00) or 72½. As the market price is higher than this hypothesized value, the stock stands in a relatively overpriced position in the long-term investment perspective.

Example 2

Determine the investment value of Company A if a 7 percent return is acceptable while all other hypotheses remain as in Example 1. Will purchase of the stock at 78 provide the required return of 7 percent?

In the 7 percent Tables, find the capitalizer corresponding to the same conditions. It is 16.9, which places value at (16.9) (5.00) or 84½ per share. Since market price is below hypothesized value, the purchase will provide the required return and the stock will stand out as being substantially underpriced on a schedule of relative stock values.

Example 3

An important aspect of the Tables is the information they provide concerning the significance of the current market price in terms of the rate and duration of growth which the price implies.

Suppose the current market price of stock B is 82. Given its 1965 normal earnings as $3.60, an investor seeking an 8 percent return wishes to know what rates and durations of growth justify the price.

The normalized value is 82/3.60 or 22.8. Looking into the 8 percent return Tables, the growth conditions satisfying this figure are:

Projected Growth Rate	Constant Growth Period	Diminishing Growth Period
8%	16 Yrs.	14 Yrs.
9	10	16
10	10	10
11	6	16
13	6	10

The investor then has the job of evaluating these projections. His appraisal of their realism can serve as a guide for market action.

Valuations of the 30 DJIA Stocks

To make our illustrations of the practical use of the Tables as objective as possible, we sent questionnaires and work sheets to research heads of numerous financial institutions with requests to have them filled by analysts specializing in the various security groups represented by the DJIA. The requested information consisted of per-share earnings estimates for each of the Average's thirty component stocks for the years 1965 and 1966 as well as their projected growth rates.

The growth rate figures shown in our Exhibits are therefore a reflection of representative composite opinions of highly trained and experienced men.

The record of the movements of earnings of each of the thirty stocks during the last three decades is summarized by the accompanying charts. In these charts, the trends were fitted, by the method of least squares, to the earnings of selected periods. The periods were chosen by judgment based on the entire evidence of the movements of the earnings—not on any set number of years.

Besides obtaining an insight into the typical behavior of each stock's earnings, an important purpose of the painstaking work in drawing well-fitting earnings trend lines was to find for each of the thirty DJIA stocks its current level of normal earnings. It serves as the capitalization base to which the multipliers found in the Tables may be applied.[4] For a large proportion of the thirty stocks, the 1965 earnings trend line points were used as capitalization bases. However, this was not done blindly. When recent developments seemed to call for it, we used estimates of normal earnings power instead of trend line points.

It will be seen that the earnings charts of the thirty stocks are not presented in the alphabetical order of their corporate names. Economy of graphical space controlled the arrangements of the charts.

We should not underestimate the power of these little charts. They are road maps of long-term earnings trends of each of the 30 stocks. They offer guidance as to the probable future development of both the rates and dependability of growth trends. Judgment, of course, has to be used. The rejuvenation of Chrysler, or the presence of political uncertainties in Anaconda's case, must find a reflection in the level of normal earnings and/

---

[4] "Valuation Bases" in Nicholas Molodovsky, *op. cit.*

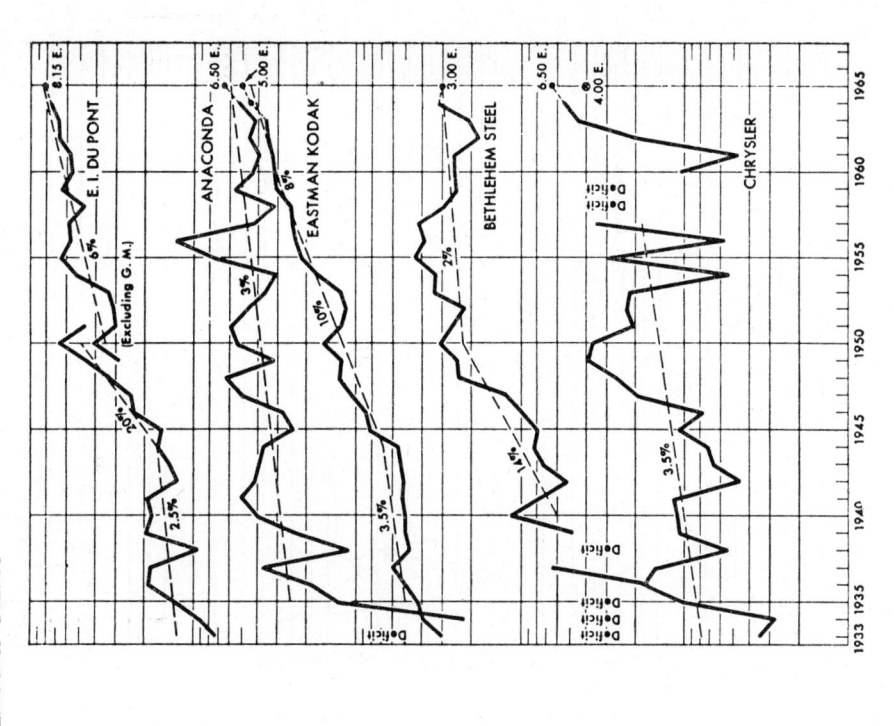

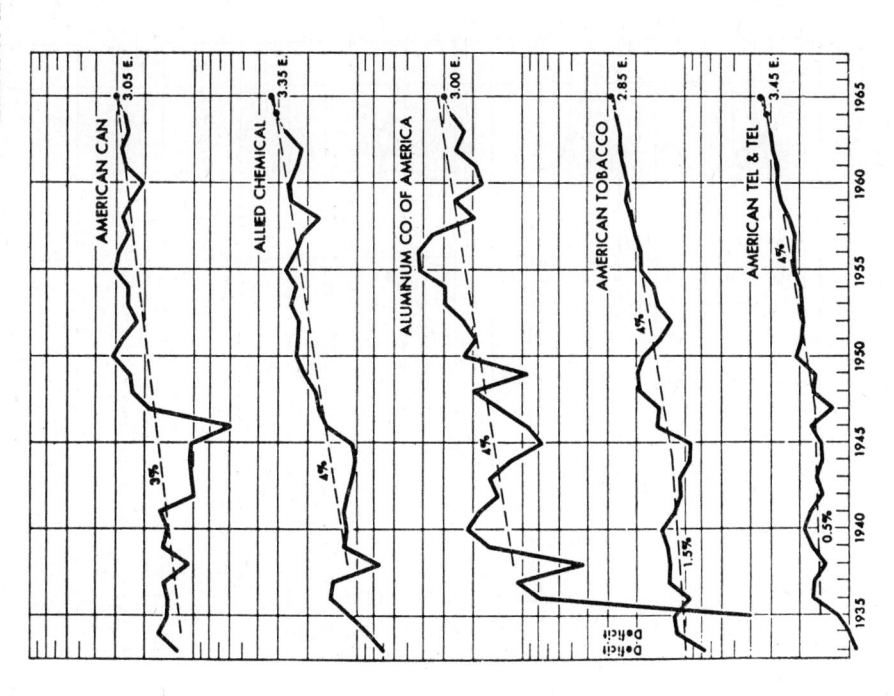

Earnings and Earnings Trends

Earnings and Earnings Trends—*Continued*

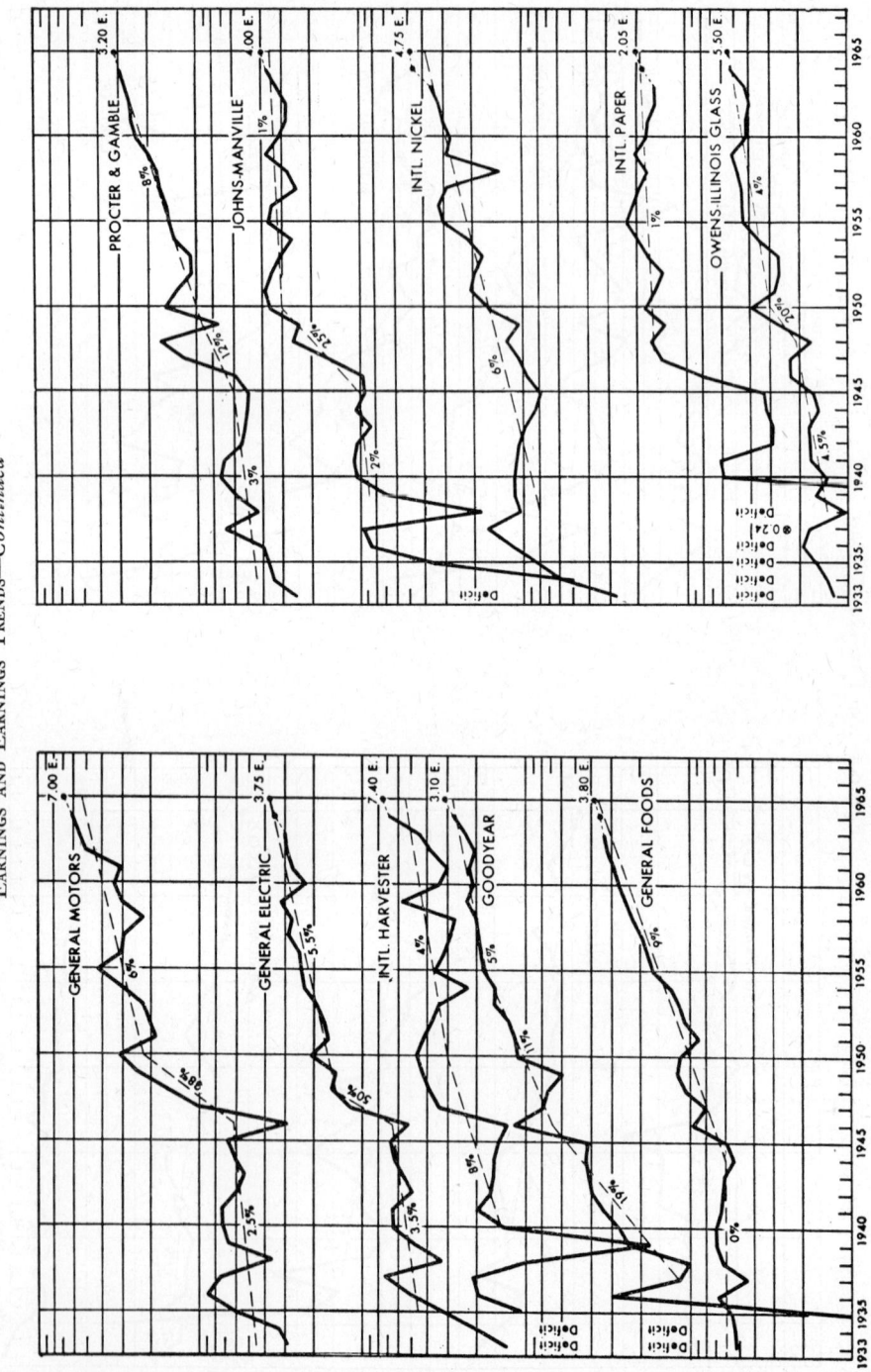

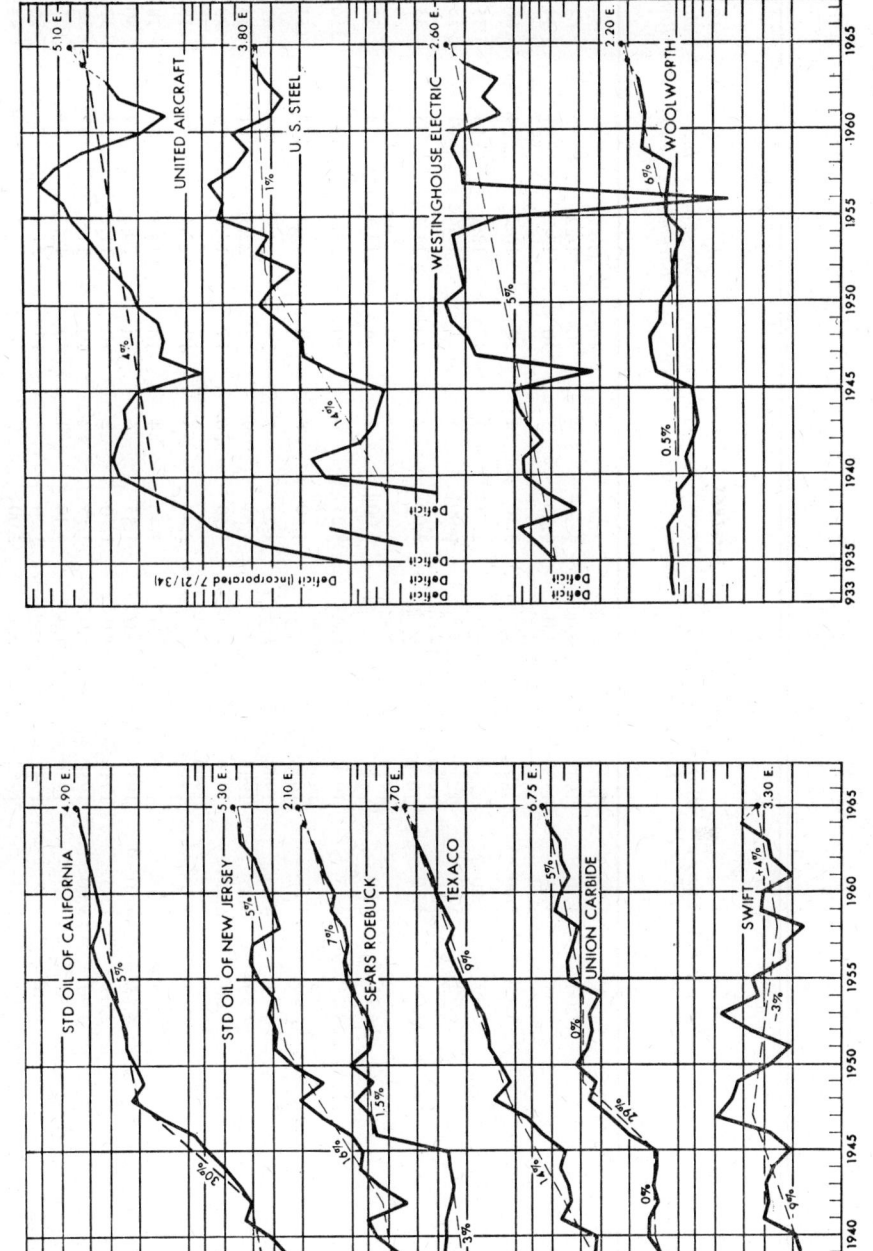

Earnings and Earnings Trends—*Continued*

EXHIBIT ONE

	Estimated Per-Share Earnings		Past Ann. Growth of Earnings Trend		Est. 1965 Normal Earnings	Projected Growth of Earnings Trend		8% Rate of Return		2/10/65 Closing Price
	1965	1966	Years	%		%	No. Yrs.	Present Worth of \$1.00 Earnings*	Invest. Value	
Allied Chemical	3.35	3.50	1938–65	4.0	3.25	5	16	16.7	54	54¾
Alcoa	3.00	3.10	1938–65	4.0	3.20	4	30	16.2	52	63⅞
American Can	3.05	3.15	1934–65	3.0	3.00	3	30	13.7	41	43¼
A T & T	3.45	3.60	1935–47 1947–65	0.5 4.0	3.30	4	30	16.2	54	66¾
American Tobacco	2.85	2.80	1944–65	4.0	2.75	3	17	12.8	35	35⅛
Anaconda	6.50	5.80	1935–65	3.0	6.00	3	1	10.6	63	58⅛
Bethlehem Steel	3.00	3.10	1940–50 1950–65	14.0 2.0	3.00	2	30	11.7	35	35⅝
Chrysler	6.25	6.00	1933–57 1957–65	3.5 — ‖	4.00‖	5	8	14.4	58	57½
E.I. duPont†	8.15	8.25	1950–65	6.0	8.25	6	30	23.8	196	256½
Eastman Kodak	5.00	5.25	1944–59 1959–65	10.0 8.0	4.50	8	30	33.4	150	153¾
General Electric‡	3.75	4.00	1948–65	5.5	3.75	7	23	25.9	97	97⅝
General Foods	3.80	3.85	1944–65	9.0	3.65	9	8	22.3	81	83¼
General Motors	7.00	6.25	1950–65	6.0	5.40	6	13	18.1	98	98⅛
Goodyear T. & R.	3.10	3.20	1946–55 1955–65	11.0 5.0	2.80	5	19	17.3	48	48⅝
Int'l. Harvester	7.40	6.85	1950–65	4.0	5.40	4	16	14.5	78	78⅛
Int'l. Nickel	4.75	4.50	1938–65	6.0	3.85	6	20	20.6	79	80
Int'l. Paper	2.05	1.95	1948–65	1.0	1.90	2	30	11.7	22	32⅝
Johns-Manville	4.00	3.80	1950–65	1.0	3.55	2	30	11.7	42	58
Owens-Ill. Glass	5.50	5.65	1950–65	4.0	5.40	4	30	16.2	88	107⅝
Procter & Gamble	3.20	3.45	1949–65	8.0	3.20	8	15	23.8	76	76⅞
Sears, Roebuck§	2.10	2.25	1952–65	7.0	2.00	7	30	29.2	59	64¼§

Std. Oil (Calif.)	4.90	5.05	1948–65	5.0	4.70	5	10	15.0	71	70½
Std. Oil (N.J.)	5.30	5.50	1951–65	5.0	4.95	5	18	17.1	85	84½
Swift	3.30	3.35	{1947–58 1958–65}	−3.0 4.0	3.30	4	30	16.2	54	63¼
Texaco	4.70	5.10	1948–65	9.0	4.75	7	6	16.7	79	80
Union Carbide	6.75	6.85	1954–65	5.0	6.60	5	30	19.5	129	133½
United Aircraft	5.10	5.25	1938–65	4.0	4.30	4	18	14.8	64	64
U.S. Steel	3.80	3.90	{1939–52 1952–65}	14.0 1.0	3.75	1	30	10.0	38	51½
Westinghouse El.	2.60	2.75	1935–65	5.0	2.40	5	28	19.2	46	46⅞
Woolworth	2.20	2.45	{1933–54 1954–65}	0.5 6.0	2.10	6	1	13.0	27	27

NOTE: To simplify, it was assumed that it will take 20 years for the indicated annual earnings growth rates to decline from the projected final year of indicated growth to zero growth.

* Capitalizers of Normal Earnings.
† Excluding ½ Sh. GM distributed 1/4/65.
‡ Before anti-trust payment—96% paid by end of 1964.
§ Adjusted for 2:1 split (Record date 2/11/65).
∥ Estimated. It is too early to determine true trend after recent changes of management and control.

or the horizon of projections which may be different from the lessons of the past.

The drawing of such charts is costly and time consuming. We hope to offer an earnings chart collection as a companion booklet to our Tables when they are published in final form. Earnings charts are helpful; but the Tables can be also used without them. Financial analysts and experienced investors will have no difficulty in appraising normal earning power and projecting growth rates into the future. In all phases of valuation investors deal with estimates and approximations.

Rates of Return

It is essential to bear in mind that every single number appearing in our Tables is a present value figure determined by discounting the entire future stream of dividends at the indicated rate of return. It shows the present value of dividends to be received beginning with the current year to perpetuity. This rate of return should not be confused with current dividend return, which is merely a ratio of current dividend to current price.

The 9 percent return from common stocks for the period 1926–60 (Fisher and Lorie) and the 7.8 percent (or approximately 8 percent return) for the period 1871–1963 (Molodovsky) both show average historical relations. We can use our Tables to find the return implied by current stock prices. Since they represent the longest historical experience, we shall first experiment with the 8 percent Tables, remembering that discount rate and investment return are equivalent expressions.

Exhibit One brings together the necessary figures. The estimates of 1965 per-share earnings and the projected rates of growth of earnings trend lines were borrowed from the representative opinions of experts mentioned earlier in this paper. Exhibit One also summarizes the graphic information given by the charts.

Exhibit One shows how many years of the projected growth rate would be necessary for each of the 30 DJIA stocks to arrive at an investment value equating as nearly as possible the stock's current price. It reveals that even the use of the longest time horizon for projections of constant growth rates into the future available in our present Tables, i.e., 30 years, is insufficient in the case of many DJIA stocks to come anywhere near their current prices. And yet, in each case, this 30-year projection is extended by an additional 20-year period during which the growth rate in question slowly declines to zero, i.e., to constant earnings per share, which are continued to perpetuity. Only some of the 30 stocks allow sufficiently short-term projections to make an 8 percent rate of return seem reasonably realistic.

There is, therefore, no point in attempting to use the 9 percent rate of return Tables for appraising the current level of common stocks. It would inevitably result in evidence of steep overpricing by the market.

The lowest rate of return in our present Tables is 6 percent. Should we use it, instead of 8 percent, in order to approach current prices, we shall find that the number of years needed is now much smaller. In many cases, it would not exceed a single year. The majority of the 30 stocks produce

EXHIBIT TWO

(Investment Values Based on a 7 Percent Return)

	Est. 1965 Normal Earnings	*Projected Growth of Earnings Trend*		*Present Worth of $1.00 Earnings**	*Invest. Value*	*2/10/65*	
		%	*No. Yrs.*			*Closing Price*	*% Price is of Value*
Allied Chemical	3.25	5	10	17.8	58	54¾	94
Alcoa	3.20	4	10	15.8	51	63⅞	125
American Can	3.00	3	10	14.0	42	43¼	103
A T & T	3.30	4	30	19.8	65	66¾	103
American Tobacco	2.75	3	8	13.7	38	35⅛	92
Anaconda	6.00	3	2	12.4	74	58⅛	79
Bethlehem Steel	3.00	2	8	12.3	37	35⅝	96
Chrysler	4.00†	5	10	17.8	71	57½	81
E. I. duPont	8.25	6	12	21.2	175	256½	147
Eastman Kodak	4.50	8	14	29.9	135	153¾	114
General Electric	3.75	7	14	24.6	92	97⅝	106
General Foods	3.65	8	10	25.9	95	83¼	88
General Motors	5.40	6	10	20.1	109	98⅛	90
Goodyear	2.80	5	8	17.0	48	48⅝	101
Int'l. Harvester	5.40	4	6	14.7	79	78⅛	99
Int'l. Nickel	3.85	6	10	20.1	77	80	104
Int'l. Paper	1.90	2	10	12.5	24	32⅝	136
Johns-Manville	3.55	2	10	12.5	44	58	132
Owens-Ill. Glass	5.40	4	10	15.8	85	107⅝	127
Procter & Gamble	3.20	8	14	29.9	96	76⅞	80
Sears, Roebuck	2.00	7	20	28.5	57	64¼‡	113
Std. Oil (Calif.)	4.70	5	8	17.0	80	70½	88
Std. Oil (N.J.)	4.95	5	8	17.0	84	84½	101
Swift	3.30	4	10	15.8	52	63¼	122
Texaco	4.75	6	8	20.8	99	80	81
Union Carbide	6.60	5	10	17.8	117	133½	114
United Aircraft	4.30	4	6	14.7	63	64	102
U.S. Steel	3.75	1	8	11.1	42	51½	123
Westinghouse El.	2.40	5	10	17.8	43	46⅛	107
Woolworth	2.10	4	8	15.2	32	27	84

NOTE: To simplify, it was assumed that it will take 20 years for the indicated annual earnings growth rates to decline from the projected final year of indicated growth to zero growth.

* Capitalizers of Normal Earnings.

† Estimated. It is too early to determine true trend after recent changes of management and control.

‡ Adjusted for 2:1 split (Record date 2/11/65).

the impression of being underpriced on the basis of a 6 percent rate of return.

Both the 8 percent and the 6 percent rates of return are off the target of current stock market prices. They fall short or overshoot.

We shall change the procedure in Exhibit Two. No attempt is made to find the number of years of projection into the future that will bring investment values close to current prices. We shall use our own judgment for projecting forward the analysts' rates of growth for as many years as seem reasonable to us and shall read off in the 7 percent Tables the corresponding capitalization multipliers. These will then be applied to estimated normal earnings and the resulting investment values confronted with current prices. Seven percent is an assumed desired rate of return which is consistent with available returns at current market levels.

Needless to say, readers who disagree with the analysts' projections of growth rates and/or our own projections of the duration of growth are free to use other figures. By using the Tables in the Appendix, they will come up with correspondingly different investment values.

VALUATION AND FINANCIAL ANALYSIS

We do not wish to create the impression that by taking analysts and investors down to the arid plain of present worth, we encourage them to leave all the green landscapes of life behind them. It is true that the common denominator of business is money. Even the quality of management can be expressed by raising or lowering the rate of projected earnings growth and extending or shortening the number of years of its projection into the future. It matters little whether the company makes steel or spaghetti. A *Fortune* article, featuring Bethlehem Steel, once opened with a forthright statement of the company's controller:

We're not in business to make steel, we're not in business to build ships, we're not in business to erect buildings. We're in business to make money.

It is clear, nevertheless, that the use of valuation tables must be preceded and has to rely on competent security analysis. This condition is just as essential for finding in the Tables the capitalizers as the capitalization bases to which they should be applied. Corporate developments have to be constantly scrutinized. Various events and new facts can affect the projections of future earnings as well as of normal earning power. Typically, for instance, new capital investment will change the magnitude of gross operating assets and the appraisals of the levels and projections of earnings.

Our Tables cannot and are not aimed to substitute for the vital and indispensable work of financial analysis. Their function is merely to place stocks on the common denominator of value after the difficult task of analysis and resulting projections has been already accomplished. Their principal merit is to take a step forward by resolving many assumptions through their computer generated figures. They ask the investor to make only the most vital judgments drawn from conclusions arrived at by security analysis.[5]

In fact, the quality of analysis—which must precede any attempt at valuation—depends itself, to a very marked degree, on the range of contacts and personal ability of the seniors who direct it. The appraisal of the management of a corporation is often the key to the accuracy of earnings projections; and the quality of top management may be better fathomed by its peers in the investment counsel and investment or commercial banking worlds.

---

[5] Nicholas Molodovsky, "Tables of Stock Values," an Investment Analysis Review, *Financial Analysts Journal*, September–October, 1964.

Stock Values and Stock Prices

Our Tables show the investment values of common stocks. They determine the relative attractiveness of stocks by comparing their values with their current prices. If the earnings projections are reasonably accurate, we may assume that market prices will move in the direction of values until they are joined. Yet the market's traveling speed towards that goal will be conditioned by the degree and timing of investors' sanction of the projections as well as by the cyclical convolutions of the road.

Besides cyclical influences, stocks are responsive to many other pricing impulses. The "market," i.e., the consensus of countless investors and traders who compose it, gives varying treatment, in terms of earnings capitalizers, to stocks belonging to different groups. Some of such special attitudes of the market are long-established habits; others are quickly changing "fashions," lasting a season or two. The latter belong to the important subject of timing, which lies outside the scope of this paper.

The Tables can give us no timing help. However, they do not leave us without direction. Our Exhibits have shown that we should not expect to obtain from common stocks, at their present price levels, more than a long-term 7 percent return. Historically, stock prices are high and most stocks produce much smaller returns than the historical averages of 8 percent to 9 percent. The ranges of stock fluctuations are typically wide; sharp downward swings may be expected.

Stock Yields and Bond Yields

At the turn of the century, Charles H. Dow believed that stock values were based on current dividend returns to investors. This approach does not lack followers today.

Most of the thinking about the differences in stock and bond yields has been none too clear. Quite often, the yields to maturity of bonds are compared with current returns on stocks. From this comparison investment conclusions of doubtful merit are drawn.

In his admirable book on interest rates, bond yields and stock prices, Frederick Macaulay was probably the first economist to emphasize that, in referring to returns from stocks as rates of current dividends to current prices, "it is highly undesirable to call the function a 'yield' and thus, by the use of terms, insidiously to suggest that it is of the same nature as the . . . yield of a bond."[6]

Bond yields are based on an assumption of payments through a given maturity. The assumption may or may not materialize. However, it introduces the element of time which enters into a mathematical relationship with all the other factors that are part of the concept. Our stock

---

[6] Frederick R. Macaulay, *Some Theoretical Problems Suggested by the Movements of Interest Rates, Bond Yields and Stock Prices in the United States since 1856* (National Bureau of Economic Research, 1938), p. 133.

value Tables use the same principle. The returns on common stocks are thereby made truly comparable with returns on bonds.

In confronting the yields *to maturity* of bonds with the yields *in perpetuity* of common stocks, no correction seems called for to adjust for the greater exposure of investments in equities to risk. In fact, bonds appear more vulnerable because of erosion of the purchasing power of the monetary unit and uncertainties of its stability as a standard of value.

The risks attaching to common stock investments are of a different nature. They stem from the necessity of projecting into the future the unknown duration and rates of earnings growth or decline. It seems consistent with the nature of the economic factors contained in this uncertainty to adjust for it by modifying the estimates of the factors themselves, i.e., duration and rate whenever new information becomes available. A range of estimates may be used as an alternative.

Practical Investment Policy

Stock prices can stray away from values for extended periods. Timing studies, even though their margin of error is frequently wide, can be helpful. The senior author's clients will attest to his finding that stock prices were extremely "oversold" by the middle of December and that early new highs seemed probable. The technique used for making this forecast was described in a study entitled "It's Good to Own Growth Stocks!" published in the *Financial Analysts Journal* of March–April, 1963.

In the light of the preceding analysis, a 7 percent rate of return from common stocks is a realistic expectation. Investors should decide what proportion of their funds they are satisfied to hold in common stocks offering an expectation of a long-term return of 7 percent. Having determined this ratio, they could then use our 7 percent Tables to select equities endowed with the most generous values. Investment values of numerous stocks can be quickly assembled and compared to respective market prices.

Depending upon the type of the investor, the rest of the total fund could then be carried in government, municipal and corporate bonds, and notes of varying maturities. Eventual declines of stock prices would create opportunities to replenish the portfolio's stock fund when sufficiently attractive rates of return become available once more.

Not in Final Form

The Tables in the Appendix are a usable tool, but represent only the first computer run designed to check whether the principles underlying their construction are workable in practice.

More variables may be allowed to enter the basic regression equation relating payout ratios and earnings growth. Statistical enrichments, such as using trend growth rates rather than simple year-to-year growth, would also improve the basic relation.[7] This basic relationship was derived from broad industrial aggregates. It represents the norm rather than the particular. As such, it loses some significance in the evaluation of firms displaying unusual dividend payout behavior. A finer breakdown with corresponding dividend payout and earnings growth relationships for each stratum might be helpful. Adjustment factors for the different strata are being compiled.

Income tax adjustment factors and the consideration of growth patterns other than illustrated by Figure 1 also merit investigation. The number of Tables based on different rates of return should be enlarged to include both lower and higher rates.

Summary and Conclusions

Not current dividends but the entire stream of future dividends determines both value and return from common stocks. The Tables were developed from this premise. Through statistical techniques, dividends were replaced by earnings growth rates as the operational input. This allowed for efficient practical use while maintaining a sound theoretical structure.

The Tables can be used to determine investment values from desired investment returns and estimates of the future growth of earnings. They can also be used to test the reasonableness of current market prices. By means of appropriate processing, set up to meet specific requirements, they could serve for portfolio planning of private and institutional investors.

An inestimable advantage of the Tables lies in the speed with which they can be read to find the investment value of a stock. Any change of opinion or projection can be at once reflected in a different valuation figure. A range of projections can be expressed by a range of values.

These Tables are not racing forms designed for picking the winners of the next stock market run. They were built to find stocks which are the most rewarding holdings for long-term investors.

We earnestly feel that our Tables, especially when they are in final form, will be an increasingly useful tool for financial analysts and investors. Their usefulness could approach the services rendered by tables of bond yields.

---

[7] See Footnote 3 above and "Rising Levels," as well as Footnote 8, in Nicholas Molodovsky, *op. cit.*

APPENDIX

INVESTMENT VALUES OF NORMAL EARNINGS OF $1 AT 6% RETURN

PROJECTED EARNINGS GROWTH RATE

1.0%

Years Constant Growth	YEARS DIMINISHING GROWTH									
	2	4	6	8	10	12	14	16	18	20
2	11.9	12.0	12.1	12.2	12.3	12.3	12.4	12.5	12.5	12.6
4	12.1	12.2	12.3	12.4	12.4	12.5	12.6	12.6	12.7	12.7
6	12.3	12.4	12.5	12.6	12.6	12.7	12.7	12.8	12.8	12.9
8	12.5	12.6	12.6	12.7	12.8	12.8	12.9	12.9	13.0	13.0
10	12.7	12.7	12.8	12.8	12.9	13.0	13.0	13.0	13.1	13.1
12	12.8	12.9	12.9	13.0	13.0	13.1	13.1	13.2	13.2	13.2
14	12.9	13.0	13.0	13.1	13.1	13.2	13.2	13.3	13.3	13.3
16	13.1	13.1	13.2	13.2	13.3	13.3	13.3	13.4	13.4	13.4
18	13.2	13.2	13.3	13.3	13.4	13.4	13.4	13.5	13.5	13.5
20	13.3	13.3	13.3	13.4	13.4	13.4	13.5	13.5	13.5	13.6
22	13.4	13.4	13.5	13.5	13.5	13.5	13.6	13.6	13.6	13.6
24	13.4	13.5	13.5	13.5	13.6	13.6	13.6	13.7	13.7	13.7
26	13.5	13.5	13.6	13.6	13.6	13.7	13.7	13.7	13.7	13.7
28	13.6	13.6	13.6	13.7	13.7	13.7	13.7	13.7	13.8	13.8
30	13.6	13.7	13.7	13.7	13.7	13.8	13.8	13.8	13.8	13.8

2.0%

Years Constant Growth	YEARS DIMINISHING GROWTH									
	2	4	6	8	10	12	14	16	18	20
2	12.2	12.4	12.6	12.7	12.9	13.1	13.2	13.3	13.5	13.6
4	12.6	12.8	13.0	13.1	13.3	13.4	13.6	13.7	13.8	13.9
6	13.0	13.2	13.4	13.5	13.6	13.8	13.9	14.0	14.1	14.2
8	13.4	13.6	13.7	13.8	14.0	14.1	14.2	14.3	14.4	14.5
10	13.8	13.9	14.0	14.2	14.3	14.4	14.5	14.6	14.7	14.8
12	14.1	14.2	14.3	14.5	14.6	14.7	14.8	14.9	15.0	15.0
14	14.4	14.5	14.6	14.7	14.8	14.9	15.0	15.1	15.2	15.3
16	14.7	14.8	14.9	15.0	15.1	15.2	15.3	15.3	15.4	15.5
18	14.9	15.0	15.1	15.2	15.3	15.4	15.5	15.5	15.6	15.7
20	15.2	15.3	15.3	15.4	15.5	15.6	15.6	15.7	15.8	15.9
22	15.4	15.5	15.5	15.6	15.7	15.8	15.8	15.9	16.0	16.0
24	15.6	15.6	15.7	15.8	15.9	16.0	16.0	16.1	16.1	16.2
26	15.8	15.8	15.9	16.0	16.0	16.1	16.2	16.2	16.3	16.3
28	15.9	16.0	16.1	16.1	16.2	16.2	16.3	16.4	16.4	16.5
30	16.1	16.2	16.2	16.3	16.3	16.4	16.4	16.5	16.5	16.6

3.0%

Years Constant Growth	YEARS DIMINISHING GROWTH									
	2	4	6	8	10	12	14	16	18	20
2	12.5	12.8	13.0	13.3	13.6	13.8	14.1	14.3	14.5	14.7
4	13.1	13.4	13.7	13.9	14.2	14.4	14.6	14.9	15.1	15.3
6	13.8	14.0	14.3	14.5	14.8	15.0	15.2	15.4	15.6	15.8
8	14.4	14.6	14.9	15.1	15.3	15.5	15.7	15.9	16.1	16.3
10	14.9	15.2	15.4	15.6	15.8	16.0	16.2	16.4	16.6	16.7
12	15.5	15.7	15.9	16.1	16.3	16.5	16.7	16.9	17.0	17.2
14	16.0	16.2	16.4	16.6	16.8	17.0	17.1	17.3	17.4	17.6
16	16.5	16.7	16.9	17.1	17.2	17.4	17.5	17.7	17.8	18.0
18	16.9	17.1	17.3	17.5	17.6	17.8	17.9	18.1	18.2	18.4
20	17.4	17.5	17.7	17.9	18.0	18.2	18.3	18.5	18.6	18.7
22	17.8	17.9	18.1	18.2	18.4	18.5	18.7	18.8	18.9	19.0
24	18.1	18.3	18.5	18.6	18.7	18.9	19.0	19.1	19.2	19.3
26	18.5	18.7	18.8	18.9	19.1	19.2	19.3	19.4	19.5	19.6
28	18.8	19.0	19.1	19.2	19.4	19.5	19.6	19.7	19.8	19.9
30	19.2	19.3	19.4	19.6	19.7	19.8	19.9	20.0	20.1	20.2

4.0%

Years Constant Growth	YEARS DIMINISHING GROWTH									
	2	4	6	8	10	12	14	16	18	20
2	12.7	13.1	13.5	13.9	14.3	14.6	15.0	15.3	15.6	15.9
4	13.7	14.0	14.4	14.8	15.1	15.5	15.8	16.1	16.4	16.7
6	14.6	14.9	15.3	15.6	16.0	16.3	16.6	16.9	17.2	17.5
8	15.4	15.8	16.1	16.5	16.8	17.1	17.4	17.7	18.0	18.3
10	16.2	16.6	16.9	17.3	17.6	17.9	18.2	18.4	18.7	19.0
12	17.0	17.4	17.7	18.0	18.3	18.6	18.9	19.2	19.4	19.7
14	17.8	18.1	18.4	18.7	19.0	19.3	19.6	19.9	20.1	20.3
16	18.5	18.9	19.2	19.5	19.7	20.0	20.3	20.5	20.8	21.0
18	19.3	19.6	19.9	20.1	20.4	20.7	20.9	21.2	21.4	21.6
20	19.9	20.2	20.5	20.8	21.0	21.3	21.5	21.8	22.0	22.2
22	20.6	20.9	21.2	21.4	21.7	21.9	22.1	22.4	22.6	22.8
24	21.2	21.5	21.8	22.0	22.3	22.5	22.7	22.9	23.1	23.3
26	21.9	22.1	22.4	22.6	22.8	23.1	23.3	23.5	23.7	23.9
28	22.4	22.7	22.9	23.2	23.4	23.6	23.8	24.0	24.2	24.4
30	23.0	23.2	23.5	23.7	23.9	24.1	24.3	24.5	24.7	24.9

6% Table (Continued)
Projected Earnings Growth Rate

5.0%

Years Constant Growth	2	4	6	8	10	12	14	16	18	20
				YEARS DIMINISHING GROWTH						
2	13.0	13.5	14.0	14.5	15.0	15.5	15.9	16.4	16.8	17.2
4	14.2	14.7	15.2	15.7	16.2	16.6	17.1	17.5	17.9	18.4
6	15.4	15.9	16.4	16.8	17.3	17.8	18.2	18.6	19.0	19.4
8	16.5	17.0	17.5	18.0	18.4	18.9	19.3	19.7	20.1	20.5
10	17.6	18.1	18.6	19.1	19.5	19.9	20.4	20.8	21.2	21.6
12	18.8	19.2	19.7	20.1	20.6	21.0	21.4	21.8	22.2	22.6
14	19.8	20.3	20.8	21.2	21.6	22.1	22.5	22.9	23.2	23.6
16	20.9	21.4	21.8	22.3	22.7	23.1	23.5	23.9	24.2	24.6
18	22.0	22.4	22.8	23.3	23.7	24.1	24.5	24.9	25.2	25.6
20	23.0	23.4	23.9	24.3	24.7	25.1	25.5	25.8	26.2	26.6
22	24.0	24.4	24.8	25.3	25.7	26.0	26.4	26.8	27.1	27.5
24	25.0	25.4	25.8	26.2	26.6	27.0	27.4	27.7	28.1	28.4
26	25.9	26.4	26.8	27.2	27.5	27.9	28.3	28.6	29.0	29.3
28	26.9	27.3	27.7	28.1	28.5	28.8	29.2	29.5	29.9	30.2
30	27.8	28.2	28.6	29.0	29.4	29.7	30.1	30.4	30.8	31.1

7.0%

Years Constant Growth	2	4	6	8	10	12	14	16	18	20
				YEARS DIMINISHING GROWTH						
2	13.6	14.3	15.1	15.9	16.6	17.3	18.1	18.8	19.5	20.3
4	15.3	16.1	16.9	17.7	18.4	19.2	19.9	20.7	21.4	22.2
6	17.1	17.9	18.7	19.5	20.3	21.1	21.8	22.6	23.3	24.1
8	19.0	19.8	20.6	21.4	22.2	23.0	23.7	24.5	25.3	26.0
10	20.8	21.7	22.5	23.3	24.1	24.9	25.7	26.5	27.3	28.0
12	22.7	23.6	24.4	25.2	26.1	26.9	27.7	28.5	29.3	30.1
14	24.7	25.5	26.4	27.2	28.1	28.9	29.7	30.6	31.4	32.2
16	26.6	27.5	28.4	29.3	30.1	31.0	31.8	32.6	33.5	34.3
18	28.7	29.6	30.4	31.3	32.2	33.1	33.9	34.8	35.6	36.4
20	30.7	31.6	32.5	33.4	34.3	35.2	36.1	36.9	37.8	38.6
22	32.8	33.7	34.7	35.6	36.5	37.4	38.3	39.1	40.0	40.9
24	34.9	35.9	36.8	37.8	38.7	39.6	40.5	41.4	42.3	43.2
26	37.1	38.1	39.0	40.0	40.9	41.9	42.8	43.7	44.6	45.5
28	39.3	40.3	41.3	42.2	43.2	44.2	45.1	46.0	47.0	47.9
30	41.6	42.6	43.6	44.6	45.5	46.5	47.5	48.4	49.4	50.3

6.0%

Years Constant Growth	2	4	6	8	10	12	14	16	18	20
				YEARS DIMINISHING GROWTH						
2	13.3	13.9	14.6	15.2	15.8	16.4	17.0	17.6	18.1	18.7
4	14.6	15.2	15.9	16.5	17.1	17.7	18.3	18.9	19.4	20.0
6	15.9	16.5	17.2	17.8	18.4	19.0	19.6	20.2	20.7	21.3
8	17.2	17.9	18.5	19.1	19.7	20.3	20.9	21.5	22.1	22.6
10	18.5	19.2	19.8	20.4	21.0	21.6	22.2	22.8	23.4	23.9
12	19.8	20.5	21.1	21.7	22.3	22.9	23.5	24.1	24.7	25.2
14	21.1	21.8	22.4	23.0	23.7	24.3	24.8	25.4	26.0	26.6
16	22.5	23.1	23.7	24.4	25.0	25.6	26.2	26.7	27.3	27.9
18	23.8	24.4	25.0	25.7	26.3	26.9	27.5	28.0	28.6	29.2
20	25.1	25.7	26.4	27.0	27.6	28.2	28.8	29.4	29.9	30.5
22	26.4	27.0	27.7	28.3	28.9	29.5	30.1	30.7	31.2	31.8
24	27.7	28.3	29.0	29.6	30.2	30.8	31.4	32.0	32.5	33.1
26	29.0	29.7	30.3	30.9	31.5	32.1	32.7	33.3	33.9	34.4
28	30.3	31.0	31.6	32.2	32.8	33.4	34.0	34.6	35.2	35.7
30	31.6	32.3	32.9	33.5	34.1	34.7	35.3	35.9	36.5	37.0

8.0%

Years Constant Growth	2	4	6	8	10	12	14	16	18	20
				YEARS DIMINISHING GROWTH						
2	13.8	14.7	15.7	16.6	17.5	18.4	19.3	20.2	21.1	22.0
4	15.9	16.9	17.8	18.7	19.7	20.6	21.5	22.5	23.4	24.4
6	18.1	19.0	20.0	21.0	22.0	22.9	23.9	24.9	25.9	26.8
8	20.3	21.3	22.3	23.3	24.3	25.4	26.4	27.4	28.4	29.4
10	22.6	23.7	24.7	25.8	26.8	27.9	28.9	30.0	31.0	32.1
12	25.0	26.1	27.2	28.3	29.4	30.5	31.6	32.7	33.7	34.8
14	27.5	28.7	29.8	30.9	32.1	33.2	34.3	35.4	36.6	37.7
16	30.1	31.3	32.5	33.6	34.8	36.0	37.2	38.3	39.5	40.7
18	32.8	34.0	35.3	36.5	37.7	38.9	40.1	41.3	42.6	43.8
20	35.6	36.9	38.1	39.4	40.7	41.9	43.2	44.5	45.7	47.0
22	38.5	39.8	41.1	42.5	43.8	45.1	46.4	47.7	49.0	50.3
24	41.5	42.9	44.3	45.6	47.0	48.3	49.7	51.1	52.4	53.8
26	44.7	46.1	47.5	48.9	50.3	51.7	53.1	54.6	56.0	57.4
28	47.9	49.4	50.8	52.3	53.8	55.3	56.7	58.2	59.7	61.1
30	51.3	52.8	54.3	55.9	57.4	58.9	60.4	62.0	63.5	65.0

6% Table (Continued)
Projected Earnings Growth Rate

9.0%

Years Constant Growth	2	4	6	8	10	12	14	16	18	20
				YEARS DIMINISHING GROWTH						
2	14.1	15.2	16.2	17.3	18.4	19.4	20.5	21.6	22.7	23.9
4	16.5	17.6	18.7	19.9	21.0	22.1	23.3	24.5	25.6	26.8
6	19.1	20.2	21.4	22.6	23.8	25.0	26.2	27.4	28.7	29.9
8	21.7	23.0	24.2	25.5	26.7	28.0	29.3	30.6	31.9	33.2
10	24.6	25.9	27.2	28.5	29.9	31.2	32.6	33.9	35.3	36.7
12	27.6	28.9	30.3	31.7	33.1	34.6	36.0	37.5	38.9	40.4
14	30.7	32.2	33.7	35.1	36.6	38.1	39.7	41.2	42.8	44.3
16	34.1	35.6	37.2	38.7	40.3	41.9	43.5	45.2	46.8	48.5
18	37.6	39.3	40.9	42.6	44.2	45.9	47.6	49.3	51.1	52.8
20	41.4	43.1	44.8	46.6	48.3	50.1	51.9	53.8	55.6	57.4
22	45.3	47.1	49.0	50.8	52.7	54.6	56.5	58.4	60.4	62.3
24	49.5	51.4	53.4	55.3	57.3	59.3	61.3	63.4	65.4	67.5
26	53.9	56.0	58.0	60.1	62.2	64.3	66.4	68.6	70.8	72.9
28	58.6	60.8	62.9	65.1	67.3	69.6	71.8	74.1	76.4	78.7
30	63.6	65.8	68.1	70.5	72.8	75.2	77.5	79.9	82.4	84.8

10.0%

Years Constant Growth	2	4	6	8	10	12	14	16	18	20
				YEARS DIMINISHING GROWTH						
2	14.4	15.6	16.8	18.0	19.3	20.6	21.9	23.2	24.5	25.9
4	17.2	18.4	19.7	21.1	22.4	23.8	25.2	26.6	28.1	29.5
6	20.1	21.5	22.9	24.3	25.8	27.2	28.7	30.3	31.8	33.4
8	23.3	24.8	26.3	27.8	29.4	30.9	32.6	34.2	35.9	37.6
10	26.7	28.3	29.9	31.6	33.2	35.0	36.7	38.5	40.3	42.1
12	30.4	32.1	33.8	35.6	37.4	39.3	41.1	43.1	45.0	47.0
14	34.3	36.2	38.1	40.0	41.9	43.9	45.9	48.0	50.1	52.2
16	38.6	40.6	42.6	44.7	46.8	48.9	51.1	53.3	55.6	57.9
18	43.2	45.3	47.5	49.7	52.0	54.3	56.6	59.0	61.5	63.9
20	48.1	50.4	52.8	55.2	57.6	60.1	62.6	65.2	67.8	70.5
22	53.4	55.9	58.5	61.0	63.7	66.3	69.1	71.8	74.7	77.5
24	59.2	61.9	64.6	67.4	70.2	73.1	76.0	79.0	82.0	85.1
26	65.3	68.2	71.2	74.2	77.2	80.3	83.5	86.7	90.0	93.3
28	72.0	75.1	78.3	81.5	84.8	88.1	91.5	95.0	98.5	102.1
30	79.2	82.5	85.9	89.4	92.9	96.5	100.2	103.9	107.7	111.6

11.0%

Years Constant Growth	2	4	6	8	10	12	14	16	18	20
				YEARS DIMINISHING GROWTH						
2	14.7	16.1	17.4	18.8	20.3	21.8	23.3	24.9	26.5	28.2
4	17.8	19.3	20.8	22.3	23.9	25.5	27.2	28.9	30.7	32.5
6	21.2	22.8	24.4	26.1	27.9	29.7	31.5	33.4	35.3	37.3
8	24.9	26.7	28.5	30.3	32.2	34.2	36.2	38.3	40.4	42.6
10	29.0	30.9	32.9	34.9	37.0	39.2	41.4	43.7	46.0	48.4
12	33.4	35.6	37.7	40.0	42.3	44.6	47.0	49.5	52.1	54.7
14	38.3	40.7	43.0	45.5	48.0	50.6	53.3	56.0	58.8	61.7
16	43.7	46.2	48.9	51.5	54.3	57.1	60.1	63.1	66.1	69.3
18	49.6	52.4	55.2	58.2	61.2	64.3	67.5	70.8	74.2	77.7
20	56.0	59.1	62.2	65.5	68.8	72.2	75.7	79.3	83.0	86.8
22	63.1	66.5	69.9	73.5	77.1	80.8	84.7	88.6	92.7	96.9
24	70.9	74.5	78.3	82.2	86.2	90.3	94.5	98.9	103.3	107.9
26	79.4	83.4	87.6	91.8	96.2	100.7	105.3	110.1	115.0	120.0
28	88.7	93.1	97.7	102.3	107.1	112.1	117.1	122.4	127.7	133.2
30	98.9	103.8	108.8	113.9	119.2	124.6	130.1	135.8	141.7	147.7

12.0%

Years Constant Growth	2	4	6	8	10	12	14	16	18	20
				YEARS DIMINISHING GROWTH						
2	15.0	16.5	18.1	19.7	21.3	23.0	24.8	26.7	28.6	30.6
4	18.5	20.1	21.9	23.7	25.5	27.4	29.4	31.5	33.6	35.9
6	22.3	24.2	26.1	28.1	30.2	32.3	34.6	36.9	39.3	41.8
8	26.6	28.7	30.9	33.1	35.4	37.8	40.3	42.9	45.5	48.3
10	31.5	33.8	36.2	38.7	41.2	43.9	46.7	49.6	52.6	55.7
12	36.8	39.4	42.1	44.9	47.7	50.7	53.8	57.1	60.4	63.8
14	42.8	45.7	48.7	51.8	55.0	58.3	61.8	65.4	69.1	73.0
16	49.5	52.7	56.1	59.5	63.1	66.8	70.7	74.7	78.9	83.2
18	57.0	60.6	64.3	68.2	72.2	76.3	80.6	85.1	89.8	94.6
20	65.3	69.3	73.5	77.8	82.3	86.9	91.7	96.7	101.9	107.3
22	74.6	79.1	83.7	88.6	93.6	98.8	104.1	109.7	115.5	121.5
24	85.0	90.0	95.2	100.6	106.2	112.0	118.0	124.2	130.6	137.3
26	96.6	102.2	108.0	114.0	120.2	126.7	133.4	140.3	147.5	155.0
28	109.6	115.8	122.3	129.0	135.9	143.1	150.6	158.4	166.4	174.8
30	124.0	131.0	138.2	145.7	153.5	161.5	169.9	178.5	187.5	196.8

6% TABLE (CONTINUED)
PROJECTED EARNINGS GROWTH RATE

13.0%

Years Constant Growth	2	4	6	8	10	12	14	16	18	20
					YEARS DIMINISHING GROWTH					
2	15.3	17.0	18.7	20.5	22.4	24.4	26.5	28.6	30.9	33.3
4	19.2	21.0	23.0	25.1	27.2	29.5	31.8	34.3	36.9	39.6
6	23.5	25.7	27.9	30.2	32.7	35.2	37.9	40.7	43.7	46.7
8	28.5	30.9	33.5	36.1	38.9	41.8	44.8	48.0	51.4	54.8
10	34.1	36.9	39.8	42.8	46.0	49.3	52.7	56.3	60.1	64.1
12	40.5	43.7	46.9	50.4	54.0	57.7	61.7	65.8	70.1	74.6
14	47.8	51.4	55.1	59.0	63.1	67.4	71.8	76.5	81.4	86.5
16	56.1	60.1	64.4	68.8	73.4	78.3	83.4	88.7	94.2	100.0
18	65.5	70.1	74.9	79.9	85.2	90.7	96.5	102.5	108.8	115.4
20	76.2	81.4	86.9	92.6	98.6	104.8	111.4	118.3	125.4	132.9
22	88.3	94.3	100.5	107.0	113.8	120.9	128.3	136.1	144.3	152.8
24	102.1	108.9	115.9	123.3	131.1	139.1	147.6	156.5	165.7	175.4
26	117.8	125.5	133.5	141.9	150.7	159.9	169.5	179.6	190.1	201.1
28	135.6	144.3	153.5	163.0	173.0	183.4	194.4	205.8	217.8	230.3
30	155.9	165.8	176.1	187.0	198.3	210.2	222.6	235.6	249.2	263.4

14.0%

Years Constant Growth	2	4	6	8	10	12	14	16	18	20
					YEARS DIMINISHING GROWTH					
2	15.6	17.5	19.4	21.4	23.6	25.8	28.2	30.7	33.4	36.2
4	19.9	22.0	24.2	26.6	29.0	31.7	34.4	37.3	40.4	43.7
6	24.8	27.2	29.8	32.5	35.4	38.4	41.6	45.0	48.5	52.3
8	30.5	33.3	36.3	39.4	42.7	46.2	49.9	53.8	57.9	62.3
10	37.0	40.3	43.7	47.4	51.2	55.3	59.5	64.0	68.8	73.8
12	44.6	48.4	52.4	56.6	61.0	65.7	70.6	75.9	81.4	87.2
14	53.4	57.8	62.4	67.2	72.4	77.8	83.5	89.5	95.9	102.6
16	63.6	68.6	73.9	79.6	85.5	91.8	98.4	105.4	112.7	120.5
18	75.3	81.2	87.3	93.8	100.7	107.9	115.6	123.7	132.2	141.2
20	88.9	95.7	102.8	110.3	118.3	126.6	135.5	144.8	154.7	165.1
22	104.6	112.4	120.7	129.4	138.6	148.3	158.5	169.3	180.7	192.7
24	122.8	131.8	141.4	151.4	162.1	173.3	185.1	197.6	210.8	224.7
26	143.8	154.3	165.3	177.0	189.2	202.2	215.9	230.4	245.6	261.7
28	168.2	180.2	193.0	206.5	220.7	235.7	251.5	268.2	285.9	304.5
30	196.3	210.3	225.0	240.6	257.0	274.4	292.7	312.1	332.4	353.9

15.0%

Years Constant Growth	2	4	6	8	10	12	14	16	18	20
					YEARS DIMINISHING GROWTH					
2	15.9	17.9	20.1	22.3	24.8	27.3	30.1	33.0	36.1	39.4
4	20.6	23.0	25.5	28.1	31.0	34.0	37.2	40.7	44.3	48.2
6	26.1	28.9	31.8	35.0	38.3	41.9	45.7	49.7	54.0	58.6
8	32.6	35.8	39.3	43.0	46.9	51.1	55.6	60.3	65.4	70.8
10	40.2	44.0	48.1	52.4	57.1	62.0	67.3	72.8	78.8	85.1
12	49.1	53.6	58.4	63.6	69.0	74.8	81.0	87.6	94.6	102.0
14	59.6	65.0	70.6	76.6	83.1	89.9	97.2	104.9	113.2	121.9
16	72.0	78.3	85.0	92.0	99.6	107.6	116.2	125.3	135.0	145.4
18	86.6	94.0	101.8	110.2	119.1	128.5	138.6	149.4	160.8	172.9
20	103.8	112.5	121.7	131.5	142.0	153.1	165.0	177.6	191.1	205.4
22	124.0	134.2	145.1	156.6	169.0	182.1	196.1	210.9	226.7	243.6
24	147.8	159.8	172.6	186.2	200.7	216.2	232.6	250.1	268.7	288.5
26	175.8	189.9	205.0	221.0	238.1	256.3	275.6	296.2	318.1	341.4
28	208.8	225.4	243.1	262.0	282.1	303.5	326.2	350.5	376.3	403.7
30	247.6	267.1	288.0	310.2	333.8	359.0	385.8	414.4	444.7	477.0

16.0%

Years Constant Growth	2	4	6	8	10	12	14	16	18	20
					YEARS DIMINISHING GROWTH					
2	16.3	18.4	20.8	23.3	26.0	28.9	32.0	35.4	39.0	42.8
4	21.4	24.0	26.8	29.8	33.0	36.5	40.3	44.3	48.6	53.2
6	27.5	30.6	34.0	37.6	41.5	45.6	50.1	54.9	60.1	65.6
8	34.8	38.5	42.6	46.9	51.5	56.5	61.9	67.6	73.8	80.4
10	43.5	48.0	52.8	58.0	63.6	69.6	76.0	82.9	90.3	98.2
12	54.0	59.4	65.2	71.4	78.0	85.2	92.9	101.1	110.0	119.5
14	66.6	73.0	79.9	87.4	95.4	103.9	113.1	123.0	133.6	145.0
16	81.6	89.3	97.6	106.5	116.1	126.3	137.4	149.2	161.9	175.6
18	99.6	108.9	118.8	129.4	140.9	153.2	166.4	180.6	195.8	212.1
20	121.2	132.2	144.2	156.9	170.6	185.3	201.2	218.1	236.4	255.9
22	147.1	160.3	174.5	189.8	206.2	223.9	242.8	263.1	285.0	308.4
24	178.0	193.9	210.9	229.2	248.8	270.0	292.7	317.0	343.1	371.2
26	215.1	234.0	254.4	276.4	299.9	325.2	352.4	381.5	412.8	446.4
28	259.4	282.2	306.6	332.8	361.0	391.3	423.9	458.8	496.3	536.5
30	312.6	339.8	369.1	400.5	434.3	470.5	509.5	551.3	596.2	644.4

6% Table (Continued)
Projected Earnings Growth Rate

17.0%

Years Constant Growth	2	4	6	8	10	12	14	16	18	20
				YEARS DIMINISHING GROWTH						
2	16.6	19.0	21.5	24.3	27.3	30.6	34.1	38.0	42.1	46.6
4	22.1	25.0	28.2	31.6	35.2	39.2	43.5	48.2	53.3	58.8
6	28.9	32.4	36.2	40.4	44.9	49.7	55.0	60.7	66.8	73.5
8	37.1	41.4	46.1	51.1	56.6	62.5	68.9	75.8	83.4	91.5
10	47.2	52.4	58.1	64.2	70.9	78.1	85.9	94.3	103.5	113.4
12	59.4	65.8	72.7	80.2	88.3	97.1	106.6	116.9	128.0	140.1
14	74.3	82.1	90.5	99.6	109.5	120.2	131.8	144.3	157.9	172.6
16	92.5	102.0	112.2	123.3	135.3	148.4	162.5	177.8	194.3	212.2
18	114.6	126.1	138.6	152.1	166.8	182.7	199.9	218.5	238.7	260.5
20	141.6	155.6	170.8	187.3	205.1	224.5	245.4	268.1	292.7	319.3
22	174.4	191.5	210.0	230.1	251.9	275.4	301.0	328.6	358.6	390.9
24	214.4	235.3	257.8	282.3	308.8	337.5	368.8	402.3	438.8	478.2
26	263.2	288.6	316.0	345.8	378.1	413.1	451.0	492.1	536.5	584.6
28	322.6	353.5	387.0	423.3	462.6	505.2	551.4	601.4	655.5	714.1
30	395.0	432.6	473.4	517.6	565.5	617.5	673.7	734.6	800.6	872.0

19.0%

Years Constant Growth	2	4	6	8	10	12	14	16	18	20
				YEARS DIMINISHING GROWTH						
2	17.2	20.0	23.1	26.4	30.2	34.3	38.8	43.8	49.2	55.3
4	23.8	27.2	31.1	35.4	40.0	45.2	50.9	57.2	64.1	71.7
6	32.0	36.4	41.2	46.6	52.5	59.0	66.2	74.1	82.8	92.4
8	42.3	47.9	54.0	60.7	68.2	76.4	85.5	95.4	106.4	118.5
10	55.4	62.4	70.1	78.6	88.0	98.3	109.7	122.3	136.1	151.3
12	71.8	80.6	90.4	101.1	112.9	126.0	140.3	156.2	173.6	192.8
14	92.6	103.7	115.9	129.4	144.4	160.8	178.9	198.9	220.8	245.0
16	118.7	132.7	148.1	165.2	184.0	204.7	227.5	252.7	280.3	310.8
18	151.6	169.3	188.7	210.2	233.9	260.0	288.8	320.5	355.4	393.8
20	193.1	215.4	239.9	267.0	296.8	329.7	366.9	405.9	449.9	498.3
22	245.4	273.5	304.4	338.5	376.1	417.6	463.3	513.6	569.0	630.1
24	311.4	346.7	385.7	428.6	476.1	528.3	585.9	649.4	719.2	796.1
26	394.5	439.0	488.1	542.3	602.0	667.9	740.5	820.4	908.5	1005.4
28	499.2	555.3	617.2	685.5	760.8	843.8	935.1	1036.0	1147.0	1269.1
30	631.2	701.9	779.9	865.9	960.8	1065.5	1180.8	1307.8	1447.6	1601.6

18.0%

Years Constant Growth	2	4	6	8	10	12	14	16	18	20
				YEARS DIMINISHING GROWTH						
2	16.9	19.5	22.3	25.4	28.7	32.4	36.4	40.8	45.5	50.8
4	22.9	26.1	29.6	33.4	37.6	42.1	47.1	52.5	58.4	64.9
6	30.4	34.3	38.7	43.4	48.5	54.2	60.3	67.0	74.4	82.4
8	39.7	44.5	49.9	55.7	62.1	69.1	76.7	85.1	94.2	104.1
10	51.1	57.2	63.8	71.1	79.0	87.6	97.1	107.4	118.7	131.0
12	65.3	72.9	81.1	90.0	99.8	110.6	122.3	135.1	149.1	164.3
14	83.0	92.3	102.4	113.6	125.7	139.0	153.5	169.4	186.7	205.6
16	104.8	116.3	128.9	142.7	157.8	174.2	192.2	211.9	233.3	256.8
18	131.8	146.1	161.7	178.8	197.5	217.9	240.2	264.6	291.2	320.2
20	165.4	183.1	202.4	223.6	246.7	272.0	299.7	329.8	362.8	398.8
22	206.9	228.9	252.8	279.1	307.7	339.1	373.3	410.7	451.6	496.1
24	258.4	285.6	315.3	347.8	383.3	422.2	464.6	511.0	561.6	616.8
26	322.2	355.9	392.7	433.0	477.0	525.2	577.8	635.2	697.9	766.3
28	401.3	443.0	488.7	538.6	593.1	652.8	718.0	789.1	866.8	951.7
30	499.2	551.0	607.5	669.4	737.0	810.9	891.7	979.9	1076.2	1181.3

20.0%

Years Constant Growth	2	4	6	8	10	12	14	16	18	20
				YEARS DIMINISHING GROWTH						
2	17.6	20.5	23.9	27.6	31.7	36.2	41.3	47.0	53.2	60.2
4	24.6	28.4	32.7	37.4	42.7	48.5	55.0	62.3	70.3	79.2
6	33.6	38.5	44.0	50.0	56.8	64.3	72.6	81.9	92.2	103.6
8	45.2	51.4	58.4	66.2	74.8	84.5	95.2	107.0	120.2	134.9
10	60.0	68.0	77.0	86.9	98.0	110.3	124.0	139.3	156.2	174.9
12	78.9	89.2	100.7	113.5	127.7	143.5	161.1	180.6	202.2	226.3
14	103.2	116.2	131.2	147.5	165.7	186.0	208.5	233.5	261.2	292.1
16	134.4	151.3	170.2	191.2	214.5	240.4	269.3	301.3	336.9	376.4
18	174.3	196.0	220.2	247.1	277.0	310.2	347.2	388.3	433.9	484.5
20	225.5	253.2	284.3	318.7	357.1	399.7	447.1	499.7	558.1	623.0
22	291.1	326.8	366.4	410.6	459.7	514.3	575.0	642.5	717.4	800.5
24	375.1	420.9	471.7	528.3	591.2	661.2	739.0	825.5	921.5	1028.0
26	482.9	541.5	606.6	679.2	759.8	849.5	949.2	1060.0	1183.0	1319.5
28	620.9	696.0	779.5	872.5	975.9	1090.8	1218.6	1360.6	1518.1	1693.2
30	797.8	894.1	1001.1	1120.3	1252.8	1400.1	1563.9	1745.8	1947.8	2172.1

Investment Values of Normal Earnings of $1 at 7% Return

Projected Earnings Growth Rate

1.0%

Years Constant Growth	2	4	6	8	10	12	14	16	18	20
				YEARS DIMINISHING GROWTH						
2	10.2	10.3	10.4	10.4	10.5	10.6	10.6	10.7	10.7	10.7
4	10.4	10.5	10.5	10.6	10.6	10.7	10.7	10.8	10.8	10.9
6	10.6	10.6	10.7	10.7	10.8	10.8	10.9	10.9	10.9	11.0
8	10.7	10.8	10.8	10.9	10.9	11.0	11.0	11.0	11.0	11.1
10	10.8	10.9	10.9	11.0	11.0	11.1	11.1	11.1	11.2	11.2
12	10.9	11.0	11.1	11.1	11.1	11.2	11.2	11.2	11.2	11.2
14	11.0	11.1	11.2	11.2	11.2	11.3	11.3	11.3	11.3	11.3
16	11.1	11.2	11.2	11.3	11.3	11.3	11.3	11.4	11.4	11.4
18	11.2	11.2	11.3	11.3	11.4	11.4	11.4	11.4	11.4	11.4
20	11.3	11.3	11.3	11.4	11.4	11.4	11.4	11.5	11.5	11.5
22	11.3	11.4	11.4	11.4	11.5	11.5	11.5	11.5	11.5	11.5
24	11.4	11.4	11.5	11.5	11.5	11.5	11.5	11.6	11.6	11.6
26	11.4	11.5	11.5	11.5	11.5	11.6	11.6	11.6	11.6	11.6
28	11.5	11.5	11.5	11.6	11.6	11.6	11.6	11.6	11.6	11.6
30	11.5	11.6	11.6	11.6	11.6	11.6	11.6	11.6	11.6	11.6

2.0%

Years Constant Growth	2	4	6	8	10	12	14	16	18	20
				YEARS DIMINISHING GROWTH						
2	10.4	10.6	10.7	10.9	11.0	11.1	11.3	11.4	11.5	11.6
4	10.8	11.0	11.1	11.2	11.3	11.4	11.6	11.6	11.7	11.8
6	11.1	11.3	11.4	11.5	11.6	11.7	11.8	11.9	12.0	12.1
8	11.4	11.6	11.7	11.8	11.9	12.0	12.1	12.1	12.2	12.3
10	11.7	11.8	11.9	12.0	12.1	12.2	12.3	12.4	12.4	12.5
12	12.0	12.1	12.2	12.3	12.3	12.4	12.5	12.6	12.6	12.7
14	12.2	12.3	12.4	12.5	12.5	12.6	12.7	12.7	12.8	12.8
16	12.4	12.5	12.6	12.6	12.7	12.8	12.8	12.9	12.9	13.0
18	12.6	12.7	12.7	12.8	12.9	12.9	13.0	13.0	13.1	13.1
20	12.8	12.8	12.9	13.0	13.0	13.1	13.1	13.2	13.2	13.3
22	12.9	13.0	13.1	13.1	13.2	13.2	13.3	13.3	13.3	13.3
24	13.1	13.1	13.2	13.2	13.3	13.3	13.4	13.4	13.4	13.4
26	13.2	13.3	13.3	13.3	13.4	13.4	13.5	13.5	13.5	13.6
28	13.3	13.3	13.4	13.5	13.5	13.5	13.6	13.6	13.6	13.6
30	13.4	13.5	13.5	13.5	13.6	13.6	13.6	13.7	13.7	13.7

3.0%

Years Constant Growth	2	4	6	8	10	12	14	16	18	20
				YEARS DIMINISHING GROWTH						
2	10.7	10.9	11.1	11.4	11.6	11.8	11.9	12.1	12.3	12.4
4	11.2	11.5	11.7	11.9	12.1	12.3	12.4	12.6	12.7	12.9
6	11.8	12.0	12.2	12.4	12.5	12.7	12.9	13.0	13.2	13.3
8	12.3	12.4	12.6	12.8	13.0	13.1	13.3	13.4	13.5	13.7
10	12.7	12.9	13.1	13.2	13.4	13.5	13.7	13.8	13.9	14.0
12	13.1	13.3	13.5	13.6	13.7	13.9	14.0	14.1	14.2	14.3
14	13.5	13.7	13.8	14.0	14.1	14.2	14.3	14.4	14.5	14.6
16	13.9	14.0	14.2	14.3	14.4	14.5	14.6	14.7	14.8	14.9
18	14.2	14.3	14.5	14.6	14.7	14.8	14.9	15.0	15.1	15.2
20	14.5	14.6	14.8	14.9	15.0	15.1	15.2	15.3	15.3	15.4
22	14.8	14.9	15.0	15.1	15.2	15.3	15.4	15.5	15.6	15.6
24	15.1	15.2	15.3	15.4	15.5	15.6	15.6	15.7	15.8	15.8
26	15.3	15.4	15.5	15.6	15.7	15.8	15.8	15.9	16.0	16.0
28	15.5	15.6	15.7	15.8	15.9	16.0	16.0	16.1	16.2	16.2
30	15.8	15.8	15.9	16.0	16.1	16.1	16.2	16.3	16.3	16.4

4.0%

Years Constant Growth	2	4	6	8	10	12	14	16	18	20
				YEARS DIMINISHING GROWTH						
2	10.9	11.2	11.5	11.9	12.1	12.4	12.7	12.9	13.2	13.4
4	11.7	12.0	12.3	12.6	12.9	13.1	13.4	13.6	13.8	14.1
6	12.4	12.7	13.0	13.3	13.5	13.8	14.0	14.2	14.5	14.7
8	13.1	13.4	13.7	13.9	14.2	14.4	14.6	14.8	15.0	15.2
10	13.8	14.0	14.3	14.5	14.8	15.0	15.2	15.4	15.6	15.8
12	14.4	14.6	14.9	15.1	15.3	15.5	15.7	15.9	16.1	16.3
14	15.0	15.2	15.4	15.7	15.9	16.1	16.3	16.4	16.6	16.8
16	15.5	15.8	16.0	16.2	16.4	16.6	16.7	16.9	17.1	17.2
18	16.1	16.3	16.5	16.7	16.9	17.0	17.2	17.4	17.5	17.7
20	16.6	16.8	17.0	17.1	17.3	17.5	17.6	17.8	17.9	18.1
22	17.0	17.2	17.4	17.6	17.7	17.9	18.0	18.2	18.3	18.5
24	17.5	17.6	17.8	18.0	18.1	18.3	18.4	18.6	18.7	18.8
26	17.9	18.1	18.2	18.4	18.5	18.7	18.8	18.9	19.0	19.2
28	18.3	18.4	18.6	18.7	18.9	19.0	19.1	19.3	19.4	19.5
30	18.7	18.8	19.0	19.1	19.2	19.3	19.5	19.6	19.7	19.8

7% Table (Continued)
Projected Earnings Growth Rate

5.0%

Years Constant Growth	2	4	6	8	10	12	14	16	18	20
2	11.1	11.6	12.0	12.4	12.8	13.1	13.5	13.8	14.1	14.5
4	12.1	12.5	12.9	13.3	13.7	14.1	14.4	14.7	15.0	15.3
6	13.1	13.5	13.9	14.2	14.6	14.9	15.3	15.6	15.9	16.2
8	14.0	14.4	14.8	15.1	15.5	15.8	16.1	16.4	16.7	17.0
10	14.9	15.3	15.6	16.0	16.3	16.6	16.9	17.2	17.5	17.8
12	15.8	16.1	16.5	16.8	17.1	17.4	17.7	18.0	18.3	18.6
14	16.6	17.0	17.3	17.6	17.9	18.2	18.5	18.8	19.0	19.3
16	17.4	17.7	18.1	18.4	18.7	19.0	19.2	19.5	19.7	20.0
18	18.2	18.5	18.8	19.1	19.4	19.7	19.9	20.2	20.4	20.7
20	18.9	19.2	19.5	19.8	20.1	20.4	20.6	20.9	21.1	21.3
22	19.6	19.9	20.2	20.5	20.8	21.0	21.3	21.5	21.7	21.9
24	20.3	20.6	20.9	21.2	21.4	21.7	21.9	22.1	22.3	22.5
26	21.0	21.3	21.5	21.8	22.0	22.3	22.5	22.7	22.9	23.1
28	21.6	21.9	22.2	22.4	22.6	22.9	23.1	23.3	23.5	23.7
30	22.3	22.5	22.8	23.0	23.2	23.4	23.6	23.8	24.0	24.2

6.0%

Years Constant Growth	2	4	6	8	10	12	14	16	18	20
2	11.4	11.9	12.4	12.9	13.4	13.9	14.3	14.8	15.2	15.6
4	12.6	13.1	13.6	14.1	14.6	15.1	15.5	15.9	16.4	16.8
6	13.8	14.3	14.8	15.3	15.8	16.2	16.7	17.1	17.5	17.9
8	15.0	15.5	16.0	16.5	16.9	17.4	17.8	18.2	18.6	19.0
10	16.2	16.7	17.1	17.6	18.1	18.5	18.9	19.3	19.7	20.1
12	17.3	17.8	18.3	18.7	19.2	19.6	20.0	20.4	20.8	21.2
14	18.4	18.9	19.4	19.8	20.3	20.7	21.1	21.5	21.9	22.3
16	19.6	20.0	20.5	20.9	21.3	21.8	22.2	22.5	22.9	23.3
18	20.6	21.1	21.5	22.0	22.4	22.8	23.2	23.6	23.9	24.3
20	21.7	22.2	22.6	23.0	23.4	23.8	24.2	24.6	25.0	25.3
22	22.8	23.2	23.6	24.0	24.4	24.8	25.2	25.6	25.9	26.3
24	23.8	24.2	24.6	25.0	25.4	25.8	26.2	26.6	26.9	27.2
26	24.8	25.2	25.6	26.0	26.4	26.8	27.2	27.5	27.9	28.2
28	25.8	26.2	26.6	27.0	27.4	27.7	28.1	28.4	28.8	29.1
30	26.7	27.2	27.6	27.9	28.3	28.7	29.0	29.4	29.7	30.0

7.0%

Years Constant Growth	2	4	6	8	10	12	14	16	18	20
2	11.6	12.2	12.8	13.5	14.1	14.6	15.2	15.8	16.3	16.9
4	12.9	13.5	14.1	14.8	15.4	15.9	16.5	17.1	17.6	18.2
6	14.2	14.8	15.4	16.1	16.6	17.2	17.8	18.4	18.9	19.5
8	15.5	16.1	16.7	17.3	17.9	18.5	19.1	19.7	20.2	20.8
10	16.8	17.4	18.0	18.6	19.2	19.8	20.4	21.0	21.5	22.1
12	18.1	18.7	19.3	19.9	20.5	21.1	21.7	22.3	22.8	23.3
14	19.4	20.0	20.6	21.2	21.8	22.4	23.0	23.6	24.1	24.6
16	20.7	21.3	21.9	22.5	23.1	23.7	24.3	24.9	25.4	25.9
18	22.0	22.6	23.2	23.8	24.4	25.0	25.6	26.1	26.7	27.2
20	23.3	23.9	24.5	25.1	25.7	26.3	26.9	27.4	28.0	28.5
22	24.6	25.2	25.8	26.4	27.0	27.6	28.2	28.7	29.3	29.8
24	25.9	26.5	27.1	27.7	28.3	28.9	29.5	30.0	30.6	31.1
26	27.1	27.8	28.4	29.0	29.6	30.2	30.8	31.3	31.9	32.4
28	28.4	29.1	29.7	30.3	30.9	31.5	32.1	32.6	33.2	33.7
30	29.7	30.4	31.0	31.6	32.2	32.8	33.4	33.9	34.5	35.0

8.0%

Years Constant Growth	2	4	6	8	10	12	14	16	18	20
2	11.8	12.6	13.3	14.0	14.8	15.5	16.2	16.9	17.6	18.2
4	13.6	14.3	15.1	15.8	16.6	17.3	18.0	18.7	19.4	20.1
6	15.3	16.1	16.9	17.6	18.4	19.1	19.8	20.6	21.3	22.0
8	17.2	17.9	18.7	19.5	20.2	21.0	21.7	22.5	23.2	23.9
10	19.0	19.8	20.6	21.4	22.1	22.9	23.7	24.4	25.2	25.9
12	20.9	21.7	22.5	23.3	24.1	24.9	25.6	26.4	27.2	27.9
14	22.8	23.6	24.4	25.2	26.1	26.9	27.6	28.4	29.2	29.9
16	24.7	25.6	26.4	27.2	28.1	28.9	29.7	30.5	31.3	32.0
18	26.7	27.6	28.4	29.3	30.1	30.9	31.8	32.6	33.4	34.1
20	28.7	29.6	30.5	31.4	32.2	33.0	33.9	34.7	35.5	36.3
22	30.8	31.7	32.6	33.5	34.3	35.2	36.0	36.9	37.7	38.5
24	32.9	33.8	34.7	35.6	36.5	37.4	38.2	39.1	39.9	40.8
26	35.0	36.0	36.9	37.8	38.7	39.6	40.5	41.3	42.2	43.0
28	37.2	38.2	39.1	40.0	40.9	41.8	42.7	43.6	44.5	45.4
30	39.4	40.4	41.4	42.3	43.2	44.2	45.1	46.0	46.9	47.7

7% Table (Continued)
Projected Earnings Growth Rate

9.0%

Years Constant Growth	2	4	6	8	10	12	14	16	18	20
2	12.1	12.9	13.8	14.6	15.5	16.3	17.2	18.0	18.9	19.7
4	14.1	15.0	15.9	16.7	17.6	18.5	19.4	20.3	21.1	22.0
6	16.2	17.1	18.0	18.9	19.9	20.8	21.7	22.6	23.5	24.4
8	18.3	19.3	20.3	21.2	22.2	23.1	24.1	25.0	25.9	26.9
10	20.6	21.6	22.6	23.6	24.6	25.5	26.5	27.5	28.5	29.5
12	22.9	24.0	25.0	26.0	27.0	28.1	29.1	30.1	31.1	32.1
14	25.3	26.4	27.5	28.6	29.6	30.7	31.7	32.8	33.8	34.9
16	27.9	29.0	30.1	31.2	32.3	33.4	34.5	35.6	36.7	37.8
18	30.5	31.6	32.8	33.9	35.1	36.2	37.3	38.5	39.6	40.7
20	33.2	34.4	35.6	36.8	37.9	39.1	40.3	41.5	42.7	43.8
22	36.0	37.2	38.5	39.7	40.9	42.2	43.4	44.6	45.8	47.1
24	38.9	40.2	41.5	42.8	44.0	45.3	46.6	47.9	49.1	50.4
26	41.9	43.3	44.6	45.9	47.3	48.6	49.9	51.2	52.5	53.8
28	45.1	46.5	47.8	49.2	50.6	52.0	53.3	54.7	56.1	57.4
30	48.3	49.8	51.2	52.6	54.1	55.5	56.9	58.3	59.7	61.2

10.0%

Years Constant Growth	2	4	6	8	10	12	14	16	18	20
2	12.3	13.3	14.3	15.3	16.3	17.3	18.3	19.3	20.3	21.3
4	14.6	15.6	16.7	17.7	18.8	19.8	20.9	22.0	23.1	24.1
6	17.0	18.1	19.2	20.3	21.4	22.6	23.7	24.8	26.0	27.1
8	19.6	20.8	21.9	23.1	24.3	25.4	26.6	27.8	29.0	30.2
10	22.3	23.5	24.8	26.0	27.2	28.5	29.7	31.0	32.3	33.6
12	25.2	26.5	27.8	29.1	30.4	31.7	33.0	34.4	35.7	37.1
14	28.2	29.6	30.9	32.3	33.7	35.1	36.5	37.9	39.3	40.8
16	31.4	32.8	34.3	35.7	37.2	38.7	40.2	41.7	43.2	44.7
18	34.8	36.3	37.8	39.4	40.9	42.5	44.0	45.6	47.2	48.8
20	38.4	40.0	41.6	43.2	44.8	46.5	48.1	49.8	51.5	53.2
22	42.1	43.8	45.5	47.3	49.0	50.7	52.5	54.2	56.0	57.8
24	46.1	47.9	49.7	51.5	53.4	55.2	57.1	58.9	60.8	62.7
26	50.3	52.2	54.1	56.1	58.0	59.9	61.9	63.9	65.9	67.9
28	54.8	56.8	58.8	60.9	62.9	64.9	67.0	69.1	71.2	73.3
30	59.5	61.6	63.8	65.9	68.1	70.2	72.4	74.6	76.8	79.1

11.0%

Years Constant Growth	2	4	6	8	10	12	14	16	18	20
2	12.6	13.7	14.8	15.9	17.1	18.2	19.4	20.6	21.9	23.1
4	15.2	16.3	17.5	18.8	20.0	21.3	22.5	23.8	25.2	26.5
6	17.9	19.2	20.5	21.8	23.2	24.5	25.9	27.3	28.7	30.1
8	20.9	22.3	23.7	25.1	26.6	28.0	29.5	31.0	32.5	34.1
10	24.2	25.7	27.2	28.7	30.2	31.8	33.4	35.0	36.6	38.3
12	27.7	29.2	30.9	32.5	34.2	35.8	37.6	39.3	41.1	42.9
14	31.4	33.1	34.9	36.6	38.4	40.2	42.0	43.9	45.8	47.8
16	35.4	37.3	39.1	41.0	42.9	44.9	46.9	48.9	51.0	53.0
18	39.8	41.7	43.7	45.8	47.9	50.0	52.1	54.3	56.5	58.7
20	44.4	46.5	48.7	50.9	53.1	55.4	57.7	60.0	62.4	64.8
22	49.4	51.7	54.1	56.4	58.8	61.2	63.7	66.2	68.8	71.4
24	54.8	57.3	59.8	62.3	64.9	67.5	70.2	72.9	75.7	78.5
26	60.6	63.3	66.0	68.7	71.5	74.3	77.2	80.1	83.1	86.1
28	66.9	69.8	72.7	75.6	78.6	81.6	84.7	87.8	91.0	94.3
30	73.6	76.7	79.8	83.0	86.2	89.5	92.8	96.2	99.6	103.1

12.0%

Years Constant Growth	2	4	6	8	10	12	14	16	18	20
2	12.8	14.0	15.3	16.6	17.9	19.3	20.7	22.1	23.5	25.0
4	15.7	17.1	18.4	19.9	21.3	22.8	24.3	25.9	27.5	29.1
6	18.9	20.4	21.9	23.4	25.0	26.6	28.3	30.0	31.8	33.5
8	22.4	24.0	25.7	27.3	29.1	30.9	32.7	34.6	36.5	38.4
10	26.2	28.0	29.8	31.6	33.5	35.5	37.5	39.5	41.6	43.8
12	30.4	32.3	34.3	36.3	38.4	40.6	42.8	45.0	47.3	49.6
14	35.0	37.1	39.3	41.5	43.8	46.1	48.5	51.0	53.5	56.1
16	40.0	42.3	44.7	47.1	49.6	52.2	54.8	57.5	60.3	63.1
18	45.5	48.0	50.6	53.3	56.1	58.9	61.7	64.7	67.7	70.8
20	51.5	54.3	57.2	60.1	63.1	66.2	69.3	72.6	75.9	79.3
22	58.1	61.2	64.3	67.5	70.8	74.2	77.6	81.2	84.8	88.5
24	65.3	68.7	72.1	75.6	79.3	82.9	86.7	90.6	94.6	98.7
26	73.2	76.9	80.7	84.6	88.5	92.6	96.7	101.0	105.3	109.8
28	81.9	86.0	90.1	94.3	98.6	103.1	107.6	112.3	117.1	121.9
30	91.4	95.9	100.4	105.0	109.8	114.6	119.6	124.7	129.9	135.3

7% Table (Continued)

Projected Earnings Growth Rate

13.0%

Years Constant Growth	2	4	6	8	10	12	14	16	18	20
2	13.1	14.4	15.8	17.3	18.8	20.4	22.0	23.6	25.3	27.1
4	16.3	17.8	19.4	21.0	22.7	24.4	26.2	28.1	30.0	32.0
6	19.9	21.6	23.3	25.1	27.0	29.0	31.0	33.0	35.2	37.4
8	23.9	25.8	27.7	29.8	31.9	34.0	36.2	38.5	40.9	43.4
10	28.4	30.5	32.7	34.9	37.2	39.6	42.1	44.7	47.4	50.1
12	33.4	35.7	38.1	40.7	43.3	45.9	48.7	51.6	54.5	57.6
14	38.9	41.5	44.3	47.1	50.0	52.9	56.0	59.2	62.5	66.0
16	45.1	48.1	51.1	54.2	57.4	60.8	64.2	67.8	71.5	75.3
18	52.0	55.3	58.7	62.2	65.8	69.5	73.3	77.3	81.4	85.7
20	59.8	63.4	67.2	71.1	75.1	79.2	83.5	87.9	92.5	97.3
22	68.4	72.4	76.6	81.0	85.4	90.1	94.9	99.8	104.9	110.2
24	78.0	82.5	87.2	92.0	97.0	102.2	107.5	113.0	118.7	124.6
26	88.7	93.7	98.9	104.3	109.9	115.7	121.6	127.8	134.1	140.7
28	100.6	106.3	112.1	118.1	124.3	130.7	137.4	144.2	151.3	158.6
30	113.9	120.2	126.7	133.4	140.3	147.5	154.9	162.6	170.5	178.7

14.0%

Years Constant Growth	2	4	6	8	10	12	14	16	18	20
2	13.3	14.8	16.4	18.0	19.7	21.5	23.4	25.3	27.3	29.4
4	16.9	18.6	20.4	22.2	24.2	26.2	28.3	30.5	32.8	35.1
6	20.9	22.9	24.9	27.0	29.2	31.5	33.9	36.3	38.9	41.6
8	25.5	27.7	30.0	32.4	34.9	37.5	40.2	43.0	46.0	49.0
10	30.7	33.2	35.8	38.5	41.4	44.3	47.4	50.6	53.9	57.4
12	36.6	39.5	42.4	45.5	48.7	52.1	55.5	59.2	63.0	66.9
14	43.3	46.6	49.9	53.4	57.1	60.8	64.8	68.9	73.2	77.7
16	51.0	54.6	58.4	62.4	66.5	70.8	75.3	80.0	84.9	90.0
18	59.6	63.8	68.1	72.6	77.3	82.2	87.3	92.6	98.1	103.9
20	69.4	74.1	79.0	84.1	89.5	95.0	100.8	106.9	113.1	119.7
22	80.6	85.9	91.5	97.3	103.3	109.6	116.2	123.1	130.2	137.6
24	93.2	99.3	105.6	112.2	119.0	126.2	133.7	141.4	149.5	158.0
26	107.6	114.4	121.6	129.1	136.9	145.0	153.5	162.3	171.5	181.1
28	123.9	131.7	139.8	148.3	157.1	166.4	176.0	186.0	196.4	207.3
30	142.4	151.2	160.5	170.1	180.1	190.6	201.5	212.9	224.8	237.1

15.0%

Years Constant Growth	2	4	6	8	10	12	14	16	18	20
2	13.6	15.2	17.0	18.8	20.7	22.7	24.8	27.1	29.4	31.9
4	17.5	19.4	21.4	23.5	25.7	28.1	30.5	33.1	35.8	38.6
6	22.0	24.2	26.5	29.0	31.5	34.2	37.0	40.0	43.1	46.4
8	27.2	29.8	32.4	35.3	38.2	41.3	44.6	48.0	51.6	55.4
10	33.3	36.2	39.3	42.4	45.9	49.5	53.3	57.3	61.5	65.8
12	40.2	43.6	47.2	50.9	54.9	59.0	63.4	68.0	72.8	77.9
14	48.3	52.2	56.3	60.6	65.2	70.0	75.0	80.3	85.9	91.7
16	57.6	62.1	66.8	71.8	77.1	82.6	88.5	94.6	101.0	107.8
18	68.3	73.5	79.0	84.8	90.9	97.3	104.0	111.1	118.5	126.3
20	80.7	86.7	93.1	99.8	106.8	114.2	121.9	130.1	138.7	147.7
22	95.0	102.2	109.3	117.0	125.1	133.7	142.6	152.1	162.0	172.4
24	111.6	119.6	128.1	137.0	146.4	156.2	166.6	177.5	188.9	200.9
26	130.7	140.0	149.8	160.0	170.9	182.2	194.2	206.8	220.0	233.9
28	152.8	163.5	174.8	186.6	199.2	212.3	226.1	240.7	256.0	272.0
30	178.3	190.7	203.7	217.4	231.9	247.1	263.0	279.8	297.5	316.0

16.0%

Years Constant Growth	2	4	6	8	10	12	14	16	18	20
2	13.9	15.7	17.6	19.6	21.7	24.0	26.4	29.0	31.7	34.6
4	18.1	20.2	22.5	24.9	27.4	30.1	32.9	35.9	39.1	42.5
6	23.2	25.6	28.3	31.1	34.0	37.2	40.5	44.1	47.8	51.8
8	29.1	32.0	35.1	38.4	41.9	45.6	49.5	53.6	58.1	62.7
10	36.0	39.4	43.1	46.9	51.0	55.4	60.0	64.9	70.1	75.6
12	44.2	48.2	52.5	57.0	61.8	66.9	72.4	78.1	84.2	90.7
14	53.8	58.5	63.5	68.9	74.5	80.5	86.9	93.7	100.8	108.4
16	65.0	70.6	76.5	82.8	89.4	96.5	104.0	111.9	120.4	129.3
18	78.3	84.8	91.8	99.2	107.0	115.3	124.1	133.4	143.3	153.8
20	93.9	101.6	109.7	118.4	127.6	137.3	147.7	158.6	170.3	182.6
22	112.2	121.2	130.8	141.0	151.8	163.2	175.4	188.3	202.0	216.5
24	133.7	144.3	155.6	167.5	180.2	193.7	208.0	223.2	239.2	256.2
26	159.0	171.5	184.7	198.8	213.7	229.5	246.3	264.1	283.0	303.0
28	188.7	203.4	218.9	235.5	253.0	271.6	291.3	312.3	334.5	358.0
30	223.6	240.9	259.2	278.6	299.2	321.1	344.3	368.9	394.9	422.6

7% Table (Continued)
Projected Earnings Growth Rate

17.0%

Years Constant Growth	2	4	6	8	10	12	14	16	18	20
2	14.1	16.1	18.2	20.4	22.8	25.4	28.1	31.0	34.2	37.5
4	18.8	21.1	23.6	26.3	29.2	32.3	35.5	39.0	42.8	46.8
6	24.3	27.1	30.1	33.3	36.8	40.4	44.3	48.5	53.0	57.8
8	31.0	34.3	37.9	41.7	45.8	50.2	54.9	59.9	65.3	71.0
10	39.0	43.0	47.2	51.8	56.7	62.0	67.6	73.6	80.0	86.8
12	48.5	53.3	58.4	63.8	69.7	76.0	82.7	89.8	97.5	105.7
14	59.9	65.6	71.7	78.2	85.2	92.7	100.7	109.3	118.5	128.3
16	73.5	80.3	87.6	95.4	103.8	112.8	122.3	132.6	143.6	155.3
18	89.8	97.9	106.7	116.0	126.0	136.7	148.2	160.4	173.5	187.6
20	109.2	119.0	129.4	140.6	152.6	165.4	179.1	193.7	209.4	226.1
22	132.5	144.1	156.6	170.0	184.3	199.6	216.0	233.5	252.3	272.3
24	160.3	174.2	189.2	205.1	222.3	240.6	260.2	281.1	303.5	327.5
26	193.5	210.2	228.1	247.2	267.6	289.5	313.0	338.0	364.8	393.4
28	233.3	253.3	274.6	297.4	321.9	348.1	376.1	406.0	438.1	472.3
30	280.8	304.7	330.2	357.5	386.8	418.1	451.6	487.4	525.7	566.6

18.0%

Years Constant Growth	2	4	6	8	10	12	14	16	18	20
2	14.4	16.5	18.8	21.3	23.9	26.8	29.9	33.2	36.9	40.7
4	19.4	22.0	24.8	27.8	31.0	34.5	38.3	42.4	46.8	51.5
6	25.6	28.7	32.1	35.7	39.7	43.9	48.5	53.5	58.8	64.6
8	33.1	36.9	41.0	45.4	50.2	55.4	61.0	67.0	73.5	80.5
10	42.2	46.8	51.8	57.2	63.0	69.3	76.1	83.4	91.3	99.8
12	53.2	58.8	64.9	71.5	78.6	86.2	94.5	103.4	113.0	123.3
14	66.7	73.5	80.9	88.9	97.5	106.8	116.8	127.7	139.4	151.9
16	83.0	91.3	100.3	110.0	120.5	131.8	144.0	157.2	171.4	186.7
18	102.9	113.0	124.0	135.8	148.5	162.3	177.1	193.1	210.4	229.0
20	127.1	139.4	152.7	167.1	182.6	199.3	217.4	236.8	257.8	280.5
22	156.5	171.5	187.7	205.1	224.0	244.3	266.3	290.0	315.5	343.1
24	192.3	210.5	230.2	251.4	274.3	299.1	325.8	354.6	385.7	419.2
26	235.8	258.0	281.9	307.7	335.6	365.7	398.2	433.2	471.0	511.7
28	288.7	315.7	344.8	376.2	410.1	446.2	486.2	528.8	574.8	624.3
30	353.1	385.9	421.2	459.4	500.7	545.2	593.3	645.1	701.0	761.2

19.0%

Years Constant Growth	2	4	6	8	10	12	14	16	18	20
2	14.7	16.9	19.4	22.1	25.1	28.3	31.8	35.6	39.7	44.2
4	20.1	23.0	26.0	29.4	33.0	37.0	41.3	46.0	51.1	56.7
6	26.9	30.4	34.2	38.3	42.8	47.8	53.1	58.9	65.3	72.1
8	35.3	39.6	44.3	49.4	55.0	61.1	67.7	74.9	82.7	91.2
10	45.6	50.9	56.8	63.1	70.0	77.5	85.7	94.6	104.3	114.8
12	58.4	65.0	72.2	80.0	88.6	97.9	108.0	119.0	131.0	144.0
14	74.2	82.4	91.3	101.0	111.6	123.1	135.6	149.2	164.0	180.1
16	93.8	103.9	114.9	126.9	140.0	154.2	169.7	186.5	204.8	224.8
18	118.0	130.5	144.1	159.0	175.1	192.7	211.9	232.7	255.4	280.0
20	147.9	163.4	180.3	198.6	218.6	240.4	264.0	289.8	317.8	348.3
22	185.0	204.1	224.9	247.6	272.4	299.3	328.6	360.5	395.1	432.8
24	230.8	254.4	280.2	308.3	338.9	372.2	408.4	447.8	490.7	537.3
26	287.4	316.7	348.6	383.3	421.1	462.3	507.2	555.9	608.9	666.6
28	357.5	393.7	433.1	476.1	522.9	573.8	629.3	689.6	755.2	826.5
30	442.2	489.0	537.7	590.9	648.8	711.8	780.3	854.9	936.0	1024.2

20.0%

Years Constant Growth	2	4	6	8	10	12	14	16	18	20
2	14.9	17.4	20.1	23.1	26.3	29.9	33.8	38.1	42.9	48.0
4	20.8	23.9	27.3	31.1	35.1	39.6	44.6	50.0	55.9	62.5
6	28.2	32.1	36.4	41.1	46.3	51.9	58.1	64.9	72.4	80.6
8	37.6	42.5	47.8	53.7	60.2	67.3	75.1	83.7	93.1	103.4
10	49.3	55.4	62.2	69.6	77.8	86.7	96.6	107.3	119.2	132.1
12	64.0	71.8	80.3	89.6	99.9	111.1	123.5	137.0	151.9	168.2
14	82.6	92.3	103.0	114.8	127.7	141.8	157.4	174.4	193.1	213.6
16	105.9	118.2	131.6	146.4	162.6	180.4	200.0	221.4	244.9	270.7
18	135.3	150.7	167.6	186.1	206.5	229.0	253.5	280.5	310.1	342.5
20	172.2	191.5	212.8	236.2	261.8	290.0	320.9	354.9	392.1	432.9
22	218.6	242.9	269.7	299.1	331.4	366.8	405.7	448.5	495.2	546.5
24	277.0	307.6	341.2	378.2	418.8	463.4	512.3	566.0	624.9	689.4
26	350.4	388.9	431.3	477.7	528.8	584.9	646.4	713.9	788.0	869.1
28	442.8	491.2	544.4	602.9	667.1	737.7	815.1	900.0	993.1	1095.2
30	558.9	619.9	686.8	760.3	841.1	929.8	1027.2	1134.0	1251.1	1379.5

Investment Values of Normal Earnings of $1 at 8% Return

Projected Earnings Growth Rate

1.0%

Years Constant Growth	\multicolumn{10}{c}{YEARS DIMINISHING GROWTH}
	2	4	6	8	10	12	14	16	18	20
2	8.9	9.0	9.1	9.1	9.2	9.2	9.3	9.3	9.3	9.4
4	9.1	9.1	9.2	9.2	9.3	9.3	9.4	9.4	9.4	9.5
6	9.2	9.3	9.3	9.4	9.5	9.4	9.5	9.5	9.6	9.6
8	9.3	9.4	9.4	9.5	9.6	9.5	9.6	9.6	9.6	9.7
10	9.4	9.5	9.5	9.6	9.6	9.6	9.6	9.7	9.7	9.7
12	9.5	9.6	9.6	9.6	9.7	9.7	9.7	9.7	9.7	9.8
14	9.6	9.6	9.7	9.7	9.7	9.7	9.8	9.8	9.8	9.8
16	9.7	9.7	9.7	9.8	9.8	9.8	9.8	9.8	9.8	9.9
18	9.7	9.8	9.8	9.8	9.8	9.8	9.9	9.9	9.9	9.9
20	9.8	9.8	9.8	9.9	9.9	9.9	9.9	9.9	9.9	9.9
22	9.8	9.9	9.9	9.9	9.9	9.9	9.9	9.9	9.9	9.9
24	9.9	9.9	9.9	9.9	9.9	9.9	10.0	10.0	10.0	10.0
26	9.9	9.9	9.9	10.0	10.0	10.0	10.0	10.0	10.0	10.0
28	10.0	10.0	10.0	10.0	10.0	10.0	10.0	10.0	10.0	10.0
30	10.0	10.0	10.0	10.0	10.0	10.0	10.0	10.0	10.0	10.0

2.0%

Years Constant Growth	\multicolumn{10}{c}{YEARS DIMINISHING GROWTH}
	2	4	6	8	10	12	14	16	18	20
2	9.1	9.3	9.4	9.5	9.6	9.7	9.8	9.9	10.0	10.0
4	9.4	9.6	9.7	9.8	9.9	10.0	10.0	10.1	10.2	10.3
6	9.7	9.8	9.9	10.0	10.1	10.2	10.3	10.3	10.4	10.5
8	10.0	10.1	10.2	10.2	10.3	10.4	10.5	10.5	10.6	10.6
10	10.2	10.3	10.4	10.4	10.5	10.6	10.6	10.7	10.7	10.8
12	10.4	10.5	10.6	10.6	10.7	10.7	10.8	10.8	10.9	10.9
14	10.6	10.7	10.7	10.8	10.8	10.9	10.9	11.0	11.0	11.0
16	10.7	10.8	10.9	10.9	11.0	11.0	11.0	11.1	11.1	11.2
18	10.9	10.9	11.0	11.0	11.1	11.1	11.2	11.2	11.2	11.3
20	11.0	11.1	11.1	11.1	11.2	11.2	11.3	11.3	11.3	11.3
22	11.1	11.2	11.2	11.2	11.3	11.3	11.3	11.4	11.4	11.4
24	11.2	11.3	11.3	11.3	11.4	11.4	11.4	11.4	11.5	11.5
26	11.3	11.4	11.4	11.4	11.4	11.5	11.5	11.5	11.5	11.6
28	11.4	11.4	11.5	11.5	11.5	11.5	11.6	11.6	11.6	11.6
30	11.5	11.5	11.5	11.5	11.6	11.6	11.6	11.6	11.6	11.7

3.0%

Years Constant Growth	\multicolumn{10}{c}{YEARS DIMINISHING GROWTH}
	2	4	6	8	10	12	14	16	18	20
2	9.3	9.5	9.7	9.9	10.1	10.2	10.4	10.5	10.6	10.8
4	9.8	10.0	10.2	10.3	10.5	10.6	10.8	10.9	11.0	11.1
6	10.3	10.4	10.6	10.7	10.9	11.0	11.1	11.2	11.3	11.4
8	10.7	10.8	11.0	11.1	11.2	11.3	11.5	11.6	11.7	11.7
10	11.0	11.2	11.3	11.4	11.5	11.7	11.8	11.8	11.9	12.0
12	11.4	11.5	11.6	11.7	11.8	11.9	12.0	12.1	12.2	12.3
14	11.7	11.8	11.9	12.0	12.1	12.2	12.3	12.3	12.4	12.5
16	11.9	12.1	12.2	12.2	12.3	12.4	12.5	12.6	12.6	12.7
18	12.2	12.3	12.4	12.5	12.5	12.6	12.7	12.8	12.8	12.9
20	12.4	12.5	12.6	12.7	12.7	12.8	12.9	12.9	13.0	13.0
22	12.6	12.7	12.8	12.9	12.9	13.0	13.0	13.1	13.1	13.2
24	12.8	12.9	13.0	13.0	13.1	13.1	13.2	13.2	13.3	13.3
26	13.0	13.1	13.1	13.2	13.2	13.3	13.3	13.4	13.4	13.5
28	13.2	13.2	13.3	13.3	13.4	13.4	13.5	13.5	13.5	13.6
30	13.3	13.4	13.4	13.5	13.5	13.5	13.6	13.6	13.6	13.7

4.0%

Years Constant Growth	\multicolumn{10}{c}{YEARS DIMINISHING GROWTH}
	2	4	6	8	10	12	14	16	18	20
2	9.5	9.8	10.1	10.3	10.6	10.8	11.0	11.2	11.4	11.6
4	10.2	10.4	10.7	10.9	11.2	11.4	11.6	11.7	11.9	12.1
6	10.8	11.1	11.3	11.5	11.7	11.9	12.1	12.2	12.4	12.6
8	11.4	11.6	11.8	12.0	12.2	12.4	12.6	12.7	12.9	13.0
10	11.9	12.1	12.3	12.5	12.7	12.9	13.0	13.2	13.3	13.4
12	12.4	12.6	12.8	13.0	13.1	13.3	13.4	13.6	13.7	13.8
14	12.9	13.1	13.2	13.4	13.5	13.7	13.8	13.9	14.1	14.2
16	13.3	13.5	13.6	13.8	13.9	14.0	14.2	14.3	14.4	14.5
18	13.7	13.9	14.0	14.1	14.3	14.4	14.5	14.6	14.7	14.8
20	14.1	14.2	14.3	14.5	14.6	14.7	14.8	14.9	15.0	15.1
22	14.4	14.5	14.7	14.8	14.9	15.0	15.1	15.2	15.3	15.4
24	14.7	14.8	15.0	15.1	15.2	15.3	15.4	15.5	15.5	15.6
26	15.0	15.1	15.2	15.3	15.4	15.5	15.6	15.7	15.8	15.8
28	15.3	15.4	15.5	15.6	15.7	15.8	15.8	15.9	16.0	16.1
30	15.5	15.6	15.7	15.8	15.9	16.0	16.1	16.1	16.2	16.2

8% Table (Continued)
Projected Earnings Growth Rate

5.0%

Years Constant Growth	2	4	6	8	10	12	14	16	18	20
				YEARS DIMINISHING GROWTH						
2	9.7	10.1	10.4	10.8	11.1	11.4	11.6	11.9	12.2	12.4
4	10.6	10.9	11.2	11.6	11.9	12.1	12.4	12.7	12.9	13.1
6	11.4	11.7	12.0	12.3	12.6	12.9	13.1	13.4	13.6	13.8
8	12.2	12.5	12.8	13.0	13.3	13.6	13.8	14.0	14.2	14.4
10	12.9	13.2	13.5	13.7	14.0	14.2	14.4	14.6	14.9	15.0
12	13.6	13.9	14.1	14.4	14.6	14.8	15.0	15.2	15.4	15.6
14	14.2	14.5	14.7	15.0	15.2	15.4	15.6	15.8	16.0	16.2
16	14.8	15.1	15.3	15.5	15.8	16.0	16.1	16.3	16.5	16.7
18	15.4	15.7	15.9	16.1	16.3	16.5	16.7	16.8	17.0	17.1
20	16.0	16.2	16.4	16.6	16.8	17.0	17.1	17.3	17.5	17.6
22	16.5	16.7	16.9	17.1	17.3	17.4	17.6	17.7	17.9	18.0
24	17.0	17.2	17.4	17.5	17.7	17.9	18.0	18.2	18.3	18.4
26	17.4	17.6	17.8	18.0	18.1	18.3	18.4	18.6	18.7	18.8
28	17.9	18.1	18.2	18.4	18.5	18.7	18.8	18.9	19.1	19.2
30	18.3	18.5	18.6	18.8	18.9	19.0	19.2	19.3	19.4	19.5

6.0%

Years Constant Growth	2	4	6	8	10	12	14	16	18	20
				YEARS DIMINISHING GROWTH						
2	9.9	10.4	10.8	11.2	11.6	12.0	12.3	12.7	13.0	13.4
4	11.0	11.4	11.8	12.2	12.6	13.0	13.3	13.7	14.0	14.3
6	12.0	12.4	12.8	13.2	13.6	13.9	14.3	14.6	14.9	15.2
8	13.0	13.4	13.8	14.1	14.5	14.8	15.2	15.5	15.8	16.1
10	13.9	14.3	14.7	15.0	15.4	15.7	16.0	16.3	16.6	16.9
12	14.9	15.2	15.6	15.9	16.2	16.6	16.9	17.2	17.4	17.7
14	15.7	16.1	16.4	16.8	17.1	17.4	17.7	18.0	18.2	18.5
16	16.6	16.9	17.3	17.6	17.9	18.2	18.5	18.7	19.0	19.2
18	17.4	17.7	18.1	18.4	18.7	18.9	19.2	19.5	19.7	20.0
20	18.2	18.5	18.8	19.1	19.4	19.7	19.9	20.2	20.4	20.6
22	18.9	19.3	19.6	19.8	20.1	20.4	20.6	20.9	21.1	21.3
24	19.7	20.0	20.3	20.5	20.8	21.0	21.3	21.5	21.7	22.0
26	20.4	20.7	20.9	21.2	21.5	21.7	21.9	22.2	22.4	22.6
28	21.1	21.3	21.6	21.9	22.1	22.3	22.6	22.8	23.0	23.2
30	21.7	22.0	22.2	22.5	22.7	22.9	23.2	23.4	23.6	23.8

7.0%

Years Constant Growth	2	4	6	8	10	12	14	16	18	20
				YEARS DIMINISHING GROWTH						
2	10.1	10.6	11.2	11.7	12.2	12.6	13.1	13.5	14.0	14.4
4	11.4	11.9	12.4	12.9	13.4	13.9	14.3	14.7	15.2	15.6
6	12.6	13.2	13.7	14.1	14.6	15.1	15.5	15.9	16.3	16.7
8	13.9	14.4	14.9	15.3	15.8	16.2	16.7	17.1	17.5	17.9
10	15.1	15.6	16.0	16.5	17.0	17.4	17.8	18.2	18.6	19.0
12	16.3	16.7	17.2	17.7	18.1	18.5	19.0	19.4	19.8	20.1
14	17.4	17.9	18.4	18.8	19.2	19.7	20.1	20.5	20.8	21.2
16	18.6	19.0	19.5	19.9	20.3	20.8	21.2	21.5	21.9	22.3
18	19.7	20.1	20.6	21.0	21.4	21.8	22.2	22.6	23.0	23.3
20	20.8	21.2	21.7	22.1	22.5	22.9	23.3	23.7	24.0	24.4
22	21.8	22.3	22.7	23.1	23.5	23.9	24.3	24.7	25.0	25.4
24	22.9	23.3	23.8	24.2	24.6	25.0	25.3	25.7	26.0	26.4
26	23.9	24.4	24.8	25.2	25.6	26.0	26.3	26.7	27.0	27.3
28	25.0	25.4	25.8	26.2	26.6	26.9	27.3	27.6	28.0	28.3
30	26.0	26.4	26.8	27.2	27.5	27.9	28.2	28.6	28.9	29.2

8.0%

Years Constant Growth	2	4	6	8	10	12	14	16	18	20
				YEARS DIMINISHING GROWTH						
2	10.3	10.9	11.6	12.2	12.7	13.3	13.9	14.4	14.9	15.5
4	11.6	12.2	12.8	13.4	14.0	14.6	15.2	15.7	16.2	16.8
6	12.9	13.5	14.1	14.7	15.3	15.9	16.4	17.0	17.5	18.0
8	14.2	14.8	15.4	16.0	16.6	17.2	17.7	18.3	18.8	19.3
10	15.4	16.1	16.7	17.3	17.9	18.4	19.0	19.5	20.1	20.6
12	16.7	17.4	18.0	18.6	19.1	19.7	20.3	20.8	21.4	21.9
14	18.0	18.6	19.2	19.8	20.4	21.0	21.6	22.1	22.6	23.2
16	19.3	19.9	20.5	21.1	21.7	22.3	22.8	23.4	23.9	24.4
18	20.6	21.2	21.8	22.4	23.0	23.6	24.1	24.7	25.2	25.7
20	21.9	22.5	23.1	23.7	24.3	24.8	25.4	26.0	26.5	27.0
22	23.1	23.8	24.4	25.0	25.6	26.1	26.7	27.2	27.8	28.3
24	24.4	25.0	25.7	26.3	26.8	27.4	28.0	28.5	29.1	29.6
26	25.7	26.3	26.9	27.5	28.1	28.7	29.3	29.8	30.3	30.9
28	27.0	27.6	28.2	28.8	29.4	30.0	30.5	31.1	31.6	32.1
30	28.3	28.9	29.5	30.1	30.7	31.3	31.8	32.4	32.9	33.4

8% Table (Continued)
Projected Earnings Growth Rate

9.0%

Years Constant Growth	2	4	6	8	10	12	14	16	18	20
					Years Diminishing Growth					
2	10.5	11.2	12.0	12.7	13.4	14.0	14.7	15.4	16.0	16.7
4	12.3	13.0	13.7	14.4	15.1	15.8	16.5	17.2	17.9	18.5
6	14.0	14.8	15.5	16.2	16.9	17.7	18.4	19.0	19.7	20.4
8	15.8	16.6	17.3	18.1	18.8	19.5	20.2	20.9	21.6	22.3
10	17.6	18.4	19.2	19.9	20.7	21.4	22.1	22.8	23.6	24.2
12	19.5	20.3	21.1	21.8	22.6	23.3	24.1	24.8	25.5	26.2
14	21.4	22.2	23.0	23.8	24.5	25.3	26.1	26.8	27.5	28.2
16	23.3	24.1	24.9	25.7	26.5	27.3	28.1	28.8	29.6	30.3
18	25.3	26.1	26.9	27.8	28.6	29.3	30.1	30.9	31.7	32.4
20	27.3	28.1	29.0	29.8	30.6	31.4	32.2	33.0	33.8	34.5
22	29.3	30.2	31.0	31.9	32.7	33.5	34.3	35.1	35.9	36.7
24	31.4	32.3	33.1	34.0	34.9	35.7	36.5	37.3	38.1	38.9
26	33.5	34.4	35.3	36.2	37.0	37.9	38.7	39.6	40.4	41.2
28	35.7	36.6	37.5	38.4	39.3	40.1	41.0	41.8	42.7	43.5
30	37.9	38.8	39.7	40.6	41.5	42.4	43.3	44.1	45.0	45.8

10.0%

Years Constant Growth	2	4	6	8	10	12	14	16	18	20
					Years Diminishing Growth					
2	10.7	11.6	12.4	13.2	14.0	14.8	15.6	16.4	17.2	18.0
4	12.7	13.6	14.4	15.3	16.1	16.9	17.8	18.6	19.4	20.2
6	14.7	15.6	16.5	17.4	18.3	19.1	20.0	20.8	21.7	22.5
8	16.9	17.8	18.7	19.6	20.5	21.4	22.3	23.2	24.1	25.0
10	19.1	20.0	21.0	21.9	22.8	23.8	24.7	25.6	26.5	27.5
12	21.3	22.3	23.3	24.3	25.3	26.2	27.2	28.1	29.1	30.1
14	23.7	24.7	25.8	26.8	27.8	28.8	29.8	30.8	31.8	32.7
16	26.2	27.2	28.3	29.3	30.4	31.4	32.5	33.5	34.5	35.5
18	28.7	29.8	30.9	32.0	33.1	34.2	35.2	36.3	37.4	38.4
20	31.4	32.5	33.6	34.8	35.9	37.0	38.1	39.2	40.3	41.4
22	34.1	35.3	36.5	37.6	38.8	40.0	41.1	42.3	43.4	44.6
24	36.9	38.2	39.4	40.6	41.8	43.0	44.2	45.4	46.6	47.8
26	39.9	41.2	42.4	43.7	45.0	46.2	47.4	48.7	49.9	51.1
28	42.9	44.3	45.6	46.9	48.2	49.5	50.8	52.1	53.3	54.6
30	46.1	47.5	48.9	50.2	51.6	52.9	54.2	55.6	56.9	58.2

11.0%

Years Constant Growth	2	4	6	8	10	12	14	16	18	20
					Years Diminishing Growth					
2	10.9	11.9	12.8	13.7	14.7	15.6	16.6	17.5	18.4	19.4
4	13.2	14.2	15.1	16.1	17.1	18.1	19.1	20.1	21.1	22.1
6	15.5	16.6	17.6	18.6	19.7	20.7	21.8	22.8	23.9	25.0
8	18.0	19.1	20.2	21.3	22.4	23.5	24.6	25.7	26.8	28.0
10	20.6	21.8	22.9	24.1	25.3	26.4	27.6	28.8	30.0	31.1
12	23.4	24.6	25.8	27.1	28.3	29.5	30.8	32.0	33.3	34.5
14	26.3	27.6	28.9	30.2	31.5	32.8	34.1	35.4	36.7	38.1
16	29.4	30.8	32.1	33.5	34.9	36.2	37.6	39.0	40.4	41.8
18	32.7	34.1	35.5	37.0	38.4	39.9	41.3	42.8	44.3	45.8
20	36.1	37.6	39.1	40.7	42.2	43.7	45.3	46.8	48.4	49.9
22	39.7	41.3	43.0	44.6	46.2	47.8	49.4	51.1	52.7	54.4
24	43.6	45.3	47.0	48.7	50.4	52.1	53.8	55.6	57.3	59.0
26	47.6	49.4	51.2	53.0	54.8	56.6	58.5	60.3	62.1	64.0
28	51.9	53.8	55.7	57.6	59.5	61.4	63.4	65.3	67.2	69.2
30	56.5	58.5	60.5	62.5	64.5	66.5	68.5	70.6	72.6	74.7

12.0%

Years Constant Growth	2	4	6	8	10	12	14	16	18	20
					Years Diminishing Growth					
2	11.2	12.2	13.2	14.3	15.4	16.5	17.6	18.7	19.8	20.9
4	13.7	14.8	15.9	17.0	18.2	19.4	20.5	21.7	22.9	24.2
6	16.3	17.5	18.7	20.0	21.2	22.5	23.7	25.0	26.3	27.6
8	19.2	20.5	21.8	23.1	24.4	25.8	27.2	28.5	30.0	31.4
10	22.3	23.7	25.1	26.5	27.9	29.4	30.9	32.3	33.9	35.4
12	25.6	27.1	28.6	30.1	31.7	33.2	34.8	36.4	38.1	39.7
14	29.2	30.8	32.4	34.1	35.7	37.4	39.1	40.8	42.6	44.3
16	33.0	34.8	36.5	38.3	40.1	41.9	43.7	45.6	47.4	49.3
18	37.2	39.0	40.9	42.8	44.7	46.7	48.6	50.6	52.7	54.7
20	41.6	43.6	45.6	47.7	49.8	51.8	54.0	56.1	58.3	60.5
22	46.4	48.5	50.7	52.9	55.1	57.4	59.7	62.0	64.3	66.7
24	51.6	53.9	56.2	58.6	61.0	63.4	65.8	68.3	70.8	73.4
26	57.1	59.6	62.1	64.6	67.2	69.8	72.4	75.1	77.8	80.5
28	63.1	65.7	68.4	71.2	73.9	76.7	79.5	82.4	85.3	88.3
30	69.5	72.3	75.2	78.2	81.1	84.1	87.2	90.3	93.4	96.6

8% Table (Continued)
Projected Earnings Growth Rate

13.0%

Years Constant Growth	2	4	6	8	10	12	14	16	18	20
2	11.4	12.5	13.7	14.9	16.1	17.4	18.6	19.9	21.3	22.6
4	14.1	15.4	16.7	18.0	19.3	20.7	22.1	23.5	25.0	26.5
6	17.2	18.5	19.9	21.4	22.8	24.3	25.9	27.4	29.0	30.7
8	20.5	22.0	23.5	25.1	26.7	28.3	30.0	31.7	33.5	35.2
10	24.1	25.8	27.4	29.2	30.9	32.7	34.5	36.4	38.3	40.3
12	28.1	29.9	31.7	33.6	35.5	37.5	39.5	41.5	43.6	45.8
14	32.4	34.4	36.4	38.5	40.6	42.7	44.9	47.2	49.4	51.8
16	37.2	39.3	41.6	43.8	46.1	48.5	50.9	53.3	55.8	58.4
18	42.4	44.8	47.2	49.6	52.2	54.7	57.4	60.0	62.8	65.6
20	48.1	50.7	53.3	56.0	58.8	61.6	64.5	67.4	70.4	73.5
22	54.3	57.2	60.1	63.0	66.0	69.1	72.3	75.5	78.8	82.1
24	61.2	64.3	67.4	70.7	74.0	77.4	80.8	84.3	87.9	91.6
26	68.6	72.0	75.5	79.1	82.7	86.4	90.1	94.0	97.9	102.0
28	76.8	80.6	84.4	88.2	92.2	96.2	100.4	104.6	108.9	113.3
30	85.8	89.9	94.0	98.3	102.6	107.0	111.6	116.2	120.9	125.7

14.0%

Years Constant Growth	2	4	6	8	10	12	14	16	18	20
2	11.6	12.9	14.2	15.5	16.9	18.3	19.8	21.3	22.9	24.5
4	14.7	16.1	17.5	19.0	20.5	22.1	23.8	25.5	27.2	29.0
6	18.1	19.6	21.2	22.9	24.6	26.4	28.2	30.1	32.0	34.0
8	21.8	23.6	25.4	27.2	29.2	31.1	33.2	35.3	37.4	39.6
10	26.1	28.0	30.0	32.1	34.2	36.4	38.7	41.0	43.4	45.9
12	30.8	32.9	35.2	37.5	39.9	42.3	44.8	47.4	50.1	52.8
14	36.0	38.4	40.9	43.5	46.1	48.9	51.7	54.6	57.5	60.6
16	41.8	44.5	47.3	50.2	53.1	56.2	59.3	65.5	65.8	69.3
18	48.4	51.4	54.4	57.6	60.9	64.3	67.8	71.4	75.1	78.9
20	55.6	58.9	62.4	65.9	69.6	73.4	77.3	81.3	85.4	89.6
22	63.7	67.4	71.2	75.2	79.3	83.5	87.8	92.3	96.9	101.6
24	72.7	76.8	81.1	85.5	90.1	94.7	99.6	104.5	109.6	114.9
26	82.7	87.3	92.1	97.0	102.1	107.3	112.7	118.2	123.9	129.8
28	93.9	99.0	104.3	109.8	115.5	121.3	127.2	133.4	139.8	146.3
30	106.3	112.1	118.0	124.1	130.4	136.8	143.5	150.4	157.5	164.7

15.0%

Years Constant Growth	2	4	6	8	10	12	14	16	18	20
2	11.8	13.2	14.7	16.1	17.7	19.3	21.0	22.7	24.6	26.4
4	15.2	16.7	18.4	20.1	21.8	23.7	25.6	27.6	29.6	31.8
6	19.0	20.8	22.6	24.5	26.5	28.6	30.8	33.0	35.3	37.8
8	23.3	25.3	27.4	29.6	31.9	34.2	36.7	39.2	41.8	44.6
10	28.2	30.5	32.8	35.3	37.9	40.6	43.3	46.2	49.2	52.3
12	33.7	36.3	39.0	41.8	44.7	47.8	50.9	54.2	57.6	61.1
14	40.0	42.9	46.0	49.2	52.5	55.9	59.5	63.2	67.1	71.1
16	47.1	50.5	53.9	57.5	61.3	65.2	69.2	73.4	77.8	82.3
18	55.2	59.0	62.9	67.0	71.2	75.7	80.3	85.0	90.0	95.1
20	64.3	68.6	73.1	77.7	82.6	87.6	92.8	98.2	103.8	109.6
22	74.7	79.6	84.7	89.9	95.4	101.0	106.9	113.1	119.4	126.1
24	86.5	92.0	97.8	103.7	109.9	116.3	123.0	130.0	137.2	144.7
26	99.8	106.1	112.6	119.3	126.4	133.7	141.3	149.1	157.3	165.8
28	115.0	122.1	129.4	137.1	145.1	153.3	161.9	170.9	180.2	189.8
30	132.1	140.2	148.5	157.2	166.3	175.6	185.4	195.5	206.0	217.0

16.0%

Years Constant Growth	2	4	6	8	10	12	14	16	18	20
2	12.0	13.6	15.1	16.8	18.6	20.4	22.3	24.3	26.4	28.6
4	15.7	17.5	19.3	21.2	23.2	25.3	27.5	29.8	32.3	34.8
6	19.9	22.0	24.1	26.3	28.6	31.0	33.6	36.2	39.0	42.0
8	24.8	27.1	29.6	32.1	34.8	37.6	40.5	43.6	46.9	50.2
10	30.4	33.1	35.9	38.9	42.0	45.2	48.6	52.1	55.9	59.8
12	36.9	40.0	43.3	46.7	50.2	54.0	57.9	62.0	66.3	70.8
14	44.4	48.0	51.7	55.6	59.8	64.1	68.6	73.3	78.3	83.4
16	53.1	57.2	61.5	66.0	70.7	75.7	80.9	86.4	92.1	98.1
18	63.0	67.8	72.7	78.0	83.4	89.2	95.2	101.5	108.1	115.0
20	74.5	80.0	85.7	91.8	98.1	104.7	111.6	118.9	126.5	134.4
22	87.8	94.1	100.7	107.7	114.9	122.6	130.6	138.9	147.7	156.9
24	103.1	110.4	118.0	126.0	134.4	143.2	152.4	162.1	172.2	182.8
26	120.7	129.2	138.0	147.2	156.9	167.0	177.7	188.8	200.5	212.7
28	141.1	150.8	161.0	171.6	182.8	194.5	206.8	219.6	233.1	247.2
30	164.6	175.8	187.5	199.8	212.7	226.2	240.4	255.2	270.7	287.0

8% Table (Continued)

Projected Earnings Growth Rate

17.0%

Years Diminishing Growth

Years Constant Growth	2	4	6	8	10	12	14	16	18	20
2	12.3	13.9	15.7	17.5	19.4	21.5	23.7	26.0	28.4	31.0
4	16.3	18.2	20.2	22.4	24.7	27.1	29.6	32.3	35.2	38.2
6	20.9	23.2	25.6	28.1	30.8	33.6	36.6	39.8	43.1	46.7
8	26.4	29.1	31.9	34.9	38.0	41.3	44.9	48.6	52.5	56.6
10	32.9	36.0	39.3	42.8	46.5	50.4	54.5	58.9	63.5	68.3
12	40.5	44.1	48.0	52.1	56.4	61.0	65.8	70.9	76.3	82.0
14	49.3	53.6	58.2	63.0	68.1	73.4	79.1	85.1	91.4	98.1
16	59.8	64.8	70.1	75.8	81.7	88.0	94.7	101.7	109.2	117.0
18	72.0	77.9	84.2	90.8	97.8	105.2	113.0	121.3	130.0	139.2
20	86.4	93.3	100.7	108.4	116.6	125.3	134.5	144.2	154.4	165.2
22	103.2	111.4	120.1	129.1	138.7	148.9	159.7	171.1	183.1	195.8
24	123.0	132.6	142.7	153.4	164.7	176.6	189.3	202.6	216.7	231.6
26	146.2	157.4	169.3	181.9	195.1	209.2	224.0	239.7	256.2	273.7
28	173.5	186.6	200.6	215.3	230.9	247.3	264.7	283.1	302.6	323.1
30	205.4	220.9	237.2	254.5	272.8	292.1	312.6	334.1	357.0	381.0

18.0%

Years Diminishing Growth

Years Constant Growth	2	4	6	8	10	12	14	16	18	20
2	12.5	14.3	16.2	18.2	20.4	22.7	25.1	27.7	30.5	33.5
4	16.8	19.0	21.2	23.6	26.2	29.0	31.9	35.0	38.4	41.9
6	22.0	24.5	27.2	30.1	33.2	36.5	40.0	43.7	47.7	51.9
8	28.2	31.2	34.4	37.9	41.5	45.5	49.6	54.1	58.8	63.9
10	35.5	39.1	43.0	47.1	51.5	56.2	61.2	66.5	72.1	78.2
12	44.3	48.6	53.2	58.1	63.4	69.0	74.9	81.3	88.0	95.2
14	54.8	60.0	65.5	71.3	77.6	84.2	91.3	98.9	107.0	115.6
16	67.3	73.5	80.0	87.0	94.5	102.5	110.9	120.0	129.6	139.9
18	82.3	89.6	97.5	105.8	114.7	124.2	134.3	145.1	156.6	168.9
20	100.1	108.9	118.3	128.2	138.9	150.2	162.3	175.2	188.9	203.5
22	121.4	131.9	143.1	155.0	167.7	181.2	195.6	211.0	227.4	244.8
24	146.9	159.4	172.7	186.9	202.1	218.2	235.4	253.8	273.3	294.2
26	177.2	192.2	208.1	225.0	243.1	262.4	283.0	304.9	328.2	353.1
28	213.5	231.3	250.3	270.5	292.1	315.1	339.7	365.8	393.7	423.4
30	256.8	278.0	300.7	324.8	350.6	378.1	407.4	438.6	471.9	507.3

19.0%

Years Diminishing Growth

Years Constant Growth	2	4	6	8	10	12	14	16	18	20
2	12.7	14.7	16.7	19.0	21.3	23.9	26.7	29.7	32.8	36.3
4	17.4	19.8	22.3	25.0	27.9	31.0	34.3	38.0	41.8	46.0
6	23.1	25.9	29.0	32.3	35.8	39.6	43.6	48.0	52.7	57.8
8	30.0	33.4	37.1	41.1	45.4	50.0	54.9	60.3	66.0	72.1
10	38.4	42.5	47.0	51.9	57.1	62.7	68.7	75.1	82.1	89.5
12	48.5	53.6	59.1	64.9	71.2	78.0	85.3	93.1	101.6	110.6
14	60.9	67.0	73.7	80.8	88.4	96.7	105.5	115.0	125.3	136.2
16	75.9	83.3	91.4	100.0	109.3	119.3	130.1	141.6	154.0	167.4
18	94.1	103.1	112.9	123.4	134.7	146.8	159.9	173.9	189.0	205.1
20	116.1	127.2	139.0	151.7	165.4	180.2	196.0	213.1	231.4	251.0
22	143.0	156.3	170.7	186.2	202.8	220.7	240.0	260.6	282.8	306.7
24	175.5	191.8	209.2	228.0	248.2	269.9	293.3	318.4	345.4	374.3
26	215.0	234.8	255.9	278.7	303.3	329.7	358.0	388.5	421.2	456.4
28	263.0	287.0	312.7	340.4	370.2	402.2	436.6	473.6	513.4	556.1
30	321.3	350.3	381.6	415.2	451.3	490.2	532.0	577.0	625.2	677.0

20.0%

Years Diminishing Growth

Years Constant Growth	2	4	6	8	10	12	14	16	18	20
2	13.0	15.0	17.3	19.7	22.4	25.2	28.3	31.7	35.3	39.3
4	18.0	20.6	23.3	26.3	29.6	33.1	37.0	41.1	45.6	50.5
6	24.2	27.4	30.8	34.5	38.6	42.9	47.6	52.8	58.3	64.3
8	31.9	35.8	40.0	44.6	49.6	55.0	60.8	67.2	74.0	81.4
10	41.4	46.2	51.4	57.1	63.2	69.9	77.1	84.9	93.4	102.5
12	53.1	59.1	65.5	72.5	80.1	88.3	97.2	106.8	117.3	128.6
14	67.6	74.9	82.9	91.5	100.8	111.0	122.0	133.9	146.8	160.8
16	85.5	94.5	104.3	115.0	126.5	139.0	152.6	167.3	183.2	200.5
18	107.5	118.7	130.8	143.9	158.2	173.6	190.4	208.5	228.2	249.5
20	134.7	148.5	163.5	179.7	197.3	216.3	237.0	259.5	283.7	310.0
22	168.3	185.4	203.8	223.8	245.5	269.1	294.6	322.3	352.3	384.8
24	209.8	230.8	253.6	278.3	305.1	334.2	365.7	399.9	436.9	477.0
26	261.0	287.0	315.1	345.6	378.7	414.6	453.5	495.7	541.4	590.9
28	324.3	356.3	391.0	428.7	469.5	513.9	561.9	614.0	670.4	731.5
30	402.3	441.9	484.7	531.2	581.7	636.4	695.7	760.0	829.7	905.1

Investment Values of Normal Earnings of $1 at 9% Return

Projected Earnings Growth Rate

1.0%

Years Constant Growth	2	4	6	8	10	12	14	16	18	20
2	7.9	8.0	8.0	8.1	8.1	8.2	8.2	8.2	8.3	8.3
4	8.1	8.1	8.2	8.2	8.2	8.3	8.3	8.3	8.4	8.4
6	8.2	8.2	8.3	8.3	8.3	8.4	8.4	8.4	8.4	8.5
8	8.3	8.3	8.4	8.4	8.4	8.4	8.5	8.5	8.5	8.5
10	8.4	8.4	8.4	8.5	8.5	8.5	8.5	8.6	8.6	8.6
12	8.4	8.5	8.5	8.5	8.6	8.6	8.6	8.6	8.6	8.6
14	8.5	8.5	8.6	8.6	8.6	8.6	8.7	8.7	8.7	8.7
16	8.6	8.6	8.6	8.7	8.7	8.7	8.7	8.7	8.7	8.7
18	8.6	8.6	8.7	8.7	8.7	8.7	8.7	8.7	8.7	8.7
20	8.7	8.7	8.7	8.7	8.7	8.7	8.8	8.8	8.8	8.8
22	8.7	8.7	8.7	8.7	8.8	8.8	8.8	8.8	8.8	8.8
24	8.7	8.7	8.8	8.8	8.8	8.8	8.8	8.8	8.8	8.8
26	8.7	8.7	8.8	8.8	8.8	8.8	8.8	8.8	8.8	8.8
28	8.8	8.8	8.8	8.8	8.8	8.8	8.8	8.8	8.8	8.8
30	8.8	8.8	8.8	8.8	8.8	8.8	8.8	8.8	8.8	8.8

2.0%

Years Constant Growth	2	4	6	8	10	12	14	16	18	20
2	8.1	8.2	8.3	8.4	8.5	8.6	8.7	8.7	8.8	8.9
4	8.4	8.5	8.6	8.7	8.7	8.8	8.9	8.9	9.0	9.0
6	8.6	8.7	8.8	8.9	8.9	9.0	9.1	9.1	9.2	9.2
8	8.8	8.9	9.0	9.1	9.1	9.2	9.2	9.3	9.3	9.3
10	9.0	9.1	9.2	9.2	9.3	9.3	9.4	9.4	9.4	9.5
12	9.2	9.2	9.3	9.4	9.4	9.4	9.5	9.5	9.5	9.6
14	9.3	9.4	9.4	9.5	9.5	9.5	9.6	9.6	9.6	9.6
16	9.5	9.5	9.5	9.6	9.6	9.6	9.7	9.7	9.7	9.7
18	9.6	9.6	9.6	9.7	9.7	9.7	9.8	9.8	9.8	9.8
20	9.6	9.7	9.7	9.8	9.8	9.8	9.8	9.8	9.9	9.9
22	9.7	9.7	9.8	9.8	9.9	9.9	9.9	9.9	9.9	9.9
24	9.8	9.8	9.9	9.9	9.9	9.9	9.9	10.0	10.0	10.0
26	9.9	9.9	9.9	9.9	9.9	10.0	10.0	10.0	10.0	10.0
28	9.9	9.9	10.0	10.0	10.1	10.0	10.0	10.1	10.1	10.1
30	10.0	10.0	10.0	10.0	10.1	10.1	10.1	10.1	10.1	10.1

3.0%

Years Constant Growth	2	4	6	8	10	12	14	16	18	20
2	8.3	8.5	8.6	8.8	8.9	9.0	9.2	9.3	9.4	9.5
4	8.7	8.9	9.0	9.1	9.3	9.4	9.5	9.6	9.7	9.8
6	9.1	9.2	9.4	9.5	9.6	9.7	9.8	9.9	10.0	10.0
8	9.4	9.6	9.7	9.8	9.9	10.0	10.1	10.1	10.2	10.3
10	9.7	9.8	9.9	10.0	10.1	10.2	10.3	10.4	10.4	10.5
12	10.0	10.1	10.2	10.3	10.4	10.4	10.5	10.6	10.6	10.7
14	10.2	10.3	10.4	10.5	10.6	10.6	10.7	10.7	10.8	10.8
16	10.5	10.5	10.6	10.7	10.7	10.8	10.9	10.9	11.0	11.0
18	10.7	10.7	10.8	10.9	10.9	11.0	11.0	11.1	11.1	11.1
20	10.8	10.9	10.9	11.0	11.1	11.1	11.1	11.2	11.2	11.3
22	11.0	11.0	11.1	11.1	11.2	11.3	11.3	11.4	11.3	11.4
24	11.1	11.2	11.2	11.3	11.3	11.3	11.4	11.4	11.4	11.5
26	11.2	11.3	11.3	11.4	11.4	11.4	11.5	11.5	11.5	11.5
28	11.4	11.4	11.4	11.5	11.5	11.5	11.6	11.6	11.6	11.6
30	11.4	11.5	11.5	11.6	11.6	11.6	11.6	11.7	11.7	11.7

4.0%

Years Constant Growth	2	4	6	8	10	12	14	16	18	20
2	8.4	8.7	8.9	9.1	9.3	9.5	9.7	9.8	10.0	10.1
4	9.0	9.3	9.5	9.6	9.8	10.0	10.2	10.3	10.4	10.6
6	9.6	9.8	10.0	10.1	10.3	10.4	10.6	10.7	10.8	11.0
8	10.0	10.2	10.4	10.6	10.7	10.8	11.0	11.1	11.2	11.3
10	10.5	10.7	10.8	11.0	11.1	11.2	11.3	11.4	11.5	11.6
12	10.9	11.0	11.2	11.3	11.4	11.6	11.7	11.8	11.9	11.9
14	11.3	11.4	11.5	11.6	11.8	11.9	12.0	12.1	12.1	12.2
16	11.6	11.7	11.8	11.9	12.0	12.1	12.2	12.3	12.4	12.5
18	11.9	12.0	12.1	12.2	12.3	12.4	12.5	12.6	12.6	12.7
20	12.2	12.3	12.4	12.5	12.5	12.6	12.7	12.8	12.8	12.9
22	12.4	12.5	12.6	12.7	12.8	12.8	12.9	13.0	13.0	13.1
24	12.7	12.7	12.8	12.9	13.0	13.0	13.1	13.1	13.2	13.3
26	12.9	12.9	13.0	13.1	13.1	13.2	13.3	13.3	13.4	13.4
28	13.1	13.1	13.2	13.3	13.3	13.4	13.4	13.5	13.5	13.5
30	13.2	13.3	13.4	13.4	13.5	13.5	13.6	13.6	13.6	13.7

9% Table (Continued)
Projected Earnings Growth Rate

5.0%

Years Constant Growth	2	4	6	8	10	12	14	16	18	20
2	8.6	8.9	9.2	9.5	9.8	10.0	10.2	10.4	10.6	10.8
4	9.4	9.7	9.9	10.2	10.4	10.7	10.9	11.1	11.3	11.4
6	10.1	10.3	10.6	10.8	11.0	11.3	11.5	11.6	11.8	12.0
8	10.7	11.0	11.2	11.4	11.8	11.8	12.0	12.2	12.3	12.5
10	11.3	11.5	11.8	12.0	12.2	12.3	12.5	12.7	12.8	13.0
12	11.9	12.1	12.3	12.5	12.7	12.8	13.0	13.1	13.2	13.4
14	12.4	12.6	12.8	13.0	13.1	13.3	13.4	13.6	13.7	13.8
16	12.9	13.1	13.2	13.4	13.5	13.7	13.8	14.0	14.1	14.2
18	13.3	13.5	13.7	13.8	13.9	14.1	14.2	14.3	14.4	14.5
20	13.7	13.9	14.0	14.2	14.3	14.4	14.6	14.7	14.8	14.9
22	14.1	14.3	14.4	14.5	14.7	14.8	14.9	15.0	15.1	15.2
24	14.5	14.6	14.7	14.9	15.0	15.1	15.2	15.3	15.4	15.4
26	14.8	14.9	15.0	15.2	15.3	15.4	15.5	15.5	15.6	15.7
28	15.1	15.2	15.3	15.4	15.5	15.6	15.7	15.8	15.9	16.0
30	15.4	15.5	15.6	15.7	15.8	15.9	16.0	16.0	16.1	16.2

6.0%

Years Constant Growth	2	4	6	8	10	12	14	16	18	20
2	8.8	9.2	9.5	9.9	10.2	10.5	10.8	11.1	11.4	11.6
4	9.7	10.1	10.4	10.8	11.1	11.4	11.6	11.9	12.1	12.4
6	10.6	10.9	11.3	11.6	11.9	12.1	12.4	12.7	12.9	13.1
8	11.4	11.7	12.1	12.3	12.6	12.9	13.1	13.4	13.6	13.8
10	12.2	12.5	12.8	13.1	13.3	13.6	13.8	14.1	14.3	14.5
12	12.9	13.2	13.5	13.8	14.0	14.3	14.5	14.7	14.9	15.1
14	13.7	13.9	14.2	14.4	14.7	14.9	15.1	15.3	15.5	15.7
16	14.3	14.6	14.8	15.1	15.3	15.5	15.7	15.9	16.1	16.2
18	14.9	15.2	15.4	15.6	15.9	16.0	16.2	16.4	16.6	16.8
20	15.5	15.8	16.0	16.2	16.4	16.6	16.8	16.9	17.1	17.2
22	16.1	16.3	16.5	16.7	16.9	17.1	17.3	17.4	17.6	17.7
24	16.6	16.8	17.0	17.2	17.4	17.6	17.7	17.9	18.0	18.2
26	17.1	17.3	17.5	17.7	17.9	18.0	18.2	18.3	18.4	18.6
28	17.6	17.8	18.0	18.1	18.3	18.4	18.6	18.7	18.8	19.0
30	18.1	18.2	18.4	18.6	18.7	18.8	19.0	19.1	19.2	19.3

7.0%

Years Constant Growth	2	4	6	8	10	12	14	16	18	20
2	9.0	9.4	9.9	10.3	10.7	11.1	11.4	11.8	12.1	12.5
4	10.1	10.5	10.9	11.3	11.7	12.1	12.5	12.8	13.1	13.4
6	11.1	11.6	12.0	12.4	12.7	13.1	13.4	13.8	14.1	14.4
8	12.2	12.6	13.0	13.4	13.7	14.1	14.4	14.7	15.0	15.3
10	13.2	13.6	13.9	14.3	14.7	15.0	15.3	15.6	15.9	16.2
12	14.1	14.5	14.9	15.2	15.6	15.9	16.2	16.5	16.8	17.0
14	15.1	15.4	15.8	16.1	16.4	16.7	17.0	17.3	17.6	17.9
16	15.9	16.3	16.6	17.0	17.3	17.6	17.9	18.1	18.4	18.6
18	16.8	17.1	17.5	17.8	18.1	18.4	18.6	18.9	19.2	19.4
20	17.6	18.0	18.3	18.6	18.9	19.1	19.4	19.7	19.9	20.1
22	18.4	18.7	19.0	19.3	19.6	19.9	20.1	20.4	20.6	20.8
24	19.2	19.5	19.8	20.1	20.3	20.6	20.8	21.1	21.3	21.5
26	19.9	20.2	20.5	20.8	21.0	21.3	21.5	21.7	22.0	22.2
28	20.6	20.9	21.2	21.5	21.7	21.9	22.2	22.4	22.6	22.8
30	21.3	21.6	21.9	22.1	22.4	22.6	22.8	23.0	23.2	23.4

8.0%

Years Constant Growth	2	4	6	8	10	12	14	16	18	20
2	9.1	9.7	10.2	10.7	11.2	11.7	12.1	12.5	13.0	13.4
4	10.4	11.0	11.5	12.0	12.4	12.9	13.4	13.8	14.2	14.6
6	11.7	12.2	12.7	13.2	13.7	14.1	14.6	15.0	15.4	15.8
8	13.0	13.5	14.0	14.5	14.9	15.4	15.8	16.2	16.6	17.0
10	14.2	14.7	15.2	15.7	16.1	16.5	17.0	17.4	17.8	18.1
12	15.4	15.9	16.4	16.8	17.3	17.7	18.1	18.5	18.9	19.3
14	16.6	17.1	17.6	18.0	18.4	18.9	19.3	19.7	20.0	20.4
16	17.8	18.3	18.7	19.2	19.6	20.0	20.4	20.8	21.1	21.5
18	18.9	19.4	19.8	20.3	20.7	21.1	21.5	21.9	22.2	22.6
20	20.1	20.5	21.0	21.4	21.8	22.2	22.6	22.9	23.3	23.6
22	21.2	21.6	22.0	22.5	22.9	23.2	23.6	24.0	24.3	24.7
24	22.2	22.7	23.1	23.5	23.9	24.3	24.7	25.0	25.4	25.7
26	23.3	23.7	24.1	24.6	24.9	25.3	25.7	26.0	26.4	26.7
28	24.4	24.8	25.2	25.6	26.0	26.3	26.7	27.0	27.4	27.7
30	25.4	25.8	26.2	26.6	27.0	27.3	27.7	28.0	28.3	28.6

9% Table (Continued)
Projected Earnings Growth Rate

9.0%

Years Constant Growth	2	4	6	8	10	12	14	16	18	20
2	9.3	9.9	10.5	11.1	11.7	12.3	12.8	13.3	13.9	14.4
4	10.6	11.2	11.8	12.4	13.0	13.5	14.1	14.6	15.1	15.6
6	11.9	12.5	13.1	13.7	14.2	14.8	15.3	15.9	16.4	16.9
8	13.1	13.7	14.3	14.9	15.5	16.1	16.6	17.1	17.7	18.2
10	14.4	15.0	15.6	16.2	16.8	17.3	17.9	18.4	18.9	19.4
12	15.7	16.3	16.9	17.5	18.0	18.6	19.1	18.9	20.2	20.7
14	16.9	17.5	18.1	18.7	19.3	19.9	20.4	20.9	21.5	22.0
16	18.2	18.8	19.4	20.0	20.6	21.1	21.7	22.2	22.7	23.2
18	19.5	20.1	20.7	21.3	21.8	22.4	22.9	23.5	24.0	24.5
20	20.7	21.3	22.0	22.5	23.1	23.7	24.2	24.7	25.3	25.8
22	22.0	22.6	23.2	23.8	24.4	24.9	25.5	26.0	26.5	27.0
24	23.3	23.9	24.5	25.1	25.6	26.2	26.7	27.3	27.8	28.3
26	24.5	25.1	25.8	26.3	26.9	27.5	28.0	28.5	29.1	29.6
28	25.8	26.4	27.0	27.6	28.2	28.7	29.3	29.8	30.3	30.8
30	27.1	27.7	28.3	28.9	29.4	30.0	30.5	31.1	31.6	32.1

10.0%

Years Constant Growth	2	4	6	8	10	12	14	16	18	20
2	9.5	10.2	10.9	11.6	12.3	12.9	13.6	14.2	14.8	15.4
4	11.2	11.9	12.6	13.3	14.0	14.7	15.3	16.0	16.6	17.3
6	13.0	13.7	14.4	15.1	15.8	16.5	17.2	17.8	18.5	19.1
8	14.8	15.5	16.2	16.9	17.7	18.3	19.0	19.7	20.4	21.0
10	16.6	17.3	18.1	18.8	19.5	20.2	20.9	21.6	22.3	22.9
12	18.4	19.2	19.9	20.7	21.4	22.1	22.8	23.5	24.2	24.9
14	20.3	21.1	21.9	22.6	23.4	24.1	24.8	25.5	26.2	26.9
16	22.2	23.0	23.8	24.6	25.3	26.1	26.8	27.5	28.2	28.9
18	24.2	25.0	25.8	26.6	27.3	28.1	28.8	29.6	30.3	31.0
20	26.1	27.0	27.8	28.6	29.4	30.2	30.9	31.7	32.4	33.1
22	28.2	29.0	29.8	30.7	31.5	32.3	33.0	33.8	34.5	35.3
24	30.2	31.1	31.9	32.8	33.6	34.4	35.2	36.0	36.7	37.5
26	32.3	33.2	34.1	34.9	35.7	36.6	37.4	38.2	38.9	39.7
28	34.5	35.4	36.2	37.1	37.9	38.8	39.6	40.4	41.2	42.0
30	36.6	37.6	38.4	39.3	40.2	41.0	41.9	42.7	43.5	44.3

11.0%

Years Constant Growth	2	4	6	8	10	12	14	16	18	20
2	9.7	10.5	11.3	12.1	12.8	13.6	14.4	15.1	15.9	16.6
4	11.6	12.5	13.3	14.1	14.9	15.7	16.5	17.2	18.0	18.8
6	13.6	14.5	15.3	16.2	17.0	17.8	18.6	19.5	20.3	21.1
8	15.7	16.6	17.5	18.4	19.2	20.1	20.9	21.8	22.6	23.4
10	17.9	18.8	19.7	20.6	21.5	22.4	23.3	24.1	25.0	25.9
12	20.1	21.1	22.0	23.0	23.9	24.8	25.7	26.6	27.5	28.4
14	22.4	23.4	24.4	25.4	26.3	27.3	28.2	29.2	30.1	31.0
16	24.9	25.9	26.9	27.9	28.9	29.9	30.9	31.8	32.8	33.8
18	27.4	28.4	29.5	30.5	31.5	32.6	33.6	34.6	35.6	36.6
20	29.9	31.0	32.1	33.2	34.3	35.4	36.4	37.5	38.5	39.5
22	32.6	33.8	34.9	36.0	37.1	38.2	39.3	40.4	41.5	42.6
24	35.4	36.6	37.8	38.9	40.1	41.2	42.4	43.5	44.6	45.7
26	38.3	39.5	40.8	42.0	43.2	44.3	45.5	46.7	47.8	49.0
28	41.3	42.6	43.8	45.1	46.3	47.6	48.8	50.0	51.2	52.4
30	44.4	45.7	47.0	48.3	49.6	50.9	52.2	53.4	54.7	55.9

12.0%

Years Constant Growth	2	4	6	8	10	12	14	16	18	20
2	9.9	10.8	11.7	12.5	13.4	14.3	15.2	16.1	17.0	17.9
4	12.0	13.0	13.9	14.9	15.8	16.7	17.7	18.6	19.5	20.5
6	14.3	15.3	16.3	17.3	18.3	19.3	20.3	21.3	22.2	23.2
8	16.7	17.8	18.8	19.9	20.9	22.0	23.0	24.1	25.1	26.2
10	19.3	20.4	21.5	22.6	23.7	24.8	25.9	27.0	28.1	29.2
12	22.0	23.2	24.3	25.5	26.6	27.8	29.0	30.1	31.3	32.5
14	24.8	26.1	27.3	28.5	29.7	31.0	32.2	33.4	34.7	35.9
16	27.8	29.1	30.4	31.7	33.0	34.3	35.6	36.9	38.2	39.5
18	31.0	32.4	33.7	35.1	36.5	37.8	39.2	40.6	42.0	43.3
20	34.4	35.8	37.2	38.7	40.1	41.6	43.0	44.5	45.9	47.4
22	37.9	39.4	40.9	42.5	44.0	45.5	47.0	48.6	50.1	51.6
24	41.6	43.2	44.8	46.4	48.1	49.7	51.3	52.9	54.5	56.1
26	45.6	47.3	49.0	50.7	52.4	54.1	55.8	57.5	59.2	60.9
28	49.7	51.5	53.3	55.1	56.9	58.7	60.5	62.3	64.1	65.9
30	54.1	56.0	57.9	59.8	61.7	63.6	65.5	67.4	69.3	71.2

9% Table (Continued)

Projected Earnings Growth Rate

13.0%

Years Constant Growth	2	4	6	8	10	12	14	16	18	20
2	10.1	11.1	12.0	13.0	14.0	15.1	16.1	17.1	18.2	19.2
4	12.5	13.5	14.6	15.7	16.8	17.8	19.0	20.1	21.2	22.4
6	15.1	16.2	17.3	18.5	19.7	20.8	22.0	23.2	24.4	25.7
8	17.8	19.1	20.3	21.5	22.8	24.0	25.3	26.6	27.9	29.2
10	20.8	22.1	23.5	24.8	26.1	27.5	28.9	30.3	31.7	33.1
12	24.0	25.5	26.9	28.3	29.8	31.2	32.7	34.2	35.7	37.2
14	27.5	29.0	30.5	32.1	33.6	35.2	36.8	38.4	40.0	41.6
16	31.2	32.8	34.5	36.1	37.8	39.5	41.2	42.9	44.6	46.4
18	35.2	36.9	38.7	40.5	42.3	44.1	45.9	47.8	49.6	51.5
20	39.5	41.4	43.3	45.2	47.1	49.0	51.0	53.0	55.0	57.0
22	44.1	46.1	48.1	50.2	52.3	54.4	56.5	58.6	60.8	63.0
24	49.0	51.2	53.4	55.6	57.8	60.1	62.4	64.7	67.0	69.3
26	54.4	56.7	59.0	61.4	63.8	66.2	68.7	71.1	73.6	76.1
28	60.1	62.6	65.1	67.7	70.2	72.8	75.5	78.1	80.8	83.5
30	66.2	68.9	71.6	74.4	77.1	79.9	82.8	85.6	88.5	91.4

14.0%

Years Constant Growth	2	4	6	8	10	12	14	16	18	20
2	10.3	11.3	12.4	13.6	14.7	15.9	17.0	18.3	19.5	20.7
4	12.9	14.1	15.3	16.5	17.8	19.1	20.3	21.7	23.0	24.4
6	15.8	17.1	18.4	19.8	21.1	22.5	23.9	25.4	26.9	28.4
8	19.0	20.4	21.9	23.3	24.8	26.3	27.9	29.5	31.1	32.7
10	22.5	24.0	25.6	27.2	28.8	30.5	32.2	33.9	35.7	37.5
12	26.3	28.0	29.7	31.5	33.3	35.1	36.9	38.8	40.7	42.7
14	30.5	32.3	34.2	36.1	38.1	40.1	42.1	44.1	46.3	48.4
16	35.0	37.0	39.1	41.2	43.3	45.5	47.7	50.0	52.3	54.6
18	40.0	42.2	44.5	46.8	49.1	51.5	53.9	56.4	58.9	61.5
20	45.4	47.9	50.3	52.8	55.4	58.0	60.7	63.4	66.1	68.9
22	51.4	54.0	56.7	59.5	62.3	65.1	68.0	71.0	74.0	77.1
24	57.9	60.8	63.8	66.8	69.8	73.0	76.1	79.4	82.7	86.0
26	65.0	68.2	71.4	74.7	78.1	81.5	85.0	88.5	92.1	95.8
28	72.8	76.3	79.8	83.4	87.1	90.8	94.6	98.5	102.4	106.5
30	81.4	85.2	89.0	93.0	97.0	101.1	105.2	109.4	113.8	118.1

15.0%

Years Constant Growth	2	4	6	8	10	12	14	16	18	20
2	10.5	11.6	12.9	14.1	15.4	16.7	18.1	19.5	20.9	22.4
4	13.4	14.7	16.0	17.4	18.9	20.3	21.8	23.4	25.0	26.6
6	16.6	18.1	19.6	21.1	22.7	24.4	26.1	27.8	29.5	31.4
8	20.2	21.9	23.6	25.3	27.0	28.9	30.7	32.7	34.6	36.6
10	24.3	26.1	28.0	29.9	31.8	33.9	35.9	38.1	40.3	42.5
12	28.7	30.8	32.9	35.0	37.2	39.4	41.8	44.1	46.6	49.1
14	33.7	36.0	38.3	40.7	43.1	45.6	48.2	50.9	53.6	56.4
16	39.3	41.8	44.4	47.0	49.7	52.5	55.4	58.3	61.4	64.5
18	45.5	48.3	51.1	54.1	57.1	60.2	63.4	66.7	70.1	73.5
20	52.3	55.5	58.7	61.9	65.3	68.8	72.3	76.0	79.7	83.6
22	60.0	63.5	67.0	70.7	74.4	78.3	82.2	86.3	90.5	94.8
24	68.5	72.4	76.3	80.4	84.6	88.9	93.3	97.8	102.4	107.2
26	78.0	82.3	86.7	91.2	95.9	100.7	105.6	110.6	115.8	121.1
28	88.6	93.4	98.3	103.3	108.5	113.8	119.2	124.8	130.6	136.5
30	100.3	105.7	111.1	116.7	122.5	128.4	134.5	140.7	147.1	153.7

16.0%

Years Constant Growth	2	4	6	8	10	12	14	16	18	20
2	10.6	11.9	13.3	14.7	16.1	17.6	19.1	20.7	22.4	24.1
4	13.8	15.3	16.8	18.4	20.0	21.7	23.5	25.3	27.1	29.1
6	17.5	19.1	20.8	22.6	24.5	26.4	28.3	30.4	32.5	34.7
8	21.5	23.4	25.4	27.4	29.5	31.6	33.9	36.2	38.6	41.1
10	26.2	28.3	30.5	32.8	35.2	37.6	40.2	42.8	45.5	48.3
12	31.4	33.8	36.3	38.9	41.6	44.4	47.3	50.2	53.3	56.5
14	37.4	40.1	42.9	45.9	48.9	52.0	55.3	58.7	62.2	65.8
16	44.1	47.2	50.4	53.7	57.2	60.7	64.4	68.2	72.2	76.3
18	51.7	55.2	58.9	62.6	66.5	70.5	74.7	79.0	83.5	88.2
20	60.4	64.3	68.4	72.7	77.1	81.7	86.4	91.3	96.4	101.6
22	70.2	74.6	79.3	84.1	89.1	94.3	99.6	105.2	110.9	116.9
24	81.2	86.3	91.6	97.0	102.7	108.6	114.6	120.9	127.4	134.2
26	93.8	99.5	105.5	111.7	118.1	124.7	131.6	138.7	146.1	153.7
28	108.0	114.5	121.3	128.3	135.5	143.0	150.8	158.9	167.2	175.9
30	124.1	131.5	139.1	147.1	155.3	163.8	172.6	181.7	191.2	201.0

9% Table (Continued)

Projected Earnings Growth Rate

17.0%

Years Constant Growth	2	4	6	8	10	12	14	16	18	20
2	10.8	12.3	13.7	15.3	16.9	18.5	20.3	22.1	24.0	26.0
4	14.3	15.9	17.6	19.4	21.2	23.2	25.2	27.3	29.5	31.8
6	18.3	20.2	22.1	24.2	26.3	28.5	30.8	33.3	35.8	38.5
8	22.9	25.1	27.3	29.7	32.1	34.7	37.4	40.2	43.1	46.1
10	28.2	30.7	33.3	36.0	38.8	41.8	44.9	48.1	51.5	55.0
12	34.4	37.2	40.2	43.3	46.6	50.0	53.5	57.2	61.1	65.2
14	41.4	44.7	48.1	51.7	55.5	59.4	63.5	67.8	72.2	76.9
16	49.5	53.3	57.3	61.4	65.7	70.3	75.0	79.9	85.0	90.4
18	58.9	63.3	67.8	72.6	77.6	82.8	88.2	93.9	99.8	106.0
20	69.7	74.7	80.0	85.5	91.2	97.2	103.5	110.0	116.8	124.0
22	82.1	87.9	94.0	100.1	106.9	113.8	121.0	128.6	136.4	144.6
24	96.4	103.1	110.1	117.4	125.0	132.9	141.3	149.9	159.0	168.5
26	112.9	120.6	128.7	137.1	145.8	155.0	164.6	174.6	185.0	195.9
28	131.9	140.8	150.1	159.7	169.8	180.4	191.4	203.0	215.0	227.6
30	153.8	164.1	174.7	185.9	197.5	209.7	222.4	235.7	249.5	264.0

18.0%

Years Constant Growth	2	4	6	8	10	12	14	16	18	20
2	11.0	12.6	14.2	15.9	17.6	19.5	21.5	23.6	25.8	28.1
4	14.8	16.6	18.5	20.5	22.5	24.7	27.1	29.5	32.1	34.8
6	19.2	21.3	23.5	25.8	28.3	30.9	33.6	36.4	39.5	42.6
8	24.4	26.8	29.4	32.2	35.0	38.0	41.2	44.6	48.1	51.8
10	30.5	33.3	36.4	39.5	42.9	46.4	50.2	54.1	58.2	62.6
12	37.6	40.9	44.5	48.2	52.2	56.3	60.7	65.3	70.1	75.2
14	45.9	49.8	54.0	58.4	63.0	67.8	73.0	78.4	84.0	90.0
16	55.7	60.3	65.1	70.3	75.7	81.4	87.4	93.7	100.4	107.4
18	67.1	72.5	78.2	84.2	90.6	97.2	104.3	111.7	119.5	127.7
20	80.5	86.8	93.5	100.6	108.0	115.8	124.1	132.8	141.9	151.5
22	96.2	103.6	111.5	119.7	128.4	137.6	147.3	157.5	168.2	179.5
24	114.6	123.3	132.5	142.2	152.4	163.2	174.5	186.4	199.0	212.2
26	136.2	146.4	157.2	168.5	180.5	193.1	206.3	220.3	235.0	250.5
28	161.5	173.4	186.1	199.4	213.4	228.1	243.7	260.1	277.3	295.5
30	191.1	205.1	219.9	235.5	251.9	269.2	287.5	306.7	326.9	348.2

19.0%

Years Constant Growth	2	4	6	8	10	12	14	16	18	20
2	11.2	12.9	14.6	16.5	18.5	20.6	22.8	25.1	27.7	30.3
4	15.3	17.3	19.4	21.6	23.9	26.4	29.1	31.9	34.9	38.1
6	20.2	22.5	25.0	27.6	30.4	33.4	36.6	39.9	43.5	47.3
8	26.0	28.7	31.7	34.8	38.2	41.7	45.5	49.5	53.7	58.3
10	32.8	36.2	39.7	43.4	47.4	51.6	56.1	60.9	66.0	71.3
12	41.1	45.0	49.2	53.7	58.4	63.5	68.8	74.5	80.5	86.9
14	50.9	55.6	60.6	65.9	71.5	77.6	83.9	90.7	97.9	105.5
16	62.5	68.1	74.1	80.5	87.2	94.3	102.0	110.0	118.6	127.7
18	76.4	83.1	90.2	97.8	105.8	114.4	123.4	133.1	143.3	154.1
20	93.0	101.0	109.5	118.5	128.1	138.2	149.0	160.5	172.7	185.6
22	112.8	122.3	132.4	143.1	154.5	166.7	179.5	193.2	207.7	223.2
24	136.3	147.7	159.7	172.5	186.1	200.6	215.9	232.2	249.5	267.9
26	164.3	177.9	192.3	207.5	223.7	241.0	259.3	278.7	299.3	321.2
28	197.9	214.0	231.1	249.3	268.6	289.1	310.9	334.1	358.7	384.8
30	237.8	257.0	277.4	299.0	322.0	346.5	372.5	400.1	429.4	460.5

20.0%

Years Constant Growth	2	4	6	8	10	12	14	16	18	20
2	11.5	13.2	15.1	17.1	19.3	21.7	24.2	26.8	29.7	32.8
4	15.8	18.0	20.3	22.7	25.4	28.2	31.2	34.5	37.9	41.7
6	21.2	23.8	26.5	29.5	32.7	36.1	39.8	43.7	47.9	52.5
8	27.6	30.7	34.1	37.7	41.6	45.8	50.2	55.0	60.1	65.5
10	35.4	39.2	43.3	47.7	52.4	57.4	62.8	68.6	74.8	81.4
12	44.9	49.5	54.5	59.8	65.5	71.6	78.1	85.1	92.6	100.6
14	56.4	62.0	68.0	74.4	81.3	88.7	96.6	105.1	114.2	123.9
16	70.3	77.1	84.3	92.1	100.5	109.5	119.1	129.3	140.3	152.1
18	87.1	95.4	104.2	113.6	123.8	134.6	146.3	158.7	172.1	186.3
20	107.6	117.5	128.2	139.7	152.0	165.1	179.2	194.3	210.5	227.8
22	132.3	144.4	157.4	171.3	186.1	202.1	219.2	237.5	257.1	278.0
24	162.3	177.0	192.7	209.5	227.6	246.9	267.6	289.8	313.5	339.0
26	198.7	216.5	235.5	255.9	277.8	301.2	326.3	353.2	382.0	412.8
28	242.8	264.3	287.4	312.1	338.6	367.0	397.5	430.1	464.9	502.3
30	296.2	322.3	350.3	380.3	412.4	446.8	483.7	523.2	565.5	610.7

30
RECENT STUDIES OF P/E RATIOS*
Nicholas Molodovsky, C.F.A.

In the July–August 1960 issue of the *Financial Analysts Journal*, S. Francis Nicholson, who was then vice president of the Provident National Bank in Philadelphia from which he retired some two years ago, published a study which made a deep impression on financial analysts. It is included in the list of Recommended Readings of the 1967 Study Guide for Examination II of the Institute of Chartered Financial Analysts and reprinted, as Article 33, in the book of C.F.A. Readings in Financial Analysis.

The Nicholson study opens with the following three paragraphs:

WITHIN THREE TO TEN YEARS, will the better price performance be in common stocks, with the current price earnings multiples of over 25 times, or in those under 12 times?

Answers to this question as posed to sophisticated Financial Analysts and business men, in the past year, have been nearly ten-to-one in favor of the high multiples. It is assumed they are bought for growth, and the low multiples only for income.

The results of certain studies, covering data for past years, would indicate a contrary conclusion; i.e., that on the average the purchase of stocks with low price-earnings multiples will result in greater appreciation in addition to the higher income provided.

Mr. Nicholson's article contains two statistical explorations. They reach identical conclusions.

Nicholson's Study #2 is limited to a sample consisting of only 29 stocks, all belonging to the chemical industry. Moreover, out of these 29 stocks, 7 were not available for all of the 18 years of the period used. In their own right, industry studies are of great interest. However, Nicholson attempts to prove an investment principle of overall significance, and, for this purpose, the sample is too small. A mitigating circumstance may be mentioned. In Mr. Nicholson's demonstration, Study #2 plays only a supporting role. The cast of leading statistical characters appears in Study #1. We shall accordingly concentrate our critical attention on that study.

Study #1 is based on a sample of 100 predominantly industrial issues of trust investment quality. It covers the time span 1939–1959, divided into 11 subperiods. The 100 stocks are arranged into five groups in the

---

* Reprinted by permission of the *Financial Analysts Journal* (May–June 1967).

ascending order of their respective P/E ratios at the beginning of each subperiod and show the price appreciation in each subperiod according to P/E ratio groups. The 20 lowest multiple stocks had larger price gains than the 20 highest multiple stocks in all 11 subperiods. Accordingly, Nicholson draws the conclusion that investors should do substantially better by buying low P/E ratio stocks. Our reservations will be noted later in this article.

In a paper, published in *The Commercial & Financial Chronicle* of September 16, 1965, in which he reviewed a number of statistical methods for selecting undervalued stocks, Professor Paul H. Cootner of M.I.T. referred to the Nicholson study. He pointed out that Mr. Nicholson wrote it in 1960. All his 100 stocks were high grade; they had been selected from the vantage point of that year. His selections might have been quite different if they had been made at the beginning of the entire period, i.e., in 1939. Many of such stocks would possibly no longer have been in Nicholson's 1960 sample by losing, in the meantime, their high investment rating, and thus dropping out. Dr. Cootner thought that if there is a fallacy in Mr. Nicholson's results, it is likely to arise from the use of hindsight in determining what is a high-grade stock.

Professor Cootner's concern does not imply that the validity of the experiment is dependent on a high investment rating of a sample's component stocks. His fear that the results might be biased—and even biased quite substantially—was undoubtedly aroused by the possibility that large losses could have been conceivably suffered by stocks which might have descended to a low grade status. Many of such possible losses could have occurred in the highest P/E group, which, by its very nature, is the most vulnerable.

One of the observations made by Nicholson in connection with his Study #1 reads as follows:

If an investor bought the 20 lowest multiples in 1939, changed in 1944 to the 20 lowest in that year, and again in 1949, and 1954, his investment would have appreciated in 1959 to 14.7 times his original investment. Similar procedure with the 20 highest multiples in these years would have brought the value to 4.5 times the original investment. (These figures are, of course, not adjusted for broker commissions and taxes.)

We ignore, as Nicholson does, the caveat placed by him in parentheses. Yet the splendor of the magnificent cumulative profits achieved by purchasing the lowest multiple stocks and consistently periodically reinvesting the effectively (or hypothetically) realized proceeds of a terminal year into stocks whose multiples had at that time become the lowest, was, to say the least, impressive. The results exceeded better than 3:1 an analogous procedure applied to stocks with the highest multiples. In the terminal year of each subperiod, the proceeds realized from the previous purchase of stocks with the highest multiples were reinvested into an equal number of stocks whose P/E ratios still were, or had become, the highest at that time.

Other Tests of P/E Ratios as Investment Guides

The distinguished investment banking firm, Drexel & Co. of Philadelphia, which recently became, through merger, Drexel Harriman Ripley Incorporated, applied the price-earnings ratio criterion to the highest and lowest multiple stocks within the DJIA 30-stock sample. The stocks were held for one year, the starting and the target date being June 30 of each year. To make the experiments more conclusive, two sets of computations were made, based respectively on the actually reported earnings of the preceding year and the estimated earnings of the year still in progress. These studies show that the lower multiple groups consistently outperform the higher multiple groups—especially the highest—by a wide margin.

The work done by Drexel & Co., using the 30 DJIA stocks, was described in an article by James D. McWilliams to which we shall again refer in this study:

> Another significant study was done by Drexel & Co. in the winter and spring months of 1963. (The first study mentioned by McWilliams is that done by Nicholson—*Ed. note*). They divided the Dow–Jones Industrial Average stocks into three categories on an annual basis: The lowest, middle, and highest P-E ratio stocks. The results were described in their publication *Monthly Review*. Again, as in the Nicholson study, the lowest price-earnings ratio stocks outperformed the middle and higher P-E ratio stocks. The Drexel study showed that $10,000 invested in June, 1936, and annually reinvested in the 10 highest P-E ratio stocks found in the Dow–Jones Industrial Average each year, would have grown to $25,347 by June, 1962. Had the investor invested in the stocks that were classified as middle price-earnings ratio stocks, the original $10,000 would have grown to $43,672 over the same period. Finally, had our hypothetical investor put his $10,000 into the 10 lowest price-earnings ratio stocks each year from 1936 through June of 1962, his fund would have grown to $66,866.

Drexel Harriman Ripley investigations of the relative action of the lowest and highest P/E ratio stocks have continued, from time to time, over the last several years. The recent studies are more sophisticated than the earlier. All calculations are made by an electronic computer.

The September 20, 1966 issue of *The Commercial & Financial Chronicle* contains a paper by Paul F. Miller, Jr., C.F.A., and Ernest R. Widman, respectively, Senior Vice President (now President), and Economist of Drexel Harriman Ripley Incorporated. The article is entitled "Price Performance Outlook for High & Low P/E Stocks."

The co-authors describe a study which they did recently. They took data from 1948 through 1964 for industrial companies in the COMPUSTAT tapes with annual sales exceeding $150 million, grouping the stocks with similar P/E ratios into five classes. The selection was confined to companies with fiscal years ending between September 30 and January 31. Companies showing no earnings or registering deficits were excluded.

The number of such companies increased from 110 in 1948 to 334 in 1964.

P/E ratios were computed using year-end prices and fiscal year earnings. Then an average price performance was derived for each P/E quintile. Price performances were compared for all one-year, three-year, and five-year segments within the 1948–1964 period. To quote the authors, "the low price-earnings group has consistently outperformed the high price-earnings group. In fact, there is a distinct tendency for the groups to fall in a pattern of inverse rank correlation with the height of the P/E ratio."

To make sure that the better performance of the low P/E group is not caused by a few stocks making unusually wide gains offsetting the possibly poor performance of the rest of the group, the authors examined the statistical distribution of stock price performance in the lowest and highest P/E quintiles. They found that the distributions of both quintiles were almost identical.

There was a statistical difference between the early and the later Drexel studies. The early investigations of the investment results of the 30 DJIA stocks were conducted on a cumulative periodic basis determined by the differential P/E approach. However, the major portion of the work using the 30 DJIA stocks was a straight measurement of price changes over specified time periods. This latter method was also used in subsequent studies dealing with broader stock samples.

None of these studies were open to the question of a possible hindsight bias which Dr. Cootner raised in commenting on Mr. Nicholson's paper. The 30 DJIA stocks are blue chips with an established history. The 334 stocks, used by Drexel Harriman Ripley in their study's terminal year of 1964, probably did not all deserve the highest investment rating. All were, nevertheless, undoubtedly quality stocks. Only stocks of companies with a large dollar volume of sales were admitted into the sample, while all companies showing deficits, or even a lack of earnings, were denied representation.

Supporting Evidence

Additional evidence supports the Nicholson–Drexel conclusions. It may be found in the work done by James D. McWilliams, Investment Officer in the Trust Department in charge of computer approaches to common stock analysis and portfolio selections for the Continental Illinois National Bank and Trust Company of Chicago. In an article which appeared in the May–June 1966, issue of the *Financial Analysts Journal*, Mr. McWilliams evaluates the usefulness of the P/E ratio as an analytical tool. He uses COMPUSTAT tapes from which he extracts a sample of 390 industrial stocks. The study covers the period from 1953 through 1964. It reveals a better investment performance of a portfolio composed of low P/E ratio stocks as contrasted to a portfolio made up of high P/E ratio stocks.

The McWilliams investigation employs many statistical techniques and constraints. In constructing his sample, McWilliams admitted into its universe only those listed industrial stocks which had a complete 12-year history of April 30th prices and had calendar fiscal years. Unlisted stocks were not admitted. The P/E ratios were calculated by dividing April 30th prices by per share earnings for the fiscal year ending the preceding December 31. The data were classified into P/E deciles, and mean returns as well as standard deviations about the means were computed. The study was done on an IBM 7010 machine using the Fortran language.

Ten thousand dollars were hypothetically invested, as of April 30, 1952, into each P/E decile, and continually reinvested on an annual basis. In this respect, Mr. McWilliams apparently followed Mr. Nicholson's method of periodic cumulative reinvestment, reclassifying stocks each year in accordance with the then prevailing P/E criterion.

It was found that the $10,000 originally invested in the highest P/E ratio decile stocks would have grown to $45,329 by April 30, 1964. The same $10,000 originally invested in the lowest P/E ratio decile stocks, and continually reinvested on an annual basis, would have grown to $103,960 during the same period.

In no case was any adjustment made for commissions that would have been incurred in actually implementing these original investment and annual reinvestment techniques. Had commissions been allowed for, adds McWilliams, the results would have been substantially poorer in all of the P/E deciles.

Growth Expectations

It is, of course, clear that when investors are willing to pay more for one dollar of current earnings of some stocks, as contrasted with other stocks, they expect to derive investment benefits from this premium. The most common expectation is that of faster relative growth of future earnings. This expectation may be reinforced by another: The assumption that the more rapid earnings growth could also prove to be more stable around the basic trend.

John E. Hammel and Daniel A. Hodes submitted this double expectation to an empirical verification in "Factors Influencing P/E Multiples," which was published in the January–February 1967 issue of the *Financial Analysts Journal*. Their findings were based on a comprehensive statistical study which used correlation-regression techniques and computer processing to analyze the financial data of over 400 major companies. The analysis related selected measures of growth and variability in earnings per share to the P/E multiples of the companies studied. This double analysis of the authors shows that variability in past earnings is a fairly important factor in the influence it has on the P/E multiple and that expected growth in earnings influences the multiple strongly.

It stands to reason that prices of stocks with characteristically high earnings multipliers are more fragile. Only confidence that earnings growth will be sustained at high compounding rates for an extended period can keep them aloft. When investors lose faith that a high flying stock will continue to make money at a rapidly growing rate, the same thing happens as when an aircraft loses speed: It starts falling.

The stock of a company enjoying a rapid earnings growth is bound to suffer more from unrealized growth expectations. As long as the expectation is fulfilled, it strengthens the anticipation of a continued favorable trend. This widens the differential spread of the earnings capitalizer of this stock compared to capitalizers of stocks whose profits are growing slower. But when confidence begins to wane, the rate of decline of a stock's price will bear a relation to its anticipated rate of earnings growth.

Since, by definition, the gap between current price and current earnings widens when the P/E ratio rises, a group consisting of the highest P/E ratio stocks will obviously contain within itself a larger proportion of coming disappointments of investment hopes than groups with lower P/E ratios. The comparison of the relative action of high and low P/E groups will be distorted when stocks included in all the groups are of good quality and when equities showing even temporary deficits are excluded. This tends to strengthen the performance of the lowest P/E group by eliminating from it stocks with flat or negative earnings trends which may often account for the very existence of a low multiple. The wider the groups of constituent stocks, the greater should then be the probabilistic incidence of relative price fragility and firmness of the high and low P/E groups.

Needless to say, not all stocks will perform alike. In the high P/E group the hope of rapid future earnings growth may be vindicated or even exceeded. Similarly, the more modest expectations of rising earnings, which are characteristic of the low multiple samples, may reveal some pleasant surprises. The reverse may also occur in either group. It seems unlikely that, in any case, the average group performance will be greatly affected. Under conditions of stock selection stipulated by the studies described above, there is good reason to expect that the group of the highest P/E ratio stocks will number the greatest proportion of price casualties. And the probabilities will gain time to work themselves out when the period of the experiment is extended. Empirical verification is welcome, but simple reasoning is pointing to its likely outcome. The reasoning is strengthened when it is applied to the cumulative periodic reinvestment process.

Structure of P/E Ratios

There are 10 possible combinations in the respective changes of prices and earnings that can bring about a rise or a decline of a P/E ratio. Three combinations can cause it to remain unchanged.

A P/E ratio will rise under five sets of conditions:

1. When both prices and earnings are rising, but prices are rising relatively more than earnings.

2. When prices are rising, but earnings remain stationary.
3. When prices are rising, but earnings are declining.
4. When prices remain stationary, but earnings are declining.
5. When both prices and earnings are declining, but prices are declining relatively less than earnings.

A P/E ratio will decline under five sets of conditions also. These will be symmetrically inverse to the above classification.

A little probing will show the three possible combinations under which there would be no change in the direction of the ratio.

When an original amount is invested into a group of stocks characterized by the highest P/E ratios and periodically cumulatively reinvested—be it at annual, three-year, or five-year intervals—into those stocks whose P/E ratios have, in the meantime, become the highest, what result will be achieved? Such a high P/E ratio group is becoming increasingly vulnerable to a price setback after each successive reinvestment. Each time, stocks eliminated from the group are replaced by others whose prices have outdistanced earnings even more than in the case of all, or some, of the stocks that were contained in the original sample, which was already from the outset selected because its P/E ratios were the highest. Cumulatively, earnings fall further and further behind prices thereby compounding the exposure to any loss of confidence in the mounting demands which are made by this procedure on earnings growth rates. The group is also rendered systematically weaker in the defense it can offer to any random market shock because its earnings base is evermore shrinking in size in relation to price.

On the opposite side of the spectrum, the group with the lowest P/E ratios is growing in strength all the time. The earnings base of the lowest P/E ratio group is being enlarged at the time of each successive reinvestment. Those equities, which will fall by the wayside at the time of each periodic revision of the composition of the lowest P/E group, will be replaced by others whose earnings have demonstrated stronger action than their respective prices. In this group relative weakness is consistently eliminated in favor of strength, while in the highest P/E group strength invariably yields to weakness. Once again, individual exceptions will occur in all the groups classified by their respective P/E ratios. They are unlikely to alter the average group effect.

This process, if cumulatively repeated when the sequence of each group's portfolio redistribution comes round to its next terminal point, contains its own forecast of investment results. They cannot fail to be confirmed by the use of an electronic machine.

Investment Strategy

Nobody can deny that the most profitable investment results will be secured by paying the lowest possible multiple for earnings which will grow in the future at a rapid rate. A successful investment strategy can be developed by purchasing low multiple stocks—which means paying less for each dollar of their respective per share earnings—and selling them when their multiples reach heights which, in the judgment of the investor, exceed acceptable risks of further holding. Such a policy, however, must be quite flexible at both ends of its operation.

When the original investment is made, it may be desirable to set some limit on the P/E ratio at the time of the acquisition. It should not be applied, however, in an iron clad manner. It should be extended to a higher multiple if the earnings trend of a particular stock warrants such a decision.

Investment criterion constraints should be provided with respect to earnings. Only those stocks should be included among the candidates for purchase which have demonstrated a consistently high and enduring earnings growth rate for several years and which offer, in addition, persuasive evidence that growth is unlikely to fall off in the reasonably visible future.

In such a strategy, there should be no time limitations for the period of holding. If an upper P/E limit is set as a selling signal it must remain flexible. It can only serve as a target for re-examination. No fixed rule can supersede constant surveillance and analysis. If the rule is applied mechanically, the portfolio will never contain any holdings of AVP, GLW, LIT, IBM, PRD, or XRX.

We find no kind words to say about the application of investment policy based on P/E ratios for periods shorter than one year. A tabulation in the November 1966 issue of *The Cleveland Trust Company Business Bulletin* has shown that low P/E multiples were no protection during the decline of stock prices in 1966. Since the turn in the stock market came early in October, the November 1966 issue of *The Bulletin* encompasses the entire bear market. *The Bulletin's* tabulation is limited to the 30 DJIA stocks. But as they represent the market's core, they offer an important illustration. The Cleveland study shows that from their 1965 highs to their 1966 lows, the tendency has been for stocks with low P/E ratios to fall the furthest. They exhibited a tendency to decline more in price than the stocks with higher P/E ratios. *The Bulletin* remarks that this experience was contrary to the record of most years. Few years, however, witnessed declines as drastic as the break which overtook the market in 1966. If the low P/E ratios offered no protection when it was most needed, the rule can hardly be confirmed by this exception.

To be fair, we should recognize that many stocks in the DJIA are sensitive to cyclical influences. Still, in dealing with ratios of current prices to current earnings, we must remember that we are in the presence of a complex measurement. Any analyst who uses current P/E ratios must have a clear insight into their structure and meaning.

CURRENT P/E RATIO AS INVESTMENT CRITERION

It is completely futile, and even quite misleading, to conduct elaborate studies of the action of P/E ratios, as is smetimes done, without relating them to a comparative analysis of the movements of stock prices and earnings. The latter are independent economic variables. P/E ratios have no existence of their own. As their name implies, they are nothing but quotients reflecting any of the 13 possible different combinations of the numerator and the denominator.

Attempts are made to average P/E ratios; or to construct intriguing, but irrelevant, patterns of their bull and bear swings. None of these things can be done without making sure that prices and earnings are in significantly related phases. Otherwise, we shall be playing meaningless arithmetic games instead of engaging in effective investment research.

To illustrate, we shall plagiarize slightly ourselves. ("For the Record," *Financial Analysts Journal*, May–June 1964). We shall do so by using the case of the 1957 bear market in stock prices and their bull market of 1958.

From its July high to its October low, the DJIA lost, in 1957, 100 points. Soon thereafter, it not only retraced the entire decline, but established, by an impressive margin, new and then unprecedented highs. The progress of this new bull market was looked upon with much distrust. Fear gripped many investors' minds. Stock prices seemed to have lost all contact with any reasonable measure of value. The P/E ratios were high and kept rising, while earnings went from bad to worse.

Not only individual investors but commentators and investment advisory organizations reacted in much the same way to rising stock prices. To place them within a framework of reference, let us remind ourselves that, in terms of the DJIA, the bull market took off, in October 1957 from a low of 416.15 and proceeded to a high of 688.21, which it reached in January 1960.

Throughout the winter of 1957–58 and the spring and summer of the latter year, bearish opinions reigned. As late as July 31, 1958, when the DJIA had advanced some 90 points from the 1957 low to the level of about 505, a famous service wrote:

> Some of the old line fundamentals about price-earnings ratios and other traditional measures of proper prices for the time being, at least, do not seem to be doing people much good.

In August, as the DJIA was reaching again towards its 1957 high, a financial writer of *The New York Times*, surveying the collapsing earnings reported for the first two quarters, commented that the securities markets are caught in one of the most confusing economic experiences of recent history. He even found it apropos to quote from Macbeth. "For the moment," he said, "the ticker tape is spinning out what seems to be best describable as 'a tale told by an idiot, full of sound and fury, signifying nothing.' . . . The babel of prices coming from the securities ticker is so incongruous that there is little of extravagance in the statement that today in Wall Street nobody seems to have any definite idea of what an investment grade common stock is really worth."

"Many Are Mystified by Continued Rise of Stock Prices" asserted a headline in mid-September 1958 in the financial pages of *The New York Herald Tribune*. The article was accompanied by photographs of customers in a brokerage office. The mood predominant among them was described by the caption "Market Baffles Tape Watchers."

Two days prior to this report, an editorial in *The Wall Street Journal*, entitled "Puzzle at Broad and Wall," stated that "if you look at the usual statistics—the relationship of earnings to stock prices, for example—the booming market makes little sense."

This statement notwithstanding, there was no mystery about the "strange" action of P/E ratios. Changes in P/E ratios may be the result of a time lag in the respective movements of stock prices and earnings. In 1958 prices were already rising while earnings were still declining. This confused many people who were anxiously watching the action of P/E ratios. Actually, P/E ratios were then only in part capitalization factors. They carried a substantial superstructure which was the arithmetical reflection of the numerator and denominator moving in opposite directions.

The price of a stock could make no sense and would be no more than a meaningless number if it did not represent an attempt to express the stock's value, i.e., its capital worth.

Capital is a store of wealth. Current earnings do not offer a broad-enough basis for erecting on it a capital structure. Capital is substantial. Its income-producing mass cannot be appraised or estimated from so slim an indication as the current earnings of a single year. And, to repeat, current P/E ratios may reflect in each case a different mix of prices and earnings.

Nevertheless, despite the fact that the ratios of stock prices to current earnings are, by their nature, quite unsuitable for such a role, in practice they are often treated as capitalizers. This attitude toward them has developed out of their ready handiness as financial yardsticks, even though these yardsticks are vacillating and uncertain in the extreme.

Much of the work being done in Wall Street measures up to high standards and is constantly improving. Some of the reports prepared by competent financial analysts, especially when they have a training in science and engineering, make impressive reading. Some firms have built their business and reputation on exhaustive studies which may take many months of research.

Yet business life moves fast and, to keep up with it, Wall Street often resorts to shortcuts. This applies particularly to quick daily financial "intercom." Just as the telegraphic language has to be succinct, a rapid-fire communication uses abbreviated financial concepts.

When individual ratios of prices to current earnings are computed for quick ready reference, they carry a limited meaning with respect to the outlook for future earnings. To acquire greater significance, they must be dissected with a surgeon's skill.

The first problem which the analyst faces in dealing with current earnings is to determine their relation to basic earning power. When a company's current earnings stand below its estimated normal earning power, the price-to-current-earnings ratio will rise to compensate for the deviation from the norm. When current earnings rise above the basic earning power, the ratio will fall.

This compensating mechanism produces another phenomenon: the counter movements of current earnings and P/E ratios. Their existence confirms the presence of a valuation process in the stock market. The principle of compensation and the rule of counter-movements were studied by us in great detail in *The Analysts Journal* of November 1953. The article was entitled "A Theory of Price-Earnings Ratios."

Increasingly, analysts avoid using price-to-current earnings ratios. Whatever label they may apply to it, they reason in terms of basic earning power. As an example, we quote a passage from an article, "The Stock Market—From One Viewpoint" by Waid R. Vanderpoel, Vice President of the First National Bank of Chicago. It appeared in the May 30, 1966 issue of the *Investment Dealer's Digest:*

> Does it follow that many groups are now attractive due to the combination of price decline and earnings rise? Before we meet this question head on, let us look at the price-earnings ratio relationship from another viewpoint. If we include 1966, earnings will have risen for five consecutive years. Yet a study of past results would indicate rather frequent variance. It is our contention that investors must take average earnings, or what we call 'trend line' earnings, into consideration. Dow–Jones Industrial Average earnings have advanced about 60 percent from the 1955/62 plateau. What is the relationship between current market levels and five-year average earnings? On this basis, stocks are still high—higher than in late 1961 from which level the Dow–Jones Average plunged more than 25 percent. Since late 1964, stocks have commanded a higher multiple of five-year avearge earnings than at any even reasonably prosperous time since 1929.

A more advanced concept of the P/E ratio was introduced into financial literature by W. Edward Bell, past President of The Security Analysts of San Francisco. In "The Price-Future Earnings Ratio," a paper published in *The Analysts Journal* of August 1958, Mr. Bell made a significant contribution by bringing into the conventional P/E ratio the dimension of time, which is an essential element of all investments. He looks at the ratio as the number of years of current earnings included in the current price. The concept of the price-future earnings ratio indicates the number of years of *future* earnings included in the market price, assuming a constant annual growth rate of earnings per share. This concept can be adapted to show the time span of future earnings increasing at different constant growth rates. Bell's article contains a table showing the corresponding P/E and price-future earnings ratios for various assumed constant annual earnings growth rates. Except for the absence of the rate of discount, Bell's concept comes close to that of present worth.

The current P/E ratio is too deeply imbedded in financial practice to allow the hope that its use may soon disappear. We should learn at least to understand more clearly its theoretical nature and its practical limitations. It would be still better if we could train ourselves to use capitalization *rates* instead of capitalization multipliers. They would tie in better with rates of discount and rates of return on common stocks which are the pillars of valuation and sound investment thinking. It is a remarkable fact that such famous treatises as "The Valuation of Property" by James C. Bonbright, who was professor of finance at Columbia University,[1] and "Financial Policy of Corporations" by Arthur Stone Dewing, who was Professor of Finance at Harvard University,[2] do not even mention the term "price-earnings ratio." Nor can the term be found in the respective Indexes of their two-volume works. Yet both these scholars devote considerable space in their books to discussions of the appraisal of common stocks.

In our opinion, the best solution to the problem of valuation of common stocks lies in methods which completely sidestep the use of P/E or E/P ratios. We must reconfirm once more our faith in a doctrine that is not of our creation, but which we have defended many times on the pages of this *Journal*. It is the thesis which holds that the value of a common stock is the present worth of its future stream of dividends. This method is completely free from any injection into the yardstick of price itself, which is the very thing investors seek to measure in their search for cheap stocks.[3]

Sometimes, the validity of this method is questioned by short-sighted critics who claim that it necessarily implies projections into an unreasonably distant future. They ignore the countervailing force of discount, which makes distant contributions to value quite negligible.

It is true that stock prices can stray from values for extended periods. Timing studies can be of assistance. In the present state of timing techniques, their margin of error is high. In the future, timing uncertainty can be reduced by the use of computers. Models will be developed for independent variables forecasting price movements towards the orbit of value, which measures the differential between a stock's price and its real present money worth.

Postword

We do not wish to leave the readers under the impression that the eminent professionals who engaged in recent studies of low and high P/E

---

[1] McGraw-Hill Book Company, Inc., New York, 1937.

[2] The Ronald Press Company, New York, 5th Ed., 1953.

[3] See, in particular, Nicholas Molodovsky, "Valuation of Common Stocks," *The Analysts Journal* (February 1959). This article was reprinted in Eugene M. Lerner's "Readings in Financial Analysis and Investment Management," Richard D. Irwin, Inc., 1963. Also: Nicholas Molodovsky, Catherine May, and Sherman Chottiner, "Common Stock Valuation: Principles, Tables, and Application," *Financial Analysts Journal* (March–April 1965).

ratios had relied blindly on the conclusions to which they led. In their investment practice these analysts also use other tools.

An unpublished study on P/E ratios dated March 26, 1963, which S. F. Nicholson distributed to his bank's clients and correspondents and which indirectly came to our attention, ends with a summary stating:

> The evidence is clear that the low price-earnings ratio stocks have shown much more appreciation than the other groups; that a larger proportion of the low ratio stocks have exceeded average results; and that a smaller proportion of the low ratio items had large losses or losses of any size. Likewise, the middle group has had better results than the high ratio group.

This summary is followed by a caveat:

> *Caution!*
> In observing the significance of data in this report as in previous price-earnings studies, attention is called to the need for analytical judgments on factors other than earnings ratios; and the preference for good earnings in relation to prices should not lead to using price-earnings ratios as an all-conclusive formula for sound investment.

In the course of a brief correspondence with Paul F. Miller, Jr. last August, Mr. Miller wrote to the author:

> Please don't misunderstand our emphasis on these studies. We have never claimed that selection by P/E ratios is a substitute for earnings growth in determining investment success. In fact, several studies which we have conducted prove conclusively that there is no substitute for earnings growth in successful investment selection. However, I am somewhat wary of earnings projections and even short-term earnings estimates. I think you will agree that even one-year estimates of earnings can be woefully inadequate and inaccurate. . . .
>
> You will notice in our more recent studies that we have shown that the market tends to be correct in appraising high price-earnings ratio and low price-earnings ratio stocks as groups, that is, the high P/E stocks do indeed tend to have better earnings growth over a period of time than do the low P/E stocks. Quantifying this very roughly, it appears that approximately 65 percent of the issues in the high P/E categories do turn out to have superior trends; likewise, 65 percent of the stocks in the low P/E categories tend to have drab or declining earnings trends. It is the balance of the 35 percent that makes the difference in the average price performances of the two groups. In the high P/E ratio group, 35 percent of the issues proved to be disappointments, and evidently record substantial losses. In the low P/E ratio group, 35 percent of the issues turned out to have very good earnings trends, and, of course, record substantial investment profits. Of the 65 percent of the issues in the high P/E group that turn out well from an earnings standpoint, profits are normally realized at an above-average rate; and in the 65 percent of the low P/E stocks that experienced drab or declining earnings, the market results are below average although not, as a rule, very heavily in the negative column.
>
> It is evidently the penalty concept as it applies to the high P/E stocks, and the reward concept applied to the low P/E stocks, both in those cases where surprises occur that causes the advantage on average to be in favor of the low P/E ratio issues.
>
> We have never said that the odds favor investment in any one low P/E

stock versus any one high P/E stock or even a select group of low P/E stocks versus high P/E stocks. All we have commented on is the action of relatively large groups of stocks in these P/E ratio categories. . . .

At the end of his article which we discussed in this paper, Mr. James D. McWilliams also limits the significance of his conclusions. Rearranging his samples into the best performing stocks, he finds that the very best performing common stocks can be found in any P/E ratio decile. He does not, however, obtain the same result by rearranging the stocks by the poorest performers. The latter predominate in the highest P/E decile. McWilliams remarks in this connection:

> Weaving the results of the extremely good and the extremely poor performers together in the analytical decision-making process, it appears that we can find good performers anywhere, but if you are looking at high P/E stocks, great care must be exercised to determine that the company is going to keep on growing. This is the area where it appears that the investor frequently bids multiples and prices up too sharply in relation to actual growth and the investor is subsequently disappointed.

We couldn't agree more.

In sum, the method used by S. Francis Nicholson, which consists in a periodic cumulative reinvestment into the highest and lowest P/E ratio stocks, when it is effected on a group basis, magnifies the overpricing and underpricing of the respective groups. Nicholson's method influenced, in this respect, some of his followers.

Even in those studies which had no recourse to the cumulative reinvestment method the results would have been more convincing if no limitations had been placed on the selection of stocks. All listed stocks should be included, as was done for a different purpose by James H. Lorie and Lawrence Fisher. Recent studies of P/E ratios merely confirmed empirically the rather obvious fact that, on the average, investors naturally profit more by paying less for one dollar of sound earnings.

Excellent values may be found among the highest P/E ratio stocks as well. The 50th issue of *"Vickers Favorite 50"* presents data, as of December 31, 1966, garnered from the common stock holdings of about 500 investment companies with combined assets of close to $50 billion. Ranked by dollar value, the two largest holdings of these funds were IBM and PRD. Among the 15 largest holdings, we also find EK, XRX, MMM, ITT, GEN and AVP. We leave it to our readers to figure the P/E ratios of these stocks based on either their reported 1966 earnings or the projected earnings of 1967.

'RECENT STUDIES OF P/E RATIOS'—A REPLY*

Paul F. Miller, Jr., C.F.A. and Thomas E. Beach

We appreciate the courtesy extended by Mr. Molodovsky in permitting us to comment on his article entitled *Recent Studies of P/E Ratios*. We certainly have no quarrel with his very fair summary of our methodology and conclusions. We would, however, like to reply to Mr. Molodovsky's apparent reservations about the low P/E concept and expand somewhat our position regarding the usefulness of the low price-earnings ratio approach in stock selection and portfolio management.

Mr. Molodovsky's only disagreement with the students of the low P/E approach stems, as we see it, from the use of the periodic cumulative reinvestment technique in some studies. He cites in his article the striking results which we and others achieved by utilizing this approach, and implies that its use is the essential reason that security analysts should not be overwhelmed by the attributes of the low P/E concept for stock selection.

In replying, our first comment would be that the majority of our efforts did not rely on the periodic cumulative reinvestment approach. As we understand it, Mr. Molodovsky's definition of periodic cumulative reinvestment is as follows: A sample list of stocks is arranged on the basis of P/Es and then divided into several groups. Equal amounts of money are invested in each stock in each group and the subsequent appreciation (or depreciation) of each group is measured for a given time period. At the completion of this period (usually one, three, or five years), the list is rearranged on the basis of the changed P/Es of the companies composing it. New P/E categories are formed so that the companies in the low P/E group, for examle, will not all be the same as under the original grouping. The proceeds of the initial appreciation (or depreciation) for each P/E group are then reinvested in the stocks now composing that group, and appreciation is again measured over a period of time. This process is

* Reprinted by permission of the *Financial Analysts Journal* (May–June 1967).

repeated periodically, with the proceeds of each P/E group being cumulatively reinvested. Finally, the results of investing a given sum in various P/E groups can be measured to determine which produces the greatest appreciation.

Mr. Molodovsky correctly implies that we did not make the mistake of following this cumulative reinvestment approach in the most comprehensive of our studies. He outlines our basic methodology and conclusions on page 402 of this book. It should be noted that our methodology involved no reinvestment procedure. We simply averaged the price changes of the stocks in each of our five P/E groups (quintiles). We measured price changes over one-year periods in one study and three-year periods in another. It was then possible to determine which P/E categories (high, low, or in between) performed the best in each of the 17 test periods from 1948 to 1964. Our finding of an inverse rank correlation of price performance and P/E ranking, which is referred to in the Molodovsky article, is illustrated in the following two tables.

PERFORMANCE OF STOCKS RANKED IN QUINTILES BY P/E
AT EACH YEAR-END
(1948–1964 incl.)

PERFORMANCE DURING SUBSEQUENT ONE-YEAR PERIODS

P/E Quintile	\multicolumn{5}{c}{Number of Years in which Price Performance Ranked:}
	First	Second	Third	Fourth	Fifth
First (high P/E)	1	3	2	3	8
Second	1	1	2	11	2
Third	1	5	7	1	3
Fourth	2	7	4	2	2
Fifth (low P/E)	12	1	2	0	2

PERFORMANCE DURING SUBSEQUENT THREE-YEAR PERIODS

P/E Quintile	\multicolumn{5}{c}{Number of Periods in which Price Performance Ranked:}
	First	Second	Third	Fourth	Fifth
First (high P/E)	2	1	1	2	9
Second	0	1	0	10	4
Third	1	3	8	2	1
Fourth	2	8	3	1	1
Fifth (low P/E)	10	2	3	0	0

The channel drawn on both tables is the perfect rank correlation channel. That is, if each quintile had had a price performance which correlated in an exact correlative way (inverse to the height of the price-earnings ratio), the numbers appearing in the channel would have equalled the number of years involved in the tests (17 in the one-year test and 15 in the three-year test). For example, in the first table the fifth quintile would have performed best in 17 years, the fourth quintile would have performed second best in 17 years, the third quintile would have performed third best in 17 years, etc. While the correlation is not perfect, it is certainly very good since the largest numbers in every column fall within the perfect correlation channel.

As the tables indicate, the low P/E quintile had an average price performance which ranked first among all quintiles in both the one- and three-year samples. The low P/E group ranked first in 12 out of 17 years and last in only one year when price performance was measured over one year; it ranked first in 10 out of 15 years and last in only two years when price performance was measured over three years. The success of the low P/E approach over an interval of several years is particularly interesting. Early critics had believed that longer time periods would provide an opportunity for the earnings growth of high P/E stocks to make itself felt enough in their stock prices to outperform the low P/E group.

We believe these results, which in no way assume periodic cumulative reinvestment, provide reasonably good evidence that, on average, a group of low P/E stocks is apt to outperform a group of high P/E stocks.

One of our earlier studies did utilize the periodic cumulative reinvestment approach to dramatize the application of the low P/E theory in portfolio management. While this study may be vulnerable to Mr. Molodovsky's critique, we are not convinced that periodic cumulative reinvestment introduces a meaningful bias. He believes that an inevitable weakening of the high P/E groups and strengthening of the low P/E groups results from the process of cumulative reinvestment which is carried out periodically. The high P/E groups are supposedly weakened each time the reinvestment procedure is performed because, as he states, "stocks eliminated from the sample (the high P/E category), are replaced by others whose prices have outdistanced earnings even more than in the case of all or some of the stocks that were contained in the original sample." Conversely, in the lowest P/E group the stocks eliminated by each reinvestment "will be replaced by others whose earnings have demonstrated stronger action than their respective prices."

This observation is certainly a correct one if we are considering only current earnings and stock prices. However, we believe its usefulness is somewhat reduced when the time dimensions of price-earnings ratios are considered. A stock on which the current multiple rises more (or falls less) than that of another stock from one period to another is not necessarily in a "weaker" position. The changed P/E relationship may simply reflect improved future earnings prospects for the former stock relative to the latter. For example, the former may have discovered a rich mineral deposit on its property which caused an abrupt upward multiple revision based on current earnings. Based on future earnings, however, the multiple may well be unchanged or even lower.

Our evidence indicates that the low P/E concept works not so much because the preponderance of stocks in the high P/E group is "weak," but because the minority, which indeed does prove disappointing from the standpoint of earnings growth, is penalized severely. The Molodovsky article contains on pages 412 and 413 a summary of our conclusions in this regard with some attempt at quantifying the results. These disappointments in the high P/E group typically suffer such precipitous price declines that the entire group's performance is materially affected. An opposite situation characteristically occurs in the low P/E group.

We would like to make one final point about periodic cumulative reinvestment as a criticism of the low P/E approach. While it may have some validity, periodic cumulative reinvestment can ony be an explanation of why the low P/E approach works so well. That is, if the higher P/E categories are continuously weakened and the lower P/E categories are strengthened by cumulative reinvestment, it follows quite logically that investors would do well to direct their attention to the groups of stocks with lower multiples.

In summary, we do not believe that Mr. Molodovsky's observations materially alter our earlier conclusions regarding low P/E stocks; namely that, on average, the prices of groups of stocks with low price-earnings ratios have outperformed the prices of groups of stocks with high price-earnings ratios. We would, however, like to re-emphasize the qualifications which we consider important in applying the low P/E approach.

The major practical application of the low P/E concept, in our opinion, is as one tool available to a research director in determining how research time can best be spent. Our studies of high and low P/E stocks indicate that the market's appraisal of industries with apparent lackluster earnings prospects is sometimes in error, and that low multiple stocks in these industries may turn out to be the future market leaders. Research undertaken with the objective of finding these industries is both more positive and apt to yield better results than that aimed at making sure the growth prospects of high multiple stocks have not changed.

32
SOME REFLECTIONS ON TECHNIQUES FOR APPRAISING GROWTH RATES*

Douglas A. Hayes, C.F.A.

In recent years, several articles in the *Financial Analysts Journal* and elsewhere have formulated some basic quantitative techniques for appraising secular growth rates in earnings per share. These techniques have undoubtedly improved the analytical arsenal of the penetrating analyst, but certain questions have emerged as to their implementation in practice. It is the objective of this article to review some significant contributions in this respect and to suggest supplementary techniques which, it is hoped, may assist in implementing the methodology which has been developed for the purpose of estimating potential growth rates.

SMITH: THE ORIGINAL GROWTH STOCK THEORY

To develop and orient the questions, a brief review of some major contributions on the subject may be helpful. First, while an assessment of cause and effect in historical events is always open to debate, a strong case can be made that the recognition of common stocks as a respectable long-term investment medium, as contrasted to a trading vehicle, dates from the research and conclusions embodied in Edgar Lawrence Smith's *Common Stocks as Long Term Investments* published in 1924. And perhaps the most important conclusion which directed attention to the clear superiority of common stocks was that they had shown a strong tendency to appreciate in value over a period of years in accordance with the principle of compound interest. This tendency, it was further found, was not restricted to periods of secular inflation but had operated during periods of falling price levels as well.

Although the fact has never obtained wide recognition in subsequent literature, it was for this reason that Smith begins his book by describing it as "the record of a failure."[1] In view of its subsequent impact on investment theory and management, this allegation seems clearly inappro-

---

*Reprinted by permission of the *Financial Analysts Journal* (July–August 1964).

[1] E. L. Smith, *Common Stocks as Long Term Investments* (New York: Macmillan Co., 1924), Introduction, p. v.

priate. But in reality the statement turns out to be a technique for emphasizing the superior long-term results (over several business cycles) obtained on common stocks because the "failure" turns out to be that the evidence disproved the original hypothesis that common stocks would show the better long-term results during secular inflationary periods, whereas bonds would be superior during deflationary periods. With one minor exception, the entire empirical evidence clearly proved the superiority of stocks under both conditions if they were held for periods of about 20 years.

With inflation ruled out as the fundamental cause of long-term appreciation in common stocks, it was necessary to find another reason for their performance. The reason became the original expression of the growth stock theory; the practice of corporations retaining a reasonable proportion of earnings into earned surplus which are then put into "productive operation." While not specifically stated, there is the inference that retained earnings put into such productive operations results in increases in earnings and dividends.[2] The natural consequence, of course, was an appreciation in the market prices of the related common stocks according to Smith's "Law of Increasing Stock Values and Income Return." This held that "over a period of years, the principal value of a well diversified holding of common stocks of representative corporations, in essential industries, tends to increase in accordance with the operation of compound interest."[3]

The purpose of relating the conclusions from this milestone in the theory and practice of investment management is not to recount the conclusions which undoubtedly are familiar to all practicing analysts. It is rather to indicate the reasoning upon which the conclusions were predicated and the consequent implications for financial analysis techniques concerned with appraising growth rates in per-share earnings. The crucial point to which attention is directed is that the growth in common stock values was implied to be a function of *increments* to per-share earnings derived from *increments* to net worth. From this view, it would seem that a reasonable inference could be drawn from this original statement of the growth stock theory that analysis should emphasize obtaining some clue to the *marginal rates of return* that a company might be able to obtain on successive increments to the common stock equity.

Recent Techniques for Estimating Growth Rates

It is surprising, therefore, to note that this concept has not been introduced on a systematic basis into either the leading books on security analysis or articles dealing with the problem of estimating growth rates. For example, the most recent edition of Graham, Dodd, and Cottle,

---

[2] Ibid., pp. 77–78.
[3] Ibid., p. 79.

Security Analysis, has an excellent section on alternative techniques for projecting potential per-share earnings. Indeed, one such technique is referred to as "the return-on-investment method," but while a marginal approach can perhaps be implied in certain comments, the emphasis is principally on the *average* rate of return obtained on total capital during a plausible past period, adjusted for such trends as are discernible in profit margins and capital turnover ratios.[4]

Again Robert Cummin in the article entitled "The Mechanics of Corporate Growth" emphasizes the importance of the rate of return on investment to an appraisal of growth rates. But like Graham, the analysis does not go beyond indicating the possible importance of differential rates of return on total accumulated investment or net worth. There is, however, an implication of the need for marginal analysis in the comment that in some instances added investment might not produce the same rate of return as that obtained on existing capital.[5] Several other articles give a similar implication; in fact as far back as 1947 Jeremy Jenks strongly implied the need for a separate analysis of earnings obtained on recent increments to capital with the observation that:

> It is frequently worth watching fairly closely the development of earning power in relation to invested capital ... since changes in rates of return, either upward or downward, may signalize a change in the growth trend.[6]

This observation clearly suggests that the analyst should find a means of appraising the magnitudes of possible long-term changes in the rate of return (as contrasted to cyclical or random variations of a temporary nature) brought about by the commitment of new capital at higher or lower rates than obtained on existing resources. However, while recognition of the nature of any analytical problem represents a major step in its solution, there remains the question of pertinent techniques to obtain an insight into the absolute and relative dimensions of the developments which are being "watched."

The Sauvain Formula

Finally, the writings of Dr. Harry C. Sauvain of Indiana University provided the essential structural framework for an analysis of estimating growth rates via an examination of the fundamental economic factors which have a causative effect on the dynamics of corporate earnings. In an article dealing with the potential levels of common stock prices in the sixties, it was shown that the growth rate of earnings per share is a function of the rate of return on the equity on the one hand and the

---

[4] Graham, Dodd, and Cottle, *Security Analysis* (New York: McGraw-Hill Book Co.), 1962, pp. 462–63.

[5] Robert I. Cummin, "The Mechanics of Corporate Growth," *Financial Analysts Journal*, August, 1957, pp. 25–28.

[6] Jeremy C. Jenks, "Investing in Growth Stock," *Financial Analysts Journal*, 2nd Quarter 1947, pp. 44–45.

payout ratio on the other. The Sauvain formula for expressing the relationship is as follows:[7]

$$Rg = \frac{Re(1 - PO)}{1 - Re(1 - PO)}$$

Rg = Rate of growth
Re = Rate of earnings on equity capital
PO = Payout ratio

In short, this formula gives the formal means of computing growth rates from a review of rates of return obtained on the equity combined with an estimate of the probable dividend policy. Thus if a company shows evidence of earning a consistent 10 percent on its equity and its payout record shows a tendency to distribute about 50 percent of earnings, its per-share earnings growth rate should approximate 5 percent. This result is obtained from the use of the numerator in the formula alone. It is true of course that the growth rate literally should be slightly greater than 5 percent because the retained earnings are continuously accumulated through time, and in this sense there are earnings on earnings within a given year. The denominator of the formula is designed to give recognition to this compounding effect and for strict accuracy it is a useful concept. However, because the results are only slightly different from those obtained from the use of the numerator alone and because its usefulness is for estimation purposes only, it is felt that as a practical matter the numerator of the formula alone is sufficiently informative for most analytical purposes. In this connection, it is interesting to note that Messrs. Block and Kisor, presumably acting independently, have published recent articles in the same issue of the *Financial Analysts Journal* using the numerator alone of the Sauvain formula to express the functional expression of the growth rate.[8]

These articles, along with Sauvain's work, deserve the most serious attention of common stock analysts because they bring into focus on a fairly precise basis the relative importance of the basic financial factors which bring about growth in per-share earnings and common stock values and prices. By making logical estimates of the magnitudes of these factors the analyst can appraise in a much more tangible way the desirability of a given common stock at its prevailing price. Alternatively or supplementary, the analyst can employ the range approach to these several factors to obtain some impression as to the probable range of value embodied in a stock.

---

[7] Harry C. Sauvain, "Common Stock Prices in the Sixties," *Business Horizons*, Bureau of Business Research, Indiana University, Bloomington, Ind., Fall, 1960, p. 36.

[8] Frank E. Block, "The Place of Book Value in Common Stock Evaluation;" and Manown Kisor, Jr., "The Financial Aspects of Growth," *Financial Analysts Journal*, March–April, 1964, p. 30 and p. 48.

Importance of Marginal Approach to the Rate of Return

In all of these recent articles, it is agreed, the element of primary importance in determining the growth rate is the expected rate of return on equity. Alternatively the rate of return on capital is also used to give recognition to the importance of a change in financial leverage to the growth potential. But while there is sometimes passing reference to the value of retained earnings being dependent upon the rate of return at which they may be put to work (an implied marginal approach), the illustrations used invariably assume a constant rate of return on equity or total capital as the case may be. This assumption would seem to ignore an important problem in a dynamic analysis, namely that the rate of return is usually not constant through time. Moreover, what is more important, a relatively minor change in the total rate of return on equity over a period of years may be associated with a highly significant change in the marginal rate of return obtained on increments to net worth in the form of retained earnings. Thus it may appear that the assumption of a constant rate of return does not appear to be seriously in error when in fact it may be quite misleading indeed.

An Example of Marginal Analysis: National Dairy

To illustrate, Table 1 shows the essential data on earnings, dividends, and rates of return on net worth for National Dairy Products for the years 1955–63 inclusive. In this analysis it might be noted that a simple one-year lag effect is assumed between retained earnings and an increase in earnings. For example, the retained earnings of $1.38 per share of 1955 are assumed to be causally related to the $.04 increase in earnings of 1956, and the total retained earnings of $11.68 per share between 1955 and 1962 inclusive relates to the $.76 increase in earnings from the level prevailing in 1955 through 1963.

Further, as earnings declined between 1960 and 1962 and only increased beyond their 1960 levels in 1963, the incremental concept requires the view that total 1960–62 retained earnings were required to obtain the earnings increase in 1963 from the 1960 result. The important point, however, to note is that earnings on net worth have varied between about 14 percent in 1955 to 10.7 percent in 1963 with an overall nine-year average rate of return of 12.2 percent. From these figures, which represent those emphasized by the several analysts mentioned above, one might obtain the impression that the rate of return to be used in the growth formula should approximate 11 percent at least. After all the company has constantly earned at least 10.7 percent on its equity and has shown an average rate of return on equity of 12.2 percent over the entire period.

The trend, however, has been downward but not at an alarming rate, so the actual quantitative implications of the trend might well be ignored on the grounds that it represents a relatively minor factor in the long-

TABLE 1
Marginal Rates of Return on Retained Earnings
National Dairy Products

	1955	1956	1957	1958	1959	1960	1961	1962	1963	Totals 1955–63
Earnings per share	2.98	3.02	3.18	3.27	3.51	3.59	3.51	3.57	3.74	—
Dividend per share	1.60	1.75	1.80	1.80	1.95	2.00	2.00	2.05	2.20	—
Retained earnings	1.38	1.27	1.38	1.47	1.56	1.59	1.51	1.52	—*	11.68
Increase in earnings	—	.04	.16	.09	.24	.08	—	—	.15†	.76
Increase—retained earnings, previous year or years	—	2.9%	12.6%	6.5%	16.3%	5.1%	—	—	3.3%‡	6.5%
										Average 1955–63
Earnings, percent of common equity	13.9	12.9	12.9	12.1	12.6	12.0	11.2	11.2	10.7	12.2
Payout ratio	54%	58%	57%	55%	56%	56%	57%	57%	59%	56%

* Excluded in calculations as assumed affects 1964 earnings.
† From previous high in 1960.
‡ Based on total retained earnings of 1960–62 inclusive.

Incremental Rate: $Rg = .065(1 - .56) = 2.86\%$
Average Rate: $Rg = .122(1 - .56) = 5.37\%$

term outlook for the company. But as a matter of actual fact, this apparently minor decline in the rate of return on the total equity has been associated with, or perhaps better caused by, a substantially reduced marginal rate of return obtained on increments to net worth over the 1955–63 period. The table shows that the marginal rate of return on such increments has averaged only 6.5 percent over these years. Therefore, based on the approximate payout ratio of about 56 percent the actual growth rate for National Dairy has been in actual fact only about 2.9 percent annually. This growth rate, it should be emphasized, is substantially different than the 5.4 percent rate obtained from the use of the average return on equity for this period. To be sure there have been some estimates that National Dairy may show a substantial increase in earnings in 1964, to as much as $4.50 per share, but even allowing for such material increase in earnings, the incremental rate of return over the 1955–64 period would be about 10 percent or significantly lower than the average rate of more than 12 percent.

Factors Causing Changes in Rate of Return

It is quite true, of course, that other significant trends and developments should be examined to supplement the above indication of the earnings potentials on additional retained earnings. These would include (1) the rate of growth of sales, (2) the trend of capital turnover, (3) the trend of profit margins, and (4) developments with respect to financial leverage. However, as Graham, Sauvain, Block, and Kisor have among them fully covered the importance and interpretation of these items, this phase of the analytical process need not be repeated here. However, in passing it might be noted that in the case of National Dairy, the annual growth rate in sales has approximated 6 percent, but profit margins and capital turnover have decreased moderately. These developments suggest competitive pressures have become more intense. Although as mentioned estimated 1964 results are expected to be favorable, it remains uncertain whether the future longer-term growth potential on additional retained earnings may resemble the 1955–63 incremental rate (6.5 percent) rather than the average rate of return on equity (12.2 percent) for the same period. Also relevant to this question is the fact that the percentage of funded debt in the capital structure decreased from about 25 percent in 1955 to 18 percent in 1963, which suggests that some improvement in the incremental rate of return might be obtained from the use of additional debt to finance a substantial proportion of any future asset requirements. As the debt ratio is conservative for a company of this stature and stability characteristics, additional debt financing would seem to be a reasonable probability assuming continuing capital needs.

Need to Analyze a Significant Span of Years

A comment might also be appropriate on the substantial year-to-year variations in the incremental rates of return. In a relatively stable company, such as National Dairy, the magnitude of fluctuations in the marginal rate of return may appear surprising, ranging from a negative position (a decline in earnings) to a return of 16 percent. Apparently even in quite stable situations minor changes in economic and industry conditions or perhaps costs associated with start-ups of new projects or product lines can have major marginal effects on any single year's earnings, although the impact of the total earning power may be modest. The existence of such fluctuations suggests that year-to-year comparisons of marginal rates of return are probably not of great significance. Rather it is the accumulated marginal results over a considerable span of years that would seem analytically significant such as the eight-year period shown above. Further, it would seem highly desirable for the beginning base year to represent conditions in the economy and industry as similar as possible to the terminal year because the objective is to measure long-term trend potential; the dimensions of any trend, of course, can be obscured by unusual factors relevant only to either the beginning or terminal year.

OTHER PROBLEMS IN MARGINAL ANALYSIS APPROACH

There is, however, another major problem in the use of marginal analysis as a means of estimating the potential rates of return on retained earnings. When increases in earnings of one year are related to retained earnings of the previous year, there are the implicit assumptions that: (1) all major increases in the common stock equity arise from retained earnings, and (2) that the proportion of fixed income securities in the capital structure has not increased by a material amount during the period under survey. If either of these assumptions is not valid, then the growth may be the consequence of an ability of the company to issue new stock on which earnings per share are greater than on existing shares or reflect the results of a major change in the financial leverage position.

To illustrate the nature of the problem in this connection, Table 2 shows the same type of marginal analysis for Charles Pfizer and Company as was presented in Table 1 for National Dairy. The problem here arises from developments in 1962 when Pfizer issued almost 660,000 new shares to acquire two existing companies and the related earnings acquired were slightly in excess of $2.00 per share. Therefore, in 1962 the increase of some $.19 per share was in some part due to these acquisitions and not the consequence of the normal incremental process. The unusual feature of these transactions, so far as rate of return analysis is concerned, is that a marginal computation (which assumes the earnings increase was solely due to retained earnings of the previous year) suggests that the rate of return on equity increased in 1962, whereas in fact it actually decreased after giving effect to the value of the new shares in the total equity. Therefore, because of this development, it would seem dubious to conclude that Pfizer can average a rate of return on increments to net worth derived from retained earnings of the magnitude of 18.7 percent shown

TABLE 2

MARGINAL RATES OF RETURN ON RETAINED EARNINGS
Charles Pfizer and Company

	1955	1956	1957	1958	1959	1960	1961	1962	1963	Totals 1955–63
Earnings per share	.98	1.15	1.41	1.47	1.52	1.58	1.74	1.93	2.07	—
Dividend per share	.51	.58	.70	.75	.80	.80	.85	.95	1.05	—
Retained earnings	.47	.57	.71	.72	.72	.78	.89	.98	—*	5.84
Increase in earnings	—	.17	.26	.06	.05	.06	.16	.19	.14	1.09
Increase—retained earnings, previous year	—	36.2%	45.6%	8.5%	6.9%	8.3%	20.5%	21.3%	14.3%	18.7%

										Average 1955–63
Earnings, percent of common equity	13.9	15.8	17.9	17.2	15.9	15.3	15.7	14.8	14.9	15.7
Payout ratio	52%	50%	50%	51%	53%	51%	49%	49%	51%	51%

* Excluded from calculation on assumption that effects are on 1964 earnings.

for the years 1955–63 inclusive. If 1962 is completely excluded by eliminating both the earnings increase and retained earnings for that year from the computation, the incremental rate of return on the average falls to about 18 percent, which amount still exceeds the 15.7 percent shown as the average rate of return on total net worth for the period. In this case, therefore, the past quantitative data might be interpreted to suggest that the possible rate of return which might be obtained on retained earnings might range from about 15 percent to 18 percent, and these alternatives might be used in the formula computation of prospective growth rates.

Effects of New Stock Issues on Growth Rates

However, this growth rate might well be exceeded if the company continues to acquire in the future other companies wherein the acquired earnings divided by the new shares issued exceed the existing per-share earnings on the prior outstanding shares. This means of achieving some acceleration in the growth rate is closely analogous to the ability of some companies, particularly electric power utilities, to obtain an increase in per-share earnings via selling new common shares in the market from time to time at a substantial premium above book value.[9] In these cases, it should be recognized, the formula suggested by Sauvain and others for measuring the growth rate results in an inaccurate picture of the growth potential. The inaccuracy results because there are two additional factors in these instances influencing the growth rate which are not embodied in the formula: (1) the amount of the premium over book value obtained on the new issues, and (2) the percentage through time of new stock issues related to the common stock outstanding at the beginning of the period.

To illustrate the absolute and relative significance of these additional factors on the growth rate, Table 3 shows three hypothetical situations which, it is assumed, have occasion to sell new common stock in the market. In the illustration it is assumed that the marginal rate of return on new equity capital will equal the average rate of return obtained on the existing equity. It may be noted, however, that this second assumption is not necessary, and a different marginal rate based on analytical judgment could be used to appraise the effect on earnings per share of new stock issues. But to isolate specifically the relative effects of the two additional factors mentioned above, the assumption of a constant rate of return factor seems desirable.

Company A, it is presumed, has occasion to sell additional shares amounting to 5 percent of the existing outstanding shares at a premium over book value of 100 percent. Under these circumstances, it is shown that earnings per share will increase from $5.00 to $5.24 at a constant rate of return on equity of 10 percent, or the percentage increase will be about 4.8 percent. The same 100 percent premium over book value is assumed

---

[9] Jeremy C. Jenks, *op. cit.*, pp. 45–46.

TABLE 3
Effects of New Common Stock Issues on Per-Share Earnings

	Co. A	Co. B	Co. C
No. of shares outstanding	100,000	100,000	100,000
Book value per share	$50	$50	$50
Total book value	$5,000,000	$5,000,000	$5,000,000
Rate of return	10%	10%	10%
Total earnings	$500,000	$500,000	$500,000
Earnings per share	$5.00	$5.00	$5.00
Price of new shares	100	100	150
No. of new shares	5,000	10,000	5,000
Total proceeds	500,000	1,000,000	750,000
Rate of return on new shares (assumed)	10%	10%	10%
Earnings obtained	50,000	100,000	75,000
Total earnings after sale	550,000	600,000	575,000
Per share after sale	$5.24	$5.44	$5.47

for Company B, but here the increase in new shares is 10 percent of outstanding shares; the result is per-share earnings advance to $5.44 or by 8 percent. Company C, on the other hand, is presumed to increase its shares by the same 5 percent as for Company A but the premium is assumed to be 200 percent of book value rather than 100 percent. In this case per-share earnings will advance to $5.47 or by about 9 percent. The illustration clearly shows, therefore, that the amount of potential increase in earnings per share associated with the sale of new stock is a function of (1) the percentage premium over book values obtained on the new shares, (2) the percentage that the number of new shares bears to the existing shares, and (3) our old friend the marginal rate of return expected on the new funds.

Algebraic Expression of Effects of New Stock Issues

There remains the question of what is the formal general relationship between these variables which can be used to compute the potential increase resulting from any combination of circumstances actually encountered in practice. At this point it was necessary to seek the assistance of a qualified mathematician, and Professor Richard M. Duvall of the Graduate School of Business, University of Michigan, worked out the following algebraic representation of the phenomena which would have general applicability.

Definition of symbols:

N_1 = Number of existing shares outstanding
P_1 = Existing book value per share
r_1 = Rate of return on existing equity
N_2 = Number of new shares
P_2 = Price of new shares
r_2 = Marginal rate of return on new funds
$N_1 P_1$ = Total book value prior to sale = V_1
$N_2 P_2$ = Proceeds on new sale = V_2

Then

Earnings per share after sale = $\dfrac{r_1 V_1 + r_2 V_2}{N_1 + N_2}$

Earnings per share before sale = $r_1 P_1$

Ratio of earnings after sale to earnings before sale = $\dfrac{r_1 V_1 + r_2 V_2}{N_1 + N_2} \div r_1 P_1$ which simplified to $\dfrac{V_1 + V_2}{P_1(N_1 + N_2)}$ if $r_1 = r_2$ (rate of return on existing equity equals marginal rate expected on new issue).

To illustrate the use of the formula, the data for Company A in Table 3 would work out as follows:

$$V_1 = 100,000 \times 50 = 5,000,000$$
$$V_2 = 5,000 \times 100 = 500,000$$
$$P_1 = 50$$
$$N_1 = 100,000$$
$$N_2 = 5,000$$
$$r_1 = r_2 = 10\%$$

$$\dfrac{5,000,000 + 500,000}{50(5,000 + 100,000)} = \dfrac{5,500,000}{5,250,000} = 1.0476$$

The coefficient of 1.0476 represents the multiple by which earnings per share would increase as a consequence of a new common stock issue of the relative magnitude and at the price-book value relationship shown in Table 3 for Company A. Thus the $5.00 per-share earnings multiplied by 1.0476 results in new per-share earnings of $5.238, which approximates the $5.24 in Table 3.

Essentially the same formula can be used to compute the effects on earnings per share of mergers or acquisitions consummated through exchanges of stock. In this case, the earnings of the acquired companies would be substituted for $r_2 V_2$ above, and the remainder of the computation would remain the same. The problem here is that the earnings data on the acquisitions may not be readily available especially if they are not publicly owned and/or do not publish financial statements. Such was the case in fact for several of the Pfizer acquisitions referred to above.

SUMMARY OF TECHNIQUES SUGGESTED FOR GROWTH RATE ANALYSIS

In summary, it has been argued that in estimating growth rates via the technique of relating rates of return on equity to the payout ratio, it might often be desirable to examine the marginal rates of return that have been obtained on retained earnings over a significant span of years. To date, however, the several articles on the subject have indicated that average total rates of return on equity be used. At least a supplementary marginal approach seems advisable because a small change in the total annual rate of return either upward or downward may in fact reflect marginal rate of returns on retained earnings which are substantially different from the indicated total rates. In addition, it was pointed out that the above technique involves the implicit assumption that additions to the common stock equity come from retained earnings only. This assumption is probably valid for the great majority of industrial companies today where internally generated funds have been quite sufficient to meet capital expansion requirements.

However, if new common stock of any significant proportions is issued, either for cash or to acquire other companies, then the growth rate may well differ from that computed via concentrating solely on the payout ratio and the rates of return indicated on retained earnings. Therefore, while perhaps applicable only to the minority of companies, it is felt that a means of estimating the effects of new issues on per-share earnings is desirable. Therefore, a formula for this purpose was suggested in the above discussion.

33

CURRENT GROWTH STOCK VALUATION METHODS*
General Motors—An Illustration

Paul J. Wendt

Most modern stock valuation techniques are based upon the present value theory, which was first set forth in detail by John B. Williams in his *Theory of Investment Value*. Building on the earlier theoretical foundations found in Marshall, Bohm Bawerk, and Irving Fisher, Williams argued that the present value of a share of stock is equal to the summation of all dividends expected to be received from it, discounted to the present at an appropriate rate of interest.[1] He argued that tangible income to the investor, dividends, was the only appropriate base for consideration in the valuation of stocks. More recently, others have argued that it does not matter whether one capitalizes dividends or earnings, since price changes in stocks would discount earnings and potential future dividends and since investors could elect to receive income either as dividends or by the sale of stock.[2]

Although most recent writers on the theory of stock valuation have continued to favor the capitalization of future dividends, they have accorded increasing attention to capitalization of earnings for rapidly growing enterprises.[3] The purpose of this article is to describe briefly some of the current growth stock valuation techniques and to illustrate the differences in methods, assumptions, and resultant valuations by reference to the valuation of General Motors common in mid-1964.

The three methods described briefly in the first part will not be

---

* Reprinted by permission of the *Financial Analysts Journal* (March–April 1965).

[1] Alfred Marshall, *Principles of Economics* (8th ed.; London, 1925), Vol. 5, chaps. IV, VI, XV. Irving Fisher, *The Nature of Capital and Income* (New York, 1906). John B. Williams, *The Theory of Investment Value* (Cambridge, 1938).

[2] F. Modigliani and M. H. Miller, "Dividend Policy, Growth and the Valuation of Shares," *Journal of Business*, October, 1961.

[3] James E. Walter, "Dividend Policies and Common Stock Prices," *Journal of Finance*, March, 1956, pp. 29–42. B. G. Malkiel, "Equity Yields and Structure of Share Prices," *The American Economic Review*, December, 1963, pp. 1004–31. See also *American Economic Review*, December, 1964, "Comment and Reply," pp. 1029–51.

illustrated because of lack of data, similarity to other techniques, or because of other limitations. The seven techniques illustrated in the second part, for which published information is available in sufficient detail to permit calculation, have been selected to provide indication of the range of values which results from alternative assumptions and objectives.

PART I

Building directly on Williams' theoretical foundations, Walter developed the following formula for valuation of the future dividend stream expected from a stock and illustrated its application to growth, intermediate, and so-called creditor stock categories. By his definition, a growth stock is one for which the rate of return on marginal investment (after adjustment for preferential tax treatment of capital gains) was larger than the company's cost of capital or capitalization rate.[4]

$$V_c = \frac{D + \frac{R_a}{R_c}(E - D)}{R_c}$$

Where:

D = Annual cash dividends expected per share
E = Earnings per share
R_a = Rate of return corporation will earn on additional investment
R_c = Market capitalization rate
V_c = Value per share

Malkiel, writing in *The American Economic Review* for December, 1963, sets forth a formula for calculating the present value of future dividends which is closely similar to the methods employed by Williams and Walter and to some of the techniques illustrated below. His formula implies the use of the reciprocal of a standard multiplier as a discount rate.[5]

$$P = \frac{D(1+g)}{(1+r)} + \frac{D(1+g)^2}{(1+r)^2} + \frac{D(1+g)^N}{(1+r)^N} + \frac{M_s E(1+g)^N}{(1+r)^N}$$

Where:

M_s = Standard earnings multiplier S&P averages
D = Dividend in dollars
g = Company's growth rate as a percentage
E = Earnings in dollars
r = Standard rate of growth S&P averages or the apparent marginal efficiency of the representative standard share
N = Number of years forecasted
P = Present value of future stream of receipts

---

[4] Walter, *op. cit.*

[5] Malkiel, *op. cit.* See also Sanford L. Margoshes, "Present Value Techniques of Common Stock Valuation," *Financial Analysts Journal* (March–April, 1961), pp. 37–42.

Current Growth Stock Valuation Methods: General Motors

The *Value Line Survey*, which might be credited with initiating the econometric analysis of the relationship between stock prices, dividends, and earnings at the practitioner level, is based upon a multiple regression analysis of dividend payments, earnings, and lagged market prices for a large sample of individual issues. Arnold Bernhard, President, describes the evolution of techniques employed by his firm in his book, *The Evaluation of Common Stocks*. Revisions in technique are published in the "Commentary" to the financial service. The Value Line technique seeks to establish a so-called Quality Rating for each of 1,100 individual issues, a Potential Value five years hence, and a Current Value. Using General Motors common stock as an illustration, the author illustrates the technique for establishing these value concepts (pp. 61–76). The most recently published analysis of General Motors common stock published on July 24, 1964, indicated an expected potential value in 1967–69 of $90 based upon an estimated eight-year growth rate of 6.3 percent. This valuation appears to be based upon the equation $V = 8 \times$ 5-year moving average Cash Earnings. (See the "Commentary" of April 3, 1964, describing the revised method of ranking stocks for the next three to five years.)

The estimated normal current value in July, 1964, was $70 per share based upon estimates of earnings of $5.75 and dividends of $4.10 for the year ending September, 1965. The regression formula used in order to obtain the above normal value was:

$$\log \text{Normal Value} = 1.168 + .750 \log (.68 \text{ Earnings} + \text{Dividends})$$

The constant (1.168) incorporated General Motors' long-term trend and logged price factors.

PART II

The earnings per share of General Motors (shown in Chart I), have been growing at an annual rate of about 5.3 percent for the last 10 years. The dividend growth, however, was almost 9 percent per annum. Why this difference? In the early years of the last decade the pay-out ratio was only about 50 percent. In 1963 General Motors reported earnings of $5.56 per share and paid a dividend of $4.00, equivalent to a pay-out ratio of approximately 70 percent. It is to be expected that future dividend growth will be more in line with earnings growth. In the following illustrations, the assumption is made that dividend and earnings growth will be about 5.3 percent for the next 10 years.

The seven valuation techniques which follow are associated with the writings of John C. Clendenin; W. Scott Bauman; Nicholas Molodovsky; Graham, Dodd, Cottle, and Tatham; Jeremy C. Jenks; Robert Ferguson; and William Kurtz. Although the author has endeavored to follow these various techniques as described in the *Financial Analysts Journal* and elsewhere, it must be emphasized that the assumptions have been made by the author, and the resultant valuations represent his interpretation of the values resulting from the application of the different techniques illustrated. Messrs. Clendenin, Bauman, Jenks, Ferguson, Molodovsky, and my colleague, Professor M. J. Keenan, made many helpful comments and suggestions on the final draft of this article.

Technique No. 1—Clendenin

John C. Clendenin has developed a method for determining the justifiable price-dividend multiplier for a growth stock, given alternative assumptions as to rates of growth, duration of growth, and discount rates.

CHART I

GENERAL MOTORS: EARNINGS, DIVIDENDS, CASH GENERATED, AND PRICE RANGE PER SHARE, AND PRICE/EARNINGS RATIO

Actual 1954–63; Estimated 1964–73

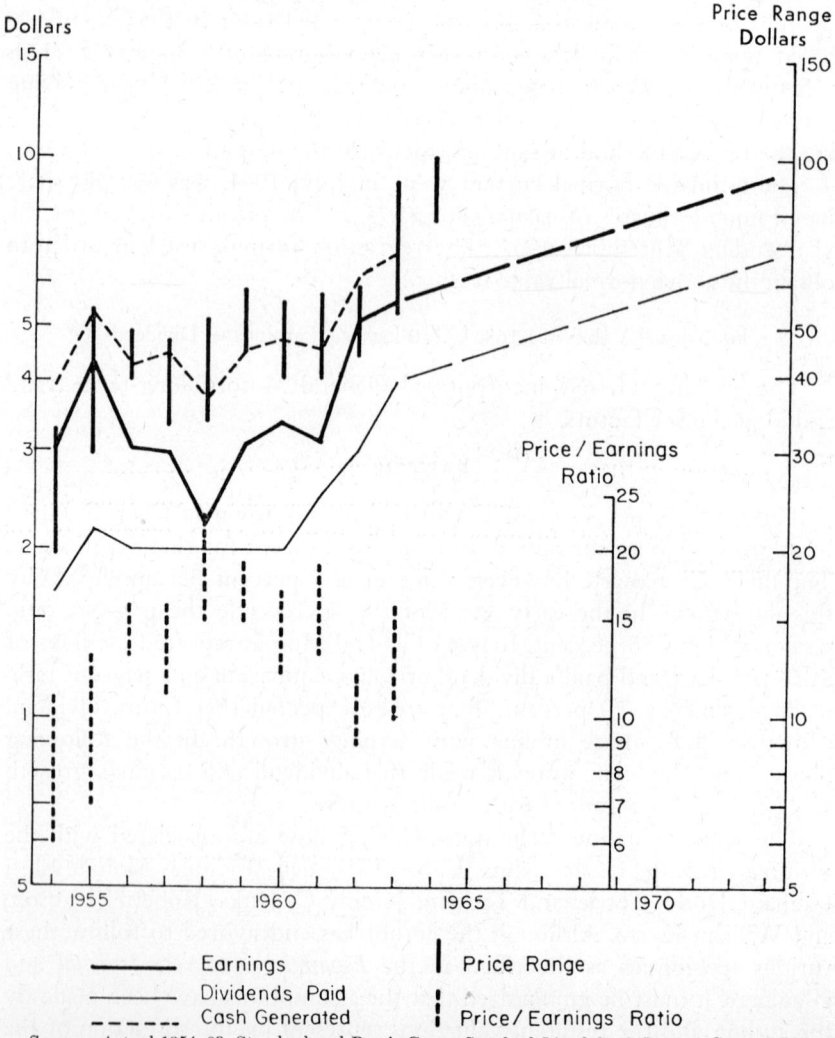

——— Earnings
——— Dividends Paid
- - - - Cash Generated
| Price Range
¦ Price/Earnings Ratio

SOURCE: Actual 1954–63, Standard and Poor's Corp., *Standard Listed Stock Reports*, General Motors November 20, 1964. Estimates 1964–73, estimated by the author, see text.

He presents a series of present value tables (see Appendix A) which can be used either to determine the assumptions concerning growth rate and duration which are implicit in the current market value of a stock, or for determining the investment value of a stock, given certain assumptions about growth and appropriate discount rates.

Following Williams' theory, Clendenin states:

> Basic theory asserts that the value of a share of stock to a long term investor is contained entirely in the future dividends the share (or its successors following mergers, stock dividends, or spin-offs) may pay, plus the value of occasional rights or small miscellaneous distributions which do not dilute the basic equity.[6]

In describing the use of his technique, Clendenin shows that it can be applied to short-term investment as well. A person who plans to hold a share of stock for only three years, for example, will arrive at today's value by discounting to its present value (a) the dividends he expects to receive during the next three years, and (b) the price he expects to receive at the time of sale, which will be determined by all future dividends the stock is expected to yield from year 3 to infinity.

Three factors are basic to Clendenin's valuation method: (1) the rate of dividend growth, (2) the duration of the growth trend, and (3) the discount or capitalization rates (or yield rates as he calls them). Cautioning investors concerning overoptimism about growth rates and duration, he advocates a system of progressively higher discount rates (with a maximum of 7 percent) to be applied to expected dividend returns in the distant future. (See Appendix A.)

Clendenin suggests that 20 years are "not beyond the scope of reasonable estimation in the case of well-established concerns." Beyond that time he advises caution but illustrates that the largest part of the value of any stock attaches to the dividends of the first 20 years because of the increasing effect of discounting as time progresses. He also suggests application of the method to groups of stocks rather than single issues, to obtain greater reliability in long-term projections.

The analyst using Clendenin's method of growth stock valuation still faces a major task, namely that of deciding what values to assign to Clendenin's basic three factors: growth rate, duration, and discount rates. The author offers limited help on how to estimate future growth rate duration. He arrives at a discount rate by checking what the norm is among high-grade stocks, adds 1 percent to expected real terms growth rate to take into account average inflationary forces, and suggests a discount rate which depends on the quality of the corporation whose stock is considered. Clendenin avoids being any more specific in assigning

---

[6] John C. Clendenin, "Theory and Technique of Growth Stock Valuation," Occasional Paper No. 1 (Bureau of Business and Economic Research, U.C.L.A., 1957).

values to his factors because, "In all instances the investor has a subjective analysis to make. . . ."

Application of Technique No. 1 to General Motors Common Stock

Reading from Clendenin's Table I in Appendix A (extrapolating to 5.3 percent growth rate) and assuming that growth will continue for only 10 years and that earnings remain stable for the ensuing 90 years; General Motors stock is worth:

$$\text{Multiplier} \quad \text{Dividend}$$
$$25.40 \quad \times \quad \$4.00 \quad = \quad \$101.60$$

Its closing price on July 17, 1964, was 94 3/8.

It can be seen from Appendix A that the multiplier rises rapidly as the growth rate and growth period assumed increase. It is interesting to observe from Appendix A that at the July 17, 1964, price of 94 3/8, General Motors common appeared to discount an approximate 4 percent growth rate for 10 years capitalizing future dividends at the rates shown (i.e., 23.04 × $4.00 = $92.16).

Technique No. 2—Bauman—(Variable Discount Rate Method)[7]

Bauman uses, as did Clendenin, the present value concept of arriving at a stock value by discounting at an appropriate yield rate all future cash incomes or dividends. He spells out the factors that determine future dividend income, namely, the growth rate and the growth duration, and argues that a company with a growth rate in excess of the average shown in an industry will sooner or later find its growth rate declining to the average level. How long this "transitional" period lasts depends on the company, the industry, product, competition, etc. A guide to follow is to determine the probable position of the company in its life cycle. For example, if a company has been experiencing an abnormally high growth rate, Bauman suggests, ". . . unless there is sufficient evidence to the contrary, the best earnings and dividend projection is probably one based on a decreasing rate of growth," until it eventually approximates the secular growth rate for the majority of companies in the economy. This secular growth rate of dividends and also earnings plus noncash charges was found to have been about 4 percent during the last 36 years. For reasons of convenience, and for lack of evidence to the contrary, Bauman makes the assumption in his model that the growth rate will decline by equal amounts over the span of the transitional period.

According to Bauman, therefore, in order to make a good estimate of future dividends, the investor must ascertain (*a*) the current growth rate of dividends (and earnings), and (*b*) how long it will take until the

---

[7] W. Scott Bauman, "Estimating the Present Value of Common Stocks by the Variable Rate Method," Michigan Business Reports No. 42 (Bureau of Business Research, University of Michigan, 1963).

growth rate has declined to the 4 percent growth rate average typical for the majority of corporations.

Once the investor has determined the pattern for future dividend incomes, he must discount them to arrive at a present value. What shall be the discount rate? Bauman offers guidelines of from 6 to 10 percent, depending on the risk involved.

The discount rate applied to the first year's expected dividends is usually the lowest, and it increases with time as incomes of more distant years become more and more uncertain. That is, the risk premium added to the discount rate increases with time. Although he does not advise the investor exactly on how much higher future discount rates should be than initial rates, he gives a very strong clue by showing what rates were representative for a majority stock average. The Standard and Poor's Index was shown to be comprised mainly of large companies with medium to high quality. An initial discount rate of 6.5 percent was held to be reasonable. The average price-dividend ratio for the period 1949–62 was 24.2, giving an average dividend yield of 4.13 percent with a 4 percent annual growth rate. Based on these relationships and using trial and error method, it was mathematically consistent to have the first year's dividend income discounted at 6.5 percent followed by the second year's dividend income discounted at 6.54875 percent, the third year's by 6.59750 percent, with each succeeding year's discount rate increased in a linear manner by the amount of 0.04875 percentage points.

Bauman relies heavily upon historical data, and believes this action is justified by absence at present of any indicators which point to large changes ahead. He reminds the investor, however, to be on guard constantly to recognize signs of changes.

Application of Technique No. 2 to General Motors Common Stock

How is the present value actually determined by Bauman's method? The same figures for General Motors are applied with the following assumptions:

1. According to Bauman, a discount rate of 6 percent is applied to the dividend in the first year for a company with a high quality rating. Consequently, this rate is used for General Motors in the first year. Because the discount rates applicable to dividend income in succeeding future years are higher, the average discount rate over the first 10-year period applicable to dividend income is actually 6.2 percent.

2. The transitional period should be 10 years, since dividends grow at 4 percent per year beyond the 10 years.

3. Bauman's tables assume that the annual growth rates during the transitional period gradually decrease to 4 percent. Since we assume that the average annual growth rate over the 10 years is 5.3 percent, a weighted average of approximately 5.3 percent is obtained if an initial growth rate of 6 percent is selected.

4. The residual growth rate used will be 4 percent (as Bauman recommends).

From Variable Rate Table B-6 in Appendix B, the price-dividend ratio applicable for General Motors is found to be 29.9.

The present value of General Motors is then $4.00 × 29.9 = $119.60.

Again, it would appear that the stock is underpriced at 94 3/8. Based on Bauman's Table B-6, shown in Appendix B, if the assumed initial dividend growth rate of 6 percent declines to 4 percent over a 10-year period, and if an initial discount rate of 7 percent is used, General Motors would provide an approximate average yield from dividends of 7.24 percent at the price of 94 3/8 (i.e., 23.8 × $4.00 = $95.20).

Technique No. 3—R. Ferguson[8]

Robert Ferguson presents a method of determining justifiable price/earnings ratios for growth stocks as compared with some standard. His objectives are to answer the following questions:

(*a*) How many years of the present high growth rate are assumed by today's market price before the growth rate of the company will drop to the "standard" rate?

(*b*) What price/earnings ratio is justified given a certain rate of growth which is higher than the standard rate for a certain number of years?

The standard can be of any sort, depending upon the kind of company analyzed. The Dow-Jones Industrial Average and Standard and Poor's serve as good examples.

Ferguson takes the market price as a base and then tries to determine what estimates of the basic factors (growth rate and growth duration) the market makes. He then leaves the investor to decide whether these estimates are too low or too high in his judgment. Ferguson develops a nomograph which eliminates the need for complicated calculation on the part of the investor (see Appendix C). The nomograph is a graphical solution to the equation:

$$\frac{P_a}{P_a^1} = \frac{(1+R_a)^n}{(1+R_b)^n}$$

---

[8] Robert Ferguson, "A Nomograph for Valuing Growth Stocks," *Financial Analysts Journal* (May–June, 1961), pp. 29–34. A similar technique was presented by W. Edward Bell in "The Price Future Earnings Ratio—A Practical Guide to Stock Valuation," *Financial Analysts Journal* (August, 1958), pp. 25–28. The author contends that his nomograph is not intended as a "theory of value," but simply as a means of determining current price-earnings ratios which are consistent with assumptions about earnings growth and going market P/E ratios. The author also rejects my view that an adjustment for dividends would represent double counting. My colleague, Professor Michael Keenan, to whom I am indebted for his careful review of this and other points, has pointed out to me that this does not exactly involve double counting, but rather a *very important difference* as to what the price of a share does and does not incorporate. He says, "It seems much more likely to me that the current market price does incorporate some notion of dividend payments but my empirical evidence is not very strong here."

Where:

P_a = Some standard price/earnings ratio
P^1_a = Growth stock price/earnings ratio
R_a = Standard growth rate assumed
R_b = Rate of growth assumed for growth stock

Although it appears that Ferguson ignores the discount rate, closer examination reveals that the use of a standard growth rate in the denominator of his equation (as in Malkiel referred to above), implies that investors will apply uniform discount rates to all common stock earnings, and that differences in price/earnings ratios arise *only* from differences in assumed growth rates and duration.

A further assumption is made implicitly that the quoted growth rates stay on the same level until period T and then drop off suddenly to a rate equivalent to the "standard rate." An analysis based on the foregoing assumption differs, of course, very strongly from Bauman's Variable Rate Method, which assumes evenly declining growth rates and increasing discount rates for incomes with longer futurity. Molodovsky's most recent techniques also assume evenly declining growth rates, as will be observed elsewhere in this *Journal*.

In the last paragraph of his article describing the nomograph, Ferguson states:

> We have not considered the fact that many stocks pay dividends which are an important source of profit, in addition to price appreciation. This is especially true in situations where the growth rate is of the same order of magnitude as the dividend yield. In these instances, the neglect of dividends may well result in an incorrect calculation. An approximate adjustment for dividend income, useful in many instances, would be to add the yield to the per share earnings growth rate and use the resultant figure in place of the growth rate.

This implicitly assumes that the current market price of stocks completely disregards dividend payments. In my view this procedure would represent double counting and overstate justifiable price/earnings ratios for growth stocks, since dividend payout, in my opinion, is already implicitly reflected in the standard price/earnings ratio used in his equation. (See note 8.)

Application of Technique No. 3 to General Motors Common Stock

1. To determine length of "transitional" period we use 4 percent as the standard DJIA growth rate, and assume a standard P/E ratio of 15. For General Motors the P/E is 17, and the growth rate is, of course, 5.3 percent.

The following instructions are used in the application of the nomograph in Appendix C:

(*a*) Locate the columns marked "standard growth rates." Choose the one with a growth rate equal to that of the standard, in this case, the $R = 4$ percent column (by interpolation).

(b) Go up this column until you come to the rate of growth of the company being analyzed, in this case, 5.3 percent (by interpolation). Then, move horizontally to the right until you reach the vertical "R line." Mark this spot.

(c) Locate the columns marked "standard price/earnings ratios." Choose the one with the price/earnings ratio equal to that of the standard, in this case, the $P/E = 15$ column.

(d) Go down this column until you come to the price/earnings ratio of the company being analyzed, in this case, 17. Then, move horizontally to the left until you reach the vertical "P/E line." Mark this spot, too.

(e) Connect these two marks with a straight line and read the number where the line intersects the diagonal "time line," in this case, 9. This is the length of time, in years, discounted by General Motors' price/earnings ratio (17).

General Motors' present market price therefore assumes the current 5.3 percent growth rate to continue for at least nine years, before it will drop to the 4 percent average rate as evidenced by the DJIA.

2. To determine the maximum price/earnings ratio which should be paid for the 5.3 percent growth rate of General Motors as compared with the DJIA rate of 4 percent if maintained for 10 years:

(a) Locate the number 10 on the "time line." Mark this spot.

(b) Locate the columns marked "standard growth rates." Choose the one with a growth rate equal to that of the standard, in this case $R = 4$ percent column (by interpolation).

(c) Go up this column until you come to the rate of growth of General Motors, in this case 5.3 percent (by interpolation). Then, move horizontally to the right until you reach the vertical "R line." Mark this spot, too.

(d) Connect these two marks with a straight line and extend the line until it intersects the "P/E line." Note the point of intersection.

(e) Locate the columns marked "standard price/earnings ratios." Choose the one with a price/earnings ratio of $P/E = 15$.

(f) Move horizontally to the right from the point noted in (d) until you come to the standard price/earnings ratio column chosen in (e). Read off the price/earnings ratio, in this case 18.5. This is the maximum price/earnings ratio that should be paid for General Motors.

Since the earnings base assumed is $5.56, the maximum price one should pay for General Motors currently (under the growth assumptions stated above) is 18.5 × $5.56 = $102.86.

It can be noted that the alternative selection of a standard price/earnings multiplier of 20 would have resulted in a price/earnings ratio for General Motors of approximately 23 and a resultant value of approximately $128.

Technique No. 4—Molodovsky[9]

Nicholas Molodovsky has written several articles on the subject of growth stock valuation. He has made a comprehensive historical analysis

---

[9] Nicholas Molodovsky, "Valuations of Common Stocks," *Financial Analysts Journal* (February, 1959), "Stock Values and Stock Prices—Part I" (May–June, 1960) and "Dow-Jones Industrials—A Reappraisal" (March–April, 1961).

of the Standard & Poor's and Cowles Commission indexes, and used them as the standard with which to compare all stocks. From the figures of the above mentioned stock indexes (which were carefully adjusted to make them as representative as possible for the 1871–1959 period studies) the author developed basic historical parameters. The historical growth rate of dividends and earnings has been about 2.5 percent. The average yield for the period as evidenced by the "Stock Averages" has been about 5 percent. These two figures combine to show a total effective yield per year of 7.5 percent, which Molodovsky consequently used as the discount rate in the present value formula in studies contributed to the *Financial Analysts Journal* through 1960. Including later years through 1963, the above parameters respectively changed to about 2.7 percent, 4.9 percent, and 7.8 percent.

Molodovsky always took great pains to emphasize that any standardized selections of future periods, such as 10 years, for instance, could serve illustrative purposes only. He stressed that in actual analytical practice, projections of future earnings trends of different stocks would have to be made for whatever varying periods might be specifically indicated. Such characteristics of appropriate valuation parameters were already noted, in no uncertain terms, in his 1959 and 1960 studies. He developed his thinking a bit further in his later papers. His article, "The Many Aspects of Yields," which appeared in the March–April, 1962, issue of this *Journal*, contained the following statement:

> It is clear that the nature of the industry to which a given company belongs—as well as that corporation's particular characteristics—should in reality determine both the length of the period for which earnings are projected into the future and also the delicate process of the "splicing" with an overall historical rate. Depending on each individual case, such a transition may well take the form of mathematical curves with very different gradations of diminishing rates of growth.

Such gradual transitions can be easily performed by a computer, which could also carry out the valuation formula's requirement of an infinite time horizon. According to Molodovsky, this latter condition can be easily met by combining the compound interest formula used for computing a bond's yield to maturity with the expression of a geometric progression for an infinite number of terms which constitutes a mathematical description of a common stock's natural *habitat*. The requisite formulae may be found in any high school textbook of aglebra.

It so happens that this issue of the *Financial Analysts Journal* [See reading number 32, above, pages 414–450.] carries an article by Molodovsky and two of his associates discussing the valuations of the DJIA and of its thirty component stocks. Since General Motors is one of the prominent members of this club, I shall let Molodovsky and his associates speak for themselves regarding the valuation of GM.

Technique No. 5—Graham, Dodd, Cottle, and Tatham[10]

Messrs. Graham and Dodd, in the most recent edition of their text, also get on the "Present-Value Bandwagon," which by now seems to be *"the"* basic principle in all major stock valuation models.

The authors are probably the most conservative of all the writers mentioned in this study so far, because of the limitations placed on growth projections. The maximum growth period which they consider in any of their techniques is 10 years. In one method they even bring the limit down to seven years.

The authors present two methods of their own described below and in their text (pp. 536–38). Following Molodovsky, they assume a single discount rate of 7.5 percent for all companies no matter whether high, medium, or low quality, an assumption criticized by Bauman. The authors also follow Molodovsky in assuming a normal price/earnings ratio. The authors assume a normal pay-out ratio of 60 percent. They mention, however, that this ratio is fairly high for good growth companies. The higher the growth rate the smaller the pay-out ratio usually becomes. For this reason, the authors do not follow the other writers in capitalizing dividends. Dividends become almost meaningless for good growth stocks, and they consider earnings as much more representative of such a firm's current and future income potential.

Method A. This approach, referred to as their "preferred method," projects earnings growth for only the next seven years. A multiplier is applied to the average of the next seven years' earnings, that is to the fourth year's earnings. The multiplier, of course, depends on the expected rate of growth for the next seven years, but will lie within the range of 13 to 20 because of the limits on the growth rate from 3½ percent to 20 percent set by the authors.

The following table, illustrated in their text *Security Analysis,* was developed on the basis of the above parameters:

TABLE 39–4

Expected Rate of Growth (Four Years)	Multiplier of Average (4th Year Earnings)	Multiplier of Current Earnings
3.5%	13×	15×
5.0	14×	17×
7.2	15×	20×
10.0	16×	23½×
12.0	17×	27×
14.3	18×	31×
17.0	19×	35½×
20.0	20×	41½×

---

[10] B. Graham, D. L. Dodd, and S. Cottle, *Security Analysis* (New York: McGraw-Hill Book Co., 1962), chap. 39.

Method B. Graham and Dodd advance two other formulas which yield similar results.

(B-1) Value = 8.6T plus 2.1, where T is the tenth-year compound amount of $1.00 of present earnings growing at any assumed rate. The reader may be reminded that we still work under the assumption of .60 pay-out and 7.5 percent discount rate. The growth period in this method is assumed to be 10 years.

A 2.5 percent growth rate will yield T = $1.28, and here the multiplier is
$$(8.6 \times 1.28) + 2.1 = 13.1$$
and a 10 percent growth rate will show a multiplier of 24.4 times.
$$(8.6 \times 2.59) + 2.1 = 24.4$$

(B-2) Value = current "normal" earnings $\times$ (8.5 + 2G), where G is the average annual growth expected for the next 7 to 10 years. "Normal" earnings are those as they would appear on a smoothed-out earnings curve or "trend line." The authors have arrived at this formula from the finding that a multiplier of 8.5 is appropriate for a company with zero expected growth, and a 2½ percent growth rate calls for a multiplier of 13.5.

A 10 percent growth rate will show a multiplier of 8.5 + (2 $\times$ 10) = 28.5, as compared with 24.4 in the first formula.

As mentioned before, Graham and Dodd's methods for valuing growth issues bear evidence of extreme conservatism in recommending the use of short periods of anticipated growth and relatively low residual growth rates and multipliers. Other writers express conservatism in different ways. Clendenin and Bauman assign a higher discount rate to years in the distant future, rather than limit estimates to 10 years. Graham and Dodd, on the other hand, disregard any higher than "average" growth rate later than 10 years hence.

As with other analysts cited, Graham and Dodd do not advise the reader on how to select the proper growth rate. Whereas past trends definitely are an important factor to consider, they should not be the sole factor. Simple projection of past trends can also lead to results far too optimistic.

Application of Technique No. 5 to General Motors Common Stock

Method A. A 5.3 percent growth rate calls for a multiplier of about 14.2 to be applied to the fourth year's earnings, or a multiplier of about 17.4 applied to current earnings (according to Table 39–4 shown above).

17.4 $\times$ $5.56 = $96.74 is the intrinsic value.

Method B.

(B-1) 8.6T + 2.1
    8.6 (1.68) + 2.1 = 14.45 + 2.1 = 16.55
    Value = 16.55 $\times$ $5.56 = $92.02 value

(B-2) Current earnings $\times$ (8.5 + 2G)
    (I assume that $5.56 is the current normal earnings figure)
    $5.56 $\times$ (8.5 + 10.6)
    $5.56 $\times$ 19.1 = $106.20 value

Technique No. 6—Jeremy C. Jenks[11]

Jeremy C. Jenks, associated with C. J. Lawrence and Sons, a New York Stock Exchange member firm, criticizes existing methods of comparative valuation because they are either based on price/earnings ratios or on price/dividend ratios. He argues that "no *one* approach will give satisfactory results in a wide variety of common stocks . . . because there are *two* "investment" reasons for owning common stocks . . . dividend income and hope of capital appreciation if the company grows." Thus there really is no sharp dividing line between an "income stock" and a "growth stock."

In this technique, two different multipliers are computed (as in Walter), one to be applied to the dividend from one set of factors, and another multiplier from another set of factors, to be applied to the earnings retained in the business. The two resultant values are added together in order to obtain "the value" of the stock.

The dividend multiplier is based on the assumption that the value of a dividend is a function of:

(1) The yield on high grade, money rate, taxable bonds (Lawrence uses governments);
(2) The quality of the dividend.

For quality classifications, the author uses rating scales from A to F (similar to ratings of bonds) applied as follows:

The best dividend is worth 1 percent current return basis less than long-term Government bond yields. Each graduation in quality is marked down an additional ½ percent. (Page 9 of booklet)

A dividend's quality is determined by the following five factors:

(1) Debt + Pref. as percent of Capital
(2) Debt + Pref. as percent of Working Capital
(3) Pay-out (in percent)
(4) Drop in the Net Earnings in 1958 from the 1956–57 peak
(5) Total Plow Back as percent of Equity

For the ratings which are assigned by these five factors the author has developed tables (see page 5 of C. J. Lawrence booklet).

The price/earnings multiples used at various levels of yields for long Governments are as follows:

Yield, Long Governments

Rating	3%	3½%	4%	4½%	5%	5½%
A	27.5	25	22.2	20	18.2	16.7
B	25	22.2	20	18.2	16.7	15.4
C	22.2	20	18.2	16.7	15.4	14.3
D	20	18.2	16.7	15.4	14.3	13.3
E	18.2	16.7	15.4	14.3	13.3	12.5
F	16.7	15.4	14.3	13.3	12.5	11.8

---

[11] C. J. Lawrence, "Comparative Valuation of Common Stocks," a booklet published by Cyrus J. Lawrence & Sons, New York, 1959.

He used an average of several of the long Government issues. The following bonds seemed representative to him at the time of his writing:

			Yield	
		12/10/58	10/23/59	1/7/60
3¼%	May, 1985............3.73		3.92	4.39
3½%	February, 1990.........3.83		4.05	4.43
3%	February, 1995.........3.59		3.81	4.11

The Retained Earnings Multiple is based on the growth prospects of the business. Lawrence employs three measurements:

(1) The historic rate of growth in earnings. Any large fluctuations are corrected by sales trends.
(2) The 3-year average plow back as a percent of equity is designed to show the company's ability to finance growth internally.
(3) The 3-year average expansion factor is intended to measure the company's efforts to grow.

By averaging these three factors the authors hope to get some indication of the growth potential of a company.

The following table of multipliers is derived which corresponds to certain growth rates:

GROWTH FACTOR—PRICE—RETAINED EARNINGS MULTIPLES

0............ 8.9×	8%.........14.0×	16%.........22.1×
1%......... 9.5×	9%.........14.8×	17%.........23.4×
2%.........10.0×	10%.........15.7×	18%.........24.8×
3%.........10.5×	11%.........16.7×	19%.........26.2×
4%.........11.1×	12%.........17.6×	20%.........27.8×
5%.........11.7×	13%.........18.6×	25%.........37.0×
6%.........12.4×	14%.........19.6×	30%.........48.0×
7%.........13.2×	15%.........20.9×	35%.........90.0×

Jenks develops retained earnings multiples by use of compound interest tables but making a 2 percent negative adjustment.

The Jenks (Lawrence) method employs a final adjustment factor to each valuation, based largely upon the size and relative importance of the company in its industry. In the illustration below, it can be seen that the adjustment factor for General Motors was 130 percent.

APPLICATION OF TECHNIQUE NO. 6 TO GENERAL MOTORS COMMON STOCK

An application of the Jenks valuation approach to the stock of General Motors follows: The following valuation can be compared with a 1961 valuation of General Motors by Cyrus J. Lawrence & Sons, which, using a dividend multiplier of 18.1 and an earnings multiplier of 8.6, and applying these to estimated annual earnings of $3.11 for 1961 and $4.00 for 1962, resulted in estimated valuations of $50.50 and $58.10 before adjustment and $65.70 and $75.50 after adjustment.[12]

---

[12] C. J. Lawrence and Sons, *General Motors Corporation in the World Automobile Market* (New York, May, 1962).

	Government Yield Basis		
Dividend Rating	%	Rating	4% *Multiple*
Debt is pfd. percent cap. (1963 figure)..... 7.6		B	20
Debt is pfd. S.C. (1963 figure).......... 14.6		B	20
Current payout—(1963)................. 72.2		E	15.4
Drop in net 1961–62 to 1963............ 0		A	22.2
Average plow back percent equity....... 6.0		D	16.7
Average......................			18.9

Growth Rating	%	*Multiple*
Growth in earnings............................ 5.3		11.9
Average plow back percent equity................ 7.0		13.2
Average expansion factor........................ 7.9		13.9
Average..		13.0
Consistency factor..........................		70
Adjusted multiple..........................		9.1

No. of Shares (12/31/63)—Total 286,653,007 Shares

Earnings	*Actual 1963*	*Estimated 1964*
Gross plant.....................	7,967 mil.	7,967 mil.
Sales to gross plant.................	2.08	2.26
Sales...........................	16,495 mil.	18,000 mil.
Net income......................	1,592 mil.	2,140 mil.
Pfd. div........................	13 mil.	13 mil.
Net for common..................	1,578 mil.	2,127 mil.
Net per share....................	$5.56	$6.00
Div. per share...................	$4.00	$4.80
Retained per share...............	$1.56	$1.50
Div. cap. at *18.9*..................	$75.60	$85.05
Retained cap. at *9.1*...............	14.2	13.65
Estimated values..................	89.8	98.70
Adjusted est. values*.............	116.7	129.30

* Net income over 200 million. The estimated values are multiplied by 130 percent.

It can be seen that the application of the Jenks technique results in an adjusted value for General Motors of $129.30.

Technique No. 7—William Kurtz

William Kurtz of Hemphill Noyes and Co., has developed a somewhat different adaptation of the present value method described in a company memorandum entitled "Valuation Standards for Investments," which involves three steps:

(1) A price/earnings multiple of 14 as a normal ratio for a nongrowth stock.

(2) A growth rate adjustment (five-year compound interest factor at the assumed growth rate) which is multiplied by the standard (14).

(3) An investment quality rating which rates issues as Premium quality (1.33), Standard (1.00), and Discount (.67) and permits intermediate quality rating multipliers.

Application of Technique No. 7 to General Motors Common Stock

Based on these elements, the value of General Motors common, assuming a 5.3 percent growth factor (for five years as the maximum growth period allowed) might be estimated as follows:

> 14.0 × 1.28 (compound amount of $1 for 5 years at 5.3%) × 1.10 (quality adjustment factor for General Motors) = $109.58.

This technique has the simplifying advantage of eliminating the selection of a growth period, assuming a standard maximum of five years. Its disadvantage, of course, lies in this very assumption, and in the subjective determination of a quality rating. Others may take issue with the assumed normal price/earnings ratio of 14 for a nongrowth issue.

SUMMARY

Virtually all the techniques examined have been directed toward the estimation of "intrinsic" value, although some of the methods were more directly aimed toward the determination of price/earnings or price/dividend ratios. Most of the methods require that the analyst make a separate and in most cases a subjective estimate of future growth rates. Jenks' technique is somewhat distinctive in that he relies entirely upon historical data and short-run estimates of current earnings.

A wide range of growth assumptions are illustrated in the several techniques discussed, in many cases without providing any guidance for the analyst as to the method of selecting a growth rate to be applied to a particular issue. So-called residual or normal growth rates range from 2.5 percent to 4 percent and residual multipliers vary from 13 to 17.1. These differences are frequently the principal factors accounting for the relatively wide range of valuations established by using the various methods shown in Table A, which provides a review of the assumptions and valuation results.

The highest valuations resulted from the methods of Bauman, Jenks, and Kurtz, whereas the Value Line approach and the Graham and Dodd methods resulted in the lowest estimated values. Bauman's high figure is a result of three factors, a long "transitional" period, a not very high (the second lowest) discount rate, and a high (the highest of all methods) residual growth rate. A 10-year transitional period with an initial growth rate of 6 percent was used in order to have a 5.3 percent average growth rate as in the other methods. A relatively high normal, nongrowth price/earnings ratio and the subjective quality rating multiplier account for Kurt's high estimate.

Two of the techniques (Clendenin and Bauman) are based upon the use of a multiplier applied to future dividends, three methods are based on earnings, while the third, Jenks' uses a combination of earnings and dividends. The techniques examined reveal an implied pay-out ratio in the dividend multipliers similar to that for General Motors (70 percent). It is obvious that the differences in the resultant valuations would have been greater if the pay-out ratio on General Motors were subsequently different. The important question appears to be, not whether a multiplier should be applied to earnings or dividends, but whether it can anticipate

TABLE A

COMPARISON OF ASSUMPTIONS AND VALUATIONS FOR
SEVEN GROWTH STOCK VALUATION TECHNIQUES

Technique	Growth Rate (%)	Growth Duration (Years)	Discount Rate	Residual Growth Rate (%)	Value
1. Clendenin	5.3	10	4%, 5%, 6%, 7%	None	$101.60
2. Bauman	5.3	10 (trans. period)	6.2%	4	119.60
3. Ferguson	5.3		Current market P/E multiplier		102.86 (maximum)
4. Molodovsky	See text of Molodovsky's article in this issue. [No. 32, pages 414–450, above]				
5. Graham & Dodd Method A	5.3	7	7.5%	3.5	96.74
Method B-1 $(8.6T + 2.1)$	5.3	10	7.5%	2.5	92.02
Method B-2 $(8.5 + 2G)$	5.3	10	7.5%	2.5	106.20
6. Lawrence (Jenks)	5.3		Variable rates for dividends and retained earnings		129.30
7. Kurtz	5.3	5	Basic market multiplier of 14 × earnings		109.58

the relative weight which will be given to dividends and earnings in the market.

It should be pointed out that the discount rates shown in Table A are not strictly comparable, since in some cases (Molodovsky, Graham and Dodd), they apply to both dividend income and price appreciation, while in others (Clendenin and Bauman), they apply only to dividend income. In the case of the Ferguson and Kurtz models, the multipliers are applied to total earnings and represent the reciprocals of discount rates.

The Ferguson technique makes no explicit assumptions about growth rate, growth duration, or discount rates. Ferguson merely examines the growth rate and duration inherent in the current market price and compares them with the components contained in a standard such as the DJIA. By his method, realtive to the standard, General Motors' growth potential warrants a maximum price of $102.86, slightly more than $8 over the current market price. Much depends, in his method, upon the so-called standard growth rate assumed.

Jenks' method also does not lend itself to a simple check on the basic assumptions as the majority of approaches do, since it is largely based on historical data. Since his technique is not based upon long-term projections, the method does not employ present value techniques. It can be noted that the so-called adjustment factor used in the Lawrence technique adds $25 to $30 to the resultant share value. This factor adds an important element of subjectivity to Jenks' technique. Mr. Jenks reports that new simplified valuation methods have been developed by his firm using Standard and Poor's Compustat tapes.

CONCLUSIONS

It is apparent that widely differing values can be assigned to growth stocks by varying the assumptions concerning future growth rates and duration of growth and by applying different discount rates to future dividend returns. None of the valuation techniques discussed provide any accurate method for estimating future growth rates or duration.

What then is the operational usefulness of these techniques? It can be argued that the application of these valuation methods will provide rough guidelines to a "range of values" for growth stocks under consistent assumptions. Assuming that an analyst is prepared to establish his own discount rates and time horizon for estimating future growth, the range of indicated values will be relatively narrow, as can be noted in Table A. The values for General Motors assuming a 10-year growth period at 5.3 percent per annum and a 7.5 percent discount rate are in a very close range. The differences noted are due to the varying assumed residual growth rates, which will influence the multipliers applied to earnings at the conclusion of the growth period. This element of prediction involves a high degree of uncertainty, since it not only requires judgment with respect to long-term growth, but also implies that the analyst can forecast price/earning ratios which will prevail in the distant future. Graham and Dodd maintain that the use of a short-growth period and a long-term average multiplier for residual earnings adds a "safety factor" to security analysis, which by its very nature involves a high degree of uncertainty.

Viewing the difficulty of forecasting long-term future corporate earnings, it would appear that the weight of evidence should favor the use of growth periods of 10 years or less. This has the further advantage that it should make less uncertain and difficult any forecast of residual growth rates and multipliers, since it brings them closer. The assumption of a gradual rather than an abrupt decline in growth rates, as Bauman and Molodovsky recommend, also seems warranted. It must be recognized, however, that adherence to these relatively conservative assumptions leaves the more distant future to be eyed with varying degrees of optimism by professional and amateur crystal gazers, and thus leaves the final judgment as to over- or undervaluation to the market place.

The recent availability of Standard and Poor's Compustat tapes has opened up new horizons for multiple regression analysis of stock market data. Economists at the Bank of New York and Trust Company have assumed a leading role in cross-sectional multiple regression analysis of stock prices, earnings, and dividends based on the Compustat tapes. Whitbeck and Kisor describe this analytical technique in the *Financial Analysts Journal* for May–June, 1963.[13] Regressing current average market price/earnings ratios on estimated growth rates, dividend pay-out (supplemented by indexes of stability and marketability), they derive an average multiple regression equation for 135 representative issues. Using the coefficients from this equation, they derive theoretical price/earnings ratios for individual issues, based upon their current estimates of growth, dividend payout, etc. By comparing these with actual prevailing price/earnings ratios (assuming "normalized" earnings), they derive indexes of relative under- or overpricing in the market for individual stocks.

The most significant potential for stock valuation techniques embodied in this cross-sectional multiple regression analysis of stock prices (and price/earnings ratios) lies in the comparison of changes over time in the relative weights accorded in the market to expected growth in earnings and dividend payout. It is of further consequence, of course, to examine the relationship between price/earnings ratios, estimated growth rates and dividend payout by individual industries or groups of industries to shed further light upon the diversity of investor expectations over time and among different stock groups. This should provide a test of the validity of the valuation technique described above. Such analysis may pave the way to greater insight into the behavioristic characteristics of security investors over time and shed more light on the never-ending academic discussions concerning the relative weight attached by investors to dividends versus earnings.

---

[13] Volkert S. Whitbeck and Manown Kisor, Jr., "A New Tool in Investment Decision Making," *Financial Analysts Journal*, Volume 19, No. 3 (May–June, 1963), pp. 55–62. The authors illustrate the derivation of a theoretical price/earnings ratio and an estimated value for General Motors Common Stock ($51), based upon estimated market parameters as of June 8, 1962 (p. 58).

APPENDIX A

TABLE I

Approximate present values of all future dividends on a stock now paying $1.00 per annum, if the dividend is expected to increase at the indicated compound rate for the indicated period of years and then remain stable until 100 years from today, and if the payments of the first decade are discounted at 4 percent, those of the second at 5 percent, those of the third at 6 percent, and those of the remaining 70 years at 7 percent.

Growth Period	\multicolumn{5}{c}{Annual Growth Rates}
	5%	4%	3%	1%	0%
None...........	$17.01	$17.01	$17.01	$17.01	$17.01
10 years.........	24.85	23.04	21.37	18.37	17.01
20 years.........	31.21	27.51	24.27	19.12	17.01
30 years.........	35.97	30.55	26.08	19.51	17.01
40 years.........	39.65	32.67	27.22	19.69	17.01
50 years.........	42.63	34.23	27.99	19.80	17.01

TABLE II

Approximate present values of the future dividends on a stock now paying $1.00 per annum, if the dividends are expected to grow at the indicated rates for 20 years and then remain stable for the next 80 years, and if the dividends of the first decade are discounted at 4 percent, those of the second at 5 percent, those of the third at 6 percent, and those of the remaining 70 years at 7 percent.

Growth Rate per year	\multicolumn{5}{c}{Present Values}
	First Decade	Second Decade	Third Decade	Next 70 Years	Total
6 percent........	$10.85	$11.36	$7.36	$5.96	$35.53
5 percent........	10.35	9.84	6.09	4.93	31.21
4 percent........	9.87	8.53	5.03	4.08	27.51
3 percent........	9.40	7.37	4.14	3.36	24.27
2 percent........	8.96	6.39	3.41	2.76	21.52
1 percent........	8.53	5.52	2.80	2.27	19.12
0 percent........	8.11	4.74	2.30	1.86	17.01

NOTE: These tables and similar Appendix tables are calculated on the assumption that each year's dividend is received at the year end, and that it contains the full year's growth element. The shortcut calculation methods which were used may underestimate some of the values by as much as 1½ percent. Slide rule computations were used.

APPENDIX B

VARIABLE RATE TABLE B-6

10-Year Transitional Period
Price-Dividend Ratios

Initial Growth Rates (Percent)	5%	6%	6½%	7%	8%	9%	10%	12%
Depressed:								
0	29.6	22.4	20.0	18.1	15.1	13.0	11.4	9.1
1	31.1	23.6	21.0	18.9	15.8	13.5	11.9	9.5
2	32.6	24.7	22.0	19.8	16.5	14.2	12.4	9.9
3	34.3	25.9	23.1	20.8	17.3	14.8	12.9	10.3
Constant:								
4	36.0	27.2	24.2	21.7	18.1	15.5	13.5	10.8
High:								
5	37.8	28.5	25.3	22.8	18.9	16.2	14.1	11.2
6	39.7	29.9	26.5	23.8	19.8	16.9	14.7	11.7
8	43.6	32.8	29.1	26.1	21.6	18.4	16.0	12.7
10	48.0	36.0	31.9	28.6	23.6	20.1	17.4	13.7
12	52.7	39.4	34.9	31.3	25.8	21.9	19.0	14.9
14	57.9	43.2	38.2	34.2	28.2	23.8	20.6	16.1
16	63.4	47.3	41.8	37.4	30.7	26.0	22.4	17.5
18	69.5	51.7	45.7	40.8	33.5	28.2	24.3	18.9
20	76.1	56.5	49.9	44.5	36.5	30.7	26.4	20.5
25	95.1	70.3	61.9	55.2	45.0	37.8	32.4	24.9
30	118.2	87.1	76.6	68.1	55.4	46.3	39.6	30.3
35	146.1	107.4	94.3	83.7	67.8	56.6	48.2	36.6
40	179.9	131.8	115.5	102.4	82.8	68.8	58.5	44.2
50	268.7	196.0	171.3	151.6	121.9	100.9	85.3	63.8
60	394.8	286.7	250.2	220.8	176.9	145.8	122.7	91.1
70	570.7	413.2	359.8	317.1	253.1	207.9	174.4	128.6

Current Growth Stock Valuation Methods: General Motors 453

APPENDIX C

Growth Stock Nomograph

34

EARNINGS GROWTH AND PRICE CHANGE IN THE SAME TIME PERIOD[*]

Joseph E. Murphy, Jr., C.F.A.

Frequently, the most important determinant of the rate of return in equity investments is the rate and direction of price change.[1] Success in investments, if it not be due to chance, is largely a function of the ability to predict price changes. The importance of predicting price changes has led to a number of studies aimed at discovering the determinants of price change. These studies may be conveniently classified into three groups: first, those studies that sought to predict future price changes from past price changes; second, those investigations that attempted to predict price changes from price ratios, such as the price/earnings ratio; and third, those studies which sought to predict price changes from past changes in other variables, such as earnings.

In the last decade a score of studies were made which attempted to discover whether future price changes could be predicted from past price changes. The results were generally disappointing. It was found that successive price changes tended to be independent; the price change of a stock in one period had little bearing on the price change in the next period. Moreover, the relative price change of a stock (relative to other stocks) in one period was not indicative of the relative price change of that stock in the next period.[2]

---

[*] Reprinted by permission of the *Financial Analysts Journal* (January–February 1968).

[1] All references to price changes or to earnings changes are to rates of change. This study was made possible through the assistance of the Numerical Analysis Center of the University of Minnesota, which provided time on its Control Data 1604 computer, and also through the assistance of the School of Business Center of the University of Minnesota. All of the data used refers to per share data.

[2] Studies presenting this evidence are contained in P. H. Cootner, ed. *The Random Character of Stock Prices*, M.I.T. Press, 1964. Independence of successive earnings changes may be the cause of independence in stock price changes. See J. E. Murphy, "Relative Growth of Earnings Per Share—Past and Future," *Financial Analysts Journal*, November–December 1966, pp. 73–76. A. C. Rayner and I.M.D. Little, *Higgledy Piggledy Growth Again*, Basil Blackwell, Oxford, 1966. Richard A. Brealey, "Statistical Properties of Successive Changes in Earnings," an address delivered to the Seminar in Security Prices, Chicago, March 1967.

Although the full import of the results of these studies is not yet clear, the studies certainly have important implications for financial analysis. Some have concluded that the results call into question the very utility of fundamental financial analysis.[3] This conclusion was certainly premature and may be questioned, as will be shown below.

The results of the second and third groups of studies were only partly encouraging. The correlation between price ratios and future price changes, though promising, was frequently neither significant nor positive, and price changes in one period tended to be independent of earnings changes in the preceding period.[4]

None of the studies were devoted to the question of the relation between relative earnings changes and relative price changes in the same period. This question should probably have been examined first. Even though previous earnings growth was unrelated to present changes in prices, perhaps percentage changes in prices and earnings in the same period were highly correlated. Per share earnings growth could still have a substantial influence on simultaneous price changes. If there were little connection between relative earnings changes and price changes in the same period, then the ability to predict relative earnings changes might be of limited value. If, on the contrary, there were high correlation between relative earnings changes and relative price changes in the same period, then the ability to predict relative earnings changes would be extremely important.[5] The purpose of this article is to report the results of a study of the influence of rates of growth of per share earnings on percentage changes in stock prices in the same period.

Test Procedure

In this study prices were defined as the average of the monthly high and low stock price during the calendar year. Earnings per share are reported earnings during the same year, adjusted to exclude the effect of nonrecurrent charges or income.[6] The sample consisted of 203 companies from 10 different industries. Separate tests were made for each industry. The industries tested were auto parts (12 companies), building materials

---

[3] E. F. Fama, "Random Walks in Stock Market Prices," *Financial Analysts Journal*, Sept.–Oct. '65, pp. 55–58.

[4] H. A. Latane, "Price Changes in Equity Securities," *Journal of Finance*, September 1951, pp. 252–264. J. D. McWilliams, "Prices, Earnings, and P-E Ratios," *Financial Analysts Journal*, May–June 1966, pp. 137–142. S. F. Nicholson, "Price-Earnings Ratios," *Financial Analysts Journal*, July–August 1960, pp. 43–46. H. S. Schneider, "Two Formula Methods for Choosing Common Stocks," *Journal of Finance*, June 1951, pp. 221–237. M. FG. Scott, "Relative Share Prices and Yields," *Oxford Economic Papers*, October 1962, pp. 218–250. D. L. Tuttle, "An Analysis of Annual Changes in Prices of Equity Securities," unpublished Ph.D. dissertation, University of North Carolina, 1965.

[5] The data is taken from The Value Line Investment Survey, Arnold Bernhard & Co., Inc., New York, N.Y.

[6] See Footnote 2 above.

(25), chemical (20), drug (13), electric machinery and electronics (16), electric utility (44), machinery (17), natural gas (25), petroleum (19), and steel (12).

The tests were designed to determine whether the companies experiencing the highest percentage growth in earnings per share in one period also recorded the highest percentage increase in price during the same period.

To provide reasonable coverage of different time periods, tests were made for each of five different time periods: one year, two years, three years, four years, and five years. To eliminate the effect of unusual years, 10 tests were made for each of the five time periods. All periods tested ended in one of the ten years 1955, 1956, . . . 1963, 1964. Five hundred separate tests were made altogether.

In conducting a test for one period for one industry, all companies in the industry were ranked in order of percent growth of earnings in that period. Then the companies were classified into five equal groups, or quintiles. The companies recording the highest growth of earnings per share were placed in the first quintile; the companies recording the next highest growth in earnings per share were placed in the second quintile, etc. Those companies with the lowest increases in earnings per share were placed in the fifth quintile. When the above steps had been completed, the percentage change in price was computed for each company in each quintile. Then, for each quintile the average percentage change in price was found.

Results of the Tests

In five-year periods, and also in four-year periods, the quintile with the highest rate of earnings growth tended to achieve the greatest price increase in the same period. This was true of all 10 industries tested, without exception. While the tables for individual industries are not presented here, the aggregate results for all industries are shown in Table I. As that table reveals, of the 100 tests on five-year periods, the first quintile in five-year earnings growth ranked in the first quintile in price appreciation in 15 tests and last in price appreciation in no tests. The lowest quintile in earnings growth over a five-year period ranked lowest in price appreciation in the same five-year period in 82 of 100 tests. The lowest quintile in earnings growth ranked first in price appreciation in only one test. These tests indicate that price changes and earnings changes in the same five-year periods were highly correlated.

A very high, but slightly lower, correspondence between relative growth of per share earnings and simultaneous price appreciation characterizes four-year periods in all industries. To a lesser extent percentage changes of per share earnings and prices are highly correlated in all industries in concurrent three-year periods.

In one- and two-year periods relative earnings growth and price appreciation still show a high degree of correlation in the aggregate. As may be

TABLE I
EARNINGS GROWTH AND PRICE CHANGE (10 INDUSTRIES)

EARNINGS CHANGE IN 1 YEAR AND PRICE CHANGE IN THE SAME YEAR

Earnings Growth Quintile	\multicolumn{5}{c}{Number of Years in Which Price Change Ranked}
	First	Second	Third	Fourth	Fifth
First (High Growth)	50	25	18	5	2
Second	18	38	21	14	9
Third	12	15	30	31	12
Fourth	12	13	23	28	24
Fifth (Low Growth)	6	9	8	22	53

EARNINGS CHANGE IN 5 YEARS AND PRICE CHANGE IN THE SAME 5 YEARS

Earnings Growth Quintile	Number of Years in Which Price Change Ranked				
	First	Second	Third	Fourth	Fifth
First (High Growth)	75	17	5	3	0
Second	16	54	25	4	1
Third	4	19	52	21	4
Fourth	4	7	14	62	13
Fifth (Low Growth)	1	3	4	10	82

TABLE II
CONCURRENT ANNUAL RATES OF CHANGE IN PRICES AND EARNINGS

Earnings Growth Quintile	1 Year Period		5 Year Period	
	Price	Earnings	Price	Earnings
First (High Growth)	17.4%	37.3%	18.3%	14.2%
Second	13.5	16.5	13.4	8.2
Third	10.7	8.4	11.1	5.2
Fourth	7.5	1.0	7.8	1.7
Fifth (Low Growth)	3.2	−13.8	3.9	−3.8

seen in Table I, the top earnings growth quintile in one-year periods ranked in the first price change quintile in 50 of 100 tests, in the second quintile in 25 tests, and in the bottom price change quintile in only two tests. The lowest quintile in earings growth was last in price change in 53 tests and first in only 8 tests.

In some industries the correlation between earnings growth and price change in one-year periods was much higher than in other industries. Earnings growth and price change in the same one-year period are highly correlated in the chemical, drug, natural gas, and electric utility industries. The correlation between simultaneous one-year earnings growth and price appreciation is somewhat lower in the building materials and the electric machinery and electronics industries. The relationship is very low in one-year periods in the auto parts, machinery, petroleum, and steel industries. In all industries the correlation increases between earnings growth and price appreciation in the same period as the time period is increased from one to five years.

Average annual rates of change of prices and earnings for one-year and five-year periods are shown in Table II. In one-year periods the average rate of price change was 17.2 percent for companies in the highest earnings growth quintile. Companies in the lowest earnings growth quintile averaged a 3.2 percent increase in price. Results for the five-year periods are similar. Companies in the highest earnings growth group recorded an average annual increase in price of 18.3 percent. Companies in the lowest earnings growth quintile recorded a mean increase in price of 3.9 percent.

Conclusion

The results of above tests indicate that there is a very high correlation between relative growth of per share earnings and relative percentage changes in stock prices in the same period. Those companies recording the highest rates of growth of earnings per share show the greatest gains in market price in the same period. Companies recording the lowest earnings growth, or greatest declines of per share earnings, record the smallest price appreciation or the steepest percentage declines in price. This correspondence was true of all 10 industries studied over extended periods—four to five years—and of most industries studied over shorter periods—one to two years.

These results reaffirm one of the basic premises of traditional security analysis: that fundamental variables, such as earnings growth, have a substantial bearing on changes in market prices. When combined with an earlier result—independence of relative past and future rates of earnings change[7]—the high correlation between rates of changes of earnings and prices in the same period provides a partial explanation of randomness in stock prices. If relative past and future rates of earnings change are independent and rates of earnings change are highly correlated with rates of price change, then successive relative percentage price changes would tend to be independent. A further possibility suggested by the results obtained in these tests is that relative price/earnings ratios would tend to be highly stable: The companies with relatively high price/earnings ratios would always tend to have relatively high price/earnings ratios and vice versa. This suggestion stems from the mathematical fact that if prices and earnings of individual stocks tend to move in the same direction at the same relative rates, their relative price/earnings ratios would tend to remain unchanged. From the viewpoint of the practicing analyst, the most important aspect of the results described above is that superior market performance will come from selecting those stocks which will record relatively superior earnings gains. Therefore, the primary effort of the analyst should be not merely to project future earnings of individual companies, but to project relative future performance so as to distinguish those companies which will show the highest percentage earnings gains from those which will record the lowest percentage gains. In this sense, the tests substantiate what is practiced by many analysts today.

[7] See Footnote 2 above.

RANDOM WALKS IN STOCK MARKET PRICES*

Eugene F. Fama

For many years economists, statisticians, and teachers of finance have been interested in developing and testing models of stock price behavior. One important model that has evolved from this research is the theory of random walks. This theory casts serious doubt on many other methods for describing and predicting stock price behavior—methods that have considerable popularity outside the academic world. For example, we shall see later that if the random walk theory is an accurate description of reality, then the various "technical" or "chartist" procedures for predicting stock prices are completely without value.

In general the theory of random walks raises challenging questions for anyone who has more than a passing interest in understanding the behavior of stock prices. Unfortunately, however, most discussions of the theory have appeared in technical academic journals and in a form which the nonmathematician would usually find incomprehensible. This article describes, briefly and simply, the theory of random walks and some of the important issues it raises concerning the work of market analysts. To preserve brevity some aspects of the theory and its implications are omitted. More complete (and also more technical) discussions of the theory of random walks are available elsewhere; hopefully the introduction provided here will encourage the reader to examine one of the most rigorous and lengthy works listed at the end of this article.

COMMON TECHNIQUES FOR PREDICTING STOCK MARKET PRICES

In order to put the theory of random walks into perspective we first discuss, in brief and general terms, the two approaches to predicting stock prices that are commonly espoused by market professionals. These are (1) "chartist" or "technical" theories and (2) the theory of fundamental or intrinsic value analysis.

The basic assumption of all the chartist or technical theories is that history tends to repeat itself, i.e., past patterns of price behavior in

---

* Reprinted by permission of the *Financial Analysts Journal* (September–October 1965).

individual securities will tend to recur in the future. Thus the way to predict stock prices (and, of course, increase one's potential gains) is to develop a familiarity with past patterns of price behavior in order to recognize situations of likely recurrence.

Essentially, then, chartist techniques attempt to use knowledge of the past behavior of a price series to predict the probable future behavior of the series. A statistician would characterize such techniques as assuming that successive price changes in individual securities are dependent. That is, the various chartist theories assume that the *sequence* of price changes prior to any given day is important in predicting the price change for that day.[1]

The techniques of the chartist have always been surrounded by a certain degree of mysticism, however, and as a result most market professionals have found them suspect. Thus it is probably safe to say that the pure chartist is relatively rare among stock market analysts. Rather the typical analyst adheres to a technique known as fundamental analysis or the intrinsic value method. The assumption of the fundamental analysis approach is that at any point in time an individual security has an intrinsic value (or in the terms of the economist, an equilibrium price) which depends on the earning potential of the security. The earning potential of the security depends in turn on such fundamental factors as quality of management, outlook for the industry and the economy, etc.

Through a careful study of these fundamantal factors the analyst should, in principle, be able to determine whether the actual price of a security is above or below its intrinsic value. If actual prices tend to move toward intrinsic values, then attempting to determine the intrinsic value of a security is equivalent to making a prediction of its future price; and this is the essence of the predictive procedure implicit in fundamental analysis.

The Theory of Random Walks

Chartist theories and the theory of fundamental analysis are really the province of the market professional and to a large extent teachers of finance. Historically, however, there has been a large body of academic people, primarily economists and statisticians, who adhere to a radically different approach to market analysis—the theory of random walks in stock market prices. The remainder of this article will be devoted to a discussion of this theory and its major implications.

Random walk theorists usually start from the premise that the major security exchanges are good examples of "efficient" markets. An "efficient" market is defined as a market where there are large numbers of rational profit-maximizers actively competing, with each trying to predict future market values of individual securities, and where important current information is almost freely available to all participants.

---

[1] Probably the best-known example of the chartist approach to predicting stock prices is the Dow Theory.

In an efficient market, competition among the many intelligent participants leads to a situation where, at any point in time, actual prices of individual securities already reflect the effects of information based both on events that have already occurred and on events which, as of now, the market expects to take place in the future. In other words, in an efficient market at any point in time the actual price of a security will be a good estimate of its intrinsic value.

Now in an uncertain world the intrisnic value of a security can never be determined exactly. Thus there is always room for disagreement among market participants concerning just what the intrinsic value of an individual security is, and such disagreement will give rise to discrepancies between actual prices and intrinsic values. In an efficient market, however, the actions of the many competing participants should cause the actual price of a security to wander randomly about its intrinsic value. If the discrepancies between actual prices and intrinsic values are systematic rather than random in nature, then knowledge of this should help intelligent market participants to better predict the path by which actual prices will move towards intrinsic values. When the many intelligent traders attempt to take advantage of this knowledge, however, they will tend to neutralize such systematic behavior in price series. Although uncertainty concerning intrinsic values will remain, actual prices of securities will wander randomly about their intrinsic values.

Of course intrinsic values can themselves change across time as a result of new information. The new information may involve such things as the success of a current research and development project, a change in management, a tariff imposed on the industry's product by a foreign country, an increase in industrial production, or any other *actual or anticipated* change in a factor which is likely to affect the company's prospects.

In an efficient market, *on the average*, competition will cause the full effects of new information on intrinsic values to be reflected "instantaneously" in actual prices. In fact, however, because there is vagueness or uncertainty surrounding new information, "instantaneous adjustment" really has two implications. First, actual prices will initially overadjust to changes in instrinsic values as often as they will underadjust. Second, the lag in the complete adjustment of actual prices to successive new intrinsic values will itself be an independent, random variable with the adjustment of actual prices sometimes preceding the occurrence of the event which is the basis of the change in intrinsic values (i.e., when the event is anticipated by the market before it actually occurs) and sometimes following.

This means that the "instantaneous adjustment" property of an efficient market implies that successive price changes in individual securities will be independent. A market where successive price changes in individual securities are independent is, by definition, a random walk market. Most simply the theory of random walks implies that a series of stock price changes has no memory—the past history of the series cannot be used to predict the future in any meaningful way. The future path of the price level of a security is no more predictable than the path of a series of cumulated random numbers.

It is unlikely that the random walk hypothesis provides an exact description of the behavior of stock market prices. For practical purposes, however, the model may be acceptable even though it does not fit the facts exactly. Thus although successive price changes may not be strictly independent, the actual amount of dependence may be so small as to be unimportant.

What should be classified as unimportant depends, of course, on the question at hand. For the stock market trader or investor the criterion is obvious: The independence assumption of the random walk model is valid as long as knowledge of the past behavior of the series of price changes cannot be used to increase expected gains. More specifically, if successive price changes for a given security are independent, there is no problem in timing purchases and sales of that security. A simple policy of buying and holding the security will be as good as any more complicated mechanical procedure for timing purchases and sales. This implies that, for investment purposes, the independence assumption of the random walk model is an adequate description of reality as long as the actual degree of dependence in series of price changes is not sufficient to make the expected profits of any more "sophisticated" mechanical trading rule or chartist technique greater than the expected profits under a naïve buy-and-hold policy.

Empirical Evidence on Independence

Over the years a number of empirical tests of the random walk theory have been performed; indeed, so many that it is not possible to discuss them adequately here. Therefore in describing the empirical evidence we limit ourselves to a brief discussion of the different approaches employed and the general conclusions that have evolved.

The main concern of empirical research on the random walk model has been to test the hypothesis that successive price changes are independent. Two different approaches have been followed. First there is the approach that relies primarily on common statistical tools such as serial correlation coefficients and analyses of runs of consecutive price changes of the same sign. If the statistical tests tend to support the assumption of independence, one then *infers* that there are probably no mechanical trading rules or chartist techniques, based solely on patterns in the past history of price changes, which would make the expected profits of the investor greater than they would be with a simple buy-and-hold policy. The second approach to testing independence proceeds by testing directly different mechanical trading rules to see whether or not they provide profits greater than buy-and-hold.

Research to date has tended to concentrate on the first or statistical approach to testing independence; the results have been consistent and impressive. I know of no study in which standard statistical tools have produced evidence of *important* dependence in series of successive price changes. In general, these studies (and there are many of them) have tended to uphold the theory of random walks. This is true, for example, of the serial correlation tests of Cootner [4],[2] Fama [5], Kendall [9], and Moore [10]. In all of these studies, the sample serial correlation coefficients computed for successive price changes were extremely close to zero, which is evidence against important dependence in the changes. Similarly, Fama's [5] analysis of runs of successive price changes of the same sign, and the spectral analysis techniques of Granger and Morgenstern [8], and Godfrey, Granger, and Morgenstern [7] also support the independence assumption of the random walk model.

We should emphasize, however, that although the statistical techniques mentioned above have been the common tools used in testing independence, the chartist or technical theorist probably would not consider them adequate. For example, he would not consider either serial correlations or runs analyses as adequate tests of whether the past history of series of price changes can be used to increase the investor's expected profits. The simple linear relationships that underlie the serial correlation model are much too unsophisticated to pick up the complicated "patterns" that the chartist sees in stock prices. Similarly, the runs tests are much too rigid in their manner of determining the duration of upward and downward movements in prices. In particular: in runs-testing, a run is considered as terminated whenever there is a change in sign in the sequence of successive price changes, regardless of the size of the price change that causes the change in sign. The chartist would like to have a more sophisticated method for identifying movements—a method which does not always predict the termination of the movement simply because the price level has temporarily changed direction.

These criticisms of common statistical tools have not gone unheeded, however. For example, Alexander's filter technique [1, 2] is an attempt to apply more sophisticated criteria to the identification of moves. Although the filter technique does not correspond exactly to any well-known chartist theory, it is closely related to such things as the Dow Theory. Thus, the profitability of the filter technique can be used to make inferences concerning the potential profitability of other mechanical trading rules.

A filter of, say, 5 percent is defined as follows: if the daily closing price of a particular security moves up at least 5 percent, buy and hold the security until its price moves down at least 5 percent from a subsequent high, at which time simultaneously sell and go short. The short position is maintained until the daily closing price rises at least 5 percent above a

---

[2] See References at article's end.

subsequent low, at which time one should simultaneously cover and buy. Moves less than 5 percent in either direction are ignored.

It is, of course, unnecessary to limit the size of the filter to 5 percent. In fact, Professor Alexander has reported tests of the filter technique for filters ranging in size from 1 percent to 50 percent. The tests cover different time periods from 1897 to 1959 and involved daily closing price for two indices, the Dow-Jones Industrials from 1897 to 1929 and Standard and Poor's Industrials from 1929 to 1959. In Alexander's latest work [2], it turns out that even when the higher broker's commissions incurred under the filter rule are ignored, the filter technique cannot consistently beat the simple policy of buying and holding the indices for the different periods tested. Elsewhere I have tested the filter technique on individual securities. Again the simple buy-and-hold method consistently beats the profits produced by different size filters. It seems, then, that at least for the purposes of the individual trader or investor, tests of the filter technique also tend to support the random walk model.

IMPLICATIONS OF THE RANDOM WALK THEORY FOR CHARTIST AND INTRINSIC VALUE ANALYSIS

As stated earlier, chartist theories implicitly assume that there is dependence in series of successive price changes. That is, the history of the series can be used to make meaningful predictions concerning the future. On the other hand, the theory of random walks says that successive price changes are independent, i.e., the past cannot be used to predict the future. Thus the two theories are diametrically opposed, and if, as the empirical evidence seems to suggest, the random walk theory is valid, then chartist theories are akin to astrology and of no real value to the investor.

In an uncertain world, however, no amount of empirical testing is sufficient to establish the validity of a hypothesis beyond any shadow of doubt. The chartist or technical theorist always has the option of declaring that the evidence in support of the random walk theory is not sufficient to validate the theory. On the other hand, the chartist must admit that the evidence in favor of the random walk model is both consistent and voluminous, whereas there is precious little published discussion of rigorous empirical tests of the various technical theories. If the chartist rejects the evidence in favor of the random walk model, his position is weak if his own theories have not been subjected to equally rigorous tests. This, I believe, is the challenge that the random walk theory makes to the technician.

There is nothing in the above discussion, however, which suggests that superior fundamental or intrinsic value analysis is useless in a random walk–efficient market. In fact the analyst will do better than the investor who follows a simple buy-and-hold policy as long as he can more quickly identify situations where there are nonnegligible discrepancies between actual prices and intrinsic values than other analysts and investors, and if he is better able to predict the occurrence of important events and evaluate their effects on intrinsic values.

If there are many analysts who are pretty good at this sort of thing, however, and if they have considerable resources at their disposal, they help narrow discrepancies between actual prices and intrinsic values and cause actual prices, on the average, to adjust "instantaneously" to changes in intrinsic values. That is, the existence of many sophisticated analysts helps make the market more efficient, which in turn implies a market which conforms more closely to the random walk model. Although the returns to these sophisticated analysts may be quite high, they establish a market in which fundamental analysis is a fairly useless procedure both for the average analyst and the average investor. That is, in a random walk–efficient market, on the average, a security chosen by a mediocre analyst will produce a return no better than that obtained from a randomly selected security of the same general riskiness.

There probably aren't many analysts (in fact, I know of none) who would willingly concede that they are no better than the "average" analyst. If all analysts think they are better than average, however, this only means that their estimate of the average is biased downward. Fortunately, it is not necessary to judge an analyst solely by his claims. The discussion above provides a natural benchmark with which we can evaluate his performance.

In a random walk–efficient market at any point in time the market price of a security will already reflect the judgments of many analysts concerning the relevance of currently available information to the prospects of that security. Now an individual analyst may feel that he has better insights than those that are already implicit in the market price. For example, he may feel that a discrepancy between market price and intrinsic value exists for some security, or he may think the intrinsic value of the security is itself about to change because of some impending piece of new information which is not yet generally available.

These "insights" of the analyst are of no real value, however, unless they are eventually borne out in the market, that is, unless the actual market price eventually moves in the predicted direction. In other words, if the analyst can make meaningful judgments concerning the purchase and sale of individual securities, his choices should consistently outperform randomly selected securities of the same general riskiness. It must be stressed, however, that the analyst must *consistently* produce results better than random selection, since, by the nature of uncertainty, for any given time period he has about a 50 percent chance of doing better than random selection even if his powers of analysis are completely nonexistent. Moreover, not only must the analyst do consistently better than random selection, but he must beat random selection by an amount which is at least sufficient to cover the cost of the resources (including his own time) which are expended in the process of carrying out his more complicated selection procedures.

What we propose, then, is that the analyst subject his performance to a rigorous comparison with a random selection procedure. One simple, practical way of comparing the results produced by an analyst with a random selection procedure is the following: Every time the analyst recommends a security for purchase (or sale), another security of the same general riskiness is chosen randomly. A future date is then chosen at which time the results produced by the two securities will be compared. Even if the analyst is no better than the random selection procedure, in any given comparison there is still a 50 percent chance that the security he has chosen will outperform the randomly selected security. After the game has been played for a while, however, and the results of many different comparisons are accumulated, then it will become clear whether the analyst is worth his salt or not.

In many circumstances, however, the primary concern is with the performance of a portfolio rather than with the performance of individual securities in the portfolio. In this situation one would want to compare the performance of the portfolio in question with that of a portfolio of randomly selected securities. A useful benchmark for randomly selected portfolios has been provided by Fisher and Lorie [6]. They computed rates of return for investments in common stocks on the New York Stock Exchange for various time periods from 1926 to 1960. The basic assumption in all of their computations is that at the beginning of each period studied the investor puts an equal amount of money in each common stock listed at that time on the Exchange. This amounts to random sampling where the sampling is, of course, exhaustive. Different rates of return are then computed for different possible tax brackets of the investor, first under the assumption that all dividends are reinvested in the month paid, and then under the assumption that dividends are not reinvested.

A possible procedure for the analyst is to compare returns for given time periods earned by portfolios he has managed with the returns earned for the same time periods by the Fisher-Lorie "randomly selected" portfolios. It is important to note, however, that this will be a valid test proceudre only if the portfolios managed by the analyst had about the same degree of riskiness as the Fisher-Lorie "market" portfolios. If this is not the case, the Fisher-Lorie results will not provide a proper benchmark. In order to make a proper comparison between the results produced by the analyst and a random selection policy, it will be necessary to define and study the behavior of portfolios of randomly selected securities, where these portfolios are selected in such a way that they have about the same degree of riskiness as those managed by the analyst.

If the claims of analysts concerning the advantages of fundamental analysis have any basis in fact, the tests suggested above would seem to be easy to pass. In fact, however, the only "analysts" that have so far undergone these tests are open end mutual funds. In their appeals to the public, mutual funds usually make two basic claims: (1) because it pools the resources of many individuals, a fund can diversify much more effectively than the average, small investor; and (2) because of its management's closeness to the market, the fund is better able to detect "good buys" in individual securities. In most cases the first claim is probably true. The second, however, implies that mutual funds provide a higher return than would be earned by a portfolio of randomly selected securities. In a separate paper [5] I reported the results of a study which suggest that if the initial loading charges of mutual funds are ignored, on the average the funds do about as well as a randomly selected portfolio. If one takes into account the higher initial loading charges of the funds, however, on the average the random investment policy outperforms the funds. In addition, these results would seem to be consistent with those of the now famous Wharton study of mutual funds [11].

These adverse results with respect to mutual funds have tended to lead random walk theorists to feel that other financial institutions, and most professional investment advisers as well, probably do no better than random selection. Institutions and analysts can only dispel such doubts by submitting their performance to a rigorous comparison with a random selection procedure.

Conclusion

In sum the theory of random walks in stock market prices presents important challenges to both the chartist and the proponent of fundamental analysis. For the chartist, the challenge is straightforward. If the random walk model is a valid description of reality, the work of the chartist, like that of the astrologer, is of no real value in stock market analysis. The empirical evidence to date provides strong support for the random walk model. In this light the only way the chartist can vindicate his position is to *show* that he can *consistently* use his techniques to make better than chance predictions of stock prices. It is not enough for him to talk mystically about patterns that he sees in the data. He must show that he can consistently use these patterns to make meaningful predictions of future prices.

The challenge of the theory of random walks to the proponent of fundamental analysis, however, is more involved. If the random walk theory is valid and if security exchanges are "efficient" markets, then stock prices at any point in time will represent good estimates of intrinsic or fundamental values. Thus, additional fundamental analysis is of value only when the analyst has new information which was not fully considered in forming current market prices, or has new insights concerning the effects of generally available information which are not already implicit in current prices. If the analyst has neither better insights nor new information, he may as well forget about fundamental analysis and choose securities by some random selection procedure.

In essence, the challenge of the random walk theory to the proponent of fundamental analysis is to show that his more complicated procedures are actually more profitable than a simple random selection policy. As in the case of the chartist, the challenge is an empirical one. The analyst cannot merely protest that he thinks the securities he selects do better than randomly selected securities; he must demonstrate that this is in fact the case.

REFERENCES

1. ALEXANDER, SIDNEY S. "Price Movements in Speculative Markets: Trends or Random Walks," *Industrial Management Review*, Vol. II (May, 1961), pp. 7–26.

2. ALEXANDER, SIDNEY S. "Price Movements in Speculative Markets: Trends or Random Walks, Number 2," *Industrial Management Review*, Vol. V (Spring, 1964), pp. 25–46.

3. COOTNER, PAUL H. (ed.). *The Random Character of Stock Market Prices*. Cambridge: M.I.T. Press, 1964.

An excellent compilation of research on the theory of random walks completed prior to mid-1963.

4. COOTNER, PAUL H. "Stock Prices: Random vs. Systematic Changes," *Industrial Management Review*, Vol. III (Spring, 1962), pp. 24–45.

5. FAMA, EUGENE F. "The Behavior of Stock Market Prices," *Journal of Business*, Vol. XXXVIII (January, 1965), pp. 34–105.

6. FISHER, L., AND LORIE, J. H. "Rates of Return on Investments in Common Stocks," *Journal of Business*, (January, 1964), pp. 1–21.

7. GODFREY, MICHAEL D.; GRANGER, CLIVE W. J.; AND MORGENSTERN, OSKAR. "The Random Walk Hypothesis of Stock Market Behavior," *Kyklos*, Vol. XVII (January, 1964), pp. 1–30.

8. GRANGER, CLIVE W. J., AND MORGENSTERN, O. "Spectral Analysis of New York Stock Market Prices," *Kyklos*, Vol. XVI (January, 1963), pp. 1–27.

9. KENDALL, M. G. "The Analysis of Economic Time Series," *Journal of the Royal Statistical Society* (Series A), Vol. XCVI (1953), pp. 11–25.

10. MOORE, ARNOLD. "A Statistical Analysis of Common Stock Prices," unpublished Ph.D. dissertation, Graduate School of Business, University of Chicago (1962).

11. "A Study of Mutual Funds," prepared for the Securities and Exchange Commission by the Wharton School of Finance and Commerce. Report of the Committee on Interstate and Foreign Commerce. Washington: U.S. Government Printing Office, 1962.

36

CONCEPTUAL FOUNDATIONS OF TECHNICAL ANALYSIS*

Robert A. Levy

The stock market fundamentalist relies upon economic and financial statistics and information. He investigates corporate income statements, balance sheets, dividend records, management policies, sales growth, managerial ability, plant capacity, and competitive forces. He looks to the daily press for evidence of future business conditions. He analyzes bank reports and the voluminous statistical compilations of the various government agencies. Taking all these factors into account, he projects corporate earnings and applies a satisfactory earnings multiplier (price-earnings ratio, capitalization rate) to arrive at the intrinsic value of the security under observation. He then compares this intrinsic value to the existing market price and, if the former is sufficiently higher, he regards the stock as a purchase candidate.[1]

The term "technical" in its application to the stock market means something quite different than its ordinary dictionary definition. It refers to the study of the market itself as opposed to the external factors reflected in the market. Technical analysis is, in essence, the recording of the actual history of trading (including both price movement and the volume of transactions) for one stock or a group of equities, and deducing the future trend from this historical analysis.[2]

Various tools of technical analysis have evolved over the years. Time and space preclude a discussion of these numerous tools; rather, they will simply be identified. The interested reader is encouraged to consult one or more of the cited publications for more complete information.[3] The precursor of all technical principles was the Dow Theory, which evolved

---

* Reprinted by permission of the *Financial Analysts Journal* (July-August 1966).

[1] Robert D. Edwards and John Magee, *Technical Analysis of Stock Trends* (Springfield, Mass.: John Magee, 1958), p. 3.

[2] *Ibid.*, p. 5.

[3] See particularly: *Encyclopedia of Stock Market Techniques*, Investors Intelligence, Inc., Larchmont, N.Y., 1963; Garfield A. Drew, *New Methods for Profit in the Stock Market* (Boston: The Metcalf Press, 1954); and Joseph E. Granville, *A Strategy of Daily Stock Market Timing for Maximum Profit* (Englewood Cliffs, N.J.: Prentice-Hall, Inc., 1960).

as a result of the work of Charles H. Dow, editor of *The Wall Street Journal* from 1889 to 1902, and his followers. Other technical tools or indicators include the Elliott Wave Principle, Barron's Confidence Index, odd lot statistics, short interest ratios, breadth (advance—decline) indexes, statistics on new highs and lows, upside-downside volume data, bar charts and point-and-figure charts (which picture price and volume movements), moving average trend-lines, relative strength measures, and statistics on debits and credits of brokerage balances—to name a few of the more important ones.

Technical theory can be summarized as follows:

1. Market value is determined solely by the interaction of supply and demand.

2. Supply and demand are governed by numerous factors, both rational and irrational. Included in these factors are those that are relied upon by the fundamentalists, as well as opinions, moods, guesses, and blind necessities. The market weighs all of these factors continually and automatically.

3. Disregarding minor fluctuations in the market, stock prices tend to move in trends which persist for an appreciable length of time.

4. Changes in trend are caused by the shifts in supply and demand relationships. These shifts, no matter why they occur, can be detected sooner or later in the action of the market itself.[4]

The basic assumption of technical theorists is that history tends to repeat itself. In other words, past patterns of market behavior will recur in the future and can thus be used for predictive purposes. In statistical terminology, the stock market technician relies upon the dependence of successive price changes.

The assumption of the fundamental analyst is quite different. He believes that each security has an intrinsic value which depends upon its earning potential, and that actual market prices tend to move toward intrinsic values. If his belief is correct, then determining the intrinsic value of a security by capitalizing future earnings is equivalent to predicting the security's future price.[5]

THE CASE FOR TECHNICAL ANALYSIS

Robert D. Edwards and John Magee, two outspoken advocates of the technical school, argue that:

> It is futile to assign an intrinsic value to a stock certificate. One share of United States Steel, for example, was worth $261 in the early Fall of 1929, but you could buy it for only $22 in June of 1932! By March 1937, it was selling for $126 and just one year later for $38. . . . This sort of thing, this wide divergence between presumed value and actual value, is not the exception; it

---

[4] Edwards and Magee, *op. cit.*, p. 86.

[5] Eugene F. Fama, "Random Walks in Stock Market Prices," *Financial Analysts Journal*, XXI, No. 5 (September–October 1965), p. 55.

is the rule; it is going on all the time. The fact is that the real value of a share of U.S. Steel common is determined at any given time solely, definitely, and inexorably by supply and demand, which are accurately reflected in the transactions consummated on the floor of the New York Stock Exchange.

Of course, the statistics which the fundamentalists study play a part in the supply-demand equation—that is freely admitted. But there are many other factors affecting it. The market price reflects not only the differing value opinions of many orthodox security appraisers but also all the hopes and fears and guesses and moods, rational and irrational, of hundreds of potential buyers and sellers, as well as their needs and their resources—in total, factors which defy analysis and for which no statistics are obtainable, but which are nevertheless all synthesized, weighed, and finally expressed in the one precise figure at which a buyer and seller get together and make a deal (through their agents, their respective brokers). This is the only figure that counts.

. . . In brief, the going price as established by the market itself comprehends all the fundamental information which the statistical analyst can hope to learn (plus some which is perhaps secret from him, known only to a few insiders) and much else besides of equal or even greater importance.

All of which, admitting its truth, would be of little significance were it not for the fact, which no one of experience doubts, that *prices move in trends* and trends tend to continue until something happens to change the supply-demand balance.[6]

The technical analyst justifies his activities in several ways. First, he contends that short-term market fluctuations are more important than long-term trends, where importance is judged by the profit potential in trading. Certainly the trader who buys at the bottom of each short-term movement and sells at the top will realize greater profits than the investor who benefits only from the major trend. Second, the technician contends that information on fundamental conditions comes too late for maximum profit. The fundamentalist is forced to wait for statistics on sales, orders, earnings, dividends, and similar factors. By the time information of this sort is made publicly available, the market may have already discounted its effect and commenced a substantial upward or downward move. The technical trader, however, can act instantaneously on any change in stock prices whether or not the news underlying the change has been made public. The technician believes that the movement of the market precedes the movement of other economic series, rather than vice versa.[7] (In this regard, he has the support of the National Bureau of Economic Research which, in its study of business cycles, has listed stock market prices as one of 12 leading indicators.)[8]

It is admitted by technicians that some fundamental analysts may be able to forecast the trend of business quite accurately; they may even

---

[6] Edwards and Magee, *op. cit.*, pp. 5–6.

[7] George L. Leffler and Loring C. Farwell, *The Stock Market* (New York: The Ronald Press Company, 1963), p. 574.

[8] Julius Shiskin, "Business Cycle Indicators: The Known and the Unknown," *Business Cycle Developments* (Washington: U.S. Department of Commerce, Bureau of the Census, September 1963), Appendix H.

know exactly what present economic conditions are, and what future conditions will be; moreover, they may be absolutely correct in their earnings projections for a given company. Yet, even assuming all of this to be true, their projections of stock market action could be grossly in error.[9] It is only technical analysis which can detect the buying and selling pressures caused by psychological and emotional, rather than economic and financial, factors. Only the market action itself reflects the existence of inside information not made publicly available. This important fact has been relied upon by all technicians, and written about by George A. Chestnutt, Jr., the manager of a mutual fund which depends heavily on technical methods.

There are so many factors, each having its own effect on the price fluctuations of any individual stock, that it is practically impossible to analyze them *separately* and give each its proper weight in an attempt to estimate the stock's future market action. Often the essential information is known only to insiders. It is not released to the public until it is too late to act upon it.

Fortunately, we do not need to know *why* one stock is stronger than another in order to act profitably upon the knowledge of the fact. The market itself is continually weighing and recording the effects of all the bullish information and all the bearish information about every stock. No one in possession of inside information can profit from it unless he buys or sells the stock. The moment he does, his buy or sell orders have their effect upon the price. That effect is revealed in the market action of the stock.[10]

The argument of the technical analyst, in a nutshell, is that stock price moves are caused by the interaction of supply and demand, and that the flow of funds into and out of various securities is first detected by the various technical market indicators, not by the analysis of fundamental economic and financial statistics.[11]

A Critique of the Intrinsic Value Approach

Technicians agree that trends and patterns evolve, for the most part, as a result of market action taken by those persons who have, or think they have, some superior knowledge of underlying fundamental factors. The obvious corollary, which fundamentalists are quick to point out, is that the possessors of this superior knowledge are in the best position to maximize their profits from stock market transactions. Since fundamental knowledge, so the argument goes, is the "stuff" which even technical analysts must ultimately rely upon to produce the trends and patterns which they study, so it must therefore be a better foundation for security appraisal.

---

[9] Joseph E. Granville, *New Key to Stock Market Profits* (Englewood Cliffs, N.J.: Prentice-Hall, Inc., 1963), p. 20.

[10] George A. Chestnutt, Jr., *Stock Market Analysis: Facts and Principles* (Larchmont, N.Y.: American Investors Corporation, 1965), p. 19.

[11] Joseph E. Granville, *A Strategy of Daily Stock Market Timing for Maximum Profit, op. cit.,* p. 9.

In fact, *there is little justification for denying that properly performed fundamental analysis is superior to technical analysis.* The technician must wait until those persons who have critical information, which others do not have, make their move in the market. Even though the technical analyst may be able to act before critical information is publicly available, nevertheless he will be later in his actions than will be the "insiders" who are first aware of the underlying fundamental factors. The conclusion must be, therefore, that investment analysis will be most successful when the analyst is among the first to gain and correctly evaluate the necessary superior knowledge.

But the technician still has a strong argument. First, it is possible that properly performed fundamental analysis could lead to unsatisfactory investment results. The opinion of the fundamentalist regarding the intrinsic value of a given security, even if correct, must be shared by other investors who control substantial financial resources and are willing to place these resources in the market place. Only when opinions are converted into action, and only when a sufficient amount of capital is involved, will the market price move toward intrinsic value. Thus, the fundamental analyst may find himself heavily invested in a security for a considerable length of time before market support develops. Of course, this lowers his rate of return by tying up funds which could have been invested elsewhere. The technician, however, purports to avoid this potential problem by delaying his investment until market support for a particular stock has already appeared. It is conceivable that the sacrifice in profits resulting from late selection is no greater than the opportunity cost of unproductive capital arising from early selection.

Second, and of greater importance, how many investors are able to successfully engage in fundamental analysis? How many are capable of being among the first to recognize and evaluate critical information? How many have the necessary nonmonetary resources (primarily time and reliable statistical information)?

Assume, for the sake of argument, that all investors are capable, and that they have sufficient time to analyze the economic and financial factors affecting any given security. These investors will then attempt to project the earnings of a particular company and capitalize these earnings in order to arrive at some estimate of intrinsic value. The most important of the statistical data upon which the investors will rely are the company's financial statements. Under these circumstances, how successful will the fundamentalist be in his analysis? The question could be posed in a more direct manner: How complete and reliable are the corporate financial reports which are the major source of information for the fundamental analyst?

The purpose of published annual reports is to convey information to present and prospective stockholders about the operations of the corporate entity. This information should include all that is relevant (both qualitative and quantitative) to enable the investor to make a rational and informed judgment as to the investment worth of the company. Consequently, published annual reports should be designed for the use of the skilled financial analyst. Only then can they possibly include information in sufficient volume and detail as to provide for an efficient allocation of capital resources through investment selection.

The Securities and Exchange Commission, through Regulation S-X, has prescribed the form and content of financial reports filed with the SEC. The Securities Acts Amendments of 1964 extended these filing requirements to most over-the-counter companies, thereby matching the requirements which theretofore had been imposed only upon listed firms. Prior to 1964 the SEC's filing requirements had only an indirect effect (through public pressure) on the form and content of published annual reports to stockholders. The published reports could, and often did, differ from the Form 10-K annual reports filed with the SEC. Differences were both as to dollar amounts and as to the extent of the information provided. However, in May 1964 the SEC adopted Rule 14a–3 which prescribed, among other things, that any material differences between the methods of reporting to the SEC and the methods of reporting to stockholders must be noted in the published annual report along with a reconciliation of the differences. Consequently, subsequent to 1964, published annual reports did not differ in dollar amount from the Form 10Ks. Nevertheless, there are still considerable differences in the extent and volume of information in the two reports. Many corporations publish no more than a summary balance sheet, income statement, and statement of retained earnings for a one-year, or perhaps two-year period. Needless to say, this is unsatisfactory to the fundamental analyst.

Some of the information which is badly needed in published reports, but which is seldom available, includes: (1) production in units; (2) sales in units; (3) rate of capacity operated; (4) breakdown of operations as between domestic and foreign; (5) division of sales as between intercompany and outsiders; (6) wages, wage rates, hours worked, and number of employees; (7) state and local taxes paid; (8) amount and details of selling and general expenses; (9) amount and details of maintenance expenditures; (10) details of capital expenditures; (11) details of inventories; (12) details of properties owned; (13) number of stockholders; (14) sales by product line and by consuming industry; (15) research and development costs; (16) details of long-term lease arrangements; (17) details of stock option and pension plans; (18) more complete disclosure of depreciation policies; and (19) orders booked and unfilled orders.[12] And this is by no means an all-inclusive list.

The American Institute of Certified Public Accountants has com-

---

[12] Benjamin Graham, David L. Dodd and Sidney Cottle, *Security Analysis* (New York: McGraw-Hill Book Company, Inc., 1962), pp. 80–82.

mented extensively upon the adequacy of information in published reports. Of particular importance are the remarks appearing in three of the *Accounting Research Studies*, covering the accounting ramifications of financial leases, business combinations, and pensions, respectively.[13] In these studies, investigations of annual reports revealed gross inadequacy of information.

The sparse quantity of information is only one of the problems of the fundamentalists, however. Of equal importance is the question of reliability. Presumably, when the financial statements of a company are accompanied by the unqualified approval of an independent certified public accountant, investors and creditors may be assured of the fairness and integrity of the reports. The auditor's report indicates whether he feels that the financial position of the company and the results of its operations are presented fairly, in conformity with generally accepted accounting principles. The audit supposedly eliminates, or at least discloses, unintentional errors by corporate accountants, bias on the part of corporate management, deviations from generally accepted accounting principles, and deliberate falsification. The audit also determines whether the financial statements have been prepared on a basis consistent with that of the prior year and whether they fully disclose all material facts.[14]

In practice, there are many reasons why the auditor's certificate is of less-than-desirable significance. First, the auditor's examination is limited to a program of tests which are not infallible in detecting errors. Second, such concepts as "fairness," "materiality," "full disclosure," and "consistency" are subjective in nature and cannot be objectively verified.[15] Third, and fortunately least frequent in occurrence, there may be outright dishonesty by the independent auditor or collusion between the accounting firm and its corporate client. Fourth, and of greatest importance, there are no truly generally accepted accounting principles. The accounting profession is in a state of flux. In some cases, there are a multiplicity of acceptable procedures, while in other cases, those principles which have been applied for so many years are now being subjected to serious reanalysis and skeptical reevaluation.

Questions as to both fairness and objectivity of financial reporting were raised in five of the *Accounting Research Studies*.[16] The specific

---

[13] John H. Myers, "Reporting of Leases in Financial Statements," *Accounting Research Study No. 4* (New York: American Institute of Certified Public Accountants, 1962); Arthur R. Wyatt, "A Critical Study of Accounting for Business Combination," *Accounting Research Study No. 5* (New York: American Institute of Certified Public Accountants, 1963); and Ernest L. Hicks, "Accounting for the Cost of Pension Plans," *Accounting Research Study No. 8* (New York: American Institute of Certified Public Accountants, 1965).

[14] Walter B. Meigs, *Principles of Auditing* (Homewood, Ill.: Richard D. Irwin, Inc., 1959), pp. 1–2.

[15] *Ibid.*, pp. 14–17.

[16] Robert T. Sprouse and Maurice Moonitz, "A Tentative Set of Broad Accounting Principles for Business Enterprises," *Accounting Research Study No. 3* (New York:

problems included asset valuation, treatment of leases, business combinations, adjustments for changes in price level, and pensions. In each of these areas there is considerable doubt as to the propriety of presently employed accounting principles (particularly as to the appropriateness of historical cost valuations).

Additional accounting problems exist in the following areas: (1) matching revenues and expenses (e.g., direct versus absorption costing, installment sales, long-term construction contracts, stock options, depreciation, the investment credit, and deferred taxes); (2) distinguishing between several acceptable accounting methods and determining the effect of using one as opposed to another (e.g., depreciation, the investment credit, and inventory valuation); and (3) estimating various factors which are relevant to the accounting process (e.g., depreciable lives and bad debt expense).

Financial ratios, while potentially useful to the fundamentalist, can be no better than the figures from which they are derived. And these figures, in turn, are only as good as the underlying accounting principles. Year-to-year comparisons and trends are suspect because the flexibility of accounting procedures permits manipulation of the financial data. Inter-company comparisons are also unreliable because of the wide choice of permissible accounting methods.

The end-result is that the analyst, using publicly available information, has an extremely difficult task in trying to reconstruct a corporation's financial statements in order to get some picture of the company's earning power.

Nor does the analyst's problems terminate upon the evaluation of recent financial statements. This only provides him with an approximation of current and historical earnings. Now he must project these into the future. Moreover, a one-year projection is not adequate. As stated in a widely respected text on fundamental analysis:

> Typically, these . . . studies rest on a careful but too abbreviated forecast of probable future earnings for a company—covering generally only the next 12 months or less.
> . . . While such a measurement is important, it is hardly sufficient for an investment recommendation, since value cannot soundly be established on the basis of earnings shown over a short period of time.[17]

And that isn't all of the fundamentalist's trials and tribulations. Determining current and historical earnings is a difficult task indeed. Projecting these earnings for a number of years into the future is even more difficult. But now comes the most difficult job of all: selecting an appropriate

---

American Institute of Certified Public Accountants, 1962); Myers, *op. cit.*; Wyatt, *op cit.*; Accounting Research Division, "Reporting the Financial Effects of Price-Level Changes," *Accounting Research Study No. 6* (New York: American Institute of Certified Public Accountants, 1963); and Hicks, *op. cit.*

[17] Graham, Dodd and Cottle, *op. cit.*, p. 434.

price-earnings multiple (or capitalization rate). The problems inherent in this last step are reflected in the following statement by Graham, Dodd and Cottle, commenting upon a 1953 estimate by the Value Line Investment Survey of the 1956–1958 prices of the stocks in the Dow Jones Industrial Average.

... although the earnings estimates were wide of the mark in several instances ... the aggregate earnings estimate for the 29 stocks was very close to the actual. ... By contrast, the aggregate market value estimate for 1956–1958 was significantly less accurate—missing by more than 22 percent the three-year mean price. ... This tends to confirm our view that earnings can be predicted with more confidence than can the capitalization rate or multiplier, which to a major degree will reflect the market psychology existing at the time.[18]

Reference to the historical relationship between market price and *current* earnings is to no avail. Graham, Dodd and Cottle compared, over the 25-year period, 1935–1959, the quarterly earnings (on an annualized basis and seasonally adjusted) of Standard and Poor's 500 Composite stock group with the quarterly average stock-price index. They found that in 46 out of the 100 quarters stock prices moved counter to the change in earnings (i.e., earnings increased while prices declined, or vice versa).[19]

Granville emphasized this same important point by demonstrating the lack of correlation between prices and earnings as uncovered in his examination of hundreds of stocks. He found that price-earnings ratios fluctuated widely and that this fluctuation "dilutes the widely held belief that good earnings are a necessary accompaniment to advancing stock prices."[20]

With all of these difficulties (determining current earnings, projecting future earnings, and selecting an appropriate capitalization rate) it might be expected that even the best fundamental analysts can be far wide of the mark. This expectation would be justified by the facts. The 1965 range of the Dow Jones Industrial Average was 840.59 to 969.26, and the average of the 1963–1965 DJIA annual high-lows was 813.60.[21] But in March of 1961 Naess and Thomas projected the 1965 Average at 688; and Value Line, in January of 1961, suggested that the mean for 1963–1965 would be 705.[22] Errors of this size are not unusual. Graham, Dodd and Cottle, in the 1962 edition of their book, *Security Analysis*, stated that "careful consideration of this problem ... led us to increase our 1951 valuation standards by an arbitrary 50 percent."[23] Such arbitrariness certainly bespeaks unreliability.

---

[18] *Ibid.*, p. 439.
[19] *Ibid.*, p. 719.
[20] Granville, *New Keys to Stock Market Profits, op. cit.*, p. 21.
[21] "Statistical Section," *Barron's*, XLVI, No. 24 (June 13, 1966), p. 57.
[22] Graham, Dodd and Cottle, *op. cit.*, p. 418.
[23] *Ibid.*, p. 421.

It is clear that fundamental analysis, even when performed by so-called experts, can be quite inaccurate. The question remains as to whether technical analysis offers any better possibilities. At least one prominent author believes that it does.

There have been frequent occasions when technical analysis was the *only* thing that could possibly have given the correct answer to the future trend of the market. This was true, for example, in the spring of 1946. If any investor had then possessed a crystal ball which would have shown him what corporate earnings were to be a year later, he could only have concluded that stock prices would be considerably higher. Instead, they were substantially lower in the face of record earnings and dividends.

There was nothing in the "fundamentals"—either in 1946 or 1947—to explain why prices had collapsed in the meantime. But there was considerable evidence of a weak *technical* situation in the market beforehand. . . . The investor who acted on technical grounds did not need to concern himself with *why* the market should seem to be acting irrationally, whereas the analyst of business facts and probabilities—unable to find a "reason"—was forced to conclude that the market could not do what it actually did.

* * * * *

In a broad sense, the experience of the past 10 years has very clearly demonstrated that the price-to-earnings ratio is a much more important factor than the actual level and/or trend of earnings themselves. Since the ratio is determined by investment psychology, the study of technical market action has, on the whole, been more fruitful than fundamental analysis.[24]

Major Criticisms of Technical Analysis

There are at least four major criticisms of technical analysis. The first three are closely interrelated. First, it is contended that the behavior of the stock market in the past may not be indicative of its behavior in the years to come. That is to say, even assuming that technical analysis would have been successful over the last decade, there is no guarantee that it will be successful over the next decade. Typical of the response to this criticism is the following denial by Edwards and Magee.

. . . all the new controls and regulations of the past several years, the new taxes which have placed a heavy handicap on successful investors, the greatly augmented and improved facilities for acquiring dependable information on securities, even the quite radical changes in certain portions of our basic economy, have not much altered the "pattern" of the stock market.[25]

The second contention of the critics is that technical traders acting on the results of their studies tend to create the very patterns and trends which they claim have predictive significance. In other words, the market action may be a reflection of the chart action instead of the reverse. Technicians recognize that this possibility exists. However, they argue that the habits and evaluative methods of individuals are so deeply ingrained that the same kinds of events continually produce the same kinds

---

[24] Drew, *op. cit.*, pp. 242–244.
[25] Edwards and Magee, *op. cit.*, p. 1.

of market responses. Since these habits and methods are extremely durable, and since fundamental analysts greatly outnumber the technicians, it is unlikely that technical trading alters the response of the fundamentalists to external factors; and hence the actions of technicians probably do not have a major influence on the behavior of a competitive market.[26]

This second criticism inevitably leads to a third—that, if technical analysis is continually successful, an influx of technical traders will neutralize whatever profit potential exists. An analogy can be offered in the field of horse racing. If someone were to perfect a system of wagering on horses, and if he were to publicize this system so as to make it available for everyone's use, the amount of betting on the highest rated horses would change the odds sufficiently to offset the profitability of the system. There are several reasons why this criticism is not fatal to the art of technical analysis. First, it is quite possible that extremely successful technical "systems" have been developed but, for this very reason, have not been publicized or made available for general use. Second, it is likely that those who are not engaged in technical analysis would be reluctant to believe the claims of successful technicians. Third, to the extent that technical analysis may depend in part upon the use of electronic computers and sophisticated mathematical techniques, both the expense and the requisite training and knowledge will prevent its exploitation by the majority of the investing public. Fourth, and most important, is the following argument given by Granville:

> There is no danger that the revelation of new techniques will so enlighten the masses as to render them (the techniques) useless. The application of such things requires time and work, and human nature is such that most people will neither have the time, patience, or desire to do the work necessary to achieve the results which might be had when these things are done.[27]

Finally, the fourth major criticism of technical analysis is its subjectivity. Advocates of the technical school contend that their methods preclude the somewhat arbitrary determinations which accompany fundamental analysis (e.g., selection of a capitalization rate). Critics, however, maintain that the technician's favorite tool, the chart of stock price movements, is subject to a wide variety of interpretations. Without debating the validity of this criticism, it may be noted that the recent use of the computer for purposes of analyzing price and volume movements would tend to reduce the subjectivity which might otherwise be inherent in technical analysis.

IMPLICATIONS OF THE RANDOM WALK THEORY

The most critical indictment of technical analysis, thereby giving indirect support to the fundamentalists' side of the debate, is the random

---
[26] *Ibid.*, pp. 391–392.
[27] Granville, *New Key to Stock Market Profits, op. cit.*, p. 11.

walk theory. This theory restates the above-mentioned criticisms in slightly different context. It argues that the activities of chart readers, if successful, would help to produce the independence of successive stock price changes. But this independence, once established, renders chart reading an unprofitable activity. On the other hand, fundamentalists who consistently evaluate the effect of new information on intrinsic values will be able to realize larger profits than those who can not.[28]

There is nothing . . . which suggests that superior fundamental or intrinsic value analysis is useless in a random walk-efficient market. In fact, the analyst will do better than the investor who follows a simple buy-and-hold policy as long as he can more quickly identify situations where there are non-negligible discrepancies between actual price and intrinsic values than other analysts and investors, and if he is better able to predict the occurrence of important events and evaluate their effects on intrinsic values.

If there are many analysts who are pretty good at this sort of thing, however, and if they have considerable resources at their disposal, they help narrow discrepancies between actual prices and intrinsic values and cause actual prices, on the average, to adjust "instantaneously" to changes in intrinsic values.[29]

The random walk theory, while refuting the concepts of technical analysis and neither proving nor disproving those of fundamental analysis, presents an empirical challenge to both schools of thought. The challenge to the technician is a direct one. If the random walk model is valid, as suggested by empirical evidence to date, then future price movements cannot be predicted by studying the history of past price movements alone. Consequently, the work of the chartist may be useless. To vindicate himself, the technician should not restrict himself to verbalizing about trends and patterns; rather, he should demonstrate their predictive significance empirically. The challenge to the fundamentalist, while still empirical, is indirect. The random walk theory is based on the premise of an "efficient" market where actual stock prices at any given time are likely to be close approximations of intrinsic values. The fundamental analyst must therefore demonstrate that his methods consistently result in the detection of discrepancies between actual prices and intrinsic values when these discrepancies exist.[30]

CONCLUSIONS

The analysis of financial and economic fundamentals must ultimately be the underlying foundation for security appraisal. Market prices will, in the long run, tend to move toward intrinsic values. Thus, the determination of value is the critical factor in investment selection. The criticisms of fundamental analysis presented in this paper are directed at practicabil-

---

[28] Eugene F. Fama, "The Behavior of Stock Market Prices," *The Journal of Business*, XXXVIII, No. 1 (January 1965), p. 39.
[29] Fama, "Random Walks in Stock Market Prices," *op. cit.*, p. 58.
[30] *Ibid.*, p. 59.

ity rather than theory. It is the inability of most investors to *properly apply* fundamental techniques which is the basis for skepticism. As the art of fundamental analysis is further developed and properly applied, it will provide a sounder basis for investment evaluation.

Nevertheless, there is conceptual justification for contending that, except for the most sophisticated of the professional analysts, technical stock analysis may be as satisfactory, or perhaps more satisfactory, than fundamental analysis. Moreover, there is conceptual support for recommending technical analysis as a supplement to fundamental analysis for even the top professionals.

However, conceptual reasoning is not enough. There is a vast amount of empirical evidence which supports the random walk model of stock market behavior and thus denies the value of technical analysis. In order to attain recognition from serious students of the stock market, technicians must combine existing conceptual support with empirical evidence which has been heretofore lacking.

37

APPRAISING MANAGEMENTS*

Townsend Hoopes

In evaluating managements there are two distinctive situations in which the security analyst might be in need of advice—namely, the newly organized small company engaged in a specialized service or in making technical products, and the large, established company that has suffered a decline and has just installed new management.

Aside from the subjective determination of the individual's capabilities, which the analyst has the opportunity and should have the ability to make, are there any other bench marks or clues that would enable the analyst to detect an impending reversal before the fact?

The most natural way for me to answer this question is to tell you how Cresap, McCormick and Paget approaches the problem of judging managements, for the appraisal of men in relation to the tasks which confront them is one of the most important functions performed by the professional management consultant.

First, I doubt if anyone is *completely* qualified to appraise management. Certainly the management consultant would be better qualified if he were also a practicing psychologist. Conversely, an industrial psychologist would be better qualified if he had the broad experience in matters of planning, organization, personnel selection, motivation, and control possessed by the qualified consultant.

If you will accept the premise, then, that no one is completely qualified to appraise management, I will try to explain how we do it at Cresap, McCormick and Paget. I will not deal with the fiscal or physical aspects of a corporate evaluation; we shall assume that these points have been checked, and that management appraisal per se is the remaining task at hand.

In appraising, say, the top five or six men in a corporation, we like to start at the top and work downward. We do this because we have found that many times the unsatisfactory performance of a subordinate is caused by the inadequacy or obtuseness of his superior. All of us here, I know, have seen situations in which it is almost impossible for anyone to do a

---

* An address before The New York Junior Society of Security Analysts; November 28, 1962. Mr. Hoopes was a member of Cresap, McCormick and Paget at that time.

good job because of the inadequacy or irrationality of the chief executive officer. By moving from the top down, we can weigh the conditions, favorable and unfavorable, that the key men may be working under.

Starting with the chief executive, we usually build the interview around the subjects of planning, organization, personnel selection, motivation, and control, without necessarily mentioning these by name; for some men who are very well qualified in these matters think about them in different terms. Then, too, these terms have a somewhat abstract and technical connotation. And indeed they are often properly associated with the unfortunate jargon of management science.

Ernest Dale, a Professor of Business and Public Administration at Cornell, and also a practicing consultant, has bluntly warned us in the July *Atlantic* against the easy assumption that a knowledge of the techniques of management science alone make a manager or are a substitute for an encyclopedic knowledge of the business and a steadfast attention to detail. He has written scornfully that "the true manager is a generalist and can easily hire specialists to get the facts for him. How he can separate the experts from the charlatans if he himself has no knowledge of the subject matter is not disclosed."

This is an important truth, for the techniques standing alone without relevant knowledge are like a skeleton without the flesh and blood of substance. Yet we have nevertheless found, in management appraisals, that a manager's knowledge of his job is usually best obtained by questioning him about his approach to management techniques. In a sense, this is a necessary device for consultants, and also I would think for security analysts, for neither of us can hope to have comprehensive, detailed knowledge of any particular business. What we can acquire is a working knowledge of management principles, and these can serve as a means of opening up communications with the manager we are seeking to evaluate.

We try to test each executive's knowledge and application of these five elements of management.

PLANNING

The word "planning," insofar as the top man is concerned, is a synonym for setting objectives. It concerns his ability to think about the future of his company.

Rather than talk in terms of plans, objectives, growth, or similar shopworn terms, we like to discuss the future of the company with the No. 1 man by asking this kind of question: "What do you think you can do with this company over the next five years?" If we have surprised him with our question, or get an answer such as, "Well, I hope I can earn enough money to maintain the dividend," we know the man has rather little understanding of planning or hasn't really explored the future of the business in his own mind. Furthermore, it is a good guess that his subordinates don't know what he is trying to do, and are probably precluded from helping him because he hasn't given them any clear idea of where he wants to go, or when he hopes to get there. We have found that it is almost impossible for subordinates to set authoritative goals in spite of the boss or without his knowing it. Yet detailed planning is absolutely dependent on objectives.

If, on the other hand, a chief executive warms up to the question, and begins explaining his objectives in terms of products, markets, and technological developments; if he shows us a projected profit and loss statement and a balance sheet for a five-year period, then we know we are in the presence of a man who at least thinks about the future. We must wait, however, until we talk to the second and third levels of management before we can evaluate the quality of the actual planning.

Incidentally, we have found no adequate substitute for the projected income statement and balance sheet as a means of thinking through and stating future goals. A planning exercise which culminates in such documents can be much more than a pro forma fiscal exercise. It can be an excellent means of forcing responsible people at several levels to think comprehensively and realistically about their business situation, to identify problems and requirements, and to determine the time and cost involved in meeting such requirements.

The need for a sound estimate of future sales volume, for example, leads directly to a study of products, markets, and competitors. Similarly, the need to estimate the cost of sales leads to studies of facilities, equipment, processes, and procedures. Such studies have implications for both the projected income statement and the projected balance sheet.

Thus, in asking a chief executive the simple question, "What do you think you can do with this business over the next five years?" we may get an answer that will cause us to give him a 0 or 100 percent rating on his competence as a planner. If we give him a low mark we are probably correct in concluding that he is:

A man of little imagination.

One who is more interested in the defensive elements of his job (namely, costs and expenses) than in the offensive elements (sales, merchandising, product development, and diversification).

A man whose subordinates are likely to be frustrated and who cannot help him very much because they do not know what he is trying to do.

When we reach conclusions about a man's ability to deal with the future of his company, either in his own mind or in written plans, we can weigh the importance of planning to the particular corporate situation we are considering.

ORGANIZATION

Organization is essentially orderliness. In the business context, it is the orderly arrangement of responsibilities, authorities, and relationships in the accomplishment of manifold, continuing tasks. Planning and organization are obviously related, for it is naturally difficult to organize men, materials, and money if the objectives of the enterprise have not been carefully thought through and clearly stated.

In evaluating a chief executive on his knowledge of organization, we usually ask for an organization chart. His answer may be, "Oh, we are just one happy family here" or, again, he may bring forth a complete organization manual, with charts and position descriptions covering everyone in the first five or six levels of management.

Detailed documentation is pro forma evidence that some thought has been given to organization, but it is by no means conclusive. A bulky organization manual may have been meticulously prepared five years ago and not looked at since. It may thus not at all reflect the realities of the current situation. On the other hand, the absence of formal documentation does not always mean the lack of sound organizational arrangements, particularly in smaller companies.

What is important to determine is the way the top men *think* about organization; how the chief executive conceives of his responsibility, how he sees himself in relation to the Board of Directors, the extent to which he delegates authority and in what areas, and the pattern of reporting relationships he has developed.

Here are some things to look for in judging a key executive's understanding of organization.

1. *Whether he grasps the importance of well-defined responsibilities.* Lack of precision and clarity on the question of who does what usually leads to confusion, wasted efforts, and negative consequences in the management group. It also encourages the flowering of unhealthy political situations, for poorly defined responsibility creates a fertile field for the empire builder, and usually an unfavorable environment for the talented, but more scrupulous, person to grow in.

2. *Whether he can distinguish clearly between the tasks to be performed and the people to perform them.* Some executives have great difficulty in separating the problem of function from that of personnel. If Joe Smith was responsible for both engineering and manufacturing when the company was doing $1 million a year, some bosses see no reason for separating these responsibilities now that the company is doing $25 million a year, and even though Joe isn't doing a very good job at either engineering or manufacturing. While organization must always be modified in a specific situation by the quality and personality of the people involved, it is the mark of a sound organizational thinker that he first defines the tasks to be performed without reference to people, and then assigns responsibility for their performance in a manner that seeks to make the best use of available or obtainable talent.

3. *Whether he can distinguish between delegation and abdication.* Some executives have difficulty in determining this difference. It seems a

particular problem in companies which have been recently "divisionalized" and have delegated profit responsibilities to a series of division general managers. A classic example of this difficulty was the sad unfolding at General Dynamics a year or so ago when very heavy losses were incurred, in large part because corporate headquarters chose not to question or override the assumptions and decisions of a particular division management—even though the consequences of divisional error were clearly of a magnitude that would affect the basic position of the entire company.

One final word to put this matter of organization in perspective.

The durability, the morale, and the earning power of a company depend importantly on good organization; and an understanding of organizational principles is a basic requirement in a top executive officer. Yet I would fully agree with William H. Whyte, author of *The Organization Man*, that it is a necessary condition of personal and also of corporate health to avoid a deification of organizational concepts, and especially of any particular organizational pattern. Organization is a tool for men and not the other way around.

PERSONNEL DEVELOPMENT AND MOTIVATION

In judging a chief executive in this area, we do not, certainly, expect him to be a technician in personnel administration; but we are very interested in the quality of the people he has brought into the company or has developed from within; also, how he thinks about their development and motivation.

One quick means of appraising the chief executive in this area is to check the rate of executive turnover in his company. If it has been abnormally high, this would cast a basic doubt on his ability to gather, build, and retain a first-rate management team. Such was the case at Fruehauf Trailer a few years ago when that company was being run as if it were some sort of oriental dynasty. There was a constant rise and fall of "court favorites" and a corresponding rate of executive turnover that debilitated both morale and corporate efficiency. I am happy to say that a far more rational, secure, and professional environment has now been created, with results that can be read in the record of corporate sales and profits.

Determination of the quality of subordinates can be made of course only by meeting and observing the subordinates. But the executive's approach to their selection, development, and motivation can be uncovered by appropriate questioning. Three aspects are especially important to probe.

1. *Whether the executive understands the necessity of selecting younger men for special development rather early in their careers.* It is frequently considered undemocratic to say so, yet the fact is that serious management development cannot apply to "everybody." Companies must

make provision for the continuity, and hopefully for the increasing competence, of their managements, and this necessarily involves selection and choice. Choice based on performance and intrinsic merit conform in fact to the democratic ideal. Indeed to forego choice and blur distinctions is to cultivate mediocrity. It is important therefore to determine whether the chief executive is sufficiently tough-minded to have made the difficult choices regarding succession to key posts, or whether he is, out of a misplaced concern for the democratic process, failing to provide for the future management of the company.

2. *Whether he is aware of the executive's basic responsibility for continually coaching and counselling his subordinates.* No matter how much formal management training is offered, the real learning of how to manage is done on the job, in real situations where mistakes are made and accounted for. It is important to determine the executive's attitude toward on-the-job training and development of his younger men.

General Lucius Clay, Chairman of the Continental Can Company, said once that "A top manager must always be available to discuss problems with young executives in an atmosphere in which arguments are encouraged and prolonged to bring out the facts. Always, the discussion should be pointed to the final decision's being made by the responsible junior and not by top management."

An indication of the chief executive's personal efforts to coach and counsel his key subordinates is an important element in judging the future quality of the management team.

3. *Whether he is aware of the need to stimulate and inspire his subordinates to their best effort.* The goals of the company as a whole and the challenge of work in various executive positions must be a continuing concern of top management. Nothing much happens without vision; and in the business world, many companies stagnate because top management cannot seem to develop and persuasively expound an illuminating vision of future possibilities. Yet only large goals are able to get people's eyes off the ground, and give them a real faith in what they are doing. It is important therefore to judge the leadership qualities of the top men by the scope and conviction of the leadership effort, and by the quality of response, as measured by the morale and productivity of the younger men.

CONTROL

Control is usually exercised through a variety of devices including periodic status reports, progress reports, graduated authority to spend the company's money, and frequent meetings between the top man and his principal subordinates. Control is both simplified and strengthened if sound plans have been developed, for actual performance can be measured against such plans. Control is also enhanced by sound organizational relationships. Thus where there is good planning and good organization, we can expect to find good control. If we find either of these to be defective, we explore the control devices very carefully.

COMPLEMENTARY TALENTS

It is also important to look for balance and diversity of talent in a management team, for a business with staying power is not usually a one-man show. Emerson said: "Idea and execution are seldom found in the same head," which may explain why an architect is seldom a builder, a design engineer seldom a production man, and an inventor almost never a good business executive. In our experience, the violation of Emerson's maxim in the business community is the key to much frustration, failure, nervous breakdown, and worse. It is sad to see a man who has been a real success in metallurgical research, for example, put in charge of a large steel works; or a man who should be captain of a steamship trying to head up advertising.

But it is also good to find what may be called complementary talents at the top of a corporation, and you would be surprised how many large and successful enterprises are so blessed, and owe their success to such a blessing. What I mean is the combination of a highly imaginative, creative man and a solid administrator in the number one and two positions. Usually the creative thinker is number one and the administrator his invaluable right arm; but sometimes the roles are reversed. Yet it seems true that these distinctive types of mind gravitate toward each other in large undertakings. Usually they work well together and respect each other.

Having thus described the way in which Cresap, McCormick and Paget approaches the appraisal of managements, it seems only fair to acknowledge the positional advantages usually enjoyed by a management consultant as distinguished from a security analyst. We are called in to examine a situation in depth, and we have the opportunity to observe men and their operating methods over a period of weeks or months. Because we are trying to help these men solve their problems, there is not much reason for them to hide their weaknesses from us. You, on the other hand, must be content with a far more superficial exposure and must be on your guard against the quite natural tendency of managements to give you only the rosiest impression of their situation.

A good example of our relative advantage occurred two years ago on the West Coast when our San Francisco partner and a reputable security analyst visited the same company on the same day. They were exposed to the same information and the same management forecasts, and both went away with a feeling of exhilaration about the prospects of a glamorous growth company.

About four months later, they met again. The view of the security analyst had not changed, and indeed there was no external information to indicate any altered prospect for the company. My partner, on the other hand, had in the interim made a thorough examination of the company's organization its market position, its products, and its manufacturing efficiency, and had been led to some distressing conclusions.

He found, for example, that the company's major product line had been in a seller's market for years, but was on the brink of a buyer's market. He found the products overpriced for the coming market conditions. Furthermore, he found that the company was not selling its products so much as it was offering them to its customers with the attitude of doing them a favor.

He found that many of the company's new products were over-engineered, and would probably have to be redesigned in order to remain competitive, because they were causing high production costs and serious storage problems.

He found that the company's organization planning was chaotic, but that management felt the constant changes in concept and in shifts in personnel were the unavoidable consequences of rapid growth. On the surface, and on the basis of all available published information, the company continued to look outstanding; but a close, thorough-going professional examination had revealed serious flaws and a prospective decline in performance.

Another kind of situation in which security analysts are probably at a natural disadvantage concerns mergers. Today the business community seems full of promoters who are pushing mergers and acquisitions with a zeal that reminds one of a mother trying to get her daughter married. Unfortunately too little attention is paid to making them work. Serious inefficiencies are concealed in combined statements, which in the aggregate show "growth."

This is a field where waste is frequently scandalous, and stockholders should be more concerned about it. While the stock market usually regards a merger optimistically, management consultants who are often in the middle of them are somewhat more pessimistic. Obviously, many mergers are sound undertakings, but a good many are not well implemented.

This matter of mergers is germane to our subject today because the waste in implementation occurs most frequently in people and in customer relationships. These are almost always the most precious assets possessed by a company. The dollars and the bricks and mortar and machines are usually treated with great care, but the people are often handled awkwardly, and the internal adjustments involving these people weaken the company's market position.

What exactly happens to the people in a merger? Too often they are treated as if they were impervious to change, as if a new environment, altered motives, new working relationships, changed and perhaps reduced incentives, and opportunities, have no effect. They are frequently put together in a new team arrangement that completely changes their role or gives a new meaning to their jobs (not always as favorable in their eyes). Unfortunately, these internal, somewhat intangible conditions are usually beyond the ken of the security analyst, but they may have an adverse effect on corporate performance through a protracted transitional period.

*****

By way of summary:

First, we should be fairly humble about our ability to appraise managers with complete accuracy, on the basis of relatively brief exposure;

Second, questions designed to bring out a manager's understanding of such techniques as planning, organization, personnel selection, motivation, and control will tend to reveal his basic competence, even though a grasp of such techniques is not a substitute for comprehensive knowledge of the business;

Third, an interview built around questions pertaining to these techniques is a sound approach, for such questions should indicate whether and what he thinks about the future, whether he possesses a sense of order, whether he understands the importance of selecting, developing and motivating people, and whether he can control his operations and resources;

Fourth, the management consultant has certain basic positional advantages in appraising people not normally possessed by the security analyst;

Fifth, a management's competence to deal with the personnel problems of a merger should be most carefully appraised, for the awkward handling of such problems is perhaps the greatest single cause of disappointing performance following the merger.

I might suggest a brief checklist of things to look for when you are seeking to evaluate corporate situations in their entirety. These are really in addition to, but not wholly separate from, the management appraisals we have been discussing.

Look for:

1. Cost-plus contracts. Companies thriving on these have developed some of the most wasteful organizational practices conceived in our time.
2. Hastily designed facilities. These may fail to anticipate new product development and hence will soon be outgrown.
3. Wasteful production methods, perhaps caused by the over-engineering of products by eager young scientists.
4. Product boners prematurely released to the market, and hastily called back for re-engineering.
5. Over-organization. The frequent springing up of new departments, divisions, and endless changes in reporting relationships.
6. Too many staff people. A large payroll of methods and systems personnel attempting to undo basic organizational errors made in the front office.
7. Mergers where the lesser company unwittingly gets stripped of some of its key people, basic drives, incentives, and customer relationships.

38

THE FINANCIAL ANALYST AND MANAGEMENT*

Harlow J. Heneman

The first question is very basic. How sound is "analysis" which devotes as little attention to management as financial analysts appear to do? How deeply do analysts penetrate in seeking to learn about the caliber of the management of corporations whose stocks they recommend?

Traditionally, financial analysts have been interested in capitalization, the strategy of financing, return on investment, dilution in the value of equities, earnings, financial and dividend trends, and future profit prospects, and have formed their judgments of management by applying yardsticks such as these. Some analysts have close contact with the management of individual corporations. There also are occasions when analysts' firms will participate in selecting the top management of a corporation and when they may be represented on its board of directors. Certainly, investment firms and analysts are interested in the results produced by good management. It is of significance to note that many financial analysts are showing greater interest in a broader understanding of management and that they are searching for indicators of evaluation to supplement those they traditionally have used.

But do analysts systematically evaluate management? When an officer or a member of the research staff of an investment firm has a close contact with a particular management, is this a planned program or approach, or is this merely the result of an individual's interest or connections? What do the research departments and the analysts say to investors about management?

Recently, I reviewed 72 reports on various corporations from five well-known investment firms. These reports ranged from 2 to 12 printed pages in length and were selected at random. Not one of these 72 reports has an underscored heading or other prominent identification directing attention to the subject of management. Fewer than half of them have any reference at all to management and then only in two or three brief

---

* Reprinted by permission of the *Financial Analysts Journal* (September–October 1967).

sentences. The conclusion usually drawn is that management is good if earnings per share have been increasing.

The literature in investment journals on industries and on corporations is singularly lacking in the treatment of the subject of management and the evaluation of sound business administration.

There may be some significance regarding the attitude toward management evaluation in the fact that members of the New York Society of Security Analysts are asked to indicate their fields of competence or interest from 36 itemized for selection purposes, and management is not listed as an area of specialization.

Based on the available information which financial analysts disseminate to the investor, either through reports or in the professional literature, it would appear that the subject of management is seldom dealt with systematically or in depth. If financial analysts have extensive knowledge of management and how to evaluate it, they do not appear to be making this information available to the prospective investor.

What Is Management and Who Are Managers?

Before proceeding further, it might be desirable to pause here and consider what management is. In management literature, there is no agreement upon a single definition. However, many of the same elements or factors occur repeatedly in the many definitions which have gained wide acceptance.

For many years, students looked upon management as the art of working with and through people to accomplish certain predetermined goals or objectives. Others have said that management is the process of planning and organizing means to attain given ends. Still another definition regards management as the process of planning and organizing the use of people, money, materials, and facilities, to attain pre-established objectives.

In a publication entitled, *Identifying and Developing Managers—Worldwide Shortages and Remedies* (June 1965), the National Industrial Conference Board stresses as elements of management the ability to plan, to organize, to lead, and, above all, to decide.

Some insight into what management is can be gotten from what organizations look for when selecting top managers. First of all, they look for persons who know how to plan, how to establish policies and set goals, how to organize, how to select good people, and how to develop an effective management team. They look for persons who know how to arrive at decisions objectively. They want persons with intellectual toughness who know how to use ideas, who want to get ideas, and who are capable of decision-making. They look for persons who can communicate with the second and third levels of management and with the work force regarding policies, objectives, and the means to attain these objectives. They want persons who know how to create conditions that are conducive to effective and efficient operations. These factors involve far more than the ability to use money and materials for they involve questions of morale, loyalty, social values, and faith in the rewards and objectives. It should be apparent that there is great room in management for art as well as science.

The NICB has stated that good management results from good managers. Good managers, it is said, are characterized by high moral standards and integrity, by imagination and creativity, by ambition and initiative, by dedication and loyalty, by administrative ability, by competence in planning and policymaking, by competence in organization of work, by unusually successful traits in personnel relations, and by successful on-the-job experience.

It should go without saying that the same qualities may not be required in all top managers. There are differences in emphasis, or in degree, depending upon the type of organization or enterprise which is being managed. The characteristics and abilities which may make a successful manager in an operation which is essentially that of an assembly line type may not be well suited to the effective management of an electronic or medical research organization.

Great strides have been made in introducing scientific techniques and methods to obtain information needed for decision-making. Mathematical formulas, electronic processing of data, and other methods and systems are making contributions that already have affected and in the future will have even a greater impact upon planning, the establishment of objectives, and on administration. However, the decisions involved in determining what use is to be made of the information obtained, and the impact on personalities and personnel all require judgments which involve arts and skills for which there may be no pure scientific substitute.

Attempts at Objective Ratings

Some attempts have been made to apply "scientific" techniques in evaluating corporate management. There has been considerable research, both of a theoretical and an applied nature, in this area. Attempts even have been made to apply a rating or scoring system to corporate managements. Illustrative of this approach are the Management Audit reports published by the American Institute of Management. It is of interest to note that in a typical Management Audit report, the following factors are evaluated: economic function, corporate structure, health of earnings, service to stockowners, research and development, directorate effectiveness, fiscal policies, production efficiency, sales vigor, and executive quality.

Under the AIM approach, each of these factors is assigned a certain number of rating points as an optimum. For each factor there is a rating scale which indicates the minimum to be attained for excellence. Actual rating points are then assigned to each factor. The total is used to determine whether overall, and in respect to which particular categories, the corporation may or may not have attained or exceeded the minimum excellence.

Caution in Rating Management

An evaluation procedure, such as that briefly described above, focuses attention on certain factors which are important components of management and undoubtedly there are advantages in forcing some form of reasonably objective review and analysis of present policies and practices for the purpose of evaluating them. However, it is doubtful whether it is possible at the present time to use a scoring system to make a hard and fast distinction between good and bad managements.

Even in his own territory the financial analyst should exercise great care in the use of traditional yardsticks. For example, the *quality* of dividends paid is very important. Are they earned dividends or are they paid out of accumulated surplus? Does a history of increased earnings per share really mean that there is good management? Two cases immediately come to mind that reveal the dangers of relying on this yardstick unquestioningly. One concerns a business enterprise whose product was so successful that for some years financial success covered very inefficient management practices which were ignored until the effects of inflation and competition made corrective action a necessity. In the case of another corporation, where the management was mediocre, the very existence of the corporation was threatened until one of its research chemists discovered a new process for making a product which gave the corporation marketing advantages and great profitability for some years. The high earnings brought complacency and cloaked the deficiencies of management. Clearly, the earnings per share yardstick reflects the past and, to some degree, the present, but it does not forecast the future or reflect the quality of management in all cases.

Although the limitations in any rating plan should be kept in mind, this is not to say that managements cannot be evaluated. The management counseling profession is engaged in the evaluation of management, directly or indirectly, and has been so engaged for many years. However, the outstanding firms among management consultants would be the first to admit that they have not found or established foolproof methods of rating management scientifically. Notwithstanding these limitations, financial analysts might be interested in what the management analyst looks for. The financial analyst may find something he can use in his own profession.

The environmental conditions in which management functions today have changed in many respects from the conditions which prevailed in the past. This has resulted from government regulation, through public policy, from labor contracts, and from scientific discoveries and developments. These influences would appear to have introduced a number of common ground rules making for a certain degree of uniformity. However, there still are marked variations and different managements act dissimilarly in response to the same conditions.

Suggested Factors for Use in Evaluating Management

Some of the factors which management analysts have found useful in forming judgments regarding corporate management are summarized in the paragraphs which follow. These suggestions should be examined by financial analysts to determine whether they, or variations of them, have any value for the investment analyst.

Can management make money when the economy has leveled off or turned downward as well as in more favorable circumstances? Many managements are cyclical in character and look good in fair weather but look quite ordinary under adverse economic conditions.

What does an *analysis of trends* reveal with respect to the quality of management? Whatever trends are analyzed, be they sales, net profits, or quality of product, they should be based upon a comparison of the organization's performance with itself as well as with its competitors.

Do the trends reflect an *effectiveness in the use of its own resources* as well as an ability to catch up with or to pass competitors? This two-way evaluation is important because the ability to catch up with a competitor who is slipping does not necessarily reflect improved internal management.

Has the business or enterprise a future? What are its future prospects? Through policies, organization, personnel appointments, and financial support, *management should show a capacity to anticipate future changes and to prepare for them.*

Are the *objectives and goals clearly defined?* Have they not only been clearly established but have they been subdivided into manageable segments and communicated to the various parts of the organization? There may be trouble in the future if the objectives are not of the kind that can command the loyal support of junior executives and the work force.

Is there sound medium and long-range *planning* to assess the validity of established objectives? Has proper provision been made for the flow of information to the long-range planning function? Do the results of the work of the planners get to the decision-makers and to the doers? Objectives must be reviewed continuously in order to make certain that they are in accord with actual conditions. The production of unwanted or outmoded products should not be started or allowed to continue. Not every corporation can afford an Edsel.

Is the *organization structure for management* a sound one and suited to meet the needs in that particular industry or of that particular corporation? Does the organization structure facilitate analysis, planning, and decision-making? Whether the organization be along product lines, geographic lines, or a combination of both, *are unnecessary layers of manage-*

ment eliminated? Is provision made for organization planning so that the organization may have the *capacity to grow* and have flexibility to meet new and unforeseen conditions?

Along with good organization it is necessary to have *sound management practices.* Are the lines of responsibility and accountability clear? Are there delegations which permit flexibility and the exercise of initiative and imagination, or does everything have to come to the top and does the presidential level tend to become a bottleneck? Are there delegations or decentralization with adequate controls? Or, have delegations been made without the necessary controls so that top management is unaware of and cannot affect in time what is being done at a lower level? A prominent aircraft and aerospace corporation failed to observe sound practices in this regard and almost became a fatal casualty before its management picture was corrected.

The *quality of leadership* is vital. This is true not only at the top but at the second and third levels as well. Who are the persons on the board of directors; are they "names" or can they make an effective contribution to policy and to top management? Is the board dominated by lawyers and bankers without particular experience as managers or knowledge of a given industry? Is there diversity in the talents and points of view reflected in the board of directors?

At the chief executive or presidential level, *is leadership timid or aggressive;* is it basically defensive-minded or is it innovative? Can top management make decisions or does it drift? If the business is scientific and technical, has top management the technical knowledge of its industry or is management dependent upon others for that knowledge? Is top management close to the business or is it absentee management with actual operating responsibilities left to lower level executives?

What are the *kinds and qualities of the persons in top management* positions? Has nepotism been a factor in staffing important positions? Have persons in top positions qualities of integrity, leadership, imagination, ability to inspire and warmth? Has the management shown social and political awareness? Does it combat and oppose social and political change or has it shown an ability to adapt to change?

What are *the ages of persons in managerial positions?* Is management growing old together or have younger persons been brought along and are the ages of persons in important positions staggered so that a whole layer of management will not be lost at one time?

Is there a sound *executive development* program? Has the enterprise shown the capacity to promote from within or has it been necessary to go outside to replace its top managers? What is the depth of good personnel? Are there personnel policies and practices which attract good men and are they retained?

If the organization is acquisition or merger-minded, has its management shown good *judgment in making acquisitions or mergers?* Do the actions reveal planned expansion or haphazard diversification? Are the acquisitions properly assimilated?

If it is a growth industry, does management show itself to be *adaptable and farsighted?* Has it shown the capacity to meet demands created by expansion in the form of new organization arrangements, alterations in staffing for management, and in techniques and procedures involving delegations and controls?

Is it important that the firm organize for, staff, and spend substantial sums on *research and development?* How much interest is shown in the encouragement of research? What percentage of income is allocated to research and are the trends in financing the research effort upward, level, or downward? Have the *results of research* increased the reputation or profitability of the business? Has there been imagination and ingenuity in translating the *results of research* into new products, new services, or in the development of new markets?

Is top management quality-minded and does the business have modern systems of *quality control?* Does the company's product compare favorably with the product of competitors?

With respect to *marketing and sales* efforts, is management close to its market, to the public, and to its customers? Are advertising and promotion sound, intelligent, and beneficial to the public image of the corporation? Has management introduced sound and effective sales development and sales incentive programs? Is provision made to maintain awareness of competitive developments?

Does management have available sound *analytical controls* in order to shape operations? Are there accurate data, and is use made of available information concerning unit costs, output per human or machine unit, per dollar in plant and equipment, per square foot of plant, and other yardsticks? Is management alert to possible financial "leaks," such as changes in the size of inventory in the case of level or declining prices?

Are equipment and facilities modern and up to date? Is provision made to introduce *new equipment and techniques* or does management follow outmoded practices with out-of-date equipment? Are facilities properly planned and laid out to meet the needs of the corporation? Are the facilities and equipment in a state of good repair for efficiency of operations? How much is being spent on plant maintenance and equipment repair?

In the case of organizations where *labor relations* are important, has management organized and staffed to deal effectively in this field? What kind of a record does management have in its relationships with its work staff and with unions?

What inducements are there to maintain investor interest in the corporation? What is the payout or return to investors? Does management pursue a sound and imaginative policy in governing its relationships with stockholders, investors, and the general public? Is there good communication with the financial community and with stockholders? *Are the annual reports informative* or are they secretive and obscure?

Finally, *what do other managements think of the management?* Alert management studies the management of competitors. The evaluations by competitors may be very significant indeed if they can be obtained.

Summary

The purposes of this article are two-fold. The first is to raise a question as to the soundness of the evaluation of management by financial analysts who have relied primarily upon financial yardsticks for their conclusions. If financial analysts are in the possession of a greater fund of knowledge than that obtainable from the application of these traditional yardsticks, they do not appear to make this information known to potential investors. This observation appears to be supported by the gaps in professional literature and, even more pointedly, by the content of the industry and corporate reports distributed by investment houses.

The second purpose of this article is to suggest that the financial analyst might be able to borrow from the management analyst and to apply certain of the factors and techniques used by management consultants to evaluate management. The management consulting profession does not have definitive answers to the problem of evaluating management, but the profession has accumulated a great deal of experience. It is hoped that this article will stimulate continuing investigation and study and that financial analysts will review the evaluation methods presented in this paper for possible adaptation to their own requirements.

Part Four
Portfolio Management

39

PERFORMANCE AND PORTFOLIO MANAGEMENT*

George C. Briggs, C.F.A.

It is of interest to trace the probable origin of the emphasis now being placed on investment performance. In the late 1940's common stocks were out of favor with investors. The direction of postwar adjustments and their effect on the general U.S. economy presented many uncertainties. Yields from good quality common stocks (Dow Jones Industrials) averaged over 6 percent from 1948 to 1950. By comparison, high grade corporate bonds, influenced by Treasury price supports, yielded less than 3 percent. In retrospect, the yield spread between these two investment areas provided far more than adequate compensation to the stock investor for the risks he assumed in stock ownership. Five years later, rising equity prices had caused Dow Jones Industrial Average yields to decline to around 5 percent; bond yields during that period changed little and the yield spreads continued to favor stock investors by over 2 percent.

By the late 1950's, however, a further rise in stock prices had caused stock yields to move into a negative relationship with bonds; in 1959 the yield spread favored the bond investor by over 1 percent. The demand for equities continued strong in the early 1960's. The yield spread remained between 1 percent and 1¼ percent as impressive gains were scored in earnings and dividends. A sharp reversal in stock prices in 1962 threatened to return the old bond-stock yield relationships. However, stock prices soon recovered, and by 1963 the bond-stock yield spread had widened again so as to favor the bond investor by well over 1 percent. Since that time the income return from bonds has exceeded the return obtainable from good grade stocks by amounts ranging from 1 percent to 2 percent.

The most common explanation for the change in the bond-stock yield relationship is that it reflects a desire on the part of investors to place greater emphasis on stock ownership in order to protect funds from a long-term erosion in the value of the dollar. Indeed, in tracing the loss in

---

* Reprinted by permission of the *Financial Analysts Journal* (September–October 1967).

purchasing power over a period of years, we find that the 1900 dollar (adjusted to changing wage levels) would purchase only 75 cents worth of goods in 1916, 50 cents worth in 1921, 25 cents worth in 1938, and a mere 8 cents worth in 1966. By comparison, dividend income distributed by Dow Jones Industrial Stocks, for the most part, has kept pace with rising wages. In 1966 dividend income was 109 percent of wage income, using 1900 as a base year.[1]

There have been other causes contributing to these changing yield relationships. From the early 1930's to the late 1940's, a modest number of entrants to the investment field, an after effect of the 1929 market collapse, caused the available supply of trained investment personnel to be spread thin. Competition for important investment posts was relatively light. This situation, plus haunting reminders of the 1929 stock market decline and fear of a possible repetition, caused investors to place a high value on the security of bond income and guaranteed principal repayments. In the past decade, a greater number of trained investment personnel have been more willing to accept the responsibility of enlarging equity commitments.

Along with the additions of trained personnel, methods of security analysis have advanced rapidly in recent years. The use of computers has enabled a vast amount of statistical information to be usefully correlated. Projections of sales and earnings have improved with a rapport between investor and company management on a widespread basis that has never before existed. The talent of applying appropriate price-earnings multipliers to companies with varying growth rates has improved considerably. Progress along these lines has been aided by the well-coordinated development of the Financial Analyst Federation and more recently by the Chartered Financial Analyst courses. The FAF's influence on corporate reporting procedures is currently being felt and is likely to produce many beneficial changes in future years.

Coincident with the emergence of a large number of investment specialists and techniques has been a growing confidence in the ability of Federal Reserve System members and administration economic advisers to take steps which would prevent the recurrence of a 1929 type depression. This confidence is by no means complete. It has developed slowly as the United States weathered a series of postwar recessions, and has been given support by a greater understanding on the part of the public of the economic problems faced by this country.

Superimposed upon this series of developments have been widespread efforts by investors to participate in the growth of small firms which can become the General Motors, General Electrics, and IBMs of tomorrow. Litton, Xerox, and Texas Instruments are representative of this type of

---

[1] Source: "Selected Financial Data," 1967 ed., First National Bank of Chicago, Table 34.

situation. Much concentration of investment wealth in 1967 is being focused on a number of such companies which are currently undergoing rapid rates of expansion. The list of names enlarges with the availability of good research information and may include any firm with publicly owned shares. In many cases, share prices have advanced to the point where investors are exposed to considerable price risk due to a miscalculation of future prospects.

Influence on Portfolio Management

To the portfolio manager, the concept of measuring performance is not new. Mutual fund selection has been based on relative performance for many years. Indeed, considerable concern developed in 1962 when a majority of reporting funds were unable to better the results of the Dow Jones Industrial Average during a sharp market setback. To the funds credit, however, were some highly commendable results during the 1966 market decline.

Managers of numerous state pension funds have adopted a policy of investing in common stocks over the past 15 to 20 years to improve their investment results. Many college funds have moved in the same direction, some with very successful consequences. Fiduciaries have enlarged what they consider prudent equity proportions in accounts to give improved performance. Common funds have evolved in a large number of institutions, partly to provide a performance record for their organizations. Little wonder there has been price escalation in stocks with favorable future expectations, or that institutional holdings of common equities, as measured by issues traded on the New York Stock Exchange, have increased year after year.

Performance, if it is defined as the measurement of relative investment results, is being discussed with increasing frequency by owners of securities as well as portfolio managers. Taken in broad context the emphasis on performance reflects an evolution in attitudes toward securities investment from a position of conservation to one of relative enhancement of asset values. The current trends present clear evidence that the institutional investor is responding to the benefits provided from rising earnings and dividends in an expanding economy by focusing large portions of investable assets in equities.

In recent years, emphasis on performance has caused an increasing amount of attention to be directed toward the proper weighting of stock market indexes. The growing popularity of the Standard & Poor's and New York Stock Exchange Averages versus the various Dow Jones indexes are evidence of this trend. As a consequence, the portfolio manager is susceptible to seeing his results compared to price changes in the generally accepted security market averages at almost any time. Either the Standard and Poor's 500 Stock Average or the NYSE Composite Index are a reasonable gauge for measuring the performance of portfolios entirely invested in common stocks, providing no unusual emphasis is being placed on producing a high rate of income or maximum capital appreciation where high risk securities are involved.

Approaches to Portfolio Management

If we accept the accent on investment performance as an outgrowth of an enlarged number of common stock investors with added confidence for buying common stocks and the research capabilities to support intelligent revisions in security holdings, what developments can we foresee in the area of portfolio management? To consider this point, let us review several steps which are normally covered to establish a meaningful relationship between a portfolio manager and his client. It is first necessary for a manager to determine the following:

1. What is the specific investment objective of each account—capital appreciation, current income or a combination of both?
2. What is the temperament of the client—whether individual or committee? How does he react to holding securities with large risks of asset depreciation even though these risks may no more than offset the probable potential for capital appreciation?
3. If a price decline occurs in a security without sound reasons, will a client exert pressure to sell out his holding?
4. Is adequate information available on all security holdings? What is the degree of relative marketability of each security?
5. How frequently should each account be reviewed on a formal basis? An informal basis?
6. What information is available on ages, tax brackets, and other asset holdings?
7. What is the degree of flexibility in the handling of each account—can action be taken instantly when desired?
8. Will new funds flow into each account from time to time?

When these several factors have been determined, particularly when the account objective has been accurately established, how may a portfolio manager proceed to accomplish the objective in the light of performance standards. Initially, let us consider the investor seeking primarily capital gains.

1. Here standards may be very important. What does this investor expect as a rate of return from his capital? What does the manager believe he can accomplish along this line? Are these two goals far apart? Should the client have no specific return on his investment in mind, then perhaps the stock indexes can be used as a minimum performance standard.

2. Again, temperament is important in investing funds. Is the investor willing to undergo the disillusionment which may result from a sharp price decline even though an investment situation is building intrinsic value? An example is the company whose sales are exhibiting a strong

uptrend but whose earnings are below normal because of conservative accounting practices or a series of unusually large expenses. A stock market which places great emphasis on reported earnings can easily fail to recognize the improvement in intrinsic value in such an instance. Textron in the early 1960's offers a case in point. Many electronics companies in the late 1950's serve as an example as does the experience of several companies in the computer field earlier in this decade.

3. Is sufficient stress placed on growth areas of the economy in making individual security selections. Changes in population groupings have offered outstanding investment opportunities, such as soft drink stocks in the late 1950's and hospital supply companies in the early 1960's. New developments in education and technology have presented excellent buying opportunities in the publishing and information systems industries in recent years.

4. Are principal product line and management changes weighed as to their effect on individual holdings? Are major acquisitions considered in a similar light?

5. May each security holding in the portfolio be classified as underpriced in relation to the stock market as a whole? Can reasons be supplied if necessary in support of this position?

6. Are adequate reserve funds maintained to take advantage of general price weakness?

7. Is sufficient consideration given to moving in and out of the stock market as monetary conditions change? While such opportunities may present themselves infrequently, a manager can enhance his results by acting on signals which forecast a substantial easing or tightening of bank credit.

Next, consider the investor to whom a high degree of current income is important.

1. Bonds may be used in a period of relatively high interest rates. In this instance, have various maturity areas been considered?

2. Is sufficient consideration given to the use of convertible bonds and preferred stocks? Often the chance to obtain a high rate of income as well as capital appreciation exists during original offerings of convertible securities. Periods of heavy capital financing accompanied by tight money conditions have presented the most attractive time for purchasing such issues. In making use of convertibles, care should be exercised to assure their sale or conversion when a price increase reduces the income return at market value.

3. Are high income stocks being employed effectively? At almost any period, opportunities exist to purchase depressed stocks which are paying an above-average return and whose negative factors are overdiscounted by the market place. History is replete with examples of such opportunities—growth utilities in the early 1950's when federal interference in rate handling was overemphasized; rubber stocks in the mid-1950's when labor

problems were overplayed and volume growth was underestimated; international oils in 1960 when a selling climax occurred following the Suez crisis a few years earlier; auto stocks in the early 1960's when valid sales projections were classified as overly optimistic, and aerospace stocks in the mid-1960's prior to a massive buildup in U.S. defense capabilities.

4. On several occasions in the past, stocks in rapidly growing companies have proved to be the most rewarding incomewise to the patient investor. IBM purchased in 1958 provides a yield at cost of 6.3 percent on today's dividend rate; Merck purchased in 1961, a yield of 5.6 percent; Xerox, Eastman Kodak and Coca-Cola all yield 5 percent on their average 1962 prices. These securities, at the same time, have given their owners several hundred percent price appreciation. There are often periods during general market weakness when such stocks may be purchased at historically attractive valuations and the merit of their inclusion in the income-oriented portfolio should not be underestimated.

Some investors seek account management assistance which places an equal emphasis on the potential for capital appreciation and the amount of current income being produced.

1. In this instance, it is also necessary to ask if each security is meeting the objectives of the portfolio. It is not enough to say a security holding qualifies for investment if it offers neither above-average income nor above-average growth prospects. On the contrary, the portfolio with securities having one characteristic or the other may well show the best results—for example, high-yielding bonds and low-yield growth stocks.

2. Several considerations outlined for the capital gains conscious investor apply to the stock list owned by the account with a combined growth-income objective. It may be particularly important in a large portfolio to shift holdings from time to time in order to place continuing emphasis on growth areas of the economy.

3. The convertible security which offers a larger current return than its common stock counterpart may be especially suited to this type of portfolio.

4. Nonconvertible bonds may serve a very definite purpose when used in sufficiently large quantity in order to take advantage of trading opportunities offered by changing interest rate patterns.

The above review of approaches to portfolio management indicate why it is important to follow individual investment situations closely in order to obtain favorable results. A portfolio manager, therefore, requires sources of information he regards highly for this purpose. Frequently, a company's progress is best followed through liaison with officials of the firm itself. Of particular importance is likely to be a manager's rapport with knowledgeable representatives of small, rapidly growing firms which will enable him to obtain the necessary information to maintain (or change) his client's investment position when it is most advantageous to do so.

It is well to bear in mind that portfolio management is not an exact science but an art frequently requiring a hedged position. Subjective judgment is necessary in selecting securities to meet account objectives, considering appropriate switches in investment holdings under a myriad of circumstances and determining the use of reserve funds. A portfolio manager is called upon to find attractively priced equities at almost any given time. During a period when considerable energy is being directed toward measuring investment performance, portfolio management results are being examined more closely than ever before. In this atmosphere the portfolio manager has a great opportunity to enhance his relationship with his clients by accurately interpreting complex trends in our economy and applying his judgment successfully in the many areas of the securities market.

Conclusion

The modern emphasis on performance probably traces its origin to a period following the late 1940's, when a yield spread favorable to stock investors over bond investors began to reverse itself as a result of expanded buying in common stocks. The principal reason that vast amounts

Year	Yield on Mean Price—D.J. Ind. Stock Average	Yield on High Grade Corp. Bonds	Stock Bond Yield Difference
1966	3.5%	5.09%	−1.63%
1965	3.1	4.53	−1.45
1964	3.1	4.37	−1.31
1963	3.3	4.24	−0.96
1962	3.5	4.29	−0.79
1961	3.2	4.36	−1.20
1960	3.3	4.41	−1.14
1959	3.1	4.38	−1.29
1958	3.7	3.80	−0.08
1957	4.3	3.91	0.40
1956	4.0	3.40	0.61
1955	4.3	3.04	1.23
1954	5.0	2.87	2.09
1953	5.9	3.18	2.69
1952	5.6	2.95	2.70
1951	6.3	2.84	3.46
1950	7.5	2.59	4.91
1949	7.1	2.64	4.46
1948	6.4	2.80	3.60
1947	5.3	2.58	2.72
1946	4.0	2.51	1.49
1945	3.9	2.61	1.24
1940	5.3	2.92	2.38
1935	3.7	3.61	0.09
1930	4.9	4.71	0.19
1925	3.0	4.93	−1.93
1920	3.9	6.18	−2.28

SOURCE: "Selected Financial Data," 1967 ed., First National Bank of Chicago, Table 29.

of savings were directed into the stock market was a growing desire on the part of investors to protect funds against the decline in the purchasing power of the dollar. Other factors have contributed importantly to this trend, however, such as an emerging sophistication in security analysis, a rapidly growing number of younger men in positions of investment responsibility, many of whom invest aggressively in common stocks, and a slowly developing confidence in the ability of Federal Reserve officials and administration authorities to control periods of economic adjustment. Also influencing market prices of shares have been widespread efforts by investors to find small companies whose growth potential is sufficiently impressive as to qualify them to become giant corporations in future years. In certain cases, the shares of these companies have been bid up in price to levels where they are considerably vulnerable in the event long-range forecasts do not materialize.

In effect, the performance era, which is not new, reflects a shift in investment goals from the preservation of asset values to the enhancement in these values to the point where they will at least maintain their purchasing power. In many cases, these goals have been carried a step further as more and more investors seek maximum capital gains from investing in the stock market. Such developments have resulted in the use of measurement techniques which facilitate comparison of investment results. In this respect, they have created new challenges for the portfolio manager.

Several factors have been reviewed as essential in the management of investment portfolios, such as clearly determining the investment objective as well as the temperament of a customer and gathering pertinent data on ages, tax brackets, outside asset holdings, cash flow, and account flexibility. In making security selections, it is necessary to have a reliable source for information on company activities as well as an understanding of the degree of the marketability of securities being used. Frequency of review is often determined by the nature of the investment holdings. Employment of reserve funds may be very important at certain intervals as is keeping a watchful eye on bank credit availability and trends of growth in various sectors of the U.S. economy. Each security in an investment portfolio should meet the established investment objectives of that particular account.

The portfolio manager's role continues to call for highly subjective judgments despite advances in computer techniques in the field of investment analysis. The availability of computers, however, has resulted in improved methods for measuring portfolio performance and focused attention on investment results. In this respect, accomplishments in the area of portfolio management are likely to be well recognized in future years, thereby offering great opportunity to the successful manager of security portfolios.

40

ELEMENTS OF PORTFOLIO CONSTRUCTION*

Frank E. Block, C.F.A.

Among the weakest sectors in the literature of investing are the elements involved in the structuring of a portfolio and the methods of implementing portfolio strategy. A great deal has been written by practitioners on the subject of portfolios. Yet when the folklore and subjective commentary are swept away, the view is pretty barren. Some progress has been made in the academic community as a result of a few brilliant contributions by mathematically oriented scholars, most notably Markowitz.[1] In addition, many of the elements of a portfolio theory have been known and discussed for years. The problem is that a general theory of *continuous* portfolio management has not yet evolved.

Basic Elements

The familiar elements involved in portfolio construction include return, risk, diversification, volatility, and time horizon. All of these terms are used frequently in discussing portfolio strategies. For a basic theory of portfolio structuring, such elements must be rigorously defined, but at present they are used loosely and have different meanings to different users. Without the disciplines of both definition and quantification, they are too vague to be assembled into a formal, logical structure.

The practitioners hold a considerably different view of the investment process than that of their academic counterparts. One example is the question of risk. The academic community is almost uniform in the view that risk is measured by variability of rate of return, which they express in such familiar statistical terms as standard deviation, variance, semivariance, and so on. The practitioner accepts variability of return as a *part* of risk, but maintains that there are many kinds of risk, some of which are subjective and most of which are not easily represented by traditional statistical measures. Thus, the practitioners are critical of the risk input used in a Markowitz type of portfolio model.

---

* Reprinted by permission of the *Financial Analysts Journal* (May–June 1969).
[1] Markowitz, Harry M., *Portfolio Selection: Efficient Diversification of Investments* (John Wiley & Sons, New York, 1959).

The practitioner finds further fault with the idea that the investor's expectations, which are used as the inputs of the academicians' portfolio models, are well handled. The literature seems to say that the returns of portfolios tend to fall under normal or log normal distribution curves, whereas the empirical evidence is that they do not.[2] These "normal" curves appear regularly in the physical sciences and in certain types of random samples where systemic consistency is present. In such cases, the random errors and deviations provide nice symmetrical heaps of data. But, in the market place, there are systemic inconsistencies which provide an unpredictable skewness. Perhaps the inconsistencies represent the waves of belief and doubt that characterize the "herd instinct." As more and more institutions introduce performance measurements techniques into their computers, portfolio managers are increasingly impressed by the absence of aesthetically and statistically pleasing "bellshaped" curves.

The practitioner is often puzzled by what seems to be an unstated assumption in the Markowitz-type portfolio models that prices are made by the impact of the market's probability distribution of return expectations. Yet many practicing market observers are convinced that prices are set by marginal sellers and marginal buyers.[3] Price expectations are a part of return expectations. There does not appear to be much evidence that price distributions set by marginal opinion would cause the sort of probability distributions of return, or variability of returns, for that matter, that would result from the influence of total market expectations.

Similarly, practitioners cannot agree with those academic views which assume the presence of markets which are "in equilibrium"[4] and "efficient markets"[5] (the latter idea tends to lead to the former). Either concept would tend to support the random walk adherents' belief that investment analysis can obtain no better than random results without inside information or other special advantages. The practitioners believe that they are observing every day a market which is rather inefficient. They respond to the random walk theorists with such remarks as, "The results of almost any natural law look like Brownian motion until the observer understands the law."

The practitioner's attitude is typified by Robert Cummins' view that

---

[2] Breen, W. and Savage, J., "Portfolio Distributions and Tests of Security Selection Models," *Journal of Finance*, Vol. XXIII, No. 5 (Dec. 1968), pp. 805–819.

[3] Smith, R. G. E., "The 'Marginal Opinion' Theory of Stock Price," *Financial Analysts Journal* (November–December 1967), pp. 127–132.

[4] Sharpe, W. F., "Capital Asset Prices: A Theory of Market Equilibrium Under Conditions of Risk," *Journal of Finance*, Vol. XIX, No. 3 (September 1964), 425–442. See also, "Risk-Aversion in the Stock Market: Some Empirical Evidence," *Journal of Finance*, Vol. XX, No. 3, pp. 416–422; Treynor, J. L., "How to Rate Management of Investment Funds," *The Harvard Business Review* (January/February, 1965), Vol. 43, No. 1, pp. 63–75.

[5] Cootner, P. H., *The Random Character of Stock Market Prices* (Cambridge, Mass.: M.I.T. Press, 1964).

investors have different amounts of information, different abilities to interpret it, and different degrees of conviction and motivation.[6]

Occasionally, portfolio managers are startled to read an academic paper which seems to say that a particular mechanism may be used to accomplish something the portfolio manager is striving to avoid. An example would be Sharpe's statement that if rates of return from efficient portfolios were perfectly correlated then "diversification enables the investor to escape all but the risk resulting from swings in economic activity—this type of risk remains even in efficient combinations."[7] The portfolio manager may accept that diversification cannot remove entirely the influence of market movements, industry, and so on—which are presumably part of "economic activity"—but he probably does not consider this to be the main objective of diversification. He does not wish to escape the unique characteristics of his portfolio holdings; he wants to participate in that uniqueness—that is why he purchased those particular securities. The portfolio manager wishes to use true diversification to reduce the external influences of market and economic vagaries. For this reason, he is much more fascinated with those studies which suggest ways to participate more intensively in the future of particular companies, such as recent volatility studies by Treynor, Priest, Fisher, and Higgins.[8] Portfolio managers generally agree that true diversification is obtained through Markowitz's covariance route, but there seems to be some disagreement between the theoretical and practicing groups as to which fluctuations diversification is trying to remove.

Further examples of this intellectual dichotomy abound, but it is not our purpose to appear as an advocate of the practitioner's viewpoint. It would be easier to attack the typical portfolio manager for his ignorance. However, this article can be more useful if it remarks on those ideas and concepts which are receiving increased attention by the more advanced practitioners who are seeking and finding new tools with which to work. This may not be of much help in bridging the educational gap of the financial analyst, but it might narrow the communications gap with the academic community.

TIME HORIZON

One of the most interesting concepts under discussion today by many portfolio managers is that of time horizon. As usual, the phrase is used loosely and means only what the speaker or writer intends it to mean at that particular time.

---

[6] Cummins, R. I., "Knowledge and Insight," *Financial Analysts Journal* (July-August, 1966).

[7] Sharpe, W. F., "Capital Asset Prices . . . ." *Op. cit.*

[8] Treynor, J. K., Priest, W. W., Fisher, L., Higgins, C. A., "Using Portfolio Composition to Estimate Risk," *Financial Analysts Journal* (September–October 1968). Also, Tunnicliff, L., "Volatility Index as a Leading Indicator of Stock Prices," unpublished study, 1968, for the Citizens and Southern National Bank.

Time horizon is of importance to portfolio managers in a number of ways. It plays a part not only in the rate of return and its variability, but also in risk and diversification.

One commonly used meaning of the concept time horizon is the *anticipated holding period* of a security or portfolio. Other time horizons are the *period over which investment results are to be measured* and the *time in which a specific objective is expected to be attained*. The time horizon is often related to the length of life of the account. Within a portfolio, the securities may have a variety of time horizons quite different from that of the whole portfolio.

Many portfolio managers adopt multiple time horizons for a single portfolio or for single securities. These time horizons may be related to objectives or to expectations—to the achievement of specific goals or to the sequence of possible events.

The "efficient portfolios" suggested by Markowitz have certain implications for the time horizon of the investor. It is not hard to imagine the designing and construction of an efficient portfolio at a given point in time. Yet, the moment that either prices or expectations change, one no longer has a perfect portfolio. Purchases and sales would have to be made continuously. Even though a portfolio were initially based on longer term expectations, the manager would find that its time horizon had collapsed to virtually zero and that its turnover was nearly infinite. Oddly enough, there would be no guarantee of success, even if all of the original longer range expectations and projections were ultimately correct. This is true because the portfolio would not be held long enough for those expectations to be realized. Shorter term market influences would be the controlling factors. Yet, logically, the Markowitz concept would certainly seem to demand that one stay in the most efficient portfolio at all times. At present, the Markowitz approach presents great difficulties in the *continuous* management of portfolios.

The conflict between the very short time horizon implied by the need to stay in the perfect portfolio (or perhaps only in those stocks on the "Purchase List") and the much longer expectational time horizon is a serious one. Experience has taught most practitioners that the expectational time horizon should be roughly the same length as the planned holding period. If one invests for a year, the important expectations are those which should influence prices and dividends for that year, and these are largely short-term expectations. Where a longer holding period is planned, the short-term predictions are useful only for timing purposes, and the main consideration becomes the longer term outlook.

Obviously, the shorter the holding period, the less likely is the possibility of the unsuspected dramatic event, which may result in disaster or rich rewards. Over a succession of short holding periods, the ultimate occurrence of the unpredictable major event approaches a certainty.

The time horizon for a portfolio is not necessarily the same as for the individual securities in the portfolio. The obvious example is the temporary investment of funds in U.S. Treasury bills awaiting a more permanent resting place. Clearly, the return and variance expectations for the U.S. Treasury bills are for a relatively short period of time, while the portfolio might quite properly have a very long time horizon. Investors often buy stocks, not to hold, but to turn over for a quick profit, regardless of the longer term perspective of the total portfolio.

THE PRESSURE FOR PERFORMANCE

A particular problem of modern day investing is the pressure for short-term performance. Many accounts are priced monthly or quarterly and reviewed by the customer or a committee to see how they have performed in such brief periods of time. Mutual funds are priced daily, and mutual fund managers almost face the question: "What have you done for me this morning?"

The increasing demand for short-term investment performance may force upon the portfolio manager a time horizon which is unsuited to the needs of the account and to the abilities of the portfolio manager. The very worst investing is done by those who attempt to invest in a way for which they are poorly equipped. Highly aggressive short-term investing requires a special set of inputs and an environment of great flexibility. A large organization having a cumbersome committee system and handling thousands of accounts must adopt a realistic time horizon that reflects the speed with which it can act and react.

The time perspective of a security analyst must be a factor in determining the holding period for his recommendations. If he is skilled at picking stocks which will move, but weak on fundamentals, he may be quite valuable in one organization and downright dangerous in another.

In view of the potential importance of the time perspective, both absolute and expectational, it seems strange that the time horizon has received no recognition on the campus, other than being hidden away in some hypothetical investor's utility curve.

DIVERSIFICATION

A substantial change in thinking about diversification has resulted from Markowitz's remarkable book *Portfolio Selection*. Markowitz pointed out that the returns from investments do not necessarily move simultaneously in the same direction and with the same magnitude, but rather are somewhat uncoordinated. In short, they do not have perfect positive *covariance*. Markowitz's contribution was the recognition that true diversification consists of a group of securities which have low covariance in their rates of return. This type of diversification minimizes the variability of the portfolio's return.

Admittedly, all common stocks are susceptible, to some degree, to general moves in the market. Various studies have indicated that perhaps half of the fluctuations in the price of individual common stocks may be accounted for by fluctuations in the market as a whole. The remainder of the stock's fluctuations must be attributed to a large variety of factors, including the market action of the industry,[9] the company's own income and dividend patterns, expectations for the company's future, quality, and so on. The fluctuations of companies engaged in a wide variety of businesses are likely to cancel one another to some extent, i.e., some may have low or even negative covariance. For example, an increase in electricity rates may have an unfavorable effect on the profits of many companies which use electricity, but at the same time it would benefit the electric utility companies which receive the rate increase.

If diversification is carried out successfully, the "risk" of a portfolio will turn out to be substantially less than the weighted average risk of the individual securities in it. The result is that there is a clear difference between portfolio risk and the risk of the portfolio's individual securities. The risk of a security is reduced by the fact that it will be part of a "diversified" portfolio. How much it is reduced depends on how the security is used.

The Markowitz theory seeks the *best* diversification. If no external constraints were put on the theory, it might result in a portfolio consisting of 90 percent in a single stock and 10 percent in U.S. Treasury bills. It offers no justification for having a fixed size for investment units.

The traditional diversification view is that concentrations are to be avoided. It tends to favor overdiversification, using "proper" (equal) investment units. In the continuous managing of portfolios, the traditional attitude about the appropriateness of size often tends to force the portfolio manager to sell part of those stocks which have done the best and to add to those that have performed poorly. More often than not, both moves turn out to be mistakes.

It has been argued, in defense of using a large number of stocks, that the portfolio manager should give his security analysts enough chances to be right. Since even the best batter has a slump once in a while, his batting average should be based on a full season and not just a few times at bat.

This introduces, through the back door, the question of time horizon again. Fifty stocks selected for a holding period of one year are, indeed, equal to 50 "times at bat." But, similarly, 25 stocks bought for a six month holding period, at the end of which time the portfolio manager again selects 25 stocks, are also 50 times at bat. The shortening of the holding period—or time horizon—increases the number of opportunities over the full period.

---

[9] King, B. F., "Market and Industry Factors in Stock Price Behavior," *Journal of Business*, Vol. XXXIX, No. 1, Part II (January 1966). Also, Breen, W., "Low Price-Earnings Ratios and Industry Relatives," *Financial Analysts Journal* (July-August 1968), and unpublished studies by J. H. Willis, Summer 1966, for the Citizens and Southern National Bank.

The investor with the "buy and hold forever" philosophy may find himself at a great disadvantage with 100 stocks in his portfolio. The manager of a more aggressive portfolio might use a smaller number of stocks—say 10 or 20—and rearrange them frequently. Over a period of time, such a portfolio manager may have 1,000 times at bat. He has the additional advantage of being in his top 10 or 20 selections rather than his top 100 selections. If security analysts are worth their salt, it must be assumed that their favorite 20 stocks will perform better than their favorite 100.

In short, we want enough times at bat, and we want also to use the maximum selectivity by staying only in those stocks in which we have the greatest faith.

There are ways to use existing probability measurements to determine the ideal number of stocks for use in a portfolio.[10] Suppose that a study of the recommendations of security analysts shows that they pick three winners and one loser out of every ten recommendations and that the other six selections perform more or less in line with the market. We shall assume: (1) that there is no covariance between the securities, (2) one winner will offset one loser, and (3) a successful portfolio is one which will at least equal or better the performance of the market over some time interval. How many stocks would be required to be reasonably certain of accomplishing this goal? Probability analysis results in the following table:

Probability of Success	Number of Stocks in the Portfolio
90 %	15
95	25
98	38
99	49
99.9	86

The table suggests that a Trust Department with 1,000 accounts would have only one unsuccessful account over the standard time period if 86 stocks were used in each account. But this assumes that a portfolio manager could pick 86 stocks with a "batting average" that was equal to his success ratio in picking, say, his favorite 15 stocks. Practical experience suggests that this is not likely and that the 86 stocks are much more likely to be the equivalent of "buying the market."

However, consider the possibility of reducing the standard time interval—that is, reducing the time horizon. The 15 stock portfolio has a 10 percent chance of being unsuccessful over a single standard time interval. The likelihood of it being unsuccessful *in two consecutive time intervals* is only 1 percent, or a 99 percent success ratio. The 15 stock portfolio

---

[10] A sophisticated approach to this problem is found in "Diversification and the Reduction of Dispersion: An Empirical Analysis" by Evans and Archer, *Journal of Finance*, Vol. XXIII, No. 5 (December 1968).

might be totally unsuited for an account whose life expectancy is one standard time interval, but might be ideal for accounts which could invest aggressively for a series of short or intermediate holding periods.

The point of the above example is two-fold. First, existing mathematical methods can probably give us guidance for the proper number of stocks to use in a portfolio; and, second, *the amount of diversification needed is a function of the time horizon.* We submit that both of these are major considerations in devising a general portfolio strategy.

Volatility

The volatility of a security may not be an official element of a basic theory of portfolio management, but it is one of the most intriguing tools that has fallen into the hands of portfolio managers in many years. The Treynor articles, referred to in footnotes (8) and (4), present the basic idea of volatility for both individual securities and for portfolios. The security or the portfolio has variance of rate of return which can be broken down into market variance and residual variance. In the case of an individual security, market variance is simply that portion of the fluctuation of the security which correlates with moves in the market as a whole. If the stock tends to move more rapidly than the market, its volatility can be expressed simply as a coefficient greater than 1, which is applied to the moves of the market. The residual variance is very appealing, since this would be a characteristic unique to the individual security. The Treynor research indicated that the residual variance shows a fair amount of stability over time. Thus, past residual variance may have some value in predicting future residual variance. The investor may have some control of the degree to which he invests purely in those characteristics of the security which are unaffected by general movements in the stock market.

At the same time, the volatility, or market variance, can be used to advantage in the structuring of portfolios. If participation in a market move were desired, a stock of high volatility could be chosen to do the job with a smaller number of dollars than would be required if the volatility were lower. If the portfolio manager also wanted to participate in the individual characteristics of a stock, he would be able to determine the degree of participation by selecting a stock with a high residual variance in comparison with the norms for a large population of securities.

While this seems to be one of the most exciting areas in portfolio management at the moment, it appears that on the campus the effort seems to be the elimination of the residual variance.

What the portfolio manager would like to have is a system which would permit him to select the volatility (or market variance) that pleased him and to participate as deeply as he wished in the destiny of certain companies. There would be great appeal in portfolio structuring devices which would subdivide the total variance of a portfolio into (1)

Elements of Portfolio Construction

market variance of the desired volatility, (2) a nonmarket economic activity variance, and (3) a residual variance that represented the company only. Sharpe (see footnote 4) and Lerner and Carlton[11] have implied the existence of great difficulties in accomplishing this result, but the rewards would be large.

Volatility is not merely a function of quality. It is true that volatile earnings and volatile prices tend to go together. At the same time, the volatility of a stock is closely tied to its floating supply in the market and the volume of trading. Price is also a factor since the floating supply tends to change with price. Certainly the psychology of the market, fadism, and the impact of transactions triggered by market technicians are major influences on volatility. Today's volatile stocks may be tomorrow's stable stocks. These influences are dynamic rather than static. That part of covariance which is tied to the volatility of the stock must also be dynamic.

Variability of Rate of Return

A number of investment organizations have attempted to test Markowitz's theory, employing computers for the complex calculations required. Some have also explored the simplifications offered by Sharpe.[12] It would appear that most of these efforts have encountered difficulties because of the aggregation of all risks into a single term—the variability of the rate of return.

Economic history is a succession of significant events. Some events could have been predicted with specific probabilities, while others fell in the categories of rude or joyous surprises, some of which were never even imagined in advance. The ideal portfolio strategy will require that specific probabilities be placed on specific events (those that lend themselves to anticipation). Diversification efforts should be designed to exploit favorable events and protect against unfavorable happenings. The unexpected events will remain "residual uncertainty," or "statistical noise."

Theoreticians have developed a system of probability distributions for rates of return. We submit that similar probability distributions could be created for specific events. Since a large number of economic events can be anticipated, a sort of spectral analysis of the portfolio would be the necessary input to reflect these expectations. The impact of each of these economic events upon a specific security must be estimated so that the weight of the event can be measured in terms of its effect on the total portfolio.

As in the Markowitz analysis of the securities in a portfolio, the

---

[11] Lerner, E. M. and Carlton, W. D., *A Theory of Financial Analysis* (Harcourt Brace and World, Inc., 1966).

[12] Sharpe, William F., "A Simplified Model for Portfolio Analysis," *Management Science* (January 1963), pp. 277–93; "Addendum to A Simplified Model for Portfolio Analysis," *Management Science* (April 1963), p. 498.

covariance between economic events should not be neglected. For example, if the economic problem to be handled were an unbalanced budget, political decisions might favor higher taxes, lower government spending, or a mixture of both. There would be a negative covariance between the two economic events, revenue and spending, since the larger the increase in taxes, the smaller the necessary reduction in expenditures to reach a balanced budget.

A general investment strategy must provide some help in the handling of these specific events. It must provide for the quantification and impact of each, simply because the covariance between the securities in the portfolios is a function of those events which actually occur or are recognized by the market as possible occurrences. In effect we are suggesting that the analysts' expectations about the interrelationship between rates of return of two or more securities must also weigh heavily the effect of major predictable events on their covariance.

Sub-Strategies

Somewhere, room must be left for the portfolio manager to introduce those sub-strategies which he believes will be effective in maximizing the rate of return of the portfolio.

Portfolio managers have their own pet sub-strategies for use within a broad portfolio strategy. They believe, correctly or not, that they have developed special abilities to accomplish certain things within the portfolio, even though those actions involve different time horizons and risk/return ratios than have been adopted for the portfolio as a whole. While they may accept the covariance type of diversification as being the most desirable approach, they do not feel that theoretical limitations should prevent them from taking advantage of what they consider to be specific opportunities for which they are uniquely adapted. If they see an opportunity to play the copper cycle, and consider that because of their personal knowledge of the nature of such a cycle there is less risk for them than for other investors, they are not easily convinced that they should forego an opportunity merely because of failure of copper stocks to show the proper covariance characteristics.

There are probably as many sub-strategies in existence as there are portfolio managers. Perhaps it would be useful if a number of these strategies could be classified as "cyclical plays," "follow through," "market fads," "turnarounds," "arbitrages," "specific events," and so on, for further study.

The point is that the portfolio manager cannot be expected to forego what he considers to be opportunities to improve the results of an account simply because the characteristics of an investment fail to meet the requirements of an "efficient" portfolio.

At the other end of the spectrum, the Markowitz supporters would say that each of these opportunities could be expressed in terms of return and variability of return, and that such investments are undesirable if they fail to make the portfolio an efficient portfolio. Perhaps this hiatus in viewpoint is merely a reflection of the ignorance of the portfolio manager. On the other hand, there is a possibility that the portfolio manager is more intensely conscious of time as an element in rates of return, and that the Markowitz model does not apparently provide for a variety of time horizons for individual investments within the portfolio.

Perhaps a part of the problem is that the academicians take a relatively long-term investment viewpoint, based on the discounted present value of all future payments. This view is not very popular in today's intensely performance oriented environment. Consider how one obtains a rate of return. The income from today's securities appears to be relatively certain in comparison with market action. Dividends from a well-diversified portfolio seldom show a decline, and interest payments are even more certain. On the other hand, the return provided by changes in market value are subject to wide swings, and cause most of the variability in rate of return which the academicians abhor. Between point X and point Y in time, a stock may go from a price of 20 to a price of 18. The academic view of rate of return would tend to reflect a 10 percent decline in market value, less whatever dividends were paid. From the portfolio manager's viewpoint it is much more important that he may have had an opportunity to sell the stock at 26, and at 14, in the interim between points X and Y. The portfolio manager may well value the wide fluctuation in market price between 14 and 26, since a good feel of the market might have gotten him out of the stock at, say, 24, for a 20 percent return, excluding dividends. Not only would this be a profit in the price, rather than a loss, it would have occurred in a shorter period of time than that from X to Y. Thus, the *rate* of return could be relatively high simply because of the short time span over which the security was held. The rate of return from the dividend could be relatively small in relation to the return from market action.

Linear or Nonlinear Returns?

If markets were really efficient, then academic concepts about rates of return would be much more acceptable to practicing portfolio managers. The academicians often present analyses which assume that return on an investment or a portfolio consists of a pure interest rate for riskless assets plus an incremental increase in return for each unit of risk. Even where academicians have assumed a nonlinear relationship, a relatively smooth curve is assumed.

The practitioner believes that he sees something entirely different in the market and wishes to take advantage of it. At times, he believes that he can obtain substantial increases in return in certain risk areas, with only a modest increase in risk. At other times, he believes that he can reduce his risk substantially with only a slight decline in return.

Typical examples of such opportunities appear frequently during the interest rate cycle, placing the yields of both low-grade and high-grade bonds quite close together when confidence is high, and spreading them rather widely when confidence is low. The intelligent portfolio manager upgrades his bonds when the yield spread is narrow and downgrades his holdings when the yield spread is large. Similarly, as a matter of portfolio strategy, he attempts to shift his stock portfolio to lower quality and higher volatility when common stock return spreads are large and the market seems undervalued. He sees the risk/return relationship as being an irregular one which constantly offers opportunities rather than threats. This is true whether he is thinking in terms of portfolios generally, efficient portfolios, or specific securities.

A Gambling Analogy

What happens when an investor constantly cuts back his more successful holdings in order to keep a "balanced" portfolio? An analogy can be drawn from the world of gambling and its many popular systems "guaranteed" of success. One of these is to double the bet each time one loses so that, when one finally wins, all previous losses are recouped and the system shows a profit equal to the original bet. To illustrate, an investor might bet a dollar on a matter of even chance. If he lost, he would be $1.00 in the hole and would then bet $2.00. If he lost again, his losses would be $3.00 and he would bet $4.00. If he wins his $4.00 bet, he has recouped his $3.00 of losses and made a profit of $1.00. If he loses, he will go on to bet $8.00, $16.00, $32.00, and so on. The system sounds great until the bettor has a run of bad luck. If he loses 10 times in a row, he will find that he has to risk perhaps $1,000 to recoup his losses and make a tiny profit of $1.00. At some point, he will run out of capital (or nerve), which is why proprietors of gambling casinos love to see gamblers who have a system. If the bettor has inexhaustible funds, he bears no risk of being wiped out. But it is difficult to visualize a J. Paul Getty spending all summer trying to win a dollar.

Gamblers are generally aware of the mathematical appeal of "doubling their bets." Professional investors occasionally adopt strategies or formula plans which force them to "halve their bets."

Consider the gambler who wishes to bet heavily, but wants never to run entirely out of money. Perhaps his assumption is that if he never goes broke, he is bound to make a killing sooner or later. Thus, he adopts a brilliant strategy of wagering exactly 50 percent of whatever he has at any stage of his gambling operation. Let him wager six times on an even bet, and assume that he wins three times and loses three times. It does not matter in which order the bettor receives his three wins and his three losses. The facts say that on three occasions he will end up with 150 percent of his previous balance and on three occasions he will have 50 percent of his previous balance. The product of these bets would be

$(150\%)^3 \times (50\%)^3$, or a final balance of 42.1875 percent of the amount with which the bettor started. In order to assure that he will never lose *all* of his money, the bettor's strategy demands a high price—a virtual guarantee of substantial losses if he plays long enough. Clearly, the development of a general portfolio strategy requires that the pure mathematics of risk taking be either neutral or working for the investor—not against him. Thus, the continuous portfolio strategy must not fall into the same trap as a few poorly thought out formula plans have.

CONCLUSION

This article has shown that portfolio elements are deeply intertwined. It seems impossible to discuss any single element without considering the interrelationship with several of the other elements. Our understanding of these interrelationships is tentative and fragmentary at today's state of the art. Initial efforts to define the elements and their relationships will necessarily be a halting, error-filled experience, but there is a glimpse of light here and there that gives hope for much better understanding in the future.

The elements in the academic portfolio theories include return, risk (expressed as variability of return), diversification (oriented toward the covariance concept), investor utility curves, and fairly efficient markets.

Practitioners are concerned with a different set of elements, although there is some overlap. These elements include return, a broader concept of risk, time horizon, volatility, sub-strategies, imperfect markets and an economic framework that is made up of a succession of specific events.

The dichotomy between practitioners and academicians is not merely the usual education and communications problem. It appears to be more a question of what portfolio management is trying to accomplish and which tools are involved in accomplishing it. The professional portfolio manager expects to hear theoretical approaches from the campus. He values theory as a structure of thinking around which he can build an approach to investing. However, when such large differences in concept and omissions of basic elements exist, he is inclined to ignore truly valuable contributions from the campus and go his own way.

The solution would appear to be a greater effort on campuses to create concepts which do include *all* of the basic elements, even if the result is highly theoretical. Hopefully, from this there will evolve a theory of continuous portfolio management which will be both intellectually satisfying and useful at the practicing level.

41
INVESTMENT POLICY FOR A GROWING PENSION FUND*

Edmund A. Mennis, C.F.A.

Investment policy for a pension fund can best be understood if it is examined within the framework of the entire investment decision-making process. Although the individual points made in this paper are well known, their organization into a logical approach to investment decisions may be useful. This paper will also indicate decisions that first must be made by the trustee and then the action that can appropriately be referred to the investment specialist. The emphasis will be on the trustee's decisions in the setting of objectives, determining fixed income-equity ratios, and selecting suitable investment media.

Technically, in a pension fund any one of several arrangements may be made for trusteeing the funds. Often a committee selected by the company, or by the company and the labor union, assumes legal responsibility for administering and investing the funds. The trustees then may call on professional investment advisers to help in making investment decisions. Another possible arrangement is to have a bank or other investment institution named sole trustee or co-trustee, with the company committee reserving the right either to approve or direct specific investments.

In this paper, the word "trustee" is used to mean whoever has the primary responsibility for setting the objectives and investment policy of a pension fund. The more technical and professional aspects of investment that flow from the trustee's decisions are performed by what will be designated "the investment adviser." Thus, the distinction between the two will be made on the practical basis of investment decision-making rather than on the legal distinction of who bears the ultimate responsibility.

DEVELOPMENT OF THE INVESTMENT DECISION

Chart I gives a graphic portrayal of the investment decision process applicable to any investment portfolio. Initially, the investment objectives of the particular portfolio must be established. These investment objectives are determined independently of the investment environment; they

---

* Reprinted by permission of the *Financial Analysts Journal* (March–April 1968).

CHART I
Development of the Investment Decision

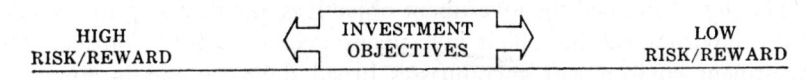

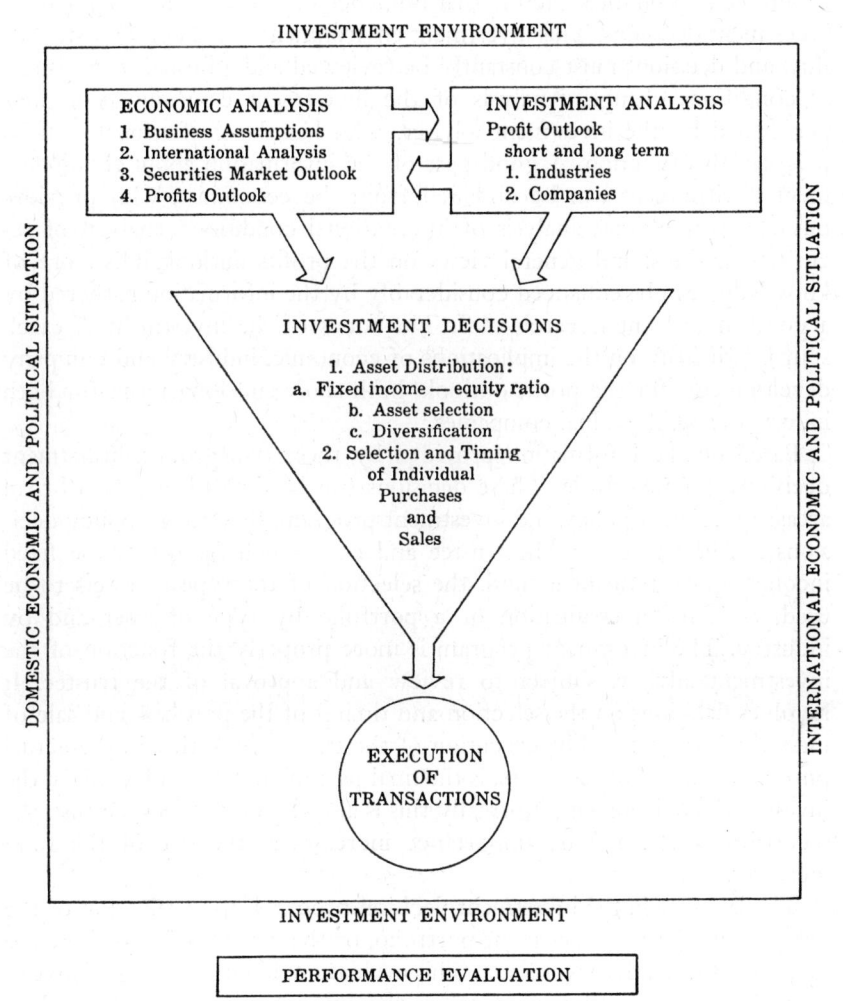

HIGH RISK/REWARD ⇐ **INVESTMENT OBJECTIVES** ⇒ LOW RISK/REWARD

INVESTMENT ENVIRONMENT

DOMESTIC ECONOMIC AND POLITICAL SITUATION | INTERNATIONAL ECONOMIC AND POLITICAL SITUATION

ECONOMIC ANALYSIS
1. Business Assumptions
2. International Analysis
3. Securities Market Outlook
4. Profits Outlook

INVESTMENT ANALYSIS
Profit Outlook
  short and long term
1. Industries
2. Companies

INVESTMENT DECISIONS
1. Asset Distribution:
   a. Fixed income — equity ratio
   b. Asset selection
   c. Diversification
2. Selection and Timing of Individual Purchases and Sales

EXECUTION OF TRANSACTIONS

INVESTMENT ENVIRONMENT

PERFORMANCE EVALUATION

Prepared by Republic National Bank of Dallas.

change only as the needs of the investor change. The trustee must determine the degree of reward that he seeks to obtain and the risk he is willing to incur, considering the need for current income, safety of principal, the desire for capital appreciation, and the requirements for liquidity. Tax considerations are important in some investment portfolios, but in tax-exempt pension funds little attention need be paid to this requirement.

Having established the investment objectives, the next step to consider is the environment in which investment decisions will be made. The investment environment encompasses broad domestic and international economic and political factors that influence day-to-day and longer term investment decisions. This investment environment is in a constant state of flux, and decisions must constantly be reviewed and adjusted if necessary as conditions change. Analysis of the investment environment is best performed by the investment adviser, who has the professional staff to perform this function. A good part of the information about the investment environment can be obtained from the economist, who provides business assumptions, analysis of international conditions, analysis of securities markets, and general views on the profits outlook. His store of knowledge can be enhanced considerably by the information gathered by a good investment research staff. The focus of the investment research staff is primarily on the implications of economic, industry and company developments for the profit outlook, both short and long term, for both industries and individual companies.[1]

Based on the information provided by these two groups, investment decisions must be made. These decisions can be divided into two broad areas: investment policy and investment program. Investment policy decisions are best made by the trustee and cover such factors as the fixed income-equity ratio of a fund, the selection of the type of assets to be used, and the diversification of a portfolio by type of asset and by industry. The investment program is more properly the function of the investment adviser, subject to review and approval of the trustee. It involves decisions on the selection and timing of the purchase and sale of individual securities. The execution of the transactions, that is, the actual purchase and sale of securities, is the final part of the work affected by the investment environment. Normally this is also the work of a specialist, the securities trader, and his importance increases as the size of the fund increases.

The last step in the investment decision process is the evaluation of the performance of the investment portfolio, or the measurement of how the investment objectives were met. This evaluation, like the setting of investment objectives, is independent of the investment environment. This function can be performed by the trustee, the investment adviser, or some independent third party, but its review is a primary responsibility of the trustee.

With this overview of the investment decision process, the focus of the

---

[1] For a more complete discussion of the interrelationships of economic and investment analysis, see Edmund A. Mennis, "Economics and Investment Management," *Financial Analysts Journal*, Volume 22: Number 6 (November–December 1966), pp. 17–23.

remainder of this paper will be on setting investment objectives and determining asset distribution in a growing pension fund. These are of primary importance to the trustee and are areas where his particular and intimate knowledge can be brought most effectively to bear on the investment decision process. The remaining parts of the investment process are more the province of the specialist who is best equipped to render advice within the framework set by the trustee. It is assumed in this discussion that the pension fund is growing, that is, that annual contributions are in excess of benefit payments. Obviously in a mature or wasting pension fund, a different policy than that described here is called for.

SETTING INVESTMENT OBJECTIVES

General Objectives

The general objectives of any pension fund can be stated in terms of the broad rewards expected and risks assumed in any investment. Ordinarily the reward for a relatively new fund is considered to be the accumulation of a sufficient amount to meet the contractual obligations of the plan in the future. However, these obligations may change, as may the contributions to the fund. From an investment viewpoint, the reward can be stated more accurately as obtaining the maximum return on the dollars invested consistent with conservation of principal.

The risks are essentially three-fold:

Purchasing Power Risk. This risk is incurred if investments are made only to conserve the fixed-dollar principal and if only fixed-dollar income is received. The risk involved here is the loss of purchasing power due to long-run inflation and the consequent depreciation in the purchasing power of benefits ultimately paid.

Interest Rate Risk. This risk is created by the uncertainties of the business environment, which affect the price and yield of fixed-income investments. This risk is peculiar to fixed-income securities, because the return is set contractually. Therefore, in a period of rising interest rates, the market value of securities with a previously set rate of return will decline to adjust to prevailing interest rate levels. This is not necessarily true in equity type investments, where the market price may not decline because dividends can increase and thus compensate for higher returns available elsewhere.

Financial Risk. This risk is caused by the uncertainties of the business environment and reflects the possibility that both income and principal may decline in value or disappear entirely.

Specific Objectives

Having recognized the general objectives with respect to reward and to the uncertainties created by the three major risk factors, the specific investment objectives must be reviewed in the light of the trust agreement and the plan under which the trustees operate. Obviously it is impossible to anticipate in any agreement all future events that may affect the investments of a plan. Designation of the specific types of investments that can be made is especially burdensome. Even operation under the freedom presumably given by the Prudent Man Rule may be unnecessarily restrictive.[2] A plan can be of maximum advantage to the beneficiaries if maximum latitude is permitted in the selection of investments.

The Actuarial Method. A particularly troublesome point in pension plans is the actuarial method used to compute required benefits. One commonly accepted method is to use a current yield concept, which recognizes only the annual cash income from dividends, interest, and other payments related to the cost of the assets. This procedure recognizes only a portion of the investment return, namely, the current income. Another method is to use a total yield concept, which recognizes income plus realized capital gains, but makes no allowance for unrealized appreciation. Use of this method may lead to injudicious investment actions in order to achieve a specific yield in a given year. Other methods make some allowance for unrealized appreciation by adjusting the book value of the fund upward each year by some selected percent. One of the more forward looking approaches is the earnings method of determining yield.[3] This method recognizes earnings rather than dividends as the proper measure of yield. The rate of investment return on common stocks would be the current year's earnings divided by the sum of the original purchase price plus the earnings that were retained in prior years. This procedure not only incorporates an orderly annual increment in the fund that ultimately should be recognized in market price, but also divorces the investment decision from the actuarial value of the fund's assets and avoids pressure to make purchases or sales in order to achieve some predetermined annual yield level.

Tax Considerations. Another factor to be considered in a pension plan is its peculiar tax position. Pension funds are generally tax exempt, which means that both income and capital appreciation can be considered alike, and investment decisions can be made apart from the tax consequences that so frequently are important to the individual investor. The tax exempt feature also indicates that tax-exempt securities or those with special tax advantages (for example, preferred stocks that are more suitable investments for tax-paying corporations) are not attractive for such funds.

Liquidity Needs. Inasmuch as this paper considers only a fund with no near-term payouts, the liquidity requirements of the investments for

---

[2] See Shackford O'Connor McSwain, "A Modern Analysis of the Prudent Man Rule," *Trusts and Estates* (August 1967), pp. 742–750.

[3] See *The Investment Return on Common Stocks—The Earnings Method of Determining Yield,* published by Arthur Stedry Hansen, Consulting Actuaries, Lake Bluff, Illinois, April 25, 1966.

the purpose of meeting payouts are not an important consideration. It does not necessarily follow, however, that the fund therefore should seek a significantly lower liquidity position in order to obtain a somewhat higher current return. Liquidity has advantages beyond meeting near-term payout requirements. An illiquid investment is one that cannot easily be disposed of and consequently one that by its very nature becomes almost a permanent part of the investment portfolio until the investment matures. The disadvantage of this lack of liquidity is the resulting lack of flexibility as economic and market conditions change. Interest rates on mortgages and private placements that looked relatively attractive several years ago have lost some of their luster compared with long-term interest rates available in late 1967. Consequently, the return to the investor on illiquid investments should be sufficiently greater than the current or prospective return from other more marketable investments in order to compensate for this loss of liquidity.

SETTING INVESTMENT POLICY

Having reviewed the investment objectives and restrictions of the fund, the next step to be considered is setting investment policy, which involves the determination of the fixed income-equity ratio in the fund, the selection of suitable investment media, and the diversification of assets.

Fixed-Equity Ratio

The establishment of the fixed-equity ratio is probably the most important single investment decision that the trustee must make. This decision should be made on a logical basis after an examination of the economic and investment environment, rather than on a basis of reviewing what is the generally accepted procedure in similar funds. Years ago, because of the contractual nature of the obligation to the beneficiaries, nearly all of the investments in pension funds were made in fixed income securities in order to protect against any financial risk that would endanger the ultimate payments. During the postwar years, however, the fallacy of this approach has been recognized because trust funds have been penalized by exposure to both the purchasing power risk and the interest rate risk. Consequently, some equity investments were made, and now higher and higher equity ratios are seen, with aggressively managed funds as high as 50–60 percent in equities. However, a brief review of the economic and investment environment at least raises the question of whether the maximum equity ratio could not be even higher.

Economic Environment

Chart II is the first of several charts that present the economic environment for the past 50 years and consider the outlook for the next 10 to 15 years. The bottom portion of Chart II shows the path of Gross National Product in the interwar period from 1919 to 1939. The top portion of that chart shows Gross National Product for the postwar period 1946 through 1966. The data are plotted on a semilogarithmic grid, so that the rates of change are emphasized rather than absolute dollar amounts.

A comparison of these two periods reveals three significant factors.

CHART II
GROSS NATIONAL PRODUCT POSTWAR PERIOD VERSUS INTERWAR PERIOD

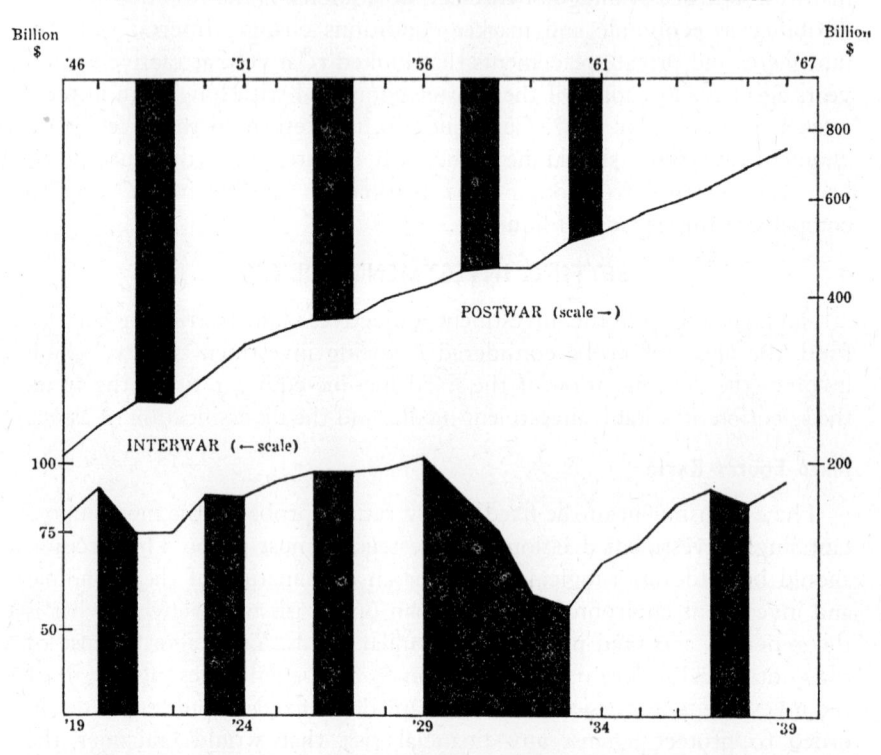

SOURCE: Department of Commerce; National Bureau of Economic Research.
Prepared by Republic National Bank of Dallas.

The first, and most striking, is that the interwar years from 1919 to 1939 can best be classified as a period of economic stagnation, whereas the postwar period has been one of economic growth. From 1919 to 1939 Gross National Product increased at a compound annual rate of only 1.2 percent per year, whereas in the postwar period the rate of increase was 5.5 percent a year.

The shaded sections of the chart represent periods of economic contraction. The second point observed is that the interwar years had longer periods of more severe business contractions than the postwar years. Only 58 percent of the months in the interwar period were months of expansion; postwar, more than 83 percent of the months were periods of expansion.

The third factor that differentiates these two periods was the pattern of prices. During the interwar period prices declined at a compound annual rate of 1.6 percent per year. In marked contrast, in the period since 1946, prices advanced at the rate of 2.3 percent a year. Clearly the economic environment since 1946 has been quite different from that between the two World Wars. Any investment policy that is geared for the earlier rather than the later period is definitely outmoded.

So much for the past. What can be said about the future? Chart III presents Gross National Product in current dollars for 1946 through 1966

CHART III

Gross National Product 1946–1980

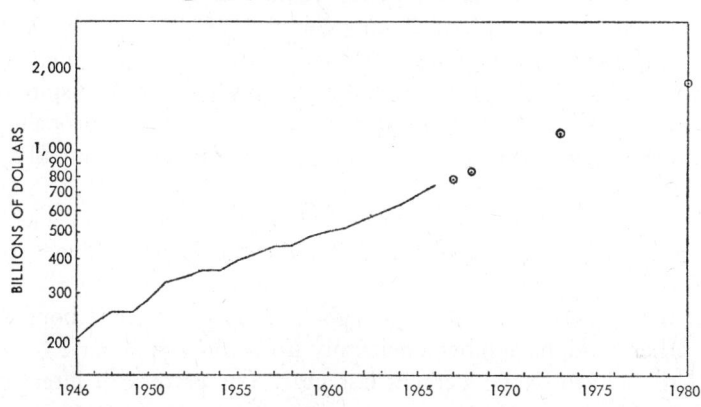

Source: Department of Commerce; Projections by Townsend–Greenspan & Co. Prepared by Republic National Bank of Dallas.

together with estimates for 1967 and 1968, and projections for 1973 and 1980. (The projections were prepared for us by the economic consulting firm of Townsend–Greenspan and Co. in New York). The 1980 Gross National Product projection is $1,751 billion, which represents a compound annual growth rate of 6.4 percent from 1966. This figure, of course, is not a precise forecast, but it does indicate that given the people and the resources of this great nation and a continuation of postwar trends, such a figure is attainable.

Attainment of this growth is made possible by factors other than just population growth and physical resources. Beginning with the passage of the Employment Act of 1946, a commitment has been made on the part of the federal government to adopt policies to promote economic growth. Moreover, the economic tools and knowledge at our disposal permit a much better use of policies designed to foster this growth. In addition, a political judgment could be made that the American people would much prefer a policy of continued growth with some moderate inflation rather than price stability or price declines accompanied by periods of severe business contractions. Therefore, a reasonable economic judgment about the future indicates the greater probability of continued growth rather than a return to the stagnation of the interwar period.

Securities Market Environment

With this economic backdrop, what has been the security market environment in the postwar period? Just as the economy has grown, so have corporate earnings and dividends, but security prices have increased at an even faster rate. As a matter of fact, security prices moved from a position of relative undervaluation of earnings after World War II to an historically high valuation in the past several years. The price-earnings ratio, which in the immediate postwar years was between 7 and 8 times, has fluctuated between 16 and 21 times since 1958. It seems reasonable to conclude, therefore, that a repetition of the rate of price increases in equities since 1947 will not be repeated in the years ahead in spite of the economic growth expected. In the future, stock prices probably will move more nearly with earnings rather than increase substantially faster than earnings.

What about fixed income securities? The patterns of stock yields and bond yields are in marked contrast. Stock yields generally have trended downward from about 6½ percent in 1949 and 1950 to a range of 3 percent to 3½ percent in 1959 through 1966. Highest grade bond yields, on the other hand, have moved generally upward from about 2½ percent in 1947 to 1950 to over 5 percent last year. The pattern of interest rates moved even higher in 1967.

What about the future of stock and bond yields? Will the negative yield spread that has prevailed since 1958 continue? This is obviously the subject for another paper at another time. However, to summarize briefly the consensus of investment wisdom at the moment, given the expected rate of economic growth and the substantial demands for equity securities, primarily from institutional investors, plus the likelihood of little increase in supply, a significant increase in stock yields should not be expected. Moreover, a return to the artificially depressed interest rates of the immediate postwar years also is not probable, and interest rates closer to the levels of last year are generally anticipated in the future.

Investment Results

To illustrate past investment results and future expectations more concretely, what would have been the results of an assumed $100,000 investment in 1947 through 1966 with income reinvested each year in both AAA bonds and in Standard and Poor's Composite Stock Average? The results are shown on Chart IV. As the chart illustrates, the compound annual growth rate of the bond investment from 1947 to 1966 would have

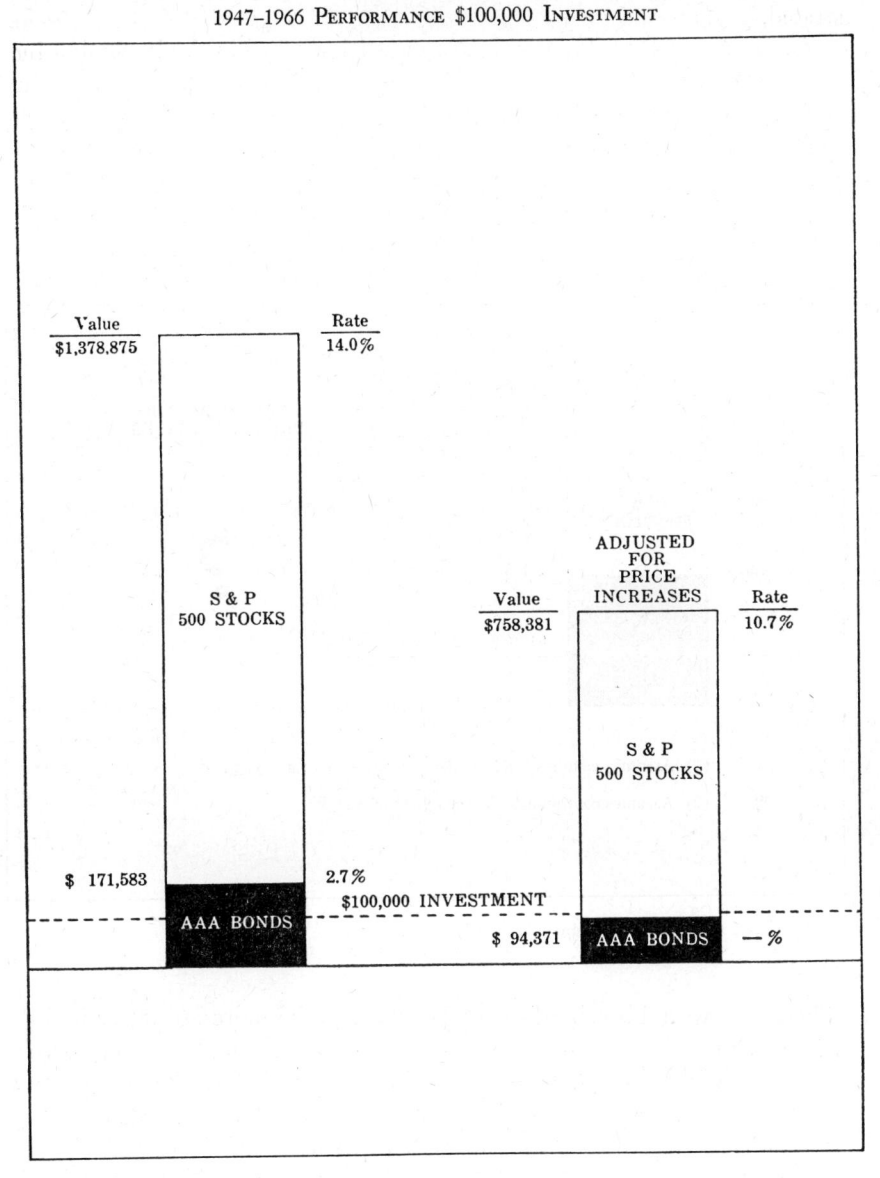

CHART IV
1947–1966 PERFORMANCE $100,000 INVESTMENT

	Value	Rate			Value		Rate
S & P 500 STOCKS	$1,378,875	14.0%		ADJUSTED FOR PRICE INCREASES S & P 500 STOCKS	$758,381		10.7%
AAA BONDS	$171,583	2.7%	$100,000 INVESTMENT	AAA BONDS	$94,371		—%

Prepared by Republic National Bank of Dallas.

been about 2.7 percent a year compared with a return of 14.0 percent per year compounded in common stocks. If these returns are adjusted for the rise in consumer prices over this period, the bond return would have been less than the original $100,000 but the stock return would have resulted in a 10.7 percent compound annual growth rate. Clearly the superiority of a stock investment over a bond investment during this period is demonstrated.

Of course, 1947 to 1966 was most unusual, marked in the beginning by well-deflated stock prices and artificially low bond yields. During the succeeding 20 years, these abnormal conditions have readjusted. High-quality bonds are now available at the highest yields in more than 45 years, while stocks are providing a much lower and more modest return.

CHART V
1967–1986 Projected Performance $100,000 Investment

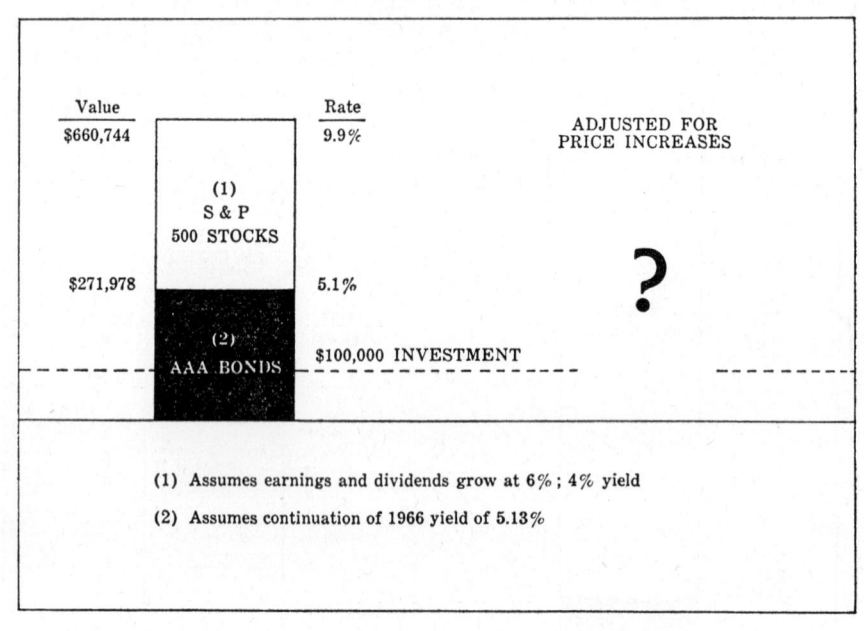

Value		Rate	
$660,744	(1) S & P 500 STOCKS	9.9%	ADJUSTED FOR PRICE INCREASES
$271,978	(2) AAA BONDS	5.1%	?
		$100,000 INVESTMENT	

(1) Assumes earnings and dividends grow at 6%; 4% yield
(2) Assumes continuation of 1966 yield of 5.13%

Prepared by Republic National Bank of Dallas.

Therefore, would not bonds in today's market be more attractive investments than stocks? Chart V is designed to give a rough answer to this question. Assuming $100,000 invested in bonds in 1967 at the interest rate prevailing on average for AAA bonds in 1966, and assuming further that interest is reinvested each year at the same high rate, the original $100,000 would grow to about $272,000 in 20 years for a compound annual growth rate of slightly over 5 percent. Assuming the $100,000 were invested in a stock with an overall rate of return of 10 percent (for example, in a utility where earnings and dividends are expected to grow at 6 percent per year and the current yield is about 4 percent), the original investment in 20 years would become about $660,700 for a compound annual growth rate of 9.9 percent. Assuming a continuation of postwar inflationary trends, the comparison would be even more favorable for stocks.

These figures suggest the superiority of equity investment for growth and inflation protection, even allowing for current yield differentials. Of course, underlying this conclusion is the assumption that the economy will continue to grow and that periods of business contraction, although not abolished, will be relatively short in duration and moderate in intensity. Also assumed is no significant reversal in the stock market evaluation of corporate earnings. If these conclusions are correct, however, the investor must answer the challenge of whether funds with no near-term payouts should not have a maximum equity ratio higher than 50 percent–60 percent. At any particular time, of course, the equity portion of the portfolio might be less than this maximum, depending on current economic and market conditions.

Selection of Investment Media

Having made the major decision of the fixed-equity ratio, the next question facing the trustee is the selection of investment media. Table I has been designed to compare and contrast the risk and rewards available from various fixed-income and variable-income investments in today's markets and also to indicate the general liquidity of these types of investments. A favorable position for an investment is marked by a "+," and unfavorable by a "–"; and a "0" indicates a neutral influence.

TABLE I
Risks and Returns for Various Investment Media

Type of Security	Purchasing Power Principal	Purchasing Power Income	Interest Rate Principal	Interest Rate Income	Financial Principal	Financial Income	Liquidity	(%) Current Yield
Fixed income:								
Savings and loan shares	–	0	+	0	+	+	+	4½–5
Real estate mortgages	–	–	+	–	0	0	–	6¾–7¼
Bonds:								
Private placements	–	–	+	–	+	+	–	6½–7
Marketable	–	–	–	–	+	+	+	6¼–6¾
Preferred stocks	–	–	–	–	+	+	0	6 –6½
Variable income:								
Real estate	+	+	NA	0	0 to –	0 to –	–	7–10
Mutual funds	+	+	NA	0	0 to –	0 to –	+	2.0–3.0
Stocks	+	+	NA	+	0 to –	0 to –	+	3–5

Legend:
+ = Favorable   0 = Neutral
– = Unfavorable   NA = Not applicable
Prepared by Republic National Bank of Dallas.

The table indicates that the purchasing power risk in fixed-income securities is greater than in equity type investments. Among fixed-income securities, only savings and loan shares have some flexibility because their dividend rates can be adjusted as conditions change. The interest rate risk is also higher in marketable fixed-income securities than in nonmarketable securities and has a limited impact on equity securities. The financial risk, of course, is greater in equity securities than in fixed-income securities. However, many portfolios today are invested to protect primarily against financial risks, which is a minor factor in the current economic and investment environment, and presumably can be avoided by skillful security analysis. The purchasing power risk is often overlooked, as is the interest rate risk. However, in the world today, rather than that of 20 years ago, protection against these two risks would seem to be more important.

With respect to liquidity of investments, ownership of real estate, real estate mortgages, and private placements involves limited liquidity and, as mentioned previously, such a lack of liquidity should be amply rewarded by a higher return because of the limited flexibility to adapt to changing conditions.

The current yield is also shown on the table to indicate ranges of returns generally available from investments of each type in the markets of late 1967. These yields have to be reviewed constantly in order to make comparisons of relative attractiveness among types of investments. High yields ordinarily indicate greater risk, as well as less potential appreciation.

Diversification

The third major area of investment policy involves diversification, that is, the selection of amounts to be invested in particular types of investments and also the industry emphasis within the stock portion of a portfolio. This determination is essentially a function of the allocation of resources to those areas that appear most attractive at any particular time. This point is not discussed at length here because skilled investment advice can be most useful to the trustee in such selection and because it flows logically from a detailed consideration of the prevailing economic and investment environment.

CONCLUDING RECOMMENDATIONS

The main ideas stressed in this paper can be summarized as follows:

1. The trustee must make definite decisions on objectives, policy, and performance measurement. Skilled investment advice is available to the trustee in economic and investment analysis to guide him in appropriate diversification, to help him select particular investments, and to assist him in executing transactions. Although he cannot avoid ultimate responsibility for these decisions, he can most effectively judge their suitability if he

has concentrated on setting the objectives of the fund and making fundamentally sound policy judgments.

2. In the current economic environment, the purchasing power and interest rate risks are greater than the financial risk. Moreover, the financial risk can be minimized by careful investment analysis, which has gained significantly in sophistication in the postwar period. The purchasing power and interest rate risks, however, are the results of economic forces that the investor must adapt to rather than change. Higher equity ratios than those currently prevailing might well be more appropriate in the future.

3. In a pension fund both current yield and the appreciation potential must be considered. If the trustee considers only current yield in establishing the actuarial method and setting investment policy, he has missed a significant portion of the investment return available to the trust.

4. Liquidity is important, not only to anticipate payouts but also to permit adaptation to changing economic and investment circumstances.

42
PORTFOLIO SELECTION AND INVESTMENT PERFORMANCE*

Irwin Friend and Douglas Vickers

The recent literature on the assessment of portfolio management has tended to confuse two closely related but separate concepts: first, *portfolio selection*, an *ex ante* concept which is concerned with the choice of securities to be included in a portfolio at a given *point* of time, considered in the perspective of specified criteria for distinguishing between more and less desirable portfolios; and second, *investment performance*, an *ex post* concept which is concerned with the results realized from holding a portfolio over a given *period* of time.

The assessment of portfolio selection at a point of time has increasingly turned on precise measures of the degree to which the portfolio satisfies the criteria of maximizing returns and minimizing risk on the grounds that these two objectives are basic to the optimization of investors' expected utility.[1] These measures generally have been based on the past record of the securities in the portfolio, and a portfolio at a point of time has typically been termed optimal if return in the past (or anticipated return based on past return) has been the highest obtainable for given risk, or risk in the past has been the lowest obtainable for given return. A good example of this type of analysis is provided by Farrar's interesting recent work, which applies such portfolio selection techniques to a sample of mutual funds.[2]

The theoretical criteria for distinguishing between superior and inferior investment performance, or for assessing the actual experience of a portfolio over a period of time, again include both return maximization and risk minimization under the usual assumptions as to the nature of the investors' utility functions. In actual practice, studies of investment performance have tended to concentrate on precise measures of return rather than on precise measures of risk, partly as a result of the unsatisfactory nature of the risk measures generally used, but to some extent also because

---

* Reprinted by permission of *Journal of Finance* (September 1965).

[1] See especially Harry M. Markowitz, *Portfolio Selection* (New York: John Wiley, 1959). Difficulties in the usual measures of risk are discussed subsequently.

[2] Donald E. Farrar, *The Investment Decision under Uncertainty* (Englewood Cliffs, N.J.: Prentice-Hall, 1962).

of a feeling that, at least within broad classes of equity securities, investors are primarily concerned with differential return rather than differential risk. Allowance is typically made for at least the major differences in risk, however, when comparisons are made between average returns realized on portfolios of different types, or portfolios structured to meet different investment objectives. A recent example of this type of analysis is presented in *A Study of Mutual Funds*, in which both authors of this paper participated.[3]

In recent work in this area there has been some tendency to use measures of the optimality of portfolio selection in the assessment of the overall efficiency of portfolio management, and even in the measurement of investment performance, perhaps partly as a result of the fact that the literature on portfolio selection has seemed to use more refined techniques than that on investment performance. This is done to some extent by Farrar and more directly by Shapiro in a review of our study of mutual funds.[4] What seems to be overlooked in these instances as well as elsewhere is that the ultimate assessment of portfolio management or of portfolio selection must lie in the investment performance realized. The only justification for the usual criteria for assessing optimality of portfolio selection, based on average security returns and variances in return over some past period of time, is that the past is believed to be indicative of the future. The test of this hypothesis, however, lies in measures of investment *performance*. There is therefore no logical basis for using measures of portfolio selection as a substitute for, or supplement to, measures of performance.

This paper has several objectives. First, it brings into focus the fact that portfolio optimization on the basis of the kind of selection criteria already referred to does not necessarily imply anything about investment performance. Second, it demonstrates that, contrary to the position taken by Shapiro, the model used by Farrar to assess the portfolio selection of mutual funds has been misinterpreted and has no implications for the performance of mutual funds. Third, it spells out the implications of various measures of investment performance in the light of different investment objectives and opportunities. Fourth, it points out that a Markowitz-type model, such as that used by Farrar, may be not only misleading but even self-defeating if future estimates of average return and risk (or, more accurately, uncertainty) are based simply on past values of these variables. And finally, but most important, it presents in terms of alternative models new substantive tests of the performance of the common stock section of mutual fund portfolios which do allow explicitly for two dimensions of performance—average realized return

---

[3] Irwin Friend, F. E. Brown, Edward S. Herman, and Douglas Vickers, *A Study of Mutual Funds* (Washington, D.C.: U.S. Government Printing Office, 1962). See pp. 16–21 and 294–358.

[4] Eli Shapiro, *American Economic Review* (March, 1964), pp. 198–203.

and risk measured by the dispersion of return around the average. It will be clear that the same type of approach could be applied to the rest of the portfolio of mutual funds and to other groups of investors.

I. RECENT CONTROVERSY AND THE MARKOWITZ-FARRAR MODEL

The points at issue stem from a much publicized result of *A Study of Mutual Funds*. It was there stated that the investment performance of the funds on the average during the period studied "did not differ appreciably from what would have been achieved by an unmanaged portfolio consisting of the same proportion of common stocks, preferred stocks, corporate bonds, Government securities, and other assets as the composite portfolios of the funds."[5] An unmanaged portfolio of common stock, which accounted for approximately 75 percent of the total net assets of these funds, was assumed to be reasonably represented by the Standard and Poor's Composite Common Stock Index. This index gives equal weight to each dollar of outstanding stock issues included in the index and covers a high proportion of the value of stock listed on the New York Stock Exchange,[6] which in turn largely constitutes the medium for common stock investment by mutual funds. The *Study* also pointed out that there did not seem much to choose between mutual funds in the aggregate and the index, or "random" average, performance in year-to-year volatility, again when the results are adjusted for the major classes of securities held by mutual funds.

Another result which has received some attention in the literature—most recently in the review of *A Study of Mutual Funds* by Eli Shapiro—is the analysis by Farrar leading to the conclusion that "it is also encouraging to note (somewhat facetiously perhaps) that professional portfolio managers are capable of providing a substantially higher expected yield, at little or no extra risk, than could be obtained by the random selection of assets."[7] This finding is based on an analysis of the portfolios of 23 mutual funds as of September, 1956, and has been construed as casting some doubts on the rather different conclusion quoted above from *A Study of Mutual Funds*. In this connection, Shapiro states:

> Farrar has put forth an alternative test of performance. He has shown that if the desirability of portfolios is judged according to their rate of return and risk (price variance) then the various classes of mutual funds hold nearly optimum portfolios. Thus one can optimize a portfolio at a given moment of time in the light of the past average returns and variance of the securities irrespective of whether they were held or were just acquired.

It is clear that the Wharton study rejects this definition of performance. In

---

[5] *A Study of Mutual Funds*, p. x.

[6] The coverage amounted to about 50 percent until 1957 and was close to 90 percent thereafter.

[7] Farrar, *op. cit.* p. 76. On the basis of this analysis, Herbert F. Ayres concludes "Farrar also shows that . . . randomly selected portfolios give much poorer results than the funds." See Paul H. Cootner, (ed.), *The Random Character of Stock Market Prices*, M.I.T. Press, 1964, p. 499.

this reviewer's judgment these views need not be alternatives but complementary. For an investor should be interested both in what the fund accomplished in the past and in what it is currently holding.[8]

To measure investment performance requires, of course, an investment objective. If the average return, including capital gains as well as dividends,[9] is the sole focus of investor interest, then there is little need for introducing any other dimension of performance, such as risk. The need for a measure of risk as well as average return arises from the strongly entrenched notion that investors as a whole have a risk aversion; that is, they will accept lower average return to reduce risk.[10] We shall therefore assume for the purpose of this paper that the objective of investors in general and of mutual fund investors in particular is to maximize average return but only for given risk. This latter we shall generally define, consistent with common current practice, as the standard deviation of returns around the average.

If the realized annual return for the common stock portfolio of mutual funds (and perhaps for most other groups of professional portfolio managers[11]) is pretty much the same year in and year out as for the Standard and Poor's Common Stock Index or some other overall measure of return on New York Stock Exchange issues, then a legitimate question to raise under the assumption of risk aversion is whether investors might not prefer to put their money into a fund which duplicates the mean return of the index without *any* dispersion around that average. This could for all practical purposes be accomplished by a sizeable mutual fund by holding minimal round lots (100 shares if necessary) of the smallest issues measured by dollar value outstanding and proportionately more round lots of the larger issues for all issues included in the index.[12] Such an investment approach would ensure an average return with minimal variance around that of the index or of New York Stock Exchange issues as a whole—and with negligible transactions costs. Mutual funds achieve this same average return at least approximately, but, as might be expected, with a fairly substantial dispersion around this average.[13]

---

[8] Shapiro, *op. cit.*, p. 202.

[9] This should be on an after-tax basis, but this complication is not relevant for our analysis.

[10] We have some new results, which will be published subsequently, casting some doubt on this assumption for investors in equity securities.

[11] E.g., see *Investment Trusts and Investment Companies, Report of the Securities and Exchange Commission*, Part II, 1940, where it is concluded (p. 489) that for the period 1930-37 "no substantial differences in performance between the typical closed-end and open-end companies [appeared]. Both types had about the same performance, virtually identical with the index (Standard Statistics Company Index of 90 common stocks)."

[12] The size of fund necessary to be able to purchase 100 shares in issues as low as $5 million in size at the end of 1957 and an equivalent relative amount (in dollar value) of the other issues on the New York Stock Exchange was roughly $200 million.

[13] For the 1953-58 period covered by *A Study of Mutual Funds*, see pp. 294-311.

This available alternative, however, ensuring that each mutual fund obtains the average return of the market as a whole (or some predominant sector in that market), may not be satisfying to either the investor or the manager of the fund. Some funds (as might be expected roughly half) have had average returns higher than the market, and while *A Study of Mutual Funds* found no evidence of systematically better than average performance for individual funds, this result may very well reflect the brief time span covered by the statistical analysis. It is unlikely that all mutual funds would be willing, through more complete diversification, to forego the possibility of superior performance by offering a somewhat different and distinctive sales package, or that all investors would find a homogeneous package attractive. In addition, for the smaller funds, particularly those with substantial turnover, more complete diversification might raise transaction costs significantly.

A question that may be raised therefore is whether, given the degree of diversification that mutual funds undertake to provide, they do in fact provide lower risk for given returns or higher returns for given risk. Farrar attempts to answer this question by applying a Markowtiz type of approach to appraising the quality of the portfolios held by mutual funds as of September, 1956. He classifies the portfolios of each of the 23 funds covered into a number of major classes of securities (including industrial groupings for common stock) and then collects monthly index data, on market prices and dividends paid, for each of these classes of securities for the period January, 1946 to September, 1956 inclusive. His initial classification of securities included 51 industry groupings for common stock and 7 groupings for the rest of the portfolio, but to reduce collinearity he finally cuts down the number of classes of securities to 7 industrial groupings for common stock and 4 groupings for the rest of the portfolio. He then obtains expected returns for the next period for each of these 11 groupings by simple projection of the most recent trends, taking as the appropriate trend pattern for each of the groupings of securities the one which would have provided the best fit (least squares test) if it had been used as a predictive mechanism throughout the postwar period covered.

As Farrar's argument was presented in terms of an expected utility maximization model, the expected utility derived from portfolio holdings was shown as dependent not only on returns thus derived, but on the portfolio risk (variance) and a risk aversion coefficient. By varying the value of the risk aversion coefficient it is then possible to generate a series of so-called optimal portfolios, each one of which will be distributed in certain proportions over some or all of the 11 portfolio groupings in such a way as to minimize the variance of the portfolio for the expected return. The risk variable for the portfolio is derived from the historically generated covariance matrix of the securities in question, based on the period 1946 to 1956. Having obtained in this way the mean and variance (return and risk) characteristics of 100 "optimal portfolios" for given risk aversion values, the locus of such mean-variance coordinates is understood to form the boundary of an "efficient set" of portfolios. Farrar then compares with this locus (i) the mean-variance data describing the actual fund portfolios as distributed among the same 11 portfolio groupings, and (ii) the corresponding characteristics of 100 random portfolios, again so distributed.

There are, however, two serious flaws in this procedure which Farrar does not recognize, at least explicitly, and which Shapiro clearly overlooks. These are flaws which typically characterize other applications of Markowtiz's approach to portfolio selection, though they are not necessarily inherent in that approach. If the expected measures of future average return and variance are based on the past, there is clearly the danger that the analysis will not provide adequately for the tendency of the price mechanism to adjust over time (and perhaps to overadjust) to whatever relevant information is contained in past trends and fluctuations in average return. Thus, if a security has been underpriced in the past in the sense that its return was higher than average or its variance lower than average, it is less likely to be underpriced currently, assuming for the moment that the past is relevant to the future.

More fundamentally, however, the procedure followed by Farrar is concerned with criteria which are essentially irrelevant to the assessment of investment performance, and probably also to most people's conception of portfolio selection. Only in a trivial sense is there any interest in the ability of management to choose stocks which performed well in terms of past average return or past average risk, or some desired combination of these two criteria for assessing investment performance. It is *future* return and the risk associated with that return in which the investor is interested. As a matter of fact, if he were interested in the Farrar type of optimality, it would be extremely simple to set up a mechanical mutual fund which would replace the "nearly optimum" performance of mutual funds to which Shapiro refers by "completely optimum" performance. Just as it is easy enough to select stocks with the highest average returns in the past, it is almost equally easy (though the arithmetic is a little more involved) to select stocks—or more meaningfully a portfolio in view of the covariance of stock returns—with the lowest average dispersion in the past, or to combine these two investment attributes mechanically in any desired fashion.

II. AN ALTERNATIVE MODEL OF INVESTMENT PERFORMANCE

In light of the discussion following the publication of our earlier results in *A Study of Mutual Funds*, we shall now consider explicitly what seems to us to be the really meaningful question in assessing portfolio performance, once it is assumed that investors are concerned with risk avoidance as well as average return. That is the question whether, given the degree of diversification that mutual funds undertake to provide, investment in such funds at any point of time necessarily implies that *for the future* the performance outcome will provide higher returns for given risk or lower risk for given returns. Availability of resources permitted us to undertake only a small number of limited tests of the analysis designed to clarify this question, but they do at least have the advantage of relevancy. The essence of our first test is to take a sample of mutual fund portfolios and a sample of random portfolios as of a point of time, measure the return of each of the fund and random portfolios over a subsequent period of time, and then obtain and compare the average and dispersion (or standard deviation) of returns for the funds and random portfolios separately.

For purposes of this test, the common stock portfolios of 50 mutual funds were taken and 50 random common stock portfolios were generated as of the end of 1957, and annual as well as cumulative returns were computed thereafter until the end of 1963.[14] The 50 funds accounted for 47 percent of the value of all common stock held by mutual funds as of December 1957. The beginning of this period was selected partly to be close to that chosen by Farrar and partly to permit us to measure average return over the period following that covered by *A Study of Mutual Funds*. Attention was confined to the common stock sections of mutual fund portfolios to save effort. In a further attempt to conserve resources, the common stock portfolios of mutual funds were classified into 27 industry groups and each industry group was treated as though it were an individual stock. In this limited respect, the analysis resembles Farrar's (though it does not attempt to compress the number of industry groups on the basis of the type of statistical analysis he utilized). Since the random portfolios also treated these industry groups in the same manner, no bias is introduced into the analysis, though the resulting test of performance is one of industry selection and not of stock selection within industries. Both fund and random portfolios are assumed to be held throughout this period so that the test is one of the quality or performance of the stocks held at the beginning of the period.[15]

---

[14] The sample of 50 mutual funds was selected in the following manner. It was found that of those funds currently offering shares to the public, portfolio data were readily available for 78 whose annual or quarterly fiscal dates coincided with December 31, or fell within one month either side of that date. These 78 funds were arrayed by order of net asset values as of December, 1961. Ten funds held assets in excess of $300 million, 17 held assets between $100 million and $300 million, and 51 held assets of less than $100 million. The sample included the ten largest funds, and a random selection of ten from the middle size class and 30 from the smallest size class.

[15] The concept of "holding period" used in the tables and text refers to the results which would have been achieved by holding unchanged, through the periods indicated, the portfolios held as of the beginning of the periods, i.e., as of the end of 1957, 1958, or 1961, depending on the analysis. In this connection see the following discussion of mutual fund portfolio turnover rates and the caveats regarding portfolio shifts and timing referred to in our conclusions. In Part IV of this paper an approach to portfolio returns and risk differing from that in the present context will be explored.

The random portfolios were generated by assuming that each of these portfolios would have the same number of issues as one of the funds which might be considered its counterpart. The random selection process gave each dollar of stock in the different industries represented on the New York Stock Exchange as well as in two major over-the-counter industries in which mutual funds invest (banks and insurance companies) an equal probability of being included. Standard and Poor's price and yield indexes were used to measure performance for each of the 27 industry groups. (See Appendix for details of construction of random portfolios and performance relatives.)

TABLE 1

CUMULATIVE MEAN PERFORMANCE RELATIVES AND DISPERSION OF PERFORMANCE RELATIVES FOR 50 MUTUAL FUNDS AND 50 RANDOM PORTFOLIOS, FOR SIX HOLDING PERIODS, 1957 THROUGH 1963

	\multicolumn{6}{c}{Holding Period 1957 Through}
	1958	1959	1960	1961	1962	1963
Cumulative Mean Performance						
Mutual Funds	145.9	159.8	158.9	202.6	184.3	223.4
Random Portfolios	142.8	158.9	158.4	205.6	189.0	231.3
Standard Deviation*						
Mutual Funds	3.8	6.8	7.9	12.7	10.3	13.2
Random Portfolios	1.7	2.7	4.6	6.7	4.6	5.6
Range						
Mutual Funds	15.6	28.2	46.0	72.5	55.6	81.8
Random Portfolios	6.6	12.6	24.7	33.3	20.8	28.3

* Adjusted for degrees of freedom.
Note: Portfolios, for both mutual funds and random portfolios, are assumed unchanged throughout the periods indicated.

The overall results of this specific test of the comparative investment performance of mutual fund and random portfolios, as summarized in Table 1, are rather striking. For the six-year period as a whole, from the end of 1957 through 1963, the random portfolios experienced a slightly higher average return than the mutual funds.[16] For the one year holding period, the superior performance of the mutual funds was statistically significant at the 1 percent level, but none of the other differences in the

---

[16] It should be noted that neither management fees nor sales charges are reflected in these performance measures for mutual funds. The construction of the performance relatives is explained in the Appendix, and such relatives are employed in most tables in this paper as indications of portfolio rates of return. Briefly, a performance relative for a specific security for a given year is measured as the ratio of (1) the market value of the security at the end of the year plus the dividends paid during the year, to (2) the market value of the security at the beginning of the year. Portfolio performance relatives are computed analogously, as appropriately weighted averages of such yield-adjusted performance relatives of individual securities or groups of securities. Holding-period performance relatives are obtained by multiplying together the portfolio performance relatives for each of the years comprising the holding period.

mean performance relatives was significant until the sixth period, by which time the gradually improving performance of the random portfolios made their superiority statistically significant at the 1 percent level.[17]

The entire difference in average return of the funds and random portfolios for the period as a whole is attributable to the years 1961–63, since the average return of the two groups for the years 1958–60 was almost identical. It could be argued that a period of six years is too long to assess the performance of a portfolio, particularly for mutual funds where annual turnover of the stock portfolio amounts to approximately 20 percent. However, the point is not too important, since all the burden of proof in the annual comparisons here and later in this paper, and also in *A Study of Mutual Funds* and elsewhere, is that there is no significant difference in the average return achieved by mutual funds from that realized by a random selection of issues.

In connection with the comparison of mean performance relatives, it will be recalled that a one-to-one correspondence was maintained between random and fund portfolios by giving to each random portfolio the same number of holdings as an actual fund. It was possible, as a result, to test the number of instances out of 50 for each holding period in which a random portfolio had a better performance relative than its corresponding fund portfolio. The results conform to the pattern established in Table 1: the number of instances in which a random portfolio outperformed its corresponding fund portfolio were, for the respective holding periods, 16, 24, 27, 30, 32, and 38. If it is assumed that there exists an *a priori* probability of 0.5 that in any observation a random portfolio would outperform a fund portfolio, the proportion of superior fund performances is significantly different from expectation in only the first and sixth holding periods, and the two significant results are in opposite directions.

A more troublesome result of the test summarized in Table 1 is the significantly larger dispersion of average return associated with investment in mutual funds as compared with the specified type of random investment. For each of the six holding periods the difference between the standard deviations is significant at the 1 percent level. To this extent, it could be argued that the performance of mutual funds is somewhat inferior to that intrinsic in a process of random selection of issues (if the assumption of risk avoidance is maintained).

The result is more complicated, however, and requires further explana-

---

[17] It is of interest to note that the mean performance of the 50 random funds corresponds closely with that of the universe of securities from which the sample was drawn. As a test of this correspondence, an aggregate dividend-adjusted index was computed for all Standard and Poor's stocks included in our 27 groups. For the six holding periods the corresponding performance relatives for this combined index were 142.10, 158.73, 163.333, 209.71, 190.84, and 232.83. These relatives for the middle two holding periods (ending in 1960 and 1961) are higher than the average for the 50 random portfolios, but for the other four periods the two measures are virtually identical.

tion. Part of the answer is that individual mutual funds when investing in a specified number of securities deliberately concentrate in certain industries to a greater degree than would be implied by random selection. This may be because they feel they cannot investigate all industries as closely as they should before committing funds for investment. Or it may be because of the relative investment merits of such specialized security holdings as the fund managers see them, with actions by one fund not

TABLE 2

Cumulative Mean Performance Relatives and Dispersion of Performance Relatives for 18 "Growth" Funds, 32 "Mixed" Funds, and Corresponding Random Portfolios, for Six Holding Periods, 1957 through 1963

	Holding Period 1957 Through					
	1958	1959	1960	1961	1962	1963
1. *Growth Funds*						
a. *Cumulative Mean Performance*						
Mutual Funds	144.9	159.4	156.7	198.0	179.7	218.3
Random Portfolios	143.1	159.3	159.7	208.0	191.6	234.5
b. *Standard Deviation**						
Mutual Funds	3.3	7.2	10.0	15.9	13.7	14.5
Random Portfolios	1.7	2.6	5.5	7.9	4.0	4.1
2. *Mixed Funds*						
a. *Cumulative Mean Performance*						
Mutual Funds	146.6	160.1	160.2	205.2	186.9	226.2
Random Portfolios	142.7	158.6	157.7	204.2	187.6	229.5
b. *Standard Deviation**						
Mutual Funds	3.9	6.7	6.2	9.8	6.8	11.7
Random Portfolios	1.7	2.8	3.9	5.7	4.3	5.6

* Adjusted for degrees of freedom.
Note: Portfolios, for both mutual funds and random portfolios, are assumed unchanged throughout the periods indicated.

wholly independent of the climate of opinion in the industry. Or it may conceivably be to some extent because the funds desire to distinguish themselves for selling purposes from the market as a whole and from other funds. Such industry concentration does of course tend to raise the dispersion of returns and hence our measure of risk.

In view of these results, it was thought desirable to classify the 50 mutual fund portfolios into two groups, on the basis of the investment objectives announced by the management of the funds. For this purpose the funds were classified in accordance with the criteria adopted in *A Study of Mutual Funds*. On this basis, the present sample contained 18 funds announcing a "growth" objective and 32 announcing varying combinations of "income" and other objectives. In Table 2 these funds are referred to as "growth" and "mixed" funds respectively. The results indicated in Table 2 conform generally to those for the 50 portfolios as a whole. Mean performance relatives for the mutual funds and the corresponding random portfolios are closely comparable, and standard deviations are still sharply lower for the random portfolios in both sets of comparisons.

The main respect in which a slight difference occurs between these results and those of Table 1 is that in the former case, with the 50 funds combined, the random portfolio mean performance relative did not pull ahead of that of the mutual funds until the fourth holding period, 1961. In the present case, however, the random portfolios pull ahead of their corresponding "growth" funds one holding period earlier, 1960, and in the case of the "mixed" funds one holding period later, 1962. In the earlier time periods, moreover, the small margin of superior performance of the mutual funds is less in the case of the growth funds than for the mixed funds, while in the later periods the small margin of superior performance of the random portfolios is less in the case of mixed funds than for growth funds. Thus this evidence suggests some superiority in performance of mixed over growth funds for the 1958–63 period covered, both in terms of somewhat higher returns and somewhat lower dispersion. However, this is at least in part a function of the time period studied. Our earlier study showed that over the 5¾ year period ending in the third quarter of 1958 the growth stock funds did have a higher average cumulative performance relative than the other types of funds.

As might be expected from the nature of the funds, the standard deviations of the growth fund performances in Table 2 are generally larger than those for either the mixed funds or the random portfolios. A test for statistical significance, however, showed that only in the 1962 holding period was the dispersion of the growth fund relatives significantly different from the dispersion of the mixed fund relatives. Perhaps of more interest, the usual tests of significance reveal that the difference between the mean performance relatives of the growth and mixed funds was not statistically significant in any of the six holding periods. Finally, in only the first holding period was the mean performance of the mixed funds significantly different from the random portfolios, and in only the last two of the holding periods was this true in the case of the growth funds, with the fund performance higher in the first case and lower in the second.

A classification of all 50 mutual funds by stock portfolio size as of December, 1957 indicates a moderate tendency for the large funds to select portfolios which, if held for the time periods in the present tests, would have experienced lower average returns than the smaller funds (Table 3).[18] This finding again might be compared with that of the *Study of Mutual Funds*, which showed that, after adjustment for portfolio com-

---

[18] An F-test on these results indicated that the mean performance differences were statistically significant at the 1 percent level in the third, fourth, and fifth holding periods, 1960, 1961, and 1962.

position, the cumulative average returns were negatively related to size of fund for the common stock fund, except for the very small funds with assets of less than $10 million. The negative relation between size of fund and mean performance relative evidenced in Table 3 is accompanied by a similar relation between fund size and standard deviations of returns. Investment in small funds may frequently earn higher average returns, but at a higher average level of risk.

TABLE 3

Cumulative Mean Performance Relatives and Dispersion of Performance Relatives for 50 Mutual Funds in Different Size Groups, for Six Holding Periods, 1957 through 1963

Size of Common Stock Portfolio ($ million) and Performance Characteristic	No. of Funds	1958	1959	1960	1961	1962	1963
Cumulative Mean Performance							
Greater than 100	9	144.7	157.0	151.3	190.9	175.1	212.6
15 to 100	16	147.0	161.2	160.2	203.9	184.4	223.5
Less than 15	25	145.8	160.0	160.9	206.0	187.6	227.1
Standard Deviation*							
Greater than 100	9	2.2	2.9	3.3	6.1	7.1	6.9
15 to 100	16	3.9	5.8	3.9	10.4	7.8	10.6
Less than 15	25	4.1	7.9	8.5	13.0	10.5	14.0

* Adjusted for degrees of freedom.
Note: Portfolios, for both mutual funds and random portfolios, are assumed unchanged throughout the periods indicated.

III. APPLICATIONS OF THE MODEL IN OTHER PERIODS

The same type of model was employed to test the performance of the common stock portfolios held by the identical sample of 50 mutual funds as of the end of 1958. Employing the same weighted probability randomization device, 50 new random portfolios were generated on the basis of the market value weights existing at the end of 1958. The number of holdings in each random portfolio was again such as to preserve a one-to-one correspondence between the random and actual portfolios. While it is not deemed necessary to present the results of this second test in full, their relationship to those of the previous test is interesting and will be summarized briefly.

The second test provided observations for five holding periods between the end of 1958 and the end of 1963, as indicated in Table 4. In this case it was found that in each of the five periods the mean performance relative of the random portfolios was significantly greater (at the 1 percent significance level) than the mean relative of the mutual funds. And, again as before, the standard deviation of the mutual fund relative in each of the five periods was significantly greater than that for the random portfolios. It might be noted also that the consistency of superior outcomes for the random portfolios is confirmed by a proportions test similar to that previously adopted. In all five holding periods the proportion of instances out of the 50 comparisons in which a random portfolio outperformed its corresponding mutual fund was significantly greater than one-half. The proportion again increased regularly during each period, as had been the case in the earlier six-period test, this time rising from 35/50 in the first period to 49/50 in the last period.

TABLE 4

Cumulative Mean Performance Relatives and Dispersion of Performance Relatives for 50 Mutual Funds and 50 Random Portfolios, for Five Holding Periods, 1958 through 1963

	Holding Period 1958 Through				
	1959	1960	1961	1962	1963
Cumulative Mean Performance					
Mutual Funds	109.2	108.6	138.3	126.3	152.8
Random Portfolios	110.7	110.7	143.6	132.7	162.1
Standard Deviation*					
Mutual Funds	2.6	4.7	8.1	7.2	7.2
Random Portfolios	1.3	2.4	4.1	3.2	3.8
Range					
Mutual Funds	10.6	28.9	47.6	40.3	37.7
Random Portfolios	6.2	10.3	17.4	15.9	18.4

* Adjusted for degrees of freedom.

Note: Portfolios, for both mutual funds and random portfolios, are assumed unchanged throughout the periods indicated.

As another application of the model, a further set of 50 random portfolios was generated on the basis of data as of the end of 1961. The same 50 mutual fund common stock portfolios were again classified into the 27 industry groups as of the end of 1961, a one-to-one correspondence between random and actual portfolios being preserved. The results are summarized in Table 5. In the two holding period observations available in this case, the mean performance relative of the mutual funds was very slightly higher in the first period, 1962, with the random portfolios moving ahead of the funds again in the second period, 1963. Neither of these differences, however, is statistically significant. But once more statistically significant differences do emerge between the standard deviations of the random portfolio performance relatives and those of the mutual fund relatives. As in previous cases, a smaller dispersion of performance occurs in the random portfolios.

The results of these further tests confirm, therefore, the general conclusions based on the earlier time period analysis: namely, even if portfolio selection by mutual funds is close to optimal in the Farrar sense, i.e., on the basis of historical return and variance characteristics, there is no logical reason to believe that such a portfolio possesses any inherent qualities which will result in better than random performance over a period of time in the future. It is of course results over time, not characteristics at a point in time, which are relevant to the assessment of performance.

Several other interesting observations emerge from our analysis. First, the mutual funds had higher average return than the random portfolios in

TABLE 5

Cumulative Mean Performance Relatives and Dispersion of Performance Relatives for 50 Mutual Funds and 50 Random Portfolios, for Two Holding Periods, 1961 through 1963

	Holding Period 1961 Through 1962	1963
Cumulative Mean Performance		
Mutual Funds	91.7	111.3
Random Portfolios	91.6	112.0
*Standard Deviation**		
Mutual Funds	2.6	3.7
Random Portfolios	1.6	2.1
Range		
Mutual Funds	13.3	21.4
Random Portfolios	6.9	10.1

* Adjusted for degrees of freedom.
 Note: Portfolios, for both mutual funds and random portfolios, are assumed unchanged throughout the periods indicated.

the first year of the initial six-period test, a year in which the stock market moved sharply upwards; they did not show any superiority over the random portfolios in the first year of the next test, a year in which the market did not move sharply but fluctuated moderately about the level reached after the 1958 price rise; and in the first year of the final test, 1962, the funds again recorded a slightly superior mean performance, the market having moved sharply downwards during the year, recovering only part of that movement by the end of the year. While too much should not be made of the meager evidence available in this connection, the possibility exists that in taking the portfolio positions they did at the end of 1957, the mutual funds may have set something of a behavior pattern in security market trading, and that some kind of follow-the-leader market vogue could have been partly responsible for pushing relevant stock prices to higher levels during the next year.[19] The slightly superior mean performance during 1962 of the portfolios held by the funds at the end of 1961 might be explained in part by similar reasoning,

---

[19] To some extent, of course, if the industry pattern of mutual fund stock purchases in 1958 followed that of their end of 1957 portfolio, their own activity may have contributed to the result observed.

but the difference between the fund and random portfolios was not significant during this period. The point just raised, of course, can not be regarded as more than the most tenuous evidence of some kind of market price formation process, the existence of which would require investigation and testing against very different kinds of models from those employed in this paper. Some analysis of this type was incorporated in our earlier *A Study of Mutual Funds* (pp. 359 ff).

However, much more statistically significant and much more puzzling than any evidence of an initial positive price impact of mutual funds on the securities which they are accumulating or have accumulated, is the evidence in this paper that in the longer run such securities perform worse than the market as a whole. One possible rationalization is that the funds' tendency to concentrate on certain issues may drive their prices to levels which leave little scope for further appreciation. If this were true, however, a more consistently favorable performance in the early years of our tests might have been expected.

TABLE 6

Cumulative Mean Performance Relatives and Dispersion of Performance Relatives for 50 Mutual Funds and 50 Random Portfolios, for the Two-Year Period 1958 through 1959

	Random Portfolios	Mutual Fund Portfolios Unchanged for 2 Years	Mutual Fund Portfolios Managed Once in 2 Years
Mean Performance	158.9	159.8	159.4
Standard Deviation*	2.7	6.8	6.5

* Adjusted for degrees of freedom.
Note: Portfolios, for both mutual funds and random portfolios, are assumed unchanged throughout the periods indicated.

A final observation of considerable significance can be drawn from the results already discussed. In the course of applying our model to portfolios as of the end of 1957 and, subsequently, the end of 1958, data were gathered on what would have been the performance results of the 50 mutual funds in the two-year period from the end of 1957 to the end of 1959 if the funds could be regarded as holding their end of 1957 portfolio through 1958, and then holding their end of 1958 portfolio through 1959. It was thus possible to construct a set of two-year cumulative performance relatives for the funds by chaining (multiplying) together the 1958 relative for any given fund from the first test and the 1959 relative for the same fund from the second test. These two-year relatives could then be compared with the two-year performance relatives of the random portfolios obtained from the first of our tests. In this way the question can be asked as to how the cumulative mean performance of random portfolios held unchanged for two years compares with the corresponding two-year performance of mutual funds which have had the opportunity to switch, or manage, their portfolios once during the two-year period. The results are summarized in Table 6. Neither of the mutual fund mean performance relatives is significantly different from the random portfolio mean, but both of the mutual fund standard deviations are significantly different (at the 1 percent level) from the corresponding statistic for the random portfolios. No appreciable difference appeared in the mutual fund's two-year performance relative under the assumption that the portfolios were managed once during the two-year period, compared with what it was for unchanged portfolios. The question of actual fund performance, taking account of the actual degree of management or switching of the funds, has been examined at length in *A Study of Mutual Funds*, and the point is not directly germane to the principal objectives of this paper.

IV. ANOTHER ALTERNATIVE MODEL

An objection that can be raised to the basic model of investment performance which we have presented in this paper is that the risk measure we have used essentially assumes that the relevant risk is inability to ensure the average performance of the group, i.e., risk is measured as the degree of dispersion from such average performance. For the mutual funds, this procedure may be regarded as supplying a measure of industry risk, with all funds considered as homogenous in this respect.

Another approach to the measurement of prospective risk associated with mutual fund and random portfolios is to take samples of such portfolios as of any point of time, derive the annual return of each of these portfolios over a subsequent period, and then measure risk for each portfolio as the standard deviation (or other measure of dispersion) of annual returns over the period. This second approach is closer to that followed by Farrar but it still retains an important advantage of our first approach. In a significant sense the measure of risk thus derived relates to prospective, rather than retrospective, risk.

In the Farrar and other models in the existing literature, it is customary to consider prospective returns, envisaged at a point in time, in conjunction with variances measured *retrospectively* from the same point in time. Both our models measure returns and risk as determined by actual performance *subsequent* to that point of time. This second approach to risk measurement which we are adopting in this section, providing as it does a measure of risk for each portfolio based on the year-to-year variability in its actual performance, is in some respects preferable to that adopted in the first part of the paper. However, in other respects it does not provide nearly so significant a measure of risk, since reliance on year-to-year fluctuations is likely to attach too much weight to cyclical and random factors and too little weight to the longer-run risk characteristic of the industry.

Table 7 summarizes the results of this second type of test of the comparative investment performance of mutual fund and random portfo-

TABLE 7

I. Average Annual Returns* and Dispersion of Returns for 50 Mutual Funds and 50 Random Portfolios, for Time Periods Indicated, Compared with Market Data

| | Six-Year Period, 1958–1963 ||||| Five-Year Period, 1959–1963 |||||
| | Mean Values |||| | Mean Values |||| |
	Average Annual Returns	Standard Deviations	Coefficients of Variation	Range of Average Annual Returns		Average Annual Returns	Standard Deviations	Coefficients of Variation	Range of Average Annual Returns
Mutual Funds	15.8	18.4	117.0	7.0		9.7	13.5	141.6	5.8
Random Portfolios	16.3	17.4	106.9	2.3		11.0	13.8	125.5	2.6
Common Stock Market†	16.3	16.8	102.8	—		11.2	13.3	118.8	—

* Annual return is here measured as the ratio of (i) dividends received plus appreciation of market value during the year, to (ii) market value at the beginning of the year.

† The annual return on the common stock market is the weighted composite return (dividends paid plus market appreciation) on all stocks included in this study, namely the Standard and Poor's 500 plus the over-the-counter stocks (banks and insurance companies) as referred to in the Appendix.

II. Comparison of Performance Results of 50 Mutual Funds and Corresponding Random Portfolios, for Time Periods Indicated

| | Number of Instances ||
	1958–1963	1959–1963
Number of instances in 50 comparisons in which:		
(A) i. Average Annual Return: R greater than MF‡	34	46
ii. Standard Deviation of Returns: R less than MF	32	20
iii. Coefficient of Variation of Returns: R less than MF	39	40
(B) Ai and Aii both occur	18	17
Ai and Aiii both occur	27	37

‡ R = Random Portfolio, MF = Mutual Fund.
Note: Portfolios, for both mutual funds and random portfolios, are assumed unchanged throughout the periods indicated.

lios. The analysis covers two time periods: the six-year period from the end of 1957 through 1963, assuming the end of 1957 portfolios were held throughout the period; and the five-year period, 1958 through 1963, employing comparable assumptions. As shown previously in Tables 1 and 4, the random portfolios experienced slightly higher average returns than the mutual funds in both time periods. However, unlike the results of this earlier type of test, the new measures point to only moderately different dispersion or risk (as indicated by the standard deviation, coefficient of variation or range) for the mutual funds compared with the random portfolios. If each of the mutual funds and random portfolios is classified both by standard deviation and average return, the random portfolios seem to have performed somewhat better than the mutual funds, i.e., for given return risk tended to be lower, and for given risk returns tended to be higher for the random portfolios. The relationship for the 1958–1963 period is shown in Chart 1. Another interesting implication of these

CHART 1
Average Annual Return and Standard Deviation of Returns for the Period 1958 Through 1963 for 50 Mutual Funds and 50 Random Portfolios

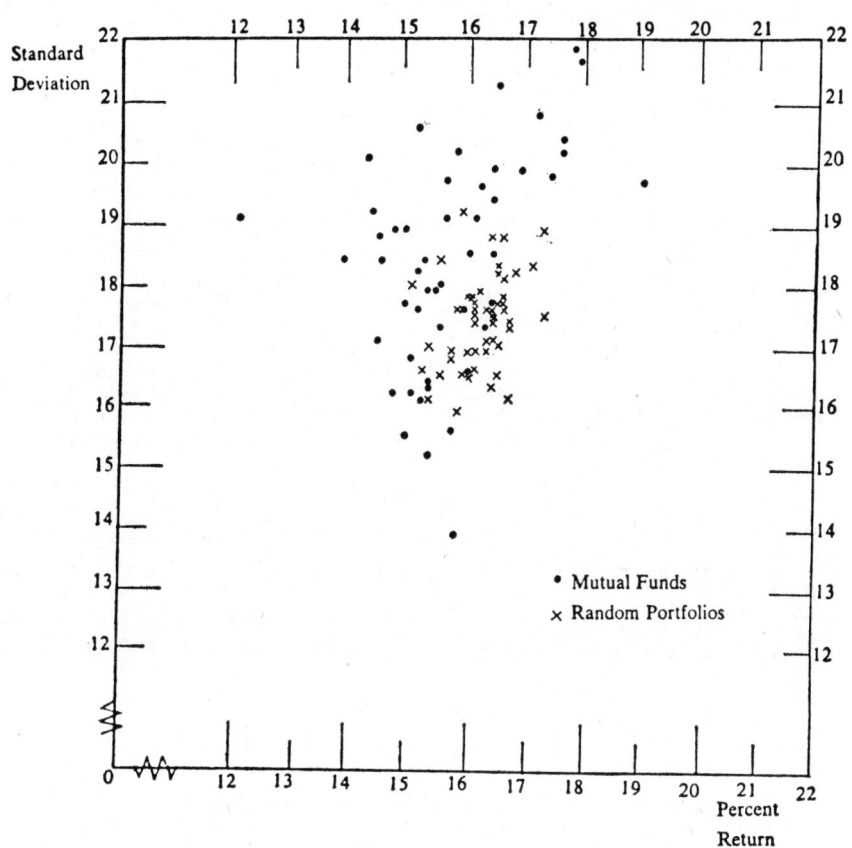

results is the relatively low correlation between risk and return over this period. If a similar analysis is made of the comparative investment performance of mutual funds and random portfolios held at the end of 1958 over the five-year period to the end of 1963, identical qualitative results are obtained although the relative performance of the random portfolios is slightly improved. If the coefficient of variation is substituted for the standard deviation as a measure of risk, the relative performance of the random portfolios would be somewhat improved for both time periods (see Table 7).

In the first of our tests it was found (see Table 3) that for the holding periods examined there appeared to be a moderate negative relation between the size of the mutual funds' common stock portfolios as of December, 1957, and both their average returns and their dispersion of returns. Smaller funds tended to give better returns, but at a higher degree of risk. As in the first analysis, Table 8 indicates that the average annual returns over the six-year and five-year periods increased steadily as the size class of mutual fund decreased. The inverse correlation between size of fund and risk, however, is no longer clear. The returns on the random portfolios were higher than those on the corresponding mutual funds for each size class in each comparison. As in the other tests reported in this

TABLE 8

AVERAGE ANNUAL RETURNS AND DISPERSION OF RETURNS FOR 50 MUTUAL FUNDS AND 50 RANDOM PORTFOLIOS, FOR TIME PERIODS INDICATED, COMPARED WITH MARKET DATA

Mutual Funds by Size of Common Stock Portfolio ($ millions) and Corresponding Random Portfolios	No. of Funds	Six-Year Period, 1958–1963			Five-Year Period, 1959–1963		
		Mean Values		Range of Average Annual Returns	Mean Values		Range of Average Annual Returns
		Average Annual Returns	Standard Deviations		Average Annual Returns	Standard Deviations	
Mutual Funds							
Greater than 100	9	14.8	18.2	1.7	9.1	13.6	2.7
15 to 100	16	15.8	18.7	4.0	9.7	13.5	2.3
Less than 15	25	16.1	18.3	7.0	9.9	13.5	5.8
Corresponding Random Portfolios							
Greater than 100	9	16.3	17.3	2.0	11.1	13.8	2.6
15 to 100	16	16.3	17.4	1.6	11.0	14.0	1.5
Less than 15	25	16.4	17.5	2.3	11.0	13.7	2.6
Common Stock Market		16.3	16.8	—	11.2	13.3	—

Note: Portfolios, for both mutual funds and random portfolios, are assumed unchanged throughout the periods indicated.

section, however, there appeared only a moderate difference in the dispersion of returns—lower for the random portfolios in the six-year period and higher in the five-year period, if the mean values of the standard deviations are compared, but generally lower dispersion among the random portfolios if attention is centered on the range of variation of the returns.

There is interest, of course, not only in the quality of the end-of-1957 and end-of-1958 portfolios as measured by subsequent return and risk characteristics over the period (six and five years respectively) through the end of 1963, but also as measured by return and risk over one year holding periods. For this purpose the same measures of risk were assumed to apply to the one year periods as to the longer holding periods starting with that year. The results presented graphically in Charts 2 and 3 imply that the quality of mutual fund portfolios was somewhat superior to that

CHART 2

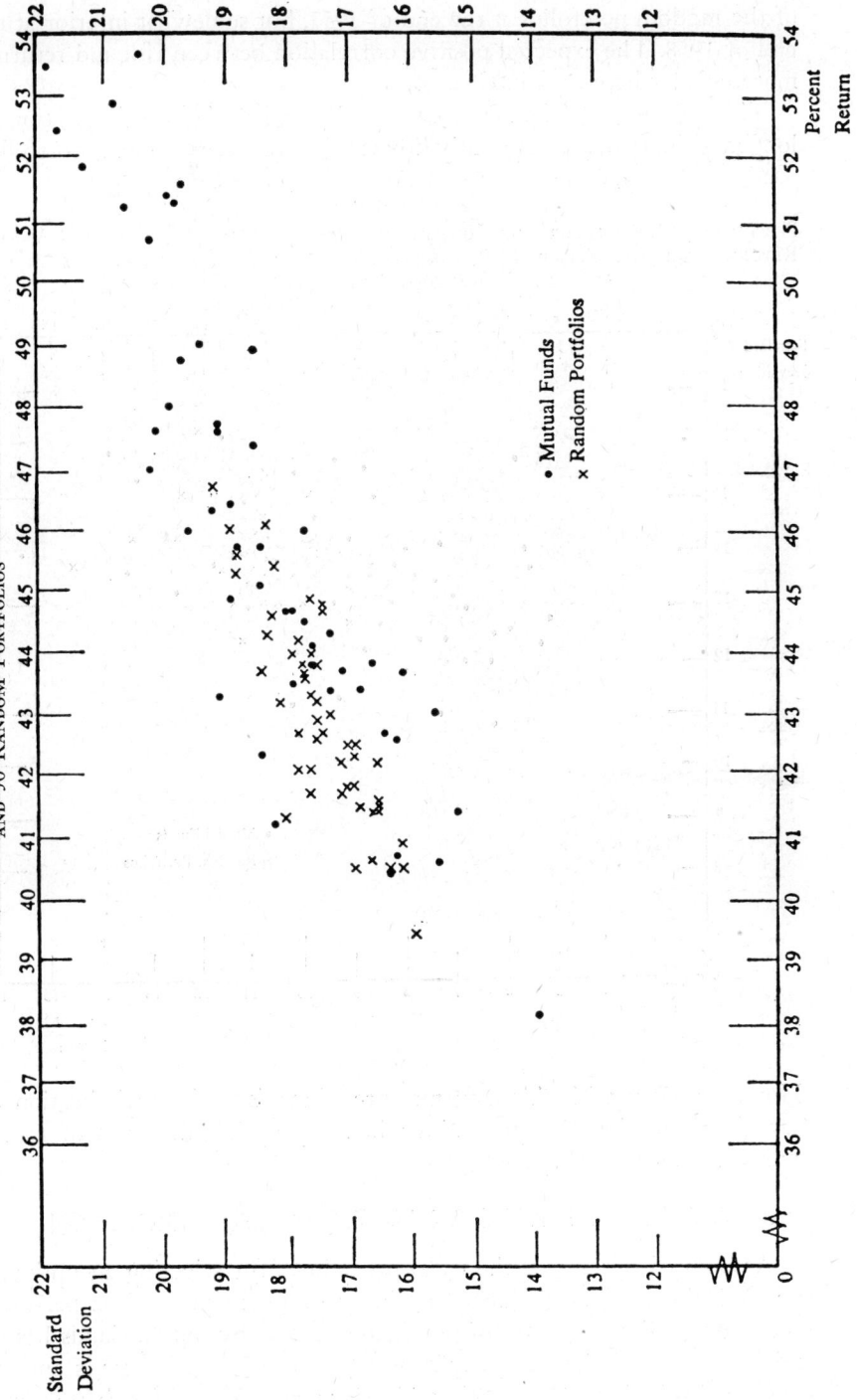

Percentage Return for the Year 1958 and Standard Deviation of Annual Returns for the Period 1958 through 1963 for 50 Mutual Funds and 50 Random Portfolios

of the random portfolios at the end of 1957, but somewhat inferior at the end of 1958. The expected positive correlation between risk and return is more evident here than in Chart 1.

The utilization of the new measure of risk described in this section no longer points to a consistently lower risk for the random portfolios.

CHART 3

PERCENTAGE RETURN FOR THE YEAR 1959 AND STANDARD DEVIATION OF ANNUAL RETURNS FOR THE PERIOD 1959 THROUGH 1963 FOR 50 MUTUAL FUNDS AND 50 RANDOM PORTFOLIOS

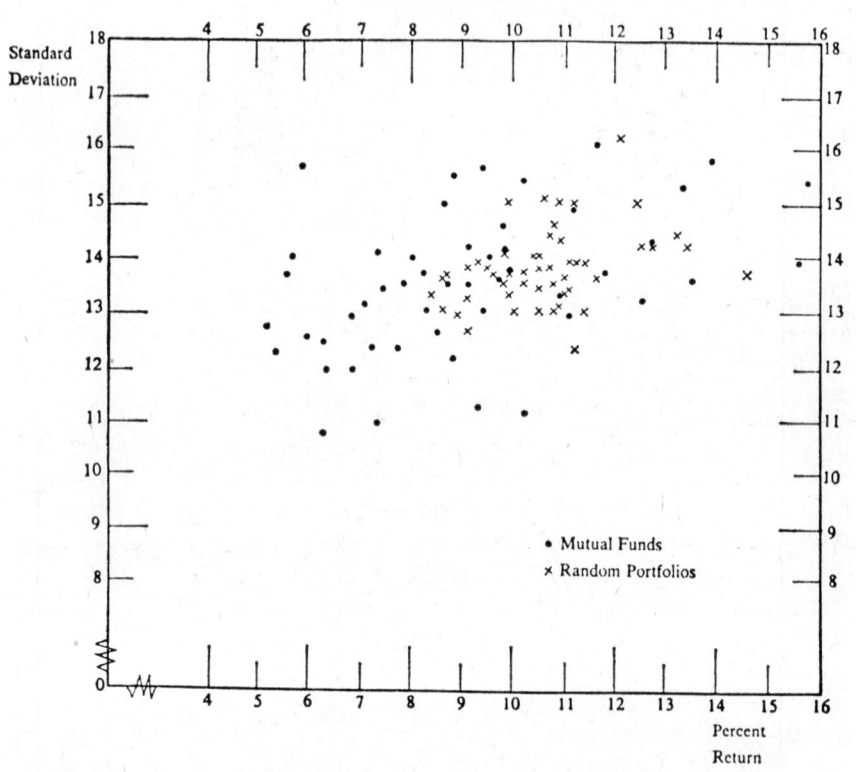

However, even with this new measure, there is again no indication of superiority of the fund portfolios when appropriate measures of return and risk are employed.

V. A FURTHER NOTE ON PORTFOLIO RANDOMIZATION

As pointed out above, the usual procedures for selecting an optimum portfolio have little relation to attaining optimum investment performance, so that Farrar's study of portfolio selection by mutual funds has no relevance to their investment performance. In addition, there is another potentially significant respect in which his procedures differed from ours. His random portfolios were generated in such a way as to give each of eleven classes of assets—seven common stock groupings, three senior securities, and cash—an equal probability of being selected, so that a much higher degree of "conservatism" could be expected to appear in such random portfolios than in the mutual funds. Consequently, any comparison of the mean return-variance characteristics of mutual fund and random portfolios might be biased in favor of the funds. As Farrar's findings show, such random portfolios could display sharply lower average returns than the funds.

TABLE 9

Cumulative Mean Performance Relatives and Dispersion of Performance Relatives for 50 Mutual Funds and 50 Uniformly Distributed Random Funds, for Six Holding Periods, 1957 through 1963

	\multicolumn{6}{c}{Holding Period 1957 through}
	1958	1959	1960	1961	1962	1963
Cumulative Mean Performance						
Mutual Funds	145.9	159.8	158.9	202.6	184.3	223.4
Uniformly Distributed Random Funds	149.1	165.6	167.1	217.9	190.1	234.2
Standard Deviation *						
Mutual Funds	3.8	6.8	7.9	12.7	10.3	13.2
Uniformly Distributed Random Funds	1.8	3.4	4.0	6.6	5.0	7.2

* Adjusted for degrees of freedom.
Note: Portfolios, for both mutual funds and random portfolios, are assumed unchanged throughout the periods indicated.

It was in recognition of the unsatisfactory implications of such a randomization procedure that the alternative models outlined in this paper gave each of the 27 industry groups in the funds' common stock portfolios a probability of appearing in a randomized portfolio proportional to their relative importance in the value of the universe of securities from which the portfolios were drawn. Such a procedure not only maintains a reasonable and consistent relationship with the Standard and Poor's index—which measures market behavior by similarly giving an equal weight to each dollar of stock issues included—but it represents also what seems to be an empirically reasonable alternative method by which actual funds might make their security selections. It seemed to be of some interest, however, to adapt our initial model to generate random common stock portfolios chosen from our 27 industry groups by a randomization procedure similar to that employed by Farrar. The mean performance relatives and standard deviations of such portfolios are compared with the corresponding results for the mutual funds in Table 9. The random portfolios are referred to in the table as "uniformly distributed random funds."

The principal point of interest in the comparison is that the random funds now outperform the mutual funds (higher means and lower standard deviations) in each of the six holding periods under observation. This is contrary to the finding in Farrar's study, where the random portfolios showed sharply lower expected returns and only moderately lower risk.

The difference in results may be due in part to the relatively high degree of inherent "conservatism" in his random portfolios. Probably more important, however, the present result, like our preceding findings, refers to the actual experience of holding a portfolio over a period of time, and not to a simple comparison of historical characteristics at a point of time.

VI. CONCLUSIONS

The objectives and significance of the models we have developed, as well as their principal findings, have already been made clear. A few brief summary observations might be offered at this point. First, in the matter of randomization, it could of course be argued that, in the first type of model we presented, the appropriate standard with which to compare a mutual fund which concentrates in certain industries, at least to a greater than average extent, is a random portfolio invested in these same industries. It is conceivable that a reasonable standard could be formulated which would fully eliminate the negative risk differential in favor of the random portfolios. This type of reasoning, however, can easily lead to the *reductio ad absurdum* that a mutual fund can properly be compared only with a portfolio which is identical with its own. Nonetheless, when the second type of model, which largely avoids this difficulty, was tested there no longer was a consistent negative risk differential in favor of the random portfolios, though such portfolios still have fully as favorable return and risk characteristics as the mutual funds.

On the assumption, then, that all mutual fund investors have the same average return-risk preferences, the mutual funds as a whole clearly do no better than the random portfolios in their common stock industry selection. A study of mutual fund investors gives some support to the thesis that most mutual fund investors have the same general set of preferences, though there are obviously some differences among investors in this respect.[20] On the other hand, to the extent that mutual funds each cater to investors with different average return-risk preferences, it is possible that the assortment of investment media they offer is superior to the random portfolios. However, there is as yet no convincing evidence that this is so. To the extent that Farrar's evidence is relevant to investment performance, a new group of mechanically selected portfolios can be constructed which is superior to the funds. Our findings above, however, cast doubt on the prospective as opposed to the retrospective relevance of the Farrar analysis.

If average return and variance are the relevant investment characteristics to an investor, it seems to us that our tests are completely appropriate. If, contrary to most theoretical writing on the subject, variance is irrelevant—i.e., investors make their decisions exclusively on the basis of expected average return—then both *A Study of Mutual Funds* and the analysis in this paper indicate that the investment performance of

---

[20] *Report of Special Study of Securities Markets of the Securities and Exchange Commission*, Part 4, 1963, pp. 282–9.

mutual funds as a whole is not superior to that obtainable by random selection of stock issues. If investors are risk averters and have the same general average return-risk preference, this conclusion might be made even stronger on the basis of the preceding analysis. If investors prefer to incur risk—which is especially dubious for mutual fund owners—there clearly are more straightforward ways of satisfying such an investment preference.

We conclude, therefore, that there is still no evidence—either in our new or old tests, or in the tests so far carried out by others—that mutual fund performance is any better than that realizable by random or mechanical selection of stock issues. The two significant caveats to this conclusion are that because of resource limitations we have not yet been able to carry out an average return-variance analysis for individual securities, as against classes of securities, held in mutual fund portfolios, or to measure the degree of success achieved by mutual funds in timing their portfolio shifts between common stocks and other investments.

Nothing in this conclusion or in this paper gainsays the useful role played by mutual funds in our economy in providing diversification of risk in stock investment to many investors who would not have achieved the same degree of diversification on their own behalf and, to some extent, in lowering the cost of equity financing and in the process stimulating economic growth.[21] Neither this paper nor *A Study of Mutual Funds* reflects on the wisdom of mutual fund investment for many investors. They both, however, raise interesting questions about the apparent inability of professional investment management on the average to outperform the market.[22]

This paper, in addition, points up the dangers of using past measures of return and variance as a basis for portfolio selection, or of assuming that the procedures for portfolio selection outlined by Markowitz provide any clues to future investment performance. Such procedures simply provide a useful, systematic approach to selecting desired combinations of future return and variance when both future return and variance are known. When these values are known, the Markowitz procedures provide an efficient approach to the selection of optimal portfolios which can be followed mechanically without resort to professional management. The potential conbribution of professional management is not in its ability to approximate mechanical formulas any more than it is in its ability to follow random selection devices. Any such contribution must rest basically on ability to pick securities with greater than average return for given risk (assuming risk aversion), or lower than average risk for given return.

---

[21] A significant number of investors would not have entered the market at all without the selling efforts of the mutual funds, and would therefore not have participated in the generally favorable return achieved. See *Report of Special Study of Securities Markets of the Securities and Exchange Commission*, Part 4, 1963, p. 358.

[22] As noted earlier, available data do not permit definitive statements to be made about the ability of individual funds to outperform the market.

APPENDIX

CONSTRUCTION OF RANDOM PORTFOLIOS AND PERFORMANCE RELATIVES

The random portfolios were generated in the following manner. A decision was made firstly on the classification of portfolios into 27 industry groups as referred to in the text. These groupings were made by combining into reasonably economically homogeneous groups the more than 80 sub-groups of stocks included in the Standard and Poor's Common Stock Index, and the over-the-counter sections of banks and insurance company stocks, for each of which price indexes, and in most cases dividend yields, are published. This was done in order that dividend-adjusted yield indexes could subsequently be constructed for each of the 27 groups by combining, in appropriately weighted form, the relevant data for the more than 80 subgroups. By this means the following 27 industry groups were obtained:

1. Aerospace
2. Amusement
    Motion Pictures
    Radio and TV Broadcasters
3. Auto and Auto Accessories
    Autos
    Auto Accessories
    Trucks
4. Building Equipment
5. Chemicals, Soaps, and Fertilizers
6. Drugs
7. Electrical Equipment, etc.
    Electrical Equipment
    Electrical Household Appliances
    Electronics
    Radio and TV Electronics
8. Food and Beverages
    Food—Composite
    Beverages—Brewers
                Distillers
                Soft Drinks
    Confectionery
    Sugar
    Vegetable Oil
9. Machinery
    Machine Tools
    Machinery—Agriculture
                 Composite
10. Mining and Metal Fabricating
    Aluminum
    Coal
    Metal Containers
    Copper, Gold, Sulphur, Lead
    Metal Fabricating
    Mining and Smelting
11. Office Equipment
12. Paper and Publishing
    Paper Containers
    Paper
    Publishing
13. Oil
14. Retail Stores—Composite
15. Rubber and Tires
16. Steel
17. Textiles and Clothing
    Apparel
    Carpets and Rugs
    Rayon and Acetate
    Shoes
    Textile Weavers
18. Tobacco
    Tobacco and Cigarettes
    Cigars
19. Railroad Equipment and Shipbuilding
    Railroad Equipment
    Shipbuilding
20. Other Transportation
    Air Transportation
    Shipping
21. Finance and Small Loan
    Finance Companies
    Small Loan
22. Miscellaneous (except AT&T)
23. Railroad Index
24. Utilities (except Communications)
25. Communications (including AT&T)

26. Banks, etc.
    New York City Banks
    Banks outside New York
    Savings and Loan Assns.

27. Insurance
    Fire and Casualty
    Life

Next, the total market value of each of the 27 groups was obtained as of the end of 1957 by aggregating the total market value of all the stocks included in the Standard and Poor's index sub-groups combined as above in our respective industry groups. It was then decided that each random portfolio should contain the same number of security holdings as an actual fund portfolio as of the end of 1957, thus maintaining a one-to-one correspondence between the actual and random portfolios (a characteristic of the model utilized in the subsequent significance tests). For example, one large fund had 135 separate common stock holdings at the benchmark date, spread over our 27 groups. A random portfolio containing 135 holdings was therefore generated. The randomization device selected the appropriate number of holdings for each random portfolio in such a way that for each random selection the probability of selecting any one of the 27 groups was equal to the percentage importance of the total market value of the stocks in that group relative to the total market value of all stocks in the 27 groups as a whole. The performance measure for each industry group for any period is then a weighted average of the yield-adjusted performance of each Standard and Poor's stock included in it. The performance relative for each portfolio is the weighted average of the performance relatives for each of the 27 groups included in it, weighted by the proportionate importance in the portfolio of each such group. The cumulative performance relative of a portfolio for any desired holding period is found by chaining (multiplying) together the annual performance relatives of the portfolio. In the initial test, the results of which are summarized in Table 1 of the text, the portfolios (both actual fund and random) were held constant as of the starting date, December, 1957, and the performance relatives reported in that table therefore refer to the cumulative outcome for each of the six holding periods, one year, two year, etc., 1957 through 1963.

43

RISK AND PERFORMANCE*

Frank E. Block, C.F.A.

With increasing frequency investment managers find themselves in need of accurate measurement, evaluation, and interpretation of the performance of investment portfolios. Requests have come particularly often from corporate customers who, quite properly, want to know how their pension and profit sharing funds are progressing. Of greater ultimate importance has been the gradual recognition that accurate measurement of performance may permit the management of an investment organization to pinpoint its areas of greatest weakness or strength. Without careful analysis of the performance figures, it is not possible to tell whether apparently good investment results were due to nimble investment timing, superior selection of individual issues, or merely a string of good luck.

Fortunately, mathematical techniques are available to measure past performance with great precision. Less fortunate is the fact that these mathematical techniques have concentrated almost exclusively on measuring rates of return. Among risk elements, only price fluctuation has received much attention. There are many other types of risk which have been given no quantitative consideration at all. Yet performance figures are of limited value unless one knows what risks have been taken to accomplish the performance.

It is necessary to select proper standards against which to measure performance. These standards should provide an opportunity to compare various timing and investment policy alternatives. The standards should be both objective and meaningful. Finally, the acid test of investment management is the effectiveness of investment policies in meeting predetermined investment objectives—assuming that these objectives are the proper ones and that they have been recognized in advance.

In discussing this subject, we will appear to emphasize the performance of pension funds, but this is largely because the pressures are strongest upon us to prove ourselves to our corporate customers. The principles involved apply to the full gamut of investment accounts.

---

* Reprinted by permission of the *Financial Analysts Journal* (March–April 1966).

Who Is the Better Investor?

The following example may be useful in pointing out some of the difficulties in measuring performance, not of a portfolio alone, but of the *investment management*.

In our example, a corporation turns over equal amounts of cash to two investment advisors. The first advisor is ultracautious and keeps his money invested entirely in U.S. Treasury bills. He bears virtually no risk, since he can always hold the bills until maturity, even if the return is low. However, by adept trading from one maturity to another, he manages to achieve a total increase in assets of 6 percent by the end of the year.

The second advisor sticks the money under his mattress and forgets about it for 11 months. Then, suddenly remembering his duties, he flies to Monte Carlo, places a few casual and random bets at the Casino, and returns home happily with a 20 percent enhancement in the assets.

In measuring the end results there is no question that the dilettante gambler has achieved more than the overly conservative but able investor. While it is painful to think of the novice roulette player laughing all the way down to the *caissier*, the numbers are undeniable.

Despite Biblical authority to the contrary (the "Parable of the Talents"), the more conservative investor has done a better job of investment management. At no time was his capital at risk to any serious degree and he provided an acceptable rate of return. On the other hand, the gambler was facing "house odds" which are quite unfavorable and guaranteed that he would be wiped out if he played long enough. The fact that he won in this particular year was mere happenstance. A loss was the greater probability—ultimately a certainty—and its likelihood could have been calculated with a high degree of precision.

This extreme example is offered to emphasize that investment management can not be judged without consideration of risk. The adequacy of investment results is not determinable without knowledge of the original requirements of the account. The amount of risk which could reasonably have been accepted is as much a part of these requirements as is the rate of return needed. The example also suggests that the period of time over which the performance of a fund is being studied can have a significant influence on the conclusions reached.

The crux of the question of a rational investment process is whether or not, and to what degree, the cumulative probabilities of success (or "payoff" odds) are greater than the cumulative probabilities of failure. If this relationship is favorable for each individual investment and we make enough investments, success can move from a probability to a near certainty. Having "enough" investments really means a combination of diversification *at all times* plus sufficient time for the investment mechanism to work its wonders. The time element is part of the number of investment transactions because *we buy our portfolio every day*, in the sense that each day we make a decision, consciously or not, to retain or to change each of our holdings. If the time and diversification elements were large enough, the mathematics would permit a reduction of effective risk (in the traditional sense of risk) to the vanishing point.

Betting on a horse which had only a 1 in 20 chance of winning, but offered a payoff of 100 to 1, is both risky and, statistically, a "good" bet. But if it were possible to make a large number of bets on different races, with the same probabilities, the total return would be five times the total amount bet. The racetrack does not offer enough of these 100 to 20, or 5 to 1, advantages at any given moment, and therefore the bettor would have to cull the racetracks of the world for years in order to find a sufficient supply of opportunities to reduce risk to certainty. This introduces the time element; if he felt that a thousand bets were needed to eliminate risk effectively, and could find only one suitable betting opportunity per week, his 5 to 1 return would become an annual *rate of return* of 8.7 percent! This is more in line with the overall returns we expect on common stocks than the thrilling five times multiplication of capital with which we started.

Fortunately, we investors do not have to wait 19.2 years to get adequate diversification, but we do need time to construct our original portfolio and to find a continuous stream of new opportunities to replace those stocks which have failed us, or which have fulfilled their promise to the limit of our past and present expectations. Similarly, time is a requisite for the economic process of internal development of the individual company and for market recognition of these internal changes.

Probability for an investment consists of a multidimensional matrix of likelihoods and consequences, which even the most sophisticated econometric models are unable to duplicate. Yet a bad bet and a bad investment have the same underlying defect—however expressed, the odds are against it, and ultimately its class will fail even if the individual transaction succeeds!

It is a perverse fate that permits the gambler to enjoy the advantage of having only two simple alternatives for each spin of the wheel—either complete success or complete failure! The poor traditional investor endures an infinite parade of possible good and bad consequences, the distribution and probabilities of which are not subject to neat calculations. Yet neither should place money at risk unless the odds of success favor him.

What Is Risk?

We regret that we are unable to present here an acceptable definition of risk.

Risk has generally been discussed, and reflected mathematically, in terms of fluctuations in market price. Markowitz in his remarkable work, "Portfolio Selection," recommended *semivariance* as an excellent measure of market risk.[1] He mentioned also that variance, standard deviation, and the "largest loss" over a period of time could be useful measures. Any of these approaches would have been effective in measuring the risk of our gambling friend, but there are many other types of risk which must be considered.

Risk is a subjective matter which quite often seems poorly adapted to quantitative representation. Risk might be described vaguely as the likelihood and intensity of adverse developments—but one man's calamity could be another's fondest dream.

Risk to the *income* beneficiary of a trust might well be fear of a reduction in dividends, or failure of the income to protect him against inflation. At the same time, the *remaindermen* may not harbor the slightest concern about income, but would be quite deeply concerned about the ultimate market value of the trust if there were a break in the stock market, for they will someday receive the portfolio itself. At the same time, a bear who had sold stocks short would view such a stock market crash, not as the risk he feared, but as the reward for which he had hoped.

A life insurance company is always deeply concerned about the prompt payment of bond principal and interest, but is not too worried about fluctuations in bond prices because these need not be reflected in those company statements which are available to the public. Yet the same life insurance company must carry common stocks at market value and therefore feels intensely the pangs of unfavorable market action in equities. (Note: Revision of these rules is being studied for 1966.)

If marketability were one of the characteristics which an investor desired in each of his holdings, loss of this marketability could be a severe blow to him. If tax-exempt bonds were held, the investor would view certain types of changes in our tax laws with considerable alarm. The trauma of the recent Atlas decision is still showing its effect on some insurance company executives. Holders of bonds which sell above call prices constantly bear the risk of call, while holders of stocks subject to assessment have sometimes had nervous moments (e.g., American Express!). These risks are not related to price, per se, although price may eventually be involved in some of them.

When money is invested by individuals, certain satisfactions are anticipated which, it is hoped, will more than offset the possible bother and worry of subjectively unfavorable developments. Most professional investors have run across nervous persons who seem totally unsuited to equity investments because they obviously pay a price in emotional torture

---

[1] Markowitz, Harry M., *Portfolio Selection* (John Wiley & Sons, New York, 1959), pp. 15, 193–194.

which far exceeds any satisfactions they may reasonably expect to gain from owning stocks. Some investment advisors even hold that a satisfied customer is the best measure of performance.

Thus, when we realize that risk is whatever event the particular investor fears or most despises, it becomes clear that we must find a variety of ways to express, quantitatively, the *various risks of each characteristic of the securities involved*. These characteristics might include price, income, marketability, liquidity, maturity, cost of trading, redemption, volatility, taxability, protection against inflation, etc., not to mention the probabilities and distribution patterns of adverse changes in each of these characteristics. In addition, we must gauge the intensity of the aversion of the particular investor to deleterious changes in each of these characteristics if we are to create a correct mathematical model.

The availability of computers and steadily improving statistical techniques offer great hope for the development of new yardsticks to measure the various types of risk against actual or expected performance. These devices may result some day in much higher levels of proficiency in portfolio construction and management. Older techniques, however, have related performance expectations to risk by such devices as a "return-to-risk ratio," or considering "net return," after deduction of a reserve for risk.[2] These approaches may be valid, but they are successful methods of handling only a very restricted variety of risk which is related exclusively to market price.

Standards of Measurement of Performance

Hopefully, it is clear now that risk must be recognized as a factor in setting investment objectives and in measuring performance, and that it cannot be handled in one of the conventional mathematical ways. If so, it is possible to proceed to the question of how one may best go about the measuring of actual performance.

In the past year, several good papers have been written on the subject of calculating the overall rate of return earned on pension funds, mutual funds, and similar types of portfolios. Most large banks and other investment management organizations have developed methods of measuring performance of pension and profit sharing accounts and frequently the methods have been applied to many other types of accounts. Depending upon the seriousness with which the need for performance measurements is viewed, a wide spectrum of sophistication is used in the forms and methods of measurement.

Because the subject has been so thoroughly discussed by McCandlish,[3]

---

[2] Hicks, J. R., *Value and Capital* (Oxford University Press, 1939), p. 126.

[3] McCandlish, R. W., Jr., "Some Methods for Measuring Performance of a Pension Fund," *Financial Analysts Journal* (November–December 1965).

Simons,[4,5] Wood,[6] Sieff, and others[7] in the past year, there will be no discussion of the mathematics involved in calculating the rate of return earned by a portfolio. It does seem in order, however, to caution the reader about three points:

1. It is possible to construct a hypothetical portfolio consisting of like purchases or sales of, say, the Moody's AA Bond Index and the DJIA, so that a model portfolio could be compared with an actual portfolio. This is a popular method, but it incorporates all of the actual portfolio's policy mistakes (such as untimely shifts in equity percentages) into the model portfolio.

2. Regardless of the method used to calculate results, it seems desirable to limit the error in the calculated effective yield to a few basis points.

3. Even with the most precise methods of calculating rates of return, any system which tends to judge a period of time by its beginning and ending points is certain to miss all that happened in between those points. Suppose during the period under consideration, the market value of a common stock in the portfolio increased by $1 million and then returned abruptly to its former value. In effect, the investor made and lost $1 million in that stock. He was responsible for an extra $1 million of market value (as a result of wise investments) but, as a result of poor decisions, he managed to lose it. This represents an erratic performance, but such an aberration would pass unnoticed in an examination which considered only the beginning and ending market values.

Not What, But How

Agreeing that accurate calculation of performance is necessary for valid measurement, one may move on to the question of the comparisons and some of their implications. If the comparison is against some popular index, then the criterion of success is likely to become "beating the Dow."

---

[4] Simons, Walter J., Treas., Chrysler Corp., "Measurement of the Comparative Investment Performance of Investment Funds," Address before the 46th Mid-Winter Trust Conference of the American Bankers Association in New York City, Feb. 8, 1964.

[5] "True Equivalent Annual Yield Tables," Treasurer's Office, Chrysler Corp., (not publicly distributed), 1964.

[6] Wood, R. Norman, "Measuring the Investment Yield of Pension Funds," Alexander and Alexander, Inc., Nov. 1964 (privately distributed). Also "Analysis of Pension Trust Investment Performance," a speech delivered Oct. 5, 1965 before the Conference of Actuaries in Public Practice Annual Meeting in New Orleans, La.

[7] Sieff, J. A., "Measurement of the Investment Results of Retirement Funds," *Commercial and Financial Chronicle*, Jan. 14, 1965. See also: Seal, Hilary L., "Pension & Profit Sharing Digest," *Trust and Estates* (Nov., 1956); Tyson, David O., "Can Pension Fund Investment Be Measured?," *The Weekly Bond Buyer* (Dec. 28, 1964 and Jan. 4, 1965); Graham, F. William and Bower, Richard C., "Corporate Responsibility in Pension Fund Management," *Financial Executive* (June 1965); Bowles, Thomas P., Jr., "Investment Management of Retirement Plan Trust Funds" (privately distributed by Bowles & Tillinghast, Actuaries.)

Many portfolios are judged by comparison with funds of a similar type. This places each investment advisor on notice that his days are numbered if he fails to keep up with his competitors or with some designated standard. There is a danger that, in the fury of the race with its pervasive atmosphere of "win or perish," the advisor with a below average record may select an investment strategy displaying excessive market courage. The worse his past performance, the more deeply will he feel the necessity to gamble in order to catch up!

Assume the existence of an account which has managed to beat the averages, or similar accounts. The record must be viewed in the light of *how* it was made. It might have been accomplished by using stocks of more than average volatility during a period of rising stock prices. If this were done knowingly, as a part of an investment policy of controlling volatility in order to beat the market, then one must tip his cap to such astute timing. However, if the high volatility were accidental, one's admiration should be more restrained. It is not difficult to select stocks of lesser or greater than average volatility by using simple statistical techniques, or merely by applying the market knowledge of an experienced investor. Shifting from cyclical to stable stocks and back again is a common way of "playing the business cycle" to gain this effect. However, the precise measuring techniques previously mentioned would not reveal whether the use of highly volatile stocks was intentional or accidental. In fact, they would reveal nothing about volatility at all!

MEASUREMENT OF VOLATILITY

The relationship of performance to volatility of a common stock portfolio has been recognized for some time. More than a decade ago, The Bank of New York[8] in annual surveys of the investment companies declared that the volatility of the shares of a given investment company varied with (1) the proportion of assets held in common stocks, (2) the inherent volatility of the stocks held, and (3) the leverage of the capital structure of the investment company. The August 1959 report said, "obviously, a high volatility, irrespective of its cause, is to be associated with a relatively high degree of risk, even though in a rising market a high volatility is likely to lead to a superior average annual appreciation."

At approximately the same time, several banks were using linear regression equations to measure the volatility of common stock portfolios in relation to some standard of market performance—generally the Dow Jones Industrial Average. Such a regression equation might typically read:

$$Y_c = 1.1 X + 0.04$$

---

[8] "Survey of the Investment Companies," The Bank of New York, Aug., 1959 (privately distributed.)

Where Y_c = the percent change in the common stock portfolio (expressed as a decimal figure); and X = the actual percent change (expressed as a decimal) in some standard, such as the Dow Jones.

The above equation, shown as a solid line in Figure 1, would indicate that, for each period of time, the common stock portfolio under consideration would move up or down 1.1 times as fast as the Dow Jones Industrial Average plus an additional 4 percent. If the Dow rose 25

FIGURE 1

VOLATILITY AND BIAS OF A PORTFOLIO RELATIVE TO DJIA

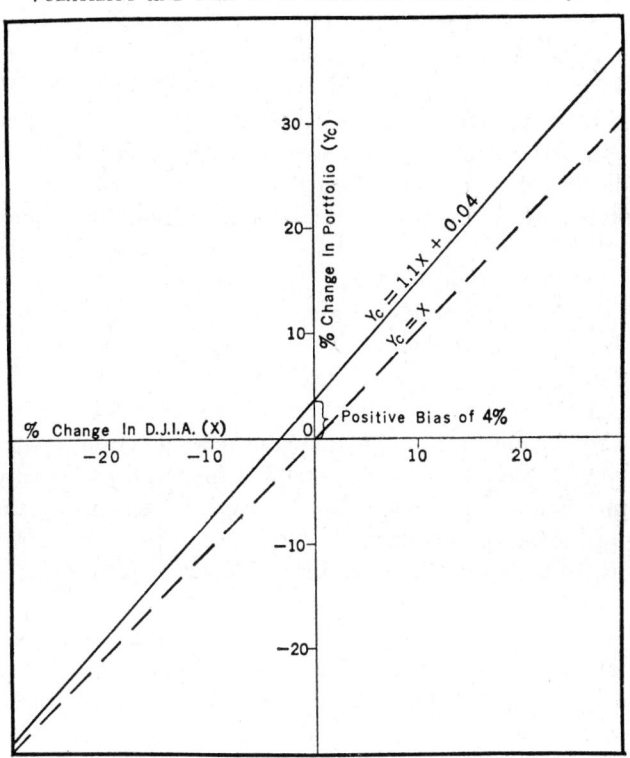

percent, the portfolio would be likely to rise 1.1 x (0.25) + 0.04, or 31.5 percent. If the Dow dropped 6 percent, the portfolio should drop 1.1 x (−0.06) + 0.04, or −2.6 percent. The 4 percent positive bias is highly significant in indicating the ability of the security analyst to find stocks which outperform the market because of merit (or value) rather than volatility. In short, the quality of investment research may be determined by the positive or negative bias of the equation.

The 1.1 coefficient of X, or *volatility*, may reveal something of investment policy, since it can show shifts of emphasis from stocks of higher volatility to lower volatility, or vice versa. Shifting to lower volatility stocks would have results much like a cutback in the percentage of the total portfolio invested in common stocks. Increasing the volatility of common stock holdings would be desirable near a market low—very much similar in action to an increase in the percentage of the total fund invested in common stocks. In measuring the soundness of investment policy, consideration should be given both to shifts in the volatility of the common stocks in the portfolio and to shifts in the percentages invested in equities.

The coefficient of X, or volatility, is the slope, or tangent, of a line. When it is equal to 1, the common stock portfolio will move parallel to changes in the market standard. (This is represented as a dashed line in Figure 1, rising at a 45° angle from $x = 0$, $y = 0$.) The positive or negative bias shows as the remainder, or vertical intercept. When the coefficient of X is greater than 1, the volatility of the common stock portfolio is greater than that of the standard, while a coefficient less than 1 would indicate greater stability than that of the standard.

It is interesting to experiment with various kinds of common stock portfolios as measured against a standard. If one believes that the stock market is due to rise sharply, it may be worthwhile to move into a high volatility group of stocks despite a negative bias for the entire group of stocks! The steepness of the line, reflecting a high volatility index, could more than offset the loss from the negative bias.

If price volatility is identified as being the same as risk, the ratio of the portion of total equity return (income plus market action of the common stocks) from positive bias to the total return minus the positive bias is clearly a measure of the effectiveness of selectivity versus the effectiveness of timing of the use of volatility.

There is no certainty that volatility, defined as the coefficient of X, should be considered as being the same as risk. Volatility is a characteristic of a security, or group of securities, *at a given time*. The author once prepared a 14-year study of the 30 DJIA stocks using certain ratios in the hope of discovering in each year the 10 most desirable stocks for the subsequent 12 months. It happened that the 10 "attractive" stocks were consistently of above-average volatility, relative to the volatility of the DJIA. Yet, over the 14 years, 25 of the 30 stocks in the DJIA were found in the more desirable group at least once and most showed up more than once. During the years when they failed to meet the statistical criteria, their volatility declined sharply, so that the stocks would have to be reclassified as "stable" stocks for at least a short while.

This suggests that some thought should be given to the question of the linearity of our volatility index. In the real stock market stocks are fast movers only for a while; and then the fickle public loses interest in the faded ladies and moves on to fresh and exciting new favorites. The tendency of prices to overshoot the mark, once momentum is gained, could indicate a more erratic pattern of behavior than a straight line.

There is also some doubt that a group of stocks having a volatility index of 2 would actually drop 100 percent if the Dow Jones were to drop 50 percent. It seems more likely that the high volatility stocks would find a floor, perhaps somewhere around half of their liquidating value. Despite the possibly defective linearity, the construction of an experience line by the method of least squares, or even roughly sketched in by eye, would appear to offer some help in measuring the degree to which the market action of a common stock portfolio is due to the faster or slower speed of movement—or to a favorable or unfavorable bias.

One problem that plagues the reviewer of investment management is the rather limited sample available for construction of a multiple regression equation. If 10 quarterly periods were under study, our sample would consist of 10 pairs, which is not sufficient to provide a high confidence factor. If investment results could be studied for 10 years by quarters, the sample would rise to 40 pairs and the confidence index would improve rather rapidly. On the other hand, a requirement that the study cover at least 10 years brings on further problems because 10 years is a long time to expect the investment philosophy, vitality, experience, and quality of personnel, etc., to remain constant. It seems much more likely that there would be some changes, for better or worse, but these changes would be difficult to detect until a sufficiently large sample of additional years or quarters was available to bring the index of confidence back to a respectable level. Thus, while the statistical methods are available to solve the problem of measuring volatility and related aspects of performance, practical considerations suggests that one be alert to changes in personnel and investment philosophy.

It is possible to subdivide longer periods into shorter periods of time—say a year into months or weeks—in order to get more samples. Yet this action merely increases the accuracy of the measurement of short-term investment performance, while our true interest is in long-term results. Once again, a measure of old-fashioned judgment seems necessary.

Obviously one is more confident when there are ten consecutive years of good results than when the record shows nine dreary years mixed with one of magnificent success. Consistency counts. Also, small regular increments compound faster than large irregular gains.

The interested reader may pursue the subject of volatility by reading the recent article "How to Rate Management of Investment Funds" by Jack L. Treynor.[9] Mr. Treynor devotes considerable attention to volatility and related matters.

How to Beat the Dow

Now we can consider in better perspective such a remark as "My stocks beat the Dow." Considering the splendid overall record of the 30

---

[9] Treynor, Jack L., "How to Rate Management of Investment Funds," *Harvard Business Review* (Jan.–Feb. 1965).

stocks in the Dow Jones Industrial Average, this is no mean claim. However, our previous discussion indicates that one should respond quickly with the question, "What kind of stocks did you own?" before rushing out to duplicate the successful portfolio. It may have outpaced the Dow in any number of ways, including: (1) the right sort of volatility for the period under discussion, (2) a positive bias, (3) proper timing in shifting in and out of the market, (4) general good luck, (5) use of "hot issues," (6) one or two uniquely successful stocks (the Polaroids and Xeroxes), (7) use of leverage, or (8) some combination of the above or other factors.

It is intriguing to consider what the characteristics of high volatility can do for the portfolio manager. If he selected stocks with twice the volatility of the Dow Jones, but invested only half the normal number of dollars, he could have the same results as he would have achieved with a full portion of common stock money invested in the DJIA. Instead of putting, say, 80 percent of his account in the DJIA, he could obtain the same effect by investing 40 percent in a group of stocks *that worked twice as hard*. And he could keep 60 percent of his money invested in very low risk fixed-income securities, rather than 20 percent. In a major bear market, the investor could lose twice as much of his capital using the high-quality Dow Jones stocks as he could in a portfolio using lesser "quality" but highly volatile stocks. In effect, the market risk would be twice as great in the portfolio using stable (safe) stocks as the one using volatile (risky) stocks!

Timing and Size of Contributions

Because the sizes of net contributions and withdrawals are significant factors in investment performance, the final results of an investment portfolio may be a reflection merely of good or bad luck rather than good or bad investment management. If an investment manager made only one or two right decisions on matters involving large amounts of money (typically upon the receipt of large net contributions) and made all of his mistakes on matters involving small amounts, his overall results could be quite good despite a poor batting average. On the other hand, one big mistake might wipe out dozens of correct moves, even though the size of the transaction was beyond the investment manager's control.

If the reader doubts the impact of the size and timing of net additions, he might compute the effect of receiving a large pension fund contribution at the end of 1961 as compared with the same amount delayed six months in the mail. Almost regardless of policy, an aggressive account would have fared better losing six months' income and, with it, the opportunity to suffer the worst of the 1962 stock market break. Outright refusal to buy equities or actual sale of equities are about the only policies in which the earlier receipt of the addition would have helped the account. A large majority of advisors would have bought *some* common stocks, regardless of when the funds were received. Customers seldom understand why they should pay advisors a fee to recommend purchase of U.S. Treasury bills.

Diversification

Another question of undue investment risk has to do with diversification. Once again we fall back on Markowitz to guide us. Markowitz'[10] most important contribution on diversification has been pointing out that a relatively small number of stocks will provide adequate diversification if the covariance between the stocks is small. In layman's language, this means that to obtain true diversification stocks must not be dependent on the same independent variables (such as Consumer Disposable Income, Index of Industrial Production, Gross National Product, or some other massive economic force) to determine their market action. The reader will be fascinated with newly developed input-output tables which show the interdependence of various industries.[11]

The variations in each stock should be as independent as possible from the influence of variations in the other stocks. This is an important investment rule—almost a fundamental law—stating that we must diversify our common stocks not by names or industries but rather by the influences which make them fluctuate. It would not be surprising in a few years to see stocks classified as to their dependency on various independent variables. A properly diversified common stock portfolio should meet disaster only if every segment of consumption and production meets disaster.

Diligence in Pruning

R. Norman Wood[12] suggests the desirability of measuring the "proportion of mean market value sold" as a measure of the investment manager's efforts to weed out unsatisfactory securities. This is a two-headed coin. It is true that good investment managers are vigorous in the pruning of their investment portfolios. Better investment managers have less to prune.

Investment Policy

Timing is probably the most elusive, undefined and poorly handled area of investments. Selecting securities is no more than half of the job of portfolio management.[13] Often the game is won or lost on a few key decisions to change investment posture at the right moment. Most of the literature on timing has been the output of market technicians whose interests appear to center on the smaller swings in the market. The

---

[10] Markowitz, H. M., *op. cit.*, Chap. 5.

[11] Leontief, Wassily W., "The Structure of the U.S. Economy," *Scientific American*, Vol. 212, No. 4 (April 1965).

[12] Wood, *op. cit.*

[13] For a contrary view, see Sieff, J. A., *op. cit.*

technician's approach may not suit the needs of the average long-term investor. However, even the most conservative of investors will freely recognize that key timing decisions are a major part of investment management and that the effete "buy and hold" approach is an admission of inability to detect those underlying values which constitute the basis for the fundamentalist's claim to investment know-how.

Yet timing is only a part of investment policy. Timing is ordinarily defined as "when to buy or sell equities." Investment policy is far broader, involving such matters as the kinds of stocks to buy or sell, shortening maturities, increasing call protection, upgrading or downgrading quality, shifting from discount to current coupon bonds, etc. Such a broad conglomerate of individual investment decisions seems impossible of statistical or visual display. Yet one indulges the hope that at least a part of the picture can be painted in a meaningful fashion.

Dr. Peter O. Dietz of Northwestern University has made a very complete study and analysis of pension fund timing and investment policies. Dr. Dietz has invented several ingenious ratios and graphic methods for reporting actual policy changes against a stock market background of "defer," "neutral," and "accumulate" periods.[14] A visual approach has much to commend it, when used with a suitable history of overall performance plus separate results of the equity and fixed income portfolios.

Borrowing selectivity from Dr. Dietz' approach, we have prepared the chart shown in Figure 2. While our presentation is crude, the reader may recognize the opportunities for further refinement to reflect whatever information is deemed necessary to interpret investment achievement.

The chart is drawn against the Standard & Poor's 500 Stock Index. The obvious "buy" areas of 1960 and the latter half of 1962 are shaded lightly. A period in 1961–62 which might have been favorable for deferring purchases or for making actual sales is shaded more heavily. While a "sell" area may also have existed in 1964, this is not yet clear to the writer and is not so designated.

Six sets of information are shown on the chart, using an actual pension fund's performance:

1. The Standard & Poor's 500 Stock Index is plotted against an index composed of the common stocks actually held in the account. The stocks in the fund "beat the S & P 500"—partly due to volatility and partly to a modest positive bias. The linear correlation is essentially the same as shown by the solid line in Figure 1.

2. The second group of lines shows, first, the "Stated Equity Policy" as reflected in letters from the investment advisor; second, the actual percent of the total fund invested in common stocks at market value ("Actual Equity Policy"); and, third, the percent of net additions which

---

[14] Dietz, Peter O., *Pension Funds: Measuring Investment Performance* (The Free Press, Inc., New York, 1966), Chap. 7.

FIGURE 2

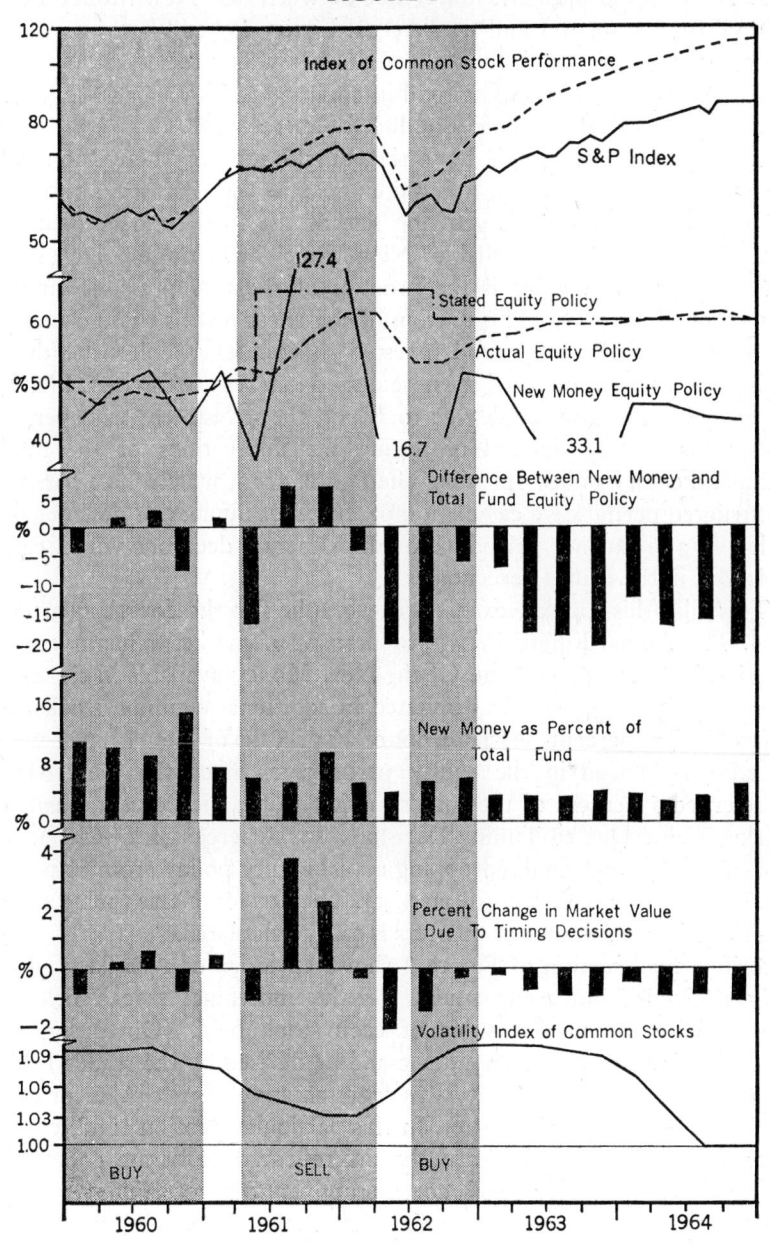

Figure showing Index of Common Stock Performance, S&P Index, Stated Equity Policy (127.4), Actual Equity Policy, New Money Equity Policy (16.7, 33.1), Difference Between New Money and Total Fund Equity Policy, New Money as Percent of Total Fund, Percent Change in Market Value Due To Timing Decisions, and Volatility Index of Common Stocks, from 1960 to 1964, with BUY, SELL, BUY periods marked.

was invested in equities during the quarter ("New Money Equity Policy"). Departures from Stated Policy, and the vacillating Stated Policy itself, indicate a weak application of the propounded attitudes toward equities. The changes in Stated and Actual Policy were badly timed.

3. A bar graph shows the difference between the "New Money Equity Policy" for the quarter and the "Actual Equity Policy" based on market values, for the total fund. In effect, a plus bar would reflect an attempt to increase the percentage of the fund in common stocks, at market, while a minus bar would be an effort to reduce the percentage.

4. The second bar graph shows the net additions, or "New Money," as a percent of the total fund. It is quite apparent that a seasonal pattern of contributions existed. The growing size of the total fund gradually reduced the ability of the available "New Money" to change policy.

5. The final bar chart is the product of the two previous ones described in (3) and (4). This portion of the chart reveals those changes in the percent of the total fund invested in equities which were due to timing decisions, as opposed to those due to market fluctuations. In effect, these final bars show the degree to which the investment manager controlled his destiny, instead of letting the fluctuations of the market command equity policy for him. The figures from which these bars were constructed permit easy calculation of the exact number of dollars gained or lost in a given time period, through deliberate decisions which caused variations in the equity percentages.

To make this clearer, examine the graphs for the fourth quarter of 1964. The Actual Equity Policy, or percent of market value invested in equities, had been 61 percent. Of the New Money available in the fourth quarter, only 41 percent was invested in additional common stocks. The difference (61 percent—41 percent) of 20 percent of New Money was an effective reduction in the equity percentage. Since the New Money represented 5 percent of the fund's market value, the Percent Change in Market Value Due to Timing Decisions was 5 percent x (−20%), or 1 percent of the total fund, (dropping actual equity policy from 61 percent to 60 percent in an unchanged market). The impact of this timing change on results in the subsequent quarters is easily calculated.

6. The final section of Figure 2 shows an index of volatility, empirically derived from prior studies of the individual stocks held and weighted by the market value of each stock held. (Obviously other methods of creating such an index could be devised by the reader.) Thus, the weighted average volatility was representative of past behavior of the stocks held during each quarter. In this particular pension fund, changes in volatility were made consciously and reflected deliberate policy. The timing was surprisingly good, considering the mediocre timing reflected in the actual and stated equity policy shown elsewhere in Figure 2.

The charts in Figure 2 have little meaning without information on overall results—and even less without the application of judgment. Information would certainly be required on the specific investment objectives of the account—for no two accounts are alike. Doubtless, the reader will think of a substantial catalog of additional data which could be helpful in judging the effectiveness of the investment management. An example is the advisor's freedom from pressure from the customer, which was a strong factor in the Figure 2 example.

Once a satisfactory system of measuring performance has been developed, the question becomes *what to do with the results of the measurements*. The suggestion that they be shown to customers brings defensive automatic objections that "roughly half of the customers will have below average performance even though they may all be beating the market nicely." No customer would be happy with his account being "below average." Obviously there are public relations problems here, but many of them have been created by rather unprofessional claims to investment omnipotence. If we are really professional investors, we shall have to reflect to our customers the same humility which we expect from all other honest professions.

Several investment management organizations plan, or have, regular computer created performance histories for all accounts. Each investment account manager is, or will be, measured and judged by the results of his accounts. Particular attention will be paid to the causes of differences in results. If the customer's account is of sufficient size and he specifically requests performance data, the figures will be given to him—occasionally with forced joviality, no doubt.

Farsighted managers already prepare detailed performance reports for each security and industry as a test of their securities analysts. In addition, summary breakdowns are made based on responsibility areas (consumer nondurables, services, raw material industries, etc.). A certain amount of effort is also being devoted to overall reports for guiding policy and setting goals.

There is little doubt that accurate performance studies will offer opportunities for the conscientious investment management organization to pinpoint its strong and weak points, alter its training programs, shift individual personnel, and make whatever other adjustments seem necessary to correct those problems which are revealed by performance analyses. Yet it becomes increasingly clear that comparing rates of return is only the starting point. ". . . There is a fair amount of evidence to suggest that most people are behaviorally innocent of the calculus of probabilities,"[15] and people make investment markets. Meaningful comparisons will embrace a full spectrum of media, objectives, relationships, policies, timing, markets, and organizations. The conclusions drawn will be closer to diagnosis than to mere measurement. The end product should provide quite satisfying internal and external improvements in the investment process.

---

[15] Luce, R. Duncan and Raiffa, Howard, *Games and Decisions* (John Wiley & Sons, Inc., New York, 1957), p. 373.

44
HOW TO RATE MANAGEMENT OF INVESTMENT FUNDS*

Jack L. Treynor

Investment management has become an important industry in the United States. The responsibilities of investment managers are enormous, and their potential rewards are great. In order to reward management for good performance in this field, however, it is necessary to be able to recognize it. Unfortunately, pension funds, trust funds, and mutual funds all share one serious problem: to the extent that they are heavily invested in common stocks, the return achieved in any one period is subject to wide fluctuations which are beyond the control of investment management. The result has been that, although many believe the quality of investment management is important, no one has devised a satisfactory way to measure its impact on performance.

In this article we shall look at a new way to rate the performance of a fund's investment managers. The comprehensiveness of this rating is a question for the reader to decide for himself, depending on how he thinks about the "quality" of investment management. Most readers are likely to agree, however, that at least one dimension—and a critical one—of the quality of the investment management is analyzed by this new method.

ANALYZING RISK

It is almost ironic that the presence of market risk should pose such a serious problem. The assets controlled by investment managers are remarkably liquid. To a degree almost unmatched in other enterprises, the investment manager is free to act independently of the investment decisions of his predecessors. Furthermore, although there are varying institutional restrictions placed on the investment manager's decisions, by and large he competes directly with other investment managers, buying and selling securities in the same market. If it were not for the problems created by market risk, therefore, performance comparisons in the investment management industry would be more meaningful than in many other industries.

* Reprinted by permission of the *Harvard Business Review* (January–February 1965). © 1964 by the President and Fellows of Harvard College; all rights reserved.

Actually, of course, there is more than one kind of risk in a diversified fund. There is a risk produced by general market fluctuations—the volatility of the stock market. There is also a risk resulting from fluctuations in the particular securities held by the fund. In any event, here are important practical consequences of either or both of these risks:

(1) The effect of management on the rate of return on investments made in any one period is usually swamped by fluctuations in the general market. Depending on whether, during the period in question, the general market is rising or falling, the more volatile funds (stock funds) will look better or worse than the less volatile funds (balanced funds). As the Wharton Report points out, the difficulty is not solved by averaging return over a number of periods.[1] For any sample interval of reasonable length, average return is still dominated by market trends.

(2) Measures of average return make no allowance for investors' aversions to risk. The importance of fluctuations in one or a few stocks from the investor's point of view is apparent when one considers that, after all, if this kind of risk were not important, investors would not diversify. It is sometimes argued that because the importance attached to risk varies from investor to investor, no absolute measure of fund performance is possible.

OVERCOMING DIFFICULTIES

In order to have any practical value, a measure of management performance in handling a trust fund invested in equities or in handling pension or mutual funds must deal effectively with both problems. It should tend to remain constant so long as management performance is constant—even in the face of severe market fluctuations. Also, it should take into account the aversion of individual shareholders or beneficiaries to investment risk. The method to be described here overcomes both difficulties.

This article has three parts. The first describes a simple graphical method for capturing the essence of what is permanent and distinctive about the performance of a fund, including the effects of fund management. The second develops a concept of fund performance which takes investment risk into account. The third develops a measure for rating fund-management performance which can be applied directly, using the graphical technique developed in the first part. For the statistician, an Appendix details certain of the relationships used.

THE CHARACTERISTIC LINE

The first main step to obtaining a satisfactory performance measure is to relate the expected rate of return of a trust, pension, or mutual fund to the rate of return of a suitable market average. The device for accom-

---

[1] In discussing the cumulative performance of investment funds between January 1, 1953, and September 30, 1958, the report says "... the interpretation of the net result is to be made against the background of the movements in security market prices during this period ... general fund performance and comparisons among funds of different types might be quite different in other time periods ...," *A Study of Mutual Funds* (Washington, Government Printing Office, 1962), p. 308.

plishing this is the *characteristic line*. Let us examine its nature and significance.

Application to Funds

If the rate of return—taking into account both market appreciation and dividends—is plotted for a fund invested substantially in common stocks, wide swings from period to period are often evident. It is not generally known, however, that most managed funds actually demonstrate a remarkably stable performance pattern over time when viewed in terms of the simple graphical device which I call the characteristic line.

Exhibit I summarizes the performance history of four actual managed funds:

The horizontal and vertical axes in these figures are measured in terms of percent rate of return. (For both individual funds and market averages, rate of return is computed by dividing the sum of dividends, interest, and market appreciation on the funds available at the beginning of the year by the value of the funds available at the beginning of the year. Any increase in asset value during the year due to infusion of new funds is eliminated, as is any reduction due to distributions to beneficiaries or shareholders. Rates of return defined in this way are obviously approximations, because the value of funds available for investment typically fluctuates more or less continuously throughout the year.)

The horizontal axis measures the corresponding rate of return recorded for a general *market* average (the Dow-Jones Industrial Average); the vertical axis shows the rate of return for the *fund*.

Each point represents a year in the ten-year interval ending January 1, 1963. The points asterisked represent the five years in the latter half of the ten-year interval; the dots, the years in the former half.

Although the funds exhibited wide swings in rate of return over the ten-year interval, the rate of return in each year fell into a straight-line pattern which remained virtually fixed throughout the ten-year interval. This line—the characteristic line—can be fitted by eye or by statistical methods. The significant thing about it is that it tends to be stationary over time, despite wide fluctuations in short-term rate of return.

Information Revealed

The characteristic line contains information about both expected rate of return and risk. The slope of the line measures volatility. Thus, a steep slope means that the actual rate of return for the fund in question is relatively sensitive to fluctuations in the general stock market; a gentle slope indicates that the fund in question is relatively insensitive to market fluctuations.

The slope angle of the characteristic line obviously provides a more refined measure of a fund's volatility than the usual categories of "balanced fund," "stock fund," or "growth fund." The range of volatilities observed in actual practice is enormous. Among mutual funds, for example, I have found that volatilities range from roughly one-third to about two. A volatility of two means that a 1 percent increase (or decrease) in the rate of return demonstrated by the Dow-Jones Average is accompanied, on the average, by a 2 percent increase (or decrease) in the rate of return demonstrated by the particular fund in question.

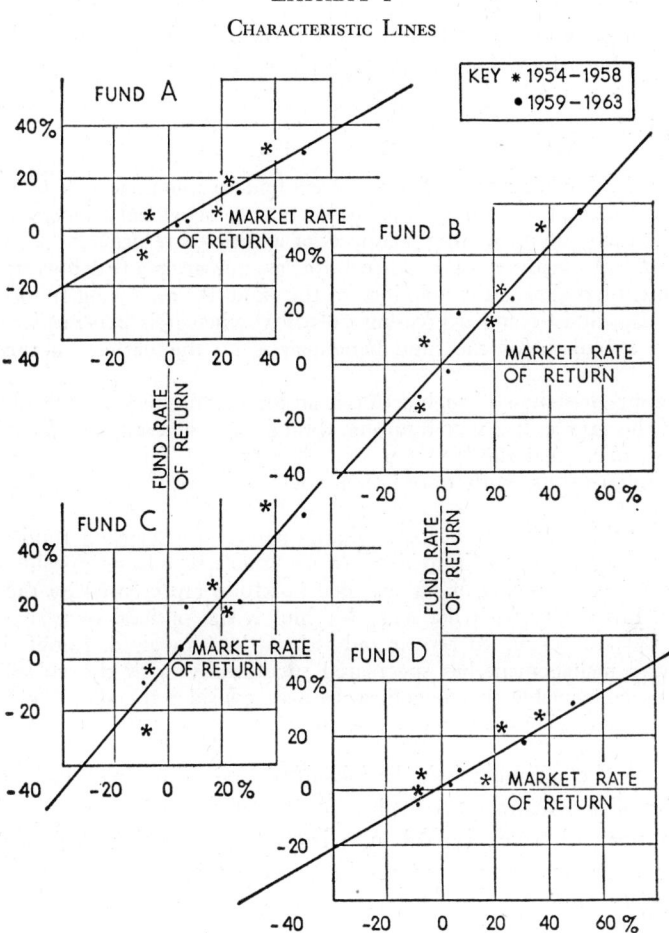

EXHIBIT I
CHARACTERISTIC LINES

[Figure: Four scatter plots labeled FUND A, FUND B, FUND C, and FUND D, each showing Fund Rate of Return vs. Market Rate of Return with characteristic lines fitted. Key: * 1954-1958, • 1959-1963]

For any individual investor who is risk-averse, the observed differences in volatility are surely large enough to be worth measuring. The differences also disclose important contrasts in management policy.

WHAT DEVIATIONS MEAN

As users of the characteristic-line method will discover, the plotted points in a typical chart will not all lie on the characteristic line. What this means is that not all of the risk in the fund in question is explained by fluctuations in the general market level.

As pointed out earlier, one can consider that investment risk in a diversified fund is the sum of responses to (1) general market fluctuations and (2) fluctuations peculiar to the particular securities held by the fund. If a fund is properly diversified, the latter risk, which tends to be causally unrelated one security from another, tends to average out. The former risk, being common to all common stocks in greater or lesser degree, does not tend to average out.

If the management of a fund attempts to maintain a constant degree of volatility, then the slope of the characteristic line will tend to measure that volatility. If there are excessive deviations from the characteristic line, we have a strong indication that:

Either the fund is not efficiently diversified to minimize risk unrelated to the general market (in which case the owner or beneficiary incurs additional risk without any compensating prospects of additional return).

Or, perhaps inadvertently or perhaps as a matter of deliberate policy, management has altered the volatility of the fund. By increasing fund volatility when it is optimistic and decreasing volatility when it is pessimistic, management can speculate for the fund beneficiaries on fluctuations in the general market.

The appropriateness of such action is an interesting question but outside the scope of this article. It is worth noting, though, that in a sample I have taken of 54 American mutual funds, 4 out of 5 demonstrate fairly clear-cut characteristic-line patterns, with correlation coefficients equal to or exceeding 90 percent.

Possibly this pattern indicates wide agreement that causing fund volatility to vary greatly leaves the individual owner unable to rely on a stable estimate of the risk in the portion of his personal portfolio represented by the fund in question. His ability to strike what for him is the optimal over-all portfolio balance between expected return and risk is then impaired. But if, in retrospect, fund management has speculated successfully with the volatility of a fund, it is conceivable that beneficiaries may consider the disadvantage more than offset by the improved rate of return.

Suppose the characteristic line itself shifts? This may happen when fund volatility remains constant but fund performance varies widely from year to year. A sweeping change in the personnel constituting fund management, for example, might be accompanied by a sudden shift in fund performance.

Comparing Performance

The characteristic line also contains information about management's ability to obtain a consistently higher return than the competition's. If, for example, two trust or mutual funds demonstrate precisely the same volatility, their respective characteristic lines would have the same slope, but one line would be consistently higher than the other (unless they coincide). For instance, suppose a certain fund had exactly the same slope as Fund A in Exhibit I. If its characteristic line were plotted on the chart, it would run parallel to Fund A's but higher or lower. The fund with the higher line would demonstrate consistently higher performance—in good years and bad.

Although the problem of comparing performances of fund managements is obviously not so simple when the slopes differ, the characteristic line does contain, as we shall see presently, the informaton necessary to make such comparisons.

IMPLICATIONS FOR CONTROL

The characteristic line has implications for management control, too. No matter how widely the rate of return for a fund may fluctuate, management performance is unchanged so long as the actual rate of return continues to lie on the characteristic line. One can establish control limits on either side of the line; points falling within these limits are assumed to represent a continuation of past management performance, while points falling outside the limits require special scrutiny. Without the characteristic line it is virtually impossible to tell whether the rate of return demonstrated in a given year represents a real change in the quality of fund management. With it, early detection of important changes becomes possible.

In summary, therefore, the graphical method provides a simple test of:

1. The extent to which a fund has adhered, purposely or not, to a single characteristic line.
2. The degree of volatility associated with the fund.
3. The success of fund management in maintaining a high rate of return under a variety of market conditions.

PERFORMANCE MEASURE

We turn now to a second line. This one deals not with an individual fund but with a *portfolio* containing a certain fund. The purpose of the line is to relate the expected return of a portfolio containing the fund to the portfolio owner's risk preferences. This line can be called the *portfolio-possibility* line. We shall see that the slope of this line is a measure of fund performance which transcends differences in investors' attitudes toward risk.

RISK PREFERENCE

Whether the performance pattern of a given fund rates high or low should depend on whether individual investors choose it in preference to the pattern demonstrated by other funds. During the last few years we have witnessed the rapid development of a theory of rational choice among portfolios.[2] The theory is too complex to be reviewed here in

---

[2] See, for example, H. M. Markowitz, *Portfolio Selection: Efficient Diversification of Investments* (New York, John Wiley & Sons, 1959); and D. E. Farrar, *The Investment Decision Under Uncertainty* (Englewood Cliffs, Prentice-Hall, Inc., 1962).

detail, but certain fragments of it provide the basis for a concept of fund-management performance.

It is interesting to note that when one talks about the historical performance pattern of a fund, he is looking at the past; but when he considers the preferences of individual investors and their choices among funds, he is talking about their appraisal of the future. We shall continue to talk about the performance of funds in terms of historical performance patterns, even though actual investor choices among funds are necessarily based on expectations regarding future performance patterns. The implication is that a good historical performance pattern is one which, if continued into the future, would cause investors to prefer it to others.

Economists sometimes study the investor's choice among possible portfolios in terms of a risk-return diagram (like that in Exhibit II):

The vertical axis in the exhibit measures the return which the investor would expect to get, on the average, from a given portfolio. The horizontal axis is some appropriate measure of risk.

(As a technical note for those interested in detail, let me add that it is traditional to measure the respective axes in terms of *expected rate of return*, where the rate is a weighted mean of possible future outcomes, and *standard error*, where standard error is a statistical measure of potential variability around the expected performance. Under certain assumptions regarding the nature of investment uncertainty, expected return and standard error completely characterize a given portfolio. These assumptions seem to fit actual stock-market experience fairly well. When the performance pattern of a mutual fund is clustered closely around the characteristic line, the slope of this line, which is our graphical measure of risk, is statistically an excellent measure of the standard error.)

The rate of return is for a standard time period—perhaps a month, quarter, or year—per dollar of the individual investor's initial capital.

The curved lines in the diagram are called indifference curves for the reason that the investor is indifferent to portfolio choices lying on a particular indifference curve; that is, he would just as soon have, say, 5 percent more return at 4 percent more risk as 8 percent more return at 6½ percent more risk, and so on (see the curve at right of chart).[3]

There is a useful analogy between the investor's relative preference, as shown by indifference curves, and relative heights as shown by contour lines on a topographical map—that is, lines along which elevation is constant. The arrows in the figure show the direction in which one moves to go from less to more desirable portfolios (or, to complete the topographical analogy, uphill).

Portfolio Choices

What kinds of portfolio choices are available to the investor? The assets he can include in his portfolio consist of two fundamentally different kinds:

---

[3] For elegant mathematical proof of the validity of indifference curves, see James Tobin, "Liquidity Performance as Behavior Towards Risk," *Review of Economic Studies*, February 1958, p. 65; a subsequently written, unpublished manuscript by the author carries the discussion further.

Money-fixed claims, such as checking deposits; savings deposits; government, municipal, and corporate bonds.

Equity assets, including equity in personal business and partnerships and corporate common stocks.

The investor who holds money-fixed claims is subject to the risk of changes in both the interest rate and price level. Although both risks are real, in American financial history they have been small compared to the

EXHIBIT II

INVESTORS' INDIFFERENCE CURVES

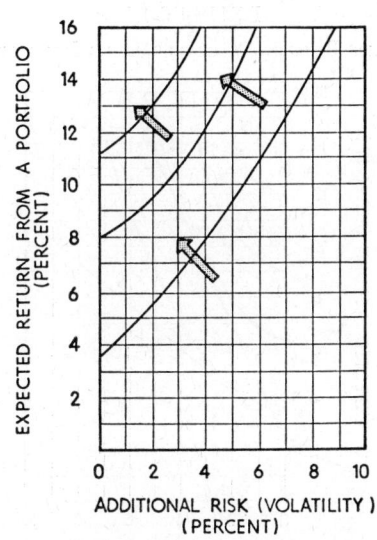

risk entailed in owning equities. The relative insignificance of market risk in money-fixed claims is reflected in the narrow range of net returns available in such claims. We shall simplify slightly and represent all assets of this type by a single point on the vertical axis of the risk-return diagram (point B in Exhibit III).

If the investor wants to raise the expected rate of return of his over-all portfolio above the rate offered by money-fixed claims, he must undertake some equity risk. On the risk-return diagram in Exhibit III, the investor has available to him the opportunity to invest in shares in a particular balanced or growth fund, Fund A, as well as the opportunity to invest in money-fixed claims, B. If he is free to vary the investment in each outlet more or less continuously, then the locus of portfolio combinations available to him is the straight line—viz., the portfolio-possibility line—joining points A and B. The combination which is best for him will lie at point D along the line which is farthest "uphill" as indicated by the "contour lines" on his indifference map. The preferred combinations for other investors will differ, depending on the precise shape of their indifference curves.

Now consider a second investment, Fund C (top right of Exhibit III). The line BC is the locus of possible portfolios made available to our investor by the existence of this investment. As in the case of locus BA, there will, in general, be a single point, E, along BC, which is the farthest "uphill" for the investor.

The significant fact is that, although the location of the points of optimum balance along lines BC and BA will differ from one investor to another, the optimum point D along line BA will always be superior for a given investor to the optimum point E along line BC. For every possible

EXHIBIT III

RISK-RETURN DIAGRAM FOR AN INVESTOR

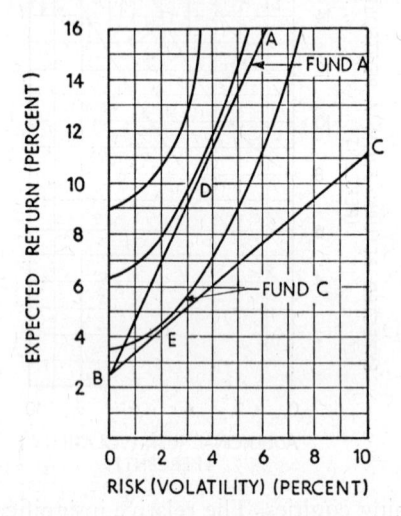

level of risk an investor might choose, the return on a combined portfolio containing Fund A is greater than the return on a portfolio containing Fund C, which provides the same level of risk. This ensures that, whatever the optimum point along line BC may be for a particular investor, the point on BA directly above it (that is, with the same risk) will have a greater expected return. This will be true for every investor who is risk averse, quite independently of the precise shape of his indifference curve.

But if, for every risk-averse investor, line BA is superior to line BC, then, in terms of the portfolio possibilities this line makes available to investors, Fund A is absolutely superior to Fund C. Now it is apparent from Exhibit III that lines BA and BC differ only in slope. Line BA, which is superior to line BC, slopes upward more sharply, showing that the rate of gain from shifting the investor's portfolio in the direction of greater risk is greater for Fund A than for Fund C. *The steepness of the portfolio-possibility line associated with a given fund is thus a direct measure of the desirability of the fund to the risk-averse investor.* The force of the preceding argument is not diminished by the fact that many investment funds contain money-fixed claims as well as equities.

Pension and Trust Funds

All very well for mutual funds, you may say. After all, the investor in mutual funds is free to adjust the fraction of his portfolio invested in each one pretty much as he pleases. But what about cases involving pension funds and trust frunds, in which the individual beneficiary has no freedom whatever to alter the fraction of his total assets which are managed by the fund? To answer this question, let us take an illustration:

Suppose a man has a certain fraction of his assets invested in a pension fund. Suppose further that the management performance of the pension fund (measured in terms of the slope of the portfolio-possibility line) ranks just equal to the performance of a certain mutual fund. A certain segment of the portfolio-possibility line for the mutual fund will be unavailable to the investor if part of his funds are irrevocably committed to the pension fund, since he is not free to convert all his assets to money-fixed claims. Within the range of the portfolio-possibility line available to him, however, he can achieve the same portfolio behavior with part of his capital committed to the pension fund as he could achieve if he were free to compose the risky portion of his portfolio entirely from the mutual fund in question. If his attitude toward portfolio risk leads him to choose a portfolio in this range, then he will be indifferent as to a choice of a pension fund or a mutual fund with an equal performance ranking. If, on the other hand, his choice lies outside this range, then the pension fund is less useful to him than a mutual fund with similarly sloped portfolio-possibility line.

Quantitative Measure

The performance demonstrated by a fund can be measured by the tangent of the slope angle, symbolized by the figure α. (For instance, the slope angle for Fund C in Exhibit III would be the difference between the slope of line BC and a horizontal line going through B; the slope angle for Fund A, which is larger, is the difference between BA and a horizontal.)

The formula for tangent α follows directly from the geometry of Exhibit III. As detailed in the Appendix, it is:

$$\text{tangent } \alpha = \frac{\mu - \mu^*}{\sigma}$$

where μ equals the expected fund rate of return at a particular market rate of return, μ^* is measured from a horizontal line through a point that would represent a fund consisting only of fixed-income securities, and σ is the symbol for volatility (which can serve as an approximate measure of investment risk as plotted on the horizontal axis of Exhibit III).

RATING MANAGEMENT

We are now ready to begin with the practical application of the concepts previously described. We will see how performance ratings can be read directly from the characteristic line.

Relative Ranking

In order to plot a fund, and the associated portfolio-possibility line, on a risk-return chart of the type discussed in the last section, one needs both an expected rate of return and an appropriate measure of risk. A measure of risk is provided by the slope of the characteristic line. The characteristic line also enables management to estimate the expected rate of return. In order to obtain a value for the expected rate of return for the fund, however, it is necessary to assume a rate-of-return value for the market. Depending on the choice of market rate of return, expected return for the fund—hence the slope of the opportunity locus—will vary. The effect of changing the assumed market rate is illustrated in Exhibits IV and V as follows:

Exhibit IV portrays a sample of characteristic lines for 20 actual managed funds based on rate-of-return data for the years 1953 through 1962. By making specific assumptions about the market rate of return, the characteristic lines for these funds can be transformed into points on the risk-return charts shown in Parts A and B of Exhibit V. (The term "volatility" on the horizontal axes of these charts, as indicated before, refers to the amount of risk in the fund due to fluctuations in the general market.)

Part A of Exhibit V was plotted by assuming a market return of 10 percent. (The characteristic line for each fund is inspected to determine its pattern of return when the market's return is 10 percent, and this pattern is converted to a point reflecting risk and return.) Given this assumption, the funds in question can easily be ranked visually; by drawing straight lines from Point Q to these points, one can obtain the portfolio-possibility lines for the funds in question. The problem is, of course, that the market-return assumption is arbitrary and other returns depend on it.

Part B results when a market rate of return of 30 percent is assumed instead. Although the risk values for the individual funds are unchanged, the expected rates of return are affected, and a new set of portfolio-possibility lines results.

Inspection shows that the ranking of the funds is unchanged in Parts A and B of Exhibit V. For example, the highest- and lowest-ranking funds in Part A are, respectively, the highest- and lowest-ranking funds in Part B, despite the fact that the two diagrams are based on widely differing assumptions about the expected rate of return for the general market. This illustrates what is actually a quite general result: although the absolute position of funds on a risk-return chart (and their corresponding portfolio-possibility lines) may vary with the level of market rate of return assumed, *the ranking of funds with respect to each other does not.*

EXHIBIT IV
Comparison of 20 Managed Funds

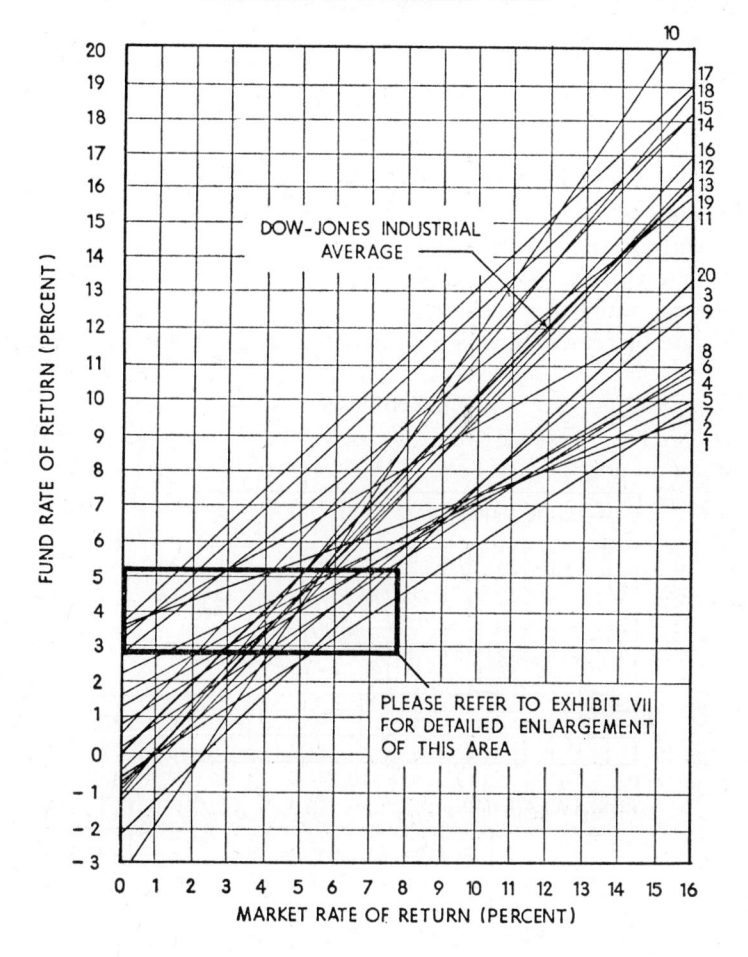

Numerical Measure

What is desired, therefore, is a number which will measure the relative ranking of a fund—preferably without being affected by changes in the absolute level of rate of return of the kind illustrated by Parts A and B of Exhibit V. It happens that there is a number which has these properties: it is the level of rate of return for the general market at which the fund in question will produce the same return as that produced by a fund consisting solely of riskless investment. As Exhibit VI shows, its value can be read directly from the characteristic line:

A horizontal line is drawn so as to intersect the vertical axis at a point representing the rate of return available on money-fixed claims. In Exhibit VI the horizontal line is drawn at 4 percent. (The choice of rate within the range of 3½ percent to 5 percent is somewhat arbitrary, but not especially critical as regards its effect on performance ratings.) The point at which the horizontal line intersects the characteristic line determines the rating of the fund, which is read off the horizontal axis as a percentage. The lower this percentage, the higher the rating of the pension, trust, or mutual fund. For those interested in a formal proof that the number just defined will have the special properties desired, the Appendix sets forth the steps in the reasoning.

In order to demonstrate the practical significance of the rating technique, let us refer back to Exhibit IV. Each of the performance ratings of the 20 funds whose characteristic lines are shown in this chart could be read directly from the figure if a horizontal line corresponding to the rate of return on a riskless portfolio (here 4 percent) were added. The performance rating for each fund could be determined by the value of market rate of return at which its characteristic line intersects the hori-

EXHIBIT V

FUND RANKINGS UNDER DIFFERENT MARKET CONDITIONS

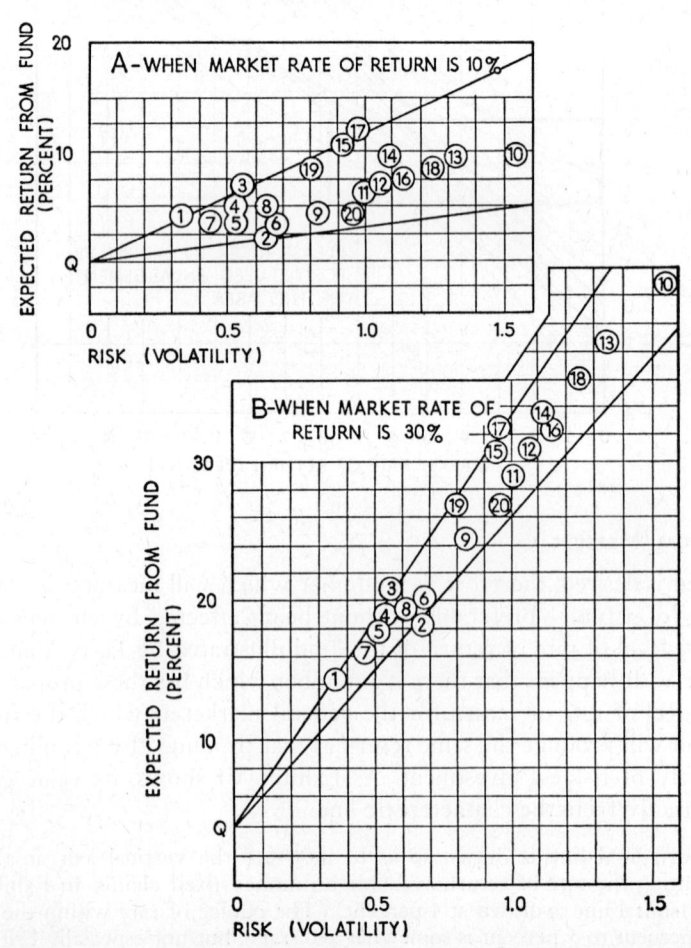

EXHIBIT VI
Ranking Number of a Fund

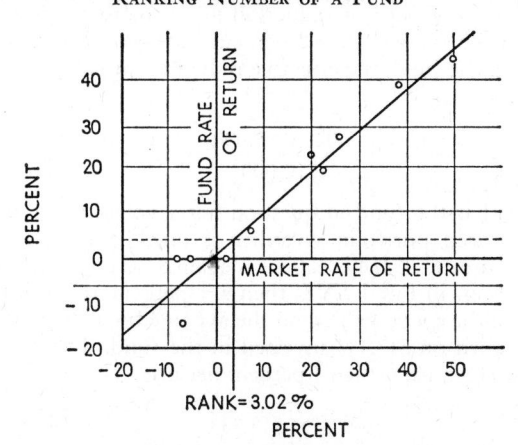

zontal 4 percent line. Now see Exhibit VII. The characteristic lines are the same as the ones in Exhibit IV, but a 4 percent horizontal has been added, and the area of intersection with it has been expanded for ease in reading. Note that the performance ratings for the 20 funds (read off the horizontal axis) range from less than 1 percent to more than 7 percent.

EXHIBIT VII
Performance of Funds

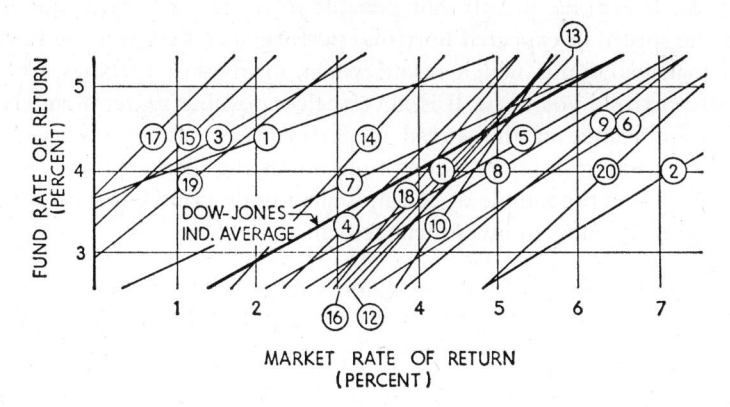

Differences Important?

Is the difference between the best and worst rated fund in Exhibit VII large enough to be significant to an investor? Let us take an illustration:

Suppose that an investor specifies his portfolio volatility should be equal to one. The amount of "riskless" investment or borrowing which he undertakes will depend on the volatility of the fund. Let us say that Fund XYZ has a volatility of two. Since the desired portfolio volatility is one, then the portfolio must be blended of equal parts (in terms of dollars invested) of the fund and riskless investment. If, for example, the beneficiary's capital is initially worth $10,000, then, since a 1 percent reduction in the market rate of return will be accompanied on the average by a 2 percent reduction in the rate of return on $5,000 invested in the fund, the effective reduction in *portfolio* rate of return is 1 percent since:

$$\frac{.02 \times \$5,000}{\$10,000} = .01$$

Now assume that the fund in question has a volatility of three-quarters. If the investor's desired portfolio volatility is one, he must invest an amount exceeding his own capital. If his capital is again $10,000, and he borrows $3,333 and invests that sum in Fund XYZ, then a 1 percent reduction in the market rate of return will be accompanied on the average by a .0075 percent reduction in the rate of return on $13,333 invested in the fund. The effective reduction in *portfolio* rate of return is then 1 percent because:

$$\frac{.0075 \times \$13,333}{\$10,000} = .01$$

In both cases the portfolios have a volatility equal to one—the value specified—but the differing fund volatilities necessitate quite different investment strategies.

Is the significance of rating differences for a sample of funds influenced by market conditions? It is to a certain extent. We have already seen that one cannot employ characteristic-line data to obtain an expected rate of return for a fund without first assuming a value for the market rate of return. It is consequently not possible to make categorical statements about the spread in expected portfolio performance between the best and worst managed funds which results when an investor specifies a certain level of portfolio volatility. It is nevertheless possible to get a rough idea of the significance of the spread in performance ratings observed in a sample by making different assumptions about the market. If we take the extreme cases in the sample of 20 funds already described, for instance, we find these differences in investment return:

Expected market rate of return	10%	30%
Return of highest-ranked fund	13.6%	33.4%
Return of lowest-ranked fund	6.6%	26.6%

These figures suggest the following conclusions about differences in ratings:

(1) In the range of normal market rate of return, the difference in portfolio rate of return between funds ranked high and low is substantial.

(2) The difference seems relatively less important, the higher the performance of the general market is. Hence the consequences of rating differences for portfolio performance will be relatively more significant in a normal market than during the bull market of recent history.

CONCLUSION

In this article we have seen that there is a good way of cutting through the confusion of facts and figures in the marketplace to compare the performance of individual trust, pension, and mutual funds. The new method described is surely not a perfect answer to the needs of fund managers and investment analysts, for it requires the making of certain assumptions about fund performance with which not all men will completely agree (e.g., the desirability of a fund's holding to a consistent investment policy). But the method goes at least part of the way, I believe, to providing answers that have long eluded executives in the investment business.

We have seen that, consistent with any specified level of the market rate of return, there is associated with each fund a range of combinations of expected portfolio return and risk. The slope of the portfolio-possibility line measures the rate at which the individual investor increases the expected rate of return of his portfolio as his burden of portfolio risk increases. A comparison of slopes among funds provides a means of rating funds which transcends variations in individual investors' attitudes toward risk. Although the slopes vary just as the market rate of return varies, it can be proved that the ranking of the funds represented remains unchanged. The relative rankings can be read directly from the characteristic lines of funds to be compared.

Differences in ranking based on the characteristic lines can be quite significant for individual investors, even though they take varying attitudes toward risk. Also, the differences are independent of market fluctuations. Because the ranking measure has these properties, it provides a useful basis for reviewing the performance of fund management.

APPENDIX

Figure A shows the characteristic line for a typical fund. For each possible value of the market rate of return, the characteristic line predicts the corresponding rate of return for the fund pictures. The slope of the characteristic line is measured by tangent B; the vertical intercept is h. For the particular market rate of return D, the expected fund rate of return is μ. A horizontal line drawn a distance μ^* above the horizontal axis depicts the behavior of a fund consisting solely of fixed income securities. The ranking measure r is determined by the intersection of the characteristic line and the horizontal line at height μ^*.

The question is whether the ranking measure r has the properties specified; that is, whether it will—

. . . rank funds in the order of their respective values of tangent $\propto$ (the slope of the opportunity locus as discussed earlier in the article);

. . . have the same value for a given fund, independently of fluctuations in the market rate of return.

FIGURE A
Characteristic Line and Value for a Typical Fund

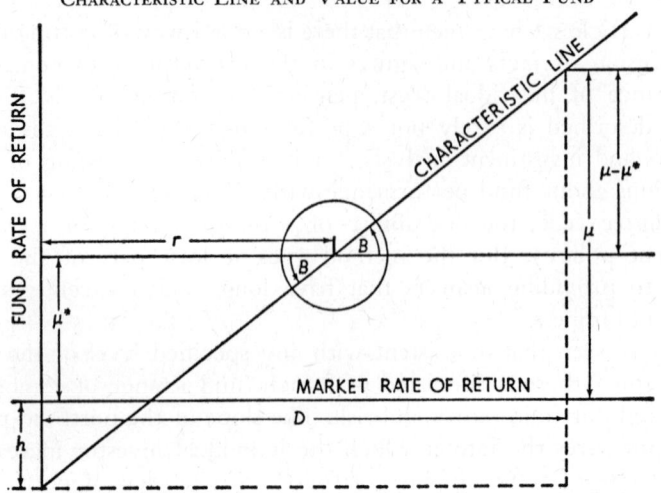

A moment's reflection shows that no number can have both properties simultaneously unless the general result alluded to in the main text holds true; that is, unless the *relative* ranking of funds—in terms of the slope of the portfolio-possibility line—is unaffected by fluctuations in the general market. Inasmuch as the proof demonstrates that the number in question does indeed have both properties, the general result follows.

From the geometry of the diagram, we have for the volatility:

$$\sigma = \text{tangent } B = \frac{\mu - \mu^*}{D - r}$$

Solving for r, we obtain:

$$r = D - \left(\frac{\mu - \mu^*}{\sigma}\right).$$

The expression in parentheses is the ranking measure discussed in the section on portfolio-possibility lines (see "Performance Measure," p. 67), with the volatility, σ, serving as the approximate measure of investment risk. We conclude that, for any given level of market rate of return D, r is uniquely related to the ranking fraction.

$$\frac{\mu - \mu^*}{\sigma} \text{ (which equals tangent } \alpha\text{)}.$$

We note that a relatively large value of r signifies a relatively low level of performance for fund management. A second important property of r is obtained when the following relationship, based on the geometry of the diagram, is substituted in the previous expression for r:

$$\mu = D \text{ tangent } B + h = D \alpha + h.$$

Substituting for μ, we find that:

$$r = \frac{\mu^* - h}{\sigma}.$$

Now μ^* is the same for all funds and independent of market fluctuations; and h and σ are the intercept and slope, respectively, of the characteristic line. It is clear in this formulation that r is independent of D, the market rate of return. Hence r tends to have the same value independently of fluctuations in the general market.

45

SOME METHODS FOR MEASURING PERFORMANCE OF A PENSION FUND*

Randolph W. McCandlish, Jr.

The problems of measuring pension fund performance are more apparent than their solutions. Because the pension field is a relatively new one (at least for common stock investment), the amount of experience that can be brought to bear is limited, and much of it has been colored by the strong bull market in which it occurred. When equity investment of pension funds was in its infancy, say in 1952, the Dow-Jones Industrial Average was at about 275. Since then, the market has risen at an average annual rate of 10 percent. This rise was undoubtedly caused, partly, by the growth of pension funds, although many equity portfolios have themselves been hard put to achieve commensurate growth. On the other hand, even 10 percent may be an inadequate minimum performance in view of a recent University of Chicago study[1] which suggests that a 9.0 percent return could have been obtained (with cash dividends reinvested) by random selection.

Among the factors which complicate the measurement of fund performance or qualify comparisons with capital aggregations such as mutual funds (apart from a basic difference in function) are varying dates of inception, inconsistencies in the timing of contributions and pension payments, and variations in the relative size of contributions and benefits. Thus, some pension funds have negligible contributions and substantial payouts, others the reverse. Some receive contributions monthly or even more frequently, others once a year or less. Most pensions pay monthly, some do not. Some of these variations may be consequences of over- or under-funding, new or mature plans, the employer-corporation's financial condition or actuarial-financial factors such as locked in split funding or other insurance considerations. They may be wholly political in the sense of deriving from the corporate attributes of the employer or the trustee, or from some aspect of the relationship between the two, or they may be

---

* Reprinted by permission of the *Financial Analysts Journal* (November–December 1965).

[1] L. Fisher, and J. H. Lorie, "Rates of Return on Investments in Common Stocks," the *Journal of Business* (January, 1964), Graduate School of Business, University of Chicago.

inherent. As a result, pension funds may have widely divergent needs for liquidity or income, or if not, may still vary widely in ability to hold equity or other high-risk investments, to adapt to market conditions, or to vary objectives in the light of changing financial, actuarial, and other circumstances.

Nevertheless, pension funds are tax-free entities and, in a sense, all assets held are repurchased every day. They are wholly reinvestable at all times without regard to any need other than to pay pensions: there are no "holds"—only "buys" and "sells." Thus, in *theory*, all pension funds are directly comparable; in practice, they have individual characteristics, and no wholly satisfactory method has yet been found to compensate for these characteristics in a usable technique which measures overall performance. A partial solution, of course, is to measure performance frequently enough so that some individual divergencies can be averaged out.

Theoretical problems involved in the measurement of performance are so-called because theoreticians often state them without trying to, or being able to, offer useful solutions. On a sophisticated level, they may have significance; as a practical matter, they are normally overlooked. For example, there is the question whether common stocks may be said to "perform" at all. The so-called "random walk" theory[2] asserts, in effect, that market prices have no real trend and that each price change is an isolated event in the universe of occurrences. A mere portfolio manager cannot hope to cope with this theory except in pragmatic language: if it looks like a duck, and acts like a duck, it's a duck.

A similar problem is the statistical weakness of indices such as the Dow-Jones Industrial Average, Standard & Poor's Stock Average, and others.[3] To the extent these indices are flawed, of course, their use as a basis of comparison is necessarily suspect, but a portfolio manager must use what is practicable. While he may recognize the questionable validity of such objective standards, he also knows they do the job about as well as anything yet devised and serve their function, if only because almost every investor looks to them as an expression of the market.

Traditional units of measure have also been questioned. For example, Walter J. Simons, Treasurer of Chrysler Corporation, asserts, with some justification, that normal compound interest calculations can introduce a

---

[2] See, for example, Sidney S. Alexander, "Price Movements in Speculative Markets: Trends or Random Walk," *Industrial Management Review*, May, 1961 (II).

[3] For a discussion of the defects of market averages, the reader is referred to Eugene M. Lerner, *Readings in Financial Analysis and Investment Management* (Homewood, Ill.: Richard D. Irwin, Inc., 1963). Mr. Lerner's book includes three excellent articles on this subject: "A Security Check on the Dow Jones Industrial Average," by Hartman L. Butler, Jr., and Martin G. Decker; "Found a Realistic Market Measure," by Saul A. Smerling; and "Which Is the Best Stock Average from a Practical Standpoint?" by Anthony Gaubis.

significant distortion in the measurement of performance.[4] His staff has therefore devised *True Equivalent Annual Yield Tables*[5] as a more precise tool. In the same vein, an arithmetic expression of a performance trend has an absolute upward bias; a geometric expression, a downward bias.[6] In theory these are strong arguments, but, on the other hand, does it matter whether an expression of performance is distorted or biased if it is consistently applied? The portfolio manager is not really concerned with ultimate truth. He is concerned only with relatives, with comparative truths, and with—most of all—improved performance. His real goal is to maximize dollars for, ultimately, the best performance is the one that generates—at the lowest cost to the employer—the funds needed to pay pension liabilities as they occur.

In selecting a measurement technique, the employer-corporation is normally interested both in total performance and, where the situation exists, the individual performance of each fund segment managed by a separate trustee. This will tell the employer, first, whether the fund is performing its intended function, and second, whether one trustee is doing his part of the job as well as another. A third consideration, not at all inconsequential in this competitive field, is whether or not a trustee is doing his job as well as some insurance company or other investment adviser might.

Compound Rate of Return

Since a pension fund derives, basically, from an invested accumulation of net contributions (and in this context is meant the total fund held by a particular trustee) the efficiency of the trustee's use of these contributions can be expressed in terms of compound interest:

$$M_2 = C_1 (1+i)^n + C_2 (1+i)^{n-1} \cdots + C_n (1+i)$$

where ending market value (M_2) is equated to a series of net contributions (C) over several time periods (n) by means of an (unknown) compound interest rate (i). This measurement, in effect, tells the employer corporation whether or not he would have done better to deposit his contributions in a savings bank or with an insurance company. By itself it does not define *perform* in terms that can be directly compared with the performance of anything but another pension fund, but even so, trustees often use this method because it produces a readily comprehensible result and involves a minimum of input data.

In the illustration of this method in Table I, the particular trust

---

[4] The reader is referred to "Measurement of the Comparative Investment Performance of Investment Funds," an address by Walter J. Simons, Treasurer of Chrysler Corporation, presented at the 46th Mid-Winter Trust Conference of the American Bankers Association in New York City on February 8, 1965.

[5] Published by Chrysler Corporation, copyright 1965.

[6] See Lawrence Fisher, "Abstract of 'Two New Sets of Common Stock Indexes for the New York Stock Exchange as a Whole and for Industry Groups'" (1965).

receives contributions annually about the middle of the year; pensions are paid monthly. To simplify the approach, *net* contributions are therefore assumed to be received at midyear exactly. Hence, at every year-end, the net contribution for that year has been held for one-half year; the prior year's contribution for three half-year periods, etc. To determine the compounded rate (i), which, when applied to all net contributions for the periods held, would have produced the market value of the trust at December 31, 1964, nominal annual rates of interest, compounded semiannually, are tested by trial and error, and the final result is then restated in terms of a compound annual rate. A standard edition of compound interest tables has been used:

TABLE I

R & R COMPANY PENSION TRUST

Year Ended December 31	Net Contributions	Semi-annual Periods Held	Accumulation at Nominal Annual Rate if Compounded Semiannually 5¼%	5⅜%
1952	$ 1,066	25	$ 2,037.45	$ 2,068.70
1953	1,134	23	2,057.96	2,086.98
1954	981	21	1,690.38	1,712.14
1955	2,227	19	3,643.60	3,685.99
1956	1,050	17	1,631.15	1,648.12
1957	1,025	15	1,511.89	1,525.76
1958	1,031	13	1,443.94	1,455.42
1959	807	11	1,073.14	1,080.36
1960	936	9	1,181.83	1,188.32
1961	883	7	1,058.60	1,063.12
1962	328	5	373.37	374.51
1963	554	3	598.78	599.88
1964	(414)	1	(424.87)	(425.13)
Market Value at 12/31/64	$17,900		$17,877.22	$18,064.17

By linear interpolation the approximate nominal annual rate, compounded semiannually, works out to 5.265 percent. If compounded *annually* the same rate is 5.3345 percent.

INCOME ON INCOME

Another technique sometimes used by actuaries[7] to measure performance in terms of a compound interest rate necessarily achieves substantially the same result but is clumsy to apply because it involves a complicated process of calculating income on income:

$$A = C(i) + I_{n-1}(i)^2 + I_{n-2}(i)^3 \cdots + I(i)^n$$

where A represents the difference between ending market value and accumulated net contributions, and C and I are the amounts of net contributions and income available for investment in each successive period.

---

[7] R. Norman Woods, "Measuring the Investment Yield of Pension Funds," Alexander and Alexander, Inc., 1964.

The basic premise is that net contributions earn income for one-half year in the year of receipt, thereafter for each full year; income earned in one year earns income on itself in each subsequent year, but earns nothing further in the year of receipt (Table II).

TABLE II
R & R Company Pension Trust

Year Ended Dec. 31	Net Contributions	i	i^2	i^3	i^4	i^5
1952	$ 1,066	$ 533i				
1953	1,134	1,066	$ 533i^2			
		567				
1954	981	2,200	533	$ 533i^3		
		491	1,633			
1955	2,227	3,181	2,166	533	$ 533i^4	
		1,113	2,691	2,166		
1956	1,050	5,408	4,857	2,699	533	$ 533i^5
		525	4,294	4,857	2,699	
1957	1,025	6,458	9,151	7,556	3,232	533
		513	5,933	9,151	7,556	3,232
1958	1,031	7,483	15,084	16,707	10,788	3,765
		515	6,971	15,084	16,707	10,788
1959	807	8,514	22,055	31,791	27,495	14,553
		404	7,998	22,055	31,791	27,495
1960	936	9,321	30,053	53,846	59,286	42,048
		468	8,918	30,053	53,846	59,286
1961	883	10,257	38,971	83,899	113,132	101,334
		441	9,789	38,971	83,899	113,132
1962	328	11,140	48,760	122,870	197,031	214,466
		164	10,698	48,760	122,870	197,031
1963	554	11,468	59,458	171,630	319,901	411,497
		277	11,304	59,458	171,630	319,901
1964	(414)	12,022	70,762	231,088	491,531	731,398
		(207)	11,745	70,762	231,088	491,531
Totals	$11,608	$94,322$i$	$384,357$i^2$	$1,024,469$i^3$	$1,945,548$i^4$	$2,742,523$i^5$

By application of the formula:

$$\$17{,}900 - 11{,}608 = \$94{,}322i + 384{,}357i^2 + 1{,}024{,}469i^3 + 1{,}945{,}548i^4 + 2{,}742{,}523i^5 + 2{,}931{,}303i^6 \quad [8]$$

After testing by trial and error: $6,292 = $5,027.78 + 1,092.10 + 155.16 + 15.71 + 1.18 + .07 if $i = 5.33044\%$

Average Return

A simpler method—applicable to segments as well as to total funds, but generally useful for short periods only—is to determine average performance by relating total earnings to a base investment. A typical formula[9]

---

[8] This last expression is not included in Table II, but since each expression in the formula is a mere progression from the preceding one, the reader can readily work out the derivation for himself.

[9] See Hilary L. Seal, "Pension and Profit-Sharing Digest: How Should Yield of a Trust Fund Be Calculated," *Trust and Estates*, Vol. XCV (November, 1956).

underlying this technique defines the change in market value between two points of time ($M_2 - M_1$) as total earnings (E) plus net contributions (C). Thus to measure performance for one year:[10]

$$(1) \quad M_2 - M_1 = E + C \text{ or } C = M_2 - M_1 - E$$

It is then assumed that the rate of return (i) applicable to E can be stated as:

$$(2) \quad E = M_1(i) + \tfrac{1}{2} C(i)$$

and therefore that:

$$(3) \quad i = \frac{E}{M_1 + \tfrac{1}{2}C}, \text{ or by substitution in (1):}$$

$$(4) \quad i = \frac{E}{M_1 + \tfrac{1}{2}(M_2 - M_1 - E)} \text{ or}$$

$$i = \frac{E}{\tfrac{1}{2}(M_2 + M_1 - E)}$$

A series of performances can be measured by applying the latter formula to successive years (Table III).

TABLE III
R & R COMPANY PENSION TRUST

Year Ended Dec. 31	Market Value M_2	Increase in Market Value $E + C$	Net Contributions C	Earnings E	$\tfrac{1}{2}(M_2 + M_1 - E)$	Rate of Performance (i)
1952	$1,092	$1,092	$1,066	$ 26	$ 533	4.88%
1953	2,299	1,207	1,134	73	1,659	4.40
1954	3,604	1,305	981	324	2,789.5	11.61
1955	6,067	2,463	2,227	236	4,717.5	5.00
1956	6,941	874	1,050	(176)	6,592	(2.67)
1957	8,088	1,147	1,025	122	7,453.5	1.64
1958	9,859	1,771	1,031	740	8,603.5	8.60
1959	10,967	1,108	807	301	10,262.5	2.93
1960	12,225	1,258	936	322	11,435	2.82
1961	14,345	2,120	883	1,237	12,666.5	9.77
1962	14,318	(27)	328	(355)	14,509	(2.45)
1963	16,764	2,446	554	1,892	14,595	12.96
1964	17,900	1,136	(414)	1,550	16,557	9.36

An overall compound rate of return can be obtained from the above results by "chaining" the annual rates of performance and deriving the annual rate that would increase 1.00 to 1.9299 (1.0488 × 1.044 × 1.1161 ... × 1.0936) over a 13-year period. In the above table the result would be 5.15%.[11]

---

[10] If this method is used to measure performance for a number or fraction of years, n, the resulting rate of return can be annualized (approximately) by multiplying i by $1/n$.

[11] See F. W. Graham and R. C. Bower, "Corporate Responsibility in Pension Fund Management," *Financial Executive*, June, 1965.

Trend of Value

Another technique measures performance in terms of the trend of a fund's market values, either through a series of compound or average rates of return, or by fitting a curve to the trend of market values directly (after compensating for the serial addition of net new money). Any such method will produce approximately the same result. An acceptable formula, using exponential least squares, is:

$$\log (1 + i) = \frac{\Sigma n (\log M - \log C)}{\Sigma n^2}$$

where i represents the trend over a number of time intervals (n) of a series of market values (M) undistorted by net contributions (C).

This technique summarizes the direction and degree of change in a fund's market value and thus accounts both for where a fund is and where it has been. (A disadvantage of the compound rate of return method is that it does not indicate, currently, what past performance has been except by a series of separate calculations.) Essentially, least squares describes the secular trend of a time series along a curve from which the squared deviations of the given data are least with a measurement which is directly comparable to similar measurements of other performances, regardless of the units of measure or the magnitude of the figures. Thus it is an apt method for comparing a fund's performance with an economic index such as the Gross National Product or the trend of Consumer Prices.

However, to the extent a fund has net cash contributions or distributions, the trend of market values alone will embrace—and therefore be distorted by—the trend of such cash changes. This trend can be compensated for by expressing market values in terms of accumulated net cash changes from the base period. Thus, each market value (M) is divided by the net cash contributions or payouts to date (C) to establish an arithmetic index of changes in market values resulting from investment decisions alone. Expressed in terms of exponents, the logic of this method seems clear:

$$\log M/C = \log M - \log C$$

Table IV applies this approach to the R & R Company Pension Trust.

Equivalents

A widely used technique measures performance in terms of "equivalents." Accuracy is difficult to achieve by this method, however, and the results obtained can never be wholly valid since, whatever equivalents index is used, it cannot—almost by definition—correspond exactly to a pension fund either in functions or objectives. In view of the variety of possibilities, no illustration of the method has been included. One solution that has been experimented with is to construct an index out of popular averages for bond and stock prices in proportions corresponding to the pension fund's own mix. Another solution, somewhat simpler but perhaps not as satisfactory, is to use a balanced no-load mutual fund as index. In either case, contributions to the pension fund are "invested" in equivalent units as they are received, and units are "sold" as benefit payouts are

TABLE IV

Year	Value of n	Market Value	Net Contributions For Year	Accumulation	Market Value ÷ Accum. Contributions	Log M − Log C	n (Log M − Log C)
1952	−6	$ 1,092	$1,066	$ 1,066	1.02439	.0104638	−.0627828
1953	−5	2,299	1,134	2,200	1.045	.01912	−.0956
1954	−4	3,604	981	3,181	1.13298	.0542224	−.2168896
1955	−3	6,067	2,227	5,408	1.12186	.0499368	−.1498104
1956	−2	6,941	1,050	6,458	1.07479	.0313239	−.0626478
1957	−1	8,088	1,025	7,483	1.08085	.0337685	−.0337685
1958	0	9,859	1,031	8,514	1.15798	.0637024	0
1959	1	10,967	807	9,321	1.17659	.0706283	.0706283
1960	2	12,225	936	10,257	1.19187	.0762319	.1524638
1961	3	14,345	883	11,140	1.2877	.109818	.329454
1962	4	14,318	328	11,468	1.24852	.096392	.385568
1963	5	16,764	554	12,022	1.39444	.1443964	.721982
1964	6	17,900	(414)	11,608	1.54204	.1880916	1.1285496
Σn^2	182				Σn (log M − log C)		2.1671466
					log $(1 + i)$		.0119074
					i		2.78%

required. Adjustments for income and commissions have to be made (index income is reinvested in units just as fund income is presumably reinvested in itself and fund transactions are ordinarily stated on a gross cost basis[12]), but even so, this type of comparison is biased against the actual fund because no allowance can be made for the day-to-day problems a portfolio manager has in making real (as opposed to hypothetical) investments. In other words, the decision to buy or sell a security is only the first step. Without trying to detail all of the problems that may be encountered before settlement, it is clearly not always as easy to trade, for instance, a stock in size on the over-the-counter market at a satisfactory price, or to settle for a particularly involved private placement, as it is to "buy" a unit of the Standard & Poor's 500 Stock Average or Moody's Aa Industrial Bonds.

Portfolio Performance

In measuring the performance of a pension fund *segment*, typically the equity portion of a mixed fund, most of the methods discussed can be applied only with difficulty because they depend upon "new cash" flow—which cannot be readily distinguished from realized gains and cash in-

---

[12] An index, of course, doesn't have to pay commissions or transfer taxes.

come as sources of investable funds. It is impracticable to try to follow the direct application of contributions to individual segments of a fund, but an indirect approximation can be made (at what sacrifice in accuracy it is difficult to determine) if it is assumed that the income and gains derived from the portfolio being analyzed, which are reinvested in that portfolio, do not represent significant new investments, but simply the retention of self-generated funds. Hence, any other increase in book value represents a proportion of net contributions to which one of the basic formulas can be applied.

Thus, to measure the average annual rate of return of a common stock portfolio at December 31, 1964, it is necessary to determine what "new money" (defined as a portion of net contributions—or proceeds from the sale of fixed income securities where net contributions were insufficient) was invested in common stocks each year (Table V).

TABLE V
R & R COMPANY PENSION TRUST

			Subtract		Net Contributions	
Year	Book Value of Commons at Year-end	Increase in Book Value[13]	Dividends	Realized Gains	Total	"New Money" Allocated to Commons
1952	...	...	...	...	$1,066	...
1953	...	...	...	...	1,134	...
1954	$ 478	$ 478	$ 21	...	981	$ 457
1955	880	402	44	$ 3	2,227	355
1956	1,222	342	63	...	1,050	279
1957	1,489	267	73	...	1,025	194
1958	2,013	524	85	...	1,031	439
1959	2,519	506	109	6	807	391
1960	3,157	638	126	...	936	512
1961	5,790	2,633	169	364	883	2,100
1962	6,966	1,176	270	6	328	900
1963	7,954	988	256	55	554	677
1964	8,526	572	282	728	(414)	(438)

At December 31, 1964, the market value of the R & R Company Pension Trust was:

Fixed Income and Cash..........$ 7,877
Common Stocks................ 10,023
Total........................$17,900

As indicated in Table I, the compound annual rate of return for the total fund at December 31, 1964, was 5.33 percent. The return on common stocks alone, measured in terms of the yearly allocation of "new money," was 10.42 percent. On fixed income securities it was 2.88 percent. (The relationship between these three rates reflects the weighted proportion of net contributions invested in the two portfolios—approximately 68½ percent fixed income, 31½ percent commons—over the life of the trust.)

---

[13] A similar technique, which achieves substantially the same result, defines "new money" in any period as the net of purchases and sales less dividends received. See Graham and Bower, *op. cit.*

Another technique often used for portfolio segments, chiefly because it is less complicated, applies the equivalents method not directly to contributions (although this could be done) but to specific transactions. That is, as actual purchases and sales are made, they are simultaneously paralleled by the purchase or sale of equivalent units at then current values. This does not measure the performance of the portfolio, of course, but only the success of individual and aggregate investment decisions. Nor does it eliminate the problem of commissions, or actual versus hypothetical transactions, and it aggravates the problem of income, because (with its different objectives) the equivalents index used will generate more or less income than the portfolio itself, which index income cannot itself be reinvested since only the portfolio income is used for that purpose.

* * * * *

The several methods discussed involve a variety of techniques, but all are adaptable to computer programing. Whatever the method, however, the usefulness of the result depends upon the quantity as well as quality of input. Here there are no guidelines except utility, practicality, and consistency. Some trustees measure performance daily—possibly because mutual funds do. In most cases once a quarter, or once a year, suffices. Decisions as to method, frequency, or detail, whether to compound on a quarterly or annual basis or to use seven-place rather than five-place logarithms, all these may affect the results obtained, but the significance of their effect is a matter for individual judgment.

The final test of performance is the comparison of one with another. The nearest and best comparison, of course, is intramural. In spite of disparate characteristics, the performance of one pension fund can most usefully be compared with the performance of another; the performance of one (common stock) portfolio in a pension fund may best be compared with a common stock portfolio in another (or the same) fund. Any allowance for differences in investment philosophies, flexibility, or willingness to assume risk then emerges as little more than an excuse for "coming in second." A methodology which purports to quantify risk, for instance, may or may not satisfy an employer-corporation (a recent Northwestern University study[14] suggests it might), but it will scarcely justify a pension trustee whose competence demands maximum return consistent with the ability to pay pensions. And since risk can be accurately measured only after the fact, it is at least questionable whether employer-corporations will ever care as much about defining past risks as they will about getting the most mileage out of their pension fund contributions. If the risks turn out to have been small, so much the better.

---

[14] Peter O. Dietz, *Pension Funds: Measuring Investment Performance* (New York Free Press, Inc., 1966).

Thus, at the present moment in the history of pension funds, the compound rate of return is probably the best expression of performance, because it indicates the one important thing the employer wants to determine: whether and to what extent his fund is outperforming its own actuarial assumptions. A better method may eventually come to light, but the subject requires considerable objective attention; for, as long as pension liabilities continue to grow at their current rate, employer-corporations, who must bear this burgeoning expense, will need most of all to know how to measure, control and, ultimately, to reduce it.

46

A MANAGEMENT SUMMARY OF MEASURING THE INVESTMENT PERFORMANCE OF PENSION FUNDS

For the purpose of Inter-Fund Comparison*

Bank Administration Institute

CONCLUSIONS OF THE STUDY

The major conclusions of the study are the following:

1. Performance of a pension fund should be measured by computing the actual rates of return on the fund's assets.

2. These rates of return should be based without exception upon determination of the *market value* of the fund's assets at different points in time, taking proper account of payments to and from the fund in whatever form. A fund's ability to provide benefits is determined by the market value of its assets and not by the book value. Therefore, measurement of performance must be based on market value.

3. The "internal rate of return," a commonly used measure often given other names including "yield to maturity," "discounted rate of return," and "average compounded rate of return," offers an excellent gauge of the rate of growth in the market value of a fund, taking into consideration the combined impact of principal and income and taking into consideration the cash flows that occur between the trustor and the fund and between the fund and its beneficiaries. A fund's results as measured by the internal rate arise, however, both from investment decisions which the fund manager makes and decisions about the amounts and timing of the cash flows which the fund manager typically does not make. It is possible, in fact, for two fund managers who follow identical investment policies, in the sense that they hold the same assets in the same proportions, to realize substantially different internal rates of return simply because they experi-

---

* Reprinted by permission of Bank Administration Institute. This article is only an excerpt from *The Management Summary* and summarizes the findings of the study. The full study is 224 pages in length, and in addition to the in-depth analysis it contains several worthwhile appendixes.

ence different cash flow patterns. If measurement were limited to this method, the manager of the fund might be blamed unfairly for poor results or applauded without justification for good results.

To illustrate that the internal rate of return will not serve as a tool to measure the effectiveness of the fund manager, assume two fund managers, each of whom keeps his fund fully invested in the same single security. Assume further that this security increased its market value (including dividends) at an annual rate, with continuous compounding, of 1 percent during the first half of the year and of 29 percent during the second half.

Both managers in the illustration begin the year with funds of $1,000,000, and no payments are made from the funds during the year. During the year, Manager A receives no contributions from the trustor, but Manager B receives $1,000,000 at the beginning of the second half.

The internal rates of return expressed as annual rates assuming continuous compounding are 15 percent for Manager A and 19.5 percent for Manager B.

While the internal rate of return would cause one to assume that Manager B had done a better job, he has not. The performance of Manager B was neither better nor worse than that of A. The inflow of an additional $1,000,000 was beyond his control and is what gave rise to the larger return.

4. While the internal rate of return will continue to be valuable in measuring a fund's performance for purposes such as judging its ability to meet its obligations, another rate of return, one that eliminates the influence of cash flows, is needed to measure the performance of the managers or trustees of the fund. Such a rate is the "time-weighted rate of return." The time-weighted rate of return measures fairly the investment results achieved by different fund managers because it removes the effect of decisions about cash flow amounts and timing. Different managers who follow identical policies by holding the same assets in the same proportions always will earn identical time-weighted rates of return. When cash flows do not occur, the time-weighted rate is the same as the internal rate.

The time-weighted rate of return perhaps is best known in connection with mutual fund performance measurement. Except for the treatment of dividends, the rate of change in net asset value per share commonly calculated for a mutual fund is the fund's time-weighted rate of return.

The time-weighted rate of return is computed ideally by dividing the period of time under study into subperiods whose boundaries are the dates of cash flows into and from the fund, and by computing the internal rate of return for each subperiod. The time-weighted rate of return is then the average of the rates for these subperiods with each rate being given a weight proportionate to the length of time in its subperiod.

In the illustration presented above, the internal rate of return of the fund handled by Manager A, 15 percent, is the same as the time-weighted rate because there was no cash flow into or out of the fund during the year. For Manager B's fund which had a cash flow, the time-weighted rate of return is the average of the between-cash-flow rates of 1 percent and 29 percent, with equal weight given to each, or 15 percent. Both managers thus achieved the same time-weighted rate because they followed identical investment policies. It is in this manner that the time-weighted rate allows a valid comparison of management results.

5. To calculate an exact internal or time-weighted rate, you must know the time and amount of each cash flow and know the fund's value at the beginning and end of the period under consideration. You need additional information, however, to complete your calculation of the exact time-weighted rate; you must know the fund's value at the time of each cash flow. If you measure rates of return every quarter, for example, quarterly fund valuation always will suffice for the internal rate, but calculation of an exact time-weighted rate will be possible only if the fund is valued whenever a cash flow occurs.

For most funds the cost of making a fund valuation at the time of each cash flow may seem prohibitive. Therefore, the Institute's research included an extensive investigation to devise and test computational methods of approximating the time-weighted rate when some of the required fund valuations are not available. This investigation, based upon studies with historical data from 390 pension funds and one profit-sharing fund, led to the conclusion that satisfactory accuracy may be achieved in either of two ways: with *monthly* fund valuations and a relatively simple approximation method called the "linked internal-rate-of-return method," or with *quarterly* valuations and a more complex approximation method called the "regression method."

6. While the time-weighted rate of return reveals one aspect of a pension fund manager's performance, complete evaluation of the manager's performance must include examining a measure of the degree of risk taken in achieving that rate of return.

The concept of risk is related to the concept of uncertainty or unpredictability in future events. Saying one security is more risky than another implies that future values of the first security are believed to be somehow more uncertain or unpredictable than future values of the second. Many different definitions of risk based upon this general idea are possible.

One of the best documented propositions in the field of finance is that investors, *on the average*, can receive a higher rate of return by assuming greater risk. It has been found, for example, that low-grade bonds on the average produce a greater return than high-grade bonds, stocks on the average produce a greater return than bonds, and low-grade stocks on the average produce a greater return than high-grade stocks. The committee members do not know any serious research, covering extended periods of time, that suggests the proposition is not true.

The fact that most investors do not invest entirely in relatively risky assets shows that most investors prefer to avoid risk and must be paid for assuming it. Indeed, a wise fund manager should not necessarily shift his fund to more risky assets in the pursuit of higher returns because in so doing he may subject his fund to an unacceptably great chance of large declines in return or an unacceptably great chance of the fund's failure to meet its obligations in the future.

If the trustees or trustors of different funds prefer to have investments made in such a way that different degrees of risk are assumed by these funds, then both risk and rate of return must be measured to permit a valid comparison of the investment skill exhibited by different fund managers. A superior fund manager is one who obtains a high rate of return for the particular degree of risk he has assumed or is permitted by policy to assume.

7. While it is recognized that additional research is needed on the subject of risk measurement, at the present time, it appears that the most satisfactory was to estimate the degree of risk assumed by a fund manager is to measure the variability in the fund's time-weighted rate of return from quarter to quarter, and that a number called the "mean absolute deviation" is the best measure of such variability.

Much evidence shows a direct correlation between variability in rate of return and degree of risk. For example, the rate of return for low-grade bonds is more variable on the average than that for high-grade bonds and the variability of returns from stocks is greater on the average than that from bonds. The available evidence demonstrates almost without question that variability in rate of return is related to risk in the short run; the longer run relationship, however, is questionable and deserves special attention in future research.

Mean Absolute Deviation

Although the "mean absolute deviation" sounds formidable, in fact it is an extremely simple measure. To illustrate, assume a fund's time-weighted rates of return for 4 consecutive quarters to be -2 percent, 10 percent, 20 percent, and -8 percent. The simple average of these rates is 5 percent $[(-2 + 10 + 20 - 8) \div 4 = 5]$, and the deviations of the rates from their average are $-2 - 5 = -7$ percent, $10 - 5 = 5$ percent, $20 - 5 = 15$ percent, and $-8 - 5 = -13$ percent. Attention should be paid only to the size of each deviation, ignoring whether the deviation has a plus or minus value. In this illustration the average size of a deviation is 10 percent $[(7 + 5 + 15 + 13) \div 4 = 10]$. Thus, 10 percent is the mean absolute deviation of the rates for the 4 quarters considered.

In order to illustrate further the measurement of time-weighted rates of return and their mean absolute deviations, performances over 10- and 20-year periods of three securities listed on the New York Stock Exchange are summarized in Figure 1.

Note that in this particular example an increase in the rate of return for the period is accompanied by a corresponding increase in the mean absolute deviation of quarterly rates of return, implying a corresponding increase in the amount of risk assumed by an investor for the period. In the time span 1946–1965, for instance, an investor who selected Texas Instruments from among the three securities shown would have achieved the highest rate of return, 16.5 percent per annum, but also would have experienced the highest degree of variability in quarterly rates of return, 62.9 percent per annum, indicating he would have assumed the highest degree of risk. In actual applications, of course, these measurements are made for entire funds rather than for individual securities.

FIGURE 1

TIME-WEIGHTED RATES OF RETURN AND MEAN ABSOLUTE DEVIATIONS FOR THREE NYSE SECURITIES

Security	1946–1965 [1]Time-Weighted Rate of Return	1946–1965 [2]Mean Absolute Deviation	1956–1965 [1]Time-Weighted Rate of Return	1956–1965 [2]Mean Absolute Deviation
Texas Instruments	16.5	62.9	28.1	59.0
American Distilling Company	10.1	38.4	14.6	34.9
American Telephone & Telegraph Company	8.8	14.8	11.6	19.9

[1] For the entire period and expressed in percent per annum, compounding continuously. These rates were computed assuming the investor reinvested dividends, paid no taxes, and paid no fees or commissions.

[2] Mean absolute deviation of the time-weighted rates for calendar quarters, expressed in percent per annum. For example, 62.9 is the mean absolute deviation of the 80 quarterly time-weighted rates achieved by Texas Instruments during the period 1946 to 1965.

8. The circumstances under which fund managers must operate vary so greatly that indiscriminate comparisons among funds might reflect differences in these circumstances rather than in the abilities of managers. This problem may be dealt with by agreeing to compare a fund only with other funds that operate under similar circumstances.

Taking into account the degree of risk assumed was discussed above. Other circumstances that might be taken into account include the purpose of the fund, the contractual arrangements between trustor and trustee, and technical characteristics of the fund.

It is proposed that allowance be made for differences in purpose and in contractual arrangements by establishing fund categories so that similar funds will be assigned to the same category and compared only with one another. Different purposes may be recognized by having separate groupings for "partitioned pension funds" that are managed in part by a bank and in part by an insurance company, other pension funds, and profit sharing funds. Different contractual arrangements may be recognized by having separate groupings based on the variation from one extreme in which the trustee has sole decision-making authority on investments to the other extreme in which the trustor retains sole decision-making authority.

Preliminary research on the effect of differences in fund technical characteristics, such as size, age, rate of growth, and unpredictability of cash flows, has not shown whether these characteristics significantly influence fund performance. Consequently, categories based on such differences are not proposed at this time.

Divide Assets into Categories

9. Often it is helpful to subdivide the assets of a fund into categories and then measure the performance of each asset category. Such categorization may reveal differences in the skill with which a manager handles different parts of a fund and may speed the detection of changes in the fund's performance.

If one decides to measure the performance of categories of assets, he must remember that comparisons of results achieved by different funds or different fund managers should focus attention on the fund as a whole and not on some portion of the fund, such as the equity portion. This is so because when risk is taken into consideration the best portfolio is not necessarily obtained by selecting those particular assets that individually are thought to be most desirable.

To illustrate the danger of comparing results for portions of funds, consider a hypothetical case involving two funds—call them A and B. Suppose both funds assumed about the same degree of risk while fund A earned a higher rate of return and so was the better performer. Suppose further the manager of fund A maintained a higher ratio of equities to nonequities, but to compensate for the higher risk accompanying a higher percentage of equities he selected more conservative equities than the manager of fund B. It would be easy to conclude erroneously that the manager of B did a better job of selecting equities than the manager of A.

10. As pointed out above, for the purpose of measuring investment performance an asset's market value always should be used. If the market value of an asset is not available, as is true, say, for privately placed investments, the appropriate valuation method is to estimate what the market value would be. The complete research report contains a thorough discussion of procedures for valuing pension fund assets.

RECOMMENDATIONS

The research and resulting conclusions have led to recommendations that are believed to permit valid comparisons of the performance of different funds and of different fund managers. As experience is accumulated, improved methods probably will emerge.

Management Summary of Measuring Performance of Pension Funds

The major recommendations are as follows:

1. The performance of pension funds should be measured in two dimensions: rate of return and risk.

2. Rates of return should be based on income and on changes in the market value of assets held. Both the time-weighted rate of return and the internal rate of return should be computed. The time-weighted rate of return measures the results of investment decisions made by a fund manager. It is not affected by decisions about the timing and amounts of cash flows—decisions which the fund manager typically does not make. The internal rate of return measures a fund's total investment performance, regardless of the source of decision-making, and is helpful in determining the adequacy of the fund to meet its obligations. Rates of return should be expressed as annual rates, compounded annually.

In those instances in which the fund's value is not known at the time of every cash flow, the time-weighted rate cannot be computed exactly. However, the time-weighted rate can be estimated with a high degree of accuracy by either of two methods: the linked internal-rate-of-return method with monthly fund valuations or the regression method with quarterly fund valuations.

3. Rates of return should be calculated for calendar quarters as well as for longer periods of time. Performance comparisons for longer periods are the more important comparisons.

4. Until future research indicates a better way, it is recommended at the outset that the degree of risk taken in a fund be estimated by calculating the mean absolute deviation of the time-weighted rate of return. Such calculation should be based on quarterly rates of return beginning with the start of the process of systematic evaluation.

5. To make comparisons more meaningful, individually administered funds should be divided into three groups: pension funds excluding partitioned funds, partitioned pension funds, and profit sharing funds. For each group the following categories should be established and comparisons be made only within these categories:

   a) Funds for which the trustee is solely responsible.
   b) Funds for which the trustor is solely responsible.
   c) Funds for which the trustor and trustee are jointly responsible.
   d) Funds whose trustees are required to maintain a specified ratio of equities to nonequities.
   e) All other.

In addition, commingled funds should be analyzed separately with individual categories for equity funds, fixed income funds, mortgage funds, special situation funds, and balanced funds.

6. The most important measures of rates of return and of risk are those relating to total portfolios. For diagnostic purposes, however, it will be useful to have measures of performance for the following classes of assets:

a) Common stocks and warrants.
b) Assets convertible into common stocks.
c) Cash and temporary investments, including all fixed income investments with less than one year to maturity from the date of valuation.
d) Intermediate and long-range fixed income assets.
e) Assets purchased or held at the direction of the trustor.
f) Other (such as real estate and commodities).

7. Since it is believed that interfund comparisons will be more valuable if there is a pooling of data for funds administered by different managers, it is recommended that plans be developed for collecting such data from banks and that the analysis of pooled data be made available to participating banks. The Bank Administration Institute is available to work out such a pooling program with interested institutions.

8. While the research on which this report is based has been sound and thorough, it should not be considered as final. Additional research could yield beneficial results in areas, such as risk measurement, the applicability of principles established herein to other classes of funds, and the refinement of procedures for interpreting performance after it has been measured.

47
BOND INVESTMENT POLICY FOR PENSION FUNDS*

Sidney Homer

My talk will fall into three parts: (I) The special characteristics of pension funds which permit and encourage them to be more flexible in their investment policies than almost any other type of institution; (II) The legal, accounting, and self-imposed conventional barriers which prevent many pension funds from taking much or any advantage of this opportunity; and (III) Bond investment policies which should be adopted by completely flexible and unrestricted pension funds.

I. OPPORTUNITIES

There are five reasons why a pension fund is the ideal medium for the application of flexible, dynamic, and imaginative long-term investment policies.

1. Most pension funds are, in effect, perpetual with no need to prepare for near-term or medium-term liquidation. Therefore, the greater part of their assets need not provide marketability, stability, liquidity, or even maturity. While these attributes, if inexpensive, may be independently desirable to provide flexibility and better long-term performance, they are not forced on the portfolio manager regardless of cost. He is investing only for the dim distant future.

2. Most pension funds enjoy steady and unusually rapid growth. This means that unfortunate investment policies, if applied to any one year's contributions, will not do large permanent damage and, conversely, even if they turn out very well cannot be of great permanent benefit. The manager can count on a flow of new funds to facilitate policy changes and to correct any temporary imbalance in his total portfolio.

3. The investment objective of pension funds is extremely simple: maximum enrichment over a period of 20–30 years. This enrichment can come from accumulated income, or from amortized discounts, or from straight capital gains. Twenty years hence no one will know whether an extra dollar came from income, or amortization, or gains. Unrealized

---
* Reprinted by permission from Salomon Brothers & Hutzler, New York, New York. Copyright 1964.

capital gains will be as valuable as realized gains. It is only the total dollars in the fund at average future market value which will count.

4. Pension funds are tax-free and hence every dollar of income, or profit, counts the same as 100 cents. Portfolio transactions need not be dictated and distorted by tax considerations. Realized gains are not shared with Uncle Sam and hence are as good as and no better than unrealized gains. Realized losses are not shared with Uncle Sam and hence are no better or worse than unrealized losses.

5. A pension fund, unlike most funds, is not pressed to create and disburse maximum current income. Its current income is mostly accumulated and so is undistinguishable in the long run from capital gain.

Because of this structure the performance of a pension fund during any one year is not a matter of moment—only the long run counts. No pension fund portfolio manager is entitled to congratulate himself because of this year's good income or market appreciation, and no manager should be criticized because of this year's lower income or market depreciation. These transitory statistics will, in part, be determined by the market and not by investment policies. Policies should be appraised only by their results over a long period of years. An effort to handle 30-year investments with an eye to a good showing "this year" is illogical and is apt to be highly prejudicial to long-term performance.

Pension funds are fiduciary in character. They have come to be the ultimate refuge of millions of Americans to cushion or to finance their later years of life. The success or failure of one pension fund will to many mean the difference between poverty and comfort. This fact imposes a heavy fiduciary responsibility on the portfolio manager.

This fiduciary responsibility unfortunately sometimes leads to a negative attitude: an effort to hoard dollars so as to be sure to be able to hand them back. However, both the beneficiaries and the employer are correctly depending on a large increase, not just the return of principal. A dollar not made is as bad as a dollar lost. Therefore, negative inaction on the part of the manager is as costly as reckless action. In fact in the history of American pension funds, inaction (disguised under the ambiguous term conservatism) has been far more costly than reckless investment.

For the pension fund manager, there is no safe refuge in pat formulae and conventional procedures. He has an immense responsibility to do the right thing, not just not to do the wrong thing. There is no simple book of rules which will tell him just what should be done. There is no formula which can be a substitute for basic personal, irrevocable decisions.

Because of the special attributes which I have summarized, pension funds can appropriately be more flexible in their choice of investment media than almost any other type of institution. It is hard, in fact, to make a case for excluding permanently any form of investment from pension fund portfolios. At any one point of time many forms of investment are relatively unattractive, while a few are very attractive. However, the roster of attractive and unattractive investment media changes almost every year; therefore, as many as feasible should be authorized so that they can always be candidates for consideration.

II. RESTRICTIONS

In the light of this exceptional latitude pointed to very long-term objectives, which suggests or demands great ingenuity and flexibility, it is disappointing to review the actual limitations of many American pension funds today, especially those serving Government employees.

1. Legislation often limits the investment of such pension funds to a very small fraction of the suitable outlets. In this way the funds not only lose the most favorable investment opportunities, but they often become captive buyers in highly unattractive markets. Such legislation often seems designed to protect these funds from mismanagement rather than to give encouragement to, or even permit, good management.

2. Legislation again often forces undue diversification and limits the size of commitments in an imprudent manner—for example, it may limit the size of holdings in the American Telephone Co. to the same size as holdings in another company $1/100$th its size. More important, legislation often puts fixed maximum limits on the proportions of specific types of securities which stay the same when these types are most attractive as when they are most unattractive.

3. Legislation often enforces detailed investment standards which rapidly become obsolete. I can remember the day when New York, New Haven & Hartford junior mortgage bonds were legal in New York State, but American Telephone bonds were not. The laws, of course, have been improved since then, but I do not doubt that today's investment standards will seem ridiculous 10 years hence.

The basic fact is that we cannot legislate prudent investment. There is an effort to regulate some pension fund investments so closely that the manager cannot go wrong no matter how hard he tries and whoever he is. This basic distrust of our public servants is costly. There is no substitute for high caliber portfolio management, and high caliber management is sure to require freedom of action.

4. Conventional accounting procedures make an artificial distinction between coupon income, amortization of discounts (although discounts are guaranteed by the same creditor), and capital appreciation. The manager is sometimes rated on only one of these three objectives: income. For example, a 4½ percent coupon, bought to yield 4.30 percent, may be credited with yielding *4.35 percent* because that is the current yield at cost, and a 3 percent coupon, bought to yield 4.50 percent, may be credited with yielding only *3.75 percent* because the sure 20 points appreciation is ignored.

5. Pension fund accounting also often ignores continuity of income. A pension fund, when it accepts a contribution, undertakes to earn and pay interest on this contribution for 20 or 30 years ahead—sometimes at a fixed minimum rate but always striving for the highest safe return. It is the average rate over this long period of years which counts, not the rate earned during the first year. The fund's earnings during the first year are not decisive or even important—they are, indeed, only $\frac{1}{20}$–$\frac{1}{30}$ of the objective. And yet its books are often kept in such a way that only this year's income is recorded. Therefore, a promise to receive $4\frac{3}{4}$ percent for one year is made to look better than a far more valuable promise to receive $4\frac{1}{2}$ percent for thirty years.

6. Another bookkeeping handicap imposed on most pension fund managers is an artificial inhibition against realizing capital losses. Since values within the bond market often change dynamically, this year's bargain may next year command an excessive price; indeed, this year's buyer hopes this will happen. If so, when next year's bargains are offered, he can switch into them with a double advantage. But such switching sometimes involves realizing capital losses: Suppose Bond A, purchased at 100, sells down in some future year to 98 at a time when the market for similar issues had declined 10 points. This is a very good performance indeed and implies both that Bond A was underpriced against the market when bought at 100 and may now be overpriced at 98. If so, it should be switched into similar bonds selling at 90 or lower. Alas, how about the 2-point realized loss?

Common sense tells us that if in fact Bond A, bought at 100, is sold at 98, and the funds are reinvested in nearly identical bonds bought at 90, the transaction itself involves not a 2-point loss but an 8-point gain. Bond A, although it declined to 98, turned out to be a much better investment than Bond B, bought at 100, which sold up to 102 at a time when the market for similar issues had advanced 10 points. Few methods of accounting would reflect this fact. Accounts are kept by comparison with cash, not by comparison with a fluctuating norm like the bond market.

Unfortunately our system of keeping our books makes a sharp distinction between realized and unrealized gains and losses. Even though on the night of a switch from Bond A at 98 into its equivalent at 90 a fund owns 8 percent more par value of almost identical bonds than it owned that morning, with 8 percent more annual income, it is sometimes said that it has taken an unnecessary loss of 2 percent of principal and that it will take, say, six years before the extra income will make up the loss. This kind of calculation, while technically true, is highly misleading; it is not descriptive of the real results of such a transaction. This dilemma arises from the custom of carrying portfolios at amortized cost; it results in frozen portfolios, usually at the very time when switching opportunities are most plentiful and obvious.

Every transaction should be forward looking, none should be backward looking. A switch should be judged on the future contributions of the alternatives, not on the past cost of the portfolio item sold. Every well-run portfolio that realizes gains and losses freely will probably average out with more gains than losses. There is no advantage per se in realizing a gain and no disadvantage per se in realizing a loss.

Thus far here I have tried to make two points:

Pension funds lend themselves better than almost any other type of institutional portfolio to wide latitude in selection, maximum flexibility of policy, and portfolio changes for large advantage, and

In fact many pension funds, particularly in the public sector, are hedged about with rigid restrictions created by legislation, or by accounting practice, or by custom, and thus are prevented from exploiting their great natural advantages of tenure, continuity, and growth.

III. BOND INVESTMENT POLICIES FOR A WELL-MANAGED FLEXIBLE PENSION FUND

At this point I will try to outline a few investment policies for a completely uninhibited and unrestricted pension fund. I realize this will seem to you like a dim and distant mirage far removed from the real world in which you carry on your daily tasks. However, it is sometimes useful to talk in terms of ideal conditions towards which we can move, albeit slowly. I will assume only good management.

1. Credit Risk

First let me mention quality standards. For many decades, my own published studies have chiefly dealt with prime money market securities; from this fact I fear many of my friends have drawn the conclusion that I am a "credit snob" looking only at Aaa bonds. If so, I will now shock them. I believe that there should be no rigid limitations at all on the credit rating of bonds eligible to be bought by well-run pension funds. My emphasis would be on picking good portfolio management, not on spelling out credit standards for unknown managements.

Just to make my point clear, I would go so far, under favorable circumstances, as to include selected defaulted bonds as a suitable medium for pension funds. There were many times in the 1940's, and the 1930's, and early in the century when strong well-secured bonds went into default and sold down to prices which made them, in a sense, safer than most bonds in good standing. Why should pension funds be permitted to buy a bond at 100 or at 90 and be forbidden to buy the same bond at 50? A certain bond can be very precarious at a price of 100, suitable at a price of 75, and as safe as the "Bank of England" at a price of 50—the coverage by the same earnings and the same assets has doubled merely because the price is down.

Today this suggestion is almost moot. There are few good values among second-grade bonds. Except for railroad bonds such issues are enormously popular and far from depressed. Today the extra reward for taking business risk in industrial bonds is at its lowest in my lifetime. Yield spreads have declined or vanished. Mediocre credits are being preferred to prime credits for a reward of 10–20–40 basis points in yield where a while back the spreads would have been 50–100–200 basis points. Therefore, the best values today are in the highest quality issues; today the opportunity for upgrading at little or no cost is almost unprecedented.

Nevertheless, this will not always be so. As a long-range policy I would be entirely open-minded on risk bonds. All insurance companies, in writing policies, take risks. Indeed, they seek risks and they expect to take losses. However, they try to make sure that they are paid for these risks, and that the risk premiums absorb the losses and leave a good net gain. All investment is also risk taking. Now to take a real risk for 20 basis points extra yield is not prudent: Translated into price this is just $\frac{1}{5}$ a point a year price advantage which will add up to just 1 extra point in 5 years, whereas the extra risk in a second-grade bond may be at least 25 points in price if things get worse for the creditor.

For this reason a little extra yield, particularly from a callable bond, is a poor reward for credit risk. Even 100 basis points extra yield is only 1 extra point in price per year, which may be a poor reward for the risk. I would prefer then to have my reward for taking credit risk in potential price recovery rather than in extra income. I would prefer to buy second-grade bonds at large discounts. If I have the risk of 25 points principal loss, I should have the opportunity of 25 points principal gain.

You will see that while I started out on the topic of quality boldly with a recommendation that you approve second-grade bonds, even defaulted bonds, I have now qualified the procedure with such demands for reward that in today's market I would rarely accept much credit risk.

2. Maturity

Next let me deal with maturity. Since most pension funds are incurring liabilities of the very longest term, the longest maturities of bonds are usually the most appropriate.

This, however, should not be a fixed rule. Bond yields usually rise and fall dynamically, and these fluctuations by themselves, provide rich opportunities for improving yield and price performance. Thus if long bonds are at any one time selling to yield 4 percent, and shorts are offered at 3 percent, and if in the following year or two longs and shorts both move to 5 percent, a present purchase of shorts at 3 percent (a seeming yield sacrifice of 1 percent) with reinvestment in a year or two in longs at 5 percent (noncallable) would be very advantageous indeed: In one case the return for 25 years would be 4 percent, in the other case it would be an average return of 4.84 percent.

Now, of course, you may object that although my mathematics are irrefutable, my logic is fallible since we never know what yields will be a year or two hence. I entirely agree that we do not know future yields, but from this basic fact of life I would not argue, as some do, that we should therefore ignore market trends and follow a rigid maturity formula such as spaced maturities or dollar averaging.

Long-term contracts should dominate pension fund portfolios most of the time, but not always and not completely. Pension fund investing is always risk taking and one legitimate risk is the manager's judgment that future yields will be higher or lower. We are not seeking sure things—we are seeking probabilities. We can afford to make mistakes in maturity selection if we do not risk too much of the fund on any one judgment.

A fund manager who is constantly making small judgments on the outlook (not indulging in sweeping convictions) and backing up each small judgment with some action (not with sweeping portfolio revisions) can afford to be wrong from time to time; he can lean on the law of averages and will be right more often than he is wrong.

Actions based on judgments of the bond market outlook should always be weighted by the present level of the market. We know when yields are historically very high and very low. At such times the level of yields should dominate our policy—not the outlook. When yields are historically very low, as in the 1940's, we can pretty much ignore the outlook which will probably favor low yields and seek as much as possible an early repayment of our money. When yields are historically very high we can also ignore the outlook, which will probably favor higher yields, and seek as much as possible to place our funds permanently, even if we have to accept less than maximum yield in order to get noncallable contracts.

Most of the time, however, yields are neither very high nor very low, and then the outlook assumes great importance. If yields are at such a median level and the outlook favors rising yields, what should a portfolio manager do about it? At such a time, I would never favor disinvesting a large part of the fund and running the risk of ruin if yields unexpectedly declined. However, some sales of less attractive longs should be made, or all of one year's contributions or perhaps more—depending on growth rate—should be held aside in 1–5 year paper, to be reinvested in longs on a scale down if and when yields rise importantly, or if and when the outlook changes.

I am aware that this procedure proved highly unprofitable to a number of institutions in the 1930's and early 1940's when stubborn waiting for good yields, year after year, turned out to be very costly. But those were exceptional times. We cannot invest in bonds as though 1920 or 1946 were always in the offing. It is worth taking these small risks for the benefits which accrue most of the time.

I am suggesting, then, that the manager set up a maturity preference schedule and plan his actions to bring the fund gradually into line with this schedule. He will, of course, from time to time revise the schedule, and it will not be practical to make as frequent or as big revisions of the maturity structure of the fund. These schedules will, however, provide him with an objective towards which to move. At one time this schedule might show, for example: Shorts 20 percent of bond fund, mediums 20 percent, and longs 60 percent; this is a defensive schedule for a pension fund. At another time it might show shorts 0, mediums 0, longs 100 percent; this is an aggressive schedule. It is the schedule I would favor at the present good level of yields.

Before the portfolio manager decides what proportion of shorts he wants to hold, he should forecast his growth two years ahead. This inflow of new funds will serve exactly the same purpose as shorts and should be so classified. He can add his two years anticipated growth to short-term holdings and also to total funds, use this ratio to compare with his preference, and thus decide whether he should build up shorts further or reduce them.

By holding some shorts, pension funds can protect themselves from, and, indeed, benefit from periods of rising yields. There is no corresponding technique, however, for exploiting prospective periods of low yields. If low yields are in prospect shorts should be converted into longs, callable bonds should be weeded out in favor of noncallables, medium-maturity bonds should be transferred into long-term bonds, and non-marketables should often be switched into marketables. However, all of these measures together will not solve the problem of investing future contributions at a time of low yields. Real hardships for pension funds come from periods of low yields—in spite of capital gains—and not from periods of high yields—in spite of capital losses.

In applying maturity policy to pension funds, my preference is usually to play shorts against longs and ignore medium-maturity bonds altogether. There are exceptional periods when there is an inverse or humped yield curve and mediums are very attractive, but most of the time medium maturities in the 5- to 10-year range can be left to the banks. They do not promise a return long enough ahead to be permanent holdings; they will be inappropriate in five years. In bear bond markets, mediums often decline in price as much as long-term bonds, and so little is gained by holding them to be switched into longs in a lower market. In bull bond markets they are apt to advance only half as much as noncallable long-term bonds, and they rapidly become too short. However this much can be said for mediums: in both a bull bond market and a bear bond market a 10-year noncallable medium may act better than a 5-year deferred call long. Usually, however, I would tend to sell off bonds when maturity has been moved back by the passage of time to 10 years or less, and reinvest the proceeds in longs or shorts according to my maturity preference.

3. Continuity of Income and Call Protection

It has sometimes been cynically said that military establishments are usually prepared to fight the last war, not the next war. However this might be, we investors are frequently guilty of looking backwards and of planning as though trends of the last decade or so will continue for the next decade or so. If stock prices have been declining on balance most of the time for 10 years, stocks are apt to be very unpopular with almost everybody, but if they have been rising most of the time for one or two decades they are apt to be enormously popular. The same is true of long-term bonds. At times like the present, when prime bond prices are down sharply from their level of 15 or 20 years ago and when yields are historically good, bonds are unpopular. There is very little expectation of future low yields and, therefore, very little concern about possible future redemptions. Conversely, when bond prices have been rising over a long period of years, investors are acutely aware of the danger of call. Let me give you some examples from history.

In 1900 the bond market was at a high level, with prime yields typically at 3.25 percent. Indeed, New York Central First 3½'s then sold up to 112. Our high-grade bond market had been rising in price most of the time for 25 years. Consequently, long-term bonds were enormously popular, even though they yielded substantially less than most short-term bonds. Investors, looking backwards, regretted that they had held few prime and really long-term bonds in their portfolios. Most of the Civil War and post-Civil War bond issues had been of moderate maturity in the range of 10–20 years, and many had been redeemable at the end of five years; of course, all these 5 percent and 6 percent bonds had been redeemed if they were prime or had probably defaulted if they were not prime.

Thus, very few investors had really benefited by this great bull bond market. To remedy this situation investors, at around the turn of the century, demanded or accepted the longest possible maturities and insisted there should be no call price. This was the era when so many railroads issued 100-year noncallable bonds, like Atchison General 4's of 1995, which are still outstanding.

For the next 20 years bond yields rose and bond prices declined. Calls were very rare. By 1920 this bad market experience led many investors to prefer shorter maturities. Gradually call prices came into fashion and were accepted by investors. Early call terms were attached to almost all the high coupon bonds offered in the 1920's. In the 1930's, of course, almost all of these issues were either called, or lost status, or defaulted.

In recent years, with yields again historically high, many investors have been willing to accept callable corporate bonds in preference to noncallable corporate or Government bonds at very small yield differentials. Lately there has been little or no noticeable yield difference between callable new issues and deferred call new issues. In other words, since yields have been rising most of the time for the last two decades, many investors have ceased to worry about the danger of future redemption.

I would suggest that pension funds today should give major attention to call price. Five-year protection is not enough. They should so far as possible hold only noncallable bonds or deep discount bonds which are, in effect, noncallable. Yields today, while not at peak levels, are historically well above average.

As I have mentioned, pension funds incur a liability to accumulate interest over several decades and eventually to pay it out. This fact should determine the nature of the bulk of their assets. If they are obliged to run the full market risk of buying bonds which mature in twenty or thirty years, they should have the assurance of contractual income for a similar length of time. There are plenty of bonds offered in the market today which do, in fact, give this assurance. Let me give you some examples.

Atchison, Topeka, & Santa Fe General 4's of 1995 sell at about 93 to yield 4.40 percent, and they are prime noncallable bonds. This is a promise to pay not $40 per $1,000 bond but 30 times this sum, i.e., $1,200 interest per $1,000 bond plus $70 eventual capital gain. Similarly, U.S. Treasury 4¼'s of 1987–92, selling around 101, promise to pay not $42.50 interest per $1,000 bond but 22 times this sum, i.e., $935 interest per $1,000 bond. Again, Telephone 3¼'s of 1984, selling at 85 to yield 4.40 percent, will pay not $32.50 per $1,000 bond but 20 times this sum or $650 interest per $1,000 invested plus $150 capital gain.

These three issues are all ideal pension fund investments in the area of prime bonds, since the income will hold up whatever the level of interest rates is in the future and will more than compensate the fund for decades ahead for its own liability to earn and accumulate income.

In contrast, let us look at more popular issues such as American Telephone 4¾'s of 1992 selling at 104 to yield 4.50 percent. It is true this bond promises to pay $47.50 per year per $1,000 bond—a higher annual rate than the other three bonds I cited. But for how long does it promise to pay? Only for one year. This is a promise to pay, not *$1,200* interest per $1,000 bond or *$935* or *$650* but only *$47.50*. And we can be sure that when they are called, reinvestment will be possible only at low rates.

These comparisons again show the fallacy of our system of accounting. Our bookkeeping seems to ignore a pension fund's greatest asset—the claims it holds to sure future income—and measures its rate of return only in terms of last year's income.

4. Choice of Investments

I have already suggested that a very wide range of investment media is suitable for pension funds. None of us can tell what will be the most attractive outlets for pension money a year or two ahead, much less a decade ahead and, therefore, permanent authorization should be as broad as possible. We should not wait until a given medium is outstandingly attractive before we start the long task of getting authority to buy. Especially we should not wait until this medium has become generally acceptable and popular; it almost surely will not then be a bargain.

Therefore instead of basing requests for authority on what should now be bought we should request authority for every suitable medium which might some day be attractive. In any one year probably only one or two departments of the market out of a potential dozen will be attractive, but the next year it may be another one or two, and so on.

I shall now comment on some of the investment media which seem potentially appropriate for pension fund investing, even though most of these may not be attractively priced today.

(*a*) U.S. Government bonds set the standard for all bond investing. These dominated pension fund investing 20 years ago and because of restrictions and conventions they absorbed an unduly large proportion of pension fund money at low yields. All this has been reversed. Government bonds are now often overlooked. They are considered somehow effete or unimaginative. As a consequence, their yields have risen more than the yields of any other type of bond and today are very close to the yields of not only the best corporate bonds but to the yields of risk bonds. They are noncallable and, therefore, are ideally suited to pension funds. At today's high yields they represent my first choice among suitable outlets for pension funds.

(*b*) High-grade corporate bonds of all types and maturities are potentially appropriate for pension funds. This includes good-grade bank debentures. Today I would buy only long-term noncallable corporate bonds, or deep discount issues, or current coupon issues with call protection of at least 10 years. At other times, however, when yields are low, callable issues, or even high coupon issues selling above call price, are potentially attractive. Today the very long maturities are the best; at other times short or medium maturities are the best.

(*c*) I have already said that carefully selected second-grade corporate bonds are suitable if they offer an adequate reward. Today this is a generally unattractive area of the market, although there always are a few exceptions.

(*d*) Private placements of corporate bonds are suitable for pension funds. They provide wider diversification than the public market and sometimes better call protection. They used to provide much better yields than similar marketable issues, but the yield premiums have become lower and lower and lately have almost vanished. For giant pension funds, private placements are, nevertheless, attractive because they are available in size.

For small- and medium-sized funds, private placements at no worthwhile yield advantage today offer little attraction. Market levels and values change, and marketable issues can be switched in the years ahead to great advantage, but private placements, while often salable at a price, sometimes cannot be sold advantageously at the very time it is highly desirable to do so.

Within the private placement area many novel forms of obligations have been developed during recent years, including leasebacks, conditional sale contracts, and many combinations of ownership with debt. While these require a high degree of selectivity and sophistication on the part of the buyer, he should have wide latitude regarding the form of contract he is authorized to accept.

(e) Obligations of smaller corporations are inappropriate for most pension funds because the funds do not have the facilities to investigate. Such loans seem to imply a banker-client relationship which is feasible for banks and even for some insurance companies but not for most pension funds. I can see no reason, however, why larger pension funds, willing to employ a highly paid and experienced staff, should not develop some of this type of business; it certainly offers compensations for risk and wide diversification and could be valuable in hard times when prime rates are low and risk is well advertised.

(f) Convertible bonds are an appropriate field. They can be substitutes for straight bonds if they sell at low bond premiums and substitutes for equities if they sell at low stock premiums. Today most convertibles are of medium and second grade which is not now an attractive department of the bond market, and today most good issues sell at high premiums, and thus offer few advantages. However, there always are exceptional issues which offer good value.

(g) Preferred stocks are entirely appropriate for pension funds. Some are identical in quality with prime bonds, only lacking a maturity; others are close in quality to commons; most are in between. Today, because of the tax advantages of preferreds for corporations, they are high in price compared with bonds, and thus most are unattractive to pension funds. However, deep discount preferreds or noncallable preferreds have a good chance of being refunded into debentures at premiums of 10 percent or so over market, and thus a diversified portfolio of high-grade issues of this sort could be worthwhile.

(h) Common stocks are discussed elsewhere on this program. They are entirely appropriate for pension funds. Today as a group they are relatively less attractive compared with most other media than at any time for several decades, but nevertheless there are always some attractive issues. As a group they have unique advantages, and there will be many times when they are outstandingly attractive.

(i) Foreign dollar bonds are appropriate for pension funds if the yields compensate for the risk. The foreign exchange and political problems of the debtor should always be considered and, therefore, they cannot rank with prime domestic issues and should yield more. The first consideration should be the will and tradition of the voting population of the debtor country to pay its debts even when payment is painful.

(j) Foreign currency bonds are also potentially appropriate for pension funds. The yield, of course, should be far higher than that of the dollar bonds of the same debtor to compensate for the exchange risk. The exchange risk must be weighed carefully, but it is no more of a risk than that properly run by pension funds in buying many other forms of investment. The political integrity of the debtor people is, of course, the prime consideration. To compensate for exchange risk, the promise of high income should run for a long period of years, and there should be a corresponding opportunity for capital gains.

(*k*) Insured real estate mortgages, which are discussed elsewhere on this program, are appropriate for pension funds. However, insured mortgage yields have declined sharply during recent years and now are at an inadequate spread over bond yields, so this is not as attractive a medium today as it usually has been. Furthermore, mortgages are redeemable and their average life is not very long so that there is a large return flow of funds from this form of investment. At present level of yields I do not think this return flow should be sought. However, whenever bond yields decline sharply mortgage yields tend to stay high, and a return flow of principal then becomes desirable. Therefore, insured mortgages are a very attractive outlet in periods of low interest rates.

(*l*) Conventional mortgages are theoretically a suitable medium for larger pension funds. They are not very attractive today because the field has been reaped, and winnowed, and gleaned by just about everybody, and terms are bad, and rates are down, and risk is high. Furthermore, this is a specialized business which requires a large, expert staff. Nevertheless, it is potentially a very valuable outlet.

(*m*) Municipal bonds are generally unsuitable for pension funds because their tax exemption reduces their yield. However, very occasionally there is an exceptional issue with yields high enough almost to compete with attractive corporate bonds of the same quality and maturity. In such cases I believe pension funds can appropriately buy municipals: there is a good chance that the value of the tax exemption to others will permit resale at a good premium sometime before maturity.

I shall not comment on many other forms of investing which are entirely appropriate. These include such short-term investments as Federal Agencies, Commercial Paper, Certificates of Deposit, and Acceptances.

5. Investment Policy

The portfolio manager, with such a wide range of investment outlets from which to choose, should usually concentrate at any one time on the most attractive departments of the market. As much as possible he should let the market determine his choice and not adhere to any predetermined rigid schedule of diversification. He should not only place his new funds in the most inviting areas of investment, but to some extent he should switch old funds out of the currently least attractive areas into the currently most attractive areas. Of course, he must consider diversification and cannot revolutionize his entire portfolio every time relative values change. But neither must he worship diversification. Every year presents a new challenge to his acumen in seeking out the best values the market affords. The investment of new money is a pressing problem but the content of the total portfolio is far more important than the new money flow and deserves the greater part of his attention.

Giant pension funds are often frozen into their past purchases. This is a serious disadvantage. Smaller funds should capitalize on their maneuverability. A constant flow of pension fund assets out of popular overpriced areas into unpopular depressed areas will improve overall performance far more than the mere careful allocation of new funds. This is so because the size of existing assets almost always far exceeds one year's new money.

In addition to moving from one department of the market towards another, the manager should be alert to switching opportunities within each department. These occur every year within many departments of the market: new bargains appear just when seasoned issues are bid up to full prices. Shifts in supply and demand factors are usually responsible—not changes in quality. I have estimated from experience that in a typical year almost one quarter of a corporate bond portfolio can be advantageously switched without making important changes in quality or maturity. At times a government bond portfolio can be improved even more rapidly.

All bonds purchased should be suitable to hold to maturity. However, none need or should be held to maturity. This year's bargains will probably be relatively overpriced at some point in the next few years, and there will be new bargains. Thus, oddly enough, equities are often suitable for long-term holding, but high-grade long-term bonds more often lend themselves to periodic portfolio changes. Such a program of constant improvement, of course, requires freedom to realize gains and losses and requires that the manager should not be bound by predetermined and rigid proportions.

A flexible program, of course, places a great burden on the versatility and wisdom of the portfolio manager. Too many of us permit a proper sense of humility to lead us to seek escape from investment judgments. Such devices as rigid spaced maturity programs, whereby we never have to choose between long, medium, or short maturities, or rigid dollar averaging, whereby we never have to make timing judgments and never sell, are appealing because they seem to offer reasonable escapes from fallible decisions. Some pension fund managers similarly seek escape from decisions by a sampling technique whereby they buy a little of almost everything.

In this dangerous world such defensive procedures seem at least safe, although admittedly they cannot produce superior results. It is a little like living out our days in a storm cellar—safe but unproductive. The portfolio manager may subsist for years in such a defensive posture, but I do not believe his beneficiaries will in the long run profit by negative protective policies.

The job of managing an investment portfolio consists of making decisions—not avoiding decisions. Errors are to be expected. We can be sure that a portfolio devoid of all errors has had a mediocre performance. As I suggested earlier, the manager who makes a multitude of small decisions (rather than a few sweeping decisions) can lean on the law of averages and expect to do a better than a routine job.

To sum up, the pension fund has the ideal institutional investment structure for versatile and imaginative portfolio management. Many pension funds, unfortunately, are so hedged about by legal, accounting, and conventional restrictions that they lose most or all of their natural advantages. I hope and expect that in the years ahead these legal restrictions will be gradually removed, the accounting distortions will be increasingly understood and ignored, and the conventional limitations will evaporate in the light of fuller understanding.

48

RELATIVE PRICE PERFORMANCE AMONG COUPON AREAS IN CORPORATE BONDS*

Neil Zaentz

After many years, investors in corporate bonds are becoming increasingly conscious of price performance. Once content to look solely at the average yield of the bond portfolio, many now are closely examining price action. This change has resulted from a severe and protracted decline in bond prices as well as the new "performance" orientation in common stocks. However, even though price action is becoming a new standard of judgment, yield cannot be ignored.

Unfortunately, many problems exist in measuring performance in a bond portfolio. There is no commonly accepted method of measurement. The price and/or yield indices (such as those of Moody's, Standard & Poor's & Salomon Bros. & Hutzler) which are available for measuring performance cannot be applied to most portfolios. Since various types of investors have different maturity, quality, and cash income requirements and their holdings vary accordingly, a single price and/or yield index would be applicable to only a relatively small number of portfolios. A second difficulty is that neither a price nor a yield standard of performance reflects the possibilities of retaining high-yielding bonds over a long period of time. This is a function of protection against call and cannot be assigned a specific value. A third is that good yield performance can mean bad price performance and vice versa. Another difficulty is that prices used in valuing a bond portfolio at any one time are approximate and do not reflect accurately where issues could be actually sold. Therefore, an individual portfolio could show a variety of performances depending upon how and by whom it was appraised.

Even if performance in the bond portfolio cannot be measured accurately, steps can be taken to improve price performance while maintaining high yield. One of the better methods for achieving good performance is the selection of attractive Coupon Areas. Coupon Areas are groups of

---

* Reprinted by permission of the *Financial Analysts Journal* (July-August 1969).

bonds with similar coupons which sell at approximately the same price and yield-to-maturity. Selection of Coupon Areas can affect performance because bond issues in each Coupon Area offer different yields and degrees of price volatility.

Investors in corporate bonds have many options available in selecting what should be bought at a given time. The purpose of this analysis is to determine which Coupon Areas are most attractive in light of potential price changes which could result from a change in the level of interest rates. No attempt is made to determine whether a given type (Utilities, Industrials, Finance, etc.), maturity range, or quality (Aaa, Aa, A, Baa, etc.) is most attractive. The discussion is limited to long maturity Aa rated utility bonds, probably the largest and most homogenous area of the entire bond market. However, the conclusions are broadly applicable to other quality ratings and types of corporate bonds.

Application of these conclusions will vary for different portfolios. Corporate bond investment portfolios can be divided roughly into two types whose selections can differ while holding the same view of the market and the same investment objectives. First, there is the Holding Portfolio which only gives up an issue when it matures or is called. Second is the Trading Portfolio which will move in and out of issues to improve the portfolio—increasing income, appreciation potential, or downside protection. Selection for both types of investors will be treated.

COUPON AREAS

Coupon Areas are groups of bonds with similar coupons which sell at approximately the same price and yield-to-maturity. The price at which a bond sells is determined by its yield-to-maturity. Since bonds of the same quality with similar coupons and maturities will sell at similar yields and prices, the demarcation between Coupon Areas is a function of price level. No matter what the level of interest rates, bonds can be typed into the following price areas or Coupon Areas:

1. Premium Bonds—highest coupon issues whose prices are approximately 2 or more points above 100.
2. Current Coupon Bonds—high coupon issues whose prices are about 2 points on either side of 100.
3. Moderate Discount Bonds—lower coupon issues with prices ranging from the upper 90's to upper 80's.
4. Deep Discount Bonds—lowest coupon issues with prices in the mid-80's or lower.

As bond prices change, individual bond issues will move from one Coupon Area to another.

YIELDS AND YIELD SPREADS

In this study many references are made to changes in interest rates. To simplify understanding of the yield changes in various Coupon Areas, certain terms and methods will be used. (1) Yield will always mean yield-to-maturity. (2) Changes in the *level of interest rates* will be shown in terms of New Issue yields. A New Issue will mean a bond selling at 100. Since yield on selling at 100 is the same as the coupon, reference to a market change (i.e., change in the level of interest rates) of 50 basis points (1 basis point equals .01% in coupon income or yield) would mean that the coupon rate on New Issues had changed by 50 basis points. (3) Yield changes in Coupon Areas will be referred to specifically. Thus, a 50 basis point change in Deep or Moderate Discount Bonds would mean that the yield in those categories had changed by .50%. (4) In comparing different bond issues or Coupon Areas, the measure is the difference between yields: i.e., Yield Spread. Thus, two bonds selling at 7.00% and 6.50% yields would have a Yield Spread of 50 basis points.

As the level of interest rates change, bond prices change and bond issues that were in one Coupon Area will move into another Coupon Area. The yield changes that take place as bond issues move from one Coupon Area to another when the level of interest rates advances or declines will be shown in two ways. One is the change in Yield Spread of the several Coupon Areas from New Issues. The other is as a greater or lesser change in yield than the change in New Issue offering yields.

For a clearer understanding of these statements, two examples are offered. If the level of interest rates changes and New Issue offering yields decline from 7.00% to 6.50%, bond issues that were Current Coupons at the 7.00% yield level might move to a 6.60% yield (price 105.20) and become Premium Bonds. The yield change would be described as a widened Yield Spread between issues that were Current Coupons and New Issues from 0 (7.00 − 7.00 = 0) basis points to 10 (6.60 − 6.50 = 10) basis points. It can also be said that the yield decline in issues that were Current Coupons (40 basis points) was almost the same as the decline in New Issues (50 basis points). Similarly, if New Issue yields rose from 7.00% to 7.50%, bond issues that were Current Coupons at the 7.00% yield level might move to a 7.25% yield (price 96.96) and become Moderate Discounts. The change in yield would be described as a widened Yield Spread between issues that were Current Coupons and New Issues from 0 (7.00 − 7.00 = 0) basis points to 25 (7.50 − 7.25 = 25) basis points. It can also be said that the yield rise in issues that were Current Coupons (25 basis points) was less than in New Issues (50 basis points). These examples also illustrate that a change in the level of interest rates will move bond issues from one Coupon Area to another.

Since New Issues are the base for computing Yield Spread, a distinction must be made between positive and negative Yield Spreads. If New Issues yield less than a particular Coupon Area, it is termed a negative Yield Spread; if New Issues yield more, it is a positive Yield Spread. Premium Bonds generally sell at a negative Yield Spread, and Moderate and Deep Discounts at a positive Yield Spread.

DETERMINANTS OF PRICE VOLATILITY

Price performance in bonds is a function of coupon volatility, the transition from one Coupon Area to another, and changing Yield Spreads between various Coupon Areas.

Coupon Volatility

Bonds sell on the basis of yield-to-maturity, a concept which determines the present value (or price) of all future payments (principal and coupon income) at a given rate of return (yield-to-maturity). The yield-to-maturity concept in pricing bonds results in different prices for issues with different coupons and maturities. It also means that for a given change in yield, price changes will vary for bonds with different coupons. The table below shows the price changes which would result from a 50

TABLE I
Price Changes for 50 Basis Point Yield Change
(30 year bonds)

Coupon	Yield-to-Maturity Price—100	50 Basis Point Yield Change Yield	50 Basis Point Yield Change Price	Change from 100 Points	Change from 100 Percent
7.00%	7.00%	7.50%	94.07	5.93	5.9
6.00	6.00	6.50	93.44	6.56	6.6
5.00	5.00	5.50	92.69	7.31	7.3
4.00	4.00	4.50	91.81	8.19	8.2

Coupon	Yield-to-Maturity Price—85	50 Basis Point Yield Change Yield	50 Basis Point Yield Change Price	Change from 85 Points	Change from 85 Percent
7.00%	8.39%	8.89%	80.37	4.63	5.4
6.00	7.23	7.73	79.93	5.07	6.0
5.00	6.10	6.60	79.21	5.79	6.8
4.00	4.97	5.47	78.95	6.05	7.1

basis point increase in yield. To examine coupon volatility, bonds with different coupons are used. Further, to show relative volatility of bonds with the same coupon at different price levels, bonds with the same coupon are examined at two prices—100 and 85. For a 7.00% bond at 100 the price change is 5.93 points (5.9%) while it is 8.19 points (8.2%) for a 4.00% bond. From an 85 price level the change for a 7.00% coupon is 4.63 points (5.4%) and 6.05 points (7.1%) for a 4.00% coupon. In other words, the lower the coupon, the greater the price volatility for a given change in interest rates. Conversely, the higher the coupon, the lower the price volatility for a given change in interest rates. (However, any issue will have greater volatility for a given change in yield when it is selling around par than when it is selling at prices below par. A 50 basis point move for a 7.00% coupon selling at 100 is a 5.9% price decline and a 5.5% decline if the same 7.00% coupon bond were selling at 85; for a 4.00% coupon the price decline is 8.2% from 100 and 7.5% from 85.) These characteristics will be referred to as "coupon volatility."

Transition from One Coupon Area to Another

If coupon volatility were the only factor affecting price volatility, the bond market would be much easier to understand. Unfortunately, it is not. Issues of similar quality rating and maturity but with different coupons do not sell at the same yield. The main reason for this is differences in call protection. There is always a price for protection against being forced into a lower yielding bond, because a changed market enables issuers to refund outstanding high coupon bonds at lower interest rates. Retention of yield is a function of call protection. This can be obtained through either indenture provisions restricting retirement of an issue or by purchasing a bond issue whose coupon is sufficiently low that the prospects for refunding are slight. As interest rates decline, it is understandable that lower coupon bonds are less likely to be refunded than higher coupon issues. The market recognizes this and yield becomes a function of price level or call protection. The lower the price level, the lower the yield; the higher the price level, the higher the yield.

In regard to the effect of call protection on yield, a corollary point should be made. Appreciation potential in any bond is the difference between its present market price and call price. Call price is used as a ceiling because bonds usually do not sell much above this level. Usually, the lower the price of a bond, the greater the appreciation potential. While it is not possible to place a precise value on appreciation potential, lower yields on Moderate or Deep Discount Bonds are also a reflection of the greater appreciation potential in bonds far from their call price.

Differences in yield among Coupon Areas is a function of call protection and appreciation potential. Premium Bonds generally have higher yields than New Issues because they offer less call protection and appreciation potential. Current Coupon Bonds have about the same yields as New Issues because both have about the same call protection and appreciation potential. Moderate Discount Bonds yield somewhat less than New Issues because they possess somewhat more call protection and appreciation potential. Deep Discount Bonds yield a good deal less than New Issues because they possess a good deal more call protection and appreciation potential. In a market with New Issues at 6.50 percent a typical pattern might have a Premium Bond with a 7.25% coupon yielding 6.69% (price 107.25); a Current Coupon Bond with a 6.50% coupon yielding 6.50% (price 100); a Moderate Discount Bond with a 6.00% coupon yielding 6.40% (price 94.69); and a Deep Discount Bond with a 5.00% coupon yielding in the 6.05–6.25% area (price 85.55–83.16).

Since bond prices (and call protection) change as interest rates move from one level to another, the movement from one Coupon Area to another will result in different changes in yields for bonds with different coupons. If New Issue offering yields declined from 6.50% to 5.50%, a 7.25% Premium Bond would remain in Premium status and the yield would be unchanged because it is not likely to sell above call price. A 6.50% Current Coupon would move into Premium status and the yield change would be about 50 basis points. The Moderate Discount 6.00% coupon would move into Premium status and the yield change would be about 80 basis points. The Deep Discount 5.00% would move into Moderate Discount status and the yield change would be 70–100 basis points. Thus, the transition from one Coupon Area to another can have a significant effect on the price action of a bond.

CHANGING YIELD SPREADS

Price volatility is also a function of changing Yield Spreads between New Issues and the various Coupon Areas. As interest rates rise or decline, yields in the various Coupon Areas do not necessarily experience

TABLE II
Price Change in a 30-Year 5.00 Percent Bond

New Issue Yield	Constant Yield Spread			Yield Spread: Narrowing as Yields Decline Widening as Yields Rise			Yield Spread: Widening as Yields Decline Narrowing as Yields Rise		
	Spread	Yield	Price	Spread	Yield	Price	Spread	Yield	Price
7.00%	.25	6.75%	77.61	55	6.45%	80.87	25	6.75%	77.61
6.50	.25	6.25	83.16	25	6.25	83.16	55	5.95	86.78
.50% Change	0	.50%	5.55 7.2%	30	.20%	2.29 2.8%	30	.80%	9.17 11.8%

the same yield change as New Issues. As a result, the Yield Spreads between New Issues and the various Coupon Areas can widen or narrow. Widening and narrowing Yield Spreads describe the change in yield of a Coupon Area in relation to the change in New Issue yields. The table above (Table II) shows the effect of changing Yield Spreads on price volatility for a 30-year 5.00% coupon bond.

Several points should be made. As the New Issue yield level declines (from 7.00% to 6.50%), price appreciation is reduced to 2.8% by a narrowing (55 to 25 basis points) Yield Spread and increased to 11.8% by a widening (25 to 55 basis points) Yield Spread. As the New Issue yield level rises (from 6.50% to 7.00%) price depreciation is reduced to 2.8% by a widening (25 to 55 basis points) Yield Spread and increased to 11.8% by a narrowing (55 to 25 basis points) Yield Spread. This also can be stated in another way and can be applied to positive, negative, or between positive and negative Yield Spreads. If the yield change of a Coupon Area is close to or greater than the yield change in New Issues, price change is large. If the yield change of a Coupon Area is less than the yield change in New Issues, price change is small.

The importance of changing Yield Spreads has the greatest bearing on Deep Discount Bonds. The fluctuation in Yield Spreads from New Issues is greater in Deep Discounts than in any other Coupon Area. Yield Spreads between New Issues and Deep Discounts have ranged from about 25–55 basis points during the 1967–69 period of high-yield levels and were 10–20 basis points at lower levels of interest rates several years ago. The degree of predictability of future yields in Deep Discounts at various market levels is substantially less than in any other Coupon Area.

At narrow Yield Spreads from New Issues, Deep Discounts are considered attractive and at wide spreads unattractive. Using the above table, ranges of price advance and decline from a narrow and wide Yield Spread can be shown:

Initial Yield Spread From New Issues	Rising Yields: Price Decline Range	Declining Yield: Price Rise Range
Narrow 25 basis points	2.8%– 7.2%	7.2%–11.8%
Wide 55 basis points	7.2%–11.8%	2.8%– 7.2%

Deep Discounts have better appreciation potential and downside protection at narrow Yield Spreads from New Issues than at wide Yield Spreads from New Issues. It should also be noted that if Yield Spreads remain constant there is little difference in price change at narrow (25 basis points) or wide (55 basis points) yield spreads.

In selecting Coupon Areas it is extremely important to determine the attractiveness of each Coupon Area in relation to New Issues as well as the changes in Yield Spread from New Issues which could occur as a result of market change.

CREATION OF MARKET MODELS

One of the greatest difficulties encountered in analyzing the bond market is the lack of good statistical information. There are a number of yield and price averages available, but averages obscure changing relationships between coupon and maturity areas. Salomon Brothers & Hutzler comes closest to providing the needed information on Coupon Areas by concentrating on the Aa Utility area. The manpower required to provide similar information for each rating (Aaa, Aa, etc.), in every market segment (Industrials, Finance, etc.) makes it unlikely that such information ever will be available. However, by using the S.B. & H. figures as a base and applying market experience, it is possible to provide a reasonably accurate guide to the various coupon and maturity characteristics of the market.

Price/yield models for various coupons at different market levels can be designed. The Model in Table III is based on the past history of yield relationships among the various Coupon Areas at different New Issue yield levels. Yield patterns in the table reflect valuation for call protection so that yields are higher on Premium Bonds than on Moderate or Deep Discount Bonds. It should be noted that the Model is a reflection of what the market has considered to be justifiable yield differentials for call protection in the past and is not an attempt to place an intrinsic value on call protection. Prices have been taken from a bond basis book for

TABLE III
MARKET MODELS
Yields and Prices for 30 Year, Aa Utility Bonds at Various Levels of Interest Rates

COUPON		7% YIELD %	PRICE	6 1/2% YIELD %	PRICE	6% YIELD %	PRICE	5 1/2% YIELD %	PRICE
7 1/4-NR	(P)	7.05	102.49	6.69	107.25*	6.69	107.25*	6.69	107.25*
7 1/4		7.20	100.61	6.85	105.07	6.69	107.25*	6.69	107.25*
7 -NR		7.00	100.00	6.60	105.20	6.48	107.00*	6.48	107.00*
7	(C)	7.15	98.16	6.80	102.55	6.48	107.00*	6.48	107.00*
6 3/4-NR		6.90	98.11	6.55	102.61	6.25	106.75*	6.25	106.75*
6 3/4		7.00	96.88	6.70	100.64	6.30	106.03	6.25	106.75*
6 1/2-NR		6.90	94.96	6.50	100.00	6.10	105.48	6.03	106.50*
6 1/2		6.95	94.36	6.65	98.06	6.25	103.37	6.03	106.50*
6 1/4-NR	(M)	6.75	93.60	6.40	98.01	6.05	102.75	5.81	106.25*
6 1/4		6.75	93.60	6.50	96.72	6.20	100.68	5.85	105.63
6 -NR		6.75	90.41	6.40	94.69	6.00	100.00	5.60	105.78
6		6.75	90.41	6.45	94.06	6.15	97.96	5.70	104.29
5 3/4-NR		6.75 / 6.45	87.21 / 90.76	6.25	93.26	5.90	97.90	5.55	102.91
5 3/4		6.75 / 6.45	87.21 / 90.76	6.25	93.26	6.00	96.54	5.65	101.44
5 1/2-NR		6.75 / 6.45	84.01 / 87.46	6.25 / 5.95	89.89 / 93.74	5.75	96.45	5.50	100.00
5 1/2	(D)	6.75 / 6.45	84.01 / 87.46	6.25 / 5.95	89.89 / 93.74	5.85	95.08	5.60	98.55
5		6.75 / 6.45	77.61 / 80.87	6.25 / 5.95	83.16 / 86.78	5.75 / 5.55	89.34 / 92.01	5.25	96.24
4 1/2		6.65 / 6.35	72.21 / 75.33	6.15 / 5.85	77.53 / 81.01	5.65 / 5.45	83.47 / 86.04	5.25 / 5.05	88.73 / 91.55

* Maximum price at call price.
COUPON AREAS: (P) = Premium bonds (M) = Moderate discount bonds
(C) = Current coupon bonds (D) = Deep discount bonds

individual coupon issues. The percent price change (price advance) from one market level to another has been calculated (Table IV). In addition, a second calculation combining price change plus one year's coupon income has been made (Table IV).

It is not possible to draw precise models, because these relationships are not fixed and can change over time. Furthermore, at every market level pockets develop which do not fit a rational pattern. The rationale presented here will facilitate drawing new models that reveal prospects for the various Coupon Areas in different markets.

All issues in the Tables are assumed to have a 30-year maturity and a call price of 100 plus the coupon rate. Issues designated "NR" have five-year indenture protection against call. Although bonds with call protection sometimes will trade somewhat above call price, call price has been used as the upper price limit on all issues. In the Deep Discount area

TABLE IV
Percent Price Change

MODERATE YIELD DECLINE

COUPON		7.00–6.50% PRICE	PRICE PLUS COUPON	6.50–6.00% PRICE	PRICE PLUS COUPON	6.00–5.50% PRICE	PRICE PLUS COUPON
7 1/4-NR	(P)	4.6	11.7	4.6	11.7	4.6	11.7
7 1/4		4.4	11.6	2.1	9.0	2.1	9.0
7 -NR		5.2	12.2	1.7	8.4	1.7	8.4
7	(C)	4.5	11.6	4.3	11.2	4.3	11.2
6 3/4-NR		4.6	11.5	4.0	10.6	4.0	10.6
6 3/4		3.9	10.8	5.4	12.1	0.7	7.0
6 1/2-NR		5.3	12.2	5.5	12.0	1.0	7.1
6 1/2		3.9	10.8	5.4	12.0	3.0	9.3
6 1/4-NR		4.7	11.4	4.8	11.2	3.4	9.5
6 1/4	(M)	3.3	10.0	4.1	10.6	4.9	11.1
6 -NR		4.7	11.4	5.6	11.9	5.8	11.8
6		4.0	10.7	4.1	10.5	6.5	12.6
5 3/4-NR		6.9 / 2.8	13.5 / 9.1	5.0	11.1	5.1	11.0
5 3/4		6.9 / 2.8	13.5 / 9.1	3.5	9.7	5.1	11.0
5 1/2-NR		7.0 / 7.2 (2.8)	13.5 / 13.5 (9.1)	7.3 / 2.9	13.4 / 8.8	3.7	9.4
5 1/2		7.0 / 7.2 (2.8)	13.5 / 13.5 (9.1)	5.8 / 1.4	11.9 / 7.3	3.6	9.4
5	(D)	7.2 / 7.3 (2.8)	13.6 / 13.5 (9.0)	7.4 (4.4) / 6.0	13.4 / 11.8 (10.3)	7.7 / 4.6	13.3 / 10.0
4 1/2		7.4 / 7.5 (2.9)	13.6 / 13.5 (8.9)	7.7 (4.6) / 6.2	13.5 / 11.8 (10.2)	6.3 (3.1) / 6.4	11.7 / 11.6 (8.4)

Price Performance among Coupon Areas in Corporate Bonds

TABLE IV—Continued

MAJOR YIELD DECLINE

COUPON		7.00-5.50% PRICE	PRICE PLUS COUPON	7.00-6.00% PRICE	PRICE PLUS COUPON	6.50-5.50% PRICE	PRICE PLUS COUPON
7 1/4-NR	(D)	4.6	11.7	4.6	11.7	4.6	11.7
7 1/4		6.6	13.8	6.6	13.8	2.1	9.0
7 -NR	(C)	7.0	14.0	7.0	14.0	1.7	8.4
7		9.0	16.1	9.0	16.1	4.3	11.2
6 3/4-NR		8.8	15.7	8.8	15.7	4.0	10.6
6 3/4		10.2	17.2	9.4	16.4	6.1	12.8
6 1/2-NR		12.2	19.0	11.1	17.9	6.5	13.0
6 1/2		12.9	19.8	9.5	16.4	8.6	15.2
6 1/4-NR		13.5	20.2	9.8	16.5	8.4	14.8
6 1/4	(M)	12.9	19.5	7.6	14.2	9.2	15.7
6 -NR		17.0	23.6	10.6	17.2	11.7	18.0
6		15.4	22.0	8.4	15.0	10.9	17.3
5 3/4-NR		18.0 / 13.4	24.6 / 19.7	12.3 / 7.9	18.9 / 14.2	10.3	16.5
5 3/4		16.3 / 11.8	22.9 / 18.1	10.7 / 6.4	17.3 / 12.7	8.8	14.9
5 1/2-NR		19.0 / 14.3	25.6 / 20.6	14.8 / 10.3	21.4 / 16.6	11.2 / 6.7	17.4 / 12.5
5 1/2	(D)	17.3 / 12.7	23.9 / 19.0	13.2 / 8.7	19.7 / 15.0	9.6 / 5.1	15.8 / 11.0
5		24.0 / 19.0	30.4 / 25.2	15.1 / 13.8 (10.5)	21.6 / 20.0 (16.7)	15.7 / 10.9	21.7 / 16.7
4 1/2		22.9 / 21.5 (17.8)	29.1 / 27.5 (23.8)	15.6 / 14.2 (10.8)	21.8 / 20.2 (16.8)	14.4 / 13.0 (9.5)	20.3 / 18.6 (15.1)

NOTES: (1) Percentage price changes are price advances as interest rates decline: i.e., from 7.00 percent to 6.50 percent. They are based on the figures in Table III. The figures in parentheses (9.1) are the smallest possible percentage change and show the effect of a narrowing yield spread as interest rates decline.

(2) *Coupon areas:*
(P) = Premium bonds (M) = Moderate discount bonds
(C) = Current coupon bonds (D) = Deep discount bonds

a range of yields (and prices) has been used, because Yield Spreads from New Issues can vary widely. The figures in parentheses in Table IV are the smallest possible percent changes and show the effect of a narrowing Yield Spread as interest rates decline. Creation of Market Model Tables will not always be required. Knowledge of markets and typical yields available in each Coupon Area usually will be sufficient for evaluation of appreciation potential and downside protection.

PRICE VOLATILITY OF COUPON AREAS

The Market Models provide a basis for certain generalizations about the relative price performance (percentage change) of the different Coupon Areas in rising and falling markets. It should be recalled that for bonds selling at a discount (and lower yields than New Issues), as interest rates decline price volatility is decreased by a narrowing Yield Spread and increased by a widening Yield Spread. When interest rates rise the process is reversed. The conclusions expressed in this section are based on typical market patterns. Atypical issues and Coupon Areas which can occur will be covered in another section. Below are descriptions of relative price change that individual bond issues in each Coupon Area will experience as the level of interest rates declines and rises.

I. DECLINING YIELDS (RISING PRICES)

A. Moderate Decline (50 Basis Points)

1. Premium Bonds. There will be no change in Coupon Area status. Upward price movement will be less than any other category, because Premium Bonds have the least number of points to their call price, lowest coupon volatility, and experience a small decline in yield relative to New Issues (decreasing price volatility).

2. Current Coupon Bonds. Almost all Current Coupons will move to Premium status. In doing so their yields will decline more than Premiums and almost as much as New Issues. Therefore price volatility is fairly high and greater than in Premiums. For this reason and because of greater room to call price than Premium Bonds, upward price movement will be greater than in Premium Bonds. Call-protected (NR) issues will do somewhat better than those lacking protection, because their yield decline will be closer to that in New Issues.

3. Moderate Discount Bonds. Most Moderate Discounts will remain in the same category, but those with higher coupons will move to Current Coupon or Premium status. Appreciation will be greater than Premiums, because Moderate Discounts have more room to call and their yield decline is closer than Premiums to that of New Issues. As a group, appreciation is somewhat less than Current Coupons, because their yield decline is not as great as the yield decline in Current Coupons. Call-protected (NR) issues will do better than those without protection.

4. Deep Discount Bonds. Higher coupons will move into Moderate Discount status and lower coupons will still be Deep Discounts. On the basis of highest coupon volatility, room to call and the possibility of a yield decline almost as great as New Issues, appreciation potential is greater than any category. However, the major complication in dealing with Deep Discounts is their tendency to sell at varying Yield Spreads from New Issues. If the Yield Spread from New Issues is maintained or widened (increasing volatility), appreciation will be the greatest of any category. If this spread narrows (decreasing volatility) appreciation could be the same or worse than any category. Issues moving into Moderate Discount status may do poorly if the Yield Spread between Moderate

Discounts and Deep Discounts narrows (decreasing volatility). Call protection (NR) has no appreciable effect on performance, because the low coupons provide a good deal of call protection.

B. Major Decline (100–150 Basis Points)

1. Premium Bonds. There will be no change in Coupon Area status. Appreciation will be worse than any other area, because they have the fewest points to call price.

2. Current Coupon Bonds. These issues will move into Premium status. Their yield decline will be fairly small in relation to the change in New Issues, reducing volatility. Appreciation will be greater than Premiums due to more room to call, but will not be as great as the two Discount areas due to fewer points to call. There will be little difference between issues with or without call protection.

3. Moderate Discount Bonds. Almost all Moderate Discounts will move into Current Coupon or Premium status. Their yield decline will be closer to that of New Issues than that of Current Coupons. For this reason and because they have more room to call, appreciation will be greater than Current Coupons. Overall appreciation is less than Deep Discounts, because the yield decline in Deep Discounts is likely to be closer to that of New Issues than that of Moderate Discounts. Call-protected (NR) issues will do better than those without protection.

4. Deep Discount Bonds. Depending upon coupon, most Deep Discounts will move to Moderate Discount or Current Coupon status and few will remain unchanged. Overall, the great amount of room to call, highest coupon volatility and a yield decline closest to that of New Issues will produce the greatest appreciation of any Coupon Area. If Deep Discounts were at a very wide Yield Spread from New Issues and the Yield Spread narrows greatly (decreasing volatility), appreciation might not be as good as Moderate Discounts. In Deep Discounts call protection (NR) has little bearing on performance, but it can provide better appreciation in higher coupon Deep Discounts.

II. RISING YIELDS (DECLINING PRICES)

A. Moderate Rise (50 Basis Points)

1. Premium Bonds. Most Premium Bonds will not change in status and a few will move to Current Coupon status. Their yield rise will be the smallest of any category relative to New Issues. This and lowest coupon volatility will result in the best downside protection of any category. Issues without call protection will provide somewhat better downside protection, because their yield change will be very small relative to New Issues.

2. Current Coupon Bonds. These will go into Moderate Discount status. Their yield rise will be the second smallest of any category relative to New Issues. This and low coupon volatility will result in downside protection that is exceeded only by Premiums. Issues without call protection will provide somewhat better downside protection, because their yield rise will be smaller relative to New Issues.

3. *Moderate Discount Bonds.* Most will not change status, but lower coupon issues can become Deep Discounts. The yield rise in Moderate Discounts will be fairly close to that of New Issues. This and higher coupon volatility will result in greater price declines than in the higher Coupon Areas. Lowest coupon Moderate Discounts can experience good downside protection, if the Yield Spread between New Issues and Deep Discounts is wide. Call protection is of little significance.

4. *Deep Discount Bonds.* Deep Discounts will remain in the same category. Price performance will depend on changes in Yield Spread from New Issues. No change or a narrowing (increasing volatility) Yield Spread combined with highest coupon volatility will produce the greatest price declines of any category. A substantial widening of Yield Spread can mean better protection than in Moderate Discounts. Call protection is of little significance.

B. Major Rise (100–150 Basis Points)

1. *Premium Bonds.* Most Premium Bonds will move into Current Coupon or Moderate Discount status. (Only a very few either will not change or go into Deep Discount status.) They will experience the smallest yield rise relative to New Issues. This and the lowest coupon volatility will result in the least price decline of any category. As in a Moderate Rise, issues without call protection will provide somewhat better downside protection.

2. *Current Coupon Bonds.* Most will move into Moderate Discount status and a few into Deep Discount status. They will experience the second smallest yield rise relative to New Issues. This and low coupon volatility provide downside protection second only to Premiums. A wide Yield Spread between the Discount Areas and New Issues would serve to further moderate price decline. As in Premiums, issues without call protection will provide somewhat better downside protection.

3. *Moderate Discount Bonds.* Most of these will become Deep Discounts. Their yield rise will be fairly close to the rise in New Issues. This and high coupon volatility will produce greater declines than in Premiums and Current Coupons. If there is a narrow Yield Spread between Deep Discounts and New Issues, price declines will be almost as severe as that for Deep Discounts. If it is wide, price declines may approach that of Current Coupons. Call protection is of no significance.

4. *Deep Discount Bonds.* These will experience no change in status. Their rise in yield is likely to be closest to the rise in New Issues. This and highest coupon volatility will produce the greatest price declines of any Coupon Area, if Yield Spreads between New Issues and Deep Discounts are maintained or narrowed. Should the Yield Spread between New Issues

and Deep Discounts widen, price declines would be close to those in Moderate Discounts.

TIME PERIOD OF THE MOVE

The length of time involved in a move from one level of interest rates to another has an important bearing on the attraction of various Coupon Areas. Table IV shows that when one year of coupon income is added to the percentage price change for each issue, the percentage change in total return (price change plus income) among Coupon Areas is not as divergent as the percentage change in price alone. If the time period is short, the income differential between various coupons is of little significance. In longer time periods, coupon income differentials become more significant. This is simply the result of the relative weighting of coupon income versus price change. The longer the time period, the more important the coupon income is in relation to price change.

Two other factors affecting price performance should be noted. The first relates to call price. Most call prices decline annually. Typically, the reduction is $1/29$ of the call premium in each year for a 30-year bond. Annual reductions in call price for a 7.00% coupon would be 0.24 points, a 6.00% coupon by 0.21 and a 5.00% coupon by 0.17. The second factor is annual "appreciation" in discount bonds which results from the yield-to-maturity concept. A 30-year 6.00% bond at a 6.75% basis has a price of 90.41 and after passage of one year is worth 90.51 at the same 6.75% basis, a price increase of 0.10. A 30-year 5.00% at 6.75% has a price of 77.61 and at 29 years it has a price of 77.86 at a 6.75% basis, a price increase of 0.25 points. This change in dollar price is accrual of income.

The influence on Coupon Area selection of declining call prices and annual appreciation is small, but they have great bearing on selection of issues within each Coupon Area. Coupon income differentials can affect Coupon Area selection, if the time period of an anticipated market move approaches a year or more.

ATYPICAL YIELDS AND ISSUE SELECTION

In every market there are typical yields for each Coupon Area. However, it is possible to find Coupon Areas or individual bond issues that are "out of line" with the market. This is often caused by a slow reaction to changes in the level of interest rates in Discount Bonds. By being aware of the usual, the unusual can be discerned. Frequently, Deep Discounts will sell at Moderate Discount yields and Moderate Discounts at Current Coupon yields. Purchases of issues out of line with the market, especially if they are in an attractive Coupon Area, can offer greater than usual appreciation potential and/or downside protection. They also present trading opportunities in the event that sale at a yield more in line with their coupon becomes possible. An attractively priced issue in an undesired Coupon Area can often present a better opportunity than another issue selling in line with the market in a desired Coupon Area.

A Coupon Area whose yields are the same as a lower Coupon Area (for example, Moderate Discounts at the same yield as Deep Discounts) contains a large degree of downside risk and a small degree of appreciation potential. The reason for this is the likelihood of a return to more typical Yield Spreads and the possibility that yields will move out of line in the opposite direction. A more frequent occurrence is an out-of-line yield on a specific issue and the same analysis of attraction is applicable.

The best and the most frequent opportunities for finding attractive issues occur in initial offerings on New Issues. Almost every New Issue is in the Current Coupon Area. When a New Issue cannot be sold at original offering price and suffers a price decline, it often yields as much as a higher coupon New Issue which has fewer points to call price. For example, when a 7.125% New Issue is available at 100, callable at 107⅛, a broken 7.00% New Issue, callable at 107, might sell at 98⅜ to yield the same 7.125%. The broken issue would be considered more attractive, because it has 1½ points more call protection than the 7⅛% New Issue. Such price breaks are temporary phenomena which correct themselves as issues are distributed and the supply of bonds is reduced. Once distributed, the broken issue would tend to sell at about 5 basis points less yield than another New Issue at 100 in order to reflect the additional call protection. In Current Coupons, 1 or 2 extra points of call protection has been valued at 5–10 basis points. Thus, when a 7.00%–NR issue sells at 100, a 6.75%–NR would tend to sell at about 6.90% yield, price 98.11.

The yield differential for five-year call protection provided by the indenture has fluctuated between 15 and 25 basis points at the 6.00%–7.00% New Issue levels. At a 4.00%–5.00% level for New Issues, five-year call protection was worth 10–15 basis points. This is the additional yield offered on a New Issue bond without call protection to make it competitive with call-protected issues. The reason why the yield differential for call protection declines as prices go below 100 and widens above 100 has been explained. Depending upon market outlook, yield differential and points to call, a broken issue without call protection can be a better purchase than a call-protected New Issue.

Another area of opportunity lies in the deepest discounts. A substantial amount of long maturity Treasury Bonds are still held in many bond portfolios. The Yield Spread between these discount long Treasuries and discount long Corporates invites switching out of Treasuries. More often than not the demand for discount corporates which can be exchanged par-for-par for Treasuries results in out-of-line yields and prices. For the holder of corporate issues, it invites a switch into somewhat higher priced discount issues which have higher yields.

In judging the relative attractiveness of individual issues the following procedure can be used:

1. Make a projection of the probable change in interest rates.
2. Establish a New Issue yield level that seems likely to be reached.

3. Estimate the likely yields on the issues under consideration at the anticipated yield level.
4. Calculate prices for the bond issues from a bond basis book using call price as a ceiling.
5. Relate the estimated time required for the market change to the income produced and price change.
6. Using the same process, estimate the risk factor if the market moves in the opposite direction.
7. Select the issue offering the combination of best price/yield performance if the market projection is correct and good protection if the market projection turns out wrong.

SELECTION OF COUPON AREAS

Once the characteristics of various Coupon Areas are understood, they can be utilized to improve price/yield performance. Attractive areas of the market can be located. The portfolio manager can gain maximum advantage from an anticipated market move. In periods of market uncertainty (more usual than unusual) a method is provided for finessing the question of whether or not to buy long maturity bonds. As pleasant as it is to buy last month's new issues down 2 or 3 points, many portfolio managers are reluctant to risk purchasing these issues 2–3 points higher than they were recently. Selection of specific bond issues for purchase is facilitated. A description of various courses of action for Holding and Trading Portfolios under different market assumptions is outlined below. (Of course if rising yields (declining prices) are anticipated, it would be best not to buy long bonds.)

I. HOLDING PORTFOLIO—NEW MONEY

A. DECLINING YIELDS (RISING PRICES)

1. Moderate Decline (50 basis points). Ignore Premium Bonds and consider the relative merits of call-protected Current Coupons and Deep Discounts. Call-protected (NR) Moderate Discounts might be used at particularly attractive Yield Spreads from New Issues.

2. Major Decline (100–150 basis points). Ignore Premium Bonds and Current Coupons and use the more attractive of either call-protected (NR) Moderate Discounts or Deep Discounts.

B. RISING YIELDS (DECLINING PRICES)

1. Moderate Rise (50 basis points). Ignore Deep Discounts and Moderate Discounts and use Current Coupons without call protection. It would be best to ignore Premium Bonds too, because once purchased the Holding Portfolio cannot restructure them for a period of Declining Yields.

2. Major Rise (100–150 basis points). While Premium Bonds would seem best, non call-protected Current Coupons should be stressed in view of the inability to restructure for a changed outlook.

C. Hedged Position

The best hedge is a broken New Issue with call protection (NR) when declining yields are more likely and without call protection when rising yields are more likely. A Moderate Discount with a small Yield Spread from New Issues would also be good. Both possess good upside potential and reasonable downside protection.

II. TRADING PORTFOLIO—NEW MONEY AND RESTRUCTURING OF EXISTING HOLDINGS

A. Declining Yields (Rising Prices)

1. Moderate Decline (50 basis points). Deep Discounts should be the first choice and Moderate Discounts the second choice, if their Yield Spreads are attractive. Otherwise, call-protected Current Coupons are indicated. Move out of Premium and Moderate Discounts without call protection.

2. Major Decline (100–150 basis points). Deep Discounts should be the first choice and Moderate Discounts the second choice, if their Yield Spreads are attractive. Otherwise, use call-protected (NR) Current Coupons and replace them with other call-protected (NR) Current Coupons as they move close to call price. Move out of Premium Bonds and non-call-protected Moderate Discounts.

B. Rising Yields (Declining Prices)

1. Moderate or Major Rise (50–150 basis points). Premium Bonds could be used. However, Current Coupons without call protection would seem better, because they would eliminate the need for a trade into another area when the market outlook changed. Move out of Deep Discounts and Moderate Discounts if Yield Spreads permit it.

C. Hedged Position

The best hedge would be a broken New Issue with call protection (NR) when declining yields are more likely and without call protection when rising yields are more likely. A Moderate Discount with a small Yield Spread from New Issues would also be good. Both possess good upside potential and reasonable downside protection.

Several points should be made in regard to these suggested courses of action. First, in most instances, Premium Bonds should be avoided. Their immediate advantage of price protection is offset by inability of the Holding Portfolios to restructure for a changed market outlook and the need for the Trading Portfolio to make an extra trade. Second, broken New Issues offer more benefits under a variety of market outlooks than any other category of coupon. The ability to anticipate and capitalize upon such price breaks can be a great aid to good performance. Third, the Trading Portfolio must emphasize marketability in purchases. Action is impossible unless holdings can be sold and frustrated if sale is possible only on a bid far from the offered side of the market. Even with marketable issues, a wide spread between bid and offered can wipe out the benefits of an indicated course of action. Fourth, one of the crucial judgments required is the relative attractiveness of Moderate and Deep Discounts. Their yield change relative to market change can alter an anticipated price move based solely on coupon volatility. Fifth, in deciding which Coupon Area is most likely to give maximum price performance one must apply a risk/reward attitude and seek the best combination of downside protection and appreciation potential. Finally, coupon behavior is only one of numerous criteria for deciding what to buy or sell in the market. Others would include the relative attractiveness of market areas (Industrials, Utilities, Finance, etc.), quality areas (Aaa, Aa, etc.), and maturity areas.

SUMMARY

Bond portfolios are being judged increasingly on the basis of price performance rather than only on yield performance. One method for improving price performance while maintaining yield is based on a knowledge of the relative price performance of Coupon Areas. Coupon Areas are groups of bonds with similar coupons which sell at approximately the same price and yield-to-maturity. Selection of Coupon Areas can affect performance because individual bond issues and Coupon Areas offer different yields and degrees of price volatility. In the bond market, yield-to-maturity is a function of call protection and appreciation potential. Call protection can be obtained either through an indenture provision or through a low coupon selling at a discount from 100. Usually, the greater the call protection and appreciation potential, the lower the yield. Price action in bonds is a function of coupon volatility, the transition from one Coupon Area to another, and changing Yield Spreads among Coupon Areas. The relative price volatility of the various Coupon Areas was examined as well as the importance of the time period required for an anticipated market move. Possible courses of action have been indicated for both the Holding Portfolio and the Trading Portfolio. With this information the portfolio manager will be able to select areas of the market and individual issues which offer the best appreciation potential and/or downside protection in light of anticipated market change. Also, methods of operating in uncertain markets and reducing the risks involved in not buying were provided. These strategies make it possible to achieve a significant improvement in price and/or yield performance for the bond portfolio.

A PRIMER ON INSTITUTIONAL TRADING*

Carter T. Geyer

During recent years, a certain mystique has developed regarding institutional trading activity. Whenever we read an article on "the market" in magazines or newspapers, some reference is certain to be made as to what the institutions are doing. Government officials have become extremely conscious of the increasing participation of institutions in the market, and public outcries against the real or imagined evils resulting from this increased participation are frequent.

Institutional trading activity has, of course, increased dramatically over the past five years. Although part of this sharp increase is attributable to the fact that institutions manage an ever larger share of the total assets earmarked for investment in equities, the activity is also due in large measure to rising turnover in once staid portfolios. The conservative institution that 10 years ago followed the policy of buying and holding until the brink of disaster might now show a 30 percent to 40 percent turnover annually in the same portfolio. The emphasis on investment performance has forced today's money managers to be equipped to trade quickly and in large volume.

Somewhere, hidden away in the labyrinths of the aggressive institutions that are pursuing the goal of investment performance are the men who are responsible for putting investment policies "on the tape"—the institutional traders. Although a lot has been written and said about institutional trading activity, almost nothing has been written about institutional traders and the new trading techniques they have developed in order to cope with modern, active, volatile institutional investment policies.

The purpose of this article is to provide a fundamental introduction to institutional trading for the benefit of portfolio managers, analysts, and other members of the investment community who depend on their traders to translate ideas into positions. We shall examine, in basic terms, the

---

* Reprinted by permission of the *Financial Analysts Journal* (March–April 1969).

functions of an institutional trader, various trading techniques, trading terminology, and the most effective means of coordinating an institutional trading capability with the other parts of the investment team.

WHAT IS AN INSTITUTIONAL TRADER?

In simplest terms an institutional trader is the man responsible for the marketing of all equity acquisition or sale programs for a particular institution. Because marketing problems have become increasingly complex, a number of highly talented, knowledgeable institutional traders have established themselves as respected professional members of the investment industry. In so doing they have established a new profession within the industry. Five years ago, the investment team was pictured as a two-part affair: financial analyst and portfolio manager. The successful investment team of today is structured much like a three-legged stool: financial analyst, portfolio manager, and trader. Each leg relates to, complements, and depends on the other two.

The importance of the trading function is attested to most clearly by the fact that in most major banks and mutual funds the head trader is one of the more senior officers of the investment division, with a title comparable to that of the head of research or portfolio management. The "order clerk" has become an anachronism. The demands imposed by modern methods of institutional investing are responsible for the rapid evolution of the professional institutional trader. Without the services of a competent institutional trader, many investment policies simply could not be brought to fruition.

FUNCTIONS OF AN INSTITUTIONAL TRADER

The primary function of an institutional trader is, of course, the successful and efficient execution of equity acquisition and sale programs for his institution. At first glance, this sounds simple—buy 'em and sell 'em, preferably buying at the low and selling at the high. However, as the execution process is examined in greater detail, particularly the execution of blocks, this function will lose its mechanical connotations and look more like an art. Many professional money managers contend that good traders are born, not made. Although this is debatable, there is no doubt that an institutional trader who can provide consistently good executions is an extremely valuable commodity.

One of the most difficult aspects of the execution process is the fact that the institutional trader is almost invariably forced to ply his trade under extreme pressure. When his institution is making a new commitment in an issue, there is an excellent chance that other institutions will get the same "story" and be clamoring for the same stock. When the fundamentals of an issue suddenly turn sour and it is time to get out fast, others want to get out as well. Even under normal conditions the institutional trader is expected to make one decision after another, often "on the line" in a matter of seconds, during the five and a half hours that the market is open. With situations often open in 30 or more different issues at the same time, it can feel like running a 50-yard dash for 50 miles.

Efficient handling of blocks (units of 2,000 shares or more, depending upon the issue) has become one of the most critical aspects of modern institutional trading. Nearly all aggressive institutions concerned with superior investment performance now do their trading in blocks. While block trading was the exclusive province of a handful of mutual funds only a few years ago, this technique of trading has now spread to all types of institutions. It is my opinion that block trading is the only logical equity marketing method for most institutions. Institutions lacking a trading operation capable of handling block executions efficiently will be left by the wayside in the quest for investment performance.

A secondary, but extremely important, function of the institutional trader is to provide market information for his portfolio managers and analysts. In effect, the trader should function as the "eyes and ears" of the investment team at the supply and demand level of the market. Because of his intimate relationship with the supply and demand picture, a good trader can view the market, industry groups, and specific issues in a perspective alien to his portfolio managers and analysts. In addition, an institutional trader with good contacts can often pick up bits of information or notice peculiarities in price movements long before they become common printed knowledge. Through the proper integration of the trading operation into the investment team, information provided by the trader can be an extremely valuable tool to portfolio management and research.

Another function of the institutional trader involves dealer relations. An institutional trader is faced with the most sensitive aspect of the relations between his institution and the brokers serving his institution: The trader is the man who places the orders that generate the commissions. This can often place the trader in a delicate position, because there is probably no such thing as the broker who has received "enough" business. However, through fair and honest practices and a constant effort to maintain good relations, it is usually possible for an experienced and capable institutional trader to perform his job properly without too many major crises involving dealer relations.

MARKETS WITHIN "THE MARKET"—A BRIEF REVIEW

Before examining the specific techniques of institutional trading, it is necessary to understand the environment of the markets in which the trader operates, some of the terminology used in trading, and the background preparation the trader must perform prior to making a trade. Most professional investors are familiar with many or all of these topics, so they will be reviewed only very briefly. The most fundamental area with which the institutional trader is concerned, and the first topic that we will examine, is the various markets for equities.

I. The New York Stock Exchange and American Stock Exchange

The New York Stock Exchange and the American Stock Exchange are considered the "primary" markets for the securities listed on each of the two exchanges. The two exchanges operate in a very similar fashion, although the physical layout of their trading floors is different to some degree. Both exchanges are based on the "auction market" (bid price and offered price) system, in contrast to the "bourse" concept on which most European exhanges function.

In addition, both exchanges use the "specialist" system. It is the function of the specialist to maintain a "fair and orderly market" in his stocks within the framework of the auction market. Each specialist is responsible for a small number of stocks, has stringent capitalization requirements that allow him to take sizable positions in those stocks if necessary, and in effect makes or creates the market in an issue when there is no close market due to the absence of a close current bid or offer. Unfortunately, due to the antics of a very few bad specialists, specialists are often maligned as a group. Most specialists handle their issues extremely well, lend stability to the market, and provide a definite measure of liquidity to listed issues. Always bear in mind that specialists, like all other businessmen, are in business to make money rather than lose it. When a specialist takes a risk position, it is a well-calculated risk. Specialists should not be thought of as super-heroes who have been put on earth simply to bail out investors in times of crisis.

II. The Over-the-Counter Market

The over-the-counter market is a vast network of securities dealers who "make markets" in securities that are not listed on the major stock exchanges. These dealers buy and sell securities for their own account, again within an auction framework established by supply and demand factors, hoping to profit by buying low (at the bid price) and selling higher (at the offered price). Most of these dealers trade actively. Some dealers quote hundreds of different issues and make their profit by turning a high volume on only a fractional markup per trade. The magnitude of the over-the-counter market is vast in comparison to the "listed" market, both in terms of the number of issues traded and the volume of trading.

A listing of actively traded over-the-counter issues, arranged alphabetically by issue and showing the dealers making markets in those issues, is published daily by The National Daily Quotation Service. Known as the "Pink Sheets" because of the pink paper on which it is printed, this listing is the trader's guide to the primary markets in over-the-counter issues. Although prices quoted in the "Pink Sheets" are the current markets as of the publishing deadline and therefore are subject to change, marked discrepancies between quoted markets can often give an indication that one broker might be a better seller than buyer, or vice versa.

III. Regional Stock Exchanges

Regional stock exchanges were originally established in a number of major cities to provide "listed" pricing and orderly markets for local or regional securities. The regional exchanges were conceived as an alternative to the over-the-counter market for smaller companies whose stock was not actively traded on a nationwide scale. As time passed, regional exchanges grew both in terms of the number of issues listed and the volume of trading and became important members of their financial community.

As regional exchanges flourished, many companies whose stocks were listed on the New York Stock Exchange had their stocks listed on regional exchanges as well. These issues became known as "dually listed" securities. Today a large percentage of the issues listed on the New York Stock Exchange are also listed on one or more regional exchanges. The result is that regional exchanges have become a very important "secondary" market in Big Board issues as well as a primary market in local issues. Major regional exchanges are the Midwest (in Chicago), the Pacific Coast (with trading floors in both Los Angeles and San Francisco), the Boston, and the Philadelphia–Baltimore. Others include the Detroit, Pittsburgh, Cincinnati, and Salt Lake City, which specializes in Western mining shares.

IV. The "Third" Market

The "Third" Market is composed of a small number of dealers who *make markets* in *listed* securities, trading these issues for their own account in much the same manner as an over-the-counter dealer. "Third" Market dealers charge no commissions as such and are generally not members of any exchange. Generally trading as principal rather than as agent, they trade an issue on a price based around the current last sale on the exchange, usually bidding ¼-point below the last sale and offering ¼-point above the last sale. Their profit, like the over-the-counter dealer's, lies in their ability to be "long" or "short" in their positions at the right time and in the spread between the "bid" and "offered" prices.

V. The Block "Matchmakers"

The trend among institutions to do their trading in "blocks" has grown dramatically over the past few years. Because of this trend, it has become important for the large, aggressive institutions to seek out brokers who specialize in trading blocks by "finding the other side," that is, matching buyer with seller. Most institutionally oriented brokers claim to have developed this specialized trading ability. Some of them (the minority) actually do and have become well known for it.

The crucial need for block trading ability has recently led to the emergence and immediate success of a small number of brokers whose trading concept is completely new to the institutional brokerage business. For lack of a better name, we shall call them "matchmakers." While methods of operation differ among the very few firms of this type, the pattern is usually the same. The firms are small, not members of any exchange, and are staffed by highly experienced block traders, many of whom have had prior experience as institutional traders themselves and understand the problems of institutional trading from "both sides of the desk."

The single speciality of these firms is to put blocks together by matching buyer and seller, negotiating a price agreeable to both sides, and consummating the trade *over-the-counter* for a *negotiated* commission which is usually one half to one third the equivalent commission were the trade transacted "on board" by brokers who are exchange members. The ability of "matchmakers" to consummate trades in this manner lies in the experience of their traders to "feel" what their institutional accounts are doing, find the other side without disturbing the market, and put the two sides together by being able to judge the price at which the trade could be made. Single trades involving hundreds of thousands of shares have been transacted in this manner without a ripple in the market, no print on a tape to announce to the investment community that a trade has been made, and with an enormous savings in commissions to the institutions making the trade.

With all of the current turmoil between the New York Stock Exchange, the Department of Justice, and SEC concerning commissions, it is interesting to note that such "matchmakers," few in number and small in size, are already operating for negotiated commissions and providing a critical, specialized service for the institutions they serve. Yet they have received little of the limelight and their abilities and services remain largely unappreciated, unknown, and often even regarded with suspicion by many institutional investors.

COMMON TYPES OF ORDERS[1]

An understanding of the basic types of orders an institutional trader might use when buying or selling listed securities is necessary before discussing trading techniques and order handling. Many institutional investors are not aware of the differences between the various types of orders that can be given a broker. Although this review will be limited to only the more common orders, explaining each briefly, most member firms will provide your institution with booklets explaining the more obscure types of orders.

---

[1] Since this writing, most exchanges have adopted some form of volume discount on commissions. Any member firm should be able to inform you of the new requirements for entering orders under the volume discount rules and give you a detailed explanation of the circumstances in which volume discount would apply.

I. The "Market" Order

A "market" order means just that. Your broker is required to consummate your trade at the "market price" and must at least participate in all trades in an issue until the order is completed. You are "holding him to the tape." For example, you give your broker an order to buy 700 shares of XYZ "at the market." The last sale of XYZ is 49¾. The current market is 49½ bid, offered at 50. On the specialist's book, there are 200 shares bid for (at 49½) and 400 shares offered (at 50). This is the current market and "size." Let's also assume that an additional 300 shares are offered at 50¼ on the specialist's book. Unless another seller enters the market at the same time you go in to buy and is willing to sell his stock at a price lower than the current offer, or unless the specialist is willing to complete your order at 50 for his own account, your broker would be obligated to fill your order at the then current market. Your execution would be: 400 shares at 50; 300 shares at 50¼; completes. There are exceptions, of course, to this example. One common case is when the specialist agrees to "stop" you on the last 300 shares at 50¼ and tries to improve your price. In this case, you are protected on 300 shares at 50¼ but have a chance of getting a better price on all or part of that 300 shares.

II. The "Or Better" Order

Suppose in this case you gave your broker an order to buy 700 shares of XYZ at "49¾ or better." The last previous sale is still 49¾, and the current market and size before your order goes in is still 49½ at 50, 200 shares by 400 shares. Your broker is obligated to place your *entire* order on the specialist's book at 49¾. The market and size then becomes 49¾ at 50, 700 shares bid for (your 700) by 400 shares offered. If a seller came into the market, you would be entitled to any sale made at 49¾ until your order was completed. Under normal circumstances, the stock would not trade down below 49¾ until your order was filled. However, if another buyer came into the market bidding higher than you, you would not participate in any trades higher than 49¾. By making your order "or better," you have not given your broker the discretion to buy stock at higher prices if the market suddenly moves away from you.

III. The "Not Held" Order

An order marked "Not Held" means that you are "not holding" your broker to every print on the tape. In effect, you are giving him discretion to judge the market and execute your order in the manner he deems most wise. With a "Not Held" order, your broker's floor partner can make the most efficient use of his knowledge and experience.

There are a number of different ways using a "Not Held" order. You may, for example, instruct your broker to buy 1,000 shares of XYZ "at the market, *not held.*" This differs from a straight market order in that you are in effect saying that you wish to buy the stock at current market prices, but are giving the broker discretion as to how the order will be filled. He is not held to participate in every trade in XYZ and may drop out of the bidding for a period of time if he feels the stock is dropping. Conversely, he may be quite aggressive if he sees large buyers coming into the stock.

You may give your broker an order to buy or sell a certain number of shares of stock at a specific price, "not held." For example, you may wish to buy 2,000 shares of XYZ at a price not exceeding 50 but may not want to give the broker an order at "50 or better," because you don't want your entire buying interest to show on the specialist's book. In this case, you would give an order to buy 2,000 shares of XYZ "at 50, *not held*." This tells the broker that you do not want to pay more than 50 and would probably like to have some participation at 50, but gives him the discretion to scale back your bid if he feels the stock is coming too easily. Typically, to use the market in XYZ, he might buy the 400 shares offered at 50, but might choose to then bid only 49¾ for an additional 600 rather than putting the entire bid for 1,600 on the book at 50.

A variation on this type of order is to instruct the broker to buy 2,000 shares of XYZ "at 50 not held, with ¼-point discretion for size." In this case, the broker would handle your order in much the same manner as in the previous example. However, he would have the discretion to pay up to 50¼ if a seller of any size (typically 1,000 shares or so, but you can be specific as to what you mean by "size") comes into the market and offers stock at that level.

Always bear in mind that when you give your broker a "Not Held" order, you are giving him the authority to exercise his discretion in handling the order. Usually, a broker can perform a better job for you if he is allowed to exercise his judgment. After all, he is on the trading floor where the action is, and you are not. However, brokers are human beings, too, and cannot always be right. Sixty percent is a pretty good batting average in the floor trading business. If your broker does make an error in judgment, do not cry, complain, write letters to the exchange, or otherwise be obnoxious. After all, *you* gave the broker the authority to exercise his own judgment.

There are, of course, many other types of orders that your trader may use. There are also many exceptions to the examples I have outlined above. A discussion of all the orders and all the exceptions would fill a volume by itself. The orders described above are not only the most common, but they are probably also the most commonly misunderstood. They are also the most necessary for you to know in order to understand how your institutional trader might work an order.

KNOWING THE ISSUE

Experienced institutional traders with a number of years behind the desk have had to work in many different stocks. A competent trader can develop a "feel" for most of the issues he works in and will subconsciously commit all of the facts and characteristics related to the trading of a specific stock to his memory. Often an institutional trader is called upon to work a stock that he has not traded for a year or more. A good trader can immediately recall all of the pertinent data concerning that issue and begin to trade it with the same confidence and "feel" he had a year before.

One of the most important parts of knowing an issue is developing a sixth sense. In addition to that intangible trader's "feel" for a stock, many very tangible things will concern a trader as he attempts to "know the issue" before attempting to trade it. For example, he will want to know the trading pattern of the stock. Is it a fairly stable issue, with an even, narrow, daily trading range or is it a volatile "swinger" that can easily move five or more points in a day? What does the chart pattern look like? Although very few traders of my acquaintance are all-out chartists, most good traders will always want to review a price chart in an unfamiliar stock to see what it has been doing not only by itself, but also in relation to its group and the market in general.

The trader will also need to know, of course, where the stock is traded. In the case of a listed stock, it is important to know whether the stock is dually listed on any of the regional exchanges, and, if so, on what regionals it is listed and how does it trade on each exchange. Curiously, some issues may be medium traders on the big board, light traders on one regional exchange, and fairly heavy traders on another regional exchange. An experienced trader will also want to know which specialist "makes" the stock on the big board. Specialists differ in the way they will handle a stock. Knowing the specialist and the way he works can be a very decisive factor in how a trader will handle his order.

VOLUME CONSIDERATIONS

An adequate position in a stock for the common trust fund of a small bank or the equity portfolio of a small insurance company may be only 3,000 shares. However, an adequate position in the same stock for a major mutual fund might be from 300,000 to 500,000 shares. Needless to say, although it is almost always possible to acquire 3,000 shares of any issue, it can be impossible to acquire 300,000 shares of a small, thinly traded security.

It is critical for an analyst, when reviewing a stock for a purchase recommendation, to examine the trading volume of the stock. At times, the number of shares outstanding can be misleading. A stock with 3,000,000 shares outstanding can have a large number of those shares closely held. The actual trading "float" conceivably could be only 100,000 shares or less. It is helpful, if the stock is listed, to check the trading volume in the stock for the previous six months. In any case, some consultation with your trader is advisable when examining trading volume. Half a position often can be worse than no position.

CHOOSING THE BROKER

It has been my experience that institutions often shackle their traders too closely when it comes to choosing brokers. All institutions expect their traders to execute orders well. Yet, all too often they force their traders to deal with brokers who simply cannot handle the job properly. In order to achieve satisfactory executions, an institutional trader must be given discretion in choosing a broker. The trader knows, far better than any other member of the investment team, the strengths and weaknesses of various brokers when it comes to executing orders.

Block trading makes the process of broker selection even more critical. Of the number of brokers who claim they can handle blocks properly (roughly 99.9 percent of all brokers in existence), only a small number are really proficient and experienced at block trading. Your trader should have the freedom to maintain good contacts with these houses, know what they are doing, and know what they can do for your institution. A good block trading house can make the difference between a beautiful execution and a half-finished abortion.

An institutional trader will take many things into consideration before choosing a broker to handle a particular order. He will determine whether the stock is relatively difficult or easy to trade, whether he should spend time trying to "find the other side" before "going to the floor" to start working the stock, whether he will be working solely on the New York or American Stock Exchanges, or whether he will be working regional exchanges simultaneously. A good trader keeps an accurate record of all buying and selling interests shown to him and can often determine from his files that a broker only a day or two previously disclosed an interest in the stock under consideration. Frequently, that interest can be "freshened up," and a trade can be made. At times, your trader may have to execute large orders in a stock of strong regional interest and may choose a broker with particular strength in that region. Often your trader will know that a certain broker has an unusual amount of activity in a certain issue. This might be due to an investment banking relationship, research work, or just simple coincidence.

Sometimes an institutional trader must simply rely on his intuition when choosing the broker. But whatever reasons he may use for choice of broker, the odds are 20 to 1 that he can do a better job than you when it comes down to the wire. Although traders are realistic enough to understand that there are peripheral considerations in choosing brokers, the execution is their responsibility. Institutions desiring a superior trading capability must always remember that their trader is the expert on executions. With respect to the choice of broker, the preferences of other members of the investment team or sales or commercial banking relationships should not be so extreme as to force your trader into making the wrong choice.

DISCRETION

Discretion is probably the single most delicate subject concerning an institutional trading operation. Some institutions give their trader full and complete discretion in the handling of his orders. Others allow no discretion at all. The majority lie somewhere in the middle but are not really sure where.

One of the best solutions to this problem is a somewhat modified approach: Have the research department or the portfolio manager set a limit on each stock on the buy list *based on the top level at which the stock is still attractive on a fundamental basis.* The limit, then, has its foundation in the fundamental outlook for the issue rather than the day-to-day ups and downs of the stock, the price at which it is now trading, or the size of the order. The trader can exercise full discretion in handling his order as long as he does not exceed that limit. The limit changes only when the fundamentals of the stock change or when a revision of multiples occurs, for example, for that particular industry group.

A trader must be allowed discretion in order to perform an effective job for his institution. The hypothetical case of the purchase of 50,000 XYZ which follows below is a pretty fair example of what a trader can do if he is allowed to handle the order himself and is given a reasonable degree of discretion. Your trader lives with the tape and each move of your stocks for five and a half hours a day, day after day. Above all, do not try to mastermind him or second guess him. Trust him and give him your confidence and support. When you mastermind an order from a distance, you are probably going to perform a disservice to your institution.

INQUIRIES

In institutional trading terminology, an "inquiry" is an indication to a broker that you have an interest in buying or selling a particular stock. Generally, an indication of the size of your interest is incorporated with the inquiry. The subject of inquiries is very delicate. As I was trying to learn the institutional trading ropes, it was very difficult for me to realize that I had to choose a broker and give out inquiries. For fear of disturbing the market, I was afraid to let any broker know what I was doing and simply hoped that some broker would come to me with an indication of interest in selling the stock I wanted to buy.

Over the years, it became obvious that I had to open up more, albeit with discretion and selectivity, in order to get the job done. Perhaps I have gone full circle, but it is my opinion that too many institutions force their traders to be too secretive. For fear of criticism, or "blowing an order," some traders are intimidated into mummy-like silence. Discreet inquiries are the commodity on which the block trading business is based.

An institutional trader simply cannot expect the specialized block trading houses to continue to show him their inquiries forever if he never shows an inquiry to them.

BLOCK TRADING TECHNIQUES

Before discussing how a typical order might be handled, some time should be devoted to the subject of special techniques used in institutional block trading. The art of block trading is something that cannot be learned from a textbook, even if there were one on the subject. It requires time, experience, and plenty of honest errors in judgment to become adept and confident at marketing large blocks of stock. However, there are certain special techniques encountered often in block trading that can be covered briefly.

I. Negotiations

The art of successful negotiation is one of the most important aspects of block trading. A competent institutional trader may have open buy orders, in size, in 25 or more different stocks at any given time. The chances are he has a different "feeling" about each of those stocks. He may feel aggressive about some and want to lay back and do nothing on others, with various shades of grey in between. The important thing is that at any given time he can react quickly to take what he feels is the proper approach should stock be offered to him and negotiations begin.

A good trader takes many things into consideration when starting to negotiate a block trade. For example, as a buyer, he is concerned with whether the stock has been acting weak or strong, what other selling interests he has seen in the stock, the size of the seller, who the seller might be and how he acts, the proficiency of the broker involved and the ability of that broker to handle large blocks. The sum of these considerations guides the trader in deciding how to negotiate.

An experienced institutional trader will not start negotiating if he is not really interested in buying stock. Extreme discount bids made simply for giggles are not part of the game. In making his initial bid the trader will probably start at a level which, although it *may* be at a discount to the last previous sale, is close enough to the last sale to indicate that he is a "real" buyer. The seller, if he is also a competent institutional trader, will have considered the same factors as the buyer. In addition, he will know how badly his institution wants to sell the stock. Although he will generally make a counter-offer somewhat higher than the initial bid rather than hitting the bid immediately, he, like the buyer, will have a pretty firm idea in mind of the price at which the trade should be made. The broker's job, of course, is to help bring the two sides together to an equitable conclusion.

There seems to be a marked trend in block trading for blocks to trade closer and closer to the last sale, particularly prenegotiated crosses. Large block trades at gross discounts are rapidly becoming a rarity. However, extreme discount bids and premium offerings are still overused and abused at many institutions. Obviously this kind of attitude results in many excellent buying and selling opportunities that are missed when negotiations collapse. It also means, and this is important, that an institution known for unrealistic negotiation practices goes straight to the bottom of a broker's contact list when he has an inquiry in a stock. These institutions see the merchandise last.

Many portfolio managers and analysts are unaware of the recent trends in block trading and the directions negotiations have taken. Often they interfere with the judgment of their trader because they still believe that if a seller in size comes into the market, that seller should readily accept a gross discount bid for his stock. On the other hand, when the same portfolio managers or analysts discuss selling a large block of stock themselves, that block suddenly becomes a very valuable piece of merchandise that should draw a premium in the market. With this kind of attitude, negotiation becomes a ludicrous fandango resulting in nothing except frayed tempers and frustration.

II. Crossing

A "crossed" block generally refers to a block trade, either on or off board, in which the buyer and seller have been matched, with the sale price prenegotiated in the manner just described. In a "pure cross," the broker will have matched both sides of the trade and handled all negotiations between buyer and seller. At times a block trading house will go "long" or "short" a small amount of stock to accommodate one party to the trade and effect the cross. At times, the specialist will perform this function, either through orders already on his book or for his own account.

III. Clean-ups

A "clean-up bid" can mean one of two things, depending on whether an institution or a broker is using the term. Often an institutional trader is shown a very large block of stock for sale, perhaps 300,000 shares. His institution may only need 50,000 shares but *does* want to buy the stock. Obviously, the trader does not want to step up and buy 50,000 shares and leave 250,000 shares overhanging the market. The tactic he will take is to determine roughly at what price the stock might trade, and if that price is agreeable, indicate to the broker that his institution has a firm buying interest in 50,000 shares on a "clean-up" basis. The broker will then attempt to find other buyers willing to "circle" the remainder of the block on the same basis. The block, of course, is considered "cleaned-up" and traded when buyers are found for the full 300,000 shares.

However, if the broker is only able to find buyers for 290,000 shares, he, himself, may make a "clean-up" bid for the remaining 10,000 shares, positioning the stock for his own account in order to make the trade. Because the broker has an obligation to his buying customers, as well as to his own purse, he will generally make every effort to scale the 10,000 shares out gradually at higher prices rather than dumping them on the market immediately.

IV. POSITIONING

During the past year or two, many brokers heavily involved in institutional trading have not only tried to establish a block trading capability, but they have also set aside a portion of their firm's capital that their block traders may use to "position" stocks. A broker will sometimes use that capital to make a "position bid" (for the broker's own account) for a block of stock an institutional customer wishes to sell if the broker is unable to find a buyer for the stock within a reasonable period of time.

The subject of position bidding is highly complex and emotional. Obviously there is a need for position bidding. Personally, however, I feel that position bidding is overdone in many respects. While many brokers claim that they will position blocks, only a few will continually step up to the line and do the job with style and class. The institutional investment community owes these brokers an obligation to come to them with business not only in times of crisis when they are asked to be heroes and risk large amounts of capital, but to favor them with an occasional easy order as well.

By the same token, many institutions tense up when faced with selling a large block and ask for and accept a position bid at a large discount to the market when the block could probably be crossed at a much better price if given a little more time and effort. A position bid is rarely, if ever, as good as the bid a bona fide buyer would make under the same conditions. In most cases, the position bid is made at a fairly hefty discount to the last previous sale.

V. USING REGIONAL EXCHANGES

From time to time, large blocks of dually listed issues are crossed on regional exchanges rather than on the New York Stock Exchange. Frequently, this is done for purposes of reciprocity. At other times, it is done because a specialist or the orders on a specialist's book may "break-up" a cross. For example, a cross of 50,000 shares of XYZ is arranged at a prenegotiated price of $49\frac{1}{4}$. The last sale of XYZ is $49\frac{3}{8}$, and the stock has had a high of 50 and a low of 49. The current market is $49\frac{1}{4}$ at $49\frac{3}{8}$, and there are 3,000 shares bid for and 800 offered. If the cross were put up at the prenegotiated price of $49\frac{1}{4}$, the book would have precedence over the buyer of the 50,000 shares. Three thousand shares would have to be sold to fill the orders on the book, and the buyer would wind up with only 47,000 shares. In addition, the specialist may, if he wishes, step in and buy stock for his own account, again pre-empting the buyer. When situations like this arise, the trade, by agreement of both buyer and seller, is generally taken to a regional exchange to be crossed without interference.

There are, of course, many other techniques and devices used in block trading. Often specialists will make excellent bids for and offers of stock trading for their own account or making use of orders on their books. Secondary distributions are often used to market large blocks of stock on very short notice, particularly when retail absorption is required to handle the size involved. Exchange Distributions, Special Bids, and other special marketing methods have been developed by the New York Stock Exchange, and any member firm can supply you with a booklet explaining these methods. Such methods, however, usually involve payment of a higher than normal commission.

HANDLING A TYPICAL ORDER

Now that we have examined some of the background involved in institutional trading, let's invent a hypothetical case and see exactly how a typical order might be handled. To define our terms, let us suppose that we have been given an order to buy 50,000 shares of XYZ. The company is headquartered in Chicago. The stock is listed on the New York, Midwest, and Pacific Coast Stock Exchanges, has 7,000,000 shares outstanding, trades an average daily volume of 7,500 shares on the big board and 3,000 on the Pacific Coast and Midwest combined, with occasional flurries in volume from time to time on the Midwest. The specialist on the Big Board has a reputation for being fair and cooperative, but is not known for his heroics. Currently trading around 50, XYZ has been in a gradual decline along with the other stocks in the same industry group but shows good support at 45/46 where it becomes historically cheap on a P/E basis. Although XYZ was as high as 62 earlier in the year during a stronger market, it is now fairly quiet and usually trades within a one point daily range. XYZ is of "institutional quality" and attracted a lot of interest earlier in the year when it was in the high 50's. There are no Third Market dealers trading the issue. There have been no recent sizable selling inquiries shown to you.

With the stock in a gradual decline, there would be no reason to rush into the market. A more sensible approach would be to show the buying inquiry to either a nonmember "matchmaker" (in order to benefit from substantially cheaper, negotiated commissions) or to a member firm with a capable block trading operation having an ability to "find the other side." The inquiry should be shown on an "exclusive" basis for at least a day. There is little point in providing price support for the stock without first allowing some time to be spent in trying to find another institution or large holder who might be willing to sell the stock in size.

Toward the end of the first day, the broker to whom you have given the inquiry calls and says he has a seller of 10,000 to 20,000 shares on the line and thinks that the seller "might have more stock behind." Let's assume that the broker is a true "matchmaker" and not a member of any exchange, so that any trade consummated will be done for a negotiated commission. XYZ, which opened at 50, has dropped to a last sale of 49½ and has had an intraday low of 49.

While the broker holds the seller on the line, you bid 49 net (no commission) for 10,000 shares and tell the broker that you would *improve* your bid for more size. This bid is really a starting point for negotiations, and you must let the broker know that you are flexible as to price and would like to see a counter-offer. The bid is definitely low, but is within the trading range and close enough to show that you are "real" and want to do business. More importantly, the bid has been designed to induce the seller to show his full size.

When shown the bid (keep in mind that both buyer and seller are holding on separate telephone lines to the broker) the seller replies that he really has 27,000 shares for sale and counters by offering the 27,000 shares at 49½ net. You and the seller are now ½ point apart, but are only really starting to bargain. After a little more banter, with the broker acting as the negotiator between both sides, you both agree to split the difference and trade at 49¼. As buyer, you negotiate commission with the broker and agree to pay him an eighth of a point per share. The seller, for his part, does the same. As buyer, you now have 27,000 shares of XYZ at a price of 49¼ plus ⅛ or a net cost of 49⅜. With the normal commission of $43.63[2] per 100 shares at a price of 49¼, you would have had to buy the stock at a price of 48⅞ on an exchange to beat the price of 49⅜ net. In effect, you have bought the stock at a price lower than the low for the day by cutting the commission to less than one third of a normal commission.[3]

You now have a good foothold on your position, having filled over half your order at a good price. Remember, the stock was 50 when you got the order. It's time to go to work buying a little "on board." In choosing a broker to represent you on board, you decide on Glotz & Co. Glotz, while not spectacular on "finding the other side," has a good trading operation; is a member of the New York, Midwest, and Pacific Coast Stock Exchanges; and from prior experience you know that his floor partner on the New York has been able to work well with the specialist who "makes" XYZ.

When you call Glotz with the order, you make it clear that he does not have the order on an exclusive basis. You inform him that you have

---

[2] Under the volume discount plan now in effect, the commission would be $27.63 per 100 after the first 1,000 shares. The volume discount is most substantial on lower priced issues and gradually diminishes as the price of the issue increases. There is no discount on commissions for stocks selling at 90 or above, under normal circumstances.

[3] Less than one half the normal commissions when compared to the minimum commission of $27.63 applicable under the volume discount plan.

already taken down a good chunk of stock, that any large potential sellers have already been shown your buying interest (the matchmaker has performed this function), and that you wish him only to represent you on the floor. In addition, you tell him that you want him to be particularly careful to look for any sizable offerings on the Midwest Stock Exchange, as small blocks of 2,000 to 5,000 sometimes show up there before being taken to New York.

With 23,000 shares left to buy, you show Glotz the full size of your buying interest and give him an idea of the approach you want to take in buying stock. In this case, with the stock still showing signs of being soft, you tell Glotz that you do not want to be an aggressive buyer. Your approach is to scale in without lending excessive support to the stock. You do make a particular point to inform Glotz that you would like to see any offerings in size of XYZ that show up either in the book or on the floor during the normal course of trading.

During the next three trading days, you buy a total of 16,000 shares of XYZ on the Big Board, 11,000 of which was bought in small lots of from 200 to 600 shares at prices ranging from $48 \frac{3}{4}$ to $47 \frac{5}{8}$. Five thousand shares were bought in one piece at 48. The small block had showed up on the floor, and Glotz's floor partner immediately had their trading department inform you of the block, which you bought "on the line." Nothing, as yet, has appeared in any size on the regional exchanges.

However, with only 7,000 shares left to buy to complete the order, the stock is showing definite signs of firmness. It was quite noticeable during the third day that the stock seldom dipped below 48 and your low bid was hardly hit at all. Moreover, you had missed a lot of stock that traded in the $48 \frac{1}{4}$ area. All indications were that you had to be more aggressive to fill the order before the stock started to get away too fast.

Prior to the opening on the fourth day, you inform Glotz that you want to be more aggressive and are willing to pay up to $48 \frac{3}{8}$ for XYZ on the opening. The stock had closed the day before at $48 \frac{1}{8}$. XYZ opens at $48 \frac{3}{8}$ on 2,000 shares. A few minutes after the opening, Glotz comes back with a bit of ominous news: a report that you bought only 1,000 shares at $48 \frac{3}{8}$ and the information that there is another buyer on the floor who bought the other 1,000 and looks aggressive. You suggest that Glotz approach the floor trader representing the other buyer and offer to split sales with him and work together. With only 6,000 shares left to buy, you are willing to participate with the other buyer and split sales at a level of his choosing.

By the middle of that afternoon you have bought an additional 2,000 shares splitting sales with the other buyer, but the stock is now up to $49 \frac{1}{8}$. Suddenly Glotz comes in and shows you 3,500 shares for sale on the Midwest Stock Exchange at $49 \frac{3}{8}$. Although it is out of range for the day so far, you buy it immediately before the other buyer sees it. At the same time, you tell Glotz to buy the remaining 500 shares on board at the market whether the other buyer wants to go along or not. The 500 shares are purchased at 49½ completing the order.

This order, of course, was purely a hypothetical case. It had to be; it just went too smoothly and simply. It is intended merely as one example of how an institutional trader might approach and work such an order. I'm sure that many institutional traders who read this might disagree with the particular approach used and the oversimplification of the example. To them I can only offer my apologies in advance along with a sincere appreciation of the technique they might have used. Each trader has a different style and technique in handling his orders and each, in turn, has made a contribution to all of us. We learn from each other.

CONCLUSION

The struggle for investment performance among institutions becomes more difficult each year. In the constant search for improved performance, institutions have sought every possible competitive edge. An increasing number of institutions have found that an effective trading operation can give them that edge. Within a very short time, what is now a competitive edge will become an operational necessity. In the future an institution lacking a competent, professional trading ability will simply be unable to compete. The finest investment decision becomes moot if it cannot be translated from an idea into a position. Today's new breed of professional institutional traders are the men you will rely on to perform that function.

The purpose and intent of this article has been to acquaint portfolio managers, analysts, and other professional money managers who are not directly involved with trading with what an institutional trader does and what he can do for his institution. Space considerations have precluded the discussion of many technical points, and the subjects covered have been presented in only the briefest and most basic terms. The opinions and attitudes I have expressed are solely my own and are the reflection of my experience as an institutional trader. As such, they are entirely subjective and probably will be the object of debate, disagreement, and correction. The only defense I can offer is that traders are not generally known to be overly prolific writers and someone had to start somewhere. With that in mind, any traders, brokers, officials of the New York Stock Exchange, et. al. who may wish to disagree with my opinions may take some small measure of satisfaction from knowing that the object of their criticism is the only literary masochist of the institutional trading profession.

50
MATHEMATICAL ANALYSIS OF PORTFOLIO SELECTION: PRINCIPLES AND APPLICATION*

William J. Baumol

1. Purpose of the Markowitz Analysis

It should be made clear to begin with that no mathematical procedure and no computer routine offer any prospect of providing final and completely rational portfolio decisions. There is a rich body of information, much of it hardly tangible, which necessarily influences the recommendations of an investment counselor, but which the computer is not able to take into account. Knowledge about the personality of a retiring company president, or about the implications of current Defense Department discussions for the saleability of a company's products is surely important, but there is no way in which it can be taken into account automatically and mechanically in accord with predeveloped mathematical formulae.

Thus, mathematical analysis of portfolio selection, no matter how successful it may become, does not threaten the investment analyst with technological unemployment. Routinized patterns of portfolio selection can be simulated by computers. Clarkson[1] achieved a remarkable degree of success in getting a computer to predict the investment recommendations of an investment trust officer. He spent some time studying the investment officer's decisions and programmed into the computer the criteria used by the officer in choosing his portfolios and so ended up with a good description of the actual selection process which, given the requirements of the investor, often succeeded in picking the same companies as those selected by the investment manager and in recommending the same number of shares. Yet ultimately, portfolio decisions must remain an art, employing at its best a fine balance of experience, judgment, and intuition, all of which only a good analyst can supply. Nev-

---

* Reprinted by permission of the *Financial Analysts Journal* (September–October 1966).

[1] Clarkson, Geoffrey P. E., *Portfolio Selection: A Simulation of Trust Investment* (Prentice-Hall, Englewood Cliffs, New Jersey, 1962).

ertheless, a successful mathematical analysis can potentially offer him invaluable assistance. For, as will be shown next, the portfolio selection problem is like an iceberg in that only a small portion of its bulk is normally visible. Because of the sheer magnitude of the problem, the analyst must consciously or otherwise adopt questionable shortcuts in his decision-making process, shortcuts that mean he is unlikely to come up with a truly optimal portfolio. The role of mathematical analysis is to cut this problem down to size and to present the alternatives to the analyst in a way that really permits him to exercise his judgment most effectively.

The unseen complexity of the portfolio selection problem is a result of what the mathematician describes as its combinatorial character. Suppose the analyst is trying to select a portfolio of two securities out of three possible stocks, say Monsanto (M), General Motors (G), and Raytheon (R). Then, neglecting the proportion of shares to go into each portfolio, he has open to him the following three alternative portfolios: MG (Some Monsanto and some GM), MR, and GR. These are the three alternatives to be compared and weighed against one another.

Now suppose, instead, that he is trying to pick a portfolio of two stocks from among five candidate companies A, B, C, D, and E. The possible portfolios are now the following: AB, AC, AD, AE, BC, BD, BE, CD, CE, and DE. Thus, with the addition of two new candidate securities, the number of possible portfolios rises from 3 to 10! In general, the number of possibilities increases far more rapidly than the number of stocks to be considered and soon grows astronomical. It can be shown that if one is looking for a portfolio of 10 stocks out of 100 possible securities (a very modest number in practice), the number of alternative portfolios exceeds 17 billion!

No unaided human mind can hope to weigh all these alternatives and balance off their relative advantages and disadvantages. Even if one were to attempt to do so in the preceding illustrative case, and one were to work at it seven days a week, 12 hours a day, devoting no more than one second to each of the possible portfolios, some simple arithmetic shows that it would take over a million years for the analyst to arrive at his decision—by which time his information on the stocks might be somewhat obsolete.

Faced with comparisons of this order of complexity, how does one usually arrive at portfolio recommendations in practice? The answer is that the analyst employs conventional groupings, rules of thumb, and a variety of shortcuts. All of these imply that many of the 17 billion alternative portfolios are not even considered. Indeed, one can be quite sure that most of them are almost totally ignored in the decision process.

Thus, no matter how successful the portfolio selected by the analyst, one cannot help suspecting that some better possibilities (some of them perhaps vastly better) simply never entered into his deliberations. In effect then, the analyst can be presumed rarely, if ever, to pick the optimal portfolio. Even if he is a very good man, the best that one can expect of him in light of the huge number of possibilities is that he will come up with something that performs reasonably well.

Mathematical analysis and the computer do offer some prospect for something closer to optimal portfolio selection. This they can accomplish by culling out the bulk of the possibilities on the ground that they are clearly nonoptimal, in the sense that will be defined presently, and by providing to the analyst a systemized listing in terms of relative riskiness of the remaining possibilities among which he can then make his choice.

2. Nature of the Markowitz Approach

To see how the Markowitz procedure attacks this problem we will proceed on the basis of a highly oversimplified example, recognizing the extreme injustice this does to the sophistication and subtlety of his portfolio selection analysis.

Suppose for some given security, A, we have somehow obtained the following predictions: That it is most likely to provide a return of 7 percent on investment (its expected return) and that, in any event, its minimum yield is not likely to go below 4 percent (the return floor). Suppose some other stock, B, offers an expected return of 9 percent and a return floor of 2 percent.

Let us now consider the expected return and return floor for a portfolio, 50 percent of which is invested in A and 50 percent in B. The expected return will be the average of the anticipated returns on the two securities, i.e., it will be $1/2 \ (9 + 7) = 8$ percent. However, the return floor of the portfolio will usually be slightly higher than the 3 percent average of the two individual return floors. For, if the two stocks are in unrelated industries and if there is no drop in the stock market as a whole, it is extremely unlikely that if the one stock happens to hit its floor, the same will simultaneously occur to the other. Consider, for example, the case where one security is that of an automobile producer and the other that of a government contractor in a depressed area. During years of poor automotive sales when the securities of the auto manufacturer may be close to the return floor, the earnings of the government contractor are likely to be relatively high. Thus, we may suppose that the floor of our portfolio is not the average of the 4 and 2 percent floors for our individual stocks, but is a somewhat higher figure, say 3½ percent.

We may represent the relevant data for our portfolio, on the following graph (Figure 1). Here we see that point P_1 corresponds to an expected earnings level of 8 percent, and a floor of 3½ percent, and so P_1 can be taken to represent our portfolio made up half and half of stocks A and B. Similarly, dots P_2 and P_3 represent two other possible portfolios.

We should note the relationships of these points to one another. First compare P_1 and P_2. We see that the latter is the safer portfolio (its return floor is 5 percent) but its expected return (6 percent) is relatively low. Hence, P_1 would tend to be preferred by an investor with some willing-

FIGURE 1

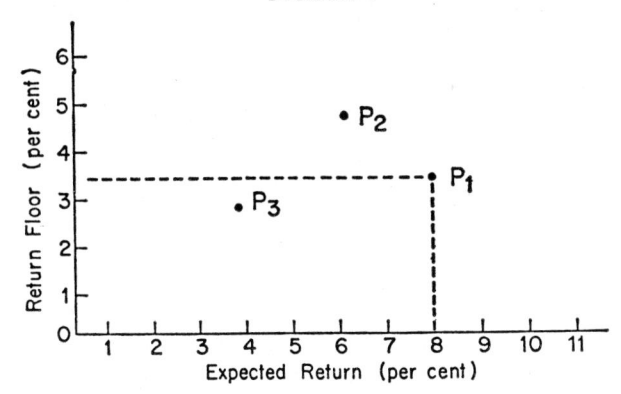

ness to gamble but would appeal only to a more conservative investor. Thus, we see that: If one portfolio point lies above and to the left of another, it will represent the more conservative investment.

Now let us compare P_2 and P_3. A moment's reflection will show that if both of these are available, no rational investor will ever select P_3 because it involves both a lower expected return and a greater risk (a lower floor) than does P_2. We say that: A portfolio is "inefficient" (it is certainly not optimal) if some other portfolio point lies above it and to its right.

In Figure 2, a large number of portfolio points are indicated. Suppose these are all the possible portfolios. The light dots, such as point L, are all inefficient portfolios while the heavy dots, such as D, are the so-called efficient portfolios. That is, there are no dots lying above and to the right of an efficient portfolio point, such as D, so that it is impossible to go from D to another portfolio which offers a higher return with no increase in risk.

One concludes that once the possible portfolios have been arrayed in this fashion one can with a clear conscience rule out the bulk of the possibilities—those corresponding to the light inner dots, such as L. This is already a major piece of progress.

FIGURE 2

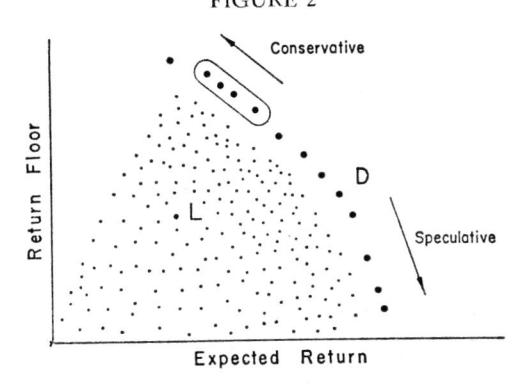

However, such an array of portfolio points accomplishes still more. It will be observed that even after the inefficient portfolios have been ruled out, one is still left with a substantial number of possibilities—there are quite a few heavy dots. How can one hope to choose among them? The answer is not as difficult as it may seem. For, as we have seen, the efficient portfolios are arrayed from left to right in order of their degree of conservatism. The most speculative portfolios are represented by the heavy dots toward the right, while the safest investments are those toward the left.

Thus, suppose the analyst wishes to select a fairly conservative portfolio but one that is not the ultimate in conservatism. He might then consider only the four alternative portfolios represented by the heavy dots in the circle and he can exercise his full judgment in selecting among them. In practice he would probably want to examine a wider range of possibilities, but that would not alter the relevant principle.

What the Markowitz procedure does then, in effect, is to produce with the computer just such an array of dots as is shown in our figure. Its potential utility for portfolio selection in practice should now be quite clear.

3. Computational Procedure and Data Requirements

To obtain this result the Markowitz procedure utilizes a nonlinear programming calculation. Because of its mathematical properties, a *linear* programming calculation is not used since it is unable to take risk fully into account. It would have a tendency to select portfolios consisting of a small number of securities because it does not take cognizance of the risk of putting all of one's eggs into one basket.

On the basis of information that will be described presently, a nonlinear programming determines for each level of expected earnings that portfolio which offers the lowest attainable level of risk (the highest return floor). Any such portfolio clearly must be efficient (it must be among those represented by a heavy dot in our diagram). By considering all possible expected earnings levels and finding the least risky portfolio corresponding to each of these, one finds the full set of efficient portfolios (all the heavy dots). A programming calculation is used for the purpose because, by definition, linear or nonlinear programming is the mathematical method for finding the minimal value of some variable (the risk) when the alternative possibilities are limited by some sort of resource restriction (the amount of money available for investment in the portfolio). Without going into very great technical detail, it is not possible to say much more than this about the workings of the method. (See Markowitz[2] and [3]).

---

[2] Markowitz, Harry, "Portfolio Selection," *The Journal of Finance*, Vol. VII (March 1952).

[3] Markowitz, Harry, *Portfolio Selection, Efficient Diversification of Investments* (John Wiley and Sons, New York, 1959).

Let us see next what information this approach requires to produce its answer. For each security to be considered, two numbers must be provided: its expected (average) return (consisting of dividends and capital gains), and the *variance* of its return. The variance is a statistical measure of the volatility of the returns to that security—it indicates whether these returns are fairly dependable or are likely to vary widely. Thus, the variance is an indicator of riskiness—a security whose earnings and stock price exhibit a low variance is relatively safe, all other things being equal.

More specifically, the variance of a set of numbers is defined as the average squared deviation from the arithmetic average of these numbers. Thus, for example, consider the numbers 10 and 20. The average of the two numbers is 15. Hence, the 10 deviates from the average by -5, and the 20 deviates from this average by $+5$. If we tried to average these two decisions they would simply cancel out (-5 and $+5 = 0$). However, the squares of these deviations are $+25$ and $+25$, which do not cancel out when averaged. This average squared deviation ($+25$) is the variance of our two numbers 10 and 20. Notice that if our two numbers had been closer together their variance would have been smaller. For example, the numbers 13 and 17 also have an average value of 15, but their variance (the average of $(+2)^2$ and $(-2)^2$) is only 4. Hence, the more widely scattered a set of numbers (such as company earnings statistics), the larger is their variance.

In addition to the expected earnings and variance for each security, the Markowitz analysis requires yet another datum for each *pair* of securities. Given any two securities under consideration, it is necessary to have a figure giving their *covariance*. The covariance is a number that measures the degree of parallelism in the movement of the values of any two variables. If when one goes down or up and the other moves correspondingly their covariance will be high, while if the two variables bear a nearly random relationship to one another their covariance will be low. For example, statistics on the number of penguins born in different years of the 18th century (if they were available) and number of theater tickets sold annually in London during the same period would probably have a low covariance, while the covariance of the level of per capita income with educational attainment levels in various counties of the United States is presumably higher—high income areas generally contain a large proportion of well-educated persons. Similarly, steel and automotive stock prices are likely to exhibit a high covariance, while that between automobiles and residential electric utilities is likely to be much lower.

The covariance measure is important in determining the true value of the diversification present in a portfolio. Two stocks do not contribute much more safety than one if their covariance is very high for, whenever one of them dips, the chances are that the other will also decline and so the loss on one will not be offset by independent behavior of the price of the other.

These three sets of data, the expected return and the variance of each security and the covariance of each pair of securities, constitute all the information required by the Markowitz analysis. From these it is a straightforward matter to set under way the nonlinear programming calculation that eliminates all inefficient portfolio possibilities and which ranks all the remaining alternatives, the efficient portfolios, in the order of their riskiness and prospective returns.

4. Implementation Problems

Why then has such an apparently simple and helpful analysis not been very widely utilized? The idea is undeniably attractive, and the imperfections of purely intuitive portfolio selection seem beyond question. Yet there are two serious problems: the cost of the Markowitz calculations and the difficulty of supplying the requisite data.

The computational problem is by no means critical, but it is not negligible either. The cost of a simplified portfolio calculation involving 1500 securities has been estimated to lie between $150 and $350 for a single run in computer time alone, and it has been suggested that a single run of the complete Markowitz calculations might come to as much as 50 times these orders of magnitude.[4] This is not as much as it may seem, for a single portfolio calculation can suffice to assist in the selection of portfolios for as many investors as one wishes. Thus, even though one may desire to undertake frequent updating calculations, the cost per portfolio can be quite low in terms of the magnitude involved, if it is undertaken by a company handling a large number of accounts or by an investor with a very large amount of money at his disposal. But it is clear that this sort of calculation is not an attractive proposition for the small investor who manages his own funds.

The second difficulty, the data problem, is far more serious—it is the basic difficulty inhibiting wider utilization of the analyses. First of all, the sheer volume of statistics involved is considerable. The number of expected earnings and variance figures will, of course, vary proportionately with the number of securities considered. These are two numbers for each security. But the number of covariances grows disproportionately with the number of securities. Three securities A, B, and C can be divided into three pairs, AB, AC, and BC so that three covariance figures will be involved. However, with four securities, A, B, C, and D, there will be six covariances corresponding to the six security pairs AB, AC, AD, BC, BD, and CD. In an analysis of 1000 securities, 499,500 covariance figures have to be gathered, and if 2000 securities are to be analyzed nearly two million covariance figures are called for! Clearly this is likely to constitute a formidable job of data gathering.

---

[4] Sharpe, William F., "A Simplified Model for Portfolio Analysis," *Management Science*, Vol. 9 (January 1963), pp. 277 and 290.

But the problem is apt to be more serious yet. Most of the requisite figures cannot be gathered by straightforward statistical calculation because what the method requires is not past figures on previous earnings and their variances and covariances, but good *forecasts* of their likely future values. Anyone experienced in the behavior of securities knows how dangerous it is to attempt to predict the future price and yield of a stock by sheer extrapolation of its past performance. There just is not much regularity in the behavior of these variables for any individual security. As a matter of fact, in the past few years, a series of highly sophisticated statistical calculations have suggested strongly that the behavior of a statistical series of the prices of an individual stock is indistinguishable from what the statistician calls a "random walk."[5] This means that while a knowledge of the company and general know-how about the ways of the stock market may permit successful prediction of the future value of a stock, sheer statistical analysis of its past prices can give no better information about prospective changes in its price than would a purely random device such as the rolling of a set of dice! Thus, there is at least at present no purely objective and statistical method for supplying all the figures needed by the Markowitz calculation.

At present, therefore, many of the figures which are collected for the portfolio computation are purely impressionistic numbers supplied by security analysts on the basis of their judgments. This clearly is not a fully satisfactory state of affairs, for it predicates a complex and sophisticated calculation on a set of admittedly impressionistic and necessarily inaccurate figures.

Yet the situation is not quite as bad as it might appear at first glance. There is some reason to suspect that while expected return figures cannot be supplied statistically, relatively acceptable variance and covariance figures can be derived by statistical means. For while a stock which brought in 7 percent on its price last year may well do far better or far worse this year, it is quite plausible that, except where the nature of the company has changed, the degree of volatility of a security's price in the past is a rather reliable indicator of its prospective volatility. A stock whose price has not varied much from its trend (relative to the market average) in the past may plausibly be expected to be comparatively stable in the future. AT&T is likely to be far more stable in the future than, say, Raytheon. Similarly, covariances are also likely to prove rather stable. Thus, while the analysts themselves will probably have to continue to supply some of the statistics needed for a mathematical portfolio analysis they may only have to provide a relatively small proportion of this information.

In any event, a computation based on analyst estimates is far from

---

[5] Cootner, Paul H., *The Random Character of Stock Market Prices* (Massachusetts Institute of Technology Press, Cambridge, Massachusetts, 1964).

useless. It can be extremely helpful for the analyst to be able to use this means to determine the full implications of his views about the values of individual stocks—to be shown just what these views indicate about the relative merits of the vast number of possible portfolio combinations. Experience shows that without such a calculation, the decision-maker may well end up with choices not fully consistent with the implications of his own judgments. For even if the individual data were all known, the portfolio selection calculation in which they are utilized is hardly simply and intuitively obvious.

Part Five

Ethical Considerations

51

RESEARCH REPORT ETHICS*

Louis J. Zitnik, C.F.A.

The public image of the securities analyst is influenced to a greater extent by the research reports of broker-dealer firms than by all other means of communications. While it is obviously impossible to list precise topics that should be included in a research report and their precise method of treatment, it seems desirable to discuss general areas where guidelines can be established in order to improve the calibre of the reports.

THE CRITICS

Among the critics of the average quality of research reports are the Securities and Exchange Commission and Graham, Dodd and Cottle.[1] The Report of Special Study of the Securities Markets of the Securities and Exchange Commission[2] states:

> The preparation and dissemination of printed advisory matter has become an ordinary part of conducting a successful retail securities business today and plays an important part in sales promotion. The most common forms taken by broker-dealer published material are the market letter, sent daily or weekly; the research report, devoted to recommending a specific company or group of companies and sent regularly or occasionally; a monthly report and special securities reports, often in finished magazine form. Some of this material contains detailed and extensive evaluations of the merits, risks, and prospects of the securities considered. Far more of it does not purport to make any detailed analysis to support the recommendations. It generally classifies the securities in terms of investment goals, but omits any consideration of adverse data or uncertainties. Overwhelmingly the recommendations are to purchase; recommendations to sell securities are few, and for the most part deliberately avoided, even with respect to securities previously recommended whose prospects may have changed. The core of the recommendation is generally a projection, which often is in the form of an estimate of future earnings but which sometimes involves an outright prediction of a future market price well in excess of the present market. Ordinarily, little information is given concerning the ex-

---

* Reprinted by permission of the *Financial Analysis Journal* (January–February 1966).

[1] Graham, Dodd and Cottle, *Security Analysis*, 4th Ed. (McGraw-Hill Book Company, Inc., 1962), pp. 106–7.

[2] Report of Special Study of Securities Markets of the Securities and Exchange Commission, Part 5, (U.S. Government Printing Office, 1963), pp. 56–60.

tent or method of research and about the person responsible for the recommendation. Moreover, usually there is no indication of any interest in or intentions as to the securities recommended on the part of the distributing broker-dealer firm, since few disclosures of these facts go further than an unrevealing boilerplate hedge clause.

By its very nature, the market letter is primarily confined to capsule comments and summaries on particular industries and companies. Such letters should contain the statement that additional information is available upon request. The discussion herein will be confined to the research report prepared for the average investor. The so-called institutional report is designed for a sophisticated analyst or investor who should be entirely competent to appraise incompleteness or shoddy work.

PRESENT REGULATION

The New York Stock Exchange,[3] the National Association of Securities Dealers, Inc.,[4] and the State of California, Division of Corporations[5] have established rules concerning research reports and other advertising for those firms coming under their respective jurisdictions. Such rules are usually quite general, but basic in nature, and are recommended reading for all students of this topic.

Rules of the regulatory bodies prohibit statements which are "promissory, exaggerated, flamboyant, or contain unwarranted superlatives." They are particularly thorough in covering the matter of disclosures of special interests of a broker-dealer regarding such matters as trading markets, securities held (including options), and participation in recent underwritings of the subject company's securities. The regulatory authorities cited all require that the date of issuance of the research report be clearly stated, as well as the market price on the release date. Yet some firms presently do not include the date (or if so, in code) in order that the report may be used for a longer length of time. This is obviously a flagrant violation.

There are other areas that are not covered by specific rules where the policy of reasonable prudence requires proper treatment. The quality of an issue should be clearly stated in terms which the layman will understand. Admittedly, research reports are used for sales purposes, but it would be as wrong to leave the impression that Communication Satellite common stock has the stability of American Telephone & Telegraph common as it would be to represent by indirection that a Volkswagen was comparable to a Cadillac.

There are three separate and distinct meanings for the word invest-

---

[3] *New York Stock Exchange Guide*, Vol. 2 (Commerce Clearing House, Inc., Nov. 1964), pp. 4025–4031.

[4] National Association of Securities Dealers, Inc., Manual, 1965. Advertising Interpretations, G-19–G-22.

[5] State of California, California Administrative Code, Title 10, Investment, Article 24, Advertising 92.10–94.1, Published by Office of Administrative Procedure, Department of Finance, State of California.

ment: (1) investment meaning purchase, (2) investment meaning securities or equities, and (3) investment meaning high quality as opposed to speculation. It is suggested that the first two meanings be avoided in research reports in order that there can be no misinterpretation by the reader.

SINS OF OMISSION

Perhaps the greatest abuses in research reports occur in failure to discuss adequately the negatives in a situation (the sins of omission). It is all too easy to gloss over a marginal trade position and the financial size and resources of competitors in fields with changing technologies. The cyclical nature of an industry should be explained. The thinness of trading markets for certain securities and their volatile nature should be fully discussed, where appropriate.

EARNINGS

The summary of the profit and loss statement for a number of years is regarded as standard in virtually all research reports. A 10-year summary would seem to be desirable, since any recent 10-year period will cover at least two recessions. The latest five-year period—1960–1964—has an optimistic bias, since 1960 was a recessionary period and each subsequent year was one of prosperity. However, it cannot be denied that the SEC requires only five years' results (plus interim periods) in a prospectus which can probably be considered as meeting the minimum requirement for a research report. Obviously, nonrecurring gains should be excluded from the earnings tabulation (though they can be covered by footnotes) and any marked changes in a corporation's tax rate from year to year should be explained.

The proper use of the term "cash flow" has been fully delineated by a committee of the Financial Analyst Federation, and its report has been reproduced in the *Financial Analysts Journal*. The use of the term "cash earnings" in place of "cash flow" is highly misleading to the average investor, and in the writer's opinion should never be used in a research report.

Compound growth rates or absolute rates of increase can also be quite misleading, depending upon the period chosen. It is not easy to suggest a precise formula to use in this regard but common sense should be the rule. A small growth company, for example, could have an average 40 percent compound growth rate for a five-year period because of the small base used, whereas the growth in the last year or two could be 10 percent or less. Using a depressed base for a cyclical company also gives a highly erroneous impression.

BALANCE SHEET

Balance sheet statements should be included in a research report, at least in abbreviated form or in text. The summary of current assets and current liabilities is usually sufficient for a well-established company, but a low cash and account receivable position should be mentioned, if appropriate. The long-term debt and preferred should be enumerated. All potential dilution to the common stock from convertibles, warrants, and options should be clearly indicated. Employee stock options should be commented upon if the quantity is material. It is worth noting that several securities firms are adjusting current year earnings per share estimates for potential dilution rather than merely stating that conversion of senior securities and/or exercise of warrants would result in a dilution of "x" percent.

PROJECTIONS

The use of earnings projections could be the topic of a separate paper as there seems to be a wide divergence of opinion on the matter. It is interesting to observe that the rule of the California commissioner of corporations states: "Estimated earnings, dividends, and profits will ordinarily not be allowed unless based upon a past earnings record and are for a reasonable period in the future. Such estimates must be supported by data filed with the commissioner upon which the reasonableness of the estimate may be determined."

A limited but increasing number of corporate executives are forecasting earnings for their respective companies for as much as one to five years into the future, while others are publicly stating their earnings goals. When such statements are available, the analyst should reveal the source in order to give authority to the report as well as proper credit to the spokesman. On the other hand, the analyst has a responsibility to evaluate independently the prospects for attaining such performances and should avoid inclusion of unrealistic goals in his report regardless of the source.

While a five- or even a ten-year earnings forecast for utility common stock might come close to eventual results, the margin of error in forecasting earnings more than a year ahead for companies with rapid past growth is so great that the use of such projections is to be questioned without considerable qualifications. Many of the enthusiastic growth stock analysts are indeed continuing to be embarrassed by many of their projections of 1961.

COMPARISONS

Comparison of one company with another in the same field is another area of potential abuse unless the differences between the two companies and their equity issues are fully described. On this point, the California commissioner of corporations has ruled that "comparisons with alleged analogous situations and the use of statistics of successful companies ordinarily will be disapproved unless the comparison is supported by a record of operating history sufficient to justify the comparison."

A PROBLEM?

Many research reports are short in nature, being purposely so tailored for the busy individual who wants the salient points without involved details. Nevertheless, this "busy individual" deserves and requires the minimum coverage of the facts, both positive and negative, in the general manner discussed above. This minimum basic information can be covered in two standard size pages which should be short enough for even the busiest individual who will take savings and purchase a security on the basis of the information.

It does not seem practical to include a biography of the report writer (even a short one), though his name should be listed at the conclusion of the study followed by the designation C.F.A., if appropriate. If the writer is truly an industry specialist (closely following one or two groups rather than twenty), this could also be stated.

The regulatory agencies have been diligent in pointing out that many organizations have consistently maintained high standards in research reports. Undoubtedly, there are many research department executives who have devoted considerable time and effort to upgrading the printed output of their respective organizations from an ethical standpoint. It would seem desirable to obtain the benefit of the conclusions of such experts on this matter in general and on specific areas where improvements can be achieved.

52

THE LAW OF CORPORATE INFORMATION*

Alan R. Bromberg

Law is just coming to recognize what analysts have known for a long time: that information is valuable. This article traces briefly the law's evolution, considers in considerable detail the present status, and projects some possible future developments. The emphasis is on the position of the analyst, although many specific points concerning him are treated more thoroughly in Corporate Disclosure and Insider Information, a transcript of the panel interview with Philip A. Loomis, Jr., SEC General Counsel, at the Oct. 7, 1968 meeting of the Financial Analysts Federation.

1. HISTORY

1.1 Misrepresentation. Falsification of information—misrepresentation—has for centuries been a legal wrong. The victim of the misrepresentation could sue for damages, if he proved that he was injured. But he usually had to show that the misrepresentation was intentionally made and that he relied on it. This was often so difficult that the victim failed to get any relief.

Particularly after the 1929 crash revealed the extent of overenthusiastic salesmanship in the securities industry, many legislatures passed laws making it easier for the victim of misrepresentation to recover his losses. The most important of thse provisions were Section 11 of the Securities Act of 1933 (under which *BarChris*[1] was decided) and Section 12(2). Other parts of the same act made misrepresentation in the sale of securities a criminal offense.

1.2 Nondisclosure. Nondisclosure of information, in contrast to falsification, was generally not a violation before this kind of legislation. The contrary result was reached in a few cases where an insider dealt face to face with a security holder, for example, buying shares from him without disclosing very favorable information about the company. But this principle of "fiduciary duty" did not apply to open market trades, on a stock exchange or over the counter.

---

* Reprinted by permission of the *Financial Analysts Journal* (March–April 1969).
[1] Escott v. BarChris Construction Corp., 283 F. Supp. 643 (S.D. N.Y. 1968).

Some older cases recognized that misrepresentation and nondisclosure might lie very close together. Thus, a statement that the company's earnings averaged $1 a share for the last three years might be true. But failing to say that they declined from $1.50 to $1 to 50 cents would give a highly misleading impression of the investment character of the company's securities. The 1933 Act, and some state laws, codified this principle, treating alike a misrepresentation and an omission of "a material fact necessary in order to make the statements [made], in the light of the circumstances under which they were made, not misleading."

But there was nothing here that applied when no statement at all was made, i.e., to complete nondisclosure. Coverage of this has evolved by court and SEC decisions interpreting SEC Rule 10b–5 which prohibits, in very broad terms, "any act, practice, or course of business which operates or would operate as a fraud or deceit upon any person." The first of the interpretations was a little noticed investigative report by the SEC in 1943 concluding that 10b–5 was violated when insiders bought shares of Ward LaFrance Truck Corp. with knowledge of an undisclosed 6-fold increase in earnings.[2] In 1961 the SEC found Cady, Roberts & Co. guilty of a violation by selling shares of Curtiss–Wright with knowledge of a 40 percent reduction in the dividend which had not yet been publicly announced.[3] The most recent of these decisions was by the U.S. Court of Appeals for the Second Circuit, with jurisdiction over New York and other Eastern states, in August 1968, in a civil suit by the SEC against Texas Gulf Sulphur Co. and several of its executives, directors, and employees.[4]

2. SOME ISSUES DECIDED IN TEXAS GULF SULPHUR

2.1 Violation by Trading with Material Inside Information. The Texas Gulf Sulphur decision confirmed judicially the Cady, Roberts rule that trading with material inside (undisclosed) information violates 10b–5. The information was preliminary data on what turned out to be the tremendous Kidd Creek mine. Moreover, the court adopted the SEC's test that the obligation to disclose (or refrain from trading) rests on anyone in a relationship giving access, directly or indirectly, to information intended to be available only for a corporate purpose and not for the personal benefit of anyone.

2.2 Violation by Tipping Material Inside Information. The TG decision made new law by holding that tipping—the selective transmission of material inside information—is a violation of 10b–5. An injunction against Glen Alden Corp. at almost the same time established the same proposi-

---

[2] Ward LaFrance Truck Corp., 13 S.E.C. 373 (1943), reprinted in A. Bromberg, Securities Law: Fraud 305 (1968).

[3] Cady, Roberts & Co., 40 S. E. C. 907 (1961), reprinted in Bromberg at 315.

[4] SEC v. Texas Gulf Sulphur Co., 401 F. 2d 833, CCH Federal Securities Law Reports par. 92,251 (2d Cir. Aug. 13, 1968).

tion, but was entered by consent and was not contested.[5] (Glen Alden had a long-pending registration statement at the SEC and was probably in no position to fight the injunction.) The principle has been extended to tippers who are not officers, directors, or employees of the company to which the information relates. The SEC (pursuant to an offer of compromise) has held that Merrill Lynch and some of its employees violated 10b–5 by passing on to selected customers the information it had received from Douglas Aircraft (as prospective underwriter for Douglas) that Douglas earnings were taking a nosedive.[5.1]

2.3 Violation by Negligent Press Release. The Texas Gulf decision opened the possibility that a company may violate 10b–5 by issuing a negligent press release. The case was returned to the lower court to determine whether the release was negligent. The release in question was the one TG published to scotch the rumors which were circulating about its discovery. It said that more work was needed to evaluate the mineral prospect, and that the rumors were exaggerated. Four days later the company announced a major discovery. The legal issue here is whether this was a kind of misrepresentation, i.e., whether it was in fact misleading to a reasonable investor.

2.4 Information Equalization Policy. The court in TG stated that the overriding policy of 10b–5 (and of the Securities Exchange Act of 1934 under which it was promulgated) is one of the relatively equal access of investors to material information and to rewards of securities transactions.

TG and the individual defendants are seeking an appeal to the Supreme Court. If it is granted, new rules may be laid down. While this kind of forecasting is extremely hazardous, I would expect the Supreme Court to write much the same kind of opinion that the 2d Circuit has. In any event, the 2d Circuit's decision is law unless or until it is changed.

3. SOME ISSUES NOT DECIDED IN TEXAS GULF SULPHUR

Many questions are raised by the 2d Circuit decision, but not answered. Two are especially significant.

3.1 Violation by Tippee. The court did not decide whether a tippee violates by trading with material inside information. No tippees were named as defendants in the suit, so there was no need for the court to rule on this point. However, the court took occasion to note that trading by tippees "could be equally reprehensible." This expression reinforces the SEC's holding that Cady, Roberts (a tippee) violated by its trading. And there is a 1967 federal district court decision[6] holding persons liable in damages for their purchases in a closely held company on several alternative grounds, e.g., that they were insiders or tippees. Thus, it is amply

---

[5] SEC v. Glen Alden Corp., CCH Federal Securities Law Reports par. 92,280 (S.D. N.Y. Aug. 8, 1968).

[5.1] Merrill Lynch, Pierce, Fenner & Smith, Inc., Securities Exchange Act Release No. 8459, CCH Federal Securities Law Reports par. 77,629 (Nov. 25, 1968).

[6] Ross v. Licht, 263 F. Supp. 395 (S.D. N.Y. 1967).

clear that a tippee is at least a quasi-insider, and his trading can be a violation, but we do not yet know under just what circumstances it will be. Some of these may be developed in the SEC administrative proceeding against Merrill Lynch and various mutual funds and hedge funds, which allegedly sold large quanities of Douglas Aircraft on hearing from Merrill Lynch of a sharp drop in Douglas earnings, which Merrill Lynch had learned as underwriter for a pending Douglas issue.[7] Without going into detail, my belief is that the factors controlling tippee violation should include:

(1) Specificity of the information; the less specific it is, the less chance there should be of violation.

(2) Knowledge that the information comes from a company source; without this, there should be no violation.

(3) Degree of diffusion of information; the tippee should be entitled to regard the information as public (and to use it) if it is fairly common knowledge in the market.

(4) The probability that the information is true or that the event (such as a merger or tender offer) will occur; the lower the probability, the less likely a violation.[8]

3.2 Monetary Liability for Trading or Tipping. There is a distinction between violation (which may lead to injunction, license revocation, etc.) and liability (to pay money damages). The liability issue has not yet been reached in the TG case; the parties agreed that this phase should be postponed until the violation questions were decided. Many private damage suits are pending against TG and its insiders.

Normally, a violation results in liability if someone was injured by the violation. Logically, this would be the seller to (or buyer from) the insider. Such a causal connection may be very difficult to establish in open market trading where purchasers and sellers cannot be easily paired and where the outsiders were willing buyers or sellers at the prevailing price. Indeed, if the information is favorable and the insider is buying, it is arguable that the outsider-seller gets a better price because of the demand from the insider-buyer. (Conversely, if the information is unfavorable and the insider is selling.) But these arguments lose their strength if you look at the price which would prevail if the inside information were public; the outsider would not be willing to trade at the former price, and would have been injured if he had.

Even apart from causation of loss, it is quite possible that an insider trading with material information will be held liable to his company on the theory that he has used his corporate position or information for personal gain. A New York court has ruled, under state law, that the

---

[7] SEC Order for Public Proceedings, CCH Federal Securities Law Reports par. 77,596 (Aug. 26, 1968). The case against Merrill Lynch and its employees was settled; see above at n. 5.1. The proceeding continues against the other parties.

[8] For a fuller discussion, See Bromberg, Corporate Information: Texas Gulf Sulphur and Its Implication, 22 Southwestern Law Journal —— (No. 5; Dec. 1968).

corporation may recover in this situation without showing damage to itself.[9]

An even more complex question is whether the tipper can be held liable for the trades of the tippee, on some such theory as conspiracy or aiding and abetting. The 2d Circuit in TG laid the predicate for this by saying of one tipper that his "violations encompass not only his own purchases but also the purchases by his son-in-law [the tippee, who happened to be a broker] and the customers of his son-in-law, to whom the material information was passed."

3.3 Criminal Liability for Trading or Tipping. TG was a civil case. Criminal penalties ($10,000 or two years) are specified in the 1934 Act for willful violation of the act and rules (like 10b–5) issued under it. Past criminal prosecutions under 10b–5 have been sparse and limited to aggravated behavior. It seems unlikely that indictments will be brought in the future against insiders who trade or tip. But once these acts are clearly established as violations, the possibility exists, and should serve as a strong deterrent.

4. SOME ISSUES LEFT IN DOUBT BY TEXAS GULF SULPHUR

4.1 Materiality. (See 7 below.)

4.2 When Is Information Disclosed or Public? Since nondisclosure is at the center of violation by use of inside information, it is crucial to know when and how information becomes disclosed. The 2d Circuit gave only a partial answer in TG: A press release is only the first step in the dissemination, which is not complete before the information appears on the broad tape. Whether further time for absorption is necessary, the court did not say, although it suggested that the SEC might promulgate a rule on this. The SEC has been reported to be considering a rule that would consider the disclosure complete, for purposes of insider trading, when the information appears in morning newspapers. Meanwhile the N.Y. Stock Exchange thinks a trading halt of 15 minutes, after appearance of important news on the tape, accomplishes adequate disclosure for the public to trade. But it counsels insiders to wait until the news appears in "the press," typically the afternoon papers.

One thing is clear from TG. When the insider places his order is the critical time, not when it is executed. Thus, he must wait for disclosure to occur—whenever that is—before he calls his broker. An order to buy as soon as something comes out on the tape would be a violation.

5. EFFECT ON THE FLOW OF INFORMATION

5.1 Time of Release. A company need not release information at any particular time, even if it is material. The TG decision confirmed that the

---

[9] Diamond v. Oreamuno, 29 A.D. 2d 285, 287 N.Y.S. 2d 300 (1968), appeal pending.

information may be withheld for business reasons. But the decision did increase the pressure to release news at an early date; otherwise it may leak or be used by insiders, leading to embarrassment as well as violations. The N.Y. Stock Exchange has strengthened its recommendations for early disclosure. At the same time, the TG decision created contrary pressures against early release of information by its holding that the first TG press release may have violated 10b–5 because of negligent preparation or interpretation of events. The corporate world feels that it is being pulled in opposite directions. Companies have reacted differently, some clamming up entirely, others pouring forth trivia.[10] The analysts have played a constructive role in trying to keep the communication channels open.[11]

5.2 Method of Release. The TG decision establishes two points in this area. First, when material information is released, it must be released widely, i.e., to the public. Selective disclosure is dangerous if not illegal. Second, the information must be full and factual, with such careful conclusions as may be warranted. The court has set a "due diligence" standard for the preparation of releases.

Companies cannot properly give material information to analysts on a selective or confidential basis (except, of course, for a company purpose, as where the analyst is employed by the company to help fashion a merger proposal). This will be true even if any serious inquirer could get the same information.

Material information can be given to meetings of analysts (or to individual analysts) if, and only if, it is simultaneously released to the public. A speech to an analysts society is not itself public dissemination, although the presence of the press and wire services may lead to the necessary publication. There is nothing to prevent analysts from asking questions about the information that is publicized.

On the other hand, nonmaterial information can be disclosed and discussed freely by company officials. The difficulty—and it's a crucial one discussed below—is in knowing what is material and what is not.

5.3 Kinds of Information. When the tensions are resolved, I think it will be in favor of earlier release of information in greater detail. Smaller companies will probably be less close-mouthed than they have been. Larger companies will be even more effusive. It will be harder to sift the significant from the insignificant. There will be more preliminary information which will be modified by later developments. Some apparently promising mineral prospects which would have been kept quiet, will be

---

[10] For surveys, see *Wall Street Journal,* Oct. 9, 1968, p. 1, col. 6; *N.Y. Times,* Nov. 10, 1968, sec. 3, p. 5, col. 1.

[11] See, e.g., Financial Analysts Federation, Public Statement Concerning Corporate Disclosure and Insider Information (Sept. 1968); George S. Bissell, Statement on Corporate Disclosure and Insider Information (Sept. 19, 1968); *N.Y. Times,* Sept. 20, 1968, p. 67, col. 2.

publicized and later turn out to be unattractive or worthless. So will some new products. We are already seeing acquisition negotiations being announced at a furious rate, many of them falling through when the parties really get down to bargaining.[12] Premature announcement may help kill the deal.[13] Early publication will probably be a boon for the analyst, with his superior capacity to evaluate not only the value of the transaction but the probability of its consummation. The ordinary investor, less sophisticated, may be in for a harder time; for example, buying on a rise following the announcement and being caught in a fall when the cancellation is publicized.

5.4 Problems of Forecasts. Companies will probably be more reticent than before in one area: forecasts, particularly of earnings. The Texas Gulf Sulphur decision (although it deals only with other kinds of information) is probably precedent for saying that forecasts—because reasonable investors rely on them—may have sufficient "connection" with securities transactions to be within the scope of 10b–5. Moreover, the case intimates that, unless prepared with "due diligence," the forecasts may be violations. This poses not only the threat of SEC injunction actions but the possibility of damage suits by hordes of investors who claim that they were misled if the forecasts turn out to be either too high or too low. In this legal situation, most companies would be rash to predict earnings more than a few months ahead. By contrast, projections of sales or capital expenditures—which are subject to fewer variables than earnings and which have a less direct impact on investor judgment—are safer and will probably continue to be made for periods up to several years.

6. THE LEGAL POSITION OF THE ANALYST

How do these various legal principles apply to analysts? The answers must come mainly by analogy, since the decided cases have said little about analysts. (In the Merrill Lynch proceeding, the heaviest penalty—censure and 60 days suspension without pay—for an individual employee of the firm was imposed on an industry specialist in the research division, but the SEC's opinion does not indicate exactly what his misconduct was.) The tentative answers depend in part on the particular analyst's role.

6.1 As Adviser to the Company. If the analyst is engaged by a company, say to evaluate an acquisition offer by or for the company, the information he receives in that capacity is inside information except insofar as the information has been released to the public. If the information is material and he uses it for his personal trading, he violates 10b–5 and may be liable for damages. If he passes on the information to other clients, employers, or friends, they are tippees and potential violators; he

---

[12] See, e.g., *Wall Street Journal*, Nov. 15, 1968, p. 1, col. 6; *N.Y. Times*, Oct. 23, 1962, p. 59, col. 2; *id.* Nov. 17, 1968, sec. 3, p. 1, col. 6.

[13] See *Wall Street Journal*, Nov. 21, 1968, p. 1, col. 6.

and they may be liable for their trading. In short, he is an insider, little (if any) different from officers and directors of the company.

6.2 As Adviser to Outsiders. More commonly, the analyst has no formal connection with the company, but is acting for a broker-dealer, fund manager, or other client. He may have an informal relation with a particular company, arising from personal acquaintance and prior inquiries. His employer or client may have a relationship with the company as underwriter, financial adviser, or major security holder. He is a tippee if he receives material inside (nonpublic) information about the company through such a relationship, and perhaps even if he receives it apart from such a relationship. As such a quasi-insider, the legal limitations on his use of the information are not fully developed. My guess (and hope) is that they will turn on the factors noted in 3.1 above. It would be risky for him to assume that he is free to use the information for his own trading *or* for recommendations to his clients (who become tippees when he tells them). The wiser course is to bury the information until the company releases it. A recommendation to the company to release may be a sound move. (Release by the analyst without company authorization would create more problems than it would solve.) The longer the analyst has the information before publication, the more likely it is to color his judgments about the company even if he is scrupulously trying not to use it, and the more likely he is to be accused of using it. The analyst should regard material nonpublic information as a hot potato, and try to avoid receiving it. In particular, he shouldn't ask for it. Unlike other hot potatoes, you can't get rid of this kind by giving it to someone else.

In the present state of affairs, the analyst should be wary about using material nonpublic information which comes to him from someone outside the company, but which he has reason to believe emanates from the company. Although less risky than information coming directly from the company, it still carries possible violation and liability.

A true insider cannot legally use inside information until some time after it appears on the tape. An outside analyst who obtains inside information can probably use it as soon as the tape carries it.

6.3 His Own Analysis. There is nothing to prevent an analyst from making his own "perceptive analysis of generally known facts." By hypothesis, no material inside information is involved. This principle was generally stated in Cady, Roberts and reiterated in Texas Gulf. Moreover, there are few restrictions on the personal use or selective dissemination of his analysis. The only well recognized limitation is that he may not "scalp" by trading in anticipation of the market effect of his recommendation.[14] However, the SEC is moving against discrimination among clients, for example when some clients receive telegraphic advice while others get the same advice by mail. In the Merrill Lynch opinion, the SEC

---

[14] SEC v. Capital Gains Research Bureau, Inc., 375 U.S. 180 (1963).

found a violation in giving inside information to institutional customers but not to retail customers; the former sold while some of the latter bought. Indeed, the 2d Circuit laid the groundwork in Texas Gulf by its broad statement that one of the purposes of the federal securities laws is to prevent informational inequities in the market. (See 2.4 above.)

Apart from the limitations just mentioned, the analyst is free to exercise to the fullest his professed expertise as an evaluator of information. He can properly forecast earnings, although he may find it difficult to get from the company any kind of confirmation or rejection of his figures. For his own protection he will want to specify the basis of his forecast, and be sure that it is carefully prepared, especially if it is publicly disseminated through an advisory service or market letter.

6.4 Who Might Sue? The analyst should realize that he is a possible target of many different plaintiffs, although the law has not sufficiently evolved to say with any certainty which of them may succeed. The SEC may initiate proceedings before the commission itself (for license revocation, etc.) or in court (for injunction) if the analyst is registered as an investment adviser or is employed by a registered adviser, broker-dealer or investment company. His own clients might sue for misleading advice or for discrimination in advice. If he uses material inside information about a company, the company or its shareholders may claim that he misappropriated company property (the information). Buyers and sellers of the company's securities at the time he has the information may allege that they were damaged by his use of the information, e.g., if he recommended confidentially to a few persons. In many of these situations, the analyst would be only one of several defendants, but this may give him little comfort.

As a practical matter, the analyst should realize that his most successful recommendations—those quickly and dramatically confirmed by market action—are the ones most likely to be challenged in the "bright gleam of hindsight," on the ground that he had material inside information.

6.5 Precautions. Precautions are difficult to fashion for the analyst beyond counselling him not to seek material inside information. Careful records, showing the time, source, and character of information received, may be some help if there is later litigation. If an analyst has material inside information on a security, it is almost a practical necessity to cut off all comment on that security or company until the information is publicized. Records showing the basis of recommendations should be as complete as possible. So should records showing distribution of the analyst's advice and recommendations. If the analyst has a small number of clients, he might do well to reach an understanding with them that he has no obligation to give all of them the same data and recommendations. If he has numerous subscribers, any differences in communicating with them should be clearly stated as part of the contract.

7. WHAT IS MATERIAL INFORMATION?

Current legal developments swirl around the use of material inside information. Inside means nonpublic and can be fairly easily classified according to whether a formal public announcement has been made (although information can become public in other ways). Far greater problems inhere in the classification of information as material or nonmaterial. On this point the Texas Gulf Sulphur decision of the 2d Circuit has contributed confusion rather than clarity.

7.1 The Reasonable Investor Test. Materiality has been an issue in dozens of 10b–5 cases. The courts have used a wide variety of definitions, but they have had a common core of reference to the objective standard of the investment judgment of a reasonable man[15]—however difficult that may be to apply in a particular situation. When the issue arises for a publicly held security, which typically fluctuates in response to the decisions of many different investors in the market, the most logical test is one which would attempt to predict how the market would react to the information. (After all, this measures the value of the information and therefore the advantage of the insider who trades with the information.) Materiality in such cases should require a predictable market effect which is itself material, i.e., large enough to distinguish from the relatively random fluctuations which constantly occur.

The 2d Circuit began its discussion of material information by quoting Arthur Fleischer's idea that it is "essentially extraordinary," and likely to have a "substantial effect" on the market. But the court quickly went on to talk about "not only information disclosing the earnings and distributions of a company, but also those facts which affect the desire of investors to buy, sell, or hold." The court gives this concept a further stretch by including speculators among the reasonable investors used for the hypothetical measure of materiality.

The two sets of ideas are inconsistent, and we will be plagued by doubts as a result. The net effect of the court's opinion is—in view of the way market professionals and short-term traders sometimes react to relatively slight bits of information—to set a very low threshhold of materiality. I find it dangerously low from the viewpoint of persons who honestly want to know if they have information which imposes legal restrictions on them. The very fact that they worry about the problem is an indication that some investors' judgments are being affected, and that the information may be within the court's zone of materiality.

SEC staff members continue to indicate that the problem area is very important information, not run of the mill items. I hope they are right. But they seem to ignore the literal language of the TG opinion. Also,

---

[15] See Bromberg, sec. 8.3, p. 521.

while SEC interpretations may limit the cases the SEC brings, they are not binding on the courts in private suits for damages. If the courts follow a low standard of materiality, incalculable damages may be awarded for trading with relatively insignificant pieces of information, and confusion will reign among those who are trying to comply.

7.2 *Probability; Relation to Company Activity.* The 2d Circuit in TG introduced into the materiality test a probability element: "whether facts are material . . . when the facts relate to a particular event . . . will depend at any given time upon a balancing of both the indicated probability that the event will occur and the anticipated magnitude of the event in light of the totality of the company activity." The court does not refine the probability factor any further; we cannot tell whether it has in mind a better than 50–50 chance, or 75–25, or something else. A probability approach realistically simulates investor judgment, which is probabilistic in some degree. But the court gives no indication of the relevant odds, and creates a test which will be difficult to apply fairly and which lends itself easily to distortion by hindsight if the event does in fact occur.

The court quite reasonably measures materiality against the total activity of the company. The same oil discovery might be trivial for Standard of Jersey but highly material for a small wildcatter with a string of dry holes.

7.3 *Use by Insiders (Cut-your-own-Throat).* A prominent indicator of materiality in TG was the use of the information by the insiders. They and their tippees spent more than $100,000 buying the stock during the period when the mining information was accumulating. More significantly they (most of whom had never owned calls before) bought calls on 10,000-plus shares.

Whenever an insider trades, he is creating evidence against himself of the materiality of whatever information hindsight shows that he had when he traded. If the amount of trading is slight, so is the evidence. If it is heavy, so is the evidence. Trading by the tippees will presumably be counted too. While this kind of test has rough justice and logic to it—the proof of the pudding argument—it is not very helpful in planning to avoid violations. If the person holding the information refrains from trading, he has solved his legal problems (except as to tipping). Indeed, the court may have emphasized the use-of-information element of materiality as a deterrent.

7.4 *Some Examples.* The cases already mentioned offer illustrations of information which has been held material, or alleged to be material by the SEC. They are worth collecting for reference:

Preliminary indication of a major mineral find—TG.
Forty percent dividend cut—Cady, Roberts.
Five-year sales, earnings, and cash flow projections for company and divisions—Glen Alden.
Sharp drop in earnings—Merrill Lynch.

Most acquisitions are material, although the relative size of the companies and the terms of the deal have some bearing. In terms of time, an acquisition plan probably becomes material when preliminary agreement is reached on major terms (e.g., the exchange ratio of the securities) and may be material when the negotiations begin. Indeed, the knowledge that negotiations are in prospect might conceivably be material.

7.5 Some Unanswered Questions. Among the many uncertainties about material information, two are especially noteworthy.

Is information about a company material if it would be important to an analyst—because of his knowledge of trends, relationship, company, and industry—but not to the average investor? If the legal standard is the ordinary investor, the answer should be no. There is no reason to penalize the analyst because of his superior research and understanding or his ability to reach a shrewder judgment by coupling the information in question with other data. But the answer is far from clear. If the analyst acts on the information, or gives it to clients or others who act on it, this is some evidence of materiality. In any given case where an analyst has nonpublic information about a company and trades its securities (or advises others to do so), he will have a hard time showing that he acted on something beside the nonpublic information.

Is market information material inside information? This might include an impending tender offer or large institutional purchase or sale. Consider a tender offer by X Co. for Y Co. All the law now on the books involves information generated by the company whose securities are traded. Extrapolating this principle, X's tender offer for Y would not be material information about Y unless X had agreed to support the offer or was otherwise involved in the transaction. The tender offer would probably be inside information about X since X is generating the information by planning the offer. But the law so far has not dealt with a case of trading in securities of Y with inside information of X.[16] The law may recognize the tie: buying Y shares with the expectation of selling them to X under the tender offer, or of reselling them in the market at the higher price the tender offer is expected to induce. In any event, the trend (as emphasized in the 2d Circuit TG opinion) seems to be against informational inequities in the market, regardless of niceties of source.

---

[16] Nondisclosure of market information by broker-dealers to customers has often been held a violation. See Bromberg, sec. 5.2. The close prior relationships in these cases make it doubtful that they are precedent for open market trading.

53

CORPORATE DISCLOSURE AND INSIDER INFORMATION*

A Panel Interview with
Philip A. Loomis, Jr., General Counsel
The Securities and Exchange Commission

Financial Analysts Federation

MR. BLOCK:† We have had a good deal of excitement for the financial analysts in the last couple of months. It all shows up in the headlines. They say things like: "Crisis in disclosure"; "shell-shocked security analysts"; "inhibited insiders"; "corporate misinformation"; "SEC cracks down"; "anxious attorneys," and "unequal customers."

Well, this is what this program is about, and we are quite fortunate in having a man who can give us a better and clearer view of the solutions to some of the problems which recent court cases and S.E.C. actions have headlined. He is Philip A. Loomis, Jr., the General Counsel of the SEC. That position, of course, is the senior staff position in the SEC, and if you will ask almost any knowledgeable attorney about him, he will tell you that Mr. Loomis is one of the outstanding attorneys in the United States. He is going to be quizzed by a panel of three officials of the Financial Analysts Federation.

Tom Lenagh is Chairman of our Government Relations Committee, Past President of the F.A.F. and Treasurer of the Ford Foundation.

Ben V. Wright, Jr., is the Chairman of the F.A.F. Corporate Information Committee; and Vice-President, Model, Roland and Co., Inc.

C. Reed Parker is the Treasurer of Financial Analysts Federation and Vice-President of Duff, Anderson & Clark, Inc.

They are going to ask prepared questions of Mr. Loomis; Mr. Loomis is going to give informal, conversational answers.

---

* A Panel Interview presented at the Fall Conference of the Financial Analysts Federation held in Atlanta, Georgia, October 7, 1968. Reprinted by permission of the Financial Analysts Federation.

† Mr. Block, the Executive Vice-President of the Financial Analysts Federation and Vice-President of the Citizens & Southern National Bank was the Moderator for the Panel Interview.

Mr. Lenagh: I wish first to thank Mr. Loomis for coming at a considerable personal sacrifice.

The cooperation between the SEC and the Government Relations Committee of the Financial Analysts Federation has been excellent over the years, and I want to start off by saying that they have seen us and listened to us on every occasion we have asked to be heard, and the cooperation of SEC, the commissioners and staff, with the Financial Analysts Federation has been and is excellent.

We know that, as analysts, the flow of information from some corporations has been either slowing down or shut off in this recent period. We know that most of us, particularly those practicing field analysts, have been quite concerned. We know that corporate management has been confused, and that in many cases the legal counsel of corporations have been advising the corporations to do and say nothing in this period of uncertainty. It seemed, therefore, that if we could get the top attorney from the SEC to address us that we might dispel some of the existing confusion. That's the essence and the background of why we are having this part of the program. It seems very clear also to us that the attorney who advises the corporation and corporation management will pay more attention to the General Counsel of the SEC in regard to this matter than probably anyone else in the country. And he agreed to come. I again want to thank him for it.

I would like to start off, Mr. Loomis, by calling your attention to a pamphlet which I recommend all of you to get if you do not have it, called *Expanded Policy on Timely Disclosure,* put out by the New York Stock Exchange in July of this year.

The first sentence in this pamphlet states: "A corporation whose stock is listed on the New York Stock Exchange is expected to release quickly to the public any new information which might reasonably be expected to materially affect the market for securities."

The FAF must, and wholeheartedly does, endorse the concept of timely and adequate disclosure. Such information is important and even vital to assist us in fulfilling our role in the investment process—a role we believe is vital to a healthy functioning of the capital markets and in turn capitalism as we know it in this country. Yet for some time in the past, Mr. Loomis, and particularly in the last few months, analysts have become confused and alarmed at the interruption in the flow of corporate information as the result of genuine confusion on the part of corporate management and especially their legal advisers as to how they should proceed.

As a result of this, the Federation, through our President, George Bissell, decided to hold our first public press conference last month. I would just like very briefly to go over part of the statement released then as a prelude to the first question:

"The Financial Analysts Federation is concerned about the effect on the corporate reporting process resulting from the recent events related to so-called 'inside information.' . . . Indeed, the Federation notes rapidly growing confusion and doubt on the part of both corporate executives and financial analysts as to their appropriate role in fulfilling their obligations to shareholders and the investing public in general.

"A number of cases already have been reported by members of the Federation where the flow of legitimate corporate information has declined sharply, or even has been eliminated. Verbal communication by means of interviews, or scheduled management appearances before investment audiences, seem to have been most affected. In a few instances this reflects the fact that the present unsettled environment presents a ready excuse for reluctant corporate executives to hide from the spotlight of shareholder inspection and evaluation. For the vast majority of corporate management, however, in the light of these new and conflicting views about appropriate conduct concerning dissemination of information to the public at large, the current atmosphere poses the question 'Have previous moral, ethical, and legal standards in disseminating corporate information changed, and if so, by what rules am I now to be guided?' "

Mr. Loomis, the first question I would like to ask is if you care to make some general comments as to the disclosure process which might help to clear up some of this current confusion, and then we might proceed to more specific questions.

Mr. Loomis: I think, at the outset, I should make the standard disclaimer. The Commission, as a matter of policy, disclaims responsibility for any private publication of any of its employees. The views that I will express hereafter are mine and do not necessarily reflect the views of the Commission or of my colleagues upon the staff of the Commission. Turning now to my comments, we are in entire agreement with the New York Stock Exchange disclosure statement. The keystone of that seems to be, first, that corporations have an obligation to make public disclosure of material facts—and I mean important facts—as soon as this is practicable.

Secondly, that the corporations should continue to meet the analysts and answer their questions in an appropriate way, and I recently advised several large corporations whose people called me up to ask if they should go forward with their meetings with analysts, and I said, "Yes. You may proceed."

The problem has revolved, to some degree, around the concept of what use can be made of inside information. Now, in the first place, the question is, "What is inside information?" The Commission's cases and proceedings so far involved information having several characteristics: It is undisclosed, and, generally, it is of sharp and immediate significance. It is not merely one link in a chain of analytical information and that is, of course, your basis of judgment. Thirdly, it is, according to the person who has it, be he a corporate executive, an underwriter, or what have you, information received in confidence for a purpose other than to use it for the person's own advantage and to the disadvantage of the investing public in the market.

Your ordinary work as analysts, as I understand it from talking to analysts, does not involve slinking around trying to get this kind of information and get an edge on somebody, make a quick killing on the market. Your ordinary function—and it is a very important one—is to, by all available means, including analysis of economic trends, published material, and personal impressions of management, arrive at informed judgments and to communicate these to whomever you are working with. This is a very important process.

Mr. Lenagh: Mr. Loomis, as analysts we sense that many corporate executives are uncomfortable about being uncommunicative with analysts but are being advised by their inside or outside counsel that saying nothing is the easier policy to defend in this period. One corporate president recently told me, "I don't like what my attorney's telling me; it's silly, but as long as I'm hiring him I guess I have to follow his advice."

In your opinion, has the legal profession overreacted to the recent events related to the corporate reporting process?

Mr. Loomis: The tendency of legal counsel is to be cautious. With caution, you don't get into any trouble, and this is particularly true when you are in a state of some uncertainty. But I do think that in some instances some counsel, at least, have overreacted.

Mr. Lenagh: Has your office been consulted in any meaningful way by corporate officials or their attorneys as to what the SEC would consider proper conduct and improper conduct?

Mr. Loomis: As I say, several corporate executives called me up with respect to the subject, and last week certain distinguished corporation lawyers from New York met with myself and my associates and we spent most of the morning talking about these problems.

Mr. Lenagh: In other words, these were fairly recent developments. Initially, that was not the case; is that right?

Mr. Loomis: Not right away, no. You people were almost the first ones to see us about it.

Mr. Lenagh: I have a very specific question, here. If a major corporation—or any corporation—sent out this sort of notice to analysts, and I quote: "Due to the current uncertainty as to the propriety of furnishing information to financial analysts, I have been advised by my senior management for the time being to limit my comments to matters already on the public record."

If this corporate official or his counsel called your office, what would be your answer to that question?

Mr. Loomis: I would say that he did not have to so limit himself, that it's a matter of judgment. The type of inside information which you are concerned with is a rare commodity, and all of you know that you don't often get it in answer to your questions.

Mr. Lenagh: Mr. Loomis, if a corporation agreed to appear before one of our Analysts' societies but because of the present situation said that "We prefer not to have a question and answer period," and then called you and said, "Do you think a question and answer period is proper?" What would be your reply?

Mr. Loomis: It is proper.

Mr. Lenagh: Mr. Loomis, is your office prepared to, or are you preparing any guidelines for corporate management to clarify the present confusion, or do you prefer to be asked on each specific question?

Mr. Loomis: We don't prefer to be asked each specific question. On the other hand, general guidelines which have the advantage that analysts may use them in all cases are beyond our means at the moment. I think that once the fundamental principles become better understood, capable people will be able to see if there is a problem and work it out within the organization.

Mr. Lenagh: Interviews with management play an increasingly important role in the evaluation and interpretation of the financial affairs of listed companies. Annual reports, quarterly reports, and any similar releases cannot by their nature provide all the financial and statistical data that should be available to the investing public. The New York Stock Exchange recommends that corporations observe an "open door" policy in their relation to security analysts, financial writers, shareowners, and others interested in investment in the stock market. In your judgment, has anything happened in the past few months which would make that recommendation inappropriate today?

Mr. Loomis: No.

Mr. Lenagh: And do you concur with its substance?

Mr. Loomis: Yes, I do.

Mr. Lenagh: Thank you very much.

Ben, I will turn this over to you.

Mr. Wright: Mr. Loomis, I would like to ask a series of very short questions covering the general subject of meetings between company officers, individual shareholders, investors, analysts, and others. And with your permission I would like to confine these questions to the subject of the meetings between corporate officers and analysts and leave the questions of the substance of what is said to the second series of questions.

The first question, is it proper for a company officer to address a group of financial analysts at a luncheon meeting?

Mr. Loomis: Yes, certainly it is. I would like to say that there are occasionally some questions of policy as to who should be admitted to these luncheons, but these are questions of policy, I think, and not of law.

Mr. Wright: Is it proper for a company officer to appear at a private luncheon or dinner meeting where the attendance is restricted to 10 or 20 people?

Mr. Loomis: Certainly, there is no legal inhibition on that.

Mr. Wright: Is it proper for a company officer to appear before a group of investment people who are industry specialists?

Mr. Loomis: Surely.

Mr. Wright: Is it proper for a company officer to meet with an individual investor, analyst, or stockholder?

Mr. Loomis: It certainly is. It's quite proper.

Mr. Wright: How about telephone calls?

Mr. Loomis: I gather that in your business everybody calls everybody on the telephone, and we certainly have no objections to it.

Mr. Wright: Is there any reason to change the practice of the last several years under which company officers meet with investment groups informally and formally on a fairly frequent basis?

Mr. Loomis: No, there is not, and, in fact, I think that is a good thing for the securities market to have this flow of information.

Mr. Wright: Next, Mr. Loomis, I would like to discuss the general area of questioning that might occur between a security analyst or investor and a company officer.

Is it proper for the company officer to discuss industry conditions at such a meeting? And by "industry conditions" I mean such things as the volume of imports of steel, the projected volume of imports next year, the possibility of import quotas, the plans of the industry to secure protection for their markets against the rising volume of imports? There are, of course, similar situations in other industries.

Mr. Loomis: I would say that all of these are proper subjects for discussion. Of course, the corporate officer has to watch a little what his answers are. But generally I think he's entirely proper, and he really doesn't have to worry about anything except to be accurate.

Mr. Wright: When you say "except be accurate," I want to remember that in response to this next question. Is it proper for a company officer to discuss industry volume projections for next year and normal growth rates of demand for the industry's product?

Mr. Loomis: Well, this raises the question of predictions, though this isn't the type of prediction that we are most concerned with. The Commission normally has not permitted use of projections of sales or earnings in a prospectus. This policy long antedates my time. It's based, I believe, upon the assumption that ordinary investors who read a prospectus as distinct from the experts, will be overly impressed with these projections and will think they are certain to come true.

Also, over the years we have encountered an unscrupulous fringe among promoters whose predictions are pretty far out. We don't want them going out under our auspices.

On the other hand, we are aware that projections legitimately prepared and analyzed critically by someone, such as a skilled analyst, are regarded as a useful tool in your trade, and in that context I see no reason why they could not be used for that purpose.

Mr. Wright: Thank you, sir. Is it proper to discuss projected levels of capital expenditures for the industry?

Mr. Loomis: Yes. In fact, we do that in our capital expenditure survey.

Mr. Wright: Is it proper to discuss the projected level of industry demand in relation to industry capacity as indicated by announced new facilities?

Mr. Loomis: I would think that it would be perfectly proper to discuss that.

Mr. Wright: Is it proper to discuss the competitive impact of one new major entry into an industry or one new major plant in a small geographical area?

Mr. Loomis: I see no reason why not. It would presumably be of interest to the analyst.

Mr. Wright: Is it proper to discuss the impact on industry demand of a significant change in styling? And I have in mind, here, the shoes that the pretty little girls in the short skirts are wearing these days?

Mr. Loomis: It's certainly an interesting subject. How you may base an analysis on it is beyond my comprehension, but I see no reason why you shouldn't try.

Mr. Wright: Is it proper to discuss the competitor's new model or new marketing plans and its impact on the remainder of the industry?

Mr. Loomis: Surely.

Mr. Wright: Is it proper to discuss the company's industry penetration, or share of market, either actual or expected?

Mr. Loomis: Yes, subject, of course, to the problem of expected penetration which you people have to view, perhaps, with a critical eye. It may be a little overoptimistic.

Mr. Wright: I think "may be" is perhaps the understatement of the morning.

How about the labor situation, sir, the emergence of a new union, the struggle within the union for now vacant posts of president, the impact of a recent settlement by an allied union with another industry or another company—these kinds of subjects?

Mr. Loomis: They're surely proper subjects for discussion. In fact, we attempt to get, whenever there are significant developments in this area, a discussion of the new developments in a prospectus.

Mr. Wright: Would any of the subjects that I have asked questions on in the last few minutes be the kind of information that would require a public disclosure to the press, or is this background information of the kind that is helpful only to a careful student and hence is not necessary to be disseminated widely? Also, in my opinion, some of these things are the kind of material, sir, that a company officer doesn't want to be quoted on.

Mr. Loomis: Well, it seems to me that this is a type of question your group is really better qualified to answer than I am. Obviously some of this information is important; on the other hand, some of it, I suspect, is not, so to speak, suitable for general dissemination to the press, nor would the press in some instances be interested in it. The problem is that of drawing the line between the type of information which any individual must recognize as significant and make use of it and the type which takes some of the skills which you have. And I would guess that much of this is in the latter category.

Mr. Wright: For the last few minutes we have been talking about industry matters, and now I address myself to some specific questions that have been asked of company officers about their own company.

Is it proper to discuss projected capital expenditures by that particular company?

Mr. Loomis: Surely it is.

Mr. Wright: Projected depreciation levels?

Mr. Loomis: Surely.

Mr. Wright: Levels or maximum levels of expected bank borrowing?

Mr. Loomis: Surely.

Mr. Wright: Inventory accumulation plans, if any?

Mr. Loomis: Surely. Again, some of this is the type of thing we try to get into the hands of the public by reports, prospectuses, and so forth.

Mr. Wright: Unfortunately, from the investors' standpoint, there are a number of industries where price competition is a serious factor. Can a company officer discuss realized prices in relation to list prices?

Mr. Loomis: If he wants to, I'm sure he can.

Mr. Wright: Is it proper for a company officer to discuss these matters in relation to a competitor's new plant?

Mr. Loomis: If he knows enough about it.

Mr. Wright: Can a company officer discuss discounts from listed prices that are being offered for spot purchases of a basic raw material? Here I have in mind such things as aluminum pig, crude oil, pulp, et cetera.

Mr. Loomis: I would think so. I think so. I think this is the kind of thing that, as I have gathered from my conversations, analysts in this particular industry find significant, and consequently I don't think it should be withheld from them, although somehow, I, like some other investors, didn't appreciate the importance until some expert tells me the significance of it.

Mr. Wright: How about the difference in the price level between the world price and the domestic price in some basic commodity?

Mr. Loomis: Surely.

Mr. Wright: Is it proper for a company officer to discuss the impact on the industry earnings of any of the above price pressures on his product?

Mr. Loomis: Yes. But this is a somewhat more sensitive area. As I mentioned earlier, projections of what the company's earnings are going to be are both important and delicate, because investors can be badly hurt if they get an improperly prepared projection of earnings which they take as gospel, while you people, I presume, do not take it as gospel, and make a useful filter for it.

Mr. Wright: Thank you, sir, for that plug.

Now, with regard to future earnings, quite often company officials will, at the time of the annual meeting, express the belief or perhaps hope that the earnings for the then current year will be somewhat more than the earnings that have been reported for the year just finished. Later on in the year would it be proper for an investor, shareholder, or analyst to discuss with the management operating conditions in the light of those expected at the time that statement was made at the annual meeting?

Mr. Loomis: Yes, and I think it could well be useful.

Mr. Wright: Would it be proper for a company officer to discuss the implications on earnings of a volume of business somewhat larger than that forecast at the time of the annual meeting?

Mr. Loomis: Yes, provided they don't go overboard.

Mr. Wright: How about discussing the implications on earnings of a disappointing level of business?

Mr. Loomis: Surely, if they want to.

Mr. Wright: Could they properly discuss the rising cost of overhead and the increased volume needed to maintain their earnings at the level of the recent past?

Mr. Loomis: I think they could, and, again, I welcome this.

Mr. Wright: Can one properly discuss break-even points?

Mr. Loomis: Yes, and people do, as I understand. We've never objected.

Mr. Wright: Quite often a company officer will be asked by someone who is making estimates, "I am estimating $5 per share this year. Am I in the ball park?"

Mr. Loomis: I gather this deals with a situation where the analyst has made his own estimate and he wants to cross-check with the company to see that it is not too far out of line. That, I think, is entirely proper and might provide a useful check on the analyst's work. On the other hand, as the stock exchange points out, the company should be careful not to underwrite the analyst's projections as their own, unless they are in a position, by reason of knowledge of how good it is and what he has done, to be sure that it is a reasonable estimate.

Mr. Wright: Now, just one question, sir, and I'm through. In the January–February issue of the *Harvard Business Review*, 1967, Arthur Fleischer, Jr. wrote an article "Corporate Disclosure/Insider Trading," which I recommend that you all read. In this article he said: "Company officials, however, are often confronted with projections made by brokerage firms and investment banking houses and asked to confirm these figures. Here again, I think the conservative course of action would be to decline comment on the projection. At the same time, it would be appropriate to call the analyst's attention to any egregious error in his assumptions or calculations."

I am wondering about a hypothetical case where several people are publishing estimates that are far off the mark. Would it be proper for the company officer to call to the attention of these people the exuberance of these estimates?

MR. LOOMIS: This is the same thing that I was discussing earlier. I can see how Art Fleischer would suggest the cautious course for company management so as to dissociate themselves as far as possible from the projections when they do not know how they were arrived at. On the other hand, I do feel that a service might be done by corporate management in calling attention through the appropriate channels to the institution whose forecasts have been circulated around the market that, in the opinion of management, that is just plain wrong.

MR. WRIGHT: Mr. Loomis, my thanks to you for a very enlightening session.

And now, I will turn this microphone over to Reed Parker.

MR. PARKER: It seems that there are a number of factors involved in trying to come up with any definition of what is "inside information?" And perhaps I could list some of these and see whether you agree or not.

In the first place, the "inside information" we're talking about—it is certainly something that is not widely known in the investment community. Would you agree?

MR. LOOMIS: Yes. In fact, in most of the cases of inside information that we have had, it's not only not widely known but the company's policy has been for some business reason to keep it from being known at all in the investment community.

MR. PARKER: Secondly, were it to be widely known, it would have a substantial and immediate effect on the price of the publicly traded securities of the company in question.

MR. LOOMIS: Well, that, of course, is a matter of judgment. It's very hard to tell what impact on the market would occur and how fast, because you can't be sure what the market is going to do on the day it comes out. Nevertheless, the cases we have been involved in have included the element of market impact, which could be anticipated to be fairly significant and immediate, although the immediate part may be followed by a delayed reaction on the part of others often of greater dimensions over the ensuing days and weeks, as the case may be.

MR. PARKER: So that here we have two more words, "substantial" and "immediate." "Substantial," I suppose is not subject to a precise definition or the same definition for all securities, but shouldn't this involve in general a price change perceptibly in excess of the given security's day-to-day or week-to-week trading norms—in percentages of market value terms?

Mr. Loomis: We have not endeavored to lay down any hard and fast rules in terms of the relation of the expected market impact to the ordinary fluctuations of the security. But, nevertheless, I think there is considerable merit in this analysis. It would normally be expected to have an impact rather more than the usual day-to-day or even week-to-week fluctuations.

Mr. Parker: As to the term "immediate"—and assume here dissemination of the inside information were quite rapid and pervasive—would immediate mean within a trading day or two after dissemination?

Mr. Loomis: Well, again, this concept has not been elucidated so far in any of the cases or Commission decisions. I think the cases which we have brought were all cases which had this characteristic, and I am inclined to feel that we are looking for something in that general area, and that this is a useful, though not an official, analysis.

Mr. Parker: Now, let's move on to some of the apparent "conflict of interest" problems that arise for a person who has inside information and who has competing obligations—one to hold the inside information confidential and the other to act upon it for the benefit of others. First, let us suppose that should there be some inside information concerning Company A which has been received by an underwriter in his capacity as underwriter for Company A. What does he do with this versus his obligation to his firm's investment advisory and brokerage customers?

Mr. Loomis: Well, before I try to get into that specific and difficult question, I would like to point out another characteristic of inside information. As it has so far developed in the cases, although you can find language in law review articles and speeches and, perhaps, even in court decisions, which suggest a broader rule, in most instances, inside information not only has the characteristics that were outlined a minute ago which basically go to its materiality, its importance. There is also the question of how it was received by the person who gets it. In most instances—for example, in the Cady Roberts case, the information was received by the persons in question because of their relationship to the company, the relationship of a director in that instance. They would not have received it had they not had that relationship. It was given to them for a corporate purpose or use in the conduct of the corporation's business, not for the purpose of making a profit on it in the stock market. And in the cases we have so far seen, those that we have brought—this actually has been so or has allegedly been so—and I don't want to get into the facts of any pending cases. But this characteristic is alluded to in the court's opinion in the Texas Gulf case. That is information acquired pursuant to a relationship and not for use in making a profit in the market.

Now, turning to this underwriter's situation, I would think that if information was imparted to a prospective underwriter because the company had a duty to him and to the public to make sure that this information got into the prospectus which would be forthcoming shortly, and he knew that that was the only reason that he got it so that he could produce an accurate prospectus as required by law, then he shouldn't use it to try to make a quick market profit before the prospectus comes out, either for himself or for his customers.

MR. PARKER: Somewhat the same kind of question. Suppose inside information concerning Company A has been received by a commercial bank in its capacity as a lender to Company A. What should the lending institution do in fulfilling its fiduciary obligation to the bank's investment advisory and trust customers?

MR. LOOMIS: We have never had that question, and it is difficult for me to answer it because of the fact that our relationships with the banks are not on the same level as they are with other institutions. Banks are largely exempt from our substantive regulations and are regulated by the banking authorities. So I don't know enough about banking practice to give you a definite answer. But I would suspect that the situation with respect to truly inside information received by a bank in its capacity as a lender might be not too dissimilar from the position of the underwriter.

MR. PARKER: Suppose that an analyst in the process of visiting Company A, just in the normal pursuit of his duties, somehow or other does receive inside information. What does he do with this in relation to his obligations to his employer and the customers of his employer?

MR. LOOMIS: This is a problem that really hasn't been answered yet. One would hope that it wouldn't happen very often. Indeed, I think it is desirable for analysts to avoid, by whatever means they can, putting themselves in this situation. They should not seek to encourage corporate officers to give them inside information of the type that I have referred to —something that is being kept confidential for a corporate purpose. If it comes to them by reason of plain mistake or stupidity on the part of a corporate official, I would think that legally they perhaps are not doing anything wrong, but they are, nevertheless, going to get themselves and the company in some trouble, because people with nasty minds will suspect that there was some conspiracy going on around here. Consequently, it might be prudent at least for them to arrange for the release of this information before making use of it, though I'm not suggesting that if they don't they have violated the law. That has not yet been generally determined in that context.

MR. PARKER: Suppose the analyst receives, again, truly inside information in the context that we are talking about here about Company A from a source outside Company A, perhaps from a competitor or perhaps at the corner bar or some place outside the company.

MR. LOOMIS: It has been our view—I think it is still our view—that because of the absence of the analyst's participating in a breach of duty which may have occurred somewhere along the line, the analyst is home free, so to speak, in that situation.

MR. PARKER: Now, in terms of the kind of relationships we have just been talking about—particularly the underwriter versus the broker's business, and the bank as lender versus the bank as a trustee, we have been talking about inside information in what is a fairly stringent definition of that term. What about all the rest of the information, *non-inside* information, gained by the underwriter as he works with Company A, or the bank as he works as a lender with Company A; what amount of this information is it reasonable to have flow over to the other side of the business?

Mr. Loomis: Well, I suppose if you analyzed this thing in a simple, logical way, if it is non-inside information by definition it is non-inside information, and consequently the firm may use it in the course of its business. On the other hand, this assumes the ability to separate inside information from non-inside information in the mind, and I doubt if they are necessarily that divided into water-tight compartments. On the other hand, I am aware that not only by reason of these underwriting type relationships but in the regular course of your business as analysts, you receive a great deal of information of various types that the public probably doesn't have, mainly because the public isn't interested in it and doesn't understand its significance. And if this is information which, as the stock exchange points out, the company would give to any person having a legitimate interest who asked for it—analyst, stockholder, and so forth —then I know of no inhibitions on its use.

Mr. Parker: A public relations executive has recently suggested publicly that no company management representative should talk to an analyst outside the presence of legal or public relations counsel. What do you think of such a suggestion?

Mr. Loomis: I don't think that it is in any way necessary. It looks as if the public relations counsel was looking for a job. But, aside from that, some companies do have a policy where a transcript is made of every meeting with analysts, of having company counsel review it and see if there is anything there which shouldn't be there, and if that can be done without inconveniencing anyone, it may be a desirable safeguard.

Mr. Parker: What would you suggest that an analyst or a stockholder could do when he is confronted with the problem of a company management who states that "On advice of counsel, we can't talk with you"— first, let us say, "at all?"

Mr. Loomis: Well, as I have said earlier, I believe that advice is incorrect. Your association has already, I gather, announced publicly that in their view it's incorrect; I concur.

Mr. Parker: I suspect maybe the answers are the same as if the company should say, "I can't talk about anything that's not already been communicated to our stockholders," or to some broad segment of the public?

Mr. Loomis: That is a very nice and cautious course, but I don't think the law requires it. Again, the test that the stock exchange suggests is "Is this confidential information which the company wouldn't give to a person who came in and asked for it? Are they slipping it to this particular analyst because they expect something in return?" Then, you've got a problem.

But aside from that, I don't think the mere fact that it has not already been disseminated—perhaps because the company doesn't want to send their stockholders something the size of a telephone book—makes it improper for them to tell an analyst.

Mr. Parker: Would *not* make it improper?

Mr. Loomis: That's right.

Mr. Parker: Or suppose the management says, "We can't talk without the advice of counsel about earning prospects?"

Mr. Loomis: Well, there, as you know, we are on more sensitive ground. I think that a corporation has no legal obigation to decline to talk to a competent and responsible analyst about earning prospects, provided they don't go overboard and are not trying to give their stock a little jiggle. And it's up to the analyst to tell the difference, and I suspect most of you can.

Mr. Parker: Or if the management should say, "We can't talk about the trends in our business prospects?"

Mr. Loomis: I think they can and should.

Mr. Parker: What should the analyst do in a situation where he has received some information and he really can't tell for sure whether it's inside information or not within the context of this very narrow definition, but perhaps his experience suggests that it is?

Mr. Loomis: Well, again, this assumes that he just somehow came across it without having set about deliberately to obtain inside information, and he has no reason to believe that someone is slipping it to him in the hope of receiving a benefit in return; then, I don't think he is inhibited. As I said earlier, if he hears it in a bar, well, that's okay. His only problem here is that while he may not have actually violated anything, his story that he just somehow came upon it has to be a creditable one, or else there may be a problem.

Mr. Parker: If the management were to discover that inside information on a specific subject is beginning to leak out, or is likely to leak out in the near future, what steps should that management take?

Mr. Loomis: The New York Stock Exchange says in the statement referred to that, in such a contingency, management should promptly release the information to the public, even if it would otherwise prefer not to, and I would agree.

Mr. Parker: Many bankers and brokers, including some security analysts, are on boards of directors of publicly held corporations. Because of their positions as directors, they receive inside information on a regular basis. Do you think that this is too dangerous a position for such a person to be in, and what should he do about it?

MR. LOOMIS: This, I think, is a matter of individual judgment and decision. There are risks in this relationship, particularly for a brokerage firm. It can make the firm uncomfortable if they have information which they know their customers could use, but they can't give it to them. The Stock Exchange, again, discusses this point in their statement and says that where a director who also is affiliated with a brokerage firm receives inside information in his capacity as director, it is his duty to the corporation of which he is director not to make use of that information to the market advantage of his firm and his customers, that it is his duty not to make use of it and to keep it quiet. And that is just the position he is in. It may be an uncomfortable one.

On the other hand, many firms think it useful for themselves and their customers to be represented on boards of directors. There is certainly no law against it, but it is, I think, highly important that a representative of a brokerage firm who assumes a directorship recognizes not only the risks that are inherent but is particularly aware of and sensitive to his responsibilities as a director.

MR. PARKER: Many analysts and their employers have large numbers of customers with widely divergent objectives. Where the analyst has reached a conclusion based on *non-inside* information, does it seem logical for him to advise all of his customers of his conclusions, even though the recommendations may be inappropriate for many of them?

MR. LOOMIS: That really isn't a problem of inside information, as I see it; maybe I am misunderstanding it. It's more a problem of the responsibilities of someone who undertakes to advise his customers as to their investments, and I think that if the analyst feels that for some particular customers a particular security may be undesirable or unsuitable, then he shouldn't do anything which would lead to their buying it.

MR. PARKER: Since the world is made up of imperfect human beings, it is not unusual for a company or an analyst to guess wrong on the importance of a piece of information. And management certainly sometimes fails to recognize the significance of a piece of information and the impact that it will have on the market place. These estimates may turn out to be either on the side of overemphasis or underemphasis of the significance of the matter. Similarly, analysts can make the same sort of mistakes. Are corporate managements and security analysts to be judged by what *subsequently* happens in the market place as to what is and what is not inside information?

MR. LOOMIS: This was discussed at considerable length by the District Court in the Texas Gulf case, and the Court of Appeals agreed that there is a certain danger in these cases of judging people by hindsight, and obviously, I don't think this should be done. It is sometimes hard to avoid it. In the Texas Gulf proceedings, it was suggested by the Court of Appeals that the market movement which, in fact, resulted from the dissemination of this information, is evidence as to its materiality. I don't think there is any way of denying that. On the other hand, the fact that the market reaction was, as it sometimes seems, illogical and perhaps either under or over what could reasonably have been expected logically, should not affect the result. It's a question of looking at the thing at the time you had the problem, not in the light of hindsight.

MR. BLOCK: That is the list of formal questions which we had prepared to offer Mr. Loomis. The remaining questions have been handed in by the audience.

The first question I would like to ask—and this one is really my own—is the relationship between someone who provides investment services and the customer. The customer relationship, as viewed by many people, is a continuing one. A typical example might be an investment counseling house that gives a "hot" issue to the first 10 names on his alphabetical customer list, because that's all of the stock he got on this "hot" issue. Then on the next "hot" issue he goes down the alphabet and gives it to the next several customers and tries to treat them equally *over a period of time*, as opposed to dividing up his 400 shares, one share each to 400 accounts and still having 200 accounts he can't give any to.

Would you say anything about that?

MR. LOOMIS: I recognize that this is a practical problem for counseling firms which they deal with in various ways. I think that probably all I can say is, they should inform their customers of what their procedures are in this regard so the customer knows what he is getting into, and that insofar as is reasonable and practicable, these procedures should not be designed to favor particular customers over other customers.

MR. BLOCK: Thank you.

Our next question is, "Is the SEC in the midst of establishing a new policy, or is it merely enforcing existing policies?"

MR. LOOMIS: We believe that this is not a new policy. The doctrine that insiders can't trade on inside information has its roots in the common law back in the 19th century, though it was not very well developed then. It was picked up almost immediately after the Exchange Act was passed and the rule was adopted in cases going back into the early 40's.

Of course, our securities markets are changing. Somewhat more sophisticated questions and more sophisticated institutions are around now, and the law, as it always does, develops and changes to meet the changing circumstances, and the courts do a little more of that than we do, frankly. I don't think, however, that the foundations of what is being done are at all new, though some of the implications are.

MR. BLOCK: The next question is, "Do you expect these recent events, such as the Merrill Lynch matter and court decisions, such as the Texas Gulf Sulphur case, will result in companies being more open with information or more closed?"

MR. LOOMIS: Well, I don't want to talk about the Merrill Lynch case. I'm not sure that really presents this problem, anyhow, because allegedly the information was about to be disclosed, and it was four days later. But, as I understand it, we believe it likely that when the dust settles, corporations will be a little more apt to disclose material facts promptly in order to avoid embarrassment for insiders and others.

MR. BLOCK: Here is a question that is very important. You have already had two questions asked you about analysts in bars, and as it was answered, one suspects that you may be encouraging them to visit bars more often. This question says, "Do I correctly understand from your answer that information which is one degree removed from the insider is not inside information; that is, heard in a bar or from another analyst?"

MR. LOOMIS: The problem there is, is it good and reliable information from a reliable source?

As to another analyst, we haven't moved this far, as I attempted to convey. There is, I think, I do not guarantee, in these cases some element of the person who receives information having reason to believe that he is getting it because somebody is breaching his duty, and if you get it from another analyst, well, you may have no basis for such an assumption.

MR. BLOCK: "As an analyst, is it proper to inform some investors—institutions, for example—of an opinion or recommendation in advance of broad dissemination to the client as a whole?"

I think that's really the Merrill Lynch case.

MR. LOOMIS: Well, again, I want to stay away from the Merrill Lynch case. However, we have encountered situations, where some well-known investment advisory firms whose recommendations carry weight, the mere fact that X & Co. says that the stock is a buy is likely to lead not only X & Co.'s numerous customers but the market generally to react. In those situations, we have raised a question about the practice of such a firm in sending out advance telegraphic notations to a few clients as to what it's going to recommend next, and sending the rest of them the same recommendations by second-class mail. In this situation are they sure that the less favored customers are entirely aware of what's going on?

MR. BLOCK: "What about the corporate official who is obviously on the so-called 'insider's' list who unknowingly buys and sells stocks a few days before the release of information of some importance?"

MR. LOOMIS: There is no such thing as an insider's list, that I know of. Particularly in the Texas Gulf case, and the Commission in the Cady Roberts case indicated a disposition not to have any such lists. As I recall, in Texas Gulf there were one or two people who we thought knew about the mineral strike, but the evidence didn't show that they did, and upon the basis of that they got off.

MR. BLOCK: "There is a fairly standard clause in most underwriting agreements that calls for the company to furnish continuing information periodically to the underwriting organization. Should this information be considered inside information?"

Mr. Loomis: That, of course, depends on what it is. I think, however, that there is a problem developing in the practice of underwriters, particularly underwriters who bring a new company to the market and who have very considerable bargaining power, to insist that all types of information be furnished them before being disseminated to the public. Now, they are running a risk in collecting information which might put them in an embarrassing position.

Mr. Block: "The thought that the analyst is home free on inside information from *non-company sources* is not clear, particularly with reference to the Texas Gulf case."

Mr. Loomis: Well, I don't know if I—

Mr. Block: We may be back in the bar again.

Mr. Loomis: I think we may be back in the bar again. And in any event, in the Texas Gulf case we did not charge the so-called tippee with anything, but the Court in its opinion remarked that while it expressed no view as to whether their conduct was illegal, it may have been equally reprehensible. I think what was meant by that—and any lawyer can have his opinion—is that if there is some sort of a conspiracy going on so that the person who gets the information knows that it is not intended for him, and the person who gave it to him shouldn't have given it to him, then the Court regards acting on it as reprehensible. On the other hand, if there is no ground for such concern—and I may be wrong—the analyst is probably home free.

Mr. Block: "Please discuss the propriety of an analyst's personal transactions in the securities which he follows or recommends to his customers, and do you have any suggested policy on this?"

Mr. Loomis: This is not an inside information question. This is a question of an analyst's, and particularly an investment adviser's, duties as an investment adviser. The Supreme Court of the United States, in the Capital Gains case, affirmed the Commission's view that it is a fraud for an investment adviser to trade on the market impact of his own advice. I think it may very well be equally wrong for an adviser to endeavor to make a profit by giving himself the benefit of his recommendations first.

Mr. Block: "Since insiders are required to report their purchases and sales of stock, should they be required to report sales of put and call options?"

Mr. Loomis: Yes, they should, and if we haven't adopted a proposed rule that would require that, I'm not quite sure whether we have, but I think so, and we should.

Mr. Block: "What questions are not appropriate for an analyst to ask management?"

Mr. Loomis: I don't think I can answer it at all without knowing what questions analysts do ask. I have been told by my friends in this group that it's not regarded as ethical practice for an analyst to try to pick up advance information on something like a dividend cut or a merger, by bringing pressure to bear on the company to give this information to him before they give it to anybody else, and I think that's right.

MR. BLOCK: "The corporate president tells the analyst that a significant piece of news has been released to the Dow Jones News Service and proceeds to tell the analyst about it. Must the analyst wait until that information appears on the broad tape before releasing it to his office or customers?"

MR. LOOMIS: Well, that question, at least the essential question was discussed in the Texas Gulf opinion. The question is when the inside information ceases to be inside information because it has been disseminated to the public. The Court declined to lay down any general, broad rule and gave us the suggestion that we assume the pleasant task of providing one. But the Court did suggest that it was improper to put in your buy or sell order after the information had been given to Dow Jones but knowing that it had not yet appeared.

MR. BLOCK: "If a company is aware that current quarterly earnings will be disappointing, may this be disclosed to an analyst without simultaneous public disclosure?"

MR. LOOMIS: If the company knows or is quite sure that its earnings are going to be significantly disappointing, whether or not it is illegal to tell an analyst before disseminating it, it would I think, be contrary to the Stock Exchange's policies, with which we agree.

MR. BLOCK: "If the brokerage firm recommends a security, and an officer of the firm is a director of the company and is aware of inside information at the time of the recommendation, how can that officer prove he was not guilty of passing on inside information to his research department?"

MR. LOOMIS: Well, he will just have to try to figure out where they got it from and document that information. That is one of the hazards of the relationship.

MR. BLOCK: "Didn't the New York Stock Exchange statement indicate that any information given to an analyst shall also be disclosed to the public at the same time?"

MR. LOOMIS: I think not, except, of course, that as to material information one of the overriding aspects of their policy is that it shall be given to everybody just as promptly as possible.

MR. BLOCK: "Announcements of merger discussions between Company A and a privately owned company for an undisclosed amount of stock are being made with increasing frequency. At what point is it incumbent upon Company A to make such information available publicly?"

MR. LOOMIS: This is a very difficult problem. The Stock Exchange's statement that was referred to contains a good discussion of it. I think that when a proposed acquisition reaches a stage where it's fairly definite, the company would be called on by the Stock Exchange to make some announcement. In any event, insiders might be prohibited from trading on the basis of their knowledge that this is what the deal is going to be. We have a case pending in the District Court which raises precisely that point. On the other hand, just to make life difficult for all of us, there are some companies which like to stir up a little excitement by announcing a contemplated acquisition which somehow never occurs. It's not an easy question and really requires an analysis of the facts in each case.

Mr. Block: "Assume a major publicly owned company with sales exceeding a hundred million dollars and listed on the New York Stock Exchange introduces a new product. The analyst studies the potential impact of this product on sales and earnings and then, for the first time, meets with company management and discusses his conclusions, which are that the product will have a major impact on earnings per share. The company recognizes the estimates as being quite good and accurate. At this point, no other release regarding the earnings impact of the product has been made. Does the confirmation of the analyst's projections at that time constitute inside information?"

Mr. Loomis: I don't know from whose viewpoint you are looking at this. Is the analyst inhibited because his previously made computations were verified by the company? I think he should not be. On the other hand, if the company knows that the analyst is going to put this out and some people are going to get it, and it is all that important, I think under the Stock Exchange policy and for the benefit of all concerned, it's time for the company to make an announcement.

54

PUBLIC STATEMENT CONCERNING CORPORATE DISCLOSURE AND INSIDE INFORMATION*

Financial Analysts Federation

The Financial Analysts Federation is concerned about the effect on the corporate reporting process resulting from the recent events related to so-called "inside information" (i.e., the current Securities & Exchange Commission investigation of Merrill Lynch, Pierce, Fenner & Smith's alleged misuse of information received from Douglas Aircraft in 1966, and the recent Second Circuit Court of Appeal's decision of the Securities & Exchange Commission's suit against Texas Gulf Sulphur Company relating to major mineral discoveries in 1963–64). Indeed, the Federation notes rapidly growing confusion and doubt on the part of both corporate executives and financial analysts as to their appropriate role in fulfilling their obligations to shareholders and the investing public in general.

A number of cases already have been reported by members of the Federation where the flow of legitimate corporate information has declined sharply, or even has been eliminated. Verbal communication by means of interviews or scheduled management appearances before investment audiences seem to have been most affected. In a few instances, this reflects the fact that the present unsettled environment presents a ready excuse for reluctant corporate executives to hide from the spotlight of shareholder inspection and evaluation. For the vast majority of corporate management, however, in the light of these new and conflicting views about appropriate conduct concerning dissemination of information to the public at large, the current atmosphere poses the question, "Have previous moral, ethical, and legal standards in disseminating corporate information changed, and if so, by what rules am I now to be guided?"

While the answers in specific detail to the legal standards have not been finally determined by clear legal precedent, The Financial Analysts Federation wishes to state its strong belief in this area. It urges corporate

---

* Position paper adopted by The Financial Analysts Federation stating the views of George S. Bissell, C.F.A., President of the Federation, in respect to the various cases dealing with disclosure of insider information, September 19, 1968.

management to maintain an "open-door policy" by communicating continuously to all segments of the investment community, whether in writing or verbally. Needless to say, this should be done in a manner indicated by existing levels of individual investor comprehension and interest. Furthermore, in our view, full and complete discussions by management of current operations and future expectations is most appropriate. If extraordinary facts exist, which if they were in the public domain, would have an immediate and substantial impact on the price of the company's securities, they should be publicly disclosed by management. By following such an "open-door policy" management will contribute to the investing public's better understanding of their companies' intrinsic value relative to the myriad of other available investment opportunities in the market place today.

The Financial Analysts Federation also wishes to reassert its fundamental position that the financial analyst represents one of the most valuable vehicles for effective and meaningful communications with the investing public. Since there is nothing in the recent judicial action that prohibits the discussions by management and analysts of available information which has traditionally occurred, the Federation feels that analysts should continue to seek substantive, but not privileged, information by all appropriate means. Such a policy contributes to sound investment decisions which lend strength and stability to the market place and tends to place all buyers and sellers of securities on an equal footing—a long-term objective of the Securities and Exchange Commission, the New York Stock Exchange, and The Financial Analysts Federation.

The Federation further urges management, if in doubt concerning specific conduct in regard to flow of information, to contact the Securities and Exchange Commission for comment and guidance. It is obvious that under current circumstances the Commission and staff are unable to discuss certain key issues that are now before the courts. Nevertheless, as a public agency, this body has an obligation to all interested parties to discuss their views of appropriate conduct concerning flow of information and disclosure. Furthermore, Federation officials are gratified to find that this agency continues to be most helpful in our deliberations on ethical standards and conduct.

The Federation also suggests that management contact the New York Stock Exchange on this subject. We are particularly impressed with its July 18, 1968 pamphlet concerning "timely disclosure," and urge all interested parties to familiarize themselves with it.

Within the Federation, a substantial number of inquiries have been received by its officers as to what is the currently appropriate conduct of a financial analyst. They ask: "Should we continue to follow our professional responsibility for ascertaining all appropriate information in order to fully analyze and evaluate securities for the investing public?" "Is our code of ethics still applicable?" "Are corporate contacts, either personal or by phone, still appropriate?" "Should we still invite corporate executives to analysts' meetings to discuss corporate progress and prospects?" "How about small luncheons and dinner meetings?" The Financial Analysts Federation is telling its members that the answers to all the above inquiries continue to be, "Yes."

The Financial Analysts Federation itself wishes to point out that in the proper exercise of their professional responsibilities, analysts seek only appropriate information. The Federation, its 41 constituent societies in the United States and Canada and their 11,800 members, all subscribe to a code of ethics concerning their professional conduct.

The Financial Analysts Federation also wishes to emphasize the basic role of the financial analyst. First he must gather and digest published information, such as annual and quarterly reports and interim releases which by their very nature cannot provide all the data that should be available to the investing public. Secondly, he must interpret and evaluate all pertinent information available to him from any source, whether published or by personal interview. For example, specific areas of analyst interest might include how various operating costs, such as labor, materials, and selling, and administrative expenses vary in relation to volume changes, how revenues and earnings relate to investment in plant and working capital, and how all of these factors relate to economic data for the company and its industry. Finally, based on personal contact he must judge managerial capabilities in order to arrive at an informed investment decision.

If such thorough analysis and professional evaluation by the trained financial analyst were not available, raw information released could be misunderstood and misinterpreted. Furthermore, the resulting uninformed decisions derived from this confusion and uncertainty in the market place could contribute to severe market price volatility.

The Financial Analysts Federation feels that the expanding professional advice and guidance of the past three decades has significantly contributed to the reduction of incidence and effects of disturbing elements in the market place, such as tips and rumors. Today's market conditions are in sharp contrast with the unhealthy financial atmosphere which led to the securities legislation of the 1930's. At that time, public knowledge of corporate happenings was almost nonexistent, and trained professional interpretation was not generally available to the investing public. Accordingly, there was no effective way to prevent dislocations in securities markets from tips and rumors. To contribute to a return to the circumstances of those days by substantially reducing the flow of appropriate corporate information is unconscionable, and The Financial Analysts Federation wishes to do its share to see that such a development does not reoccur.

55

TROUBLE AT QUIGBY*

Financial Analysts Journal

Bill and Joe were sitting in the Officer's Lounge at the Quigby National Bank discussing a Trust Investment Committee meeting held earlier that afternoon. Emotions had been high and the disputes vigorous. Bill's annoyance was easily detected in his voice even though the meeting had ended more than two hours earlier.

BILL: One of these days I'm going to brain Ed right in the middle of the meeting. He hasn't the faintest notion of our obligation to our customers and he must have never heard of trustees being surcharged. I just don't understand him.

JOE: Ed may be a little cautious, but you've got to admit that the main reason you wanted to sell that stock was because of that five-year projection you saw in the loan officer's meeting. You can't say that wasn't inside information—only four banks know about it, and it hasn't been published anywhere.

BILL: How do you know only four banks know about it? The stock is down three points since Monday, and that's about 15 percent. Somebody knows about it. But that isn't the point. Our customers hire us because they think we'll do our very best for them. If we know the company is in trouble, it's immoral and illogical not to get out of it. Our customers depend on us, and I say it would be breach of trust if we didn't use every available piece of information we had to get the best investment results for our accounts.

JOE: But Bill, you reached your conclusion entirely on that five-year projection which was given to the bank purely as an application for a term loan—not for the Trust Department. The cash squeeze was there in the figures. That was your only motivation for selling it.

BILL: I don't see how you can equate motivation and inside information. Every investment action has to start with a motivation of some sort. It was my interpretation of the figures that motivated me to recommend selling.

JOE: Yes, but wouldn't any other good analyst have reached the same conclusion?

---

* Reprinted by permission of the *Financial Analysts Journal* (July–August 1969).

BILL: Do you mean to tell me that it's improper for me to reach a conclusion because there are other security analysts around who aren't too bright? I'm all for this equalitarian bit, but when the time comes that a good analyst has to wait for bad analysts to catch up before he can make an honest recommendation, it's time we quit the field altogether. None of us would have gotten into financial analysis if we felt that initiative and hard work wouldn't be rewarded. If stupidity and ignorance—and even laziness—are to get equal rewards, then this country is really in a mess.

JOE: That wasn't Ed's point at all. He was just saying that you had some information that we couldn't use because it was material and undisclosed.

BILL: Who is to say what is material and what isn't? I've read all those court cases that talk about "reasonable men." The only catch is that the reasonable man is one who turns out to be right by hindsight, and if he turned out to be wrong he was unreasonable. You know very well that the average businessman wouldn't have picked up the implications of that cash flow projection if he had studied it for 10 years. Some security analysts would have and others wouldn't.

If you are going to define material as a quick change in market price when the information is released, who is to say in advance what's material. I happen to think that the cash flow projection was a good reason for us selling the stock, but I'm not convinced that the market would recognize it if it were printed in every newspaper in the country tomorrow morning. Yet how many newspaper readers would sit down and project the quarterly cash balance of a company, making their own seasonal adjustments, from a five-year set of annual figures. That's analysis—not inside information.

Also, who's to say whether the release of the information would move the stock at all. You and Ed said you didn't know what the market would do if the company were to publish the five-year cash flow figures.

JOE: You had one supporter in Jack. Jack said that he thought it would be all right for us to sell the stock on that sort of information, but he wouldn't want to defend us in court if we used that sort of information to make a "buy" decision.

BILL: Buy, sell, I don't see that it makes any difference. We've got the same obligation to do our best for our customers, or it's just plain breach of trust. I'd like to see Ed get up as a witness in front of a jury and explain that our Trust Department knew that Amalgamated Nutmeg was going to pieces, but we didn't do anything about it. I'd much rather face an SEC hearing or something, and to argue that it wasn't our having the cash flow figures, but our analysis of those figures that caused us to sell the stock.

JOE: Well, all that stuff has been settled in the courts already. You can't use inside information. There's nothing in the state or federal law that says a trustee has to break the law in order to be loyal to his customers.

Just take a look at the estates we've handled over the past 20 years. We've had brothels, counterfeit plates, one-armed bandits, and Lord knows what else. You don't think trust law demands that we continue operating a brothel just because it's the most productive use of the account's assets, do you?

BILL: I'm not talking about that sort of asset at all. I'm talking about the common stock of a company which we've been analyzing for years and which we decided to sell because our reasoning told us that we could put the money to work more profitably in some other common stock. It's not the same thing at all.

JOE: But that recommendation was based on information that the general public didn't have. The SEC says that the public has a right to have just as much information as insiders and that if the public doesn't have it, the insiders can't use the information.

BILL: The SEC is living in a dream world. In the first place, there's no practical way to get all of the information to all of the people who might conceivably be interested in making an investment decision based on that information. You can't make the *Wall Street Journal* print something if they don't think it's news, and how can some kid reporter know which facts and figures are significant and which ones aren't. They are no analysts.

Also, the SEC is pretty naïve in even imagining that the average investor would know what to do with the information if he got it. First, he probably wouldn't read it. Second, he'd probably just see that sales were going up if he read it, and would want to buy the stock instead of sell it. Third, the impact of the information on the market is a matter of opinion. Sometimes management and analysts think a piece of information is going to move the stock up, and it goes through the floor. Just look at some of the recent merger announcements to show how far off base management can be sometimes.

JOE: Well, maybe you haven't given them enough time. One of the SEC people said that the information could be material if the price went up either immediately or some time later.

BILL: I don't see where they get that "delayed action effect" argument. If some information is really material, the market will react to it immediately and not 10 years later. Isn't price supposed to discount the entire future of a company? I can understand an exceptional case where there might be a time lag due to the analytical problem—say, consulting some geologists to find out the magnitude of a new mineral find—but on the average, it's ridiculous to say that something is material if it doesn't move the stock within at most a week. I certainly wouldn't go with any notion that materiality depended on what the stock did in the next six months. Most stocks fluctuate 10 or 20 percent in six months anyhow, and how could anyone prove that a particular move of that magnitude over six months was due to a particular piece of inside information and not just to normal fluctuations or some general change for the company.

JOE: Well, regardless of all that, you've got to admit that it's unethical to break the law, whatever the law is.

Bill and Joe were so concerned with the complexities and implications of their Trust Investment Committee meeting that they decided to tape their own private bull session in order to get further reactions from others outside of the Quigby National Bank. They sent copies of the tape to a lawyer, a fellow financial analyst, and to an SEC representative.

The responses form a series of critiques presented in the following pages.

CRITIQUES ON 'TROUBLE AT QUIGBY'

FROM THE VIEWPOINT OF A LAWYER

DODSON & FOGG
ATTORNEYS AT LAW
225½ South Broad Street
Peculiar, Missouri

ELIHU DODSON
ELIJAH FOGG

ELMER FOGG

Telephone: PEculiar 758–5252
Cable Address: Foggydod

June 20, 1969

Quigby National Bank
Quigby, Missouri

Attention: Bill and Joe—Officer's Lounge

Dear Bill and Joe:

To start off with, it's certainly good to hear from you again. After that last job I did for you I thought you had gone out of business because you never paid my fee. Now you send me a tape recording of a bull session that you two were holding awhile back in the Officer's Lounge and ask me for my candid opinion as to who is right. By that I assume that you don't want one of those long-winded legal dissertations like the ones that come out of those fancy New York law factories. As you know, I haven't hired anyone from the *Harvard Law Review* to write my opinion letters like those folks do and I can't pay $15,000 a year for some smart aleck neophyte from an Ivy League college to tell me what the law is.

Anyway, you want my opinion—so I'll get right to the point.

My opinion is that, although Bill may be a fine banker, Joe is probably right as far as the law goes. I know that Bill's reply to this is probably going to be that this means that it is against the law to be a fine banker.

Maybe so. If he goes to jail for violating the law, he may find that he has some very good company because some pretty sharp operators are pulling down stiff sentences these days (I'm not going to mention any names, but you probably know who I am referring to) so Bill will at least have someone who can talk his kind of language.

One of Bill's main points seems to be that since he has a duty to his customers to act in their best interests he shouldn't be held for any violation of federal law if he uses this information about cash flow projection for selling stock to protect his customers. I'm afraid that Bill's just out in left field on this one. Back in 1961 there was a case involving Cady, Roberts & Co., 40 SEC 907, which involved this very point. In that case, like yours, there was some unfavorable information (a decision to reduce the dividend on Curtiss–Wright stock) and the news was "leaked" to a brokerage firm by one of its registered representatives who happened to be a director of Curtiss–Wright. You should read that opinion. It was written by a law professor they brought down from Columbia University up in New York City to serve as Commission Chairman. Now I don't usually believe what law professors say—especially the ones from the big universities where there is all that talk about theory and sociology and the students are rioting all the time—but frankly this opinion in the *Cady, Roberts & Co.* case has become very widely recognized as stating the basic law on insider trading. In fact, whenever a federal court wants to talk about basic principles these days, it always seems to go back to this one case. For example, you can read that long-winded set of opinions in SEC v. Texas Gulf Sulphur Co., 401 F. 2d 833, 848 (2d Cir. 1968) ("en banc" as the French say) and if that doesn't endorse *Cady, Roberts* as being the law, I don't know what does. At least it's convinced all of *us* and, as you know, we're from Missouri.

Now to get to the point. In the *Cady, Roberts & Co.* case the broker argued, as Bill is doing, that he had a duty to his customers to sell and so that should let him off the hook as far as the SEC was concerned. Chairman Cary more or less flattened him on this one, if I can quote a bit:

> Moreover, while Gintel [the broker] undoubtedly occupied a fiduciary relationship to his customers, this relationship could not justify any actions by him contrary to law. Even if we assume the existence of conflicting fiduciary obligations, there can be no doubt which is primary here. On these facts, clients may not expect of a broker the benefits of his inside information at the expense of the public generally.

What Chairman Cary is saying, then, is that the duty to the public, not to trade on the basis of inside information, comes first. This is a duty which arises under federal law, and federal law is primary in this area.

Bill raises the question of whether he might be violating state law if he obeys the federal law which prevents him from selling. His point is a good one. I don't know of any state cases saying that a bank officer may be surcharged in this situation, but then again, I don't know of any cases saying that he can't be held accountable. Awhile back I read an article in the *Bankers Magazine* (Vol. 150, No. 1, Winter 1967, p. 37) which discusses this very point. The article is written by a professor so maybe you should take what he says with a grain of salt (although he has recently published a book on *Federal Regulation of Insider Trading* so he *may* qualify as knowing at least something about the subject). He concludes that:

> Whether in that situation it may be a defense in the state court that the director's inaction was due to his paramount duty to refrain from disclosure until a public announcement of the news is an open question, which the state courts may resolve differently depending upon the strictness of a jurisdiction's particular fiduciary standards.

In other words, we really don't know the answer. It depends on state law and maybe on the particular judge that tries the case. Personally, I would say that any state judge who held a trustee accountable under state law for *not* violating federal law would be best advised not to run again for office when his term expires. We may be states' righters down here in Missouri, but this would be going too far.

Bill was right, however, on one point. When Jack suggested that it would be all right to sell the stock on the basis of the cash flow information but that it might be improper to use such "inside" information to make a "buy" decision, Bill replied, "Buy, sell, I don't see that it makes any difference." Although I don't agree with the rest of what Bill said, I do agree that if the information really is "inside" information, and undisclosed, it doesn't make any difference whether the information is used in a "sell" situation or in a "buy" situation. The *Cady, Roberts & Co.* case already referred to illustrates that it is improper to use the information in a "sell" situation and the recent *Texas Gulf* opinion speaks eloquently about the "buy" point. I suppose that what Jack had in mind was something rather basic, namely, that if a person in a fiduciary relationship has "inside" information that the ship has sprung a leak and will go down shortly, he has a duty to start unloading the passengers. This seems to make sense as far as the law of fiduciaries is concerned, but when you move into the federal area and talk about the law relating to the marketplace in securities, what the SEC and the courts seem to be saying rather clearly is that you can't begin to unload passengers until the news has been broadcast over the public address system. Of course, the customer is going to be angry as all get out when he later learns that his investment advisor knew that something was seriously wrong and didn't do something about it. The answer to this one may be that, although the customer's anger is a perfectly normal reaction under the circumstances, he must somehow be brought to realize that he is not entitled to insist that his investment advisor violate federal law to protect his own interests. To soothe the customer's ruffled feelings somewhat we might tell him that there may be certain situations where his investment advisor can use undisclosed "inside" information to protect him. Professor Painter, whom I have already referrred to, in his book on *Federal Regulation of Insider Trading* (pp. 140–41) suggests that a broker who has favorable information may still execute *unsolicited* purchase or sell orders on behalf of a client and may advise customers who wish to sell that they should not do so. But he should not tell them why he advises against selling, because if he did, they might use the information to go out and buy. That would clearly be improper. Where a broker has unfavorable information and his customer wants to buy, then the broker may advise against it but again, he may not tell the customer the real reason for the advice he is giving. If he did, the customer might go to another broker and start "shorting" the stock. Although there are no cases supporting Professor Painter's views, his reasoning seems to be that the broker can act within this limited area because the undisclosed "inside" information is not being used as a basis for either a purchase or sale. In the first situation (where the customer just happened to suggest the right course of action on his own) the transaction was not motivated by the "inside" information. In other words, the broker can act for his customer as long as he does not use the information to solicit the transaction, and of course, he must not disclose it to the customer. In the other situations the customer is merely being advised *not* to do something which otherwise he might do. This harms no one as far as the public is concerned and no one has used the "inside" information to buy or sell.

Let me get on to another point that Bill was making which seems to me to be a very basic one. He took the view that it was his "interpretation" of the cash flow figures which motivated him to recommend the selling and that such an "interpretation" was "analysis—not inside information." In the *Cady, Roberts & Co.* case, Chairman Cary implied that a buy or sell order which was arrived at "as a result of perceptive analysis of generally known facts" would not violate the law. In the majority opinion in the *Texas Gulf* case the Court of Appeals for the Second Circuit agreed with this approach and stated as follows:

> Nor is an insider obligated to confer upon outside investors the benefit of his superior financial or other expert analysis by disclosing his educated guesses or predictions. (3 Loss, *op. cit.*, supra at 1463.) The only regulatory objective is that access to material information be enjoyed equally, but this objective requires nothing more than the disclosure of *basic facts* so that outsiders may draw upon their own evaluative expertise in reaching their own investment decisions with knowledge equal to that of the insiders. SEC versus Texas Gulf Sulphur Co., 401 F. 2d 833, 848–49 (2d Cir. 1968) (emphasis supplied).

I have emphasized the words "basic facts" in the above quotation because in the case we are discussing it seems fairly clear that the five-year cash flow projection would fall into the category of a "basic fact." Unless it is disclosed, it cannot be used as a basis for buying or selling. Once disclosed, then it's any man's game. As Bill says, he is free to sell on the basis of his *interpretation* of the figures and that his interpretation may be miles ahead of that of some other security analyst. But he misses the main point —although the law does not prevent him from interpreting and analyzing all he wants, he cannot take action on the basis of such interpretation or analysis unless the *basic facts* (i.e., the cash flow figures) have been publicly disclosed. This is what the court in the *Texas Gulf* case said in no uncertain terms—the "basic facts" there were the information relating to a particularly promising drill hole in Timmins, Ontario.

Well, as I said before, I don't want this opinion to get long-winded, but there are two more points which I think I should mention: Bill raises the question of whether anyone would be able to tell "whether the release of the information would move the stock at all." Here again the recent *Texas Gulf* majority opinion provides a rough guide. The opinion states that information is not "material" unless its disclosure would be "reasonably certain to have a substantial effect on the market price of the security." (401 F. 2d 833, 848). It also states that "material" information is not merely confined to information which would be of interest to the average prudent investor. In other words, as the court says:

The speculators and chartists of Wall and Bay Streets are also "reasonable" investors entitled to the same legal protection afforded conservative traders. (*Id.* at p. 849)

The lesson which can be gathered from the above is that the courts are going to require that the information, if disclosed, would be "reasonably certain" to have a substantial market effect (although the court at another point uses the phrase "*might* affect the value") but also that the "materiality" test is going to be quite broadly construed to protect speculators as well as bankers like you. This means that if there is any question about something being considered "material," you'd better play it safe and assume that it *is* material. Even though it might not be relevant to a banker's decision, it might be relevant to the investment plans of a speculator. If so, then it's "material."

The second point Bill raises relates to the time period within which the market must react in order to gauge the "substantial market effect" of the information on the market. I want to call your attention to an interesting footnote in the *Texas Gulf Sulphur* decision, footnote 18 on page 854. There the court is discussing the question of how long an insider must wait after disclosure of the news before he can resume trading. The court said:

Where the news is of a sort which is not readily translatable into investment action, insiders may not take advantage of their advance opportunity to evaluate the information by acting immediately upon dissemination.

It then went on to suggest that the SEC might well make some rules in this area about what is a proper "waiting period." In any case, the answer to Bill's problem is not an easy one. The only thing one can say is that the market reaction time to be taken into account in order to measure "substantial market effect" will vary with the kind of news involved. Thus, news of increased earnings could be expected to have a more or less immediate market effect and insiders *might* be able to trade as soon as the news comes out over the Dow-Jones ticker, although they would be wise to wait, possibly for 24 hours or until the news has come out in next morning's newspapers. On the other hand, news of a complex merger involving a conglomerate acquisition, a one bank holding company, or the use of what people are calling "funny money" or "Castro convertibles" might require a considerably longer market reaction time. I know that this is not a very satisfactory answer, but I can't do any better on this one than Judge Waterman, who wrote the majority opinion.

I know that there are all sorts of other questions which came up in your bull session, such as what happens when the financial press simply neglects or refuses to publish the news (to my knowledge no one has answered this one—you'd better check with the people down at the SEC if this situation comes up) and whether the average investor ever reads or understands the financial news. Perhaps the important thing is that there are those (such as you and the financial analysts) who do read and understand this information and that, as a result, the market is likely to reflect its dissemination to the public, even though the "public" may not always be able or willing to understand it.

That's about all I can add at this point. I'll send you my bill later. Maybe you can get the Financial Analysts Federation to pick up the tab from the profits they make out of publishing the *Financial Analysts Journal*. At any rate, they should at least post bond for you if you get indicted for using "inside" information. I know the American Automobile Association will do this for a fellow. Anyway, if they refuse, give me a ring and I'll come right over. Maybe we can also have a round or two of golf and you could give me some tips on the market. This law business gets rough sometimes and a little inside information could come in handy in a pinch.

Elihu Dodson

From the Viewpoint of an Analyst

Frontier National Bank
Frontier, Missouri

TRUST DEPARTMENT

June 24, 1969

Quigby National Bank
Quigby, Missouri

Attention: Bill and Joe—Officer's Lounge

Dear Bill and Joe:

Thank you very much for sending me a tape of the "bull session" you two have had regarding some ethical and legal questions in making investments. Although we are major competitors, you certainly have hit at some common problems, and I hope we can be of some help. At best, however, I can only give you our own position here in the bank. Even that is just our best judgment of the ethical considerations and our layman's understanding of some of the current laws and regulations on the subject. The legalities we must leave to the SEC, the courts, and the lawyers.

Just dealing with the ethics of the problem, the most obvious comment is that, at the moment, the rules and guidelines in this area are extremely fuzzy. Consequently, it is perfectly possible for highly ethical analysts to disagree violently with each other about what should be done in a particular case. Therefore, although we might have views with which you might disagree, please do not think I am accusing you people of behaving in an unethical manner. Until the fuzziness is cleared up, we will never quite be sure what is appropriate.

Taking up the questions that you have raised, I am inclined to believe that we would not permit the kind of action that Bill recommended. Information given on a confidential basis by a company to the Loan Committee of a commercial bank is certainly inside information and, in our judgment at least, should not be available to Trust Department officers at all. As a matter of fact, we have a written rule which must be initialed by each member of our Trust Investment Division that states they will not seek financial information about commercial customers, nor will they have access to any of the credit files in the bank. This does not preclude our investment people from talking with commercial officers to get a "feel" of certain industries or to ask about the quality and caliber of the management of a company or something of that sort. However, financial information is considered privileged and not available for investment use.

Whether this position would help the bank in a law suit or not, I really don't know. I have been told by my legal friends that the courts have held that any information made available to any officer of the bank is assumed available to all officers, because we all live "under one roof." Consequently, literally interpreted, if the commercial side of the bank should make a loan to a company on the basis of privileged financial information, we might be held guilty of knowing about it even though we might not have ever seen it. Whether our initialled memorandum and its enforcement would keep us out of jail or not, I can't guess.

I also disagree with Bill's comment that the cash projection information must be well known because the stock is off 15 percent. I don't think he would press this point too hard, because we all could think of a lot of reasons why a stock would go off 15 percent. Certainly, in and of itself, this would be no evidence that information you had in your possession was more widely spread than you thought. Moreover, although Bill is quite right in arguing that his interpretation of the figures gave him the rewards of superior analytical ability, I do not think he overcomes the objection that his use of the figures in the first place is of doubtful ethical merit, at least as we view it.

The next question you raise is the definition of "material." I admit we have been given some guidelines that are more infuriating than helpful. For example, something is material if it moves the price and, therefore, we will not know whether it is material until after the price moves. But how much of a change is a price "move"? Is it relative or absolute? Moreover, we don't know whether the price move has to be immediate or whether it can occur over a period of time in the future. Apparently this relates to how complex the information is. It seems virtually impossible with the "help" we have been given thus far to make any objective determination in advance of what is material. You will only find this out retrospectively and then you may be in trouble. From the ethical point of view of an analyst, I think each man has to make his own decision. Certainly a good analyst should be able to answer the question of whether a piece of information would cause him to buy or sell a security. If it would, I think he has provided the answer to the question of whether it is material or not.

Of course, this brings up the question of inside information that may have been obtained by other than the rather clear-cut way you have described. Suppose, for example, you inadvertently receive some inside information, either because one of your broker friends calls you up or because it is passed on to you from one of the bank officers or bank customers who is not aware that, by giving you this inside information, he promptly ties your hands. I think it is fairly clear from an ethical point of view, and from the point of view of the SEC as well as the law, that if this inside information is used to buy a stock, you are guilty not only of unethical conduct but also of illegal conduct. I wish I could be as sure in my own conscience that there is no difference between a "buy" and a "sell" decision. For example, if you get some adverse information about a company that is material, and you hold the stock in trust accounts, what do you do? The SEC's position is known. You may not use this information to sell the stock. However, if you are a trust officer or if you are in a fiduciary capacity, you know very well that a rather imposing number of state law cases decree that you must discharge your fiduciary responsibilities for the benefit of these customers, and you might reasonably argue that your responsibility to these customers takes precedence over the guy you sell to, whom you don't know and to whom you really have no obligation at all.

I have consulted our counsel about this, and he is not particularly encouraging. He agrees completely that should a buy decision be made on the basis of inside information, it would be illegal. On the sell side, however, if I don't seek the inside information but do happen to come in possession of it, the best I can get from our lawyers is the assurance that the law on the matter is somewhat fuzzy, but they would be glad to defend me in court should I make the decision to sell! (As a matter of interest, I am enclosing a memo from our counsel on the subject.) From an ethical point of view, I know that the directors of our bank, with whom I have discussed this, feel instinctively that our responsibilities to our customers should take precedence and I am inclined to go along with them. This may some day be held *illegal*, but you have asked me about my *ethical* judgment.

I guess it all boils down to what is ethical, and the best answer is that the more you try to refine it and define it, the less successful you are likely to be. As one of my good friends once put it, if you want to build a house with a roof that won't leak merely put that statement in the contract. The more you spell out the kind of material and detailed specifications of the roof to insure that it won't leak, the more likely you are to have the builder fix it up so that he will meet the specifications and you will have water all over the floor. There is also some argument that trust men, or others who act in a fiduciary capacity, are held to a higher ethical standard than the ordinary analyst or investment manager. I am afraid my attitude would be that the ethics of the situation are the same for all people in the investment area; it is only the penalties that are more severe when a fiduciary relationship is involved.

To sum it up then, our view would be that using five-year loan projections or other confidential information submitted to a bank is clearly off base. From an ethical viewpoint, we do not permit in it our own organization. Whether the information is really not that confidential or whether the interpretation of the figures really leads to the investment conclusion does not, from an ethical point of view, seem to be relevant. The basic point is that the information was not obtained in a proper manner. When you get to the less clear-cut case of inside information obtained otherwise, I think there is a distinction between a buy and sell decision, with the buy decision being outlawed but, from an ethical viewpoint at least, the sell decision is indicated. As to what is "material" information, I think the current guidelines are useless and you must say subjectively "material" is what would move you as an analyst to an investment decision.

I'm not sure that everything I have said is legal and proper, nor can I assure you that we won't change as further guidelines are given us by the courts. Like you, we do our honest best and hope that the penalties, if any, won't be too severe.

Sincerely,

J. Wellington Smythe
Senior Vice President

Enclosure

LEAD, KINDLY AND LIGHT
ATTORNEYS AT LAW
INTEROFFICE MEMORANDUM

To: J. Wellington Smythe, Senior Vice President, Frontier National Bank
FROM: Joshua Lead
SUBJECT: Use of Inside Information in Selling Securities Held in Trust

In answer to your recent inquiry, I would make the following observations:

1. *Cady, Roberts & Co.*, 40 S.E.C. 907, is not a legal decision by a court but is a statement of policy by the SEC. When this problem is finally resolved, the impact of *Cady, Roberts* may be weakened.
2. The reason that *Cady, Roberts'* impact may be weakened is because it was a "sell" case and the buyer was a member of the public, a person to whom under existing legal principles the brokerage firm owed no duty and to whom it had no fiduciary responsibility.
3. The practical effect of *Cady, Roberts* is to impose a whole new legal obligation which has never existed before—a legal obligation to the whole world. For the first time, it makes every man "his brother's keeper." Nothing in the law has ever gone this far before. It would make the trust officer's obligation to the public greater than the trust officer's obligation to the beneficiary of the trust. I am not sure that the courts will finally make into law this principle of "brotherly love."
4. Furthermore, *Cady, Roberts* cannot be categorized as a new development. It has been published for almost eight years and was practically ignored until the *Texas Gulf* decision. The *Texas Gulf* decision does not on its facts confirm *Cady, Roberts* because the *Texas Gulf* decision was a "buy" case in which corporate management bought from its own stockholders, persons to whom a fiduciary duty was owed.

In my opinion, a logical extension of the principle of *Cady, Roberts* would create havoc in financial circles. Its logical extension is that no person can act in the purchase and sale of securities until all persons have the same information.

Except for *Cady, Roberts*, which is not a legal decision, I am not aware of any holding by any agency or court to the effect that a trust officer (as distinguished from a broker) must jeopardize the interest of the beneficiary of the trust by failing to act until he is sure that the whole world has the same information he has.

FROM THE VIEWPOINT OF AN S.E.C. REPRESENTATIVE

The following represents an extract from a letter to Bill and Joe by a friend of theirs at the SEC.

The Securities and Exchange Commission, as a matter of policy, disclaims responsibility for any private publication by any of its employees. The views expressed herein are those of the author and do not necessarily reflect the views of the Commission or of the author's colleagues upon the staff of the Commission.

At the outset, it seems altogether likely that, assuming the information contained in the five-year projection is material and that it is undisclosed to the public, its use by the bank's trust department in selling securities would violate Rule 10b–5. As the courts and the Commission have said, anyone who has access, directly or indirectly, to information intended to be available only for a corporate purpose and not for the personal benefit of anyone may not take advantage of such information.

The information in question was given to the bank by the corporation for a corporate purpose, i.e., to assist it in obtaining a loan, and the bank obtained it by reason of its relationship to the corporation as a source of credit.

I recognize that this type of restriction creates a problem for the bank in view of its obligations to its trust accounts. A similar problem was presented to the commission in the *Cady, Roberts* case, where it was held that clients of a broker may not expect from him the benefits of his inside information at the expense of the public generally or, in other words, that clients cannot expect even a fiduciary to violate the law for their benefit.

In order to avoid placing fiduciaries, such as bank trust departments, brokers handling discretionary accounts, and other persons managing the money of others, in an intolerable position, there can only be one of two alternative rules in this area. Either a money manager cannot take advantage of material undisclosed inside information for the benefit of his clients and consequently he is not required to do so, or alternatively he is required to do so by his obligations to his clients, and consequently he is entitled to. If one accepts the premise that an insider, however defined, cannot trade for his own account on the basis of material inside information and that the primary purpose of this restriction is to provide fairer markets and to prevent overreaching of investors who do not have access to such information, it would seem logically to follow that the first rule is the correct one. The contrary result would mean that clients of fiduciaries, and only clients of fiduciaries, would be able indirectly to buy or sell on the basis of material inside information. Such an exception has no relationship to the primary purpose of the existing restrictions. It is true that clients of a fiduciary in this situation are not guilty of anything involving personal misconduct unless, perchance, they choose their money manager on the basis of his access to inside information which, incidentally, they might be tempted to do. But the main purpose of the restrictions on insider trading is not to punish anyone for misconduct but, as indicated, for the primary purpose of protecting investors and the markets.

The most difficult and novel question presented by the example is whether the information involved was, in fact, "material" within the meaning of the act and rule. There are two aspects to this: first, whether the projections are reliable, and secondly, whether the information they provide is material for purposes of the restrictions on insider trading. As to the first aspect, Bill, Joe, and Ed all proceed on the assumption that the projections are reliable and that they reflect what in fact is going to happen to the company. If this assumption is correct—and I do not think it is necessarily correct about projections generally—the inquiry turns to the significance of the information. It would appear, based on the conversation, that the significance of the information relates to future cash flow and that, in Bill's opinion, this will have a serious adverse impact on the company. It also appears that in all probability the average investor or businessman would not have recognized this significance, and some security analysts would and others wouldn't. No case has occurred where information having these characteristics has been claimed to be "material" inside information; and certain language in the *Cady, Roberts* opinion indicates that it might not be. It was there indicated that "perceptive analysis of generally known facts" is not inside information. On the other hand, as the art of financial analysis improves, ethics and, perhaps ultimately the law, may extend insider trading restrictions to information which any good analyst would regard as highly significant. This is particularly true if, as a result of increased reliance by investors on the talents of analysts, information of this character comes to in fact have a significant market impact.

Index

INDEX

A

Accelerated depreciation, 16–18
Accounting
  audits of corporate accounts, 47–53
  divisional, 40–41
  inflation period, field test for, 24–33;
    see also Inflation, accounting for
  pension fund, procedures for, 617–18
  principles in; *see* Accounting principles
  problems in, 475–76
  product-line; *see* Diversification, of product-lines
  product-line sectors, 40–41
Accounting principles, 3–23
  basic guidelines for, 22–23
  comparability of data utilized, 3–4, 6, 23
  conflict in, 6–9
  consistency in application of, 3–6, 23
  depreciation, treatment of, 14–16
  income determination, 6–13
  Interstate Commerce Commission, 50
  investment analysis and, 3–23
  investment credit deduction, 18–20
  lease commitments, 21–22
  objectives, 51
  procedures distinguished, 5–6
  railroads, 50
    accelerated depreciation, 16–18
  reliability of data, 3
  subsidiary earnings, recognition of, 9–13
  tax regulations versus, 13–16
Affiliates; *see also* Subsidiaries
  consolidation of earnings, 10–11
  defined, 10
Agricultural machinery, 159–61
AICPA; *see* American Institute of Certified Public Accountants
Aircraft-space industries, 159–61
Alexander, Sidney S., 463–64
American Institute of Certified Public Accountants (AICPA), 7, 474
American Smelting & Refining Co., 337, 340–41
American Stock Exchange, 651
Anaconda earnings, 338–39

Analyst; *see* Financial analyst
Analysts Handbook, 133
Appraisal of management; *see* Management
Assets
  product-line analysis of, 43
  real versus financial, 94
  value of, 48–49
Assumptions; *see* Forecasts and forecasting
Atchison, Topeka & Sante Fe Railway Company, 17
Atkinson, Thomas R., 125
Audits of corporate accounts, 47–53
  balance sheet, purpose of, 48
  methods of accounting, 49–50
  objectives to be kept in mind, 51
  shareholders furnished with accounts, 51–52
  value of assets of large business, 48–49

B

Balance of payments accounts
  categories of, 281
  defined, 281
  economic measures of, 282–84
  goods and services, 281
  government, 282
  interpretation of, 281–84
  liquidity balance, 282–83
  miscellaneous, 282
  nature of, 281
  official settlements balance, 282–84
  private capital, 281–82
Balance sheet; *see also* Statement of financial position
  balance required on, 103–4
  defined, 96–97
  financial assets, 94
  generalized for single sector of economy, 93–96
  net worth, 94–95
  real assets, 94
  research reports to include, 679–80
Balanced budget sector, 101
Ballooning effect in inflation, 29
Bank Administration Institute, 614
Bank credit; *see* Monetary policy

Bankers Trust Company
  flow of funds analysis of bond yields, 125
  flow of funds analysis study, 118-24, 127
Banking, 83
Barron's Confidence Index, 470
Bauman, W. Scott, 433, 436-38
Bawerk, Bohm, 431
Bell, W. Edward, 410
Bench mark, 35-36
Bernhard, Arnold, 433
Block, Frank E., 421, 424
Block trading of securities; see Institutional investing
Blue chip securities, 290
Boeing Company airliner contract, 206-7
Bonbright, James C., 411
Bond investment policy for pension funds; see Pension funds
Bond portfolios
  appreciation potential, 634, 647
  atypical yields, 643-45
  call protection, 634-35, 647
  coupon areas
    classification of, 631
    defined, 631, 647
    price volatility of, 639-40
    selection of, 645, 647
    time period of move from one interest level to another, 643
    transition from one to another, 634-35
  coupon volatility, 633-34
  current coupon bonds, 640-42
  declining yields (rising prices)
    holding, 645
    major decline, 641
    moderate decline, 640-41
    trading, 646
  deep discount bonds, 640-43
  difficulties in measuring performance of, 630
  holding, 631, 646-47
    declining yields (rising prices), 645
    hedged position, 646
    rising yields (declining prices), 645-46
  issue selection, 643-45
  market models, creation of, 636-39
  moderate discount bonds, 640-42
  new money, 645-46
  pension fund investments, 625-26
  performance measurement in coupon areas, 630-47
  premium bonds, 640-41
  price performance among coupon areas in, 630-47
  price volatility determinants, 633-36, 639-40

Bond portfolios—Cont.
  restructuring of existing holdings, 646
  rising yields (declining prices)
    holding, 645-46
    major rise, 642-43
    moderate rise, 641-42
    trading, 646
  trading, 631, 646-47
    declining yields (rising prices), 646
    hedged position, 646
    rising yields (declining prices), 646
  volatility, 633-36, 639-40
  yield spreads and changes, 632, 635-36
  yields defined and classified, 631-32
Bond yields; see Interest rates and Bond portfolios
Book value of common stock, 352-62
  distortion of, 352
  dividend payout, 355-57
  fundamentalist approach, 360-61
  growth in earnings, 355
  growth in market price, 355
  hypothetical illustrations, 353-55
  long-term growth, 353
  percent earned, calculation of, 352-53
  postwar period, 352
  present day analysis, 352-53
  price-earnings ratio, 357-62
  rate of return, 353
  relationships in analysis of, 355
  significance of, 361
Borrowing, 96-99, 112
  defined, 107n
Brown, Murray, 151n
Budget surplus, 103
Built-in stabilizers, 276-77
Bureau of the Census, 70, 80-82
Bureau of Employment Statistics, 70
Bureau of Labor Statistics, 194-95
Bureau of the Budget, 131, 195
Burroughs Corporation, 11-12
Business Cycle Developments, 82, 170
Business cycles, 239-42
  money, influence of, 251-55
  money supply in, role of, 237-55
  reference cycles, 239
Business forecasts, 84-87; see also Forecasts and forecasting
Butters, J. Keith, 140

C

Cacy, J. A., 209 ff.
Cady, Roberts & Co. case, 683, 721 ff.
California Division of Corporations, 678-79
Canadian restricted list of securities, 325
Capital expenditures, 99-101
  defined, 99
Capital markets, 292-94
Capital turnover defined, 153n

Index

Capitalization rates, long-run projection of, 275–78
Carleton, W. T., 300
Carter, Anne P., 202
Cash dividends, 31–32
Census, 70; *see also* Bureau of the Census
Chase, Samuel, 209 ff.
Chestnutt, George A., Jr., 472
Clay, Lucius, 487
Clendenin, John C., 433–36
Commercial & Financial Chronicle, The, 401–2
Commercial banks, 252–53
Commodity prices, 263–65
Common stocks; *see also* Securities
  book value in evaluation of; *see* Book value of common stock
  diversification in portfolio, 513–14
  economic analysis of investment in, 83
  equivalent, 56–58
  growth rate of; *see* Growth rate analysis
  input-output analysis, 193–208; *see also* Input-output analysis
  institutional investment in, 287–88
  long-term investment medium, 418–19
  pension fund investment in, 503, 626
  price-earnings ratio; *see* Price-earnings ratio
  trading medium, 418
  valuation methods; *see* Growth stock valuation
  valuation tables; *see* Stock valuation tables
  values, determination of, 301–2
  volatility of portfolio of; *see* Portfolio management and selection
Common Stocks as Long Term Investments, 418
COMPUSTAT data base, 344; *see also* Computer-aided financial analysis
  growth stock valuation, 449–50
  price-earnings ratio studies, use in, 402–3
Computer-aided financial analysis
  applications of, 342–44
  caveats in, 342–51
  comparability among companies, 346
  compilation procedures, 348–49
  comprehensiveness, 348
  COMPUSTAT data base, 344 ff.
  data bases for, 342, 344
    limitations of, 344–46
  data retrieval operations, 343
  definitions, 348–49
  First Financial Language (FFL), 342
  implications for, 350–51
  lack of qualitative and descriptive disclosures, 347

Computer-aided financial analysis—*Cont.*
  Language for the Aid of Financial Fact Finders (LAFFF), 342
  languages for, 342–43
  limitations of the data base, 344–45
    compilation procedures, 345–46, 348–49
    definitions, 345–46, 348–49
    reporting format, 345–46
    source data, 345
  noncomparable data, 346
  non-quantitative disclosures, 347
  portfolio management and selection, use in, 343, 502, 508, 666–68
  reliability, 349–50
  research, 344
  stock valuation and selection, 343
  uniformity, appearance of, 346
Conglomerate defined, 35; *see also* Diversification, of product-lines
Consolidated financial statements
  corporate profits, treatment of, 138–39
  necessity of, 9n
  subsidiary earnings, recognition of, 9–13
Consumer durables, 159–61
Consumer end products, 159–61
Consumer intermediate products, 159–61
Continental Illinois National Bank and Trust Company (Chicago, Ill.), 403
Convertible bonds, 626
Cootner, Paul H., 401, 403
Copper industry study
  actual consumption versus estimated demand, 331
  earnings breakdown for 1964 versus 1966, 337
  forecasting by probabilities, 327–41
  free world production by geographic origin, 330
  ingredients for forecast, 331, 333, 338
  mine needs, 330
    mine capacity versus, 335
    operating rate, 335
  partial probability tree, 333
  price forecast, effect of, 336–37
  primary needs, 334
  probabilistic forecasting approach, 332–36
  refined copper prices, 336
  single point forecasting technique, 331–32
    problems with, 332
  supply and demand elements, 329–30
  traditional forecasting approach, 331–32
    problems with, 332
Cornfield, Jerome, 194
Corporate accounts; *see* Accounting
Corporate bonds; *see* Bond portfolios

INDEX

Corporate diversification; *see* Diversification, of product-lines
Corporate earnings; *see* Corporate profits
Corporate information
  adverse, 727
  analyst's position, 688–90
  cash flow information, 717–31
  conflict of interest problems, 704–5
  criminal liability for trading or tipping, 686
  customer relationship, 709, 717–20
  disclosure of
    competitive reasons for refusal to make, 13, 45
    diversified product lines, income of, 13, 45
    Exchange Act requirements, 317–18
    federal income tax law requirement, 50
    lease commitments, 21
    net income determination, 8–9
    risks of, steps to avoid, 707–8
    statutes relating to, 315
    timely and adequate, 695
    when and how, 686
  equalization policy, 684
  ethical considerations, 725–28
  Financial Analysts Federation policy statement, 714–16
  industry demand versus industry capacity, 700
  insider, 696–97, 704–5, 717–31
  labor situation, 700
  law of, 682–93
  leakage of, 721
  legal position of analyst, 688–90
  market effect of, 724–25
  materiality of, 686, 691–93, 727, 731
    illustrations, 692–93
    insiders' use, 692
    probability, 692
    reasonable investor test, 691
    relation to company activity, 692
    unanswered questions, 693
  meetings with investment groups, 699
  misrepresentation, 682–83
  monetary liability for trading or tipping, 685–86
  negligent press release, 684
  nondisclosure, 682–83
  non-inside, 706
  open-door policy, 715
  panel discussion regarding, 694–713
  policy of Securities and Exchange Commission, 709–11
  predictions and projections, 699–700, 702–3
  price competition, 701–2
  question and answer period, 698

Corporate information—*Cont.*
  release of
    forecast problems, 688
    kinds of information, 687–88
    method, 687
    time, 686–87
  Texas Gulf Sulphur case, 683–93, 714
  tippee's trading with material inside information, liability for, 684–85
  tipping material inside information, 683–84
  trading with material inside information, 683
  value of, 682
Corporate profits
  additional uses of new data, 191–92
  adjustments in, 184–86
  after-tax analysis, 139
  aggregate measures of, 131–35
  analysis of, 174–92
  consolidated reporting, 138–39
  contrasts and change in, 148–73
  cyclical upswing, 148
  deductions for tax purposes, 138
  definition, 174–75
  depletion, types of, 137, 140, 143
  depreciation methods, 137, 140–41, 143
  domestic, 183–85
  econometric model, 188n
  economic analysis of, 89–91
  economic variables affecting, 174–92
  expenses, treatment of, 138
  financial component of, 185
  First National City Bank of New York, data of, 149, 152
  foreign earnings, 138–40
  future estimates, 186–91
    advantages of, 191–92
  gains and losses on property transactions, 137–38, 140
  government agencies data, 149, 152
  income concepts applicable, 137–39
  income items, 138
  income statistics, 136–37
  industrial classification, 131–32
  installment sales, 137–38, 140–41
  inventory valuation adjustment, 185–86
  level of, 148–64; *see also* Manufacturing corporations
  long-run projection, 274–75
  manufacturing corporations, 148–73; *see also* Manufacturing corporations
  national income concept, 174–75
  nonfinancial gross corporate product; *see* Nonfinancial gross corporate product
  reports on, series of, 131–35
    comparisons of, 134
    limitations of, 132

Corporate profits—*Cont.*
  reports on—*Cont.*
    recommendations for the financial analyst, 132–33, 135
  research, 89–91
  Stanford Research Institute data, 149, 152
  structure of, 148–49, 165–73; *see also* Manufacturing corporations
  tax return versus book data, 136–47
    findings for 1964, 141–43
    income concepts, differences in, 137–39
    industry comparisons, 141–43
    measurement of differences, 139–41
    pilot study of Schedule M-1, 143–46
  total, 185–86
Corporation Records, 133
Cost analysis, 179–83
Cost of goods sold, 169–71
Cowles Commission, 364, 441
Cowles Magazines and Broadcasting Inc., 7–8
Credit agencies, book profits versus tax return profits, 141
Credit availability, changes in, 254
Cresap, McCormick and Paget, 482
Crude petroleum and natural gas industry, book profits versus tax profits, 141
Cummin, Robert, 420, 510–11
Current expenditures defined, 99
Current transactions, 102–5

D

Dale, Ernest, 482
Davis, Richard G., 209 ff.
Deficit sector, 101, 104–5, 107
  dishoarding by, 111
  financial markets, significance of, 108
Definitions; *see specific terms*
Demand deposits, 107n
Department of Commerce, 131–34
  input-output analysis, research on, 194
  National Income Accounts of, 92
  series for study of corporate profits, 174 ff.
Depletion
  corporate profits on tax return and on books, 137, 140–41, 143
  cost, 137, 140
  percentage, 137, 140–41
Depreciation
  accelerated, 16–18
  consistency in method of treatment, 16
  corporate profits on tax return and on books, 137, 140–41, 143
  diversification of product-lines, 37

Depreciation—*Cont.*
  manufacturing corporations
    earnings affected by, 151
    rate of return adjustments, 155
    structure of profits, 169–71
  methods used, 49, 51
  steel companies' treatment, 14–16
  tax regulations versus accounting principles, 14–16
Dewing, Arthur Stone, 411
Dietz, Peter O., 574
Directory of Companies Filing Annual Reports with the Securities and Exchange Commission under the Securities Exchange Act, 325
Disclosure of corporate information; *see* Corporate information
Diversification
  in portfolio management, 511, 513, 573
    "buy and hold forever" philosophy, 515
    common stocks, 513–14
    factors, 514
    Markowitz-type portfolio model, 513–14, 573
    mutual funds, 559
    pension fund investments, 534
    probability measurement, 515–16
    risk versus, 514
    time horizon function, 516
    traditional view, 514
  of product-lines, 34–36
    balance sheet, 36–37
    definition, 34–35
    depreciation, 37
    development, 34
    external versus internal, 37–38
    financial statement breakdowns, need for, 36
    income statement, 13, 36–37
    market-based prices, 41–45
    product-line sectors, 40–41
    readiness and willingness of management to engage in, 39–40
    reporting for firm engaged in, 36–38
    reporting requirements, 34
    transfer pricing, 41–45
    unprofitable operations in early stages of, 38–40
Diversified operations defined, 35
Diversifying company defined, 37
Divisional accounting, 40–41
Dow, Charles H., 377, 470
Dow-Jones Industrial Averages, 90, 438, 501–3, 596–97
  how to beat, 571–72
Dow Theory, 460n, 463, 469–70
Drexel & Co. (Philadelphia, Pa.), 402–3
Drexel Harriman Ripley Incorporated, 402–3

Durable goods industries, 159–61
Duvall, Richard M., 428

E

Earnings available for total capital defined, 153n
Earnings estimates, preparation of, 90–91
Earnings margin
 defined, 153n, 165
 manufacturing corporations profits, structure of, 165–72
Earnings of corporations; see Corporate profits
Earnings per share
 changes in relation to price changes, 454–58
 early method of computing, 54–56
 fully diluted determination of, 56, 60–63
  alternative method, 60–63
  treasury stock method, 60
 historical background to computing method, 54–56
 primary, determination of, 56–60, 63
  common stock equivalent, 56–58
  treasury stock method, 58
  warrants outstanding, 58–59
  weighted average of common stocks, 58–59
 residual security concept, 55–56
Economic analysis
 banking community, use in, 83
 common stock investment field, use in, 83
 computer use in, 344
 corporate profits research, 89–91
 earnings estimates, preparation of, 90–91
 forecasting function, 84–87
 foreign developments, 88–89
 increased use of, 83
 international developments, 88–89
 investment field, use in, 83–84
 money market trends, 87–88
 price trends, 89
 profit margins, 89
 sales trends, 89
 tax structure changes, 90
Economic forecasts, 84–87
Economic growth
 accuracy of rates of, 74–76
 base year, selection of, 76–77
 conceptual problem involved, 77–78
Economic statistics
 cyclical movements in, 80–81
 errors in; see Errors in economic statistics
 irregular movements in, 80–82
 month-to-month movements, 81

Economic statistics—*Cont.*
 Months for Cyclical Dominance (MCD) as measure of, 81
 improvement in, need for, 82
 seasonal patterns, 80–81
 trend-cycle movements, 80–81
Economist, 84–87
Economy, 93
Edwards, Robert D., 470, 478
Efficient markets, 460–61
Einstein, Albert, 68
Eiteman, David, 302
Elliott Wave Principle, 470
Employment statistics; see Bureau of Employment Statistics
EPS; see Earnings per share
Equity price changes, 126–27
Errors in economic statistics
 additional information regarding, 78–80
 canceling out, 68–69
 economic growth rates
  accuracy of, 74–76
  base year, selection of, 76–77
  conceptual problem involved, 77–78
 evasive answers, 68
 foreign versus domestic statistics, 69
 functional speciousness, 70
 international comparisons, 72–73
 lies as basis, 68
 machines, use of, 68
 margin of, 67–68
 measurement of extent of, 81
 national income estimates, 71–72
 nations compared with one another, 72–73
 past versus present statistics, 69
 publication of, need for, 78–79
 reduction in, 82
 sources of, 68–69
 Soviet Union statistics, 73
 specious accuracy, tendency toward, 69–72
 unemployment, determination of, 70–71
Escott v. BarChris Construction Corp., 682
Ethical considerations, 677 ff.
Evans, W. Duane, 194
Ex-Cell-O Corporation, 13n
Exchange Act; see also Securities and Exchange Commission filings
 registration, 318–19
 requirements, 317–18

F

Farrar portfolio model, 537–41
Federal Communications Commission, 324

Index

Federal income tax
  corporate profit data on return versus on company books, 136–47; *see also* Corporate profits
  disclosure of information requirements, 50
  inflation period, rates for, 31
  Schedule M-1 for corporate profits, study of, 139–46
Federal Open Market Committee, 231
Federal Power Commission, 324
Federal Reserve Bank, 252–53
Federal Reserve Board, 117
  flow of funds analysis, 118–24
Federal Reserve Bulletin, 118, 120, 131, 134
Federal Reserve Index of Industrial Production, 87
Federal Reserve Notes, 107n
Federal Reserve System
  avoidance of depression, steps for, 502, 508
  flow of funds accounts of, 92
Federal Trade Commission, 131–34
Feedback of money market to business analysis, 88
Ferguson, Robert, 433, 438–40
FFL; *see* First Financial Language
Fiber glass manufacturing, 38–40
Finance industry, book profits versus tax return profits, 141, 146
Financial accounting; *see* Accounting *and* Accounting principles
Financial analysis
  computer-aided, 342–51; *see also* Computer-aided financial analysis
  stock valuation tables, use of, 376
Financial analyst
  adviser to company, 688–89
  adviser to outsiders, 689
  corporate information sought by, 715
  legal position of, 688–90
  management, interest in and evaluation of, 491–98; *see also* Management
  own analysis, 689–90
  precautions to be taken by, 690
  who might use, 690
Financial Analysts Federation, 502
  corporate information disclosure, policies on, 714–16
Financial Analysts Journal, 378, 400, 403–4, 408, 410–11, 421, 441
Financial assets
  changes in, 96–99
  defined, 94
Financial markets
  deficit sectors, importance to, 108
  defined, 107
  economic function of, 107

Financial markets—*Cont.*
  gross national product in relation to, 108
  importance of, 107–8
  interest rates in relation to, 109–12
  loanable funds as product of, 109
  sources and uses of funds statement, 109–12
Financial reporting of product-lines, 41–42
  diversification; *see* Diversification, of product-lines
  materiality standards, need for, 46
  transfer pricing, 42
Financial statements
  auditor's certificate of approval, significance of, 475
  balance sheet; *see* Balance sheet *and* Statement of financial position
  consolidated; *see* Consolidated statements
  diversified companies, 34
  footnotes to, 23
  general price-level in inflation periods, 25
    conventional statements distinguished, 25
    feasibility of, 32
    historical-dollar, 25, 27
  inadequacy of information from, 474–76
  product line breakdowns, need for, 36
  purpose of, 22
  responsibility for preparation, 23
  Securities and Exchange Commission requirements, 321–22
Financial use of funds defined, 97
First Financial Language (FFL), 342
First National City Bank of New York, 131–34, 149, 152, 157
Fiscal policy, 265, 268
Fisher, Irving, 225, 431, 466
Fisher, Lawrence, 364, 374, 413
Fleischer, Arthur, Jr., 702–3
Flow of funds accounts
  borrowing, 96–99
  defined, 93, 105
  Federal Reserve System, 92
  financial markets, 107–12
  flow of funds matrix for whole economy, 105–7, 113–16
  generalized income statement for single sector, 102–3
  generalized sector balance sheet, 93–96
  gross national product in relation to financial markets, 107–8
  hoarding, 96–99
  importance of, 92
  interest rates in relation to financial markets, 108–12

Flow of funds accounts—*Cont.*
 investment defined, 99–101
 lending, 96–99
 National Income Accounts distinguished, 92–93, 116
 nature of, 93
 potential usefulness of, 116
 saving defined, 99–101
 scope of, 116
 sectoring in, 116
 sectors of economy, 93
 sources and uses of funds statement, 93–94, 97–98, 100–105
Flow of funds analysis
 Bankers Trust Company study, 118–24, 127
 bond men's use of, 117–18
 commercial banks included in residuals, 128
 deliberate residuals, 127
 equity price changes, 126–27
 federal agency operations, 123
 Federal Reserve study, 118–24
 forecasting, use for, 120–21
 foreign investment, inclusion of, 127–28
 "Individuals and Others" residuals, 126–28
 interest rate trends, divergences in, 124–26
 limitations of, 117–30
 market sectors, breakdown for, 125–26
 money and capital markets, 119–22
 mortgage borrowing, 120
 persons making use of, 117
 quarterly basis, 124
 residuals, 127–29
  commercial banks, 128
  defined, 127
  deliberate, 127
  forecasting market conditions, 127
  foreign investments, 128
  "Individuals and Others," 128
  interest rates versus, 129
  unavoidable, 127
  unavoidable errors and discrepancies, 128–29
 Salomon Brothers and Hutzler study, 118–24
 seasonally adjusted quarterly figures, 124
 semi-annual basis, 124
 special problems in preparation of, 123
 studies available, 118–24
 tight money policy, 121
 time periods of less than one year, 124
 Treasury's actual demand for funds, 121–23
 unadjusted raw data, use of, 124
 unavoidable residuals, 127

Flow of funds analysis—*Cont.*
 usefulness of, 129–30
 uses of, 117–30
Flow of funds matrix, 105–7, 113–16
FMC Corporation, 13
Footnotes in financial statements, 23
Forecasts and forecasting
 corporate profits, 186–91
 details to be included in data for, 87
 flow of funds analysis used for, 120–21
 function of economist in making, 84–87
 gross national product, 237
 industry sales through input-output analysis, 205–6
 institutional investing, 294–95
 interest rate trends, 256–70; *see also* Interest rates
 interest rates, 117; *see also* Flow of funds analysis
 investment field, use in, 85–87
 long-run projections; *see* Long-run economic and financial projections
 probabilities, 327–41; *see also* Copper industry study
Foreign dollar bonds, 626–27
Foreign investment, 127–28
Foreign profits, 138–40
Foreign subsidiaries
 consolidation of earnings, 11–13
 earnings recognition, 9–10
Four-digit industry, 35–36
Freuhauf Trailer, 486
Friedman, Milton, 230n
Friedman lag, 228–30
Fundamental stock analysis; *see also* Technical stock analysis
 accounting problems of, 476
 assumptions of, 470
 financial reports, completeness and reliability of, 473–75
 functions involved, 469
 inaccuracy of, 478
 price-earnings multiple, selection of, 476–77
 superiority of, 472–73
 technical analysis distinguished, 471
 unsatisfactory investment results, 473

G

Gains and losses
 accounting principles governing determination, 6–9
 corporate profits on tax return and on books, 137–38, 140
 general price-level, 25
  inflation periods, 31
 inconsistent treatment of, 7–8
 pension funds, treatment for, 618–19
 purchasing power, 25

General Electric Corporation, 347, 350
General Motors Corporation, 431–53; see also Growth stock valuation
General price-level financial statements, 25; see also Inflation, accounting for
conventional statements distinguished, 25
feasibility of, 32
Generalized income statement for single sector, 102–3
GNP; see Gross national product
Goldman, Morris R., 207–8
Government agencies, 149, 152
Graham, Dodd, and Cottle, 419–20, 424
Graham, Dodd, Cottle, and Tatham, 433, 442–43
Gramley, Lyle, 209 ff.
Granville, Joseph E., 469, 477, 479
Great Depression, 151, 247, 682
steps to avoid, 502, 508
Gross national product (GNP)
corporate profits as part of, 174–75
financial markets in relation to, 108
forecast data to include details of, 87
forecasts of, 237
growth rates
accuracy of, 74–76
base year, selection of, 76–77
conceptual problem involved, 77–78
implicit price deflator, 26–27
input-output analysis, 199
manufacturing corporations' level of profits, 151–52
margins of error in estimates of, 71–72
pension fund investment policy considerations, 527–30
projection to 1975, 271–72
Growth rate analysis, 418–30; see also Rate of return
average rate of return, 420
Block and Kisor technique, 421, 424
changes in, factors causing, 424
Charles Pfizer and Company illustration, 425–27
Cummin technique, 420
economic factors, examination of, 420–21
Graham, Dodd, and Cottle technique, 419, 424
intrinsic value theory, 459–60
investment versus trading of common stock, 418–19
Jenks technique, 420
long-term appreciation in common stocks, 419
long-term investment medium, 418–19
marginal approach, 419, 429–30
example, 422–24
importance of, 422
problems in, 425–27

Growth rate analysis—Cont.
National Dairy Products illustration, 422–25
new stock issues, effects of, 427–28, 430
algebraic expression of, 428–29
original theory, 418–19
price-earnings multipliers, application of, 502
recent techniques, 419–20
retained earnings, 425–27
return-on-investment method, 420
Sauvain formula, 420–21, 424
separate analysis, 420
span of years, measure of, 424–25
technical approach; see Technical stock analysis
techniques for, 418–30
Growth stock defined, 432
Growth stock valuation, 431–53
Bauman technique, 436–38, 447
chartist, 459–60
Clendenin technique, 434–36, 447
comparison of assumptions and valuations for seven techniques, 448
COMPUSTAT, use of, 449–50
Ferguson technique, 438–40, 449
formula for, 432
future dividend stream expected from stock, 432, 451
future dividends, 451
General Motors illustration, 431–53
Graham, Dodd, Cottle, and Tatham technique, 442–43, 447, 477
intrinsic, 459–60, 464–67, 472–78
Jenks technique, 444–47, 449
justifiable price-dividend multiplier
determination of, 434–36
standard, comparison with, 438–40
Kurtz technique, 446–47
methods, 431–53
Molodovsky technique, 440–41
nomograph developed for, 438–40, 453
potential for, 450
present value concept, 434–38, 442, 451
price-dividend ratios, 452
retained earnings multiple, 445
technical analysis of; see Technical stock analysis
Value Line technique, 433, 447, 477
variable discount rate method, 436–38, 452
Gurley, John G., 213

H

Hammel, John E., 404
Harbrecht, Paul, 285
Hemphill Noyes and Co., 446
Historical-dollar financial statements, 25, 27

Hoarding, 96–99, 111–12
Hodes, Daniel A., 404
Hoffenberg, Marvin, 194
Homer, Sidney, 126

I

Income determination; *see also* Net income
  basis for, 49
  breakdown on income statement, 13
  conflict in accounting principles, 6–9
  diversified product-lines, 13
  subsidiary earnings, recognition of, 9–13
  tax regulations versus accounting principles, 13–16
Income effects, 252
Income statement
  balance required on, 103–4
  depreciation of steel companies, treatment of, 14–16
  diversification of product-lines, 13, 36–37
  generalized for single sector, 102–3
  product line analysis of, 44
Income tax; *see* Federal income tax *and* Tax regulations
Industrial classification, 131–32
Inflation
  accounting for, 24–33
    cash dividends, 31–32
    federal income tax rates, 31
    field test, 24–33
    gains and losses
      general price level, 31
      purchasing power versus general price-level, 25
    general prive-level financial statements
      conventional statements distinguished, 25
      feasibility of, 32
    gross national product implicit price deflator as measure, 26–27
    net income, 28
      ballooning effect, 29
      company operations, nature of, 30
      comparisons between companies, 30
      crosscurrents caused by restatement of, 29–30
      understatement and overstatement, 27, 29
      wide variation between general price-level and historical-dollar basis, 27
    rate of return, 32
  manufacturing corporations' earnings, 151, 155

Information; *see* Corporate information
Inland Steel Company, 14–16
Input-output analysis
  applications of concept, 194–95
  basic methodology, 195
  countries adopting, 208
  criticism of, 207–8
  definitions of terminology, 193–94
  direct coefficients to measure demand, 199, 206–7
  estimating application of
    industry sales, 205–6
    capital equipment orders, 206–7
  final demand, 193
  gross national product in relation to, 199
  historical background of concept, 194–95
  industry sales forecast, construction of, 205–6
  input, 193
  interindustry flows, 195–98
  intermediate output, 193
  inventory problem, 207–8
  inverse coefficients, 199–200, 204, 207
  labor productivity, 202
  limitations in use of, 208
  1958 study by Office of Business Economics, 195 ff.
  output, 193
  Pan American contract, 206–7
  short-term application, 204–6
    inventory problem in, 207–8
    timing problem in, 207–8
  stock analysis
    adjustments necessary, 200–201
    application to, 200–206
    changing structure of inputs, 202–4
    equation to translate input-output flows into revenue flows, 204–5
    inverse coefficients, 204
    long-term technological change, 201–2, 204
    short-term effects, anticipation of, 201, 204–6
  tables arranged as matrices, 195–99
  technological changes affecting interindustry flows, 202
  tables to measure, 204
  timing problem, 207–8
  tracing product flows, 195, 199
  value added, 193
Insider information; *see* Corporate information
Insider trading, 310, 321
Installment sales, 137–38, 140–41
Institutional investing
  American Stock Exchange, 651
  auction market versus bourse concept, 651

Institutional investing—*Cont.*
  block "matchmakers," 652–53
  block trading, 290, 650
    broker selection, effect upon, 657
    clean-up bids, 660–61
    crossing, 660
    negotiations, 659–60
    position bidding, 661
    regional exchanges, use of, 661–62
    techniques of, 659–62
  broker selection, 657
  capital markets, impact on, 292–94
  commission business, complexity of, 292
  common stock, 287–88
  competition in, 286
    increase of, 294
  concentration in portfolios of, 289
  dealer relations, 650
  discretion involved in, 658
  diversification, 294
  equities, 503
  fundamental introduction to, 648–65
  future trends, 294–95
  growth of, 285
  importance of, 285–86
  increase in, 648
  inquiries, handling of, 658–59
  institutional trader
    defined, 649
    functions of, 649–50
    importance of, 649
    professionalism of, 649
  knowledge of issues, 655–56
  market information, providing of, 650
  markets within "the market," 650–53
  mutual funds, 288–89
  New York Stock Exchange, 651
    trading patterns on, 289–92
  orders, handling of, 662–65
  orders, types of, 653
    "market," 654
    "not held," 654–55
    "or better," 654
  over-the-counter market, 651–52
  patterns of, 287–90
  pension funds, 287–88
  performance
    definition of, 286–87
    demonstration of, 286–87, 295
  portfolios of, 287–90
  records kept, 657
  regional stock exchanges, 652
  Salomon Brothers and Hutzler analysis, 293
  size of funds involved, 285–86
  stock exchange institutions, impact on, 290–92
  third market, 291, 652
  trading volume of, 289, 656

Institutional investing—*Cont.*
  trends in, 285–95
  turnover of holdings in portfolio, 289
Institutional investor; *see* Institutional investing
Institutional trader; *see* Institutional investing
Institutional trading; *see* Institutional investing
Insurance industry, book profits versus tax return profits, 141
Interest rates
  bonds, divergences in, 124–26
  defined, 111
  determination of, 111
  financial markets in relation to, 109–12
  forecasting of, 117; *see also* Flow of funds analysis
  loanable funds, price of, 110
  trends
    cyclical 259–68
      commodity prices and unemployment, 263–65
      fiscal policy, 265, 268
      monetary policy, 265, 268
      price fluctuations, 261–62
      supply and demand for credit, 264–67
      tentative economic model for year ahead, 260–63
    divergences in, 124–26
    forecasting
      in 1966 boom year, 268–70
      techniques for, 256–68
    long term, 257–59
    medium-term, 259–68
    seasonal, 257
    secular, 257–59
    short-term, 257
Internal Revenue Service, 131–34
International Harvester Corporation, income statement breakdown, 13
Interstate Commerce Commission, 324
  accelerated depreciation, treatment of, 16–18
  accounting principles, 50
  uniform system of accounts, inflexibility of, 16–18
Intrinsic value approach to stock valuation, 459–60, 464–67, 472–78
Inventories, methods of stating, 49–51
Invested capital, rate of return on; *see* Manufacturing corporations
Investment; *see also* Portfolio management and selection
  defined, 99–100
  foreign, 127–28
  institutional, 285–95; *see also* Institutional investing
  meanings of, 678–79

Investment—*Cont.*
 price-earnings ratio as guides for, 400–404, 407–11
 stock valuation tables, use of, 378
Investment adviser, 522
 best suited for portfolio management and selection, 563–64
Investment analysis
 accounting principles involved, 3–23; *see also* Accounting principles
 common stock values, determination of, 301–2
 computer programs, usefulness of, 299
 conflict currently extant in, 299–303
 conventional techniques versus elaborate mathematical models, 300–301
 forecast results, use of, 87
 growth yields, tables of, 302
 iso-yield curves, series of, 302
 potential economic values, appraisal of, 299–300
 potential risks, estimating techniques of, 300
 potential stream of earnings and dividends, 301
 present-value techniques, 301–2
 prospective price performance, 302
 random walk theory, 300
 values in absolute or relative terms, 301
Investment Company Act, 323
Investment credit deduction, federal tax treatment of, 18–20
Investment decision; *see* Investment analysis *and* Portfolio management and selection
Investment management
 analyzing risk, 578–79
 basis for policy of, 87
 characteristic line, 579, 593–95
  application to funds, 580
  comparison of performance, 582–83
  defined, 579–80
  deviations, 581–82
  implications for control, 583
  information revealed, 580–81
 economic analysis in, use of, 83–91; *see also* Economic analysis
 forecasts, use of, 85–87
 foreign developments, 88–89
 how to rate performance of, 478–95
 importance of, 578
 international developments, 88–89
 overcoming difficulties in, 579
 performance measure, 583–87
 performance ratings, 588
  differences, importance of, 591–93
  numerical measure, 589–91
  relative ranking, 588–89, 594

Investment management—*Cont.*
 portfolio-possibility line, 583, 593
  choices, 584–87
  pension funds, 587
  quantitative measure, 587
  risk preference, 583–84
  trust funds, 587
 risk in, 578
  types of, 579
"Investment Outlook, The," 118
Investment performance
 assessment of, 536–37
 measure of, 537
 mutual funds; *see* Mutual funds
 objective, requirement of, 539
 portfolio selection distinguished, 536–38
Investment policy
 bonds for pension funds; *see* Pension funds
 changes in versus stock market, 574–77
 elements in, 574
 pension funds; *see* Pension funds
 timing, 573–74
Investment recommendations; *see* Securities and Exchange Commission filings
Investment team, past and present, 649

J

Jenks, Jeremy C., 420, 433, 444–46
Journal of Finance, 117

K

Kareken, John H., 209 ff.
Kendall rank correlation, 247n, 248n
Kennecott Copper earnings, 338–39
Keynes, John Maynard, 220, 222, 225 ff., 303
Khrushchev, Nikita, 73
Kimberly-Clark Corporation, 10–11
Kisor, Manown, Jr., 421, 424, 450
Korean war, 153, 186
Kurtz, William, 433, 446–47
Kuznets, Simon, 71–72

L

Labor statistics; *see* Bureau of Labor Statistics
Labor supply, long-run projection, 273
LAFFF; *see* Language for the Aid of Financial Fact Finders
Language for the Aid of Financial Fact Finders (LAFFF), 342
Law of increasing stock values and income return, 419
Lawrence, C. J., and Sons, 444
Lease commitments
 accounting principles governing, 21–22

Index

Lease commitments—*Cont.*
  disclosure of information relating to, 21
Lending, 96–99, 112
  defined, 107n
Leontief, Wassily, 194
Leontief inverse coefficients, 199–200, 204, 207
Lerner, Eugene M., 300
Level of profits; *see* Manufacturing corporations
Liquidity effects, 252n
Liquidity needs of pension funds, 526–27, 534–35
Litton Industries, 502
Loanable funds
  demand for, 109–12
  financial markets, product of, 109
  rate of interest as price of, 110
  supply of, 110–12
Long-run economic and financial projections, 271–80
  basic growth forces, 273–74
  capitalization rates, 275–78
  gross national product in constant prices to 1975, 271–72
  industry outlook, 278–79
  labor supply, 273
  market outlook, 278
  price-earnings ratio, 275–78
  prices, 274
  productivity, 273–74
  profits, 274–75
  sales, 274
  stock prices, 275–78
  total real gross national product, 273–74
  unemployment, 273
Lorie, James H., 364, 374, 413, 466
Losses; *see* Gains and losses

M

Macaulay, Frederick, 377
McWilliams, James D., 403–4, 413
Magee, John, 470, 478
Malkiel, B. G., 432
Management
  appraisal of, 482–90
    complementary talents, 488–90
    control, 487–88
    five elements of, 483 ff.
    mergers, 489
    method of, 482–83
    organization, 484–86
    personnel development and motivation, 486–87
    planning, 483–84
    summary, 490
  criteria for, 492–93

Management—*Cont.*
  definition, 492–93
  evaluation of, 491–92
    ages of persons, 496
    analytical controls, 497
    caution in, 494–95
    development program, 496
    factors involved in, 493–94
    judgment in acquisitions and mergers, 496–97
    labor relations, 497
    leadership, quality of, 496
    limitations of, 494–95
    Management Audit reports, 493
    marketing and sales efforts, 497
    objectives and goals, 495
    opinion of other management, 498
    organization structure, 495–96
    quality control, 497
    research and development programs, 497
    sound practices, 496
    suggested factors for use in, 495–98
    techniques of, 493–94
  financial analyst's interest in, 491–92
  investments; *see* Investment management
  pension funds, 587
  portfolio selection; *see* Portfolio management and selection
  qualities required for, 492–93
Management Audit reports, 493
Managers; *see* Management
Manufacturing corporations
  book profit versus tax return profit, 143
  levels of profits, 148–49
    after-taxes figures, 150
    amount earned in dollars, 149–53
    depreciation factor, 151
    distortion of, 150
    Great Depression, recovery from, 151
    gross national product in relation to, 151–52
    growth rates, 150
    inflation, 151
    1947–1964 earnings, 153–57
    1964 earnings, 162–64
    postwar period, 152–53
    rate of return on invested capital, 149, 152–57
    war years, 151
  postwar analysis of profits of, 153–64
  profit margin increase, 148
  rate of return on invested capital, 149, 152–57
    adjustments due to inflation and depreciation changes, 155
    definitions of terms used, 153n

Manufacturing corporations—*Cont.*
   rate of return on invested capital—*Cont.*
      disaggregation of manufacturing sector, 157–59
      durable versus nondurable goods groups, 158–59, 161
      long-term perspective, 155–57
      major components, comparative performance by, 159–62
      period-by-period analysis, 162–64
      postwar and prewar comparison, 156
      postwar eras, 153–55
      Stanford Research Institute sample, 157–58, 161
   structure of profits, 148–49, 165–73
      change over last three decades, 165–67
      changes which occurred in, 172–73
      cost of goods sold, 169–71
      depreciation, 169–71
      earnings margin, 165–72
      net operating income ratio, 171–72
      research and development costs, 171
      selling, general and administrative expenses, 169, 171
      total operating expense ratio, 169–70
      turnover of principal asset categories, 168–69
      turnover of total capital, 165–72
Marginal approach to growth rate analysis, 419, 422–27, 429–30
Market letter; *see* Research reports
Market prices, 41–45
Markowitz, Harry M., 509, 517
Markowitz-Farrar portfolio model, 537–41
Markowitz-type portfolio model, 509–10
   computational procedure, 670–72
   data requirements, 670–72
   diversification of holdings, 513–14, 573
   efficient portfolios suggested, 512
   implementation problems, 672–74
      computational, 672
      data, 672–74
   nature of, 668–70
   nonlinear programming calculation, 670–72
   purpose of, 666–68
   time horizon, 512
Marshall, Alfred, 431
Mathematical analysis of portfolio selection, 666–74; *see also* Markowitz-type portfolio model
MCD; *see* Months for Cyclical Dominance
Mergers, 489
Merrill Lynch case, 685, 714
Metal industries, book profit versus tax return profit, 143

Miller, Herbert E., 22
Miller, Paul F., Jr., 402, 412
Molodovsky, Nicholas, 364, 374, 433, 440–41
Monetarist thesis; *see* Monetary policy
Monetary analysis, development of, 209
Monetary base, 231–33
Monetary growth, cyclical fluctuations of, 210, 219–25
Monetary liabilities, 107n
Monetary policy
   application of economic analysis to financial markets and institutions, 212n, 218–19, 235
   bank credit, effect upon, 217
   banks' behavior, consideration of, 211, 215–16
   business conditions in relation to, 245–46
   Cacy, views of, 209 ff.
   countercyclical policy, 230–35
   criticisms of established procedures, 209
   cyclical behavior of, money in relation to, 245–46
   cyclical fluctuations in monetary growth, 210, 219–25
   Davis, views of, 209 ff.
   defense of established procedures, 209–12
   Federal Open Market Committee interpretation, 231
   Gramley-Chase, views of, 209 ff.
   indicator problem, 233–35
   interest rate trends, forecasting of, 265, 268
   interpretation of, 230–35
   Kareken, views of, 209 ff.
   lags in effects of, 248–51
   Monetarist thesis, 209, 235–36
      cyclical fluctuations in monetary growth, 220–21
      empirical theories, 214–15
      examination of New View money supply theory, 216–19
      Friedman lag, 228–30
      income-expenditure approach, 226–27
      money supply processes, 214
      rejection of, 210–11
      strong, 227–30
      weak, 225–27
   monetary dynamics, analysis of, 227–28
   money stock, effect upon, 217
   New View, 236
      analysis of medium of exchange function, 214n
      money supply theory, 216–19

Monetary policy—*Cont.*
  New View—*Cont.*
    nature of, 213
    research strategy, 212n, 213-14
    specific conjectures of, 212n, 216-19
    traditional view versus, 210-12
  public's behavior, consideration of, 211, 215-16
  relevance with respect to economic activity, 225-30
  role of, 209-36
  target problem, 234-35
  Wicksell-Keynes mechanism, 220, 222
Money
  behavior affecting behavior of economy, 237
  business cycles, role in, 237-55
  cycles in, 239-42
    monetary policy in relation to, 245-46
    severity of, 246-48
  defined, 237
  growth rate
    cycles in, 239-42
    cyclical contractions in, 247-48
    maintenance of, 238
    monetary policy, relevance of, 245-46
  importance as determinant of business conditions, 237-38
  income effects, 252
  influence of business on, 242-45
    balance of payments, 243
    complexity of, 244
    Federal Reserve member banks' borrowing, 243
    gold imports or exports, 243
    monetary policy, 245-46
    ratio of bank excess reserves to deposits, 244
    ratio of public holding of coin and currency to bank deposits, 243
  influence on business, 251-55
    measuring lags in, 248-51
  liquidity effects, 252n
  market trends
    feedback to business analysis, 88
    research in, phases of, 88
    uses of, 87
  printing of, 95, 101n, 105n, 107n
  portfolio balance, 252n
  relevance with respect to economic activity, 225-30
  role of, 209-36
    business cycles, 237-55
    substitution effects, 252-53
    wealth effects, 252
Money stock; *see* Monetary policy
Money supply; *see* Money
Monthly Economic Letter, 131-34

Months for Cyclical Dominance (MCD)
  improvement in, need for, 82
  measure of economic statistics, 81
Moody's Manuals, 135
Moore index, 247n
Mortgages
  flow of funds analysis, 120
  pension fund investment in, 627
Municipal bonds, pension fund investment in, 627
Murphy, 302
Mutual funds
  alternative models of investment performance, 541-47, 551-56
  application in other periods, 547-51
  classification by stock portfolio size, 546-47
  construction of random portfolios and performance relatives, 560-61
  controversy concerning, 538-41
  diversification of risk, 559
  holding period concept, 542n, 543n
  institutional investment in, 288-89
  Markowitz-Farrar portfolio model, 537-41
  objective of investors in, 539
  portfolio selection and investment performance distinguished, 536-38
  random walk theory, 467
  randomization, 556-58
  role played by, 559
  selection of, basis for, 503
  study of, 536 ff.

N

National Association of Securities Dealers, Inc., 678-79
National Bureau of Economic Research (NBER), 471
  reference cycles of, 239-40
National Cash Register Company, 11-12
National Daily Quotation Service, The, 651
National Dairy Products, 422-25
National debt concept, 95-96
National income; *see* Gross national product
National Income Accounts
  Department of Commerce, 92
  familiarity with, 92
  flow of funds accounts distinguished, 92-93, 116
  importance of, 92
  sectoring in, 116
  sectors of economy, 93
  scope of, 116
National Industrial Conference Board, 492-93
National Planning Association, 195

INDEX

Nazi Germany, unemployment in, 70
NBER; *see* National Bureau of Economic Research
Net income; *see also* Income determination
  all-inclusive concept, 6–7
  current operating performance concept, 6–7
  disclosure of information, 8–9
  inflation, accounting for, 27–30; *see also* Inflation, accounting for
Net operating income ratio, 171–72
Net worth, 94–95
  addition to, 103
  changes in, 99–101
  defined, 100, 103
  increase in, 100
New York Society of Security Analysts, 492
New York Stock Exchange, 503
  guideposts for securities recommendations, 305–6
  institutional investing, 651
  institutional investment
    estimate, 286
    trading patterns, 289–92
  research reports, rules governing, 678–79
NFGCP; *see* Nonfinancial gross corporate product
Nicholson, S. Francis, 400–440, 412–13
Nondurable goods industries, 159–61
Nonfinancial gross corporate product (NFGCP), 175–78, 184–85
  cost analysis, 179–83
  defined, 175–76
  future estimates, 188–91
    advantages of, 191–92
  historical analysis, 176–78
  labor costs, 179–83
  nonlabor costs, 179–80
  price deflator for, 176

O

Office of Business Economics, 194–95
  input-output analysis of common stocks, 195 ff.
Office of Statistical Standards, 195
Official Summary, 325
Olin Mathieson Chemical Company, 13
Organization Man, The, 486
Over-the-counter securities, 474
  Exchange Act requirements, 317–18
  institutional investing in, 651–52

P

Pan American World Airways
  contract for 747 airliners, 206–7
  investment credit deduction, 19

Pension funds
  accounting procedures, 617–18
  average return, 600–601
  bond investment policy for, 619, 627–29
    call protection, 622–24
    choice, 624–27
    continuity, 622–24
    credit risk, 619–20
    maturity, 620–22
    selection, 624–27
  cash flows, 609
  characteristics of, 615–17
  comparison of one with another, 605
  compound rate of return, 598–99, 606
  division of assets into categories, 612
  equivalents, 602–3, 605
  fiduciary responsibility for, 616
  flexibility in investment of, 616–17
  gains and losses, treatment of, 618–19
  growth rate of, 615
  income on income, 599–600
  institutional investment in, 287–88
  interest rate divergences, 125–26
  internal rate of return, 607–8
  investment policy for, 522–35
    actuarial methods to compute benefits, 526
    arrangements for, 522
    common stock, 503
    development of the investment decision, 522–25
    diversification, 534
    economic environment, consideration of, 527–30, 535
    establishment of, 527–34
    financial risk, 525
    fixed-equity ratio, 527
    gross national product considerations, 527–30
    interest rate risk, 525
    investment adviser versus trustee, 522
    liquidity needs, 526–27, 534–35
    media selection, 533–34
    objectives
      general, 525
      specific, 525–27
    performance results examined, 530–33
    Prudent Man Rule, 526
    purchasing power risk, 525
    rewards expected, 525
    risks assumed, 525
    securities market environment, 530
    stock-bond yield patterns, 530, 535
    tax considerations, 526
    timing, 574–77
  legislative limitations, 617
  linked internal-rate-of-return method, 609

Pension funds—*Cont.*
  long-run nature of, 616
  management of, 587
  mean absolute deviation, 610–11
  measurement of performance of, 587, 596–606
    management summary of, 607–14
    recommendations for, 612–14
  media for investment of, 624–27
  objective of, 615–16
  partitioned, 611–12
  portfolio performance, 603–4
  rates of return, 607–14
  regression method, 609
  restrictions imposed upon, 617–19
  risk measurement, 609–10
    mean absolute deviation, 610–11
  tax-free, 616
  time-weighted rate of return, 608–9
  trend of value, 602
  variations in, 596–97
Petroleum refining industry, book profits versus tax return profits, 141
Pfizer, Charles, and Company, 425–27
Phelps Dodge earnings, 338, 340
"Pink Sheets," 651
Pittsburgh Plate Glass Company, 38–40
Planned transactions, 112
Portfolio balance, 252n
Portfolio management and selection; *see also specific topics*
  approaches to, 504–8
  assessment of, 536
  basic elements of, 509–21
  bond-stock yield relationship, change in, 501–3, 507–8
  bonds; *see* Bond portfolios
  computer-aided selection, 343, 502, 508, 666–68
  conservative manager, 563–64
  considerations of portfolio manager in, 504–8
  contributions to, timing and size of, 572–73
  Cummin's view, 510–11
  depression, avoidance of, 502, 508
  development of investment decision, 522–25
  dichotomy between practitioners and academicians, 521
  distribution curves, appearance of, 510
  diversification, 511, 513–16
  Dow Jones averages, how to beat, 571–72
  elements of, 509–21
  gambling analogy, 520–21, 563–64
  institutional investor; *see* Institutional investing
  investment adviser best suited for, 563–64

Portfolio management and selection—*Cont.*
  investment performance
    distinguished, 536–38
    since 1940's, 501–3
  investment policy, 573–77
  Markowitz-type model; *see* Markowitz-type portfolio model
  mathematical analysis of, 666–74
  mutual funds; *see* Mutual funds
  optimality of, 537
  pension funds; *see* Pension funds
  performance measurement, 501–3, 562–77
    comparisons of techniques, 567–68
    influence of, 503–4
    standards of, 566–67
  pressure for short-term performance, 513
  price expectations, 510
  probability measurement, 515–16
  pruning of portfolios, diligence in, 573
  random errors and deviations, 510
  random selection, 466
  random walk theory, 510–11
  randomization, 556–58; *see also* Mutual funds
  rate of return variability, 509, 517–18
    linear or nonlinear return, 519–20
  risk elements, 509, 562–77
    characteristics of securities, 566
    defined, 564–66
    diversification versus, 514
    techniques for measurement of, 566
  security analysis methods, advancement in, 502, 508
  short-term performance, 513
  small firms, participation in growth of, 502–3, 508
  stock market indexes as guide, 503–4
  structuring theory, 509–21
  sub-strategies, 518–19
  time horizon, 511–13
  trained investment personnel, additions of, 502
  variability of rate of return, 509, 517–18
  volatility, 511, 516–17
    measurement of, 568–71
Postwar period
  book value of common stock, 352
  manufacturing corporations
    level of profits, 152–53
    profitability, 153–64
    rate of return on invested capital, 153–55
Preferred stocks, 626
Price
  changes in relation to earnings changes, 454–58

752 INDEX

Price—Cont.
  common stock; see Stock prices
  long run projection, 274
  trends, 89
Price-earnings ratio
  book value of common stock, 357–62
  built in stabilizers, 276–77
  changes in, 408–9
  COMPUSTAT data use, 402–3
  growth expectations, 404–5
  high versus low, 404–6, 411–17
  investment guides, use as, 400–404, 407–11
  investment policy or strategy based on, 406–7
  long-run projections, 275–78
  periodic cumulative reinvestment approach, 413–17
  risk premium, 276–77
  stock prices in relation to, 409–11
  structure of, 405–6
  studies of, 400–413, 414–17
  usefulness of, 414–17
  value in use of, 411–13
Primary industry operations, 39
Probabilities, 327–41; see also Copper industry study
Producer equipment, 159–61
Producer intermediate products, 159–61
Producer materials, 159–61
Product line
  analysis of assets by, 43
  analysis of income statement by, 44
  diversification of; see Diversification, of product-lines
  general sector in accounting for, 42–45
  loss shown for, 46
  sectors of; see Product-line sectors
Product-line sectors
  divisional structure versus, 40
  interrelationships, 40–41
  transfer pricing, 41–45
Profit and loss statement, 679
Profit margins, 89
  defined, 153n, 165
Profits of corporations; see Corporate profits
Projections 1970: Interindustry Relationships, Potential Demand, Employment, 279
Provident National Bank (Philadelphia, Pa.), 400
Proxy requirements, 320–21
Prudent Man Rule of investments, 526
Public utilities, book profits versus tax return profits, 141, 143
Public Utility Holding Company Act, 323
Publicly owned securities; see Securities and Exchange Commission filings

Q

Quality growth stocks, 290
Quarterly Financial Report for Manufacturing Corporations, 131–34

R

Railroads
  accounting principles, 50
  uniform system of accounts, inflexibility of, 16–18
Random sampling, 466
Random walk theory, 300, 459–68, 597
  basis of, 460–61
  challenges presented by, 467–68, 480
  competition, effect of, 460–61
  Dow Theory, 460n, 463
  efficient markets, 460–61
  empirical evidence on independence, 462–64
  filter technique, 463
  implications of, 479–80
    chartist and intrinsic value analysis, 464–67
  importance of, 467
  independence of price changes, 461–62
  mutual funds, 467
  nature of, 459
  portfolio construction, 510–11
  statistical techniques, 462–63
  techniques for predicting stock market prices, 459–60
  testing of, 462–64
Rate of interest; see Interest rates
Rate of return; see also Growth rate analysis
  book value of common stock, 353
  changes in relation to price changes, 454–58
  inflation, accounting for, 32
  manufacturing corporations; see Manufacturing corporations
  pension funds, 598–99, 607–10
  portfolio construction, variability in, 509, 517–18
    linear or nonlinear return, 519–20
  stock valuation tables, 367, 374–78
  on total capital defined, 153n
Real assets
  acquisition of, 99–101
  changes in, 99–101
  defined, 94
  increase in, 100
Realized transactions, 112
Regional stock exchanges, 291, 652
  block trading by institutional investors, 661–62

Index

Regulation S-X, 321–22
Report of the Special Study of Securities Markets, 304–6
Reports, inadequacy of information in, 474–75
Research; *see* Economic analysis
Research and development costs, 171
Research Project on the Structure of the American Economy, 194, 202
Research reports
 balance sheet in, 679–80
 comparison of companies, 680
 criticisms of, 677–78
 earnings projections, 680
 earnings summary in, 679
 ethics of, 677–81
 expert opinion on improvement of, 681
 guidelines for improvement of, 677
 investment, meanings of word, 678–79
 market letter, 677–78
 profit and loss statement, 679
 projections of earnings, 680
 regulation of, 678–79
 rules governing, 678–79
 sins of omission in, 679
Residual defined, 127
Residual security defined, 55
Residuals; *see* Flow of funds analysis
Retained earnings, 103
Return on total capital defined, 165n
Revenue Act of 1962, 18–20
Revenue Act of 1964, 18–19
Ripley, William Z., 48
Risk; *see* Pension funds *and* Portfolio management and selection

S

Sales
 long-run projection, 274
 trends, 89
Salomon Brothers and Hutzler, 293, 636
 flow of funds analysis, 118–24
Sauvain, Harry C., 420–21, 424
Sauvain formula, 420–21
Saving defined, 100, 103
SEC; *see* Securities and Exchange Commission
SEC News Digest, 325
Sector defined, 93
Securities; *see also* Common stock
 block "matchmakers," 652–53
 block trading of; *see* Institutional investing
 blue chip, 290
 buying and selling of, 108–10
 commercial bank purchases of, 252–53
 defined, 108n
 Federal Reserve purchases of, 252–53
 price changes, effects of, 126–27

Securities—*Cont.*
 quality growth, 290
 selection of; *see* Investment analysis
 speculative, 290
Securities Act Amendments of 1964, 304–5, 317, 474
Securities Act of 1933, 9
 registration statements, 315–16
 Regulation A filings under, 316–17
Securities and Exchange Commission (SEC), 131–34
 commissions for stock transactions, 292
 investment credit, treatment of, 19
 net income determination, principles governing, 7
 regional offices, 317n
 research reports, criticism of, 677–78
Securities and Exchange Commission filings, 304–26
 adequacy of investigation underlying a recommendation, 304–14
 analysis of information contained in, 313–14
 annual reports, 322–23
 banks, 323
 basis for recommendations by professional, 305, 307–9
 best or only available source of information, illustrations of, 309–14
 Canadian restricted list, 325
 content and use, 315–26
 copies of filed documents, availability of, 313
 copies of information, inspecting or obtaining, 324
 disclosure requirements in, 309
 Exchange Act
  registration, 318–19
  requirements, 317–18
 exempt issuers, 323–24
 financial statements, 309–10, 321–22
 forms
  commonly used, description of, 326
  consulted prior to recommendations, 312–13
  periodic reports, 319–20
  Securities Act registration statements, 316
  Securities Act Regulation A, 316–17
 full disclosure requirements, 311–12
 guideposts of New York Stock Exchange, 305–6
 inadequacies of, 474
 information necessary for, 307–8
 insider securities transactions, 310, 321
 insurance companies, 323–24
 investigation to be made by professional, 306–7
 investment companies, 323

754 INDEX

Securities and Exchange Commission filings—*Cont.*
  listed companies, 317
  management changes, 310–11
  miscellaneous material available as information sources, 324–25
  misrepresentations, 311
  OTC registered companies, 317–18
  over-the-counter companies, 305, 317–18
  periodic reports, listing of, 319–20
  persons who make use of, 304
  prospectus, 315–16
  proxy requirements, 320–21
  public utility holding companies, 323
  red herring prospectus, 316
  Regulation S-X, 321–22
  relevance of information in, 309
  Report of the Special Study of Securities Markets, 304–6
  reports required by the Securities and Exchange Commission, 322–23
  reports to security holders, 322–23
  responsibility of persons making recommendations, 312
  Section 15(d) companies, 318
  Securities Act amendments of 1964, 304–5, 317
  Securities Act of 1933
    registration statements, 315–16
    Regulation A, 316–17
  special classes of issuers, 323–24
  standard financial manuals, use of, 308
  statutes relating to, 315
  use to professional analyst, 304–14
  voluntary company reporting in addition to, 308
Security analysis; *see* Financial analysis
Selling, 169, 171
Shapiro, Eli, 537 ff.
Shareholders
  profits, 175
  purpose of furnishing accounts to, 51–52
Sharpe, William F., 511, 517
Shaw, Edward F., 213
SIC Code; *see* Standard Industrial Classification Code
Simons, Walter J., 597
Smith, Edgar Lawrence, 418–19
Smith, Dan Throop, 140
Social accounting, 92
Soldofsky, 302
Sources and uses of funds; *see* Flow of funds analysis
Sources and uses of funds statement
  current transactions, 102–5
  financial markets in relation to interest rates, 109–12
  flow of funds system component, 93–94, 97–98, 100–105

Soviet Union
  statistics of, defects in, 73
  unemployment in, 70
Spearman rank correlation, 247n, 248n
Speculative securities, 290
SRI; *see* Stanford Research Institute
Stable goods, 159–61
Stalin, 73
Standard and Poor's, 90, 133, 364, 438, 441, 503, 597; *see also* COMPUSTAT data base
Standard Industrial Classification, 195
Standard Industrial Classification Code, 35–36
Standard Industrial Classification Manual, 131
Stanford Research Institute (SRI), 149, 152, 157–58, 161
Statement of financial position; *see also* Balance sheet
  diversification of product-lines, 36–37
  importance of, 20
  nature of, 48–53
  objectives of, 20
  purpose of, 48–53
Statistical information; *see* Errors in economic statistics
Statistics of Income, 131–34
  corporate profits, data on, 136–37, 139–40, 146
Steel companies, 14–16
Stock exchanges
  auction market versus bourse concept, 651
  commissions, 292
  institutional investing, impact of, 290–92
  regional, 291, 652
    block trading by institutional investors, 661–62
  specialist system, 651
  third market, 291, 652
Stock market averages, weakness and defects in, 597
Stock market indexes, weighting of, 503–4
Stock prices
  chartist theories for predicting, 459–60
  Dow Theory of predicting, 460n
  long-run projections, 275–78
  price-earnings ratio, 409–11
  random walks in; *see* Random walk theory
  stock valuation tables, use of, 377
  technical analysis of; *see* Technical stock analysis
  techniques for predicting, 459–60

Stock valuation
  adjustments required in use of, 378–79
  advantage of, 379
  basis of, 363
  bond yields, 377–78
  component stocks illustrated (1965–1966), 368–74
  constant growth period, 366
  diminishing growth period, 366–67
  discount rate, 364
  dividend model, 363
  dividend payouts, 364
  earnings charts, 369–73
  financial analysis based on, 376
  form not final, 378–79
  growth pattern used, 365–66
  illustrations in use of, 367–68
  need for, 363
  normal earnings, 366
  operational model, 364–65
  practical investment policy, 378
  projected growth rate of earnings, 366
  rate of return, 367, 374–76
  relationship between dividends and earnings, 364
  reproduction of, 380 ff.
  stock prices indicated by, 377
  stock yields, 377–78
  tables, 380–99
  use of, 366–67, 379
  valuation principles, 363–64
  variables to enter into, 378–79
Stocks; *see* Securities
Strumilin, S. G., 73
Study of Mutual Funds, A, 537 ff.
Subsidiaries; *see also* Affiliates
  accounting principles applicable, 9–13
  controlling financial interest defined, 9
  earnings, recognition of, 9–13
  foreign; *see* Foreign subsidiaries
Substitution effects, 252–53
Supply and demand
  copper industry, 329–30
  interest rate trends, forecasting of, 264–67
"Supply and Demand for Credit," 118–19
Surplus sectors, 101, 104–5, 107
  hoarding by, 111
Survey of Current Business, The, 120, 151n, 174

T

Tax regulations
  corporate taxable income, computation of, 13–16
  depreciation, treatment of, 14–16
Tax value; *see* Corporate profits
Taxable and Business Income, 140

Technical stock analysis, 469–81
  advocates of, 470–72
  Barron's Confidence Index, 470
  conceptual foundations of, 469–81
  criticisms of, 478–79
  defined, 469
  Dow Theory, 469–70
  Elliott Wave Principle, 470
  fundamentalist view distinguished, 469–70; *see also* Fundamental stock analysis
  intrinsic value approach, criticisms of, 472–78
  justification for use of, 471–72
  random walk theory, implications of, 479–80
  summary of theory of, 470
  tools of, 469–70
Texas Gulf Sulphur case, 683–93, 714, 722 ff.; *see also* Corporate information
Texas Instruments, 502
Theory of Investment Value, 431
Third market, 291, 652
Tight money, 121
  cause and effect of, 88
Time horizon in portfolio management, 511
  defined, 512
  diversification, function in, 516
  expectational versus planned, 512
  Markowitz-type portfolio, 512
  multiple, 512
  types, 512
  U.S. Treasury bills, 513
Tobin, James, 213
Total capital defined, 153n
Total operating expense ratio, 169–70
Townsend-Greenspan and Co. (New York), 529
Trade and Securities Statistical Manual, 133
Transfer pricing
  market-based prices for, 41–45
  product-line sectors, 41–45
Transportation companies, book profits versus tax return profits, 141, 143
Treasury stock, 58, 60
Treynor, Jack L., 571
True Equivalent Annual Yield Tables, 598
Turnover of principal asset categories, 168–69
Turnover of total capital, 165–72

U

Unemployment
  determination of extent of, 70–71
  frictional, 70
  hidden, 70

Unemployment—*Cont.*
  interest rate trends, forecasting of, 263–65
  long-run projection, 273
  Nazi Germany, 70
  Soviet Union, 70
U.S. government bonds, pension fund investment in, 625
U.S. Treasury bills
  interest rate divergences, 125
  time horizon for, 513
U.S. Treasury Bulletin, 120
Unprofitable operations
  diversification of product-lines, 38–40
  primary industry, 39

V

Value
  assets, 48–49
  common stock, 301–2; *see also* Book value of common stock *and* Stock valuation
  tax versus book; *see* Corporate profits
Value Line Survey, 433, 477

Vanderpoel, Waid R., 410
Vickers Associates report, 288–89
Vickers Favorite 50, 413
Volatile goods, 159–61
Volatility in portfolio management, 511, 516–17
  corporate bonds, 633–36
  measurement of, 568–71

W

Walter, James E., 432
War years, manufacturing corporations' earnings, 151
Ward LaFrance Truck Corp. case, 683
Wealth effects, 252
Wharton Report, 288, 467
Whitbeck, Volkert S., 450
Whyte, William H., 486
Wicksell, Knut, 220, 222, 225
Williams, John B., 431–32
Wood, R. Norman, 573

X

Xerox Corporation, 502